WO

GERMAN
DICTIONARY

GERMAN-ENGLISH/ENGLISH-GERMAN
(American English)

Compiled by
PAUL H. GLUCKSMAN, Ph.D.

Edited by
HERBERT RODECK, Ph.D., *and* T. C. APPELT, Ph.D

with a
TRAVELER'S CONVERSATION GUIDE
Containing hundreds of expressions
and items of information
useful to tourists and students alike

NEW WIN PUBLISHING, INC.

Printing Code
16   17   18   19   20

Library of Congress Catalog Card Number: 82-81061

ISBN 0-8329-9687-4 Paper
ISBN 0-8329-0144-X Thumb Indexed, Cloth

Printed in the United States of America

A Tool for Travelers and Students

"Our world is shrinking." Modern means of travel and communication have shortened distance and time to an astounding degree and facilitated contacts between people and nations. This "shrinking" is placing renewed emphasis on the value of foreign-language learning for a deeper appreciation of other cultures and a more rewarding experience in communication.

This dictionary will be a valuable aid in the study of German and English. Its more than 40,000 entries have been carefully and scientifically selected on the basis of frequency and with a view to its greatest usefulness for both students and travelers. Besides accurate meanings in various synonymous and semantic shadings of the listed words, a large number of the entries include derivations and compounds of the words and illustrate their use in many idiomatic phrases. Thus the German word *Glocke* is interpreted by three English words: "bell; (glass) shade; clock." This is followed by the phrase **etwas an die grosse Glocke hängen,** with its meaning: "to make a big fuss about something." Seven compounds with their equivalents in English complete the entry. The same procedure is followed for English words. In this way the book becomes a most useful tool not only for the interpretation of material written in either of the two languages, but also for guidance in correct and enriched expression in speaking and writing.

A feature which definitely enhances the value of this dictionary is the listing and interpretation of many modern expressions like *aerial, airborne, apple-pie-order, feedback, filter-tip, intercom, long-playing, overdrive, photo finish, picture window, strip-tease,* and many quite recent terms that have come from the area of science and the international scene, such as *air lift, anti-missile, anti-missile missile, count-down, cyclotron,* ICBM, IRBM, *microgroove, spaceship, summit conference, turbojet, tranquilizer.*

With respect to the manner of listing it should be noted that both compounds and derivatives are listed under their first element. German nouns derived from adjectives or participles are given in the form required for the nominative when preceded by the definite article.

GERMAN PRONUNCIATION

A proper pronunciation of foreign words is best acquired by imitation. The following statements will be helpful for German.

Vowels and Diphthongs

Vowels are either long or short. A vowel is long when followed by a single consonant, when doubled, or when followed by *h*. Examples: *sagen, Haar, Jahr*. A vowel is short when followed by more than one consonant. Ex.: *Mann, Kappe, wenn*. In some short words the vowel is short even if followed by only one consonant: *in, am, um, mit, das*.

a, aa, ah long, like *a* in *father*. Examples: *Vater, Aal, Jahr*.
a short, like *a* in *artistic*, but shorter. Ex.: *Mann, Land, Park*.
ä, äh long, like *ai* in *air*. Ex.: *Mädchen, mähen, Mähne*.
ä short, like *e* in *let*. Ex.: *Kälte, Bälle*.
e, ee, eh long, like *ay* in *gay*. Ex.: *den, See, sehr*.
e short, like *e* in *let*. Ex.: *Bett, nett, Emma*.
e in unaccented syllables, like the slurred *e* in *open*. Ex.: *Frage, Glocke*.
i, ie, ih long, like *ee* in *meet*. Ex.: *wir, Bier, Wien, ihr*.
i short, like *i* in *it*. Ex.: *mit, Finger, Wind*.
o, oo, oh long, like *o* in *note*. Ex.: *oder, wo, Grossvater*.
o short, like *u* in *fun*. Ex.: *Gott, kommt*.
ö, öh long, like the vowel sound in *her* or *hurt*. Ex.: *hören, Röhre*.
ö short, like the vowel sound in unaccented *-ter* in *Walter*, but quite short.
  Ex.: *können, zwölf*.
u, uh long, like *oo* in *boot*. Ex.: *gut, rufen, Schuh*.
u short, like *oo* in *foot*. Ex.: *Butter, Busch, und*.
ü, üh long, like *ee* with lips rounded for long *oo* (in *boot*). Ex.: *Mühle, über*.
ü short, like short *i* with lips rounded for short *oo* (in *foot*). Ex.: *Rücken, Glück*.
y is pronounced like *ü*.
au like *ou* in *out*. Ex.: *Haus, laufen*.
ei, ai, ay, ey like *y* in *my*. Ex.: *Ei, mein, Mai, Bayern, Mayer, Meyer*.
eu, äu like *oi* in *oil*. Ex.: *heute, Deutschland, Fräulein*.

Consonants

b, d, f, g, h, m, n, p, ph, t, and *x* are pronounced as in English. When *b, d,* and *g* are in final position they are pronounced like *p, t, k*. Ex.: *gab* (like *gap*), *Kind* (like *Kint*), *Tag* (like *Tak*). *g* before a vowel is always pronounced hard as in English *go*, never soft as in *gem*. In the final syllables *-ig, -igst, -igt* the *g* is pronounced like *ch*. Ex.: *ewig, billigst, verewigt*.

4

c is retained only in words of foreign origin. It is pronounced like *ts* before
  e, ä, i, y, otherwise like *k*.
ch like the *h* when whispering English *huge*. Ex.: *ich, weich, euch*. When
  preceded by *a, o, u, au*, it is produced by forcing the breath between the
  tongue and the uvula. Ex.: *ach, doch, Tuch, auch*. In some words of
  Greek origin *ch* is pronounced like *k*. Ex.: *Chor, Christus*.
chs like *ks* or *x*. Ex.: *Fuchs, Sachsen*.
j like *y* in *yes*, never like English *j*. Ex.: *ja, jung*.
kn like *k* followed by *n*; the *k* is pronounced; not like English *knee*. Ex.: *Knie*.
l not like English *l*. The tip of the tongue is placed at the base of the upper
  teeth. Ex.: *leben, lang*.
ng like the *ng* in *sing*, not like *finger*. Ex.: *singen, Finger*.
pf like *p* followed by *f*; both *p* and *f* are pronounced. Ex.: *Pferd, Pfund*.
ps like *p* followed by *s*, not like *ps* in English *psalm*. Ex.: *Psalm, Psychologie*.
qu like *qv*. Ex.: *Quelle, quitt*.
r is produced either by the uvula vibrating against the tongue, or by trilling
  with the tip of the tongue. The latter is easier.
s like *z* in *zone*. Ex.: *sagen, Sonne*. At the end of a word or syllable, *s* is pronounced like *s* in *son*. Ex.: *das, was, Gras, Wasser*.
ss or *sz* like *s* in *son*. Ex.: *gross* or *grosz*.
sch like *sh* in *shine*. Ex.: *schon, scheinen*.
sp and *st* at the beginning of a word or syllable sound like *shp* and *sht*. Ex.:
  sprechen, stehen.
th like *t*, never like English *th*. Ex.: *Theke, Thomas, Goethe*.
z, tz like *ts* in *fits*. Ex.: *zu, zeigen, sitzen*. *z* is never pronounced like English *z*.
v like *f* in *father*. Ex.: *Vater, von*.
w like *v* in *very*. Ex.: *wer, wo, wie, was*.

The Glottal Stop

In English there is a tendency to permit words to "run together," as
when *not at all* is spoken as *notatall*; the glottis or opening between the vocal
chords remains open. In German the glottis is closed before a word or syllable
beginning with an accented vowel; every word or syllable of this type is
enunciated separately. Ex.: *Wo ist er?* In English this may also occur in
emphatic expressions, as e.g. "It's awful!"

Accent

German words are accented on the stem syllable; generally, this is the
first syllable: *le'ben, Fräu'lein*. In words compounded with prefixes (syllables
placed before the stem) the prefix is accented except for the following: *be-,
emp-, ent-, er-, ge-, ver-, zer-*. These prefixes are never stressed. Ex.: *ge'hen,
aus'gehen, bege'hen, verge'hen, zerge'hen*.

The end-syllable (suffix) *-ei* is always stressed. Ex.: *Fischerei'*.

Words of foreign origin are generally accented on the last syllable:
Student', Papier'. In some foreign words the accent is on the next-to-last
syllable: *Charak'ter*.

STRONG AND IRREGULAR VERBS

In the following table compound verbs are included only where the corresponding simple verb does not occur, or where it is very uncommon. Where the stem vowel changes in the present indicative, the change is indicated in parentheses following the infinitive. When the auxiliary of the perfect is a form of *sein*, it is indicated by the word *ist*. When transitive forms using *haben* also occur, *ist* is enclosed in parentheses (*ist*). *Verbs marked with an asterisk (*) sometimes have weak forms.*

Infinitive	Past	Past Participle
backen (ä)	buk	gebacken
befehlen (ie)	befahl	befohlen
befleissen	befliss	beflissen
beginnen	begann	begonnen
beissen	biss	gebissen
bergen (i)	barg	geborgen
*bersten (i)	barst	ist geborsten
*bewegen	bewog	bewogen
biegen	bog	gebogen
bieten	bot	geboten
binden	band	gebunden
bitten	bat	gebeten
blasen (ä)	blies	geblasen
bleiben	blieb	ist geblieben
braten	briet	gebraten
brechen (i)	brach	gebrochen
brennen	brannte	gebrannt
bringen	brachte	gebracht
denken	dachte	gedacht
*dingen	dang	gedungen
dreschen (i)	drasch, drosch	gedroschen
dringen	drang	gedrungen
dürfen	durfte	gedurft
empfehlen (ie)	empfahl	empfohlen
erbleichen	erblich	ist erblichen
erlöschen (i)	erlosch	ist erloschen
*erschrecken(i)	erschrak	ist erschrocken

Infinitive	Past	Past Participle
essen (i)	ass	gegessen
fahren (ä)	fuhr	ist gefahren
fallen (ä)	fiel	ist gefallen
fangen (ä)	fing	gefangen
fechten (i)	focht	gefochten
finden	fand	gefunden
flechten (i)	flocht	geflochten
fliegen	flog	ist geflogen
fliehen	floh	ist geflohen
fliessen	floss	ist geflossen
fressen (i)	frass	gefressen
frieren	fror	gefroren
gären	gor	gegoren
gebären (ie)	gebar	geboren
geben (i)	gab	gegeben
gedeihen	gedieh	ist gediehen
gehen	ging	ist gegangen
gelingen	gelang	ist gelungen
gelten (i)	galt	gegolten
genesen	genas	ist genesen
geniessen	genoss	genossen
geschehen (ie)	geschah	ist geschehen
gewinnen	gewann	gewonnen
giessen	goss	gegossen
*gleichen	glich	geglichen
*gleissen	gliss	geglissen
*gleiten	glitt	ist geglitten

6

Infinitive	Past	Past Participle
*glimmen	glomm	geglommen
graben (ä)	grub	gegraben
greifen	g iff	gegriffen
haben (hat)	hatte	gehabt
halten (ä)	hielt	gehalten
hangen (ä)	hing	gehangen
hauen	hieb	gehauen
heben	hob	gehoben
heissen	hiess	geheissen
he.fen (i)	half	geholfen
kennen	kannte	gekannt
kiesen	kor	gekoren
*klimmen	klomm	ist geklommen
klingen	klang	geklungen
kneifen	kniff	gekniffen
kommen	kam	ist gekommen
können (kann)	konnte	gekonnt
kriechen	kroch	ist gekrochen
küren	kor	gekoren
*laden (ä)	lud	geladen
lassen (ä)	liess	gelassen
laufen (äu)	lief	ist gelaufen
leiden	litt	gelitten
leihen	lieh	geliehen
lesen (ie)	las	gelesen
liegen	lag	gelegen
lügen	log	gelogen
mahlen	mahlte	gemahlen
meiden	mied	gemieden
*melken (i)	molk	gemolken
messen (i)	mass	gemessen
misslingen	misslang	ist misslungen
mögen (mag)	mochte	gemocht
müssen (muss)	musste	gemusst
nehmen (nimmt)	nahm	genommen
nennen	nannte	genannt
pfeifen	pfiff	gepfiffen
*pflegen	pflog	gepflogen
preisen	pries	gepriesen
quellen (i)	quoll	ist gequollen
raten (ä)	riet	geraten
reiben	rieb	gerieben
reissen	riss	gerissen
reiten	ritt	ist geritten
rennen	rannte	ist gerannt
riechen	roch	gerochen
ringen	rang	gerungen
rinnen	rann	ist geronnen
rufen	rief	gerufen
salzen	salzte	gesalzen
saufen (äu)	soff	gesoffen
*schaffen	schuf	geschaffen
*schallen	scholl	geschollen
scheiden	schied	ist geschieden
scheinen	schien	geschienen
schelten (i)	schalt	gescholten
schieben	schob	geschoben
schiessen	schoss	geschossen
schinden	schund	geschunden
schlafen (ä)	schlief	geschlafen
schlagen (ä)	schlug	geschlagen
schleichen	schlich	ist geschlichen
*schleifen	schliff	geschliffen
schleissen	schliss	geschlissen
schliefen	schloff	ist geschloffen
schliessen	schloss	geschlossen
schlingen	schlang	geschlungen
schmeissen	schmiss	geschmissen
*schmelzen (i)	schmolz	ist geschmolzen

Infinitive	Past	Past Participle
schneiden	schnitt	geschnitten
*schrauben	schrob	geschroben
*schrecken (i)	schrak	ist erschrocken
schreiben	schrieb	geschrieben
schreien	schrie	geschrieen
schreiten	schritt	ist geschritten
schweigen	schwieg	geschwiegen
*schwellen (i)	schwoll	ist geschwollen
schwimmen	schwamm	ist geschwommen
schwinden	schwand	ist geschwunden
schwören	schwur	geschworen
sehen (ie)	sah	gesehen
sein	war	ist gewesen
senden	sandte	gesandt
	sendete	gesendet
*sieden	sott	gesotten
singen	sang	gesungen
sinken	sank	ist gesunken
sinnen	sann	gesonnen
sitzen	sass	gesessen
sollen (soll)	sollte	gesollt
speien	spie	gespieen
spinnen	spann	gesponnen
sprechen (i)	sprach	gesprochen
spriessen	spross	ist gesprossen
springen	sprang	ist gesprungen
stechen (i)	stach	gestochen
*stecken	stak	gesteckt
stehen	stand, stund	gestanden
stehlen (ie)	stahl	gestohlen
steigen	stieg	ist gestiegen
sterben (i)	starb	ist gestorben

Infinitive	Past	Past Participle
stieben	stob	(ist) gestoben
stinken	stank	gestunken
stossen (ö)	stiess	gestossen
streichen	strich	gestrichen
streiten	stritt	gestritten
tragen (ä)	trug	getragen
treffen (i)	traf	getroffen
treiben	trieb	getrieben
treten	trat	(ist) getreten
*triefen	troff	getroffen
trinken	trank	getrunken
trügen	trog	getrogen
tun	tat	getan
*verderben (i)	verdarb	(ist) verdorben
vergessen (i)	vergass	vergessen
verlieren	verlor	verloren
wägen	wog	gewogen
waschen (ä)	wusch	gewaschen
weben	wob	gewoben
weisen	wies	gewiesen
wenden	wandte	gewandt
	wendete	gewendet
werben (i)	warb	geworben
werden (i)	wurde, ward	ist geworden
werfen (i)	warf	geworfen
wiegen	wog	gewogen
winden	wand	gewunden
wissen (weiss)	wusste	gewusst
wollen (will)	wollte	gewollt
zeihen	zieh	geziehen
ziehen	zog	(ist) gezogen
zwingen	zwang	gezwungen

8

* The following verbs are always weak when used in the meanings indicated: bewegen (move physically); pflegen (be accustomed to); schaffen (to work, do); schleifen (drag); schmelzen (melt something); schrecken (frighten); schwellen (make larger); sieden (seethe); stecken (stick, put)

GERMAN—ENGLISH

DEUTSCH—ENGLISCH

ABBREVIATIONS

abbr.	abbreviation	*m.*	masculine
adj.	adjective	math.	mathematics
adv.	adverb	mech.	mechanics
avi.	aviation	med.	medicine
agr.	agriculture	mil.	military
anat.	anatomy	min.	mining, minerals
arch.	architecture	mus.	music
art.	article	*n.*	noun
ast.	astronomy	naut.	nautical
auto.	automobile	*neu.*	neuter
bibl.	biblical	opt.	optical
biol.	biology	orn.	ornithology
bot.	botany	phil.	philosophy
chem.	chemistry	phot.	photography
coll.	colloquial	phy.	physics
com.	commerce	physiol.	physiology
conj.	conjunction	*pl.*	plural
dent.	dentistry	poet.	poetry
dial.	dialectal	pol.	politics
eccl.	ecclesiastic	*p.p.*	past participle
educ.	education	*prep.*	preposition
elec.	electricity	*pron.*	pronoun
ent.	entomology	rad.	radio
f.	feminine	rail.	railway
fig.	figurative(ly)	rel.	religion
geog.	geography	rhet.	rhetoric
geol.	geology	*sing.*	singular
geom.	geometry	sl.	slang
gram.	grammar	theat.	theater
hort.	horticulture	TV	television
ichth.	ichthyology	typ.	typography
interj.	interjection	*v.*	verb
interr.	interrogative	zool.	zoology
lit.	literature		

GERMAN — ENGLISH

A

Aachen *neu.* Aix-la-Chapelle
Aal *m.* eel
aalglatt *adj.* elusive, slippery
Aar *m.* (poet.) eagle
Aas *neu.* carcass, carrion; bait, lure
ab *adv.* away, down, from, off; — **und zu** to and fro, now and then; **von nun —** henceforth
abändern *v.* to alter, to modify; to amend
Abänderung *f.* alteration; modification
Abart *f.* variety
Abbau *m.* cutting down, reduction; discharge; (min.) working; exhaustion; demolition
abbauen *v.* to cut down, to reduce; to discharge; (min.) to work; to demolish
abbekommen *v.* to get a share of; to get hurt
abberufen *v.* to recall; to call away
abbestellen *v.* to countermand; to cancel
abbiegen *v.* to bend off; to branch off
Abbild *neu.* copy, image, likeness
abbilden *v.* to copy, to portray, to delineate
Abbildung *f.* picture, illustration
abbinden *v.* to untie, to tie off
Abbitte *f.* apology
abbitten *v.* to apologize for; to beg off
abblasen *v.* to blow off (*oder* away); to sound retreat; to cancel, to call off
abblättern *v.* to strip off (leaves); to shed (leaves), to exfoliate, to peel off
abblenden *v.* to dim, to screen, to shade
abblühen *v.* to cease blooming; to fade, to wither
abbrechen *v.* to break off; to tear down, to interrupt suddenly; to cut short; to drop (a subject)

abbrennen *v.* to burn down; to fire off
abbringen *v.* to lead away; to dissuade
Abbruch *m.* breaking off; rupture, demolition; — **tun** to damage, to injure, to disparage; **auf —** **verkaufen** to sell as scrap
abbruchreif *adj.* dilapidated
abbüssen *v.* to atone for, to expiate; (law) to serve a sentence
abdachen *v.* to slope, to slant
abdämmen *v.* to dam off; to embank
abdampfen *v.* to cease to evaporate; (coll.) to depart, to steam away
abdanken *v.* to resign, to abdicate; to discharge; (mil.) to cashier
abdecken *v.* to flay, to skin; to turn down (bed); to clear (table); to pay (debts)
abdienen *v.* to pay in service
abdrehen *v.* to switch (*oder* turn, twist) off
abdrosseln *v.* (mech.) to throttle, to choke
Abdruck *m.* copy; impression, print; cast, mark, stamp; **-srecht** *neu.* copyright
abdrucken *v.* to print, to imprint, to stamp
Abend *m.* evening, night; **am —** in the evening, at night; **gestern —** yesterday evening, last night; **heute —** this evening, tonight; **es wird —** it's getting dark; **-andacht** *f.* evening prayer; **-anzug** *m.* full dress; **-blatt** *neu.* evening paper; **-brot** *neu.*, **-essen** *neu.* supper; **-dämmerung** *f.* dusk, evening twilight; **-land** *neu.* occident; West; **-mahl** *neu.* Lord's Supper; **-röte** *f.* sunset glow; **-schule** *f.* evening classes; **-sonne** *f.* setting sun; **-stern** *m.* evening star
Abenteuer *neu.* adventure

Abenteurer m. adventurer

aber adv. again; — conj. but, yet; however; **-mals** adv. once more; **-malig** adj. repeated

Aberglaube m. superstition

abergläubisch adj. superstitious

abfahren v. to depart; to start; (skiing) to glissade; to sever by driving over; to wear out by driving; — **lassen** to snub

Abfahrt f. departure; (skiing) glissade

Abfall m. falling off; slope, declivity; refuse, garbage; (fig.) revolt, apostasy

abfallen v. to fall off, to slope; to lose (weight); to apostatize; to be wasted; to fail; to be snubbed

abfällig adj. sloping; adverse; disparaging

abfangen v. to intercept; to snatch, to catch

abfärben v. to lose color; to stain; — **auf** to influence

abfassen v. to draw up; to compose, to write; (coll.) to catch, to arrest

abfertigen v. to dispatch; to forward; (coll.) to snub

abfeuern v. to fire off, to discharge

abfinden v. to compensate; to pay off; to satisfy; **sich** — **mit** to come to terms with; to resign oneself to (oder with)

abflachen v. to flatten, to level

Abflug m. (avi.) take-off, start

Abfluss m. flowing off; discharge; **-graben** m. drain; **-rohr** neu. drain pipe

abfragen v. to interrogate, to examine, to inquire of

abfressen v. to eat off, to consume

Abfuhr f. removal, carting off; rebuff

abführen v. to lead (oder carry) away; (med.) to purge

Abführmittel neu. laxative, purgative

Abgabe f. delivery; duty, tax; **-n** pl. fees

Abgang m. departure; exit; retirement; loss, offal; **-sprüfung** f. final examination

Abgas neu. exhaust (oder waste) gas

abgeben v. to deliver; to share (oder deal) with; **sich** — **mit** to occupy oneself with

abgebrannt adj. burned down; (fig.) stone-broke

abgebrüht adj. scalded; (fig.) callous

abgedroschen adj. trite, hackneyed, commonplace

abgegriffen adj. thumbed; worn out by handling

abgehen v. to depart; to deviate; to retire; to exit; to branch off; to be missing; to relinquish; (med.) to be discharged; **gut** — to end well; **sich nichts** — **lassen** to deny oneself nothing

abgelebt adj. decrepit, worn out

abgelegen adj. remote, distant

abgemacht adj. settled; — interj. agreed! all right!

abgemessen adj. measured; slow; formal

abgeneigt adj. disinclined; averse to

Abgeordnete(r) m. representative, deputy

abgerechnet adv. deducted; — **davon** aside from

abgerissen adj. ragged, shabby; torn off; abrupt, disjointed

Abgesandte(r) m. delegate, messenger; ambassador, envoy

abgeschieden adj. secluded; deceased

abgeschmackt adj. in bad taste; absurd, silly

abgesehen prep. apart from, without regard to

abgespannt adj. exhausted, tired

abgestumpft adj. blunted; dull, indifferent

abgewöhnen v. to wean from; **sich etwas** — to give up the habit of something

Abglanz m. reflection

Abgott m. idol

Abgötterei f. idolatry

abgrenzen v. to mark off, to demarcate; to define

Abgrund m. abyss; precipice

Abguss m. cast, copy

abhalten v. to hold (oder keep) off; to hinder, to restrain; **Versammlung** — to hold a meeting

abhandeln v. to get (by bargaining); to discuss, to debate

abhanden adv. missing, lost; **-kommen** to get lost

Abhandlung f. treatise, essay

Abhang m. slope, declivity

abhängen v. to take off; — **von** to depend on

Abhängigkeit f. dependence

abhärmen v. **sich** — to languish, to pine away

abhärten v. to harden; to toughen

abhaspeln v. to reel off

abhauen v. to chop off; (sl.) to scram

abheben v. to lift off; to withdraw; to cut (cards); **sich** — **von** to contrast with

abhelfen v. to help, to remedy, to redress

abhold adj. ill-disposed, disinclined

abholen v. to pick up, to call for; to collect

abhören v. to overhear; to hear (lesson)

abirren v. to deviate; to go astray

abjagen v. to override, to overdrive; to snatch away

abkanzeln v. (coll.) to rebuke, to scold

abkaufen v. to buy from

abkehren v. to sweep from; to turn away; **sich** — **von** to withdraw assistance

Abklatsch m. stereotype plate, proof; (fig.) poor imitation

abknappen, abknapsen v. to stint, to curtail

abknöpfen v. to unbutton; jemand etwas — to do someone out of something

abkommandieren v. (mil.) to detach, to detail, to order away

Abkomme, Abkömmling m. descendant; derivative

Abkommen neu. agreement; origin; decline

abkommen v. to deviate, to digress; to drop; to get off (oder away); to become obsolete

abkratzen v. to scratch off; (sl.) to kick the bucket

abkühlen v. to cool, to chill, to refrigerate

Abkunft f. descent, origin, extraction

abkürzen v. to shorten, to abbreviate; to curtail

abladen v. to unload, to discharge

ablagern v. to deposit, to store; to season, to mature

Ablass m. (eccl.) indulgence

ablassen v. to drain off; to cease, to desist; to reduce (prices)

Ablauf m. running off; course; expiration; start; sink; (com.) maturity

ablaufen v. to run off (oder down); to expire; to start; to wear out; gut — to pass off well

ableben v. to die

ablegen v. to put away; to file; to render (account); to make (confession); to pass (examination); to take (oath); to bear (witness)

Ableger m. (bot.) slip, shot; (fig.) branch

ablehnen v. to decline, to refuse

Ablehnung f. refusal, rejection

ableiten v. to turn aside, to divert; to drain; to derive

ablenken v. to distract; to deflect; to avert; to diffract; to divert

ablesen v. to read off; to pick off, to gather

ableugnen v. to deny, to disclaim

abliefern v. to deliver, to hand over

ablösen v. to loosen; to remove, to detach; (mil.) to change (oder relieve) guards

abmachen v. to undo, to remove, to detach; to settle, to arrange for

Abmachung f. arrangement, settlement; agreement

abmagern v. to reduce (oder lose) weight

Abmarsch m. marching off; start

abmelden v. to give notice of departure

abmessen v. to measure, to gauge; to survey; seine Worte — to weigh one's words

abmühen v. sich — to exert oneself

Abnahme f. taking off; sale; decrease;

decline; loss (in weight); (astr.) wane

abnehmen v. to lose weight; to take off; to decrease, to diminish; to subside; to gather; to buy; to cut (cards); (astr.) to wane

Abnehmer m. buyer, customer

Abneigung f. aversion, dislike; antipathy

abnutzen, abnützen v. to wear out

Abnutzung f. wear and tear; attrition

Abnutzungsvergütung f. depletion allowance

Abonnement neu. subscription

Abonnent m. subscriber

abonnieren v. to subscribe for

abordnen v. to delegate, to deputize

Abort m. toilet, latrine; (med.) abortion

abpassen v. to watch for; to measure; to lie in wait for

abplacken, abplagen v. sich — to drudge

abprallen v. to rebound, to recoil; (mil.) to ricochet; to glance off

abputzen v. to clean, to polish; to roughcast

abquälen v. to torment; sich — to worry oneself; to toil

abraten v. to dissuade; to warn (against)

abräumen v. to take (oder clear) away; to remove

abrechnen v. to deduct; to settle

Abrechnungsstelle f. clearing house

Abrede f. agreement; in — stellen to deny, to dispute

abreden v. to dissuade (from)

abreiben v. to rub off (oder down); to scour

Abreise f. departure

abreisen v. to depart; to leave (for)

abreissen v. to tear off; to pull down, to demolish; to wear out

abrichten v. to train, to break in (animals)

Abriss m. sketch, draft; summary

abrollen v. to roll off; to unwind (film)

abrücken v. to move off (oder away); (mil.) to march off; to depart

abrufen v. to call off (oder away); (rail.) to call out

abrunden v. to round off; to make round

Abrüstung f. disarmament

absägen v. to saw off; (coll.) to discharge

Absatz m. paragraph; pause, stop; heel; sale, circulation; (stairs) landing; —gebiet neu. market

abschaffen v. to do away with; to abolish

abschätzen v. to evaluate, to appraise

Abschaum m. scum

abscheiden v. to separate; to refine; von der Welt — to die

Abscheu m. aversion; loathing; abhorrence

abscheulich adj. abominable, atrocious

abschicken v. to send off, to dispatch

abschieben v. to deport; to shove (*oder* move) off; (coll.) to back out of

Abschied m. parting; dismissal; — nehmen to take leave, to say goodbye; seinen — bekommen to be dismissed; seinen — nehmen to resign; -sbesuch m. farewell visit

abschiessen v. to fire; to shoot off; (*oder* down); den Vogel — to take the cake

abschinden v. to skin; sich — to drudge

Abschlag m. fall (in price); auf — by installments, on account

abschlagen v. to beat (*oder* knock) off; to refuse, to deny; (mil.) to repel

abschlägig adj. negative

abschleifen v. to grind, to polish

abschleppen v. to drag off; to tow away; (fig.) to tire oneself out

abschliessen v. to lock up; to balance (account); to strike (bargain); to finish (work); sich — to seclude oneself; -d adj. conclusive, definitive, final

Abschluss m. conclusion; settlement; balancing (account); -prüfung f. final examination

abschmieren v. (mech.) to lubricate, to grease; (coll.) to copy carelessly

abschminken v. to remove make-up; (sl.) to desist from

abschneiden v. to cut off (*oder* short), to clip; gut — to come off well

Abschnitt m. cut; division; period; (com.) coupon; (lit.) part, paragraph, chapter

abschrecken v. to deter, to di hearten

Abschreckung f. deterrence; -swaffe f. deterrent weapon

abschreiben v. to copy; to plagiarize; (com.) to deduct; (educ.) to crib

abschreiten v. to pace

Abschrift f. copy, duplicate, transcript

abschüssig adj. steep, precipitous

Abschusstisch, Abschussturm m. launching pad

abschwächen v. to weaken, to diminish, to soften

abschweifen v. to stray; to digress

abschwören v. to deny upon oath; to recant

absehbar adj. within sight; in -er Zeit before long

absehen v. to learn by observation; to copy; — von to desist from; to disregard; es — auf to aim at

abseits adv. and prep. apart, aside, away from; (sport) offside

absenden v. to send off (*oder* away); to dispatch, to forward

Absender m. sender, shipper

absetzen v. to put down, to deposit; to

depose; to remove; to sell; to pause; to deduct

Absicht f. intention, purpose; in böser — with malice; in der — with the intention; mit — on purpose

absichtlich adj. intentional; — adv. on purpose

absitzen v. to dismount; to serve (sentence)

absolvieren v. to absolve, to acquit, to finish (studies)

absondern v. to detach, to isolate; to secrete; sich — to seclude oneself

abspannen v. to unbend, to unharness, to uncock; to relax

abspenstig adj. disloyal; — machen to alienate, to estrange

absperren v. to bar, to lock; to shut off; to block; to isolate, to separate

abspielen v. sich — to take place; vom Blatt — to play at sight

abspringen v. to jump (*oder* leap) off, to crack off; (avi.) to bail out;

Absprung m. jump; (avi.) parachute jump

abstammen v. to descend; to be derived (from)

Abstand m. distance; interval; difference, contrast; — nehmen von to desist from; -sgeld neu., -ssumme f. indemnity, compensation

abstatten v. to make, to give, to render; to return (thanks); to pay (visit)

abstechen v. to pierce, to stab; to trump; — von to contrast with, to stand out against

Abstecher m. excursion, side-trip; digression

abstecken v. to unpin; to trace, to stake out

absteigen v. to descend; to dismount; to alight; to put up (at a hotel)

abstellen v. to put down; to stop, to turn off; to park; to abolish;

absterben v. to die away (*oder* out); to fade

Abstieg m. descent

abstimmen v. to tune (in); to vote; — lassen to put to a vote

abstossen v. to knock (*oder* push, rub) off; to repel; -d adj. repellent, repulsive

abstrahieren v. to abstract

abstrakt adj. abstract; metaphysical; -e Kunstrichtung abstractionism

abstreichen v. to deduct; to remove

abstreiten v. to deny; to dispute

Abstufung f. gradation; shading

abstumpfen v. to blunt; to dull; sich — gegen to become insensible to

Absturz m. crash; precipice; zum — bringen to bring (*oder* shoot) down

abstürzen v. to fall precipitately; (avi.) to crash

absuchen v. to search; to scour

Abt m. abbot; **-ei** f. abbey

Abteil neu. (rail.) compartment

abteilen v. to divide: to partition off

Abteilung f. department, section; (med.) ward; (mil.) detachment

abtragen v. to wear out; to carry (oder clear) away; to pull down; to level

abtreiben v. to drive away (oder off); to dispossess; (med.) to cause abortion; (avi.) to yaw

abtrennen v. to detach, to separate; to rip off

abtreten v. to resign; to retire; to abdicate; to exit; to yield; to tread off

Abtritt m. toilet; (theat.) exit

abtrudeln v. (avi.) to auger

abtrünnig adj. apostate; disloyal; faithless

Abtrünnige m. deviationist

abwägen v. to weigh; to consider carefully

abwälzen v. to roll away (oder down, off); to shirk (responsibility), to shift (blame)

Abwandlung f. (gram.) declension; conjugation

abwarten v. to await; to wait and see

abwärts adv. and prep. down, downward(s)

abwechselnd adj. alternating, intermittent; — adv. alternately; by turns

Abwechslung f. change, variety; alternation; zur — for a change

Abweg m. wrong way; auf **-e** geraten to go astray

abwehren v. to keep off; to defend; to parry

Abwehrgeschoss neu. anti-missile

Abwehrrakete f. interceptor missile

abweichen v. to deviate; to differ

abweisen v. to refuse, to reject; to repulse; (law) to dismiss; (mil.) to repel

abwenden v. to avert, to prevent; to turn away

abwendig adj. alienated; — machen to estrange

abwerfen v. to throw (oder cast) off; to shed; (avi.) to drop (bombs); to yield (profit)

abwesend adj. absent; (fig.) absent-minded

abwickeln v. to unwind; (fig.) to finish

abzahlen v. to pay off; to pay by installments

abzehren v. to waste (away); to consume

Abzeichen neu. badge; stripe; — pl. insignia

abzeichnen v. to copy, to draw; sich — to stand out against

Abziehbild neu. decalcomania

abziehen v. to take off; to strip; to skin; to strop; to draw off; to distill; to print; to subtract, to deduct; (sl.) to move off

Abzug m. departure, retreat; outlet; (com.) allowance, deduction, discount, rebate; (mech.) trigger; (phot.) print; (typ.) proof; **-skanal** m. drain, sewer, culvert

ach! interj. ah! oh! alas! — so! I see! — was! — wo! nonsense! not at all!

Achse f. axle; axis

Achsel f. shoulder; auf die leichte — nehmen to take it easy; die **-n** zucken to shrug one's shoulders; über die — ansehen to look down on; **-höhle** f. armpit

Achte f. eighth; **-eck** neu. octagon; **-el** neu. eighth; **-elnote** f. quaver; **-er** m. eighth

Acht f. attention, care; ban; ausser — lassen to disregard; in die — erklären to outlaw; sich in — nehmen to beware

acht adj. eight; heute in — Tagen a week from today; **-mal** adv. eight times; **-zehn** adj. eighteen; **-zig** adj. eighty

acht: **-bar** adj. respectable; **-en** v. to esteem, to regard, to respect; **-geben** (or **-haben**) v. to pay attention, to take care; **-los** adj. careless, negligent; **-sam** adj. attentive, careful

Achtung f. esteem, regard; **—!** interj. attention! beware! look out!

achtungsvoll adj. respectful

ächzen v. to groan, to moan

Acker m. field, soil; acre; **-bau** m. agriculture; **-bestellung** f. tillage; **-boden** m. arable soil; **-gerät** neu. agricultural implement; **-knecht** m. farmhand; **-smann** m. farmer

ackern v. to plow, to till

addieren v. to add (oder sum) up

Ade! neu. (coll.) adieu! goodbye! farewell!

Adel m. aristocracy, **-stand** m. nobility; in den **-stand** erheben to ennoble

Adelbert m. Ethelbert

Adelheid f. Adelaide

ad(e)lig adj. noble, titled; blueblooded

Ader f. vein; (min.) lode, seam; (wood) grain

Adler m. eagle; **-nase** f. aquiline nose

Adress: **-at** m. addressee; (com.) consignee; **-buch** neu. directory; **-e** f. address; per **-e** care of

adressieren v. to address

Adria f. Adriatic Sea

Aerodynamik f. aerodynamics

Affe m. ape, monkey

Affekt m. affection, passion, impulse

äffen v. to mock. to mimic; to fool

After m. anus, posterior, behind; **–kritiker** m. would-be critic, **–miete** f. subletting

Agentur f. agency

Ägypten neu. Egypt

Ahle f. awl

Ahn, Ahnherr m. ancestor, forefather; **–frau** f. ancestress

ahnen v. to anticipate, to foresee

ähnlich adj. resembling, similar

Ahnung f. presentiment, foreboding; **er hatte keine** — he had no idea

ahnungslos adj. unsuspecting; without misgivings

ahnungsvoll adj. full of foreboding; ominous

Ahorn m. maple

Ähre f. (bot.) spike; ear

Akademiker m. academician

akademisch adj. academic(al); **–e Freiheit** academic freedom

Akazie f. acacia

Akkord m. agreement, contract; (mus.) chord; **–arbeit** f. piece work

Akt m. action; act; (art) nude; **–en** pl. deeds, documents, records, files; **zu den –en legen** to pigeonhole; **–enmappe** f. brief case

Aktie f. share, stock; **–ngesellschaft** f. stock company

Aktionär m. shareholder

Aktiva neu. pl. assets

aktivieren v. to activate

Akustik f. acoustics

Alarm m. alarm; **blinder** — false alarm; **–bereitschaft** f. (mil.) alert; **–start** (mil.) scramble

albern adj. foolish, silly

Albrecht m. Albert

Aleutischen Inseln f. pl. Aleutian Islands

Alge f. seaweed

Algerien neu. Algeria

Alimente neu. pl. alimony

Alkohol m. alcohol; **–iker** m. alcoholic, drunkard; **–schmuggler** m. bootlegger

alkoholfrei adj. nonalcoholic

all adj. all, entire, whole; each, every, any; **–e Tage** every day; **–e Welt** everybody; **auf –e Fälle** in any case; **in –er Eile** in great hurry; **ohne –en Grund** for no reason at all; **trotz –em** in spite of everything; **vor –em** above all; **–bekannt** adj. notorious; **–enfalls** adv. possibly, perhaps, if need be; **–esamt** adv. altogether; **–gegenwärtig** adj. omnipresent; **–gemein** adj. universal; general; **in –em** in general; **–jährlich** adj. annual, yearly; every year; **–mächtig** adj. omnipotent; **–mählich** adj. gradual; **–mählich** adv. gradually, by degrees; **–seitig** adj. all-round; universal; **–täg-**

–lich adj. daily, everyday; commonplace, trivial; **–überall** adv. everywhere; **–wissend** adj. omniscient; **–zu(viel)** adv. too (much); too much by far; **–zeit** adv. at all time, always

All neu. universe; **–gemeinheit** f. generality, universality; **–heilmittel** neu. panacea, universal remedy; **–macht** f. omnipotence; **–tag** m. working day; daily life

Allee f. avenue, parkway

allein adj. alone, apart, single; solitary; — adv. by oneself; — conj. but, however; **von** — without assistance, of one's own account; **–ig** adj. exclusive, sole; **–stehend** adj. detached; isolate; single

Allein-: **–besitz** m. sole ownership; **–betrieb** m. sole management; **–handel** m. monopoly; **–herrschaft** f. absolutism, autocracy; **–sein** neu. loneliness, solitude

aller-: **–dings** adv. certainly, to be sure; **–hand** adj. of all kinds (oder sorts); **–lei** adj. diverse, of all kinds; **–liebst** adj. most charming

Allergie f. allergy

Allerlei neu. hodge-podge; miscellany; medley

Allerweltskerl m. smart fellow

Alliierte m. ally

allumfassend adj. omnibus

Alm f. Alpine meadow (oder pasture)

Almosen neu. pl. alms; **–büchse** f. poor box; **–empfänger** m. pauper

Alp f. mountain (meadow); **–en** pl. Alps; **–englühen** neu. alpenglow; **–enveilchen** neu. cyclamen

Alpen pl. Alps

alphabetisch adj. alphabetic(al)

als conj. as, but, than, when, like; for; **— ob** as if (oder though); **kein and(e)rer** — none other than; **sobald** — as soon as; **sowohl** — as well as; **–bald** adv. at once, forthwith; **–dann** adv. then, thereupon

also adv. thus, so; — conj. therefore, hence, consequently

alt adj. old; ancient; stale; worn; **alles beim –en lassen** to leave things as they were; — **angesessen** long-established; **–backen** adj. stale; (fig.) old-fashioned; **–bewährt** adj. of long standing; **–ern** v. to age, to grow old; to decline; **–erschwach** adj. decrepit, senile; **–ertümlich** adj. antique; archaic; **–hergebracht** adj. customary, traditional; **–klug** adj. precocious; **–modisch** adj. old-fashioned

Alt m. (mus.) alto; **–istin** f. alto singer

Alteisen neu. scrap iron

Alter neu. age; epoch; **bibilisches** — a

great age; blühendes –er prime of life; –sgenosse *m.* one of the same age, contemporary; –sgrenze *f.* age limit; –sschwäche *f.* senility; –sversorgung *f.* old age insurance; –tum *neu.* antiquity; –tumsforschung *f.* archeology

älter *adj.* older; elder, senior

Altpapier *neu.* waste paper

Altwaren *f. pl.* Secondhand goods

am: an dem *prep.* at (*oder* by, in, on) the

Amateurrennwagen *m.* hot-rod

Amboss *m.* anvil

Ameise *f.* ant; –nsäure *f.* formic acid

Amerika *neu.* America; –ner *m.* (male) American; –nerin *f.* (female) American

amerikanisch *adj.* American

Amme *f.* wet nurse

Amöbenruhr *f.* amoebic dysentery

amputieren *v.* to amputate

Amsel *f.* blackbird

Amt *neu.* office, charge, employment; post, appointment; duty; board; seines –es walten to officiate; von –s wegen officially; –salter *neu.* seniority; –sbefugnis *f.* competence; –sbereich *m.* jurisdiction; –sbewerber *m.* candidate; –sgeheimnis *neu.* official secret; –shandlung *f.* official act; –sgericht *neu.* district court; –sniederlegung *f.* resignation; –sschimmel *m.* red tape

amtieren *v.* to officiate

amtlich *adj.* official

amüsant *adj.* amusing

amüsieren *v.* to amuse; to enjoy oneself

an *prep.* at, by, in, on; along, near; up to; about; against; — der Arbeit sein to be at work; es ist — mir it is my turn; — *adv.* onward, upward; von nun — henceforth

analog *adj.* analogous

Analphabet *m.* illiterate

Analyse *f.* analysis

analysieren *v.* to analyze

Analytiker *m.* analyst

analytisch *adj.* analytic(al)

Ananas *f.* pineapple

anbahnen *v.* to embark on, to start out

Anbau *m.* (agr.) cultivation; (arch.) annex, wing

anbauen *v.* (agr.) to cultivate, to grow, to till; (arch.) to build on

anbei *adv.* herewith, enclosed

anbeissen *v.* to bite into; (coll.) to take the bait

anberaumen *v.* to appoint (day *oder* time)

anbeten *v.* to adore; to worship; to idolize

Anbetracht, Anbetreff *m.* concern; in — der Lage considering the situation

anbieten *v.* to offer

anbinden *v.* to tie to; (coll.) to pick a

quarrel with; kurz angebunden sein to be blunt (*oder* curt)

Anblick *m.* sight, view

anbrechen *v.* to commence; to open; der Tag bricht an the day is dawning

anbrennen *v.* to kindle; to catch fire; to burn

anbringen *v.* to bring in; to fix; to make; to settle; to sell, to dispose of; gut angebracht appropriate, suitable; schlecht angebracht out of place, unsuitable

Anbruch *m.* beginning, opening; — des Tages daybreak; — der Nacht nightfall

Andacht *f.* devotion; prayers

andächtig *adj.* devout, pious; (fig.) attentive

Anden *pl.* Andes

Andenken *neu.* remembrance; souvenir, keepsake; zum — an in memory of, as a souvenir of

ander *adj. and pron.* (an)other; different; am — en Morgen next morning; –er Meinung sein to be of a different opinion; ein –es Mal another time; ein ums –e Mal repeatedly; etwas –s somewhat different; nichts –es als nothing but; unter –em among other things; –nfalls *adv.* or else, otherwise; –nteils *adv.* on the other hand; –wärts, –weit *adv.* elsewhere

ändern *v.* to alter, to change

anders *adv.* otherwise; differently; else; — sein als to be different from; — werden to change; –denkend *adj.* dissenting; –gesinnt *adj.* of a different mind; –gläubig *adj.* of a different faith; –wo *adv.* elsewhere

anderthalb *adj.* one and a half

andeuten *v.* to indicate, to hint

Andrang *m.* rush, press; congestion

andrängen, andringen *v.* to crowd, to jam

Andreas *m.* Andrew

andrehen *v.* to turn on; (mech.) to cause to start; (sl.) to trick, to hoax

Androsteron *neu.* (männliches Hormon) androsterone

aneignen *v.* to adopt, to appropriate

aneinander *adv.* together; against one another; — geraten to come to blows

anekeln *v.* to disgust

Anerbieten *neu.* offer, proposal

anerkennen *v.* to acknowledge, to admit; to appreciate; to honor (a bill); to recognize

anfachen *v.* to blow (into a flame); to kindle; (fig.) to stimulate, to incite

anfahren *v.* to drive (*oder* bring) up to; to collide, to run into; (naut.) to call (at a port); (coll.) to address gruffly

Anfall *m.* assault; (med.) fit

anfallen v. to assail, to attack

Anfang m. beginning, start; **von — an** from the very beginning; **–sbuchstabe, m.** initial letter; **–sgründe** m. pl. fundamental principles (oder elements); rudiments

anfangen v. to begin; to do; to contrive

Anfänger m. beginner

anfänglich adj. initial, incipient; — adv. in the beginning, at first

anfassen v. to handle, to touch; to take hold of; to set to work; **mit —** to lend a hand

anfechten v. to contest, to dispute; (law) to attack; (rel.) to tempt; to trouble

Anfeindung f. hostility, persecution

anfertigen v. to make, to manufacture

anfeuchten v. to dampen, to moisten

anfeuern v. to inflame; to encourage

anflehen v. to implore

anfliegen (Flugplatz) v. to make a pass

Anflug m. (avi.) approach; (fig.) tinge, touch, trace; (min.) efflorescence; **–splatz** m. (avi.) landing field

Anforderung f. claim, demand; **grosse –en stellen** to expect great things

anfragen v. to inquire; to question; **bei einem —** to ask someone

anfressen v. to gnaw (oder nibble) at; to corrode, to decay

anführen v. to lead, to command; to cite, to quote; to cheat, to trick

Angabe f. assertion, declaration, statement; instruction; boast; **nach seinen –n** according to him; **nähere –n** particulars

angängig adj. feasible, permissible

angeben v. to state, to indicate, to specify; to declare; to denounce; to boast; **Ton — to set the fashion**; to give the keynote; (cards) to deal first

Angeber m. informer, spy; **zum — werden** to turn state's evidence; **–ei** f. denunciation

angeblich adj. ostensible, alleged

angeboren adj. congenital; innate

Angebot neu., bid, offer, tender; **— und Nachfrage** supply and demand

Angegriffenheit f. nervous (oder delicate) state of health; physical exhaustion, strain

angehen v. to concern, to apply to, to ask for; to be feasible; **das geht nicht an** that will not do; **–d** adj. beginning, incipient

angehörig adj. belonging to; related to

Angehörige m. relative, next of kin

Angeklagte m. the accused, the defendant

Angel f. fishing-rod; (mech.) hinge

Angelegenheit f. affair, concern

angeln v. to angle, to fish; (coll.) to hook

angeloben v. to promise solemnly; to vow

angemessen adj. adequate, appropriate; suitable; **der Zeit nicht — out of season,** untimely

angenehm adj. acceptable, agreeable; **du bist mir immer — you are always welcome**; **sehr —! pleased to meet you!**

angesäuselt adj. (coll.) tipsy

angeschlagen adj. groggy; knocked out

angesehen adj. esteemed; respected

Angesicht neu. face; **dem Tod ins — schauen** to face death; **im Schweisse deines –s** in the sweat of thy brow; **von — zu — face to face**

angesichts prep. in view of, considering

angestammt adj. hereditary

Angestellte m. employee

angewachsen adj. increased; grown together; rooted; **wie — rooted to the ground**

angewandt adj. applied

angewiesen adj. assigned; **— auf dependent on**

angewöhnen v. to accustom; **sich etwas — to get in the habit of something**

Angewohnheit f. habit, custom

angleichen v. to assimilate

angreifbar adj. assailable, vulnerable

angreifen v. to take hold of, to seize; **to undertake; to attack; to affect; to exhaust**; **–d** adj. exhausting, trying

Angreifer m. aggressor, assailant; invader

angrenzen v. to border on, **–d** adj. adjacent

Angriff m. attack; **in — nehmen** to begin, to take in hand; **zum — vorgehen** to take the offensive; **–skrieg** m. offensive war

angriffslustig adj. agressive

Angst f. anguish, anxiety; fear; **–hase, –meier** m. coward; **–schweiss** m. cold sweat

ängstigen v. to distress; to frighten; **sich — to feel anxious, to worry; sich — vor** to be afraid of

ängstlich adj. afraid, frightened

anhaben v. to have on, to wear; **einem etwas — to accuse (oder harm) someone**

anhaften v. to stick, to cling to

Anhalt m. support; foothold; **–spunkt** m. clue; proof, evidence

anhalten v. to stop; to spur on; **— um to propose to**; **–d** adj. continuous

Anhang m. appendix, supplement; adherents, followers; (sport) fans

anhangen v. to adhere, to stick to

anhängen v. to add, to append; to hang on; (tel.) to hang up; **jemand etwas —** to slander someone

Anhänger *m.* disciple, follower; partisan; (auto.) trailer; (jewelry) pendant

anhänglich *adj.* attached; faithful

anhäufen *v.* to accumulate; to hoard

anheben *v.* to lift, to raise; (fig.) to begin

anheimeln *v.* to remind one of home; **–d** *adj.* cozy, snug

anheimfallen *v.* to pass into possession of

anheimstellen *v.* to leave (*oder* submit) to

Anhöhe *f.* elevation, hill, rising ground

anhören *v.* to listen to; **sich — wie** to sound like

Anis *m.* anise; **–samen** *m.* aniseed

Ankara *neu.* Angora

Ankauf *m.* acquisition; purchase

Anker *m.* anchor; **vor — gehen** to anchor; **vor — liegen** to ride at anchor; **–mast** *m.* mooring mast; **–winde** *f.* windlass, capstan

ankern *v.* to anchor, to moor

Anklage *f.* accusation; indictment; impeachment; **eine — erheben** to bring (*oder* make) a charge; **–bank** *f.* dock; **–schrift** *f.* indictment

anklagen *v.* to accuse; to indict; to impeach

Ankläger *m.* accuser; prosecutor

Anklang *m.* reminiscence; (mus.) accord; **—finden** to meet with approval

ankleben *v.* to glue (paste, *oder* stick) on; to adhere (*oder* cling) to; **–d** *adj.* adhesive

ankleiden *v.* to attire, to dress

anklingeln *v.* to ring (doorbell); (tel.) to call

anknüpfen *v.* to fasten (*oder* tie) to; **eine Bekanntschaft —** to strike up an acquaintance; **Verbindungen —** to establish connections

ankommen *v.* to arrive; **darauf — to** depend on; **darauf soll es nicht —!** never mind that! **es darauf — lassen** to chance (*oder* risk) it; **gut — to** be well received

Ankömmling *m.* newcomer; stranger

ankünd(ig)en *v.* to announce, to advertise

Ankunft *f.* arrival, coming

ankurbeln *v.* to start, to stimulate; to boost

Anlage *f.* grounds, park; plant, works, installation; investment; (letter) enclosure; talent; tendency; **–kapital** *neu.* stock, funds

anlangen *v.* to arrive; to concern

Anlass *m.* cause, occasion; **ohne allen —** for no reason at all

anlassen *v.* to leave on; to start; to turn on (water); to temper (metal); to rebuke, to snub; **sich gut —** to promise well

Anlasser *m.* (auto.) starter

Anlauf *m.* run, start; attack, onset; (avi.) take-off run; **einen — nehmen** to take a running start

anlegen *v.* to apply; to put on; to establish; to lay out (*oder* against); to take in hand; to invest; (dog) to tie up; (gun) to aim; (naut.) to moor; **Fesseln — to** put in chains; **Feuer — to** commit arson; **Trauer — to** go into mourning

anlehnen *v.* to lean against; to find support in; **Tür — to** leave the door ajar

Anlehnung *f.* imitation; **in — an** in imitation of, with reference to

Anleihe *f.* loan

anleiten *v.* to guide; to instruct

Anliegen *neu.* request; desire; concern

anliegend *adj.* adjacent, adjoining; neighboring; **— adv.** enclosed (in a letter)

anlocken *v.* to allure, to entice

anmachen *v.* to attach, to fix; **to mix** (*oder* dress salad); to light (fire)

anmassen *v.* **sich — to** arrogate; to presume; to pretend; **–d** *adj.* arrogant; presumptuous

anmelden *v.* to announce; to register

anmerken *v.* to jot down; to perceive

Anmut *f.* charm, grace; (fig.) sweetness

anmutig *adj.* charming, graceful

annähern *v.* to approximate; to approach

Annahme *f.* acceptance; assumption, hypothesis

Ännchen *n.* Nancy

annehmbar *adj.* acceptable

annehmen *v.* to accept, to receive; **to** assume; to suppose; to adopt; **to** contract (habit)

Annehmlichkeit *f.* amenity, comfort

Annonce *f.* advertisement

annoncieren *v.* to advertise; to announce

anodisieren *v.* to anodize

anordnen *v.* to direct; to arrange; to regulate

anpacken *v.* to grasp, to seize; to work

anpassen *v.* to fit; to suit; to adjust; **sich — to** adapt oneself to; to adjust

Anpassung *f.* adaptation; adjustment; **kulturelle — acculturation; –sfähigkeit** *f.*, **–svermögen** *neu.* adaptability

anpflanzen *v.* to plant, to cultivate

Anprall *m.* collision; impact

anpreisen *v.* to commend, to praise

anprob(ier)en *v.* to fit (*oder* try) on

anraten *v.* to advise, to recommend; **dringend — to** urge

anrechnen *v.* to charge; **hoch — to** value greatly; **zuviel — to** overcharge

Anrecht *neu.* claim, title; **— haben auf** to be entitled to

anreden *v.* to address, to accost

anregen *v.* to incite, to stimulate; to suggest; **–d** *adj.* interesting, stimulating

anreihen *v.* to add to; to rank with; to join; **sich —** to stand in line

Anreiz *m.* incitement; stimulus; incentive

anrichten *v.* to prepare; to serve up; to cause

anrüchig *adj.* disreputable

anrücken *v.* to draw near; to approach

Anruf *m.* appeal; shout; (tel.) call

anrufen *v.* to appeal to; to hail; (tel.) to call

anrühren *v.* to touch, to mix, to stir

ansagen *v.* to announce; (cards) to bid

Ansager *m.* (rad.) announcer; (cards) bidder

ansammeln *v.* to accumulate; to collect

ansässig *adj.* resident; settled

Ansatz *m.* start; tendency; incrustation; (math.) statement; (mus.) mouthpiece

anschaffen *v.* to buy; to provide, to procure

anschauen *v.* to look at; to contemplate

anschaulich *adj.* descriptive; graphic

Anschauung *f.* view; perception; contemplation

Anschein *m.* appearance; **den — erwekken** to make believe; **es hat den — it seems as if; sich den — geben** to pretend that

anscheinend *adj.* apparent, seeming

anschicken *v.* **sich —** to prepare, to set about

Anschlag *m.* poster, placard; stroke; plot; (com.) estimate; (law) assault; (mus.) touch; **in — bringen** to take into account; (gun) to aim; **–breit** *neu.* bulletin board; **–geschwindigkeit** *f.* impact velocity

anschlagen *v.* to affix, to post; to take effect; (orn.) to sing; (zool.) to bark; **einen anderen Ton —** to change tone

anschliessen *v.* to annex; to chain; to join; to follow, to accompany; to fit close; (mil.) to close ranks; **–d** *adj.* following

Anschluss *m.* annexation; joining; supply; connection; **— suchen** to seek company; **–dose** *f.* (elec.) junction box

anschmieren *v.* to smear, to daub; (coll.) to cheat

anschnauben, anschnauzen *v.* to snub, to snort at

anschneiden *v.* to begin to carve (*oder* cut); (fig.) to broach a subject

Anschnitt *m.* first cut (*oder* slice)

anschreiben *v.* to write down; to charge; to score; to chalk up; **— lassen** to take on credit; **bei jemand gut angeschrieben sein** to stand high in a per-

son's favor

Anschrift *f.* (letter) address

anschuldigen *v.* to charge with, to accuse of

anschwärzen *v.* to blacken; (coll.) to slander

anschwellen *v.* to swell; to increase

anschwemmen *v.* to wash up (*oder* ashore)

Anschwemmung *f.* alluvium

anschwindeln *v.* to swindle; to bamboozle

ansehen *v.* to look at; to take for; to esteem

Ansehen *neu.* appearance; authority; esteem; **dem — nach** to all appearance; **ohne — der Person** without respect of persons; **sich ein — geben** to give oneself airs; **von — kennen** to know by sight

ansehnlich *adj.* considerable; imposing

Ansicht *f.* sight, view; opinion; **nach meiner — in** my opinion; **zur — on** approval; **–skarte** *f.* picture postcard

ansiedeln *v.* to colonize, to settle

anspannen *v.* to stretch; to harness; to strain

anspielen *v.* to begin to play; (cards) to have the lead; (tennis) to serve; **— auf** to hint at, to allude to

anspitzen *v.* to point, to sharpen

Ansporn *m.* spur, stimulus

anspornen *v.* to spur on, to stimulate

Ansprache *f.* address, speech

ansprechen *v.* to speak to; to accost; to appeal to, to please; **–d** *adj.* attractive

anspringen *v.* to jump at; (motor) to start

Anspruch *m.* claim, demand; **— haben auf** to be entitled to; **— machen auf** to lay claim to; **in — nehmen** to take up (time)

anspruchslos *adj.* modest, unassuming

anspruchsvoll *adj.* fastidious; presumptious

anstacheln *v.* to spur on; to incite; to stimulate

Anstalt *f.* establishment, institution; inst

tute; **–en treffen** to make arrangements

Anstand *m.* decency; decorum; **— nehmen** to doubt, to hesitate; **ohne — without** hesitation; **–sbesuch** *m.* formal call; **–sgefühl** *neu.* tact

anständig *adj.* decent, respectable; proper

anstatt *conj.* and *prep.* instead of

anstechen *v.* to prick; to tap

anstecken *v.* to fasten to, to pin on; to light, to kindle; (med.) to contaminate, to infect; **–d** *adj.* catching, contagious

anstellen *v.* to place against; to appoint, to employ; to draw (comparison); to undertake; (mech.) to start; (rad.) to turn on; **sich —** to behave; to feign; to make a fuss

anstellig *adj.* able, handy

Anstieg *m.* ascent

anstiften *v.* to cause, to incite to; to plot

Anstifter *m.* instigator

anstimmen *v.* to begin to sing; to strike up

Anstoss *m.* collision; impulse; (football) kickoff; **— erregen** to offend, to shock; **— nehmen** to take offense; **ohne —** fluently; without delay; **Stein des —es** stumbling block

anstossen *v.* to bump (*oder* knock) against; to nudge; to stammer; to clink (glasses); to adjoin, to border on; **—d** *adj.* adjacent

anstössig *adj.* improper, obnoxious, offensive

anstreichen *v.* to score; to paint; **jemand etwas —** to make someone pay for something; **weiss —** to whitewash

Anstreicher *m.* house painter

anstrengen *v.* to exert, to strain; **Prozess —** to bring action against

Anstrich *m.* paint; color; appearance; tinge

anstürmen *v.* to assail, to rush headlong

Anteil *m.* portion; share; **— nehmen** to sympathize (with), to take an interest (in)

Antenne *f.* aerial; antenna

Antike *f.* antiquity

Antiquar *m.* dealer in antiques (*oder* secondhand books)

Antlitz *neu.* face; countenance

Anton *m.* Anthony

Antrag *m.* proposal, proposition; motion; **einen — stellen** to make a motion

antreten *v.* to start, to take possession of

Antrieb *m.* impulse; impetus, stimulus; incentive, motive; drive, propulsion

Antriebsrakete *f.* booster rocket

Antritt *m.* accession; **—srede** inaugural address

antun *v.* to put on; to do, to inflict; to harm; **es einem —** to bewitch someone

Antwerpen *neu.* Antwerp

Antwort *f.* answer, reply

antworten *v.* to answer, to reply

anvertrauen *v.* to confide in, to entrust with

anverwandt *adj.* related to

anwachsen *v.* to grow on (to); to take root; to rise, to swell; to augment, to increase

Anwalt *m.* attorney; counsel

Anwandlung *f.* attack, fit; touch (of pity)

anweisen *v.* to direct; to instruct, to assign

Anweisung *f.* direction; instruction; order

anwendbar *adj.* applicable; practicable

anwenden *v.* to apply; to employ, to use

anwerben *v.* to recruit (troops); to enlist

anwerfen *v.* (motor) to start

Anwesen *neu.* estate; **—den** *m. pl.* those present; **—heit** *f.* presence

anwesend *adj.* present

anwidern *v.* to disgust

Anzahl *f.* number; quantity; **—ung** *f.* payment on account

anzapfen *v.* to tap

Anzeichen *neu.* indication, sign, symptom; omen

Anzeige *f.* advertisement; announcement; notice; (law) denunciation

anzeigen *v.* to advertise; to announce; to notify; to inform against, to denounce

anzetteln *v.* to plot, to scheme

anziehen *v.* to draw; to tighten; to absorb; to dress, to put on; to quote; to rise; to approach; to attract, to interest; (chess) to move first; **—d** *adj.* attractive

Anzug *m.* dress; suit; (chess) opening move; **im — sein** to approach; to be imminent; **Raum—** space suit

anzünden *v.* to light; to kindle

Anzünder *m.* lighter

apart *adj.* uncommon, distinctive

apathisch *adj.* apathetic(al)

Apfel *m.* apple; **in den sauren — beissen** to swallow a bitter pill; **—mus** *neu.* applesauce; **—wein** *m.* cider

Apfelsine *f.* orange

Apotheke *f.* pharmacy; **—r** *m.* pharmacist

Apparat *m.* apparatus, appliance; instrument; telephone; (coll.) camera; **am — bleiben** (tel.) to hold the line

Appell *m.* (mil.) roll-call; (fig.) appeal

appellieren *v.* to appeal (to); to move for a new trial

appetitlich *adj.* appetizing; dainty

Aprikose *f.* apricot

Aquarell *neu.* aquarelle, water color painting

Äquator *m.* equator

Ära *f.* era

Arabien *neu.* Arabia

Arbeit *f.* work, job; **—geber** *m.* employer; **—nehmer** *m.* employee; **—samt** *neu.* employment bureau; **—seinstellung** *f.* strike; **—sfeld** *neu.* sphere of action, province; **—slohn** *m.* wages; **—slosenunterstützung** *f.* unemployment compensation; **—slosigkeit** *f.* unemployment; **—ssperre** *f.* lockout; **—szeit** *f.* working hours; **—szeug** *neu.* tools

arbeiten *v.* to work; to make; (agr.) to cultivate

Arbeiter *m.* worker, laborer; **geistiger —**

brainworker; –bund *m.*, –gewerkschaft *f.* labor union; –mangel *m.* labor shortage; –schaft *f.* working class

arbeitsam *adj.* diligent, industrious

arbeitsfähig *adj.* able-bodied

arbeitslos *adj.* unemployed

arbeitsunfähig *adj.* disabled, unfit for work

Arche *f.* ark

Archipel *m.* archipelago

Archiv *neu.* archives, public records; –ar *m.* archivist

arg *adj.* bad, evil; mischievous, severe; (coll.) awful, very; –es Versehen gross mistake; –listig *adj.* crafty, cunning; –los *adj.* harmless, unsuspecting; –willig *adj.* malevolent; –wöhnen *v.* to suspect; –wöhnisch *adj.* suspicious

Argentinien *neu.* Argentine

Ärger *m.* anger; vexation; –nis *neu.* annoyance, vexation; scandalous behavior

ärgerlich *adj.* angry, annoying, provoking

ärgern *v.* to make angry, to vex, to annoy

Arie *f.* (mus.) air, aria

aristokratisch *adj.* aristocratic(al)

arktisch *adj.* arctic

arm *adj.* poor; indigent; needy; piteous; –selig *adj.* beggarly, miserable, wretched

Arm *m.* arm; branch; die –e frei haben to have elbowroom; unter die –e greifen to give assistance; –band *neu.* bracelet; –banduhr *f.* wristwatch; –binde *f.* armband; (med.) sling; –höhle *f.* armpit; –leuchter *m.* chandelier; candlestick; –sessel *m.* armchair, easy chair

Armee *f.* army; –befehl *m.* army order

Ärmel *m.* sleeve; aus dem — schütteln to do easily; –aufschlag *m.* cuff

Ärmelkanal *m.* English Channel

Armen *m. pl.* (the) poor; –anstalt *f.* poorhouse; –viertel *neu.* slum

Armesündergesicht *neu.* hangdog look

ärmlich *adj.* miserable; needy, shabby

Arm- und Beinamputierte *m.* (med.) basket case

Armut *f.* poverty; — schändet nicht poverty is no disgrace; sich ein –szeugnis ausstellen to show one's incapacity

arretieren *v.* to arrest

Art *f.* manner, mode; kind, sort; race, breed; species; way; aus der — schlagen to vary from type; einzig in seiner — unique

Arterie *f.* artery; –nverkalkung *f.* arteriosclerosis

artig *adj.* well-behaved; gallant; pretty

Artikel *m.* article; commodity

Arznei *f.*, **Arzneimittel** *neu.* medicine, drug; –kunde *f.* pharmacology; –ver-

schreibung *f.* prescription

Arzt *m.* physician, doctor

ärztlich *adj.* medical

As *neu.* ace; (mus.) A flat

Asche *f.* ash(es); in — legen to burn down; in — verwandeln to reduce to ashes, to incinerate; –nbecher *m.* ash tray; –nbrödel *neu.* scullion; Cinderella

asch: –fahl *adj.*, –farben *adj.*, –farbig *adj.*, –grau *adj.* ash-colored, ash gray

Aschermittwoch *m.* Ash Wednesday

Asien *neu.* Asia

Ast *m.* branch; –loch *neu.* knothole; –werk *neu.* branches, boughs

ästhetisch *adj.* aesthetic(al)

Astrobiologie *f.* astrobiology

Astrolog *m.* astrologer; –ie *f.* astrology

Astronom *m.* astronomer; –ie *f.* astronomy

Astronaut *m.* astronaut

Astrophysik *f* astrophysics

Asvl *neu.* asylum, refuge, shelter

Atelier *neu.* studio

Atem *m.* breath; — anhalten to hold one's breath; — holen to breathe; bis zum letzten –zug to one's last breath

Äther *m.* ether; celestial space; mit — betäuben to put under ether, to etherize

ätherisch *adj.* ethereal; (rad.) etheric(al)

Äthyl *neu.* (chem.) ethyl

Atlas *m.* atlas; (fabric) satin

atmen *v.* to breathe

Atmungsapparat *m.* resuscitator

Atom *neu.* (phys.) atom; –bombe *f.* atom(ic) bomb, A-bomb; –gewicht *neu.* atomic weight; –kern *m.* nucleus; –krieg *m.* atomic war; nuclear war; –säule *f.* atomic pile; –zertrümmerer *m.* atom smasher

atomisch *adj.* atomic(al)

atomisieren *v.* to atomize

Attentat *neu.* assault, assassination

Attrappe *f.* mock-up

auch *conj.* also, too; likewise; even; — nicht einer not a single one

Audionröhre *f.* detector tube

auf *prep.* on, upon; at; in; for; to, towards; — *adv.* up, upwards; aloft; alle bis — einen all but one; — Dein Wohl here's to you; — dem Meere at sea; — dem nächsten Wege by the nearest way; — der Stelle on the spot; — der Strasse on the street; — Deutsch in German; — einen Augenblick for a moment; — einmal suddenly; — Erden on earth; — jeden Fall in any case; — meine Bitte at my request; — und davon laufen to run away, to make off; es geht — neun it is getting on to nine; von klein — from childhood on

aufarbeiten *v.* to work open; to use up; to finish; to refurbish

aufatmen *v.* to breathe again; to feel relieved

aufbahren *v.* to put on the bier

Aufbahrung *f.* lying in state

Aufbau *m.* erection; construction; plot

aufbäumen *v.* to rear, to prance; to rebel

aufbekommen *v.* to get open; (educ.) to be assigned; to eat up

aufbessern *v.* to mend; to improve; to raise

aufbewahren *v.* to keep; to preserve; to store

aufbieten *v.* to cite, to summon; to publish (banns); (mil.) to call up; alles — to make every possible effort

aufbinden *v.* to untie; to tie on; to impose on; er lässt sich alles — he swallows everything; jemand einen Bären — to hoax someone

aufblähen *v.* to swell, to puff up; to inflate

aufblasen *v.* to inflate; to raise (dust)

aufbleiben *v.* to remain open; spät — to stay up late

aufblicken *v.* to look up; to raise the eyes

aufblühen *v.* to begin to blossom; to flourish

aufbrauchen *v.* to use up; to consume

aufbrausen *v.* to bubble up, to effervesce; to roar; to flare up

aufbrechen *v.* to break (*oder* burst) open; to crack; to depart, to set out

aufbringen *v.* to get open; to rear; to raise; to provoke, to irritate

Aufbruch *m.* break-up, departure

aufdecken *v.* to uncover; to disclose; (cards) to show one's hand

aufdrängen *v.* to push open; to obtrude upon

aufdrehen *v.* to unravel; to unscrew; to wind up; to turn on

aufdringlich *adj.* importunate; obtrusive

aufdrücken *v.* to press on (*oder* open)

aufeinander *adv.* one upon (*oder* after) another; successively

Aufeinanderfolge *f.* succession; series

Aufenthalt *m.* sojourn, residence; delay, stop

auferlegen *v.* to inflict; to impose; to enjoin

Auferstehung *f.* resurrection

auffädeln *v.* to thread, to string

auffahren *v.* to ascend, to rise; to jump up; to flare up; to run aground

Auffahrt *f.* ascent; ramp

auffallend, auffällig *adj.* striking, remarkable; conspicuous, showy

auffangen *v.* to catch; to intercept; to parry

auffassen *v.* to catch; to apprehend; falsch — to misconceive; leicht — to be quick-witted

Auffassung *f.* comprehension; conception, view; interpretation; -sgabe *f.* perceptive faculty

auffliegen *v.* to fly up (*oder* open); to explode

auffordern *v.* to call upon; to demand; to invite; to challenge, to summon

auffrischen *v.* to freshen up; to revive; to renew; (art) to touch up; (coll.) to brush up on

aufführen *v.* to erect; to behave; (theat.) to act, to perform; einzeln — to itemize

Aufgabe *f.* duty, task; problem; resignation; posting; -schein *m.* receipt of delivery

Aufgang *m.* ascent; stairs; (sun) rising

aufgeben *v.* to give up, to abandon; to resign; to post; to set (task)

Aufgebot *neu.* public notice; banns of marriage; levy; mit — aller Kräfte with might and main

aufgebracht *adj.* angry, furious

aufgeh(e)n *v.* to come up; to open; to get loose; to rise; to break up; to take root; to be spent; (math.) to leave no remainder; -in to be absorbed in; die Augen gehen mir auf it dawns on me

aufgeklärt *adj.* enlightened

aufgeknöpft *adj.* unbuttoned; (coll.) approachable

aufgeräumt *adj.* high-spirited

aufgeweckt *adj.* awake; alert, intelligent

aufgiessen *v.* to pour upon; to infuse; Tee — to make tea

aufgreifen *v.* to catch; to snatch up

aufhaben *v.* to have open, to wear (hat); wir haben zuviel auf we have too much homework

aufhalten *v.* to hold open; to stop; to delay, to retard; den Strom — to stem the tide; sich — to stay; to find fault; sich unnütz — to waste one's time

aufhängen *v.* to hang up; jemandem etwas — (coll.) to play a trick on someone

aufhäufen *v.* to heap up; to accumulate

aufheben *v.* to lift, to pick up; to preserve; to annul; to cancel; die Tafel — to rise from the table; ein Urteil — to quash a sentence; eine Belagerung — to raise a siege; eine Sitzung — to adjourn a meeting; eine Verlobung — to break an engagement to marry; Handelsgenossenschaft — to dissolve partnership; gut aufgehoben well taken care of

aufheitern *v.* to cheer up; to clear up

aufhelfen *v.* to help up; to aid

aufhellen *v.* to brighten, to clear up

aufhören *v.* to cease, to stop; to discontinue; **da hört sich alles auf!** that's the limit!

aufkaufen *v.* to buy up, to forestall

aufklappen *v.* to open

aufklären *v.* to clear up; to clarify; (mil.) to reconnoiter; to enlighten; to solve (mystery)

Aufklärungsflug *m.* reconnaissance flight

aufkommen *v.* to come (*oder* get) up; to approach; to rise; (med.) to recover; **— für** to be responsible for; **nicht — gegen** to be no match for

aufkündigen *v.* to give notice; to retract; to renounce; **Freundschaft —** to break (*oder* sever) friendship; **Gehorsam — to** refuse obedience; **Hypothek —** to call in a mortgage

aufladen *v.* to load; to charge; **sich Verantwortung —** to take responsibility

Auflage *f.* edition; duty, tax

auflassen *v.* to let rise; to leave open

auflauern *v.* to lie in wait (*oder* ambush)

Auflauf *m.* mob; commotion; riot; soufflé

aufleben *v.* to revive

auflegen *v.* to lay on, to apply; to publish; to inflict; **gut aufgelegt** in a good mood; **Karten —** to spread one's cards

auflehnen *v.* to lean against; **sich —** to rebel

auflesen *v.* to pick up, to gather; to glean

aufliegen *v.* to lie (*oder* lean) on; to be on show; to be exposed; to develop bedsores

auflockern *v.* to loosen

auflösbar *adj.* (dis)soluble; solvable

auflösen *v.* to loosen; to undo; to analyze; to dissolve; to solve; to disband

Auflösung *f.* (dis)solution; dispersal; (mil.) disbandment; **-szeichen** *neu.* (mus.) natural

aufmachen *v.* to open; to undo; to set out

aufmerken *v.* to pay attention to; to heed

aufmerksam *adj.* attentive; polite

aufmuntern *v.* to cheer up; to encourage

Aufnahme *f.* admission, enrollment; reception; photograph; **— von Geld** loaning

aufnehmen *v.* to take up; to receive; to admit; to take (picture); to absorb; (law) to draw up; (geog.) to map out; **als Beleidigung** (*or* **Scherz**) **—** to take as an insult (*oder* joke); **Arbeit wieder —** to resume work; **es — mit** to cope with; **Geld —** to borrow money

aufopfern *v.* to sacrifice; to devote

aufpassen *v.* to adapt; to be attentive, **to** watch

aufpeitschen *v.* to whip up; to stimulate

aufpflanzen *v.* to fix (*oder* set) up; to plant

aufprallen *v.* to bounce against, to rebound

aufputzen *v.* to polish; (coll.) to spruce up

aufraffen *v.* to snatch up; **sich — to** pull oneself together; (med.) to recover from

aufragen *v.* to tower up, to stand up

aufräumen *v.* to clear away; to tidy up; to set in order; (coll.) to make a clean sweep of

aufrecht *adj.* erect, upright; **-erhalten** *v.* to keep up, to maintain, to preserve

aufregen *v.* to excite; to arouse

Aufregung *f.* excitement, agitation

aufreiben *v.* to rub open; to chafe; (mil.) to annihilate; **sich —** to wear oneself out

aufreissen *v.* to burst (*oder* tear) open; to open wide, **den Mund —** to gape; **eine alte Wunde —** to reopen old sores

aufreizen *v.* to incite, to provoke, **to stir up**

aufrichten *v.* to raise, to set up; to comfort; to erect; **sich —** to sit upright; **sich wieder —** to recover from

aufrichtig *adj.* frank, sincere; candid

Aufriss *m.* draft, sketch; (arch.) elevation

aufrollen *v.* to roll up; to coil; to unroll; to raise (curtain); to broach (question**)**

Aufruf *m.* call; proclamation; (law) appeal, summons

aufrufen *v.* to call up (*oder* upon); **namentlich —** (mil.) to call the roll

Aufruhr *m.* rebellion, insurrection, mutiny, riot; uproar; **in hellem —** in open revolt

aufführen *v.* to stir up; to inflame; **alte Geschichten wieder —** to rake up old grievances; **Erinnerungen —** to revive memories

Aufrührer *m.* insurgent, mutineer, rebel, rioter; agitator

Aufrüstung *f.* rearmament

aufrütteln *v.* to shake; to rouse

aufsagen *v.* to recite; **Dienst —** to give notice to quit a position (*oder* job)

aufsässig *adj.* hostile; rebellious

Aufsatz *m.* composition, essay, **article;** treatise; centerpiece, head-piece, **crest**

aufsaugen *v.* to absorb, to suck up

aufscheuchen *v.* to scare up, to startle

aufschieben *v.* to push open; to defer, **to** postpone; to adjourn

Aufschlag *m.* bounce; (cloth) facing, **revers;** (price) advance; (tennis) service; **-geschwindigkeit** *f.* impact velocity

aufschlagen *v.* to break open; to bounce, to rebound; to open (eyes, books); to advance (prices); to pitch (tent); (ten-

nis) to serve
Aufschluss *m.* disclosure, explanation; —
geben to throw light on; — erbitten to
ask for full particulars
aufschneiden *v.* to cut open, to carve; to
boast, to brag; to exaggerate
Aufschneider *m.* boaster, braggart
Aufschnitt *m.* (act of) cutting open;
(med.) incision; **kalter** — cold cut
(meat)
aufschrecken *v.* to startle; to frighten
Aufschrei *m.* scream, shriek; outcry
aufschreiben *v.* to write down; (cards) to
score; (com.) to enter, to charge
Aufschrift *f.* address; inscription; epitaph
Aufschub *m.* delay, deferment; postponement
aufschwatzen *v.* jemand etwas — to talk
a person into a thing
Aufschwung *m.* upswing; soaring; progress; prosperity; **plötzlicher** — (com.)
boom
Aufsehen *neu.* surprise; scandal, sensation; **wenig** — machen to attract little
attention
Aufseher *m.* custodian; foreman, inspector
aufsetzen *v.* to put on, to set up; to draw
up; to make out (account); **seinen
Kopf** — to be obstinate
Aufsicht *f.* supervision; guardianship;
custody; **-srat** *m.* board of directors
aufsitzen *v.* to sit up(on); to mount
(horse)
aufspannen *v.* to stretch; to mount; to
open (umbrella); to spread (sails);
(mus.) to string
aufsperren *v.* to unlock; to open wide
aufspielen *v.* to strike up (tune); **sich** —
to pose as, to swagger, to put on airs
aufspiessen *v.* to impale; to gore
aufspringen *v.* to jump up; to chap, to
crack
aufspüren *v.* to trace, to track down
aufstacheln *v.* to goad; to spur on; to
incite
Aufstand *m.* insurrection, rebellion; uproar
aufstechen *v.* to prick open; (med.) to
lance
aufstecken *v.* to stick on; to pin up;
jemand ein Licht — to enlighten a
person
aufstehen *v.* to get up; to arise; to stand
open; — **gegen** to rebel
aufsteigen *v.* to ascend; to rise; to climb
aufstellen *v.* to set up; to expose; to
erect; (pol.) to nominate; (mil.) to
activate
Aufstieg *m.* ascent; rise

Aufstiegmessgerät *n.* (avi.) climb indicator
aufstossen *v.* to push open; to belch
aufstreichen *v.* to spread on; (mus.) **to**
start to play
aufsuchen *v.* to seek for; to look up, **to**
visit
auftauchen *v.* to emerge, to appear suddenly
auftauen *v.* to thaw; to become communicative
auftischen *v.* to serve up; to regale with;
alte Geschichten — to warm up old
tales
Auftrag *m.* commission; charge, mission,
order; **im** — **von** by order of, in behalf
of; **-geber** *m.* consignor; employer;
customer
auftragen *v.* to serve up; to commission;
to wear out; **dick** — to lay it on thick,
to exaggerate
auftreiben *v.* to drive upward; to rouse
(game); to obtain with difficulty;
(med.) to distend
auftrennen *v.* to ravel out
auftreten *v.* to appear; to behave; **to open**
by stepping on
Auftritt *m.* appearance; (theat.) scene
auftrumpfen *v.* to stamp; to trump
auftun *v.* to open; to disclose
auftürmen *v.* to pile up, to rise aloft
aufwachen *v.* to awake, to wake up
aufwachsen *v.* to grow up
aufwärmen *v.* to warm up; (coll.) **to re-**
hash
aufwarten *v.* to wait on; to serve; **to visit**
Aufwärterin *f.* waitress, stewardess
aufwärts *adv.* upwards; uphill
aufwecken *v.* to rouse, to wake up
aufweichen *v.* to soften; to soak
aufweisen *v.* to exhibit; to show
aufwenden *v.* to spend upon
aufwerfen *v.* to throw open (*oder* up);
aufgeworfene Lippe pouting lip; **aufgeworfene Nase** turned-up nose
aufwiegeln *v.* to incite, to stir up
aufwiegen *v.* to counterbalance; **to com-**
pensate
aufwieglerisch *adj.* inflammatory, sedi-
tious
aufwinden *v.* to reel; to hoist (with windlass); to untwist; to weigh (anchor)
aufwirbeln *v.* to whirl up; **Staub** — **to**
raise dust; to make a great stir
aufwühlen *v.* to root (*oder* stir) up; to
agitate
aufzählen *v.* to count up; to enumerate
aufzäumen *v.* to bridle
aufzehren *v.* to consume; to use up
aufzeichnen *v.* to note down; to sketch;
to record

aufziehen v. to pull up (*oder* open); to
wind up (watch); to stretch on; to
approach; to string; to rear; to cultivate, to breed; (coll.) to tease; **andere
Seiten —** to adopt a different tone
Aufzug m. attire; pageant; parade; crane;
elevator; (theat.) act
Augapfel m. eyeball; (poet.) darling
Auge neu. eye; (bot.) bud; (cards) spot;
sight; **aus den –n verlieren** to lose sight
of; **ein — zudrücken** to connive; **ganz
— sein** to be all eyes; **im — behalten**
to keep in mind; **kein — zutun** to sleep
not a wink; **mit blossem —** with the
naked eye; **unter seinen –n** under his
very eyes; **unter vier –n** privately;
–narzt m. ophthalmologist; **–nblick** m.
moment; **–nbraue** f. eyebrow; **–nhöhle**
f. eye socket; **–nlicht** neu. eyesight;
–nmass neu. sense of proportion;
–nmerk neu. attention; **–nschein** m. appearance; **in –nschein nehmen** to inspect; **–nspezialist** m. oculist, ophthalmologist; **–nspiegel** m. ophthalmoscope;
–ntäuschung f. optical illusion; **–nweide**
f. eye-catcher; **–nwimper** f. eyelash;
–nzeuge m. eyewitness
augen: –blicklich adj. instantaneous;
momentary, at present; **–fällig** adj.,
–scheinlich adj. apparent, evident, obvious
Aula f. auditorium
aus prep. by, for, from, of, out of; in, on,
on account of, upon; **—** adv. over, finished; **— dem Kopfe** by heart; **— freier
Wahl** by free choice; **— Furcht vor** for
fear of; **— Gold** made of gold; **— Neugier** out of curiosity; **— Unwissenheit**
through sheer ignorance; **die Kirche ist
— church** is over; **mit ihm ist es —** he
is done for; **von mir —** for my part
ausarbeiten v. to work out; to elaborate
ausarten v. to degenerate; (mil.) to escalate
ausatmen v. to exhale
Ausbau m. extension; completion
ausbauen v. to complete, to develop; to
enlarge
ausbedingen v. to stipulate; to reserve
(right)
ausbessern v. to mend, to repair; to correct
Ausbeut: –e f. gain; profit, yield; **–ungs-
vergütung** f. depletion allowance; **–en** v.
to exploit; to take advantage of
ausbieten v. to offer for sale; to bid
ausbilden v. to educate; to develop; to
drill, to train; **sich —** to improve one's
mind (skills)
ausbitten v. **sich —** to ask for; to insist

ausblasen v. to blow out; **das Lebenslicht
—** to kill
ausbleiben v. to stay away; to fail to
appear (*oder* take place)
Ausblick m. outlook, view; prospect
ausbrechen v. to break out; to escape;
(med.) to vomit; **in Lachen —** to burst
out laughing
ausbreiten v. to spread; to extend; (mil.)
to escalate; to display; to disseminate;
to promulgate; to propagate
ausbrennen v. to burn out; (med.) to
cauterize
ausbringen v. to bring out, to get off;
(naut.) to hoist out; **Gesundheit —** to
toast
Ausbruch m. outburst; eruption; escape
ausbrüten v. to hatch out; to brood on;
to plot
ausdauern v. to hold out; to persevere
ausdehnen v. to expand, to extend; to
stretch
ausdenken v. to think through; to contrive; to devise; **sich etwas —** to imagine; to invent
ausdrehen v. to switch (*oder* turn) off
Ausdruck m. expression; phrase, term
ausdrücken v. to press (*oder* squeeze) out;
to express; **sich klar —** to speak clearly;
sich kurz — to be brief
ausdrücklich adj. explicit; strict
ausdruckslos adj. inexpressive, blank
ausdrucksvoll adj. expressive
ausdunsten, ausdünsten v. to sweat out,
to exhale; to evaporate
auseinander adv. apart, separately; **–bringen** v. to separate; **–fliegen** v. to fly in
different directions; **–gehen** v. to part
company, to disband, to diverge;
–halten v. to keep separate, to distinguish; **–nehmen** v. to take to pieces, to
dismount; **–setzen** v. to set apart; to
explain; to analyse; to discuss
auser: –koren adj. selected, elect; **–lesen**
adj. choice, exquisite; **–sehen** v. to
choose, to select; **–wählen** v. to single
out, to destine
ausfahren v. to go (*oder* take, drive) out;
(min.) to ascend; (naut.) to put to sea
Ausfahrt f. drive, excursion; gateway
ausfallen v. to fall out; to be deducted
(*oder* omitted); (mil.) to attack, to
make a sally; to fail to take place; **gut
—** to turn out well; **–d** adj. aggressive;
insulting
ausfertigen v. to draw up, to make out;
to issue
Ausfertigung f. execution; issue; **in
zweifacher —** in duplicate
ausfinden, ausfindig machen v. to find

out, to discover

ausfliegen v. to fly out; to leave home; to make a trip; to escape

ausfliessen v. to flow out; to emanate

Ausflucht f. loophole; excuse; evasion; pretext

Ausflug m. excursion, outing

Ausflügler m. excursionist; hiker

ausforschen v. to investigate, to inquire into; to sound out

ausfragen v. to quiz; to question closely; (coll.) to pump

ausfressen v. to corrode; (coll.) to eat up; to make mischief

Ausfuhr f. export

ausführ: -bar adj. exportable; feasible, practicable; -en v. to lead out; to export; to execute; to perform; to finish; to explain; -lich adj. detailed, full

Ausführung f. execution, performance; statement

ausfüllen v. to fill up (oder in); to pad

Ausgabe f. expenditure, expense; outlay; edition, issue; delivery

Ausgang m. going out; outlet; exit; result, upshot; day off; -spunkt m. starting point

ausgeben v. to give out; to issue; to spend; (cards) to deal; to distribute; sich — für to pretend to be

ausgeh(e)n v. to go out; to come (oder fall) out; to fade; to run short; to end, to terminate; — auf to aim at; leer — to get nothing, to be left out in the cold

ausgelassen adj. exuberant, frolicsome

ausgemacht adj. agreed on; settled; ein -er Gauner a complete scoundrel; eine -e Sache an established fact

ausgenommen adv. except, save; with the exception of; niemand — bar none

ausgeprägt adj. pronounced, distinctive

ausgerechnet adv. precisely; that very

ausgeschlossen adj. locked out; excluded; impossible; out of the question

ausgeschnitten adj. cut out; low-necked (dress)

ausgesprochen adj. pronounced; decided, marked; — adv. especially

ausgestalten v. to shape; to develop; to arrange; to elaborate

ausgesucht adj. choice, select, exquisite

ausgezeichnet adj. excellent; distinguished

ausgiebig adj. abundant; plentiful; rich

ausgiessen v. to pour out; to vent; to diffuse

Ausgleich m. agreement; settlement; compromise; equalization; (com.) balance; (tennis) deuce

ausgleichen v. to equalize; to compromise,

to settle; to compensate; to balance; sich — mit to become reconciled with

ausgleiten, ausglitschen v. to slip, to slide

ausgraben v. to dig out; to excavate; to disinter; Leiche — to exhume

ausgreifen v. to take long strides; -d adj. far-reaching

Ausguck m. lookout; watch

Ausguss m. outpouring; gutter; sink; spout

aushalten v. to hold out, to last, to bear, to endure; nicht zum — beyond endurance

aushändigen v. to hand over; to deliver up

Aushang m. display; placard; notice

aushängen v. to hang out; to unhinge; to post

Aushängeschild neu. signboard; best product; pretense

ausharren v. to hold out; to persevere

aushauchen v. to exhale; die Seele — to expire, to die

aushauen v. to hew out; to excavate; to carve out; to thin (forest); to flog

ausheben v. to lift out; to unhinge; (mil.) to draft; (police) to raid; sich die Schulter — to dislocate one's shoulder

aushecken v. to hatch; to concoct, to plot

ausheilen v. to heal up; to cure completely

Aushilfe f. temporary aid; stopgap

aushöhlen v. to hollow out; to excavate

ausholen v. to raise the arm (for striking, throwing); to sound out; to spar; weit — to be circumstantial; zum Sprung — to take a running start to jump

aushorchen v. to sound out; to pump

aushungern v. to famish, to starve out

aushusten v. to expectorate

auskennen v. sich — to be well qualified; to know what's what; sich nicht — to be at wit's end

auskleiden v. to undress; to line, to coat

Auskleideakt m. striptease

ausklopfen v. to beat out, to dust

ausklügeln v. to puzzle out

auskneifen v. (coll.) to slip off; to run away

auskochen v. to extract by boiling; to scald; (coll.) to plot

auskommen v. to come (oder break) out; to escape; to manage with; to become public; gut (or schlecht) — to be on good (oder poor) terms

Auskommen neu. livelihood; subsistence; es ist kein — mit ihm nobody can get along with him

auskosten v. to taste thoroughly; to enjoy.

auskratzen v. to scratch (oder scrape) out; (coll.) to run off; (med.) to curette

auskundschaften v. to explore; (mil.) to

reconnoiter; (coll.) to discover, to spy out

Auskunft f. information; **-sbüro** neu., **-sstelle** f. information office; **nähere —** particulars

auskuppeln v. to throw out of gear

auslachen v. to laugh at

ausladen v. to unload; to lighten (ship); to disembark; (arch.) to project; **-de Geste** sweeping gesture

Auslage f. (com.) advance; disbursement, outlay; (show window) display

Ausland neu. foreign country; **im Inland und —** at home and abroad

Ausländer m. foreigner, alien

ausländisch adj. foreign, alien; outlandish

auslassen v. to let (oder leave) out; to omit; (cooking) to render; **sich —** to explain oneself; to give vent to

auslaufen v. to run (oder set) out; to end; to diverge; to clear (oder leave) port; to leak

Ausläufer m. errand boy; (bot.) runner, sucker; (geol.) spur; (fig.) branch

ausleeren v. to empty; to drink up; to clear out; to drain; (med.) to purge

auslegen v. to lay (oder spread) out; to display, to expose for sale; to advance, to pay; to inlay, to tile; to expound, to interpret

ausleihen v. to lend out, to loan; **sich etwas —** to borrow something from

auslernen v. to finish learning (oder studying)

Auslese f. selection; choice wine

auslesen v. to choose, to select; to sort; to pick out, to cull; to finish reading

ausliefern v. to hand over; to deliver up; to give up; to surrender, to extradite

auslöffeln v. to spoon (oder ladle) out; **etwas —** to pay for one's mistake

auslosen v. to draw lots for; to raffle

auslöschen v. to put (oder blot) out, to extinguish, to erase

auslösen v. to loosen; to ransom; to cause

Auslöser m. (phot.) release, trigger

ausmachen v. to constitute, to make up; to extinguish; to take out; to husk, to shell; to agree on, to decide, to settle; **nichts —** it does not matter

ausmalen v. to paint; to color, to emblazon, to illuminate; to imagine (in detail)

Ausmass neu. degree, extent

ausmerzen v. to eliminate; to expurgate

ausmessen v. to measure, to survey

ausmisten v. (agr.) to clear of manure; to clean up a mess

Ausnahme f. exception; **-fall** m. exceptional case; **-zustand** m. state of emer-

gency

ausnahmsweise adv. exceptionally

ausnehmen v. to take out; to draw (fowl); to exempt; to except; **sich gut —** to look well; **-d** adj. exceptional; **-d** adv. exceedingly

ausnutzen, ausnützen v. to wear out, to utilize; to make the most of; to exploit

auspfeifen v. to hiss; to catcall, to condemn

ausplaudern v. to divulge, to blab

ausprägen v. to coin, to impress

auspressen, ausquetschen v. to squeeze out; to extort

ausprob(ier)en v. to test, to try; to taste

Auspuff m. exhaust; **-klappe** f. exhaust valve; **-rohr** neu. exhaust pipe; **-topf** m. muffler

auspumpen v. to pump out (oder dry); to exhaust; to produce a vacuum

ausquartieren v. to dislodge; to quarter out

ausradieren v. to erase

ausräuchern v. to smoke out; to fumigate

ausräumen v. to clear away, to empty

ausrechnen v. to calculate, to compute; **falsch —** to miscalculate

Ausrede f. excuse, pretext; evasion; **faule —** bad excuse

ausreden v. to finish speaking; to speak freely; to dissuade, to argue (oder talk) out of; to exculpate; (coll.) to wriggle out of

ausreichen v. to suffice; **-d** adj. sufficient

Ausreise f. departure; journey abroad

ausreissen v. to tear out; to pull up; to burst; (coll.) to bolt, to desert

ausrenken v. to dislocate

ausrichten v. to straighten out; to execute; to accomplish, to perform; **Grüsse — to** give regards to; **nichts —** to fail

ausringen v. to wring out; **er hat ausgerungen** his struggles are over; **he is dead**

ausroden v. to root out; to grub up; to clear

ausrotten v. to eradicate, to exterminate

ausrücken v. to march off; to decamp; to throw out of gear

Ausruf m. outcry, shout; exclamation; proclamation; **-ungszeichen** neu. exclamation mark

ausrufen v. to call (oder cry) out; to ejaculate, to exclaim; to proclaim

ausruhen v. to rest; to repose; to relax

ausrüsten v. to equip, to fit out; to endow

ausrutschen v. to slide, to slip, to skid

aussäen v. to sow; to disseminate

Aussage f. assertion, declaration, statement; (law) deposition; (gram.) predicate

aussagen *v.* to state, to give evidence

Aussatz *m.* leprosy, Hansen's disease

Aussätzige *m.* leper

aussaugen *v.* to suck dry (*oder* out); to drain, to exhaust; to bleed; to impoverish

ausschachten *v.* to deepen, to excavate, to sink

ausschalten *v.* to switch off; to disconnect; to eliminate, to remove

Ausschank *m.* retailing of liquor; bar, tavern

Ausschau *f.* lookout; — **halten** to watch for

ausscheiden *v.* to separate; to resign; to eliminate; to excrete, to secrete

ausschelten *v.* to scold, to abuse

ausschenken *v.* to pour out; to retail liquor

ausschiffen *v.* to put to sea, to set sail; to land, to disembark; to unload; to discharge

ausschimpfen *v.* to revile, to cuss out

ausschlachten *v.* to cut up (for sale); (fig.) to broaden

auschlafen *v.* to sleep amply; **Rausch** — to sober up

Ausschlag *m.* (mech.) amplitude, deflection; (med.) eruption, rash; (fig.) issue (of events), **einer Sache den** — **geben** to clinch the matter

ausschlagen *v.* to beat (*oder* thrash) soundly; to knock out; to trim, to line; (bot.) to bud, to sprout; (mech.) to deflect, to turn; (med.) to erupt; (fig.) to decline, to refuse

ausschliessen *v.* to lock out; to exclude; to disqualify

ausschliesslich *adj.* exclusive

Ausschluss *m.* exclusion; disqualification; (typ.) justification; **mit** (*or* **unter**) — **der Öffentlichkeit** behind closed doors

ausschmücken *v.* to adorn, to decorate; to embellish; (coll.) to deck out

Ausschnitt *m.* cut(ting) out; clipping; (arch.) bay; (dress) low neck; (math.) sector

ausschöpfen *v.* to bail, to scoop; to exhaust

ausschreiben *v.* to write out; to copy; to announce, to proclaim, to advertise; (tax) to impose

ausschreien *v.* to shout out; to proclaim; **sich die Kehle** — to strain one's voice

ausschreiten *v.* to step out; to go too far

Ausschuss *m.* board, committee; refuse; wastepaper; **–sitzung** *f.* committee meeting; **–waren** *f. pl.* damaged goods, remnants

ausschütten *v.* to pout out; **Dividende** — to distribute dividends; **sich vor Lachen** — to split one's sides with laughing

ausschweifen *v.* to digress, to ramble; **to** lead a dissolute life; **–d** *adj.* dissolute

ausschwitzen *v.* to exude; to sweat out

aussehen *v.* to appear; to look out; **gesund** — to look well; **nach Regen** — to look like rain

Aussehen *neu.* appearance, aspect, look

aussen *adv.* outside; out-of-doors; **nach** — outward; **von** — **betrachten** to judge from the outside

Aussen: –bordmotor *m.* outboard motor; **–dienst** *m.* foreign (*oder* outdoor) service; **–handel** *m.* export trade, **–minister** *m.* Minister for Foreign Affairs; **–politik** *f.* foreign policy; **–seite** *f.* outside; surface; **–seiter** *m.* outsider; **–stände** *m. pl.* outstanding claims; **–welt** *f.* external (*oder* visible) world

ausser *prep.* beside(s), outside of; out of; beyond; except; — **acht lassen** to neglect, to overlook; — **sich sein** to be beside oneself; — **Bereich** beyond reach; — **der Zeit** out of season, at the wrong time; — **Dienst** off duty; out of employment; — **Frage** beyond all doubt; — **Kurs setzen** to withdraw from circulation; — **Landes gehen** to go abroad; — *conj.* but, except, save, unless; — **dass** except that; **–amtlich** *adj.*, **–dienstlich** *adj.* unofficial, private; **–dem** *adv.* moreover; **–ehelich** *adj.* illegitimate; **–gerichtlich** *adj.* extrajudicial; **–gesetzlich** *adj.* unlawful; **–gewöhnlich** *adj.* extraordinary, unusual; **–halb** *prep.* outside; **–ordentlich** *adj.* extraordinary, amazing; **–stande** *adv.* unable (to)

äusser: –e *adj.* outer, outward; external, exterior; **–lich** *adj.* external; superficial; **–n** to manifest, to show; to express, to utter; **–st** *adv.* extremely, exceedingly; **–ste** *adj.* outermost, ut(ter)most

Aussicht *f.* view; prospect; expectation

aussichtslos *adj.* hopeless; without prospects

aussöhnen *v.* to reconcile

aussondern, aussortieren *v.* to select, to single out; to sort out; to cull

ausspannen *v.* to unharness; to extend, to stretch; to relax, to rest

aussperren *v.* to lock (*oder* shut) out; (typ.) to space out

ausspielen *v.* to play to the end; to play for (prize); (cards) to lead; **einen gegen den andern** — to play off one against the other

ausspionieren *v.* to ferret (*oder* spy) out

Aussprache *f.* pronunciation; articulation; brogue, accent; discussion, talk

aussprechen *v.* to finish speaking; to pronounce; to articulate; to declare; to express; Urteil — to pass a sentence

Australien *neu.* Australia

Ausspruch *m.* utterance; remark; (law) decision, finding, sentence, verdict

ausspülen *v.* to rinse out; to wash away

ausspüren *v.* to trace; to track down

ausstaffieren *v.* to equip, to fit out; to trim

Ausstand *m.* outstanding debt; strike

ausständig *adj.* outstanding (debt); in arrears; on strike

ausstatten *v.* to equip, to fit out; to establish, to set up; to give (dowry); to endow

aussteh(e)n *v.* to be exposed (for sale); to stand out; to bear, to endure; **nicht —**
können to be unable to stand

aussteigen *v.* to get out, to alight from; (naut.) to land; (rail.) to leave (train)

ausstellen *v.* to exhibit; to display; — an to find fault with; to issue

Ausstellung *f.* exhibition, show; **–en**
machen to raise objections, to find fault

aussterben *v.* to die out, to become extinct (*oder* desolate)

Aussteuer *f.* dowry; trousseau; endowment

ausstopfen *v.* to stuff; to pad, to wad

ausstossen *v.* to push out; to expel; to eject, to oust; to banish, to excommunicate; (gram.) to drop, to elide; (med.) to excrete; Fluch — to swear; Schrei — to scream, to yell; Worte — to ejaculate, to utter

ausstrahlen *v.* to radiate, to emit rays

ausstreichen *v.* to cross (*oder* strike) out; to cancel; to smooth out; to obliterate

ausstreuen *v.* to scatter, to disseminate; to circulate

ausströmen *v.* to flow, to stream forth; (phys.) to emanate, to escape

aussuchen *v.* to pick out, to select

austauschen *v.* to barter, to exchange

austeilen *v.* to dole out; to distribute; to allot; (eccl.) to administer; Befehle — to give orders

Auster *f.* oyster; **–nbank** *f.* oyster bed; **–nfang** *m.* oyster catching (*oder* dredging)

austilgen *v.* to obliterate; to exterminate; to eradicate; to wipe out (guilt, debt)

austoben *v.* sich — to sow one's wild oats; to cease raging; Jugend muss sich — youth must have its fling

austreiben *v.* to drive out; to eject; to dislodge; to evict; to cast out, to ex-

orcise

austreten *v.* to step out; to withdraw; to resign; to wear out by treading; (mil.) to fall out; to overflow; to go to the toilet

austrinken *v.* to drink up, to empty

Austritt *m.* resignation, withdrawal; inundation, overflow; emergence

ausüben *v.* to exercise (authority); to practice; to commit (crime)

Ausverkauf *m.* clearance sale

ausverkaufen *v.* to sell out; to clear of stock

Auswahl *f.* selection; assortment; anthology

auswählen *v.* to choose, to select; to pick out

auswandern *v.* to emigrate

auswärtig *adj.* foreign; abroad

auswärts *adv.* outward(s); outside of

auswechseln *v.* to change for; to exchange

Ausweg *m.* way out; evasion, loophole; keinen — mehr wissen to be at wits' end

ausweichen *v.* to make way for, to turn aside; to evade, to elude

ausweinen *v.* to have a good cry; sich die Augen — to cry one's eyes out

Ausweis *m.* proof of identity; certification

ausweisen *v.* to expel, to deport; to show, to prove; sich — to identify oneself

ausweiten *v.* to widen, to stretch; to scoop out

auswendig *adj.* outward, external; by heart

auswerfen *v.* to throw out (*oder* overboard); to eject; to vomit; to allow, to grant

auswerten *v.* to evaluate; to make full use of

auswirken *v.* to work out; to effect; to obtain; to procure

Auswuchs *m.* excrescence; (med.) hump; tumor; Auswüchse *pl.* abuses

Auswurf *m.* scum, refuse; garbage, rubbish; (med.) expectoration, discharge; — der Menschheit dregs of humanity

auszacken *v.* to indent; to notch; to scallop

auszahlen *v.* to pay out; to disburse

auszählen *v.* to count out; to score

Auszehrung *f.* wasting away; (med.) phthisis

auszeichnen *v.* to mark out; to decorate; (com.) to label, to ticket

ausziehen *v.* to draw out, to take off; to disrobe; to extract; to move away; to stretch

Auszug *m.* moving out; departure; emigration; summary; extract; quintessence: abstract; (rel.) exodus

Auto *neu.* auto(mobile), (motor) car; **–bahn** *f.* freeway; **–biographie** *f.* autobiography; **–didakt** *m.* self-taught person; **–droschke** *f.* taxi-(cab); **–falle** *f.* police trap; **–gramm** *neu.* autograph; **–heber** *m.* jack; **–mat** *m.* automat

Autor *m.* author, writer; **–enschaft** *f.* authorship; **–ität** *f.* authority

autorisieren *v.* to authorize; to license

Avancen machen *v.* to make a pass

Axt *f.* ax, hatchet

B

Bach *m.* brook, creek; **–stelze** *f.* wagtail

Back: –fisch *m.* fried fish; teen-age girl; bobby-soxer; **–obst** *neu.* dried fruit; **–ofen** *m.* oven; **–pulver** *neu.* baking powder; **–stein** *m.* brick

Back: –e *f.* cheek; **–enbart** *m.* side whiskers; **–enknochen** *m.* jawbone; **–enzahn** *m.* molar; **–pfeife** *f.*, **–enstreich** *m.* box on the ear

backen *v.* to bake

Bäcker *m.* baker; **–ei** *f.* bakery; pastries; **–laden** *m.* bakery

Bad *neu.* bath; spa, health resort; **–eanstalt** *f.* baths; bathing establishment: **–eanzug** *m.* swim suit; **–ekur** *f.* treatment at medicinal springs; **–emantel** *m.* bathrobe; **–er** *m.* barber; (lit.) surgeon; **–estrand** *m.* beach; **–ewanne** *f.* bathtub; **–ezimmer** *neu.* bathroom

baden *v.* to bathe

Bagage *f.* luggage; baggage; (coll.) rabble

Bagger *m.* dredger

baggern *v.* to dredge

Bahn *f.* road, track, way; course; career; railway; orbit; **–brecher** *m.* pioneer; **–g(e)leis(e)** *neu.* railway track; **–hof** *m.* station, terminal; **–linie** *f.* line; **–netz** *neu.* railway system; **–steig** *m.* train platform; **–übergang** *m.* railway crossing

bahnbrechend *adj.* pioneering; epoch-making

bahnen *v.* to open up (path); to pioneer; to prepare; einen Weg — to force one's way

Bahre *f.* stretcher; von der Wiege bis zur — from the cradle to the grave

Bai *f.* bay

Bakkalaureus *m.* bachelor (B.A., B.S., etc.)

Bakteri: –e *f.* bacterium; **–ologie** *f.*, **–enforschung** *f.*, **–enkunde** *f.* bacteriology

Balance *f.* balance; equilibrium

bald *adv.* soon; presently; almost

Baldachin *m.* canopy

Balg *m.* skin; slough; bellows; (coll.) brat

balgen *v.* to scuffle, to wrestle, to tussle

Balken *m.* beam, rafter; joist; girder

Balkon *m.* balcony; **–tür(e)** *f.* French window(s)

Ball *m.* ball; globe; dance; **–anzug** *m.* full dress; **–kleid** *neu.* evening dress; **–saal** *m.* ballroom; **–schläger** *m.* racket; bat; batter

Ballen *m.* bale; packet, bundle; (anat.) bunion

ballen *v.* to form a ball; to bale; to conglomerate; die Faust — to clench one's fist

Ballon *m.* balloon; **–korb** *m.* nacelle

balsamieren *v.* to embalm

Bambus *m.* bamboo

banal *adj.* banal; commonplace

Banane *f.* banana

Band *neu.* band, ribbon; tape; ligament, tetters; (mech.) hoop; link, bond, tie; laufendes — conveyor belt; **–eisen** *neu.* hoop (oder strap) iron; **–erole** *f.* revenue stamp; **–mass** *neu.* tape measure; **–säge** *f.* band saw; **–wurm** *m.* tapeworm

Band *m.* binding, cover; volume

Bande *f.* band; gang, pack; (billiards) cushion; **–nkrieg** *m.* guerrilla warfare

bändigen *v.* to subdue, to tame; to break in

bange *adj.* alarmed, anxious, frightened; **–n** *v.* to be afraid, to tremble for, to worry about

Bank *f.* bench, seat; pew; reef; auf die lange — schieben to put off, to delay

Bank *f.* bank; die — sprengen to break the bank; **–abschluss** *m.* balance sheet; **–beamte** *m.* bank clerk; **–ier** *m.* banker; **–konto** *neu.* bank account

Bänkelsänger *m.* ballad singer, rhymester

Bankett *neu.* banquet

bankrott *adj.* bankrupt

Bann *m.* ban; constraint; spell; excommunication; **–fluch** *m.* anathema; **–kreis** *m.*, **–meile** *f.* sphere of influence, spell; **–ware** *f.* contraband

bannen *v.* to fascinate; to conjure; to banish; to exorcise; to excommunicate

Banner *neu.* banner, flag, standard; **–träger** *m.* standard bearer

bar *adj.* bare, naked; devoid of; pure, unmixed; — bezahlen to pay in cash; **–e Münze** face value; **–er Unsinn** sheer nonsense; **–es Geld** ready cash

Bär *m.* bear; Grosser — (ast.) Big Dip-

per; –in *f.* female bear
Baracke *f.* barracks; shed
Barbar *m.* barbarian; –ismus *m.* barbarism
barbarisch *adj.* barbaric
Barbier *m.* barber
barbieren *v.* to shave; (coll.) to cheat
Barbitursäure *f.* barbiturate
Barett *neu.* beret. biretta
barfuss, barfüssig *adj.* barefoot(ed)
barhäuptig *adj.* bareheaded
barmherzig *adj.* merciful; charitable; compassionate; — **Samariter** good Samaritan
Baron *m.* baron; –esse *f.*, –in *f.* baroness
Barriere *f.* barrier
Barsch *m.* (ichth.) perch
barsch *adj.* gruff, rude, tart
Bart *m.* beard; whiskers; wattle; (key) bit; in den — brummen to mutter to oneself; jemanden um den — gehen to flatter someone
bärtig *adj.* bearded, whiskered; barbed
Base *f.* female cousin; (chem.) base
Basis *f.* base, basis; foundation
Bass *m.* (mus.) bass; –geige *f.* bass viol; –ist *m.* bass singer
Bassin *neu.* basin; reservoir
Bast *m.* bast, inner bark
basta! *interj.* that will do! that's enough!
basteln *v.* to put together; to work at a hobby; to potter
Batterie *f.* battery
Bau *m.* building, construction; structure; build; (agr.) cultivation; (min.) working; (zool.) lair; den; burrow; –art *f.* style of architecture; –fach *neu.* architecture, building trade; –gerüst *neu.* scaffold(ing); –holz *neu.* timber; –kasten *m.* set of building blocks; –meister *m.* architect; –platz *m.* –stelle *f.* building lot (*oder* site)
Bauch *m.* belly, abdomen; –fellentzündung *f.* peritonitis; –landung *f.* (avi.) bellylanding; –redner *m.* ventriloquist; –speicheldrüse *f.* pancreas; –weh *neu.* (coll.) belly-ache; colic
bauen *v.* to build, to construct; (agr.) to cultivate; (min.) to work; to rely (*oder* count) on
Bauer *neu.* bird cage, aviary
Bauer *m.* builder, constructor; farmer, peasant, rustic; yokel, boor; (cards) knave, jack; (chess) pawn; –nbursche *m.* country lad; –ndirne *f.* country girl; –nfänger *m.* swindler; crook; –nhof *m.* farm
Bäuerin *f.* peasant woman; farmer's wife
bäuerlich *adj.* rural, rustic; (fig.) boorish
baufällig *adj.* dilapidated

Baum *m.* tree; beam; boom; –schule *f.* tree nursery; –stamm *m.* trunk; –wolle *f.* cotton
bäumen *v.* to prance; (horse) to rear
Bayern *neu.* Bavaria
Bazillus *m.* bacillus; germ
beabsichtigen *v.* to intend; to mean to do
beacht: –en *v.* to take notice; to observe; –enswert *adj.*, –lich *adj.* noteworthy, remarkable
Beamte *m.*, **Beamtin** *f.* official; public officer; officeholder; –nherrschaft *f.* bureaucracy; –nschaft *f.*, –ntum *neu.* civil service; officialdom; –wirtschaft *f.* redtape methods
bean: –spruchen *v.* to claim, to demand; Zeit –spruchen to take up time; –standen to demur; to object, to contest; –tragen to move, to propose; to apply; –worten to answer, to reply
beängstigen *v.* to make anxious; to alarm
bearbeiten *v.* to work (on); to fashion; (agr.) to cultivate; (lit.) to adapt; to revise; to rewrite; jemanden — to belabor someone
beaufsichtigen *v.* to supervise; to control; to inspect
beauftragen *v.* to charge (with), to commission, to empower
bebauen *v.* to build (up)on; (agr.) to cultivate
beben *v.* to quiver, to quake, to tremble
Beben *neu.* quivering; earthquake
Becher *m.* cup, goblet; beaker; mug, tumbler; dice-box; calyx
Becken *neu.* basin, bowl; (anat.) pelvis; (mus.) cymbal
bedacht *adj.* thoughtful, wary; intent on; –sam considerate; (coll.) a bit slow
bedächtig *adj.* considerate, circumspect
Bedarf *m.* need, requirement; –sartikel *m.* requisites, utensils
bedauerlich *adj.* deplorable, regrettable
bedauern *v.* to pity, to deplore; to regret
Bedauern *neu.* pity; sympathy; regret
bedecken *v.* to cover, to screen; to protect; to escort; der Himmel ist bedeckt the sky is overcast
bedenken *v.* to consider, to mind; to provide; sich anders — to change one's mind; sich — to hesitate
Bedenken *neu.* doubt, scruple; hesitation
bedenklich *adj.* doubtful, serious; critical
Bedenkzeit *f.* time for reflection; respite
bedeut: –en *v.* to mean, to signify; to indicate; es hat nichts zu –en it is of no consequence; –end *adj.* significant; notable; –end *adv.* by far, considerable; –sam *adj.* significant, meaningful
Bedien: –stete *m.* employee; –te *m.* serv-

ant; footman; **–ung** f. service; attendance, servants

bedienen v. to attend, to serve; to wait on; (mech.) to operate; (cards) to follow suit; **sich —** to help oneself

Bedienungsturm m. (Rakete) gantry

bedingen v. to stipulate; to involve

bedingt adj. conditional; limited; qualified

Bedingung f. condition; restriction; terms

bedrängen v. to press hard; to oppress; to vex

bedrohen v. to menace, to threaten

bedrücken v. to press upon; to depress

bedürfen v. to need; to be in want of

Bedürfnis neu. need, want; necessity; **–anstalt** f. comfort station

bedürftig adj. needy, poor

beeiden v. to confirm by oath; to swear

beeilen v. to hasten, to hurry; to hustle

beeinflussen v. to influence

beeinträchtigen v. to impair; to injure

beend(ig)en v. to end, to finish; to terminate

beerben v. to inherit, to be heir to

Beerdigung f. burial, interment; funeral

Beere f. berry

Beet neu. (agr.) bed, border

befähigen v. to enable; to qualify

befähigt adj. capable, talented; fit

befallen v. to befall, to happen (to); to attack

befangen adj. shy; biased, prejudiced; embarrassed, confused

befassen v. to touch, to handle; **sich — mit** to concern (oder occupy) oneself with

Befehl m. command; order; decree; **zu — stehen** to be at the service of

befehlen v. to command; to order; to decree

Befehlsausgabe f. briefing

befehlshaberisch adj. imperious; dictatorial

befestigen v. to attach, to fasten, to fix; to stiffen, to harden; to fortify

befeuchten v. to moisten, to wet

befinden v. to deem, to consider; **sich —** to be present; to feel (ill, well, etc.)

Befinden neu. opinion; condition; health

beflecken v. to soil, to spot, to stain; to contaminate, to pollute; to sully

befleiss(ig)en v. **sich —** to apply oneself to; to take great pains to

beflissen adj. diligent; zealous

beflügeln v. to add wings to; to accelerate

befolgen v. to follow, to obey; to observe

befördern v. to forward, to transport; to convey; further, to promote; to favor

befragen v. to interrogate; to consult

befreien v. to liberate; to release; to free

befremdend, befremdlich adj. odd, strange

befreunden v. **sich — mit** to befriend, to become friends; to reconcile oneself to

befrieden v. to pacify; to bring peace to

befriedigen v. to satisfy; to gratify; to appease; **schwer zu —** hard to please; **–d** adj. satisfactory

befruchten v. to fructify, to impregnate; to fecundate, to fertilize

Befugnis f. authority; warrant; competence

befühlen v. to feel, to finger, to touch

Befund m. finding; condition, state; diagnosis

befürchten v. to fear, to dread; to suspect

befürworten v. to recommend; to advocate; to back, to support

begabt adj. gifted, talented

Begabung f. gift, talent; capacity, endowment

Begebenheit f. event, occurrence; happening

begegnen v. to meet, to come upon, to run across; to happen; to obviate

begeh(e)n v. to walk (tracks); to celebrate, to commemorate; to commit, to perpetrate

begehren v. to desire, to covet, to crave; to demand, to request; **–swert** adj. desirable

begeistern v. to inspire; to fill with enthusiasm

Begier(de) f. longing, eagerness; desire; lust; appetite; cupidity

begierig adj. eager, desirous; lustful; covetous; **— zu erfahren** anxious to learn

begiessen v. to water, to wet; to baste

Beginn m. beginning; commencement; origin; **–en** neu. undertaking, enterprise

beginnen v. to begin, to commence

beglaubigen v. to attest, to certify; to authenticate; to accredit

Begleit: –er m. companion; attendant; accompanist; (ast.) satellite; **–erscheinungen** f. pl. circumstances, symptoms; **–ung** f. accompaniment; attendants, suite; escort, convoy

begleiten v. to accompany; to escort

beglückwünschen v. to congratulate

begnad(ig)en v. to pardon; to amnesty

begnügen v. **sich — mit** to be content (oder satisfied) with

Begräbnis neu. burial, interment; funeral; **–platz** m. burial ground

begreifen v. to finger, to handle, to touch; to comprehend, to grasp; **das Haus ist**

im Bau begriffen the house is being built; im Anmarsch begriffen to be on the way; nicht zu — incomprehensible, inconceivable

begreiflich *adj.* comprehensible, conceivable; **–erweise** *adv.* understandably, naturally

begrenzen *v.* to bound, to limit; to confine

Begriff *m.* concept, idea; abstraction; im — sein to be about (*oder* on the point of); schwer von — sein to be slow of comprehension; **–sbestimmung** *f.* definition; **–svermögen** *neu.* intellectual capacity, comprehension

begründen *v.* to base (*oder* found); to establish; to prove, to substantiate

begrüssen *v.* to greet, to welcome; to salute

begünstigen *v.* to favor; to promote

Begünstigte *m.* favorite; protégé

begutachten *v.* to give an opinion on; to judge

begütert *adj.* rich, wealthy

begütigen *v.* to appease, to placate, to soothe

behaart *adj.* hairy; hirsute

behäbig *adj.* corpulent; easy, comfortable

behaftet *adj.* afflicted with; subject to

behagen *v.* to please, to suit

behaglich *adj.* comfortable, cozy, snug; es sich — machen to feel at home (*oder* at ease)

behalten *v.* to keep, to retain; to maintain; to remember; für sich — to keep secret

Behälter *m.* container, reservoir; box; tank

behandeln *v.* to handle; to deal with; to manage; (med.) to treat, to dress

beharren *v.* to persevere, to persist; to insist (*oder* hold) on, to continue

beharrlich *adj.* persevering, constant, tenacious

behaupten *v.* to assert, to affirm; to maintain; sich — to hold one's own (*oder* out)

Behausung *f.* lodging; home, dwelling

Behelf *m.* expedient, shift; device

behelfen *v.* sich — to make shift; sich mit wenigem — to get along with a minimum

behelligen *v.* to annoy, to bother, to importune

behend(e) *adj.* agile, nimble

beherbergen *v.* to harbor, to shelter, to lodge; to accomodate

beherrschen *v.* to govern, to rule; to dominate; to master; to sway; sich — to control (*oder* restrain) oneself

beherzigen *v.* to take to heart; to consider

well; to heed

behexen *v.* to bewitch; to charm, to enchant

behilflich *adj.* helpful; serviceable; — sein to lend a hand; to render assistance

Behörde *f.* governmental authorities

behutsam *adj.* careful, cautious; wary

bei *prep.* at, by, near; amid, among; in, on; to, with; in connection with; upon; — aliedem for all that; — Gelegenheit on occasion; — gutem Wetter if the weather permits; — guter Gesundheit in good health; — hellem Tage in broad daylight; **–m** ersten Anblick at first sight; — seinen Lebzeiten during his lifetime; — sich behalten to keep to oneself; — Sicht on presentation; — weitem nicht far from it; dicht — close to; nicht — Geld sein to be short of cash

Beiblatt *neu.* supplement; extra sheet

beibringen *v.* to bring forward; to produce; to adduce; to inflict; to teach, to impart

Beicht: –e *f.* confession; **–vater** *m.* father confessor; **–kind** *neu.* penitent; confessor

beichten *v.* to confess

beide *adj.* and *pron.* both; either; alle — both of them; wir — we two; **–mal** *adv.* both times; **–rlei** *adj.* both kinds, of either sort; **–rseitig, –rseits** *adv.* on both sides; mutually, reciprocally

beieinander *adv.* together

Beifall *m.* assent; approbation; applause

beifolgend *adj.* enclosed; herewith

beifügen *v.* to add; to append; to enclose

Beigabe *f.* something added; supplement

beigeben *v.* to add

beikommen *v.* to come (*oder* get) at; to equal; jemandem — to get hold of somebody; sich — lassen to take into one's head; to dare

Beil *neu.* hatchet; axe

Beilage *f.* enclosure; supplement; side dish

beiläufig *adj.* incidental; approximate; *adv.* incidentally; by the way

beilegen *v.* to add, to enclose; to ascribe to, to impute; to confer; to settle; (naut.) to heave to; sich — to assume (name)

beiliegen *v.* to be enclosed; (naut.) to lie to

beimengen, beimischen *v.* to add to, to admix

beimessen *v.* to ascribe, to attribute, to impute

Bein *neu.* leg; bone; auf die –e bringen to get (*oder* set) going; das — stellen to trip up; **die –e in die Hand nehmen** to take to one's heels; **es geht durch Mark und —** it sends thrills through one; **immer auf den –en sein to be always on the go; sich auf die –e machen** to leave; **sich kein — ausreissen** to take one's time; **wieder auf die –e kommen** to convalesce; **–kleider** neu. pl. trousers, pants

beinahe adv. almost, all but; nearly; **— umkommen** to have a narrow escape

Beiname m. surname; nickname; epithet

beiordnen v. to co-ordinate; to adjoin

beipflichten v. to agree, to assent; to espouse

beisammen adv. together; **dicht —** close to each other; **seine Gedanken — haben** to have one's wits about one

Beischlaf m. cohabitation

Beisein neu. presence

beiseite adv. apart, aside; **–bringen** v. to purloin; to spirit away

Beispiel neu. example; instance; **als — anführen** to quote as a precedent; **zum — for** example

beispiellos adj. unprecedented, unheard of

beispringen v. to run to assist; to give aid

beissen v. to bite; to burn; to prick (conscience); **in den sauren Apfel —** to swallow the bitter pill; **ins Gras — to** bite the dust, to die; **–d** adj. mordant; sarcastic, pungent

Beistand m. support; assistance; aid, help; assistant; **— vor Gericht** legal counsel

beistehen v. to render aid; to back up, to side with; to plead (oder speak) for; to comfort; **Gott stehe ihm bei!** God help him!

Beisteuer f. contribution; subsidy; collection

beistimmen v. to agree to (oder with); to concur (with); to accede to

Beitrag m. contribution; quota, share; premium

beitragen v. to contribute to(wards); to be instrumental in; to promote

beitreten v. to join (club, etc.); to assent to; to concur (with); to espouse

Beitritt m. joining (club, etc.); accession to

Beiwagen m. sidecar

Beiwerk neu. accessories

beiwohnen v. to attend; to be inherent; to cohabit

beizeiten adv. betimes, early; in good time

beizen v. to corrode; to tan; to etch (copper); to stain; to cauterize

bejahen v. to affirm; to assent to, to accept; **–d** adj. (in the) affirmative

bejahrt adj. aged; elderly

bejammern v. to deplore. to lament

bekämpfen v. to combat, to resist; **to** strive against; to oppose; to overcome

bekannt adj. (well-)known, renowned; familiar (with); **–lich** adv. as everybody knows; **–machen** to advertise, to publish; to announce; **sich –machen to** acquaint one of (oder with)

Bekanntschaft f. acquaintance

bekehren v. to convert, to evangelize

bekennen v. to admit, to confess, to acknowledge; (law) to plead guilty; (tel.) to profess; **Farbe —** (cards) to follow suit

Bekenntnis neu. confession; (rel.) denomination; **–schule** f. denominational school

beklagen v. to lament, to deplore; to commiserate; to regret; **sich — to** complain about; **–swert** adj. deplorable, pitiable

Beklagte m. accused; defendant

beklatschen v. to applaud, to clap; **to** gossip

bekleben v. to paste on (oder over); **mit Zettel —** to label

bekleckern, beklecksen v. to bespatter, **to** spot

bekleiden v. to clothe, to dress; to cover, to drape; to face, to line; to veneer, to wainscot; **ein Amt —** to hold office

beklommen adj. anxious, uneasy; depressed

bekommen v. to get, to receive; to obtain; **einen Korb —** to meet with a rebuff (oder refusal); **einen Schnupfen — to** catch cold; **es fertig —** to bring about; **es wird ihm schlecht —** he will fare badly with it

beköstigen v. to board, to feed

bekräftigen v. to confirm, to corroborate

bekränzen v. to wreathe; **mit Lorbeer —** to crown with laurel

bekreuz(ig)en v. (rel.) to make the sign of the cross upon; to cross oneself

bekritteln v. to criticize, to carp at

bekümmern v. to grieve, to trouble; **to** afflict; **sich — um** to concern oneself with, to meddle with

bekunden v. to depose, to state; to manifest

beladen v. to burden (oder load) with; **—** adj. encumbered, weighed down, burdened

Belag m. anything laid on (oder upon); sandwich meat; coating; film (teeth)

belagern v. to beleaguer, to besiege

Belang m. importance; **von —** important; **nicht von —** of no consequence

belang: –en v. to concern; (law) to sue;

to prosecute; **–los** *adj.* insignificant, of no consequence; **–reich** *adj.* important

belasten *v.* to burden, to load; to accuse, to incriminate; to debit

belästigen *v.* to bother, to importune, to molest

Belastung *f.* burden(ing); load; debit, charge; **–szeuge** *m.* witness for the prosecution

belaufen *v.* sich — to amount (*oder* come up) to

belauschen *v.* to overhear; to spy out

beleben *v.* to animate, to enliven; to cheer

belebt *adj.* animated, lively; crowded

Belebungsmittel *neu.* restorative

Beleg *m.* proof; document; voucher; **–schaft** *f.* personnel, staff; (min.) gang; **–stelle** *f.* quotation, authoritative passage

belehren *v.* to inform, to instruct; **eines Besseren** — to set right, to correct

beleibt *adj.* corpulent, stout; portly, plump

beleidigen *v.* to affront, to insult, to offend; **tätlich** — to assault; **–d** *adj.* offensive

beleuchten *v.* to light up, to illuminate; to elucidate, to examine

Beleuchtung *f.* illumination; elucidation; **–skörper** *m.* lighting fixture

Belgien *neu.* Belgium

belichten *v.* (phot.) to expose to light

belieb: –en *v.* to be pleasing; to condescend; **–ig** *adj.* optional; anything, no matter what; **–t** *adj.* liked, popular; beloved; favorite; sich **–t machen** to ingratiate oneself (with); **wie –t?** what did you say?

bellen *v.* to bark, to bay; to yelp

Belobigung *f.* commendation, praise

belohnen *v.* to recompense, to reward; to remunerate; **–swert** *adj.* deserving a reward

belustigen *v.* to amuse, to entertain

bemächtigen *v.* sich — to seize; to take over by force

bemalen *v.* to paint (*oder* daub) over

bemannen *v.* to man

bemerkbar *adj.* observable, perceptible

bemerken *v.* to notice, to observe, to perceive; to note; to mention, to remark

bemitleiden *v.* to pity; to be sorry for

bemittelt *adj.* prosperous, wealthy; well-to-do

bemoost *adj.* mossy; **–es Haupt** old stager

bemühen *v.* to trouble; sich — um to take pains; to endeavor, to strive; to seek to promote

benach: –bart *adj.* neighboring; adjacent;

–richtigen to advise (*oder* inform) of; to notify; **–teiligen** to prejudice; to damage; to injure; to put at a disadvantage

benebelt *adj.* foggy, cloudy; tipsy

benehmen *v.* to take away from; to make impossible; sich — to behave (*oder* conduct) oneself

Benehmen *neu.* behavior, conduct; bearing; **feines** — good manners

beneiden *v.* to envy, to begrudge; **–swert** *adj.* enviable

Bengel *m.* (coll.) rude fellow; rascal

benommen *adj.* benumbed, giddy

benutzen *v.* to use, to utilize; to employ; to profit by, to take advantage of

Benzin *neu.* benzine; gasoline

beobachten *v.* to observe, to watch; to shadow

Beobachtung *f.* observation; observance

bequem *adj.* comfortable; convenient; easygoing

Bequemlichkeit *f.* comfort(ableness); convenience; ease

beraten *v.* to advise; to settle by conference; sich — to deliberate; **–d** *adj.* consultative

Beratung *f.* advice; consultation; conference

berauben *v.* to rob; to deprive of; **des Augenlichts beraubt** (poet.) blind

berauschen *v.* to intoxicate; to enchant

berechnen *v.* to calculate, to compute; to charge; to estimate; **–d** *adj.* calculating; scheming

berechtigen *v.* to authorize; to entitle

bereden *v.* to persuade, to talk over; to gossip

Beredsamkeit *f.* eloquence

Bereich *m.* and *neu.* range, sphere; province

bereichern *v.* to enrich; to enlarge

bereit *adj.* prepared, ready; disposed (to); **–en** *v.* to get (*oder* make) ready; to prepare, to ride over, to inspect on horseback; to break in (horse); **–s** *adv.* already; previously; **–willig** *adj.* ready (*oder* willing) to do

bereuen *v.* to regret, to repent; to be sorry

Berg *m.* mountain; hill; **das Haar stand ihm zu –e** his hair stood on end; **er ist über alle –e** he took to his heels; **goldene –e versprechen** to promise pie in the sky; **hinter dem — halten** to keep in the dark; **über den — sein** to be out of the woods; **–ahorn** *m.* sycamore, maple; **–arbeit** *f.* mining; **–arbeiter** *m.* miner; **–bau** *m.* mining; **–bewohner** *m.* highlander, mountaineer; **–geist** *m.* gnome; **–gewerkschaft** *f.* miner's union; **–gipfel** *m.* mountain top; **–kessel** *m.*

gorge; **–kette** *f.* mountain range; **–knappe** *m.* miner, pitman; **–kristall** *m.* rock crystal; **–land** *neu.* highland; **–mann** *m.* miner; mountaineer; **–predigt** *f.* Sermon on the Mount; **–rutsch** *m.* landslide; **–schlucht** *f.* ravine; **–spitze** *f.* peak, summit; **–steiger** *m.* mountain climber; **–stock** *m.* alpenstock; **–werk** *neu.* mine
Berg- und Talbahn *f.* switchback
berg: **–ab** *adv.* downhill; **–an** *adv.* uphill; **–en** *v.* to save, to salvage; to rescue; **–ig** *adj.* mountainous
Bericht *m.* account, report; (rad.) commentary; **–erstatter** *m.* reporter, correspondent; (rad.) commentator
berichten *v.* to report, to inform, **falsch —** to misinform
berichtigen *v.* to adjust, to correct, to rectify; to settle
Beringstrasse *f.* Bering Strait
Bernstein *m.* amber; **schwarzer —** jet
bersten *v.* to burst; to split; to crack
berüchtigt *adj.* notorious
berück: **–en** *v.* to enchant, to fascinate; **–end** *adj.* fascinating, bewitching; **–sichtigen** to consider, to regard; to take into account
Beruf *m.* occupation, profession, business; vocation; **–sberatung** *f.* vocational guidance; **–sspieler** *m.* (sports) professional; **–ung** *f.* appointment, call; (law) appeal; **unter –ung auf** with reference to
beruf: **–en** *v.* to call; to appoint; to convoke; to convene; (law) to appeal, to summon; **sich –en auf** to cite a precedent, to refer to; **–en** *adj.* competent; celebrated; **–lich** *adj.* professional; **–stätig** *adj.* employed
beruhen *v.* to be based (*oder* rest) on; **etwas auf sich — lassen** to let it pass
beruhigen *v.* to calm, to pacify
Beruhigungsmittel *neu.* (med.) sedative; tranquillizer
berühmt *adj.* celebrated, famous
berühren *v.* to touch; to come in contact with
besänftigen *v.* to assuage, to soothe, to appease
Besatzung *f.* garrison; crew; **–sheer** *neu.* occupation army
beschädigen *v.* to damage, to injure
beschaffen *v.* to procure, to supply; **—** *adj.* conditioned; qualified
Beschaffenheit *f.* condition; constitution; character, disposition
beschäftigen *v.* to engage, to employ; to occupy
beschämen *v.* to put to shame, to make

ashamed; **–d** *adj.* disgraceful
beschauen *v.* to look at; to examine, to inspect; to contemplate
Beschauer *m.* looker-on, spectator; inspector
Bescheid *m.* answer; decision, information; **abschlägiger —** negative reply, refusal; **— geben** to inform; (coll.) to give a piece of one's mind; **bis auf weiteren —** until further notice; **über alles — wissen** to know what's what
bescheiden *v.* to allot; to inform, to instruct; **sich —** to resign oneself; **zu sich — to send for; —** *adj.* modest, unassuming; humble
bescheinigen *v.* to attest, to certify; **Empfang —** to acknowledge receipt
beschenken *v.* to present
bescheren *v.* to distribute gifts; to bestow
Bescherung *f.* distribution of gifts; **das ist eine schöne —!** what a mess!
beschimpfen *v.* to insult, to revile, to abuse
beschirmen *v.* to protect, to shield
beschlafen *v.* to sleep on; to consider over night
Beschlag *m.* (glass) moisture; (horse) shoe; (mech.) mounting, fittings; (chem.) efflorescence; **in — nehmen, mit — belegen** to confiscate, to seize; **–nahme** *f.* confiscation, seizure
beschleunigen *v.* to accelerate; to speed up
Beschleunigungsmesser *m.* accelerometer
beschliessen *v.* to conclude; to resolve
Beschluss *m.* conclusion; decree; resolution
beschmutzen *v.* to soil, to dirty; to pollute
beschneiden *v.* to clip; to prune; to circumcise
beschönigen *v.* to gloss over; to extenuate
beschränken *v.* to confine, to limit, to restrict; to curb; to curtail
beschränkt *adj.* dull; weak-minded; limited
beschreiben *v.* to describe; to write upon
beschreiten *v.* to walk on; to step over into; **den Rechtsweg —** to go to court
beschuldigen *v.* to accuse, to charge (with)
beschützen *v.* to protect, to defend
Beschwerde *f.* grievance; complaint
beschweren *v.* to burden, to charge; **sich — to complain of
beschwerlich *adj.* troublesome; **— fallen** to be a burden (*oder* trouble)
beschwichtigen *v.* to appease; to allay; **sein Gewissen —** to silence one's conscience
beseh(e)n *v.* to look at; to examine, to

inspect

beseitigen *v.* to eliminate; to remove

Besen *m.* broom; **-stiel** *m.* broomstick

besessen *adj.* possessed, fanatic; raving

besetzen *v.* to occupy, to garrison, to border; to people; (naut.) to man; to distribute; to edge, to trim (cloth); to garnish; to engage, to fill; to reserve

Besetzung *f.* occupation; (theat.) cast-(ing)

besichtigen *v.* to inspect; to view

besiedeln *v.* to settle, to colonize

besiegeln *v.* to seal

besiegen *v.* to defeat, to conquer

besinnen *v.* to consider, to reflect on; **sich eines anderen** — to change one's mind; **sich auf etwas** — to recollect

Besinnung *f.* consciousness; **jemand zur — bringen** to bring one to his senses; **zur — kommen** to recover consciousness

besinnungslos *adj.* senseless; unconscious

Besitz *m.* possession, property; estate; **-er** *m.* owner, proprietor; **-ergreifung** *f.* seizure; occupation, usurpation; **-recht** *neu.* legal possession; **-tum** *neu.*, **-ung** *f.* property

besitzen *v.* to possess; to own

besoffen *adj.* (coll.) drunk, tipsy

besohlen *v.* to sole

besolden *v.* to pay wages, to remunerate

besondere *adj.* particular; peculiar; separate

besonders *adv.* especially; exceptionally; separately

besonnen *adj.* prudent, considerate, thoughtful

besorgen *v.* to take care of; to manage; to procure; to fear

besorgt *adj.* alarmed, apprehensive; anxious

besprechen *v.* to discuss; to talk over; to review; to conjure; **sich — mit** to confer with

Besprechung *f.* conference; discussion; review

besser *adj.* better; **umso —** so much the better

bessern *v.* to improve; to correct; to reform; to advance; **nicht zu —** incorrigible

Besserungsanstalt *f.* reformatory

Bestand *m.* continuation, duration; amount (*oder* stock) on hand; **-(s)aufnahme** *f.* inventory; **-teil** *m.* ingredient; component

beständig *adj.* constant, steady, continual

bestärken *v.* to confirm; to fortify

bestätigen *v.* to confirm; to okay; to ratify; **to verify; sich —** to prove true

bestatten *v.* to bury, to inter

bestauben, bestäuben *v.* to cover with dust, to spray; (bot.) to pollinate

beste *adj.* best; **auf das —** in the best way; **etwas zum -n geben** to treat, to entertain with; **zum -n haben** to tease; **-nfalls** *adv.* at best, at most; **-ns** *adv.* as well as possible

Beste *neu.* (the) best; **der erste —** the firstcomer; **zu Ihrem -n** in your interest

bestechen *v.* to bribe, to corrupt

bestehen *v.* to undergo; to stand; to overcome; to exist; to subsist, to continue; to pass (examination); **— auf** to insist on; **— aus** to consist of; **nicht —** to fail

bestehlen *v.* to steal from; to plagiarize

besteigen *v.* to ascend; to mount; (naut.) to board

bestellen *v.* to order, to send for; to appoint; to set in order; to deliver (greetings); (agr.) to till; **es ist schlecht mit ihm bestellt** he is in a sad plight

besteuern *v.* to tax

Bestie *f.* beast; brute

bestimmen *v.* to determine; to appoint; to define; to evaluate; **to analyze; jemand — etwas zu tun** to induce a person to do something; **über etwas —** to dispose of

bestimmt *adj.* decided; certain; definite; **— nach** bound for; **— sein für** to be destined for

Bestimmung *f.* determination; destiny, vocation; definition; evaluation; **amtliche -en** regulations

bestrafen *v.* to punish

bestrebt *adj.* endeavored; **— sein** to exert oneself, to strive

bestreichen *v.* to spread over, to smear, to butter; (mil.) to sweep

bestreiten *v.* to contest; to deny, **to pay for**

bestricken *v.* to ensnare

bestürmen *v.* to storm, to assail, to importune

bestürzt *adj.* dismayed; amazed; confused

Besuch *m.* call, visit; visitor(s); attendance

besuchen *v.* to visit; to attend; to frequent

betagt *adj.* aged, elderly

betätigen *v.* to practise, to put in action; **sich —** to be busy, to take active part in

betäuben *v.* to deafen; to stun; to anesthetize; to stupefy

beteiligen *v.* to give a share (*oder* interest) in; **sich —** to take part in

beten *v.* to pray, to say one's prayer

beteuern *v.* to assert; to swear to

Beton *m.* concrete

betonen *v.* to stress, to accent, to emphasize

Betracht *m.* account, consideration, respect; **in — ziehen** to take into account

betrachten *v.* to consider, to regard; to reflect on; **Dinge im rosigen Lichte —** to look at things through rose-colored glasses

beträchtlich *adj.* considerable

Betrag *m.* amount

betragen *v.* to amount to; **sich — to behave**

betrauen *v* to entrust with

betrauern *v.* to mourn for, to deplore

Betreff *m.* reference; **in — with regard to,** in respect of, concerning

betreffen *v.* to concern, to affect; to fall upon; **-d** *adj.* concerning, concerned

betreiben *v.* to carry (*oder* urge) on; to pursue

betreten *v.* to set foot on, to enter, to mount; **— adj** perplexed, embarassed

betreuen *v.* to take care of; to attend to

Betrieb *m.* factory, plan; workshop; business; **in — setzen** to set in motion; **-sjahr** *neu.* fiscal year; **-skapital** *neu.* working capital; **-skosten** *f. pl.* operating expenses; **-sleiter** *m.* manager, superintendent; **-sstockung** *f.*, **-sstörung** *f.* breakdown

betrieb: -sam *adj.* active, industrious; **-sfertig** *adj.* ready for service; **-ssicher** *adj.* foolproof

betrübt *adj.* sad, dejected

Betrug *m.* fraud, deceit; swindle

betrügen *v.* to cheat, to deceive, **to defraud**

Betrüger *m.* cheat, deceiver; swindler

Bett *neu.* bed; **das — hüten** to be confined to bed; **-decke** *f.* coverlet; blanket; **-laken** *neu.*, **-tuch** *neu.* sheet; **-stelle** *f.* bedstead; **-wäsche** *f.* bed linen

betteln *v.* to beg; to plead continuously

bettlägerig *adj.* bedridden

Bettler *m.* beggar; **-sprache** *f.* beggars' argot

beugen *v.* to bend; to lower; (gram.) to inflect; **sich — to** humble oneself, to submit

Beule *f.* boss, bump; boil, tumor, lump

beunruhigen *v.* to alarm, to disquiet; to harass

beurlauben *v.* to give leave, to furlough; **sich — to** withdraw, to take leave

beurteilen *v.* to judge, to criticize; to review

Beute *f.* booty, prey; **auf — ausgehen** to go plundering; **-macher** *m.* looter

Beutel *m.* bag, pouch; purse; **-ratte** *f.* opossum; **-schneider** *m.* cutpurse, pick-

pocket

bevölkern *v.* to populate; to people

Bevölkerung *f.* population, people, inhabitants

bevollmächtigen *v.* to empower; to authorize

bevor *conj.* before; **— adv.** beforehand; **-munden** to act as guardian; to prevent autonomous action; **-zugen** to favor

bewachen *v.* to watch over; to guard; to shadow

bewaffnen *v.* to arm

bewahren *v.* to keep, to preserve; **— vor** to guard against; to protect from; **Gott soll mich —!** Heaven forbid!

bewähren *v.*, **sich — to** stand the test, to prove true

bewandert *adj.* versed, skilled

bewässern *v* to irrigate

beweg: -en *v.* to move, to keep in motion; to agitate, to excite; to induce; **sich — to** move; **sich um etwas — to** revolve round; **-end** *adj.* moving; **-lich** *adj.* mobile, agile

Beweggrund *m.* motive

Bewegung *f.* motion, movement; stir; agitation; emotion

beweinen *v.* to deplore

Beweis *m.* proof; sign, evidence; **-führung** *f.* demonstration

beweisen *v.* to prove; to show, to demonstrate

bewerben *v.* **sich — to** apply for; to compete, to solicit; to court, to woo

bewerkstelligen *v.* to accomplish, to effect

bewilligen *v.* to grant, to concede

bewirken *v.* to bring out; to cause; to effect

bewirten *v.* to entertain, to regale, to treat

bewohnen *v.* to inhabit, to occupy; to reside in

bewölkt *adj.* cloudy, overcast

bewundern *v.* to admire; **-swert** *adj.* admirable

bewusst *adj.* conscious; known; intentional; **die —e Sache** the matter in question; **sich — sein** to be aware of; **-los** *adj.* unconscious

Bewusst: -heit *f.* consciousness, knowledge; **-losigkeit** *f.* unconsciousness; insensibility; **-sein** *neu.* consciousness, awareness

bezahlen *v.* to pay; to compensate for; **mit gleicher Münze — to** give tit for tat

bezähmen *v.* to tame; **sich — to** control (*oder* restrain) oneself

bezaubern *v.* to bewitch, to charm; **-d** *adj.* charming, enchanting

bezeichnen *v.* to designate; to mark; to indicate; **-d** *adj.* characteristic, significant

bezeugen *v.* to testify; to bear witness

beziehen *v.* to cover; to occupy; to draw, to receive. to obtain, to get; to procure; (bed) to change; (mus.) to string; **Lager — to encamp; sich — to become cloudy; sich — auf** to relate to

Beziehung *f.* relation; **in dieser —** in this respect; **in freundschaftlichen –en stehen** to be on good terms

beziehungsweise *adv.* respectively

Bezirk *m.* district

Bezug *m.* cover(ing); supply; reference, relation; (mus.) set of strings; **Bezüge** *pl.* income, salary; **— nehmen auf** to refer to; **in — auf** in regard to

bezweifeln *v.* to doubt, to question

bezwingen *v.* to overcome, to subdue; to master; **sich —** to control (*oder* restrain) oneself

Bianca *f.* Blanche

Bibel *f.* Bible

Biber *m.* beaver

Bibliothek *f.* library

biblisch *adj.* biblical

biegen *v.* to bend, to bow; to decline, to inflect; **um die Ecke —** to turn the corner

biegsam *adj.* flexible; yielding

Biene *f.* bee; **–nkönigin** *f.* queen bee; **–nkorb** *m.*, **–nstock** *m.* beehive; **–nzüchter** *m.* beekeeper

Bier *neu.* beer; **helles — ale; –brauerei** *f.* brewery; **–fass** *neu.* beer barrel, keg; (coll.) paunch; **–hefe** *f.* yeast; **–idee** *f.* stupid idea; **–krug** *m.*, **–seidel** *m.* beer mug, stein

bieten *v.* to offer; to bid; **das lässt sich niemand —** nobody will take that; **sich alles — lassen** to put up with everything

Bild *neu.* picture, portrait, illustration, representation; view; idea; symbol; metaphor; **auf der –fläche erscheinen** to come into view; **im –e sein** to understand; **lebendes —** tableau; **–erschrift** *f.* hieroglyphs; **–hauer** *m.* sculptor; **–nis** *neu.* portrait, likeness; **–seite** *f.* (coin) face; **–ung** *f.* education, culture; formation

bilden *v.* to form, to shape; to constitute; to educate, to cultivate; **to fashion –de Künste** fine arts

bildlich *adj.* figurative

Billet *neu.* ticket; note

billig *adj.* cheap; fair, just; moderate

billigen *v.* to approve, to sanction

Billion *f.* billion; (Am.) trillion

binär *adj.* binary

Binärziffer *f.* binary digit

Binde *f.* band; bandage; (neck)tie; (arm)

sling; **–gewebe** *neu.* connective tissue; **–glied** *neu.* connecting link; **–strich** *m.* hyphen, dash; **–wort** *neu.* conjunction

binden *v.* to bind; to fasten, to tie; to hoop (cask); (cooking) to thicken; **–d** *adj.* obligatory

Bindfaden *m.* string, twine; **es regnet —** (coll.) it is raining cats and dogs

Binnen: –gewässer *neu.* inland water(s); **–handel** *m.* domestic trade; **–land** *neu.* interior; **–meer** *neu.* inland sea

Biogenese *f.* biogenesis

biogenetische Grundgesetz *neu.* biogenesis

Biometrie *f.* biometry

Birke *f.* birch

Birne *f.* pear; (elec.) bulb

bis *prep.* as far as, down (*oder* up) to; till, until; (even) to; **— conj.** till, until; **alle — auf einen** all but one

Bisam *m.* muskrat

Bischof *m.* bishop; **–shut** *m.*, **–smütze** *f.* mitre; **–ssitz** *m.* episcopal see; **–sstab** *m.* crosier; **–sstuhl** *m.* episcopate

Biss *m.* bite, sting; **–en** *m.* mouthful; snack, morsel; **guter –en** tidbit

bissig *adj.* biting, snappish; sharp

Bitt: -e *f.* request, petition; supplication; entreaty; **–e!** *interj.* please! you're welcome! **–gang** *m.* pilgrimage; **–schrift** *f.* petition; **–steller** *m.* petitioner

bitten *v.* to ask; to beg; to entreat; to invite; to request; **darf ich Sie —?** may I trouble you? **für jemanden —** to plead for someone; **um Aufträge —** to solicit orders; **wie bitte?** what did you say?

bitter *adj.* bitter; (fig.) severe, grievous; **–böse** *adj.* very angry (*oder* wicked)

Bittersäure *f.* acerbic acid

blähen *v.* to inflate, to swell; **sich —** to boast; to swell; **–d** *adj.* flatulent

blamieren *v.* to expose, to ridicule; **sich — to** disgrace oneself

blank *adj.* bright, polished, shining; bare

Blas: -e *f.* bubble; bladder; flaw (in metal, glass); (sl.) gang, lot; **–ebalg** *m.* bellows; **–instrument** *neu.* wind instrument; **–rohr** *neu.* blow pipe

blasen *v.* to blow; (mus.) to sound

blass *adj.* pale

Blatt *neu.* leaf; sheet; blade; newspaper; (cards) hand; **das — hat sich gewendet** the tide has turned; **das steht auf einem anderen —** that's another matter; **vom — singen** (*or* spielen) to sight-read

Blattern *f. pl.* smallpox

blättern *v.* to turn over the leaves; to leaf

blau *adj.* blue; **— machen** (coll.) to stay away from work; **–e Bohne** *f.* (coll.) bullet; **–e Jungs** *m. pl.* sailors; **–ge-**

schlagenes Auge black eye; der **—e Rock** military service
Blau *neu.*, **Eläue** *f.* color, dye; **das —e vom Himmel herunterreden** to talk a blue streak; **Fahrt ins —e** trip to an unknown destination; **—papier** *neu.* carbon paper; **—stift** *m.* blue pencil
bläulich *adj.* bluish
Blech *neu.* sheet-metal, tin plate; (coll.) nonsense; **—instrument** *neu.* brass instrument; **—kanne** *f.* tin can; **—schmied** *m.* tinsmith
blechen *v.* (coll.) to pay, to fork out
blechern *adj.* tin
blecken *v.* **Zähne —** to show one's teeth
Blei *neu.* lead; plummet; **—kugel** *f.* bullet; **—stift** *m.* pencil; **—stiftanspitzer** *m.* pencil sharpener
bleiben *v.* to remain, to stay; to fall (in battle); **— lassen** to let alone; **dabei muss es —** there the matter must rest; **es bleibt dabei** agreed; **—d** *adj.* permanent, lasting
bleich *adj.* pale; **—en** *v.* to bleach
Bleichsucht *f.* chloremia
blenden *v.* to blind; to dazzle
Blick *m.* look; glance, view
blicken *v.* to look; **sich — lassen** to appear
blind *adj.* blind; dull; blank; **—anflug** *m.* instrument approach
Blind: —darm *m.* appendix; **—darmentzündung** *f.* appendicitis; **—darmoperation** *f.* appendectomy; **—ekuh** *f.* blindman's buff; **—enanstalt** *f.* home for the blind; **—flug** *m.* instrument flight
blinke(r)n *v.* to gleam, to glitter, to twinkle; (naut.) to signal with lights
Blinkfeuer *neu.* blinker; intermittent light
blinzeln *v.* to blink, to wink
Blitz *m.* lightning, flash; **—ableiter** *m.* lightning rod; **—funk** *m.* radiotelegraphy; **—licht** *neu.* (photo.) flashlight; **—lichtlampe** *f.* flash bulb; **—schlag** *m.* stroke of lightning; **—strahl** *m.* flash of lightning; **—zug** *m.* (rail.) flyer
blitz: —blank *adj.* spick and span; **—en** *v.* to lighten, to flash, to sparkle; **—sauber** *adj.* very pretty; **—schnell** *adj.* quick as lightning
Block *m.* block; log; pad; stocks; (pol.) bloc; **—haus** *neu.* log cabin
blöde *adj.* imbecile, stupid
Blödsinn *m.* imbecility; nonsense
blond *adj.* blond(e), fair
bloss *adj.* bare, naked; plain, simple; mere; **—** *adv.* barely, merely, only; **—legen** *v.* to lay bare; **—stellen** *v.* to expose, to compromise
Blösse *f.* bareness, nakedness; weak point
Blossstellung *f.* exposure

blühen *v.* to bloom, to blossom; to flourish; **—d** *adj.* blooming; flourishing
Blume *f.* flower; aroma, bouquet, flavor; **durch die — sprechen** to speak in metaphors; **—nbeet** *neu.* flower-bed; **—nblatt** *neu.* petal; **—nerde** *f.* gardenmold; **—händler** *m.* florist; **—nkohl** *m.* cauliflower; **—nstrauss** *m.* bouquet; **—nzucht** *f.* floriculture
Bluse *f.* blouse
Blut *neu.* blood; lineage, race; **böses — machen** to arouse angry feelings; **das liegt im —(e)** it runs in the blood; **—ader** *f.* blood vessel; **—armut** *f.* anemia; **—bad** *neu.* massacre; **—druck** *m.* blood pressure; **—egel** *m.* leech; **—erguss** *m.* hemorrhage; **—schande** *f.* incest; **—sturz** *m.* violent hemorrhage; **—sverwandtschaft** *f.* blood relationship; **—vergiessen** *neu.* bloodshed; **—vergiftung** *f.* blood poisoning; **—wasser** *neu.* lymph, serum; **—zeuge** *m.* martyr
blut: —arm *adj.* anemic; very poor; **—durstig, —rünstig** *adj.* bloodthirsty; **—en** *v.* to bleed; to suffer; **—ig** *adj.* bloody; **—jung** *adj.* very young; **—wenig** *adj.* very little
Blüte *f.* blossom, bud; bloom; prime of life; **—nstaub** *m.* pollen; **—zeit** *f.* efflorescence
Bock *m.* ram; (coachman's) box; side horse; (mech.) jack; **den — zum Gärtner machen** to set the wolf to mind the sheep; **einen — schiessen** to blunder, to slip; **—springen** *neu.* leapfrog; **—sprung** *m.* caper, gambol
bock: —(bein)ig *adj.* obstinate, stubborn; **—en** *v.* to butt; to prance; (coll.) to balk
Boden *m.* ground, soil; base; floor; bottom; attic, loft; **—gymnastik** *f.* setting-up exercises; **—radarpeilung** *f.* ground control; **—satz** *m.* grounds; sediment
bodenlos *adj.* bottomless; (coll.) vast
Bodensee *m.* Lake Constance
bodenständig *adj.* deeply rooted, indigenous
Bogen *m.* bow, bend; curve; arc(h); sheet (of paper); **—gang** *m.* arcade; **—lampe** *f.* arc lamp; **—schütze** *m.* archer
Böhmen *neu.* Bohemia
Bohne *f.* bean; **blaue —** (coll.) bullet; **keine — no** idea; **keine — wert** not worth a straw; **—nkaffee** *m.* pure coffee
bohnen *v.* to polish, to wax
bohren *v.* to bore, to drill
Bohrer *m.* borer, drill, gimlet
Boje *f.* (naut.) buoy
Bolzen *m.* bolt; pin; rivet; heater (of **an** iron)
bomb(ardier)en *v.* to bomb(ard), to shell
Bombe *f.* bomb, shell; bombshell; **—ner-**

folg *m.* (theat.) hit, huge success;
-nflugzeug *neu.* bomber; -zielgerät *n.*
bombsight
bombensicher *adj.* bombproof; quite certain
Bonze *m.* (coll.) big shot; bigwig
Boot *neu.* boat; -sanlegestelle *f.*, -shafen
m. marina; -smann *m.* boatswain
Bord *m.* border, edge, rim; (naut.) board;
über — werfen to jettison; -buch *neu.*
logbook; -funker *m.* (avi. *und* naut.)
radio operator; -schwelle *f.* curb
borgen *v.* to borrow
Borke *f.* bark, rind
borniert *adj.* narrow-minded; conceited
Börse *f.* purse; stock exchange; -nkurs
m. rate of exchange; -nmakler *m.*
stockbroker
börsenfähig *adj.* negotiable, marketable
Borste *f.* bristle
Borte *f.* border, braid, lace
bösartig *adj.* malicious, malignant, virulent
böse *adj.* bad, evil, wicked; angry, sore
(wound); er meint es nicht — he means
no harm; in -n Ruf bringen to bring
into disrepute
Böse *m.* devil, fiend; — *neu.* evil; -wicht
m. villain
boshaft *adj.* malicious
Botanik *f.* botany; -er *m.* botanist
botanisch *adj.* botanic(al)
Bote *m.* messenger; -ngang *m.* errand
Botschaft *f.* message; embassy; -er *m.*
ambassador
Böttcher *m.* cooper; -ei *f.* cooperage
Bottich *m.* tub, vat; barrel
Bowle *f.* bowl; spiced wine
boxen *v.* to box
Brand *m.* burning; fire(brand); (bot.)
blight, mildew; (med.) gangrene; ardor;
in — geraten to catch fire; in — setzen
(*or* stecken) to set on fire, to commit
arson; -blase *f.* blister; -bombe *f.* incendiary bomb; -mal *neu.* brand, scar;
stigma; -mauer *f.* fireproof wall; -sohle
f. inner sole; -stifter *m.* arsonist;
-stiftung *f.* arson
Brandung *f.* surf
Branntwein *m.* brandy, whisky; -brennerei *f.* distillery
Brasilien *neu.* Brazil
Brat: -en *m.* roast meat; den -en riechen
to smell a rat; -enwender *m.*, -sp.ess
m. turnspit; -fisch *m.* fried fish; -huhn
neu. roast chicken; -kartoffeln *f. pl.*
fried potatoes; -pfanne *f.* frying pan,
skillet; -wurst *f.* sausage for frying
braten *v.* to fry, to grill, to roast
Bräu, Gebräu *m.* and *neu.* brew

Brauch *m.* custom, usage; use
brauchbar *adj.* serviceable, useful
brauchen *v.* to use; to need, to require
Braue *f.* eyebrow
brauen *v.* to brew
Brauer *m.* brewer; -ei *f.* brewery
braun *adj.* brown; tanned; tawny
bräunlich *adj.* brownish
Braunschweig *neu.* Brunswick
brausen *v.* to bluster, to rage, to storm;
to roar, to rush; to shower; to effervesce
Braut *f.* bride; fiancée; -ausstattung *f.*
trousseau; -führer *m.* best man; -jungfer *f.* bridesmaid; -kleid *neu.* wedding
dress; -paar *neu.* engaged couple;
-schatz *m.* dowry; -schleier *m.* bridal
veil
Bräutigam *m.* bridegroom; fiancé
brav *adj.* honest; good, well-behaved
brechen *v.* to break, to fracture; to
quarry; to vomit; to vi late to vomit;
(flower) to pick; (phy.) to refract
Brei *m.* mush, porridge; -masse *f.* pulp
breit *adj.* broad; wide; -beinig *adj.*
straddle-legged; -schlagen (coll.) to
induce; -treten (coll.) to dilate upon
Breite *f.* breadth, width; diffuseness;
-ngrad *m.* degree of latitude
Brems: -e *f.* gadfly; brake; -fallschirm
m. drag chute, drogue; -klappe *f.* (avi.)
flap; -klotz *m.* chock; -rakete *f.* retrorocket; -schuh *m.* brake shoe (*oder*
block); -strahlung *f.* bremsstrahlung
bremsen *v.* to brake, to apply the brakes
Brenn: -er *m.* burner; distiller; -holz
neu. firewood; -kammer *f.* combustion
cham'er; -kraftmotor *m.* combustion
engine; -material *neu.* fuel; -ofen *m.*
kiln; -punkt *m.* focus
brennen *v.* to burn; to brand; (bricks) to
bake; (chem.) to distill; (coffee) to
roast; (hair) to wave; (med.) to cauterize; (wounds) to sting
Bretagne *f.* Brittany
Brett *neu.* board, plank; am schwarzen
— on the bulletin board; die -er
betreten to go on the stage; mit -ern
vernagelt that's the end of it; -er *pl.*
ski; -erbude *f.* shed
Bre(t)zel *neu.* pretzel
Brief *m.* letter; eingeschriebener — registered letter; -beschwerer *m.* paper
weight; -bote *m.*, -träger *m.* letter
carrier, mailman; -einwurf *m.*, -kasten
m. mailbox; -fach *neu.* pigeonhole;
-geheimnis *neu.* privacy of correspondence; -marke *f.* postage stamp; -ordner
m. letter file; -papier *neu.* writing
paper; -porto *neu.* postage; -post *f.*
first-class mail; -tasche *f.* billfold,

pocketbook, wallet; **–taube** *f.* carrier pigeon: **–umschlag** *m.* envelope; **–waage** *f.* postage scale; **–wechsel** *m.* correspondence

brieflich *adj.* and *adv.* by letter

brillant *adj.* brilliant; diamond

Brille *f.* glasses, spectacles; goggles; **–nschlange** *f.* cobra

bringen *v.* to bring, to convey; to escort; **an sich —** to acquire: **es mit sich —** to involve; **es zu etwas —** to achieve something; **Gewinn —** to yield profit; **nach Hause —** to see one home; **Opfer —** to make sacrifices; **Schaden —** to cause injury; **um etwas —** to deprive of; **ums Leben —** to murder; **Zinsen —** to bear interest; **zu Fall —** to ruin; **zu Papier —** to put (*oder* write) down; **zustande —** to bring about, to accomplish

Brise *f.* breeze

Britannien *neu.* Britain

bröck(e)lig *adj.* crumbly, friable

Brocken *m.* crumb; fragment; scrap

Brokat *m.* brocade

Brom *neu.* bromine; **–beere** *f.* blackberry

bronchiale Lungenentzündung *f.* bronchopneumonia

Brosam *m.*, **–e** *f.* (poet.) crumb, scrap

Brosche *f.* brooch

broschiert *adj.* paper-bound

Broschüre *f.* brochure, pamphlet

Brot *neu.* bread; loaf; (fig.) livelihood; **sein —** verdienen to earn one's living; **–aufstrich** *m.* spread; **–erwerb** *m.* making a living; **–herr** *m.* employer; **–korb** *m.* dem **–korb** höher hängen to keep (one) on short rations; **–röster** *m.* toaster; **–studium** *neu.* professional study

Brötchen *neu.* roll; **belegtes —** sandwich

Bruch *m.* breach, break; fold, crease; (law) violation; (math.) fraction; (med.) fracture, rupture; **in die Brüche gehen** to come to naught; **–band** *neu.* truss; **– landung** *f.* crash landing; **–strich** *m.* division (*oder* fraction) sign; **–stück** *neu.* fragment; **–teil** *m.* fraction

Brücke *f.* bridge; dental arch; small rug

Bruder *m.* brother; friar

brüderlich *adj.* brotherly, fraternal

Brüderschaft *f.* brotherhood; fraternity

Brühe *f.* broth; consommé

brühen *v.* to scald

Brügge *neu.* Bruges

brüllen *v.* to roar; to bellow; to howl

brummen *v.* to growl, to grumble; to snarl; to be grouchy; (sl.) to be in jail; **in den Bart —** to mutter; **mir brummt der Kopf** my head is spinning, I feel dizzy

Brunnen *m.* fountain; spring; well; spa; mineral (soda) water

Brunst *f.* ardor; heat; lust, rut; **–schrei** *m.* bell; **–zeit** *f.* rut

brünstig *adj.* ardent; lustful; (zool.) in heat

Brüssel *neu.* Brussels

Brust *f.* breast, chest; **sich in die — werfen** to put on airs; **–bonbon** *m.* cough drop; **–fellentzündung** *f.* pleurisy; **–schwimmen** *neu.* breast stroke; **–warze** *f.* nipple

brüsten *v.* sich — to boast, to brag

Brut *f.* brood; (ichth.) fry, spawn; **–apparat** *m.* incubator; **–henne** *f.* sitting hen; **–stätte** breeding place; hotbed

brüten *v.* to brood, to hatch

Brutto: –betrag *m.* gross amount; **–einnahme** *f.*, **–ertrag** *m.* gross receipts (*oder* earnings); **–gewicht** *neu.* gross weight

BTU (britische Wärmeeinheit) *f.* British Thermal Unit, BTU

Bube *m.* boy; (cards) jack; (coll.) rascal; **–nstreich** *m.* knavish trick

Buch *neu.* book; ein — **herausgeben** (*or* verlegen) to publish a book; **ein — bearbeiten** (*or* revidieren) to edit a book; **–binder** *m.* bookbinder; **–druck** *m.* printing; **–druckerkunst** *f.* typography; **–halter** *m.* bookkeeper; **–haltung** *f.* bookkeeping; **–handel** *m.* bookselling trade; **–handlung** *f.* bookstore; **–stabe** *m.* letter (of alphabet); type; **–umschlag** *m.* jacket; **–ung** *f.* entry; (travel) reservation

Buch: –e *f.* beech; **–ecker** *f.*, **–el** *f.* beechnut; **–weizen** *m.* buckwheat

buchen *v.* to enter, to book

Bücher *neu. pl.* books; **–abschluss** *m.* balancing (*oder* closing) of books; **–brett** *neu.* bookshelf; **–ei** *f.* library; **–freund** *m.* bibliophile; **–kunde** *f.* bibliography; **–revisor** *m.* auditor; **–schrank** *m.* bookcase

Buchsbaum *m.* boxtree; **–holz** *neu.* boxwood

Büchse *f.* box, case; can; rifle; **–nfleisch** *neu.* canned meat; **–nöffner** *m.* can opener; **–nschütze** *m.* rifleman

buchstabieren *v.* to spell; **falsch —** to misspell

buchstäblich *adj.* literal, verbal, exact

Bucht *f.* bay, creek, inlet

Buckel *m.* hump(back); buckle, boss, stud

buck(e)lig *adj* humpbacked

bücken *v* to stoop; to bow; to incline

Bückling *m.* smoked herring; bow. curtsy

Bude *f.* booth, stall; den

Büffel *m.* buffalo

büffeln *v.* to drudge, to slave;

Büf(f)ett *neu.* sideboard; bar, counter

Bug *m.* bow (of a ship)

Bügel *m.* handle; coat hanger; **–brett** *neu.* ironing board; **–eisen** *neu.* flatiron; **–falte** *f.* crease

bügeln *v.* to iron; to press

buhlen *v.* to make love to; to strive (for); to vie (with)

Bühne *f.* stage; platform; **–nanweisung** *f.* stage direction; **–nausstattung** *f.* scenery; **–nbild** *neu.* stage background; **–dichter** *m.* playwright, dramatist; **–nleiter** *m.* stage manager

Bull: –auge *neu.* porthole; **–e** *m.* (zool.) bull; **–e** *f.* (rel.) bull; **päpstliche –e** papal bull

Bumm: –el *m.* stroll; **–elei** *f.* loafing, laziness; **–elzug** *m.* slow train; **–ler** *m.* bum, tramp

Bund *m.* alliance; band; — *neu.* bundle; **–esgenosse** *m.* ally; **–eslade** *f.* Ark of the Covenant; **–estag** *m.* Lower House (of Federal Government)

Bündel *neu.* bundle; bale

bündig *adj.* concise; convincing; **sich kurz und — ausdrücken** to speak to the point

Bündnis *neu.* alliance, union; treaty

bunt *adj.* multi-colored; mixed; stained; topsy-turvy; gay; **–gefleckt**, **–gesprenkelt** *adj.* speckled, spotted

Bürde *f.* burden, load

Burg *f.* castle, citadel; (fig.) refuge

Bürge *m.* guarantor; bailsman

bürgen *v.* to guarantee; to furnish bail

Bürger *m.* citizen, commoner; **–krieg** *m.* civil war; **–kunde** *f.* civics; **–meister** *m.* mayor; **–steig** *m.* sidewalk; **–wehr** *f.* militia

bürgerlich *adj.* civic, civil; middle-class; **–es Gesetzbuch** code of civil law

Bürgschaft *f.* bail; surety; sponsorship

Büromaschinen-Bit *neu.* binary digit

Bursche *m.* lad, fellow; (coll.) guy

Bürste *f.* brush; **–nbinder** *m.* brushmaker; **–nabzug** *m.* (typ.) galley

bürsten *v.* to brush

Busch *m.* bush; **auf den — klopfen** to beat about the bush; **hinter dem –e halten** to hesitate; **sich seitwärts in die Büsche schlagen** to slip away; **–werk** *neu.* shrubbery

Büschel *neu.* bunch, tuft

buschig *adj.* bushy, shaggy

Busen *m.* bosom, breast; bay, gulf, sound

Busse *f.* penance; atonement; repentance

büssen *v.* to atone for; to expiate

Büsser *m.* penitent

bussfertig *adj.* penitent, repentant, contrite

Büste *f.* bust; **–nhalter** *m.* brassiere

Büttel *m.* beadle, bailiff, jailer

Butter *f.* butter; **–blume** *f.* buttercup; **–brot** *neu.* (slice of) bread and butter; **für ein –brot kaufen** to buy for a song; **–fass** *neu.* churn

C

Chaiselongue *f.* and *neu.* couch, long chair

Champagner *m.* champagne

Champignon *m.* champignon, edible mushroom

chaotisch *adj.* chaotic(al)

Character *m.* character; type; **–istik** *f.* characterization; **–losigkeit** *f.* lack of principles; **–zug** *m.* characteristic

characterisieren *v.* to characterize

characteristisch *adj.* characteristic

Chaussee *f.* highway; **–graben** *m.* roadside ditch

Chef *m.* chief; head; (coll.) boss; **–redakteur** *m.* editor-in-chief

Chemi: –e *f.* chemistry; **–ker** *m.* chemist; **–kalien** *f. pl.* chemicals

chemisch *adj.* chemical

Chemosphäre (Luftschicht 32–50 km über der Erde) *f.* chemosphere

Chiffre *f.* cipher, numeral; code

Chinin *neu.* quinine

Chirurg *m.* surgeon; **–ie** *f.* surgery

Chlor *neu.* chlorine

chloroformieren *v.* to chloroform

cholerisch *adj.* choleric

Cholesterin *neu.* cholesterol

Chor *m.* choir, chorus; **–gang** *m.* aisle; **–hemd** *neu.* surplice; **–herr** *m.* canon; **–stuhl** *m.* stall

Christ *m.* Christian; **Christ(us)** *m.* Christ; **–abend** *m.* Christmas Eve; **–baum** *m.* Christmas tree; **–enheit** *f.* Christendom; **–entum** *neu.* Christianity; **–fest** *neu.* Christmas

christlich *adj.* Christian

Chrom *neu.* chrome, chromium

Chronik *f.* chronicle

chronisch *adj.* (med.) chronic(al)

Chronist *m.* chronicler

conferencier *m.* master-of-ceremonies

Coupé *neu.* (rail.) compartment; two-door automobile

Creme *f.* cream, cosmetic cream; high society

Cypern *neu.* Cyprus

D

da *adv.* here, there; in existence, present; in that case, this being so, then; —

conj. as, when, while; because, since; — **haben wir's** there we are; — **sein** to be at hand; **von — an** (*or* **ab**) from that time, since then; **-behalten** *v.* to retain; **-bleiben** *v.* to stay

dabei *adv.* near, nearby; therewith; besides, moreover; but; as well, at the same time; — **kommt nichts heraus** nothing can be gained by it; — **sein** to be present, to take part; **ich bin —** agreed; I'll go along; **was ist —?** what does that matter? **-bleiben** *v.* to persist in

Dach *neu.* roof, shelter; **-balken** *m.* rafter; **-boden** *m.* loft; **-decker** *m.* roofer; **-fenster** *neu.* attic window; **-first** *m.* ridge (of roof); **-geschoss** *neu.* attic; **-rinne** *f.* gutter

Dachs *m.* badger; **ein frecher —** a fresh guy

dadurch *adv.* through it; thereby; by this means

dafür *adv.* for it (*oder* that); instead of it; **ich kann nichts —** I can't help it; **-halten** *v.* to be of the opinion

dagegen *adv.* and *conj.* against; in comparison with; on the contrary; on the other hand; in exchange (*oder* return) for; **nichts — haben** to have no objection to; **-halten** *v.* to compare; to put side by side

daher *adv.* thence, from that place; — *conj.* therefore, hence, accordingly, consequently

dahin *adv.* to that place (*oder* time); so far that; along, away; gone; past; (poet.) thither; **bis —** until then; **-bringen** *v.* to manage to; to induce; **-geben** *v.* to give up, to sacrifice; **-stehen** *v.* to be uncertain

dahinten *adv.* behind there

dahinter *adv.* behind it (*oder* that); **-kommen** *v.* to find out, to get to the bottom of; **es steckt nichts —** there is nothing in it

Dakron *neu.* dacron

damals *adv.* then; at that time

Damast *m.* (fabric) damask

Dame *f.* lady; dame; (cards, chess) queen; (checkers) king; **-brett** *neu.* checkerboard; **-nheld** *m.* ladies' man; **-nsattel** *f.* side-saddle

damit *adv.* and *conj.* therewith; with it (*oder* that); by it (*oder* that); **es ist nichts —** it is useless; **er ist — einverstanden** he agrees to it; **es ist — aus** it is all over; — **ist mir nicht gedient** that won't help me; — *conj.* in order to; — **nicht lest** ᵕ

dämlich *adj.* stupid, dull

Damm *m.* dam, dike; mole, pier; embankment; barrier; **auf dem — sein** to be okay

dämmen *v.* to dam up; to restrain, to stop

dämmerig *adj.* dusky, dim; uncertain; dreamy

Dämmerung *f.*, **Dämmerlicht** *neu.* twilight, dawn

Dämon *m.* demon

dämonisch *adj.* demoniac(al)

Dampf *m.* steam, vapor; **-bad** *neu.* steam bath; **-boot** *neu.* steamboat; **-druck** *m.* steam pressure; **-er** *m.* steamer; **-fleisch** *neu.* stew; **-kessel** *m.* boiler; **-kochtopf** *m.* pressure cooker; **-maschine** *f.* steam engine; **-walze** *f.* steamroller

dampfen *v.* to steam

dämpfen *v.* to dampen, to subdue; to stew

danach *adv.* after it (*oder* that); accordingly; **er sieht — aus** he quite looks it; **ich frage nicht —** I don't care

daneben *adv.* near it, next to it, close by; — *conj.* besides, also; **-gehen** *v.* to go amiss; **-treffen** *v.* to miss one's mark

Dänemark *neu.* Denmark

danieder *adv.* down; on the ground; **-liegen** *v.* to be prostrate; to be depressed

Dank *m.* thanks; reward; — **wissen** to be grateful; **zu — verpflichten** to oblige

dankbar *adj.* grateful, thankful; profitable

danken *v.* to thank; **danke!** *interj.* thank you!

dann *adv.* then; moreover; thereupon

d(a)ran *adv.* at (*oder* by, in, on, to) it (*oder* that); near it; in regard to it; **gut — sein** to be well off; **was liegt —?** what does it matter? **wir sind — it's** our turn; **-geh(e)n** *v.* to set to work; **-setzen** *v.* to risk

d(a)rauf *adv.* (up)on it, after that; **gleich — directly** afterwards; **-dringen** *v.* to demand; **-geh(e)n** *v.* to be lost; **-hin** *adv.* thereupon

d(a)raus *adv.* from it (*oder* that); **ich mache mir nichts —** I don't care

darben *v.* to suffer, to want

darbieten *v.* to offer, to present

Darbietung *f.* offering; performance

d(a)rein *adv.* into it; **-finden** *v.* **-fügen** *v.* to put up with; **-reden** *v.* to interfere; **-willigen** *v.* to consent

d(a)rin(nen) *adv.* in it; inside, within

darlegen *v.* to explain, to expose

Darleh(e)n *neu.* loan

Darm *m.* intestine, bowel, gut; **-saite** *f.* (mus.) catgut string; **-verschluss** *m.* (med.) enteritis

Darre *f.* kiln-drying, drying oven

darstellen *v.* to describe, to represent; to

exhibit; to act, to perform

Darsteller m. actor

dartun v. to demonstrate, to prove

d(a)rum adv. around; therefore; **er weiss** — he is aware of it; **es ist mir nur** — **zu tun** my only object is; **–bringen** to deprive of; **–kommen** v. to lose

das art neu. the; — pron. that. which

Dasein neu. existence; life; presence; **–skampf** m. struggle for existence

dass conj. that; **auf** — in order that; **ausser** — except that; **es sei denn** — unless

datieren v. to date

Dattel f. (bot.) date

Datum neu. (time) date

Daube f. stave (barrel, vessel etc.)

Dauer f. duration; continuance; **auf die** — in the long run; **–flug** m. nonstop flight; **–karte** f. season-ticket; **–lauf** m. endurance run; **–welle** f. permanent wave; **–wurst** f. hard sausage

dauer: **–haft** adj. durable, lasting; **–n** v. to continue, to last; **es –t mich** I am sorry for it; **–nd** adj. enduring, lasting

Dau nen n. thumb; **den** — **halten** to keep one's fingers crossed

davon adv. of it; away; off; by that; **das kommt** — that's the result; **sie sind auf und** — they left in a hurry; **–bleiben** v. to keep off, to leave alone; **–kommen** v. to escape; **–laufen** v. to take to one's heels; to desert; **–machen, sich –machen** v. to steal away, to abscond; **–tragen** v. to carry off; to win

davor adv. in front of; before; against it

dawider adv. against it

dazu adv. for (oder to) something; for the purpose of; in addition to that; **ich komme nie** — I can never find time for that; **–geben** v. to contribute to; **–gehören** v. to belong to; **–kommen** v. to come across

dazwischen adv. among, in the midst of; between (times); **–kommen** v. to intervene; **–liegend** adj. intermediate; **–treten** v. to interpose

Deck neu. deck; **–adresse** f. "in care of" address; **–blatt** neu. (bot.) bract; (cigar) wrapper; **–e** f. blanket, cover; ceiling; **sich nach der –e strecken** to adapt oneself to circumstances; **unter einer –e strecken** to conspire together; **–el** m. cover, lid; (coll.) hat; **–mantel** m. (fig.) cloak, pretense; **–name** m. pseudonym, nome de plume; **–offizier** m. (naut.) warrant officer

decken v. to cover, to protect, to secure; to reimburse; **den Tisch** — to set the table; **sich** — to coincide; to be identi-

cal (with)

defekt adj. defective, imperfect

Defekt m. defect, imperfection

definieren v. to define

definitiv adj. definite; final

Degen m. sword

dehnen v. to extend: to stretch; **to drawl**

dehnbar adj. elastic; vague

Deich m. dike

dein pron. and adj. your; (bibl.) thy, thine; **–erseits** adv. on your part; **–esgleichen** adj. and pron. such as you, thy like, your equal; **–ethalben** adv., **–etwegen** adj., **–etwillen** adv. for your sake, on your account

Dekan m. dean

deklamieren v. to recite, to declaim

deklinieren v. (gram.) to decline, to inflect; (ast.) to deviate

Dekoration f. decoration; ornament; (theat.) scenery; **–smaler** m. painter

Dekret neu. decree

delikat adj. delicate; delicious; dainty

Delphin m. dolphin

dem art. to the; — conj. whom; **–entsprechend**, **–gemäss**, **–nach** adv., **–zufolge** adv. accordingly; **–nächst** adv. shortly, soon; **–ungeachtet** conj. notwithstanding, nevertheless

Dementi neu. denial

dementieren v. to deny

demolieren v. to demolish

demonstrieren v. to demonstrate

demontieren v. to dismantle

Demut f. humility

demütig adj. humble; **–en** v. to humiliate

Denk: **–er** m. thinker; **–mal** neu. memorial, monument; **–zettel** m. reminder; punishment

denk: **–bar** adj. conceivable; **–en** v. to think; to reflect, to contemplate; to believe; to intend; **auf Mittel und Wege –en** to devise ways and means; **–en an** to remember, to think of; **sich –en** to imagine; **–würdig** adj. memorable

denn adv. and conj. because, for then; **es sei** — unless, provided that; **–(n)och** conj. nevertheless, still, though

Dentin neu. dentine

Depesche f. telegram

deponieren v. to deposit; (law) to depose

Deputierte m. deputy

der art. m. the; — pron. that, who, which; **–art** adv. in such a manner; **–artig** adj. of such kind; **–(mal)einst** adv. some day, in the future; **–einstig** adj. future; **–enthalben** adv., **–entwegen** adv., **–entwillen** adv. on her (oder their, whose) account; **–gestalt**, **–massen** adv. in such manner; **–gleichen** adv. such; **–zeit** adv.

at present; **–zeitig** *adj.* present
derb *adj.* solid, sturdy; rough, clumsy; blunt
Dermatologie *f.* dermatology
des: –gleichen *adv.* likewise; **–halb** *prep.*, **–wegen** *prep.* therefore; **–to** *adv.* the; **–to besser** all the better
Deserteur *m.* deserter
desertieren *v.* to desert
desinfizieren *v.* to disinfect
destillieren *v.* to distill
Detail *neu.* detail; retail
deut: –eln *v.* to twist (meaning); **–en** *v.* to point (at); to explain, to construe, to interpret; **–lich** *adj.* distinct, clear; intelligible
deutsch *adj.* German
Deutschland *neu.* Germany
Devise *f.* device, motto; **–n** *pl.* foreign money
Dezember *m.* December
dezimal *adj.* decimal
dezimieren *v.* to decimate
Diagnose *f.* diagnosis
Dialog *m.* dialogue
Diamant *m.* diamond
Diät *f.* diet; daily allowance
dicht *adj.* dense, thick, compact; tight, close; **–en** *v.* to tighten, to caulk
dichten *v.* (lit.) to write; (coll.) to dream up
Dichter *m.* poet, bard
Dichtung *f.* poem; poetry; epic; poetical work; fiction
dick *adj.* thick; corpulent, fat; **–e Freunde** intimate friends; **er hat es — hinter den Ohren** he is not as simple as he looks; **etwas — haben** to be fed up with; **sich — tun** to boast, to brag; **–bäckig** *adj.* chubby; **–bäuchig** *adj.* pot-bellied; **–blütig** *adj.* thick-blooded; **–fellig** *adj.* thick-skinned; callous; **–flüssig** *adj.* viscous; **–köpfig** *adj.* obstinate, block-headed; **–leibig** *adj.* corpulent
die *art. f.* the; **— pron.** that, who, which
Dieb *m.* thief, crook; **–stahl** *m.* theft
diebisch *adj.* thievish
Dietrich *m.* Theodore
Diele *f.* board, plank; floor; hall
dienen *v.* to serve; **womit kann ich —?** may I help you? **zu nichts —** to be of no use
Diener *m.* domestic, servant; bow; curtsy; **–schaft** *f.* servants, domestics
dienlich *adj.* serviceable, useful
Dienst *m.* service; duty; employment, post; good turn; **ausser — off** duty; retired; **im — in** service, on duty; **in — treten** to enter service; (mil.) to enlist; **–ablösung** *f.* relief; **–abzeichen**

neu. service badge, stripe; **–alter** *neu.* seniority; **–bote** *m.* domestic, servant; **–grad** *m.* rank; **–kleidung** *f.* livery; uniform; **–mädchen** *neu.* servant girl, maid; **–mann** *m.* porter, messenger; handyman; **–pflicht** *f.* official duty; **–stelle** *f.* headquarters; center, administrative department; **–stunden** *f. pl.* official (*oder* business) hours; **–weg** *m.* official channel, (coll.) red tape; **–wohnung** *f.* official residence; **–zeugnis** *neu.* reference (for employment); **–zwang** *m.* compulsory (*oder* military) service
Dienstag *m.* Tuesday
dies: –bezüglich *adj.* referring to this; **–e** *pron.*, **–er** *pron.*, **–es** *pron.* this; **–jährig** *adj.* of this year; **–mal** *adv.* this time; **–seitig** *adj.* on this side; **–seits** *adv.* and *prep.* on this side, here
Diktat *neu.* dictation; **–or** *m.* dictator; **–ur** *f.* dictatorship
diktieren *v.* to dictate
Diktiermaschine *f.* dictaphone
Dilettant *m.* amateur, layman
Ding *neu.* thing; matter; object; **das dumme —** the silly girl; **ein — der Unmöglichkeit** an impossibility; **guter –e sein** to be in high spirits; **vor allen –en** above all
ding: –en *v.* to hire; **–fest** *adv.*, **–fest machen** to arrest; **–lich** *adj.* real, judicial
Diözese *f.* diocese
Diplom *neu.* diploma; certificate; **–at** *m.* diplomat; **–atie** *f.* diplomacy
dir *pron.* to you, to thee
direkt *adj.* direct; **— beziehen** to buy direct (from manufacturer); **–er Zug** through train
Direktion *f.*, **Direktorium** *neu.* management; board of directors
Direktor *m.* headmaster, principal; manager
Dirigent *m.* conductor, band leader
dirigieren *v.* to conduct; to direct, to manage
Dirnd(e)l *neu.* dirndl; (dial.) girl, lass
Dirne *f.* girl; (coll.) hussy, prostitute
Diskant *m.* descant; treble, soprano; **–schlüssel** *m.* treble clef
Diskont(o) *m.* discount
diskret *adj.* discreet, tactful
Diskretion *f.* discretion
Diskurs *m.* discourse, conversation
diskutieren *v.* to discuss, to debate
Dispens *m.* dispensation; special license
dispensieren *v.* to release; to dispense
disputieren *v.* to dispute; to debate
Distanz *f.* distance

Distel *f.* thistle; **–fink** *m.* goldfinch
distinguiert *adj.* distinguished
Disziplin *f.* discipline; branch of knowledge; organized study
disziplinarisch *adj.* disciplinary
disziplinieren *v.* to discipline; to train
dividieren *v.* to divide
Diwan *m.* couch, divan, sofa
doch *conj.* and *adv.* however, nevertheless; after all; though; but, still, yet; **ja —** but of course; **nicht —**! certainly not! don't!
Docht *m.* wick
Dock *neu.* dock (yard)
Docke *f.* baluster; skein; (dial.) doll; sheaf of grain; straw torch
Dogge *f.* bulldog; **deutsch —** great Dane
Dohle *f.* jackdaw
Doktor *m.* doctor; physician, surgeon; **den — machen** to confer a doctor's degree; **–at** *neu.* doctorate, doctor's degree
dokumentieren *v.* to document
Dolch *m.* dagger; **–messer** *neu.* bowie-knife; **–stich** *m.* dagger wound; **–stoss** *m.* stab
dolmetschen *v.* to interpret
Dom *m.* cathedral; dome, cupola
Domäne *f.* domain; province
Domino *m.* domino
Dompfaff *m.* bullfinch
Donau *f.* Danube
Donner *m.* thunder; **–keil** *m.* thunderbolt; **–schlag** *m.* thunderclap; **–stag** *m.* Thursday; **–wetter** *neu.* thunderstorm; (coll.) scolding; **–wetter!** *interj.* confound it!
donnern *v.* to thunder; (gun) to boom; to fulminate; to roar
Doppel *neu.* double; duplicate; **–boden** *m.* false bottom; **–bruch** *m.* compound fracture (*oder* rupture); **–decker** *m.* biplane; **–ehe** *f.* bigamy; **–fehler** *m.* (tennis) double fault; **–flinte** *f.* double-barreled gun; **–gänger** *m.* double, second self; **–laut** *m.* diphthong; **–leben** *neu.* double life; **–punkt** *m.* (gram.) colon; **–rolle** *f.* (theat.) double part; **–sinn** *m.* double meaning; ambiguity; **–spiel** *neu.* (tennis) double; double-dealing; **–sterne** (um ein Zentrum) *m. pl.* (ast.) binary stars; **–steuerung** *f.* (avi.) dual controls
doppel *adj.* **läufig** *adj.* double-barreled; **–n** *v.* to double; **–reihig** *adj.* double-breasted; **–sinnig** *adj.* ambiguous; **–t** *adj.* double, twofold; **–te Buchführung** double-entry bookkeeping; **–t** *adv.* doubly, twice; **–wertig** *adj.* ambivalent; **–züngig** *adj.* two-faced

Dorf *neu.* village, hamlet; **–bewohner** *m.* villager; **–gemeinde** *f.* rural parish; **–krug** *m.*, **–schenke** *f.* country inn; **–leute** *f.* village folk; **–schulze** *m.* village magistrate
Dorn *m.* thorn, prickle, spine; mandrel; **ein — im Auge** a thorn in the side; **–röschen** *neu.* Sleeping Beauty
dorren *v.* to become dry; to wither
dörren *v.* to desiccate; to parch; to kiln-dry
Dörrobst *neu.* dried fruit
dort *adv.* yonder; in that place, (over) there; **bis –hin** as far as that place; **— herum** thereabouts; **–her** *adv.* from there; **–ig** *adj.* of that place; **–zulande** *adv.* in that country
Dose *f.* box; can; **–nöffner** *m.* can opener
dösen *v.* to doze, to be drowsy
Dosis *f.* dose
Dotter *m.* and *neu.* yolk; **–blume** *f.* marsh marigold, buttercup
Dozent *m.* university teacher (*oder* lecturer); **–ur** *f.* (German university) right to teach
Drache(n) *m.* dragon; serpent; kite; (coll.) termagant; **–nkopf** *m.* (arch.) gargoyle
Dragoner *m.* dragoon; (coll.) virago
Draht *m.* cable, wire; line; **–anschrift** *f.* telegraphic address; **–antwort** *f.* telegraphic reply; **–geflecht** *neu.* wire netting; **–hindernis** *neu.*, **–verhau** *neu.* wire entanglement; **–nachricht** *f.* wire, telegram; **–puppe** *f.* marionette; **–seilbahn** *f.* cable railroad, funicular railway; **–stift** *m.* wire nail; **–zaun** *m.* wire fence
drall *adj.* tight; firm, robust; buxom
Drama *neu.* drama; **–tiker** *m.* playwright; **–turg** *m.* producer
dramatisch *adj.* dramatic
dramatisieren *v.* to dramatize
Drang *m.* pressure; distress; impulse; craving; hurry; **–sal** *f.*, *neu.* affliction, distress
dränge(l)n *v.* to crowd, to press, to push, to shove; to urge, to hurry; **sich durch die Menge —** to elbow (*oder* force) one's way through the crowd; **sich in eine Ecke —** to crouch in a corner
drangsalieren *v.* to oppress; to vex, to harass
drapieren *v.* to drape
drastisch *adj.* drastic
Draufgänger *m.* daredevil; **–tum** *neu.* recklessness
Drauflosfahren *neu.* reckless driving
draussen *adv.* outside, abroad
drechseln *v.* to turn on a lathe
Drechsler *m.* ᵗ ᵘrner; **–ei** *f.* turner's craft

(*oder* workshop)

Dreck *m.* dirt, filth, mud; dung, excrement; rubbish, trash; **–fink** *m.* filthy fellow

dreckig *adj.* dirty, filthy, muddy; nasty

Dreh: **–bank** *f.* turning lathe; **–brücke** *f.* swing bridge; **–buch** *neu.* (film) scenario; **–bühne** *f.* revolving stage; **–er** *m.* turner; **–kran** *m.* derrick; **–kreuz** *neu.* turnstile; **–orgel** *f.* barrel organ; **–punkt** *m.* pivot; **–ring** *m.* swivel; **–scheibe** *f.* (potter's) wheel; turntable; **–tür** *f.* revolving door

drehbar *adj.* rotary

drehen *v.* to revolve, to turn; to twist; (avi.) to spin; (film) to shoot; **es dreht sich darum** the point is

drei *adj.* three; **–eckig** *adj.* triangular; **–erlei** *adj.* of three kinds; **auf –erlei Art** in three (different) ways; **–fach** *adj.* threefold, treble, triple; **–jährig** *adj.* three years old; **–kantig** *adj.* three-edged; **–mal** *adv.* three times; **–malig** *adj.* occurring three times; **–monatlich** *adj.* quarterly, every three months; **–saitig** *adj.* three-stringed; **–seitig** *adj.* three-sided, trilateral; **–ssig** *adj.* thirty; **–stellig** *adj.* (math.) of three places; **–stündig** *adj.* of three hours (duration); **–teilig** *adj.* in three parts; **–winklig** *adj.* triangular; **–zehn** *adj.* thirteen

Drei *f.* three; **–bund** *m.* Triple Alliance; **–eck** *neu.* triangle; **–ecklehre** *f.* trigonometry; **–einigkeit** *f.* Trinity; **–fuss** *m.* tripod; **–käsehoch** *m.* (coll.) toddler; **–königsabend** *m.* Twelfth-night; **–königsfest** *neu.* Epiphany; **–rad** *neu.* tricycle; **–sprung** *m.* hop, skip, and jump; **–zack** *m.* trident; **–zahl** *f.* triad

dreist *adj.* bold, daring, audacious; impudent

Dresch: **–e** *v.* (sl.) good beating; **–en** *neu.* threshing; **–er** *m.* thresher; **–flegel** *m.* (agr.) flail; **–maschine** *f.* threshing machine, combine

dreschen *v.* to thresh; (sl.) to beat up, to thrash

dressieren *v.* to tame, to train, to break in; to coach, to drill

Drill *m.* (mil.) drill(ing); **–bohrer** *m.* crankshaft; **–säge** *f.* hack saw

Drilling *m.* triplet; lantern pinion; three-barrelled gun

dring: **–en** *v.* to press forward; to urge, to compel; to penetrate; **–end** *adj.* pressing, urgent; **–lich** *adj.* urgently

dritt: **–e** *adj.* third; **–ens** *adv.* thirdly

Drittel *neu.* third

droben *adv.* above, on high, up there

Drog: **–e** *f.* drug; **–erie** *f.* pharmacy; **–ist** *m.* druggist

Drohbrief *m.* threatening (blackmail) letter

drohen *v.* to threaten, to menace

Drohne *f.* (ent.) drone; (coll.) idler

dröhnen *v.* to roar, to rumble; to boom

drollig *adj.* droll, funny, comical

Dromedar *neu.* dromedary; (coll.) blockhead

Droschke *f.* cab; taxi; **–nlenker** *m.* cab driver

Drossel *f.* (orn.) thrush; (mech.) throttle

drosseln *v.* to throttle

drüben *adv.* over there, yonder

Druck *m.* compression, pressure; weight; oppression; (typ.) print(ing); impression; kleiner (*or* grosser) — small (*oder* large) type; **–er** *m.* printer, typographer; **–erei** *f.* printing; print shop; **–erlaubnis** *f.* imprimatur; **–erpresse** *f.* printing press; **–erschwärze** *f.* printer's ink; **–fehler** *m.* misprint, typographical error; **–jahr** *neu.* year of issue; **–kabine** *f.* pressurized cabin; **–knopf** *m.* snap fastener; **–kombination** *f.* pressure suit; **–luft** *f.* compressed air; **–probe** *f.* printer's proof; **–sache** *f.* printed matter; **–schrift** *f.* publication

drucken *v.* to print, to impress

drücken *v.* to press; to grip, to squeeze; to pinch; to lower; to bring down (prices), to depress; to oppress; **sich** — (coll.) to sneak off, to steal away; **–d** *adj.* heavy, sultry

Drücker *m.* latch; (gun) trigger

drunten *adv.* below, down there

Drüse *f.* gland; **–nentzündung** *f.* adenitis

Dschungel *neu.* jungle

du *pron.* thou, you; **auf — und — stehen** to be on intimate terms

Dublette *f.* duplicate; doublet

ducken *v.* to duck, to stoop; to bow; to humble

Duckmäuser *m.* coward; sneak; soft-pedaler

Dudelei *f.* monotonous (*oder* poor) music

Dudelsack *m.* bagpipe

Duell *neu.* duel

duellieren *v.* to fight a duel

Duett *neu.* duet

Duft *m.* fragrance, scent

duft: **–en** *v.* to be fragrant, to smell sweetly; **–end** *adj.*, **–ig** *adj.* fragrant; airy, light

Dukaten *m.* ducat

duld: **–bar** *adj.* tolerable, endurable; **–en** *v.* to tolerate; to suffer, to endure; **–sam** *adj.* tolerant; patient; long-suffering

dumm *adj.* stupid; foolish, silly; **–dreist**

adj. impertinent; –stolz *adj.* conceited

Dummkopf *m.* blockhead

dumpf *adj.* damp, muggy, stuffy; hollow-sounding; oppressive; vague; –ig *adj.* damp, musty

Düne *f.* dune

Dung, Dünger *m.* dung, manure

düngen *v.* to fertilize, to manure

dunkel *adj.* dark, dim; sombre; suspicious; –n *v.* to grow dark (*oder* dim)

Dünkel *m.* conceit, arrogance

dünkelhaft *adj.* conceited, arrogant

Dunkelkammer *f.* (photo.) darkroom

dünken *v.* to appear; to look, to seem

dünn *adj.* thin, fine; slender; sparse; diluted, weak; rare; –bäckig *adj.* hollow-cheeked; –beinig *adj.* spiderlegged

Dunst *m.* exhalation; vapor; fume; haze; false appearance; **jemand blauen vormachen** to bamboozle (*oder* humbug) a person; –gebilde *neu.* phantom; –kreis *m.* atmosphere

dunsten *v.* to evaporate, to steam; to exhale

dunstig *adj.* vaporous; hazy, misty; damp

Duplikat *neu.* duplicate

durch *adv.* and *prep.* through; across; by (means of); because of; during; throughout; — **die Finger sehen** to overlook (someone's blunder); — **die Post** by mail; — **und** — thoroughly; — **und** — **nass** drenched to the skin; — **Zufall** by chance

durcharbeiten *v.* to work through; to study thoroughly; to elaborate

durchaus *adv.* thoroughly; throughout; in every way; quite; absolutely, positively; by all means; — **nicht** not at all

durchbilden *v.* to educate (*oder* develop) thoroughly

durchblättern *v.* to leaf (*oder* skim) through

Durchblick *m.* vista, view; penetration

durchblicken *v.* to look through; to appear; — **lassen** to hint, to give to understand

durchbohren *v.* to bore through; to pierce; to perforate

durchbrechen *v.* to break through; to pierce

durchbrennen *v.* to burn through; (elec.) to fuse; (coll.) to abscond, to flee

durchbringen *v.* to carry through; to rear; to enact (law); to dissipate, to squander; **sich** — to subsist

Durchbruch *m.* (act of) breaking through; eruption; rupture; (teeth) cutting; gap

durchdenken *v.* to think through; to ponder

durchdrängen *v.* to force through; **sich** —

to elbow one's way through

durchdring: –en *v.* to permeate; to penetrate; to prevail, to succeed; –end *adj.* penetrating; shrill, keen; –lich *adj.* penetrable

durcheinander *adv.* confusedly; promiscuously; pell-mell, topsy-turvy

Durcheinander *neu.* confusion, disorder; jumble

durchfahren *v.* to drive (*oder* pass) through; to traverse; to wear out by driving

Durchfahrt *f.* thoroughfare, passáge; driving (*oder* passing) through; gateway; channel

Durchfall *m.* falling through; (med.) diarrhea; failure, rejection

durchfallen *v.* to fall through; to fail, to be rejected; to fall flat

durchfechten *v.* to fight it out (*oder* one's way through)

durchfeilen *v.* to file through; (fig.) to polish; to give the finishing touches

durchfinden *v.* **sich** — to find one's way through

durchfliegen *v.* to fly (*oder* rush) through, to skim over

Durchflug *m.* flight through; nonstop flight

durchforschen *v.* to search through; to examine closely; to investigate

durchfressen *v.* (zool.) to eat through; to corrode; (sl.) to struggle through; to sponge on

durchfrieren *v.* to freeze completely; to chill to the bone

Durchfuhr *f.* transit; –handel *m.* transit trade; –zoll *m.* transit duty

durchführbar *adj.* practicable, feasible

durchführen *v.* to convey (*oder* lead) through; to accomplish, to execute; (mus.) to develop

Durchgang *m.* passing through; passage, thoroughfare; defile; transit; gateway; –sgüter *neu. pl.* goods in transit; –srecht *neu.* right of way; –swagen *m.* (rail.) through car

Durchgänger *m.* bolting horse; absconder

durchgängig *adj.* throughout, without exception

durchgehen *v.* to go through; to pass; to penetrate; to escape, to abscond; to examine, to peruse, to work through; (horse) to bolt

durchgeistigt *adj.* spiritual, intellectual

durchgiessen *v.* to filter, to pour through

durchglühen *v.* to heat red hot; (chem.) to calcine; (mech.) to anneal; to inflame

durchgreifen *v.* to put one's hand through; to proceed vigorously, to act decisively;

-d *adj.* decisive, sweeping, vigorous, thorough

durchhalten *v.* to hold out; to carry through

durchhauen *v.* to cut through; to cleave

durchhecheln *v.* to heckle, to criticize

durchkauen *v.* to chew through; (coll.) to repeat

durchkommen *v.* to get through; to pass; to succeed; to escape; to recover

durchkreuzen *v.* to cross, to traverse; to thwart

durchlassen *v.* to let through, to allow to pass; (phy.) to transmit

durchlässig *adj.* pervious, penetrable

durchlaufen *v.* to filter; to go through; to wear out (shoes)

durchleuchten *v.* to shine through; to flood with light; to irradiate; to X-ray

durchliegen *v.* to become bedsore

durchlochen, durchlöchern *v.* to perforate; to punch; to puncture; (coll.) to badger

durchmachen *v.* to go (*oder* pass) through; to experience; to suffer

Durchmarsch *m.* march(ing) through; (cards) grand slam

durchmessen *v.* to measure through; to traverse

Durchmesser *m.* diameter; (mil.) caliber; (opt.) aperture

durchmustern *v.* to review; to search through, to examine, to inspect, to scrutinize

durchnässen *v.* to wet through; to soak

durchnehmen *v.* to go over; to analyze; to explain; to criticise

durchpeitschen *v.* to flog (*oder* whip) soundly; to dispatch quickly

durchprügeln *v.* to beat (*oder* thrash) soundly

durchreiben *v.* to rub through; to wear out by friction; to chafe

Durchreise *f.* journey through, passage, transit

durchschauen *v.* to look through; to penetrate; to detect, to discover

durchscheinen *v.* to shine through; **-d** *adj.* transparent, translucent; diaphanous

durchschiessen *v.* to shoot through; to dash through; to interleave; (typ.) to lead

Durchschlag *m.* colander, strainer; carbon copy

durchschlagen *v.* to beat (*oder* punch) through; to penetrate; to strain, to filter; to beat soundly; to blot; to be effective; Sicherungen — to cause a short-circuit

durchschlüpfen *v.* to slip through; to have

a narrow escape

durchschneiden *v.* to cut through; to cross, to traverse; to intersect

Durchschnitt *m.* cut(ting) through; cross-section; section; profile; average

durchschnittlich *adj.* average, of medium size (*oder* quality); — *adv.* on an average, ordinarily speaking

durchsehen *v.* to see (*oder* look) through; to scrutinize; to proofread; to revise

durchseihen *v.* to filter, to strain

durchsetzen *v.* to carry through; to make one's way; to succeed; to intersperse

Durchsicht *f.* vista, correction, revision

durchsichtig *adj.* transparent; clear

durchsickern *v.* to trickle (*oder* ooze) through; to percolate

durchsieben *v.* to sift, to bolt, to screen

durchsprechen *v.* to talk over; to discuss

durchstechen *v.* to pierce through; to cut; to transfix; to perforate; to prick

durchstöbern *v.* to rummage through; to ransack

durchstossen *v.* to push (*oder* knock) through; to pierce, to stab

durchstreichen *v.* to strike out; to cancel; to roam through; (orn.) to pass through

durchstreifen *v.* to range (*oder* roam) through

durchsuchen *v.* to search; to examine closely

durchtreten *v.* to wear (*oder* step) through

durchtrieben *adj.* crafty, cunning, sly

durchwachsen *adj.* (meat) marbled; streaked

Durchwässerung *f.* (chem.) saturation

durchweben *v.* to interweave; to interlace

Durchweg *m.* through-passage; thoroughfare

durchweg *adv.* throughout; without exception

durchwirken *v.* to interweave; to have effect

durchwühlen *v.* to root up; to burrow; to rummage

durchzeichnen *v.* to trace (through paper)

durchziehen *v.* to draw (*oder* pass) through; to thread; to soak; (coll.) to criticize

durchzucken *v.* to flash through; to realize suddenly; to convulse

Durchzug *m.* passing (*oder* drawing) through; through draft

dürfen *v.* to be allowed (*oder* permitted); **darf ich?** may I?

dürftig *adj.* indigent, needy; shabby; scanty

dürr *adj.* parched, arid; withered; lean; skinny; bare, **mit -en Worten** in plain language

Dürre *f.* dryness, aridity; drought; leanness

Durst *m.* thirst

dursten, dürsten *v.* to be thirsty, to thirst

Dusche *f.* shower bath

Düse *f.* nozzle, jet; **–nbomber** *m.* jet bomber; **–nflugzeug** *n.* jet plane; (coll.) blowtorch; **–nstrahl** *m.* jet stream

Dusel *m.* (coll.) pure luck, windfall

duselig *adj.* dreamy, drowsy; dizzy

düster *adj.* dark, dusky, sombre, gloomy; sad

Dutzend *neu.* dozen; **–gesicht** *neu.* ordinary face; **–mensch** *m.* commonplace person

dutzendweise *adv.* by the dozen

duzen *v.* to address familiarly

dynamisch *adj.* dynamic(al)

D-Zug *m.* express train

E

Ebbe *f.* ebb tide; **–n** *v.* to ebb

eben *adj.* even, level; smooth; plane; **zu –er Erde** on the ground floor; — *adv.* just, quite; namely, exactly; evenly; — **erst** just now; **–bürtig** *adj.* equal (in birth); **–da** *adv.* at the same place; **–falls** *adv.* likewise, also; **–mässig** *adj.* proportionate; **–so** *adv.* just so; **–sowohl** *adv.* just as well

Eben: –bild *neu.* exact likeness, image; **–e** *f.* plain; level ground; plane; **in gleicher –e** on a level with; **schiefe –e** gradient, inclined plane; (coll.) skid row; **–mass** *neu.* symmetry, right proportion

Ebenholz *neu.* ebony

Eber *m.* wild boar

ebnen *v.* to make level, to smooth; **die Bahn —** to pave the way

echt *adj.* genuine, authentic, unadulterated, pure; real, original; fast (color)

Eck *neu.* (dial.) corner, angle, edge; **–brett** *neu.* corner shelf; **–chen** *neu.* nook; **–e** *f.* angle, corner; (arch.) quoin; **an allen –en und Enden** everywhere; **um die –e bringen** (sl.) to murder; **um die –e gehen** to turn the corner; **–stein** *m.* cornerstone; (cards) diamond; **–zahn** *m.* eye tooth

edel *adj.* noble, genteel, benevolent; precious, superior, refined; **–e Teile** vital parts; **–gesinnt** *adj.* high-minded, magnanimous

Edel: –frau *f.* titled lady; **–knabe** *m.* page; **–mann** *m.* nobleman; **–metall** *neu.* precious metal; **–mut** *m.* generosity, magnanimity; noble-mindedness; **–rost** *m.* patina; **–stein** *m.* precious stone,

jewel; **–wild** *neu.* deer

Edikt *neu.* edict

Efeu *m.* ivy

Effekt *m.* effect; **–en** *pl.* movable goods; (com.) securities; **–enbörse** *f.* stock exchange; **–enhändler** *m.* stockbroker; **–hascherei** *f.* sensationalism, playing to the gallery

egal *adj.* equal; alike, same; **das ist mir ganz —** it's all the same to me

Egel *m.* (zool.) leech

Egge *f.* (agr.) harrow

Egoismus *m.* egoism; selfishness

egozentrisch *adj.* self-centered

ehe *adv.* before, until; **–dem** *adv.* before this; **–malig** *adj.* former; **–mals** *adv.* formerly, of old; **–r** *adv.* earlier, sooner; rather, more easily; **je –r je lieber** the sooner the better; **–stens** *adv.* as soon as possible

Ehe *f.* matrimony, marriage; **wilde —** common-law marriage; **–bett** *neu.* marriage bed; **–brecher** *m.* adulterer; **–bruch** *m.* adultery; **–bund** *m.* matrimony; **–hälfte** *f.* one's "better half"; **–kreuz** *neu.* (coll.) termagant; **–krüppel** *m.* (coll.) hen-pecked husband; **–leute** *pl.* married couple; **–mann** *m.* husband; **–paar** *neu.* married couple; **–pflicht** *f.* conjugal duty; **–recht** *neu.* matrimonial law; **–scheidung** *f.* divorce; **–schliessung** *f.* contracting of marriage; **–stand** *m.* married life; **–stifter** *m.* matchmaker; **–versprechen** *neu.* promise of marriage; **–vertrag** *m.* marriage contract

ehelich *adj.* conjugal, matrimonial; (child) legitimate; **–lichen** to marry

ehelos *adj.* unmarried, single

Ehr: –abschneider *m.* slanderer; **–e** *f.* honor, praise; credit; distinction; **–furcht** *f.* awe, veneration; **–gefühl** *neu.* sense of honor; self-respect; **–geiz** *m.* ambition; **–ung** *f.* honors; **–verlust** *m.* loss of civil rights; **–würden** *f.* Reverend; Reverence

ehr: –bar *adj.* honorable, respectable; decent, decorous; reputable; **–erbietig** *adj.* respectful, reverential; **–fürchtig** *adj.* awe-inspiring, reverential; **–lich** *adj.* honest, fair dealing, loyal, true; **–los** *adj.* dishonorable; **–sam** *adj.* decent, worthy, respectable; **–vergessen** *adj.* unprincipled, base-minded; **–widrig** *adj.* disgraceful, discreditable; **–würdig** *adj.* reverent, venerable

ehren *v.* to honor; to esteem; to revere; **–amtlich** *adj.* honorary; **–haft** *adj.* honorable, high-principled; **–halber** *prep.* for honor's sake; **–rührig** *adj.* defamatory, libelous; **–voll** *adj.* honorable; **–wert** *adj.* respectable

Ehren: –amt *neu.* honorary office; position of honor (*oder* trust); **–bezeugung** *f.* ovation; proof of esteem; (mil.) salute; **–bürger** *m.* honorary citizen; **–dame** *f.* maid of honor; **–doktor** *m.* honorary doctor; **–erklärung** *f.*, **–rettung** *f.* reparation of honor; rehabilitation; **–gast** *m.* guest of honor; **–geleit** *neu.* honorary escort; **–halle** *f.* hall of fame; **–handel** *m.* affair of honor; **–klage** *f.* libel suit; **–kränkung** *f.* affront, insult, libel; **–mitglied** *neu.* honorary member; **–raub** *m.* dishonoring; **–sache** *f.* unquestionable duty; duel; **–sold** *m.* honorarium, donation; **–tag** *m.* anniversary; **–titel** *m.* honorary title; **–trunk** *m.* toast; **–wache** *f.* guard of honor; **–wort** *neu.* word of honor; (law) parole; **–zeichen** *neu.* decoration, medal

Ei *neu.* egg; **hartes —** hard-boiled egg; **kaum aus dem — gekrochen** just out of the shell; (coll.) a greenhorn; **verlorenes —** poached egg; **wie aus dem — gepellt** (*or* geschält) spic and span; **–dotter, –gelb** *neu.* yolk; **–erkuchen** *m.* omelet; **–erschnee** *m.* whipped white of eggs; **–erstock** *m.* ovary; **–weiss** *neu.* white of egg, albumin; **–weisstoff** *m.* protein

Eich: –e *f.* oak; **–el** *f.* acorn; (cards) clubs; **–horn** *neu.*, **–hörnchen** *neu.*, **–katze** *f.* squirrel

eichen *v.* to calibrate

Eichung (Gradeinteilung) *f.* calibration

Eid *m.* oath; **–brecher** *m.*, **–brüchige** *m.* perjurer; **–bruch** *m.* perjury; **–esabnahme** *f.* taking an oath; **–genosse** *m.* confederate

Eidechse *f.* lizard

eif: –ern *v.* to show zeal, to display ardor; to emulate, to vie (with); **–ern gegen** to inveigh against; **–ersüchtig** *adj.* jealous; **–rig** *adj.* eager, zealous, ardent

Eifer *m.* zeal, ardor, fervor, emulation; **–er** *m.* zealot; **–sucht** *f.* jealousy; **–süchtelei** *f.* petty jealousy

eigen *adj.* own, proper, individual; particular, special, separate; exact; peculiar; odd, strange; **sich zu — machen** to adopt; to appropriate; **–artig** *adj.* peculiar; **–händig** *adj.* with (*oder* in) one's own hand; **–mächtig** *adj.* on one's own authority; arbitrary; **–nützig** *adj.* selfish, self-interested; **–s** *adv.* expressly, purposely; **–sinnig** *adj.* stubborn, obstinate; capricious; **–tlich** *adj.* real, true; proper; intrinsic; **–tlich** *adv.* properly, exactly, really; **–tümlich** *adj.*

real, proper, specific; peculiar; characteristic; **–willig** *adj.* willful, self-willed

Eigen: –art *f.* peculiarity; **–bericht** *m.* (newspaper) special report; **–brödler** *m.*, **–brötler** *m.* quaint fellow, introvert; **–gewicht** *neu.* net weight; **–liebe** *f.* self-love, egotism; **–lob** *neu.* self-praise; **–nutz** *m.* self-interest, selfishness; **–peilung** *f.* (avi.) homing; **–schaft** *f.* attribute, property; quality; characteristic; **–schaftswort** *neu.* adjective; **–sinn** *m.* willfulness; obstinacy; **–tum** *neu.* property; ownership; **–tümer** *m.* proprietor, owner; **–tumsrecht** *neu.* proprietorship; copyright; **–tumssteuer** *f.* property tax; **–wille** *m.* willfulness

eignen *v.* **sich —** für to be suited for

Eignung *f.* qualification; aptitude; **–sprüfung** *f.* aptitude test

Eil: –brief *m.* special delivery letter; **–bote** *m.* courier; special-delivery mailman; **–e** *f.* haste, hurry; speed; **–fracht** *f.*, **–gut** *neu.* express freight; **–marsch** *m.* forced march; **–zug** *m.* express train

eil: –en *v.* to hasten, to hurry; **–ends** *adv.* hastily, quickly; **–fertig** *adj.* precipitate; hasty; **–ig** *adj.* urgent; quick, speedy

Eimer *m.* pail; bucket

eimerweise *adv.* by buckets, **in pailfuls**

ein *art.* a(n); **—** *adj.* one; **—** für alle Mal once and for all; **—** ums andere Mal alternatively; **in –em fort** continuously; **um –s** at one o'clock; **—** *pron.* a, one, some; **—** jeder each one; **–er von beiden** either one; **—** und derselbe the very same; **—** *adv.* in; **—** und aus gehen to frequent; **–ander** *pron.* one another, each other; **–armig** *adj.* one-armed; single-branched; **–äugig** *adj.* one-eyed, monocular; **–bändig** *adj.* in one volume; **–deutig** *adj.* having but one meaning, unequivocal; **–erlei** *adj.* of one kind, monotonous; **–erseits, –esteils** *adv.* on the one hand; **–fach** *adj.* simple; single; plain; frugal; (math.) indivisible, **–fache Buchführung** single entry bookkeeping; **–fältig** *adj.* silly, simpleminded; **–farbig** *adj.* one-colored, plain; monochromic; **–förmig** *adj.* uniform, monotonous; **–geboren** *adj.* native; (rel.) only begotten; **–händig** *adj.* one-handed; **–heitlich** *adj.* uniform, homogenous, centralized; **–hellig** *adj.* unanimous; **–ig** *adj.* in agreement; united; **–ige** *adj.* some; **–(ig)en** *v.* to unify, to unite; to conciliate; **sich –igen** to agree, to come to terms; **–jährig** *adj.* one-year-old; annual; **–mal** *adv.* once; formerly; at some future time; **–malig** *adj.* happening but once, one-time, unique; —mütig *adj.* unanimous; —reihig *adj.* single-breasted; —sam *adj.* solitary; lonely; —seitig *adj.* —silbig *adj.* monosyllabic; taciturn; —sitzig *adj.* singleseated; —spurig *adj.* single-railed; —stimmig *adj.* unanimous; of (*oder* for) one voice; solo; —stöckig *adj.* onestoried; —tägig *adj.* lasting one day, ephemeral; —tönig *adj.* monotonous, tedious; —trächtig *adj.* harmonious; united; —zellig *adj.* one-celled; —zig *adj.* only, single, sole; unique; —zigartig *adj.* unique, matchless

Ein: —bahnstrasse *f.* one-way street; —decker *m.* monoplane; —ehe *f.* monogamy; —er *m.* any number under ten; —erlei *neu.* uniformity, monotonv, sameness; —falt *f.* simplicity; artlessness, silliness; —faltspinsel *m.* simpleton; —geborene *m.* native; —glas *neu.* monocle; —heit *f.* unity; unit; —klang *m.* harmony; accord, un son; —maleins *neu.* multiplication table; —siedler *m.* hermit; recluse; —tracht *f.* harmony, concord, union

einarbeiten *v.* to train; **sich** — to familiarize oneself (with)

einäschern *v.* to reduce to ashes, to incinerate; to calcine

einatmen *v.* to inhale

einbalsamieren *v.* to embalm

Einband *m.* (book) binding

einbe: —dingen *v.* to include (in a bargain); —griffen *adj.* included; —halten to detain; —rufen *v.* (mil.) to call up (*oder* out); to convene; to convoke; to summon

einbiegen *v.* to bend inward; to turn into

einbilden *f.* to fancy (*oder* imagine); **sich etwas** — to be conceited

Einbildungskraft *f.* power of imagination; poetic fancy; fantasy

einblasen *v.* to blow (*oder* breathe) into; to insinuate, to prompt

einbläuen *v.* to blue; to inculcate

Einblick *m.* insight, glance into

Einbrecher *m.* housebreaker, burglar

einbrennen *v.* to burn into; to brand; (cooking) to thicken; to fumigate; to cauterize

einbringen *v.* to bring in; to yield (profits); **etwas wieder** — to make good, to retrieve

einbrocken *v.* to crumble into; **sich etwas** — to get into trouble

Einbruch *m.* housebreaking, burglary

einbürgern *v.* to naturalize; to enfranchise

eindecken *v.* to provide with; to store up

eindeutschen *v.* to Germanize

eindrängen *v.* to push in; **sich** — to intrude

eindrir gen *v.* to enter forcibly; to penetrat ; to infiltrate

eindringlich *adj.* penetrating; impressive, touching; affecting, forcible

Eindringling *m.* interloper, intruder

Eindruck *m.* impression; imprint

eindrücken *v.* to crush; to imprint; **to** impress

eindrucksvoll *adj.* emphatic, impressive

einebnen *v.* to flatten, to level, to smooth

einengen *v.* to confine, to narrow, to limit

einernten *v.* to reap, to harvest; to gain

einexerzieren *v.* to drill, to train

einfädeln *v.* to thread; to contrive

einfahren *v.* to drive in(to); to carry (*oder* bring) in; to enter; (horse) to break in; (min.) to descend

Einfahrt *f.* (act of) driving in; entry, gateway, inlet; (min.) descent

Einfall *m.* invasion; sudden idea, notion; (phys.) incidence

einfallen *v.* to fall in, to ruin; to interrupt; to occur; to invade; (mus.) to join in

einfangen *v.* to catch, to seize

einfassen *v.* to border. to edge, to trim; to enclose, to frame

einfetten *v.* to grease, to lubricate

einfinden *v.* **sich** — to appear, to arrive, to turn up

einflössen *v.* to instill, to inspire; to imbue

Einflug *m.* (act of) flying in

Einfluss *m.* influx; influence

einflussreich *adj.* influential

einflüstern *v.* to whisper to; to insinuate

einfordern *v.* to call in, to demand

einfrieren *v.* to freeze in; to be icebound

einfügen *v.* to insert; to dovetail; **sich** — to adapt oneself to; to fit in

Einfuhr *f.* import(ation); —**sperre** *f.* embargo on imports; —**zoll** *m.* import duty

einführen *v.* to import; to introduce; to install; to inaugurate; to bring in

Einführung *f.* introduction; elementary guidance

Eingabe *f.* petition; presentation; memorial

Eingang *m.* (act of) entering, entry; arrival; access; (anat.) passage; (geog.) inlet, mouth; (lit.) preface, introduction; **kein** — no admission; **nach** — on receipt

eingeben *v.* to prompt; to inspire; to give, to hand in; (med.) to administer

eingebildet *adj.* imaginary, fanciful, conceited

eingedenk *prep.* mindful of, remembering

eingefallen *adj.* sunken (eye), hollow (cheek)

eingefleischt *adj.* incarnate; inveterate

eingehen *v.* to go in; to arrive; to enter; to decay; to cease; to die; to shrink; — **lassen** to give up, to leave off; to drop; **Vergleich** — to come to terms; **Wette** — to wager; **-d** *adj.* thorough, exhaustive, in detail

Eingemachte *neu.* preserves; jam; pickles

eingemeinden *v.* to merge, to incorporate

eingenommen *adj.* prepossessed, biased, partial

Eingesandt *neu.* letter to the editor

eingeschränkt *adj.* limited, confined

eingeschrieben *adj.* registered

Eingeständnis *neu.* avowal, confession

eingestehen *v.* to avow, to confess; to concede

Eingeweide *neu. pl.* bowels, entrails, intestines

Eingeweihte *m.* initiated person; adept

eingewöhnen *v.* sich — to accustom oneself; to get used to

eingewurzelt *adj.* deep-rooted, inveterate

eingezogen *adj.* retired, secluded; confiscated; (mil.) drafted

eingittern *v.* to fence in; to rail off

eingliedern *v.* to incorporate; to embody

eingraben *v.* to dig in; to bury; to entrench; to engrave

eingravieren *v.* to engrave

eingreifen *v.* (mech.) to catch; to interlock; to gear together; (fig.) to encroach, to interfere; to intervene

Eingriff *m.* intervention; interference; encroachment; (med.) operation

einhaken *v.* to hook into; sich — to link arms

Einhalt *m.* stop, check; impediment, prohibition

einhalten *v.* to observe, to fulfill, to keep; to pause, to stop; to restrain; to hem

einhändigen *v.* to hand over; to deliver

einhauchen *v.* to breathe into; to inspire

einhauen *v.* to hew in, to cut into; (mil.) to attack, to charge; (coll.) to dig in

einheimisch *adj.* native; indigenous; homemade

einheimsen *v.* to get in, to house; (coll.) to reap; to rake in, to pocket

einher *adv.* along; **-stolzieren** *v.* to strut

einholen *v.* to bring in, to collect, to gather; to overtake; to seek; to apply for, to shop; (naut.) to haul (*oder* take) in

einhüllen *v.* to wrap up; to envelop

einimpfen *v.* to inoculate, to vaccinate; (fig.) to implant, to inculcate

einkassieren *v.* to cash; to collect

Einkauf *m.* (act of) buying; purchase; **-spreis** *m.* cost price

einkaufen *v.* to buy, to purchase; to shop

Einkäufer *m.* buyer

Einkehr *f.* short rest (*oder* stay); — **bei sich selbst** contemplation; remorse

einkehren *v.* to turn in, to enter; to stop at (an inn); to call at

einkellern *v.* to cellar; to store, to lay up

einkerkern *v.* to incarcerate; to imprison

einkitten *v.* to fix with cement (*oder* putty)

einklammern *v.* to fasten with clamps; to put in brackets (*oder* parentheses)

einkleiden *v.* to clothe; to accouter; (mil.) to provide with uniforms; (eccl.) to veil

einknicken *v.* to fold; to bend in, to double up; to give way, to break down

einkochen *v.* to boil down; to put up (preserves)

Einkommen *neu.* income; revenue; emoluments; **-steuer** *f.* income tax

einkreisen *v.* to encircle, to encompass, to surround

Einkünfte *f. pl.* income, revenue

einkuppeln *v.* to throw into gear

einladen *v.* to invite; to load in; to freight; **-d** *adj.* inviting; attractive

Einlage *f.* enclosure; insertion; deposit; (gaming) stake; (med.) arch support

einlagern *v.* to store

Einlass *m.* entrance, admission; inlet; **-ventil** *neu.* intake valve

einlassen *v.* to admit, to let in; **sich auf** (*oder* mit) **etwas** — to engage in (*oder* meddle) with something

einlaufen *v.* to arrive, to come in; to shrink; to enter (harbor); **jemandem das Haus** — to pester someone

einleben *v.* sich — to become used to; to familiarize oneself with

einlegen *v.* to put in, to enclose; to inlay; to insert; (com.) to deposit; (cooking) to preserve, to pickle; **Berufung** — to appeal; **Ehre** — to gain honor; **ein gutes Wort** — to intercede

einleiten *v.* to begin, to initiate; to introduce; (law) to institute

Einleitung *f.* introduction; preamble, preface; (mus.) prelude, overture

einlenken *v.* to turn in; to lead into; to give in; to be reasonable

einlernen *v.* to teach, to train

einleuchten *v.* to be clear (*oder* intelligible); **-d** *adj.* evident, obvious

einliefern *v.* to deliver up; to hand over

einliegend *adj.* enclosed

einlösen *v.* to redeem; to honor (bill, check)

einmachen *v.* to preserve, to pickle, to can

Einmarsch *m.* entry (of troops); marching in

einmarschieren v. to march in

einmauern v. to wall in; to immure

einmeisseln v. to chisel in

einmengen, einmischen v. to intermix, to mingle (oder meddle) with; to interfere

einmieten v. to engage lodgings; to pit (potatoes)

Einnahme f. (act of) receiving, receipt; revenue, proceeds; capture; **–quelle** f. source of revenue

einnehmen v. to take in; to receive; to collect; to capture, to occupy; to fascinate; to influence, to prejudice; **–d** adj. captivating, charming

einnicken v. to fall asleep; to nod

einnisten v. to nest(le); to establish firmly; **sich —** to insinuate oneself

Einöde f. desert

einordnen v. to put in proper order; to arrange, to classify, to file

einpacken v. to pack (oder wrap) up; (coll.) to give way

einpassen v. to fit in; to adjust

einpauken v. to drum into; to cram

einpflanzen v. to plant in; to implant

einpfropfen v. to cork up; to cram in; to engraft

einpökeln v. to pickle; to cure, to salt

einprägen v. to impress, to imprint

einpuppen v., **sich —** to change into a chrysalis (oder pupa); (coll.) to buy new clothes

einquartieren v. (mil.) to billet (oder quarter)

einrahmen v. to frame

einrammen v. to ram in

einräumen v. to put away; to store; to give up; to concede; to furnish (rooms)

Einrede f. objection, protest, remonstrance

einreden v. to make (one) believe; to urge, to persuade; to convince; to object

einreiben v. to rub in

einreichen v. to hand in, to deliver; to present

einreihen v. to arrange in a line (oder row) to range, to rank; to insert

Einreise f. entry into a country; **–erlaubnis** f. entry permit

einreissen v. to pull down, to demolish; to tear; (fig.) to gain ground, to spread

einrenken v. to set (bones oder joints)

einrennen v. to ram open, to batter into

einrichten v. to arrange; to establish; to furnish; to set (bone); **sich —** to prepare for; to economize

einrosten v. to become rusty; to rust in; to become stupid (oder dull) by inactivity

einrücken v. to enter, to march into; to insert; to advertise, to announce (in newspapers); (mil.) to join the ranks; (typ.) to indent

eins adj. one; **—** adv. the same; **— A** (coll.) A one; excellent; **— werden to** agree, to come to terms; **es kommt auf — hinaus** it amounts to the same thing

einsacken v. to put into sacks, to pocket

einsalben v. to anoint

einsalzen v. to salt, to pickle

einsammeln v. to gather, to glean; to collect; (coll.) to pass the hat

Einsatz m. insertion; stake; attachable (oder interchangeable) part; (mus.) cue; **–besprechung** (mil.) briefing (Lagebesprechung)

einsäuern v. to leaven; to pickle (in vinegar)

einsaugen v. to suck in; to absorb

einschachteln v. to put into a box; to encase

einschalten v. to insert; to put in; to interpolate; to intercalate (leap-year); to engage (gears); (elec.) to switch on

einschärfen v. to impress upon; to inculcate

einscharren v. to bury; to scrape in

einschätzen v. to assess, to estimate, to evaluate

einschenken v. to pour in; **reinen Wein — to** tell the plain truth

einschieben v. to shove in; to insert; to interpolate

Einschienenbahn f. monorail

einschiessen v. to test (gun); to shoot; (com.) to deposit, to contribute; **sich — to** practice shooting

einschiffen v. to embark; to take on board

einschlafen v. to fall asleep; to become numbed (oder dormant); to die

einschläfern v. to lull to sleep (oder security); to narcotize

Einschlag m. impact; (bomb) burst; (com.) handshake; woof; wrapper, cover, envelope; **–papier** neu. wrapping paper

einschlägig adj. relative to; competent

einschleichen v. **sich —** to sneak (oder steal) in

einschliessen v. to lock up; to enclose; to encircle; to include, to comprise

einschliesslich adj. inclusive

Einschluss m. inclusion; enclosure

einschmeicheln v. **sich —** to insinuate oneself (into); to ingratiate oneself (with); **–d** adj. engaging, winning

einschmelzen v. to melt down

einschmieren v. to grease, to oil

einschneiden v. to cut into; to notch; **–d**

adj. incisive

Einschnitt *m.* incision; cut; notch, indentation; turning point; (math.) segment

einschnüren *v.* to cord; to lace (*oder* tie) up

einschränken *v.* to restrict; to limit, to check; to confine; to reduce; **sich —** to economize, to retrench

einschreiben *v.* to write in (*oder* down); to inscribe; to enter; to register; to enroll

einschreiten *v.* to step in; to interfere, to intervene; to proceed against

einschrumpfen, (coll.) **einschrumpeln** *v.* to shrink, to shrivel up

Einschub *m.* insertion; interpolation

einschüchtern *v.* to abash; to intimidate

Einschuss *m.* capital advanced, share; woof; admixture; (bullet) point of entry

einsegnen *v.* to consecrate, to bless; to confirm

einsehen *v.* to look into; to comprehend, to realize, to understand

einseifen *v.* to soap, to lather; (sl.) to humbug, to take in

Einsender *m.* sender, transmitter, contributor

einsetzen *v.* to put (*oder* set) in; to insert; to employ, to use; to appoint, to install; to begin; to plant; to risk; **sich — für** to stand up for; to side with

Einsicht *f.* inspection, examination; view; insight, understanding, judgment

einsichtig *adj.* sensible, prudent, judicious

einsickern *v.* to trickle in; to soak into; to infiltrate

einspannen *v.* to stretch; to yoke, to harness; to enlist (help)

einsperren *v.* to lock up; to imprison

einsprechen *v.* to influence, to persuade; to inspire; **bei jemanden —** to drop in for a visit; **Mut —** to encourage

einspringen *v.* to pump (*oder* leap) in; to catch, to snap; to substitute

einspritzen *v.* to give a shot; to inject

Einspritzpumpe *f.* injection pump

Einspritzung *f.* injection, (coll.) shot

Einspruch *m.* objection, protest; **— erheben** to protest, to oppose, to interrupt

einst *adv.* in days past, at some future time; **–weilen** *adv.* meanwhile, for the time being; temporarily; **–weilig** *adj.* temporary, provisional

einstechen *v.* to dig in; to puncture; to prick

einstecken *v.* to put (*oder* stick) in; to pocket; to sheathe; **Beleidigungen —** to swallow insults; **jemanden —** (coll.) to clap someone into jail

einstehen *v.* to substitute; to answer (*oder* be responsible) for

einsteigen *v.* to get in; to embark; to break into (a house); **—!** *interj.* all aboard!

einstellen *v.* to put in; to adjust; to focus; to engage; to stop; to suspend; to set in; (mil.) to enlist; (rad.) to tune in; **Arbeit —** to strike; **Betrieb — to close down; sich —** to appear

Einstellung *f.* adjustment; hiring (workers); cessation; strike; shut-down; (mil.) enlistment; tuning-in; attitude, opinion

einstimmen *v.* to join in; to agree with, to consent to; to harmonize

einstossen *v.* to push (*oder* smash) in

einstreichen *v.* to pocket, to rake in (money)

einstudieren *v.* to study; to rehearse

einstürmen *v.* to assail; to rush upon

Einsturz *m.* collapse; cave-in

einstürzen *v.* to collapse; to tumble down

Eintänzer *m.* gigolo

eintauchen *v.* to dip in; to immerse

eintauschen *v.* to exchange, to get in exchange

einteilen *v.* to divide; to distribute; to classify; to calibrate; to budget

Eintrag *m.* earnings, proceeds, gain; damage, detriment; **–ung** *f.* entry; registration

eintragen *v.* to carry in; to enter, to register; to yield

einträglich *adj.* lucrative, profitable

eintränken *v.* to steep, to impregnate

eintreffen *v.* to arrive; to coincide; to happen, to be fulfilled

eintreiben *v.* to drive in (*oder* home); to collect (debts); to exact (payment)

eintreten *v.* to enter, to step in; to join; to occur, to take place; to intercede (for); to act as substitute; to kick in

Eintritt *m.* entering, entry; entrance, admission; commencement; setting in; (mil.) enlistment; **–skarte** *f.* admission ticket

eintrocknen *v.* to dry in (*oder* up)

eintunken *v.* to dip in; to sop; to dunk

einüben *v.* to practice; to exercise; to drill

einverleiben *v.* to incorporate, to embody

Einvernehmen *neu.* understanding; agreement; **sich ins — setzen** to bring to an understanding

einverstanden! *interj.* agreed! **— sein to** agree

Einwand *m.* objection, protest

Einwanderer *m.* immigrant

einwandern *v.* to immigrate

Einwanderung *f.* immigration

einwärts *adv.* inward(s)

einwechseln v. to change; to cash

einweichen v. to soak, to steep

einweihen v. to initiate; to ordain; to consecrate; to inaugurate

einwenden v. to object, to demur

einwerfen v. to throw in; to interject, to object

einwickeln v. to wrap up; to envelop; to curl (hair); (coll.) to cause to believe

einwilligen v. to consent; to agree; to acquiesce

einwirken v. to interweave; to influence

einwohnen v. to lodge with; **sich —** to begin to feel at home

Einwohnerschaft f. inhabitants; population

einzahlen v. to pay in, to deposit

einzäunen v. to fence in; to enclose

einzeichnen v. to draw (oder mark) in; **sich —** to enter one's name; to subscribe

Einzel: -fall m. individual case; **-haft** f. solitary confinement; **-handel** m. retail trade (oder sale); **-heit** f. singularity; detail; **-heiten** f. pl. particulars; **-spiel** neu. (tennis) singles; **-wesen** neu. individual being

einzeln adj. odd, single; individual

einziehen v. to draw (oder pull) in; to move (oder march) into; to call in; to collect; to confiscate, to seize; (naut.) to furl; to absorb, to soak

Einzug m. solemn entrance; moving

Eis neu. ice, ice cream; (mus.) E sharp; **-bahn** f. skating-rink; **-bär** m. polar bear; **-bein** neu. pig's knuckles; **-decke** f. sheet of ice; **-gang** m. drift (oder break up) of ice; **-händler** m. iceman; **-lauf** m., **-laufen** neu. skating; **-läufer** m. skater; **-maschine** f. freezer; **-meer** neu. polar sea; **-picke** f. ice pick; **-regen** m. sleet; **-scholle** f. floe; **-schrank** m. refrigerator; **-strom** m. glacier; **-zacken** m., **-zapfen** m. icicle

eis: -en v. to turn into ice; **-grau** adj. hoary with age; **-ig** adj. icy, covered with (oder cold as) ice; **-laufen** to skate

Eisen neu. iron; iron instrument; **Not bricht —** necessity knows no law; **zum alten — werfen** to scrap; **-abfälle** m. pl. scrap iron; **-beton** m. reinforced concrete; **-blech** neu. sheet-iron; **-erz** neu. iron ore; **-fresser** m. (coll.) braggart, bully; **-guss** m. iron casting; **-hammer** m. sledge hammer; **-hütte** f. iron works; forge; **-walzwerk** neu. iron rolling mill; **-ware** f. hardware

Eisenbahn f. railroad; **-abteil** neu. railroad compartment; **-er** m. railroad man; **-fahrt** f. railroad trip; **-netz** neu.

railroad system; **-schwellen** f. pl. sleepers; **-übergang** m. railway crossing; **-zug** m. train

eisern adj. iron; hard, stern; **-e Lunge** f. iron lung; **-er Bestand** reserve for emergencies

eitel adj. vain; conceited; futile, empty

Eiter m. pus, matter; **-beule** f. abcess

eitern v. to fester, to suppurate, to ulcerate

Ekel m. nausea, disgust; (coll.) nasty fellow

ekelhaft adj. nauseous; disgusting, loathsome

ekeln v. to nauseate; to loathe; **es ekelt mich** I am nauseated

Eklipse f. eclipse

Ekstase f. ecstasy

Ekzem neu. eczema

Elastizität f. elasticity

Elch m. elk

Elefant m. elephant; **-enrüssel** m. elephant's trunk; **-enzahn** m. elephant's tusk

Eleganz f. elegance

Elegie f. elegy

Elektriker m. electrician

elektrisch adj. electric(al)

elektrisieren v. to electrify; to thrill

Elektrizität f. electricity

Elektro- -lyse f. electrolysis; **-kardiogramm (EKG)** neu. electrocardiogram

Elektronenbeschleuniger m. cyclotron; **-gehirn** neu. Univac

Element neu. element; (elec.) cell

Elementar: -buch neu. primer; **-schule** f. elementary school

Elend neu. misery, distress, want; **graues —** (coll.) the blues; **-er** m. wretch

elend adj. miserable, forlorn; wretched; in distress; indigent; despicable; ill

Elf f. eleven; **-tel** neu. eleventh part

elf adj. eleven

Elfenbein neu. ivory

elfenbeinern adj. ivory

Elle f. ell (seventh part of yard); ulna

Ell(en)bogen m. elbow

eloxieren v. to anodize

Elsass neu. Alsace

Elster f. magpie

elterlich adj. parental

Eltern pl. parents

elternlos adj. orphaned

Email neu. enamel

emanzipieren v. to emancipate

Emigrant m. emigrant

Empfang m. reception; receipt; **-sapparat** m. receiver; **-sdame** f. receptionist; **-sschein** m. receipt; **-sstörung** f. (rad.) interference

empfangen v. to receive; to welcome; to conceive; to become pregnant

Empfänger m. receiver; recipient; consignee; acceptor; payee; receiving instrument

Empfängnis f. conception

empfehlen v. to commend; to give regards (to); **es empfiehlt sich** it is advisable; **sich** — to take leave; to offer one's services; **-swert** adj. commendable; worthy of recommendation

Empfehlung f. recommendation; compliments; **-sschreiben** neu. letter of introduction

empfind: **-en** v. to experience; to feel; to perceive; **übel -en** to take as an offense; **-lich** adj. sensitive; painful, touchy; **-sam** adj. sentimental, sensitive, delicate; **-ungslos** adj. unfeeling, callous

Empfindung f. feeling; perception, sensation; sentiment

Emphysem neu. emphysema

empor adv. up, upward(s); on high; aloft; **-blicken** to look up; **-ragen** to tower; **-streben** to strive upwards; to aspire

Empore f. (arch.) gallery, choir

empören v. to enrage, to excite; to rouse to anger; **sich** — to become furious; to rebel

Empörer m. rebel, insurgent

Emporkömmling m. upstart

Empörung f. insurrection; indignation

emsig adj. assiduous, industrious; active, busy

End: **-bahnhof** m. (rail.) terminal; **-e** neu. end; conclusion; aim; finale; death; (antler) point; **-ergebnis** neu. final result; **-ung** f. ending, termination; **-ziel** neu. final aim; **-zweck** m. ultimate object, main design

end: **-gültig** adj. conclusive, final, definite; **-(ig)en** v. to end, to finish; to cease; to terminate; to conclude; to expire, to die; **-lich** adj. finite; final; **-lich** adv. at last; finally; **-los** adj. endless, infinite

Energie f. energy, vigor

energisch adj. energetic, vigorous

eng adj. narrow; tight, close; intimate; **im -eren Sinne** strictly speaking; **-anschliessend** adj. tight-fitting; **-befreundet** adj. very intimate; **-brüstig** adj. asthmatic; **-herzig** adj. narrow-minded; straitlaced; **-maschig** adj. close-meshed; **-spurig** adj. (rail.) narrow-gauge

Enge f. narrowness, tightness; defile; strait; **in die** — treiben to corner

Engel m. angel; **-schar** f. host of angels; **-sgruss** m. (rel.) Hail Mary

engelhaft adj. angelic

Engländer m. Englishman; monkey wrench

englisch adj. English; **-e Krankheit** rickets

Engpass m. narrow pass, defile, strait

en gros adv. wholesale

Enkel m. grandson; **-in** f. granddaughter; **-kind** neu. grandchild

enorm adj. enormous

entarten v. to degenerate, to deteriorate

entäussern v. **sich** — to part with; to discard; to divest oneself of

entbehren v. to do without; to miss, to lack; **ich kann ihn nicht** — I cannot spare him

entbehrlich adj. dispensable; superfluous

Entbehrung f. privation, want

entbieten v. to send for, to summon; to offer, to present

entbinden v. to unbind, to untie; to release, to disengage, to absolve; to give birth

Entbindung f. dispensation; release; childbirth; **-sanstalt** f. maternity hospital

entblättern v. to strip of leaves; to defoliate

entblössen v. to bare, to uncover

Entblössung f. deprivation, destitution

entbrennen v. to catch fire, to blaze up; to be inflamed

entdecken v. to discover, to explore; to find out, to detect; **sich** — to disclose (oder reveal) oneself

Ente f. duck; (coll.) hoax

entehren v. to dishonor; to degrade, to disgrace; to deflower

enteilen v. to hurry away; to slip away

enteisen v. to de-ice

enterben v. to disinherit

Enterhaken m. (naut.) grappling iron

Enterich m. drake

entfachen v. to inflame; to kindle

entfahren v. to escape from; to slip out of

entfallen v. to fall out of; to slip from (memory); — **auf** to fall to (as share)

entfalten v. to unfold, to unfurl; to burst into bloom; to develop; to display

Entfaltung f. efflorescence

entfärben v. to discolor; **sich** — to change color; to grow pale

entfernen v. to remove; to take away; to alienate; **sich** — to go away, to withdraw, to depart, to slip away; to deviate (from)

entfernt adj. far away; remote, distant

Entfernung f. distance, range; withdrawal; removal; **-smesser** m. rangefinder

entfesseln v. to unchain; to set free

entflammen v. to inflame; to kindle

entfliehen v. to flee; to escape; to pass (time)

entfremden v. to alienate; to estrange

entführen v. to carry off; to elope (with); to kidnap

entgegen adv. and prep. towards; opposed to; against; contrary to; –arbeiten to work against; to counteract; –blicken to look towards (oder forward to); –geh(e)n to go to meet; to face (danger); –gesetzt prep. and adj. opposite, contrary; –halten to hold toward; to object to; to contrast with; –kommen v. to come to meet; to meet halfway; to obviate; –kommend adj. obliging, accommodating; –laufen v. to run towards; to oppose, to clash with; –nehmen v. to accept, to receive; –rücken v. to push towards, to march against; –sehen v. to look forward to; to expect; –setzen v. to oppose; to contrast with; –steh(e)n v. to face; to be opposed to; –stellen v. to set against; to contrast with; to oppose; –wirken v. to counteract; to check; (med.) to repel; –ziehen v. to advance, to march towards

entgegnen v. to answer, to reply; to retort

entgeh(e)n v. to escape, to elude

Entgelt neu. and m. remuneration; recompense, compensation

entgelten v. to pay (oder atone) for

entgleisen v. to derail; to make a slip (oder mistake)

entgleiten v. to slip away, to escape from

entgräten v. to bone (fish)

enthalten v. to contain, to hold; to comprise, to include; sich — to abstain from

enthaltsam adj. abstemious; continent; –keit f. abstinence

enthaupten v. to behead, to decapitate

entheben v. to remove (from office)

entheiligen v. to desecrate, to profane

enthüllen v. to unveil; to reveal, to disclose

Enthusiasmus m. enthusiasm

enthusiastisch adj. enthusiastic

entkleiden v. to undress, to disrobe; to deprive (oder divest) of

Entkleideakt m. striptease

entkommen v. to escape

entkorken v. to uncork

entkräften v. to debilitate, to enervate; to exhaust; to invalidate; to refute

entladen v. to unload; to explode, to discharge

entlang adv. along; by the side of

entlassen v. to discharge, to dismiss

entlasten v. to unburden; to relieve; to exonerate

Entlastung f. relief; exoneration; (com.) crediting; –szeuge m. witness for the defense

entlaufen v. to run away; to desert

entlausen v. to delouse

entledigen v. sich — to get rid of; sich eines Auftrages — to execute one's commission; sich eines Versprechens — to keep one's word

entleeren v. to empty; to evacuate; to void

entlegen adj. distant, remote

entlehnen v. to borrow; to lend; to plagiarize

entleiben v. sich — to commit suicide

entlocken v. to draw, to elicit, to wheedle

entmannen v. to castrate; to emasculate

entmenscht adj. inhuman; brutal

entmutigen v. to discourage, to dishearten

entnehmen v. to take out; to understand

entpuppen v., sich — to burst from the cocoon; to reveal as; to turn out to be

entraffen v. to snatch from; sich — to disengage oneself from

enträtseln v. to decipher; to solve

entreissen v. to snatch from; to rescue

entrichten v. to pay

entrinnen v. to run (oder slip) away; to escape

entrollen v. to roll down (oder away); to unroll

entrücken v. to remove from (sight); to put beyond the reach of; to enrapture

entrüsten v. to make indignant; sich — to become angry

entsagen v. to renounce; to waive; to relinquish, to abdicate

entschädigen v. to compensate, to indemnify; to reimburse

entscheiden v. to decide; to arbitrate; to pass sentence; –d adj. decisive; final; critical

entschieden adj. decided; determined, resolute

entschlafen v. to fall asleep; to pass away, to die

entschliessen v. to decide, to determine; sich — to make up one's mind

entschlossen adj. determined, resolute

entschlummern v. to fall asleep; to doze off; to die (gently)

Entschluss m. resolution; determination

entschuldigen v. to excuse; sich — to apologize; — Sie! I beg your pardon!

entschwinden v. to disappear, to vanish

entseelt adj. dead, lifeless

entsetzen v. to dismiss; to depose; to relieve; sich — to be horrified (oder terrified)

Entsetzen *neu.* terror; horror
entsetzlich *adj.* frightful, horrible, shocking
entsinnen *v.* sich — to recollect, to remember
Entspannung *f.* relaxation, easement; rest, recreation
entspinnen *v.* sich — to begin; to develop
entsprechen *v.* to correspond to, to be analogous to; **-d** *adj.* adequate, appropriate; corresponding; pertinent
entspringen *v.* to spring (*oder* arise) from; to descend from, to originate in; to escape
entstammen *v.* to descend from
entsteh(e)n *v.* to arise; to originate; to result from; to break out (fire, etc.)
entstellen *v.* to disfigure, to deform; to distort, to misrepresent, to garble
entsühnen *v.* to absolve
enttäuschen *v.* to disappoint, to disillusion
entvölkern *v.* to depopulate
entwachsen *v.* to outgrow
Entwaffnung *f.* disarmament
Entwarnung *f.* all-clear signal
entweder *conj.* either; — oder either . . . or
entweichen *v.* to escape; to flee; to vanish
entweihen *v.* to desecrate, to profane
entwenden *v.* to misappropriate, to embezzle
entwerfen *v.* to draft; to sketch; to outline
entwickeln *v.* to develop; to evolve; (mil.) to deploy; to explain
Entwickler *m.* (phot.) developer
Entwicklungsgeschichte *f.* (biol.) biogenesis
Entwicklungszeit *f.* adolescence
entwinden *v.* to wrest from; sich — to extricate oneself
entwischen *v.* to slip away, to escape
entwöhnen *v.* to wean; to disaccustom
Entwurf *m.* draft; design, plan; project
entwurzeln *v.* to uproot
entziehen *v.* to withhold, to deprive of; sich — to shun, to withdraw from
Entziehung *f.* deprivation; withholding; **-skur** *f.* treatment (for drug addicts, etc.)
entziffern *v.* to decode, to decipher
entzücken *v.* to enchant, to delight
Entzücken *neu.* rapture, delight; ecstasy
entzünden *v.* to kindle; sich — to catch fire; (med.) to become inflamed
Entzündung *f.* ignition; inflammation
entzwei *adv.* in two, asunder; broken, torn; **-en** *v.* to disunite, to estrange; sich **-en** to quarrel; to become alienated; **-geh(e)n** *v.* to break; to go to pieces; **-schlagen** *v.* to smash

Epidemie *f.* epidemic
Epik *f.* epic poetry; **-er** *m.* epic poet
epileptisch *adj.* epileptic
Epistel *neu.* and *f.* epistle
Epoche *f.* epoch
er *pron.* he; — selbst he himself
erachten *v.* to consider, to deem
Erb: **-adel** *m.* hereditary nobility; **-begräbnis** *neu.* family lot in a cemetery; **-e** *m.* heir; successor; **-e** *neu.* heritage, inheritance; **-feind** *m.* sworn foe; (fig.) devil; **-folge** *f.* hereditary succession; **-krankheit** *f.* hereditary disease; **-lasser** *m.* testator; **-recht** *neu.* right of succession; **-schaft** *f.* inheritance, legacy; **-schaftsgericht** *neu.* probate court; **-stück** *neu.* heirloom; **-sünde** original sin; **-teil** *neu.* share of an inheritance
erb: **-en** *v.* to inherit; **-eigen** *adj.*, **-lich** *adj.* hereditary
erbarmen *v.* sich — to pity; to have mercy
Erbarmen *neu.* compassion, pity; mercy
erbärmlich *adj.* miserable; contemptible
erbarmungslos *adj.* pitiless, merciless
erbauen *v.* to build, to erect; (fig.) to edify
erbeben *v.* to tremble
erbieten *v.* to offer; to volunteer
erbitten *v.* to beg (*oder* ask) for; to solicit
erbittern *v.* to embitter; to exasperate
erblassen, erbleichen *v.* to grow pale; to fade, (poet.) to die
erblicken *v.* to see; to catch sight of
erblinden *v.* to grow blind
Erbse *f.* pea
Erd: **-apfel** *m.* (dial., poet.) potato; **-arbeit** *f.* excavation, digging; **-ball** *m.* globe; **-beben** *neu.* earthquake; **-beere** *f.* strawberry; **-boden** *m.* soil; ground; **-ferne** (höchster Punkt der Raketenflugbahn) *f.* apogee; **-gas** *neu.* natural gas; **-geist** *m.* gnome; **-geschoss** *neu.* ground floor; **-kreisbahn** *f.* orbit; **-kunde** *f.* geography; **-leitung** *f.* earth connection; ground wire; **-nuss** *f.* peanut; **-öl** *neu.* petroleum; **-reich** *neu.* earth; (bibl.) Earthly Kingdom; **-rinde** *f.* earth's crust; **-rutsch** *m.* landslide; **-schluss** *m.* (elec.) ground; **-scholle** *f.* clod; **-teil** *m.* continent
erdenken *v.* to conceive; to devise, to invent
erdenklich *adj.* conceivable, imaginable
erdichten *v.* to invent; to imagine
Erdnähe *f.* (ast.) perigee
erdolchen *v.* to stab to death
erdrosseln *v.* to strangle; to throttle
erdrücken *v.* to crush; to overwhelm
erdulden *v.* to endure, to suffer
ereignen *v.* sich — to happen, to come to

pass

Ereignis *neu.* event, occurrence

ereilen *v.* to catch up with; to overtake

Eremit *m.* hermit

erfahren *v.* to hear, to learn; to experience; — *adj.* experienced; expert

Erfahrung *f.* experience; empirical knowledge; **in — bringen** to ascertain, to hear, to learn

erfahrungsgemäss *adv.* from experience

erfassen *v.* to seize, to take hold of; to comprehend

erfinden to invent; to think out, to conceive

erfinderisch *adj.* inventive; resourceful, creative; **Not macht — ** necessity is the mother of invention

Erfindung *f.* invention; fiction

erflehen *v.* to implore for; to entreat

Erfolg *m.* result, outcome; success

erfolgen *v.* to ensue; to follow (from); to result; to take place

erfolgreich *adj.* successful, effective

erforderlich *adj.* necessary, requisite

erfordern *v.* to require; to demand

Erfordernis *neu.* requirement, presupposition

erforschen *v.* to explore; to search into

erfragen *v.* to find out by questioning

erfrechen *v.* **sich — ** to have the impudence

erfreuen *v.* to delight, to gladden; to cheer; **sich — ** to rejoice, to enjoy oneself

erfreulich *adj.* gratifying; delightful, pleasing; **–erweise** *adv.* fortunately

erfrieren *v.* to freeze to death

Erfrierung *f.* frost-bite

erfrischen *v.* to refresh; to recreate

erfüllen *v.* to fulfill, to perform; to fill up; to imbue, to accomplish, to keep (promise); **sich — ** to be realized (*oder* fulfilled)

ergänzen *v.* to complete; to supplement; to replenish; to restore

Ergeb; –enheit *f.* devotion; resignation; **–nis** *neu.* result; outcome; **–ung** *f.* surrender

ergeben *v.* to yield, to prove; **sich — ** to submit; to surrender; to result from; to devote oneself to; to indulge in; to be resigned (to)

ergeh(e)n *v.* to fare (well *oder* ill); to be issued (*oder* promulgated); **sich — ** to stroll; to indulge in

ergiebig *adj.* productive; abundant; lucrative

ergiessen *v.* to pour forth (*oder* out); **sich — ** to discharge; to flow into

ergötzen *v.* to entertain, to delight; **sich**

— to enjoy oneself

ergötzlich *adj.* amusing, diverting, droll

ergreifen *v.* to seize; to arrest; to take (up); to choose (profession); to touch; **–d** *adj.* touching; gripping

ergriffen *adj.* moved (*oder* touched)

Ergriffenheit *f.* emotion

ergrimmen *v.* to become angry (*oder* furious)

ergründen *v.* to fathom; to get to the bottom of

Erguss *m.* discharge; effusion; gush

erhaben *adj.* elevated; in relief; eminent, exalted; sublime; **sich — fühlen über etwas** to feel above (*oder* superior) to something

erhalten *v.* to obtain, to receive; to preserve, to maintain, to support; **gut — in good condition** (*oder* repair); **sich — von** to subsist on

erhängen *v.* to hang; **sich — ** to hang oneself

erhärten *v.* to harden; to confirm, to corroborate

erhaschen *v.* to catch, to seize, to snatch

erheben *v.* to lift up, to heave; to elevate; to raise; to bring (suit); to collect (taxes); to extol, to praise; **sich — ** to rise; to arise; to rebel

erheblich *adj.* considerable; important; weighty

erheitern *v.* to amuse, to cheer

erhellen *v.* to illuminate; to elucidate; to become clear (*oder* evident)

erhitzen *v.* to heat; to inflame; **sich — ** to become heated; to fly into a passion

erhöhen *v.* to raise, to elevate; to increase; to exalt; (mus.) to raise by a sharp

erholen *v.* **sich — ** to recover, to improve; (com.) to rally

Erholung *f.* recovery, recreation, relaxation

erhören *v.* to give ear; to hear, to grant

Erika *f.* heather

erinnern *v.* to remind; **sich — ** to recollect, to remember

Erinnerung *f.* recollection, remembrance; reminiscence; **zur — an** in memory of

erkalten *v.* to grow cold

erkälten *v.* to chill; **sich — ** to catch a cold

erkaufen *v.* to buy; to bribe

Erkenn: –tnis *f.* cognition; knowledge, perception, understanding; (law) verdict; **–ung** *f.* recognition; (bibl.) carnal knowledge; **–ungsmarke** *f.* identification badge; **–ungswort** *neu.* watchword

erkennen *v.* to recognize; to perceive; to realize; to understand; (com.) to credit; (law) to judge; (med.) to diagnose

erkenntlich *adj.* recognizable; grateful

Erker *m.* bay window

erklären *v.* to explain; to expound, to interpret; to comment; to proclaim, to declare; **sich —** to avow; to propose (marriage)

Erklärung *f.* explanation; elucidation, interpretation, commentary; manifesto; proposal

erklecklich *adj.* sufficient; considerable

erklettern, erklimmen *v.* to climb; to clamber up; to scale; to ascend to the top

erkoren *adj.* chosen, selected

erkundigen *v.* **sich —** (nach) to inquire about

Erkundigung *f.* inquiry

erlangen *v.* to attain, to achieve; to obtain

Erlass *m.* dispensation, indulgence; remission; exemption, deduction; writ; decree, edict

erlassen *v.* to decree, to publish; to remit, to abate; to release; to exempt (from)

erlauben *v.* to allow, to permit, to license; **sich —** to dare, to presume

Erlaubnis *f.* permission; leave; dispensation; license; **-schein** *m.* permit

erläutern *v.* to explain, to elucidate; to illustrate; to comment

Erle *f.* alder

erleben *v.* to live to see; to experience

Erlebnis *neu.* experience; event; adventure

erledigen *v.* to settle, to finish; to carry through; to dispatch, to execute

erlegen *v.* to kill; to lay down; to deposit

erleichtern *v.* to facilitate, to ease; to lighten; to alleviate, to relieve; (coll.) to steal (from)

erleiden *v.* to suffer; to bear, to endure

erlernen *v.* to learn, to acquire, to master

erlesen *v.* to choose, to select; — *adj.* chosen; select, exquisite, choice

erleuchten *v.* to light up; to illuminate; to enlighten, to inspire

erliegen *v.* to be defeated; to succumb, to die

erlogen *adj.* fabricated, false, untrue; acquired by lying

Erlös *m.* proceeds; **-er** *m.* deliverer, liberator; Redeemer; **-ung** *f.* deliverance; redemption

erlöschen *v.* to go out, to expire; to cease; to die (*oder* fade) away; to lapse

erlösen *v.* to deliver, to free; to redeem

ermächtigen *v.* to authorize, to empower

ermahnen *v.* to admonish, to exhort, to warn

ermangeln *v.* to be deficient (*oder* lacking)

ermannen *v.* **sich —** to summon up courage

ermässigen *v.* to moderate; to abate; to reduce

ermatten *v.* to fatigue; to become weary

ermessen *v.* to judge; to consider; to gauge

ermöglichen *v.* to make possible (*oder* feasible)

ermorden *v.* to murder, to assassinate

ermüden *v.* to tire, to weary; to become tired (*oder* weary)

ermuntern *v.* to wake (*oder* cheer) up; to encourage, to rouse, to incite

ermutigen *v.* to encourage; to summon up courage

ernähren *v.* to nourish; to maintain, to support; **sich —** to subsist on; to make a living

ernennen *v.* to appoint, to nominate

erneue(r)n *v.* to renew, to renovate; to revive

erniedrigen *v.* to lower; to degrade, to humble; to humiliate; (mus.) to flatten

Ernst *m.* seriousness; gravity; sternness

ernst(haft) *adj.* earnest, serious; grave, stern

Ernte *f.* harvest; crop; (fig.) reward; **-dankfest** *neu.* thanksgiving; **-monat** *m.* August

ernten *v.* to harvest; to gather in; to reap

ernüchtern *v.* to make sober; to disillusion; **sich —** to sober up

erobern *v.* to conquer, to capture, to captivate

eröffnen *v.* to open; to inaugurate; to begin; to disclose; to inform

erörtern *v.* to consider; to discuss thoroughly

erotisch *adj.* erotic

erpicht *adj.* intent (upon); eager (for)

erpressen *v.* to blackmail, to extort

erproben *v.* to test, to try

erquicken *v.* to refresh, to revive, to quicken

erquicklich *adj.* refreshing; invigorating

erraten *v.* to guess, to conjecture; to solve

Erreg: -er *m.* exciter, agitator; (med.) germ; (phys.) agent; **-theit** *f.* excitement; irritation; **-ung** *f.* excitation, provocation

erregbar *adj.* excitable, irritable; sensitive

erregen *v.* to excite, to provoke; to agitate; to stir up; **-des Mittel** (med.) stimulant

erreichen *v.* to reach; to attain; to accomplish; to catch (train)

erretten *v.* to rescue, to save; to redeem

errichten *v.* to erect, to establish, to found

erringen *v.* to obtain by struggling (*oder* wrestling); to gain, to win; to achieve

erröten *v.* to blush

Errungenschaft *f.* achievement; acquisition

Ersatz *m.* reparation; compensation; substitute; replacement, reserve; **–mann** *m.* substitute, proxy; **–rad** *neu.* spare wheel (*oder* tire); **–stoff** *m.* substitute; **–stück** *neu.*, **–teil** *neu.* spare part; **–wahl** *f.* by election

ersaufen *v.* (coll.) to be drowned; to flood

ersäufen *v.* (coll.) to drown

erschaffen *v.* to create; to produce, to make

erschallen *v.* to resound; **— lassen** to spread

erschau(d)ern *v.* to shudder, to tremble (with horror)

erscheinen *v.* to appear; to be published; to seem

Erscheinung *f.* appearance; phenomenon; vision; apparition; publication; symptom

erschiessen *v.* to shoot (dead)

erschlaffen *v.* to languish; to slacken; to enervate; to relax

erschlagen *v.* to slay, to kill, to murder

erschliessen *v.* to unlock; to open; to disclose; to make accessible

erschöpfen *v.* to exhaust; (fig.) to drain

erschrecken *v.* to frighten, to alarm, to startle

erschüttern *v.* to shake; to convulse; to affect deeply, to shock

Erschütterung *f.* shaking, shock; (med.) concussion

erschweren *v.* to render difficult; to aggravate; to obstruct

erschwingen *v.* to attain with difficulty; to manage, to afford

ersehen *v.* to see; to observe, to learn; to choose, to select

ersehnen *v.* to long (*oder* yearn) for; to desire

ersetz: –bar *adj.*, **–setzlich** *adj.* reparable; **nicht –bar** irreparable; **–en** *v.* to replace; to make amends; to reimburse; to indemnify; to repair, to restore

ersichtlich *adj.* evident; obvious; clear, plain

ersinnen *v.* to think out; to contrive, to devise

ersparen *v.* to save, to spare, to economize

Ersparnis *f.*, **Ersparung** *f.* saving(s); economy

erspriesslich *adj.* profitable; beneficial

erst *adv.* (at) first; above all; just; not till; only; **–e** *adj.* first; foremost, prime, leading, der **–ere** the former; **eben —** just now; **— recht** all the more; **fürs –e** for the present; **–ens** *adv.* in the first place, to begin with; **–genannt** *adj.*

aforementioned; **–klassig** *adj.* first class; **–malig** *adj.* first-time; **–mals** *adv.* for the first time

erstarren *v.* to stiffen; to congeal, to freeze

erstatten *v.* to restore, to replace; to compensate, to recompense; **Bericht —** to make a report; **wieder —** to refund

erstaunen *v.* to astonish; to amaze; to be amazed (*oder* astonished)

Erstaunen *neu.* amazement, astonishment

erstaunlich *adj.* amazing, astonishing

erstechen *v.* to stab to death

ersteigen *v.* to ascend, to climb, to mount

ersticken *v.* to suffocate; to choke; to stifle; to suppress; **im Keime —** to nip in the bud

Erstickung *f.* asphyxiation

erstreben *v.* to aspire; to strive for; **–swert** *adj.* desirable

erstrecken *v.* to extend; to reach, to stretch

erstürmen *v.* to take by storm (*oder* assault)

ersuchen *v.* to beseech, to implore; to request

ertappen *v.* to catch, to detect, to surprise

erteilen *v.* to bestow on; to grant; to give, to impart; (rel.) to administer, to dispense

ertönen *v.* to (re)sound

ertöten *v.* to deaden; to mortify

Ertrag *m.* yield; **–sfähigkeit** *f.* productivity

Erträgnis *neu.* produce; proceeds; profit

ertragen *v.* to bear, to endure, to tolerate

erträglich *adj.* bearable, endurable, tolerable

ertränken *v.* to drown

ertrinken *v.* to be drowned

ertrotzen *v.* to get by obstinacy (*oder* under duress)

erübrigen *v.* to save, to lay (*oder* put) by; **sich —** to be superfluous (*oder* unnecessary)

erwachen *v.* to awake; to arise (to new life)

erwachsen *v.* to grow up; to spring (from); to arise, to accrue from; **—** *adj.* adult, grown-up

erwägen *v.* to ponder; to consider; to discuss

erwählen *v.* to choose, to select; to elect

erwähnen *v.* to mention; to call to notice

erwärmen *v.* to warm, to heat; **sich — für** to take a lively interest in

erwarten *v.* to await; to expect

erwecken *v.* to awaken, to rouse; to resuscitate; to stir up, to arouse

erwehren *v.* **sich —** to defend oneself (against); to restrain (tears); **ich kann**

mich des Lachens nicht — I cannot help laughing

erweichen v. to soften; to move, to touch

erweisen v. to render, to show; **jemandem einen Gefallen** — to do someone a favor; **sich** — to prove, to turn out

erweitern v. to enlarge, to widen; to expand, to extend, to amplify

Erwerb m. acquisition; gain; earnings; **–slosenunterstützung** f. unemployment compensation

erwerben v. to acquire, to earn, to gain

erwidern v. to reply, to retort; to requite; to reciprocate; to return

erwiesenermassen adv. as has been proved

erwirken v. to effect; to bring about; to procure

erwischen v. (coll.) to catch, to detect

erwünscht adj. desired; agreeable, welcome

erwürgen v. to strangle, to throttle

Erz neu. metal; ore, bronze, brass; **–ader** f. vein of ore; **–förderung** f. output of ore; **–giesserei** f. brass (oder bronze) foundry; **–grube** f. mine; **–hütte** f. smeltery; **–kunde** f. metallurgy, mineralogy

Erz: **–betrüger** m., **–gauner** m. extraordinary scoundrel; **–bischof** m. archbishop; **–bistum** neu. archbishopric; **–engel** m. archangel; **–herzog** m. archduke; **–kämmerer** m., **–kanzler** m. Lord High Chamberlain (oder Chancellor); **–tugend** f. cardinal virtue

erzählen v. to relate; to report; to narrate; (coll.) to make believe

Erzähler m. narrator; novelist; writer; story teller

erzeigen v. to show, to render; to prove

erzeugen v. to beget, to procreate; to manufacture, to produce; to generate; to breed

Erzeuger m. creator, father; producer

Erzeugnis neu. produce; product; production

erziehen v. to educate; to rear; to train

Erzieher m. educator; teacher, tutor

Erziehungsanstalt f. educational establishment

erzielen v. to obtain; to realize (profit)

erzürnen v. to anger, **sich** — to become angry

erzwingen v. to force, to extort (from)

erzwungen adj. forced, feigned, simulated

es pron. it; **er sagt** — he says so; — **gibt** there is

Esche f. ash (tree)

Esel m. donkey, ass; (coll.) blockhead, dunce; **–ei** f. stupid blunder, stupidity;

–sbrücke f. pony (students); **–sgeschrei** neu. braying; **–sohr** neu. (book) dog-ear

Espe f. aspen (tree)

Ess: **–en** neu. food; meal; dish; **–gelage** neu. banquet, feast; **–gier** f. gluttony; **–löffel** m. tablespoon; **–lust** f. appetite; **–waren** f. pl. eatables, provisions

essbar adj. edible

Esse f. chimney, flue; forge

essen v. to eat, to dine; (mil.) to mess

Essig m. vinegar; **–gurke** f. pickled cucumber; **–säure** f. acetic acid

Estland neu. Esthonia

Estrade f. platform

Estrich m. plaster (oder clay, cement) floor

etablieren v. to establish, to set up

Etage f. floor, story; **–re** f. bookshelf, whatnot

Etat m. budget, estimate; financial statement; **–sjahr** neu. financial year

Ethik f. ethics

ethisch adj. ethical

Etikette f. etiquette; — neu. label, ticket

etliche pron. some, a few; several

etwa adv. about, nearly; perhaps; **–ig** adj. eventual; contingent

etwas pron. something; — adj. some, any; — adv. somewhat; a little

Etzel m. Attila

euch pron. pl. (to) you

euer adj. pl. your; — adv. yours

Eule f. owl; **–nspiegelei** f. tomfoolery; practical joke

eur: **–esgleichen** pron. like you, of your kind; **–ethalben** adv., **–etwegen** adv., **–etwillen** adv. for your sake, on your account; **–ig** pron. yours

Europa neu. Europe

Euter neu. udder

e.V. (eingetragener Verein) m. Inc. (Incorporated)

evangelisch adj. evangelical, protestant

Evangelium neu. (rel.) gospel

eventuell adj. possible; — adv. possibly, perhaps; under certain circumstances

ewig adj. eternal; endless, perpetual; (coll.) very long; **auf** — forevermore; **der –e Jude** the wandering Jew; **immer und** — for ever and ever

Examen neu. examination

examinieren v. to examine

Exempel neu. example; problem, sum

exemplarisch adj. exemplary; excellent

exerzieren v. (mil.) to drill, to train

Exerzitium neu. (educ.) homework; (rel.) devotional exercise, meditation

Exil neu. exile

existieren v. to exist, to subsist, to be

exkommunizieren v. to excommunicate

expedieren v. to dispatch, to forward

Expedition f. expedition; dispatching, forwarding; shipping department

Experiment neu. experiment

experimentieren v. to experiment

exportieren v. to export

Extrablatt neu. special edition, supplement

Extremitäten f. pl. (anat.) extremities

exzentrisch adj. eccentric

Exzess m. excess

F

Fabel f. fable; (lit.) plot; tale, fiction

fabelhaft adj. fabulous; incredible, marvelous

Fabrik f. factory, mill, plant; **–ant** m. manufacturer; **–at** neu. manufactured product; **–ation** f. manufacturing; **–zeichen** neu. trade-mark

fabrizieren v. to manufacture, to fabricate

Facette f. facet

Fach neu. compartment, drawer, pigeonhole; branch, department; speciality; subject; line, profession, trade; **–ausdruck** m. technical term; **–gelehrte** m. specialist; **–mann** m. expert; **–ordnung** f. classification; **–schule** f. professional school; **–simpelei** f. shop talk; **–studium** neu. professional study; **–werk** neu. (arch.) framework; **–wissenschaft** f. technical knowledge; **–zeitschrift** f. technical journal

fach: **–kundig** adj., **–männisch** adj. competent, expert; **–simpeln** v. to talk shop

fächeln v. to fan

Fächer m. fan; **–palme** f. fan palm

Fackel f. torch; **–zug** m. torchlight procession

fackeln v. to flicker; to hesitate

Façon, Fasson f. fashion, manner, pattern

fad(e) adj. insipid; stale; dull, flat

Faden m. thread; string, twine; filament; fiber; (naut.) fathom; **keinen trockenen — am Leibe haben** to be wet to the skin; **–nudeln** f. pl. vermicelli

fadenscheinig adj. threadbare, shabby

Fagott neu. bassoon

fähig adj. able, capable; gifted; competent

fahl adj. pale, faded

Fahne f. flag, banner; ensign, standard, colors; vane; (feather) barbs; (typ.) galley proof; **–neid** m. oath of allegiance; **–nflucht** f. desertion; **–nflüchtige** m. deserter; **–nstange** f. flagstaff; **–nträger** m. standard bearer

Fähnrich m. (mil.) ensign; (naut.) midshipman

Fahr: **–bahn** f., **–damm** m. roadway; **–betrieb** m. traffic; **–dienst** m. railroading; **–dienstleiter** m. station master; **–er** m. driver; **–gast** m. passenger; **–geld** neu. fare; **–gelegenheit** f. conveyance; **–gestell** neu. undercarriage; chassis; **–karte** f. ticket; **–kartenschalter** m. ticket office; **–p an** m. timetable; **–rad** neu. bicycle; **–strahl** m. (avi.) gunsight beam; **–strasse** f. highway; **–stuhl** m. elevator; **–t** f. journey, trip, drive, ride; **–wasser** neu. (naut.) wake; (fig.) element; **–zeug** neu. vehicle

fahr: **–bar** adj. passable, navigable; **–en** v. to drive, to ride, to go (by train, etc.); to convey; to fare (ill, well); **aus der Haut –en** (coll.) to hit the ceiling; **–ig** adj. fickle, restless; **–lässig** adj. negligent, careless; **–planmässig** adj. on schedule, regular

Fährte f. scent, track, trail; **auf falscher — sein** to be on the wrong track (oder at fault)

faktisch adj actual, real, founded on facts

Faktotum neu. factotum; Jack-of-all-trades

Faktura f. invoice

Falke m. falcon; **–nbeize** f. falconry

Fall m. fall; waterfall; ruin; seduction; case, instance; **auf jeden —** in any event; **auf keinen —** on no account; **gesetzt den —** supposing that; **im –e in** case; **zu — bringen** to ruin; **zu — kommen** to be ruined; **–beil** neu. guillotine; **–e** f. trap; **–ensteller** m. trapper; **–gesetz** neu. law of gravitation; **–grube** f. pitfall; **–obst** neu. fallen fruit; **–reep** neu. (naut.) rope ladder, gangway; **–schirm** m. parachute; **–schirm-Sanitäts-personal** m. paramedics; **–schirmtruppen** f. pl. paratroopers; **–schirmspringer** m. parachutist; **–strick** m. snare, noose; **–sucht** f. epilepsy; **–tür** f. trapdoor

fall: **–en** v. to fall; to drop; to decrease, to go down; to be ruined (oder seduced); to die (in battle); **aus allen Wolken –en** to be thunderstruck; **in den Rücken –en** to attack from behind; to deceive; **in die Augen –en** to catch the eye; **in die Rede –en** to interrupt; **in Ohnmacht –en** to faint; **leicht** (or **schwer**) **–en** to be easy; (oder difficult); **–ieren** v. to fail; to become bankrupt; **–s** adv. if; in case; provided

fällen v. to cut, to fell; to pronounce (judgment); (chem.) to precipitate; to draw (perpendicular); to lower (bayonet); **Entscheidungen —** to make decisions

fällig adj. due; payable

falsch adj. wrong; false; incorrect; artificial; counterfeit, forged; perfidious, deceitful; — anführen to misquote; — aussprechen to mispronounce; — schreiben to misspell; — schwören to perjure; — singen to sing out of tune; —e Würfel loaded dice; –klingend adj. dissonant, discordant

Falsch neu. (poet.) falsehood; ohne — guileless; –heit f. falsity, perfidiousness, deceit(fulness); –münzer m. forger, counterfeiter; –spieler m. cheat, cardsharp

fälschen v. to falsify; to adulterate; to forge; to counterfeit

Fälscher m. forger

fälschlicherweise adj. erroneously; by mistake

Falsett neu. falsetto

Falt: –boot neu. collapsible boat; –e f. fold; pleat; crease; wrinkle; die Stirne in –en ziehen to knit one's brow; –enrock m. pleated skirt; –enwurf m. arrangement (of draperies)

falten v. to fold; to crease; to wrinkle; to pleat; to clasp (hands)

Falter m. butterfly, moth

faltig adj. pleated; wrinkled

Falz m. fold; groove, channel, rabbet; –bein neu. paper knife (oder folder)

Familie f. family; tribe; –nname m. family name, surname

famos adj. famous; fine, grand, great

Fanal neu. beacon; signal

Fanatiker m. fanatic

fanatisch adj. fanatic(al)

Fanatismus m. fanaticism

fangen v. to catch, to capture; to seize; to hook, to trap, to snare; sich — to be caught (oder entangled); to regain security

Farb: –band neu. typewriter ribbon; –e f. color, tint, shade; dye, paint, stain; complexion; (cards) suit; die –e wechseln to change sides; –e bekennen (cards) to follow suit; (fig.) to show one's true colors; –ige m. nonwhite person, Negro; –stift m. colored pencil; –ton m. tint, shade

farbecht adj. fast, fadeless

färben v. to color; to stain; to dye

farbig adj. colored; stained

Färbung f. dyeing; hue, tinge; touch, shading

Farn m., **Farnkraut** neu. fern

Fasan m. pheasant

Faschismus m. fascism

faseln v. to talk nonsense; to fuss

Faser f. fiber, filament; thread

fasern v. to fray, to ravel

Fass neu. barrel, cask; butt, tun; tub, vat; (coll.) potbelly; das schlägt dem — den Boden aus! that's the last straw! frisch vom — on draught; –bier neu. draught beer; –binder m. cooper; –daube f. stave; –hahn m. spigot; –reifen m. hoop; –spund m. bung

fass: –en v. to seize, to catch, to take hold; to comprise, to contain; to mount, to set; to comprehend, to grasp; eine Meinung –en to form an opinion; einen Gedanken –en to conceive an idea; einen Vorsatz –en to resolve; ein Herz (oder Mut) –en to summon up courage; ins Auge –en to consider; sich kurz –en to be brief; Wurzel –en to take root; –lich adi. conceivable; comprehensible, intelligible

Fassung f. setting, mounting; wording; composure, self-control; aus der — bringen to upset, to disconcert; –sgabe f., –skraft f., –svermögen neu. power of comprehension

fassweise adj. by the barrel

fast adv. almost, nearly, all but

Fast: –en neu. fasting, abstention; –enzeit f. Lent; –nacht f. Shrove Tuesday

fasten v. to fast; to abstain (from food)

faszinieren v. to fascinate

fatal adj. disagreeable, annoying, unfortunate

faul adj. rotten, putrid; mouldering; uncertain, unreliable; idle, lazy; –en v. to rot, to putrefy; –enzen v. to be idle

Faul: –heit f. idleness, laziness; –pelz m. lazybones, sluggard; –tier neu. sloth

Fäule, Fäulnis f. rottenness; putrefaction

Faust f. fist; auf eigene — on one's own responsibility; sich ins Fäustchen lachen to laugh in one's sleeve; –kampf m. boxing match; (coll.) fisticuff; –kämpfer m. boxer; –recht neu. club law; government by violence

Faxe f. tomfoolery; –nmacher m. buffoon

Fazit neu. final sum (oder result)

Februar m. February

fechten v. to fence; to fight with foil (oder rapier, sword); (coll.) to beg

Feder f. feather; pen, nib; spring; in die –n gehen (coll.) to go to bed; –ball m. badminton; –busch m. tuft of feathers, plume; (orn.) crest; –fuchser m. scribbler, ink slinger; –kiel m. quill; –kleid neu. (orn.) plumage; –kraft f. elasticity; –taschenmesser neu. switchblade; –vieh neu. poultry; –wisch m. feather duster; –wolke f. cirrus (cloud); –zange f. tweezers; –zug m. stroke of the pen; signature

feder: -(art)ig *adj.* feathered, feathery; -n *v.* to moult; to be springy (*oder* elastic); -nd *adj.* elastic, springy

Fee *f.* fairy

feenhaft *adj.* fairylike; marvelous, magical

Fegefeuer *neu.* purgatory

fegen *v.* to sweep, to clean; (coll.) to scamper

Fehl *m.* fault, blemish; -bestand *m.* deficiency, shortage; -betrag *m.* deficit; -druck *m.* misprint; -er *m.* blemish; defect, flaw; fault, error, mistake; (mech.) *m.* abort; -farbe *f.* off shade; (cards) renounce; -geburt *f.* abortion, miscarriage; -griff *m.* failure, disappointment; -schluss *m.* wrong conclusion; -tritt *m.* false step, slip; moral lapse; -zündung *f.* (mech.) misfire, backfire

fehl *adv.* amiss, wrongly; in vain; -bar *adj.* fallible; -en *v.* to miss; to err; to fail, to lack; to sin; to be absent (*oder* missing, wanting); -erhaft *adj.* faulty, defective

Feier *f.* celebration; festival; solemnity ceremony; rest; -abend *m.* cessation of work; hours of leisure; -lichkeit *f.* solemnity, ceremony; -tag *m.* day of rest, holiday

feierlich *adj.* solemn, festive

feiern *v.* to celebrate, to commemorate; to rest, to cease working

feig(e) *adj.* cowardly; faint-hearted

Feige *f.* fig

Feigheit *f.* cowardice; poltroonery

Feigling *m.* coward

feil *adj.* for sale; venal; -bieten to offer for sale; to auction; -schen to bargain, to haggle

feilen *v.* to file (*oder* rub); to elaborate

fein *adj.* fine, thin, delicate; subtle; elegant, refined; -fühlig *adj.* sensitive; -hörig *adj.* sharp of hearing; -körnig *adj.* fine-grained

Fein: -bäckerei *f.* fancy (*oder* pastry) bakery; confectioner's shop; -gefühl *neu.* delicacy; -gehalt *m.* fineness, standard; -kosthandlung *f.* delicatessen; -schmecker *m.* gourmet, epicure; -sliebchen *neu.* (poet.) sweetheart

Feind *m.* enemy, foe; adversary, opponent; (bibl.) devil; -schaft *f.* enmity; hostility; hatred; -seligkeit *f.* hostility; -seligkeiten *f.* war

feindlich *adj.* hostile; inimical

feist *adj.* fat, well-fed, plump

Feld *neu.* field; ground; plain; locale of war; sphere of action; (arch.) panel; (chess) square; das — behaupten to hold a position; das — räumen to quit

a position; ins — rücken to take a position; -arbeit *f.* agricultural labor; -arzt *m.* army surgeon; -bett *neu.* camp-bed; -blume *f.* wild flower; -dienst *m.* (mil.) active service; -flasche *f.* canteen; -funksprecher *m.* walkie-talkie; -geschrei *neu.* war cry; -herr *m.* warrior, strategist; -herrnkunst *f.* strategy; -hospital, -lazarett *neu.* field hospital; -lager *neu.* camp; -messer *m.* surveyor; -messkunst *f.* art of surveying; -prediger *m.* army chaplain; -schlacht *f.* battle; -spat *m.* feldspar; -stecher *m.* field glasses, binoculars; -stuhl *m.* folding chair; -webel *m.* sergeant; -webelleutnant *m.* warrant officer; -zeichen *neu.* military flag; -zeugmeister *m.* quartermaster; -zug *m.* campaign, crusade

Fell *neu.* hide, skin; fur; (anat.) film, ein dickes — haben to be thick-skinned; jemandem das — gerben to thrash someone; jemandem das — über die Ohren ziehen to fleece (*oder* cheat) someone; -eisen *neu.* knapsack, carpetbag

Fels, Felsen *m.* rock; cliff; crag; -block *m.* boulder; -enhöhle *f.* grotto; -enriff *neu.* reef; -(en)wand *f.* precipice

Felsengebirge *neu.* Rocky Mountains

Fenster *neu.* window; hotbed; -bogen *m.* window arch; -brett *neu.*, -sims *neu.* window sill; -brüstung *f.* window ledge; parapet; -flügel *m.* casement; -gitter *neu.* window lattice; -jalousien *f. pl.* Venetian blinds; -kitt *m.* putty; -laden *m.* window shutter; -rahmen *m.* window frame; -riegel *m.* window catch; -scheibe *f.* window pane

Ferien *pl.* vacation; (law) recess; -kolonie *f.* vacation camp

Ferkel *neu.* suckling pig; (coll.) dirty person

fern *adj.* far distant, remote; das sei von mir! far be it from me! -er *adv.* further; besides, moreover; -erhin *adv.* furthermore, henceforth; -liegen *v.* to be out of one's line; -mündlich *adj.* by telephone; -stehen *v.* to be a stranger (to)

Fern: -e *f.* distance, remoteness; -gespräch *neu.* long distance call; -glas *neu.*, -rohr *neu.* telescope; -sehen *neu.* television, video; -sicht *f.* prospect; vista; -sprecher *m.* telephone; -sprechzelle *f.* telephone booth; -steuerung *f.* remote control; -verkehr *m.* long distance traffic; -zug *m.* mainline train

Fernlenkgeschoss mittlerer Reichweite *neu.* intermediate range ballistic missile

(IRBM)

Fernlenkung *f.* space command

Fernsehgrossprogramm *neu.* spectacular

Ferse *f.* heel

fertig *adj.* ready; accomplished; finished; ready-made; **er ist —** he is ruined, he is done for; **sich —machen** to get ready; **-bringen** *v.* to accomplish, to bring about; **-en** *v.* to make, to manufacture; **-stellen** *v.* to complete, to get ready

Fertig: -fabrikat *neu.*, **-ware** *f.* manufactured (*oder* ready-made) goods; **-keit** *f.* dexterity; skill, **-stellung** *f.* completion

Fes *m.* and *neu.* fez

fesch *adj.* fashionable; stylish, smart

Fessel *f.* fetter, shackle; (anat.) pastern; **-ballon** *m.* captive balloon

fesseln *v.* to chain, to fetter, to shackle; to fascinate

fest *adj.* solid; firm; tight; fast, fixed; constant; permanent; strong, safe; **-e Nahrung** solid food; **-er Platz** fortress, stronghold; **-er Schlaf** sound sleep; **-fahren** *v.* to run aground; **-halten** *v.* to hold fast; to detain; to arrest; to portray; to write down; to adhere (*oder* cling, stick) to; **-igen** *v.* to secure; to consolidate; **-legen** *v.* to invest (money); to drop anchor; **-liegen** *v.* to be set fast (*oder* fixed to); **-machen** *v.* to fasten; to tighten; to fortify; to settle; **-nehmen** *v.* to arrest, to seize; **-setzen** *v.* to fix; to establish; to arrest; to stipulate; **sich -setzen** *v.* to gain a footing; **-sitzen** *v.* to be stuck, to be firmly fixed; **-steh(e)n** *v.* to stand firm; to be certain; **-stellbar** *adj.* capable of proof; **-stellen** *v.* to ascertain, to establish, to determine, to identify

Fest *neu.* festival; feast; holiday; **-essen** *neu.* gala dinner, banquet; **-halle** *f.* banquet hall; **-lichkeit** *f.* festivity, solemnity; **-spiel** *neu.* festival performance; **-tag** *m.* holiday, festival day

Fest: -e *f.* citadel; (bibl.) firmament; **-igkeitsgrenze** *f.* breaking point; **-körperphysik** *f.* solid-state physics; **-land** *neu.* continent; **-nahme** *f.* seizure; apprehension, arrest

festlich *adj.* festive; solemn; splendid

Festung *f.* fortress; **-sbau** *m.* fortification; **-swerk** *neu.* fortification

fett *adj.* fat; stout; greasy, rich; (agr.) fertile; lucrative; (typ.) bold-faced; **-bäuchig** *adj.* paunch-bellied; **-(halt)ig** *adj.* fatty; greasy, oily; **-leibig** *adj.* corpulent; **-wanstig** *adj.* paunchy

Fett *neu.* fat; grease; lard; **-darm** *m.* straight intestine; **-fleck** *m.* grease spot

Fetzen *m.* shred, tatter; rag, scrap

feucht *adj.* moist; damp; humid; **noch — hinter den Ohren** still wet behind the ears, inexperienced; **-emesser** (für Atmosphären) *m.* psychrometer

Feuchtigkeit *f.* moisture; dampness, humidity; **-smesser** *m.* humidistat; hygrostat

Feuer *neu.* fire; firing, bombardment; brilliance, ardor; **— fangen** to catch fire; **— und Flamme sein** to be very enthusiastic; **-bestattung** *f.* cremation; **-eifer** *m.* ardent zeal; **-haken** *m.* poker; **-leiter** *f.* fire escape; **-löschapparat** *m.*, **-löscher** *m.*, **-löschgerät** *neu.* fire extinguisher; **-mal** *neu.* birthmark; mole; scar (of burn); **-melder** *m.* fire alarm; **-sbrunst** *f.* conflagration; **-schiff** *neu.* lightship; **-stein** *m.* flint; **-ung** *f.* firing; fuel; heating; **-versicherung** *f.* fire insurance; **-wache** *f.* fire station; **-waffe** *f.* firearm; gun; **-wehr** *f.* fire department; **-wehrleiter** *f.* snorkel; **-werk** *neu.* fireworks; **-werkerei** *f.* pyrotechnics; **-zange** *f.* fire tongs; **-zeug** *neu.* lighter

feuer: -fangend *adj.* inflammable; combustible; **-fest** *adj.* fireproof; **-gefährlich** *adj.* inflammable; **-n** *v.* to burn fuel; to fire

Fiasko *neu.* fiasco, failure, break-down

Fibel *f.* primer; tibula

Fiber *f.* fiber

Fichte *f.* spruce (tree)

fidel *adj.* jolly, jovial; merry

Fieber *neu.* fever; **— messen** to take (someone's) temperature; **vom — befallen** fever-stricken; **-phantasie** *f.* delirium; **-thermometer** *neu.* clinical thermometer

fieber: -haft *adj.*, **-ig** *adj.* feverish; **-n** *v.* to be feverish (*oder* delirious, agitated)

Fiedel *f.* fiddle; **-bogen** *m.* fiddle bow

Figur *f.* figure; shape, form; image; diagram; (cards) picture card; (chess) piece

figürlich *adj.* figurative

Filet *neu.* network; netting; (meat) fillet

Filiale *f.* branch (establishment)

Filigran *neu.* filigree, filigrane

Film *m.* film; movie; **-atelier** *neu.* motion picture studio; **-aufnahme** *f.* filming, shooting; **-rolle** *f.*, **-streifen** *m.* reel; film strip; **-verleih** *m.* film exchange

Filz *m.* felt; (coll.) hat

filzig *adj.* of felt, feltlike; stingy, mean

Finanz *f.*, **-en** *pl.* finance(s); **-amt** *neu.* tax office; **-ausschuss** *m.* finance committee; **-jahr** *neu.* fiscal year; **-mann** *m.* financier; **-minister** *m.* minister of finance; secretary of the treasury

finanzieren v. to finance; to support

Findelkind neu., **Findling** m. foundling

finden v. to find; to discover; to meet; to consider; to deem; **sich — in** to resign oneself to; **wie — Sie es?** How do you like it?

Finger m. finger; **jemandem auf die — sehen** to keep strict watch on someone; **lange — machen** to steal; **sich etwas aus den —n saugen** to imagine something; **–abdruck** m. finger print; **–fertigkeit** f. manual skill, easy (oder rapid) fingering; **–hut** m. thimble; (bot.) foxglove; **–satz** m. (mus.) fingering; **–spitze** f. finger tip; **–zeig** m. hint, tip

Fink m. finch

Finne f. fin; claw (of hammer); pimple, acne

finster adj. dark, gloomy; obscure

Finsternis f. darkness, gloom; obscurity; (ast.) eclipse; (bibl.) hell

Finte f. feint; trick; excuse; deception

Firm: –a f. firm, business; **–enbuch** neu., **–enregister** neu. commercial (oder trade) directory

Firmelung f. (Catholic) confirmation

Firn m. mountain snow; **–is** m. varnish

firnissen v. to varnish

First m. ridge, roof

Fisch m. fish; **–adler** m. osprey, sea eagle; **–bein** neu. whalebone; **–brut** f., **–laich** m. fry, spawn; **–er** m. fisherman; **–erei** f. fishing, fishery; **–ereigerät** neu. fishing tackle; **–gräte** f. fish bone; **–händler** m. fishmonger; **–kunde** f. ichthyology; **–leim** m. fish glue, isinglass; **–reiher** m. heron; **–rogen** m. roe; **–schuppe** f. scale; **–tran** m. fish (oder train) oil; **–zucht** f. pisciculture; **–zug** m. catch (oder haul) of fish

fisch: –blütig adj. cold-blooded; **–en** v. to fish; **im Trüben –en** to fish in trouble waters; **–ig** adj. fishy

Fiskus m. state treasury

Fistel f. (med.) fistula; **–stimme** f. falsetto

Fix: –ierbad neu. (phot.) fixing bath; **–iermittel** neu. fixing agent; **–ierung** f. fixation; **–stern** m. fixed star; **–um** neu. fixed salary

flach ad. flat, level; shallow; insipid, dull, unoriginal; **–gedrückt** adj. flattened

Flach: –ball m. (tennis) drive; **–glas** neu. plate glass; **–land** neu. low country; **–relief** neu. bas relief

Fläche f. surface; level, plain; **–ninhalt** m. area; **–nmass** neu. square (oder plane) measure

Flachs m. flax; **–brechen** neu. flax dressing; **–hechel** f. flax comb; **–samen** m. linseed

flachsen, flächsern adj. flaxen

flackern v. to flicker; to flare

Fladen m. flat, thin cake

Flagge f. flag; colors; **die — aufziehen** (or hissen) to hoist the flag; **die — einholen** to haul down the flag

flaggen v. to display the flag

Flak f. (mil.) antiaircraft battery

Flakon neu. phial; perfume bottle

Flamingo m. flamingo

Flamme f. flame; blaze; (coll.) sweetheart; **–nwerfer** m. flame thrower

flammen v. to flame, to blaze; to flash; **–d** adj. aflame, blazing. flaming

Flanke f. flank; (tennis) side

flankieren v. to flank; (mil.) to enfilade

Flasche f. bottle; flask; **auf –n ziehen to** bottle; **–nbier** neu. bottled beer; **–nhals** m. bottleneck; **–nzug** m. block and tackle

flatterhaft adj. fickle, inconstant

flattern v. to flutter, to dangle; to wave

flau adj. feeble, weak; faint; slack; insipid

Flaum m. down, fluff; **–bart** m. downy beard

Flaus(ch) m. tuft of hair; fleecy woolen cloth

Flause f. fib; evasion; humbug

Flaute f. calm weather; poor business

Flechse f. sinew, tendon

Flecht: –e f. braid, plait, tress; (bot.) lichen; (med.) tetter, ringworm; **–er** m. braider, basket maker; **–werk** neu. wickerwork

flechten v. to braid, to plait: to interweave

Fleck m. blot, stain; place, spot; blemish, flaw; **sich nicht vom –e rühren** not to budge an inch; **–en** m. market town, village; **–enwasser** neu. stain remover

Fledermaus f. (zool.) bat

Flederwisch m. feather duster

Flegel m. flail; (coll.) boor; **–ei** f. rudeness; insolence; **–jahre** neu. pl. teens

flegelhaft adj. rude: boorish

flehen v. to implore; to beseech, to entreat

Fleisch neu. flesh; meat; pulp; (bibl.) man, humanity; **sich ins eigene — schneiden** to injure oneself; **wildes — ** proud flesh; **–beschau** f. meat inspection; **–brühe** f. meat broth; **–er** m. butcher; **–eslust** f. carnal desire; **–fresser** m. carnivore; **–gift** neu. ptomaine; **–kloss** m. meatball; **–konserve** f. canned meat; **–pastete** f. meatpie; **–ton** m. flesh tint; **–werdung** f. (rel.) incarnation; **–wolf** m. meat grinder

fleisch: –farben, adj., **–farbig** adj. fleshcolored; **–fressend** adj. carnivorous; **–geworden** adj. (rel.) incarnate; **–ig**

adj. fleshy; pulpy; **-lich** *adj.* fleshly, carnal, sensual

Fleiss *m.* diligence: application; industry; **mit —** (coll.) intentionally; on purpose

fleissig *adj.* diligent, industrious; regular

fletschen *v.* die Zähne **—** to show one's teeth

Flick: -arbeit *f.* patchwork; **-en** *m.* patch; **-schneider** *m.* job tailor; **-schuster** *m.* cobbler; **-wort** *neu.* expletive

flicken *v.* to mend, to repair, to patch; to botch; to cobble, to vamp; to darn; jemand etwas am Zeuge, **—** to find fault with someone

Flieder *m.* lilac; elder (tree)

Fliege *f.* fly; bow tie; **-n** *neu.* flight, soaring; **-nfenster** *neu.* window screen; **-nklatsche** *f.* fly swatter; **-npilz** *m.* toadstool

fliegen *v.* to fly; (coll.) to be fired; **-d** *adj.* airborne; **-des Blatt** fly leaf

Flieger *m.* aviator, pilot; **-abwehr** *f.* anti-aircraft; **-alarm** *m.* alert; **-einsatz** *m.* sortie; (unvollständig) abort; **-in** *f.* aviatrix; **-station** *f.* air station

fliehen *v.* to flee; to retreat; to avoid

Fliehkraft *f.* centrifugal force; (der Erde) G-force

Fliess *neu.* fleece; **-band** *neu.* conveyor belt; **-papier** *neu.* blotting paper

fliessen *v.* to flow; to stream; to run, to rush; **-d sprechen** to speak fluently

flimmern *v.* to glimmer, to glitter;˜to flicker; to sparkle; **-de Sterne** twinkling stars

flink *adj.* brisk, nimble; agile, alert

Flinte *f.* gun, rifle; die **— ins Korn werfen** to throw in the sponge

flirren *v.* to flit about; (air) to vibrate

Flirt *m.* flirtation

flirten *v.* to flirt

Flitter *m.* tinsel; spangle; frippery; **-glanz** *m.* false splendor, hollow pomp; **-gold** *neu.* tinsel; leaf gold; **-kram** *m.* cheap trinkets; **-wochen** *f. pl.* honeymoon

flitzen *v.* to dash (*oder* flit, shoot) along

Flocke *f.* flake; flock

Floh *m.* flea

Flor *m.* bloom, blossom; flourishing condition; crape, gauze; veil; bevy

florieren *v.* to flourish, to prosper

Floss *neu.* float, raft; **-e** *f.* fin; **-brücke** *f.* floating bridge; **-führer** *m.* raftsman

flössen *v.* to float, to raft

Flöte *f.* flute

flöten *v.* to play the flute; to whistle; to warble; **— gehen** (sl.) to be lost (*oder* broken)

Flotille *f.* flotilla

flott *adj.* floating, afloat; (fig.) nimble; dashing; fast, gay; smart; **— machen** to set afloat; **— leben** to live it up

Flotte *f.* fleet; navy; **-nschau** *f.* naval review (*oder* display); **-nstützpunkt** *m.* naval base

Fluch *m.* oath; malediction; anathema; curse

fluchen *v.* to curse; to swear

Flucht *f.* flight; escape; suite, row, sequence (arch.) alignment; (mech.) play

flüchten *v.* to flee; to escape

flüchtig *adj.* runaway, fugitive; volatile; superficial; hasty; fleet(ing), transitory

Flüchtling *m.* fugitive; refugee; deserter

Flug *m.* flying, flight; flock (of birds); **im -e** on the wing, in haste; **-abwehr** *f.* anti-aircraft defense; **-bahn** *f.* trajectory; **-ball** *m.* (tennis) volley; **-blatt** *neu.* handbill, flyer; **-bericht (nach der Landung)** *m.* debriefing; **-bericht erstatten** *v.* to debrief; **-blatt** *neu.* handbill; **-hafen** *m.* airport; **-lehre** *f.* aerodynamics; **-post** *f.* airmail; **-sand** *m.* quicksand; **-schema** *neu.*, **-schneise** *f.* flight pattern; **-schrift** *f.* pamphlet; **-stützpunkt** *m.* airbase; **-wesen** *neu.* aeronautics; **-sport** *m.* aviation

Flügel *m.* wing; leaf, casement; (army) flank; grand piano; **-adjutant** *m.* aide-de-camp; **-fenster** *neu.* French window; **-haube** *f.* cap with lappets; (motor) hood; **-mann** *m.* (mil.) file leader, flank man; **-schlag** *m.* beat of wings

flügge *adj.* (orn.) fledged; ready to start; self-supporting

Flugzeug *neu.* airplane; **-führer** *m.* pilot; **-halle** *f.* hangar; **-modell** *neu.* mock-up; **-mutterschiff** *neu.* aircraft carrier; **-rumpf** *m.* nacelle; **-schwanzflosse** *f.* empennage; **-träger** *m.* aircraft carrier

Fluor *neu.* fluorine; **-eszenz** *f.* fluorescence

Flur *f.* field, meadow; commons; **—** *m.* lobby; corridor, passage; floor

Fluss *m.* river; flow(ing); flux; fusion, melting; (med.) catarrh; menstruation; fluency; **-arm** *m.* tributary stream; **-krebs** *m.* crawfish; **-mündung** *f.* estuary; **-pferd** *neu.* hippopotamus

flüssig *adj.* fluid, liquid; flowing; fluent

flüstern *v.* to whisper

Flut *f.* flood; high tide (*oder* water); flow; deluge; **-welle** *f.* tidal wave; seiche; **-zeichen** *neu.* high-water mark

föderativ *adj.* confederate; federal

Fohlen *neu.* colt, foal

fohlen *v.* to foal

Föhn *m.* warm, humid Alpine wind in spring; hair dryer

Föhre *f.* Scotch pine (*oder* fir)

folg: -en *v.* to follow, to succeed; to obey;

–endermassen *adv.*, **–enderweise** *adv.* as follows, in the following manner; **–enschwer** *adj.* of great consequence; **–lich** *adv.* consequently; therefore; **–sam** *adj.* obedient, docile, tractable; **–ern** *v.* to conclude, to infer

Folge *f.* sequence, succession; consequence; order, series; set, suite; continuation; sequel; — leisten to comply with, to obey; **in der** — in the future; **–leistung** *f.* compliance, obedience; **–nde** *m.* follower; **–rung** *f.* conclusion; deduction; **–satz** *m.* corollary; **–zeit** *f.* time to come

Foliant *m.* folio, volume

Folie *f.* foil; mounting; (mirror) silvering

Folter *f.* torture, rack; **auf die** — **legen** (*or* spannen) to put to the rack; to keep in suspense; **–er** *m.*, **–knecht** *m.* torturer; **–kammer** *f.* torture chamber; **–qual** *f.* torture, torment

foltern *v.* to torture, to put to the rack

Fond *m.* stock; foundation; background; (auto.) back seat; **–s** *pl.* (public) funds, capital

foppen *v.* to tease; to trick, to fool

Förder: –band *neu.* conveyor belt; **–er** *m.* promoter, patron; **–korb** *m.* elevator; **–ung** *f.* promotion; **–wagen** *m.* mine railway

förderlich *adj.* useful; helpful; promoting

fordern *v.* to ask, to demand; to claim; to exact, to require; to challenge, to summon

fördern *v.* to further, to advance, to promote

Forelle *f.* trout

Forke *f.* pitchfork; manure fork

Form *f.* form, shape; figure; cut; model, pattern; good behavior, formality; (gram.) voice; (mech.) mold, block, last; **–alitäten** *f. pl.*, **–alien** *f. pl.* formalities; **–at** *neu.* size; importance; **–el** *f.* formula; **–fehler** *m.* breach of etiquette; flaw

form: –al *adj.* formal; **–ell** *adj* according to form; **–en** *v.* to form, to mold, to shape, to block; **–ieren** *v.* to form, to arrange; (mil.) to fall in line; **–ulieren** *v.* to formulate

förmlich *adj.* formal; ceremonious; real, regular; — *adv.* really, so to speak; downright

forsch *adj.* dashing; vigorous

Forsch: –er *m.* investigator, research worker; **–ung** *f.* investigation, research; **–ungsreisender** *m.* explorer

forschen *v.* to investigate, to inquire, to search

Forst *m.* forest, wood; **–hüter** *m.* forest ranger; **–mann** *m.* forester; **–wirtschaft** *f.* forestry

Förster *m.* forester; gamekeeper; ranger; **–ei** *f.* forester's district (*oder* house)

fort *adv.* forth, forward; on(ward); away, gone, off; **in einem** — continually, without interruption; **und so** — and so forth (*oder* on); **–an** *adv.* henceforth, hereafter; **–arbeiten** *v.* to continue working; **–besteh(e)n** *v.* to continue to exist; **–bewegen** *v.* to move on (*oder* forward); to keep moving; **–dauern** *v.* to continue, to last; **–fahren** *v.* to drive away, to remove; to depart; to continue; **–führen** *v.* to lead away; to carry on; **–geh(e)n** *v.* to go away (*oder* forward, on); **sich –helfen** *v.* to make a living; **–kommen** *v.* to get away (*oder* on, along); **–lassen** *v.* to allow to go; to omit; **–laufen** *v.* to escape, to run away; **–laufend** *adj.* continuous, uninterrupted; **–machen** *v.* to make off (*oder* haste); **–müssen** *v.* to be obliged to leave; **–pflanzen** *v.* to propagate; to transmit; **–schaffen** *v.* to clear away, to remove, to eliminate; **–schreiten** *v.* to advance, to proceed; to make progress; **–schrittlich** *adj.* progressive; **–schwemmen** *v.* to wash away; **–setzen** *v.* to put away, to carry on; to pursue; **–stehlen** *v.* to steal (*oder* slip) away; **stürmen, –stürzen** *v.* to rush away; **–während** *adj.* continuous, incessant, perpetual; **–weisen** *v.* to send away; **–ziehen** *v.* to move away, to leave; to march off; to migrate

Fort: –bestand *m.* continuation, duration, permanence; **–bewegung** *f.* locomotion; **–bildungsanstalt** *f.*, **–bildungsschule** *f.* continuation school; institution for higher education; **–fall** *m.* cessation; abolition; discontinuance; **–führung** *f.* continuation; pursuit; **–gang** *m.* departure, leaving; continuation; progress; **–kommen** *neu.* progress; living; **–leben** *neu.* survival; life after death; **–pflanzungsorgane** *neu. pl.* sexual (*oder* reproductive) organs; **–schritt** *m.* progress, advancement; improvement; **–schrittspartei** *f.* progressive party; **–setzung** *f.* continuation, prosecution; pursuit; (lit.) sequel

Foto *m.* (see Photo)

Fötus *m.* foetus, fetus

Fracht *f.* freight, cargo, load; freight charges; **–brief** *m.* bill of lading; **–er** *m.* freighter; shipper; **–gut** *neu.* freight, load, cargo; **–satz** *m.* freight rate

frachten *v.* to freight, to load; to ship

Frack *m.* full dress coat

frag: –en v. to ask, to question; to inquire; **nicht lange** (or **viel**) — to be quick about it; **um Rat** — to seek advice; –lich adj. questionable

Frage f. question; inquiry, query; interrogation; **in** — **stellen** to make uncertain; **nicht in** — **kommen** to be out of question; **ohne** — undoubtedly, unquestionably; –bogen m. questionnaire; –rei f. continuous (oder importunate) questioning; –stellung f. formulation of questions; –wort neu. interrogative; –zeichen neu. question mark

Fraktion f. fraction

Fraktur f. fracture; Gothic (oder Old English) type

frank adj. frank, open; — **und frei** quite frankly; –ieren v. (mail) to stamp, to send postpaid; –o adv. prepaid; all charges paid

Franken neu. Franconia

Frankreich neu. France

Franse f. fringe

fransen v. to fray (oder ravel) out

Franz m. Frank

Frass m. fodder, feed; (med.) caries; (sl.) grub

Fratze f. grimace, caricature; mask; (sl.) mug; –n schneiden to make faces

fratzenhaft adj. distorted, grotesque

Frau f. woman; wife; Mrs.; gnädige — madam; **Unsere liebe** — Our Lady; –enarzt m. gynecologist; –enkloster neu. nunnery; –enrechtlerin f. suffragette; –ensleute pl. womanfolk; –enzimmer neu. (lit.) female, woman

frauenhaft adj. womanly; feminine

Fräulein neu. single lady; Miss; saleslady

frech adj. impudent, insolent; cheeky, saucy

Frechdachs m. young rascal; saucy fellow

Frechheit f. impudence, insolence; cheek

Fregatte f. frigate

frei adj. free; independent; unrestrained, bold; candid, frank, open, unprotected; vacant; exempt from; gratis, prepaid; liberal; (law) acquitted, exonerated; **aus** –**en Stücken** of one's own free will; **aus** –**er Hand** freehand, offhand; **ich bin so** —! allow me! in –**er Luft, under** –**em Himmel** in the open air; –**en** v. to court, to woo; –geben v. to release, to set free; to give a holiday; –gebig adj. liberal; generous; –geistig adj. openminded, unbiased; –halten v. to pay for all expenses, to treat; –händig adj. offhand, freehand; –heitlich adj. liberal; –heraus adv. frankly, candidly; –herrlich adj. baronial; –lich adv. certainly, to be sure, of course; –mütig adj.

candid, frank; –sinnig adj. enlightened, liberal minded; –sprechen v. to acquit, to absolve; –stehen v. to be isolated, to be free, to be vacant; –willig adj. voluntary, spontaneous

Frei: –beuter m. freebooter, pirate; plagiarist; –billet neu. free pass, complimentary ticket; –brief m. license, permit; –er m. suitor, wooer; –denker m. free-thinker; –exemplar neu. presentation copy; –fall (avi. ohne Fallschirm) m. free fall; — frauf. baroness; –hafen m. free port; –heit f. freedom, liberty; –heitskrieg m. war of independence; –heitsstrafe f. imprisonment; –herr m. baron; –kauf m. redemption; –korps neu. volunteer corps; –kuvert neu. stamped envelope; –lauf m. free wheeling; –lichtbühne f. open-air theater; –lichtkino neu. drive-in theater; –marke f. postage stamp; –maurer m. free-·mason; –maurerei f. freemasonry; –mut m. frankness, candor, openness; –schar f. volunteers; insurgents; –spruch m. acquittal; –stelle f. scholarship; –stoss m. (sports) free kick; –tod m. suicide; –treppe f. grand staircase; –werber m. matchmaker

Freitag m. Friday

fremd adj. strange; foreign; –es Gut other people's property; **unter** –**em Namen** incognito; –artig adj. odd, strange; heterogeneous; –ländisch adj. alien, foreign; –stämmig adj. alien, of foreign birth (oder race)

Fremd: –e f. foreign country; –e m. stranger; foreigner; alien; guest; –enbuch neu. hotel register; –enführer m. tourist guide; –enlegion f. Foreign Legion; –enstube f. spare room; –herrschaft f. foreign rule; –körper m. foreign substance; –ling m. stranger; –sprache f. foreign language; –wort neu. foreign word

Frequenz f. attendance; traffic; number of persons; frequency, wave length

Fress: –en neu. food (for animals); ein gefundenes –en (coll.) windfall; –er m. glutton; –erei f. gluttony; (sl.) feast

fressen v. to eat, to feed (used only of beasts); to corrode; (fire) to spread; to devour, to gobble up

freu: –de(n)voll adj. cheerful, joyful; –destrahlend adj. beaming with joy; –detrunken adj. enraptured, overjoyed; –dig adj. cheerful, joyous, gratifying; **sich** –**en** v. to rejoice, to be glad; **sich** –**en auf** to look forward to

Freude f. gladness, joy; delight, pleasure; –nbotschaft f. glad tidings; good news:

−nfeier *f.* festival; −nfeuer *neu.* bonfire; −nhaus *neu.* disorderly house; −nmädchen *neu.* prostitute; −nrausch *m.* exultation, rapture; −nstörer *m.* killjoy; −ntag *m.* red-letter day; −ntaumel *m.* mad delight

Freund *m.* friend; −schaft *f.* friendship

freundlich *adj.* friendly, bright, agreeable

freundschaftlich *adj.* amicable, friendly

Frevel *m.* crime, trespass, infringement

frevel: −haft *adj.*, −lerisch *adj.* malicious, wanton; criminal; outrageous, sacrilegious; −n *v.* to infringe, to trespass, to blaspheme

Frevler *m.* malefactor; transgressor, blasphemer

Friderika *f.* Frederica

Fried: −e(n) *m.* peace; tranquillity; −ensbruch *m.* breach of peace; −ensrichter *m.* Justice of the Peace; −ensschluss *m.* conclusion of peace; −ensstifter *m.* pacifier, mediator; −ensvertrag *m.* peace treaty; −hof *m.* churchyard, cemetery

fried: −fertig *adj.* peaceable, pacific; −lich *adj.* peaceful; −liebend *adj.* peaceloving

Friedrich *m.* Frederick

frieren *v.* to freeze; to feel cold; to chill

Fries *m.* (arch.) frieze; (fabric) baize

Fris: −ur *f.* hairdo, coiffure; trimming; −eur *m.* hairdresser; −euse *f.* lady hairdresser; −iersalon *m.* beauty (*oder* barber) shop

frisch *adj.* fresh; brisk; new; hale, vigorous; auf −er Tat in the very act; — auf! cheer up! −e Eier newlaid eggs; −e Spur hot scent; −e Wäsche clean linen; — gestrichen! wet paint! — zu! onward! let's go! −weg *adv.* straightway

frisieren *v.* (hair) to dress, to curl

Frist *f.* set term (*oder* time); respite, grace

froh *adj.* joyful, cheerful, joyous, happy; −gelaunt *adj.* in a happy mood; −locken *v.* to exult, to triumph; −sinnig *adj.* cheerful, joyful

Froh: −locken *neu.* exult, triumph; −mut *m.*, −sinn *m.* cheerfulness, happiness; −natur *f.* cheerful disposition

fröhlich *adj.* cheerful, joyful, merry, happy

fromm *adj.* pious, devout; patient; artless; −en *v.* to benefit, to avail, to profit

Frömm: −elei *f.* bigotry; hypocrisy; sanctimoniousness; −igkeit *f.* godliness, piety; devoutness; −ler *m.* hypocrite

Fron *f.* −arbeit *f.*, −dienst *m.* compulsory (*oder* enforced) labor; drudgery; −herr *m.* feudal lord; −leichnam *m.* Corpus Christi; −vogt *m.* taskmaster

fronen *v.* to do forced labor

Front *f.* front; face; zone of battle

Frosch *m.* frog; firecracker; (mech.) bracket; −mensch *m.* frogman; −schenkel *m.* frogleg

Frost *m.* frost; chill, cold; −beule *f.* chillblain; −schutzmittel *neu.* anti-freeze

frösteln *v.* to shiver; to feel chilly

Frucht *f.* fruit; grain; crop; result, product; eingemachte Früchte preserves; −boden *m.* (bot.) receptacle; −folge *f.*, −wechsel *m.* rotation of crops; −garten *m.* orchard; −keim *m.* germ; −knoten *m.* seed bud; ovary; −lese *f.* fruit harvest

früh *adj.* early, in the morning; premature; −er *adj.* earlier, prior, sooner; former, late; −estens *adv.* at the earliest; −lingshaft *adj.* vernal, springlike; −reif *adj.* precocious; early (-ripe); −stücken *v.* to breakfast; −zeitig *adj.* early; untimely; premature

Früh: −aufsteher *m.* early riser; −e *f.* (early) morning; dawn; in aller −e before daybreak; −geburt *f.* premature birth; −konzert *neu.* matinée; −ling *m.*, −jahr *neu.* spring; −reife *f.* earliness, precociousness; −saat *f.* spring sowing; −stück *neu.* breakfast; zweites −stück lunch(eon)

Fuchs *m.* fox; chestnut horse; freshman, cunning (*oder* sly) fellow; −bau *m.* foxhole; −eisen *neu.* fox trap; −schwanz *m.* foxtail; handsaw

füg: −en *v.* to join, to fit, to regulate; to add; to ordain, to dispose; sich — to accomodate, to reconcile oneself; to acquiesce in; to submit; to happen, to coincide; −lich *adj.* convenient, just; −sam *adj.* obedient, docile, pliant, yielding, submissive

Fühl: −er *m.*, −horn *neu.* feeler, antenna; −ung *f.* touch

fühlbar *adj.* tangible, perceptible, marked

fühlen *v.* to feel, to touch, to sense; to notice, to surmise; jemand auf den Zahn — to sound someone out; Reue — to repent; sich gut — to feel well

Fuhr: −e *f.* conveyance; wagon load; −mann *m.* drayman, driver; −werk *neu.* vehicle, wagon

führen *v.* to lead; to conduct, to guide; to convey, to carry; to handle, to manage; to keep (books); to stock (goods); to bear (name, title); to show (proof); to wage (war); das grosse Wort — to brag, to boast; das Wort— to be spokesman; einen Prozess — to carry on a lawsuit; im Schilde — to intend, to plan; zum Mund — to raise to one's lips

Führer *m.* leader, guide; conductor; driver, operator; pilot; manual; guidebook; –schaft *f.* leadership, guidance; the leaders; –schein *m.* driver's license

Führung *f.* conduct, command, guidance; management, (sports) lead; behavior; –srille *f.* groove; –szeugnis *neu.* police certificate of behavior

Füll: –e *f.* fullness, abundance; plumpness; in Hülle und –e plenty and to spare; –federhalter *m.* fountain pen; –horn *neu.* cornucopia; –sel *neu.* stopgap; stuffing; –ung *f.* filling; stuffing; packing; (door) panel; –werk *neu.* padding; (arch.) rubble work; –wort *neu.* expletive

Füllen *neu.* foal, colt, filly

füllen *v.* to fill, to stuff; auf Flaschen — to bottle; in Fässer — to barrel

fummeln *v.* to fumble; to potter, to dabble

Fund *m.* find(ing); discovery; –büro *neu.* lost and found department; –grube *f.* rich mine (*oder* source); –stück *neu.* found article

Fundament *neu.* foundation, basis; –ierung *f.* laying of a foundation

fünf *adj.* five; –eckig *adj.* pentagonal; –erlei *adj.* of five kinds; –fach *adj.,* –fältig *adj.* five-fold; –mal *adv.* five times; –stöckig *adj.* five-storied; –zehn *adj.* fifteen; –zig *adj.* fifty

Fünf *f.,* **Fünfer** *m.* five; –eck *neu.* pentagon; –ling *m.* quintuplet; –tel *neu.* fifth part

fungieren *v.* to act, to officiate; to discharge

Funk *m.* wireless; radio; –e(n) *m.* spark; bit; –enfänger *m.* spark catcher; –er *m.* radio operator, wireless telegrapher; –meldung *f.* radio message; –sendung *f.* radio broadcasting; –spruch *m.* radiogram; –turm *m.* radio tower; –wagen *m.* squad car

funk: –eln *v.* to twinkle, to sparkle; –elnagelneu *adj.* brand-new; –en *v.* to radio, to broadcast; –ensprühend *adj.,* –enwerfend *adj.* sparkling, scintillating

funktionieren *v.* to function

für *prep.* for; in favor of; for the sake (*oder* on behalf) of; in return for; instead of; an und — sich in (*oder* of) itself; ein — allemal once and for all; –s Erste for the present; — sich for oneself alone; (theat.) aside; — und — forever and ever; — und wider pro and con; ich habe es — mein Leben gern I am exceedingly fond of it; Schritt — Schritt step by step; Tag — Tag day after day; –liebnehmen to put up with, to content onself with

Für: –bitte *f.* intercession; –sorge *f.* precaution, care; relief; –sorgeerziehung *f.* child welfare work; education of juvenile delinquents; –sprache *f.* recommendation; intercession; –sprecher *m.* interceder; advocate; –wort *neu.* pronoun

Furage *f.* forage, fodder

Furche *f.* furrow; wrinkle

Furcht *f.* fear, fright; dread; anxiety; in — setzen to frighten

furcht: –bar *adj.* frightful, dreadful; awful; (coll.) great, tremendous; –los *adj.* intrepid; fearless; –sam *adj.* timid, faint-hearted

fürchten *v.* to fear; to be afraid of; to dread

fürchterlich *adj.* frightful, awful, terrible

Furie *f.* fury, termagant

Furier *m.* forager

Fürst *m.* prince; sovereign; — dieser Welt (poet.) the devil, Satan; –entum *neu.* principality

fürstlich *adj.* princely

Furt *f.* ford

Fuss *m.* foot; footing; base, pedestal; bottom; auf dem –e folgen to follow close on one's heels; auf eigenen Füssen stehen to be independent; auf freien — setzen to set free; auf grossem –e leben to live in grand style; auf gutem –e steh(e)n to be on good terms; — fassen to gain a footing; stehenden –es immediately; zu — on foot; –abtreter *m.* foot scraper; –bank *f.* footstool; hassock; –boden *m.* floor(ing); –fall *m.* prostration; –gänger *m.* pedestrian; –gelenk *neu.* ankle; –gitter *n.* grille; –note *f.* footnote; –spitze *f.* point of the foot; –spur *f.,* –stapfe *f.* footprint, footstep; track; –steig *m.* sidewalk, –weg *m.* path; –tritt *m.* treadle, footboard; kick; –truppen *f. pl.,* infantry

fuss: –en *v.* to stand (*oder* depend) on; –fällig *adj* on one's knees; –frei *adj.* foot-free

futsch *adj.* (coll.) lost, gone; ruined

Futter *neu.* feed, fodder, forage; lining; casing; –beutel *m.* nosebag; –kasten *m.* corn bin; –neid *m.* (coll.) professional jealousy

Futteral *neu.* case, covering, sheath

füttern *v.* to feed; to breed; to line, to cover, to case; to stuff; to fur

Fütterung *f.* feeding; forage; lining, casing

G

Gabe *f.* gift, present; donation; talent; dose

Gabel *f.* fork; –frühstück *neu.* lunch(eon)
gabel: –förmig *adj.*, –ig *adj.* forked; **sich**
 –n *v.* to fork, to branch off; to bifurcate
gackeln, gackern *v.* to cackle
gaffen *v.* to gape, to gaze, to stare
Gaffer *m.* gaper; idle onlooker; –ei *f.* gaping
Gage *f.* salary; fee (of artist)
gähnen *v.* to yawn; –d *adj.* yawning
Gala *f.* gala; festive dress
Galan *m.* lover (of woman)
galant *adj.* gallant, courteous, courtly;
 –es Abenteuer romantic adventure
Galanterie *f.* gallantry, courtesy; **–waren**
 f. pl. costume jewelry; finery
Galeere *f.* (naut.) galley
Galgen *m.* gallows; –frist *f.* reprieve;
 –humor *m.* grim humor; –schelm *m.*,
 –strick *m.*, –vogel *m.* rogue, scoundrel,
 good-for-nothing
Gall: –apfel *m.* gallnut; –e *f.* gall, bile;
 anger, bad humor; –enblase *f.* gallbladder
Gallert *neu.*, **Gallerte** *f.* gelatine, jelly,
 glue
galoppieren *v.* to gallop
galvanisieren *v.* to galvanize, to electrolyze
Gamasche *f.* gaiter, legging
Gambe *f.* bass viol
Gamsbart *m.* beard of the chamois;
 goatee
Gang *m.* walk; errand; corridor, passage;
 course (of meal); action, motion;
 (anat.) canal, duct; (mech.) gear,
 worm; (min.) lode, vein; (naut.) gangway; (sports) round; **aus dem — bringen** (*or* setzen) to throw out of gear;
 **to disarrange; im — bleiben to stay in
 motion; im — sein** to be in operation
 (*oder* going on, in progress); **in — bringen** to set in motion; to bring into
 fashion; **in — kommen** to come into
 action; –art *f.* gait, pace; –werk *neu.*
 driving gear
Gängelband *neu.* leading strings; **jemand
 am — führen** to lead someone by the
 nose
Gans *f.* goose; **dumme —** (coll.) silly girl
Gänse *f. pl.* geese; –blümchen *neu.* daisy;
 –füsschen *neu.* quotation marks; –haut
 f. goose skin; (fig.) goose flesh, pimples;
 –küken *neu.* gosling; –leber *f.* goose
 liver; –marsch *m.* single file; –rich *m.*
 gander; –wein *m.* (coll.) water
ganz *adj.* all, entire, whole; complete,
 total; intact; **ein –er Mann** every inch
 a man; **eine –e Zahl** an integer; many;
 etwas — anderes quite a different
 thing; **— besonders** particularly; **—**

gewiss most certainly; **— und gar nicht**
 not at all; **von –em Herzen** with all my
 heart
Ganze *neu.*, **Ganzheit** *f.* whole; totality;
 im –n on the whole, generally
gänzlich *adj.* entire, full, total
gar *adj.* done, ready, finished; well
 cooked; prepared; **—** *adv.* fully, quite,
 very; perhaps; even; **— mancher** many
 a man; **— nicht** not at all; **— nichts**
 nothing at all
Garant *m.* guarantor; –ie *f.* guarantee
garantieren *v.* to guarantee
Garaus *m.* ruin; end; death
Garbe *f.* sheaf; yarrow
Garderobe *f.* wardrobe; clothes; cloakroom; –nmarke *f.* coat check
Gardine *f.* curtain; **hinter schwedischen
 –n** (sl.) in jail; –npredigt *f.* curtain
 lecture
Gärbottich *m.* fermenting vat
gären *v.* to ferment; to germinate
Garn *neu.* yarn; twine; net, snare; **ein —
 spinnen** to spin a story; **jemandem ins
 — gehen** to be tricked into something
Garnele *f.* shrimp; prawn
garnieren *v.* to trim; to garnish
Garnison *f.* (mil.) garrison
Garnitur *f.* trimming; fittings, mountings;
 equipment, outfit, set, series
garstig *adj.* nasty; filthy, indecent; ugly
Garten *m.* garden; –bau *m.* gardening,
 horticulture; –haus *neu.* summer house;
 –laube *f.* arbor, bower; –säge *f.* pruning
 saw
Gärtner *m.* gardener; –ei *f.* gardening,
 nursery
Gärung *f.* fermentation; commotion, ferment
Gas *neu.* gas; –anstalt *f.* gasworks; –anzünder *m.* gas lighter; –hahn *m.* gas
 cock; –hebel *m.* (mech.) throttle;
 –leitung *f.* gas pipes; –olin *neu.* gasoline
Gasse *f.* narrow street; lane; **eine —
 machen** to make a path; **Hans in allen
 –n** Jack-of-all-trades; –nbube *m.*,
 –njunge *m.* street Arab, gamin;
 –nhauer *m.* street (*oder* vulgar) song
Gast *m.* guest; visitor; customer; –bett
 neu. spare bed; –erei *f.*, –mahl *neu.*
 banquet, feast; –freundschaft *f.* hospitality; –geber *m.* host; –haus *neu.*,
 –wirtschaft *f.* inn, restaurant; –hof *m.*
 hotel; –spielreise *f.* (theat.) tour;
 –stube *f.* inn; guest room; –wirt *m.*
 innkeeper
gast: –frei *adj.*, –freundlich *adj.*, –lich *adj.*
 hospitable; –ieren *v.* to feast, to carouse; (theat.) to star
Gatt: –e *m.* husband, consort; –in *f.* wife;

-ung *f.* kind, breed, sort; genus, species

gatten *v.* to pair; to join; to couple, to match, **sich** — to copulate; to unite

Gatter *neu.* grating, railing

Gauk: **-elbild** *neu.* phantasm, illusion, mirage; **-elei** *f.*, **-elwerk** *neu.* hocus-pocus, trickery, magic; **-ler** *m.* juggler, magician; buffoon

gaukeln *v.* to flutter about; to juggle

Gaul *m.* horse; (coll.) nag

Gaumen *m.* palate

Gauner *m.* swindler, gangster; **-ei** *f.* swindling, trickery; **-sprache** *f.* thieve's cant; **-streich** *m.*, **-stück** *neu.* swindle, trick

Gaze *f.* gauze, gossamer

Geächtete *m.* ostracized person; outlaw

geädert *adj.* veined; grained, marbled

Gebäck *neu.* baked goods; pastry, confectionery

Gebärde *f.* bearing, air; mien; gesture; **-nspiel** *neu.* gesticulation; pantomime

gebären *v.* to bring forth, to give birth (to)

Gebäude *neu.* building, structure, system

Gebein *neu.* bony structure; skeleton; **-e** *pl.* corpse

geben *v.* to give, to present; to grant, to bestow, to yield, (cards) to deal; einen **Verweis** — to reprimand; es gibt there is (*oder* are); etwas — auf to value, to regard; **Fersengeld** — to run away; in **Druck** — to have printed; in **Verwahrung** — to deposit with; **Recht** — to agree with; **sich Mühe** — to take pains; **sich zu erkennen** — to make oneself known; **sich zufrieden** — to content oneself; **verloren** — to give up for lost; **von sich** — to express, to utter; to vomit; **Zeugnis** — to bear witness

Gebet *neu.* prayer; jemand ins — nehmen to question closely

Gebettel *neu.* begging

Gebiet *neu.* area, district, territory; sphere, field; **-er** *m.* ruler

gebieten *v.* to order, to command, to govern

gebieterisch *adj.* imperious; categorical

Gebilde *neu.* form(ation), structure; image

gebildet *adj.* educated, well-bred

Gebirg: **-e** *neu.* mountain chain; highland; **-sabhang** *m.* mountain side; **-sbewohner** *m.* mountaineer, highlander; **-sgrat** *m.*, **-skamm** *m.* mountain ridge

gebirgig *adj.* mountainous

Gebiss *neu.* teeth, denture; bridle bit

Gebläse *neu.* blower

geblümt *adj.* flowered, flowery; figured

Geblüt *neu.* blood; lineage, family; race;

es steckt im — it runs in the family

Gebot *neu.* order, command; bid(ding); **-e** *pl.* the Ten Commandments; **zu** — stehen to be at one's disposal

Gebräu *neu.* brew; (coll.) mixture, poor drink

Gebrauch *m.* use, application; custom, usage; rite; **-sanweisung** *f.* directions (for use); primitive **-sgegenstand** archeological artefact (*oder* artifact); **-sgraphik** *f.* commercial art; **-smusterschutz** *m.* registered trade mark

gebrauchen *v.* to (make) use (of), to utilize

gebräuchlich *adj.* customary; nicht mehr — obsolete

gebraucht *adj.* used, worn; secondhand

Gebrechen *neu.* want, need; (bodily) defect

gebrechlich *adj.* weak, decrepit; infirm, frail

Gebrüder *m. pl.* brothers

Gebrüll *neu.* roaring, lowing

Gebühr *f.* duty; fees, tax; due; nach — deservedly; über — excessively; wider — quite improper, contrary to custom; **-enlass** *m.*, **-ennachlass** *m.* remission of fees (*oder* taxes)

gebühr: **-en** *v.* to be due, to belong to; **sich -en** to be becoming (*oder* fit, proper); **-end** *adj.* fitting, suitable; proper, becoming, decent; **-endermassen** *adv.*, **-enderweise** *adv.* deservedly; **-enfrei** *adj.* exempt from duty (*oder* taxes); prepaid

Geburt *f.* birth; origin; product; **-enregelung** *f.*, **-sbeschränkung** *f.* birth control; **-enziffer** *f.* birth rate; **-shilfe** *f.* obstetrics; **-sland** *neu.* native country; **-sliste** *f.* register of births; **-stag** *m.* birthday; **-swehen** *f.* labor pains; **-sschein** *m.*, **-surkunde** *f.* birth certificate; **-szange** *f.* forceps

gebürtig *adj.* born in, native of

Gebüsch *neu.* bush(es); thicket; copse

Gedächtris *neu.* recollection, memory; remembrance; aus dem — from memory, by heart; im — bewahren to keep in mind; zum — in remembrance of; **-feier** *f.*, **-fest** *neu.* commemoration

Gedanke *m.* thought; conception, idea; plan, design; in **-n** sein to be engrossed (*oder* preoccupied); sich **-n** machen to worry; **-nfolge** *f.*, **-ngang** *m.*, **-nreihe** *f.* train of thought; **-nlesen** *neu.* mind reading; **-nspäne** *m. pl.* aphorisms; **-nstrich** *m.* (gram.) dash; **-nübertragung** *f.* telepathy; mental suggestion

Gedärm *neu.* intestines, entrails

gedeihen v. to prosper, to thrive, to flourish

Gedenk: −feier f. commemoration; −spruch m. motto; −stein m. monument, memorial stone

gedenken v. to mention, to remember; to intend

Gedicht neu. poem

gediegen adj. genuine, true, solid; (min.) pure

Gedränge neu. crowd, throng; scrimmage; ins — geraten (or kommen) to get into difficulties, to get into a fix

gedrängt adj. crowded; pressed, urged; concise

gedrückt adj. oppressed, held down; depressed

Gedruckte neu. printed matter

gedrungen adj. stocky, compact, concise

Geduld f. patience; forbearance; endurance

gedulden v. sich — to wait patiently

geduldig adj. patient; forbearing

gedunsen adj. bloated, turgid

geeignet adj. appropriate, suitable, fit, meet

Gefahr f. danger, peril, risk

gefährden v. to endanger, to jeopardize

gefährlich adj. dangerous, perilous; critical

Gefährt neu. vehicle

Gefährte m. associate, companion, mate

Gefallen m. pleasure; favor

gefallen v. to please, to suit; **sich etwas —** lassen (coll.) to swallow something

Gefallene m. fallen person; slain (soldier)

gefällig adj. accommodating, pleasant, kind

Gefangen: −e m. captive, prisoner; −nahme f., −nehmung f. arrest, imprisonment; capture; −schaft f. captivity, imprisonment

Gefängnis neu. jail, prison; −direktor m. warden; −strafe f. imprisonment; −wärter m. jailer

Gefäss neu. vessel, receptacle

gefasst adj. calm, composed; ready; set (jewel)

Gefecht neu. (mil.) action, combat; **ausser —** setzen to put out of action; −slehre f. tactics; −sübung f. maneuver, sham fight

Gefieder neu. feathers, plumage

gefleckt adj. speckled, spotted, freckled

geflissentlich adj. premeditated, intentional, willful; — adv. with malice aforethought

Geflügel neu. poultry; birds

geflügelt adj. winged; −e **Worte** familiar quotations, proverbial sayings

Geflunker neu. fibbing; bragging

Gefolge neu. retinue, suite, train; escort

Gefolgschaft f. followers, staff (of a firm); — leisten to follow, to obey

gefrässig adj. gluttonous, greedy, voracious

Gefreiter m. (mil.) private first class

gefrieren v. to freeze, to congeal

Gefrierpunkt m. freezing point

Gefüge neu. structure; joints; (anat.) articulation; (geol.) stratification

gefügig adj. pliant; submissive, obedient

Gefühl neu. emotion; feeling, sentiment; touch; −sart f. disposition; −sduselei f. sentimentalism; −smensch m man of keen sensibility

gefühllos adj insensitive, callous

gegebenenfalls adj. if suitable; eventually

gegen prep. against; contrary to; towards; counter; in return for, in comparison with; about; — bar for cash; — Empfang on receipt; **hundert —** eins a hundred to one; −sätzlich adj. contrary, opposite; adverse; −seitig adj. mutual, reciprocal; −ständlich adj. objective; −standslos adj. without object, to no purpose; −teilig adj. contrary; −über prep. and adv. opposite to, facing; in relation to; −überstellen v. to oppose; to confront; to contrast; −wärtig adj. and adv. present; actual, current; now-(adays)

Gegen: −angriff m. counterattack; −besuch m. return visit; −bewegung f. countermove, reaction; −forderung f. counterclaim; −gewicht neu. counterweight; −gift neu. antidote; −klage f. recrimination; −liebe f. mutual affection; −massregel f. preventive measure; retaliation; −part m. opponent; −rede f. reply, objection; −satz m. contrast, opposition; antithesis; −schrift f. refutation; −seite f. opposite side; (coin) reverse; −spieler m. opponent; antagonist; −stand m. subject; theme; −stoss m. counterattack, counterthrust; −stück neu. counterpart; −teil neu. contrary, reverse; −wart f. presence; present time; (gram.) present tense; −wehr f. defense; resistance; −wert m. equivalent; −wind m. head wind; −wirkung f. reaction; −zug m. countermove

Gegend f. region; district; surroundings; neighborhood; direction

Gegenelektrizitätsatom neu. antiproton

Gegenelektron neu. anti-electron

Gegner m. adversary, opponent; foe; −schaft f. opponents; opposition

gehaben v. sich — to be slow (oder fussy)

Gehalt m. contents; capacity; proportion;

intrinsic value; — *neu.* salary, pay, wages

gehalt: –los *adj.* empty, worthless, superficial, shallow; –reich *adj.*, –voll *adj.* of intrinsic value; substantial; solid

Gehänge *neu.* sword-belt; ears (of hunting dogs); pendants; (eccl.) drapery; (min.) slope

gehässig *adj.* malicious, spiteful

Gehäuse *neu.* (lit.) housing; case; (fruit) core; (naut.) binnacle

Gehege *neu.* game preserve; enclosure, pen; einem ins — kommen to interfere in a person's affairs

geheim *adj.* secret; concealed, hidden; private; –nisvoll *adj.* mysterious

Geheim: –nis *neu.* mystery, secret; –polizei *f.* secret police; –polizist *m.* plain-clothes man; –schrift *f.* cipher, code

Geheiss *neu.* command, order

gehen *v.* to go, to walk; to extend (to); to leave; to proceed (com.) to sell; (mech.) to run, to work; an die Arbeit — to begin to work; das Fenster geht nach Norden the window faces north; das geht nicht! that won't do! die Geschäfte — schlecht business is slack; es wird schon — it is feasible; in sich — to repent; sich — lassen to take it easy; Wie geht es Ihnen? How do you do?

Gehilfe *m.* helper, assistant, journeyman

Gehirn *neu.* brain; sense; brainpower; –lähmung *f.* cerebral palsy; –schlag *m.* apoplexy; –wäsche *f.* brain washing

Gehöft *neu.* farm, homestead

Gehölz *neu.* thicket, woods

Gehör *neu.* hearing; musical ear; — finden to obtain a hearing; jemandem — schenken to give someone a hearing; nach dem — spielen to play by ear

gehorchen *v.* to obey

gehör: –en *v.* to belong to, to be owned by; to be fitting (*oder* proper); –ig *adj.* owned by; appertaining to; appropriate, becoming, fit, proper, –ig *adv.* thoroughly, duly, properly

gehörnt *adj.* horned, horny; antlered

gehorsam *adj.* obedient, dutiful

Gehorsam *m.* obedience, dutifulness

Gehrock *m.* frock coat

Gehwerk *neu.* (mech.) movements, works; –zeuge *neu. pl.* (coll.) feet

Geier *m.* vulture; –falke *m.* gerfalcon

Geifer *m.* drivel, slaver, slobber; venom; –er *m.* venomous person

Geige *f.* violin; –r *m.* violinist

geigen *v.* to play the violin; ich werde dir etwas — I'll give you a piece of my mind

Geigerzähler *m.* geiger counter

geil *adj.* rank, lecherous, lewd; voluptuous

Geisel *m.*, *f.* hostage

Geiser, Geisir, Geysir *m.* geyser

Geiss *f.* goat; doe; –blatt *neu.* woodbine, honeysuckle; –bock *m.* billy goat; –hirt *m.* goatherd; –lein *neu.* kid

Geissel *f.* whip, lash; scourge, plague

geisseln *v.* to scourge, to castigate

Geist *m.* spirit; intellect, mind; ghost, sprite; –erglaube *m.* spirit(ual)ism; –erseher *m.* ghost seer, visionary; –erstunde *f.* witching hour; –esarbeit *f.* brainwork; –esblitz *m.* stroke of genius, brain wave; –esfunke *m.* flash of wit; –esgabe *f.* talent; –esgegenwart *f.* presence of mind; –eskraft *f.* intellectual power; –eskrankheit *f.* mental disease, insanity; –esschwäche *f.* feeblemindedness, imbecility; –esstörung *f.* mental derangement, psychopathy; –esverfassung *f.* frame of mind; –eszustand *m.* mental condition; –liche *m.* clergyman; minister, priest; –lichkeit *f.* clergy

geist: –erhaft *adj.* ghostly, spectral; –esabwesend *adj.* absent-minded; –eskrank *adj.* mentally deranged, insane; –esschwach *adj.* feeble-minded; –ig *adj.* spiritual; intellectual, mental; alcoholic, spirituous; –lich *adj.* spiritual, sacred; ecclesiastical; –los *adj.* spiritless, dull; –reich *adj.*, –voll *adj.* spirited, witty; gifted; –tötend *adj.* stupefying; monotonous

Geiz *m.* avarice; miserliness; stinginess; –hals *m.*, –kragen *m.* miser

geizen *v.* to be avaricious, to be thrifty

geizig *adj.* avaricious, miserly, stingy

Gejammer *neu.* lamentation, wailing

Gejauchze *neu.*, **Gejubel** *neu.* jubilation

Gejohle *neu.* howling, yelling

gekachelt *adj.* tiled

Gekeife *neu.* nagging, squabbling, wrangling

Gekicher *neu.* tittering, snickering, giggling

Geklatsche *neu.* clapping; gossip

Geklingel *neu.* tinkling; sounding (of bell)

Geknister *neu.* crackling; rustling

Geknurr(e) *neu.* growling, snarling

Gekose *neu.* caressing; billing and cooing

Gekritzel *neu.* scribbling; scrawl

gekünstelt *adj.* artificial; affected

Gelächter *neu.* laughter; (coll.) laughingstock

Gelage *neu.* revel, feast, drinking bout

gelähmt *adj.* paralyzed, lame

Gelände *neu.* tract of ground; terrain

Geländer *neu.* railing; balustrade, bannister

gelangen *v.* to arrive at, to reach; to attain

gelassen *adj.* calm, composed, collected

geläufig *adj.* fluent, ready; familiar

gelaunt *adj.* disposed; **gut** — in good humor; **schlecht** — cross, peevish

gelb *adj.* yellow; **–e Rübe** carrot; **–lich** *adj.* yellowish, sallow; **–süchtig** *adj.* jaundiced

Geld *neu.* money; **bares** — cash; **falsches** — counterfeit money; **kleines** — small change; **öffentliche –er** public funds; **–anlage** *f.* investment of capital; **–anweisung** *f.* money order; **–gier** *f.* avarice; **–heirat** *f.* marriage for money; **–kasten** *m.* strong box; **–leute** *pl.* financiers; **–schneider** *m.* extortioner, usurer; **–schrank** *m.* safe; **–strafe** *f.* fine; **–stück** *neu.* coin; **–tasche** *f.* purse; **–umlauf** *m.*, **–umsatz** *m.* circulation of money; **–verlegenheit** *f.* financial difficulty; **–währung** *f.* currency; **–wechselgeschäft** *neu.* currency exchange; **–wesen** *neu.* finance

Gelee *neu.* jelly

gelegen *adj.* located, situated; opportune, convenient; **–tlich** *adj.* incidental, occasional; **–tlich** *adv.* as opportunity arises; at one's convenience

Gelegenheit *f.* occasion; opportunity; **–sarbeiter** *m.* casual laborer; **–skauf** *m.* bargain; **–smacher** *m.* go-between; procurer

gelehrig *adj.* docile, tractable

Gelehrsamkeit *f.* scholarship, erudition

gelehrt *adj.* learned, scholarly, bookish

Gelehrte *m.* scholar, savant, pundit

Geleier *neu.* grind organ music; monotonous playing (singing *oder* talking)

Geleis(e) *neu.* rut; track, rails

Geleit(e) *neu.* accompaniment; safe conduct; escort; convoy; **–wort** *neu.* preface

Gelenk *neu.* joint, articulation; link; **–entzündung** *f.* arthritis; **–puppe** *f.* marionette; **–ring** *m.* swivel

gelenkig *adj.* flexible, supple; nimble

Gelichter *neu.* riffraff, gang

Geliebte *m.* or *f.* beloved, lover, sweetheart

gelind(e) *adj.* gentle, soft; lenient; slight

gelingen *v.* to succeed; to be successful

Gelispel *neu.* lisping, whispering

gellen *v.* to shrill, to yell; **–d** *adj.* shrill; piercing

geloben *v.* to promise, to vow; to pledge

Gelöbnis *neu.* pledge, promise, vow

gelockt *adj.* curly

gelt? *interr.* (dial.) right? isn't it so?

gelten *v.* to have influence (*oder* value); to be valid; to be held in esteem; to be considered; **es galt unser Leben** our lives were at stake; **es gilt!** agreed! — **für** to pass for; **sich –d machen to** assert oneself (*oder* itself)

Geltung *f.* value; recognition, validity

Gelübde *neu.* vow

gelungen *adj.* successful; (coll.) funny; good

Gelüst(e) *neu.* desire, longing; lust

gelüsten *v.* sich — **lassen** to long for, to hanker (*oder* lust) after; to covet

Gemach *neu.* room; chamber; leisure

gemach, gemächlich *adj.* leisurely, easygoing

Gemahl *m.* husband; **–in** *f.* wife

Gemälde *neu.* painting

gemäss *adj.* commensurate; agreeable, conformable; suitable; — *prep.* in accordance with

Gemäuer *neu.* masonry; **altes** — ruins

gemein *adj.* common, ordinary; vulgar; coarse, base, low, mean; **–fasslich** *adj.* **–verständlich** *adj.* easy to understand, popular; **–gefährlich** *adj.* dangerous to the public; **–gültig** *adj.* generally admitted; **–hin** *adv.* commonly, generally, customarily; **–nützig** *adj.* beneficial to the public; **–sam** *adj.* common; **–schaftlich** *adj.* in common; mutual

Gemein: **–besitz** *m.* public property; **–e** *m.* (mil.) private first class; **–geist** *m.* public spirit; **–gut** *neu.* common property; **–heit** *f.* baseness; meanness; vulgarity; **–platz** *m.* platitude; **–schaft** *f.* community; congeniality, fellowship; **–wesen** *neu.* commonwealth; **–wohl** *neu.* common welfare

Gemeinde *f.* community, municipality; congregation, parish; **–acker** *m.*, **–anger** *m.* village common; **–haus** *neu.* town hall; **–rat** *m.* municipal (*oder* town) council; **–schule** *f.* primary school, **–verwaltung** *f.* local government; **–vorstand** *m.* local board; **–vorsteher** *m.* mayor

Gemenge *neu.* mixture; affray, melee

gemessen *adj.* measured; formal, grave, sedate

Gemetzel *neu.* slaughter, massacre; carnage

Gemisch *neu.* mixture

Gemme *f.* gem

Gemse *f.* chamois

Gemunkel *neu.* mutterings, gossip, rumors

Gemurmel *neu.* murmur(ing); mumbling

Gemüse *neu.* vegetables, greens; **junges**

— (coll.) young people

Gemüt *neu.* soul; heart; sentiment; **–sart** *f.*, **–sbeschaffenheit** *f.* disposition; temper; **–sbewegung** *f.* emotion; **–slage** *f.*, **–sverfassung** *f.* mood, frame of mind; **–sleben** *neu.* inner life; **–smensch** *m.* sentimental person; (coll.) rude fellow; **–sruhe** *f.* peace of mind, composure

gemüt: –lich *adj.* cozy; homelike, informal; snug, comfortable; good-natured; **–skrank** *adj.* melancholy; **–voll** *adj.* emotional

gen *prep.* towards, to

genau *adj.* accurate, exact; precise; particular, scrupulous; sparing; close-fisted

genehm *adj.* agreeable; welcome; **–igen** *v.* to agree (to); to approve; to grant; to sanction; einen **–igen** (coll.) to take one (drink)

geneigt *adj.* inclined; favorable, disposed to

General *m.* general; **–direktor** *m.* general manager; **–feldmarschall** *m.* Field Marshall General; (coll.) five-star general; **–ität** *f.* (body of) generals; generality; **–nenner** *m.* (math.) lowest common denominator; **–probe** *f.* final rehearsal; **–stab** *m.* General Staff; **–vollmacht** *f.* general power of attorney

genesen *v.* to recover; to regain health; eines Kindes — to give birth to a child

Genever *m.* gin

Genf *neu.* Geneva

Genialität *f.* powers (*oder* gifts) of genius; creative ability, originality; geniality

Genick *neu.* nape, neck

Genie *neu.* genius; creative ability

genieren *v.* to inconvenience; to embarrass; sich — to be embarrassed, to be shy

geniessen *v.* to enjoy, to relish; to have the benefit of; nicht zu — unpalatable, unsavory; (fig.) intolerable

Genitalien *f. pl.* genitals

Genius *m.* genius; guardian angel

Genosse *m.* companion, comrade; colleague; confederate, partisan; fellow member; (law) abettor, accomplice; **–nschaft** *f.* association; c-ooperative

Genua *neu.* Genoa

genug *adj.* enough, sufficient; **—!** *interj.* enough! stop it!

Genüge *f.* sufficiency; satisfaction

genügen *v.* to suffice, to satisfy

Genugtuung *f.* satisfaction; compensation

Genuss *m.* enjoyment; indulgence; use; **–mensch** *m.* voluptuary, sensualist; **–mittel** *neu.* luxuries; **–sucht** *f.* craving for pleasure

Geographie *f.* geography

Geologie *f.* geology

Geometrie *f.* geometry

Georg *m.* George

Georgine *f.* dahlia

Gepäck *neu.* baggage, luggage; **–abfertigung** *f.*, **–aufgabe** *f.*, **–ausgabe** *f.* baggage room; **–marsch** *m.* (mil.) march with full equipment; **–träger** *m.* porter

Gepflogenheit *f.* custom, usage

Geplänkel *neu.* skirmish

Geplapper *neu.* babbling, chattering

Geplätscher *neu.* splashing, purling

Geplauder *neu.* chatting, prattle

Gepolter *neu.* rumble; loud scolding

Gepräge *neu.* coinage; impression, **stamp**

Geprahle *neu.* brag, boast

Gepränge *neu.* pageantry, pomp

Geprassel *neu.* crackling, clatter

Gequake *neu.* croaking, quacking

Gequieke *neu.* squeaking, squealing

gerad: –e *adj.* direct; erect; even; straight(forward); constant, upright; **–e** das Gegenteil the very opposite; **–e** und ungerade even and odd; ich bin **–e** gekommen I have just come; ich war **–e** dort I happened to be there; nun **–e** now more than ever; **–eaus** *adv.* straight ahead; **–eheraus** *adv.* frankly, bluntly; **–ehin** *adv.* straight on; pointblank; **–eüber** *adv.* just opposite; **–e**(s)wegs *adv.* directly, at once; **–ezu** *adv.* straight ahead; downright, plainly, flatly; **–linig** *adj.* in a straight line, rectilinear; **–sinnig** *adj.* straightforward, upright

Gerade *f.* straight line

Geranie *f.*, **Geranium** *neu.* geranium

Gerassel *neu.* clanking, clatter, rattling

Gerät *neu.* implement, tool, apparatus; **–ekammer** *f.* storeroom; **–ekasten** *m.* tool box (*oder* chest); **–schaften** *f. pl.* utensils; appliances; equipment

geraten *v.* to get into, to run into, to come upon; in Konkurs — to go bankrupt; **—** *adj.* advisable, advantageous

Geratewohl *neu.* aufs — at random

geraum *adj.* ample; considerable

geräumig *adj.* roomy, capacious, spacious

Geräusch *neu.* noise, bustle, stir

geräuschlos *adj.* noiseless, quiet

geräuschvoll *adj.* noisy, tumultuous

Geräusper *neu.* clearing of the throat; coughing

gerben *v.* to tan; den Buckel (*or* das Fell, die Haut) — (coll.) to flog severely

gerecht *adj.* just, righteous; fair; in allen Sätteln — sein to be a Jack-of-all-trades

Gerechtigkeit *f.* justice, impartiality

Gerechtsame *f.* prerogative, privilege

Gerede *neu.* empty talk; gossip, rumor

gereichen *v.* to conduce (*oder* redound) to

Gereiztheit *f.* irritation

gereuen *v.* es gereut mich I regret it

Gerhard *m.* Gerard

Gericht *neu.* court of justice, tribunal; judgment; dish; Jüngstes — (bibl.) Last Judgement; **–sbarkeit** *f.* jurisdiction; **–sbeamter** *m.* magistrate; **–sbefehl** *m.* warrant, writ; **–spräsident** *m.* presiding judge; **–sschranke** *f.* bar of justice; **–sverhandlung** *f.* trial; **–svollzieher** *m.* bailiff; sheriff

gerichtlich *adj.* judicial; forensic; legal

gerieben *adj.* grated; (coll.) cunning; sly

gering *adj.* small, light; trifling, unimportant; inferior, low; — achten to think little of; to disdain; nicht im **–sten** not in the least; ohne den **–sten** Zweifel without the shadow of a doubt; **–fügig** *adj.* insignificant, trifling; **–schätzen** *v.* to attach little value to, to despise; **–schätzig** *adj.* derogatory, disdainful

gerinnen *v.* to curdle; to clot; to coagulate

Gerippe *neu.* skeleton; framework

gerippt *adj.* corded, ribbed; fluted

gerissen *adj.* torn; cunning, sly, wily

gern *adv.* gladly, with pleasure; readily, willingly; — geschehen! don't mention it! — gesehen welcome everywhere; **–e haben** to be fond of

Gernegross *m.* would-be great; four-flusher

Geröll(e) *neu.* rubble; boulders

Gerste *f.* barley; **–nkorn** *neu.* grain of barley; sty (in eye); **–nsaft** *m.* (poet.) beer

Gerte *f.* twig; switch

Geruch *m.* (sense of) smell; odor, scent

Gerücht *neu.* rumor

geruhen *v.* to condescend

Gerümpel *neu.* old equipment; lumber, rubbish

Gerüst *neu.* scaffold(ing); platform, stage; **kran** *m.* gantry

Gerüttel *neu.* shaking, jolting

gesamt *adj.* entire, whole; total; joint, all

Gesamt: –absatz *m.* total sale; **–ausgabe** *f.* complete edition; **–begriff** *m.* general concept; **–eindruck** *m.* general impression; **–ertrag** *m.* entire proceeds; total output; **–gut** *neu.* joint property; **–haftung** *f.* joint liability; **–heit** *f.* total(ity), the whole; **–wohl** *neu.* common (*oder* public) weal

Gesandte *m.* envoy; ambassador, minister; (rel.) nuncio

Gesandtschaft *f* embassy, legation

Gesang *m.* singing; song; **–buch** *neu.* songbook; hymn book; **–lehrer** *m.* voice teacher; **–verein** *m.* choral society

Gesaufe *neu.* carousing; drinking; boozing

Gesäusel *neu.* murmurs; rustling

Geschäft *neu.* business; transaction; affair; occupation; office, shop, store; ein (natürliches) — verrichten to relieve oneself; **–sbetrieb** *m.* business management; **–sführer** *m.* business manager; **–sgegend** *f.* business district; **–smann** *m.* businessman; **–sordnung** *f.* order of business; agenda; **–personal** *neu.* staff; **–sreisende** *m.* salesman; **–sschluss** *m.* closing time; **–sträger** *m.* representative; charge d'affaires; **–sviertel** *ne* shopping center; **–szimmer** *neu.* offic

geschäft: –ig *adj.* active, busy; **–lich** *ad* relating to business; commercial; **–slo** *adj.* dull

geschehen *v.* to happen, to occur; to take place; to be done, es geschieht ihm rechtl it serves him right! es ist um mich —! I am done for! — lassen to tolerate

Geschehnis *neu.* event, happening, occurrence

gescheit *adj.* intelligent, smart; clear-headed, judicious; nicht recht — a bit cracked

Geschenk *neu.* gift, present

Geschicht: –e *f.* story, tale; narrative; history; affair, incident, occurrence; **–enbuch** *neu.* storybook; **–sbuch** *neu.* history; historical work; **–sforscher** *m.* historian

geschichtlich *adj.* historic(al)

Geschick *neu.* destiny, fate; aptitude; **–lichkeit** *f.*, **–theit** *f.* dexterity, ingenuity, skill

geschickt *adj.* dexterous, ingenious, skilled

Geschirr *neu.* vessels; crockery, dishes; harness, trappings (of horses)

Geschlecht *neu.* sex; kind; genus, species; gender; family, stock; generation; **–erkunde** *f.* genealogy; **–sfall** *m.* genitive case; **–sfolge** *f.* lineage; **–sglieder** *neu. pl.*, **–steile** *m.* and *neu. pl.* genitals; **–skrankheit** *f.* venereal disease; **–sname** *m.* family name, surname; generic name; **–sregister** *neu.* pedigree; **–sreife** *f.* puberty; **–strieb** *m.* sexual desire; **–sverkehr** *m.* sexual intercourse; **–swort** *neu.* (gram.) article

Geschmack *m.* (sense of) taste; liking; **–sache** *f.* matter of taste; **–slehre** *f.* esthetics

Geschmeide *neu.* jewelry, trinkets

geschmeidig *adj.* malleable, supple, pliant

Geschmeiss *neu.* excrement; droppings; vermin; dregs, scum

Geschmetter *neu.* (trumpets) flourish; blare

Geschnatter *neu.* cackling, gabbling; jabbering

Geschnörkel *neu.* flourishes

Geschöpf *neu.* creature; production; minion

Geschoss *neu.* missile, projectile, shell; floor, story; **–bahn** *f.* trajectory

geschraubt *adj.* screwed; affected, stilted

Geschrei *neu.* screaming, shouting; clamor; ado

Geschütz *neu.* cannon, gun; **–bedienung** *f.* gun crew; **–feuer** *neu.* barrage, cannonade; **–kunst** *f.* gunnery; **–rohr** *neu.* gun barrel; **–stand** *m.* gun emplacement

Geschwader *neu.* squadron; **–chef** *m.* commodore; **–flug** *m.* flight in formation

Geschwätz *neu.* idle talk; tittle-tattle

geschwätzig *adj.* talkative, verbose

geschwind *adj.* quick, fast, swift; nimble

Geschwind: –igkeit *f.* quickness, speed; fleetness, nimbleness; **–igkeitsmesser** *m.* speedometer; **–schritt** *m.* double-quick step

Geschwirr *neu.* whirring, whizzing, buzzing

Geschwister *pl.* brother(s) and sister(s)

Geschworene *m.* juryman; **–n** *pl.* jury; **–nliste** *f.* panel (jury)

Geschwulst *f.* swelling; tumor

Geschwür *neu.* abscess, sore, ulcer

Gesell: –e *m.* companion; pal; journeyman; fellow, chap; **–schaft** *f.* society, association; high society; company; party; **–schafter** *m.* companion; business partner; **–schaftsanzug** *m.* evening (*oder* full) dress

gesell: –en *v.* to associate with, to join; **–ig** *adj.* sociable; entertaining; **–schaftlich** *adj.* social

Gesetz *neu.* law; statute; rule; **–buch** *neu.* code; statute book; **–(es)antrag** *m.* (pol.) bill; **–geber** *m.* legislator; **–gebung** *f.* legislation; **–(es)tafeln** *f.* *pl.* (bibl.) decalogue; **–übertretung** *f.* transgression of the law

gesetz: –gebend *adj.* legislative; **–kräftig** *adj.* legal, legally valid; **–lich** *adj.*, **–mässig** *adj.* lawful, legal, statutory; **–lich geschützt** patented; **–t** *adj.* quiet, sedate; composed; **–t den Fall** supposing that; **von –tem Alter** of mature age; **–widrig** *adj.* illegal, unlawful

Gesicht *neu.* sight; face; appearance; vision, hallucination; **–er schneiden** to make faces; **zu —** **bekommen** to catch sight (of); **zweites —** second sight; **–sausdruck** *m.* features, physiognomy;

–sfarbe *f.* complexion; **–skreis** *m.* horizon; **–spunkt** *m.* point of view; aspect; **–ssinn** *m.* (sense of) sight; visual faculty; **–stäuschung** *f.* optical illusion; **–sweite** *f.* range of sight; **–szug** *m.* feature, lineament, mien

Gesims *neu.* moulding, cornice; ledge

Gesinde *neu.* domestics, servants; **–l** *neu.* rabble; scamps, rascals

gesinn: –t *adj.* disposed, minded; **gleich –t** of the same mind; **–ungslos** *adj.* unprincipled; **–ungstreu** *adj.* loyal

Gesinnung *f.* moral attitude; conviction; **edle —** noblemindedness; **seine —** **ändern** to change one's mind (*oder* sides); **–sgenosse** *m.* political friend; partisan

gesittet *adj.* well-bred, civilized

Gesittung *f.* good manners, civilization

Gespann *neu.* vehicle; draft animals; team

gespannt *adj.* stretched, taut; eager, intense, anxious; strained. tense

Gespenst *neu.* ghost, spectre; apparition

gespenst: –erhaft *adj.*, **–ig** *adj.*, **–isch** *adj.* ghostlike, spectral

Gespiele *m.* playmate; childhood companion; **—** *neu.* playing

Gespinst *neu.* spun yarn

Gespött *neu.* mockery, derision; laughing-stock

Gespräch *neu.* dialog; conversation; (tel.) call; **–sgegenstand** *m.*, **–sstoff** *m.* topic of conversation

gesprächig *adj.* talkative; communicative

gespreizt *adj.* spread; affected, stilted

gesprenkelt *adj.* flecked, speckled

Gestade *neu.* (lit.) coast, shore, beach

Gestalt *f.* form, build, stature; manner

gestalten *v.* to fashion, to shape; to create

Gestaltung *f.* formation

Gestammel *neu.* stammering, stuttering

Geständnis *neu.* confession; acknowledgment

Gestank *m.* stench, bad smell; stink

gestatten *v.* to allow, to permit

Geste *f.* gesture

gestehen *v.* to admit, to confess; to acknowledge

Gestehungskosten *f.* *pl.* prime cost; cost of production

Gestein *neu.* rock; stone; **–sgang** *m.* (min.) lode, streak

Gestell *neu.* rack, stand; frame; trestle; **–ung** *f.* appearance; presentation

gestern *adv.* yesterday; **ich bin nicht von** **—** I wasn't born yesterday, don't try to kid me

gestiefelt *adj.* booted; **der –e Kater** Puss in Boots

gestikulieren *v.* to gesticulate
Gestirn *neu.* star; constellation
Gestöber *neu.* snow flurries; storm
Gestotter *neu.* stuttering, stammering
Gesträuch *neu.* bushes, shrubbery; copse
gestreift *adj.* striped, streaky
gestrichelt *adj.* broken (line); hatched
gestrig *adj.* yesterday's, of yesterday
Gestrüpp *neu.* shrubbery; underbrush; thicket
Gestümper *neu.* botching, bungling
Gesuch *neu.* request; application, petition
gesucht *adj.* in demand, desired, sought after; affected, unnatural, artificial
gesund *adj.* healthy, sane; sound; beneficial, wholesome, salubrious; durch und durch — in the pink; frisch und — hale and hearty; –er Menschenverstand common sense; –en *v.* to convalesce; to become healthy; –heitlich *adj.* sanitary, hygienic; –machen *v.* to restore to health, to cure
Gesund: –e *m.* person in good health; –heit *f.* health; (drinking) toast; exclamation (when sneezing); –heitsamt *neu.* board of health; –heitslehre *f.* hygiene, hygienics; –heitsschein *m.* clean bill of health
Getäfel *neu.* paneling; wainscoting
Getändel *neu.* dallying, toying, trifling
Getier *neu.* (bibl.) animals; animal kingdom
Getobe *neu.* raging, raving; roaring
Getose, Getös(e) *neu.* noise; uproar; din
Getrampel *neu.* trampling, stamping
Getränk *neu.* beverage, drink; potion
Getrappel *neu.* pattering (of feet)
getrauen *v.* sich — to dare, to venture
Getreide *neu.* grain; cereals; –brand *m.* (bot.) smut; –mangel *m.* shortage of grain; –schwinge *f.* winnow; –speicher *m.* granary
getreu *adj.* exact, true
Getriebe *neu.* machinery; driving gear; bustle
getrost *adj.* confident, hopeful; — *adv.* cheerfully
Getue *neu.* affected attitude; (coll.) fuss
Getümmel *neu.* tumult, bustle
Gevatter *m.* godfather, sponsor; relative, (lit.) neighbor; talkative company
Geviert *neu.* square
Gewächs *neu.* plant; vintage; excrescence, growth; –haus *neu.* greenhouse; conservatory
gewachsen *adj.* grown; jemand — sein to be a person's equal
gewagt *adj.* risky
gewahr *adj.* aware of; –en *v.* to notice, to perceive

Gewähr *f.* guarantee; bail, surety; –smann *m.* guarantor; authority
gewähren *v.* to grant; to permit; to concede
Gewahrsam *m.*, *neu.* custody; detention
Gewalt *f.* might, power; authority; force, violence; höhere — superior force; –herrschaft *f.* despotism, tyranny; –herrscher *m.* despot, tyrant; –marsch *m.* (mil.) forced march; –massregel *f.* drastic (*oder* violent) measure; –streich *m.* bold stroke, arbitrary act
gewalt: –haberisch *adj.* despotic; –ig *adj.* powerful; gigantic; –sam *adj.* forcible, highhanded; –tätig *adj.* brutal, violent
Gewand *neu.* garment, gown; robe, vestment
gewandt *adj.* agile; skillful
gewärtig *adj.* expecting, prepared for
Gewässer *neu.* lake, pond; — *pl.* waters
Gewebe *neu.* web; fabric, textile; (biol.) tissue; –lehre *f.* histology
geweckt *adj.* alert, bright, wide-awake
Gewehr *neu.* gun, rifle
Geweih *neu.* antlers, horns
gewerb: –etreibend *adj.* industrial; manufacturing; –lich *adj.* industrial; –smässig *adj.* professional
Gewerbe *neu.* craft, trade; vocation; –ausstellung *f.* industrial exhibition; –freiheit *f.* free enterprise; –kammer *f.* Board of Trade; –schule *f.* polytechnic (*oder* trade) school
Gewerk *neu.* craft, guild; –schaft *f.* labor (*oder* trade) union
Gewicht *neu.* weight; importance, significance; — legen auf to lay stress on; ins — fallen to weigh heavily (in decision)
gewichtig *adj.* significant, weighty; serious
Gewieher *neu.* neighing; horselaugh
gewillt *adj.* willing; disposed, inclined
Gewimmel *neu.* throng, crowd, swarm, crush
Gewinde *neu.* (screw) worm; garland, festoon
Gewinn *m.* profit, yield; prize, advantage, benefit; –anteil *m.* dividend, royalty; –beteiligung *f.* profit-sharing; –er *m.* winner; –liste *f.* list of prizes; –los *neu.*, –nummer *f.* winning number
gewinn: –en *v.* to earn, to gain, to get, to win; to extract, to produce; die Oberhand — en to prevail upon, to conquer; es über sich — en to bring oneself to; –end *adj.* attractive, engaging; –süchtig *adj.* greedy, covetous
Gewinsel *neu.* whimpering, lamentation, wailing

gewiss *adj.* sure; fixed; certain; — *adv.* certainly, indeed; probably, apparently; **-enhaft(ig)** *adj.* conscientious; scrupulous; dependable; **-enlos** *adj.* unscrupulous; unprincipled; **-ermassen** *adv.* so to speak, to a certain degree

Gewiss: -en *neu.* conscience; **-ensbiss** *m.* twinge of conscience; remorse; **-ensfreiheit** *f.* freedom of conscience, religious liberty; **-enszwang** *m.* coercion of conscience; religious intolerance; **-heit** *f.* certainty, surety

Gewitter *neu.* thunderstorm; (coll.) outburst

gewitter: -n *v.* **es -t** it is thundering and lightning; **-schwer** *adj.*, **-schwül** *adj.* (air) sultry

gewitz(ig)t *adj.* taught by experience; shrewd

gewogen *adj.* well disposed, favorably inclined

gewöhnen *v.* to accustom, to habituate; **sich an etwas** — to become accustomed to (*oder* familiar with)

Gewohnheit *f.* habit, custom

gewohnheitsmässig *adj.* habitual; — *adv.* in the usual way; mechanically, routine

gewöhnlich *adj.* customary, usual; everyday, ordinary; low, vulgar

gewohnt *adj.* habitual, customary, usual

Gewölbe *neu.* (lit.) arched roof (*oder* ceiling), vault; impressive construction

Gewühl *neu.* turmoil; bustle, throng; agitation

gewunden *adj.* twisted; winding; tortuous

gewürfelt *adj.* checkered; variegated

Gewürz *neu.* spice; condiment, seasoning; **-nelke** *f.* clove; **-pflanze** *f.* aromatic herb

gezahnt, gezähnt *adj.* notched

Gezänk, Gezanke *neu.* quarreling, wrangling

Gezeter *neu.* screaming, outcry, clamor

geziem: -en *v.* to be fit, to become; **-end** *adj.*, **-lich** *adj.* decorous; becoming; proper; due

geziert *adj.* affected; dandyish, foppish

Gezirpe *neu.* chirping

Gezücht *neu.* breed, brood; (coll.) rabble

Gezwitscher *neu.* chirping, twitter, warbling

gezwungen *adj.* compulsory, forced; affected

Gicht *f.* gout, arthritis

Giebel *m.* gable; **-balken** *m.* rooftree, ridgepole; **-feld** *neu.* pediment; **-stube** *f.* attic, garret

Gier *f.* greed(iness); avidity

gieren *v.* to yaw

gierig *adj.* greedy, avaricious, covetous

Giess: -bach *m.* torrent; **-er** *m.* caster, founder, molder; **-kanne** *f.* sprinkling can

giessen *v.* to pour; to spill; to cast, to found, to mold; to water

Gift *neu.* poison, venom; virus; toxin; virulence; malice; anger; **darauf kannst du** — **nehmen!** (coll.) that is certain! **-hauch** *m.* blight; **-nudel** *f.* (coll.) cigar; **-schwamm** *m.* poisonous mushroom, toadstool; **-zahn** *m.* poison fang

giftig *adj.* poisonous, venomous; toxic; malicious, virulent

Gilde *f.* guild

Gimpel *m.* bullfinch; simpleton

Gipfel *m.* peak, summit; pinnacle; limit; **leistung** *f.* record performance; **-punkt** *m.* culminating (*oder* highest) point; limit

Gipfelkonferenz *f.* summit conference

gipfeln *v.* to culminate

Gips *m.* gypsum, plaster of Paris; **-abdruck** *m.*, **-abguss** *m.* plaster cast; **-bewurf** *m.* plastering; **-form** *f.* plaster mold

girieren *v.* (com.) to clear; to endorse

Girlande *f.* garland, festoon, wreath

Giro *neu.* endorsement; **-bank** *f.* clearing house

Gischt *m.* spray, foam; yeast

Gitter *neu.* lattice, trellis; fence, grating, railing, grid; **-fenster** *neu.* grille window; **-tor** *neu.* trellised gate

Glanz *m.* luster; gloss, polish; splendor; glory; **-leder** *neu.* patent leather; **-leistung** *f.* splendid achievement; (sports) record; **-punkt** *m.* culminating point, climax

glänzen *v.* to be bright (*oder* brilliant); to shine; to stand out, to be striking; **-d** *adj.* bright, brilliant; lustrous; excellent, splendid

Glas *neu.* glass; tumbler; **-bläser** *m.* glass blower; **-er** *m.* glazier; **-karaffe** *f.* decanter; **-kitt** *m.* putty; **-kuppel (Pilotenkanzel)** *f.* canopy; **-platte** *f.*, **-scheibe** *f.* glass pane (*oder* plate); **-schleifer** *m.* glass cutter (*oder* grinder); **-ur** *f.* glaze; icing; enamel

gläsern *adj.* of glass; glassy, vitreous

glasieren *v.* to glaze; to ice, to frost; to varnish; to enamel

glasig *adj.* glassy; **-e Augen** glazed eyes

glatt *adj.* smooth, even; slippery; slick; — *adv.* smoothly; offhand, directly, quite; entirely; plainly; **-machen** *v.* to level; eine Sache **-machen** to settle a matter; **-weg** *adj.* flatly, plainly; **-züngig** *adj.* honey-tongued

Glätte *f.* evenness, smoothness; slipperiness

Glatteis *neu.* slippery ice; **jemand aufs —
führen** to get someone into a scrape

glätten *v.* to sleek, to smooth; to calender;
to iron; to settle

Glatze *f.* bald spot (on head); bald head

glaub: -en *v.* to believe, to trust, to have
faith in; to suppose; **-haft** *adj.*, **-lich**
adj., **-würdig** *adj.* reliable; credible;
authentic

Glaube(n) *m.* belief, faith; credence;
trust; creed; **-nsheld** *m.*, **-nszeuge** *m.*
martyr; **-nslehre** *f.*, **-nssatz** *m.* dogma;
-nszwang *m.* religious intolerance

gläubig *adj.* believing, faithful

Gläubige *m.* believer; **-r** *m.* creditor

gleich *adj.* like, identical; same; even,
level, similar; uniform; equal; — *adv.*
at once, immediately; alike, equally;
an Kräften — be a match for; **es ist
ganz** — it makes no difference; — **zur
Hand** ready at hand; **von —em Werte**
equivalent; **-altrig** *adj.* of the same age,
coeval; **-artig** *adj.* of the same kind,
homogeneous; **-bedeutend** *adj.* synonymous; **-empfindend** *adj.* sympathetic;
-en *v.* to equal; to resemble, to correspond to; **-ermassen** *adv.*, **-erweise**
adv., **-falls** *adv.* and *conj.* likewise, also;
-förmig *adj.* uniform; monotonous;
-gestellt *adj.* equal in rank; co-ordinate; **-gestimmt** *adj.* in accord; tuned
to the same pitch; **-gültig** *adj.* indifferent, unconcerned; **-kommend** *adj.*
equivalent to; **-laufend** *adj.* parallel;
-mässig *adj.* equable; uniform; un-
varied; regular; **-mütig** *adj.* even-
tempered; imperturbable; **-namig** *adj.*
of the same name, homonymous; **-sam**
adv. so to speak, to a certain degree;
-setzen, **-stellen** to put on a par with;
-temperiert *adj.* isothermal; **-tun** to
compete with; to equal, to match; **-viel**
adv. all the same; no matter; **-wertig**
adj. equivalent; **-wohl** *adv.* and *conj.*
nevertheless, notwithstanding; **-zeitig**
adj. simultaneous

Gleich: -e *f.* equinox; **-e** *neu.* (the) same;
-es mit —em vergelten to give tit for
tat; **-gewicht** *neu.* balance, equilibrium,
equipoise; **-heit** *f.* equality, likeness;
-heitszeichen *neu.* (math.) sign of
equation; **-klang** *m.* accord, unison,
consonance; **-mut** *m.* equanimity; **-nis**
neu. image; comparison; parable;
-stand *m.* (tennis) deuce; **-strom** *m.*
direct (*oder* continuous) current;
-strom/Wechselstrom Transformator
m. inverter; **-ung** *f.* equation

Gleit: -bahn *f.* slideway; **-boot** *neu.* hy-

droplane; **-schutzreifen**, *m.* nonskid tire

gleiten *v.* to glide, to slide, to slip

Gletscher *m.* glacier; **-spalte** *f.* crevasse

Glied *neu.* limb, member; link; file, rank;
(bibl.) generation; (math.) term; **-er-
bau** *m.* structure; articulation; build;
-erlähmung *f.* paralysis; **-erpuppe** *f.*
marionette; **-massen** *pl.* limbs

glimmen *v.* to glimmer, to glow, to smolder

glimpflich *adj.* indulgent; mild

glitsch(r)ig *adj.* slippery

glitzern *v.* to glisten, to glitter, to twinkle

Globus *m.* globe

Glocke *f.* bell; (glass) shade; clock; **etwas
an die grosse — hängen** to make a big
fuss about something; **-nhaus** *neu.*,
-nstube *f.*, **-nstuhl** *m.* belfry; **-nklöppel**
m. bell clapper; **-nschlag** *m.* stroke of
the bell (*oder* hour); **-nspiel** *neu.*
chimes; **-nturm** *m.* bell tower, steeple

Glöckner *m.* bell ringer, sexton

Glorie *f.* glory; **-nschein** *m.* halo; aureole

glorreich *adj.* glorious, illustrious

Gloss: -ar *neu.* glossary; **-e** *f.* marginal
note, gloss; **-enmacher** *m.* commentator

glotzen *v.* to gape, to stare

Glück *neu.* fortune, luck; happiness; **auf
gut** — hopeful for the best; **Freunde
im** — fairweather friends; — **ab!** (avi.)
happy landing! — **auf!** good luck! —
wünschen to congratulate; **im** —
schwimmen to be in clover; **sein** —
machen to make one's fortune; **viel —!**
good luck! many happy returns! **zum**
— fortunately; **-sbringer** *m.* mascot;
-sfall *m.* lucky incident, stroke of good
fortune; **-sgüter** *neu. pl.* worldly pos-
sessions; **-skind** *neu.*, **-spilz** *m.* lucky
fellow; **-srad** *neu.* wheel of fortune;
-sritter *m.* fortune hunter; adventurer;
-sspiel *neu.* game of chance (*oder* hazard); **-ssträhne** *f.* stroke of luck; **-stag**
m. red-letter day; **-swunsch** *m.* congratulation

glück: -en *v.* to succeed; **-lich** *adj.* lucky,
successful; happy; glad; advantageous;
-licherweise *adv.* fortunately; **-selig**
adj. blissful; **-strahlend** *adj.* beaming
with happiness

Glucke, Gluckhenne *f.* mother hen

glucksen *v.* to gurgle; to sob; to burp

Glüh: -birne *f.* electric light bulb; **-hitze**
f. intense heat; **-lampe** *f.* incandescent
lamp; **-wein** *m.* mulled wine; **-wurm** *m.*
glowworm

glühen *v.* to glow, to be ardent (*oder*
fervent)

Glut *f.* heat; glowing embers; ardor,

fervor

Gnade *f.* mercy, pardon; favor; grace; clemency; — **für Recht ergehen lassen** to temper justice with mercy; **–nbund** *m.* (rel.) convenant of grace; **–nfrist** *f.* reprieve, respite; **–ngeschenk** *neu.* gratification

gnädig *adj.* lenient, merciful; affable, favorable; **–e Frau** (salutation) dear madam

Gockel *m.* (coll.) rooster

Gold *neu.* gold; **–arbeiter** *m.*, **–schmied** *m.* goldsmith; **–blech** *neu.* gold foil; **–finger** *m.* ring finger; **–fink** *m.* goldfinch; **–fuchs** *m.* (horse) palomino; (coll.) gold coin; **–gewicht** *neu.* troy weight; **–gräber** *m.* gold digger; **–käfer** *m.* rose beetle (*oder* chafer); **–kind** *neu.* darling; **–klumpen** *m.* gold nugget; **–legierung** *f.* gold alloy; **–macherkunst** *f.* alchemy; **–regen** *m.*, **–rute** *f.* laburnum; goldenrod; **–schaum** *m.* tinsel; **–schnitt** *m.* (book) gilt edge; **–waage** *f.* gold balance; **–währung** *f.* gold standard

Golf *m.* gulf

Golfstrom *m.* Gulf Stream

Gondel *f.* gondola; (coll.) small boat

gönnen *v.* not to begrudge, to wish well

Gönner *m.* patron, protector; benefactor

Gosse *f.* gutter, drain

Gott *m.* God; deity; gerechter (*or* grosser) —! good Heavens! — **behüte** God (*oder* Heaven) forbid! **grüss** —! good day (*oder* morning)! — **befohlen!** good-by! **um –es willen!** for goodness sake! **–esacker** *m.* churchyard; **–esdienst** *m.* divine service; **–esgelehrtheit** *f.* theology; **–eshaus** *neu.* church, chapel; **–eslästerung** *f.* blasphemy; **–esleugner** *m.* atheist; **–essohn** *m.* Son of God; **–esurteil** *neu.* ordeal; **–heit** *f.* divinity, deity

gott: **–ähnlich** *adj.* godlike; **–begnadet** *adj.* endowed with divine grace; highly gifted; **–ergeben** *adj.* resigned to the will of God; **–esfürchtig** *adj.* God-fearing; pious; **–eslästerlich** *adj.* blasphemous; **–los** *adj.*, **–vergessen** *adj.* wicked; **–selig** *adj.* godly; devout; **–verlassen** *adj.* Godforsaken

Gött: **–er** *m. pl.* gods, deities; **–erbrot** *neu.*, **–erspeise** *f.* ambrosia; **–erdämmerung** *f.* twilight of the gods; **–erlehre** *f.* mythology; **–erspruch** *m.* oracle; **–ertrank** *m.* nectar; **–in** *f.* god less

Gottfried *m.* Godfrey, Geoffrey

göttlich *adj.* divine, godlike; (coll.) droll, funny; magnificent

Götze *m.* idol, false god; **–nbild** *neu.* idol;

–ndienst *m.* idolatry

Gouvernante *f.* governess

Gouverneur *m.* governor

Grab *neu.* grave, tomb; sepulchre; **–en** *m.* ditch; (mil.) trench; **–geläute** *n.* knell; **–legung** *f.* burial, interment; **–mal** *neu.*, **–stein** *m.* tombstone; **–schrift** *f.* epitaph; **–stätte** *f.* place of burial

graben *v.* to dig; **to trench;** to engrave

Grad *m.* degree; rate; grade, rank, title, stage; (math.) power; **im gewissen –e** to a certain degree; **im hohen –e** extraordinarily

grad: **–ieren** *v.* to graduate; to alloy, to refine; **–uell** *adv.*, **–weise** *adv.* gradually; by degrees

Graf *m.* count; (England) earl

Gräfin *f.* countess

Gram *m.* grief, sorrow; **jemanden — sein** to bear a grudge against someone

grämen *v.* sich — to fret, to grieve, to worry

grämlich *adj.* morose, sullen, peevish

Gramm *neu.* gram

Grammatik *f.* grammar

grammat(ikal)isch *adj.* grammatical

Gran *neu.* (weight) grain

Granat *m.* garnet; **–apfel** *m.* pomegranate

Granate *f.* grenade, shell

grandios *adj.* grand, magnificent

Granit *m.* granite

Graphik *f.* graphic arts

graphisch *adj.* graphic

Graphit *m.* graphite, plumbago, black lead

graps(ch)en *v.* (coll.) to grab, to snatch

Gras *neu.* grass; **das — wachsen hören** to know everything better; **ins — beissen** to die; **–halm** *m.* blade of grass; **–hüpfer** *m.* grasshopper; (lit.) frog; **–land** *neu.* pasture

grasen *v.* to graze

grassieren *v.* (med.) to rage, to spread

grässlich *adj.* horrible, ghastly, hideous

Grat *m.* sharp edge; crest; ridge (pole)

Gratifikation *f.* gratuity; extra pay

Gratulant *m.* congratulator, well wisher

Gratulation *f.* congratulation

gratulieren *v.* to congratulate

grau *adj.* gray; ancient; **–braun** *adj.* dun; **–en** *v.* to turn gray, to dawn

grau: **–en** *v.* to have a horror of; **–enhaft** *adj.*, **–envoll** *adj.* horrible, gruesome; **–lich** *adj.* fearful, uncanny; **–sam** *adj.* cruel, inhuman; **–sen** *v.* to shudder; **to** dread; **–sig** *adj.*, **–slich** *adj.* dreadful, frightful, horrid

Graupe *f.* hulled barley (*oder* wheat)

Grautier *neu.* (lit.) donkey

Graveur *m.* engraver
gravieren *v.* to engrave
Gravierung *f.* rotogravure
gravitätisch *adj.* grave, solemn
Gravitationskraft (der Erde) *f.* G-force
Grazie *f.* charm, grace
graziös *adj.* graceful
Greif *m.* griffin
greifbar *adj.* seizable; on hand; palpable
greifen *v.* to catch hold of; to grasp; to
  seize, to affect; to strike (chord); aus
  der Luft gegriffen pure invention;
  ineinander — to interlock; nach jedem
  Mittel — to snatch at every straw; um
  sich — to gain ground, to spread; unter
  die Arme — to aid, to give a lift; zu
  den Waffen — to take up arms
greinen *v.* (coll.) to whine, to blubber, to
  cry
Greis *m.* old man; –enalter *neu.* old age;
  senility; –in *f.* old woman
grell *adj.* shrill; glaring; crude
Grenz: –bezeichnung *f.* demarcation; –e
  f. border, boundary, frontier; limit-
  (ation); –er *m.* frontiersman; boundary
  guard; customs officer; –linie *f.*,
  –scheide *f.* borderline; –mal *neu.*,
  –stein *m.* landmark; –stadt *f.* frontier
  town; –verkehr *m.* traffic across the
  border
grenzen *v.* to border (on); to adjoin; –los
  adj. boundless, infinite, unlimited, immense
Greuel *m.* abomination, atrocity, outrage
greulich *adj.* atrocious, frightful, horrible
gries: –grämig, –grämisch, –grämlich *adj.*
  morose, surly
Griesgram *m.* surly (*oder* morose) person
Griff *m.* grasp, grip; hold; handle, haft,
  hilt; (mil.) manipulation (of gun);
  (mus.) touch; –brett *neu.* (mus.) keyboard, finger board
Griffel *m.* slate pencil; (bot.) pistil, style
Grille *f.* cricket; caprice, whim; –nfänger
  m. whimsical person; pessimist, crank
grillenhaft *adj.* capricious, moody, surly
Grimasse *f.* grimace
Grimm *m.* grimness; fury, anger
Grimmen *neu.* gripes; — *pl.* colic
grimmig *adj.* enraged, furious; grim
Grind *m.* scab, scurf, mange
grinsen *v.* to grin; to smirk
grob *adj.* rude, rough, coarse, gross
Groll *m.* rancor, resentment; grudge
Grönland *neu.* Greenland
Groschen *m.* penny; Austrian coin; trifle
gross *adj.* great; tall, high; big, large;
  grown-up; spacious, vast; eminent;
  grand; — auftreten to assume airs; —
  denken to think nobly; — und klein

grownups and children; high and low;
  — ziehen to raise, to bring up; –er
  Buchstabe capital letter; –es Los first
  prize; sich — tun to boast, to swagger;
  –artig *adj.* grand(iose), imposing; –enteils *adv.* to a large extent, mostly;
  –herzig *adj.* generous, noble-minded,
  magnanimous; –jährig *adj.* of age,
  mature; –mächtig *adj.* high and
  mighty; giant-sized; –mäulig *adj.*
  boastful; –mütig *adj.* generous, broad-
  minded; –spurig *adj.* arrogant; –städtisch *adj.* metropolitan; fashionable;
  –tuerisch *adj.* swaggering; –zügig *adj.*
  on a large scale; broadminded
Gross: –aufnahme *f.* (film) close-up;
  –betrieb *m.* big business; –e *neu.* im
  –en wholesale, on a large scale; –eltern
  pl. grandparents; –fürst *m.* grand duke;
  –handel *m.* wholesale trade; –herzog *m.*
  grand duke; –ist *m.* wholesale dealer;
  –macht *f.* first-rate power; –mast *m.*
  mainmast; –maul *neu.* boaster; –mut *f.*
  magnanimity; –mutter *f.* grandmother;
  –sprecher *m.* braggart; –sprecherei *f.*
  boasting, bragging; –stadt *f.* metropolis; –städter *m.* urbanite; –tuer *m.*
  swaggerer; –vater *m.* grandfather;
  –wild *neu.* big game
Grösse *f.* dimension, size; amplitude;
  height; volume; celebrity; (ast.) magnitude; (math.) quantity, value;
  –nwahn *m.* megalomania
grösstenteils *adv.* chiefly, mostly
grotesk *adj.* grotesque
Grotte *f.* grotto
Grübchen *neu.* dimple
Grube *f.* excavation; cavity; hole, den;
  mine, pit; (bibl.) grave; –narbeiter *m.*
  miner; –nlampe *f.*, –nlicht *neu.* miner's
  (safety) lamp; –nwetter *neu.* firedamp
Grübelei *f.* meditation; rumination;
  brooding
grübeln *v.* to brood, to ponder, to ruminate
Gruft *f.* vault; mausoleum; (poet.) grave,
  tomb
Grum(m)et *neu.* aftermath
grün *adj.* green; verdant; immature; auf
  einen –en Zweig kommen to prosper;
  vom –en Tisch aus only in theory; –en
  v. to become green; to flourish; –lich
  adj. greenish
Grün *neu.* green; (cards) spades; im –en
  out-of-doors; –futter *neu.* green fodder;
  –kohl *m.* kale; –kramladen *m.* green-
  grocery; –schnabel *m.* inexperienced
  person
Grund *m.* ground; foundation; valley;
  bottom; estate; soil; cause, motive, rea-

son; (art) priming; **auf den — gehen** to investigate thoroughly; **auf — von** on the basis of; **aus welchem -e?** for what reason? **im -e** fundamentally; after all; **von — aus** from the very bottom, thoroughly; **-akkord *m.*** fundamental chord; **-anstrich *m.*** first coat (paint); **-begriff *m.*** fundamental idea, basic principle; **-besitz *m.*** real estate; **-buch *neu.*** legal register of real estate; **-farbe *f.*** (art) priming; **-fehler *m.*** radical fault; **-feste *f.*** (poet.) foundation; **-fläche *f.*** base; **-gedanke *m.*** fundamental idea; **-gesetz *neu.*** fundamental law; organic statute; **-kapital *neu.*** original stock; **-lage *f.*** groundwork, foundation; assumption; **-linie *f.*** base line; **-mauer *f.*** foundation wall; substructure; **-peilung *f.*** (naut.) sounding; **-rente *f.*** ground rent; **-riss *m.*** ground plan; outline; sketch; syllabus; compendium; **-satz *m.*** axiom, principle; **-schuld *f.*** mortage; **-stein *m.*** cornerstone; **-steuer *f.*** land tax; **-stoff *m.*** element; raw material; **-strich *m.*** down stroke; **-stück *neu.*** real estate; **-ton *m.*** (mus.) keynote; **-zahl *f.*** cardinal number, radix

grund: -ehrlich *adj.* thoroughly honest; **-falsch *adj.*** fundamentally wrong; **-legend *adj.*** fundamental; **-los *adj.*** bottomless; groundless, unfounded; **-verkehrt *adj.*** altogether wrong; **-verschieden *adj.*** entirely different

Gründ: -er *m.* founder; promoter; **-ling *m.*** (ichth.) groun‑fling, gudgeon; **-ung *f.*** foundation, establishment

gründlich *adj.* thorough; scrupulous; profound

grunzen *v.* to grunt

Gruppe *f.* group, section; smallest battle unit

gruppieren *v.* to group

Grus *m.* coal slack

gruselig *adj.* uncanny, creepy

gruseln *v.* es gruselt mich my flesh creeps; **— machen** to cause to shudder

Gruss *m.* greeting, salutation; regards; salute

grüssen *v.* to greet, to welcome; to give regards to; to salute

Grütze *f.* grits, groats; (coll.) brains

gucken *v.* to look, to peer

Gulasch *neu.* goulash; **-kanone *f.*** (mil.) field kitchen; (coll.) beanery

Gulden *m.* florin, guilder

gültig *adj.* valid; legal; binding; authentic

Gummi *neu.* gum; **— *m.*** rubber, eraser; **-absatz *m.*** rubber heel; **-band *neu.*** elastic band; **-mantel *m.*** rubberized

raincoat; **-reifen *m.*** rubber tire; **-schlauch *m.*** rubber hose; **-schuhe *m. pl.*** galoshes; **-stempel *m.*** rubber stamp

Gunst *f.* favor; partiality; advantage

günstig *adj.* favorable, advantageous

Günstling *m.* favorite; minion

Gurgel *f.* throat; **die — spülen** (coll.) to drink, to spray the tonsils; **-wasser *neu.*** gargle

gurgeln *v.* to gargle; to gurgle

Gurke *f.* cucumber; gherkin; (coll.) nose; **saure -n** pickled cucumbers, pickles

Gurt *m.* belt; girdle; girth; strap

Gürtel *m.* belt, girdle; zone; **-flechte *f.*, -rose *f.*** (med.) shingles

gürten *v.* to gird(le)

Guss *m.* (act of) pouring; downpour; cast(ing), founding; (cooking) icing; (typ.) font; **-eisen *neu.*** cast iron; **-stahl *m.*** cast steel; **-waren *f. pl.*** foundry goods

gut *adj.* good; beneficial; kind; considerable, useful; **— *adv.*** well; **ein -es Wort einlegen** to put in a good word; **es — haben** to be well off; **im — amicably; jemand — sein** to like someone; **kurz und —** in short; **man muss -e Miene zum bösen Spiel machen** one must grin and bear it; **nicht für Geld und -e Worte** not for love or money; **schon —!** all right! **Sie haben — lachen** it is very easy for you to laugh; **-artig *adj.*** good‑natured; (med.) benign; **-geartet *adj.*** well‑mannered; **-gelaunt *adj.*** in good spirits; **-gemeint *adj.*** well‑meant; **-gesinnt *adj.*** well‑disposed; **-gläubig in good faith; credulous; -heissen** to approve, to sanction; **-herzig *adj.*** good‑hearted, charitable; **-machen** to make amends for; **nicht wieder -zumachen** irreparable; **-mütig *adj.*** good‑natured; **-sagen** to be security (*oder* surety) for; **-schreiben** to credit; **-willig *adj.*** readily, voluntarily

Gut *neu.* farm, estate; property; merchandise; goods; **-sbesitzer *m.*** owner of an estate (*oder* farm)

Gut: -achten *neu.* expert (*oder* professional) opinion; **-dünken *neu.*** judgment, opinion; **-haben *neu.*** credit, balance due; **-schein *m.*** credit note

Güte *f.* kindness; purity; goodness, value, quality; nature

Güter *pl.* goods; **-gemeinschaft *f.*** joint property, common ownership; **-transport *m.*** freight traffic; **-wagen *m.*** truck; **-zug *m.*** freight train

gütig *adj.* affable, good, kind; charitable

gütlich *adv.* and *adj.* amicable, friendly; **sich — tun** to enjoy

Gymnasialbildung *f.* high-school (*oder* junior-college) education

Gymnasiast *m.* high-school student; college undergraduate

Gymnasium *neu.* high school; university preparatory school

Gymnastik *f.* gymnastics

gymnastisch *adj.* gymnastic

Gynäkologe *m.* gynecologist

H

Haar *neu.* hair; nap; pile; **aufs —** precisely; **das hat an einem — gehangen** it was a close shave; **ein — in etwas finden** to find a flaw in a thing; **—e lassen müssen** to suffer damages; **mit Haut und —en** entirely; **sich in die —e geraten** to come to blows; **um ein —** nearly, narrowly; **um kein — besser** not a bit better; **—ausfall** *m.* loss of hair; **—esbreite** *f.* hair's breadth; **—flechte** *f.* braid of hair; **—frisur** *f.* hairdress, hairdo; **—gefäss** *neu.* capillary; **—künstler** *m.* hairdresser; **—nadel** *f.* hairpin; **—spalterei** *f.* hairsplitting; **—tracht** *f.* hairdress, style; **—wasser** *neu.* hair tonic

haar: —en *v.* to shed one's hair; **—ig** *adj.* hairy; haired; stunning; **—klein** *adv.* minutely, with all details; **—scharf** *adj.* very sharp; hypercritical; **—sträubend** *adj.* shocking

Hab: —e *f.* belongings; property; **—enichts** *m.* penniless person; **—en** *neu.* credit, asset; **—gier** *f.*, **—sucht** *f.* greediness, avarice

haben *v.* to have, to own, to possess; to be obliged (to); **am Schnürchen —** to have at one's finger tips; **auf sich —** to signify, to mean; **da hast du's!** there you are! **etwas — wollen** to ask for, to desire; **gern —** to like; **nichts auf sich — to be of no consequence; recht (*or* unrecht) —** to be right (*oder* wrong); **sich —** to put on airs; **unter sich — to be in charge of; was hast du?** what's the matter with you?

habgierig, habsüchtig *adj.* greedy, avaricious

Habicht *m.* hawk; **—nase** *f.* hooked nose

Habilitation *f.* prerequisite for teaching at a German university

Hack: —beil *neu.*, **—messer** *neu.* chopper; hatchet; **—block** *m.* chopping block; **—brett** *neu.* chopping board; (mus.) dulcimer; **—e** *f.* mattock, hoe; **—en** *m.* heel; **—epeter** *m.* chopped raw pork; **—fleisch** *neu.* minced meat

hacken *v.* to hack; to hoe; to chop, to split; to mince; (birds) to pick

Hader *m.* dispute, quarrel; feud; (dial.) rag; **—er** *m.* quarreler; **—lump** *m.* (dial.) ragamuffin

hadern *v.* to quarrel; to argue, to dispute

Hafen *m.* harbor, port; haven, refuge; (dial.) earthenware vessel; **—arbeiter** *m.* longshoreman; **—damm** *m.* jetty, mole; **—räumer** *m.* dredge; embargo; **—platz** *m.*, **—stadt** *f.* seaport

Hafer *m.* oats; **ihn sticht der —** good luck has spoilt him; **—brei** *m.* porridge; **—flocken** *f. pl.* rolled oats; **—grütze** *f.* oatmeal; **—schleim** *m.* gruel

Haft *f.* arrest; custody; **—el** *f.* clasp, pin, hook; **—befehl** *m.* warrant (of arrest); **—pflicht** *f.* liability; responsibility; **—ung** *f.* security, bail; **mit beschränkter —ung** with limited liability; **—vollzug** *m.* imprisonment

haftbar *adj.* liable, responsible

haften *v.* to adhere (*oder* stick) to; **— für** to be liable, to vouch for

Häftling *m.* prisoner

der Haag *m.* the Hague

hageln *v.* to hail

hager *adj.* haggard, gaunt

Hahn *m.* cock, rooster; male bird; (gun) hammer; faucet, valve, tap; **danach kräht kein —** nobody pays any attention to that; **der rote — fire; — im Korb** cock of the walk; **—enbart** *m.* wattles; **—enkamm** *m.* cock's comb; **—enschrei** *neu.* cock's crowing; **—rei** *m.* cuckold

Hai(fisch) *m.* shark

Hain *m.* (poet.) grove, wood

Häkchen *neu.* small (*oder* crochet) hook

Häkelei *f.* crocheting; (coll.) teasing

Haken *m.* hook; check mark; **einen — schlagen** to dodge around a corner; to trip up; **— und Öse** hook and eye; **—kreuz** *neu.* swastika

halb *adj.* half; partial; incomplete; **— adv.** by halves; **auf —em Wege** halfway, midway; **—e Note** (mus.) semitone; **— soviel** half as much; **um — zwei** at one thirty; **—amtlich** *adj.* semiofficial; **—blütig** *adj.* half-breed, half-caste; **—entschlummert** *adj.* dozing; **—er** *prep.* for the sake (*oder* on account, by reason) of; **—fertig** *adj.* semi-manufactured; **—ieren** *v.* to halve; to bisect; **—jährlich** *adj.* semiannual; **—militarisch** *adj.* paramilitary; **—rund** *adj.* semicircular; **—wegs** *adv.* halfway; reasonably well; **—wüchsig** *adj.* adolescent

Halb: —bildung *f.* superficial education; **—bruder** *m.* stepbrother; **—dunkel** *neu.* dusk, twilight; **—e** *neu.* half; **—geschwister** *pl.* stepbrothers (*oder* sisters); **—gott**

m. demigod; **–heit** *f.* incompleteness; **–insel** *f.* peninsula; **–kreis** *m.* semicircle; **–kugel** *f.* hemisphere; **–messer** *m.* radius; **–part** machen to go halves; **–schlummer** *m.* drowsiness; **–schuh** *m.* low shoe; slipper; **–schwester** *f.* stepsister; **–schwergewicht** *neu.* light heavyweight; **–starke** *m.* beatnik; **–welt** *f.* demimonde

Hälfte *f.* half; **auf der — des Weges** halfway

Halfter *m.* halter

Hall *m.* sound, noise, reverberation

Halle *f.* hall; vestibule; lounge; lobby

hallen *v.* to sound, to resound

Halluzination *f.* hallucination

Halm *m.* blade, stalk; **–früchte** *pl.* cereals

Hals *m.* neck, throat, gullet; **aus vollem –e lachen** to split with laughter; **einer Flasche den — brechen** to drink up a bottle; **es geht ihm an den —** he is doomed; **es hängt mir zum –e heraus** I'm fed up with it; **— über Kopf** head over heels; **um den — fallen** to embrace; **vom –e schaffen** to get rid of; **–abschneider** *m.* profiteer; cutthroat; **–ader** *f.* jugular vein; **–binde** *f.* necktie; **–bräune** *f.* quinsy; **–kette** *f.* necklace; **–kragen** *m.* collar; cape; **–schmerzen** *m. pl* , **–weh** *neu.* sore throat; **–tuch** *neu.* scarf

hals: –brecherisch *adj.* dangerous, foolhardy, rash; **–en** *v.* to embrace; (naut.) to veer round; **–starrig** *adj.* headstrong; stubborn; obstinate

Halt *m.* halt, stop; hold; support; footing; **–er** *m.* holder; **–estelle** *f.* stop, station; **–ezeichen** *neu.* stop signal; **–ung** *f.* bearing, carriage; behavior, conduct

haltbar *adj.* defensible; tenable; durable

halten *v.* to hold; to check; to halt, to stop; to observe; to keep; to support; to deliver (speech); to contain; to subscribe to; **es — mit** to side with; **grosse Stücke — auf** to think highly of; **— für** to consider, to take for; **sich bereit —** to be ready; **sich — to** hold out; to endure; **was — Sie von?** what do you think of? **zu jemand —** to adhere (*oder* stick) to someone

Halunke *m.* scoundrel; rascal; rogue; swindler

Hammel *m.* wether; **–braten** *m.* roast mutton; **–sprung** *m.* (pol.) pairing off

Hammer *m.* hammer; forge; **–schlag** *m.* stroke of the hammer; hammer scales; **–werk** *neu.* forge

Hampelmann *m.* puppet; jumping jack

Hand *f.* hand; **auf der — liegen** to be obvious; **an die — geben** to supply; **an die — gehen** to assist, to help; **auf Händen tragen** to coddle; **aus bester —** from the best source; **bei der — sein** to be ready; **die öffentliche —** the government; **eine — wäscht die andere** one good turn deserves another; **einem die — geben** to shake hands; **— an sich legen** to commit suicide; **— ans Werk legen** to put the shoulder to the wheel; **— im Spiel haben** to have a finger in the pie; **unter der —** secretly; **von der — weisen** to deny, to reject; **vor der —** for the present, just now; **–arbeit** *f.* handicraft; manual labor; needlework; **–arbeiter** *m.* manual laborer; **–aufheben** *neu.* (voting) show of hands; **–beil** *neu.* hatchet; **–buch** *neu.* manual, handbook; **–feger** *m.* hand brush; **–fertigkeit** *f.* manual skill, dexterity; **–schellen** *f. pl.* handcuffs, manacles; **–feuerwaffen** *f. pl.* (mil.) small arms; **–geld** *neu.* earnest money; advance; **–gelenk** *neu.*, **–wurzel** *f.* wrist; **–gemenge** *m.* hand-to-hand fight; **–gepäck** *neu.* hand baggage; **–griff** *m.* grasp; **–habe** *f.* handle; manipulation, pretext; **–harmonika** *f.* accordion, concertina; **–karren** *m.* handcart; **–koffer** *m.* handbag, suitcase; **–langer** *m.* handy man; **–reichung** *f.* aid, assistance; **–schlag** *m.* handshake (as pledge); **–schrift** *f.* handwriting; manuscript; **–schuh** *m.* glove; **–seife** *f.* toilet soap; **–tasche** *f.* handbag; **–tuch** *neu.* towel; **–tuchhalter** *m.* towel rack; **–werk** *neu.* handicraft; trade; **–werker** *m.* craftsman; artisan

hand: –fest *adj.* robust, stalwart, sturdy; **–gemacht** *adj.* handmade; **–gemein** *adv.* at blows (*oder* close quarters); **–gerecht** *adj.* handy; **–greiflich** *adj.* palpable; obvious; **–haben** *v.* to handle, to manipulate; to manage; **–lich** *adj.* easy to use, manageable; **–schriftlich** *adj.* written, in writing (*oder* manuscript)

Händ: –edruck *m.* handshake; **–elmacher** *m.* brawler, quarreler; **–ler** *m.* trader, dealer

Handel *m.* commerce; business, transaction; trade; bargain; lawsuit; affair; **–sakademie** *f.* commercial college; **–samt** *neu.* Board of Trade; **–sbilanz** *f.* balance of trade; **–sblatt** *neu.* trade journal; **–sbuch** *neu.* ledger; **–sfirma** *f.* commercial firm; **–sflotte** *f.* merchant marine; **–sgenossenschaft** *f.* business partnership; **–sgericht** *neu.* commercial court; **–sgeschäft** *neu.*, **–sgesellschaft** *f.* commercial concern, business corporation; **–skammer** *f.* Chamber of Commerce; –sminister *m.* secretary of commerce; –ssperre *f.* embargo; –svertrag *m.* commercial treaty; –szeichen *neu.* trademark

handel: –n *v.* to act, to proceed; to trade; to traffic; –n mit to deal with (*oder* in); –n um to bargain for; es –t sich um the question is; –n von to treat of; –seinig *adj.*, –seins *adj.* agreed on terms; –treibend *adj.* trading; commercial; –süblich *adj.* usual in trade

händelsüchtig *adj.* quarrelsome

Handlung *f.* deed, act; undertaking; business house; (lit.) plot; –sdiener *m.*, –gehilfe *m.* clerk; –sweise *f.* proceeding

Hanf *m.* hemp

Hänfling *m.* linnet

Hang *m.* slope; inclination, disposition

Häng: –ebacke *f.* jowl; –ebahn *f.* suspended railroad; –ebauch *m.* paunch; potbelly; –eboden *m.* loft; –ebrücke *f.* suspension bridge; –edach *neu.* penthouse; –ematte *f.* hammock

hängen *v.* to hang, to suspend, to hook; — an to adhere (*oder* cling) to, to be fond of

Hannover *neu.* Hanover

Hans *m.* Jack

hänseln *v.* to tease, to ridicule; to hoax

Hansnarr, Hanswurst *m.* buffoon, clown

Hantel *f.* dumbbell

hantieren *v.* to handle, to manipulate

Happen *m.* mouthful; morsel, piece

häretisch *adj.* heretical

Harfe *f.* harp; –nist *m.*, –nspieler *m.* harpist

Harke *f.* rake; jemand zeigen, was eine — ist (coll.) to give somebody a piece of one's mind

Harm *m.* grief, sorrow; insult, wrong, injury

Harmon: –ie *f.* harmony, –ika *f.* accordion; –ikazug *m.* corridor train; –ielehre *f.* theory of harmony

harmlos *adj.* harmless, innocent, guileless

Harn *m.* urine; –blase *f.* (urinary) bladder

Harnisch *m.* armor; in — geraten to fly into a rage; in — jagen to infuriate

harpunieren *v.* to harpoon

harren *v.* (poet.) to wait, to hope

harsch *adj.* harsh; hard, rough

hart *adj.* hard; tough, severe; burdensome; cruel; (phy.) penetrating; –e Eier hardboiled eggs; –e Züge stern features; –er Verlust heavy loss; –gesotten *adj.* hardboiled; hardened; –herzig *adj.* hardhearted, callous; –hörig *adj.* hard of hearing; –köpfig *adj.* headstrong; –leibig *adj.* constipated; –näckig *adj.* obstinate, stubborn;

(med.) chronic

Härte *f.* hardness; harshness, sternness

Hartgeld *neu.* coined money

Hartgummi *m.* vulcanized rubber

Harz *neu.* resin; rosin

Hasardspiel *neu.* game of chance, gambling

Haschee *neu.* hash

haschen *v.* to catch, to seize; — nach to snatch at; to strive for

Hase *m.* hare; rabbit; da liegt der — im Pfeffer (*or* begraben) there's the hitch; falscher — meat loaf; –nfuss *m.* hare's foot; coward; –nklein *neu.*, –pfeffer *m.* rabbit stew

Haspe *f.* hasp, hinge; –l *f.* reel, windlass

Hass *m.* hate, hatred; –er *m.* hater

hässlich *adj.* ugly; odious; repulsive; nasty

Hast *f.* haste, hurry, precipitation

hasten *v.* to hasten, to hurry, to precipitate

hastig *adj.* hasty, precipitate

hätscheln *v.* to caress, to fondle; to pamper

Haube *f.* cap, hood; helmet; bonnet; (rail.) dome; (biol.) crest; unter die — kommen to get married; –nlerche *f.* crested lark

Hauch *m.* breath; breeze, puff (of wind); touch, trace; aspiration

hauchen *v.* to breathe, to exhale; to aspirate

hauen *v.* to hew; to chop; to strike; to lash, to whip; to cut (stone); — und stechen to cut and thrust; übers Ohr — to cheat

häuf: –eln *v.* to heap up (around plant); –en *v.* to heap (up); to accumulate, to amass; –ig *adj.* frequent, repeated

Haufe(n) *m.* heap; pile; number, crowd; etwas über den –n werfen to upset; –nwolke *f.* cumulus cloud

Haupt *neu.* head; chief, leader; aufs — schlagen to vanquish; –altar *m.* high altar; –anstifter *m.* ringleader; –bahnhof *m.* central station; –bestandteil *m.* and *neu.* chief constituent (*oder* ingredient); –buch *neu.* ledger; –büro *neu.* central office; –eingang *m.* main entrance; –fach *neu.* main subject; –gewinn *m.* first prize; –kerl *m.* head man; –leitung *f.* (elec.) main wire; –mann *m.* captain; –nenner *m.* (math.) common denominator; –post *f.*, –postamt *neu.* central post office; –probe *f.* (theat.) dress rehearsal; –quartier *neu.* headquarters; –redakteur *m.* editor-in-chief; –rolle *f.* (theat.) leading part; –sache *f.* main (*oder* most important) thing;

–satz *m.* (gram.) principal sentence; **–schiff** *neu.* central aisle; (naut.) flagship; **–schlagader** *f.* aorta; **–segel** *neu.* mainsail; **–spass** *m.* capital joke; **–stadt** *f.* capital, metropolis; **–strasse** *f.* main road; **–streich** *m.* master stroke; **–ton** *m.* principal accent; **–treffer** *m.* first prize; **–verkehrsstunden** *f. pl.* rush hours; **–versammlung** *f.* general meeting; **–wort** *neu.* noun; **–zug** *m.* main feature; principal train

Häuptling *m.* chief(tain); (coll.) leader

häuptlings *adv.* head over heels

hauptsächlich *adj.* chief, foremost, main

Haus *neu.* house; home; household; dynasty; parliamentary body; firm; das — bestellen to make a will; das — hüten to be confined to the house; ein fideles — a jolly fellow; — und Hof house and home; von –e aus originally, by birth; zu –e at home; –andacht *f.* family devotions; –angestellte *f.* domestic, servant; –arbeit *f.* indoor work; domestic work; –arzt *m.* family doctor; –besitzer *m.* landlord; –bewohner *m.* tenant; –dame *f.* housekeeper; –flur *m.* hall, vestibule; –frau *f.* housewife, homemaker; –freund *m.* family friend; –genosse *m.* fellow lodger; –gesetz *neu.* family law; –gesinde *neu.* domestics; –halt *m.* household; –hälterin *f.* housekeeper; –haltsplan *m.* budget; –haltung *f.* housekeeping; –haltungskosten *f. pl.* household expenses; –herr *m.* host; –ierer *m.* peddler; –knecht *m.* porter, handyman; –kreuz *neu.* (coll.) domestic affliction, bad wife; –lehrer *m.* family tutor; –mädchen *neu.* woman servant, maid of all work; –meister *m.* janitor; caretaker; –mittel *neu.* home remedy; –ordnung *f.* house regulations; –rat *m.* household furniture; –schuhe *m. pl.* slippers; –stand *m.* household; –suchung *f.* (police) house search; –tier *neu.* domestic animal; –tor *neu.* gate; –tür *f.* front door; –verwalter *m.* steward; –wirt *m.* landlord; –wirtschaft *f.* home management; –zins *m.* house rent

haus: –backen *adj.* home-baked; plain, prosaic; **–en** *v.* to dwell, to reside; to economize; **übel –en** to devastate, to ravage; **–halten** *v.* to manage a household; **–hälterisch** *adj.* economical; thrifty; **–ieren** *v.* to peddle

Häuschen *neu.* small house; cottage; **aus dem — sein** to be excited (*oder* beside oneself)

Häusler *m.* cottager

häuslich *adj.* domestic; housekeeping;

economical; home-loving; **–e Aufgaben** homework

Hausse *f.* rise (of prices); boom

Haut *f.* skin; hide; coat; film; membrane; **auf blosser — tragen** to wear next to one's skin; **aufgesprungene —** chapped (*oder* cracked) skin; **aus der — fahren** (coll.) to hit the ceiling; **eine ehrliche — an** honest fellow; **jemandem die — über die Ohren ziehen** to fleece someone; **mit — und Haar** completely; **mit heiler — davonkommen** to have a close shave; **–ausschlag** *m.* (med.) efflorescence; **–bläschen** *neu.* pimple; **–farbe** *f.* complexion; **–heilkunde, –lehre** *f.* dermatology

häuten *v.* to skin; to flay; **sich —** to cast off skin, to slough

Heb: –amme *f.* midwife; **–earm** *m.* leverarm; **–el** *m.* lever; **–ebühne** *f.* platform elevator; **–ekran** *m.* hoisting crane; **–er** *m.* siphon; **–ung** *f.* elevation, removal

heben *v.* to lift, to raise; to heave, to elevate; to bring up; to cancel; to improve, to favor; **sich —** to rise

hech: –eln *v.* to hackle, to carp, to gossip; **–tblau** *adj.* grayish blue; **–tgrau** *adj.* bluish gray

hecken *v.* to breed, to hatch

Heer *neu.* army; crowd, multitude, swarm; **–(es)bann** *m.* levies, military force; **–esabteilung** *f.* (mil.) division; **–esleitung** *f.* army command; **–esmacht** *f.* (mil.) forces; **–esverpflegung** *f.* (mil.) commissariat; **–esverwaltung** *f.* military administration; **–folge** *f.* military duty; **–führer** *m.* army commander; **–lager** *neu.* army camp; **–schar** *f.* (poet.) army; **–schau** *f.* army parade (*oder* review); **–strasse** *f.* broad highway; **–zug** *m.* (mil.) expedition

Hefe *f.* barm, leaven, yeast; dregs, sediment

Heft *neu.* haft, hilt; copy book; (magazine) issue; **das — in der Hand haben** to be master of a situation; **–faden** *m.* basting thread; **–klammer** *f.* paper fastener; **–pflaster** *neu.* adhesive plaster; **–stich** *m.* tack, basting

heften *v.* to stitch, to pin; to baste; to fix, to rivet; **sich an jemandes Sohlen —** to stick close to someone's heels

heftig *adj.* violent, vehement, irascible

hegen *v.* to preserve, to protect, to tend; to entertain (suspicion, hope, etc.)

Hehl *neu.* concealment; secret; **–er** *m.* receiver of stolen goods; fence; **–erei** *f.* (act of) receiving stolen goods

hehlen *v.* to conceal, to keep secret

hehr *adj.* sublime; venerable; **hoch und**

— high and mighty

Heid: -e *f.* heath; **-e** *m.* heathen, pagan; **-ekraut** *neu.* heather; **-elbeere** *f.* bilberry; **-elerche** *f.* wood lark; **-engeld** *neu.* immense sum; fortune; **-enmission** *f.* foreign mission; **-eröschen** *neu.* brier rose

heidnisch *adj.* heathenish, pagan

heikel *adj.* delicate, difficult, ticklish

heil *adj.* healthy; healed; whole; **—!** *interj.* hail! good luck! **-bar** *adj.* curable; **-bringend** *adj.* salutary; **-en** *v.* to heal, to cure; **-kräftig** *adj.* curative, healing; **-kundig** *adj.* skilled in medical arts; **-los** *adj.* (coll.) wicked; awful; tremendous; **-sam** *adj.* wholesome

Heil *neu.* welfare; luck; salvation; **-and** *m.* Saviour, Redeemer; **-anstalt** *f.* sanatorium; **-bad** *neu.* medicinal bath; spa; **-brunnen** *m.* mineral spring; **-butt** *m.* halibut; **-kraft** *f.* healing power; **-kunde** *f.* medical science, therapeutics; **-mittel** *neu.* drug, remedy; **-mittellehre** *f.* pharmacology; **-quelle** *f.* mineral spring; **-serum** *neu.* antitoxin; **-stätte** *f.* sanatorium; **-ung** *f.* cure, healing; **-verfahren** *neu.* medical treatment

heilig *adj.* holy; sacred; **-en** *v.* to hallow, to sanctify; der Zweck **-t** die Mittel the end justifies the means

Heilig: -e *m.* saint; das **-e** Abendmahl the Lord's Supper; der **-e** Abend Christmas Eve; die **-e** Schrift Holy Writ, the (Holy) Scriptures; **-enschein** *m.* halo; **-keit** *f.* sanctity; Seine **-keit** His Holiness (the Pope); **-tum** *neu.* sanctuary, relic; **-tumsentweihung** *f.*, **-tumsschändung** *f.* sacrilege

Heim *neu.* home; **-arbeiter** *m.* homeworker; **-at** *f.* native country; homeland; habitat; (law) domicile; **-atkrieger** *m.* stay-at-home soldier; **-atschein** *m.* certificate of domicile (*oder* naturalization); **-atvertriebene** *m.* displaced person; **-chen** *neu.* house cricket; tiny person; **-fahrt**, **-reise** *f.* homeward journey; **-gang** *m.* going home; death; **-gegangene** *m.* deceased; **-stätte** *f.* homestead; **-weh** *neu.* homesickness; nostalgia

heim *adv.* home(ward); **-atlich** *adj.* native; **-elig** *adj.* comfortable, snug; homey; **-fallen** *v.* to revert; **-isch** *adj.* native, indigenous; domestic; homey, accustomed; sich **-isch** fühlen to feel at home; **-kehren** *v.* to return home; **-leuchten** *v.* (coll.) to send (one) about his own business; **-suchen** *v.* to visit; to afflict; **-zahlen** *v.* to retaliate; to

repay

heimlich *adj.* clandestine, secret; snug

heimtückisch *adj.* malicious, deceitful; underhanded

Heinrich *m.* Henry

Heinzelmännchen *neu.* brownie, goblin

Heirat *f.* marriage; **-santrag** *m.* marriage proposal; **-sbüro** *neu.* matrimonial agency; **-sgut** *neu.* dowry; **-skandidat** *m.* suitor, wooer; **-sschein** *m.* marriage license; **-sstifter** *m.* matchmaker; marriage broker

heirat: -en *v.* to marry, to wed; **-sfähig** *adj.* marriageable; **-slustig** *adj.* desirous of marrying

heiser *adj.* hoarse, husky; raucous

heiss *adj.* hot; ardent, vehement; **-hungrig** *adj.* ravenously hungry; **-laufen** *v.* (mech.) to overheat

heissen *v.* to call, to name; to be called (*oder* named); to command; to designate, to signify; es heisst it is said; jemand willkommen **—** to bid someone welcome

heiter *adj.* bright, serene; cheerful, gay

Heiz: -anlage *f.* heating installation; **-er** *m.* stoker; fireman; **-kissen** *neu.* heating pad; **-körper** *m.* radiator; **-material** *neu.* fuel; **-rohr** *neu.* flue; fire tube; **-sonne** *f.* electric heater; **-ung** *f.* heating (installation)

heizen *v.* to heat; to fire; to give off heat

Hektar *neu.* hectare (2.41 acres)

Held *m.* hero; **-endichtung** *f.* epic poem; **-enrolle** *f.* (theat.) part of the hero; **-entum** *neu.* heroism; **-in** *f.* heroine

heldenhaft, heldenmütig *adj.* heroic

helfen *v.* to help; to aid, to assist; to be useful, to serve; es hilft nichts it is of no use; sicht nicht zu **—** wissen to be at wit's end

Helfer *m.* helper, rescuer, assistant; **-shelfer** *m.* (law) aider and abettor, accomplice

hell *adj.* bright, shining; fair, light; pale; smart; am **-en** Tage in broad daylight; **-es** Gelächter hearty laughter; in **-en** Haufen in great numbers; **-hörig** *adj.* keen-eared

Hell: -e *neu.* (coll.) pale beer; **-e** *f.*, **-igkeit** *f.* brightness, brilliancy; distinctiveness; **-ebarde** *f.* halberd; **-er** *m.* farthing; Austrian coin

Hellas *neu.* Greece

Helm *m.* helmet; (arch.) dome, cupola; **-busch** *m.* crest (*oder* plume) of a helmet

Helvetien *neu.* Switzerland

Hemd *neu.* shirt; chemise; jemand bis aufs **—** ausziehen (coll.) to strip someone to the skin; **–brust** f. dicky; **–chen** neu. chemisette; **–einsatz** m. shirt front; **–särmel** m. shirt sleeve

Hemm: **–nis** neu. hindrance, impediment; obstruction; **–schuh** m., brake shoe; **–ung** f. restraint, retardation; (watch) escapement; (gun) safety catch

hemmen v. to check, to stop; to retard; to curb, to restrain

Hengst m. stallion; male (of ass, camel, zebra); **–fohlen** neu., **–füllen** neu. colt

Henk: **–el** m. handle (of basket, pot, etc.); **–er** m. hangman, executioner; **–ersknecht** m. hangman's assistant; torturer

henken v. to hang

Henne f. hen

her adv. here, hither, this way, near; ago, since; from; **hin und —** to and fro; **hinter etwas —** sein to be after something; **nicht weit —** sein to live near by; to be of little importance; **um mich —** around me; **von alters —** of old, for a long time; **–bestellen** v. to send for; **–fallen** v. to fall towards; **über jemand –fallen** to pounce upon; to attack; **–geben** v. to hand over; to give away; **sich dazu –geben** to be a party to; **–gehen** v. to go on; to set about; to happen; **–halten** v. to hold forth; to bear the brunt; **–kommen** v. to come hither, to approach; to arise from; **–kömmlich** adj. traditional, customary; **–leiten** v. to lead hither; to derive; **–machen** v. to set about; to fall upon; **–nehmen** v. to obtain; (coll.) to take to task; **–richten** v. to prepare; to make ready; **–sagen** v. to recite; to repeat; **–schaffen** v. to bring hither; to provide, to procure; **–stellen** v. to set up; to produce, to manufacture; **–ziehen** v. to draw (oder march) hither; **–ziehen über jemand** (coll.) to run a person down

herab adv. down(ward); **von oben —** from above; **–drücken** v. to depress; **–lassend** adj. condescending; **–sehen** v. to look down; **–setzen** v. to lower; to disparage; to reduce; **–würdigen** v. to debase, to degrade

Heraldik f. heraldry

heran adv. along, near, on; hither; **–bilden** v. to train; to educate; **–kommen** v. to come on, to approach; **–nahen** v. to approach; **–nehmen** v. to discipline; **–rücken** v. to draw near; to advance; **–treten** v. to approach, to step up to; **–wachsen** v. to grow up; **–ziehen** v. to draw near; to educate

heraus adv. out; from within; forth; **frei** (or **offen**) **—** frankly, bluntly; **— damit!** out with it! **–bekommen** v. to get back

(change); to elicit; to puzzle out; to make out; **–bringen** v. to bring (oder find) out; **–fordern** v. to challenge; to provoke; **–geben** v. to deliver, to hand out; to give change; to publish; to issue; **–geh(e)n** v. to go out; **aus sich –geh(e)n** to become communicative; **–kommen** v. to come out; to appear; to be published (oder issued); **auf eins –kommen** to be all the same; **–nehmen** v. to take out; **sich etwas –nehmen** to venture, to presume; **–reden** v. to speak out; **–reissen** v. to tear out; **sich –reissen** to extricate oneself; **–rücken** v. to come out with; to hand over; **–rufen** v. to call forth (oder out); **–schlagen** v. to knock out; **–stellen** v. to place outside; **sich –stellen** to turn out to be; **–streichen** v. to strike out; to single out, to praise; **–treten** v. to step out, to emerge, to protrude; **–ziehen** v. to extract

herbei adj. hereto, hither; near to; **—!** come here! **–führen** v. to bring near (oder about); to cause; to give rise to; **–schaffen** v. to provide

Herberge f. lodging, shelter; inn

Herbsäure f. acerbic acid

Herbst m. fall, autumn; harvest time; **–zeitlose** f. meadow-saffron

Herd m. hearth, fireplace, kitchen range; home; focus; central (oder starting) point

Herde f. herd, flock; drove; crowd, multitude; **–nmensch** m. one of the mass of humanity; **–ntier** neu. gregarious animal

herein adv. in (here), into this place; **—!** come in! **–brechen** v. to beset; to befall; **–dringen** v. to enter forcibly; **–fallen** v. to fall into; (coll.) to be taken in; **–gehen** v. to enter; **–legen** v. to put in; (coll.) to cheat; **–schneien** v. to snow in; (coll.) to appear suddenly

Hergang m. course of events

hergebracht adj. traditional, customary

Hering m. herring

Herkunft f. derivation; descent, origin

Hermelin neu. ermine

hernach adv. afterwards, thereafter; subsequently

hernieder adv. downward

Hero: **–ismus** m. heroism; **–ld** m. herald

heroisch adj. heroic(al)

Herr m. master; owner, principal; gentleman; Sir, Mr., Lord; **als grosser — leben** to live in grand style; **— werden** to master, to overcome; **sein eig(e)ner — sein** to be independent; **–enabend** m. stag party; **–enartikel** m. gentlemen's apparel; **–enhaus** neu. manor, mansion; **-enzimmer** *neu.* study; **-gott** *m.* Lord God; **-in** *f.* mistress, lady; **-schaft** *f.* mastery, dominion; power; authority; master and mistress; **-scher** *m.* ruler, sovereign; **-schsucht** *f.* ambition

herüber *adv.* over, across; to this side

herum *adv.* (round) about, near; around; (coll.) finished, over; **hier —** hereabouts; **rings** (*or* **rund**) **—** all around; **überall —** everywhere; **-bringen** *v.* to bring around; to persuade, to induce; **-drücken** *v.* to squeeze around; **sich -drücken** (coll.) to hang around; **-irren** *v.* to wander aimlessly; **-irrend** *adj.* stray, vagrant; **-kommen** *v.* to come around; to travel about; to become known; **-kriegen** *v.* to talk over; **-reichen** *v.* to pass around; **-schnüffeln** *v.* to poke one's nose into everything; **-stöbern** *v.* to rummage about; **-streichen** *v.* to roam about; **-treiben** *v.* to drive around; **sich -treiben** to gad about; to rove around

herunter *adv.* down(ward); off; **-giessen** *v.* to pour down; **-holen** *v.* to bring down; (avi.) to shoot down; **-klappen** *v.* to turn down (collar, etc.); **-kommen** *v.* to come dówn; to decline; (coll.) to go to the dogs; **-lassen** *v.* to let down; to lower; **-reissen** *v.* to pull down; (*oder* to pieces); **-setzen** *v.* to reduce, to lower; to downgrade; to disparage

hervor *adv.* forth, forward; out; **-brechen** *v.* to break through; to emerge; **-bringen** *v.* to bring forth; to produce; to utter; to engender, to generate; **-drängen** *v.* to press forward; **-geh(e)n** *v.* to go forth; to result from; **-heben** *v.* to make conspicuous (*oder* prominent); (typ.) to display; to emphasize, to stress; **-ragen** *v.* to stand out, to project; **-ragend** *adj.* excellent, outstanding, prominent; **-rufen** *v.* to call forth; to cause; **-stechen** *v.* to stand out; to be conspi uous; **-steh(e)n** *v.* to stand out; to project; **-treten** *v.* to step forward; to be prominent; **sich -tun** to distinguish oneself; to excel; **-ziehen** *v.* to draw forth, to produce

Herz *neu.* heart; center, core; (cards) hearts; courage; **ans — legen** to enjoin, to urge; **das — auf der Zunge haben** to wear one's heart on one's sleeve; **ein Kind unterm -en tragen** to be pregnant; **ein Mann nach meinem -en** a man to my liking; **etwas auf dem -en haben** to have something on one's mind; **ins — schliessen** to become fond of; **sein — an etwas hängen** to set one's heart on something; **sich ein — fassen** to take courage; **von -en gern** with pleasure; **-ader** *f.* aorta; **-beutel** *m.* pericardium; **-blut** *neu.* lifeblood; **-blutgefässkurve** *f.* angiocardiogram; **-dame** *f.* queen of hearts; **-ensangelegenheit** *f.* love affair; **-ensbrecher** *m.* lady-killer; **-enseinfalt** *f.* simplicity; simple-mindedness; **-ensgüte** *f.* kindheartedness; **-enslust** *f.* heart's content; **-gefässbild** *neu.* angiocardiogram; **-geräusch** *neu.* heart murmur; **-kammer** *f.* heart ventricle; **-klopfen** *neu.* palpitation of the heart; **-liebste** *f.* true love; **-muskel** *m.* miocardium; **-schlag** *m.* heartbeat; apoplexy; **-weh** *neu.* heartache

herz: -allerliebst *adj.* sweet, lovely; **-bewegend** *adj.* heart-stirring, touching; **-brechend** *adj.* heart-breaking; **-en** *v.* to hug, to embrace, to caress; **-ensfroh** *adj.* very glad; **-ensgut** *adj.* very kind; **-ergreifend** *adj.* moving; **-erhebend** *adj.* heart-stirring; **-förmig** *adj.* heart-shaped; **-haft** *adj.* stouthearted, valiant, vigorous; **-ig** *adj.* charming, lovely; **innig** *adj.* heart-felt; **-lich** *adj.* hearty, cordial, affectionate; **-los** *adj.* heartless, cruel; **-zerreissend** *adj.* heart-rending

Herzog *m.* duke; **-in** *f.* duchess; **-tum** *neu.* duchy

herzu *adv.* up (to), towards

heterosexuell *adj.* heterosexual

Hetz: -blatt *neu.* (coll.) hate sheet; yellow journal; **-er** *m.*, **-redner** *m.* agitator, instigator; **-presse** *f.* yellow press; **-rede** *f.* inflammatory speech

Hetze *f.* hunt, hunting with hounds; agitation; hurry, mad race

Heu *neu.* hay; **-boden** *m.* hayloft; **-er** *m.* haymaker; **-fieber** *neu.* hay fever; **-gabel** *f.* pitchfork; **-schober** *m.* haystack; **-schrecke** *f.* grasshopper

heuch: -eln *v.* to play the hypocrite; to feign; to pretend, to simulate

Heuch: -elei *f.* hypocrisy; **-ler** *m.* hypocrite

heuen *v.* to make hay

heulen *v.* to howl, to hoot, to yelp; to cry

heute *adv.* today; nowadays; **— vor acht Tagen** a week ago today! **-abend** *adv.* tonight; **-früh** *adv.* this morning

heutig *adj.* of today; modern

heutzutage *adv.* nowadays

Hexe *f.* witch, sorceress; hag; **-nkessel** *m.* hurly-burly, hubbub; **-nkreis** *m.* magic circle; **-nkunst** *f.* witchcraft, sorcery, magic art; **-nmeister** *m.* magician, sorcerer; **-nschuss** *m.* lumbago;

–rei *f.* sorcery; black magic

Hieb *m.* blow, cut, stroke; gash, slash; hit

hier *adv.* here; — sein to be present; — **und da** now and then; in various places; **–an** *adv.* hereon; **–auf** *adv.* hereupon, on (*oder* after, at, by) this; **–aus** *adv.* from this; hence; **–bei** *adv.* hereby, herewith; enclosed; **–durch** *adv.* through here, this way; by this means; hereby; **–gegen** *adv.* against this; **–her** *adv.* this way, hither; **bis –her** so far; hitherto, up to now; **–herum** *adv.* hereabouts; **–hin** *adv.* in this direction; **–mit** *adv.* herewith; **–nach** *adv.* hereafter; according to this; **–orts** *adv.* here; **–über** *adv.* over here; concerning this; **–um** *adv.* around here; **–unter** *adv.* beneath this; among these **–von** *adv.* hereof, herefrom; **–zu** *adv.* in addition to this; moreover; **–zulande** *adv.* in this country

hiesig *adj.* of this country (*oder* place), local

Hilf- **–e** *f.* help; aid, assistance; relief; **–sarbeiter** *m.* temporary worker; **–sgelder** *neu. pl.* subsidies; **–skasse** *f.* charitable fund; **–slehrer** *m.* substitute teacher; **–smittel** *neu.* remedy, resource; expedient; **–smotor** *m.* servomotor; booster; **–sprediger** *m.* curate; **–squelle** *f.* resource; **–struppen** *f. pl.* auxiliary troops; **–s(zeit)wort** *neu.* auxiliary verb; **–szug** *m.* relief train

Himbeere *f.* raspberry

Himmel *m.* heaven; sky, firmament; canopy; **aus allen.–n fallen** to be bitterly disappointed; **–bett** *neu.* fourposter (bed); **–blau** *neu.* sky-blue, azure; **–fahrt** *f.* (rel.) Ascension; Assumption; **–reich** *neu.* kingdom of heaven; **–sgegend** *f.*, **–srichtung** *f.* quarter of the heaven, direction; point of the compass; **–skörper** *m.* celestical body; **–skunde** *f.* astronomy; **–sschlüssel** *m.* primrose, primula; **–sstrich** *m.* climate, region, zone; latitude; **–szeichen** *neu.* sign of the zodiac; **–szelt** *neu.* (lit.) celestial dome, firmament

himmlisch *adj.* heavenly, celestial; divine

hin *adv.* there, thither, toward(s); along, till; forth; (coll.) gone, lost, dead; ruined; exhausted; **aufs Ungewisse —** at random; **es zieht sich —** it drags on; **Fahrkarte —** und zurück round-trip ticket; **— ist —** there's no use crying over spilt milk; **— und her** to and fro; **— und her überlegen** to rack one's brain; **— und wieder** now and then; **— und zurück** coming and going; **überall —** in all directions; **–bringen** *v.* to bring (*oder* carry) to; to pass, to spend;

–deuten *v.* to point at; **–fallen** *v.* to fall down; **–fällig** *adj.* decaying, frail, weak; **–geben** *v.* to give away, to surrender, to sacrifice; **sich –geben** to devote oneself; **–geh(e)n** *v.* to go there; to pass away; to elapse; **–halten** *v.* to hold out; to keep in suspense; **–länglich** *adj.* sufficient; **–legen** *v.* to lay (*oder* put) down, **sich –legen** to lie down; **–nehmen** *v.* to take; to accept; to suffer; **–raffen** *v.* to cut off (by death); **–reichen** *v.* to stretch out; to hand over; to suffice; **–reichend** *adj.* sufficient; **–reissen** *v.* to overpower; to enchant, to charm; **–reissend** *adj.* charming, enchanting; **–scheiden** *v.* to die, to pass away; **–schleppen** *v.* to drag on; **–schwinden** *v.* to dwindle, to vanish; **–setzen** *v.* to set down; **sich –setzen** to sit down; **–sichtlich** *adj.* with reference to; in view of; **–stellen** *v.* to put down; to represent; **–strecken** *v.* to stretch out; to kill; **sich –strecken** to lie down, to lay low; to last; **–weisen** *v.* to refer (*oder* point) to; **–weisend** *adj.* demonstrative; **–werfen** *v.* to throw down; to sketch; **–ziehen** *v.* to draw to; to attract; to move there; **sich –ziehen** to draw out, to drag on

Hin- **–blick** *m.* glance; regard; **im –blick auf** in view of; **–fahrt** *f.* journey (*oder* voyage, trip) there; **Hin– und Rückfahrt** round trip; **–gabe** *f.* abandonment; devotion; indulgence; **–gang** *m.* decease; **–reise** *f.* journey (*oder* voyage) to; **–richtung** *f.* execution; **–sicht** *f.* respect, regard; **–weg** *m.* (the) way toward; **–weis** *m.* hint, indication; reference, allusion

hinab *adv.* down, downward(s); **den Fluss —** downstream

hinauf *adv.* up to; upward(s); **den Fluss —** upstream; **die Treppe —** upstairs; **–setzen** *v.* to raise; **–steigen** *v.* to ascend, to mount

hinaus *adv.* out(side); **—!** *interj.* get out! **hoch —** wollen to aim high; **über etwas — sein** to be beyond something; **–gehen** *v.* to go out; to exceed; **auf etwas –gehen** to end in, to aim at; **–schieben** *v.* to defer, to postpone, to put off; **–werfen** *v.* to throw out; to expel; **–ziehen** *v.* to draw out; to march (*oder* move) out(side); to protract

hindern *v.* to hinder, to impede; to obstruct

Hindernis *neu.* hindrance; impediment; obstacle; deterrence; **–rennen** *neu.* steeplechase; hurdle race

hinein *adv.* in (thither), into; **mitten–**

right into the mid le; **-arbeiten** v., **sich -arbeiten in** to work one's way into; to familiarize oneself with; **-fallen** v. to fall into; (coll.) to be taken in; **sich -finden** v. to accomodate (oder reconcile) oneself to; **-geh(e)n** v. to go in(to); to enter; **-geraten** v. to get into

hinfort adv. henceforth; in the future

hingegen adv. and conj. on the contrary; on the other hand; but, whereas

hinken v. to limp; to hobble; to drag along

hinten adv. behind; in the rear; (naut.) aft; **-über** adv. upside down, backwards

hinter adj. back; hind(er); posterior; — adv. back(wards), behind; — prep. behind, after; back of, in the rear of; — **die Sache** (or **Schliche**) **kommen** to find out something; — **die Schule gehen** to play truant; — **einer Sache her sein** to be persistent about; — **Schloss und Riegel bringen** to jail; **sich lassen** to outdistance, to outstrip; **jemand — das Licht führen** (coll.) to cheat someone; **-bringen** v. to inform (oder report) secretly; **-drein** adv. afterwards. subsequently; following; **-einander** adv. successively; one after the other; **-geh(e)n** v. to deceive, to hoodwink; **-hältig** adj. deceitful; **-her** adv. behind; subsequently; eagerly; **-lassen** v. to leave behind; to bequeath; **-legen** v. to deposit; **-listig** adj. cunning; treacherous; **-rücks** adv. from behind; deceitfully; **-st** adj. hindmost, last; **-treiben** v. to frustrate; to thwart; **-wärts** adv. backwards, behind; **-ziehen** v. to drag back; to embezzle; to defraud

Hinter: -backe f. buttock; **-bein** neu. **sich auf die -beine setzen** to strain oneself; **-bliebene** m. survivor, mourner; **-deck** neu., **-schiff** neu. sterndeck; **-gedanke** m. mental reservation; **-grund** m. background; **-halt** m. ambush; **-hof** m. back yard; **-lader** m. breechloader; **-lassenschaft** f. inheritance; estate; **-list** f. deceit, treachery; **-n** m. (coll.) buttock₃; **-pforte** f. back gate; **-reihe** f. (mil.) rear file; **-steven** m. sternpost; (sl.) buttocks; **-teil** neu. back part; hindquarter; buttock; (naut.) stern; **-treffen** neu. rearguard; **ins -treffen geraten** to be at a disadvantage; **-treppenroman** m. cheap novel; **-viertel** neu. hindquarter; loin; **-wand** f. back wall; (theat.) backdrop

hinunter adv. down(ward); **-giessen** v. (coll.) to toss off (drink); **-schlucken** v. to swallow; **-spülen** v. to wash down; **-würgen** v. to gulp down

hinweg adv. away; off; —! interj. get away! out you go! **-gerafft** adj. dead; **-gehen (über)** to overlook; **-kommen (über)** to overcome; **-sehen (über)** to shut one's eyes to; **-setzen, sich -setzen (über)** to reconcile oneself to, to ignore

hinwieder(um) adv. again, once more; on the other hand

hinzu adv. toward; near; in addition to, supplementing; **-fügen** v. to add, to annex; **-kommen** v. to come up; to be added; **-ziehen** v. to add; to include; to consult

Hiob m. Job

Hiobsbote m. bearer of ill tidings

Hippe f. scythe; billhook

Hirn neu. brain; **-gespinst** neu. fancy, notion, whim; vision, chimera; **-hautentzündung** f. meningitis; **-schädel** m., **-schale** f. skull, cranium

Hirsch m. stag; hart; **-fänger** m. hanger, bowie knife; **-geweih** neu. antlers, hart's horns; **-kalb** neu. fawn; **-kuh** f. hind, female deer; **-leder** neu. buckskin

Hirse f. millet; **-brei** m. millet gruel

Hirt(e) m. herdsman; shepherd; pastor; **-enamt** neu. shepherd's duties; pastorate; **-enbrief** m. pastoral letter; **-engedicht** neu. pastoral (oder bucolic) poem, eclogue; **-enleben** neu. pastoral life; **-enstab** m. shepherd's staff; (eccl.) crosier; **-envolk** neu. pastoral people; nomadic tribe; **-in** f. shepherdess

hissen v. to hoist, to pull up

Historiker m. historian

historisch adj. historic(al)

Hitz: -e f. heat; ardor, passion; **-egradmesser** m. pyrometer; **-eschild** (bemannte Rakete) neu. heat shield; **-kopf** m. hothead; **-schlag** m. heat stroke, sunstroke

hitzig adj. hot; heated; inflamed; angered, hotheaded; vehement; irascible

Hobel m. plane; **-bank** f. carpenter's (oder joiner's) bench; **-späne** m. pl. shavings

hoch adj. high; tall; noble, sublime; — adv. highly; greatly, very; **das ist mir zu** — that is beyond my reach; **die See ging** — the sea was rough; **es geht — her** there is much merrymaking; **Hände —!** hands up! **— angeschrieben sein** to be in great favor; **— anrechnen** to value greatly; **— leben lassen** to toast, to give three cheers for; **— spielen** to play for high stakes; **— und heilig** (or **teuer**) **versprechen** to promise solemnly; **-achtungsvoll** adj. respectfully yours; **-bejahrt** adj., **-betagt** adj. very old; **-fahrend** adj. haughty, overbearing; **-fein** adj. superfine, exquisite;

-fliegend *adj.* flying high; ambitious; -gehend *adj.* running high; rough (sea); -gemut *adj.* in good spirits; -gesinnt *adj.* noble-minded; -gespannt *adj.* high-tensioned; exaggerated: -gestimmt *adj.* high-pitched; high-minded; -gradig *adj.* to a high degree; intense; -halten *v.* to cherish, to esteem highly; -herzig *adj.* noble, high-minded, magnanimous; -klingend *adj.* high-sounding; bombastic; -mütig *adj.* haughty, arrogant; -näsig *adj.* supercilious, (coll.) stuck-up; -rot *adj.* bright red; highly inflamed; -selig *adj.* of blessed memory, late; -stämmig *adj.* tall, standard; -trabend *adj.* pompous, bombastic; -wertig *adj.* of high value, valuable

Hoch *neu.* cheer; (meteorology) high pressure area; -achtung *f.* high esteem, deep respect; -amt *neu.* (eccl.) high mass; -antenne *f.* overhead aerial; -bahn *f.* elevated railroad; -bau *m.* tall construction, skyscraper; -betrieb *m.* intensive activity, hustle; -burg *f.* stronghold; -druck *m.* high pressure; great hurry; relief printing; -ebene *f.* plateau; -(ehr)würden *m.* Right Reverend; -genuss *m.* great enjoyment; real treat; -gericht *neu.* place of execution; gallows; -gesang *m.* anthem, ode; -haus *neu.* skyscraper; -mut *m.* haughtiness; arrogance; -ofen *m.* blast furnace; -schule *f.* college; university; -sommer *m.* midsummer; -spannung *f.* (elec.) high voltage; -sprung *m.* high jump; -stapelei *f.* swindling; criminal imposture; -stapler *m.* swindler; confidence man; -verrat *m.* high treason; -wasser *neu.* high water (*oder* tide); flood; -wild *neu.* big game

höchst *adj.* highest; extreme; utmost; maximum; — *adv.* extremely, most, very; aufs -e to the last extremity; — schädlich highly injurious; -ens *adv.* at most; -wahrscheinlich *adj.* very probably, in all likelihood

Höchst: -geschwindigkeit *f.* top speed; -leistung *f.* maximum output; record performance; -preis *m.* maximum price; -mass *neu.* maximum

Hochzeit *f.* wedding, nuptials; marriage; -er *m.* bridegroom; -erin *f.* bride; -sreise *f.* honeymoon trip; -sschmauss *m.* wedding dinner; -szug *m.* bridal procession

hocken *v.* to crouch, to squat; (coll.) to stick

Höcker *m.* knoll; protuberance; hunchback; hump

Hof *m.* yard, courtyard; farm; estate;

court; (ast.) corona, halo; **den —** machen to court; -besitzer *m.* owner of an estate; -brauch *m.*, -sitte *f.* court etiquette; -burg *f.* royal residence; -dame *f.* lady in waiting; lady of the court; -dichter *m.* poet laureate; -haltung *f.* royal household; -hund *m.* watchdog; -meister *m.* private tutor; manager of an estate; -rat *m.* privy councilor; -staat *m.* princely household; court dress; -schranze *f.* courtier

Höf: -lichkeit *f.* politeness; -lichkeitsbezeigungen *f. pl.* marks of attention, compliments; -ling *m.* courtier

hoff: -en *v.* to hope, to expect; -entlich *adv.* it is to be hoped; -nungsvoll *adj.* hopeful, promising; -nungslos *adj.* hopeless

Hoff: -art *f.* haughtiness, arrogance, conceit; -nung *f.* hope; expectation; in guter -nung pregnant; -nungsschimmer *m.* gleam of hope; -nungsstrahl *m.* ray of hope, silver lining

hoffärtig *adj.* haughty, arrogant; conceited

höflich *adj.* courteous, polite

Höhe *f.* height; altitude; elevation; auf der — up to par; up to date; in the latitude (of); auf gleicher — on a level with; das ist die —! that's the limit!; Ehre sei Gott in der —! Glory to God in the Highest; -nkrankheit *f.* aeroembolism; -nmesser *m.* altimeter; -nzug *m.* mountain range; -punkt *m.* peak; zenith; climax

Hoheit *f.* sovereignty; Highness; -sgewässer *n. pl.* territorial waters

höher *adj.* higher; superior

hohl *adj.* hollow; concave; empty; flimsy; -äugig *adj.* hollow-eyed; -bäckig *adj.* hollow-cheeked; -geschliffen *adj.* hollow-ground; concave; -köpfig *adj.* empty-headed, shallow-witted, vacuous

Hohl: -bohrer *m.* post-hole digger; -heit *f.* hollowness; -kehle *f.*, -rinne *f.* (arch.) groove, channel; -kopf *m.* empty-headed fellow; -naht *f.*, -saum *m.* hemstitch; -raum *m.* hollow; cavity; -weg *m.* ravine; narrow pass; defile

Höhle *f.* cave(rn); hollow, cavity; den; -nbewohner *m.* cave dweller; troglodyte; -nforscher *m.* spelunker

Höhlung *f.* hollow; cavity; excavation

Hohn *m.* disdain; scorn; derision; -gelächter *neu.* mocking laughter

höhnen *v.* to jeer; to scorn, to deride

höhnisch *adj.* disdainful, scornful; derisive

Höker *m.* street vendor

hold *adj.* charming, graceful, lovely,

jemandem — sein to favor someone; —selig *adj.* most charming, enchanting

holen *v.* to fetch; (naut.) to lower; to haul up; — lassen to send for; sich — to catch (cold, etc.) sich Rat — to consult

Hölle *f.* hell; Himmel und — aufbieten to move heaven and earth; jemand die —heiss machen to make it hot for someone; —nangst *f.* mortal fright; —nbrand *m.* hell-fire; tremendous conflagration; —nmaschine *f.* infernal machine

höllisch *adj.* diabolical; (coll.) tremendous

holp(e)rig *adj.* rugged, rough, uneven

holpern *v.* to jolt; to stumble

Holunder *m.* elder (shrub *oder* tree)

Holz *neu.* wood; timber; forest; — sägen (coll.) to snore; —apfel *m.* crab apple; —bekleidung *f.* wooden lining, wainscoting; —bildhauer *m.* woodcarver; —birne *f.* wild pear; —bock *m.* sawhorse; (ent.) tick; —bohrer *m.* auger, gimlet; wood beetle; —essig *m.* wood vinegar; —fäller *m.*, —hacker *m.*, —hauer *m.* woodcutter, lumberman; —fäule *f.* dry rot; —frevel *m.* forest damage; —geist *m.* wood alcohol; —häher *m.* jay; —hof *m.* lumberyard; —kohle *f.* charcoal; —nagel *m.* wooden peg; —schlag *m.* forest clearing; felling of timber; —schneider *m.* wood engraver (*oder* carver); —schnitt *m.* woodcut; —schuh *m.* clog; —späne *m. pl.* shavings; auf dem —weg sein to be on the wrong track; —wolle *f.* excelsior

holz: —en *v.* to fell timber; to gather wood; (coll.) to cudgel; —ig *adj.* containing wood fibers; —reich *adj.* woody

hölzern *adj.* wooden; stiff; tedious; dull

homogen *adj.* homogeneous

honett *adj.* honorable; decent

Honig *m.* honey; — um den Mund schmieren to coax, to wheedle; to fawn; —kuchen *m.* gingerbread; —monat *m.*, —mond *m.* honeymoon; —saft *m.* nectar; —scheibe *f.*, —wabe *f.* honeycomb; —seim *m.* liquid honey

Honorar *neu.* honorarium; fee; —professor *m.* honorary professor

Honoratioren *pl.* notables; City Fathers

honorieren *v.* to honor; to pay an honorarium

Hör: —bild *neu.* sound picture; —ensagen *neu.* hearsay; —er *m.* hearer, auditor, noncredit student; (tel.) receiver; —erschaft *f.* audience; —folge *f.* (rad.) program; —saal *m.* auditorium; lecture room; —spiel *neu.* radio play; —weite *f.* earshot

hör: —bar *adj.* audible; —en *v.* to hear; to listen; to obey; to attend (lectures);

auf einen Namen —en to answer to a name; das lässt sich —en that sounds all right; Flöhe husten (*or* Gras wachsen) —en to have sharp hearing, to be keenly alert; schwer —en to be hard of hearing; von sich —en lassen to send news of oneself; to write; Berlin —en (rad.) to get Berlin; —ig *adj.* dependent; living in bondage

horchen *v.* to hearken; to eavesdrop

Horizont *m.* horizon

horizontale Luftströmung *f.* advection

Horn *neu.* horn; bugle; peak; (ent.) feeler; die Hörner zeigen to oppose vigorously; sich die Hörner abstossen to learn by experience; —bläser *m.* hornblower, bugler; —haut *f.* horny skin; callous; cornea; —hecht *m.* garfish; —isse *f.* hornet; —rabe *m.* hornbill; —signal *neu.* bugle call; —ung *m.* (poet.) February; —vieh *neu.* horned cattle; (coll.) blockhead

horn(art)ig *adj.* like horn; horny; hardened

Hörnchen *neu.* small horn, cornicle; crescent

hörnern *adj.* of horn; like horn

horrend *adj.* horrible; gruesome

Horst *m.* eyrie; bush, thicket; den, dwelling

Hort *m.* (lit.) hoard, treasure; day nursery; refuge, protection

Hortensie *f.* hydrangea

Hose *f.* trousers; shorts; panties; —nband *neu.* kneeband; (Order of the) Garter —nboden *m.* seat of trousers; sich auf den —nboden setzen to work hard; —nbund *m.* waistband; —nklappe *f.*, —nlatz *m.* fly (of trousers); —nmatz *m.* little fellow; —nträger *m. pl.* suspenders

Hospital *neu.* hospital

Hospiz *neu.* hospice

Hostie *f.* (rel.) the Host

Hotel *neu.* hotel; —ier *m.* hotel owner

Hub *m.* lift(ing), raising; (piston) stroke; —schrauber *m.* helicopter; —schrauber-Nahverkehr *m.* helibus

hübsch *adj.* pretty; handsome

Huckepack *m.* piggyback

Huf *m.* hoof; —beschlag *m.* horseshoeing; —eisen *neu.* horseshoe; —nagel *m.* horseshoe nail; —schlag *m.* hoof beat; —schmied *m.* blacksmith

Hüft: —bein *neu.*, —knochen *m.* hipbone; —e *f.* hip, haunch; —gelenk *neu.* hip joint; —nerv *m.* sciatic nerve; —schmerz *m.*, —weh *neu.* sciatica

Hügel *m.* hill; knoll; —land *neu.* hill country

hügelig *adj.* hill-shaped; hilly

Huhn *neu.* hen, chicken, pullet; **ein verrücktes —** a crazy fellow; **a silly woman**

Hühner *pl.* poultry; **-auge** *neu.* (toe) corn; **-augenoperateur** *m.* chiropodist; **-frikassee** *f.* stewed chicken; **-haus** *neu.*, **-stall** *m.* hen coop; **-hof** *m.* poultry yard; **-hund** *m.* pointer, setter; **-pastete** *f.* chicken pie; **-stange** *f.* perch, roost

Huld *f.* grace, favor, clemency; **-igung** *f.* homage; **-igungseid** *m.* oath of allegiance

huld: -igen *v.* to render homage; to indulge in; **-reich** *adj.*, **-voll** *adj.* gracious; clement

Hülle *f.* cover(ing), envelope; **in — und Fülle** in abundance; **sterbliche —** mortal frame

hüllen *v.* to cover, to wrap; to veil, to hide; **sich in Schweigen —** to remain silent

Hülse *f.* shell; pod; capsule; hull; **-nfrüchte** *f. pl.* legumes

human *adj.* humane; **-istisch** *adj.* humanistic; classical; **-itär** *adj.* humanitarian

Hummel *f.* bumble bee

Hummer *m.* lobster; **-schere** *f.* lobster claw

Humor *m.* humor; **-eske** *f.* humorous sketch (*oder* play, story); **-ist** *m.* humorist

humoristisch *adj.* humorous

Humpen *m.* bumper, goblet

Humus *m.* humus, mould

Hund *m.* dog, hound; (min.) truck; **auf dem — sein** to be down and out; **auf den — kommen, vor die -e gehen** to go to the dogs; **da liegt der — begraben** there's the rub! **ein toter — beisst nicht** dead men tell no tales; **-earbeit** *f.* drudgery; **-efutter** *neu.* dog food; **miserable meal; -ehütte** *f.* kennel; **-ekuchen** *m.* dog biscuit; **-emarke** *f.* dog tag; **-ewache** *f.* (naut.) midnight watch; **-ewärter** *m.* kennel man; **-ewetter** *neu.* bad weather; **-ezucht** *f.* breeding of dogs; **-sfott** *m.* scoundrel; cur; **-sstern** *m.* Dog Star, Sirius; **-stage** *m. pl.* dog-days; **-swut** *f.* hydrophobia, rabies

hundert *adj.* hundred; **-erlei** *adj.* of a hundred different kinds; **-fach** *adj.*, **-fältig** *adj.* hundredfold, centuple; **-jährig** *adj.* of a hundred years, centenary; **-tägig** *adj.* lasting a hundred days; **-weise** *adv.* by (*oder* in) hundreds

Hundert *neu.*, **-er** *m.* hundred; **-stel** *neu.* hundredth part

Hündin *f.* bitch

hündisch *adj.* bootlicking, servile, fawning

Hüne *m.* giant; **-ngestalt** *f.* mighty figure; **-ngrab** *neu.* prehistoric barrow, cairn

Hunger *m.* hunger; famine; predilection, eagerness; **am -tuch nagen** to suffer hunger; **-gestalt** *f.* mere skeleton; **-kur** *f.* reducing diet; **-leider** *m.* needy wretch; **-lohn** *m.* starvation wage; **-snot** *f.* famine; **-tod** *m.* death from starvation

hungern *v.* to be hungry, to suffer hunger; **— lassen** to starve; **— nach** to yearn for

hungrig *adj.* hungry

Hupe *f.* (auto.) horn, siren

hüpfen *v.* to hop, to skip, to jump

Hürde *f.* hurdle, pen; stand (for drying fruit); **-nrennen** *neu.* hurdle race

Hure *f.* prostitute; whore; **-rei** *f.* fornication

hurtig *adj.* brisk, nimble, agile

huschen *v.* to scurry, to whisk

husten *v.* to cough

Husten *m.* cough

Hut *m.* hat, round cover; **unter einen — bringen** (coll.) to reconcile; **— *f.* guard, protection; **auf der — sein** to be on one's guard; **in Gottes —** in God's keeping; **-krempe** *f.* hat brim; **-schachtel** *f.* hatbox

hüten *v.* to guard, to protect; to take care of; **das Bett —** to be confined to one's bed; **ich werde mich —!** I certainly won't do that! **sich —** to be on guard, to avoid

Hütte *f.* hut, cabin; chalet, shelter; foundry, smeltery; **-nkunde** *f.*, **-wesen** *neu.* metallurgy

Hyäne *f.* hyena

Hymne *f.*, **Hymnus** *m.* hymn; anthem

hypnotisieren *v.* to hypnotize

Hypo: -chonder *m.* hypochondriac; **-thek** *f.* mortgage; **-these** *f.* hypothesis; supposition, assumption

Hysterie *f.* hysteria

I

ich *pron.* I; **— selbst** I myself; **— Armer! — Elender!** poor me!

Ich *neu.* self; ego; **-sucht** *f.* egotism

ideal *adj.* ideal; **-isieren** *v.* to idealize; **-istisch** *adj.* idealistic(al)

Idee *f.* idea; notion, concept; (coll.) **a little** (bit); **-nverbindung** *f.* association of ideas

ideell *adj.* ideal; imaginary, fanciful

identifizieren *v.* to identify

identisch *adj.* identical

Identitätsnachweis *m.* certificate of identity

idiotisch *adj.* idiotic(al)

Idyll *neu.*, Idylle *f.* idyl

idyllisch *adj.* idyllic

Igel *m.* hedgehog; (agr.) drill-harrow; urchin

Ignorant *m.* ignoramus

ignorieren *v.* to ignore

ihm *pron.* to him, to it

ihn *pron.* him, it; –en *pron.* to them

ihr *pron.* and *adj.* to her; hers, its; — *pl.* you; theirs; –er *pron.* (of) her (*oder* them, their); –erseits *adv.* in her (*oder* their) turn; –esgleichen *adj.* of her (*oder* their) kind; like her (*oder* them); –ethalben *adv.*, –etwegen *adv.*, –etwillen *adv.* on her (*oder* their) account; for her (*oder* their) sake; as far as she (*oder* they) is (*oder* are) concerned

illegitim *adj.* illegitimate

Illegitimität *f.* illegitimacy

illoyal *adj.* disloyal

illustrieren *v.* to illustrate

Ilse *f.* Alice, Elsie

Iltis *m.* polecat, ferret

imaginär *adj.* imaginary

Imbiss *m.* snack; –halle *f.* snack bar

Imker *m.* beekeeper; –ei *f.* beekeeping

immatrikulieren *v.* to matriculate

Imme *f.* (poet.) bee

immer *adv.* always, continually; constantly; auf — forever; — mehr more and more; — und — wieder over and over again; — wieder continuing; noch — still, yet, even now; nur — zu! keep it up! wann auch — whenever; was auch — what(so)ever; wen auch — whom(so)ever; wenn auch — (although; wer auch — who(so)ever; wie auch (*or* nur) — in whatever manner; how(so)ever; wie — as usual; wo auch — where(so)ever; wohin auch — wherever; whithersoever; –dar *adv.* forever; –fort *adv.* constantly, on and on; –hin *adv.* for all that, nevertheless; –während *adj.* constant, permanent; –zu *adv.* and *interj.* continuously; go ahead!

Immobilien *pl.* real estate; immovables

immunisieren *v.* to render immune; to immunize

Immunität *f.* immunity

impfen *v.* to inoculate, to vaccinate; to graft

imponieren *v.* to impress; –d *adj.* impressive

Import *m.* importation, imports; –e *f.* imports (especially cigars); –eur *m.* importer

imposant *adj.* imposing

Impotenz *f.* impotence

imprägnieren *v.* to impregnate

improvisieren *v.* to improvise; to extemporize

Impuls *m.* impulse

impulsiv *adj.* impulsive

imstande *adv.* capable (of); — sein (coll.) to be foolish enough (to do something)

in *prep.* in, at; to, into; within

Inangriffnahme *f.* start, setting about

Inbegriff *m.* totality; embodiment; essence; (fig.) quintessence

inbegriffen *adv.* included

Inbrunst *f.* fervor. ardor

inbrünstig *adj.* ardent, fervent

indem *adv.* (mean)while; because, as, since; by

indes(sen) *adv.* meanwhile; but; nevertheless

Indien *neu.* India

indigniert *adj.* indignant

Indiskretion *f.* indiscretion; tactlessness

indisponiert *adj.* indisposed

Individu: –alismus *m.* individualism; –alität *f.* individuality; –um *neu.* individual; personality

individuell *adj.* individual

Indiz *neu.* (law) indication of guilt; –ienbeweis *m.* circumstantial evidence

Indossament *neu.* endorsement

Industri: –alisierung *f.* industrialization; –e *f.* industry; –eller *m.* manufacturer; industrialist; –estaat *m.* manufacturing country

industriell *adj.* industrial

ineinander *adv.* into each other

infam *adj.* infamous

Infamie *f.* infamy

Infant *m.* infante; –erie *f.* infantry; –in *f.* infanta; –rist *m.* infantryman, foot. soldier

Infektionskrankheit *f.* infectious disease

infizieren *v.* to infect

infolge *prep.* because (*oder* as a result) of; –dessen *adv.* consequently; therefore

Ingenieur *m.* engineer (degree of a technical university); –skunst *f.* engineering

Ingredienz *f.* ingredient

Ingwer *m.* ginger

Inhaber *m.* owner, proprietor; holder

Inhalt *m.* content(s), capacity; area, volume; subject, matter; –sangabe *f.*, –sverzeichnis *neu.* table of contents, index, summary

inhalt: –lich *adj.* as regards the contents; –los *adj.* empty, unmeaning; –reich *adj.*, –schwer *adj.*, –voll *adj.* rich; significant; full of meaning

Injurie *f.* insult

Inkarnat *neu.* flesh color

Inkasso *neu.* cashing; collection
inklusive *adj.* included, including
Inkonsequenz *f.* inconsistency; illogicalness
Inkrafttreten *neu.* coming into force
Inländer *m.* native
inländisch *adj.* indigenous, domestic
Inlett *neu.* bedtick
inn: –ehaben *v.* to possess; **–ehalten** *v.* to pause, to interrupt; to comply with; **–en** *adv.* inside, within; **–er** *adj.* inner, internal; **–erhalb** *adv.* and *prep.* inside, within; **–erlich** *adj.* inward; internal; heartfelt; **–erst** *adj.* inmost; **–ewerden** *v.* to perceive; **–ig** *adj.* heartfelt, intimate
Inn: –ere *neu.* interior; heart, soul; Minister des **–eren** Secretary of the Interior; **–erste** *neu.* innermost, core; **–ung** *f.* guild, association of craftsmen
inoffiziell *adj.* unofficial
insbesondere *adv.* above all; in particular
Inschrift *f.* inscription, legend, epigraph
Insekt *neu.* insect; **–enkunde** *f.* entomology
Insel *f.* island; **–bewohner** *m.* islander; **–chen** *neu.* islet; **–staat** *m.* insular state
Inserat *neu.* advertisement
insge: –heim *adv.* secretly; **–mein** *adv.* in general; usually; **–samt** *adv.* collectively
insofern, insoweit *adv.* so far; to that extent; — *conj.* if, in this respect; as far as
insonderheit, insonders *adv.* particularly
inspirieren *v.* to inspire
inspizieren *v.* to inspect
installieren *v.* to install
instandhalten *v.* to keep up, to maintain
inständig *adj.* imploring; urgent
instandsetzen *v.* to repair; to enable
Instanz *f.* instance; legal step (*oder* division); letzte — last resort
instruieren *v.* to direct, to instruct
instrumentieren *v.* (mus.) to score
Insulaner *m.* islander; inhabitant of an island
inszenieren *v.* to stage, to arrange
Integralrechnung *f.* integral calculus
integrierend *adj.* integral
intellektuell *adj.* intellectual
intelligent *adj.* intelligent
Intelligenz *f.* intelligence, intelligentsia
Intendant *m.* manager; superintendent; intendant
Intensität *f.* intensity, intensiveness
inter: –essant *adj.* interesting; **–essieren** *v.* to interest; sich **–essieren für** to take interest in; **–mittierend** *adj.* intermittent; **–n** *adj.* internal; **–nieren** *v.* to intern; **–pretieren** *v.* to elucidate, to interpret; **–venieren** *v.* to intervene; **–viewen** *v.* to interview
Inter: –esse *neu.* interest, advantage; **–essengemeinschaft** *f.* community of interest; pool, trust; **–essent** *m.* interested party; **–imsregierung** *f.* provisional government; **–nat** *neu.* boarding school; **–nierung** *f.* internment; **–nist** *m.* internist; **–punktion** *f.* punctuation; **–rogativ** *m.* interrogative pronoun; **–vall** *neu.* interval
interkontinentales Fernlenkgeschoss *neu.* intercontinental ballistic missile (ICBM)
intim *adj.* intimate; private
Intimität *f.* intimacy, privacy
Intimus *m.* intimate friend
intonieren *v.* (mus.) to intone
Intrige *f.* intrigue
intrigieren *v.* to intrigue, to plot
invalid *adj.* invalid, weak; disabled
Invalide *m.* invalid; disabled **person**; **–nversicherung** *f.* old-age insurance
Invent: –ar *neu.* stock; inventory; **–ur (aufnahme)** *f.* taking of an inventory
Investitur *f.* investiture
inwendig *adj.* inside, interior, inward
inwieweit *adv.* to what extent
inwohnend *adj.* inherent
inzwischen *adv.* meanwhile
Ionosphäre *f.* ionosphere
irden *adj.* earthen; made of clay
irdisch *adj.* earthly; mortal; wordly
irgend *adv.* any, some; at any time, in any way; perhaps; ever; **wenn — möglich** if at all possible; **–einer** *pron.*, **–jemand** *pron.*, **–wer** *pron.* anybody, somebody, anyone, someone; **–einmal** *adv.* any time, sometime; **–wie** *adv.* anyhow, somehow; **–wo** *adv.* anywhere, somewhere; **–woher** *adv.* from any (*oder* some) place; **–wohin** *adv.* to any (*oder* some) place
irisierend *adj.* iridescent
Irland *neu.* Ireland
Ironie *f.* irony
ironisch *adj.* ironic(al)
irr: –e *adj.* astray; wrong; confused, insane; **–e werden** to become confused (*oder* insane); **–eführen** *v.* to lead astray; to mislead; **–ereden** *v.* to rave; **–ig** *adj.* erroneous; false, incorrect; **–itieren** *v.* to irritate, to disturb; **–sinnig** *adj.* insane; **–tümlich** *adj.* erroneous, mistaken
Irr: –e *m.* insane person; **–e** *f.* mistaken course; in die **–e gehen** to go astray; **–enanstalt** *f.* mental hospital; **–gang** *m.*, **–garten** *m.* maze, labyrinth; **–glaube** *m.*, **–lehre** *f.* heresy; **–licht** *neu*

will-o'-the-wisp; **–sinn** *m.* insanity; **–tum** *m.* error, oversight, mistake; **–weg** *m.* wrong way; **–wisch** *m.* will-o'-the-wisp; boisterous child; fickle person

Ischias *neu.* sciatica

Island *neu.* Iceland

isolieren *v.* to isolate; to insulate

Isotope *f.* isotope

Italien *neu.* Italy

J

ja *adv.* yes; aye; **–wohl** *adv.* indeed

Jacke *f.* jacket; jerkin; jersey; **–tt** *neu.* short (morning) coat; jacket; das ist (mir) — wie Hose (coll.) it's six of one, half a dozen the other; die — vollkriegen (coll.) to get a spanking

Jagd *f.* hunt(ing); hunting ground; — machen to chase, to pursue; **–aufseher** *m.* gamekeeper; **–flieger** *m.* (avi.) fighter pilot; **–flugzeug** *neu.* fighter plane; **–frevel** *m.* poaching; **–gehege** *neu.* game preserve; **–geschwader** *neu.* (avi.) fighter squadron; **–gesetze** *neu. pl.* game laws; **–horn** *neu.* bugle; **–hund** *m.* hound; setter; **–rennen** *neu.* steeplechase; **–revier** *neu.* hunting ground; **–schein** *m.* hunting license; (sl.) proof of insanity; **–sportlichkeit** (*or* **–zünftigkeit**) *f.* hunting ability; **–verband** *m.* (mil. avi.) fighter unit

jagen *v.* to hunt: to chase, to pursue; to dash; to race; jemand aus etwas — to force somebody to leave

Jäger *m.* hunter, huntsman; ranger, gamekeeper; (avi.) fighter; rifleman; **–ei** *f.* profession of hunting; **–haus** *neu.*, **–hof** *m.* ranger's (*oder* gamekeeper's) house

jäh *adj.* abrupt, sudden; steep, precipitous; **–lings** *adv.* suddenly, abruptly; precipitously; **–zornig** *adj.* hottempered; quick to anger

Jahr *neu.* year; das ganze — hindurch all the year round; in den besten **–en** sein to be in the prime of life; in die **–e kommen** to grow old; schon bei **–en** sein to be advanced in years; übers — a year hence; vor — und Tag a full year ago; **–buch** *neu.* almanac, yearbook; **–esabschluss** *m.* annual balance sheet; **–esbericht** *m.* annual report; **–esrente** *f.* annuity; **–estag** *m.* anniversary; **–eszahl** *f.* year (*oder* date); **–eszeit** *f.* season; **–hundert** *neu.* century; **–markt** *m.* annual fair; **–tausend** *neu.* millenium; **–zehnt** *neu.* decade

jähr: –en *v.* sich — to have occurred a year ago; **–ig** *adj.* one year old; lasting

a year; occurring a year ago; **–lich** *adj.* annual

Jähzorn *m.* irascibility, violent temper

Jakob *m.* James, Jacob

Jalousie *f.* Venetian blind

Jamaikapfeffer *m.* allspice

Jammer *m.* distress, misery; lamentation, wailing; was für ein —! what a pity! **–bild** *neu.*, **–gestalt** *f.* pitiable figure; **–holz 'neu.** (coll.) guitar; out-of-tune piano; **–lappen** *m.* (coll.) weakling; crybaby; **–tal** *neu.* (bibl.) vale of tears

jammer: –n *v.* to lament, to moan, to wail; er **–t** mich I pity him; **–schade** *adv.* too bad! **–voll** *adj.* deplorable, lamentable, piteous

jämmerlich *adj.* miserable; pitiable, deplorable

Janhagel *m.* mob, rabble, riffraff

Januar *m.* January

Jaspis *m.* jasper

jäten *v.* to weed

jauchzen *v.* to exult, to jubilate

Jazzkapelle *f.* jazz band

je *adv.* each (time); at any time, ever; — drei und drei three at a time, three by three; — eher — lieber the sooner the better; — nachdem depending on circumstances; — und — always; from time to time; **–denfalls** *adv.* at any rate, by all means; **–der** *pron.* each, every, any; **–dermann** *pron.* everybody, everyone; **–derorts** *pron.* everywhere; **–derzeit** *adv.* at all times, always; **–desmal** *adv.* each (*oder* every) time; **–doch** *adv.* however, still, yet; **–her** *adv.* von **–her** at all times; **–mals** *adv.* at any time, ever; **–mand** *pron.* somebody; someone; irgend **–mand** anyone; **–ner** *pron.* that (one); the former; **–nseitig** *adj.* on the other side, opposite; **–nseits** *prep.* and *adj.* beyond, on the other side, across, yonder; **–weilig** *adj.* actual, respective; **–weils** *adv.* at times, at any given time

Je längerjelieber *m.* and *neu.* honeysuckle

Jenseits *neu.* the world beyond; the life to come; jemand ins — befördern to kill someone

Jesaias *m.* Isaiah

Jett *neu.* and *m.* jet, black amber

jetzig *adj.* present; existing, actual, current

jetzt *adv.* now, at present; gleich — at once; von — ab (*or* an) henceforth; from this time forward

Jetztzeit *f.* modern times; these days

Joch *m.* yoke; (mountain)ridge; crossbeam; land measure; **–bein** *neu.* cheek bone

Jockei *m.* jockey

Jod *neu.* iodine
jodeln *v.* to yodel
Johann *m.* John
Johannis: –beere *f.* currant; –brot *neu.* (bot.) carob; –käfer *m.* June bug; glowworm; –tag *m.* St. John's day; midsummer solstice; –trieb *m.* second bloom; late love; –würmchen *neu.* glowworm
Jongleur *m.* juggler
jonglieren *v.* to juggle
Joppe *f.* jacket, jerkin
Jot *neu.* letter j; –a *neu.* iota, jot, whit
Journal *neu.* journal, magazine; (comm.) daybook; –ismus *m.* journalism; –ist *m.* journalist
Jub: –el *m.* jubilation, exultation; –eljahr *neu.* year of jubilee; alle –eljahre einmal (coll.) once in a blue moon; –ilar *m.* person who celebrates a jubilee; –iläum *neu.* jubilee, anniversary
jubeln *v.* to jubilate, to exult, to rejoice
jubilieren *v.* to rejoice, to jubilate
Juchzer *m.* shout of joy
jucken *v.* to itch; to feel itchy; ihm juckt das Fell (coll.) he is itching for a fight; sich — to scratch oneself
Jude *m.* Jew; –nhetze *f.*, –nverfolgung *f.* Jew-baiting
Jugend *f.* youth; –freund *m.* friend of one's youth; school chum; –gericht *neu.* juvenile court; –herberge *f.* youth hostel; –liebe *f.* first love; –schriften *f. pl.* juvenile books; –werk *neu.* early work (of an artist)
jugendlich *adj.* youthful; juvenile
Juli *m.* July
jung *adj.* young, youthful; juvenile; immature; early, fresh; –en *v.* (zool.) to bring forth young; –enhaft *adj.* boyish; –fer(n)haft *adj.* maidenly; –fräulich *adj.* immaculate, virginal
Jung: –brunnen *m.* fountain of youth; –e *m.* boy, lad; apprentice; (cards) knave; –e *neu.* (zool.) young; –fer *f.* girl, virgin; maid; alte –fer spinster; –fernfahrt *f.* (naut.) maiden voyage; –fernkranz *m.* bridal wreath; –fernrede *f.* first public speech; –fernschaft *f.* maidenhood; virginity; –frau *f.* virgin; –geselle *m.* bachelor
Jüng: –er *m.* disciple, adherent; –erschaft *f.* discipleship; –ling *m.* youth, young man; –lingsalter *neu.* adolscence; –st(geboren)e *m.* youngest, last born; der –ste Tag doomsday; das –ste Gericht the last judgment
Juni *m.* June
Junker *m.* titled (*oder* Prussian) landowner

Jurist *m.* jurist; lawyer
juristisch *adj.* juridical, legal
Jus *neu.*, **Jura** *pl.* jurisprudence
Justiz *f.* administration of the law; –beamte *m.* officer of the law; –behörde *f.* legal authority; –minister *m.* minister of justice; Attorney General; –mord *m.* condemnation of an innocent person; judicial murder
Juwel *neu.* jewel; gem, precious stone; –en(arbeit) *f.* jewelry; –ier *m.* jeweler
Jux *m.* frolic; practical joke, lark

K

Kabale *f.* cabal, intrigue
Kabarett *neu.* cabaret; compartmented dish, Lazy Susan
Kabel *neu.* cable(gram); –jau *m.* codfish
kabeln *v.* to cable
Kabine *f.* cabin; (bathhouse) cubicle; –tt *neu.* cabinet; council (of governor); closet; –ttsfrage *f.* vital question
Kachel *f.* tile; –ofen *m.* Dutch tile stove
Kadenz *f.* cadence
Kadett *m.* cadet; –enanstalt *f.* military academy
Käfer *m.* beetle, chafer; (coll.) pretty girl
Kaff *neu.* chaff; rubbish; (sl.) poor village
Kaffee *m.* coffee; — *neu.* coffee shop; –brenner *m.* coffee roaster; –(e)rsatz *m.* coffee substitute; –grund *m.*, –satz *m.* coffee grounds; –klatsch *m.*, –kränzchen *neu.* ladies' gossip party; –maschine *f.* percolator; –mühle *f.* coffee grinder; –pause *f.* coffee break; –pflanzung *f.* coffee plantation; –schwester *f.* coffee lover, gossiper
Käfig *m.* cage
kahl *adj.* bare, bald; barren, bleak; — geschoren close-cropped; –köpfig *adj.* bald-headed
Kahm *m.* mould, scum
Kahn *m.* boat, skiff; barge; (sl.) slipper; bed
Kai *m.* quay, wharf
Kaiser *m.* emperor; –in *f.* empress; –reich *neu.* empire; –schnitt *m.* Caesarian operation
kaiserlich *adj.* imperial
Kajak *m.* kayak, Eskimo canoe
Kajüte *f.* (naut.) cabin; — erster Klasse stateroom; –njunge *m.* cabin-boy
Kakadu *m.* cockatoo
Kakao *m.* cocoa bean; cocoa
Kaktee *f.*, **Kaktus** *m.* cactus
Kalb *neu.* calf; fawn; –fleisch *neu.* veal; –sbraten *m.* roast veal; –skeule *f.* leg of veal; –skotelett *neu.* veal cutlet; –sschnitzel *neu.* veal steak

kalb: -en *v.* to calve; -ern *v.* (coll.) to frolic, to dally; -erig *adj.* silly

Kaldaunen *f. pl.* intestines, tripe

Kalender *m.* calendar, almanac

Kalfaktor *m.* (prison) trusty; toady

Kali(um) *neu.* (caustic) potash; potassium

Kaliber *neu.* caliber; capacity, level; kind

Kalif *m.* caliph

Kalk *m.* lime (chem.) calcium; **mit — bewerfen** to roughcast, to plaster; **mit — tünchen** to whitewash; **ungelöschter —** quicklime; -bewurf *m.* roughcast, plaster; -brennerei *f.* limekiln

kalk: -en *v.* to fertilize with lime; to plaster; to whitewash; -ig *adj.* chalky

Kalkulator *m.* computer

Kalligraphie *f.* calligraphy

kalt *adj.* cold; frigid; unemotional; — **machen** (coll.) to kill; — **stellen** to keep cold; (coll.) to shelve; -er **Schlag** harmless lightning flash; -blütig *adj.* cold-blooded; composed

Kälte *f.* cold(ness); indifference; frigidity

Kalzium *neu.* calcium

Kambüse *f.* caboose

Kamee *f.* cameo

Kamel *neu.* camel; (coll.) stupid person, -garn *neu.* mohair; -ie *f.* camellia

Kamera *f.* camera

Kamerad *m.* comrade; companion, chum; -schaft *f.* comradeship, camaraderie; fellowship

kameradschaftlich *adj.* companionable; — *adv.* friendly as comrades

Kamille *f.* camomile

Kamin *m.* chimney; fireplace, fireside; cleft; crevice; -sims *m.* mantlepiece

Kamm *m.* comb; crest, ridge; (meats) neck, shoulder; **alles über einen — scheren** (coll.) to treat everyone (*oder* everything) alike

Kammer *f.* chamber; small room; board; (heart) ventricle; -diener *m.* valet; -gericht *neu.* (provincial) court of appeal; -herr *m.* chamberlain; -jäger *m.* exterminator; gamekeeper of a sovereign; -jungfer *f.* woman-in-waiting; lady's maid; -musik *f.* chamber music; -ton *m.* (mus.) concert-pitch

Kampf *m.* combat; fight, battle; conflict, struggle; **— auf Leben und Tod** fight to the death; **— ums Dasein** struggle for existence; -bahn *f.* stadium; -flugzeug *neu.* fighter plane, bomber; -hahn *m.* game cock; squabbler. sorehead; -platz *m.* battlefield; -preis *m.* winning prize; -richter *m.* umpire; -spiel *neu.* tournament

kämpfen *v.* to fight; to battle; to struggle

Kampfer *m.* camphor

Kämpfer *m.* fighter; warrior; (arch.) abutment

kampieren *v.* to camp

Kanal *m.* canal; channel; conduit; sewer, drain; duct; **ich habe den — voll** (coll.) I am fed up; -isation *f.* canalization; sewer system

Kanapee *neu.* sofa; settee

Kanarienvogel *m.* canary

Kandelaber *m.* candelabrum; street lamp

Kandidat *m.* candidate; applicant; -enrede *f.* electioneering speech; -tur *f.* candidacy

kandidieren *v.* to run (*oder* stand) for office

Kandis(zucker) *m.* sugar candy

Känguruh *neu.* kangaroo

Kaninchen *neu.* rabbit; -bau *m.* rabbit burrow; -fell *neu.* rabbit skin

Kanker *m.* canker; venereal disease

Kanne *f.* can; pot; jug; tankard; -giesser *m.* pewterer; tavern polician; political babbler

Kannibale *m.* cannibal

Kanon *m.* canon; regulation. criterion; curriculum; (Holy Scriptures) authorized version; -e *f.* cannon; gun; piece of ordnance; (coll.) expert; -ier *m.* artilleryman, gunner

Kant: -e *f.* edge; margin, brim; border; selvage; **auf die hohe -e legen** (coll.) to save (money); -ine *f.* canteen, mess; -or *m.* choirmaster; cantor; church music director, organist; -schu *m.* short, thick leather whip; knout

Kanu *neu.* canoe

Kanz: -el *f* pulpit; (avi.) cockpit, turret; (educ.) chair; elevated hunting blind; -elrede *f.* sermon; -lei *f.* (government) office; office staff; -ler *m.* chancellor; -list *m.* (government) clerk

Kap *neu.* (geog.) cape

Kapaun *m.* capon

Kap der guten Hoffnung *neu.* Cape of Good Hope

Kapelle *f.* small church; chapel; band

Kapellmeister *m.* bandmaster; conductor

Kaper *m.* pirate's ship; — *f.* caper

Kapillar *neu.* capillary

Kapital *neu.* capital; principal; festgelegtes **—** invested capital; flüssiges **—** available funds, fluid capital; **— schlagen aus** to profit by; -anlage *f.* investment; -besitz *m.* cash property; -ismus *m.* capitalism; -ist *m.* capitalist; -verbrechen *neu.* capital crime

Kapitän *m.* captain; skipper

kapitulieren *v.* to capitulate

Kaplan *m.* chaplain

Kappe *f.* cap hood; cowl(ing); (shoe) tip;

etwas auf seine eigene — nehmen (coll.) to make oneself responsible for something

kappen v. to shorten; to trim, to top

Kapsel f. housing, case, capsule; (gun) cap

kaputt adj. broken, destroyed, unstrung

Kapuz: -e f. hood, cowl; -iner m. Capuchin monk; -inerkresse f. nasturtium

Karabiner m. carbine

Karaffe f. carafe, decanter

Karambolage f. collision; (billiards) carom

Karat m. carat; -gewicht neu. troy weight

Karawane f. caravan

Karbid neu. carbide

Karbolbarbitursäure f. phenobarbitol

Karbonade f. chop, cutlet

Karbunkel m. carbuncle, anthrax

Kardätsche f. carding (oder curry) comb

Kardinal m. cardinal; drink (of white wine)

Karfreitag m. Good Friday

Karfunkel m. carbuncle (gem)

karg adj. paltry; stingy; (soil) sterile; -en v. to be niggardly (oder stingy)

kärglich adj. paltry, scanty; poor

kariert adj. checkered

Karikatur f. caricature; cartoon

karikieren v. to caricature

Karl m. Charles, Carl

karmesin adj. crimson

Karmin m. and neu. carmine

Karnickel neu. rabbit; bunny; (sl.) scapegoat

Kärnten neu. Carinthia

Karo neu. square; check; (cards) diamonds

Karosse f. state coach; -rie f. (auto.) chassis, body

Karpfen m. carp

Karre f., **Karren** m. cart; (wheel)barrow; **an dem selben -n ziehen** (coll.) to be in the same boat

Karree neu. square

karren v. to cart

Karriere f. career; full gallop

Kartätsche f. case (oder canister, grape) shot; currycomb; (plastering) trowel

Kartäuser m. Carthusian monk; -likör m. chartreuse

Karte f. card; chart, map; ticket; bill of fare, menu; **die -n abheben** to cut the cards; **die -n geben** to deal the cards; **die -n legen** (or schlagen) (cards) to tell a (person's) fortune; **ein Spiel -n** a pack of cards; **jemand in die -n sehen** (cards) to look into somebody's hand; to discover someone's designs; -nbrief m. letter card; -ngeber m. (cards) dealer; -nkunststück neu. card trick;

-nschläger m. (cards) fortune teller; -nzeichnen neu. cartography; -i f. card index

Kartell neu. cartel; trust; pool

Karthago neu. Carthage

Kartoffel f. potato; (sl.) watch; -brei m. mashed potatoes; -stäbchen neu. pl. shoestring potatoes; -puffer m. potato pancake

Kartographie f. cartography

Karton m. cardboard; carton

Kartothek f. card index

Kartusche f. cartridge; (arch.) cartouche

Karussel neu. carousel, merry-go-round

Karwoche f. Holy Week (before Easter)

Karzer m. lockup; (coll.) prison

käs: -en v. to curd(le); -eweiss adj. chalk-white; -ig adj. cheesy; pale

Käse m. cheese; -blatt neu. (coll.) small newspaper, rag; -rei f. cheese factory

Kasematte f. casemate

Kaserne f. (mil.) barracks

Kasper(le) m. Punch; -theater neu. Punch-and-Judy show

das Kaspische Meer neu. Caspian Sea

Kass: -e f. cashbox; cash money; pay office; health insurance association; ticket (oder box) office; -enabschluss m. balancing (oder closing) of (cash) accounts; -enbestand m. cash balance; -enbote m. bank messenger; -enführer m. cashier; -enprüfer m., -enrevisor m. auditor; -enschrank m. safe; -enübersicht f. balance sheet; -ette f. (money) casket; cashbox; (arch.) coffer; caisson; (phot.) plateholder; -ierer m. cashier; teller

kassieren v. to take in money; (law) to annul, to invalidate; (mil.) to discharge

Kastagnette f. castanet

Kastanie f. chestnut

Kaste f. caste; class

kasteien v. to castigate, to mortify

Kastell neu. citadel; fortress

Kastrat m. eunuch

kastrieren v. to castrate

Katabolismus m. catabolism

Katakombe f. catacomb

Katalog m. catalog, list

katalogisieren v. to catalog

Katapultflugzeug n. catafighter

katastrophal adj. catastrophic

Kate f. cottage, hut

Kate: -chismus m. catechism; -gorie f. category

Kater m. tomcat; (coll.) hangover; -idee f. (coll.) crazy idea

Kathed: -er neu. (educ.) desk; -erblüte f. (educ.) malapropism, boner; -erweisheit f. academic wisdom; -rale f.

cathedral

Kathol: **–ik** *m.* Catholic; **–izismus** *m.* Catholicism

katholisch *adj.* Catholic

Kattun *m.* calico; cotton print

Katz: **–balgerei** *f.* (act of) scuffling, brawling; **–e** *f.* cat; feline; cat-o-nine-tails; money bag; **das ist für die –e** (coll.) that's futile; **die –e im Sack kaufen** to buy a pig in a poke; **–enauge** *neu.* cat's eye; (traffic) reflector light; **–enjammer** *m.* hangover; **–enkopf** *m.* box on the ear; round paving stone; **–enmusik** *f.* caterwauling; mock serenade; **–ensprung** *m.* (coll.) a stone's throw

Kätzchen *neu.* kitten; catkin

Kauderwelsch *neu.* gibberish; jargon

kauen *v.* to chew

kauern *v.* to cower, to crouch

Kauf *m.* purchase; **er ist leichten –s davon gekommen** he got off cheaply; **mit in — nehmen** to take into the bargain (*oder* the bad with the good); **–brief** *m.* bill-of-sale; **–haus** *neu.* commercial firm; department store; **–laden** *m.* shop, store; **–leute** *pl.* merchants, dealers; **–mann** *m.* shopkeeper, merchant

kauf: **–en** *v.* to buy, to purchase; to bribe; **–lustig** *adj.* keen to buy; **–männisch** *adj.* commercial, mercantile

Käufer *m.* buyer, purchaser; customer

käuflich *adj.* marketable; corruptible, venal; **—** *adv.* by purchase

Kaulquappe *f.* tadpole

kaum *adv.* barely, hardly, scarcely; just now

Kaution *f.* security; (law) bail

Kautschuk *m.* and *neu.* caoutchouc; rubber

Kauz *m.* small owl; (coll.) queer fellow

keck *adj.* bold, forward, direct; pert, saucy

Keg: **–el** *m.* cone; bowling pin, tenpin; **mit Kind und –el** with the whole family; with bag and baggage; **–elbahn** *f.* bowling alley; **–elkugel** *f.* bowling ball; **–ler** *m.* bowler

Kehle *f.* throat; gullet; fluting; gorge; (bastion) rear entrance; **aus voller —** loudly, heartily

Kehr: **–aus** *m.* last dance; **den –aus machen** to bring to a close; **–besen** *m.* broom; **–bürste** *f.* whisk broom; **–e** *f.* turn(ing), bend; **–er** *m.* sweeper; **–frau** *f.* charwoman; **–icht** *m.* sweepings; rubbish; **–reim** *m.* refrain; **–seite** *f.* reverse; (fig.) drawback; **–t** *neu.* (mil.) about-face; **–wisch** *m.* duster

kehr: **–en** *v.* to sweep; to turn around (*oder* over, back); **den Rücken –en to** cold-shoulder; **sich –en an to** mind; **–tmachen** *v.* to face about

keifen *v.* to scold; to bark; to yelp

Keil *m.* wedge; (arch.) keystone; (dress) gore, gusset; (mech.) key; (typ.) quoin; **–e** *f.* (coll.) thrashing; drubbing; **–er** *m.* mature wild boar; **–erei** *f.* scuffle, drubbing fight; **–schrift** *f.* cuneiform writing

Keim *m.* sprout, bud; germ; **im — ersticken** to nip in the bud; **–träger** *m.* (med.) carrier

keimen *v.* to germinate; to sprout, to bud

kein *adj.* no (one), none; **–er** *adj.* nobody; **–er von beiden** neither of the two; **–erlei** *adj.* not of any kind; not any; **–erseits** *adv.* on neither side; **–esfalls** *adv.* in no case, on no account; certainly not; **–eswegs** *adv.* by no means, not at all; **–mal** *adv.* not once

Keks *m.* cookie

Kelch *m.* goblet; calyx; chalice; cup

Kell: **–e** *f.* ladle; trowel; **–er** *m.* cellar; **–erei** *f.* wine cellar; **–ergeschoss** *neu.* basement; **–erladen** *m.* basement shop; **–ner** *m.* waiter; **–nerin** *f.* waitress

Kelter *m.* wine (*oder* fruit) press

keltern *v.* to press (grapes, fruits)

kenn: **–bar** *adj.* recognizable; **–en** *v.* to know, to be acquainted (with); **–en lernen** to become acquainted (with); to get to know; **–tlich** *adj.* distinguishable; conspicuous, marked; **–zeichnen** *v.* to characterize; to (ear)mark

Kenn: **–buchstabe** *m.* key letter; **–er** *m.* connoisseur, expert; adept; **–erblick** *m.* sure eye; **–ermiene** *f.* mien (*oder* attitude) of an expert; **–karte** *f.* identity card; **–tnis** *f.* knowledge, experience; acquirements; **etwas zur –tnis nehmen** to take note of something; **–ung** *f.* characteristic; (naut.) landmark; **–wort** *neu.* device, motto, password; **–zeichen** *neu.* characteristic; symptom

kentern *v.* (naut.) to capsize

Keramik *f.* ceramics; pottery

Kerb: **–e** *f.* notch; **in die gleiche –e hauen** (coll.) to pursue the same goal; **–tier** *neu.* insect

kerben *v.* to notch; (coin) to mill

Kerker *m.* (lit.) jail

Kerl *m.* fellow; chap

Kern *m.* core, nucleus; kernel, pit; (fig.) quintessence; **–frucht** *f.* stone fruit; **–gehäuse** *neu.* core; **–fleisch** *neu.* prime cut; **–holz** *neu.* heartwood; **–säure** *f.* (phy.) nucleic acid; **–schuss** *m.* bull's-eye shot; **–spaltung** *f.* nuclear fission;

–spruch *m.* pithy saying; –waffenkrieg *m.* nuclear war

kern: –en *v.* to granulate; to churn, to curdle; –gesund *adj.* thoroughly healthy; –ig *adj.* full of kernels (*oder* stones, pips); granular; substantial; strong; vigorous, pithy

Kerze *f.* candle; taper; –ngiesser *m.* candlemaker; –nhalter *m.* candleholder, candlestick; –nstärke *f.* (elec.) candle power

kerzengerade *adj.* as straight as an arrow

Kessel *m.* kettle; tank; boiler; caldron; valley; basin; –flicker *m.* tinker; –pauke *f.* kettledrum; –schmied *m.* coppersmith; boilermaker; –wagen *m.* tank truck

Kette *f.* chain; bracelet, necklace; row, series; (orn.) flock; –nbrücke *f.* suspension bridge; –nfaden *m.* warp thread; –nglied *neu.* chain link; –nhandel *m.* wholesaling; chain store; –nhund *m.* watchdog; –npanzer *m.* coat of mail; –nraucher *m.* chain smoker; –nstich *m.* chain stitch

ketten *v.* to (tie to a) chain

Ketzer *m.* heretic; –ei *f.* heresy; heterodoxy

ketzerisch *adj.* heretical; heterodox

keuchen *v.* to pant, to puff; to gasp

Keuchhusten *m.* whooping cough

Keule *f.* club; Indian club; pestle; (zool.) hind leg

keusch *adj.* chaste, pure; virginal, maidenly

kichern *v.* to snicker; to chuckle, to giggle

Kiebitz *m.* lapwing, peewit; (coll.) kibitzer

Kiefer *m.* jawbone; mandible; — *f.* pine

Kiel *m.* quill; keel; –holen *neu.* keelhauling; –raum *m.* ship's hold; –wasser *neu.* (naut.) wake

Kieme *f.* gill

Kies *m.* gravel; pyrite; –el *m.* pebble; flint; silica, silex; –grube *f.* gravel pit; –weg *m.* gravel path (*oder* walk)

Kimme *f.* notch; (gun) sight

Kind *neu.* child; offspring; an –es Statt annehmen to adopt; das — beim rechten Namen nennen to call a spade a spade; totgeborenes — stillborn child; von — auf from childhood on; –bett *neu.* childbed; –heit *f.* childhood, infancy; –taufe *f.* christening (of child); kind: –erleicht *adj.* extremely easy; –erlieb *adj.* fond of children; –isch *adj.* childish; silly, immature; –lich *adj.* childlike, naïve

Kinder *pl.* children, die –schuhe ausziehen to grow up, to mature; –art *f.*

children's way; –ei *f.* childish idea; trifle; –frau *f.*, –mädchen *neu.* nurse; governess; –gärtnerin *f.* kindergarten teacher; –jahre *neu. pl.* infancy; –lieder *neu. pl.* nursery songs; –literatur *f.* juvenile literature; –märchen *neu.* fairy tale; –mord *m.* infanticide; –spiel *neu.* child's play; trifling matter; –sprache *f.* prattle; –stube *f.* nursery; –wagen *m.* baby carriage; –zeit *f.* babyhood, childhood, infancy

Kindes: –alter *neu.* tender age; –kind *neu.* grandchild; –liebe *f.* filial affection; –not *f.*, –nöte *pl.* childbed labor; –räuber *m.* kidnapper

Kinkerlitzchen *neu. pl.* superfluous efforts; pointless overspending

Kinn *neu.* chin; –backen *m.*, –backe *f.*, –lade *f.* jaw

Kino *neu.* motion-picture theater

kippen *v.* to seesaw; to tip, to tilt; ein Glas — (coll.) to hoist one (drink)

Kirch: –dorf *neu.* village around a church; –e *f.* church; –gang *m.* churchgoing; –gänger *m.* churchgoer; –hof *m.* churchyard; cemetery; –sprengel *m.* diocese; –turm *m.* steeple, spire

Kirchen: –älteste *m.* church elder; –amt *neu.* church office; ecclesiastical function; –bann *m.* excommunication; –buch *neu.* parish register; –busse *f.* church penance; –chor *m.* church choir; –diener *m.* sexton, sacristan; –gesang *m.* congregational song (*oder* singing); –geschichte *f.* ecclesiastical history; –gesetz *neu.* canonical law; –jahr *neu.* ecclesiastical year; –lehre *f.* church doctrine; –musik *f.* sacred music; –patron *m.* patron saint of a church; –politik *f.* ecclesiastical politics; –raub *m.*, –schändung *f.* sacrilege; –sänger *m.* chorister; –steuer *f.* church tax; –streit *m.* ecclesiastical dissension; religious controversy; –stuhl *m.* pew; –vater *m.* Church Father; early Christian writer

kirchlich *adj.* ecclesiastic(al)

Kirmes *f.* annual parish fair

Kirsch: –branntwein *m.*, –geist *m.* cherry brandy; –e *f.* cherry; –rot *neu.* cerise; –wasser *neu.* cherry cordial

Kissen *neu.* cushion; pillow; –bezug *m.*, –überzug *m.* cushion cover; pillow case

Kiste *f.* box, chest, case; (sl.) auto; airplane

Kitsch *m.* trash; trumpery; gingerbread

Kitt *m.* cement; putty; lute; der ganze — the whole kit and caboodle

Kittel *m.* smock; frock

kitten *v.* to cement; to glue (together)

Kitz: –e *f.* fawn; kid; kitten; –el *m.*

tickling, titillation; pruriency; **–ler** *m.* tickler

kitzeln *v.* to tickle, to titillate

klaffen *v.* to gape, to yawn; to be ajar

kläffen *v.* to yap, to yelp; to scold, to carp

Klafter *m.* fathom; (wood) cord

klag: –bar *adj.* (law) actionable; **–elustig** *adj.*, **–süchtig** *adj.* litigious; **–en** *v.* to complain; to lament, to mourn, to wail; (law) to bring an action; to sue; **–los** *adj.* without complaint; **–los stellen** (law) to satisfy

Klage *f.* complaint; lamentation, moaning; lawsuit; **–lied** *neu.* dirge, elegy; **–punkt** *m.* (law) count of an indictment; **–schrift** *f.* (law) bill of complaints

Kläger *m.* plaintiff

kläglich *adj.* lamentable, pitiable, plaintive

Klamm *f.* ravine; gorge; **–er** *f.* clasp; clamp; paper clip; bracket, parenthesis

Klang *m.* sound, tone; **von gutem —** of good repute; **–boden** *m.* sounding board; **–farbe** *f.* timbre; **–lehre** *f.* acoustics

klangvoll, klangreich *adj.* sonorous

Klapp: *m.* slap, blow; **–bett** *neu.* folding bed; **–e** *f.* flap; lid; valve; (mus.) key, stop, damper; (sl.) mouth; **in die –e gehen** (*or* **steigen**) (coll.) to go to bed; **zwei Fliegen mit einer –e schlagen** to kill two birds with one stone; **–fenster** *neu.* trap (*oder* skylight) window; **–hornvers** *m.* limerick; **–messer** *neu.* jackknife; **–stuhl** *m.* folding chair; **–sitz** *m.* jump seat; **–tür** *f.* trapdoor

klappen *v.* to clap, to clack; **es klappt** this comes at the right moment; **zum –en kommen** to come to a head

Klaps *m.* slap, smack; **–smühle** *f.* (sl.)

klar *adj.* clear; bright; pure; (naut.) ready; shipshape; distinct; plain; obvious; **das ist — wie Klossbrühe** (coll.) that's obvious; **–legen, –machen, –stellen** *v.* to clear up, to explain

klären *v.* to purify; to clarify; to clear

Klarinette *f.* clarinet

Klasse *f.* class; rank; **das ist —** (coll.) that's tops; **–narbeit** *f.* (educ.) written exercise; **–neinteilung** *f.* classification; **–nzimmer** *neu.* classroom, schoolroom

klassifizieren *v.* to classify

Klassifizierung *f.* classification; taxonomy

Klassik *f.* classical period; **–er** *m.* (art) old master; classic

klassisch *adj.* classic(al); first-class

Klatsch *m.* slap, clap; (whip) crack; gossip; **–base** *f.*, **–maul** *neu.* gossiper, scandalmonger; chatterbox; **–e** *f.* fly swatter; gossiper; **–en** *neu.* applause;

gossiping; **–erei** *f.* gossip; **–mohn** *m.*, **–rose** *f.* (European) red field poppy

klatsch! *interj.* pop! smack! **–en** *v.* to clap, to slap; to gossip; **Beifall –en, in die Hände –en** to applaud; **–süchtig** *adj.* fond of gossip; **–nass** *adj.* soaking wet

klauben *v.* to pick out, to select, to sort; **Worte —** to split hairs

Klaue *f.* claw; fang, talon; hoof; (sl.) bad handwriting; **in den –n haben** (coll.) to have in one's grip

Klaus: –e *f.* hermitage; cell; **–ner** *m.* hermit, recluse; **–ur** *f.* secluded cloister room; written examination under supervision

Klausel *f.* clause, proviso, stipulation

Klavi: –atur *f.* (mus.) keyboard; **–er** *neu.* piano; **–erauszug** *m.* piano arrangement; **–erstimmer** *m.* piano tuner

Klebe: –bild *neu.* collage; **–mittel** *neu.*, **–stoff** *m.* adhesive; glue; **–pflaster** *neu.* adhesive tape; Band-Aid; **–r** *m.* billposter; gluten

kleben *v.* to glue, to gum, to paste; **jemandem eine —** (sl.) to box someone's ears; **–bleiben** to adhere to; to cling

kleckern, klecksen *v.* to blot(ch); to daub

Klee *m.* clover, trefoil; **über den grünen — loben** .(coll.) to praise to the skies; **–blatt** *neu.* cloverleaf; inseparable trio; **–blattkreuzung** *f.* (auto.) cloverleaf

Kleid *neu.* garment, dress, frock, gown, covering; **–er** *pl.* clothing; raiment; **–erablage** *f.* cloak room; **–erbügel** *m.* coat hanger; **–erbürste** *f.* clothes brush; **–erpuppe** *f.* clothes dummy; **–erschrank** *m.* closet, wardrobe; **–erstoff** *m.* dress material; **–ung** *f.* clothing, raiment; **–ungsstück** *neu.* garment; **–verleiher** *m.* costumer

kleiden *v.* to clothe, to dress; to become, to suit; **in Worte —** to express in words

Kleie *f.* bran

klein *adj.* little, small; young; minor; petty; humble; **ein — bisschen** (*or* **wenig**) a little bit; **gross und —** great and small; old and young; **im –en verkaufen** to retail; **–er Geist** narrow mind; **–es Geld** change; small coins; **–es Schläfchen** short nap; **kurz und — schlagen** to break into small pieces; **sich — machen** to humble oneself; **um ein –es** almost; **von — auf** from childhood; **–denkend** *adj.*, **–geistig** *adj.* narrow-minded; **–laut** *adj.* subdued, deflated; **–lich** *adj.* pedantic, fussy; **–mütig** *adj.* faint-hearted; **–städtisch** *adj.* provincial; small townlike

Klein *neu.* giblets; fragments; **–asien** *neu.* Asia Minor; **–bahn** *f.* narrow-gauge railroad; **–bauer** *m.* small farmer; **–betrieb** *m.* small business; **–bildkamera** *f.* miniature camera; **–bürger** *m.* prosaic person; philistine; **–funkgerät** *neu.* walkie-talkie; **–geld** *neu.* small coins, change; **–handel** *m.* retail business; **–holz** *neu.* wood kindling; **–igkeit** *f.* trifle; small matter; **–kind** *neu.* small child; **–kinderbewahranstalt** *f.* day nursery; **–kram** *m.* trifles; **–krieg** *m.* guerilla warfare; **–kunst** *f.* industrial arts; cabaret programs; **–mut** *m.* faintheartedness; **–stadt** *f.* small town; **–wagen** *m.* compact car; **–vieh** *neu.* rabbits, poultry

Kleinasien *neu.* Asia Minor

Kleinod *neu.* gem, jewel

Kleister *m.* paste

Klemme *f.* clamp; cramp; pinch; trouble; **in einer —** sein (*or* sitzen, stecken) to be in a fix; **–r** *m.* pince-nez

Klempner *m.* tinsmith; **–ei** *f.* tinsmith's shop

Klepper *m.* old nag, hack, jaded horse

Kleriker *m.* clergyman

Klerus *m.* clergy

Klette *f.* bur; burdock; **haften wie eine — to** stick like a bur; **–rpflanze** *f.* climber, creeper

klettern *v.* to climb; to ascend

Klient *m.* client; customer; **–el** *f.* clientele

Klima *neu.* climate; **–anlage** *f.* air-conditioning

klimatisch *adj.* climatic

Klimbim *m.* (coll.) painting the town red; fanfare; (medals) fruit salad; fuss and feathers

klimmen *v.* to climb

klimpern *v.* to jingle, to tinkle; (mus.) to strum

kling(e)ling! *interj.* ding-dong!

Klinge *f.* blade; (poet.) sword; **–nspender** *m.* blade dispenser

Klingel *f.* small bell; **–beutel** *m.* (church) ·collection bag

klingeln *v.* to pull the bell, to ring, to tinkle

klingen *v.* to sound; to clink, to tinkle; **–de Münze** hard cash

Klinik *f.* clinical hospital; clinical instructions

klinisch *adj.* clinical

Klinke *f.* latch; door handle; ratchet; switchboard plug

klinken *v.* to operate (latch); to shut (door)

Klinker *m.* clinker

klipp! *interj.* click! **— und klar** definitely and clearly; obvious; **–ig** *adj.* craggy, rocky

Klipp: –e *f.* cliff, crag; reef; **–er** *m.* (naut.) clipper; **–fisch** *m.* dried cod; **–klapp** *neu.* click-clack; flip-flap

klirren *v.* to clink, to clash, to clatter

Klischee *neu.* cliché, stereotype plate

Kloake *f.* cesspool, sewer; (zool.) cloaca

Kloben *m.* split cordwood; log; block, pulley

klobig *adj.* weighty, massive; rude, clumsy

klopfen *v.* to knock, to rap; to beat; **auf den Busch —** (coll.) to sound out; **jemandem auf die Finger —** (coll.) to reprimand someone

Klopfer *m.* beater, knocker

Klöppel *m.* club, cudgel; bobbin; drumstick; (bell) clapper

klöppeln *v.* to make (bobbin) lace

Klops *m.* meat ball

Klosett *neu.* toilet; **–papier** *neu.* toilet paper

Kloss *m.* clod, lump; dumpling

Kloster *neu.* cloister; monastery, convent; **–bruder** *m.* monk, friar; **–frau** *f.*, **–fräulein** *neu.* nun; **–wesen** *neu.* monasticism

klösterlich *adj.* conventual; monastic

Klotz *m.* block; clog; (coll.) lout

klotzig *adj.* coarse, clumsy; (sl.) enormous

Klub *m.* club; **–kamerad** *m.* clubmate, fellow member; **–sessel** *m.* lounge (*oder* club) chair

Kluft *f.* abyss, chasm; gorge, defile, ravine; (sl.) clothes; uniform

klug *adj.* intelligent; judicious; prudent; shrewd, clever; **durch Schaden — werden** to learn by experience; **ich kann nicht — daraus werden** I can't make head or tail of it

Klügelei *f.* sophistry; subtilization

klügeln *v.* to affect wisdom; to criticize

klüglich *adv.* judiciously, prudently, wisely

Klumpen *m.* clump, lump; clod; clot; nugget

klumpen *v.* to conglomerate; to clot, to lump

Klumpfuss *m.* clubfoot

klumpig *adj.* lumpy, clotted, agglomerated

Klüngel *m.* clique; **der ganze —** the whole crew

knabbern *v.* to gnaw, to nibble

Knabe *m.* boy, lad; **–nalter** *neu.* boyhood

knack: –s! *interj.* crack! snap! **–en, –sen** *v.* to crack, to snap, to break, to click; **eine harte Nuss zu –en haben** to have a tough job

Knäckebrot *neu.* rye wafer

Knall *m.* bang; (coll.) insanity; **— und**

Fall suddenly; unexpectedly; –bonbon *m.* cracker bonbon; –büchse *f.* popgun; –erbse *f.* pea-shaped firecracker

knallen *v.* to detonate, to crack; to bang

knallig *adj.* glaring (colors); crazy; goofy

knapp *adj.* tight, narrow; scarce; concise; scanty; limited; –e Mehrheit bare ma;ority; — halten to keep a tight rein; — werden to run short; mit –er Not with great difficulty; by the skin of one's teeth

knarr! *interj.* creak! –en to creak, to groan

Knaster *m.* (coll.) inferior tobacco; grumbler

knattern *v.* to rattle; to crackle

Knäuel *m.* and *neu.* (yarn) ball; entanglement, mixup; cluster; crowd

Knauf *m.* knob; (arch.) capital; pommel

Knauser *m.* niggard, miser; –ei *f.* stinginess

knaus(e)rig *adj.* niggardly, stingy; miserly

knausern *v.* to be stingy (*oder* a miser)

knautschen *v.* to crumple

knautschig *adj.* creased, crumpled

Knebel *m.* gag; toggle; short stick; –bart *m.* twisted moustache; imperial

knebeln *v.* to gag; to muzzle, to suppress

Knecht *m.* farmhand; servant; (lit.) slave; jack; — Ruprecht Santa Claus; –schaft *f.* slavery; bondage, servitude; –ssinn *m.* servile spirit

knechten *v.* to keep in servitude; to enslave

kneifen *v.* to pinch; to flinch; to shirk

Kneifer *m.* pince-nez; coward, flincher

Kneifzange *f.* tweezers; flat-nosed pliers

Kneipe *f.* (coll.) tavern, inn; –rei *f.* drinking bout, carousal

kneipen *v.* to pinch, to tipple, to carouse

kneten *v.* to knead

Knick *m.* flaw, crack; bend; hedge; –er *m.* miser, niggard; folding knife; –beine *neu. pl.* knock-kneed legs; –s *m.* curtsy

knick: –en *v.* to break, to crack, to bend; to dispirit; –(e)rig *adj.* stingy; –ern *v.* to be stingy; to crackle; –sen *v.* to curtsy

Knie *neu.* knee, bend; (mech.) elbow, joint; –band *neu.* garter; knee ligament; –fall *m.* going down on one's knees; –geige *f.* bass viol; –gelenk *neu.* knee joint; –riemen *m.* shoemaker's strap; Meister –riem *m.* (coll.) shoemaker; –rohr *neu.* elbow pipe; –scheibe *f.* knee cap; –schützer *m.* kneepad

Kniff *m.* pinch; crease, fold; dodge, knack, trick

knipsen *v.* to punch; to clip; to snip; to snap

Knirps *m.* little fellow; dwarf; (coll.) shrimp

knirschen *v.* to crunch, to gnash, to grate

knistern *v.* to crackle, to rustle; to crepitate

knittern *v.* to crackle; to ruffle; to crumple

Knoblauch *m.* garlic; –zehe *f.* garlic clove

Knöchel *m.* knuckle; ankle; (sl.) dice

Knochen *m.* bone; (sl.) house key; bis auf die — right to the core; –bau *m.* bony frame (*oder* structure); –bruch *m.* bone fracture; –frass *m.* caries; –gerüst *neu.* skeleton; –gewebe *neu.* bone tissue; –haus *neu.* charnel house; –lehre *f.* osteology; –mann *m.* (poet.) Death; –mehl *neu.* bone meal; –splitter *m.* bone splinter

knöchern *adj.* of bone, bony, osseous

Knödel *m.* dumpling

Knolle *f.*, **Knollen** *m.* bulb, tuber; clod; lump

Knopf *m.* button; stud; knob; boss; pommel; head; der — geht ihm auf (coll.) he finally gets the idea

knöpfen *v.* to button; to finger buttons

Knorpel *m.* cartilage; gristle

knorpelig *adj.* gristly; cartilaginous

knorrig *adj.* gnarled, knobby, knotty

Knospe *f.* bud; tender young person

knospen *v.* to bud, to sprout; to blossom

Knötchen *neu.* small knot; nodule, tubercle

Knoten *m.* knot; difficulty; plot; (fig.) ganglion; hier hat es einen — there's a hitch in it; –punkt *m.* junction; –stock *m.* knotty stick

knoten *v.* to knot

knotig *adj.* knobby; lumpy; crude, vulgar

Knuff *m.* ;uff, thump, push

knüllen *v.* to crumple, to crush

knüpfen *v.* to tie, to knot; ein Bündnis — to form an alliance

Knüppel *m.* club, cudgel; log; (bakery) small roll; mallet; (avi.) stick; der — liegt beim Hunde there is no choice

knüppeldick *adj.* very thick (*oder* much); er hat es — hinter den Ohren he's a very sly fellow

knurren *v.* to growl, to snarl; to grumble; (stomach) to rumble

knusp(e)rig *adj.* crisp

knuspern *v.* to crunch; to nibble

Knute *f.* knout

knutschen *v.* to crush; to cuddle

Knüttel *m.* club, cudgel; –vers *m.* doggerel

koalisieren *v.* to form a coalition

Kobold *m.* sprite, (hob)goblin, imp

Koch *m.* cook; –er *m.* cooker; cooking apparatus; –erei *f.* inferior cooking; –geschirr *neu.* pots and pans; soldiers' (*oder* campers') mess kit; **–herd** *m.* kitchen range; **–kunst** *f.* culinary art; **–löffel** *m.* ladle

kochen *v.* to cook; to boil; to stew; to scald; to seethe, to be exited; **überall wird mit Wasser gekocht** people are the same everywhere

Köcher *m.* quiver

Köchin *f.* cook

Kode *m.* code, cipher; **–x** *m.* (law) code

ködern *v.* to bait, to decoy, to lure

Koffer *m.* bag, box, suitcase, trunk; **–träger** *m.* porter, redcap; **–grammofon** *neu.* portable phonograph

Kognak *m.* cognac, brandy

Kohl *m.* cabbage; cole, kale; **aufgewärmter** — an old story; **–kopf** *m.* head of cabbage; **–rabi** *m.* kohlrabi; **–rübe** *f.*, rutabaga; **–weissling** *m.* cabbage butterfly

Kohle *f.* coal; charcoal; (elec.) carbon; **auf glühenden** — **nsitzen** to sit on pins and needles; **–narbeiter** *m.* coal miner; collier; **–nbecken** *neu.* coal field; brazier; **–nbergwerk** *neu.* coal mine; **–nblende** *f.* anthracite; **–neimer** *m.* coal scuttle; **–nflöz** *neu.* coal seam; **–ngrube** *f.* coal mine; **–nkasten** *m.* coal box; **–nkeller** *m.* coal cellar; **–nlager** *neu.* coal deposit (*oder* seam); **–nschiff** *neu.* collier; **–nstoff** *m.* carbon; **–nzeichnung** *f.* charcoal drawing

Köhler *m.* charcoal burner; coalfish; **–glaube** (**n**) *m.* blind faith, superstition

Koje *f.* (naut.) cabin, berth

Koka *f.* coca; **–in** *neu.* cocaine

kokett *adj.* coquettish; **–ieren** *v.* to flirt

Kokon *m.* cocoon

Kokos: –baum *m.*, **–palme** *f.* coconut tree; **–nuss** *f.* coconut; **–öl** *neu.* coconut oil

Koks *m.* coke; (sl.) cocaine; money

Kolben *m.* club, mace; (rifle) butt; flask; (chem.) still; soldering iron; piston; plunger; (bot.) spike, spadix

Kolibri *m.* hummingbird

Kolik *f.* colic, gripes

kollaborieren *v.* to collaborate

Kollage *f.* collage

Kolleg *neu.* (university) lecture, course; **–e** *m.* colleague; **–ialität** *f.* fellowship; **–iengelder** *neu. pl.* students' fees; **–ium** *neu.* faculty, staff, board

kollegial *adj.* harmonious; collegiate

Kollekt: –e *f.* collect(ion); **–eur** *m.* collector; **–ion** *f.* collection; **–iv** *neu.* group, association

kollektiv *adj.* collective; united

Koller *m.* choler, frenzy, rage; (horses) blind staggers; leather jerkin

kollern *v.* to roll; to rumble; to gobble

kollidieren *v.* to collide

Kollisionskurs (Rakete) *m.* collision course

Kolloquium *neu.* scientific conference

Köln *neu.* Cologne

Koloni: –alwaren *f. pl.* groceries; colonial produce; **–e** *f.* colony; **–st** *m.* settler

kolonisieren *v.* to colonize

Kolonne *f.* (mil.) column; formation

Kolor: –atur *f.* coloratura; **–ierung** *f.* coloring; **–it** *neu.* coloring

kolorieren *v.* to color

Koloss *m.* colossus

Kolportage *f.* colportage; cheap, sensational publication

kolportieren *v.* to hawk; to circulate rumors

Kolumne *f.* pillar; column

kombinieren *v.* to combine

Kombüse *f.* caboose, ship's galley

Komik *f.* funniness, comic deportment; drollery; **–er** *m.* comedian; comic actor

komisch *adj.* comical, funny, strange

Komma *neu.* comma; (math.) decimal point

Kommand: –ant *m.*, **–eur** *m.* commandant, commander; **–antur** *f.* commander's office; garrison headquarters; **–itgesellschaft** *f.* company with limited liability (*oder* membership); **–o** *neu.* command; detachment; **–obrücke** *f.* (pilot) bridge; **–ostab** *m.* commanders' baton; **–oturm** *m.* control tower

kommandieren *v.* to command

kommen *v.* to come; to approach, to arise, to result (from); to arrive; to occur; to cost; **an die Reihe** — to have one's turn; **aneinander** — to come to blows; **auf etwas** — to hit upon; to remember; **hinter etwas** — to detect something; **in Verlegenheit** — to get into trouble; — **lassen** to send for; — **seh(e)n** to foresee; **nach Hause** — to get home; **nicht dazu** — to have no time; **um etwas** — to lose (*oder* come for) something; **wie** — **Sie dazu?** How do you get it? How dare you? **zu etwas** — to acquire something; **zu kurz** — to lose out; **zu sich** — to recover

Komment *m.* students' club code; **–ar** *m.* commentary; annotation; **–ator** *m.* annotator

kommentieren *v.* to annotate

kommissarisch *adj.* provisional

Kommode *f.* chest (of drawers)

Kommun: –albeamte *m.* municipal official; **–alschule** *f.* council school; **–alsteuer** *f.* local tax; **–e** *f.* community; (coll.) Communist Party; **–ikant** *m.* (rel.) communicant; **–ion** *f.* (rel.) Holy Communion; **–ismus** *m.* communism

kommun: -al *adj.* communal; municipal; -istisch *adj.* communistic; -izieren *v.* to communicate

Komödi: -ant *m.* comedian, actor; -antentum *neu.* bohemianism; -e *f.* comedy; pretense; -enhaus *neu.* playhouse; theater (for comedies)

Kompa(g)nie *f.* company; firm

Kompagnon *m.* (com.) partner; collaborator

Kompass *m.* compass; -häuschen *neu.* binnacle; -peilung *f.* compass bearing

Komplementärfarbe *f.* complementary color

komplett *adj.* complete; -ieren *v.* to complete

Kompliment *neu.* compliment; bow

Komplize *m.* accomplice

komplizieren *v.* to complicate

kompliziert *adj.* complicated; -er Bruch compound fracture

Komplott *neu.* plot, conspiracy

komponieren *v.* to compose; to set to music

Komponist *m.* (mus.) composer; arranger

Kompott *neu.* compote; stewed fruit

Kompresse *f.* (med.) compress

komprimieren *v.* to compress; to condense

Kompromiss *m.* compromise

kompromittieren *v.* to compromise; to expose

Komtesse *f.* countess

Kondensator *m.* condenser

kondensieren *v.* to condense

Kondensstreifen *m.* (avi.) contrail

Konditor *m.* confectioner; -ei *f.* confectionery; -ware *f.* confectionery; pastries, sweets

kondolieren *v.* to condole (with)

Kondukt *m.* (funeral) procession; -eur *m.* (traffic) conductor; -or *m.* (phys.) conductor

Konfekt *neu.* confectionery, sweets; -ion *f.* ready-made clothing; -ionär *m.* outfitter

Konferenz *f.* conference; meeting; convention

konferieren *v.* to confer; to act as announcer

Konfession *f.* confession; creed; -sschule *f.* denominational school

konfessionell *adj.* denominational

konfessionslos *adj.* nondenominational

Konfirmand *m.* (rel.) person being confirmed; -enunterricht *m.* confirmation classes

konfirmieren *v.* to confirm

konfiszieren *v.* to confiscate

Konfitüre *f.* confectionery; candied fruit; preserves; marmalade

Konflikt *m.* conflict

konform *adj.* conformable; exact; -gehen to agree

konfrontieren *v.* to face; to confront

konfus *adj.* confused, muddled

König *m.* king; -in *f.* queen; -reich *neu.* kingdom; realm; -smord *m.* regicide; -stiger *m.* Bengal tiger; -streue *m.* royalist; -tum *neu.* kingship, royalty

königlich *adj.* royal; wonderful, grand, regal

konisch *adj.* conic(al)

Konjunktiv *m.* subjunctive (mood)

Konjunktur *f.* high level of business; bear market; -politiker *m.* (pol.) coattail rider

konkav *adj.* concave

konkret *adj.* concrete; real; palpable

Konkubinat *neu.* concubinage

Konkurrent *m.* competitor

Konkurrenz *f.* competition

konkurrieren *v.* to compete

Konkurs *m.* bankruptcy; failure; -erklärung *f.* declaration of insolvency; -masse *f.* bankrupt's estate; -verfahren *neu.* proceedings in bankruptcy; -verwalter *m.* trustee in bankruptcy

können *v.* to be able; to know; to be possible; to be permitted to; es kann sein it may be; nicht mehr — to be exhausted; sie — nichts dafür it wasn't their fault

Könner *m.* expert, adept

Konrad *m.* Conrad

Konsens *m.* consent, agreement

konsequent *adj.* consistent; persistent

Konsequenz *f.* consistency; consequence

Konserv: -atorium *neu.* academy of music, conservatory; -e *f.* preserve; canned food; -enbüchse *f.* tin can; -enfabrik *f.* cannery

konservieren *v.* to conserve; to preserve, to can

Konsistorium *neu.* (rel.) consistory

konsolidieren *v.* to consolidate; to make safe

Konsorte *m.* accomplice; associate member

Konsortium *neu.* syndicate

Konspiration *f.* conspiracy

konstatieren *v.* to give evidence

konstituieren *v.* to constitute; sich — als to resolve itself into

konstitutionell *adj.* constitutional; consistent with the constitution

konstruieren *v.* to construct, to design, to plan; to construe; (phil.) to establish

Konsul *m.* consul; -at *neu.* consulate; -tation *f.* consultation; counseling

konsularisch *adj.* consular

konsultieren v. to counsel; to consult
Konsum m. consumption; **-ent** m. consumer; **-verein** m. co-operative society
konsumieren v. to consume
Konter: -admiral m. Rear Admiral; **-bande** f. contraband; smuggling, smuggled goods; **-fei** neu. portrait, likeness; **-tanz** m. square dance
kontinuierlich adj. continuous, connected
Kontinuität f. continuity, connection
Konto neu. account; **-korrent** neu. current account; **-r** neu. office; **-rist** m. office clerk
Kontra neu. (car's) double; **-alt** m. contralto; **-altistin** f. contralto singer; **-bass** m. contrabass; **-hent** m. contracting party, contractor; opponent; **-punkt** m. counterpoint
kontrakt: -brüchig adj. contract-breaking; **-lich** adj. fixed, stipulated; **-pflichtig** adj. bound by contract
Kontrakt m. contract, agreement; **-bruch** m. breach of contract
kontrollieren v. to control; to check; to audit; to keep time
Kontroll-(oder Warn-)**station** f. (radio oder Radar) beacon; **-stelle** (avi. & mil.) check point
Kontur f. contour (line)
Konvent m. assembly (of clergy, student bodies, French Revolution); (eccl.) conventicle; **-ion** f. custom, tradition; convention, agreement; **-ionalstrafe** f. penalty for breach of contract
konventionell adj. conventional
Konversation f. conversation; **-slexikon** neu. encyclopedia; **-sstück** neu. society comedy
Konvertit m. convert
konzentrieren v. to concentrate, to saturate
konzentrisch adj. concentric
Konzert neu. (mus.) concert(o)
konzertieren v. to give a concert
Konzession f. concession, license, patent
Konzil neu. (eccl.) council
Köper m. twill
Kopf m. head; knob, button; top; brains; **alles auf den — stellen** to turn everything upside down; **auf seinen — bestehen, seinen — aufsetzen** to be stubborn; **aus dem -e wissen** to know by heart; **durch den — gehen (lassen)** to (let) revolve in one's mind; **er handelt nur nach seinem —** he follows no one's advice but his own; **es ist ganz nach meinem —** it's quite to my liking; **im — behalten** to remember; **im — rechnen** to compute mentally, **— an — closely packed; mit einem dicken**

— dasitzen to be overwhelmed with worries; **nicht auf den — gefallen sein** to be no fool; **nicht von seinem — abgehen, seinen — durchsetzen** to stick to one's guns; **sich den — zerbrechen** to rack one's brains; **sich etwas in den — gesetzt haben** to be obstinate; **über den — wachsen** to outgrow; **vor den — stossen** to offend; **-arbeit** f. brain (oder mental) work; **-bahnhof** m. terminal railroad station; **-ende** neu. head; **-hängerei** f. dejection; **-haut** f. scalp; **-hörer** m. headphone; **-kissen** neu. pillow; **-kissenbezug** m. pillow case; **-nicken** neu. nod; **-nuss** f. head blow; box on the ear; **-putz** m. coiffure; **-rechnen** neu. mental arithmetic; **-salat** m. head lettuce; **-schmerz** m., **-weh** neu. headache; **-sprung** m. (swiming) header; **-steuer** f. poll tax; **-stimme** f. falsetto; **-stück** neu. headpiece; (coll.) box on the ear; **-tuch** neu. head-cloth, kerchief; **-waschen** neu. shampoo; **-zerbrechen** neu. brain cudgeling
kopf: -hängerisch adj. moping; **-los** adj. headless; disconcerted, **-über** adv. head foremost, head over heels; **-unter** adv. headlong
köpfen v. to behead; to lop, to top
Kopie f. copy, facsimile; duplicate; proof sheet; reproduction; imitation; (contact) print
kopieren v. to copy; to make a contact print
Koppel f. coupling; group of dogs, train of horses; paddock, enclosure; **— neu.** sword (oder shoulder) belt
koppeln v. to couple, to link
kopulieren v. to copulate; to marry
Koralle f. coral; amber bead
Korb m. basket, hamper; creel, pannier, hive; gondola (of balloon); (coll.) refusal; **Hahn im — sein** to be cock of the walk; **-geflecht** neu. wickerwork
Kord m. corduroy; **-el** f. cord, string, twine
Korinthe f. currant
Kork m. cork; stopper; **-enzieher** m. corkscrew
korken adj. of cork; **— v.** to cork
Korn neu. grain; cereal, (Germany) rye; small particle; (coins) fine weight; (gun) sight; **auf's — nehmen** to aim at, to keep a sharp eye upon; **von altem** (or **echtem**) **Schrot und — of the good old sort; -ähre** f. spike of grain; **-boden** m., **-speicher** m. granary; silo; **-börse** f. grain exchange; **-branntwein** m. whisky; **-kammer** f. granary; bread-

basket
Kornett *neu.* (mus.) cornet; — *m.* (mil.) cornet, mounted standard bearer
Korona *f.* corona; (sl.) circle of listeners, participants
Körper *m.* bo·ly; bulk; substance; **–bau** *m.* body structure, build; **–bemalung** *f.* tattooing; **–beschaffenheit** *f.* constitution, physique; **–fehler** *m.* bodily defect, deformity; **–fülle** *f.* corpulence; **grösse** *f.*, **–wuchs** *m.* stature; **–haltung** *f.* bearing, attitude; carriage; **–inhalt** *m.* solid contents; **–kraft** *f.* physical strength; **–mass** *neu.* cubic measure; **–pflege** *f.* physical culture; **–schaft** *m.* corporation; group, association
körperlich *adj.* bodily; somatic; material
körperschaftlich, korporativ *adj.* corporate, collective
Korps *neu.* corps; (coll.) group
korpulent *adj.* corpulent, obese
Korpulenz *f.* corpulence, obesity
Korrekt: –or *m.* proofreader; **–ur** *f.* correction; proofreading; **–urabzug** *m.*, **–urbogen** *m.*, **–urfahne** *f.* printer's proof; galley proof
Korrespondenz *f.* correspondence; **–büro** *neu.* newsroom
korrigieren *v.* to correct; to proofread; to amend
Korsar *m.* corsair, freebooter; pirate ship
Korsett *neu.* corset; **–stange** *f.* corset stay
kosen *v.* to caress, to fondle; to hug
Kosename *m.* pet name
Kosmetik *f.* cosmetics; cosmetic care
kosmisch *adj.* cosmic
Kosmologie *f.* cosmology
Kosmonaut *m.* cosmonaut
Kost *f.* food; board, diet; **–gänger** *m.* boarder; **–geld** *neu.* board allowance; (law) alimony; **–probe** *f.* sample, relish; **–verächter** *m.* dainty (*oder* fastidious) person; scorner
kost: –bar *adj.* precious; costly; **–en** *v.* to cost; to take; to require; to taste; to experience the effect (of); **–enfrei** *adj.*, with free board; **–spielig** *adj.* expensive, costly
Kosten *pl.* costs, expenses; charges; **auf seine — kommen** not to regret expenditures; **–anschlag** *m.* estimate of costs; **–aufwand** *m.* expenditure; **–punkt** *m.* problem of expense
köstlich *adj.* fine, precious; delicious
Kostüm *neu.* costume; dress, clothes; jacket and skirt; **–fest** *neu.* fancy dress ball; **–probe** *f.* dress rehearsal
Kot *m.* dirt, filth; mud; excrement; **–au** *m.* kowtow; **–blech** *neu.*, **–flügel** *m.*

mudguard; fender
Kotelett *neu.* cutlet, chop
Köter *m.* cur; watchdog
Krabbe *f.* crab, shrimp; (coll.) lively girl
krabbeln *v.* to grovel, to crawl
krach! *interj.* crash! **–en** *v.* to crack; to crash
Krach *m.* crash; collapse; quarrel, scene
krächzen *v.* to caw, to croak
Kraft *f.* strength, power, force; vigor; validity; hand, laborer, worker; **ausser — setzen** to annul, to abrogate; **–anstrengung** *f.*, **–aufwand** *m.* effort; **–ausdruck** *m.* strong expression; **–äusserung** *f.* manifestation of force; **–brühe** *f.* strong broth; **–droschke** *f.* taxi; **–fahrer** *m.* motorist; **–fahrzeug** *neu.* motor vehicle; **–probe** *f.* trial of strength; **–rad** *neu.* motorcycle; **–stoff** *m.* fuel, gasoline; **–verstärker** *m.* servomotor; **–wagen** *m.* automobile; **–werk** *neu.* power plant (*oder* station)
kraft *prep.* by virtue of, on the basis of
kräftig *adj.* strong, vigorous; robust; nourishing; **–en** *v.* to strengthen, to invigorate
Kragen *m.* collar; neck; (zool.) ruff; **beim — nehmen** to collar; **es geht ihm an den —** it will cost him his neck; **–knopf** *m.* collar stud
Krähe *f.* crow, rook; **–nfüsse** *m. pl.* crow's feet, wrinkles (around eye); bad handwriting, hen tracks
krähen *v.* to crow
Krakeel *m.* brawl, aquabble, row, wrangle
Kralle *f.* claw, talon, clutch
krallen *v.* to claw, to scratch
Kram *m.* odds and ends; rubbish; (coll.) business; **–laden** *m.* hole-in-the-wall shop
kramen *v.* to rummage; to stir, to move
Krämer *m.* small shopkeeper; petty person
Krampf *m.* cramp, spasm; convulsion; fit; **–ader** *f.* varicose vein
krampf: –artig *adj.*, **–haft** *adj.* convulsive, spasmodic; **–en** *v.* to contract, to convulse, to clench; **–stillend** *adj.* antispasmodic
Kran *m.* (mech.) crane; hoist
Krangerüstturm *m.* gantry tower
Kranich *m.* (orn.) crane
krank *adj.* ill; sick; suffering; (hunting) wounded; **— am Beutel sein to be** short of money; **sich — stellen** to feign illness; **–en** *v.* to be ailing; to suffer from; **–haft** *adj.* morbid; pathological; **–heitshalber** *adv.* owing to illness
Krank: –e *m.* sick person, patient; **–heit** *f.* illness, disease; (zool.) distemper;

–heitserreger *m.* disease germ; –heits-erscheinung *f.* symptom; –heitslehre *f.* pathology; –heitsübertragung *f.* infection; –heitsurlaub *m.* sick-leave

kränk: –eln *v.* to be in poor health; –en *v.* to offend; to anger; to grieve; –lich *adj.* sickly, susceptible to illness

Kranken: –anstalt *f.*, –haus *neu.* hospital; –bericht *m.* doctor's report, bulletin; –bett *neu.*, –lager *neu.* sick-bed; –dienst *m.* care of the sick; –kasse *f.* hospitalization insurance, sick benefit fund; –kost *f.* diet; –pflege *f.* nursing; –saal *m.* hospital ward; (naut.) sick bay; –schwester *f.*, –wärterin *f.* nurse; –stube *f.* sickroom; –tragbahre *f.* stretcher; –träger *m.* stretcher bearer; –wagen *m.* ambulance; –wärter *m.* male nurse; –zimmer *neu.* sickroom

Kränkung *f.* offense; vexation, insult

Kranz *m.* garland, wreath; (arch.) cornice; –jungfer *f.* bridesmaid

Kränzchen *neu.* small wreath; kaffee-klatsch

kränzen *v.* to crown (with garlands)

Krapfen *m.* doughnut, fritter

Krater *m.* crater

Kratz: –e *f.* scraper; carding comb; –bürste *f.* wire (*oder* hard) brush; intractable person; –eisen *neu.* scraping iron; –er *m.* scraper; scratch

kratzbürstig *adj.* cross, quick-tempered

Krätze *f.* itch; –r *m.* sour wine

kratzen *v.* to scratch; to scrape; to grate

krätzig *adj.* itchy, mangy, full of scabs

kraus *adj.* curly, frizzled; dishevelled; queer; die Stirne — ziehen to knit one's brow; –haarig *adj.* curly-haired

Krause *f.* frill, ruff

kräuseln *v.* to curl, to frizzle, to ripple

Kraut *neu.* herb, plant; herbage; cabbage; weed; ins — schiessen to grow rankly

Kräuter *neu. pl.* herbs; –käse *m.* green cheese; –kunde *f.* botany

Krawall *m.* uproar, row, free-for-all fight

Krawatte *f.* cravat, necktie

Kreatur *f.* creature; favorite, minion

Krebs *m.* crayfish; crab; (ast.) Cancer; (med.) cancer; –erregende Substanz carcinogen; –erreger *m.* carcinogen; –gang *m.* crabwise movement; retrogression; –geschwür *neu.* (med.) carcinoma

Kredenz *f.* sideboard, buffet

Kredit *m.* credit; –iv *neu.* power of attorney; credentials; –or *m.* creditor

kreditfähig *adj.* (com.) solvent, sound

Kreide *f.* chalk, crayon; in die — geraten to go into debt; tief in der — stehen to be deeply (*oder* heavily) in debt

Kreis *m.* circle; orbit; district; province, sphere, ring; (biol.) phylum; –bahn *f.* orbit; –bogen *m.* arc; –elachse *m.* gyroscope; –lauf *m.* circulation, rotation; –säge *f.* circular saw; –umfang *m.*, –linie *f.* circumference, periphery

kreischen *v.* to scream, to shriek, to screech; –de Stimme shrill voice

kreisen *v.* to circulate, to circle; to revolve

Krempe *f.* (hat) brim

Krempel *m.* rubbish; — *f.* carding machine

Kremserweiss *neu.* white lead

krepieren *v.* (coll.) to die; to burst, to explode

Krepp *m.* crêpe, crape

Kresse *f.* cress; nasturtium

Krethi und Plethi *m.* riffraff; rag, tag, and bobtail

Kreuz *neu.* cross; crucifix; loins; backbone; (cards) clubs; (horse) croup; (mus.) sharp; (typ.) dagger; affliction; ans — heften (*or* schlagen) to crucify; das — auf sich nehmen to take up the cross, to be willing to bear consequences; das — schlagen to make the sign of the cross; drei –e hinter jemand machen to be glad to be rid of someone; über — legen to lay crosswise; zu –e kriechen to submit humbly; –band *neu.* crossbeam; mailing wrapper (for printed matter); –er *m.* copper coin; cruiser; –fahrer *m.*, –ritter *m.* crusader; –gang *m.* cloisters; –otter *f.* adder, viper; –schmerz *m.* lumbago; –schnabel *m.* crossbill; –ung *f.* intersection; crossbreeding; –verhör *neu.* crossexamination; –weg *m.* crossroad; Way of the Cross; –worträtsel *neu.* crossword puzzle; –zug *m.* crusade

kreuz: — und quer crisscross; in all directions; –brav *adj.* honest to the core; –en *v.* to cross, to intersect; to crossbreed; to cruise; –igen *v.* to crucify; –lahm *adj.*, –steif *adj.* lame (*oder* stiff) in the back

kribbeln *v.* to crawl, to itch, to tickle

kriechen *v.* to crawl, to creep, to sneak; to fawn; to cringe

Krieg *m.* war, feud; in den — ziehen to go to war; — führen to wage war; –er *m.* soldier, old fighter; –erverein *m.* association of war veterans; –sausrüstung *f.* armaments; –sbaukunst *f.* military engineering; –sbereitschaft *f.* preparedness for war; –sdienstverweigerer *m.* conscientious objector; –sentschädigung *f.* war indemnity; –serklärung *f.* declaration of war; –sgebiet *neu.* war zone; –gefährte *m.*, –kamerad *m.*

fellow-soldier; -sgefangene m. prisoner of war: -sgericht neu. court-martial; -sgeschrei neu. war cry; -sgewinnler m. war profiteer; -shandwerk neu. military profession; -shetzer m. warmonger; -smacht f. military forces; -srat m. council of war; -srecht neu. martial law; -sschauplatz m. theater of war; -sschiff neu. battleship, warship; -sschuld f. war guilt; war debt; -ssteuer f. war tax; -streiber m. warmonger; -szucht f. military discipline; -szug m. military campaign (oder expedition)

krieg: -en v. to wage war; to catch, to seize; to obtain, to receive; -erisch adj. bellicose; martial; -führend adj. belligerent; -spflichtig adj. liable for military service

die Krim f. Crimea

Kriminal: -beamte m. detective; -gericht neu. criminal court; -roman m. detective story; -gesetzbuch neu. criminal (oder penal) code; -wissenschaft f. penology

kriminell adj. criminal

Krimskrams m. rubbish, trash

Krippe f. crib, manger; crèche; day nursery; -nspiel neu. nativity play; -nbeisser m., -nsetzer m. (coll.) old horse (oder man)

Krise. Krisis f. crisis

Kristall m. crystal; — neu. crystal glass

Kriterium neu. criterion

Kritik f. criticism; evaluation; review; -er m. critic; reviewer; -losigkeit f. lack of judgment

kritisch adj. critical, judicious; precarious

kritisieren v. to criticize; to review

Krittelei f. carping criticism; fault-finding

kritzeln v. to scrawl; to scribble

Krokodil neu. crocodile

Kron: -e f. crown; coronet, corona; diadem; crest; (bot.) corolla; (coll.) head; -enblatt neu. petal; -engold neu. 18 carat gold; -leuchter m. chandelier; -zeuge m. material witness; prosecution's star witness

krönen v. to crown

Kropf m. (orn.) crop, craw; goiter; -taube f. pouter pigeon

Kröte f. toad; (coll.) coin; kleine — impertinent girl

Krücke f. crutch; T-shaped tool

Krug m. jug, pitcher; inn, tavern

Krume f. crumb; topsoil

krümeln v. to crumble; to crumb; to pulverize

krumm adj. crooked, bent; hooked; arched, curved; sinuous; die Hand —

machen (coll.) to beg; — ansehen v. to look askance; — liegen (coll.) to have no money; — nehmen (coll.) to take amiss; -e Wege gehen to pursue dishonest ways; -beinig adj. bowlegged; knock-kneed

Krumm: -holz neu. dwarf shrub; underbrush; -stab m. crozier

krümmen v. to bend, to curve, to crook; to wind, to meander; sich — to cringe; to stoop; to wriggle, to writhe

Krupp m. croup, diphtheria

Kruppe f. crupper

Krüppel m. cripple

krüppelhaft, krüpp(e)lig adj. crippled

Kruste f. crust; scab; -ntier neu. crustacean

Kruzifix neu. crucifix

Krypta f. crypt

Kübel m. bucket; tub; vat

kubisch adj. cubic(al)

Küch: -e f. kitchen; in des Teufels -e kommen (coll.) to be in danger of losing one's neck; kalte -e cold dinner; -enherd m. kitchen range; -enmeister m. chef; -enzettel m. bill of fare; -lein neu. small cake; chicken

Kuchen m. cake; clot; -bäcker m. pastry cook

Kuckuck m. cuckoo; -sei neu. cuckoo's egg; dubious gift

Kufe f. vat; (cradle) rocker; (sledge) runner

Kugel f. ball, sphere; bullet; (gym.) shot; -lager neu. ball bearing; -mass neu. caliber; -schreiber m. ball-point pen; -stossen neu. shot-put

kugel: -fest adj. bulletproof; -förmig adj. spherical; globular; -ig adj. round, globular; -n v. to bowl, to roll; to ballot

Kuh f. cow; blinde — blindman's buff; das geht auf keine -haut that's beyond all measure; -euter neu. cow's udder; -fladen m. cow-dung; -handel m. shady deal; -hirt m. cowboy, cowherd

kühl adj. cool, chilly; fresh; unfriendly, stiff; -en v. to cool; sein Mütchen an jemandem -en to take one's temper out on someone

Kühl: -anlage f., -haus n. cold-storage plant; -apparat m. refrigerator; -e f. coolness, freshness; unfriendliness; stiffness; -er m. cooler; radiator; -mittel neu. refrigerant; -raum m. cold storage room; -ung f. cooling; refrigeration

kühn adj. bold, daring; intrepid; audacious

Küken neu. small chicken

Kulisse f. (theat.) wing; scene; -nschieber m. scene shifter

Kult *m.* cult; **-ivierung** *f.* cultivation; **-ur** *f.* culture, civilization; forestation; (agr.) cultivation; **-urfilm** *m.* educational film; **-urpflanzen** *f. pl.* cultivated plants; **-usminister** *m.* Minister of Culture; **-relle Anpassung** *f.* (demography) acculturation

Kümmel *m.* caraway (seed); brandy

Kummer *m.* grief; worry; sorrow

kümmer: -lich *adj.* miserable; pitiful; stunted; **-lich** *adv.* barely, scarcely; **-n** *v.* to trouble, to take pains; **sich -n um** to care for; to be concerned about

Kümmernis *f.* grief; affliction; anxiety

Kum(me)t *neu.* horse collar

Kumpan *m.* companion, fellow

kund *adj.* known; **-geben** *v.* to demonstrate; to manifest; **-machen, — tun** *v.* to make known, to publish; to proclaim; **-ig** *adj.* experienced, familiar with; **-schaften** *v.* to reconnoiter

Kund: -e *m.* customer; (sl.) tramp; **— f** information, news; **-ige** *m.* well-informed person; expert; **-schaft** *f.* customers; (mil.) reconnoitering, scouting; **-schafter** *m.* scout, spy; emissary

künd: -bar *adj.* recallable, redeemable; **-en** *v* (bibl.) to announce, to make known; **-igen** *v.* to give notice; to call off; to denounce

künftig *adj.* future; later; **seine -e Frau** (coll.) his wife-to-be; **-hin** *adv.* henceforth, from now on

Kunkel *f.* distaff

Kunst *f.* art; ingenuity, skill; **das ist keine —** it's easy; **schwarze —** black magic; **volkstümliche —** folk art; **-akademie** *f.* academy of arts; **-dünger** *m.* chemical fertilizer; **-erzeugnis** *neu.* artifact (*oder* artefact); **-flug** *m.* (avi.) stunt flight; **-gärtner** *m.* horticulturist; **-gewerbe** *neu.* applied art; arts and crafts; **-händler** *m.* art dealer; **-handwerker** *m.* artisan, craftsman; **-kenner** *m.* art connoisseur; **-kniff** *m.* ruse; trick; **-lauf** *m.* figure skating; **-leder** *neu.* plastic, vinyl; **-liebhaber** *m.* amateur; **-reiter** *m.* equestrian; **-richter** *m.* art critic; **abstrakte -richtung** abstractionism; **-seide** *f.* rayon; **-springen** *neu.* diving; **-stoff** *m.* plastic; **-stück** *neu.* trick; **-tischler** *m.* cabinetmaker

kunst: -fertig *adj.* possessing artistic skill; **-gemäss** *adj.*, **-gerecht** *adj.* artistically correct; **-los** *adj.* inartistic; artless; simple; **-reich** *adj.* artistic; ingenious; **-sinnig** *adj.* appreciative of art; **-verständig** *adj.* expert in art

Künst: -elei *f.* artificiality; affectation;

-ler *m.* artist; virtuoso; **-lerwerkstatt** *f.* artist's studio

künst: -eln *v.* to elaborate, to overrefine; to attitudinize; **-lerisch** *adj.* artistic; **-lich** *adj.* artificial; arty

Kupfer *neu.* copper; **-druck** *m.* copperplate print(ing); **-stich** *m.* copperplate engraving (*oder* print); **-tiefdruck** *m.* photogravure

kupfern, kupfrig *adj.* of copper, coppery

Kuppe *f.* (nail) head; top, summit; **-l** *f.* cupola, dome; firmament

Kupp(e)lung *f.* coupling, clutch

kuppeln *v.* to couple; to make a match; to clutch

Kur *f.* cure; course of treatment; **einer Dame die — schneiden** to pay court to a woman: **-arzt** *m.* physician (at health resort); **-atel** *f.* guardianship, trusteeship; curatorship; **-ator** *m.* guardian; trustee; supervisor (at German university); **-atorium** *neu.* board of trustees; governing body; **-fürst** *m.* (German) elector; **-fürstentum** *neu.* electorate; **-gast** *m.* health resort patient; **-haus** *neu.* health resort hotel; casino; pump room; **-ort** *m.* health resort, spa; **-pfalz** *f.* Palatinate; **-pfuscher** *m.* quack

Kür *f.* choice; **-assier** *m.* cuirassier; **-bis** *m.* pumpkin; gourd; (sl.) head; **-bisflasche** *f.* calabash; **-schner** *m.* furrier

Kurbel *f.* crank; **-kasten** *m.* (coll.) movie camera: **-welle** *f.* crankshaft

kurbeln *v.* to crank

Kurie *f.* curia; (eccl.) court of justice; magistracy

Kurier *m.* courier, express

kurieren *v.* to cure

kurios *adj.* odd, strange, rare

Kuriosität *f.* oddity, rarity, curiosity

Kurrentschrift *f.* cursive writing, italics

Kurs *m.* course; currency; rate of exchange; **-abweichung (Rakete)** *f.* yaw; **ausser — setzen** to withdraw from circulation; **in — setzen** to circulate; **-bericht** *m.* stock exchange quotations; stock market report; **-buch** *neu.* train schedules, railway guide, time tables; **-schwankungen** *f. pl.* stock exchange fluctuations

kursieren *v.* to circulate

Kursivschrift *f.* italics

Kursus *m.* course (of lectures)

kurz *adj.* short; brief; **in -em soon,** shortly; **— angebunden** brusque; **— entschlossen** quickly resolved; **— fassen** to be brief; **— treten** (mil.) to mark time; **— und bündig** concise; **— und gut in a word; — und klein schlagen** to smash into bits; **über — oder lang** sooner or later; **vor -em**

recently; zu — **kommen** to come off the loser; **–atmig** *adj.* short-winded, asthmatic; **–erhand** *adv.* without hesitation, abruptly; **–fristig** *adj.* short-termed; short-dated; **–gefasst** *adj.* briefly worded, concise; **–lebig** *adj.* short-lived; **–schliessen** *v.* to handcuff; (elec.) to short circuit; **–sichtig** *adj.* nearsighted, shortsighted; **–um** *adv.* in short, in a word; **–weilig** *adj.* amusing, funny

Kurz: –geschichte *f.* short short story; feature article; **–schluss** *m.* (elec.) short circuit; **–schrift** *f.* shorthand, stenography; **–streckenläufer** *m.* sprinter; **–waren** *f. pl.* notions; haberdashery; **–weil** *f.* amusement, pastime; **–wellensender** *m.* short-wave transmitter

kürzen *v.* to shorten, to diminish, to reduce; to curtail; (math.) to simplify

kürzlich *adv.* lately, recently

Kusine *f.* cousin

Kuss *m.* kiss; **–hand** *f.* blown kiss

küssen *v.* to kiss

Küssen *neu.* kissing

kussfest *adj.* kissproof

Küste *f.* coast, shore; **–nfahrer** *m.* coaster; **–nstrich** *m.*, **–nland** *neu.* maritime country

Küster *m.* sexton, verger

Kustos *m.* custodian, curator; canon

kutschieren *v.* to drive (coach)

Kutte *f.* monk's robe, cowl

Kuvert *neu.* envelope; table setting

L

Lab: –e *f.*, **–sal** *neu.*, **–ung** *f.* refreshment; restorative; comfort; **–etrank** *m.*, **–etrunk** *m.* refreshing drink

labbern *v.* to lap; (sl.) to babble

laben *v.* to refresh; **sich —** to enjoy; to restore oneself

Laborant *m.* laboratory assistant

laborieren *v.* to work in a laboratory; **mit seiner Krankheit —** to labor with one's sickness, to/show off one's affliction

Lach: –anfall *m.*, **–krampf** *m.* laughing fit; **–e** *f.* laughter; puddle, slough; **–en** *neu.* laughter, laugh(ing); **–er** *m.* laugher; **–gas** *neu.* laughing gas, nitrous oxide; **–taube** *f.* ring dove; (coll.) gay girl

lächeln *v.* to smile, to simper, to smirk

lächerlich *adj.* laughable; ridiculous; foolish; absurd; **— machen** to ridicule

Lachs *m.* salmon; cordial made in Danzig; **–schinken** *m.* fillet of smoked ham

Lack *m.* lac; **–firnis** *m.* lacquer, varnish; **–ierarbeit** *f.* lacquered ware; **–ierer** *m.*

lacquerer; **–leder** *neu.* patent leather; **–muspapier** *neu.* litmus paper; **–schuh** *m.* patent-leather shoe

lackieren *v.* to lacquer; **da war ich lackiert** I was cheated on that

Lade *f.* box, chest, shrine; drawer; (organ) wind chest

Lade: baum *m.* boom, derrick; **–fähigkeit** *f.* tonnage; **–platz** *m.* wharf; freight platform; **–r** *m.* loader; longshoreman; **–raum** *m.* loading space, ship's hold; (gun) chamber; **–schein** *m.* bill of lading; **–stock** *m.* ramrod

Laden *m.* shop, store; shutter; **–besitzer** *m.* shopkeeper; **–dieb** *m.* shoplifter; **–hüter** *m.* dead stock, white elephant; **–kasse** *f.* till; **–preis** *m.* retail price; **–tisch** *m.* counter

laden *v.* to load; to freight; to invite; (elec.) to charge; (law) to cite, to summon

Ladung *f.* invitation; load, freight; (law) citation, summons; (elec.) charge; (mil.) volley; (naut.) cargo

Lage *f.* position, situation; condition, state; layer; round (of beer); (fencing) guard; (mus.) pitch; (naut.) broadside; (paper) quire; **bedrängte — distress; in der — sein** to be able; **in die rechte — bringen** to put into proper order; **missliche — predicament**

Lager *neu.* bed; lodging; camp; lair; stock; supply; store; (geol.) deposit, layer, stratum; (mech.) bearing; support; party, side; **auf — in stock; aufs — bringen** to store, to warehouse; **nach langem —** after a long illness; **–aufnahme** *f.* stock inventory; **–aufseher** *m.*, **–ist** *m.* storekeeper; **–feuer** *neu.* campfire; **–gebühr** *f.*, **–geld** *neu.*, **–miete** *f.* storage charges; demurrage; **–haus** *neu.* storehouse, warehouse; **–patz** *m.*, **–statt** *f.*, **–stätte** *f.* resting place; bed; (geol.) deposit; **–schein** *m.* warrant; **–ung** *f.* storage, warehousing; stratification; **–vorrat** *m.* stock; **–wache** *f.* camp watch

lagern *v.* to lie down; to rest, to camp; to store, to warehouse; to be in stock; to stratify

Lagune *f.* lagoon; **–nriff** *neu.* atoll

lahm *adj.* lame, limpid; paralyzed; (coll.) tired, tedious; **–en** *v.* to limp; to be lame; **–legen** *v.* to render ineffective

lähmen *v.* to lame; to paralyze, to enervate

Lähmung *f.* paralysis; palsy

Laib *m.* (bread) loaf; rounded mass

Laich *m.* spawn; **–zeit** *f.* spawning time

Laie *m.* layman; amateur; **–nbruder** *m.*

lay brother
Lake *f.* brine, pickle
Laken *neu.* (bed) sheet, shroud; (coll.) sail
lakonisch *adj.* laconic
Lakritze *f.* licorice
lallen *v.* to mumble, to stammer, to babble
lamentieren *v.* to lament
Lamm *neu.* lamb; **-zeit** *f.* lambing time
Lämm: -chen *neu.* lambkin; **-erhüpfen** *neu.* (sl.) teen-age dancing; hop
lammfromm *adj.* gentle as a lamb
Lamp: -e *f.* lamp; **-e** *m.*, **eins auf die -e giessen** to hoist one (drink); **-endocht** *m.* wick; **-enfieber** *neu.* stage fright; **-enschirm** *m.* lamp shade
Land *neu.* land; country, state; continent; territory; ground, soil; **ans — bringen** (*or* **setzen**) to bring ashore; **ausser -es sein** to be abroad; **das Gelobte —** the Promised Land; **des -es verweisen** to banish, to exile; **über — geh(e)n** to go overland; **Unschuld vom -e** country cousin; **vom -e eingeschlossen** landlocked; **vom -e stossen** to put to sea; **-arbeiter** *m.* farm hand; **-arzt** *m.* country doctor; **-bau** *m.* agriculture; **-bewohner** *m.* countryman; **-briefträger** *m.*, **-bote** *m.* rural mailman; **-brot** *neu.* farmer's bread; **-dienst** *m.* (naut.) duty on shore; **-enge** *f.* isthmus; **-flucht** *f.* migration from the country (to cities); **-friede** *m.* public peace; **-gericht** *neu.* country court; **-gut** *neu.* country estate; **-karte** *f.* map; **-kreis** *m.* rural district; **-macht** *f.* continental power; (mil.) land forces; **-mann** *m.* farmer; countryman; **-mark** *f.* national boundary; territory; **-marke** *f.* landmark; **-messer** *m.* surveyor; **-partie** *f.* outing, picnic; **-plage** *f.* public calamity; **-pomeranze** *f.* country bumpkin; **-post** *f.* rural mail delivery; **-stagecoach;** **-rat** *m.* district magistrate; **-ratte** *f.* (naut.) landlubber; **-recht** *neu.* common law; **-regen** *m.* steady rain; **-richter** *m.* country judge; **-rücken** *m.* ridge (of land); **-schaft** *f.* district, province; landscape, scenery; **-see** *m.* inland lake; **-sitz** *m.* country seat; **-smann** *m.* compatriot, fellow countryman; **was für ein -smann sind Sie?** What's your native country? **-spitze** *f.* cape, headland; **-steuer** *f.* land tax; **-strasse** *f.* highway; **-streicher** *m.* tramp, vagabond; **-strich** *m.* region, zone; **-ung** *f.* landing, disembarkation; **-ungsbrücke** *f.* landing stage; pier; **-vermessung** *f.* land surveying; **-wehr** *f.* militia; **-wirtschaft** *f.* agriculture, farming
land: -en *v.* to land, to disembark;

-flüchtig *adj.* fugitive; **-flüchtig werden** to flee one's country; **-fremd** *adj.* strange; foreign; **-läufig** *adj.* customary, universally known; **-schaftlich** *adj.* scenic
Länd: -erkunde *f.* geography; **-ler** *m.* slow waltz
Landes: -beschreibung *f.* topography; **-farben** *f. pl.* national colors; **-kirche** *f.* national church; **-obrigkeit** *f.* public authority; **-sitte** *f.* national custom; **-sprache** *f.* language of a country, vernacular, idiom; **-tracht** *f.* national costume; **-trauer** *f.* public mourning; **-vater** *m.* sovereign; **-verfassung** *f.* constitution of a country; **-verrat** *m.* high treason; **-verweisung** *f.* banishment, exile
landes: -kundig *adj.* familiar with a country; well-known; **-kundlich** *adj.* geographical; **-üblich** *adj.* customary in a country; **-verräterich** *adj.* treasonable
ländlich *adj.* rural, rustic; provincial
lang *adj.* long; tall; lengthy; **auf die -e Bank schieben** to put off; **auf -e hinaus** for a long time to come; **die Zeit wird mir —** time hangs heavy on my hands; **einen -en Hals machen** to crane one's neck; **ein -es Gesicht machen** to make a long face; **eine -e Nase machen** to thumb one's nose; **entsetzlich —** endless; **es ist noch — nicht fertig** it is far from done; **in nicht zu -er Zeit** before long; **— und breit** at full length; **-e Finger machen** to pilfer; **-e hin a long time yet; über kurz oder — sooner or later; — adv. for a long time; -e nicht not by far; not nearly; -atmig adj. long-winded, prolix; -en v. (coll.) to suffice; to reach for; -gespitzt adj. sharp pointed; -her adv. long ago; -hin adv. far and away; -mütig adj. forbearing, patient; -sam adj. slow, lingering; -stielig adj. long-stemmed; longhandled; -weilen v. to bore, to weary; -weilig adj. tedious, boring; -wierig adj. lengthy, protracted, chronic
Lang: -bein *m.* long-legged person; **-eweile** *f.* boredom, tedium, ennui; **-finger** *m.* pickpocket, pilferer; **-mut** *f.* forbearance; patience; **-schiff** *neu.* (church) nave; **-schläfer** *m.* late riser
läng: -lich *adj.* longish, elongated; **-s** *adv.* along; **-st** *adv.* for a long time; by far; **-stens** *adv.* at most, at the latest
Läng: -e *f.* length; duration; lengthiness; longitude; **-engrad** *m.*, **-enkreis** *m.* meridian; **-enmass** *neu.* linear measure; **-srichtung** *f.* longitudinal direc-

tion; **-sschwelle** f. (rail.) stringer; **-ststreifen** m. crossline

Lanze f. lance, spear; **eine — für jemand brechen** to go to bat for someone; **-tte** f. lancet

lapidar adj. lapidary, pithy; forceful, concise

Lappalie f. trifle, bagatelle

lappen v. to lap, to sip

Lappen m. rag, tatter; duster; (bot., zool.) lobe; wattle; flap; (dog) ear; inhabitants of Lapland; **durch die — gehen** (coll.) to escape

Läpperei f. trifle, bauble; silliness

läppern v. (coll.) to lap, to sip; **sich zusammen — (coll.)** to mount up, to accumulate

läppish adj. silly, childish, foolish

Lärm m. noise; din, clamor; **viel — um nichts** much ado about nothing

lärmen v. to clamor, to bluster, to row

Larve f. mask; larva, grub; specter

lasch adj. loose, flabby; lax; limp

Laser abbr. (Lichtverstärkung durch Strahlungsanregung unter Verwendung einer fremden Strahlungsquelle) laser

lasieren v. to glaze, to coat

lassen v. to let, to allow, to permit; to tolerate; to make possible; to cause, to effect; to leave undone (oder off, open, shut); to abandon; to deposit; to give up, to renounce; **ausser Acht —** to disregard; **das Licht brennen —** to keep the light burning; **das muss man ihm —** one must give him credit for that; **es beim alten —** to leave things as they were; **etwas sein —** to abstain from something; **holen —** to send for; **ich habe mir sagen —** I have been told; **lass das!** stop it! **lass nur!** never mind! **mit sich reden —** to be reasonable; **sagen —** to send word; **sein Leben —** to lose one's life; **sich Zeit —** to take time; **vermuten —** to give ground to believe; **zufrieden —** to let alone

lässig adj. negligent, remiss; careless; dilatory; idle, lazy; indolent

Last f. load; burden; freight, cargo, tonnage; trouble; **-en** pl. tax, impost; **einem etwas zur — legen** to make someone responsible for something; **einem zur — fallen** to be a burden (oder inconvenience) to someone; **zu -en des Käufers** paid for by the purchaser; **-enaufzug** m. freight elevator; **-igkeit** f. ship's tonnage (oder capacity); **-kahn** m. barge, lighter; **-(kraft)wagen** m. motor truck; **-schrift** f. debit; **-tier** neu. beast of burden; **-träger** m. porter

last: -en v. to weigh (on); to encumber;

to press upon; to load; **-enfrei** adj. unburdened, exempt from encumbrances; **-ig** adj. freighted; heavy, weighty; (naut.) listing, careening

läst: -erlich adj. blasphemous; abusive, slanderous; **-ern** v. to slander, to revile, to malign; **-ig** adj. troublesome; unpleasant

Laster neu. vice; bad habit; **langes —** (coll.) very tall person, stringbean; **-höhle** f. den of iniquity

Läster: -er m. blasphemer; reviler; maligner; slanderer; **-maul** neu. scandalmonger; **-ung** f. blasphemy; abuse; slander

lasterhaft adj. vicious, wicked, dissolute

Latein neu. Latin; **mit seinem — zu Ende sein** to be at the end of one's rope (oder wits)

Laterne f. lantern; street lamp; **-nanzünder** m. lamplighter; **-npfahl** m. lamp post

Latsch m. (coll.) untidy fellow; sloven; **-e** f. slipper; dwarf pine

Latt: -e f. lath; batten; (coll.) lanky person; **-enkiste** f. crate; **-enverschlag** m. latticework partition; **-enzaun** m. picket fence

Lattich m. lettuce

lau adj. lukewarm, tepid; indifferent

Laub neu. foliage, leaves; **-e** f. arbor, summerhouse; **fertig ist die -e!** ready we are! **-engang** m. arbored walk; arcade; **-baum** m. deciduous tree; **-fall** m. defoliation; **-frosch** m. tree frog; **-säge** f. fret saw; **-wald** m. deciduous forest; **-werk** neu. foliage; leafwork

Lauer f. lurking; ambush; **auf der — liegen** to lie in ambush for

Lauf m. run, race; career; (ast.) movement, speed; current; way, course; (gun) barrel; (mus.) quick run; (zool.) leg; **das ist der — der Welt** that's how it goes; that's life; **einer Sache freien — lassen** to let something take its course; **in vollem -e** at top speed; **-bahn** f. course; career; **-brett** neu. running board; **-brücke** f. plank bridge; pontoon; gangway; **-bursche** m., **-junge** m. errand boy; **-erei** f. running about; **-käfer** m. ground beetle; **-katze** f., **-kran** m. traveling (oder overhead) crane; **-pass** m. dismissal, sack; **-rädchen** neu. caster; **-riemen** m. endless belt; **-schiene** f. guide rail; **-schritt** m. (mil.) double pace; **im -schritt!** on the double! **-werk** neu. movement, wheelwork; **-zeit** f. running time; rutting season; **-zettel** m. bill of lading; handbill; circular

Laufstall *m.* play-pen
laufen *v.* to run; to rush; to flow, to pass, to leak; to continue, to go on; to strand; **in den Hafen —** to put into port; **in den Weg —** to come across; **— lassen** to let go; **Rollschuh —** to rollerskate; **Schlittschuh —** to skate; **Spiessruten —** to run the gauntlet; **Sturm —** to assault. to storm; **vom Stapel — lassen** to launch; **-d** *adj.* running, current, recurring; **auf dem -den sein** to be up to date; **-de Nummern** consecutive numbers; **-de Rechnung** open account
Läufer *m.* runner; messenger; (mech.) slider; upper millstone; hall (*oder* stair) carpet
Lauge *f.* lye, leach; (coll.) sarcasm
laun: -enhaft *adj.* capricious, changeable; **-ig** *adj.* humorous; entertaining; **-isch** *adj.* moody; cross; ill-humored
Laune *f.* mood; caprice; fancy, whim; temper; **bei guter — sein** to be in good humor
Laus *f.* louse; **-bub(e)** *m.*, **-ejunge** *m.* young rascal; rogue
lauschen *v.* to hearken, to listen, to eavesdrop
lausen *v.* to delouse; **mich laust der Affe!** (coll.) that beat's all!
lausig *adj.* lousy; (sl.) shabby, pitiful; mean
laut *adj.* loud; noisy; audible, distinct, sonorous; (mus.) forte; **— werden to** become known (*oder* public); **—** *adr.* aloud; **—** *prep.* in accordance with; **-bar** *adj.* notorious known; **-en** *v.* to sound, to run; to read, to say; **-los** *adj.* silent, inaudible
Laut *m.* sound, tone; audible noise; utterance; **-bildung** *f.* formation of sounds; **-e** *f.* lute; **-lehre** *f.* science of sound; **-schrift** *f.* phonetic writing; **-sprecher** *m.* loud-speaker
läuten *v.* to ring; to toll; to peal; **etwas — hören** to learn via the grapevine
lauter *adj.* pure, unalloyed, unsullied; flawless; genuine, true, sincere; nothing but, mere; **aus — Neid** out of sheer envy
läutern *v.* to purify; to refine; to clarify
Läutewerk *neu.* alarm bell
Lawine *f.* avalanche
lax *adj.* lax, loose; licentious
Lazarett *neu.* (mil.) hospital
Leb: -emann *m.* playboy; man about town; **-ewesen** *neu.* living being; **-kuchen** *m.* gingerbread; spice cake; **-tage** *m. pl.* days of one's life; **-(e)wohl** *neu.* farewell, goodbye
Leben *neu.* life; existence; activity, animation; reality; **am — bleiben to** survive; **am — sein** to be alive; **bei Leib und —** under penalty of death; **das — schenken** to give birth (to); to spare life; **ins — rufen** (mil.) to activate; **Kampf auf — und Tod** life and death struggle; **mit dem — davonkommen** to escape with one's life; **mit Leib und —** with body and soul; **ums — bringen** to kill; **ums — kommen to** perish; **-de** *m.* living person; **-salter** *neu.* age, period of life; **-sart** *f.* manners, good breeding; **-saufgabe** *f.* lifework; **-sbild** *neu.* biography; **-sfähigkeit** *f.* vitality; **-sfrage** *f.* vital question; **-sfreude** *f.* enjoyment of life; **-sführung,** *f.* conduct of life; **-sgefahr** *f.* mortal danger; **-sgefährte** *m.* life companion; spouse; **-sgeister** *m. pl.* animal spirits; **-sgrösse** *f.* life size; **-shaltung** *f.* standard of living; **-skraft** *f.* vital energy; **-slauf** *m.* course of life; biographical sketch; **-slicht** *neu.* lamp of life; **-sraum** *m.* essential space to subsist on; **-srente** *f.* life annuity; **-sstrafe** *f.* capital punishment; **-sunterhalt** *m.* livelihood, subsistence; **-sversicherung** *f.* life insurance; **-swandel** *m.* moral conduct; **-swasser** *neu.* water of life; (sl.) brandy; **-sweisheit** *f.* practical philosophy; wisdom of experience; **-szeit** *f.* lifetime; **-szweck** *m.* goal in life
leben *v.* to live; to be alive; to dwell, to reside; to stay; **einen (hoch) — lassen** to drink to someone's health; to cheer; **in den Tag hinein —** to lead a careless life; **nichts zu — haben** to be destitute; **-d** *adj.* living, alive; **-des Bild** tableau; **-dig** *adj.* alive, living; vivid, active; **-sfroh** *adj.* joyful; **-sgefährlich** *adj.* perilous; **-sgross** *adj.* life-sized; **-skräftig** *adj.* vigorous; **-slang, -slänglich** *adj.* lifelong; **-slustig** *adj.* jovial, merry, cheerful; **-smüde** *adj.* weary (*oder* sick) of life; **-swichtig** *adj.* vital
Leber *f.* liver; **frei von der — weg reden** to speak freely; **-fleck** *m.* freckle; mole; **-tran** *m.* cod-liver oil; **-wurst** *f.* liver sausage
lebhaft *adj.* lively, vivacious, impulsive; sprightly, brisk, vivid; acute; animated
leblos *adj.* lifeless; dull, rigid
lechzen *v.* to languish (*oder* thirst, long) for
Leck *neu.* leak, leakage; **ein — bekommen** to spring a leak
leck: -en *v.* to leak; to lick; to trickle; **-er** *adj.* tasty, delicious, appetizing, fastidious, attractive; **-ern** *v.* to nibble
Lecker *m.* licker; **-bissen** *m.* dainty mor-

sel, tidbit; **–ei** f. delicacy, sweetmeat; **–maul** neu. sweet tooth; dainty feeder
Leder neu. leather; (coll.) football; leather apron; in **—** gebunden calf-bound; vom **—** ziehen to unsheathe a weapon; **zäh wie —** as tough as leather; **–haut** f. thick skin; **–hosen** f. pl. leather breeches
ledern adj. leathery; tough
ledig adj. unmarried; vacant, empty; except (oder free) from; **—** adv. exclusively; purely, simply; **los und —** absolutely free; **–lich** adv. only, solely, quite, merely
leer adj. empty; void; vacant; unoccupied; vain; **—** ausgehen to be left empty-handed; **–e** Ausrede lame excuse; **—** laufen (mech.) to idle; **–er** Schein empty show; **–er** Vorwand idle pretext; **–en** v. to empty, to clear, to void; to vacate; to drain
Legalität f. legality
Legat m. legate; **—** neu. legacy; **–ion** f. legation
legen v. to lay; to put, to place; sich **—** to abate, to slacken; to cease; to lie (oder calm) down; an den Tag **—** to evince, to show; etwas nahe **—** to suggest; to urge; Hand an etwas **—** to turn one's hand to something; Hand an sich **—** to commit suicide; Karten **—** (cards) to tell a fortune; letzte Hand an etwas **—** to put the finishing touches to; sich ins Mittel **—** to intervene; Wert auf etwas **—** to attach value (oder importance) to something; zurecht (oder bereit) **—** to arrange, to keep in readiness
Legende f. legend
legitim adj. legitimate; **–ieren** v. to legalize; to legitimize; sich **—** to identify oneself
Legitim: –ation f. legitimation; proof of identity; **–ierung** f. legitimization; **–ität** f. legitimacy
Leh(e)n neu. fief; **–sbesitz** m. feudal tenure; **–sherr** m. feudal lord; **–smann** m. vassal; **–swesen** neu. feudalism
Lehm m. clay, loam; **–mauer** f., **–wand** f. mud wall
Lehn: –e f. chair back; rest, support; slope; **–sessel** m., **–stuhl** m. armchair, easy chair
lehnen v. to lean (against), to rest (upon) to bend (over)
Lehr: –amt neu. teacher's position; professorship; **–anstalt** f. educational establishment; school; academy; **–auftrag** m. professorship; **–buch** neu. textbook; **–bursch(e)** m., **–junge** m.,

–ling m. apprentice; **–e** f. precept; moral; doctrine; apprenticeship; (mech.) gauge; **–er** m. teacher; instructor; **–erbildungsanstalt** f. teacher's college; **–erin** f. teacher, instructress; **–erkollegium** neu., **–schaft** f. staff of teachers; **–fach** neu. teaching profession; branch of instruction; **–film** m. educational film; **–gang** m. course of studies; **–gebäude** neu. system (of science); **–geld** neu. fee for apprenticeship; tuition; **–geld bezahlen** to pay for one's wisdom; **–herr** m. master of apprentices; **–jahre** neu. pl. (years of) apprenticeship; **–körper** m. teaching body (oder staff); **–kunst** f. pedagogy; **–plan** m. curriculum; **–saal** m. classroom; **–satz** m. proposition; theorem; dogma; doctrine; **–schriften** f. pl. didactic writings; **–spruch** m. maxim, aphorism; **–stand** m. educational profession; **–stoff** m. subject matter of instruction; **–stuhl** m. academic chair; **–zeit** f. (term of) apprenticeship
lehren v. to teach, to inform, to instruct
lehrreich adj. instructive
Leib m. body; abdomen, belly; am ganzen **–e** all over; auf den **—** rücken to attack; bei lebendigem **–e** while still alive; bei **–e** nicht on no account; es ging ihm an **—** und Leben his life was at stake; gesegneten **–es** (poet.) pregnant; vom **–e** bleiben to stay away (from someone); **–arzt** m. court physician; **–binde** f. waistband, abdominal belt; sash; **–chen** neu. bodice; **–eigene** m. serf; **–eigenschaft** f. serfdom; **–esbeschaffenheit** f. constitution; physique; **–eserbe** m. heir; **–eskraft** f. aus **–eskräften** with all one's might; **–esstrafe** f. corporal punishment; **–esübungen** f. pl. gymnastics, calisthenics, physical training; **–garde** f., **–wache** f. bodyguard; **–gericht** neu., **–speise** f. favorite dish; **–haftige** m. the devil; **–rente** f. life annuity; **–schmerz** m. stomach ache, colic; **–wäsche** f. underwear
leib: –eigen adj. in serfdom (oder bondage); **–haftig** adj. embodied, incarnate; personified; real; **–lich** adj. corporeal, bodily, material; sein **–licher** Sohn his own son
Leich: –dorn m. (dial.) corn (on toe); **–e** f. corpse; cadaver; (coll.) funeral; (typ.) omission; **–enausgrabung** f. exhumation; **–enbahre** f. bier; **–enbegängnis** neu. funeral; **–enbeschauer** m. coroner; **–enbestatter** m. undertaker; **–enhalle** f. mortuary; **–enhemd** neu. shroud; **–enschändung** f. desecration of the

dead; **−enschau** *f.* inquest; **−enstarre** *f.*
rigor mortis; **−enstein** *m.* tombstone;
−enträger *m.* pallbearer; **−entuch** *neu.*
pall; shroud; **−enverbrennung** *f.* cremation; **−enwagen** *m.* hearse; **−enzug** *m.*
funeral procession; **−nam** *m.* corpse;
dead body

leicht *adj.* light; easy; mild, slight; insignificant; frivolous; — *adv.* easily,
lightly, gently; — **entzündlich** highly
inflammable; **−en Herzens** light-
heartedly; **−er Absatz** ready sale;
−blütig *adj.* sanguine; playful; **−fasslich**
easy to understand; **−fertig** *adj.* careless; frivolous; thoughtless; **−flüssig** *adj.*
mobile, easily fusible; **−füssig** *adj.* light-
footed; **−gläubig** *adj.* credulous, gullible; **−herzig** *adj.* light-hearted; **−hin**
adv. lightly, carelessly; **−lebig** *adj.*
happy-go-lucky; **−sinnig** *adj.* careless,
frivolous; **−ern** *v.* (naut.) to unload

Leicht: −er *m.* (naut.) lighter; **−fuss** *m.*
happy-go-lucky fellow; **−igkeit** *f.* light-
ness, ease, facility; **−matrose** *m.*
ordinary seaman; **−sinn** *m.* carelessness,
levity, frivolity

Leid *neu.* grief, sorrow; harm, hurt, injury; pain; **in Lieb' und —** in good and
evil days; **sich ein — antun** to commit
suicide; **−eform** *f.* passive voice; **−en**
neu. pain, torture; disease; **−enschaft**
f. passion, emotion; **−tragende** *m.*
mourner; **−wesen** *neu.* affliction; grief;
zu unserem −wesen to our regret

leid *adj.* sorrowful; painful; **es tut mir —**
I am sorry; **−en** *v.* to suffer; to bear, to
endure; to permit; to tolerate; **Ich kann
ihn nicht −en** I can't stand him; **ich
mag ihn wohl −en** I rather like him;
−enschaftlich *adj.* passionate; **−en-
schaftslos** *adj.* dispassionate; **−er** *adv.*
unfortunately; regrettably; **−er!** *interj.*
alas! **−ig** *adj.* disagreeable, troublesome;
sore; **−lich** *adj.* tolerable; mediocre

Leier *f.* lyre; (ast.) Lyra; (mech.) crank;
die alte — the same old story; **−mann**
m. organ grinder; **−kasten** *m.* grind
organ, hurdy gurdy; **−schwanz** *m.*
lyrebird

leiern *v.* to grind; to turn (a winch); to
harp on one string; (coll.) to reel off

Leih: −bibliothek *f.*, **−bücherei** *f.* rental
library; **−er** *m.* lender, borrower; **−haus**
neu. pawnshop, loan firm

leihen *v.* to lend; to loan; to borrow

leihweise *adv.* as a loan

Leim *m.* glue, size; birdlime; **auf den —
geh(e)n** to be taken in; **aus dem —
geh(e)n** to fall to pieces

leimen *v.* to glue; (coll.) to cheat, to

entrap

Lein *m.* flax(plant); **−e** *f.* line, cord, rope;
leash, rein; **an der −e haben** to have in
one's power; **−en** *neu.* linen; **−kuchen**
m. linseed cake; **−öl** *neu.* linseed oil;
−samen *m.* flaxseed, linseed; **−wand** *f.*
linen (cloth); canvas; movie screen

leinen *adj.* linen

leise *adj.* low, soft, faint, light; gentle

Leist: −e *f.* border, ledge, margin; selvage;
(anat.) groin; (book) edge; **−en** *m.*
shoemaker's last; **alles über einen —
schlagen** to treat everything alike;
−ung *f.* performance, execution; output,
effect; result; (com.) payment; **−ungs-
fähigkeit** *f.* productivity, efficiency;
(mech.) power

leisten *v.* to do, to perform; to offer, **to**
ex..nd, to provide; **einen Eid —** to take
an oath; **es sich — können** to be able to
afford; **Genugtuung —** to give satisfaction; **sich etwas —** to treat oneself to;
Vorzügliches — to achieve excellent
results

leistungsfähig *adj.* productive; efficient;
(com.) solvent

Leit: −artikel *m.* leading article; **−er** *m.*
leader; guide, conductor; manager;
principal; **−er** *f.* ladder; (mus.) scale;
−ersprosse *f.* ladder rung; **−erwagen** *m.*
rack wagon; **−faden** *m.* clue; guide, key,
manual; **−fähigkeit** *f.* conductivity;
−gedanke *m.* main thought; keynote;
−motiv *neu.* theme melody; **−regel** *f.*
guiding principle; **−schiene** *f.* switch;
−stern *m.* guiding star; polar star;
−strahl *m.* (avi.) vector; **−ung** *f.* leading,
leadership, guidance, direction, manage-
ment; pipe line; (phy. and elec.) con-
duction, circuit; **eine lange −ung haben**
(coll.) to be slow to comprehend

leiten *v.* to lead, to steer, to guide; **to**
direct, to control, to manage; to conduct

Lek: −tion *f.* lesson; lecture; reprimand;
−tor *m.* lecturer; (publisher's) reader;
−türe *f.* reading matter

Lende *f.* loin, hip; **−nbraten** *m.* roast loin;
−nschurz *m.* loin cloth

lenk: −bar *adj.* guidable; dirigible; **−en** *v.*
to drive, to steer; to govern; to guide;
to direct, to lead; to manage; to rule;
die Aufmerksamkeit −en auf to call
attention to; **−sam** *adj.* docile; manageable, flexible

Lenker *m.* driver; guide; ruler; pilot

Lenkstange *f.* handle bar; connecting rod

Lenz *m.* (poet.) spring; prime (of life)

Lerche *f.* lark; **−ngesang** *m.* song of a lark

lernen *v.* to learn; to study

Les: **–art** *f.* reading, version; **–ebuch** *neu.* reader; **–ehalle** *f.* public reading room; **–epult** *neu.* reading desk; **–er** *m.* reader; **–eratte** *f.* bookworm; **–erkreis** *m.*, **–erschaft** *f.* circulation; **–esaal** *m.* lécture (*oder* reading) room; **–estoff** *m.* reading material; **–estücke** *neu. pl.* selections for reading; **–ezeichen** *neu.* bookmark; **–ezirkel** *m.* book club; **–ung** *f.* recitation; (pol.) reading

les: **–bar** *adj.* legible; readable; worth reading; **–en** *v.* to read; to lecture; to gather, to glean; **–erlich** *adj.* legible

Lese *f.* gleaning; gathering, harvesting; vintage; culling; **–r** *m.* gleaner

Lettland *neu.* Latvia

letzt *adj.* last, final; ultimate; **der –ere** the latter; **in den –en Zügen liegen** to breathe one's last; **in –er Zeit** lately, of late; **–e ölung** (rel.) extreme unction; **–er Wille** last will and testament; **zu guter —** last but not least; **zum –en, am –en** finally, ultimately; **–hin** *adv.*, **–lich** *adv.* lately; recently; lastly, finally

Letzte *neu.* (the) last; **das ist das —** that's the limit

Leucht: –e *f.* (coll.) light; lantern; sage; luminary; **–en** *neu.* radiation, shining; glow; sparkling; **–er** *m.* candlestick, candelabra; chandelier; **–feuer** *neu.* flare; beacon; **–gas** *neu.* household gas; **–käfer** *m.* firefly; **–kraft** *f.* (phot.) saturation; **–turm** *m.* lighthouse; **–uhr** *f.* luminous clock; **–zifferblatt** *neu.* luminous dial

leuchten *v.* to light, to illuminate; to shine; to beam, to radiate

leugnen *v.* to deny; to disavow; to gainsay

Leugnen *neu.* denial; retraction

Leukoplast *neu.* adhesive tape; Band-Aid

Leukämie *f.* leukemia

Leukozyte *f.* leucocyte

Leumund *m.* reputation

Leute *pl.* peóple, persons; folk(s); (mil.) men, subordinates;. servants; public, world; **–schinder** *m.* oppressor; slave-driver, extortioner

Leutnant *m.* (second) lieutenant; (naut.) lieutenant junior grade

leutselig *adj.* affable, friendly, jovial

Lexikograph *m.* lexicographer

Lexikon *neu.* dictionary; encyclopedia

Libell *neu.* libel; **–e** *f.* dragonfly; (mech.) water level

Librettist *m.* librettist, textbook writer

Licht *neu.* light; brightness, luster; clarity; candle; eye (of game); high-light; (diamond) fire; **ans — bringen** to bring to light; **bei — besehen** to examine closely; **das — der Welt**

erblicken to be born; **einem ein — aufstecken** to set someone straight, to open someone's eyes; **in gutem –e erscheinen** to make a good impression; **ins falsche — setzen** to misrepresent; **— in etwas bringen** to clear up a matter; **mir geht ein — auf** I see the point; **–bad** *neu.* solar bath; **–bild** *neu.* photograph; **–blick** *m.* ray of hope; **–bogen** *m.* (elec.) arc; **–druck** *m.* phototype, photogravure; **–kegel** *m.* cone of light; searchlight beam; **–körper** *m.* luminary; **–mess(e)** *f.* Candlemas; **–leitung** *f.* lighting circuit; **–pause** *f.* blueprint; **–pausverfahren** *neu.* photographic printing; **–reklame** *f.* illuminated advertising; **–seite** *f.* bright (*oder* sunny) side; **–spielhaus** *neu.* motion-picture theater; **–stärke** *f.* candle power; **–strahl** *m.* ray (*oder* beam) of light; **–ung** *f.* clearing; **–zieher** *m.* candlemaker

licht *adj.* bright, light; shining; **am –en Tage** in broad daylight; **–echt** *adj.* light-fast, fadeless; **–empfindlich** *adj.* sensitive to light; (phot.) sensitized; **–en** *v.* to light (up); to clear; to thin; to lighten; to lift; to weigh (anchor); **–erloh** *adj.* blazing; flaring; **–erloh** *adv.* ablaze

Lid *neu.* eyelid

lieb *adj.* dear, beloved, cherished; agreeable, amiable; sweet, charming; **den –en langen Tag** the livelong day; **mir zu –e** for my sake; **sich — Kind machen** to ingratiate oneself; **–äugeln** *v.* to ogle; **–eln** *v.* (coll.) to dally, to flirt; **–en** *v.* to love, to like, to be fond of; **–end** *adj.* affectionate, loving; **–enswert** *adj.* worthy of love, attractive, charming; **enswürdig** *adj.* pleasing, amiable; **–evoll** *adj.* loving, affectionate, kind-hearted; **–gewinnen** to take a fancy (*oder* liking) to; **–haben** *v.* to be fond of; to like, to love; **–kosen** *v.* to caress, to fondle; **–lich** *adj.* lovely, charming; pleasing; sweet; **–los** *adj.* loveless, unkind; **–reich** *adj.* loving, benevolent; kind; **–reizend** *adj.* winning, charming, lovable

Lieb: –chen *neu.*, **–ste** *m.* and *f.* beloved, darling, sweetheart; **–e** *f.* love, affection; passion; charity; kindness; (coll.) sweetheart; love for love; **–elei** *f.* flirtation; **–esdienst** *m.* act of charity; **–esgabe** *f.* charitable gift; **–esgeschichte** *f.* love story (*oder* affair); **–eshandel** *m.* love affair; **–esheirat** *f.* love match; **–espfand** *neu.*, **–eszeichen** *neu.* love token; **–estrank** *m.* love potion; **-eswerke** *neu. pl.* charitable deeds; **-haber** *m.* lover, admirer; amateur, fancier, collector, dilettante; **-haberei** *f.* hobby; **-habervorstellungen** *f. pl.* amateur theatricals; **-kosung** *f.* caress(ing), fondling, petting; **-ling** *m.* darling, pet; favorite; **-lingsbeschäftigung** *f.* favorite occupation, hobby; **-lingssünde** *f.* besetting sin; **-reiz** *m.* charm; fascination; **-schaft** *f.* love affair

Lied *neu.* song; air, melody, tune; ballad; **das ist das Ende vom —** that's how it all came out; **immer das alte —** the same old complaint; **-chen** *neu.* short song, ditty; **-erabend** *m.* song (*oder* ballad) concert; **-erbuch** *neu.* songbook; hymnbook; **-erdichter** *m.* songwriter, lyrical poet; **-erkranz** *m.*, **-ertafel** *f.* choral society; glee club; song collection

Liederjahn *m.* wastrel; scoundrel, rake

liederlich *adj.* careless, negligent, slovenly; disorderly; dissolute; profligate; loose

Liefer: -ant *m.* seller, supplier; contractor; **-bedingungen** *f. pl.* terms of delivery; **-frist** *f.*, **-zeit** *f.* term of delivery; **-schein** *m.* delivery ticket; **-ung** *f.* delivery, supplying

lieferbar *adj.* deliverable

liefern *f.* to deliver; to furnish; to provide, to supply; to yield; to issue (in series); to fight (battle); **ans Messer —** to ruin, to kill; **er ist geliefert** he is lost

liegen *v.* to lie, to be situated; to camp; to be quartered; **es ist mir nichts daran gelegen** it is of no importance (*oder* consequence) to me; **es liegt an ihm** it is up to him; **es liegt in ihm** it's characteristic of him; **im Anschlag —** (gun) to aim; to lie in ambush; **in den Ohren —** to pester; **jemand links — lassen** to disregard someone; **— bleiben** to keep to (one's bed); (car) to break down; to be discontinued; (goods) to remain on hand; **mir ist daran gelegen** I value (*oder* esteem) it; **nach Osten —** to face east; **wem liegt daran?** who cares about it? **zutage —** to be obvious

Lift *m.* elevator; **-boy** *m.* elevator operator

Liga *f.* league; association, club

Likör *m.* liqueur, cordial

Lila *neu.* lilac

Lilie *f.* lily

lind *adj.* gentle, mild, soft; **-ern** *v.* to soften; to assuage; to mitigate; to appease

Lind: -e *f.* linden, basswood, lime tree; **-wurm** *m.* (poet.) dragon

Lineal *neu.* ruler, straightedge; (typ.) guide

Linie *f.* line, stroke; boundary; route; descent, lineage; (mil.) position; **in erster —** first of all, above all; **-npapier** *neu.* ruled paper; **-nschiff** *neu.* liner; battleship; **-nzieher** *m.* ruler

linieren *v.* to rule, to draw lines

link *adj.* left; left-handed; **-e Seite** wrong side; (coin) reverse; (com.) debit side; (naut.) port; **mit dem -en Bein zuerst aufstehen** to get up out of the wrong side of bed; **-erhand** *adv.* on the left hand (*oder* side); **-isch** *adj.* awkward, clumsy; **-s** *adv.* on (*oder* to) the left; **-s liegen lassen** to ignore; **-s stehen** to belong to the party of the left; **-s um!** turn left! **-shändig** *adj.* left-handed, counterclockwise

Linke *f.* (the) left; party of the left

Linnen *neu.* linen (see under Lein)

Linse *f.* lentil; lens; **-ngericht** *neu.* dish of lentils; (bibl.) mess of pottage

Lippe *f.* lip; **-nblütler** *m.* labiate (flower); **-nlaut** *m.* labial; **-nstift** *m.* lipstick

liquidieren *v.* to liquidate, to wind up; to clear accóunts

lispeln *v.* to lisp; to whisper

List *f.* cunning, craft; ruse, trick, stratagem; **-e** *f.* list, register, roll

listig *adj.* cunning, crafty, sly, wily, tricky

Litanei *f.* litany; (coll.) endless talk

Liter *m.* and *neu.* liter; 1.0567 liquid quarts, 0.9081 dry quart

literarisch *adj.* literary; **-er Diebstahl** plagiarism

Literat *m.* man of letters; writer; **-entum** *neu.* literary vocation; **-ur** *f.* literature

lithographieren *v.* to lithograph

Liturgie *f.* liturgy

liturgisch *adj.* liturgic(al)

Livland *neu.* Livonia

Livree *f.* livery

Lizentiat *m.* licentiate

Lizenz *f.* license, permit

Lob *neu.* praise, commendation; **-eserhebung** *f.* high praise, encomium; **-gesang** *m.* song of praise; **-hudelei** *f.* exaggerated praise; **-hudler** *m.* adulator, toady, flatterer; **-rede** *f.* eulogy; panegyric; **-spruch** *m.* eulogy

lob: -en *v.* to praise, to commend, to extol; **-esam** *adj.* (poet.) praiseworthy, upright; **-hudeln** *v.* to overpraise, to laud extravagantly; **-preisen, -singen** *v.* to extol, to glorify

löblich *adj.* laudable, praiseworthy, commendable

Loch *neu.* hole; aperture, cave, hollow; gap; (billiard) pocket; (sl.) jail; **auf dem letzten — pfeifen** (coll.) to be on one's last legs; er säuft wie ein — (sl.) he drinks like a fish; jemand ein — in den Bauch reden (coll.) to talk someone's ear off; **-er** *m.*, **-eisen** *neu.* punch, perforator

löch(e)rig *adj.* porous, perforated

Lock: -e *f.* lock, curl; **-enkopf** *m.* curly head; **-enwickel** *m.*, **-enwickler** *m.* curler, curl paper

lock: -en *v.* to curl, to wave; to allure, to entice; to decoy; **-ig** *adj.* curly, crimped

Locker *m.* tempter, seducer; decoyer; **-mittel** *neu.* bait, lure; **-ruf** *m.* bird call; siren call; **-speise** *f.* bait; **-spitzel** *m.* agent provocateur; **-vogel** *m.* decoy bird

locker *adj.* loose, not solid; slack; lax, dissolute; nicht **-er lassen** (coll.) not to give in; **-n** *v.* to loosen, to slacken; to break up (soil); to relax; Sitten **-ern** to demoralize; **-ig** *adj.* curly, crimped

lodern *v.* to blaze, to flare

Löffel *m.* spoon, ladle; (rabbit, hare) ear; jemand eins hinter die — geben (coll.) to box someone's ear; **-ente** *f.*, **-gans** *f.* shoveller

löffeln *v.* to ladle (out); to spoon

Log: -e *f.* lodge; (theat.) box; secret society; **-engang** *m.* (theat.) lobby

Logarithmus *m.* logarithm

logieren *v.* to lodge, to stay

logisch *adj.* logical

Lohe *f.* blaze, flare; tanner's bark

lchen *v.* to blaze, to flare, to tan

Lohn *m.* wages; compensation; payment; **-arbeiter** *m.* laborer, workman; hireling; **-diener** *m.* temporary servant; **-drückerei** *f.* exploitation of workers; **-empfänger** *m.* wage earner; **-satz** *m.* wage scale; **-tüte** *f.* pay envelope

lohnen *v.* to compensate, to remunerate; to be profitable; sich der Mühe — to be worth while; **-d** *adj.* advantageous, remunerative

lokal *adj.* local; **-isieren** *v.* to locate

Lokal *neu.* locale, locality; place; office; inn; **-behörde** *f.* local authority; **-ität** *f.* locality; **-kenntnisse** *f. pl.* knowledge of (*oder* familiarity with) a place; **-nachrichten** *f. pl.* local news; **-patriotismus** *m.* parochialism; narrow patriotism; **-verkehr** *m.* local traffic; **-zug** *m.* local (*oder* suburban) train

Lokomo: -bile *f.* traction engine; **-tive** *f.* locomotive; engine; **-tivführer** *m.* locomotive engineer; **-tivschuppen** *m.* engine shed

Lorbeer *m.* laurel, bay; **-kranz** *m.* crown of laurel; honor, fame

Los *neu.* lot; chance, destiny, **fate;**

(lottery) ticket; (ground) parcel, allotment; das grosse — ziehen to win first prize; to have a windfall; **-trennung** *f.* separation

los *adj.* loose; free; slack, released; dort ist der Teufel — hell broke loose there; — werden to get rid of; mit ihm ist nicht viel — he is no bargain; was ist —? what's the matter? **-arbeiten** *v.* to extricate; to work off; **-binden** *v.* to unbind, to untie; (naut.) to unfurl; **-brechen** *v.* to break loose; **-bröckeln** *v.* to crumble away; **-drehen** *v.* to twist off; **-drücken** to squeeze off; (coll.) to fire, to shoot; **-e** *adj.* loose, slack; incoherent; free; frivolous; **-en** *v.* to raffle, to draw lots; **-fahren** *v.* to drive away; to become loose; to fly off; (coll.) to blow up; **-feuern** *v.* to fire off; **-geben** *v.* to release; **-geh(e)n** *v.* to go off, to become loose; **-kaufen** *v.* to ransom, to redeem; **-lassen** *v.* to release, to unleash; **-legen** *v.* to loosen; (coll.) to set about; to inveigh (against); **-lösen** *v.* to detach; **-machen** *v.* to undo; to set free; **-reissen** *v.* to tear off; to separate; **-sagen** *v.* to break with; sich **-sagen** to renounce; **-schiessen** *v.* to fire off (*oder* away); **-schlagen** *v.* to knock off; to attack; to sell (cheaply); **-schnallen** *v.* to unbuckle; **-schrauben** *v.* to unscrew; **-sprechen** *v.* to absolve; to acquit; **-stürmen** *v.* to rush forth; **-trennen** *v.* to rip off; **-ziehen** *v.* to pull off; to start; to inveigh

lös: -bar *adj.*, **-lich** *adj.* soluble; **-en** *v.* to loosen; to relax; to free; to undo; to cancel; to unravel, to clear up; to (dis)solve; to buy (tickets)

Lösch: -blatt *neu.*, **-papier** *neu.* blotting paper; **-eimer** *m.* fire bucket; **-er** *m.* extinguisher; blotter; **-gerät** *neu.* firefighting apparatus; **-kalk** *m.* quicklime; **-mannschaft** *f.* fire brigade

löschbar *adj.* extinguishable, quenchable

löschen *v.* to extinguish, to quench, to slake; to blot (out), to cancel; (naut.) to unload

Lösegeld *neu.* ransom

Losung *f.* password; watchword; dung (of game)

Lot *neu.* lead, plummet; plumb line; one-half ounce; (geom.) perpendicular line; er ist nicht ganz im — (coll.) he does not feel quite well; **-se** *m.* pilot

Löt: -er *m.* solderer; **-kolben** *m.* soldering iron; **-lampe** *f.* blowtorch; **-rohr** *neu.* blowpipe

löten *v.* to solder

Lothringen *neu.* Lorraine

Lotterie *f.* lottery; **–los** *neu.* lottery ticket

lotterig *adj.* disorderly, slovenly, dissipated

Löw: –e *m.* lion; (ast.) Leo; **–enmaul** *neu.* lion's mouth; snapdragon; **–enzahn** *m.* lion's tooth; dandelion; **–in** *f.* lioness

Loyalität *f.* loyalty

Luchs *m.* lynx; **schlau wie ein —** very cunning

Lücke *f.* gap, hole, void; breach; omission; deficiency; **–nbüsser** *m.* stopgap

lückenhaft *adj.* gapped; defective, incomplete

Luder *neu.* carrion, bait, decoy; hussy; (sl.) sly fox; **armes —** poor wretch; **–leben** *neu.* dissolute life

Luft *f.* air, atmosphere; breeze, draft; **aus der — gegriffen** unfounded, fictitious; **das hängt in der —** it is uncertain (*oder* undecided); **dicke —** (coll.) great danger; tense atmosphere; **er ist — für mich** he means nothing to me; **in die — fliegen** to blow up, to explode; **in freier —** in the open air; outdoors; **jemand an die — setzen** to throw a person out; **sich — machen** to give vent (to one's feelings); **–akrobat** *m.* aerialist; **–angriff** *m.* air raid; **–aufklärung** *f.* air reconnaisance; **–bild** *neu.* phantom, vision; aerial photograph; **–blase** *f.* bubble; **–brücke** *f.* airlift; **–druck** *m.* atmospheric pressure; **–druckbremse** *f.* air brake; **–druckmesser** *m.* barometer; **–fahrt** *f.* aviation; **–fahrtmedizin** *f.* aeromedicine; **–fahrzeug** *neu.* aircraft; **–geschwader** *neu.* air wing; **–gespinst** *neu.* chimera; **–gewehr** *neu.* air rifle; **–heizung** *f.* air heating; **–ikus** *m.* scatterbrain; **–kanal** *m.* air passage; **–klappe** *f.* air valve; **–landetruppen** *f. pl.* airborne troops; **–linie** *f.* air line; beeline; **–loch** *neu.* air pocket; **–post** *f.* airmail; **–raum** *m.* air space, atmosphere; **–reifen** *m.* pneumatic tire; **–reiniger** *m.* air filter; **–reklame** *f.* sky writing; **–röhre** *f.* windpipe; trachea; **–röhrenentzündung** *f.* bronchitis; **–schacht** *m.* air shaft; **–schaukel** *f.* flipflap; **–schiff** *neu.* airship; **–schiffahrt** *f.* aeronautics; **–schlange** *f.* streamer; **–schlauch** *m.* inner tube; **–schraube** *f.* propeller **–schutz** *m.* air defense; **–schutzkeller** *m.* air raid shelter; **–spiegelung** *f.* mirage; **–sprung** *m.* caper, leap; **–streitkräfte** *f. pl.* air forces; **–strömungsmesser** *m.* anemometer; **–strom** *m.* air current; **–stützpunkt** *m.* air base; **— und Raumfahrt** *f.* aerospace; **–waffe** *f.* air force; **–widerstand** *m.* gust load; air resistance; **–zug** *m.* current (*oder* draft) of air

luft: –dicht *adj.* airtight; hermetical; **–gekühlt** *adj.* air-cooled; **–ig** *adj.* airy, light; breezy, aerial; **–krank** *adj.* airsick; **–leer** *adj.* airless; **–leerer Raum** vacuum; **–tüchtig** *adj.* airworthy

Lüftchen *neu.* breeze

lüften *v.* to lift; to air, to ventilate; to reveal, to unveil; **den Hut –en** to tip the hat

Lüg: –e *f.* lie, falsehood; **harmlose –e** white lie; **–en haben kurze Beine** one doesn't get far with lies; **–endetektor** *m.* lie detector, polygraph; **–enmaul** *neu.*, **–ner** *m.* liar

lüg: –en *v.* to lie, to tell stories; **–enhaft** *adj.*, **–nerisch** *adj.* lying, false

Luke *f.* dormer window; (naut.) hatch

lullen *v.* to lull, **in den Schlaf —** to sing to sleep

Lümmel *m.* hooligan, hoodlum, lout; **–ei** *f.* hooliganism, rudeness

Lump *m.* bum, scamp, ragamuffin; **–en** *m.* rag; **–engeld** *neu.* paltry sum; **–engesindel** *neu.*, **–enpack** *neu.*, **–envolk** *neu.* riffraff, rabble; **–ensammler** *m.* ragpicker; **–erei** *f.* shabby trick; meanness

lumpen *v.* to lead a dissolute life; **sich nicht — lassen** (coll.) not to act shabbily

lumpig *adj.* ragged, tattered; shabby, stingy

Lunge *f.* lung; **–n** *pl.* (zool.) lights; **–nblutung** *f.* lung hemorrhage; **–nchiale –nentzündung** bronchopneumonia; **–nkrankheit** *f.*, **–nschwindsucht** *f.* tuberculosis; **–rer** *m.* loiterer, loafer

lungern *v.* to loaf, to loiter, to idle

Lupe *f.* magnifying glass; pocket lens; **unter die — nehmen** to examine closely

Lust *f.* delight, pleasure; inclination, desire; lust; **— haben zu** to like to do; **mit — und Liebe** with heart and soul; **–barkeit** *f.* merriment, gaiety; entertainment; **–barkeitssteuer** *f.* entertainment tax; **–fahrt** *f.* pleasure trip; **–haus** *neu.* summerhouse, pavilion; **–mord** *m.* rape and murder; **–spiel** *neu.* comedy

lust: –erweckend *adj.* appetizing, savory; **–ig** *adj.* joyous, merry, gay; amusing, funny; **sich –ig machen über** to mock at; **–los** *adj.* listless; dull; **–wandeln** *v.* to stroll, to promenade

Lüst: –er *m.* chandelier; luster; gloss; (cloth) alpaca; **–ernheit** *f.* lustfulness; concupiscence; **–ling** *m.* sensualist

lüstern *adj.* lustful, covetous; lascivious

lutschen *v.* (coll.) to suck

Lüttich *neu.* Liège

luxuriös *adj.* luxurious
Luxus *m.* luxury; **-ausgabe** *f.* de luxe edition; **-waren** *f. pl.*, **-artikel** *m. pl.* fancy goods, luxuries
lynchen *v.* to lynch
Lynchgesetz *neu.*, **Lynchjustiz** *f.* lynch (*oder* mob) law
Lyrik *f.* lyric(al) poetry; **-er** *m.* lyric poet
lyrisch *adj.* lyric(al)
Lyzeum *neu.* lyceum; (Germany) high school and junior college for girls

M

Maat *m.* (naut.) mate
Mach (Geschwindigkeitsmasseinheit nach dem Physiker Ernst Mach) einmalize Schallgeschwindigkeit *f.* Mach
Mach: -enschaft *f.* machination, intrigue
machen *v.* to make, to do; to create, to manufacture; to cause; to arrange, to progress; **da ist nichts zu —** nothing can be done about it; **das macht nichts** that doesn't matter; **er macht sich jetzt** he is getting on now; **Freude —** to give pleasure; **Holz —** to split wood; **möglich —** to render possible; **Mut —** to encourage; **niemand kann es ihm recht —** nobody can satisfy him; **sich auf den Weg (*or* die Beine) —** to get on one's way; **sich aus dem Staube —** to make off; **jemand schlecht —** to defame a person; **sich viel Mühe —** to go to a lot of trouble; **Vorwürfe —** to reproach; **zu etwas —** to convert to
Macht *f.* might, force, strength, power; sovereign state, authority; army; **-befugnis** *f.* full authority (*oder* power); competence; **-bereich** *m.* sphere of influence; **-haber** *m.* ruler, dictator; **-vollkommenheit** *f.* absolute power
machthaberisch *adj.* despotic, dictatorial
mächtig *adj.* mighty, powerful; (min.) thick, rich; **seiner —** in control of himself; **— adv.** much; in great degree
machtlos *adj.* impotent, powerless
Mädchen *neu.* girl; maiden; maidservant; **-füralles** *neu.* maid-of-all-work; **-handel** *m.* white slave traffic; **-name** *m.* maiden name
mädchenhaft *adj.* girlish, maidenly
Made *f.* maggot; grub
madig *adj.* maggoty; worm-eaten; **— machen** (coll.) to run down (*oder* defame)
Magazin *neu.* storehouse; depot; magazine
Magd *f.* maid servant, housemaid; (poet.) maiden
Magen *m.* stomach; maw; **er liegt mir im** — (coll.) I am fed up with him; **seine Augen waren grösser als der —** he took more than he could eat; **-beschwerden** *f. pl.* indigestion; **-brennen** *neu.* heartburn; **-entzündung** *f.* gastritis; **-säure** *f.* gastric acid; **-schwäche** *f.* dyspepsia

mager *adj.* lean, meager; (milk) skimmed; (soil) devitalized; (wine) lacking body
Magi: -e *f.* magic; **-ker** *m.* magician; magi; **-ster** *m.* (school)master; **-strat** *m.* magistracy; city (*oder* town) council
Magnat *m.* magnate; grandee; **-en** *pl.* body of nobles
Magnet *m.* magnet; loadstone; **-ismus** *m.* magnetism; mesmerism; **-nadel** *f.* magnetic needle; **-ofongerät** *neu.* magnetic tape recorder
magnet: -isch *adj.* magnetic; hypnotic; **-isierbar** *adj.* magnetizable; **-isieren** *v.* to magnetize; to mesmerize
mähen *v.* to mow, to reap; **to bleat**
Mäher *m.* mower, reaper
Mahl *neu.* meal; **-zeit** *f.* repast; meal; **— interj.** (coll.) what a mess! **gesegnete -zeit** may your meal be blessed!
mahlen *v.* to mill, to grind; to crush
Mahn: -brief *m.* request to pay; dunning (*oder* monitory) letter; **-er** *m.* admonisher; dun; **-ung** *f.* warning; admonition
Mähne *f.* mane; (coll.) long hair
mahnen *v.* to remind; to admonish, **to dun**
Mähre *f.* mare; plug, hack
Mähren *neu.* Moravia
Mai *m.* May; **-baum** *m.* maypole; **-feier** *f.* May Day (labor) demonstration; **-fest** *neu.* May Day; **-glöckchen** *neu.* lily of the valley; **-käfer** *m.* cockchafer; **-kätzchen** *neu.* (birch) catkin
Mailand *neu.* Milan
Mainz *neu.* Mayence
Mais *m.* maize; Indian corn; **-hülse** *f.* corn husk; **-kolben** *m.* corncob, ear of corn
majestätisch *adj.* majestic(al)
Major *m.* (mil.) major; **-at** *neu.* primogeniture; entail; **-ität** *f.* majority
majorenn *adj.* of age; major
Majuskel *f.* capital letter; (typ.) small capital
Makel *m.* blemish, defect, stain, spot
mäkeln *v.* to find fault; to be fastidious
Makler *m.* broker, middleman; **-gebühr** *f.* brokerage; **-geschäft** *neu.* broker's business
Mäkler *m.* faultfinder; fastidious **person**
Makrele *f.* mackerel
Makrokosmos *m.* macrocosm
Makrone *f.* macaroon
Makulatur *f.* wastepaper; **-reden** (coll.)

to talk nonsense

Mal *neu.* mole, spot; sign; monument; (boundary) mark; (sports) base, goal; time; **das wievielte —** how many times; **manches —** often, many a time; **mit einem —** suddenly; **nicht ein einziges — not once; zum ersten —** for the first time; **zu wiederholten –en** repeatedly; again and again

mal *adv.* multiplied by; (coll.) once

male: –n *v.* to paint; to portray; to draw, to delineate; (lit.) to describe; **–erisch** *adj.* picturesque; graphic

Maler *m.* painter; artist; **–ei** *f.* (art of) painting

Malheur *neu.* misfortune, accident

Malstrom *m.* maelstrom

malträtieren *v.* to maltreat

Malz *neu.* malt; **da ist Hopfen und — verloren** (coll.) this case is hopeless

Mammut *neu.* and *m.* mammoth

Mamsell *f.* girl, miss, housekeeper

man *pron.* one, somebody; we, you; they, people

manch *pron.* and *adj.* many a (one); **–e** *pron.* some, several; **–erlei** *adj.* of several kinds, various; **–mal** *adv.* sometimes; many a time; often; now and again

Mand: –ant *m.* client; (pol.) constituent; **–at** *neu.* mandate, authorization, power of attorney

Mandarine *f.* tangerine

Mandel *f.* almond; tonsil; **–entzündung** *f.* tonsillitis

Mandoline *f.* mandolin

Mangan *neu.* manganese

Mangel *f.* mangle; **—** *m.* defect, want; lack; deficiency, scarcity; **aus — an** for want of; **— leiden** to be destitute

mangel: –haft *adj.* imperfect, incomplete; defective; **–n** *v.* to be deficient, to want, to lack; to mangle, to calender; **–s** *adv.* for want of

Mani: –e *f.* mania, craze

mani: –eriert *adj.* affected, stilted, mannered; **–erlich** *adj.* well-mannered, mannerly, civil

Manier *f.* manner, deportment; way, fashion; **–iertheit** *f.* mannerism

manifestieren *v.* to manifest, to declare

maniküren *v.* to manicure

Manko *neu.* deficiency, deficit; shortage

Mann *m.* man; male; husband; soldier; sailor, worker; **alle — an Deck** all hand on deck; **an den — bringen** (coll.) to sell; **an den unrechten — kommen** to come up against a better man; **ein — ein Wort** a man's word is his bond; **er wird seinen — schon finden** he'll find

his match; **seine Tochter an den — bringen** to marry off one's daughter; **seinen — stellen** to hold one's own, to be brave; **–e** *m.* vassal; **–esalter** *neu.* years of manhood; **–eskraft** *f.* virility; **–sbild** *neu.* male; **–schaft** *f.* body of men, personnel; (mil.) ranks; squad; (naut.) crew; (sports) team; **–sleute** *pl.* menfolk; **–(e)szucht** *f.* (mil.) discipline; **–weib** *neu.* manlike woman, amazon

mann: –bar *adj.* marriageable; **–haft** *adj.* manly; resolute; virile; **–shoch** *adj.* of a man's height; **–stoll** *adj.* man-crazy, nymphomaniac

mannigfach, mannigfaltig *adj.* various, manifold, diverse

Manöver *neu.* maneuver

manövrieren *v.* to maneuver

Manövrierfähigkeit *f.* maneuverability

Mansarde *f.* attic room; garret

Manschette *f.* cuff; **–n haben** (coll.) to be afraid; **–nknopf** *m.* shirt stud, cuff button

Mantel *m.* mantle; cloak, overcoat; (mech.) jacket, casing; (naut.) case; (tire) cover; **–kragen** *m.* (cloak) cape; **–sack** *m.* (poet.) valise

Manu: –al *neu.* manual; notebook; (mus.) keyboard; **–faktur** *f.* manufacture; factory; **–skript** *neu.* manuscript; (typ.) copy

Mappe *f.* portfolio; briefcase; file folder

Mär, Märe *f.* tale; tidings; **–chen** *neu.* fairy (*oder* folk) tale; (coll.) story, fib

märchenhaft *adj.* fabulous, wonderful, legendary

Marder *m.* marten

Marien: –fäden *m. pl.* Indian summer; gossamer; **–glas** *neu.* isinglass; **–käfer** *m.* ladybug

Marine *f.* marine, navy; **–flieger** *m.* naval airman; **–flugzeug** *neu.* seaplane; **–station** *f.* naval base; **–wesen** *neu.* naval affairs

marinieren *v.* to pickle, to marinate

Mark *neu.* marrow, pulp; core, essence; vigor **—** *f.* boundary, border country; (money unit) mark; **–stein** *m.* boundary stone; landmark

mark: –ant *adj.* striking; characteristic; **–ieren** *v.* to mark; (coll.) to simulate; to pretend; **–ig** *adj.* pithy, vigorous

Marke *f.* mark, sign; (identification) check; stamp, trademark; token; sort, quality, vintage

Marketender *m.* sutler, canteen clerk

Markise *f.* awning, blind

Markt *m.* market; trade; fair; **–flecken** *m.* small country town; **–kurs** *m.* market quotation; **–schreier** *m.* high-pressure salesman

Marmelade *f.* jam; marmalade

Marmor *m.* marble; **–bruch** *m.* marble quarry; **–platte** *f.* marble slab

Marodeur *m.* marauder

marodieren *v.* to maraud, to pillage

Marotte *f.* caprice, whim; fad, hobby

marschieren *v.* to march

Marter *f.* torment, torture; **–bank** *f.* torture rack; **–er** *m.* tormentor, torturer; **–holz** *neu.* cross of torture; **–pfahl** *m.* torture stake; **–tod** *m.* martyr's death

martern *v.* to torment, to torture

martialisch *adj.* martial; warlike

Märtyrer *m.* martyr; **–geschichte** *f.* martyrology

Martyrium *neu.*, **Märtyrertum** *neu.* martyrdom

März *m.* March

Marzipan *m.* and *neu.* marzipan; marchpane

Masche *f.* mesh; stitch (in knitting)

Maschine *f.* machine, engine; typewriter; motorcycle, bicycle; **–narbeiter** *m.* machinist; **–nbauer** *m.* mechanical engineer; **–nführer** *m.* engineer; **–nschreiberin** *f.* typist; **–nschrift** *f.* typewriting, typescript; **–nwesen** *neu.* engineering; **–rie** *f.* machinery

maschinemässig *adj.* machine-like; mechanical

Maser *f.* (wood) streak, vein; spot, speckle; **–n** *pl.* measles

Maske *f.* mask; disguise; **–nball** *m.* masked (*oder* fancy dress) ball; **–nscherz** *m.* mummery; **–rade** *f.* masquerade

maskieren *v.* to mask; to disguise

Mass *neu.* measure; proportion; degree; limit; measurement; criterion; moderation; **nach** — angefertigt tailor-made; made to measure; **über alle –en** beyond measure, exceedingly; **–arbeit** *f.* custom work; **–einheit** *f.* unit of measurement; **–gabe** *f.* proportion; **nach –gabe** in accordance with; **–nahme** *f.* measure; **–regeln** *f. pl.* measures; remedies; **gesetzliche –regeln ergreifen** to take legal steps; **–reg(e)lung** *f.* reprimand, disciplinary punishment; **–stab** *m.* scale; rule, standard; yardstick; **–verhältnis** *neu.* dimension; **–werk** *neu.* (arch.) carved work, tracery

mass: –enhaft *adj.* in masses; abundant; numerous; **–enweise** *adv.* in masses, in bulk; **–gebend** *adj.* authoritative, decisive; standard; **–halten** *v.* to keep within bounds; to observe moderation; **–ig** *adj.* massive, bulky, large; **–iv** *adj.*

massive, solid; **–los** *adj.* boundless; exorbitant; limitless; **–regeln** *v.* to take to task, to reprimand; to inflict disciplinary punishment; **–voll** *adj.* moderate, measured

Masse *f.* mass, bulk; substance; multitude; (law) assets, estate; **–nabsatz** *m.* quantity sales, bulk sales; **–narmut** *f.* pauperism; **–naufgebot** *neu.* general levy; **–nmord** *m.* massacre; **–nversammlung** *f.* rally; mass meeting

massieren *v.* to massage

mässig *adj.* moderate, temperate; reasonable; **–en** *v.* to moderate; to check, to mitigate

Mässigung *f.* moderation, restraint, control

Mast *f.* (food) mast; **–(baum)** *m.* mast; pole; **–darm** *m.* rectum; **–ix** *m.* mastic; putty; **–kalb** *neu.* fatted calf; **–korb** *m.* (naut.) masthead, top; **–kur** *f.* fattening diet

mästen *v.* to fatten

Material *neu.* (raw) material; equipment; **rollendes —** (rail.) rolling stock; **–ismus** *m.* materialism

Materie *f.* matter; substance; subject

materiell *adj.* material; real

Mathematik *f.* mathematics; **–er** *m.* mathematician

mathematisch *adj.* mathematic(al)

Matratze *f.* mattress; (gym.) mat

Mätresse *f.* (kept) mistress

Matrikel *f.* register, roll; matriculation

Matrize *f.* matrix; mold

Matrone *f.* matron

Matrose *m.* sailor

Matsch *m.* pulp, mash; slush, mud

matschen *v.* to mash; to splash, to (s)quash

matt *adj.* exhausted, feeble; faint, dim; insipid; **–setzen** (chess) to mate

Matt *neu.* (chess) checkmate

Matte *f.* (mountain) meadow, pasture

Maturität *f.* maturity

Matz *m.* little fellow; (dicky)bird

Mauer *f.* wall; **–blümchen** *neu.* wallflower; **–brecher** *m.* battering ram; **–kelle** *f.* trowel; **–stein** *m.* brick; **–werk** *neu.* stonework, masonry

mauern *v.* to build masonry, to immure; (cards) to risk nothing

Maul *neu.* (zool.) mouth; **halt's —!** shut up! **— und Klauenseuche** foot-and-mouth disease; **–esel** *m.*, **–tier** *neu.* mule; **–held** *m.* braggart, blowhard; **–korb** *m.* muzzle; **–schelle** *f.* slap in the face; **–sperre** *f.* lockjaw; **–trommel** *f.* mouth organ; **–werk** *neu.* gift of gab

maul: –en *v.* to sulk, to mope

Maulbeere *f.* mulberry

Maulwurf *m.* mole

Maure *m.* Moor

Maurer *m.* mason, bricklayer; **–handwerk** *neu.* building trade

Maus *f.* mouse; (thumb) base; **–efalle** *f.* mouse trap

maus: –en *v.* to catch mice; (coll.) to filch, to pilfer; **–etot** *adj.* dead as a doornail; stone-dead; **–farben** *adj.* mousecolored, dun; **–ig** *adj.* mousy

Maut *f.* duty, excise, toll

Maxime *f.* maxim

Mechan: –ik *f.* mechanics; **–iker** *m.* mechanic(ian); **–isierung** *f.* mechanization; **–ismus** *m.* mechanism; works

mechanisch *adj.* mechanical

meckern *v.* to bleat; (coll.) to criticize, to laugh foolishly

Medaille *f.* medal

Medaillon *neu.* medallion, locket

meditieren *v.* to meditate

Medizin *f.* medicine; art of healing; **–albeamte** *m.* medical officer; **–albehörde** *f.* Board of Health; **–algewicht** *neu.* troy weight; **–er** *m.* medical student; medical man; (coll.) medic

medizinisch *adj.* medical, medicinal

Meduse *f.* jellyfish; sea jelly

Meer *neu.* ocean, sea; **–busen** *m.* bay, gulf; **–enge** *f.*, **–esstrasse** *f.* channel, straits; **–esbrandung** *f.* surf, breakers; **–eskunde** *f.* oceanography; Museum für **–eskunde** *neu.* oceanarium; **–esspiegel** *m.* sea level; **–frau** *f.* mermaid; **–katze** *f.* long-tailed monkey; **–rettich** *m.* horseradish; **–schaum** *m.* meerschaum; **–schweinchen** *neu.* guinea pig; **–spinne** *f.* king crab

Mehl *neu.* flour, meal; dust; **–kloss** *m.* dumpling; **–speise** *f.* pastry; pudding; **–suppe** *f.* gruel; **–tau** *m.* mildew, blight

mehr *adv.* more; es dauert nicht — lange it won't last much longer; es ist nichts — da there is nothing left; immer — more and more; — als more than; noch — even more; umso — all the more; **–en** *v.* to augment, to increase; **–ere** *adj. pl.* several; **–erlei** *adj.* various, sundry; **–fach** *adj.* manifold; multiple; repeated, frequent; **–jährig** *adj.* for several years; **–malig** *adj.* repeated, frequent; **–mals** *adv.* more than once, several times; **–silbig** *adj.* polysyllabic; **–stellig** *adj.* (math.) of several places; **–stimmig** *adj.* (mus.) for several voices

Mehr: –aufwand *m.*, **–ausgabe** *f.* increased (*oder* additional) expenditure; **–bedarf** *m.* surplus demand; **–betrag** *m.* surplus amount; **–gebot** *neu.* overbid;

–heit *f.* majority; **–kosten** *pl.* additional expenses; **–ung** *f.* increase, augment; **–wert** *m.* surplus value; **–zahl** *f.* plural(ity)

meiden *v.* to avoid, to shun

Meier *m.* manager (of an estate); farm tenant; **–ei** *f.* farm(house); dairy farm; dairy

Meile *f.* mile; **–nstein** *m.* milestone

meilenweit *adj.* extending for miles, many miles away

mein *pron.* and *adj.* my, mine; gedenke — remember me; **–erseits** *adv.*, **–esteils** *adv.* for my part; **–ethalben** *adv.*, **–etwegen** *adv.*, **–etwillen** *adv.* so far as I am concerned; um **–etwillen** on my account; **–ig** *adj.* mine, my; **–tag** *adv.* as long as I live; for a long time

Meineid *m.* perjury; **–ige** *m.* perjurer

meinen *v.* to mean; to think, to suppose, to believe; to intend

Meinung *f.* opinion, meaning; intention; view, belief; jemand die — sagen to give someone a piece of one's mind; **–sverschiedenheit** *f.* difference of opinion, disagreement

Meise *f.* titmouse

Meissel *m.* chisel

meist *adj.* most; — *adv.* generally, mostly; die **–en** Menschen most of the people; **–enorts** *adv.* almost everywhere; **–ens** *adv.*, **–enteils** *adv.* mostly, in most cases; generally, usually

Meist: –begünstigung *f.* preference; **–begünstigungsklausel** *f.* most-favored-nation clause; **–betrag** *m.* maximum amount; **–bietende** *m.* highest bidder

Meister *m.* master; champion; **–schaft** *f.* mastery; championship; **–stück** *neu.*, **–werk** *neu.* masterpiece (*oder* work)

meister: –haft *adj.*, **–lich** *adj.* excellent, masterful; **–n** *v.* to master; to subdue; to excel, to outdo; (coll.) to find fault with

melancholisch *adj.* melancholy

Melasse *f.* molasses

Meld: –eamt *neu.* registration office; **–edienst** *m.* intelligence service; **–er** *m.* orderly; messenger; **–ereiter** *m.* (mil.) dispatch rider; **–estelle** *f.* local reporting station; **–ezettel** *m.* registration form; **–ung** *f.* report; announcement; information; notification; (sports) entry

melden *v.* to inform, to report; to notify; sich — lassen to send in one's name

melken *v.* to milk

Melod: –ie *f.* melody; **–ik** *f.* melodics; **–rama** *neu.* melodrama

Melone *f.* melon; derby hat

Membrane *f.* membrane; diaphragm

Memme *f.* coward; poltroon; (coll.) chicken

memorieren *v.* to memorize

Menage *f.* menage; household; housekeeping; set of dishes (*oder* cruets)

Menge *f.* quantity, multitude; heap, swarm, crowd; **eine — Geld** plenty of money

mengen *v.* to mix, to mingle, to blend; **sich in etwas —** to meddle (*oder* interfere)

Mensch *m.* human being; person; (bibl.) man; **kein —** nobody; **-enaffe** *m.* anthropoid ape; **-enalter** *neu.* generation; average age of man; **-enfeind** *m.* misanthrope; **-enfresser** *m.* cannibal; ogre; **-enfreund** *m.* philanthropist; **-engedenken** *neu.* (from) time immemorial; **-engeschlecht** *neu.* human race; mankind; **-enhandel** *m.* slave trade; **-enliebe** *f.* philanthropy; cháríty; **-enraub** *m.* kidnapping; **-enrechte** *neu. pl.* human rights; **-enscheu** *f.* unsociableness; **-enschinder** *m.* exploiter, extortioner; **-enschlag** *m.* race of men; **-ensohn** *m.* Christ; **-heit** *f.* mankind; **-werdung** *f.* incarnation

mensch: **-enfeindlich** *adj.* misanthropic; **-enfreundlich** *adj.* philanthropic; **-enleer** *adj.* deserted; **-enmöglich** *adj.* humanly possible; **-enscheu** *adj.* unsociable; **-lich** *adj.* human, humane

menstruieren *v.* to menstruate

Mensur *f.* mensuration; (fencing) distance; standard (for organ pipes); diapason

Mentalität *f.* mentality

Menü *neu.* menu

Menuett *neu.* minuet

Merk: **-blatt** *neu.* instructional pamphlet; **-buch** *neu.* notebook; **-er** *m.* marker; (poet.) critic; **-mal** *neu.* distinguishing mark; characteristic feature; **-wort** *neu.* catchword; (theat.) cue; **-zeichen** *neu.* distinctive mark

merk: **-bar**, **-lich** *adj.* noticeable, perceptible; **-en** *v.* to mark; to remember; to notice; **das werde ich mir -en** I will bear that in mind; **-en lassen** to show; **lass dir nichts -en** do not let it be seen; **-enswert** *adj.* remarkable; **-würdig** *adj.* noteworthy; strange; memorable; **-würdigerweise** *adv.* strange to say

Merkur *m.* Mercury; **—** *neu.* (chem.) mercury

Merle *f.* blackbird

Mesner *m.* (Roman Catholic) sacristan, sexton

Mess: **-amt** *neu.* celebration of the Mass; **-buch** *neu.* missal; **-e** *f.* trade fair; **Mass;** (mil.) mess; **-ebude** *f.* booth (at a fair)

Mess: **-band** *neu.* measuring tape; **-kunde** *f.* surveying; **-ung** *f.* measurement; mensuration

mess: **-bar** *adj.* measurable; **-en** *v.* to measure; to compare (with); to survey; **sich -en mit** to be a match for; to compete with

Messer *neu.* knife; **—** *m.* measurer; measuring apparatus; **-scheide** *f.* scabbard; **-schneide** *f.* knife-edge; **auf -sschneide** on the razor's edge; **-schmied** *m.* cutler; **-stecher** *m.* cutthroat

Messing *neu.* brass; **-beschlag** *m.* brass mounting

Met *m.* mead

Meta: **-morphose** *f.* metamorphosis; **-pher** *f.* metaphor; **-physik** *f.* metaphysics

Metall *neu.* metal; **edle -e** precious metals; **unedle -e** base metals; **-geld** *neu.* hard cash; **-urgie** *f.* metallurgy; **-probe** *f.* assay; **-waren** *f. pl.* hardware

metaphysisch *adj.* metaphysical

Meteor *neu.* meteor; **-it** *m.* meteorite; **-ologie** *f.* meteorology

Meter *m.* and *neu.* meter (1.0936 yards); **-mass** *neu.* metric measure

Methode *f.* method

Methodik *f.* theory of method

Metier *neu.* profession, trade

Metr: **-ik** *f.* metrics; **-onom** *neu.* metronome; **-opole** *f.* metropolis; **-um** *neu.* meter

metrisch *adj.* metrical

Mette *f.* matins

Mettwurst *f.* German Bologna sausage

Metz: **-elei** *f.* massacre; **-ger** *m.* (dial.) butcher; **-gerei** *f.* butcher's shop

metzeln, metzgen *v.* to slaughter, to massacre

Meuchelmord *m.* assassination; **-er** *m.* assassin

meuchl: **-n** *v.* to assassinate; **-erisch** *adj.* murderous, treacherous; **-ings** *adv.* insidiously, treacherously

Meute *f.* pack of hounds; (coll.) gang, crowd

Meuter: **-ei** *f.* mutiny; **-er** *m.* mutineer

meuter: **-isch** *adj.* mutinous; **-n** *v.* to mutiny

miau! *interj.* miaow! **-en** *v.* to mew

mich *pron.* me

Mieder *neu.* bodice, corselette

Miene *f.* air, expression; mien; countenance; **gute — zum bösen Spiel machen** to make a virtue of necessity; **-nspiel** *neu.*, **-nsprache** *f.* facial expression; pantomime

Miet: −e *f.* rent, hire; lease, tenancy; (theat.) season ticket; (agr.) rick, shock, pit; −er *m.* renter, tenant; −erschaft *f.* tenancy; −geld *neu.* rent; −kontrakt *m.* rental agreement; −ling *m.* hireling; −shaus *neu.* apartment house; −skaserne *f.* tenement house; −sleute *pl.* lodgers, tenants, roomers; −svertrag *m.* lease; −swohnung *f.* rented dwelling, apartment; −zins *m.* rental

mieten *v.* to rent; to hire; to charter

Miez(e) *f.* pussycat; pussy; girl's pet name

Migräne *f.* migraine; sick headache

Mikro: −be *f.* microbe; −biologie *f.* microbiology; −fon *neu.* microphone; −millimeter *m.* micron; −rillen *f. pl.* (Schallplatten) microgrooves; . −skop *neu.* microscope

Milch *f.* milk; −bart *m.* (coll.) milksop; greenhorn; −brei *m.* porridge; −brot *neu.* French (*oder* Vienna) bread; −bruder *m.* foster brother; −gesicht *neu.* baby face; immature youth; −glas *neu.* milk tumbler; opalescent glass; −händler *m.* dairyman, milkman; −kuh *f.* milk cow; −kur *f.* milk diet; −schwester *f.* foster sister; −strasse *f.* Milky Way; −suppe (avi. Nebel) *f.* soup; −wirtschaft *f.* dairy farm(ing); −zahn *m.* milk tooth

milch: −en *v.* to give milk; −ig *adj.* milky; translucent; −weiss *adj.* milk-white

Mild: −e *f.* gentleness; indulgence; benevolence; clemency; −erungsgrund *m.* mitigating circumstance

mild(e) *adj.* mild; gentle, mellow, soft; bland; indulgent; charitable; −ern *v.* to mitigate, to moderate; to soften, to soothe; to reduce; −ernde Umstände (law) extenuating circumstances; −gesinnt *adj.* of gentle disposition; −herzig *adj.*, −tätig *adj.* charitable, openhanded, kindhearted

Milieu *neu.* environment; setting; local color; background; sphere

Militär *neu.* (the) military; army; — *m.* professional soldier; −arzt *m.* army surgeon; −behörden *f. pl.* military authorities; −dienst *m.* military (*oder* active) service; −herrschaft *f.*, −ismus *m.* militarism; −kapelle *f.* military band; −polizei *f.* military police; −wesen *neu.* army affairs; war department

militärisch *adj.* military, soldierlike, martial

Miliz *f.* militia

Mill: −iarde *f.* (England) milliard; (Am.) billion; −iardär *m.* billionaire; −ion *f.* million; −ionär *m.* millionaire

Milz *f.* milt, spleen

Mim: −e *m.* mimic; −ik *f.* mimicking; mimicry; −ikry *f.* mimesis; mimicry

mimen *v.* to act; to mimic; to imitate

mimisch *adj.* mimic, acting

minder *adj.* less(er); inferior, minor; **nicht mehr, nicht** — neither more or less; −jährig *adj.* under age; −n *v.* to diminish, to slacken; to lessen; −wertig *adj.* of inferior quality

Minder: −betrag *m.* deficiency, deficit; −einnahme *f.*, −ertrag *m.* decrease of receipts; −heit *f.* minority; −jährigkeit *f.* minority (of age); −wertigkeitsgefühl *neu.* inferiority complex; −zahl *f.* minority

mindest *adj.* least, slightest, smallest; **nicht das −e** not a bit; **nicht die −e Aussicht** not the ghost of a chance; **nicht im −en** not at all, by no means; **zum −en** at least; −ens *adv.* at least

Mindest: −betrag *m.* minimum amount; −gebot *neu.* lowest bid; −gehalt *m.* lowest percentage; minimum wages; −mass *neu.* minimum

Mine *f.* mine; (pencil) refill; −nräumer *m.*, −nsucher *m.* mine sweeper; −nsperre *f.* mine blockade; −ntrichter *m.* mine crater

Mineral *neu.* mineral; −ogie *f.* mineralogy; −reich *neu.* mineral kingdom

Miniatur *f.*, **Miniaturgemälde** *neu.* miniature

minimal *adj.* minimum

Minister *m.* minister; −ium *neu.* ministry; −präsident *m.* Prime Minister; −rat *m.* Cabinet, Council

Minne *f.* (poet.) love; −sang *m.* old chivalric love song; −sänger *m.* minnesinger, troubadour

minorenn *adj.* under age, minor

Minorität *f.* minority

minus *adv.* minus

Minus *neu.* deficit; loss; −kel *f.* miniscule; −zeichen *neu.* subtraction sign

minut: −enlang *adj.* for minutes; −enlang *adv.* lasting a (*oder* for) minute(s); −iös *adj.* minute

Minute *f.* minute; −nzeiger *m.* minute hand

Minze *f.* (bot.) mint

mir *pron.* (to) me, (to) myself

Mirakel *neu.* miracle

Misch: −dünger *m.* compost; −ehe *f.* mixed marriage; −ling *m.* half-breed, mongrel, hybrid; −masch *m.* hodgepodge; medley; −rasse *f.*, −volk *neu.* mixed race; −ung *f.* mixing, mixture; combination, composition; alloy

mischen *v.* to mix; to mingle; to blend; to alloy; (cards) to shuffle; **sich in**

etwas — to interfere in something

Misere *f.* misery

miss: -achten *v.* to disregard, to despise; to undervalue; -behagen *v.* to displease; -behaglich *adj.* displeasing; uncomfortable; -billigen to disapprove, to disavow; -brauchen *v.* to abuse, to misuse; -bräuchlich *adj.* improper; -deuten *v.* to misinterpret, to misconstrue; -en *v.* to miss; to lack; -fallen *v.* to displease; -fällig *adj.* unpleasant, disparaging; -gebildet *adj.* malformed; -gestaltet *adj.*, -gestaltig *adj.* misshapen, deformed; -gestimmt *adj.* peevish, discordant, depressed; -glücken *v.* to fail; -gönnen *v.* to grudge, to envy; -günstig *adj.* envious, jealous; -handeln *v.* to maltreat; -hellig *adj.* dissonant, incongruous; -leiten *v.* to mislead; -lich *adj.* unpleasant, precarious; difficult; -liebig *adj.* unpopular; obnoxious; -lingen *v.* to fail; -mutig *adj.* ill-humored, discontented; -raten *v.* to turn out badly; -stimmen *v.* to depress, to upset; -tönend *adj.*, -tönig *adj.* discordant; -trauen *v.* to mistrust; -trauisch *adj.* distrustful, suspicious; -vergnügt *adj.* dissatisfied, malcontent; -verständlich *adj.* misleading, erroneous; -versteh(e)n *v.* to misunderstand, to misconstrue

Miss: -achtung *f.* disdain, disregard; -behagen *neu.* uneasiness; -belieben *neu.* displeasure; -bildung *f.* malformation, deformity; -brauch *m.* abuse; -erfolg *m.* failure; -ernte *f.* crop failure; -etat *f.* misdeed, crime; -etäter *m.* evildoer, criminal; -fallen *neu.* dislike; displeasure; disapproval; -geburt *f.* abortion; monster; -geschick *neu.* misfortune; mishap; -gestalt *f.* deformity; monster; -griff *m.* mistake; -gunst *f.* envy, jealousy; grudge; -handlung *f.* maltreatment; (law) assault and battery; -helligkeit *f.* difference, discord; -klang *m.* disharmony, dissonance; -laut *m.* discordant sound; -stand *m.* inconvenience; grievance; -stimmung *f.* discordance, depression; -ton *m.* dissonance; -trauen *neu.* mistrust, suspicion; -verständnis *neu.* misunderstanding, dissension; -wirtschaft *f.* maladministration, mismanagement

Mission *f.* mission; -är *m.* missionary

Mist *m.* dung, manure; (coll.) junk; (naut.) mist, fog; er hat Geld wie — (coll.) he has a lot of money; -beet *neu.* hotbed; -haufen *m.* dunghill; -käfer *m.* dung beetle

Mistel *f.* mistletoe

misten *v.* to manure; to clean (out); (naut.) to fog

mit *prep.* and *adv.* with; also, likewise; at, by; too; Böses — Gutem vergelten to return good for evil; — Absicht intentionally; — dabei sein to be one of the party; — der Zeit in time, gradually; — einem Wort in a word; — fünfzig Jahren at the age of fifty; — Namen nennen to call by name; -arbeiten *v.* to collaborate; to contribute; -beteiligt *adj.* participating; interested (in); -bewerben *v.* to compete for (*oder* with); -einander *adv.* together, jointly; -eingriffen *adj.*; -eingeschlossen *adj.* included, inclusive; -empfinden, -fühlen *v.* to sympathize; -halten *v.* to share; -helfen *v.* to assist; -hin *adv.* and *conj.* consequently, therefore; -hören *v.* to overhear; -laufen *v.* to run along with; to do as (others do); -leidig *adj.* compassionate; -machen *v.* to take part in; to follow; to go through with; -nehmen to take along with; to exhaust; to treat harshly; to profit by; -nichten *adv.* by no means; -reden *v.* to join in conversation; -samt *prep.* together with; -schuldig accessory (to crime); übel -spielen to play a trick on; -teilen *v.* to impart; to communicate; to announce; -unter *adv.* sometimes, now and then; -wirken *v.* to assist; to collaborate; to take part in; -wissen *v.* to know of, to share (secret); -zählen *v.* to count in; to take into account

Mit: -arbeiter *m.* co-worker, contributor; -besitzer *m.* joint owner; -bewerber *m.* competitor, rival; -bringsel *neu.* present, souvenir; -bürger *m.* fellow citizen; -erbe *m.* coheir; -esser *m.* (med.) blackhead; parasite; -fahrerzentrale *f.* carpool; -gefühl *neu.* compassion; sympathy; -gift *f.* dowry; -giftjäger *m.* fortune hunter; -glied *neu.* member; -gliedschaft *f.* membership; -helfer *m.* assistant; accessory, accomplice; -hilfe *f.* assistance; -inhaber *m.* copartner; -laut *m.* consonant; -leid *neu.* pity; -leidsbezeugung *f.* condolence; -mensch *m.* fellow man; -schuld *f.* complicity; -schuldner *m.* codebtor; -schüler *m.* schoolmate, classmate; -welt *f.* our contemporaries; -wirkung *f.* assistance, participation

Mittag *m.* midday, noon; south; zu — essen to dine; -brot *neu.*, -essen *neu.* dinner; -slinie *f.* meridian; -stunde *f.* noon, lunch time

mittägig, mittäglich *adj.* midday, meridional; southern

mittags *adv.* at midday, at noon

Mitte *f.* middle, center, midst; mean, medium; **das Reich der** — the Middle Kingdom, China; **die goldene** — the golden mean; **in die — nehmen to attack from both sides; to take between;** — **Vierzig in the middle forties**

Mittel *neu.* means; expedient; remedy; average, mean; medium; — *pl.* money; **kein — unversucht lassen to leave no stone unturned; sich ins — legen to** mediate; **–alter** *neu.* Middle Ages; **–arrest** *m.* (mil.) solitary confinement; neutral zone; **–mächte** *f. pl.* Central Powers; **–punkt** *m.* center; **–schiff** *neu.* middle aisle; **–schule** *f.* secondary school; **–smann** *m.* go-between; broker; mediator; **–stand** *m.* middle classes; **–strasse** *f.*, **–weg** *m.* middle course, compromise, mean; **–stufe** *f.* middle step; intermediate degree (*oder* grade); **–treffen** *neu.* center (of army); **–wort** *neu.* participle

mittel: –alterlich *adj.* medieval; (coll.) middle-aged; **–bar** *adj.* indirect; mediate; **–bar** *prep.* with the aid of; **–gross** *adj.* medium-sized; **–ländisch** *adj.* Mediterranean; **–los** *adj.* without means; destitute; **–mässig** *adj.* mediocre, average; indifferent; **–s** *prep.* by means of

Mittelmeer *neu.* Mediterranean Sea

mitten *adv.* midway, amidst; — **auf der Strasse in the open street;** — **in der Luft in midair;** — **ins Herz right into the heart; –drin** *adv.* in the center; **–durch** *adv.* right across; **–entzwei** *adv.* broken in the middle

Mitternacht *f.* midnight, north

mitternächtig, mitternächtlich *adj.* taking place at midnight; nocturnal, northern

mitternachts *adv.* at midnight

Mittler *m.* mediator; intercessor

mittler *adj.* middle, central; middling; average; medium; mediocre; **–weile** *adv.* in the meantime, meanwhile

Mittwoch *m.* Wednesday

Mixtur *f.* mixture

Möbel *neu.* piece of furniture; **–schoner** *m.* slipcover; **–spediteur** *m.* furniture mover; **–tischler** *m.* cabinetmaker; **–wagen** *m.* furniture van

mobil *adj.* mobile; active, nimble; **–isieren, –machen** *v.* to mobilize

Mobil: –iar *neu.* furniture; **–ien** *pl.* movables; personal property; **–isierung** *f.*, **–machung** *f.* mobilization

möblieren *v.* to furnish; **möbliertes Zimmer furnished apartment**

Mode *f.* mode, fashion, vogue; **–artikel** *m. pl.*, **–waren** *f. pl.* fancy goods; novelties; **–dame** *f.* lady of fashion; **–journal** *neu.* ladies' (*oder* fashion) magazine; **–schau** *f.* fashion show; **–schriftsteller** *m.* popular (*oder* fashionable) author; **–welt** *f.* world of fashion; **–wort** *neu.* slogan in vogue

Modell *neu.* model, pattern, mold; sample, draft; **–ierer** *m.* patternmaker, molder, modeller

modellieren, modeln *v.* to model; to mold, to shape, to fashion

Moder *m.* mold, mud, decay; **–geruch** *m.* musty smell

moder: –ig *adj.* moldy, musty; decaying, putrid; **–n** to decay, to putrefy, to rot; **–n** *adj.* modern, fashionable; **–nisieren** *v.* to modernize

modifizieren *v.* to modify

modulieren *v.* to modulate

Modus *m.* mode, manner; (gram.) mood

Mogelei *f.* cheating, trickery

mögen *v.* to like, to want, to desire; to be willing, to let; **das mag sein that may be so; lieber — to like better; to prefer; mag kommen was will no matter what happens; wie dem auch sein mag be that as it may**

möglich *adj.* possible, feasible, practicable; eventual; **alles –e all kinds of things; everything possible; nicht —! you don't say so! sein –stes tun to do one's utmost; so bald wie — as soon as possible; –enfalls** *adv.*, **–erweise** *adv.* possibly, perhaps

Möglichkeit *f.* possibility; potentiality

Mohär *m.* mohair

Mohn *m.* poppy; **–same(n)** *m.* poppyseed

Mohr *m.* Moor; Negro; **–enwäsche** *f.* vindication

Möhre, Mohrrübe *f.* carrot

mokieren *v.* **sich — über — to ridicule, to** mock

Molch *m.* salamander

Mole *f.* mole, jetty, pier; **–kül** *neu.* molecule

Molke *f.* whey; **–rei** *f.* dairy; creamery

Moll *neu.* (mus.) minor; **alles in — dole-** ful, sad

mollig *adj.* cozy, snug; soft; rounded

Moment *m.* moment; instant; — *neu.* momentum; impulse; **–aufnahme** *f.* snapshot

momentan *adj.* momentary, instantaneous; — *adv.* for the moment (*oder* present); just now

Monarch *m.* monarch; **–ie** *f.* monarchy

Monat *m.* month; **–abschluss** *m.*, **–bericht** *m.* monthly balance (*oder* report);

–sfluss *m.* menstruation; **–sfrist** *f.* one month's grace (*oder* time); **–sgeld** *neu.* monthly allowance; **–sgehalt** *neu.* monthly pay (*oder* salary); **–skarte** *f.* monthly ticket; **–sschrift** *f.* monthly magazine

monatelang *adj.* for months

monatlich *adj.* monthly

Mönch *m.* monk, friar; **–skappe** *f.* monk's hood; **–skloster** *neu.* monastery; **–skutte** *f.* cowl; **–sorden** *m.* monastic order; **–swesen** *neu.*, **–tum** *neu.* monasticism; **–szelle** *f.* friar's cell; **–szucht** *f.* monastic discipline

Mond *m.* moon; (ast.) satellite; (poet.) month; **den — betreffend** lunar; **–bahn** *f.* orbit; **–finsternis** *f.* lunar eclipse; **–hof** *m.* halo around the moon; **–rakete** *f.* circumlunar rocket; **–sichel** *f.* moon crescent; **–stein** *m.* moonstone; **–sucht** *f.* somnambulism

Mono: **–gamie** *f.* monogamy; **–gramm** *neu.* monogram; **–kel** *neu.* monocle; **–log** *m.* monolog; **–pol** *neu.* monopoly; **–polisierung** *f.* monopolization

monoton *adj.* monotonous

Monstranz *f.* monstrance

monströs *adj.* monstrous

Monstrum *neu.* monster

Monsun *m.* monsoon

Montag *m.* Monday

Montage *f.* mounting, fitting

Mont: –eur *m.* fitter, mounter; mechanic; **–ierung** *f.* erection, assemblage; adjusting; (mil.) equipment; **–ur** *f.* uniform

montieren *v.* to fit, to erect, to assemble

Monument *neu.* monument

Moor *neu.* bog, fen, marsh, swamp; **–bad** *neu.* mud bath; **–land** *neu.* marshy country

Moos *neu.* moss; (coll.) money

moosig *adj.* mossy

Mop *m.* (dust) mop; **–s** *m.* pug

mopsen *v.* (sl.) to pilfer; **sich —** (coll.) to be bored

Moral *f.* moral(s); morality; morale; **den –ischen haben** to feel the prick of conscience; **–pauke** *f.*, **–predigt** *f.* severe reprimand, moral lecture

moralisch *adj.* moral

moralisieren *v.* to moralize

Morast *m.* morass, marsh, swamp, slough

Mord *m.* murder; **–(io)!** *interj.* murder! **–anschlag** *m.* murderous attack (*oder* plot); **–brenner** *m.* incendiary; **–gier** *f.*, **–lust** *f.* bloodthirstiness, murderous lust; **–kommission** *f.* homicide squad; **–skerl** *m.* devil of a fellow; **–spektakel** *m.* dreadful din, hullabaloo

mord: –en *v.* to murder, to kill; **–gierig**

adj. bloodthirsty, sanguinary; **–smässig** *adj.* (coll.) enormous

Mörder *m.* murderer; **gedung(e)ner —** hired assassin; **aus seinem Herzen keine –grube machen** (coll.) to wear one's heart on one's sleeve; **to be very outspoken**

mörderisch, mörderlich *adj.* murderous; awful; terrible, cruel, enormous; deadly, fatal

morg: –endlich *adj.* matutinal; **–enfrüh** *adv.* tomorrow morning; **–ens** *adv.* in the morning; **–ig** *adj.* of tomorrow; **–enländisch** *adj.* oriental

Morgen *m.* morning daybreak; (the) morrow; acre; east; **–andacht** *f.* morning devotions; **–dämmerung** *f.*, **–grauen** *neu.* dawn, morning twilight; **–gabe** *f.* bridegroom's gift; **–land** *neu.* Orient; **–luft wittern** to scent an advantage; **–rock** *m.* negligée

Morphium *neu.* morphine

morsch *adj.* rotten; decayed; rickety; carious

Mörser *m.* mortar; **–keule** *f.* pestle

Mörtel *m.* mortar; **–trog** *m.* hod

Mosaik *neu.* mosaic

mosaisch *adj.* Mosaic

Moschee *f.* mosque

Moschus *m.* musk; **–bock** *m.* musk beetle; musk deer

Moskito *m.* mosquito

Most *m.* must; fruit wine

Motiv *neu.* motive;

motivieren *v.* to motivate

Motor *m.* motor; **–hotel** *neu.* tourist court; **–rad** *neu.* motorcycle; **–schaden** *m.* engine trouble

motorisieren *v.* to motorize

Motte *f.* moth; **Ach, Du kriegst die –n!** (coll.) holy cow! **–nfrass** *m.* damage by moths; **–npulver** *neu.* insecticide

Möwe *f.* gull, sea mew

Mucke *f.* whim, caprice; (dial.) gnat; **–r** *m.* bigot, hypocrite

Mücke *f.* gnat, midge; **–nstich** *m.* gnat bite

mucken *v.* to grumble; to mutter; to be glum

mucksen *v.* (fig.) to stir; **er darf sich nicht —** he dare not say a word

müde *adj.* tired, weary; exhausted

Muff *m.*, **–e** *f.* muff; (mech.) socket; sleeve; moldy smell; **–el** *f.* muffle

muffig *adj.* fusty, moldy; sulky, cross

muh! *interj.* moo; **–en** to moo, to low

Müh: –e *f.* trouble; toil; effort; pains; **es ist der –e wert** it's worth while; **mit –e und Not** with difficulty; **sich –e geben** to take pains; **–ewaltung** *f.* care, exertion; **-sal** f. hardship; distress

müh: -elos adj. effortless, easy; **-en** v. to labor, to toil; **-evoll** adj. difficult, hard, laborious; **-sam** adj. wearisome, intricate, tiring; **-selig** adj. toilsome, wretched, unpleasant

Mühl: -bach m. millstream; **-e** f. mill; game (played on a board); das ist Wasser auf seine **-e** that's grist for his mill; **-wehr** neu. milldam

Muhme f. (dial.) aunt; older woman

Mulatte m. mulatto

Mulde f. tray; trough; hollow, valley

Mull m. mull, muslin

Müll neu. garbage, dust, rubbish, sweepings; **-abfuhr** f. garbage collection; **-eimer** m., **-kasten** m. dustbin; **-schippe** f. dustpan; **-wagen** m. garbage van

Müller m. miller

multiplizieren v. to multiply

Mum: -ie f. mummy

Mumme: -rei f., **-nschanz** m. mummery, masquerade

mumifizieren v. to mummify

mummeln v. to mumble

Mumpitz m. nonsense, bosh

München neu. Munich

Mund m. mouth; den — halten to hold one's tongue; den — vollnehmen to brag; die Bissen im -e zählen to begrudge every morsel; im -e führen to talk constantly about; kein Blatt vor den — nehmen to speak freely; nach dem — reden to flatter; nicht auf den — gefallen sein to have a ready tongue; reinen — halten to keep a secret; sich den — verbrennen to give oneself away; sich vom -e absparen to scrimp; über den — fahren to cut short; **-art** f. dialect; **-höhle** f. oral cavity; **-sperre** f. lockjaw; **-stück** neu. mouthpiece; (cigarette) tip; **-vorrat** m. victuals, provisions; **-wasser** neu. mouthwash, gargle; **-werk** neu. (coll.) glib tongue; gift of gab; **-winkel** m. corner of the mouth

Münd: -el neu. ward, minor; **-elgeld** neu. money held in trust; **-igkeit** f. coming of age. majority

münd: -en v. to flow (oder run) into; **-lich** adj. oral; **-lich** adv. by word of mouth

mündig adj. of age

Mündung f. mouth, estuary, orifice; (gun) muzzle; outlet, terminus

Munition f. ammunition; **-slager** neu. ammunition dump; **-snachschub** m. ammunition supply

munkeln v. to mutter, to whisper; (coll.) to plot; im Dunkeln ist gut — night

covers all

Münster neu. minster, cathedral

munter adj. brisk, lively, sprightly, gay, merry; — werden to awake

Münz: -anstalt f. mint; **-e** f. coin, money, change, medal; für bare **-e** nehmen to take words at face value; klingende **-e** hard cash; mit gleicher **-e** bezahlen to give tit for tat; **-einheit** f. monetary unit; **-fernsprecher** m. telephone booth; **-fuss** m. standard of coinage; **-kunde** f. numismatics; **-prägung** f. coinage; **-recht** neu. right of coinage; **-system** neu., **-wesen** neu. monetary system; **-zusatz** m. alloy

mürbe adj. tender, mellow; well-boiled; brittle, crisp; unnerved, worn-down; — machen to break (one's) spirit; (mil.) to soften up; — werden to give in

Mürbekuchen m. shortcake

murmeln v. to murmur; to mutter; to play marbles

Murmeltier neu. marmot; wie ein — schlafen to sleep like a log

murren v. to growl; to grumble

mürrisch adj. sullen, morose; surly, sulky

Mus neu. jam, stewed fruit; purée; pap

Muschel f. mussel; shell(fish); conch; earpiece

Muse f. muse; **-nross** neu. Pegasus; **-nsohn** m. poet; university student; **-um** neu. museum

Muselman m. moslem

musi: -kalisch adj. musical; **-zieren** v. to perform music

Musik f. music, band; in — setzen to set to music; **-alienhandlung** f. music shop; **-ant** m., **-er** m., **-us** m. musician; **-antenknochen** m. funny bone; **-direktor** m. bandmaster; conductor; **-dose** f. music box; **-korps** neu. military band; **-schule** f. conservatory; **-werk** neu. music mechanism, musical work

Musk: -at m. nutmeg; **-ateller** m. muscatel wine (oder grape)

Muskel m. muscle; **-kater** m. stiffness, soreness; **-schwund** m. muscular dystrophy; **-zerrung** f. sprain

Musket: -e f. musket; **-ier** m. musketeer

muskelig, muskulös adj. muscular; sinewy

Musse f. leisure; mit -e at one's leisure

Musselin m. muslin

müssen v. to have to, to be obliged (oder compelled to); alle Menschen — sterben all men must die; sie — bald kommen they are bound to come soon; Sie — wissen you should know

müssig adj. idle, unemployed; superfluous; useless; — gehen to idle, to loaf

Müssiggänger *m.* idler, loafer; lazybones

Muster *neu.* design, model, pattern; sample, example, standard; specimen; **–bild** *neu.* ideal, paragon; **–knabe** *m.* model boy; prig; **–schutz** *m.* trademark; **–werk** *neu.* classical (*oder* standard) work; **–wirtschaft** *f.* model farm; **–zeichner** *m.* designer; **–zimmer** *neu.* sample (*oder* show) room

muster: **–gültig** *adj.* ideal, model, exemplary; standard, classical; **–haft** *adj.* and *adv.* perfectly; **–reisende(r)** *m.* traveling salesman

mustern *v.* to examine, to inspect, to review

Mut *m.* courage, boldness; valor, spirit, mood; **den — nehmen** to discourage; **den — verlieren** (*oder* sinken lassen) to become discouraged; **guten –es sein** to be full of hope (*oder* good cheer); **— fassen** to summon up courage; **— machen** to encourage; **–massung** *f.* surmise; suspicion; presumption

mut: **–ig** *adj.* fearless, brave; **–los** *adj.* discouraged; **–massen** *v.* to presume, to guess, to suppose; **–masslich** *adj.* probable, presumptive, presumable; **–willig** *adj.* playful, wanton

Mütchen *neu.* mood; **sein — kühlen** to vent one's anger (on)

Mutter *f.* mother; (mech.) nut; (zool.) dam; **–boden** *m.* native (*oder* fertile) soil; humus; **–gottesbild** *neu.* image of the Holy Virgin; **–land** *neu.* native (*oder* mother) country; **–leib** *m.* womb; **vom –leibe an** from birth on; **–mal** *neu.* birthmark, mole; **–mord** *m.* matricide; **–pferd** *neu.* mare; **–schaf** *neu.* ewe; **–schaft** *f.* maternity; **–schoss** *m.* mother's lap; **–schwein** *neu.* sow; **–söhnchen** *neu.* mother's darling; mama's boy; spoiled child; **–sprache** *f.* mother tongue

mütterlich *adj.* maternal; motherly; **–erseits** *adv.* from (*oder* on) the mother's side

mutterseelenallein *adv.* all (*oder* quite) alone

Mütze *f.* cap; **–nschirm** *m.* visor (of cap)

Myrrhe *f.* myrrh

Myrte *f.* myrtle

myst: **–eriös** *adj.* mysterious; **–ifizieren** *v.* to mystify, to dupe; **–isch** *adj.* mystical

Myst: **–erium** *neu.* mystery; **–ik** *f.*, **–izismus** *m.* mysticism

Myth: **–e** *f.* myth; **–ologie** *f.* mythology; **–os** *m.*, **–us** *m.* myth

myth: **–enhaft** *adj.*, **–isch** *adj.* mythical; **–ologisch** *adj.* mythological

N

na *interj.* now! well! **— nu?** what next?; **— und?** well, and afterward?

Nabe *f.* (mech.) nave, hub; boss

Nabel *m.* navel; **–schnur** *f.*, **–strang** *m.* umbilical cord

nach *prep.* after(wards); behind; past; according to; to(wards); along, by, from; **einer — dem anderen** one by one; **— der Reihe** in turn; **— deutchem Gelde** in German money; **— jemand ausschauen** to look out for someone; **—** *adv.* after, behind; **mir —!** follow me! **— und — little** by little; gradually; **— wie vor** now as before, as usual

nachäffen *v.* to ape, to mimic

nachahmen *v.* to imitate, to copy, to counterfeit; **–swert** *adj.* worthy of imitation

Nacharbeit *f.* additional (*oder* finishing) work

nacharten *v.* to resemble, to take after

Nachbar *m.* neighbor; **–dorf** *neu.* neighboring village; **–schaft** *f.* neighborhood; **–sleute** *pl.* neighbors; **–volk** *neu.* neighboring nation

nachbauen *v.* to build after (a model); to build subsequently

nachbestellen *v.* to repeat

nachbeten *v.* to pray after; (coll.) to parrot; to echo

Nachbeter *m.* blind adherent; satellite

nachbilden *v.* to copy, to imitate; to mold from, to counterfeit

nachbleiben *v.* to remain, behind; to be left over; to survive; **— müssen** (school) to be kept in

Nachbleibsel *neu.* remains; rest; aftereffect

nachblicken *v.* to look (*oder* gaze) after

nachdatieren *v.* to postdate

nachdem *adv.* afterward(s); **—** *conj.* after, when; **je — according to**

nachdenken *v.* to meditate (on), to reflect

nachdenklich *adj.* thoughtful, meditative

Nachdichtung *f.* free version (*oder* limitation) of a literary work

nachdrängen *v.* to press (*oder* drive) after

nachdringen *v.* to pursue; to press after

Nachdruck *m.* stress, emphasis; reprint(ing), reproduction; pirated edition; **— verboten** copyright reserved

nachdrucken *v.* to reprint; **unerlaubt — to pirate**

nachdrücklich *adj.* energetic, emphatic

Nacheiferer *m.* emulator, rival

nacheilen *v.* to hurry after; to pursue

nacheinander *adv.* one after another; **by turns; successively; –folgend** *adj.* subsequent

nachempfinden v. to feel (for); **-d** adj sympathetic, receptive

Nachen m. (poet.) skiff, fishing boat

nacherzählen v. to repeat; dem Deutschen nacherzählt adapted from the German

Nachfahr(e) m. descendant, successor

nacbfahren v. to drive (oder follow) after

nachfliegen v. to fly after

Nachfolge f. succession; disciples; — Christi Imitation of Christ; **-r** m. successor

nachfolgen v. to follow, to succeed; **-d** adj. subsequent, following

nachforschen v. to investigate, to inquire (oder search) after

Nachfrage f. inquiry, request; demand

nachfragen v. to inquire after; er fragt nicht danach he does not care about it

nachfühlen v. to feel with, to empathize; **-d** adj. sympathetic

nachfüllen v. to fill up (oder in); to add

nachgeben v. to give way (oder up); to yield; jemand nicht — to be a match for someone

nachgeboren adj. younger; posthumous

Nachgebühr f. excess postage (oder fee)

Nachgeburt f. afterbirth

nachgeh(e)n v. to follow, to pursue; to trace; (clock) to be slow; (com.) to attend to

nachgemacht adj. counterfeit, imitated, sham, artificial; **-e Waren** imitation goods

nachgerade adv. by now, by this time; after all; gradually, by degrees

Nachgeschmack m. aftertaste

nachgiebig adj. compliant; flexible; tractable, yielding; obliging; indulgent, easygoing

nachgraben v. to dig after (oder for)

nachgrübeln v. to ruminate; to ponder

Nachhall m. echo, resonance, reverberation

nachhaltig adj. enduring, lasting; persistent

nachhause adv. homewards; — gehen to go home

nachhelfen v. to help; to lend a hand; to retouch, to prompt; to push forward

nachher adv. after that; afterwards; later; **-ig** adj. later, subsequent, posterior

Nachhilfe f. help, aid, assistance

nachholen v. to recover; to finish later

Nachhut f. (mil.) rear(guard)

nachjagen v. to hunt (oder chase) after, to pursue; jemand eine Kugel — to fire a shot after someone

Nachklang m. reverberation; resonance; reminiscence

Nachkomme m. descendant; **ohne -n** without issue; **-nschaft** f. posterity, descendants

nachkommen v. to come after, to follow; to overtake; to execute, to fulfill; **Ihrem Wunsche** — in accordance with your wishes; **seinem Versprechen** — to keep one's promise

Nachkriegszeit f. postwar period

Nachlass m. legacy, heritage; estate; (com.) reduction, discount; allowance; **-en** neu. remission; reduction; relaxation; diminution; ceasing; **-enschaft** f. estate, inheritance; **-gericht** neu. probate court; **-steuer** f. inheritance tax; **-versteigerung** f. auction of an estate; **-verwalter** m. executor

nachlassen v. to leave behind; to transmit; (com.) to reduce; to grant; to relax, to give over (oder up); to yield; to diminish; to cease, to slacken, to temper

nachlässig adj. negligent, careless; remiss

nachlaufen v. to run after

Nachlese f. gleaning(s); (lit.) supplement; **-n** neu. rereading

nachlesen v. to look up again, to reread

nachmachen v. to copy, to imitate; to mimic; to counterfeit

nachmal: **-en** v. to paint after, to copy; **-ig** adj. subsequent; **-s** adv. afterward(s)

Nachmittag m. afternoon; **-svorstellung** f. afternoon performance

nachmittägig, nachmittäglich adj. taking place (oder occurring) in the afternoon

nachmittags adv. in the afternoon

Nachnahme (per) f. cash on delivery; c.o.d.; unter — paid on delivery; **-gebühr** f. collection fee

nachordnen v. to rearrange

nachplappern v. to repeat by rote; to parrot

Nachporto neu. excess postage; surcharge

nachprüfen v. to verify; to check, to test

nachrechnen v. to count again; to verify figures (oder a calculation); to audit

Nachrede f. epilogue; slander, rumor; in üble — bringen to slander; **-r** m. slanderer

Nachredner m. later speaker

Nachricht f. news; information; **ausführliche** — detailed account; **-enamt** neu., **-enbüro** neu. press agency; **-endienst** m. news service; (mil.) signals; **-entechnik** f. means of communication; **-entruppen** f. pl. signal corps; **-enwesen** neu. intelligence service; **-er** m. hangman

Nachruf m. posthumous reputation;

obituary notice, memorial poem (*oder* speech)

nachrufen v. to call after

Nachruhm m. posthumous fame

Nachsatz m. concluding sentence; postscript

nachschicken v. to forward; to send after

Nachschlag m. afterstroke; (mus.) complementary (*oder* grace) note; **-ebuch** neu., **-ewerk** neu. reference book, encyclopedia

nachschlagen v. to strike afterwards; to resemble; (mus.) to syncopate; to consult (book); to look up (word); to counterfeit (coins)

nachschleppen v. to drag after; (naut.) to tow

Nachschlüssel m. picklock; master key

nachschmieren v. to copy poorly; to relubricate

nachschreiben v. to copy; to plagiarize

Nachschrift f. copy; transcript; postscript; lecture notes

Nachschub m. supply; reinforcement

Nachschuss m. new (*oder* additional) payment

nachsehen v. to look after (*oder* for); to examine, to revise; to check, to look up; to see (whether); **jemand etwas — to overlook** (*oder* excuse) someone's faults

Nachsehen neu. revising, rereading; **das — haben** to have one's trouble for nothing; to come too late

nachsenden v. to send after, to forward; to redirect (mail); **Bitte — please** forward

nachsetzen v. to set behind (*oder* after); to pursue; to consider inferior

Nachsicht f. indulgence; forbearance; clemency; **— haben mit** to make allowances for

nachsicht: -ig adj. forbearing, indulgent; **-slos** adj. unrelenting, stern; **-svoll** adj. considerate; lenient, indulgent

Nachsilbe f. suffix

nachsinnen v. to muse, to meditate, to reflect

nachsitzen v. to be kept in

Nachsommer m. Indian summer

Nachspeise f. sweets, desert

Nachspiel neu. (theat.) afterpiece; epilogue; (mus.) postlude; (fig.) sequel

nachsprechen v. to repeat (someone's) words

nachspüren v. to track, to trace out; to investigate; to spy upon

nächst adj. next, nearest; shortest; closest; **bei der —en Gelegenheit** at the first opportunity; **mit -er Post** by return mail; **— adv.** next; soon; **— prep.** next to, after; **-beste** adj. second best; **-dem** adv. thereupon, soon; **-ens** adv. shortly, very soon; **-folgend** adj. next (in order); **-liegend** adj. nearest

Nächste m. (the) next; fellow man, neighbor; **jeder ist sich selbst der -e** everybody thinks first of himself; **-nliebe** f. charity

nachstehen v. to stand after; to be inferior to; **wie -d bemerkt** as mentioned below

nachstellen v. to place behind; (clock) **to** put back; (mech.) to adjust; to pursue

Nachstellung f. pursuit, persecution

nachstreben v. to strive after; to aspire to emulate

nachsuchen v. to search for

nachsynchronisieren v. to dub

Nacht f. night; **bei — und Nebel davongehen** to escape under cover of darkness; **mit einbrechender —** at nightfall; **über — bleiben** to stay overnight; **über — kommen** to come unexpectedly; **-essen** neu. supper; **-eule** f. screech owl; **-geschirr** neu., **-topf** m. chamber pot; **-gleiche** f. equinox; **-hemd** neu. nightgown; **-igall** f. nightingale; **-lager** neu. bed; **-lokal** neu. night club; (mit Schallplattenmusik) discotheque; **-musik** f. serenade; **-schicht** f. night shift; **-schwalbe** f. nighthawk; **-schwärmer** m. moth; night owl; **-wächter** m. night watchman; **-wandler** m. sleepwalker, somnambulist; **-zeug** neu. nightwear; overnight articles

nacht: -s adv. at (*oder* by) night; **-schlafend** adj. **zu -schlafender Zeit** when everyone sleeps; **-wandlerisch** adj. somnambulistic; **mit -wandlerischer** Sicherheit with absolute certainty

nächt: -elang adv. for nights; **-igen** v. to pass the night; **-lich** adj. nightly, nocturnal; **-licherweise** adv. at night time

Nachteil m. disadvantage, prejudice, detriment; **im — sein** to be at a disadvantage

nachteilig adj. detrimental, disadvantageous; prejudicial; disparaging; derogatory

Nachtisch m. dessert

Nachtrag m. supplement; codicil; postscript

nachtragen v. to carry after; to add; to bear a grudge; **-d** adj. resentful, vindictive

nachträglich adj. additional, supplementary; subsequent, further, later

nachtun v. to imitate; to emulate; **es**

jemandem — **wollen** to try to compete
nachwachsen to grow again (*oder* up)
nachweinen v. to mourn; to bewail, to lament
Nachweis m. proof, evidence; agency
nachweisbar, nachweislich adj. traceable, demonstrable; evident, authentic
Nachwelt f. posterity; future generations
Nachwirkung f. after-effect, consequence
Nachwort neu. epilogue; concluding remarks
Nachwuchs m. aftergrowth; (fig.) new blood
nachzahlen v. to pay extra (*oder* additionally)
nachzählen v. to recount; to count one's change
nachzeichnen v. to draw from, to copy
nachziehen v. to drag along, to pencil (eyebrow); to follow
Nachzügler m. straggler
Nacken m. (nape of) neck; **jemand auf dem — sitzen** to harass someone; **jemand den — beugen** to curb someone's wilfulness; **–schlag** m. blow from behind; mischief
nackend, nackt adj. naked, nude; bare; plain
Nadel f. needle; pin; **wie auf –n sitzen** to be on pins and needles; **–arbeit** f. needlework; **–baum** m., **–holz** neu. conifer; **–geld** neu. pin money; **–kissen** neu. pincushion; **–kopf** m. pinhead; **–öhr** neu. eye of a needle; **–stich** m. stitch, prick; pinprick
Nagel m. nail; peg; stud; spike; tack; **an den — hängen** to give up; **auf den Nägeln brennen** to be urgent; **–bürste** f. nailbrush; **–kuppe** f. nailhead; **–pflege** f. manicure; **–schmied** m. nail maker
nageln v. to nail, to spike
nagelneu adj. brand-new
nagen v. to gnaw, to nibble; to corrode
Nager m., **Nagetier** neu. gnawer, rodent
nah adj., **–e** adj. near, close; imminent; approaching; **–e** adv. nearby; **–egehen** v. to affect, to grieve; **–ekommen** v. to to come near; to get at; **–elegen** to suggest, to urge; **–eliegen** v. to be obvious; **–en** v. to approach, to draw near; **–estehen** v. to be closely connected; **–etreten** v. to come close; **jemandem –etreten** to hurt someone's feelings; **–ezu** adv. almost
Nah: **–aufnahme** f. close-up; **–kampf** m. close fight; **–verkehr** m. local traffic
Näh: **–e** f. nearness, proximity, vicinity; **in der –e** at hand, close by; **–ere** neu. particulars, details
Näh: **–erei** f. needlework, sewing; **–garn**

neu. sewing cotton; **–korb** m. sewing basket; **–maschine** f. sewing machine; **–nadel** f. sewing needle; **–zeug** neu. sewing implements
nähen v. to sew, to stitch; to suture
näher adj. nearer, closer; intimate, detailed; **–n** v. to bring (*oder* place) near; to approach
Nähr: **–boden** m. nurturing soil; culture medium; **–kraft** f. nutritive power; **–präparat** neu. patent food; **–wert** m. nutritive value; **–stand** m. (the) farmers
nähren v. to feed, to nurse; to suckle; to nourish, to entertain; **sich — von** to live (*oder* maintain oneself) on
nahrhaft adj. nourishing, nutritious, nutritive, substantial; lucrative
Nahrung f. food, nourishment; **–smangel** m. want of nourishment; **–smittel** neu. pl. provisions, food(stuff); victuals; **–s(mittel)sorgen** f. pl. cares of subsistence, struggle for livelihood
Naht f. seam; (med.) suture
naiv adj. naïve, harmless, ingenuous, artless
Name m. name; reputation; **auf meinen –n** on my account; **jemand dem –n nach kennen** to know someone by name; **wie war doch Ihr —?** may I ask your name? **–nsaufruf** m. roll call; **–ngebung** f. naming; christening; **–nliste** f., **–nverzeichnis** neu. list of names, nomenclature; **–nsvetter** m. namesake; **–nszug** m. signature
namhaft adj. renowned, notable; considerable; **— machen** to name; to specify
nämlich adj. same, very; — adv. namely
Napf m. bowl, basin; **–kuchen** m. poundcake
Narbe f. scar, cicatrice; grain; (bot.) stigma
narbig adj. scarred, grained
Narkose f. narcosis, anaesthesia
narkotisieren v. to narcotize, to anaesthetize
Narr m. fool, buffoon; **einen –en fressen an** to take a great fancy to; **zum –en machen** (*oder* halten) to dupe; **–enfreiheit** f. liberty at carnival; riotous merrymaking; **–enhaus** neu. madhouse; **–enkappe** f. fool's cap; **–enpossen** f. pl., **–enstreich** m. tomfoolery; foolish trick; **–etei** f. folly; **–heit** f. craziness
närrisch adj. foolish; mad, odd, strange
Narzisse f. narcissus; **gelbe —** daffodil
Nasch: **–erei** f., **–werk** neu. dainties, sweets; **–katze** f. sweet tooth
naschen v. to eat sweets on the sly; to have a sweet tooth
Nase f. nose; snout; (dog) scent; (coll.)

rebuke; auf der — liegen (coll.) to be ill (*oder* in trouble); das sticht ihm in die — he covets that; die — rümpfen to sneer; to fool; etwas an der — ansehen to see at a glance; immer der — nach follow your nose; straight on; jemand auf der — herumtanzen to make a fool of someone; unter die — reiben (coll.) to rub it in; **–nbein** *neu.* nasal bone; **–nbluten** *neu.* nosebleed; **–loch** *neu.* nostril; **–rücken** *m.* bridge (of nose)

naseweis *adj.* saucy, pert, cheeky

nasführen *v.* to fool, to trick, to dupe

Nashorn *neu.* rhinoceros

nass *adj.* wet, damp, moisty, rainy; **–auern** *v.* (coll.) to sponge; to cadge

Nass *neu.* liquid; (coll.) water; rain; drink

Nässe *f.* wetness, humidity, dampness

nässen *v.* to moisten, to wet

Nation *f.* nation; **–alfarben** *f. pl.*, **–alflagge** *f.* national colors (*oder* flag); **–alhymne** *f.* national anthem; **–alökonomie** *f.* political economy; **–ialität** *f.* nationality

national *adj.* national; **–isieren** *v.* to nationalize

Natter *f.* viper, adder

Natur *f.* nature; constitution; temper-(ament); in — in kind; von — aus by nature; wider die — against the grain; **–anlage** *f.* disposition; **–bursche** *m.* child of nature, unceremonious fellow; **–dichter** *m.* self-taught poet; **–ell** *neu.* temper, nature; **–erscheinung** *f.* phenomenon; **–forscher** *m.* investigator of nature; **–gabe** *f.* gift of nature, talent; **–geschichte** *f.* natural history; **–kraft** *f.* power of nature; **–kunde** *f.* natural science; **–recht** *neu.* natural right; **–reich** *neu.* kingdom of nature; **–trieb** *m.* instinct; **–volk** *neu.* primitive race; **–wissenschaften** *f. pl.* natural sciences

Natural: **–ien** *f. pl.* products of nature; natural history specimen; victuals; **–ienkabinett** *neu.*, **–iensammlung** *f.* natural history collection; **–ist** *m.* naturalist; **–leistung** *f.* payment in kind

natürlich *adj.* natural; innate, genuine; simple; **–es Kind** illegitimate child; — *adv.*, **–erweise** *adv.* of course, certainly, naturally

Navigationsraum *m.* chartroom

n. Chr. *abbr.* nach Christus A.D., after Christ

Nebel *m.* fog, haze, mist; künstlicher — smoke screen; **–fleck** *m.* (ast.) nebula; **–horn** *neu.* foghorn; **–mond** *m.*, **–monat** *m.*, **–ung** *m.* (lit.) November: **–schwaden** *m. pl.* damp fog

nebel: **–haft** *adj.* hazy; nebulous; **–ig, neblig** *adj.* foggy, hazy, misty; damp; **–n** *v.* to be foggy

neben *adv.* and *prep.* beside, near, close to; alongside; besides, in addition to; **–an** *adv.* close by, next door; **–bei** *adv.*, **–her** *adv.*, **–hin** *adv.* adjoining, alongside; by the way, incidentally; moreover; **–einander** *adv.* side by side; **–sächlich** *adj.* subordinate, unimportant, incidental

Neben: **–absicht** *f.* secondary objective; **–anschluss** *m.* (elec.) shunt; (tel.) extension; **–arbeit** *f.* extra work; **–ausgang** *m.* side exit; **–bedeutung** *f.* secondary meaning; **–beruf** *m.* additional occupation, sideline; **–beschäftigung** *f.* avocation; **–buhler** *m.* competitor, rival; **–eingang** *m.* side entrance; **–einkünfte** *pl.*, **–einnahmen** *f. pl.* additional income, perquisites; **–fluss** *m.* tributary; **–gebäude** *neu.* lean-to, annex; **–geleis** *neu.* sidetrack; **–handlung** *f.* episode; byplay; **–kosten** *pl.* incidental costs, extras; **–mann** *m.* next man; **–mensch** *m.* fellow creature; **–person** *f.* (theat.) subordinate character; **–produkt** *neu.* by-product; **–rolle** *f.* subordinate part; **–sache** *f.* side issue; **–satz** *m.* (gram.) subordinate clause; **–strasse** *f.* by-street; **–tisch** *m.* sidetable

nebst *prep.* together (*oder* along) with; besides; in addition, including

necken *v.* to tease, to banter, to fool

Neckerei *f.* teasing, banter, raillery

Neffe *m.* nephew

Neger *m.* Negro; **–in** *f.* Negress

nehmen *v.* to take; to accept, to receive; to appropriate; to remove; to seize; aufs Korn — to take aim at; die Folgen auf sich — to bear the consequences; ein Ende — to come to an end; es genau — to be pedantic; es sich nicht — lassen to insist on; etwas zu sich — to eat something; jemand beim Wort — to take someone at his word; jemand gefangen — to capture someone; — wir den Fall let us suppose; Partei — to side with; streng genommen strictly speaking; Urlaub — to take a vacation; to go on furlough; wie man's nimmt according to the way you take it; zur Ehe — to marry

Neid *m.* envy; jealousy; grudge; **–er** *m.*, **–hammel** *m.* envious person; grudger

neidisch *adj.* envious, jealous

Neig: **–e** *f.* slope; remainder; dregs, heel-tap; auf die (*or* zur) **–egeh(e)n** to decline, to run short; to come to an end; **–ung** *f.* declivity, inclination, tendency; taste; **-ungsehe** *f.* love match

neigen *v.* to bend, to bow; to incline, to slope; to lower, to dip

nein *adv.* no

Nekro: -log *m.* necrology; **-manie** *f.* necromancy

Nelke *f.* carnation, pink; clove

nenn: -bar *adj.* mentionable; **-en** *v.* to name, to call, to enter; to term; to mention; **-enswert** *adj.* worth mentioning

Nenn: -er *m.* denominator; **-ung** *f.* naming; nomination; entry; **-wert** *m.* nominal value; **zum -wert** (com.) at par; **-wort** *neu.* noun

Nerv *m.* nerve; **auf die -en fallen** (*or* gehen) to drive one mad; **-enentzündung** *f.* neuritis; **-enheilanstalt** *f.* mental hospital; **-enknoten** *m.* ganglion; **-enkrankheit** *f.* neurosis; **-enkunde** *f.*, **-enlehre** *f.* neurology; **-enschmerz** *m.* neuralgia; **-ensystem** *neu.* nervous system; **-enzelle** *f.* neuron; **-osität** *f.* nervousness

nerv: -enkrank *adj.* neurotic ; **-ig** *adj.* nervy; pithy; sinewy; **-ös** *adv.* nervous

Nerz *m.* mink

Nessel *f.* nettle; **-tuch** *neu.* unbleached muslin (*oder* calico)

Nest *neu.* nest; aerie, eyrie; (coll.) small town; **-häkchen** *neu.* nestling

nett *adj.* nice, pretty, kind

netto *adj.* net

Nettogehalt *neu.* take-home pay

Netz *neu.* net(work), trap; **in seine -e ziehen** to ensnare, to fascinate; **seine -e auswerfen** to allure, to entice; **-hemd** *neu.* mesh shirt

neu *adj.* new, fresh; recent, modern; **aufs -e, von -em** anew, again; **die -e Mode** latest fashion; **-ere Sprachen** modern languages; **-ste Nachrichten** late news; **-(ge)backen** *adj.* just baked; **-erdings** *adv.* recently, lately; **-erlich** *adj.* anew, late; **-gemacht** *adj.* renovated; **-gestalten** to reorganize; **-gierig** *adj.* curious, inquisitive; **-lich** *adv.* recently; **-modisch** *adj.* fashionable; **-vermählt** just married; **-zeitlich** *adj.* modern

Neu: -angeworbene *m.* fresh recruit; **-anschaffung** *f.* new purchase; **-auflage** *f.* new edition; **-bau** *m.* new construction; rebuilding; **-bearbeitung** *f.* revised version; **-druck** *m.* reprint; **-(e)rer** *m.* innovator; **-(e)rung** *f.* innovation, reform; **-gestaltung** *f.* reorganization; modification; **-gier(de)** *f.* curiosity, inquisitiveness; **-heit** *f.* newness, novelty; **-igkeit** *f.* news; **-igkeitskrämer** *m.* newsmonger; **-jahrsabend** *m.* New

Year's Eve; **-land** *neu.* unknown territory; new field of research; **-ling** *m.* beginner, novice; **-regelung** *f.* rearrangement; **-reiche** *m.* parvenu; newly rich; **-stadt** *f.* newest part of a city; **-vermählten** *pl.* bridal coupl ; **-zeit** *f.* modern times

neun *adj.* nine; **-erlei** *adj.* of nine kinds; **-fach** *adj.*, **-fältig** *adj.* ninefold; **-te** *adj.* ninth; **-zehn** *adj.* nineteen; **-zig** *adj.* ninety

Neunik *m.* beatnik

Neur: -algie *f.* neuralgia; **-asthenie** *f.* neurasthenia; **-ose** *f.* neurosis

neutral *adj.* neutral; **-isieren** *v.* to neutralize

Neuyork *neu.* New York

nicht *adv.* not; **auch —** not even; nor; **das — no such thing; durchaus —** by no means; **gar —** not at all; **ganz und gar — not in the least; ich auch —** nor I, either; **mit -en** not at all; **— doch** certainly not; don't; **— einmal** not even; **— verantwortlich** irresponsible; **— wahr?** isn't it? **—** wenig not a little; **nur das —** anything but that; **zu -e machen** to nullify; **zu -e werden** to become spoiled; **-ig** *adj.* null, vain, void; transitory; **für -ig erklären** to annul

Nicht: -achtung *f.* disrespect; disregard; **-befolgung** *f.* nonobservance; **-erscheinen** *neu.* nonappearance; nonpublication; **-igkeitserklärung** *f.* annulment; **-wissen** *neu.* ignorance;

Nichte *f.* niece

nichts *pron.* nothing; **es ist — damit** there is nothing to it; **fast gar —** hardly anything; **gar —** nothing at all; **mir —, dir —** without ado or ceremony; **so viel wie —** next to nothing; **-destominder** *adv.*, **-destoweniger** *adv.* nevertheless, notwithstanding; **-nutzig** *adj.* useless, naughty; **-sagend** *adj.* meaningless; insignificant; **-würdig** *adj.* worthless; base, contemptible

Nickel *m.* (coin) nickel; **—** *neu.* (min.) nickel

nicken *v.* to nod; (coll.) to doze, to nap

nie *adv.* never, at no time; **fast —** hardly ever

nieder *adj.* low, base, mean; inferior; **—** *adv.* down, low; **-beugen** *v.* to bend down; to discourage; **-brechen** *v.* to fall (*oder* break) down; **-deutsch** *adj.* low (*oder* North) German; **-drücken** to press down; to depress; **-fahren** to drive down; to descend; **-gedrückt** *adj.* depressed, dejected; **-geh(e)n** to go down; (avi.) to land; (thunderstorm) to burst;

–halten v. to keep down; to curb, to suppress; –holen v. to haul down, to lower; –kämpfen v. to subdue, to master; –knüppeln v. to club, to bludgeon; –kommen v. to descend; to be confined; –lassen v. to let down, to lower; sich –lassen to settle down; to establish; (avi.) to land; to light; –machen v. to cut down, to massacre; –metzeln v. to slaughter; –schlagen to knock down, to fell; to calm down; to quash, to stop; (chem.) to precipitate; to discourage; –schmettern v. to dash to the ground, to crush; –schreiben v. to write down; –trächtig adj. base, vile, infamous; –wärts adv. downwards; –werfen to throw down, to overcome; sich –werfen to prostrate oneself

Nieder: –fahrt f. descent; –fall m. downfall; –gang m. decline; (ast.) setting; (mech.) downstroke; –kunft f. confinement, childbed; –lage f. (com.) branch establishment; depot; (act of) depositing; defeat; –schlag m. sediment; (chem.) knockout blow; rain; result; (radioaktiv) fallout; –schrift f. writing; copy; –tracht f. baseness, infamy; –ung f. lowland, plain; –werfung f. overthrow, suppression

Niederlande pl. Netherlands

niedlich adj. pretty, neat, nice

Niednagel m. hangnail

niedrig adj. low, humble, inferior; base, mean

niemals adv. never, at no time

niemand pron. no one, nobody

Niere f. kidney; –nentzündung f. (med.) nephritis

nieseln v. to drizzle

niesen v. to sneeze

Niet m. and neu. rivet

nieten v. to rivet

Nihilismus m. nihilism

Nikotin neu. nicotine

Nilpferd neu. hippopotamus

Nimbus m. nimbus; prestige

nimmer adv. never; –mehr adv. nevermore; –satt adj. insatiable

Nimmersatt m. glutton

Nippel m. nipple

nippen v. to sip

Nippesachen f. pl. knickknacks

nirgend(s) adv. nowhere

Nische f. niche

nisten v. to (build a) nest

Nitrat neu. nitrate

Niveau neu. level, standard

nivellieren v. to level, to equalize

Nivellierwaage f. spirit level

Nix m. nix, water elf; –e f. nymph, mer-

maid

nobel adj. noble, generous, distinguished

noch adv. still, yet; besides, in addition; er hat weder Geld — Freunde he has neither money nor friends; — am gleichen Tag the very same day; — dazu in addition, into the bargain; — einmal once more; — etwas something more, anything else; — immer still; — lange nicht far from it; — nichts nothing yet; — obendrein over and above that; sei es — so klein be it ever so small; –malig adj. repeated; –mal(s) adv. again, once more

Nocke f., **Nockerl** neu. dumpling; –n m. cam

Nomade m. nomad

Nominalbetrag m., **Nominalwert** m. nominal value

Nonne f. nun; –nkloster neu. nunnery, convent

Nord m. north; (poet.) north wind; –en m. (the) North, northern region; –licht neu. northern lights, aurora borealis; –pol m. North Pole; –polfahrt f. Arctic expedition

nordisch adj. northern

nordwärts adv. northward(s)

nörgeln v. to nag, to grumble, to carp

Norm f. norm, standard; rule; criterion; –alarbeitstag m. ordinary workday; –algeschwindigkeit f. average (oder normal) speed; –algewicht neu. standard weight; –alspur f. (rail.) standard gauge; –alzeit f. mean time

norm: –al adj. normal, standard; –alisieren v. to normalize; –en v. to regulate, to standardize

Norwegen neu. Norway

Not f. want, need, necessity; distress; danger, emergency; misery; aus — from necessity; in — geraten to become destitute; mit knapper — entrinnen to have a narrow escape; von Nöten sein to be hard pressed; seine liebe — haben to have enough trouble; zur — at the worst; –anker m. sheet (oder spare) anchor; –ausgang m. emergency exit; –ausstieg m. (bemannte Rakete) escape hatch; –behelf m. makeshift; stopgap; expedient; last resource; –bremse f. emergency brake; –fall m. emergency; –kapsel (aerospace) escape capsule; –lage f. calamity; –landung f. (avi.) forced landing; –leine f. (rail.) communication cord; –lüge f. white lie; –pfennig m. savings; –ruf m., –schrei m. cry of distress; –signal neu. signal of distress; danger signal; –stand m. critical state, urgent case; –standsarbeiten *f. pl.* relief work; **–tür** *f.* fire escape; **–verband** *m.* temporary dressing; **–wehr** *f.* self-defense; **–zucht** *f.* rape

not: **–dürftig** *adj.* needy, makeshift; **–gedrungen** *adj.* compulsory, forced; **–landen** (avi.) to make a forced landing; **–leidend** *adj.* poor, distressed; **–wendig** *adj.* necessary, urgent, indispensable; **–züchtigen** *v.* to rape

Nota *f.* memorandum, bill; **–blen** *m. pl.* notabilities; **–r** *m.* notary; **–riat** *neu.* notary's office

Note *f.* note; annotation; bank note; memorandum; (pol.) communique; **nach –n** thoroughly; **nach –n singen** to sing at sight; **–nausgabe** *f.* issue of bank notes; **–nbank** *f.* issuing bank; **–nblatt** *neu.* sheet of music; **–nbuch** *neu.* music book; **–nhalter** *m.*, **–nständer** *m.* music stand; **–nschlüssel** *m.* clef; **–nsystem** *neu.* staff

notieren *v.* to note, to book, to score

Notierung *f.* quotation, notation, entry

nötig *adj.* necessary, required, indispensable; **—** **haben** to need; **–en** *v.* to compel, to force, to urge; to invite; **sich –en lassen** to need pressing; **–enfalls** *adv.* if need be

Notiz *f.* notice, note, memorandum; **–block** *m.* scratch pad; **–buch** *neu.* notebook

Notturno, Nokturno *neu.* nocturne

Novelle *f.* short story; supplementary law

November *m.* November

Novität *f.* novelty

Novize *m.* and *f.* novice

Nu *m.* and *neu.* moment; **im —** in an instant, in no time

nüchtern *adj.* sober, dry; prosy; insipid

Nudel *f.* noodle; komische **—** (sl.) funny fellow; **–holz** *neu.* rolling pin

Null *f.* zero, nought; **–punkt** *m.* zero

numerieren *v.* to number; **numerierter Platz** reserved seat

Nummer *f.* number; copy, issue; size; ticket; **auf — Sicher bringen** (coll.) to save; to put in jail; **eine grosse — sein** (coll.) to be influential; **–nfolge** *f.* numerical order; **–nscheibe** (tel.) dial; **–nschild** *neu.* license plate

nun *adv.* now, then; henceforth; **—!** *interj.* well! **— und nimmermehr** never; **–mehr** *adv.* now, by this time, since then; **–mehrig** *adj.* actual, present

nur *adv.* only, solely, merely; but, except; just; **Du weisst — zu gut** you know well enough; **— etwa** only about; **— mehr**, **— noch** only just; **— weiter! — zu!** go on! **wenn —** provided that; **wer — immer** whoever

Nürnberg *neu.* Nuremberg

Nuss *f.* nut; (mech.) tumbler; **–kern** *m.* kernel (of nut); **–knacker** *m.* nutcracker; **–schale** *f.* nutshell

Nüstern *f. pl.* nostrils

nutz, nütze *adj.* useful; **zu nichts — quite** useless; good for nothing; **zu –e machen** to utilize; **–bar** *adj.* useful; **–bringend** *adj.* profitable; **–en** *v.* to serve, to be of use; to make use of; **–los** *adj.* unprofitable, useless; **–niessen** *v.* to enjoy the profits

Nutz: **–anwendung** *f.* practical application; **–barmachung** *f.* utilization; **–en** *m.* use, profit, advantage; utility; **–garten** *m.* kitchen garden; **–holz** *neu.* timber; **–last** *f.* payload; **–ung** *f.* produce, yield, revenue

nützen *v.* to be of use; to utilize, to serve

nützlich *adj.* useful, of use, advantageous

Nymphe *f.* nymph

O

o! *interj.* oh! ah! **— weh!** oh dear!

Oase *f.* oasis

ob *conj.* whether, if; **na —!** rather! I should say so! **—** *prep.* on account of; above; **–gleich** *conj.*, **–schon** *conj.*, **–zwar** *conj.* although

Ob: **–acht** *f.* care, attention; **–acht geben** to pay attention; **–dach** *neu.* shelter; **–dachlose** *m.* homeless person; **–dachlosenheim** *neu.* house of refuge; **–hut** *f.* guardianship, protection, care; **–liegenheit** *f.* incumbency, duty; **–mann** *m.* chairman; foreman

Obduktion *f.* autopsy

oben *adv.* above, aloft, on high, on top, overhead, upstairs; on the surface; **da** (*or* dort) **—** up there; **nach —** upwards; **von — bis unten** from top to bottom; **weiter —** further (*oder* higher) up; **wie —erwähnt** as mentioned above; **–an** *adv.* at the top, in the first place; **–auf** *adv.* on top of; uppermost; on the surface; **–auf sein** to be in great form; **–drein** *adv.* over and above, into the bargain; **–erwähnt** *adj.*, **–genannt** *adj.* above-mentioned; **–hin** *adv.* superficially, perfunctorily; **–hinaus** *adv.* ambitiously

ober *adj.* upper, higher, superior; leading; **–faul** *adj.* very lazy; bad (excuse); **–flächlich** *adj.* superficial, shallow; **–halb** *adv.* and *prep.* above; **–irdisch** *adj.* above ground, overhead; **–lastig** *adj.* topheavy; **–st** *adj.* topmost, highest, supreme; first; head

Ober *m.* waiter; (cards) knave; **–appella-**

tionsgericht *neu.* High Court of Appeal; –arm *m.* upper arm; –arzt *m.* head physician; –aufsicht *f.* superintendence; –bau *m.* superstructure; –befehl *m.* supreme command; –befehlshaber *m.* commander-in-chief; –bett *neu.* coverlet; –bürgermeister *m.* Lord Mayor; –deck *neu.* (naut.) upperdeck; –e *m.* (eccl.) Father Superior; –fläche *f.* surface, area; –gericht *neu.* superior court; –geschoss *neu.* upper story; –gewalt *f.* supreme authority; –hand *f.* upper hand; predominance; –haupt *neu.* chief, head, sovereign; leader; –haus *neu.* upper house, Senate; House of Lords; –haut *f.* epidermis; –hemd *neu.* shirt; –herrschaft *f.* supremacy; –in *f.* (eccl.) Mother Superior; –kiefer *m.* upper jaw; –kellner *m.* headwaiter; –kommando *neu.* supreme command; –körper *m.* upper part of the body, torso; –land *neu.* upland, upper country; –landesgericht *neu.* Supreme Court of the country; –leder *neu.* uppers; –lehrer *m.* headmaster; –leitung *f.* top management; (elec.) overhead conveyor system; –leutnant *m.* first lieutenant; –licht *neu.* skylight; –priester *m.* high priest; –quartiermeister *m.* quartermaster general; –rock *m.* overcoat; –s *neu.* (dial.) whipped cream; –schicht *f.* upper classes; –st *m.* colonel; –schwester *f.* head nurse; –staatsanwalt *m.* attorney general; –steiger *m.* (min.) foreman; –stimme *f.* treble, soprano; –stube *f.* attic, garret; –stleutnant *m.* lieutenant colonel; –stufe *f.* upper grade; –wasser haben to have the upper hand

obig *adj.* above(-mentioned), foregoing
Objekt *neu.* object; –iv *neu.* lens; –ivität *f.* objectivity
Oblate *f.* wafer; (eccl.) host
obligat *adj.* indispensable, necessary; –orisch *adj.* obligatory, compulsory
Obrigkeit *f.* authorities, government
obrigkeitlich *adj.* official, governmental, magisterial; — *adv.* by authority
Observatorium *neu.* observatory
Obst *neu.* fruit(s); –garten *m.* orchard; –kelter *f.* fruit press
obszön *adj.* obscene
Ochse *m.* ox, bullock; (sl.) blockhead; –nbraten *m.* roast beef; –ngespann *neu.* ox team; –nschwanzsuppe *f.* oxtail soup; –nziemer *m.* horsewhip
öde *adj.* bare, bleak, deserted, desolate; dreary, dull
Öde *f.* desert, desolation; solitude
Odem *m.* (poet.) breath

oder *conj.* or; or else; — aber or instead
Ofen *m.* furnace, stove, oven; –hocker *m.* stay-at-home; –klappe *f.* damper; –loch *neu.* oven mouth; –rohr *neu.*, –röhre *f.* stovepipe; –schirm *m.* fire screen; –setzer *m.* stovemaker; –vorsetzer *m.* fender
offen *adj.* open, frank, vacant; public; candid, severe; auf –er Strecke on the open road; frei und — handeln to act straightforwardly; –e Rechnung (com.) current account; –e See high sea; –er Kredit unlimited credit; — gesagt, — gestanden frankly speaking; — lassen to leave blank; –bar *adj.* obvious, manifest, evident; –baren *v.* to disclose, to reveal, to manifest; –halten *v.* to reserve; –herzig *adj.* openhearted; frank; –kundig *adj.* notorious; public; –e Handlung overt act; –sichtlich *adj.* apparent; –stehen *v.* to stand open; to remain unpaid; to be at liberty to
öffentlich *adj.* public
Öffentlichkeit *f.* publicity, (the) public
Offerte *f.* offer, proposal, tender
Offizier *m.* officer; –smesse *f.* (naut.) wardroom; –spatent *neu.* officer's commission
öffnen *v.* to open, to uncork; (med.) to dissect
Öffnung *f.* opening, aperture, hole; mouth; gap, slit, slot; dissection
öfter *adj.* repeated, more frequent; –s *adv.*, des –en *adv.* frequently, now and then
oft(mals) *adv.* frequently, often
Oheim, Ohm *m.* uncle
ohne *prep.* without, but for, except; nicht not so bad; — weiteres without much ado; –dem *adv.*, –dies *adv.*, –hin *adv.* anyhow; besides; –gleichen *adj.* unequalled, unparalled
Ohnmacht *f.* powerlessness, weakness; faint, unconsciousness; –sanfall *m.* fainting spell
ohnmächtig *adj.* helpless, powerless, unconscious; — werden to faint
Ohr *neu.* ear; bis über beide –en (coll.) up to the eyes; die –en spitzen (coll.) to listen attentively; die –en steif halten (coll.) to keep a stiff upper lip; ein geneigtes — finden to get a favorable hearing; eins übers — bekommen to get one's ears boxed; er hat es dick hinter den –en he is a sly fellow; jemand das Fell über die –en ziehen to fleece someone; jemand übers — hauen (coll.) to cheat someone; mir klingen die –en my ears are ringing; someone is talking about me; sich aufs

— legen to take a nap; sich etwas hinter die –en schreiben (coll.) to note well; –enarzt m. ear specialist, otologist; –enbläser m. flatterer, slanderer; –enklingen neu., –sausen neu. ringing in the ear; –enschmalz neu. ear wax; –enschmaus m. musical treat; –schützer m., –enwärmer m., –klappe f. earflap, earmuff; –ring m. earring

Öhr neu. (needle) eye

ohrenzerreissend adj. earsplitting

Ökonom m. farmer, steward, housekeeper; –ie f. economy, economics, housekeeping; agriculture

ökonomisch adj. economic(al)

oktroyieren v. to impose, to dictate

Okular neu. eyepiece

okulieren v. to inoculate; to graft

ökumenisch adj. (eccl.) ecumenical

Okzident m. occident

Öl neu. oil; — auf die Wogen giessen (coll.) to pacify; — ins Feuer giessen (coll.) to add fuel to the fire; –baum m. olive tree; –berg m. (bibl.) Mount of Olives; –bild neu. oil painting; –kanne f. oilcan, oiler; –kuchen m. oilcake; –ung f. oiling, lubrication; anointment; letzte –ung extreme unction; –zweig m. olive branch

ölen v. to oil, to lubricate, to anoint; wie geölt as if oiled; very fast, very easily

ölig adj. oily; unctuous

Olive f. olive

Olympiade f., olympischen Spiele neu. pl. Olympiad; Olympic games

ominös adj. ominous

ondulieren v. to wave (hair)

Onkel m. uncle

Oper f. opera; opera house; –ette f. operetta; –nglas neu., –gucker m. opera glasses; –ntext m. libretto

oper: –ativ adj. operatic; –ieren v. to operate (on); –nhaft adj. in operatic style

Opera: –teur m. operator; operating surgeon; –tion f. operation; –tionsgebiet neu. (mil.) theater of operations

Opfer neu. sacrifice, oblation; victim; casualty; –gabe f. offering; –kasten m., –stock m. poor box; –lamm neu. sacrificial lamb; victim; –tod m. sacrifice of one's life; –trank m. libation; –ung f. sacrifice, sacrificing

opfer: –n v. to sacrifice, to immolate; –willig adj. –freudig adj. self-sacrificing

opponieren v. to oppose

Opt: –ik f. optics; –iker m. optician

optieren v. to choose

Optimismus m. optimism

optisch adj. optic(al)

Orakel neu. oracle

Orange f. orange; –nschale f. orange peel

oratorisch adj. oratoric(al)

Oratorium neu. oratory

orchestrieren v. to orchestrate

Orchidee f. orchid

Orden m. order, decoration, medal; –sbruder m. member of an order; friar, monk; –sgeistlichkeit f. regular clergy; –skleid neu. monastic garb; –sschwester f. nun; –szeichen neu. badge, order

ordentlich adj. orderly, regular; tidy, decent; respectable; good, sound; — adv. fairly, downright

ordin: –är adj. common, ordinary; low, vulgar; –ieren v. to ordain

Ordinarius m. professor in ordinary, headmaster

ordnen v. to put in order, to arrange, to classify; to regulate

Ordnung f. arrangement, regulation; order; tidiness; class; classification; der — nach in due order; –sruf m. (pol.) call to order; –sstrafe f. fine; –szahl f. ordinal number

ordnungs: –gemäss adj., –mässig adj. orderly, regular, lawful; –liebend adj. order-loving; –swidrig adj. contrary to order; illegal

Ordonnanz f. (mil.) orderly; order

Organ neu. organ; official voice (oder publication); –isation f. organization; –isator m. organizer; –ismus m. organism; –ist m. organist

organisch adj. organic

organisieren v. to organize

Orgel f. organ; –pfeife f. organ pipe

Orgie f. orgy

Orient m. orient; –ierung f. orientation; information; –ierungssinn m. sense of direction

orientalisch adj. oriental

orientieren v. to orient(ate), to locate, to inform

Original neu. original; –handschrift f. autograph; –ität f. originality, peculiarity

originell adj. original, peculiar

Orkan m. hurricane, typhoon

Ornat m. official robes

Ornithologe m. ornithologist

Ort m. place, spot, locality; (mil.) termination; am unrechten — out of place; an — und Stelle gelangen to arrive at one's destination; –sbehörde f. local authorities; –sbeschreibung f. topography; –sbestimmungsrecht neu. local option; –schaft f. village, place; –sgespräch neu. (tel.) local call; –skenntnisse f. pl. local knowledge, familiarity with a place; **–ssinn** *m.* sense of location; **–sveränderung** *f.* change of location; **–svorsteher** *m.* village magistrate; **–szeit** *f.* local time

Ortho: **–dontie** *f.* orthodontics; **–doxie** *f.* orthodoxy; **–graphie** *f.* orthography; **–pädie** *f.* orthopedics, orthopedy

ortho: **–dox** *adj.* orthodox; **–graphisch** *adj.* orthographic; **–pädisch** *adj.* orthopedic

örtlich *adj.* local

Öse *f.* loop, ring; (hook) eye; (shoe) eyelet

Ost *m.* east; (poet.) east wind; **–en** *m.* east; Orient

ostentativ *adj.* ostentatious

Oster: **–fest** *neu.,* **–n** *neu.* Easter; Passover; **–hase** *m.* Easter bunny; **–lamm** *neu.* Paschal lamb; **–mond** *m.* (poet.) April

Österreich *neu.* Austria

östlich *adj.* eastern, easterly, Oriental

Ostsee *f.* Baltic Sea

Otter *m.* otter; **—** *f.* adder

Ouvertüre *f.* overture

oval *adj.* oval

oxidieren *v.* to oxidize

Oxyd *neu.* oxide; **–dation** *f.,* **–ierung** *f.* oxidation; rusting

Ozean *m.* ocean; **–flieger** *m.* transocean airman

Ozon *neu.* ozone

P

p.A. *abbr.* per Adresse c/o, care of

Paar *neu.* pair, couple; brace

paar *adj.* some, few; even, like, matching; in pairs; **—** oder **unpaar** even or odd; **–en** *v.* to pair; to mate, to couple, to copulate; **–ig** *adj.* in pairs; **–mal** *adv.* ein **–mal** several times; **–weise** *adv.* in pairs, two by two

Pacht *f.* tenure, lease, rent; **–ertrag** *m.* rental; **–kontrakt** *m.,* **–vertrag** *m.* lease; **–zeit** *f.* term of lease; **–zins** *m.* rent

pachten *v.* to lease, to rent, to farm; (coll.) to monopolize

Pächter *m.* leaseholder, tenant, tenant farmer

pachtweise *adv.* on lease

Pack *m.* package, bundle, pile; **mit Sack und —** with bag and baggage; **—** *neu.* rabble; **–eis** *neu.* pack ice; **–en** *m.* bale; **–er** *m.* packer; **–erei** *f.* packing; **–esel** *m.* pack mule; **–hof** *m.* bonded warehouse; **–papier** *neu.* packing paper; **–raum** *m.* packing (*oder* stowage) room; **–ung** *f.* pack(ing); wrappings; **–wagen** *m.* baggage car

Päckchen *neu.* small parcel

packen *v.* to pack; to grasp, to seize; to grip; to fascinate, to thrill; **sich —** (coll.) to be gone, to clear out

Pädagoge *m.* pedagogue

Pädagogik *f.* pedagogy

paddeln *v.* to paddle, to canoe

Page *m.* page; **–nkopf** *m.* bobbed hair

paginieren *v.* to page, to paginate

Pagode *f.* pagoda

Pair *m.* peer; **–swürde** *f.* peerage

Paket *neu.* parcel, package; **–ausgabe** *f.* parcel delivery; **–boot** *neu.* (naut.) packet; **–karte** *f.* dispatch note; **–post** *f.* parcel post

Pakt *m.* pact, agreement

Palast *m.* palace

palastartig *adj.* palatial

Paletot *m.* (man's) overcoat

Palm: **–e** *f.* (bot.) palm; **–in** *neu.* coconut butter; **–wedel** *m.* palm branch

Pampelmuse *f.* grapefruit

Pamphlet *neu.* pamphlet; lampoon

Paneel *neu.* panel; wainscot

Panier *neu.* banner, standard

panieren *v.* to dress with breadcrumbs, to bread

panisch *adj.* panic

Panne *f.* breakdown; puncture; mishap

Panoptikum *neu.* waxwork exhibition

Pantine *f.* clog, patten

Pantoffel *m.* slipper; **unter dem —** **steh(e)n** to be henpecked; **–blume** *f.* slipperwort; **–held** *m.* henpecked husband

Panzer *m.* armor; coat of mail; (mil.) tank; **–abwehr** *f.* antitank defense; **–auto** *neu.* armored car; **–faust** *f.* mailed fist; antitank hand grenade; **–granate** *f.* antitank grenade; **–handschuh** *m.* gauntlet; **–hemd** *neu.* shirt of mail; **–jäger** *m. pl.* antitank troops; **–kreuzer** *m.* battle cruiser; **–platte** *f.* armor plate; **–regiment** *neu.* tank regiment; **–schiff** *neu.* ironclad; **–tür** (luftdrucksichere, army) *f.* bulkhead; **–wagen** *m.* tank; **–zug** *m.* armored train

Papagei *m.* parrot; **–enkrankheit** *f.* psittacosis

Papier *neu.* paper; (com.) securities, bonds; **–e** *pl.* identification papers; **das steht nur auf dem —** it means nothing; **zu — bringen** to put on paper, to write down; **–abfälle** *m. pl.* wastepaper; **–bogen** *m.* sheet of paper; **–brei** *m.* paper pulp; **–fabrik** *f.* paper mill; **–format** *neu.* size of paper; **–geld** *neu.* paper money; **–handlung** *f.* stationery store; **–korb** *m.* wastebasket; **–waren** *f. pl.* stationery

Papp *m.* pap; (coll.) paste; **–band** *m.*

pasteboard binding; **-e** *f.* cardboard, pasteboard; **nicht von -e** (coll.) thorough, sound, remarkable; **-enstiel** *m.* trifle; **um einen -enstiel** dirt cheap
Pappel *f.* poplar
Papst *m.* pope; **-tum** *neu.* papacy; pontificate
päpstlich *adj.* papal
Parabel *f.* parable; parabola
Parade *f.* parade; (mil.) review; parry; **-bett** *neu.* bed of state; **-platz** *m.* parade ground; **-schritt** *m.* goose step
paradieren *v.* to parade
Paradies *neu.* paradise
paradiesisch *adj.* paradisiac(al); heavenly
paradox *adj.* paradoxical
paralisieren *v.* to paralyze
parallel *adj.* parallel
Paralyse *f.* paralysis, palsy
paralytisch *adj.* paralytic(al), paralized
Parasit *m.* parasite
parat *adj.* ready
Parenthese *f.* parenthesis
Parforceritt *m.* steeplechase
Parfüm *neu.* perfume; **-erie** *f.* perfumery
parfümieren *v.* to perfume
pari *adv.* at par
Paria *m.* pariah
Park *m.* park, grounds; **-platz** *m.* parking place
Parkett *neu.* parquet; inlaid floor; (theat.) orchestra seats
Parlament *neu.* parliament; (U.S.A.) Congress; **-är** *m.* bearer of a flag of truce; **-arier** *m.* parliamentarian; (pol.) representative
parlamentarisch *adj.* parliamentary
Parodie *f.* parody
Parole *f.* parole; password; watchword
Partei *f.* party, faction; side; tenant; **— nehmen für** to side with; **sich zwischen den -en halten** to sit on the fence; **-gänger** *m.* partisan; **-gruppe** *f.* faction; **-programm** *neu.* party platform
partei: **-isch** *adj.*, **-lich** *adj.* partial, biased; **-los** *adj.* impartial, independent, neutral
Parterre *neu.* parterre, ground floor
Partie *f.* excursion, outing; game; (sport) match, set; (theat.) part; lot
Partikel *f.* particle
Partitur *f.* (mus.) score
Partner *m.* partner; **-schaft** *f.* partnership
Parzelle *f.* allotment, lot, parcel (of land)
parzellieren *v.* to divide into lots; to parcel
Pass *m.* pass(age), defile; amble, pace; passport; **-age** *f.* passage; (mus.) run; **-agier** *m.* passenger; **blinder -agier** stowaway; **-agierflugzeug** *neu.* air liner; **-agiergut** *neu.* passenger's baggage;

-ant *m.* passer-by; **-gänger** *m.* ambling horse; **-ierschein** *m.* pass, permit
pass: **-abel** *adj.* tolerable; bearable; **-en** *v.* to fit, to suit; (game) to pass; to be becoming (*oder* convenient); **-en auf** to fit on; to lie in wait for; **zueinander -en** to match; to be harmonious; **-end** *adj.* convenient, appropriate; becoming; **für -end halten** to think proper; **-ieren** *v.* to pass, to cross; to happen
passlich *adj.* convenient, suitable, fit
Past: **-e** *f.*, **-a** *f.* paste
Pastell *neu.* pastel; **-farben** *f. pl.* pastel crayons (*oder* colors)
Pastete *f.* pie; pastry; **da haben wir die — we are in a nice mess**
pasteurisieren *v.* to pasteurize
Pastille *f.* lozenge
Pastor *m.* pastor, minister, clergyman; **-at** *neu.* pastorate; parsonage
Pate *m.* godfather, sponsor; **-nkind** *neu.* godchild; **-nstelle** *f.* sponsorship
Patent *neu.* patent; **-amt** *neu.* patent office
Pater *m.* (eccl.) Father; priest; **-noster** *m.* and *neu.* Lord's Prayer; escalator
pathetisch *adj.* pathetic
Pathologe *m.* pathologist
Patient *m.* patient
Patin *f.* godmother
Patri: **-arch** *m.* patriarch; **-ot** *m.* patriot; **-otismus** *m.* patriotism; **-zier** *m.* patrician
patriarchalisch *adj.* patriarchal
patriotisch *adj.* patriotic
Patron *m.* patron; protector; fellow; **-at** *neu.* patronage
Patrone *f.* cartridge; **-ngurt** *m.* cartridge belt; **-ntasche** *f.* cartridge pouch
Patrouille *f.* patrol
patrouillieren *v.* to patrol, to go the rounds
Patsch *m.* smack, slap; **-e** *f.* dilemma, mess; **in der -e sitzen** (coll.) to be in a fix
patschen *v.* to splash; to slap, to smack
patschnass *adj.* soaked to the skin
patt *adj.* (chess) stalemate
patzig *adj.* (coll.) impudent, pert, saucy
Pauke *f.* kettledrum; **-nwirbel** *m.* roll of the kettledrum; **-rei** *f.* (coll.) duel; cramming
pauken *v.* to beat (kettledrum); (coll.) to cram
Paus: **-e** *f.* pause, intermission, break; rest; tracing, traced design; **-enzeichen** *neu.* pause signal; **-papier** *neu.* tracing paper
pausbäckig *adj.* chubby-faced
Pauschal: **-gebühr** *f.* flat rate; **-kauf** *m.*

wholesale purchase; **–summe** *f.* lump (*oder* round) sum

Pavillon *m.* pavilion

Pech *neu.* pitch; (cobbler's) wax; bad luck; **–draht** *m.* (cobbler's) thread; **–fackel** *f.* pine torch; **–strähne** *f.* run of bad luck; **–vogel** *m.* unlucky fellow

Pedal *neu.* pedal

pedantisch *adj.* pedantic

Pedell *m.* beadle; janitor; proctor

Peil: **–(funk)gerät** *neu.* radio locator; direction finder; **–kompass** *m.* azimuth compass; **–ung** *f.* direction finding, radiolocation

Pein *f.* pain, agony, torment; **–iger** *m.* tormentor, torturer; **–igung** *f.* torture

peinigen *v.* to torment, to torture, to harass

peinlich *adj.* distressing; painful, tormenting; (law) penal, criminal; pedantic, punctilious

Peitsche *f.* whip, lash, scourge; **mit der — knallen** to crack the whip; **–nhieb** *m.* lash, whip cut; **–nschnur** *f.* whip thong, lash

peitschen *v.* to whip, to flog, to lash, to scourge; **das peitschte mich auf** this stirred (*oder* stimulated) me

Pelikan *m.* pelican

Pelle *f.* peel, skin

pellen *v.* to peel, to skin, to pare

Pellkartoffeln *f. pl.* potatoes in their jackets

Pelotonfeuer *neu.* platoon firing

Pelz *m.* pelt, skin, hide; fur; **auf den — rücken** (coll.) to importune; **den — ausklopfen** (coll.) to thrash soundly; **jemandem Läuse in den — setzen** (coll.) to play a dirty trick on someone; **–futter** *neu.* fur lining; **–händler** *m.* furrier; **–jäger** *m.* fur trapper; **–verbrämung** *f.* fur trimming; **–ware** *f.*, **–werk** *neu.* furs

Pendel *m.* and *neu.* pendulum; **–schwingung** *f.* oscillation; **–verkehr** *m.* shuttle service

pendeln *v.* to oscillate, to swing

penibel *adj.* pedantic; particular; fastidious

Pension *f.* pension; boardinghouse; **–är** *m.* pensioner; boarder; **–at** *neu.* boarding school

pensionieren *v.* to pension off

Pensum *neu.* task, lesson, curriculum

per *prep.* by; **— Adresse** care of; **— Jahr** per annum, a (*oder* each) year; **— sofort** from now on

perfekt *adj.* perfect

perfid *adj.* perfidious

Pergament *neu.* parchment; **–haut** *f.* membrane

Periode *f.* period; menstruation

periodisch *adj.* periodic

Peripherie *f.* periphery; circumference

Perl: **–e** *f.* pearl, bead; bubble; **seine –en vor die Säue werfen** to waste one's talents; **–enkette** *f.* pearl necklace; **–huhn** *neu.* guinea fowl; **–muschel** *f.* pearl oyster; **–mutter** *f.* mother-of-pearl; **–schrift** *f.* (typ.) pearl

perlen *v.* to effervesce, to sparkle; to pearl

Perpendikel *m.* and *neu.* pendulum, perpendicular

perplex *adj.* perplexed

Perron *m.* (rail.) platform

Person *f.* person(age); (theat.) character, part; **in —** personally, personified; **–al** *neu.* employees; staff, personnel; servants; (theat.) performers; **–alien** *f. pl.* personal data; **–alverzeichnis** *neu.* list of employees; **–enaufzug** *m.* passenger elevator; **–enstand** *m.* state of population; **–enverzeichnis** *neu.* (theat.) cast; **–enwagen** *m.* passenger car

personifizieren *v.* to personify

persönlich *adj.* personal; **— —** *adv.* in person

Persönlichkeit *f.* person(ality)

Perspektiv *neu.* small telescope; **–e** *f.* perspective; prospect, outlook

Perücke *f.* wig

pessimistisch *adj.* pessimistic

Pest *f.*, **Pestilenz** *f.* pestilence, plague

Petersilie *f.* parsley

Petschaft *neu.* seal, signet

Petunie *f.* petunia

petzen *v.* to bear tales, to tattle, to inform

Pfad *m.* path; **–finder** *m.* pioneer; boy scout

Pfaffe *m.* (coll.) cleric; **–ntum** *neu.* clericalism

Pfahl *m.* stake, pole, post, pile, prop; **–bau** *m.* pilework; lake dwelling; **–werk** *neu.* palisade, stockade

Pfalz *f.* Palatinate; imperial palace

Pfand *neu.* pledge, security; **–brief** *m.* mortgage bond; **–gläubiger** *m.* mortgagee; **–haus** *neu.*, **–leihe** *f.* pawnshop; **–leiher** *m.* pawnbroker; **–recht** *neu.* lien; **–schein** *m.* pawn ticket; **–schuldner** *m.* mortgagor; **–verschreibung** *f.* mortgage deed

Pfänd: **–erspiel** *neu.* game of forfeits; **–ung** *f.* distraint, distress, seizure; **–ungsbefehl** *m.* warrant of distress

Pfanne *f.* pan; (anat.) socket

Pfannkuchen *m.* pancake; doughnut; omelet

Pfarr: **–amt** *neu.*, **–bezirk** *m.*, **–gemeinde** *f.* parish; **–e(i)** *f.* parsonage, pastorate; **–er** *m.* parson, pastor, minister; **–haus**

neu. parsonage; **–kind** *neu.* parishioner
Pfau *m.* peacock; **–enrad** *neu.* peacock's
fan; **–henne** *f.* peahen
Pfeffer *m.* pepper; **–streuer** *m.* pepper-
shaker; **–gurke** *f.* gherkin; **–kuchen** *m.*
gingerbread; **–ling** *m.* mushroom;
–minze *f.* peppermint; **–nuss** *f.* ginger-
(bread) nut
pfeffern *v.* to (season with) pepper; to
make spicy: (coll.) to throw
Pfeife *f.* whistle, pipe; fife; **–n** *neu.* whis-
tling; (theat.) hissing; **–nkopf** *m.* pipe
bowl
pfeifen *v.* to whistle, to pipe; (mice) to
squeak; (wind) to howl; (theat.) to hiss;
er pfeift auf dem letzten Loch he is on
his last legs; **ich pfeife darauf** I don't
give a hoot for it
Pfeil *m.* arrow, dart; **–hagel** *m.* shower of
arrows; **–spitze** *f.* arrowhead
Pfeiler *m.* pillar, post
Pfennig *m.* pfennig, penny; **–fuchser** *m.*
pinchpenny, miser; **–kraut** *neu.* money-
wort
Pferd *neu.* horse; (chess) knight; (gym.)
vaulting horse; **das — beim Schwanze
aufzäumen** to put the cart before the
horse; **zu –e** on horseback; **–ebremse**
f. horsefly; **–edecke** *f.* saddlecloth;
–ehändler *m.* horse dealer; **–eknecht** *m.*
groom; hostler; **–ekoppel** *f.* paddock;
–ekraft *f.* horsepower; **–erennen** *neu.*
horse race; **–eschwemme** *f.* horse pond;
–ezucht *f.* breeding of horses
Pfiff *m.* whistle; **–ikus** *m.* smart fellow
pfiffig *adj.* smart; artful, crafty, sly, sharp
Pfingst: –en *neu.* Pentecost, Whitsuntide;
–rose *f.* peony; **–sonntag** *m.* Whitsun-
day
Pfirsich *m.* peach
Pflanz: –e *f.* plant; **–enbutter** *f.* vegetable
butter; **–enernährungslehre** *f.* agrobiology; **–enfaser** *f.* vegetable fiber;
–enkunde *f.* botany; **–enreich** *neu.,*
–enwelt *f.* flora; **–ensaft** *m.* (bot.) sap;
–er *m.* planter, colonist, settler; **–schule**
f. nursery; **–stätte** *f.* (fig.) seminary;
source; hotbed; **–ung** *f.* plantation;
colony
pflanz: –en *v.* to plant; **–enfressend** *adj.*
herbivorous, graminivorous; **–lich** *adj.*
vegeta(b)l(e)
Pflaster *neu.* plaster; pavement; **Paris ist
ein teures — Paris** is very expensive;
–er *m.* paver; **–stein** *m.* paving stone;
–treter *m.* loafer; **–ung** *f.* paving
Pflaume *f.* plum; getrocknete (*or* ge-
dörrte) **–e** prune; **–nmus** *neu.* plum jam
Pfleg: –e *f.* care, nursing; rearing; cultivation; **–ebefohlene** *m.* ward; **–eeltern**

f. foster parents; **–ekind** *neu.* foster
child; **–emutter** *f.* foster mother; **–er**
m., **–erin** *f.* nurse, guardian, curator;
–esohn *m.* foster son; **–ling** *m.* foster
child; **–schaft** *f.* guardianship
pflegen *v.* to care for, to nurse, to foster;
to cultivate; to be accustomed, to be in
the habit; **der Ruhe — to take one's
ease; Umgang —** to associate with
Pflicht *f.* duty, obligation; **–anteil** *m.,*
–beitrag *m.* quota; **–eifer** *m.* zeal;
–gefühl *neu.* sense of duty; **–leistung**
f. performance of duty; **–teil** *m.* legitimate portion
Pflock *m.* peg, pin, plug, picket; **einen —
zurückstecken** (coll.) to moderate one's
demands
pflücken *v.* to gather, to pick, to pluck;
sie hat ein Hühnchen mit ihm zu —
she has a bone to pick with him
Pflug *m.* plow; **–schar** *f.* plowshare
pflügen *v.* to plow, to till
Pforte *f.* gate, door; Porte
Pförtner *m.* doorkeeper, janitor, porter;
(anat.) pylorus
Pfosten *m.* post; pale, stake, jamb
Pfote *f.* paw
Pfriem(en) *m.,* **Pfrieme** *f.* awl; punch,
bodkin
Pfropf(en) *m.* stopper, plug, cork, wad;
–enzieher *m.* corkscrew; **–messer** *neu.*
grafting knife; **–reis** *neu.* scion, graft
pfropfen *v.* to cork; to plug; to cram, to
stuff; (hort.) to graft
Pfründe *f.* benefice; sinecure; prebend
Pfründner *m.* beneficiary; prebendary
Pfuhl *m.* pool, puddle; (fig.) slough, pit
pfui! *interj.* phooey! phew! shame on you!
Pfund *neu.* pound; **mit seinem –e wuchern** to make the most of one's talent;
sein — vergraben to hide (*oder* bury)
one's talent
Pfusch: –erei *f.* bungling; botching; **–er**
m. botcher, bungler; quack
pfuschen *v.* to botch, to bungle; to scamp
Pfütze *f.* puddle, bog, quagmire
phänomenal *adj.* phenomenal, extraordinary
Phant: –asie *f.* imagination, fancy; fantasy; **–asiegebilde** *neu.* fantastic vision;
chimera; **–ast** *m.* dreamer, visionary;
–om *neu.* phantom
phant: –asieren *v.* to daydream; to improvise; to rave, to ramble; **–asievoll**
adj. imaginative, fanciful; **–astisch** *adj.*
fantastic, fanciful
Pharmaz: –eut *m.* pharmacist; druggist;
–ie *f.* pharmacy
Phenobarbital *neu.* phenobarbital
Phil: –anthrop *m.* philanthropist; **–anth-**

ropie *f.* philanthropy; –ologe *m.* philologist; –ologie *f.* philology; –osoph *m.* philosopher; –osophie *f.* philosophy
phil: –anthropisch *adj.* philanthropic(al); –ologisch *adj.* philologic(al); –osophieren *v.* to philosophize; –osophisch *adj.* philosophic(al)
Phiole *f.* phial, vial
Phlegma *neu.* phlegm; equanimity; –tiker *m.* phlegmatic person
Phon (Lautstärkemasseinheit) *n.* decibel
phonetisch *adj.* phonetic(al)
Photo *m.*, –apparat *m.* camera; –grametrie *f.* space control; –graph *m.* photographer; –graphie *f.* photograph(y); –montage *f.* photographic layout
photographieren *v.* to photograph
Physik *f.* physics; –er *m.* physicist
physikalisch *adj.* physical, of physics
Physio: –gnomie *f.* physiognomy; –loge *m.* physiologist; –logie *f.* physiology
physisch *adj.* physical; somatic
picken *v.* to pick, to peck
Picknick *neu.* picnic
Piedestal *neu.* (arch.) pedestal
piepen *v.* to chirp, to cheep, to squeak; bei dir piept's wohl? (sl.) Are you crazy?
Piet: –ät *f.* piety, reverence; –ätlosigkeit *f.* irreverence; –ismus *m.* pietism, bigotry
Pik *m.* pique, grudge; — *neu.* (cards) spade; –anterie *f.* piquancy, pungency
Pikkolo *m.* boy waiter; –flöte *f.* piccolo
Pil: –ger *m.* pilgrim; –gerfahrt *f.*, –gerschaft *f.* pilgrimage
pilgern *v.* to go on a pilgrimage
Pilz *m.* mushroom, fungus, agaric; giftiger — toadstool
Pinguin *m.* penguin
Pinie *f.* stone pine
pinkeln *v.* (sl.) to make water; to piddle
Pinne *f.* peg, tack; pivot; (naut.) tiller
Pinsel *m.* (paint)brush; (coll.) simpleton; –ei *f.* daubing; –strich *m.* stroke of the brush
pinseln *v.* to paint; to daub
Pinzette *f.* tweezers
Pionier *m.* pioneer; (mil.) engineer, sapper
Pirat *m.* pirate
Pirol *m.* (orn.) oriole
pirschen *v.* to hunt, to stalk game
Pistazie *f.* pistachio
Pistole *f.* pistol; –ntasche *f.* holster
Piston *m.* piston; — *neu.* (mus.) cornet
pitschnass *adj.* wet to the skin, wet through
pittoresk *adj.* picturesque
placken *v.* to torment, to drudge
Plackerei *f.* drudgery, vexation, trouble

plädieren *v.* to plead
Plage *f.* plague, affliction, torment, nuisance; –geist *m.* bore, tormentor
plagen *v.* to plague, to annoy, to pester; sich — to drudge, to toil
Plagiat *neu.* plagiarism; –or *m.* plagiarist
plagiieren *v.* to plagiarize
Plak: –at *neu.* placard, bill, poster; –atsäule *f.* advertisement pillar; –ette *f.* plaque
Plan *m.* plan, design, project, plot
plan *adj.* plain, level, flat; –ieren *v.* to plane, to level
plan: –en *v.* to plan, to project, to plot; –los *adj.* without a plan, desultory; –mässig *adj.* planned; systematic, methodical
Plane *f.* tarpaulin, awning
Planet *m.* planet; –arium *neu.* planetarium
planetarisch *adj.* planetary
Planierungsraupenfahrzeug *n.* bulldozer
Plänkelei *f.* skirmish
Plantage *f.* plantation
Planung *f.* planning
Planwirtschaft *f.* economic planning
Plapper: –ei *f.* babble, chatter; –maul *neu.*, –tasche *f.* chatterbox
plappern *v.* to babble, to chatter
plärren *v.* to bawl; to blubber, to wail
Plastik *f.* plastic art; sculpture
plastisch *adj.* plastic
Platane *f.* plane tree
Platin *neu.* Platinum
platonisch *adj.* Platonic
plätschern *v.* to splash; to murmur, to plash
platt *adj.* flat, even; insipid, dull, commonplace; die –e Wahrheit the plain truth; — heraus sagen to speak frankly; — sein (coll.) to be dumbfounded; –deutsch *adj.* Low German; –erdings *adv.* absolutely, decidedly, flatly; –füssig *adj.* flat-footed; –weg *adj.* flatly
Platt: –e *f.* plate; plateau; slab; (mus.) disk, record; (coll.) baldness; –enteller *m.* turntable; –form *f.* platform; –fuss *m.* flat foot; –fusseinlage *f.* arch support
Plätt: –brett *neu.* ironing board; –eisen *neu.* flat iron; –wäsche *f.* laundry (to be ironed)
plätten *v.* to iron, to press
Platz *m.* place; locality, site; square; seat; (sport) ground, court; am –e sein to be opportune; nicht am –e out of place; — greifen to gain ground, to spread; — machen to clear the way; — nehmen to sit down; seinen — behaupten to

stand one's ground; **–karte** f. ticket (for reserved seat); **–kommandant** m. military commandant; **–patrone** f. blank cartridge; **–regen** m. torrential rain; downpour; **–wärter** m. groundman; **–wechsel** m. change of place; (com.) local draft; (sports) change in lineup

Plätzchen neu. small place; fancy cookie

platzen v. to burst, to crack; to explode

platzraubend adj. space-stealing

Plauder: –er m. chatterer; talker; **–stündchen** neu. cozy chat; **–tasche** f. chatterbox; gossiper; **–ton** m. conversational tone

plaudern v. to chat, to chatter, to blab, to talk; **aus der Schule —** to act as talebearer

Plebejer m. plebeian

Pleite f. (coll.) bankruptcy

Plejaden f. pl. (ast.) Pleiades

Plenarsaal m. plenum chamber

Plenarsitzung f., **Plenum** neu. plenum

Pleuelstange f. connecting rod

Plombe f. lead seal; dental filling

plombieren v. to seal with lead; to fill (tooth)

plötzlich adj. sudden, unexpected; **— adv.** suddenly, abruptly, offhandedly

Pluderhosen f. pl. wide breeches

plump adj. blunt; heavy, clumsy; awkward, shapeless; **–s!** thump! **–sen** v. to plump, to plop

Plunder m. lumber, rubbish, trash

plündern v. to plunder, to pillage, to sack

Plüsch m. plush

Pneu(matik) m. pneumatic tire

Pöbel m. mob, rabble; **–herrschaft** m. mob rule

pöbelhaft adj. vulgar, low, plebeian

pochen i. to knock, to rap; to beat, to throb; **— auf** to insist on, to boast about

Pochspiel neu. poker

Pochwerk neu. stamping mill; pounding machine

Pocke f. pock; **–n** pl. smallpox; **–nimpfung** f. vaccination; **–nnarbe** f. pockmark

pockennarbig adj. pockmarked

Podex m. (coll.) buttocks

Podium neu. platform, rostrum

Poesie f. poetry

poetisch adj. adj. poetic(al)

Pointe f. point (of joke oder story)

Pokal m. goblet; cup

Pökel: –fleisch neu. salted meat; **–hering** m. pickled herring; **–rindfleisch** neu. corned beef

pökeln v. to pickle, to salt

Pol m. pole; (elec.) terminal; **–arforscher**

m. polar explorer; **–arfuchs** m. arctic fox; **–arkran** m. gantry; **–arlicht** neu. northern lights; **–arzone** f. frigid zone

polarisieren v. to polarize

polemisch adj. polemic(al)

poli: –tisch adj. political; **–tisieren** to dabble in politics; **–zeilich** adj. (of the) police; **–zeiwidrig** adj. contrary to police regulations

Police f. (insurance) policy

polieren v. to polish, to burnish

Politik f. politics; policy; **–er** m. politician

Politur f. polish; gloss; varnish

Poliz: –ei f. police; **–eibüro** neu., **–eiwache** f. police station; **–eiaufsicht** f. police supervision; **unter –eiaufsicht** on parole; **–eibeamte** m. police officer; **–eibehörde** f. police authorities; **–eikommissar** m. police inspector; **–eipräsident** m. police commissioner; **–eisspitzel** m. police informer; **–eistreife** f. police raid; **–eistunde** f. closing hour; curfew; **–ist** m. policeman

Polster neu. cushion; bolster; **–er** m. upholsterer; **–möbel** neu. pl. upholstered furniture; **–sessel** m., **–stuhl** m. easy chair; **–ung** f. stuffing, upholstery

polstern v. to stuff, to upholster, to pad

Polter: –abend m. eve before a wedding; **–er** ml blusterer; **–geist** m. hobgoblin

poltern v. to be noisy, to rumble

Polygraph m. polygraph, lie detector

Polytechnikum neu. technological school

pomadig adj. (coll.) phlegmatic

Pommern neu. Pomerania

Pomp m. pomp, ostentation

pomphaft, pompös adj. pompous, magnificent

Popanz m. bugbear; dummy

Popo m. (coll.) behind, buttocks

populär adj. popular; **— machen** to popularize

Popularität f. popularity

Pore f. pore

porös adj. porous

Portal neu. portal

Porte: –feuille neu. portfolio; **–monnaie** neu. purse; **–pee** neu. sword knot

Portier m. doorkeeper; porter; **–e** f. door curtain

Portion f. portion, helping, ration

Porto neu. postage; **–kasse** f. petty cash

portofrei adj. postpaid, prepaid

Porträt neu. portrait, likeness

Porzellan neu. porcelain, china; **–brennerei** f. porcelain manufactory; **–erde** f. kaolin; **–service** neu. set of china

Posamentier m. lacemaker; haberdasher; **–waren** f. pl. lacework; trimmings;

haberdashery
Posaune *f.* trombone; (bibl.) trumpet;
  -nengel *m.* angel with chubby cheeks
Pose *f.* pose, attitude; quill
posieren *v.* to pose, to strike an attitude
Positiv *m.* (gram.) positive degree; —
  neu. (phot.) positive; small organ
Positur *f.* posture
Posse *f.* drollery; farce, burlesque; **-n** *m.*
  prank, trick; **-nreisser** *m.* buffoon,
  jester
possenhaft *adj.* clownish, farcical
possierlich *adj.* droll, funny, quaint
Post *f.* mail; post (office); news, message;
  -amt *neu.* post office; **-anweisung** *f.*
  money order; **-beamte** *m.* post office
  clerk; **-beutel** *m.* mailbag; **-bote** *m.*
  mailman; **-kasten** *m.* mail box;
  -schliessfach *neu.* post office box;
  -stempel *m.* postmark; **-wertzeichen**
  neu. postage stamp
Postament *neu.* pedestal, base
Posten *m.* post, (com.) sum, item, entry;
  (mil.) outpost, sentry; **auf dem — sein**
  (coll.) to feel well; **-jäger** *m.* position
  hunter; **-kette** *f.*, **-linie** *f.* (mil.) outpost
  line
Postille *f.* postil, book of family sermons
post: **-alisch** *adj.* postal; **-lagernd** *adj.*
  general delivery; **-wendend** *adj.* by
  return mail
Potenz *f.* power; potency
Pott: **-asche** *f.* potash; **-fisch** *m.*, **-wal** *m.*
  sperm whale
Prä: **-dikat** *neu.* predicate; title; (school)
  mark; **-gestock** *m.* die, matrix; **-lat** *m.*
  prelate: **-mie** *f.* premium, prize; bonus;
  -parat *neu.* preparation; **-position** *f.*
  preposition; **-sens** *neu.* present (tense);
  -sent *neu.* present, gift; **-sident** *m.*
  president; chairman; **-sidium** *neu.*
  presidency; chair; **-tendent** *m.* pre-
  tender; **-teritum** *neu.* preterite, past
  tense; **-zedenzfall** *m.* precedent; **-zision**
  f. precision
prä: **-destinieren** *v.* to predestinate;
  -historisch *adj.* prehistoric(al); **-mie-**
  ren to award (prize to); **-numerando**
  adv. in advance, beforehand; **-parieren**
  v. to prepare; **-sentieren** to present, to
  offer; **-sidieren** to preside; **-zis** *adj.*
  precise; concise; punctual
Pracht *f.* magnificence, splendor, luxury;
  -exemplar *neu.* splendid specimen
prächtig, prachtvoll *adj.* magnificent,
  gorgeous
prachtliebend *adj.* ostentatious, fond of
  show
Prag *neu.* Prague
prägen *v.* to coin, to shape

prägnant *adj.* significant
Prägnanz *f.* terseness, significance
Prahl: **-er** *m.*, **-hans** *m.* boaster, braggart;
  -erei *f.* vainglory
prahlen *v.* to boast, to brag; to show off
prahlerisch *adj.* boastful; vainglorious,
  showy
prakt: **-ikabel** *adj.* practicable; **-isch** *adj.*
  practical, useful; **-ischer Arzt** general
  practitioner; **-izieren** *v.* to practice
Praktik *f.* practice; **-ant** *m.* probationer;
  -er *m.* practical person, expert
Prall *m.* collision; bounce, rebound, impact
prallen *v.* to bounce, to dash, to rebound
prangen *v.* to make a show; to shine
Pranger *m.* pillory
Prärie *f.* prairie
prasseln *v.* to crackle, to patter
prassen *v.* to carouse, to revel, to feast
Praxis *f.* practice; exercise; usage; (law)
  clients; (med.) patients
predigen *v.* to preach; to sermonize
Prediger *m.* preacher, clergyman
Predigt *f.* sermon; lecture
Preis *m.* price; prize; praise; **um jeden —**
  at any price; **um keinen —** not for all
  the world; **-angabe** *f.* quotation of
  prices; **-aufgabe** *f.* prize question; **-aus-**
  schreiben *neu.* competition, award;
  -drückerei *f.* close bargain; **-gabe** *f.*,
  abandonment, surrender; exposure;
  -richter *m.* arbiter, judge; **-schiessen**
  neu. shooting match; **-schwankungen**
  f. pl. fluctuation of prices; **-sturz** *m.*
  fall of prices; **-träger** *m.* prize winner;
  -treiberei *f.* forcing up of prices;
  -zuschlag *m.* markup
preis: **-en** *v.* to praise, to extol, to glorify;
  -geben to abandon, to surrender, to
  expose; **-krönen** to award a prize to;
  -wert *adj.* cheap; **-würdig** *adj.* praiseworthy
Preis(s)elbeere *f.* cranberry
Prell: **-bock** *m.* bulkhead, buffer; **-er** *m.*
  cheat; tosser; ricochet shot; **-erei** *f.*
  cheating, fraud; **-schuss** *m.* ricochet;
  -stein *m.* curbstone; **-stoss** *m.* drop
  kick
prellen *v.* to toss; to cheat, to swindle
Premiere *f.* (theat.) first night
Presbyterium *neu.* presbytery
Press: **-e** *f.* press; journalism; (coll.)
  crammer; **-erundschreiben** *neu.* newsletter; **-estimme** *f.* press comment;
  -etribüne *f.* press gallery, press box;
  -glas *neu.* molded glass; **-kohle** *f.*
  briquette; **-luft** *f.* compressed air
pressen *v.* to press; to squeeze; to urge
pressieren *v.* to be urgent; to dun

Preussen *neu.* Prussia

Priester *m.* priest; **−amt** *neu.*, **−schaft** *f.*, **−tum** *neu.* priesthood; **−hemd** *neu.* alb; surplice; **−herrschaft** *f.* hierarchy; **−rock** *m.* cassock; **−weihe** *f.* ordination of a priest

priesterlich *adj.* priestly, sacerdotal

Prima *f.* highest class (of a junior college); **−ner** *m.* student of the highest class (of a junior college); **−s** *m.* primate; **−t** *neu.* primacy

prima *adj.* prime; first-class; **— vista** (mus.) at first sight; (com.) payable on sight

primär *adj.* primary

Primel *f.* primrose, primula

primitiv *adj.* primitive

Prinz *m.* prince; **−essin** *f.* princess; **−gemahl** *m.* prince consort

Prinzip *neu.* principle; **−al** *m.* principal, head, boss; **−ienreiter** *m.* stickler for principles

prinzipiell *adj.* on principle

prinzlich *adj.* princely

Prior *m.* prior; **−ität** *f.* priority; **−itätsaktie** *f.* preferred stock

Prise *f.* (naut.) prize; pinch (of snuff)

Pritsche *f.* wooden sword; plank bed

privat *adj.* private; **−im** *adv.* privately; **−isieren** *v.* to free-lance, to live on one's means (*oder* resources)

Privat: −dozent *m.* university lecturer; **−mann** *m.* private person; **−recht** *neu.* civil law

Privileg(ium) *neu.* privilege

probat *adj.* proved, tried, tested

Probe *f.* trial, test, proof; sample; probation; rehearsal; **auf die — stellen** to put to the test; **auf —** on trial; **−abzug** *m.* (typ.) proof sheet; **−zeit** *f.* probation

Probier: −er *m.* assayer, tester; **−glas** *neu.* test tube; **−mamsell** *f.* (coll.) mannequin; **−stein** *m.* touchstone

prob(ier)en *v.* to test, to try; to taste; to sample; to assay; to rehearse

Problem *neu.* problem

problematisch *adj.* problematic(al)

produktiv *adj.* productive

Produzent *m.* producer

produzieren *v.* to produce; **sich —** to show off, to perform

profan *adj.* profane; **−ieren** *v.* to profane

Profess: −ion *f.* profession; trade; **−or** *m.* professor; **−ur** *f.* professorship, professioriate

Profil *neu.* profile

profitieren *v.* to profit (*oder* gain by)

Prognose *f.* prognosis; forecast

Programm *neu.* program; (pol.) platform

Projekt *neu.* project; **−il** *neu.* projectile;

−ion *f.* projection; **−ionsapparat** *m.* projector

proklamieren *v.* to proclaim

Prokur: −a *f.* procuration; **−ator** *m.* procurator; **−ist** *m.* (com.) authorized manager

Proletarier *m.* proletarian

Prolog *m.* prologue

Promotion *f.* promotion; graduation

promovieren *v.* to graduate; to take one's doctor's degree

propagieren *v.* to propagandize

Propeller-Turbinenmotor *m.* turboprop

Prophet *m.* prophet

prophetisch *adj.* prophetic(al)

proportioniert *adj.* proportionate; proportioned

Propst *m.* provost; prior

Prosa *f.* prose; **−iker** *m.*, **−ist** *m.* prose writer; prosaic person

prosaisch *adj.* prosaic

prosit! prost! *interj.* cheers! here's to your health! **— Neujahr!** happy New Year!

Prospekt *m.* prospect; prospectus; view

Prostituierte *f.* prostitute

Proszeniumsloge *f.* stage box

Protekt: −ion *f.* protection; **−ionswirtschaft** *f.* protectionism; **−or** *m.* protector; sponsor; **−orat** *neu.* protectorate; sponsorship

Protest *m.* protest; **mit — zurückkommen** (com.) to be dishonored; **−ant** *m.* Protestant; **−antismus** *m.* Protestantism

protestantisch *adj.* Protestant

protestieren *v.* to protest

Protokoll *neu.* protocol; record; minutes; **−buch** *neu.* minute book; **−führer** *m.* recording clerk

protokollarisch *adj.* in the minutes; on record

protokollieren *v.* to record

Protoplasma *neu.* protoplasm

protzen *v.* to show off; to put on airs

Proviant *m.* provisions, supplies; **−amt** *neu.* supply depot; **−kolonne** *f.* supply column

Provinz *f.* province; **−ler** *m.* provincial

Provis: −ion *f.* commission, percentagé; **−ionsreisende** *m.* salesman on commission; **−or** *m.* druggist's assistant; **−orium** *neu.* temporary arrangement (*oder* provisionsweise *adr.* on commission

provisorisch *adj.* provisional, temporary

provozieren *v.* to provoke

Prozent *neu.* per cent, percentage; **−satz** *m.* percentage; rate of interest

Prozess *m.* process; lawsuit, action; **einen — anstrengen** to sue (at law); **kurzen — machen mit** to make short work of; **−akten** *f. pl.* minutes of a law case;

pleadings; **-führer** m. litigant; **-führung**
f. conduct of a case; **-ion** f. procession;
-ordnung f. rules of court
prozessüchtig adj. litigious
prüde adj. prudish
Prüf: -er m. examiner, assayer; **-ling** m.
examinee; **-stein** m. touchstone; criterion; **-ung** f. examination; inspection;
testing; (bibl.) affliction; **-ungsaus-
schuss** m., **-ungskommission** f. board
of examiners
Prüfzählen neu. countdown
prüfen v. to examine; to inspect; to test;
to investigate; (com.) to audit, to check
Prügel m. cudgel, stick; — pl. thrashing;
-ei f. fight; free-for-all; **-knabe** m.
scapegoat; **-strafe** f. corporal punishment
prügeln v. to thrash; **sich** — to fight
Prunk m. splendor, pomp, ostentation'
prunk: -en v. to show off, to boast; **-süch-
tig** adj. ostentatious; **-voll** adj. gorgeous, splendid, sumptuous
prusten v. to sneeze, to snort; to burst out
Psalm m. psalm; **-ist** m. palmist
Pseudonym neu. pseudonym, fictitious
Psych: -iater m. psychiatrist; **-iatrie** f.
psychiatry; **-oanalyse** f. psychoanalysis; **-ologe** m. psychologist; **-ologie** f.
psychology; **-ose** f. psychosis
psych: -isch adj. psychic(al); **-ologisch**
adj. psychological; **-opathisch** adj.
psychopathic
Pubertät f. puberty
Publi: -kum neu. public; audience; **-zist**
m. journalist; **-zität** f. publicity
publizieren v. to publish
Pudel m. poodle; wie ein begossener —
crestfallen; **-mütze** f. fur cap
Puder m. powder; **-quaste** f. powder puff
pudern v. to powder
Puff m. push; bang, pop; crush; puff;
(coll.) bordello; **-ärmel** m. puffed
sleeve; **-bohne** f. horsebean; **-er** m.
potato pancake; buffer; **-spiel** neu.
backgammon
puffen v. to puff, to jolt, to nudge; to pop
Puls m. pulse; **-ader** f. artery; **-schlag** m.
pulse beat, pulsation; **-wärmer** m.
wristlet
puls(ier)en v. to pulsate
Pult neu. desk, lectern
Pulver neu. powder, gunpowder; **er hat
das** — nicht erfunden (coll.) he isn't
very bright; **sein** — unnötig verschiessen (coll.) to try in vain; **-fass** neu.
powder barrel; **-ladung** f. powder
charge
pulverisieren v. to pulverize; to demolish
Pump m. (coll.) borrowing, credit; **-e** f.

pump; -enschwengel m. pump handle;
-hosen f. pl. baggy trousers
pumpen v. to pump; (coll.) to borrow, to
loan
Punkt m. point; dot; period; place; moment; item; matter; subject; **bis zu
einem gewissen** — to some extent; —
ein Uhr at one o'clock sharp; **springen-
der** — main point; **-um** neu. period,
end; **-zahl** f. score
punktieren v. to dot; to puncture, to punctuate
pünktlich adj. punctual, prompt, exact
Punsch m. (beverage) punch
Pupille f. (eye) pupil
Puppe f. doll, puppet; chrysalis, pupa;
shock (of grain); **-nmacher** m. doll-
maker; **-nspiel** neu., **-ntheater** neu.
puppet show; **-nstube** f. doll's house;
-nwagen m. doll buggy
pur adj. pure, sheer
Pur: -itaner m. Puritan; **-itanertum** neu.
Puritanism
Püree neu. puree, mash
purgieren to purge
puritanisch adj. Puritan
Purpur m. purple
Purzelbaum m. somersault
purzeln v. to tumble
Puste f. (coll.) breath; **-rohr** neu. blowpipe
Pustel f. pustule
pusten v. too puff; to blow; to pant
Pute f. turkey hen; **-r** m. turkey cock
Putsch m. putsch, revolutionary outbreak, riot
Putz m. trimmings; ornaments; attire,
finery; (arch.) plaster, roughcast; **-er**
m. clean(s)er; **-frau** f. charwoman;
-geschäft neu. milliner's shop; **-händ-
lerin** f. milliner; **-waren** f. pl. millinery;
-wolle f. cotton waste; **-zeug** neu.
cleaning utensils
putzen v. to clean; to polish; to adorn; to
shine; (horse) to groom; (nose) to blow;
(arch.) to plaster, to roughcast; (candle) to snuff; **sich** — to dress up
Pygmäe m. pygmy
Pyjama m. and neu. pajama
Pyramide f. pyramid

Q

quabb(e)lig adj. flabby; jellylike
Quack: -elei f. silly talk; gabble; **-sal-
ber** m. quack; **-salberei** f. quackery;
malpractice
quacksalbern v. (med.) to quack
Quader m. and f. square stone; ashlar
Quadrat neu. square; **ins** — erheben to

square; **–wurzel** *f*. (math.) square root
quadratisch *adj*. square; quadratic
quadrieren *v*. to square
quaken *v*. to quack, to croak
Quäker *m*. Quaker
Qual *f*. pain; torment; agony; **–ität** *f*. quality; **–itätsware** *f*. high-class article
qual: –ifizieren *v*. to qualify; **–itativ** *adj*. qualitative
Quäl: –er *m*., **–geist** *m*. tormentor; torturer; bore; **–erei** *f*. tormenting, pestering; drudgery
quälen *v*. to torment, to torture, to harass, to worry; to anoy; **sich —** to drudge, to toil
Qualm *m*. dense smoke; fumes
qualm: –en *v*. to smoke; **–ig** *adj*. smoky
qualvoll *adj*. painful; tormenting; distressing
Quant: –entheorie *f*. quantum theory; **–ität** *f*. quantity; **–um** *neu*. quantum
Quappe *f*. tadpole, eelpout
Quarantäne *f*. quarantine
Quark *m*. curd; cottage cheese; nonsense, trifle
Quart *neu*. quart; (typ.) quarto; **–e** *f*. (mus.) fourth; (fencing) quarte; **–a** *f*. (secondary school) third grade; **–al** *neu*. quarter (of year); **–aner** *m*. (secondary school) pupil of the third grade; **–ett** *neu*. quartet
Quartier *neu*. quarters; lodging; (mil.) billet; **–meister** *m*. quartermaster
Quarz *m*. quartz
quasar, quasi-stellär *adj*. quasar
quasseln *v*. to talk nonsense, to jabber
Quast *m*. knot, tuft; **–e** *f*. tassel; brush
Quatemberfasten *neu*. Ember days
Quatsch *m*. nonsense, twaddle; rubbish
Quecke *f*. quick grass, couch grass
Quecksilber *neu*. quicksilver, mercury; **–kur** *f*. mercurial treatment; **–säule** *f*. column of mercury
quecksilberig, quecksilbern *adj*. of quicksilver, mercurial; restless, lively
Quell *m*. (poet.) spring, well; **–e** *f*. source, spring, fountain; origin
quellen *v*. to gush, to swell; to spring (from)
quer *adj*. cross, transverse, oblique; queer; **—** *adv*. across, diagonally; athwart; **–en** *v*. to traverse; **–feldein** *adv*. cross-country; **–köpfig** *adj*. stubborn, cranky; **–über** *adv*. across
Quer: –balken *m*. crossbeam; **–e** *f*. diagonal direction; **jemand in die –e kommen** (coll.) to thwart someone's designs; **–feldeinlauf** *m*. cross-country race; **–kopf** *m*. queer fellow; crank; **–pfeife** *f*. fife; **–strasse** *f*. cross street; **–strich**

m. crossline; **–treiberei** *f*. intriguing, plotting
Quetsch: –e *f*. crush; **–kartoffeln** *f*. *pl*. mashed potatoes; **–kommode** *f*. (dial.) accordion; **–ung** *f*., **–wunde** *f*. contusion; bruise
quetschen *v*. to crush, to squeeze; **to contuse**
quick *adj*. quick, alert; brisk, lively
quietschen *v*. to squeak, to creak
Quint: –a *f*. (secondary school) second grade; **–aner** *m*. (secondary school) second grade student; **–e** *f*. quinte; (mus.) fifth; **–essenz** *f*. quintessence; **–ett** *neu*. quintet
quirlen *v*. to twirl, to beat, to whisk
quitt *adj*. even, free, rid; quits; **–ieren** *v*. to acknowledge receipt; to quit, **to** abandon
Quitte *f*. quince
Quittung *f*. receipt
Quote *f*. quota, share

R

Rabatt *m*. discount; rebate
Rabbi(ner) *m*. rabbi
Rabe *m*. raven; **weisser —** rare bird; **–naas** *neu*. carrion; **–neltern** *pl*. cruel parents; **–nstein** *m*. place of execution
rabenschwarz *adj*. raven-black; pitch-dark
Rach: –e *f*. revenge, vengeance; **–egefühl** *neu*. resentment, vengefulness; **–gier** *f*., **–sucht** *f*. vindictiveness
rach: –edurstig *adj*., **–gierig** *adj*., **–süchtig** *adj*. vindictive, vengeful
Rachen *m*. throat; jaws; (coll.) mouth; (poet.) abyss; **–putzer** *m*. (coll.) sour wine; strong brandy
rächen *v*. to avenge, to revenge; **das wird sich an ihr —** it will come home to her
Räcker *m*. avenger; vindicator
Rachitis *f*. rickets
Racker *m*. rogue, rascal
Rad *neu*. wheel; bicycle; **unter die Räder kommen** (coll.) to perish; **–achse** *f*. axletree; **–bremse** *f*. wheel lock; hub brake; **–dampfer** *m*. paddle steamer; **–fahrer** *m*. cyclist; **–kranz** *m*. rim; **–ler** *m*. cyclist; **–macher** *m*. wheelwright; **–reifen** *m*. tire; **–rennen** *neu*. bicycle race; **–schaufel** *f*. paddle wheel; **–speiche** *f*. spoke; **–spur** *f*. rut; wheel track; **–zahn** *m*. cog
Radar *neu*. radar; **–gerät** *neu*. radar indicator; radio direction finder; **–auffanggerät** *neu*. lobe
radeln, radfahren *v*. to bike, to cycle
Radau *m*. noise, row

radebrechen v. to speak badly

Rädelsführer m. ringleader

Radier: –gummi m. rubber eraser; –messer neu. penknife; –nadel f. etching needle; –ung f. etching erasure

radieren v. to etch

Radieschen neu. radish

radikal adj. radical

Radio neu. radio; –apparat m. radio set; –peilung f. radio homing; –röhre f. radio tube

radioaktiv adj. radioactive

Radium neu. radium; –heilverfahren neu. radiotherapy

raffen v. to snatch, to gather

raffinier: –en v. to refine; –t adj. crafty, cunning; refined

Ragout neu. ragout, hash; hodge-podge

Rah: –e f. (naut.) yard; –segel neu. (naut.) square sail; –tau neu. (naut.) headrope

Rahmen m. frame; (shoe) welt; background; surroundings; –enantenne f. loop aerial; –sucher m. view finder

Rain m. (agr.) balk, ridge, edge

Rakete f. rocket; –nabschuss m. blast-off; ⋅–abschussbasis f. launching pad; –nabschussführungsschiene f. launching rail; –nabwehrgeschoss neu. anti-missile missile; –nbasis f. rocket base; –nbunker m. silo; –nfähre f. ferry rocket; –ngeschoss (ferngelenkt) neu. ballistic missile; –nstart m. jet-assisted take-off, jato; Rückfeuerungs– f. retro-rocket; Träger– carrier rocket

Ramm: –bär m., –block, –e f. rammer, pile driver; –ler m. ram, buck rabbit

rammen v. to ram; to drive in; to butt

Rampe f. ramp; platform; –nlicht neu. footlights

Rand m. rim; brim; edge, margin; (wound) lip; verge; ausser — und Band sein to be out of hand; halt deinen —! (coll.) shut up! –bemerkung f. marginal note

rändern v. to border, to rim; (coins) to mill

Rang m. rank; order; position; quality; (theat.) balcony; den — ablaufen to outrun; ersten –es first class; –abzeichen neu. badge of rank; –älteste m. senior in rank; –ordnung f. order of precedence

Range f. scamp, tomboy

Rangier: –bahnhof m. (rail.) switchyard; –er m. switcher; –gleis neu. (rail.) siding

rangieren v. (rail.) to switch; to rank

Ranke f. tendril; shoot; branch

Ränke m. pl. intrigues, machinations, tricks; –schmied m. intriguer, plotter, schemer

Ranzen m., **Ränzel** neu. knapsack; schoolbag

ranzig adj. rancid

Rappe m. black horse; **auf Schusters –n reiten** (coll.) to travel on foot

rappel: –n v. to rattle; **bei ihm –ts he is crazy; er –te sich auf** (coll.) he recuperated

rapportieren v. (mil.) to report

Raps m. (bot.) rape; –saat f., –samen m. rapeseed

rar adj. rare, scarce; exquisite; **er macht sich —** (coll.) one hardly sees him

Rarität f. rarity, scarcity; curiosity

rasch adj. quick, swift, hasty

rascheln v. to rustle

Rasen m. grass, lawn; turf; –mähmaschine f. lawn mower; –sprenger m. lawn sprinkler

rasen v. to rage, to rave; to speed; –d adj. raging, raving; rapid; **jemand — machen** to drive someone mad; –d adv. (coll.) very much

Raserei f. rage, raving; frenzy; speeding

Rasier: –apparat m., –messer neu. razor; –klinge f. razor blade; –pinsel m. shaving brush; –seife f. shaving soap; –zeug neu. shaving utensils

rasieren v. to shave; (mil.) to raze

räsonieren v. to reason, to argue, to grumble

Raspel f. rasp; grating iron

raspeln v. to rasp; to grate; **Süssholz —** to spoon, to flirt, to coax, to fawn

Rasse f. race; breed; –nhygiene f. eugenics; –nkreuzung f. crossbreeding; –nvermischung f. miscegenation; –nwahn m. racism

rasseln v. to rattle, to clank

rassig adj. racy, thoroughbred

Rast f. rest; repose; (mil.) halt; –losigkeit f. restlessness; –tag m. day of rest

rasten v. to rest; to repose; to relax; to halt

rastlos adj. restless, indefatigable

Rasur f. erasure, shave

Rat m. advice, counsel; counsellor; council board; deliberation; means, expedient; **keinen — mehr wissen** to be at wit's end; **mit — und Tat** by word and deed; — **schaffen** to devise a remedy; **zu –e ziehen** to consult; –geber m. adviser; –haus neu. city hall; –losigkeit f. helplessness; –schlag m. advice, counsel; –schluss m. resolution; decree; –sherr m. councilman; –skeller m. tavern in the basement of a city hall; –sschreiber m. clerk to the council

rat: −en *v.* to advise; to counsel; to guess, to solve; **−los** *adj.* helpless, embarrassed; **−sam** *adj.* advisable, expedient; **−schlagen** *v.* to deliberate

Rate *f.* rate; instalment; **in −n** by instalments

Ratifizierung *f.* ratification

Ratio: −n *f.* ration; **−nalisierung** *f.* rationalization; **−nalismus** *m.* rationalism

ratio: −nal *adj.* rational; **−nalistisch** *adj.* rationalistic; **−nalisieren** *v.* to ration; **−nell** *adj.* reasonable; rational; economical

rätlich *adj.* advisable; expedient

Rätsel *neu.* riddle, puzzle, enigma

rätselhaft *adj.* puzzling, enigmatical

Ratte *f.* rat; **−nfänger** *m.* ratcatcher

rattern *v.* to rattle, to clatter

Raub *m.* robbery; piracy; rape; prey; **−bau** *m.* wasting (of natural resources); **−gier** *f.* rapacity; **−krieg** *m.* predatory war; **−mord** *m.* murder with robbery; **−ritter** *m.* robber knight; **−tier** *neu.* beast of prey; **−überfall** *m.* predatory attack; **−zug** *m.* raid

rauben *v.* to rob; to plunder; to deprive

Räuber *m.* robber; brigand; **−ei** *f.* robbery; **−höhle** *f.* den of thieves; **−geschichte** *f.* cock-and-bull story; **−hauptmann** *m.* gang leader

Rauch *m.* smoke; **−er** *m.* smoker; **−erabteil** *neu.* smoking compartment; **−fang** *m.* chimney, flue; **−fass** *neu.* censer; **−fleisch** *neu.* smoked meat; **−zimmer** *neu.* smoking room

rauch: −en *v.* to smoke; **−geschwärzt** *adj.* smokestained; **−ig** *adj.* smoky

Räucher: −fass *neu.* censer; **−hering** *m.* kipper; **−waren** *f. pl.* smoked meat, smoked fish

räuchern *v.* to smoke, to fumigate

Rauchwerk *neu.* furs

Räude *f.* mange, scab

räudig *adj.* mangy, scabby

Rauf: −bold *m.*, **−degan** *m.* bully; rowdy; **−erei** *f.* scuffle, row; **−lust** *f.*, **−sucht** *f.* pugnacity, combativeness

Raufe *f.* rack

raufen *v.* to pluck, to pull; **sich —** (coll.) to scuffle, to fight

rauh *adj.* rough; hoarse; raw; uneven; coarse, rude; **−beinig** *adj.* caddish; **−en** *v.* to roughen

Rauhreif *m.* hoarfrost

Raum *m.* room; space; place; district; (naut.) hold; **freier —** open space; **luftleerer —** vacuum; **— geben** to give way to; to indulge in; to grant; **−ersparnis** *f.* saving of space; **−inhalt** *m.* volume; capacity; **−kunst** *f.* (art of) in-

terior decoration; **−meter** *m.* cubic meter; **−schiff** *neu.* spaceship

Räum: −lichkeit *f.* locality, premises; space; **−ung** *f.* removal, clearance, evacuation; **−ungsausverkauf** *m.* clearance sale

räumen *v.* to clear away, to remove; to make room, to evacuate; to leave, to quit

räumlich *adj.* spatial

raunen *v.* to whisper; **man raunt sich zu** there is a rumor

Raupe *f.* caterpillar; **−nantrieb** *m.* caterpillar drive; **−nfrass** *m.* damage done by caterpillars; **−nschlepper** *m.* caterpillar tractor

Rausch *m.* drunkenness, intoxication; ecstasy; **−gift** *neu.* narcotic, dope; **−gold** *neu.* brass foil, tinsel

rauschen *v.* to rush, to rustle; to roar

räuspern *v.* **sich —** to clear one's throat, to hem, to hawk

Rayon *m.* rayon; district; department; circuit

Reagens *neu.* reagent; **−glas** *neu.* test tube; **−papier** *neu.* test (*oder* litmus) paper

reagieren *v.* to react

Reaktion *f.* reaction; **−är** *m.* reactionary

reaktionär *adj.* reactionary

real *adj.* real; material, substantial; **−isieren** *v.* to realize; **−istisch** *adj.* realistic

Real: −gymnasium *neu.*, **−schule** *f.* secondary school (for modern subjects); **−injurie** *f.* (law) assault and battery; **−ismus** *m.* realism; **−ist** *m.* realist; **−ität** *f.* reality; **−wert** *m.* actual value

Reb: −e *f.* grape, vine; tendril; **−enblut** *neu.*, **−ensaft** *m.* grape juice; wine; **−enhügel** *m.* vineclad hill; **−laus** *f.* vine louse; **−stock** *m.* vine

Rebell *m.* rebel; **−ion** *f.* rebellion, mutiny

rebellieren *v.* to rebel, to revolt, to mutiny

Rebhuhn *neu.* partridge

Rebus *m.* and *neu.* rebus; picture puzzle

rechen *v.* to rake

Rechen *m.* rake; rack

Rechen: −aufgabe *f.*, **−exempel** *neu.* arithmetic problem; **−buch** *neu.* arithmetic book; **−fehler** *m.* miscalculation; **−kunst** *f.* arithmetic; **−lehrer** *m.* teacher of arithmetic; **−maschine** *f.* calculating machine; **−schaft** *f.* account; **−schieber** *m.* slide rule; **−tafel** *f.* slate

rechnen *v.* to count, to calculate, to reckon; **alles in allem gerechnet** taking all in all; **— auf** to count upon; **— zu** to include; to rank amongst; to class with

Rechnung *f.* calculation; account, bill;

auf eigene — at one's own risk; auf — setzen to charge, to put to one's account; auf seine — kommen to benefit (by); den Umständen — tragen to act according to circumstances; in — ziehen to take into account; -sab- schluss m. closing of accounts; -sführer m. accountant, bookkeeper; -sjahr neu. fiscal year; -sprüfer m. auditor

recht adj. right, correct; just; due, lawful, legitimate; real; genuine; — adv. right, well; very; quite; es geht nicht mit -en Dingen zu there is something wrong about it; es geschieht ihm — it serves him right; es ist mir — I don't mind; ich weiss nicht — wie I don't quite know how; jetzt erst — now more than ever; — behalten to be right in the end; — haben to be right; — und schlecht fairly good; wenn ich es — bedenke when I consider it properly; -eckig adj. rectangular; -en v. to litigate; -ens adv. legally; -erhand adv. on the right hand; -fertigen v. to justify; to vindicate; -gläubig adj. orthodox; -habe- risch adj. disputatious, dogmatic; -lich adj. lawful, legal; -los adj. illegal, outlawed; -mässig adj. legitimate; -s adv. at (oder on) the right; -schaffen adj. honest, righteous; -sgültig adj., -skräftig adj. legal, valid; -suml (mil.) right about! -swidrig adj. illegal; -winklig adj. rectangular; -zeitig adj. in time

Recht neu. right; privilege; claim; justice, law; allgemeines — common law; an den —en kommen to meet one's match; mit vollem — for good reasons; nach dem —en sehen to see to things; — sprechen to administer justice; sich selbst — verschaffen to take law into one's own hands; von —s wegen by rights; zu — bestehen to be legally valid; -e f. right hand; (pol.) Right; -e m. (boxing) right; -eck neu. rectangle; -gläubige m. orthodox person; -haberei f. dogmatism; -sanwalt m. lawyer, attorney; -sausdruck m. legal term; -sbeistand m. legal adviser; -schreibung f. orthography; -sgang m. legal procedure; -sgelehrsamkeit f. jurisprudence; -sgelehrte m. jurist; -sgrund m. legal argument; -sgültigkeit f. legality; -shandel m. lawsuit, legal action; -skraft f. legal force; validity; -smittel neu. legal measure; -snachfolger m. assignee; -sperson f. (law) body corporate; -sprechung f. administration of justice; -sspruch m. sentence, verdict; -sstaat m. constitutional state; -sstreit m. lawsuit; -sverfahren neu.

legal procedure; -swissenschaft f. jurisprudence

Reck neu. (gym.) horizontal bar

Recke m. hero, warrior, swordsman

recken v. to stretch, to extend; to crane (neck); -haft adj. heroic, valiant

Red: -e f. speech; talk, conversation; address; oration; rumor; davon kann keine -e sein that is out of the question; es geht die -e davon it is being rumored that; es ist nicht der -e wert it is not worth mentioning; -in die -e fallen to interrupt; jemand zur -e stellen to call someone to account; -e stehen to answer (for); -egabe f., -ekunst f. rhetoric; oratory; -ensart f. phrase, saying; expression; empty talk; -erei f. prattle; -eschwall m. verbosity; -eschwulst m. bombast; -eweise f. manner of speech, style; -ewendung f. phrase, idiom; -ner m. orator, speaker; -nerbühne f. platform

red: -ebegabt adj., -egewandt adj. fluent in speech, eloquent; -en v. to speak, to talk; to converse; mit sich -en lassen to listen to reason; das Wort -en to put in a good word for; -nerisch adj. oratorical, rhetorical; -selig adj. talkative; loquacious; garrulous

Redak: -teur m. editor; -tion f. editing; editorial staff; editorial office; -tions- schluss m. deadline

redlich adj. honest, upright, just, sincere

Redlichkeit f. honesty, integrity

reduzieren v. to reduce; to diminish

Reede f. (naut.) roadstead; -r m. shipowner; -rei f. shipping line; shipping trade

reell adj. fair, honest, good; solid

Refektorium neu. refectory

Refer: -at neu. report, lecture; -endar m. junior lawyer; -ent m. reporter, lecturer; -enz f. reference, information

referieren v. to report, to lecture

reflektieren v. to reflect; auf etwas — to have something in view

Reflex m. reflex; -bewegung f. reflex action; -ion f. reflection

Reform f. reform; -ation f. reformation; -ator m. reformer; -ierte m. member of the Reformed Church

reformieren v. to reform

Refrain m. refrain; -sänger m. crooner

Refraktor m. refractor; refracting telescope

Regal neu. (book)shelf; stand

rege adj. active, animated; brisk, lively

Regel f. rule, regulation; norm; precept; (med.) menses; in der — as a rule; -detrie f. (math.) rule of three

regel: –mässig *adj.* regular; –mässig *adv.* regularly, usually; –n *v.* to regulate; to adjust; to arrange; to settle; –recht *adj.* regular; correct; –widrig *adj.* irregular

Regen *m.* rain; **aus dem — in die Traufe kommen** to jump from the frying pan into the fire; –bogen *m.* rainbow; –guss *m.* downpour; –mantel *m.* raincoat; –schirm *m.* umbrella; –wurm *m.* earthworm; –zeit *f.* rainy season

regen *v.* to stir, to move

regendicht *adj.* rainproof, waterproof

regenerieren *v.* to regenerate

Regensburg *neu.* Ratisbon

Regent *m.* regent; –schaft *f.* regency

Regie *f.* administration, state monopoly; stage management

regieren *v.* to govern, to rule; to reign

Regierung *f.* government; reign, rule; –santritt *m.* accession (to presidency *oder* throne); –sbeamte *m.* government official; –sbezirk *m.* administrative district; –sgewalt *f.* supreme power

Regiment *neu.* government; regiment

Regionalprogramm *neu.* (rad. & TV) closed-circuit

Regist: –er *neu.* register; index; table of contents; (organ) stop; –rator *m.* registrar, recorder; –ratur *f.* registry; –rierkasse *f.* cash register; –rierung *f.* registration

registrieren *v.* to register, to record; to file

Reglement *neu.* regulations; bylaw

Regler *m.* regulator

regnen *v.* to rain; **es regnet Bindfaden** it's raining cats and dogs

regnerisch *adj.* rainy

regsam *adj.* active, agile. mobile

regulieren *v.* to regulate; to adjust; to settle

Regung *f.* motion, movement; emotion, impulse

regungslos *adj.* motionless, immovable

Reh *neu.* roe, deer; –geiss *f.* doe; –kitz *neu.* fawn; –posten *m.* buckshot

Reib: –e *f.*, –eisen *neu.* grater; –erei *f.* friction; –fläche *f.* rough (*oder* striking) surface; –ung *f.* friction; collision; conflict; –ungsfläche *f.* (fig.) source of irritation

reiben *v.* to rub, to grate; to grind; **jemand etwas unter die Nase —** to tell a person something to his face

reich *adj.* rich, wealthy; substantial, copious; –haltig *adj.*, –lich *adj.* abundant, full, copious

Reich *neu.* empire, realm, kingdom; –sautobahn *f.* German express highway; –sapfel *m.* imperial globe; –sfar-

ben *f. pl.* national flag (*oder* colors); –skleinodien *neu. pl.* imperial crown jewels

Reich: –e *m.* rich person; –tum *m.* riches, wealth

reichen *v.* to reach, to extend; to hand, to present, to pass; to suffice

Reichweite *f.* range, reach

reif *adj.* ripe; mature; mellow; –en *v.* to ripen, to mature; –lich *adj.* mature; thorough

Reif *m.* ring; circle; –eisen *neu.* hoop iron; –en *m.* ring; hoop, tire; –enpanne *f.*, –enschaden *m.* tire puncture; –rock *m.* hoop skirt, crinoline

Reif *m.* hoarfrost

Reife *f.* ripeness; maturity; –prüfung *f.* final examination

reifen *v.* to form hoarfrost, to rime

Reigen *m.*, **Reihen** *m.* round dance

reih: –en *v.* to range, to rank, to string; –enweise *adv.* by (*oder* in) rows; –um *adv.* by (*oder* in) turns, alternately

Reihe *f.* row, range, series; line, sequence; rank, file; **ausser der — out** of turn; **der — nach successively; er ist an der —** it is his turn; –nfolge *f.* succession, sequence

Reiher *m.* heron

Reim *m.* rhyme; –erei *f.* inferior poetry; –schmied *m.* poetaster; rhymester

reimen *v.* to rhyme; (coll.) to make sense

rein *adj.* pure, unalloyed, unadulterated; clean, genuine; net; mere, sheer; — *adv.* entirely, quite; –en Mund halten to keep a secret; –en Wein einschenken to tell the plain truth; –es Deutsch correct German; –es Gewissen clear conscience; — unmöglich quite impossible; –igen *v.* to clean, to cleanse, to purify; to refine; –lich *adj.* clean, neat, tidy; –rassig *adj.* purebred

Rein: –emachefrau *f.* cleaning woman; –ertrag *m.* net proceeds; –fall *m.* failure; –gewinn *m.* net gain

Reis *m.* rice; –brei *m.* rice boiled in milk

Reis *neu.* twig, scion, sprig; –ig *neu.* brushwood; –igbündel *neu.* fagot

Reise *f.* journey; trip; travel; –büro *neu.* tourist agency; –führer *m.* guide book; guide; –gefährte *m.* fellow traveler; –gepäck *neu.* baggage; –nde *m.* traveler; salesman; –scheck *m.* traveler's check; –zeit *f.* tourist season; –ziel *neu.* destination

reisen *v.* to travel, to journey; to go (to)

Reiss: –aus nehmen to take to one's heels; –brett *neu.* drawing board; –er *m.* bestseller; thriller; box-office success; –feder *f.* drawing pen; –kohle *f.*

charcoal crayon; **–nagel** *m.*, **–zwecke** *f.* thumbtack; **–verschluss** *m.* zipper; **–zahn** *m.* canine tooth; **–zeug** *neu.* drawing instruments

reissen *v.* to tear, to drag, to pull; to burst, to split; **an sich —** to snatch; to seize; to usurp; to monopolize; **ihm riss die Geduld** he lost his patience; **in Stücke —** to tear to pieces; **Possen — to clown; wenn alle Stränge —** if worst comes to worst; **Witze —** to crack jokes; **–d** *adj.* rapid, rapacious; acute; violent; **die Ware geht –d** the goods sell like hot cakes

Reit: –bahn *f.* riding academy; **–er** *m.* horseman; rider; **–erei** *f.* cavalry; **–erstandbild** *neu.* equestrian statue; **–gerte** *f.* whip, switch; **–hose** *f.* riding breeches; **–knecht** *m.* groom; **–kunst** *f.* horsemanship; **–pferd** *m.* saddle horse; **–stiefel** *m. pl.* riding boots; **–weg** *m.* bridle path; **–zeug** *neu.* riding equipment

reiten *v.* to ride, to go on horseback; **Galopp —** to gallop; **Schritt —** to amble, to pace; **Trab —** to trot; **über den Haufen —** to ride down; **vor Anker —** (naut.) to ride at anchor; **–d** *adj.* on horseback, mounted

Reiz *m.* attraction, charm; stimulus; irritation; **–mittel** *neu.* incentive; stimulant; **–stoff** *m.* irritant

reiz: –bar *adj.* irritable; sensitive; **–en** *v.* to excite, to stir up; to irritate, to provoke; to entice; to charm; (cards) to bid; **–end** *adj.*, **–voll** *adj.* attractive, charming; **–los** *adj.* insipid; unattractive

Rekapitulationstheorie *f.* biogenesis

rekapitulieren *v.* to recapitulate

rekeln, räkeln *v.* to loll about

Reklamation *f.* reclamation, protest; complaint

Reklame *f.* advertisement; publicity; **–film** *m.* advertising film; **–schild** *neu.* billboard; **–zeichner** *m.* advertising designer

rekonstruieren *v.* to reconstruct

Rekonvaleszent *m.* convalescent

Rekord *m.* record performance (*oder* event)

Rekrut *m.* recruit; **–enunteroffizier** *m.* drill sergeant; **–ierung** *f.* recruiting

rekrutieren *v.* to recruit; to be recruited

Rektor *m.* rector; headmaster; **–at** *neu.* rectorship; headmastership

Relais *neu.* relay

relativ *adj.* relative; relating to

Relegation *f.* expulsion; rustication

Relief *neu.* relief; **–karte** *f.* relief map;

–stickerei *f.* raised embroidery

Religion *f.* religion; **–sgebräuche** *m. pl.* rites

religiös *adj.* religious; pious

Religiosität *f.* religiousness; religiosity

Reling *f.* and *neu.* (naut.) main rail

Reliquie *f.* relic; **–nschrein** *m.* reliquary

Reminiszens *f.* reminiscence, recollection

Remise *f.* coach house; shed

remittieren *v.* to remit, to return

Remonte *f.* remount

Rempelei *f.* jostling; rumpus

rempeln *v.* to jostle, to push; to look for a fight; to barge (into)

Renegat *m.* renegade

renitent *adj.* obstinate, refractory

Renn: –bahn *f.* race track; **–boot** *neu.* hydroplane; **–en** *neu.* race; **totes –en** undecided race; **–er** *m.* race horse; **–fahrer** *m.* race cyclist; car racer; **–mannschaft** *f.* race crew; **–sport** *m.* racing, turf; **–tier** *neu.* reindeer; **–tierflechte** *f.* reindeer moss; **–wagen** *m.* racing car; **–ziel** *neu.* goal line

rennen *v.* to run, to rush; to race

Renommee *neu.* reputation

renovieren *v.* to renovate, to redecorate

Rent: –abilität *f.* lucrativeness, profitableness; **–amt** *neu.*, **–kammer** *f.* revenue office; **–e** *f.* revenue, income; annuity; pension; **–ier** *m.*, **–ner** *m.* pensioner; man of private means

rentabel *adj.* lucrative, profitable

rentieren *v.* sich — to be profitable; to pay

reorganisieren *v.* to reorganize

Reparat: –ion *f.* reparation; **–ur** *f.* repair(ing); **–urwerkstätte** *f.* repair shop

reparieren *v.* to repair

repatriieren *v.* to repatriate

repetieren *v.* to repeat

Repetiergewehr *neu.* repeating rifle; repeater

Replik *f.* rejoinder, reply; replica

Report *m.* (com.) extra charge; **–age** *f.* (rad.) report; **–er** *m.* reporter

Repräsentant *m.* representative

repräsentieren *v.* to represent

Reproduktion *f.* reproduction; rendering

reproduzieren *v.* to reproduce

Reptil *neu.* reptile

Republik *f.* republic; **–aner** *m.* republican

republikanisch *adj.* republican

requirieren *v.* to requisition

Requisiten *neu. pl.* requisites; (theat.) properties, props

Reserv: –ation *f.* reservation; **–e** *f.* reserve; **–oir** *neu.* reservoir; tank; **–rad** *neu.* spare wheel; **–truppen** *f. pl.* reserves

reservieren *v.* to reserve

Residenz *f.* seat (of government); residence

resignieren *v.* to resign; to give up

Resinsäure *f.* acrylic acid

resolut *adj.* resolute, determined

Resolution *f.* resolution

Resonanz *f.* resonance; **-boden** *m.* sounding board

Respekt *m.* respect, esteem; **-sperson** *f.* person held in respect; notability; notable

respekt: -abel *adj.* respectable; **-ieren** *v.* to respect, to esteem; **-ive** *adv.* respectively; **-los** *adj.* irreverent; **-voll** *adj.* respectful; **-widrig** *adj.* disrespectful

Rest *m.* rest; remainder; remnant; balance; dregs; **den — geben** to finish off; **to kill; irdische -e** mortal remains; **-auflage** *f.* remainders; **-bestand** *m.* remnant, residue; **-betrag** *m.* remainder

Restaurant *neu.* restaurant

Restauration *f.* restoration; repair; (pol.) reinstatement; restaurant

restaurieren *v.* to restore, to renew, to repair

Resultat *neu.* result; outcome

retirieren *v.* to retreat

Retorte *f.* (chem.) retort

retour *adv.* back

Rett: -er *m.* rescuer, deliverer; Redeemer; **-ungsboot** *neu.* lifeboat; **-ungsgürtel** *m.*, **-ungsring** *m.* life belt; **-ungsmittel** *neu.* remedy; expedient; last straw; **-ungsstation** *f.* first-aid post

retten *v.* to save, to rescue, to deliver; **sich —** to escape

Rettich *m.* radish

rettungslos *adj.* past help; irretrievable

retuschieren *v.* to retouch

reu: -en *v.* **es -t mich** I am sorry for it; **-ig** *adj.*, **-mütig** *adj.*, **-evoll** *adj.* repentant, remorseful; **-los** *adj.* impenitent

Reue *f.* repentance; regret; remorse; **-egeld** *neu.* forfeit, penalty

Revanche *f.* revenge; **-partie** *f.* return match

revanchieren *v.* **sich —** to revenge oneself; to return a favor

revidieren *v.* to revise; to audit, to check

Revier *neu.* hunting ground; preserve; district; quarter; (mil.) sick bay

Revis: -ion *f.* revision, revisal, auditing; (law) appeal; rehearing; **-ionsbogen** *m.* (typ.) revise; **-or** *m.* reviser; auditor, controller

Revol: -te *f.* insurrection; **-ution** *f.* revolution; **-utionär** *m.* revolutionist

Revue *f.* review; (theat.) revue

Rezens: -ent *m.* reviewer, critic; **-ion** *f.* review; critique

Rezept *neu.* prescription; recipe

rezitieren *v.* to recite

Rhapsodie *f.* rhapsody

Rhabarber *m.* rhubarb

Rhein *m.* Rhine River

Rhesusfaktor *m.* (med.) RH-factor

Rhetorik *f.* rhetoric; **-er** *m.* rhetorician

rhetorisch *adj.* rhetorical

Rheuma *neu.*, **Rheumatismus** *m.* rheumatism

Rhinozeros *neu.* rhinoceros

rhythmisch *adj.* rhythmic(al)

Rhythmus *m.* rhythm

Richt: -balken *m.* traverse beam; **-blei** *neu.* plummet; **-er** *m.* judge; adjuster; **-eramt** *neu.* judgeship, judicature; **-erspruch** *m.* sentence; judgment; **-erstand** *m.* judiciary; **-erstuhl** *m.* tribunal; judge's chair; **-kanonier** *m.* gunner; **-linie** *f.* direction; guiding principle; **-mass** *neu.* standard; guage; **-platz** *m.*, **-statt** *f.* place of execution; **-scheit** *m.* and *neu.* level, ruler; **-schnur** *f.* plumb line; guiding principle; guide; **-ung** *f.* direction; course; bearing; tendency; adjustment

richt: -en *v.* to set straight; to adjust; (mil.) to dress; (min.) to straighten; to prepare; expedient; **-en** to set; to direct, to turn; to judge, to sentence; to execute; **sich -en nach** to conform with; to be guided by; **zugrunde -en** to ruin; **-erlich** *adj.* judicial; **-ig** *adj.* right, correct; accurate; suitable, fair; genuine, real; **-ig!** *interj.* quite right! **-ig gehen** to go right; (watch) to keep good time; **-igstellen** *v.* to rectify

Riech: -er *m.* (coll.) smeller; nose; **-fläschchen** *neu.* scent bottle; **-salz** *neu.* smelling salts; **-stoffe** *m. pl.* scents; perfumes; **-werkzeuge** *neu. pl.* olfactory organs

riechen *v.* to smell, to scent; **den Braten (or Lunte) —** to smell a rat; **ich kann ihn nicht —** I can't stand him

Riege *f.* section; (gym.) squad; team

Riegel *m.* bolt, bar; (clothes) rack; (mil.) switch line; **einen — vorschieben** to bar; to hinder; **hinter Schloss und —** under lock and key

Riemen *m.* strap, thong; oar; sling; **-antrieb** *m.* belt drive; **-scheibe** *f.* pulley; **-werk** *neu.* straps, harness

Ries *neu.* ream (1000 sheets of paper)

Riese *m.* giant; ogre; **-narbeit** *f.* tremendous work; **-nerfolg** *m.* smash hit; **-nschlange** *f.* python; boa constrictor

Rieselfeld *neu.* irrigated field

rieseln *v.* to drizzle, to ripple, to trickle

riesengross, riesig *adj.* gigantic, enormous

Riff *neu.* reef

Rigorosum *neu.* (doctor's degree) examination

Rille *f.* small groove

Rind *neu.* ox, cow; horned cattle; –erbraten *m.* roast beef; –erbremse *f.* gadfly; –erbrust *f.* brisket of beef; –erhirt *m.* cowboy; –fleisch *neu.* beef; –sleder *neu.* cowhide; –vieh *neu.* bovine; (coll.) blockhead

Rinde *f.* bark; crust; rind

Ring *m.* ring; circle; (com.) pool, trust; (mech.) link; –bahn *f.* circular railroad; –finger *m.* ring finger; –mauer *f.* circular wall

Ring: –er *m.*, –kämpfer *m.* wrestler; –kampf *m.* wrestling match; –richter *m.* umpire

Ringel *m.* ringlet, curl; –blume *f.* marigold; –locke *f.* curl; –reigen *m.*, –reihen *m.* ring-around-a-rosy; –söckchen *neu. pl.* bobby socks

ringen *v.* to struggle; to wrest(le); to wring

rings *adv.* (a)round; –herum *adv.* –um(her) *adv.* all around; round about

Rinn: –e *f.* groove, gutter, channel; furrow; –sal *neu.* watercourse, rill; –stein *m.* gutter

Ripp: –chen *neu.* small rib; chop; –e *f.* rib; (arch.) groin; –enfellentzündung *f.* pleurisy; –enstoss *m.* nudge in the ribs; –enspeer *m.* sparerib

Risiko *neu.* risk

riskant *adj.* risky

riskieren *v.* to risk

Riss *m.* tear, cleft, split, scratch; fracture; sketch, plan; (fig.) schism; breach

Ritt *m.* ride; –meister *m.* cavalry captain

Ritter *m.* knight, cavalier; arme — fritters; fahrender — knight-errant; –gut *neu.* estate, manor; –orden *m.* order of knighthood; –schaft *f.* knights; knighthood; –schlag *m.* knighting, dubbing; –sporn *m.* larkspur; –tum *neu.*, –wesen *neu.* chivalry

ritterlich *adj.* knightly; chivalrous; gallant

rittlings *adv.* astride, astraddle

rituell *adj.* ritual

Ritus *m.* rite

Ritz *m.*, Ritze *f.* cleft, fissure; rift; crack; chink; scratch

ritzen *v.* to cut, to scratch, to graze, to slit

Rivale *m.* rival

rivalisieren *v.* to rival, to compete

Rivalität *f.* rivalry

Rizinusöl *neu.* castor oil

Robbe *f.* (zool.) seal; –fang *m.* sealing;

–fänger *m.* sealer; seal hunter

Robber *m.* (cards) rubber

Roboter *m.* robot

robust *adj.* robust, sturdy

röcheln *r.* (throat) to rattle, to rasp

rochieren *v.* (chess) to castle

Rock *m.* coat; skirt; –schoss *m.* coattail; front of a skirt

Rocken *m.* distaff

Rodel *f.* toboggan; –bahn *f.* toboggan run; –schlitten *m.* toboggan; bobsled

rodeln *v.* to toboggan

roden *v.* to clear land, to root out, to stub

Roggen *m.* rye

roh *adj.* raw; crude; brutal; rough, rude; vulgar uncultured

Roh: –bau *m.* bare brickwork; –einnahmen *f. pl.* gross receipts; –eisen *neu.* pig iron; –kost *f.* vegetarian food; –köstler *m.* vegetarian; –ling *m.* cruel person; brute; –material *neu.*, –stoff *m.* raw material; –metall *neu.* crude metal

Rohr *neu.* cane; reed; pipe, tube; (gun) barrel; –dach *neu.* reed thatch; –dommel *f.* bittern; –geflecht *neu.* wickerwork; –kolben *m.* (bot.) cattail; –leger *m.* pipe fitter; plumber; –leitung *f.* pipeline; –mündung *f.* (gun) muzzle; –netz *neu.* pipes, conduit; –spatz *m.* reed sparrow; wie ein –spatz schimpfen to swear like a fishwife; –stock *m.* bamboo; –stuhl *m.* basket chair; –zucker *m.* cane sugar

Röhr: –e *f.* tube, pipe; conduit; –icht *neu.* reeds; canebrake

Roll: –e *f.* roll; roller; pulley; reel, spool; calender, mangle; caster; list, register; (theat.) part; aus der –e fallen to misbehave; –enbesetzung *f.*, –enverteilung *f.* (theat.) cast; –er *m.* roller; canary; (toy) scooter; –feld *neu.* (avi.) runway; –film *m.* roll film; –kommando *neu.* raiding (*oder* murder) squad; –kutscher *m.* carrier, carter; –mops *m.* rolled pickled herring; –schiene *f.* rail; –schuhe *m. pl.* roller skates; –schuhbahn *f.* skating rink; –stuhl *m.* wheel chair; –treppe *f.* escalator; –wäsche *f.* laundry for mangling

rollen *v.* to roll; to mangle; to rumble; (avi.) to taxi; –des Material rolling stock

Roman *m.* novel; romance; –literatur *f.* fiction; –schriftsteller *m.* novelist; –tik *f.* romantic period; romanticism; –ze *f.* romance; ballad

romantisch *adj.* romantic

Römer *m.* Roman; rummer; large wineglass

römischkatholisch *adj.* Roman Catholic

Romme *neu.* rummy (game)

Ronde *f.* (mil.) round; **-ll** *neu.* round (flower) bed; round tower

röntgen *v.* to X ray

Röntgen: -aufnahme *f.*, **-bild** *neu.* X-ray photograph; **-strahlen** *m. pl.* X rays

Ros: -e *f.* rose; (med.) erysipelas; **-enkohl** *m.* Brussel sprouts; **-enkranz** *m.* wreath of roses; rosary; **-enkreuzer** *m.* Rosicrucian; **-enmontag** *m.* last Monday before Lent; **-enöl** *neu.* attar of r ses; **-enstock** *m.*, **-enstrauch** *m.* rose bush; **-ette** *f.* rosette

rosa *adj.* pink, rose-colored

rosig *adj.* rose, rosy, roseate

Rosine *f.* raisin; currant

Ross *neu.* horse, steed; **auf dem hohen — sitzen** to sit on one's high horse; **-händler** *m.* horse dealer; **-kamm** *m.* currycomb; **-kastanie** *f.* horse chestnut

Rösselsprung *m.* (chess) knight's move; riddle

Rost *m.* rust; gridiron; grate, grill; **-braten** *m.* (meat) roast; **-fleck(en)** *m.* ironmold; **-schutz** *m.* antirust

rost: -en *v.* to rust; **-frei** *adj.* (steel) stainless; **-ig** *adj.* rusty

Röstbrot *neu.* toast

rösten *v.* to roast, to grill, to toast

rot *adj.* red, ruddy; **der -e Hahn** (the) fire; **— werden** to blush; **-bäckig** *adj.* redcheeked; **-blond** *adj.* auburn; **-glühend** *adj.* red-hot; **-haarig** *adj.* red-haired; **-ieren** to rotate, to revolve; **-ten, sich zusammen -ten** to form gangs

Rot *neu.* red; **-auge** *neu.*, **-feder** *f.* (ichth.) roach; **-dorn** *m.* pink hawthorn; **-drossel** *f.* redwing; **-fuchs** *m.* bay horse; **-haut** *f.* redskin; Indian; **-käppchen** *neu.* Red Riding Hood; **-kehlchen** *neu.* robin; **-kohl** *m.* red cabbage; **-lauf** *m.* (med.) erysipelas; **-schwänzchen** *neu.* (orn.) redstart; **-spon** *m.*, **-wein** *m.* red wine; claret; port; **-stift** *m.* red pencil; **-tanne** *f.* spruce; **-welsch** *neu.* thieves' argot; **-wild** *neu.* red deer

röt: -en *v.* to redden; **-lich** *adj.* reddish; **-lichbraun** *adj.* russet

Röte *f.* redness; blush; **-l** *m.* red chalk (*oder* ochre); **-ln** *f. pl.* German measles

Rotte *f.* band, gang; troop

Rotz *m.* mucus; nasal discharge

Rou: -lade *f.* rolled meat; roulade; **-leau** *neu.* Venetian (*oder* roller) blind

Rüb: -e *f.* turnip; beet; **gelbe -e** carrot; **-enzucker** *m.* beet sugar; **-saat** *f.*, **-samen** *m.* rapeseed

Rubin *m.* ruby

Rubrik *f.* heading; rubric; column

rubrizieren *v.* to head; to arrange in columns

ruchbar *adj.* notorious, public; **— werden** to become known; to get about

ruchlos *adj.* infamous, impious, wicked

Ruck *m.* jerk, jolt; start; **auf einen —** at one pull; **sich einen — geben** to pull oneself together; **-sack** *m.* rucksack, shoulder bag

Rück: -anspruch *m.* (law) counterclaim; **-antwort** *f.*, **-äusserung** *f.* reply; **-berufung** *f.* recall; **-bleibsel** *neu.* remainder, residue; **-blick** *m.* retrospect; backward glance; **-erinnerung** *f.* reminiscence; **-fahrkarte** *f.* round-trip ticket; **-fahrt** *f.* return journey; **-fall** *m.* relapse; (law) reversion; **-gabe** *f.* restitution, return; **-gang** *m.* decrease; retrogression; recession; decline; **-grat** *neu.* backbone; **-halt** *m.* support; reserve; **-hand** *f.* (tennis) backhand; **-kauf** *m.* redemption, repurchase; **-kehr** *f.* return; **-lage** *f.* reserve fund; **-porto** *neu.* return postage; **-prall** *m.* rebound, recoil; **-ruf** *m.* recall; **-schlag** *m.* recoil; backstroke; reverse; **-schritt** *m.* regression, relapse; **-seite** *f.* back, wrong side; reverse; **-sicht** *f.* consideration, regard; **-sitz** *m.* back seat; **-sprache** *f.* consultation, discussion; **-stand** *m.* arrears, residue; **-stoss** *m.* rebuff; recoil; **-stossmotor** *m.* jet propulsion; **-tritt** *m.* retirement; resignation; **-trittbremse** *f.* coaster brake; **-vergütung** *f.* reimbursement; **-wärtsgang** *m.* reverse gear; **-weg** *m.* way back, return; **-wirkung** *f.* retroaction; reaction; **-zahlung** *f.* repayment; **-zug** *m.* retreat, withdrawal

Rückkoppelung *f.* feedback

rück: -bezüglich *adj.* reflexive; **-erstatten** to refund; **-fällig** *adj.* relapsing; (law) revertible; **-gängig machen** to cancel, to recall, to break off; **-haltlos** *adj.* unreserved; open; **-läufig** *adj.* retrograde; **-lings** *adv.* backwards, from behind; **-schrittlich** *adj.* reactionary; **-sichtsvoll** *adj.* considerate, thoughtful; **-ständig** *adj.* in arrears; old-fashioned; **-wärtig** *adj.* retrograde; rearward; behind the lines; **-wärts** *adv.* back(wards); **-wirkend** *adv.* retroactive; retrospective; **-zahlen** *v.* to repay

Rücken *m.* back; rear; ridge; (nose) bridge; **es läuft mir eiskalt über den —** my spine tingles; **in den — fallen** to attack in the rear; **jemand den — kehren** to turn one's back to (*oder* on) someone; **-flug** *m.* upside-down flying; **-lehne** *f.* (chair) back; **-mark** *neu.* spinal cord

rücken *v.* to move; to push; to draw; **an jemandes Stelle — ** to take a person's place; **ins Feld — ** to take the field; **jemand zu Leibe — ** to press someone hard; **sich nicht von der Stelle — ** not to budge an inch

Rüde *m.* male dog (*oder* fox, wolf)

Rudel *neu.* herd, troop, crowd, pack

Ruder *neu.* rudder, helm, oar; **ans — kommen** to come into power; **–bank** *f.* rower's seat; (naut.) thwart; **–boot** *neu.* rowboat; **–er** *m.* rower, oarsman; **–pinne** *f.* tiller

rudern *v.* to row; to pull an oar

Rüdiger *m.* Roger

Ruf *m.* cry, shout; call; summons; reputation; fame, name; credit; **im –e stehen to be** reputed (to be); to be generally considered (as); **er hat einen — als Professor erhalten** he has been offered a professorship; **in üblen — bringen** to defame; **Mann von —** celebrity; **–name** *m.* Christian name; **–nummer** *f.* (tel.) number; **–weite** *f.* earshot; **in –weite** within call; **–zeichen** *neu.* (tel.) call signal

rufen *v.* to cry, to shout; to call; to summon; **etwas ins Leben — ** to call something into being; **ins Gedächtnis — ** to recall to mind, to remind; **— lassen** to send for; **wieder ins Leben — ** to restore to life; **wie gerufen kommen** to appear at the right moment

Rüffel *m.* reprimand, dressing down; rebuke

Rüge *f.* rebuke, reproach, reprimand, censure

rügen *v.* to blame, to censure, to reprimand

ruh: –elos *adj.* restless, disquieted; **–en** *v.* to rest, to repose; to sleep; to be buried; **eine Sache –en lassen** to drop a matter; **es –t auf ihm** it is his duty; **–en auf** to rest on, to be based on; **–endes Kapital** dead capital; **–ig** *adj.* quiet, still, silent; composed, calm; **–ig** *adv.* with pleasure, safely

Ruhe *f.* rest, repose; quiet, silence, calm; **in aller — ** very calmly; **in — lassen** to let alone; **sich zur — setzen** to retire; **zur — bringen** to calm; to pacify; **zur — gehen** to go to bed; **–bett** *neu.* couch; **–gehalt** *neu.* pension; **–punkt** *m.* point of rest; pause; **–stand** *m.* retirement; **–stätte** *f.* resting place; **letzte –stätte** grave; **–störung** *f.* disturbance; **–tag** *m.* day off

Ruhm *m.* glory; renown; fame; **–eshalle** *f.* Hall of Fame, pantheon

ruhm: –los *adj.* inglorious; **–redig** *adj.*

vainglorious; **–süchtig** *adj.* ambitious

rühmen *v.* to praise, to extol; to glorify; **sich — ** to be proud (of); to brag

rühmlich *adj.* glorious, honorable

Ruhr *f.* dysentery

Rühr: –ei *neu.* scrambled eggs; **–löffel** *m.* ladle; **–stück** *neu.* melodrama, sob stuff; **–ung** *f.* feeling, emotion; compassion

rühr: –en *v.* to move, to stir; to touch; to beat (drum); to affect; **–t euch!** (mil.) at ease! **–end** *adj.* affecting, touching; **–ig** *adj.* active, busy; agile, alert, nimble; **–selig** *adj.* sentimental, emotional

Ruin *m.* ruin; destruction; decay; **–e** *f.* ruins, debris; (coll.) wreck

ruinieren *v.* to ruin, to destroy

Rummel *m.* bustle; hubbub; amusement park; **den — kennen** (coll.) to know what's what; **den — verstehen** (coll.) to know a trick or two

rumoren *v.* to slam-bang; to rummage; to rumor

Rumpelkammer *f.* junk closet

Rumpf *m.* trunk; body; torso; (naut.) hull; fuselage; **–versteifung** (avi.) bulkhead

rümpfen *v.* **die Nase — ** to turn up one's nose

rund *adj.* round, circular, plump; **–en** *v.* to round; to go around; (baseball) to make a run; **–heraus sagen** to speak frankly; **–herum** *adv.* all around; **–lich** *adj.* rounded, plump; **–weg** *adv.* bluntly, flatly

Rund: –bau *m.* circular building; **–blick** *m.* view all around; panorama; **–bogen** *m.* Roman arch; **–e** *f.* circle; (sports) lap; round; (coll.) party; **–erlass** *m.* circular (notice); **–fahrt** *f.* circular tour; **–frage** *f.* questionnaire; **–funk** *m.* radio, broadcasting; **–funkansager** *m.* radio announcer; **–funkempfänger** *m.* radio receiver; **–funkgerät** *neu.* radio set; **–funkhörer** *m.* radio listener; **–funksender** *m.* radio transmitter; **–funksendung** *f.* broadcasting; **–funkstation** *f.* radio station; **–funkzeitung** *f.* radio magazine; **–gang** *m.* round; stroll; **–gemälde** *neu.* panorama; **–reise** *f.* round trip; **–reisebillet** *neu.* round-trip ticket; **–schau** *f.* panorama; review; **–schreiben** *neu.* circular; **–ung** *f.* rounding; curve; roundness

Rune *f.* rune; **–nschrift** *f.* runic writing

Runkelrübe *f.* beet root

Runzel *f.* wrinkle; pucker

runzeln *v.* to wrinkle; **die Stirn — ** to frown

runzlig *adj.* wrinkled, puckered

rupfen v. to pluck, to pull up; (coll.) to fleece
ruppig adj. unkempt; unmannered; shabby
Rüsche f. frill(ing), ruche
Russ m. soot
Russe m. Russian
Rüssel m. (zool.) trunk, snout, proboscis; –käfer m. weevil
russ(art)ig adj. sooty
Russland neu. Russia
Rüst: –kammer f. armory, arsenal; –ungsanlage f., –ungsbetrieb m. munition works, armament plant; –zeug neu. tools, equipment; implements
rüsten v. to prepare; to equip; to arm
rüstig adj. robust, vigorous; active
Rute f. rod, switch, twig; tail; –nbündel neu. fasces; –ngänger m. dowser
Rutsch m. glide, slide; landslip; (coll.) short visit; –bahn f. slide, chute
rutschen v. to glide, to slide, to slip, to skid
rütteln v. to shake, to jog; to jolt; **gerüttelt voll** heaped, crammed

S

Saal m. hall, large room
Saat f. seed, sowing; young crop; –feld neu. grain field; –gut neu., –korn neu. seed grain; –krähe f. rook
Sabbat m. Sabbath
Säbel m. sabre, sword; –beine neu. pl. bow legs; –hieb m. sword cut
sabotieren v. to sabotage
Sach: –bearbeiter m. administrator; –e f. thing; matter, subject; (law) case; –en pl. goods, clothes; **bei der –e sein** to pay attention to; **nicht bei der –e sein** to be absent minded; **nicht zur –e gehören** to be irrelevant; **seine sieben –en** (coll.) all his personal effects; **seiner –e gewiss sein** to be sure of one's facts; **zur –e!** come to the point! (pol.) question! –kenner m., –kundige m. expert; –kenntnis f., –kunde f. expert knowledge; –lage f. state of affairs; –leistung f. payment in kind; –register neu. index, list of contents; –verhalt m. facts of a case; –verständige m. specialist, authority; –verwalter m. attorney; counsel; –wert m. real value
sach: –dienlich adj. pertinent, relevant; useful; –gemäss adj. appropriate; proper; –gemäss adv. in a suitable manner; –kundig adj., –verständig adj. competent, expert; –lich adj. real; objective; –lich adv. to the point
Sachsen neu. Saxony

sacht(e) adj. soft, gentle; easy-going, slow
Sack m. sack, bag; (dial.) pocket, purse; **mit — und Pack** with bag and baggage; –erlot! –erment! interj. Darn it! –garn neu. twine; –gasse f. blind alley (fig.) deadlock; –hüpfen neu., –laufen neu. sack race; –leinen neu., –leinewand f. sackcloth; –pfeife f. bagpipe; –tuch neu. (dial.) handkerchief
sacken v. to sack; to pocket; to sink
säen v. to sow
Säer, Sämann m. sower
Saft m. sap, juice; fluid, liquid; **voll — succulent; weder — noch Kraft haben** to have no energy, to be insipid
saftig adj. juicy; spicy, coarse
Sage f. legend; myth; saga; **es geht die — the story goes**
Säge f. saw; –blatt neu. saw blade; –bock m. sawhorse; –mehl neu., –späne m. pl. sawdust; –mühle f., –werk neu. sawmill
sagen v. to say, to tell; to signify; **das hat nichts zu — that does not matter; er lässt sich nichts — he will not listen to reason; gesagt, getan no sooner said than done; ich habe mir — lassen I was told; ich muss — I must admit; lassen Sie es sich gesagt sein believe me; let it be a warning to you; — lassen to send word; — wollen mit to mean by;** –haft adj. legendary, mythical
sägen v. to saw; (coll.) to snore
Sahne f. cream
Saison f. season; –arbeiter m. seasonal worker; –ausverkauf m. clearance sale
Saite f. (mus.) string, cord; **andere –n aufziehen** to change one's attitude; –ninstrument neu. stringed instrument; –nspiel neu. lyre; string music
Sakrament neu. sacrament
Sakristei f. vestry
Säkularfeier f. centennial; centenary
säkularisieren v. to secularize
Salat m. salad; **da haben wir den —!** (coll.) that's a fine mess; **grüner — lettuce**
Salb: –e f. salve, ointment; –ung f. anointment, unction
salbadern v. to wheedle, to prattle
Salbei m. and f. (bot.) sage
salben v. to anoint, to salve
salbungsvoll adj. unctuous; smug, pathetic
saldieren v. to balance, to settle
Saldo m. (com.) balance; **— ziehen to strike a balance;** –vortrag m. balance forward
Salm m. salmon
Salmiak m. sal ammoniac; –geist m. liquid ammonia

Salon *m.* drawing room; (naut.) saloon; **-held** *m.*, **-löwe** *m.* playboy; **-wagen** *m.* Pullman car

Salpeter *m.* saltpeter, sodium nitrate

Salto *m.* somersault; **-mortale** *m.* breakneck leap

Salut *m.* (mil.) salute; **-schuss** *m.* gun salute

salutieren *v.* to salute

Salve *f.* volley; salvo; (naut.) broadside

Salz *neu.* salt; (coll.) wit; **-bergwerk** *neu.* salt mine; **-fass** *neu.* salt shaker; **-gurke** *f.* pickled cucumber; **-hering** *m.* pickled herring; **-lake** *f.*, **-lauge** *f.* brine, pickle; **-lecke** *f.* salt lick; **-sole** *f.* salt water; brine

salz: **-artig** *adj.* saline; **-bildend** *adj.* saltforming; **-en** *v.* to salt, to season; **gesalzene Preise** exorbitant prices; **-ig** *adj.* salty

Säm: **-aschine** *f.* seeding machine; **-ereien** *f. pl.* seeds; **-ling** *m.* seedling

Samariter *m.* Samaritan

Same(n) *m.* seed; sperm; **-nfädchen** *neu.* spermatozoon; **-nkapsel** *f.* pod; **-nkorn** *neu.* grain of seed; **-nstaub** *m.* pollen

Samm: **-elband** *m.* (lit.) omnibus; volume; **-elbecken** *neu.*, **-elbehälter** *m.* reservoir; **-elbüchse** *f.* collecting box; **-elplatz** *m.* meeting place; **-elruf** *m.* (mil.) assembly; **-elstelle** *f.* central depot; collecting station; **-elsurium** *neu.* medley; **-elwort** *neu.* collective noun; **-ler** *m.* collector; compiler; **-lung** *f.* collection; composure, concentration

sammeln *v.* to gather, to collect; to accumulate; to assemble, to rally; to concentrate; **sich —** to compose oneself

Samstag *m.* (dial.) Saturday

samt *prep.* and *adv.* together with; **— und sonders** each and all, jointly and severally

Sam(me)t *m.* velvet; **jemanden mit -handschuhen anfassen** to handle someone very delicately

sämtlich *adj.* all (together); **—** *adv.* collectively, as a whole

Sand *m.* sand, grit; **auf — bauen** to build on an uncertain foundation; **im -e verlaufen** to come to naught; **wie — am Meer** (bibl.) innumerable; **-bahn** *f.* dirt track; **-boden** *m.* sandy soil; **-korn** *neu.* grain of sand; **-läufer** *m.* sandpiper; **-mann** *m.* sandman; **-papier** *neu.* sandpaper; **-stein** *m.* sandstone

Sandale *f.* sandal

sandig *adj.* sandy, gritty

sanft *adj.* soft, smooth; gentle, mild; slight; **-mütig** *adj.* gentle, mild, goodnatured; meek

Sanftmut *m.* gentleness, mildness

Sang *m.* song, singing; **ohne — und Klang** silently, unceremoniously

Sänger *m.* singer; songster; poet

sanieren *v.* to cure; to restore

Sanierung *f.* restoration, reorganization

sanitär *adj.* sanitary

Sanität: **-er** *m.* ambulance man; **-sbehörde** *f.* Board of Health; **-shund** *m.* first-aid dog; **-skolonne** *f.* ambulance corps; **-soffizier** *m.* medical officer; **-swache** *f.* first-aid station; **-swagen** *m.* motor ambulance

Sankt *adj.* saint; **-ion** *f.* sanction; **-ionierung** *f.* confirmation, recognition; ratification

sanktionieren *v.* to sanction

Saphir *m.* sapphire

Sarg *m.* coffin

sarkastisch *adj.* sarcastic

satanisch *adj.* satanic

Satellit *m.* satellite

Satin *m.* satin, sateen

Satire *f.* satire

satirisch *adj.* satiric(al)

satt *adj.* satisfied; satiated; deep, intense; rich; saturated; **etwas — haben** to be fed up with something; **nicht — werden** never to tire of; **nicht — zu bekommen** insatiable; **sich — essen** to eat one's fill; **-sam** *adv.* sufficiently, enough

Sattel *m.* saddle; bridge (of nose); ridge; **aus dem — heben** to unhorse; to supersede; **fest im — sitzen** to be firmly established; **in allen Sätteln gerecht sein** to have all-around experience, to be Jack-of-all-trades; **-dach** *neu.* ridged roof; **-knopf** *m.* (saddlebow) pommel; **-pferd** *neu.* saddle horse; left horse; **-zeug** *neu.* saddle and harness

sattelfest *adj.* firm in the saddle; proficient; knowing one's business (*oder* trade), mastering one's trade

satteln *v.* to saddle

sättigen *v.* to satiate, to satisfy; to saturate; **sich —** to appease one's hunger

Sättigung *f.* (chem.) saturation; **-spunkt** *m.* saturation point

Sattler *m.* saddler; **-ei** *f.* saddlery

Satyr *m.* satyr

Satz *m.* sentence; proposition, thesis, theorem; composition; phrase; bound, leap; set; sediment; (com.) rate, charge; (typ.) matter; **in — geben** to give to the typesetter; **-bau** *m.* (gram.) construction; **-bild** *neu.* (typ.) setting; **-fehler** *m.* misprint; **-gefüge** *neu.* complex sentence; **-lehre** *f.* syntax; **-spiegel** *m.* (typ.) face; page proof; **-ung** *f.* statute; ordinance; regulations; **-zei-**

chen *neu.* punctuation mark
satzungsgemäss *adj.* statutory
Sau *f.* sow; unter aller — (sl.) beneath contempt; –bohne *f.* broad bean; –kerl *m.* cad; –stall *m.* pigsty; –wetter *neu.* foul weather
sauber *adj.* clean, neat, tidy; (coll.) fine
säubern *v.* to clean, to clear, to purge
Sauce *f.* sauce; gravy
sauer *adj.* sour, acid, pickled; hard; morose; cross; –töpfisch *adj.* peevish, sour, sullen
Sauer:–ampfer *m.* (bot.) sorrel;–braten *m.* marinated beef roast; –kohl *m.*, –kraut *neu.* sauerkraut; –milch *f.* curdled milk; –stoff *m.* oxygen; (flüssig) lox; –stoffmangel *m.* anoxia; (im Blut) anoxemia; –teig *m.* sourdough
säuern *v.* to make sour; to leaven
Sauf:–bold *m.* drunkard; –en *neu.* drinking; –erei *f.*, –gelage *neu.* drinking bout; booze
saufen *v.* to drink; to booze; to carouse
Säufer *m.* drunkard; –wahnsinn *m.* delirium tremens
Saug: –er *m.* sucker; (bottle) nipple; –flasche *f.* feeding bottle; –heber *m.* siphon; –rüssel *m.* proboscis; –scheibe *f.* suction disk
Säug: –en *neu.* suckling, nursing; lactation; –etier *neu.* mammal; –ling *m.* suckling; baby; infant; –lingsfürsorge *f.* infant welfare; –lingsheim *neu.* nursery; home for infants
saugen *v.* to suck(le); to absorb; sich etwas aus den Fingern — to invent tales
säugen *v.* to suckle, to nurse
Säule *f.* column, pillar; (phys.) pile; –nfuss *m.* pedestal; –gang *m.*, –halle *f.* colonnade, arcade; portico; –knauf *m.* (arch.) capital
Saum *m.* seam, hem; border, edge; –pfad *m.* mule track; –pferd *neu.* pack horse; –tier *neu.* pack mule (*oder* horse)
säumen *v.* to hem; to border; to tarry; to hesitate; to lag behind; to delay
saumselig *adj.* tardy; lazy; negligent
Säure *f.* sourness, tartness; acidity; acid; –messer *m.* acidimeter
Saus *m.* in — und Braus leben to live riotously
säuseln *v.* to rustle, to whisper, to buzz
sausen *v.* to rush, to dash; to sough
Saxophon *neu.* saxophone
Schabe *f.* cockroach
Schabe: –fleisch *neu.* scraped meat; –r *m.* scraper; –rnack *m.* trick, hoax
schaben *v.* to scrape, to grate, to rasp; to graze; (art) to rub

schäbig *adj.* shabby; stingy; mean
schablon: –enhaft *adj.*, –enmässig *adj.* mechanical; stereotyped; –isieren *v.* to stencil
Schablone *f.* model, pattern; stencil
Schach *neu.* chess; in — halten to keep in check; — bieten to (give) check; –brett *neu.* chessboard; –feld *neu.* (chess) square; –figur *f.* chessman; –meister *m.* chess champion; –partie *f.* game of chess; –zug *m.* (chess) move; clever move
Schach: –er *m.* bargaining, jobbery; –erer *m.* haggler
Schächer *m.* (bibl.) thief; poor wretch
schachern *v.* to bargain, to haggle, to job
schachmatt *adj.* checkmated; knocked out
Schacht *m.* shaft, pit
Schachtel *f.* box; alte — old frump; –deckel *m.* box lid
Schächter *m.* (kosher) butcher
schad: –e *adj.* regrettable; dafür ist es zu –e it's too good for that; es ist –e it's a pity; wie –e! what a pity! too bad! –en to damage, to harm, to hurt; das –et dir nichts that serves you right; das –et nichts that does not matter, never mind; –enfroh *adj.* rejoicing over another's misfortune, malicious; –haft *adj.* damaged, defective, faulty; –los *adj.* undamaged; sich –los halten to indemnify; to recoup oneself
Schad: –en *m.* damage, harm, injury; defect; loss; disadvantage, detriment; mischief; durch –en wird man klug a burnt child fears the fire; jemand –en zufügen to harm someone; mit –en verkaufen to sell at a loss; –en leiden to come to grief; –enersatz *m.* compensation, indemnification; –enersatzklage *f.* action for damages; –enfeuer *neu.* destructive fire; –loshaltung *f.* indemnification
Schäd: –igung *f.* damage; prejudice; –ling *m.* noxious person (*oder* animal); vermin; parasite
Schädel *m.* skull; (fig.) head; –bohrer *m.* (med.) trepan; –bruch *m.* skull fracture
schädigen *v.* to damage, to injure, to harm
schädlich *adj.* injurious, hurtful; noxious
Schaf *neu.* sheep; weibliches — ewe; (coll.) simpleton; –bremse *f.* botfly; –bock *m.* ram; –fell *neu.* sheepskin, fleece; –fleisch *neu.* mutton; –garbe *f.* yarrow; –herde *f.* flock of sheep; –hirt(e) *m.* shepherd; –hürde *f.* sheepfold; –schur *f.* sheep shearing; –skopf *m.* sheepshead; –stand *m.* stock of sheep; –zucht *f.* sheep breeding
Schäf: –chen *neu.* lamb(kin); seine –chen

ins Trockene bringen to feather one's nest; **–chenwolke** f. cirrus (cloud); **–er** m. shepherd; **–erei** f. sheep farm; **–ergedicht** neu. pastoral, idyll, eclogue; **–erin** f. shepherdess; **–erspiel** neu. pastoral play; **–erstunde** f. lover's hour

schaffen v. to create, to produce; to work; to accomplish; to provide; to convey; to remove; **an Ort und Stelle —** to bring to the agreed place; **er weiss immer Rat zu —** he is never at a loss; **ich habe nichts damit zu —** it doesn't concern me; **jemanden aus dem Wege** (or **beiseite**) **—** to kill (oder remove) someone; **jemandem viel zu — machen** to give someone a lot of trouble; **sich zu — machen** to putter about

Schaffner m. conductor; **–in** f. housekeeper; female conductor

Schafott neu. scaffold; execution place

schäkern v. to joke, to dally, to flirt

schal adj. insipid; stale; flat, dull

Schal m. shawl, scarf, comforter; **–e** f. shell; peel, skin; hull, husk; pod; cup, dish, bowl, basin; scale; **–entier** neu. crustacean

Schäl: –hengst m. stallion; **–maschine** f. peeling machine; **–pflug** m. breastplow

schälen v. to peel, to pare; to husk, to shell; to bark; **sich —** to peel (off), to cast one's shell; to shed (bark); to scale

Schalk m. rogue, wag; jester; **–haftigkeit** f., **–heit** f. waggishness; archness; roguery; **–snarr** m. court jester

schalkhaft adj. roguish, waggish; jocular

Schall m. sound, reverberation; **–becken** neu. cymbal; **–boden** m. soundboard; **–dämpfer** m. silencer, muffler; **–explosion** f. sonic boom; **–grenze** f. sound barrier; **–lehre** f. acoustics; **–platte** f. record; **–plattenrille** f. microgroove; **–plattensammlung** f. record collection; **–rille** f. groove; **–trichter** m. bell; horn; megaphone; **–welle** f. sound wave

schall: –dicht adj. soundproof; **–en** v. to ring; to (re)sound; **–end** adj. resonant; sonorous

Schalt: –anlage f. switch gear; **–brett** neu. switchboard; dashboard; instrument panel; **–er** m. switch; ticket window, counter; **–getriebe** neu. main gearshift; **–jahr** neu. leap year; **–schlüssel** m. ignition key; **–tafel** f. switchboard; **–ung** f. gearshift; (elec.) connection

schalten v. to rule, to direct; (elec.) to switch, to connect; to put into gear; to deal with; **jemand — und walten lassen**

Scham f. shame; bashfulness, modesty; (anat.) genitals; **–bug** m. (anat.) groin; **–gefühl** neu. sense of shame; **–röte** f.

blush; **–teile** m. pl. genitals

scham: –haft adj. bashful, chaste; **–los** adj. shameless, impudent; **–rot** adj. blushing

schämen v. sich **—** to be ashamed (of)

Schand: –bube m. scoundrel; **–e** f. shame; disgrace; **–fleck** m. blemish, stain; **–gedicht** neu., **–schrift** f. libelous writing; **–geld** neu., **–preis** m. scandalous price; **–mal** neu. brand; mark of infamy; **–maul** neu. evil tongue, slanderer; **–pfahl** m. pillory; whipping post; **–tat** f. crime, misdeed, infamous action

Schän: –er m. violator; ravisher; **–lichkeit** f. infamy, baseness; **–ung** f. defamation; desecration; disfigurement; violation, rape

schandbar adj. shameful, infamous

schänden v. to dishonor, to defame; to sully, to brand; to desecrate, to profane; to rape

schändlich adj. infamous, atrocious

Schank: –sale (of liquors); **–berechtigung** f. liquor license; **–bier** neu. tap beer; **–tisch** m. bar; **–wirtschaft** f. tavern, bar

Schanz: –arbeiten f. pl. entrenchments; **–e** f. redoubt; entrenchment; **sein Leben in die –e schlagen** to risk one's life

Schar f. troop; flock; crowd; plowshare; **–führer** m. platoon leader; **–mützel** neu. skirmish; **–wache** f. watch; patrol

Scharade f. charade

scharen v. sich **—** to assemble; to flock

scharf adj. sharp, cutting; pointed; harsh, caustic; acute; shrill; keen; rigorous; **— bewachen** to watch closely; **–e Patrone** live cartridge; **–e Zucht** rigid discipline; **— reiten** to ride hard; **–sichtig** adj. sharp-sighted; penetrating; **–sinnig** adj. sagacious, ingenious

Scharf: –blick m. penetrating glance; keen eye; acuteness; **–macher** m. agitator; firebrand; **–richter** m. executioner; **–schütze** m. sharpshooter; **–sicht** f. perspicacity; **–sinn** m. sagacity, acumen, ingeniousness

Schärfe f. sharpness, acuteness; severity; pungency; precision; edge

schärfen v. to sharpen, to point; to whet; to intensify, to increase, to strengthen

Scharlach m. scarlet; **–fieber** neu. scarlet fever

scharlachfarben, scharlachrot adj. scarlet, vermilion

scharmant adj. charming, fascinating

Scharnier neu. hinge, joint

Schärpe f. sash

scharren v. to scrape, to scratch; (horse) to paw; to shuffle (feet)

schartig adj. dented, jagged, notchy

scharwenzeln v. to fawn, to toady

schatt: −enhaft adj. shadowy; unreal, ghostly; **−ieren** v. to shade, to tint; to hatch (drawing); **−ig** adj. shady, shaded

Schatten m. shade, shadow; phantom, spirit; **in den — stellen** to place (oder throw) in the shade; to eclipse; **−bild** neu. silhouette; phantom; **−könig** m. mock king, kinglet; **−reich** neu. underworld, Hades; **−riss** m. silhouette; **−spiel** neu. shadow play; phantasmagoria

Schatulle f. cash box; private fund

Schatz m. treasure, riches; hoard; darling, sweetheart; **−amt** neu. treasury; exchequer; **−anweisung** f. treasury note; **−gräber** m. treasure hunter; **−kammer** f. treasury; **−meister** m. treasurer

schätz: −bar adj., **−enswert** adj. estimable; valuable; **−en** v. to estimate; to value, to judge; to esteem; to appreciate; to respect; **−ungsweise** adv. approximately, probably

Schätzung f. estimate; appraisal, esteem; appreciation; **−swert** m. estimated value

Schau f. show, view; display, exhibition; review; **zur — stellen** to exhibit, to display; **−brot** neu. (bibl.) shewbread; **−bude** f. booth (at a fair); **−budenbesitzer** m. showman; **−bühne** f. stage, theater; **−fenster** neu. show window; **−fensterreklame** f. window display; **−gefecht** neu. sham battle; **−gerüst** neu. platform, grandstand; **−haus** neu. mortuary; morgue; **−kasten** m. showcase; **−münze** f. medal; **−packung** f. dummy; **−platz** m. scene, theater; **−spiel** neu. play; drama; spectacle, scene, sight; **−spieldichter** m. dramatist, playwright; **−spieldirektor** m. theatrical manager; **−spieler** m. actor, player; **−spielerin** f. actress; **−spielkunst** f. dramatic art; **−spieltruppe** f. touring company; **−stellung** f. exhibition, show; **−stück** neu. show piece; specimen; **−turnen** neu. gymnastic display

schau! interj. look! **−en** v. to see, to observe, to look, to gaze; **−lustig** adj. curious; **−spielern** v. to act; to sham; to play-act

Schauder m. shudder(ing), shivering; fright

schauder: −erregend adj., **−haft** adj. horrible; shocking, awful, terrible, atrocious; **−n** v. to shudder, to shiver, to feel creepy

Schauer m. shuddering; fit; awe; thrill; shower; **−drama** neu. thriller; **−leute** pl. stevedores; **−roman** m. dime novel, ghastly novel

schauer: −lich adj., **−rig** adj. awful, horrible; ghastly; **−n** v. to feel awe (for); to shudder

Schaufel f. shovel, scoop; paddle; **−rad** neu. paddle wheel

schaufeln v. to shovel

Schaukel f. swing; **−pferd** neu. rocking horse; **−stuhl** m. rocking chair

schaukeln v. to swing, to rock; **wir werden das Kind schon —** (coll.) we'll take care of the matter

Schaum m. foam, spume, froth; (soap) lather; **−gold** neu. tinsel; **−kelle** f., **−löffel** m. skimmer, skimming ladle; **−schläger** m. empty talker, windbag; **−wein** m. sparkling wine; champagne

schäumen v. to foam, to froth, to effervesce, to sparkle; (soap) to lather; **vor Wut —** to boil with rage

Scheck m. (bank) check; **−buch** neu. checkbook; **−formular** neu. blank check; **−inhaber** m. bearer

scheckig adj. piebald, dappled, speckled

scheel adj. envious; squint-eyed; askew; **−süchtig** adj. envious, jealous

Scheffel m. bushel

Scheibe f. disk; slice; (ast.) orb; honeycomb; (mech.) dial; (mil.) practice target; (potter's) wheel; (window) pane; **−ngardine** f. cafe curtain; **−nhonig** m. honey in the comb; **−nschiessen** neu. target shooting; **−nstand** m. target range; **−nwischer** m. windshield wiper

Scheich m. sheik

Scheide f. sheath, scabbard; boundary, limit; (anat.) vagina; **−blick** m. parting glance; **−brief** m. farewell letter; **−gruss** m. farewell; **−kunst** f. analytical chemistry; **−mauer** f., **−wand** f. partition; **−münze** f. small coin, change; **−weg** m. parting of ways; crossroad

scheiden v. to separate, to divide; to analyze, to divorce; **sich — to part**; to separate, to depart; **sich — lassen** to get divorced

Scheidung f. separation; divorce

Schein m. shine, light; appearance; certificate; receipt; banknote; **es ist alles nur —** it's nothing but make-believe; **sich den — geben** to feign, to pretend; **zum — as** a matter of form; **−angriff** m. sham attack; **−grund** m. pretense; sophism; **−heilige** m. hypocrite; **−könig** m. mock king; **−werfer** m. searchlight, headlight, spotlight

schein: −bar adj. seeming, apparent, pretended; **–en** v. to shine; to appear, to **seem**; **–heilig** adj. hypocritical; **–tot** adj. seemingly dead

Scheit m. and neu. log

Scheitel m. (hair) parting; vertex, summit; **–punkt** m. vertex, zenith

scheiteln v. to part (hair)

scheitern v. to run aground, to wreck, to fail

Schelle f. (small) bell; manacle; (dial.) box on the ear; **–n** pl. (cards) diamonds; **–ngeläut** neu. tinkling of bells; **–nkappe** f. fool's cap and bells

schellen v. to ring (oder pull) a bell

Schelm m. rogue; knave; **–enstreich** neu., **–enstück** neu., **–erei** f. roguery, prank

schelmisch adj. roguish; arch

schelten v. to scold, to reprimand, to abuse

Schema neu. scheme; model, patter; schedule; diagram; order, arrangement

Schenk m. (lit.) cupbearer; **–e** f. bar, inn, tavern

Schenkel m. thigh; shank; leg; (geom.) side; **–bruch** m. fracture of the thighbone

schenken v. to pour out; to retail liquor; to donate, to present, to grant; das Leben — to give birth; to grant life

Schenker m. donor

Schenkungsurkunde f. deed of gift

Scherbe f. fragment; potsherd; (sl.) monocle

Schere f. scissors; shears; clippers; claw (of crabs); **–nfernrohr** neu. periscope; **–nschleifer** m. scissors grinder; **–nschnitt** m. silhouette

scheren v. to shear, to clip; to shave; to warp; (naut.) to sheer; to bother, to disturb; **sich fort** — to be off, to go away

Schererei f. vexation; bother, trouble

Scherflein neu. mite; **sein** — **beitragen** to do one's bit

Scherge m. executioner; beadle; bailiff

Scherz m. jest, joke, pleasantry; — **treiben mit** to make fun of; **–wort** neu. joke

scherz–en v. to make merry, to jest, to joke; **–haft** adj. jocular, playful; **–liebend** adj. frolicsome, waggish; **–weise** adv. for fun

Scheu f. shyness; timidity; awe; **ohne** — bold; **–sal** neu. monster

scheu adj. shy; timid; skittish; — **machen** to intimidate; **–chen** v. to scare, to frighten

Scheuche f. scarecrow; bugbear

scheuen v. to shy (at), to avoid, to shun; **sich** — to be afraid (of), to hesitate; **keine Mühe** — to spare no trouble

Scheuer f. barn, shed

Scheuer: **–bürste** f. scrubbing brush; **–frau** f. cleaning woman; **–lappen** m. scouring cloth; **–leiste** f. baseboard

scheuern v. to scour, to scrub; to rub, to chafe

Scheune f. barn, shed

scheusslich adj. atrocious, hideous, horrible

Schicht f. layer, bed, stratum; shift; coating; class, rank; (wood) pile; **–enbildildung** f. stratification; **–meister** m. (min.) overseer; **–wechsel** m. change of shift

schichten v. to arrange in layers; to pile up; to stratify; to classify

Schick m. skill, fitness; elegance, chic; **–lichkeitsgefühl** neu. sense of propriety; tact; **–sal** neu. destiny, fate; lot; **–salsglaube** m. fatalism; **–salsschlag** m. misfortune; **–ung** f. affliction; dispensation; Providence

schick adj. chic, stylish; smart; **–en** v. to send, to dispatch; to transmit; **es –t sich** to be becoming (oder proper); **sich für** (or zu) **etwas –en** to be adapted for something; **–lich** adj. proper, decent; becoming

Schieb: **–efenster** neu. sash window; **–er** m. slide (rule); profiteer; **–etür** f. sliding door; **–karren** m. wheelbarrow; **–ung** f. profiteering

schieben v. to push, to shove; to slide; to shift; to profiteer; die Schuld auf jemand —, jemandem etwas in die Schuhe — to put the blame on someone; Kegel — to bowl

Schieds: **–gericht** neu. court of arbitration; **–smann** m., **–srichter** m arbitrator; referee; **–spruch** m. arbitration, decision

schief adj. slanting, inclined; crooked; bent; wry; **–er Winkel** oblique angle; — adv. awry; **das geht** — that fails; **jemand** — **ansehen** to look askance at someone; — **gewickelt** (coll.) in error

Schiefer m. slate; **–bruch** m. slate quarry; **–dach** neu. slate roof; **–decker** m. slater; **–tafel** f. (school) slate

schielen v. to squint; to be cross-eyed; — **nach** to leer at

Schien: **–bein** neu. shinbone; **–e** f. rail; (med.) splint; **aus den –en kommen** to derail; **–ennetz** neu. railway system; **–enstrang** m. railroad track; **–enweite** f. gauge

schier adj. pure, sheer; — adv. almost

Schiess: **–ausbildung** f. gunnery drill; **–baumwolle** f. guncotton; **–bedarf** m. ammunition; **–bude** f. shooting gallery;

—**gewehr** *neu.* gun, rifle; —**ıehre** *f.* ballistics; —**platz** *m.* firing range; —**prügel** *m.* (coll.) firearm; —**pulver** *neu.* gunpowder; —**scharte** *f.* loophole, embrasure; —**scheibe** *f.* target; —**stand** *m.* rifle range

schiessen *v.* to shoot, to fire; (sports) to score; to dart, to rush; (plants) to spring up; **die Zügel — lassen** to give rein to; **einen Bock —** to pull a boner; **einen Purzelbaum —** to somersault; **es ist zum —** it's just too funny; **hinterrücks —** to snipe; **in Samen —** to run to seed

Schiff *neu.* ship, boat; (arch.) nave; (mech.) shuttle; —**(f)ahrt** *f.* navigation; —**bau** *m.* shipbuilding; —**bruch** *m.* shipwreck; —**brüchige** *m.* castaway; —**er** *m.* skipper, sailor, navigator; —**erklavier** *neu.* (coll.) accordion; —**sbesatzung** *f.* ship's crew; —**sbrücke** *f.* pontoon bridge; —**sjournal** *neu.* logbook; —**sjunge** *m.* cabin boy; —**skörper** *m.*, —**srumpf** *m.* hull; —**sladung** *f.* ship's cargo; —**smakler** *m.* ship broker; —**sraum** *m.* hold, tonnage

schiff: —**bar** *adj.* navigable; —**brüchig** *adj.* shipwrecked; —**en** *v.* to navigate, to ship

Schikane *f.* chicanery, vexation, annoyance

schikanieren *v.* to annoy, to vex, to irritate

schikanös *adj.* vexatious

Schild *m.* shield, buckler; escutcheon; **etwas ım —e führen** to have something up one's sleeves; — *neu.* signboard; nameplate; label; peak (of cap); —**bürger** *m.* duffer; —**drüse** *f.* thyroid gland; —**erhaus** *neu.* sentry box; —**knappe** *m.* shield bearer, squire; —**kröte** *f.* tortoise, turtle; —**wache** *f.* sentry, sentinel

schildern *v.* to describe, to depict, to paint

Schilderung *f.* description, depiction

Schilf *neu.* reed, sedge; —**rohr** *neu.* reed(s)

schillern *v.* to change colors; —**d** *adj.* iridescent, opalescent

Schimäre *f.* chimera, phantom

Schimmel *m.* mildew; mold; white horse

schimmelig *adj.* mildewy, moldy, musty

Schimmer *m.* glimmer, gleam, shimmer; **er hat keinen —** he hasn't the faintest idea

schimmern *v.* to glimmer, to glitter, to glisten

Schimpanse *m.* chimpanzee

Schimpf *m.* affront, insult; disgrace; —**name** *m.* abusive name; —**wort** *neu.* invective

schimpfen *v.* to abuse, to revile, to scold

schimpflich *adj.* disgraceful, scandalous

Schindel *f.* shingle

schinden *v.* to flay, to skin; to exploit, to sweat; **sich —** to drudge, to slave

Schinken *m.* ham; (sl.) old book, bad painting

Schippe *f.* spade, shovel, scoop

schippen *v.* to shovel

Schirm *m.* umbrella; screen; peak (of cap); shelter, protection; —**dach** *neu.* penthouse; lean-to; —**er** *m.*, —**herr** *m.* patron, protector; —**herrschaft** *f.* protectorate; —**mütze** *f.* peaked cap; —**ständer** *m.* umbrella stand

schirmen *v.* to protect, to shield, to screen

schirren *v.* to harness

Schisma *neu.* schism; —**tiker** *m.* schismatic

schlabbern *v.* to slobber, to slaver; to babble

Schlacht *f.* battle, fight; —**bank** *f.* shambles; —**enbummler** *m.* camp follower; —**feld** *neu.* battlefield; —**getümmel** *neu.*, —**gewühl** *neu.* affray; melee; —**haus** *neu.*, —**hof** *m.* slaughterhouse, abattoir; —**messer** *neu.* butcher's knife; —**opfer** *neu.* victim; sacrifice; —**ordnung** *f.* order of battle; —**ruf** *m.* battle cry; —**schiff** *neu.* battleship; —**vieh** *neu.* fattened stock

schlachten *v.* to slaughter, to massacre

Schlächter *m.* butcher; —**ei** *f.* butcher shop; butchery, massacre, slaughter

Schlacke *f.* slag; cinder, dross, scum

schlacken *v.* to form slag

Schlaf *m.* sleep; **fester —** sound (*oder* deep) sleep; **im — liegen** to be asleep; —**anzug** *m.* pajamas; —**bursche** *m.* night lodger; —**enszeit** *f.* bedtime; —**gefährte** *m.*, —**genosse** *m.* bedfellow; —**gewand** *neu.* nightgown; —**lied** *neu.* lullaby; —**losigkeit** *f.* sleeplessness, insomnia; —**mittel** *neu.* soporific, sleeping pill; —**mütze** *f.* nightcap; sleepyhead; —**rock** *m.* dressing gown; —**saal** *m.* dormitory; —**sack** *m.* sleeping bag; —**stelle** *f.* night's lodging; —**stube** *f.*, —**zimmer** *neu.* bedroom; —**wagen** *m.* Pullman, sleeping car; —**wandler** *m.* sleepwalker, somnambulist

schlaf: —**en** to sleep; —**en gehen** to go to bed; —**mützig** *adj.* sluggish, sleepy; —**trunken** *adj.* drowsy; —**wandeln** to sleepwalk

Schläf: —**chen** *neu.* doze, nap, forty winks; —**er** *m.* sleeper

schläfern *v.* to feel sleepy

Schläfe *f.* (anat.) temple

schläf(e)rig *adj.* sleepy, drowsy, somnolent

schlaff *adj.* slack; flabby; loose; limp; lax

Schlag *m.* blow, stroke; slap; punch; coach door; (bird's) song; (clock) striking; (heart) beat; apoplexy; (pigeon) loft; (thunder) clap; (wood) cut; (fig.) race, kind; **ein Mann von meinem –e** a man after my own heart; **elektrischer —** electric shock; **—** drei Uhr three o'clock sharp; **–ader** *f.* artery; **–anfall** *m.*, **fluss** *m.* apopleptic stroke; **–ball** *m.* bat and ball; **–baum** *m.* turnpike; **–bolzen** *m.* firing pin; **–er** *m.* song hit; **–fertigkeit** *f.* quickness at repartee; **–holz** *neu.*, **–instrument** *neu.* percussion instrument; **–kraft** *f.* striking power; **–obers** *neu.*, **–rahm** *m.*, **–sahne** *f.* whipped cream; **–wort** *neu.* catchword; slogan; **–zeile** *f.* headline; **–zeug** *neu.* percussion instruments

schlag: –artig *adv.* all of a sudden; **–en** *v.* to strike, to beat, to hit; to knock, to kick; (birds) to sing; to coin (money); to cut (wood); **Alarm –en** to sound alarm; **ans Kreuz –en** to crucify; **ans schwarze Brett –en** to announce on the blackboard; **aus der Art –en** to vary from type; **das schlägt nicht in mein Fach** that's not in my line; **die Beine übereinander –en** to cross one's legs; **die Zinsen zum Kapital –en** to add the interest to the capital; **eine Brücke –en** to build a bridge; **ein Figur –en** (chess) to take a piece; **eine geschlagene Stunde** a whole hour; **einen Knoten –en** to tie a knot; **einen Kreis –en** to describe a circle; **ein Kreuz –en** to make the sign of the cross; **in Falten –en** to fold; **in Papier –en** to wrap up in paper; **klein –en** to break into pieces; **mit den Flügeln –en** to flap one's wings; **sich –en** to fight a duel; **sich –en zu** to side with; **Takt –en** (mus.) to beat time; **Wunden –en** to inflict wounds; **Wurzeln –en** to take root

Schläger *m.* beater, kicker, rapier, sword; bat, racket, golf club; (bird) warbler; **–ei** *f.* brawl, scuffle, free-for-all fight

Schlamm *m.* mud, ooze, slime; **–bad** *neu.* mud bath; **–beisser** *m.* mudfish

Schlämmkreide *f.* whiting, whitener

Schlampe *f.* slut, slattern, sloven; **–erei** *f.* disorder, untidiness; slovenliness; mess

Schlange *f.* snake, serpent; **— stehen** to stand in line; **–nbeschwörer** *m.* snake charmer; **–nbiss** *m.* snakebite; **–nbrut** *f.* (fig.) generation of vipers; **–nlinie** *f.* wavy line; **–nmensch** *m.* contortionist

schlängeln *v.* **sich —** to wind, to meander

schlank *adj.* slender, slim; lean, lanky; **–weg** *adv.* right away; downright, flatly

schlapp *adj.* flabby, limp, slack; tired; **— machen** (coll.) to collapse, to faint

Schlapp: –e *f.* defeat, failure, reverse; **–hut** *m.* slouch hat; **–schwanz** *m.* coward, weakling

Schlaraffe *m.* lazybones, sluggard; **–nland** *neu.* land of milk and honey; **–nleben** *neu.* life of idleness and luxury

schlau *adj.* sly; artful, crafty, cunning

Schlauch *m.* hose; tube; (leather) bag; (bot.) utricle; **–boot** *neu.* rubber dinghy

Schlauf *m.*, **Schlaufe** *f.* loop, sling, ring

schlecht *adj.* bad, wicked; inferior, poor, ill; wretched; **–e Luft** foul air; **–e Zeiten** hard times; **mir ist —** I feel ill; **— machen** to run down; **— und recht** plain and honest, somehow; **— werden** to go bad, to turn sour; **—** *adv.* badly, ill; **–erdings** *adv.* absolutely; by all means; **–gelaunt** *adj.* in bad humor; **–hin** *adv.*, **–weg** *adv.* plainly, simply, absolutely, quite

schlecken *v.* to lick; to eat dainties

Schleckermaul *neu.* sweet tooth; epicure

Schlegel *m.* drumstick; (baseball) bat; (bell) clapper; (mech.) mallet; (veal) leg

Schlehdorn *m.* blackthorn

Schleich: –er *m.* sneak; **–ware** *f.* smuggled goods, contraband; **–handel** *m.* smuggling; black market; **–händler** *m.* smuggler; black marketer; **–weg** *m.* secret path (*oder* means)

schleichen *v.* to slink, to sneak, to creep; **–d** *adj.* creeping; furtive, stealthy; **–des Gift** slow poison

Schleier *m.* veil, haze; (smoke) screen; **–eule** *f.* barn owl; **–flor** *m.* crape

schleierhaft *adj.* hazy, mysterious

Schleif: –bahn *f.* slide; **–e** *f.* bow, tie; loop, curve, bend; sledge; slide; **–er** *m.* grinder; cutter; glide (waltz); **–lack** *m.* grinding paste; enamel; **–lackmöbel** *neu. pl.* enameled furniture; **–stein** *m.* grindstone

schleifen *v.* to grind, to whet; to polish; to cut; to drag, to slide; to slur; to demolish

Schleim *m.* slime; mucus, phlegm; **–absonderung** *f.*, **–fluss** *m.* expectoration, mucous secretion; **–haut** *f.* mucous membrane; **–suppe** *f.* gruel

schlemmen *v.* to feast, to gormandize

Schlemmer *m.* glutton; gourmand, gourmet; **–ei** *f.* gluttony, revelry; gormandizing

schlendern *v.* to saunter, to stroll, to loiter

Schlendrian *m.* beaten track; old humdrum way

schlenkern *v.* to dangle, to swing, to fling

Schlepp: –dampfer *m.* tugboat; **–e** *f.* train (of dress); trail; **–enträger** *m.* train-bearer; **–er** *m.* dragger; tug; **–kleid** *neu.*

dress with a train; –lohn *m.* towage; –netz *neu.* dragnet; –tau *neu.* towrope; ins –tau nehmen to take in tow

schleppen *v.* to drag, to trail, to tug

Schlesien *neu.* Silesia

Schleswig-Holstein *neu.* Schleswig-Holstein

Schleuder *f.* sling, catapult; centrifuge; –er *m.* slinger; price cutter; –honig *m.* strained honey; –preis *m.* cut price; zum — preis dirt cheap; –sitz *m.* (avi.) ejection seat

schleudern *v.* to hurl, to sling, to fling; to swing; to undersell

schleunig *adj.* prompt, speedy, quick; –st *adv.* in all haste, immediately

Schleuse *f.* lock, sluice; –ngeld *neu.* lock charges; –nmeister *m.*, –nwärter *m.* lock keeper; –ntor *neu.* lock gate

Schlich *m.* dodge, trick; jemand auf die –e kommen to see through someone's tricks

schlicht *adj.* plain, simple; unpretentious; sleek; –en *v.* to smooth, to plane; to settle

Schlichter *m.* mediator; arbitrator; peacemaker; (mech.) dresser, sizer

Schlichtungsausschuss *m.* arbitration committee

schliessen *v.* to close, to shut; to lock; to conclude; to finish; to break up; to infer (from); to judge (by); to contract; an die Brust (*or* in die Arme) — to embrace; ein Bündnis — to form an alliance; einen Vergleich — to come to an agreement; Frieden — to make peace; geschlossen dafür sein (*or* dafür stimmen) to vote unanimously for; in's Herz — to take a great liking to; in sich — to include, to comprise

schliesslich *adj.* final, conclusive, last; — *adv.* finally, after all, at last

Schliff *m.* polish; (glass, diamonds) cut

schlimm *adj.* bad, evil; ill, sick; serious; –stenfalls *adv.* if worst comes to worst

Schling: –e *f.* sling, loop, snare, noose; sich aus der –e ziehen to get out of a difficulty; –pflanze *f.* climbing plant, creeper

Schlingel *m.* rascal, naughty boy, imp

schlingen *v.* to wind; to tie (a knot); to sling, to twist; to devour; to gulp

Schlips *m.* (neck)tie; cravat; –nadel *f.* tie pin

Schlitt: –en *m.* sled, sleigh; toboggan; sliding platform; (ship's) cradle; mit jemand –en fahren (coll.) to abuse somebody; unter den –en kommen to come off badly; –erbahn *f.* slide, shoot; –schuh *m.* skate; –schuh laufen to skate; –schuhläufer *m.* skater

Schlitz *m.* slit, slash, slot

schlitzen *v.* to slit, to slash

Schloss *neu.* (pad)lock; clasp, snap; castle, palace; ins — fallen (door) to snap to; unter — und Riegel under lock and key; –er *m.* locksmith; (mech.) fitter; –erei *f.* locksmith's workshop; –hof *m.* castle yard

Schlosse *f.* hailstone

schlott(e)rig *adj.* flabby, loose, shaky; tottery, wobbly; rickety; trembling

schlottern *v.* to hang loosely, to fit badly; to shake, to tremble, to wobble, to totter

Schlucht *f.* gorge, gully, ravine, glen

schluchzen *v.* to sob

Schluck *m.* gulp, draught, sip; –auf *m.*, –en *m.* hiccups; –er *m.* hiccups; armer –er poor wretch

schlucken *v.* to gulp, to swallow

Schlummer *m.* slumber; –lied *neu.* lullaby; –rolle *f.* round pillow, bolster

schlummern *v.* to slumber

Schlund *m.* gullet, throat; abyss

Schlupf: –loch *neu.* hiding place; loophole; –winkel *m.* hiding place, hidden corner; refuge

schlüpfen *v.* to slip, to glide, to slide

schlüpfrig *adj.* slippery; indecent, obscene

schlürfen *v.* to sip, to lap; to shuffle

Schluss *m.* closing; end, termination; closure; conclusion; –akt *m.* last act; –antrag *m.* motion for closure; –ergebnis *m.* final result; –folgerung *f.* conclusion; inference; –formel *f.* closing phrase; –licht *neu.* taillight; –rechnung *f.* final account; –rede *f.* final speech, epilogue; –runde *f.* (sports) final; –satz *m.* closing sentence; finale; –stein *m.* keystone; –verkauf *m.* clearance sale; –wort *neu.* last word, summary

Schlüssel *m.* key; spanner; cipher, code; solution; (mus.) clef; –bart *m.* key bit; –bein *neu.* collarbone; –blume *f.* (bot.) cowslip; –bund *neu.* bunch of keys; –loch *neu.* keyhole; –wort *neu.* keyword; codeword

Schmach *f.* disgrace, humiliation; shame

schmachten *v.* to languish, to pine; — nach to long for; –d *adj.* languishing, languid

schmachvoll *adj.* disgraceful, humiliating

schmackhaft *adj.* appetizing, palatable, tasty, savory

Schmäh: –er *m.* defamer, slanderer; –rede *f.* abuse, diatribe, philippic; –schrift *f.* libelous writing; –sucht *f.* abusiveness

schmäh: –en to abuse, to revile, to defame, to slander; –end *adj.* abusive, slanderous; –lich *adj.* disgraceful, humiliating

schmal *adj.* narrow, slender; slim; scanty, poor; **–brüstig** *adj* narrow-chested; **–spurig** *adj.* (rail.) narrow-gauged

Schmal: –film *m.* 8-millimeter film; **–hans** *m.* lanky fellow; **da ist –hans Küchenmeister** they are on short rations; **–spur** *f.* narrow gauge

schmälen *v.* to abuse, to scold, to chide

schmälern *v.* to diminish; to curtail; to impair, to belittle, to disparage

Schmalz *neu.* lard; drippings

schmalzen *v.* to lard, to add fat to, to grease

schmalzig *adj.* fatty, greasy; sentimental

schmarotz: –en *v.* to be a parasite, to sponge; **–erhaft** *adj.*, **–erisch** *adj.* parasitic(al)

Schmarotzer *m.* parasite; sponger; **–tum** *neu.* parasitism

Schmarre *f.* scar, gash, slash

schmatzen *v.* to smack, to buss

schmauchen *v.* (dial.) to smoke, to puff (at a pipe)

Schmaus *m.* feast, banquet; **–erei** *f.* feasting, banquet; carousal

schmausen *v.* to feast, to carous, to banquet

schmecken *v.* to taste; **— nach** to taste of

schmeich: –elhaft *adj.*, **–lerisch** *adj.* fawning, wheedling; flattering; **–eln** *v.* to flatter; to wheedle, to coax; to fawn; to fondle

Schmeich: –elei *f.* flattery, coaxing; **–elkatze** *f.* caressing girl; **–ler** *m.* toady, wheedler

schmeissen *v.* to fling, to throw, to hurl

Schmelz *m.* enamel; glaze; bloom; sweetness; **–arbeit** *f.* enamel(ing); **–e** *f.* melt(ing); **–er** *m.* smelter; **–erei** *f*, **–hütte** *f.* foundry, smeltery; **–ofen** *m.* smelting furnace; **–punkt** *m.* melting point; **–tiegel** *m.* crucible; **–wasser** *neu.* melting (*oder* melted) snow

schmelz: –bar *adj.* fusible, meltable; **–en** *v.* to melt, to fuse; to diminish; **–end** *adj.* melting; languishing; mellow

Schmerz *m.* ache, pain; grief, suffering; **–ensgeld** *neu.* damage compensation; **–enskind** *neu.* child of sorrow; **–enslager** *neu.* bed of suffering

schmerz: –beladen *adj.*, **–erfüllt** *adj.* greatly afflicted; **–en** *v.* to pain, to hurt, to ache; to grieve; to distress; **–haft** *adj.*, **–lich** *adj.*, **–voll** *adj.* painful, grievous; **–lindernd** *adj.*, **–stillend** *adj.* soothing; (med.) analgesic

Schmetter: –ling *m.* butterfly

schmettern *v.* to smash, to dash; to shatter; to throw (down); to blare; to bray; to peal, to yell; to warble; **einen —** (coll.) to drink

Schmied *m.* smith; **–e** *f.* smithy, forge; **–eeisen** *neu.* wrought iron; **–ehammer** *m.* sledge hammer

schmied: –bar *adj.* malleable; **–eeisern** *adj.* of wrought iron; **–en** *v.* to forge; to plan, to fabricate; to hatch, to plot, to concoct

schmiegen *v.* to bend; **sich —** to nestle (against); to twine around, to cling (to)

schmiegsam *adj.* flexible, pliant; supple

Schmier: –e *f.* grease; troop of strolling actors; (sl.) gaff; **–er** *m.* greaser; scribbler; dauber; **–fink** *m.* dirty fellow; **–geld** *neu.* (coll.) bribe; palm oil; **–käse** *m.* soft cheese; **–mittel** *neu.* lubricant; **–öl** *neu.* lubricating oil; **–plan** *m.* lubrication chart; **–seife** *f.* soft soap

schmieren *v.* to smear, to grease, to lubricate; (butter) to spread; to scrawl, to scribble; (art) to daub; to bribe; **jemand Honig um den Mund — to** flatter someone

schmierig *adj.* greasy; dirty, filthy; sordid

Schminkdose *f.* rouge pot; make-up set

Schminke *f.* rouge, paint; make-up

schminken *v.* to paint the face, to rouge

Schmirgel *m.* emery; **–papier** *neu.* emery (*oder* sand) paper; **–scheibe** *f.* emery wheel

schmirgeln *v.* to polish with emery

Schmöker *m.* old (*oder* trashy, trivial) book

schmökern *v.* to pore over (a book)

schmollen *v.* to pout, to be sulky

Schmorbraten *v.* stewed meat

schmoren *v.* to stew, to swelter

Schmu *m.* (sl.) unfair gain; **— machen** to swindle

Schmuck *m.* decoration, ornament; finery; jewelry; **–kasten** *m.* jewel box; **–sachen** *f. pl.* jewels; **–stück** *neu.* piece of jewelry

schmuck *adj.* neat, trim, smart, spruce

schmücken *v.* to adorn, to decorate; to trim

Schmugg: –el *m.*, **–elei** *f.* smuggling; **–ler** *m.* smuggler; **–waren** *f. pl.* smuggled goods

schmuggeln *v.* to smuggle

schmunzeln *v.* to smirk, to grin

schmusen *v.* to prattle; (coll.) **to flirt**

Schmutz *m.* dirt, filth, mud; **–blech** *neu.* mudguard; **–fink** *m.* dirty fellow; **–fleck** *m.* stain, spot; **–titel** *m.* (typ.) half title

schmutzen *v.* to soil, to get dirty

schmutzig *adj.* dirty, filthy, soiled; shabby

Schnabel *m.* beak, bill, prow; spout; (coll.) mouth; **-schuhe** *m. pl.* pointed shoes
Schnack *m.* chit-chat; twaddle; chatter, gossip
schnacken *v.* (dial.) to talk; to chatter
Schnadahüpfel *neu.* Alpine folk song
Schnalle *f.* buckle, clasp
schnallen *v.* to buckle, to fasten, to strap up
schnalzen *v.* to snap (fingers); to click (tongue)
schnappen *v.* to snap, to snatch; to clutch; **nach Luft —** to gasp for breath
Schnäpper *m.* catch, snap; (med.) lancet; (orn.) flycatcher
Schnaps *m.* schnapps, strong liquor
schnarchen *v.* to snore
Schnarre *f.* rattle
schnattern *v.* to cackle, to quack; to jabber
schnauben *v.* to snort; to puff, to blow; **nach Rache —** to breathe vengeance; **sich die Nase —** to blow one's nose; **vor Wut —** to fret and fume, to foam with rage
schnaufen *v.* to breathe heavily, to pant
Schnauzbart *m.* mustache
Schnauze *f.* snout, muzzle, spout, nozzle; **die — voll haben** (sl.) to be fed up (with)
Schnecke *f.* snail, slug; gastropod; **-nbohrer** *m.* screw auger; **-ngang** *m.* winding alley; **im -ngang** at a snail's pace; **-nhaus** *neu.* snail shell; **-npost** *f.* slow coach; **-ntempo** *neu.* snail's pace
Schnee *m.* snow; beaten egg whites; **-ball** *m.* snowball; **-brille** *f.* snow goggles; **-fall** *m.* snowfall; **-flocke** *f.* snowflake; **-gestöber** *neu.*, **-treiben** *neu.*, **-wehe** *f.* snowdrift; **-glöckchen** *neu.* snowdrop; **-grenze** *f.* snow line; **-huhn** *neu.* white grouse; **-kette** *f.* skid chain; **-könig** *m.* **sich wie ein -könig freuen** to be merry as a lark; **-pflug** *m.* snowplow; **-schläger** *m.* quick sweep; **-schuh** *m.* ski; **-sturm** *m.* snow storm; blizzard; **-wasser** *neu.* slush; **-wittchen** *neu.* Snow White
schneeig *adj.* snowy, snow-white
Schneid *m.* dash, energy
Schneide *f.* edge, blade, bit; **-bank** *f.* chopping bench; **-bohnen** *f. pl.* French beans; **-mühle** *f.*, **-werk** *neu.* sawmill; **-zahn** *m.* incisor
schneiden *v.* to cut, to carve; to mow; to trim; to intersect; **Gesichter —** to make faces; **in Streifen —** to shred; **-d** *adj.* cutting, sharp; biting, piercing; glaring; sarcastic

Schneider *m.* tailor; cutter; **-erei** *f.* tailor's business; **-in** *f.* dressmaker; **-puppe** *f.* dummy
schneidern *v.* to do tailoring (*oder* dressmaking); (coll.) to make
schneidig *adj.* sharp, cutting; dashing, smart
schneien *v.* to snow
Schneise *f.* forest aisle; (avi.) flying lane
schnell *adj.* fast, quick, rapid, speedy, swift; prompt; **-en** *v.* to jerk, to toss
Schnell- -hefter *m.* letterfile; **-igkeit** *f.* rapidity; speed; velocity; quickness; **-kraft** *f.* elasticity; **-presse** *f.* steam press: **-schritt** *m.* quickstep; **-waage** *f.* steelyard; **-zug** *m.* express train
Schnepfe *f.* snipe, woodcock
schneuzen *v.* (coll.) to trim (a wick); **sich — to blow one's nose**
Schnickschnack *m.* tittle-tattle, prank, chat
schniegeln *v.* to dress up
schnipp- -ern *v.*, **-(s)eln** *v.* to cut up; **-ig** *adj.* snappish, pert; **-(s)en** *v.* to snap, to punch
Schnippchen *neu.* snap (of fingers); **ein — schlagen** to play a trick (on)
Schnitt *m.* cut(ting), section; incision; shape, pattern; harvest, reaping; (book) edge; **einen guten — machen** (coll.) to make a good profit; **-blumen** *f. pl.* cut flowers; **-bohnen** *f. pl.* string beans; **-e** *f.* slice, cut; **-er** *m.* mower, reaper; **-lauch** *m.* chive; **-linie** *f.* intersecting line; **-muster** *neu.* dress pattern; **-punkt** *m.* point of intersection; **-waren** *f. pl.* dry goods; **-wunde** *f.* cut gash
Schnitz *m.* cut, snip; (dial.) slice; **-arbeit** *f.*, **-erei** *f.*, **-werk** *neu.* wood carving; **-er** *m.* cutter, carver; blunder, slip
Schnitzel *m.* chip; parings, shavings; **Wiener -el** breaded veal cutlet; **-jagd** *f.* paper chase
schnitze(l)n *v.* to cut, to carve, to chip
schnöd(e) *adj.* vile, base, disdainful
Schnorchel *m.* snorkel
Schnörkel *m.* scroll; flourish
schnörkelhaft *adj.* full of flourishes
schnorren *v.* (coll.) to sponge, to peddle
schnüffeln *v.* to sniff, to snuffle; to spy out, to snoop (around)
Schnupf- -en *m.* cold, catarrh; **den — bekommen** to catch a cold; **-tabak** *m.* snuff; **-tuch** *neu.* (coll.) handkerchief
schnupfen *v.* to (take) snuff
Schnuppe *f.* (candle) snuff; shooting star; **das ist mir —** (coll.) that's all the same to me
schnuppern *v.* to snuffle, to smell out

Schnur f. cord, string, line, lace; **über die — hauen** to kick over the traces

Schnür: **-band** neu. lace; **-boden** m. (theat.) loft, gridiron; **-chen** neu. thin string; **am -chen haben** to have at one's fingertips; **wie am -chen** like clockwork; **-leib** m., **-leibchen** neu. corset; **-loch** neu. eyelet; **-riemen** m. lace, strap; **-senkel** m. shoelace

schnüren v. to lace; to tie up; to cord, to rope; **sein Bündel — to depart; sich — to wear a corset**

schnurgerade adj. as straight as an arrow

schnurr! interj. buzz! whir! purr! **-en** v. to buzz; to whir; to purr; **-ig** adj. droll; funny, odd, queer

schnurstracks adv. directly, **straight** away; immediately, at once

Schnurrbart m. mustache

Schober m. barn, shed, rick, stack

Schock neu. threescore; heap, shock; **—** m. shock; **-schwerenot!** confound it!

Schöffe m. juror, juryman; **-ngericht** neu. trial by jury

Schokolade f. chocolate; **-ntafel** f. chocolate bar

Scholastik f. scholasticism; **-er** m. scholastic

Scholle f. clod, lump; (fig.) land, soil; floe

schon adv. already, so far, as yet; even, indeed; **das ist — wahr** that's true enough; **das kennen wir —** it's an old story; **es wird sich — machen lassen** it will come out all right; **— am nächsten Tage** the very next day; **— gut!** that's all right! **wenn — although; wenn — denn —** in any event

schön adj. beautiful; lovely; fine; handsome, great, considerable; **das -e Geschlecht** the fair sex; **das ist alles — und gut** that's all very fine; **das wäre noch -er!** certainly not! **das werde ich — bleiben lassen** I'll take good care to avoid it; **die -en Künste** the fine arts; **die -e Literatur** belles-lettres; **eine -e Summe** a good round sum; **sich — machen** to spruce up; **-en Dank** many thanks; **— machen** (dog) to beg; **— tun** to flirt; **-geistig** adj. aesthetic

Schon: -ung f. careful treatment; forebearance; mercy; nursery for trees; **-zeit** f. closed season

Schön: -färberei f. heightening, coloring; optimism; **-geist** m. aesthete, bel esprit; **-heit** f. beauty; **-heitsmittel** neu. cosmetic; **-heitspflege** f. beauty culture; **-heitssalon** m. beauty shop; **-heitswasser** neu. beauty lotion; **-redner** m. spouter; fine talker; **-schreibekunst** f., **-schrift** f. caligraphy; **-tuerei** f. coquet-

ting, flirting

Schoner m. schooner; antimacassar

Schopf m. top (of head); forelock, tuft; crest, crown

Schöpf: -brunnen m. draw well; **-eimer** m. bucket; **-er** m. creator; **-kelle** f., **-löffel** m. bailer, skimmer; **-rad** neu. bucket wheel; **-ung** f. creation; **-werk** neu. hydraulic engine

schöpfen v. to scoop, to ladle, to draw; to conceive; **Hoffnung — to gather fresh hope; wieder Atem — to recover one's breath**

schöpferisch adj. creative, productive

Schoppen m. half a pint; mug

Schöps m. wether; simpleton; **-enfleisch** neu. mutton; **-enbraten** m. roast mutton

Schorf m. scurf, scab

Schornstein m. chimney, smokestack; funnel; **-feger** m. chimney sweep

Schoss m. shoot, sprig, sprout; scion; lap; womb; coattail; flap; **die Hände in den — legen** to idle; **es ist ihm in den — gefallen** it just fell into his lap; **im -e seiner Familie** in the bosom of his family; **-hund** m. lap dog; **-kind** neu. darling, pet

Schössling m. offshoot, sprig

Schote f. husk, pod; **-n** pl. green peas; **-nfrüchte** f. pl. legumes

schräg(e) adj. oblique, slanting; diagonal; transversal; **-über** adv. across, aslant

Schräge f. obliquity, slope, slant, bevel

Schramme f. scratch, scar; crack

Schrank m. cupboard, wardrobe; **-koffer** m. trunk

Schranke f. barrier turnpike; (law) bar; (rail.) gate; limit, bound(s); **in die -n; fordern** to challenge; **in -n halten** to restrain; **-n setzen** to put a stop to; **-nwärter** m. (rail.) gatekeeper, signalman

schränken v. to cross (arms), to set (a saw)

schrankenlos adj. boundless; unbridled

Schranze m. and f. cringing courtier, flunkey

Schrapnell neu. shrapnel

schrappen v. to scrape

Schrat m. faun, satyr

Schraube f. screw; propeller; **bei ihm ist eine — locker** he has a screw loose; **-nschlüssel** m. wrench, spanner; **-zieher** m. screwdriver

schrauben v. to screw, to turn, to twist, to spiral; **seine Forderungen höher — to increase one's demands; seine Hoffnungen niedriger — to come down a peg**

Schraubstock *m.* vise

Schreck, Schrecken *m.* fright, horror; **in —en setzen** to terrify; **–bild** *neu.* horrible sight, bugbear; **–ensbotschaft** *f.* alarming news; **–ensherrschaft** *f.* reign of terror; **–nis** *neu.* horror; **–schuss** *m.* warning shot; false alarm; idle threat

schreck: –en *v.* to frighten, to alarm, to terrify; to startle; **–haft** *adj.* fearful, timid; **–lich** *adj.* dreadful, frightful, horrible; awful; tremendous

Schrei *m.* cry, shout, scream, shriek; **letzter —** latest fashion; **–er** *m.* crier; **–hals** *m.* crybaby; **–vögel** *m. pl.* (orn.) screechers

Schreib: –art *f.* style; spelling; **–bedarf** *m.* writing material, stationery; **–block** *m.* writing pad; **–en** *neu.* writing; letter; communication, note; **–er** *m.* writer, clerk, secretary; **–erei** *f.* writing, scribbling; **–feder** *f.* pen, nib; **–fehler** *m.* slip of the pen, error in writing; **–heft** *neu.* exercise book; **–mappe** *f.* writing case; portfolio; **–maschine** *f.* typewriter; **–papier** *neu.* writing paper; **–stube** *f.* office; (mil.) orderly room; **–tisch** *m.* desk; **–unterlage** *f.* blotting pad; **–waren** *f. pl.* stationery; **–warenhändler** *m.* stationer; **–zeug** *neu.* pen and ink set

schreib: –en *v.* to write, to spell; **mit der Maschine –en** to type; **–faul** *adj.* lazy about writing; **–fertig** *adj.* ready to write

schreien *v.* to shout, to scream, to howl; **–d** *adj.* shrill, glaring, loud; flagrant

Schrein *m.* shrine; **–er** *m.* carpenter, joiner, cabinetmaker; **–erei** *f.* carpenter's workshop

schreiten *v.* to stride, to stalk; **zum Äussersten —** to take extreme measures; **zur Entscheidung —** to proceed towards a decision

Schrift *f.* (hand)writing; work; publication; (law) writ; (rel.) Scriptures; (typ.) font, typeface; **–art** *f.* type; **–auslegung** *f.* exposition of the Scriptures, exegetics; **–bild** *neu.* (typ.) setting, face; **–deutsch** *neu.* literary German; **–führer** *m.* secretary; **–gelehrte** *m.* scribe; **–leiter** *m.* editor; **–leitung** *f.* editors, editorship; **–probe** *f.* specimen of writing (*oder* type); **–satz** *m.* composition; **–setzer** *m.* typesetter; **–steller** *m.* author, writer; **–stück** *neu.* document; **–tum** *neu.* literature; **–wechsel** *m.* correspondence; **–zeichen** *neu.* letter, type, character; **–zug** *m.* character, flourish

schrift: –lich *adj.* by letter, written; **–stellerisch** *adj.* literary; **–stellern** *v.* to do literary work

schrill *adj.* shrill; **–en** *v.* to sound shrilly

Schritt *m.* step, pace, stride, gait; **auf — und Tritt** everywhere; **den ersten — machen** to move first; **— für —** step by step; **— halten** to keep pace; **–macher** *m.* pacemaker

schrittweise *adv.* by steps, step by step

schroff *adj.* steep; harsh; abrupt, blunt

Schröpf: –eisen *neu.* cupping instrument; **–er** *m.* cupper, fleecer; **–kopf** *m.* cupping glass

Schrot *m. and neu.* small shot; crushed grain; (coin) weight; **–brot** *neu.* wholemeal bread; **–flinte** *f.* shotgun; **–mehl** *neu.* coarse flour; **–mühle** *f.* rough-grinding mill; **–säge** *f.* pitsaw

schroten *v.* to rough-grind, to crush; (casks) to lower

schrubben *v.* to scrub

Schrubber *m.* scrubber

Schrulle *f.* whim, fad, crochet, caprice

schrumpfen, schrumpeln *v.* to shrink, to shrivel; to contract; to wrinkle

Schub *m.* shoving; push, thrust; batch, heap; **–fach** *neu.*, **–kasten** *m.*, **–lade** *f.* drawer; **–karren** *m.* wheelbarrow

schüchtern *adj.* bashful, timid, shy

Schuft *m.* scoundrel, rascal; **–erei** *f.* drudgery

schuften *v.* (coll.) to drudge, to plod

schuftig *adj.* rascally, base, mean, shabby

Schuh *m.* shoe; boot; (measure) foot; **jemand etwas in die –e schieben** to pass the buck; **–anzieher** *m.* shoehorn; **–band** *neu.* (boot) lace; **–flicker** *m.* cobbler; **–knöpfer** *m.* button hook; **–krem** *m.*, **–wichse** *f.* shoe polish; **–macher** *m.* shoemaker; **–putzer** *m.* shoeblack; **–waren** *f. pl.*, **–werk** *neu.*, **–zeug** *neu.* footwear

Schul: –amt *neu.* school administration; **–arbeit** *f.* homework; **–ausgabe** *f.* school edition; **–bank** *f.* form, bench; **–behörde** *f.* Board of Education; **–bildung** *f.* educational background; **–diener** *m.* porter, janitor; **–e** *f.* school; **hinter die –e gehen, die –e schwänzen** to play truant; **höhere –e** secondary school; **–e machen** to establish a precedent; **–ferien** *pl.* school vacations; **–freund** *m.*, **–kamerad** *m.* schoolfellow, chum; **–fuchs** *m.* pedant; **–geld** *neu.* tuition; **–heft** *neu.* exercise book; **–jugend** *f.* schoolchildren; **–klasse** *f.*, **–zimmer** *neu.* classroom; **–kollegium** *neu.* teaching staff; **–lehrer** *m.* schoolteacher; **–mappe** *f.* schoolbag; **–meister** *m.* schoolmaster; pedant; **–ordnung** *f.* school regulations; **–pferd** *neu.* trick horse; **–rat** *m.* school board; school inspector; **–reiter** *m.* trick rider; **–schiff** *neu.* training ship; **–stunde** *f.* lesson; **–tafel** *f.* blackboard; **–ung** *f.* instruction, training; **–wesen** *neu.* educational system, school affairs; **–zeugnis** *neu.* school report(card)

schul: –en *v.* to school, to instruct; to train; **–meistern** *v.* to teach, to censure; **–pflichtig** *adj.* obliged to attend school

Schuld *f.* guilt, fault; debt, obligation; blame, sin; **es ist seine —** it's his fault; **jemand die — geben** to lay the blame at someone's door; **–beweis** *m.* proof of guilt; **–brief** *m.* promissory note; **–buch** *neu.* ledger; account book; **–entilgung** *f.* discharge of debts; **–forderung** *f.* claim, demand, debt; **–haft** *f.* imprisonment for debts; **–ige** *m.* guilty person; trespasser; culprit; **–igkeit** *f.* obligation; duty; **–ner** *m.* debtor; **–schein** *m.*, **–verschreibung** *f.* promissory note

schuld: –bewusst *adj.* conscious of guilt; **–en** *v.* to owe; **–enfrei** *adj.* free from debt, unencumbered; **–ig** *adj.* guilty, culpable; owing, due; **–los** *adj.* guiltless, innocent

Schüler *m.* pupil, student; disciple, follower; **–in** *f.* schoolgirl; **–schaft** *f.* discipleship

schülerhaft *adj.* schoolboylike, immature

Schulter *f.* shoulder; **–bein** *neu.* humerus; **–blatt** *neu.* shoulder blade; **–klappe** *f.*, **–stück** *neu.* shoulder strap

schultern *v.* to shoulder

Schultheiss, Schulze *m.* (lit.) village mayor

Schund *m.* rubbish, trash, junk; **–roman** *m.* cheap novel; literary trash

Schuppe *f.* scale, scurf, dandruff

schuppen *v.* to scale, to scrape, to peel off; **sich —** to form scales

Schuppen *m.* shed, garage, hangar

schüren *v.* to poke, to rake, to add fuel (to); to stir (up), to incite

schürfen *v.* (min.) to dig; to prospect; to graze, to scratch; **–d** *adj.* (fig.) thorough

Schurke *m.* scoundrel, rascal; **–nstreich** *m.*, **–erei** *f.* rascality, villainous trick

schurkisch *adj.* knavish, rascally, villainous

Schurz *m.* apron, loincloth, kilt; **–fell** *neu.* leather apron

Schürze *f.* apron; **–nband** *neu.* apron string; **–nherrschaft** *f.* petticoat government; **–njäger** *m.* woman chaser

schürzen *v.* to tie (*oder* tuck) up; **den Knoten eines Dramas —** to weave a plot

Schuss *m.* shot; rush; (bullet) wound; (bot.) shooting; **einen — abgeben to**

fire a round; **einen — Kognak** a dash of brandy; **in — kommen** to get into working order; **jemand in den — kommen** to come across someone; **weit vom — out** of danger; **–feld** *neu.* firing zone; **–waffe** *f.* firearm; **–weite** *f.* firing range; **ausser –weite** out of reach; **–wunde** *f.* gunshot wound

schuss: –bereit *adj.* ready to fire; **–fest** *adj.*, **–sicher** *adj.* bulletproof; invulnerable

Schüssel *f.* dish, tureen, basin, bowl

Schuster *m.* shoemaker; **auf –s Rappen** on foot; **–ahle** *f.* awl; **–pech** *neu.* cobbler's wax

schustern *v.* to cobble, to mend shoes

Schutt *m.* garbage, rubble; debris; **–abladeplatz** *m.* garbage dump

Schütte *f.* heap; granary

Schüttelfrost *m.* shaking chills, shivers

schütteln *v.* to shake; **sich —** to shiver, to tremble

schütten *r.* to pour; **es schüttet** the rain pours down

Schutz *m.* protection; shelter, cover, screen; safeguard; custody; **in — nehmen** to defend; to protect; **— suchen** to take shelter; **–befohlene** *m.* charge, ward, protégé; **–blech** *neu.* mudguard; **–brief** *m.* letter of safe conduct; **–brille** *f.* protective goggles; **–bündnis** *neu.* defensive alliance; **–engel** *m.* guardian angel; **–färbung** *f.* protective coloring; **–frist** *f.* term of copyright; **–gebiet** *neu.*, **–herrschaft** *f.* protectorate; **–geleit** *neu.* safe conduct, escort; convoy; **–haft** *f.* protective custody; **–heilige** *m.* patron saint; **–herr** *m.* protector, patron; **–insel** *f.* safety island; **–mann** *m.* policeman; **–männer** *m. pl.*, **–leute** *pl.* policemen; **–marke** *f.* trademark; **–umschlag** *m.* jacket, wrapper; **–wall** *m.* (Sandsäcke) revetment; bulwark

Schütz: –er *m.* protector; guardian; **–ling** *m.* protégé

Schütze *m.* rifleman; (ast.) Sagitarius; **–nfest** *neu.* shooting match; **–ngraben** *m.* (mil.) trench; **–nkönig** *m.* champion shot; **–nloch** *neu.* rifle pit

schützen *v.* to protect, to defend, to guard

Schwabe *m.* Swabian; **–nstreich** *m.* tomfoolery

Schwabe *f.* cockroach

Schwaben *neu.* Swabia

schwach *adj.* weak, feeble; frail; faint; infirm; scanty; **–e Seite** weak point; **–er Verstand** feeble intellect; **–es Gedächtnis** bad memory; **–es Licht** dim light; **–sichtig** *adj.* dim-sighted; **–sinnig** *adj.* feeble-minded; imbecile

Schwach: –heit *f.* weakness; frailty; –kopf *m.* imbecile, simpleton: –sinn *m.* imbecility; –strom *m.* low tension

Schwäch: –e *f.* weakness; debility; faintness; –lichkeit *f.* feebleness, delicacy; –ling *m.* weakling; pushover; –ung *f.* enervation, diminution: defloration

Schwadron *f.* and *neu.* squadron; –eur *m.* braggart, gasbag. swaggerer

Schwager *m.* brother-in-law

Schwägerin *f.* sister-in-law

Schwägerschaft *f.* relations by marriage

Schwalbe *f.* swallow; –schwanz *m.* swallowtail; dovetail

Schwall *m.* swell, flood; torrent (of words)

Schwamm *m.* sponge; fungus; dry rot

Schwan *m.* swan; –engesang *m.*, –enlied *neu.* swan song; (lit.) last song

Schwang *m.* vogue; im –e sein to be in fashion

schwanger *adj.* pregnant

Schwangerschaft *f.* pregnancy

schwank *adj.* flexible, pliable; slender; –en *v.* to waver, to vacillate; to sway, to totter; to fluctuate; –end *adj.* wavering, unsteady; irresolute

Schwank *m.* funny story; prank; (theat.) farce; –ung *f.* oscillation, fluctuation

Schwanz *m.* tail, end; –riemen *m.* crupper

schwänzen *v.* to play truant; to idle about

Schwäre *f.* abscess, ulcer. boil

schwären *v.* to suppurate, to ulcerate

Schwarm *m.* swarm, flock, herd; crowd, throng; (coll.) idol; –geist *m.* fanatic, reveller

schwärmen *v.* to swarm, to rove, to revel; — für to be enthusiastic (about)

Schwärmer *m.* reveller; dreamer; enthusiast; (ent.) hawk moth; (fireworks) cracker; (rel.) fanatic; –erei *f.* reverie; fanaticism

Schwarte *f.* rind, skin; old book: dass die — kracht (sl.) vigorously; –enmagen *m.* headcheese

schwarz *adj.* black; dark; dirty; das –e Brett the bulletin board; –e Kunst black magic; — sehen to take a gloomy view (of)

Schwarz: –amsel *f.*, –drossel *f.* blackbird; –arbeit *f.* scab labor; –brot *neu.* rye bread; –e *m.* Negro: devil; –e *neu.* black (color); blackness, darkness; ins –e treffen to hit the bull's eye; –fahrer *m.* joy rider: –handel *m.* black market; –künstler *m.* magician, necromancer; –schlachten *neu.* illegal slaughtering; –rock *m.* black coat; (coll.) cleric; –seher *m.* pessimist; –wild *neu.* wild boars

Schwärze *f.* blackness; printer's ink; baseness

schwärzen *v.* to blacken, to ink; to defame

Schwarzwald *m.* Plack Forest

schwatzen, schwätzen *v.* to chatter, to gossip

Schwätzer *m.* babbler, prattler, gossip

Schwebe *f.* suspense, balance; in der — sein to be undecided; –bahn *f.* suspension railway

schweben *v.* to be suspended. to hover; to dangle; to soar; to be undecided (*oder* pending); es schwebt mir auf der Zunge I have it on the tip of my tongue; in Gefahr — to be in jeopardy; –de Schulden floating debts

Schweden *neu.* Sweden

Schwefel *m.* sulphur; –bad *neu.* sulphur bath; sulphurous springs; –hölzchen *neu.* match

schwefel: –farbig *adj.*, –gelb *adj.* sulphuryellow; –(halt)ig *adj.* sulphurous; –sauer *adj.* sulphuric

Schweif *m.* tail; train; –stern *m.* comet

schweifen *v.* to rove, to roam; to curve

schweigen *v.* to be (*oder* keep) silent; to hold one's tongue; to keep mum

schweigsam *adj.* taciturn, reticent

Schwein *neu.* hog, pig, swine; — haben to be lucky; –ebraten *m.* roast pork; –efett *neu.* lard; –efleisch *neu.* pork; –ehirt *m.* swineherd; –ehund *m.* filthy dog; –ekoben *m.*, –estall *m.* pigsty; –epökelfleisch *neu.* salt pork; –erei *f.* filthiness; obscenity; –igel *m.* smutty fellow, obscene talker; (dial.) hedgehog; –igelei *f.* obscenity; –sleder *neu.* pigskin; –sschwarte *f.* rind of bacon, crackling

die Schweiz *f.* Switzerland

schweinisch *adj.* swinish, filthy; obscene

Schweiss *m.* sweat, perspiration; (hunting) blood; toil; –arbeit *f.* welding; –blätter *neu.* *pl.* perspiration guards; –er *m.* welder

schweiss: –(be)fördernd *adj.* sudorific; –en *v.* to weld; (hunting) to bleed; –ig *adj.* sweaty; perspiring; (hunting) bloody

schwelen *v.* to smoulder

schwelgen *v.* to feast, to revel, to indulge in

Schwelger *m.* epicure, glutton, reveller; –ei *f.* revelry; gluttony; debauchery

schwelgerisch *adj.* luxurious, debauched

Schwelle *f.* sill; threshold; doorstep; architrave; beam, joist; (rail.) sleeper

schwellen *v.* to swell, to rise; to bloat, to inflate; to increase, to distend

Schwemme *f.* watering place; horse pond

Schwengel *m.* swingle; clapper; (pump)

handle

schwenken v. to swing; to wave; to brandish; to rinse; to turn; to change (one's mind)

schwer adj. heavy; weighty; ponderous; hard, difficult; serious, severe; grave; etwas — nehmen to take something to heart; mit –em Herzen reluctantly; — daniederliegen to be seriously ill; — fallen to be difficult; –e See rough sea; –e Zeiten hard times; –e Zunge slow tongue; –er Atem short breath; –er Fehler great blunder; –er Junge gangster, mobsman; –er Wein full-bodied wine; –es Essen indigestible food; –es Geld round sum; –es Verbrechen atrocious crime; — verwundet mortally wounded; –betrübt adj. deeply grieved; –blütig adj. melancholy; –fällig adj. clumsy, sluggish, slow; –hörig adj. hard of hearing; –lich adv. hardly, scarcely; –mütig adj. melancholy, sad, mournful; –verständlich adj. abstruse; –wiegend adj. grave, serious

Schwer: –e f. heaviness; weight; gravity; –elosigkeit f. weightlessness; –enöter m. gay rascal; playboy; –gewicht neu. heavyweight; chief stress; emphasis; –industrie f. heavy industry; –kraft f. force of gravity; –kriegsbeschädigte m. disabled soldier; –mut m. melancholy, sadness; –punkt m. center of gravity; main point

Schwert neu. sword; –feger m. furbisher; –lilie f. iris

Schwester f. sister; registered nurse; nun; –nschaft f. sisterhood; sorority

Schwibbogen m. archway; flying buttress

Schwieger: –eltern pl. parents-in-law; –mutter f. mother-in-law; –sohn m. son-in-law; –tochter f. daughter-in-law; –vater m. father-in-law

Schwiele f. wale; callus

schwierig adj. difficult; hard; complicated; delicate, particular; fastidious; trying

Schwimm: –anstalt f. swimming establishment; –blase f. air bladder; water wings; –dock neu. floating dock; –er m. swimmer; (mech.) float; –flosse f. fin; –fuss m. webfoot; –gürtel m. life belt; –hose f. bathing trunks; –kraft f. buoyancy; –weste f. life jacket

schwimmen v. to swim, to float; to welter

Schwind: –el m. dizziness; swindle; fraud, cheat; –elei f. swindle; –elfirma f., –elgesellschaft f., –elunternehmen neu. bogus (oder fraudulent) company; –elgefühl neu. giddy sensation; –ler m. swindler, cheat, imposter; –sucht f.

tuberculosis of the lungs

schwind: –en v. to dwindle, to shrink; to vanish; –süchtig adj. consumptive

schwindel: –haft adj. causing dizziness; very high; fraudulent, swindling; –ig adj. dizzy, giddy; –n v. to swindle, to cheat; mir –t I feel dizzy

schwingen v. to swing, to oscillate, to vibrate

Schwips m. tipsiness; einen — haben to be tipsy

schwirren v. to whir, to whiz, to buzz; umher — to flit to and fro

Schwitzbad neu. Turkish bath

schwitzen v. to sweat, to perspire; to toil

schwören v. to swear, to take an oath; Rache — to vow vengeance; — auf to swear by; to have confidence in

schwül adj. sultry, oppressive, close

Schwulst m. bombast, turgidity

schwülstig adj. bombastic, turgid

Schwund m. dwindling; falling off; disappearance, shrinkage; atrophy; (rad.) fading

Schwung m. swing(ing); vault(ing); ardor; verve; flight; edler — noble strain; in — bringen to set going; –feder f. (orn.) pinion; –kraft f. centrifugal force; energy; buoyancy; –rad neu. flywheel; –seil neu. slack rope

schwunghaft adj. lively, flourishing, brisk

Schwur m. oath; –gericht neu. (law) jury

Sechs f. six; –eck neu. hexagon; –pfünder m. six pounder; –tel neu. sixth part

Sechs· adj. six; –eckig adj. hexagonal; –fach adj., –fältig adj. sixfold, sextuple; –jährig adj. six-year-old; –monatlich adj. six monthly; every six months; –te adj. sixth; –teilig adj. in six parts; –tens adv. sixthly

sechzehn adj. sixteen; –te adj. sixteenth

Sechzehn f. sixteen; –tel neu. sixteenth part

sechzig adj. sixty; –jährig adj. sixty year old; –ste adj. sixtieth

Sechzig f. sixty; –er m. sexagenarian; –stel neu. sixtieth part

See m. lake; — f. sea; an der — at the seashore; an der — gelegen maritime; auf hoher — at sea; in — stechen to put to sea; zur — gehen to go to sea; –bad neu. seaside resort; –bär m. fur seal; (coll.) old salt; –beben neu. seaquake; –dienst m. naval service; –fahrer m. seafarer, sailor; navigator; –fahrt f. cruise, navigation; –flugzeug neu. seaplane; –gefecht neu. naval action; –gesetz neu. maritime law; –gras neu. seaweed; –herrschaft f. naval supremacy; –hund m. (zool.) seal; –igel *m.* sea urchin; **–jungfer** *f.* mermaid; dragonfly; **–kadett** *m.* midshipman, naval cadet; **–karte** *f.* sea chart; hydrographic map; **–leute** *pl.* seamen; **–löwe** *m.* sea lion; **–mann** *m.* seaman, sailor; **–meile** *f.* nautical mile; **–möwe** *f.* seamew, gull; **–not** *f.* distress; **–räuber** *m.* pirate; **–rose** *f.* water lily; **–schlacht** *f.* sea battle; **–schlange** *f.* sea serpent; **–schwalbe** *f.* tern; **–stern** *m.* starfish; **–streitkräfte** *f. pl.* naval forces; **–tang** *m.* seaweed; **–teufel** *m.* devilfish; **–volk** *neu.* maritime nation; **–warte** *f.* naval observatory; **–weg** *m.* sea route; **auf dem –wege** by sea; **–zunge** *f.* sole

Seele *f.* soul; mind, heart; (gun) bore; **eine — von Mensch** a love of a man; **jemand aus der — sprechen** to guess someone's thoughts; **von ganzer —** with all one's heart; **–namt** *neu.*, **–nmesse** *f.* service for the dead, requiem; **–ngrösse** *f.* magnanimity; **–nheil** *neu.* spiritual welfare; salvation; **–nhirt** *m.* pastor; **–nleiden** *neu.* mental trouble; **–nnot** *f.*, **–npein** *f.*, **–nqual** *f.* mental distress; **–nwanderung** *f.* transmigration of souls; **–nwärmer** *m.* (coll.) comforter

seelen: –froh *adj.*, **–vergnügt** *adj.* very glad; **–voll** *adj.* soulful; sentimental

Seelsorge *f.* ministerial work; **–r** *m.* pastor; clergyman, minister

Segel *neu.* sail, canvas; **die — einziehen** (*oder* streichen) to shorten sail; to give in; **unter — gehen** to set sail; **–boot** *neu.* sailboat; **–flug** *m.* (avi.) gliding; **–flugzeug** *neu.* (avi.) glider; **–klasse** *f.* (avi. and naut.) rating; **–macher** *m.* sailmaker; **–schiff** *neu.* sailing ship; **–schlitten** *m.* iceboat; **–sport** *m.* yachting; **–stange** *f.* (naut.) yard; **–tuch** *neu.* sailcloth, canvas

Segen *m.* benediction, blessing; grace; luck; **–swunsch** *m.* benediction; good wishes

segensreich *adj.* blessed; lucky, prosperous

segnen *v.* to bless, to give benediction; to consecrate; **das Zeitliche — to die;** **gesegneten Leibes** pregnant

Seh: –en *neu.* sight; **ihm verging Hören und –en** he lost consciousness; **–enswürdigkeiten** *f. pl.* sights, objects of interest, curiosities; **–er** *m.* seer, prophet; **–feld** *neu.* field of vision; **–kraft** *f.* visual power; **–nerv** *m.* optic nerve; **–rohr** *neu.* periscope; **–schärfe** *f.* sight, focus; **ausser –weite** out of sight; **–werkzeug** *neu.* organ of sight, eye

sehen *v.* to see, to look; to notice, to perceive, to experience, to realize, **darauf — to see to, to watch; durch die Finger — to connive;** schlecht — to have poor eyesight; **— lassen** to display, to show; **–swert** *adj.*, **–swürdig** *adj.* worth seeing; remarkable

Sehn: –e *f.* sinew, tendon; (bow) string; (geom.) secant; chord; **–enverzerrung** *f.* sprain of a tendon

sehn: –en *v.* **sich –en** to long (*oder* yearn) for; **sich nach Hause –en** to be homesick

Sehnsucht *f.* longing, yearning, ardor, desire

sehr *adv.* very, much, greatly, most; **wie — auch immer** however much

seicht *adj.* shallow, flat; superficial, insipid; **–e Redensarten** platitudes

seid: –en *adj.* silk(en); **–enartig** *adj.*, **–ig** *adj.* silky

Seide *f.* silk; **–nbau** *m.* silkworm culture; **–nernte** *f.* yield of cocoons; **–nflor** *m.* silk gauze (*oder* crepe); **–nglanz** *m.* silky luster; **–npapier** *neu.* tissue paper; **–nraupe** *f.* silkworm

Seidel *neu.* beer glass; pint, mug

Seife *f.* soap; **–nblase** *f.* soap bubble; **–nflokken** *f. pl.* soap flakes; **–nlauge** *f.* soapsuds; **–nschaum** *m.* lather

seihen *v.* to filter, to strain

Seil *neu.* rope; line, cable; **— springen** to skip; **–bahn** *f.* cable railway, funicular; **–er** *m.* ropemaker; **–erei** *f.* rope-making; ropery; **–tänzer** *m.* ropewalker; **–werk** *neu.* cordage; (naut.) rigging; **–winde** *f.* rope winch; windlass; **–ziehen** *neu.* tug of war; **–zug** *m.* tackle

sein *v.* to be, to exist; **etwas — lassen** to leave something alone, to stop something; **— pron. and adj.** his, its, one's; **of him; –erseits** *adv.* on his part; with regard to him; **–erzeit** *adv.* in his (*oder* its) time; formerly; **–esgleichen** *pron.* his equals; people like him; **–ethalben** *adv.*, **–etwegen** *adv.*, **–etwillen** *adv.* for his sake; on his account; **–ig** *pron.* his, its

Sein *neu.* being, existence; essence; **–en** *pl.* his people; **–ige** *neu.* his (*oder* one's) property; his (*oder* one's) duty

seit *prep. and conj.* since; **— damals** since then; **— einigen Tagen** these last few days; **— kurzem** lately, of late; **–dem** *adv. and conj.* since then, ever since; **–ens** *prep.* on the part (*oder* side) of; **–her** *adv.* up to now, since then; **–lich** *adj.* (col)lateral, side; **–lich** *adv.* at the side; **–wärts** *adv.* toward the side, sideways, aside; laterally

Seite *f.* side; flank, wing; age; party;

(geom.) face; (math.) member; **auf die — geh(e)n** to step aside; **auf jemandes — sein** (*oder* **treten**) to side with someone; **nach allen –n** in all directions; **schwache —** weakness; **von allen –n** from every quarter; **von –n** on the part of; **zur — steh(e)n** to stand by, to help; **–nansicht** *f.* side view; profile; **–nbewegung** *f.* (avi.) yawing; **–nblick** *m.* side glance; **–nflügel** *m.*, **–ngebäude** *neu.* (arch.) wing; **–ngewehr** *neu.* side arms; bayonet; **–nhieb** *m.* side blow; sarcastic remark; **–nkulisse** *f.* (theat.) side wing; **–nlehne** *f.* arm rest; **–nschiff** *neu.* aisle; **–nsprung** *m.* side leap; evasion, escapade; **–nstück** *neu.* counterpart; **–nzahl** *f.* number of pages; page number

Sekret: **–är** *m.* secretary; desk; secretary bird; **–ariat** *neu.* secretary's office, secretariat

Sekt *m.* dry wine, champagne

Sekt: **–e** *f.* sect; **–ierer** *m.* sectary; **–ion** *f.* section; post-mortem examination; **–ionsbefund** *m.* findings of a post-mortem examination; **–or** *m.* sector

Sekund: **–a** *f.* second highest class of college; **–aner** *m.* student of the second highest class of college; **–ant** *m.* (sports) second; **–e** *f.* second; **–enzeiger** *m.* (watch) second hand

sekundär *adj.* secondary, subordinate

selbst *pron.* self, in person, myself, himself; herself, itself, themselves; **das versteht sich von —** that's a matter of course; **von —** of one's own accord, voluntarily, automatically; **—** *adv.* even; **–bewusst** *adj.* self-confident; **–gefällig** *adj.* self-satisfied; complacent; **–genügsam** *adj.* self-sufficient; **–gerecht** *adj.* self-righteous; **–herrlich** *adj.* autocratic; **–isch** *adj.* selfish, egotistic; **–los** *adj.* unselfish, disinterested; **–mörderisch** *adj.* suicidal; **–redend** *adj.* self-evident; obvious; **–sicher** *adj.* self-assured; **–süchtig** *adj.* selfish; **–tätig** *adj.* automatic; self-acting; **–vergessen** *adj.* forgetful of oneself; **–verständlich** *adj.* self-evident, natural, obvious; **–verständlich** *adv.* of course; **das ist –verständlich** that stands to reason; **–willig** *adj.* wilful

Selbst *neu.* (the) self, individuality, personality; ego; **–achtung** *f.* self-respect; **–anlasser** *m.* self-starter; **–anschluss** *m.* dial telephone; **–aufopferung** *f.* self-sacrifice; **–befleckung** *f.* masturbation; **–beherrschung** *f.* self-control; **–bekenntnis** *neu.* voluntary confession; **–bestimmung** *f.* self-determination; **–bewusstsein** *neu.* self-confidence;

–bildnis *neu.* self-portrait; **–binder** *m.* necktie; (agr.) binder; **–biographie** *f.* autobiography; **–erhaltung** *f.* self-preservation; **–erkenntnis** *f.* knowledge of oneself; **–erniedrigung** *f.* self-abasement; **–fahrer** *m.* owner-driver; **–gefälligkeit** *f.* complacency; **–gefühl** *neu.* self-reliance; **–gespräch** *neu.* monologue, soliloquy; **–herrlichkeit** *f.* sovereignty; vanity; **–hilfe** *f.* self-help; self-defense; **–kostenpreis** *m.* cost price; **–kritik** *f.* self-criticism; **–ladepistole** *f.*, **–lader** *m.* automatic pistol; **–laut** *m.* vowel; **–losigkeit** *f.* unselfishness; **–mord** *m.* suicide; **–sucht** *f.* selfishness; egotism; **–täuschung** *f.* self-deception; **–überhebung** *f.*, **–überschätzung** *f.* presumptuousness; **–überwindung** *f.* self-conquest; **–unterricht** *m.* self-instruction; **–verblendung** *f.* infatuation; **–verleugnung** *f.* self-denial; **–ständlichkeit** *f.* matter of course; foregone conclusion; **–vertrauen** *neu.* self-confidence; **–zucht** *f.* self-discipline; **–zünder** *m.* automatic lighter; **–zündung** *f.* hypergolic ignition

selig *adj.* blessed, blissful, happy; deceased, late; (coll.) tipsy; **–sprechen** *v.* to beatify

Selig: **–e** *m.* the departed; **–preisung** *f.* (bibl.) beatitude; **–sprechung** *f.* beatification

Sellerie *m.* and *f.* celery

selten *adj.* rare, scarce, extraordinary, unusual; **—** *adv.* seldom, rarely

Selterwasser *neu.* Seltzer water; soda water

seltsam *adj.* strange, odd, queer, curious

Semester *neu.* semester, term, session

Seminar *neu.* seminar, seminary; training college; **–ist** *m.* theological student

Semmel *f.* bun, roll; **–knödel** *m.* *pl.*, **–klösse** *m.* *pl.* dumplings

semmelblond *adj.* flaxen-haired

Senat *m.* senate; **–or** *m.* senator

Send: **–bote** *m.* messenger, delegate, emissary; **–brief** *m.*, **–schreiben** *neu.* open letter; **–efolge** *f.* radio program; **–er** *m.* transmitter; **–eraum** *m.* (rad.) studio; **–espiel** *neu.* radio play; **–estation** *f.*, radio station; **–estörung** *f.* (rad.) dead air; **–ling** *m.* emissary; **–ung** *f.* sending; mission; consignment; shipment; transmission; broadcast

senden *v.* to send, to forward, to transmit, to broadcast

Senf *m.* mustard; **seinen — dazugeben** (coll.) to put in one's two cents' worth; **–korn** *neu.* mustard seed

sengen *v.* to singe, to scorch, to burn

Senk: –blei *neu.*, –lot *neu.* plummet, sounding lead; –e *f.* low ground; –er *m.* (hort.) layer; –fuss *m.* flat foot; –fusseinlage *f.* arch support; –grube *f.* cesspool; –kasten *m.* caisson; –leine *f.* fathom line; –rechte *f.* perpendicular; –schnur *f.* plumb line; –ung *f.* lowering; reduction; declivity; unaccented syllable

Senkel *m.* shoelace

senken *v.* to sink, to lower; (hort.) to lay; to bow (one's head), to cast down; **sich —** to sink, to settle; to incline

senkrecht *adj.* vertical, perpendicular

Senn *m.* Alpine cowherd; –erei *f.* Alpine dairy; –erin *f.* Alpine dairymaid; –hütte *f.* chalet

Sense *f.* scythe; –nmann *m.* mower; (lit.) Death

sensibel *adj.* sensitive, touchy

Sentenz *f.* aphorism, maxim

Separatvertrag *m.* special agreement

Sept: –ember *m.* September; –ett *neu.* septet; –ime *f.* (mus.) seventh

Sequenz *f.* sequence

sequestrieren *v.* to sequestrate, to sequester

Serail *neu.* seraglio

Serbien *neu.* Serbia

Serie *f.* series; issue, set; (billiard) break

Sermon *m.* sermon; tedious lecture

Serpentine *f.* serpentine road

Serum *neu.* serum

Service *neu.* set of china

Servierbrett *neu.* tray, salver

servieren *v.* to serve, to wait (at table)

Serviette *f.* table napkin

Sesam *m.* sesame

Sessel *m.* armchair

sesshaft *adj.* established, resident; sedentary

Setz: –er *m.* (typ.) compositor; –fehler *m.* typographical error; –kasten *m.* letter case; –ling *m.* seedling; –maschine *f.* typesetting machine

setzen *v.* to set, to place, to put; to plant; (typ.) to set, to compose; to erect (monument); to stake, to wager; **alles daran —** to move heaven and earth; **ans Land —** to disembark; **aufs Spiel —** hazard, to risk, to stake; **ausser Kraft —** to annul, to invalidate; **den Fall —** to suppose; **in Angst und Schrecken —** to frighten, to terrify; **in Rechnung —** to charge (to); **in Szene —** (theat.) to stage; **in Verlegenheit —** to embarrass; **jemand auf die Strasse —** to turn someone out of doors; **Kinder in die Welt —** to beget children; **— über** to leap over; to cross

(river); **sich aufs Pferd —** to mount a horse; **sich —** to sit down; (birds) to perch; **sich zur Wehr —** to defend oneself; **unter Wasser —** to submerge, to flood

Seuche *f.* epidemic; pestilence; –nherd *m.* center of infection; –nlazarett *neu.* hospital for contagious diseases

seufzen *v.* to sigh, to groan, to moan

Seufzer *m.* sigh, groan

Sext: –a *f.* sixth (*oder* lowest) class of an undergraduate college; –aner *m.* student of the lowest class of an undergraduate college; –ant *m.* sextant; –e *f.* (mus.) sixth; –ett *neu.* sextet

sexuell *adj.* sexual

Sezier: –besteck *neu.* dissecting case; –messer *neu.* scalpel; –ung *f.* dissection

sich *pron.* himself, herself, itself, themselves; oneself; one another; each other; **an —** in itself

Sichel *f.* sickle; crescent

sicher *adj.* safe, secure; steady; sure, certain; reliable; **aus –er Hand** from good authority; **seiner Sache — sein** to be certain of something; **seines Lebens nicht — sein** to be in danger; **— geh(e)n** to make quite sure; **— stellen** to put in safe keeping; –heitshalber *adv.* for safety's sake; –lich *adv.* surely, certainly; **–n** *v.* to secure; to guarantee

Sicher: –heit *f.* safety, security; assurance; –heitskette *f.* door chain; –heitsklausel *f.* safeguard; –heitsleistung *f.* security, bail; –heitsnadel *f.* safety pin; –heitsschloss *neu.* safety lock; –heitsventil *neu.* safety valve; –stellung *f.* safeguarding, guarantee; –ung *f.* protection, safety device; (elec.) fuse; safety bolt

Sicht *f.* sight, view; visibility; **auf —, bei — at** sight; **auf lange —** long-term; –bereich *m.*, –weite *f.* visual range; –tage *m. pl.* days of grace; –vermerk *m.* visa; –wechsel *m.* sight draft

sicht: –bar *adj.* visible, apparent, evident; **–en** *v.* to sight; to sort, to sift; –lich *adv.* evidently, obviously; visibly

sickern *v.* to trickle, to ooze, to leak

sie *pron.* she; her; they; them

Sie *pron.* you

Sieb *neu.* sieve; colander, strainer; sifter

Sieb: –en *f.* seven; **böse –en** shrew, termagant; –engestirn *neu.* Pleiades; –enmeilenstiefel *m. pl.* seven-league boots; –ensachen *f. pl.* goods and chattels; –enschläfer *m.* lazybones; dormouse; –entel *neu.* seventh part; –zehn *f.* seventeen; –zig *f.* seventy; –ziger *m.* septuagenarian

sieb: –en *adj.* seven; –enerlei *adv.* of seven different kinds; –enfach *adj.*, –enfältig *adj.* sevenfold; –enjährig *adj.* septennial; –enmal *adv.* seven times; –ente *adj.* seventh; –tens *adv.* in the seventh place; –zehn *adj.* seventeen; –zig *adj.* seventy

sieben *v.* to sift, to strain; to eliminate

siech *adj.* sickly, infirm; –en *v.* to pine away

Siechtum *neu.* sickliness, long illness

Sied: –ler *m.* settler; –lung *f.* settlement, colony; –lungsgesellschaft *f.* building and loan association

Siede: –grad *m.*, –punkt *m.* boiling point

siedeln *v.* to settle, to colonize

sieden *v.* to boil, to seethe; –dheiss *adj.* boiling hot

Sieg *m.* victory; den — davontragen to win the day; — durch Zielfotografie photo finish; –er *m.* victor, winner; –esbeute *f.* victor's spoils; –esbogen *m.* triumphal arch; –eszeichen *neu.* trophy; –eszug *m.* triumphal procession

sieg: –en *v.* to be victorious; to win; –esgewiss *adj.* confident of victory; –estrunken *adj.* elated with victory; –haft *adj.*, –reich *adj.* victorious, triumphant

Siegel *neu.* seal; unter dem — der Verschwiegenheit in strict confidence; –bewahrer *m.* keeper of the seal; –lack *m.* sealing wax; –ring *m.* signet ring

siegeln *v.* to (affix a) seal

Signal *neu.* signal; bugle call; –buch *neu.* code of signals; –ement *neu.* personal description; –leine *f.* bell rope; communication cord; –mast *m.* signal mast; semaphore; –pfeife *f.* warning whistle; –wärter *m.* signalman

signalisieren *v.* to signal

Signet *neu.* collophon; printer's trade mark

Silbe *f.* syllable; –nfall *m.* (lit.) rhythm; –nmass *neu.* syllabic quantity; meter; –nmessung *f.* prosody; –nrätsel *neu.* charade; –nstecher *m.* quibbler, hairsplitter; –ntrennung *f.* syllabication

Silber *neu.* silver; silverware; –arbeiter *f.* silversmith; –geschirr *neu.* silver plate; –legierung *f.* silver alloy; –ling *m.* (bibl.) silver coin; –pappel *f.* white poplar; –plattierung *f.* silver plating; –reiher *m.* egret, white heron; –währung *f.* silver standard; –zeug *neu.* silverware

silber: –(art)ig *adj.*, –n *adj.* silvery, argentine; –hell *adj.* silvery

Silvesterabend *m.* New Year's Eve

Simili(stein) *m.* artificial gem

simpel *adj.* simple, naïve, plain

Sims *neu.* ledge; sill; cornice, molding

simulieren *v.* to simulate, to feign

simultan *adj.* simultaneous

Sinfonie *f.* symphony

Sing: –akademie *f.* singing school; –drossel *f.* (orn.) thrush; –erei *f.*, –sang *m.* singsong; –spiel *neu.* musical comedy; –stimme *f.* singing voice; vocal part; –vogel *m.* songster, warbler; –weise *f.* tune, melody

singen *v.* to sing; to carol, to warble; nach dem Gehör — to sing by ear; nach Noten —, vom Blatt weg — to sing at sight

sinken *v.* to sink; to fall, to decline, to decrease; den Mut — lassen to lose heart; die Stimme — lassen to lower one's voice; in Ohnmacht — to faint away

Sinn *m.* sense; intellect, mind; opinion; meaning; taste, wish; tendency; and(e)ren –es werden to change one's mind; bei — sein, seine fünf –e beisammen haben to have one's wits about one; seinen — auf etwas richten to turn one's attention to something; sich etwas aus dem — schlagen to dismiss something from one's mind; von –en sein to be out of one's mind; –bild *neu.* symbol, emblem; allegory; –enlust *f.* sensual enjoyment; voluptuousness; –enmensch *m.* sensualist; –enwelt *f.* material world; –esänderung *f.* change of mind; –esart *f.* character, disposition; –esorgan *neu.*, –eswerkzeug *neu.* organ of sense; –estäuschung *f.* illusion, hallucination; –gedicht *neu.* epigram; –spruch *m.* epigram; motto

sinn: –bildlich *adj.* symbolic, allegoric(al); –en *v.* to think; to speculate (upon), to reflect; to meditate, to ponder, to muse; auf etwas –en to plan, to plot; auf Mittel und Wege — to devise means and ways; –fällig *adj.* obvious; –getreu *adj.* faithful; –ig *adj.* thoughtful; ingenious; sensible; –lich *adj.* sensual; material; –los *adj.* senseless; foolish; –reich *adj.* sensible, clever; ingenious; witty; –verwandt *adj.* synonymous; –voll *adj.* significant, pregnant

sintemal *conj.* whereas, since

Sintflut *f.* deluge; (bibl.) the Flood

Sippe *f.*, **Sippschaft** *f.* kindred, kith and kin

sistieren *v.* to inhibit, to stop, to arrest

sitt: –enlos *adj.* immoral, dissolute, profligate; –enrein *adj.* morally pure, chaste; –enstreng *adj.* puritanical; –ig *adj.* well-bred, modest; –lich *adj.* moral;

-sam *adj.* modest, decent; reserved, respectable

Sitt: -e *f.* custom, habit, usage; **-en** *pl.* morals, manners; **das ist nicht mehr -e** that's out of date; **feine -en** good manners; **lockere -en** loose morals; **-engesetz** *neu.* moral code; **-enprediger** *m.* moralizer; **-enrichter** *m.* censor; **moralist; -enverfall** *m.* demoralization; moral corruption

Sittich *m.* parakeet

situiert *adj.* **gut** (*or* **wohl**) — well-off; well-to-do

Sitz *m.* seat, place; domicile, residence; fit (of clothes); **-arbeit** *f.* sedentary work; **-fläche** *f.* seat (of chair); **-fleisch** *neu.* perseverance; **er hat kein -fleisch** he can't sit still; he does not persevere; **-gelegenheit** *f.* seating accomodation; **-platz** *m.* seat; **-stange** *f.* perch; **-streik** *m.* sit-down strike; sit-in (strike); **-übungen** *f. pl.* sit-up exercises; **-ung** *f.* sitting; session; meeting; **-ungsbericht** *m.* minutes of a meeting; **-ungsperiode** *f.* (law) term; **-ungssaal** *m.* plenum chamber

sitzen *v.* to sit; (birds) to perch; to fit; to hold a meeting; to adhere, to stick fast; (coll.) to be imprisoned; **hinter Schloss und Riegel** — to sit in jail; **jemand auf dem Halse** — to be a burden to someone; — **bleiben** to remain seated; to be a wallflower; (educ.) not to pass; — **lassen** to abandon, to leave in the lurch

Skala *f.* scale; **bewegliche** — sliding scale

Skalp *m.* scalp

Skalpell *neu.* scalpel

Skandal *m.* scandal, noise, row

skandal: -ieren *v.* to abuse, to slander; **-isieren** *v.* to scandalize; **-ös** *adj.* scandalous

Skelett *neu.* skeleton

Skepsis *f.* skepticism

Skeptiker *m.* skeptic

skeptisch *adj.* skeptic(al)

Ski *m.* ski; **-lauf** *m.* skiing; **-läufer** *m.* skier; **-springen** *neu.* ski jumping

skilaufen *v.* to ski

Skizze *f.* sketch, **-nbuch** *neu.* sketchbook

skizzenhaft *adj.* sketchy

Sklave *m.* slave; **-rei** *f.* slavery

sklavisch *adj.* slavish, servile

Skonto *m. and neu.* discount

Skorbut *m.* scurvy

Skrofeln *f. pl.* scrofula

Skrupel *m.* scruple

skrupellos *adj.* unscrupulous

Smaragd *m.* emerald

so *adv.* so, thus; such; approximately; anyhow; as; **—?** *interj.* indeed? really?

— *conj.* if, therefore, then; — **auch** however; — **doch** nevertheless, yet; — **ein Mensch** such a person; — **gross wie** as big as; — oft whenever; **um** — **besser** so much the better; **-bald** *adv.* as soon as; **-dann** *adv.* then, after (*oder* upon) that; **-eben** *adv.* just now; **-fern** *conj.*, **-weit** *conj.* so far as; **-fern nur** as long as, if only; **-fort** *adv.* at once, immediately; **-fortig** *adj.* immediate; instantaneous, prompt; **-gar** *adv.* even; **-genannt** *adj.* so-called; **-gleich** *adv.* directly, promptly; **-lange** *adv.* as (*oder* s) long (as); whilst; **-mit** *adv.*, **-nach** *adv.* consequently, therefore; **-viel** *conj.* as far (*oder* much) as; the same as; **-wie** *conj.* as soon as; just as; also; **-wieso** *adv.* in any case, anyhow; **-wohl** *conj.* as well (as); not only; **-zusagen** *adv.* so to speak, as it were

Socke *f.* sock; **-nhalter** *m.* garter, suspender

Sockel *m.* base, pedestal

Soda *neu.* soda; **-wasser** *neu.* soda water

Sodbrennen *neu.* heartburn, pyrosis

Sofa *neu.* sofa; **-schoner** *m.* antimacassar

Sohle *f.* sole; bottom; (min.) floor

Sohn *m.* son; **der verlorene** — (bibl.) the Prodigal Son

Sojabohne *f.* soybean

Solawechsel *m.* promissory note

Solbad *neu.* saltwater (*oder* brine) bath

solch *pron.* and *adj.* such, the same; **-enfalls** *adv.* in such a case; **-ergestalt** *adv.* in such a form (*oder* manner, way); **-erlei** *adj.* of such a kind; **-ermassen** *adv.*, **-erweise** *adv.* to such a degree, in such a way

Sold *m.* pay, wages; **-buch** *neu.* (mil.) pay book

Soldat *m.* soldier; **-eska** *f.* gang of soldiers

soldatisch *adj.* soldierlike, military; of soldierly bearing

Söldling, Söldner *m.* hireling, mercenary

solid *adj.* solid, substantial; respectable; thorough; reliable; solvent; **-arisch** *adj.* joint; unanimous

Solid: -arität *f.* solidarity, unanimity; **-arschuldner** *m.* joint debtor; **-ität** *f.* solidity; soundness; reliability, respectability

Solist *m.*, **Solistin** *f.* soloist

Soll *neu.* debit; **-bestand** *m.* calculated assets

sollen *v.* to be obliged, to be bound to, to have to; to be supposed to; **das hat nicht sein** — that was not to be; **er hätte schreiben** — he ought to have written; **sollte er krank sein?** can he be ill? **Was soll das?** what is the use of that?

Solo *neu.* solo; **-stimme** *f.* solo part; **-tänzer** *m.* principal dancer

Sommer *m.* summer; **-aufenthalt** *m.*, **-frische** *f.* summer resort; **-fäden** *m. pl.* gossamer; **-frischler** *m.* summer vacationer; **-getreide** *neu.* spring grain; **-sonnenwende** *f.* summer solstice; **-sprosse** *f.* freckle; **-wohnung** *f.* summer residence

sommersprossig *adj.* freckled

somnambul *adj.* somnambulistic

Sonate *f.* sonata

sonder *prep.* without; **-bar** *adj.* strange, odd; peculiar; **-barerweise** *adv.* strange to say; **-gleichen** *adj.* unique, unequalled; **-lich** *adj.* particular, special, remarkable; **-n** *conj.* but; **-s** *adv.* samt und **-s** all together

Sonder: **-(ab)druck** *m.* special reprint, extract; **-berichterstatter** *m.* special correspondent; **-fall** *m.* exceptional case; **-ling** *m.* eccentric person, original; **-meldung** *f.* special announcement; **-recht** *neu.* special privilege; **-zug** *m.* special train

sondern *v.* to separate, to sever

sondieren *v.* to probe; to sound, to fathom

sonn: **-en** *v.* to (expose to the) sun; to bask; **-enklar** *adj.* clear as daylight; evident; **-(en)verbrannt** *adj.* sunburnt, tanned; **-ig** *adj.* sunny; **-täglich** *adj.* taking place on Sunday(s); **-täglich** *adv.* every Sunday

Sonn: **-abend** *m.* Saturday; **-e** *f.* sun; **-enaufgang** *m.* sunrise; **-enbad** *neu.* sunbath; **-enbahn** *f.* orbit of the sun, ecliptic; **-enblume** *f.* sunflower; **-enbrand** *m.* sunburn; **-endach** *neu.*, **-ensegel** *neu.* awning; **-enfinsternis** *f.* solar eclipse; **-enfleck** *m.* sunspot; **-enjahr** *neu.* solar year; **-ennähe** *f.* perihelion; **-enscheibe** *f.* solar disk; **-enschirm** *m.* sunshade; **-enseite** *f.* sunny side; **-enstäubchen** *neu.* mote; **-enstich** *m.* sunstroke; **-ensystem** *neu.* solar system; **-enuhr** *f.* sundial; **-enuntergang** *m.* sunset; **-enwende** *f.* solstice; **-tag** *m.* Sunday; **-tagsanzug** *m.* (clothes) Sunday best; **-tagsausflügler** *m.* week-ender; **-tagsfahrkarte** *f.* weekend ticket; **-tagskind** *neu.* person born on Sunday (*oder* under a lucky star); **-tagsstaat** *m.* Sunday finery

sonst *adv.* otherwise; else, besides, moreover; usually; before, formerly; — **nichts als** nothing but; — **nirgends** nowhere else; **wenn es** — **nichts ist** if that's all; **-ig** *adj.* other, former, remaining; **-wie** *adv.* in some other way;

-wo *adv.* elsewhere, somewhere else; **-woher** *adv.* from somewhere else; **-wohin** *adv.* to another place, somewhere else

Sopran *m.* soprano; **-ist** *m.*, **-istin** *f.* soprano

Sorg: **-e** *f.* sorrow, anxiety; concern, care; worry, trouble; lass das meine **-e** sein leave that to me; sich **-en machen** to trouble oneself (about); **-e tragen** to take care of; to see to; **-enkind** *neu.* problem child; **-enstuhl** *m.* easy chair; **-falt** *f.* carefulness, precision; care

sorg: **-en** *v.* sich **-en** to be anxious, to worry; to trouble oneself (about); **-en für** to care for, to provide for; to see to; dafür lass mich **-en** I'll take care of that; **-enfrei** *adj.* free from trouble; lighthearted; **-envoll** *adj.* careworn; worried; **-fältig** *adj.* careful; precise, scrupulous; **-lich** *adj.* careful, anxious; **-los** *adj.* careless; thoughtless; carefree; lighthearted; **-sam** *adj.* cautious, circumspect

Sort: **-e** *f.* sort, kind, species; quality, brand; **-ierer** *m.* sorter; **-iment** *neu.* assortment; retail book trade; **-imenter** *m.* bookseller

sortieren *v.* to (as)sort; to arrange, to sift

Sosse *f.* sauce, gravy

Souffleur *m.*, **Souffleuse** *f.* prompter; **-kasten** *m.* prompter's box

soufflieren *v.* to prompt

Souper *neu.* supper

Souverän *m.* sovereign; **-ität** *f.* sovereignty

sozial *adj.* social; **-isieren** *v.* to socialize; **-istisch** *adj.* socialistic

Sozial: **-demokratie** *f.* social democracy; **-ismus** *m.* socialism; **-ist** *m.* socialist; **-versicherung** *f.* social security; **-wissenschaft** *f.* sociology

Spachtel *m.* and *f.* spatula

Späh: **-er** *m.* spy, scout, secret observer; **-erblick** *m.* prying glance; **-trupp** *m.* patrol

spähen *v.* to spy, to scout, to reconnoiter

Spalier *neu.* espalier; trellis; — **stehen** to form a lane; **-obst** *neu.* wall fruit

Spalt *m.*, **Spalte** *f.* crack, gap; slit, slot; fissure; crevasse; **-e** *f.* (typ.) column; **-holz** *neu.* firewood; **-ung** *f.* splitting, fission; dissension, schism

spalt: **-bar** *adj.* cleavable, fissile; **-en** *v.* to cleave, to split; to divide; to decompose, to ferment; **-enweise** *adv.* (typ.) in columns

Span *m.* chip, splinter; **-ferkel** *neu.* sucking pig

Spange *f.* buckle; clasp; brooch; **-nschuh**

m. buckled shoe

Spanien *neu.* Spain

Spann: **-e** *f.* span; interval; **-er** *m.* boot tree, last; (ent.) looper; **-feder** *f.* spring; **-kraft** *f.* elasticity; tension; energy; **-ung** *f.* stretching; tension; strain; (arch.) span; (elec.) voltage; potential; **-ungsmesser** *m.* voltmeter; **-weite** *f.* spread; (arch.) span

spannen *v.* to stretch; to strain; to tighten; (bow) to bend; (gun) to cock; to excite; **gespannt sein** to be anxious (*oder* curious); **vor den Wagen —** to hitch to the wagon; **-d** *adj.* exciting, fascinating, thrilling

Spar: **-büchse** *f.* money box; **-einlage** *f.* savings deposit; **-er** *m.* saver, economizer; **-flamme** *f.* pilot light; **-kasse** *f.* savings bank; **-pfennig** *m.* savings, nest egg

sparen *v.* to spare, to save, to economize

Spargel *m.* asparagus

spärlich *adj.* scanty, frugal; thin, sparse

Sparren *m.* spar, rafter

sparsam *adj.* economical, thrifty; parsimonious

Spass *m.* joke, jest; fun; **— machen** to amuse; **zum —** for fun; **-macher** *m.*, **-vogel** *m.* wag, clown, buffoon; jester; **-verderber** *m.* spoil-sport

spass: **-en** *v.* to jest, to joke, to make fun; **-eshalber** *adv.* for fun; **-ig** *adj.*, **-haft** *adj.* joking, amusing, funny, droll

spät *adj.* late; **wie — ist es?** what time is it? **zu — kommen** to be late; **-er** *adj.* later; **-er** *adv.* afterwards; **-erhin** *adv.* later on; **-estens** *adv.* at the latest

Spät: **-herbst** *m.* late autumn; **-ling** *m.* latecomer; late fruit; **-obst** *neu.* late fruit

Spatel *m.* spatula

Spaten *m.* spade; **-stich** *m.* spade cut

Spatz *m.* sparrow; **das pfeifen die -en schon von den Dächern** that's the talk of the town

spazieren *v.* to walk, to stroll; **-fahren** *v.* to go for a drive; **-führen** *v.* to take out for a walk; **-geh(e)n** *v.* to go for a walk

Spazier: **-fahrt** *f.* drive; boating; **-gang** *m.* walk, stroll; **-gänger** *m.* stroller, walker, promenader; **-stock** *m.* walking stick

Specht *m.* woodpecker

Speck *m.* bacon; fat; lard; **— ansetzen** to become fat; **wie die Made im — sitzen** to be in clover; **-schwarte** *f.* bacon rind; **-seite** *f.* flitch of bacon; **-stein** *m.* soapstone

spedieren *v.* to dispatch, to forward

Spedit: **-eur** *m.* forwarding agent; **-ion** *f.* forwarding; shipping department; **-ionsgeschäft** *neu.* forwarding agency; furniture removal business

Speer *m.* spear, lance; javelin

Speiche *f.* spoke

Speichel *m.* spittle; slaver; **-drüse** *f.* salivary gland; **-fluss** *m.* salivation; **-lecker** *m.* lickspittle, toady

Speicher *m.* warehouse; storeroom; reservoir; loft; granary, accumulator; silo

speichern *v.* to store, to warehouse

speien *v.* to spit, to expectorate, to vomit

Speise *f.* food, nourishment; meal, dish; dessert; **-eis** *neu.* ice cream; **-fett** *neu.* cooking fat; **-kammer** *f.* pantry, larder; **-karte** *f.*, **-zettel** *m.* bill of fare; **-naufzug** *m.* dumb-waiter; **-nfolge** *f.* menu; **-öl** *neu.* salad oil; **-rohr** *neu.* supply pipe; **-röhre** *f.* esophagus, gullet; **-saal** *m.*, **-zimmer** *neu.* dining room; **-wagen** *m.* (rail.) diner

speisen *v.* to eat, to dine; to feed, to nourish, to supply

Spektakel *m. and neu.* noise, row, fracas

Spektrum *neu.* spectrum

Spekulant *m.* speculator

spekulieren *v.* to speculate

Spelunke *f.* den; low tavern

Spend: **-e** *f.* gift, contribution, donation; **-er** *m.* donor, benefactor; **-ung** *f.* contribution, donation

spenden *v.* to give, to contribute; to deal out; **Almosen —** to bestow alms; **das Abendmahl —** to administer the sacrament

spendieren *v.* to spend, to pay for; to treat

Spengler *m.* plumber; tinsmith

Sper: **-ber** *m.* sparrow hawk; **-ling** *m.* sparrow

Sperr: **-e** *f.* shutting, bar(ring); blockade; embargo; **-feuer** *neu.* curtain fire; **-frist** *f.* period of grace; **-gebiet** *neu.* prohibited area; blockade zone; **-gut** *neu.* bulky goods; **-haken** *m.* catch; ratchet; **-holz** *neu.* plywood; **-sitz** *m.* (theat.) orchestra seat; **-ung** *f.* stoppage; blockade; embargo; **-vorrichtung** *f.* locking device; lock

sperrangelweit *adv.* ajar; **— offen** wide open

sperren *v.* to close, to lock; to block(ade), to stop; (legs) to straddle; (typ.) to space; **sich —** to oppose

Spesen *f. pl.* charges, expenses, costs

Spezerei *f.* spice

spezial, speziell *adj.* special, particular; **-isieren** *v.* to specialize

Spezial: **-arzt** *m.* (med.) specialist; **-fach**

neu., **–ität** *f.* specialty, special branch
spezifisch *adj.* specific; **–es Gewicht** specific gravity
Sphäre *f.* sphere, range, province
Spick: –aal *m.* smoked eel; **–gans** *f.* smoked goose breast; **–nadel** *f.* larding pin
Spiegel *m.* mirror; (med.) speculum; tab, facing; (fig.) model, paragon; **–bild** *neu.* reflected image; **–ei** *neu.* fried egg; **–fechterei** *f.* jugglery, humbug; **–fern-rohr** *neu.* reflecting telescope; **–pfeiler** *m.* (arch.) pier; **–schrift** *f.* mirror writing; **–ung** *f.* reflection, mirage
spiegel: –blank *adj.* shining; **–glatt** *adj.* as smooth (*oder* slippery) as a mirror; **–n** *v.* to shine; to reflect; **sich –n** to be reflected, to look at oneself in the mirror
Spiel *neu.* play(ing), game, sport; gamble; (mus.) touch; (theat.) performance; acting; set, suit, pack (of cards); **auf dem –e stehen** to be at stake; **aufs — setzen** to hazard, to risk; **aus dem –e lassen** to leave out of question; **die Hand mit im –e haben** to have a finger in the pie; **ehrliches — fair play; leichtes — haben** to have no difficulty; **sein — treiben mit** to make game of; **–art** *f.* manner of playing; special type; (bot.) variety; **–ball** *m.* ball; (fig.) plaything; puppet; **–bank** *f.* gambling table (*oder* house); **–dose** *f.* musical box; **–er** *m.* player, gambler; actor, performer; **–erei** *f.* play, sport; trifle; **–ergebnis** *neu.* score; **–feld** *neu.* field, ground, court; **–film** *m.* feature movie; **–gefährte** *m.*, **–genosse** *m.* playmate; **–hölle** *f.* gambling den; **–karte** *f.* playing card; **–leiter** *m.* stage manager, producer; **–mann** *m.* musician; fiddler, minstrel; **–marke** *f.* chip, counter; **–plan** *m.* repertory; program; **–platz** *m.* playground; **–raum** *m.* elbowroom, free scope; **–sachen** *f. pl.*, **–waren** *f. pl.*, **–zeug** *neu.* toys; **–schar** *f.* (mus. and theat.) amateur company; **–schuld** *f.* gambling debt; **–schule** *f.* kindergarten; **–uhr** *f.* musical clock; **–verderber** *m.* killjoy; spoilsport; **–werk** *neu.* chime
spiel: –bar *adj.* (theat.) stageable; **–en** *v.* to play, to gamble; to act, to perform; to simulate; to flash; **–end** *adv.* playing; with the utmost ease
Spiess *m.* spear, pike, lance; spit; **den — umdrehen** to turn the tables on; **–bürger** *m.*, **–er** *m.* narrow-minded fellow; Philistine; **–er** *m.* stag, young buck; **–geselle** *m.* accomplice; **–rute** *f.* gauntlet; **–ruten laufen** to run the gauntlet

spiess: –bürgerlich *adj.*, **–ig** *adj.* narrow-minded; **–en** *v.* to spear, to spit
Spinat *m.* spinach
Spind *neu.* wardrobe, locker, cupboard
Spindel *f.* spindle, distaff; mandrel; axis
Spinett *neu.* spinet
Spinn: –e *f.* spider; **–er** *m.* spinner; silkworm; **–erei** *f.* spinning (mill); **–faser** *f.* synthetic fiber; **–gewebe** *neu.*, **–webe** *f.* cobweb; **–maschine** *f.* spinning jenny; **–rad** *neu.* spinning wheel; **–rocken** *m.* distaff; **–stoffindustrie** *f.* textile industry
spinnen *v.* to spin; (cat) to purr; **to be crazy**
Spion *m.* spy, scout; **–age** *f.* espionage; **–ageabwehr** *f.* counterespionage
spionieren *v.* to spy, to scout; to pry
Spiralsturzflug *m.* spiral dive
Spirit: –ismus *m.* spiritualism; **–uosen** *f. pl.* alcoholic liquors; **–us** *m.* spirit, alcohol; **–usbrennerei** *f.* distillery
Spital *neu.* hospital
Spitz *m.* Pomeranian dog; **einen — haben** (coll.) to be tipsy; **–bart** *m.* pointed beard; **–bogen** *m.* pointed arch; **–bube** *m.* thief, rascal; **–e** *f.* point; peak, top; head; (pen) nib; (tongue) tip; lace; sarcastic remark; **an der –e stehen** to act as leader; **die –e abbrechen** to take the edge off; **etwas auf die –e treiben** to carry something to extremes; **jemand die –e bieten** to defy someone; **–enbesatz** *m.* lace trimming; **–enklöppelei** *f.* bobbin lacemaking; **–enleistung** *f.* peak performance (*oder* power output); **–enlohn** *m.* maximum pay; **–entanz** *m.* toe dance; **–hacke** *f.* pickaxe; **–maus** *f.* shrewmouse; **–name** *m.* nickname
spitz *adj.* pointed, acute; sharp; sarcastic; **–bübisch** *adj.* roguish, rascally; **–en** to point; to sharpen; **den Mund –en** to purse one's lips; **die Ohren –en** to prick up one's ears; **sich –en auf** to be eager about; **–findig** *adj.* subtle; hairsplitting, captious; sophistical; **–winklig** *adj.* acute-angled
Spitzel *m.* informer, spy; police agent
spleissen *v.* to split, to splice
Splitter *m.* splinter, chip; fragment; mote
splitter: –(faser)nackt *adj.* stark naked; **–ig** *adj.* splintered, splintery; **–n** *v.* to splinter
spontan *adj.* spontaneous
Sporen *m.* spur; incentive, stimulus; **die — geben** to put spurs to
spornen *v.* to spur; to stimulate
spornstreichs *adv.* at full speed, directly
Sport *m.* sport; **–abzeichen** *neu.* sports badge; **–eln** *f. pl.* perquisites, fees;

–funk *m.* (rad.) sports news; –ler *m.* sportsman; –wagen *m.* gocart; sport car
sportlich *adj.* sportsmanlike; athletic
Spott *m.* mockery, derision, ridicule; butt; Gegenstand des –es laughingstock; seinen — treiben to make sport of; –drossel *f.* mockingbird; –geburt *f.* monstrosity; –gedicht *neu.* satirical poem; –geld *neu.*, –preis *m.* low price; trifling sum; –name *m.* nickname
spott: –billig *adj.* dirt-cheap; –en *v.* to mock, to ridicule; –lustig *adj.* satirical
Spötte–lei *f.*, –rei *f.* banter, chaff; raillery; mockery, derision, sneer; –r *m.* jeerer; mocker, scoffer; (bibl.) blasphemer
spöttisch *adj.* mocking, ironical, sarcastic
Sprach: –armut *f.* lack of words; –e *f.* speech; language, tongue; diction; articulation; jemand die –e benehmen to strike one dumb; mit der –e herausrücken to speak freely; mit der –e nicht herauswollen to beat about the bush; zur –e bringen to broach a subject; –eigenheit *f.*, –eigentümlichkeit *f.* idiomatic peculiarity; –fehler *m.* speech defect; –forscher *m.* linguist, philologist; –forschung *f.* linguistics, philology; –führer *m.* colloquial guide, phrase book; –gebrauch *m.* usage (of a language); –grenze *f.* linguistic frontier; –lehrer *m.* language teacher; –regel *f.* grammatical rule; –rohr *neu.* speaking tube; (coll.) mouthpiece, spokesman; –schatz *m.* vocabulary; –schnitzer *m.* solecism; –talent *neu.* talent for acquiring languages; –unterricht *m.* teaching of languages; –verwirrung *f.* confusion of tongues; –wissenschaft *f.* linguistics, philology
sprach: –kundig *adj.* proficient in languages; –lich *adj.* linguistic, grammatical; –los *adj.* speechless, dumb; –widrig *adj.* ungrammatical; –wissenschaftlich *adj.* philological
Sprech–er *m.* speaker, spokesman; lecturer; (rad.) announcer; –film *m.* talking motion picture; –gesang *m.* recitative; –stunde *f.* consulting hour; –stundenhilfe *f.* doctor's receptionist; –übung *f.* exercise in speaking; –weise *f.* diction; –zimmer *neu.* consultation room
sprechen *v.* to speak, to talk; to say, to discuss; ausführlich (*or* weitläufig) — to enlarge on; dafür — to speak in favor of; er ist nicht zu — he is engaged; er lässt nicht mit sich — he won't listen to reason; frei — to extemporize; to find innocent; schuldig — to find

guilty; sich herum — to be the talk of the town; — wir nicht davon don't mention it; –de Ähnlichkeit striking resemblance; –der Beweis conclusive evidence; Urteil — to pronounce judgment; vor Gericht — to plead
spreiten *v.* to spread, to extend
spreizen *v.* to spread, to stretch out, to straddle; sich — to be affected; to resist
Spreng: –bombe *f.* bomb; –er *m.* sprinkler, spray; –körper *m.* explosive shell; –ladung *f.* explosive charge; –stoff *m.* explosive; –wagen *m.* street sprinkler
Sprengel *m.* parish, diocese
sprengen *v.* to blow up, to burst open; to force; to break up (*oder* open); to sprinkle, to water; to ride at full speed
sprenkeln *v.* to speckle, to spot; to marble
Spreu *f.* chaff
Sprichwort *neu.* proverb; adage, saying
Spring: –brunnen *m.* fountain; jet (of water); –er *m.* jumper, vaulter; (chess) knight; –flut *f.* spring tide; –insfeld *m.* harum-scarum fellow; romp; –seil *neu.* skipping rope
springen *v.* to jump, to leap; to spring; to dive; (fountain) to gush, to play; to crack, to burst; in die Augen — to strike the eye; in die Bresche — to fill the breach; Seil — to skip rope; über die Klinge — lassen to put to the sword; to kill
Sprit *m.* spirit, alcohol
Spritz: –arbeit *f.* firemen's work; marbled work; –bewurf *m.* roughcast; –e *f.* fire engine, sprayer; squirt; injection, syringe; –enhaus *neu.* fire engine shed; –er *m.* splash, squirt; spot; –fahrt *f.* outing; –kuchen *m.* fritter
spritzen *v.* to squirt; to sprinkle, to spray; to spout; to inject; to gush forth
spröde *adj.* brittle; fragile, inflexible; chapped; shy, coy; prudish
Spross *m.* shoot, sprout, sprig; (stag) antler; offspring
Sprosse *f.* rung, round, step; sprout; freckle
sprossen *v.* to sprout, to shoot, to germinate
Sprössling *m.* shoot, sprout; offspring, scion
Spruch *m.* aphorism, maxim, saying; verse (of Scriptures); motto; sentence, verdict
Sprudel *m.* bubbling water, mineral spring; overflow (of humor *oder* words)
sprudeln *v.* to bubble, to gush forth, to effervesce, to sparkle; to brim (over)
sprühen *v.* to drizzle; to sparkle, to flash
Sprung *m.* leap, bound, jump; crack;

split; **auf dem —e sein zu** to be on the point of; **jemand auf die** (*or* **hinter jemandes**) **Sprünge kommen** to find someone out; **nur ein — bis dahin** only a stone's throw away; **—brett** *neu.* springboard; **—federmatratze** *f.* spring mattress; **—gelenk** *neu.* hock; **—hügel** *m.*, **—schanze** *f.* ski jump platform; **—tuch** *neu.* (life-saving) jumping net

Spucke *f.* (coll.) spittle, saliva

spucken *v.* to spit, to expectorate

Spucknapf *m.* spittoon

Spuk *m.* spook, apparition, ghost, specter; noise; **—geschichte** *f.* ghost story

spukhaft *adj.* ghostly, haunted

Spul: **—e** *f.* spool, bobbin; coil; quill; **—maschine** *f.* spooling machine, bobbin frame; **—rad** *neu.* spooling wheel; **—wurm** *m.* bellyworm

Spül: **—eimer** *m.* slop pail; **—fass** *neu.* wash tub; **—frau** *f.* scullery maid; dishwasher; **—icht** *neu.*, **—wasser** *neu.* dish water, rinsings; slops; **—kasten** *m.* flush tank; **—stein** *m.* sink

spülen *v.* to rinse, to flush, to cleanse

Spund *m.* bung, plug, stopper; faucet, tap; **—bohrer** *m.* tap borer; **—loch** *neu.* bunghole

Spur *f.* trace, scent, track, rut; footprint; (fig.) mark, sign, vestige; **jemand auf die — kommen** to be on someone's tracks; **keine —** not a bit; **—weite** *f.* (rail.) gauge

Spür: **—hund** *m.* bloodhound, pointer; (coll.) spy; **—nase** *f.* good nose; keen sense of smell; **—sinn** *m.* sagacity, shrewdness

spüren *v.* to feel, to notice, to perceive; **— nach** to track, to scent out; to search for

spurlos *adj.* trackless; **—** *adv.* without a trace

sputen *v.* **sich —** to hurry, to make haste

Staat *m.* state; government; pomp, finery; **in vollem —** in full dress; **— mit etwas machen** to parade; to show off; to boast; **—enbund** *m.* confederation; **—enlose** *m.* person without nationality; **—sakt** *m.* state ceremony; **—saktion** *f.* political event; **—sangehörige** *m.* citizen; **—sangehörigkeit** *f.* nationality; citizenship; **—sanwalt** *m.* public prosecutor; **—sanzeiger** *m.* official gazette; **—sarchiv** *neu.* government record office; **—sbeamte** *m.* government official; **—sbürger** *m.* citizen; **—sdienst** *m.* civil service; **—seinkünfte** *pl.* public revenues; **—sgefangene** *m.* prisoner of state; **—sgeheimnis** *neu.* state secret; **—sgelder** *neu. pl.* public money; **—sgewalt** *f.*

supreme power; **—shaushalt** *m.* budget, finances; **—skerl** *m.* fine fellow; **—skleid** *neu.* gala dress; **—skunst** *f.* statecraft, politics; **—smann** *m.* statesman, politician; **—sordnung** *f.* political system; **—spapiere** *neu. pl.* government bonds; **—srecht** *neu.* constitutional law; **—sschuld** *f.* national debt; **—sstreich** *m.* coup d'état; **—swesen** *neu.* state affairs; **—swissenschaft** *f.* political science; **—swohl** *neu.* general welfare; **—szuschuss** *m.* government subsidy

Stab *m.* staff, stick; rod, bar; baton; personnel; headquarters; **den — über jemand brechen** to condemn someone; **—(hoch)sprung** *m.* pole jump; **—ilität** *f.* stability; **—reim** *m.* alliteration; **—sarzt** *m.* surgeon major; **—squartier** *neu.* headquarters; **—sträger** *m.* sergeant at arms

Stäbchen *neu.* small rod; (coll.) cigarette

stabil *adj.* stable; **—isieren** *v.* to stabilize

Stachel *m.* sting, goad, tongue, spike, thorn; prick(le); (stimulus, spur; **—beere** *f.* gooseberry; **—draht** *m.* barbed wire; **—schwein** *neu.* porcupine

stach(e)lig *adj.* prickly, thorny; sarcastic

Stadion *neu.* stadium, arena

Stadium *neu.* phase, stage

Stadt *f.* city, town; **—bahn** *f.* metropolitan railroad; **—bezirk** *m.*, **—teil** *m.*, **—viertel** *neu.* city district, ward; **—bild** *neu.* panorama; city plan; **—gemeinde** *f.* municipality; **—kern** *m.* center of a city; **—koffer** *m.* suitcase; **—randsiedlung** *f.* suburban settlement; **—rat** *m.* alderman, city council; **—väter** *m. pl.* city fathers; **—verordnete** *m.* city councilor; **—verordnetenversammlung** *f.* city council; **—waage** *f.* public scales

Städt: **—ebau** *m.* city planning; **—eordnung** *f.* municipal ordinance; **—er** *m.* townsman

städtisch *adj.* municipal, urban

Stafette *f.* courier; dispatch rider; **—nlauf** *m.* relay race

Staffage *f.* accessories

Staffel *f.* rung, step; (avi.) squadron; (mil.) echelon, detachment; (sport) relay; **—ei** *f.* easel; **—lauf** *m.* relay race; **—tarif** *m.* sliding tariff; graduated wage scale

Stahl *m.* steel; **—feder** *f.* steel spring; steel pen; **—helm** *m.* steel helmet; **—kammer** *f.* strong-room; **—panzer** *m.* steel armor; **—stich** *m.* steel engraving; **—waren** *f. pl.* hardware, cutlery; **—werk** *neu.* steelworks

stählen *v.* to (convert into) steel; to harden

stählern *adj.* made of steel; steely, hard

Staken *m.* stake, pile, pole

Staket *neu.* palisade, fence, stockade

Stall *m.* stable, stall; (pig)sty; kennel, shed; **–dienst** *m.* stable work; **–geld** *neu.* stable fee; **–knecht** *m.* groom, hostler; **–magd** *f.* dairy maid; **–meister** *m.* riding master, equerry; **–ung** *f.* stables; stabling

Stamm *m.* stem, trunk, stalk; family, race, tribe, clan; breed; main part; stock; **–aktie** *f.* original share; **–baum** *m.* pedigree; **–buch** *neu.* genealogical register; album; **–eltern** *pl.* ancestors; first parents; **–folge** *f.* lineage; **–gast** *m.* regular guest; **–halter** *m.* eldest son; son and heir; **–holz** *neu.* standing timber; **–kapital** *neu.* original capital; **–kneipe** *f.*, **–lokal** *neu.* favorite pub; **–rolle** *f.* muster roll; **–sitz** *m.* ancestral estate; **–tafel** *f.* genealogical table; **–vater** *m.* ancestor; **–wort** *neu.* root word, stem

stammeln *v.* to stammer, to stutter

stammen *v.* to descend, to originate, to derive; to come (*oder* spring) from

stämmig *v.* sturdy, strong, robust, vigorous

Stammler *m.* stammerer, stutterer

stammverwandt *adj.* cognate, kindred, akin

stampfen *v.* to stamp, to pound, to ram, to crush; to trudge, to paw; (naut.) to pitch

Stampfkartoffeln *f. pl.* mashed potatoes

Stand *m.* stand(ing); position; stall, booth; condition, situation; state; profession; rank, class; **einen schweren — haben** to have a hard fight; **–bild** *neu.* statue; **–er** *m.* (mil.) pennant; **–esamt** *neu.* registrar's office; **–esbeamte** *m.* registrar; **–esehre** *f.* professional honor; **–esgenosse** *m.* equal in rank; **–esregister** *neu.* vital statistics; **–esvorurteil** *neu.* class prejudice; **–esperson** *f.* person of rank; **–geld** *neu.* booth fee; **–gericht** *neu.* court martial; **–licht** *neu.* parking lights; **–ort** *m.*, **–platz** *m.* site, station, position; garrison; **–punkt** *m.* point of view; stand; **–quartier** *neu.* permanent quarters; **–recht** *neu.* martial law; **–rede** *f.* harangue; **–uhr** *f.* pendulum clock

stand: –esgemäss *adv.*, **–esmässig** *adv.* in accordance with one's rank; **–haft** *adj.* steady, constant, firm; steadfast; **–halten** *v.* to hold out, to resist, to withstand; **–rechtlich** *adj.* according to martial law

Standarte *f.* standard, ensign

Ständchen *neu.* serenade

Ständer *m.* stand, post, pillar

ständig *adj.* permanent, constant; **— *adv.*** continuously

Stange *f.* pole, rod, perch, bar, **stake; bei der — bleiben** to persevere; **eine — Geld** a lot of money; **jemand die — halten** to back someone; **von der — ready-made**; **–nbohne** *f.* pole bean; **–spargel** *m.* asparagus served whole

Stänker *m.* stinker, quarrelsome fellow; **–erei** *f.* brawl, quarrel, squabble, slander

Staniol *neu.* tinfoil; **–streifen** (Radarstörung) *m.* (avi.) window; chaff

Stanze *f.* punch, stamp, die; (lit.) stanza

Stapel *m.* pile, heap; (naut.) slips, stocks; depot; dump; **vom — lassen** to launch; **vom — laufen** to be launched; **–lauf** *m.* launch(ing); **–platz** *m.* depot, dump

stapeln *v.* to pile up, to stack up

Star *m.* starling; (med.) cataract; (movie) star; **den — stechen** to remove a cataract; (fig.) to open someone's eyes

stark *adj.* strong, sturdy, intense; corpulent, stout; violent; considerable, numerous; voluminous; **— auftragen** to exaggerate; **–e Erkältung** severe cold; **–er Esser** hearty eater; **–e Seite** (fig.) strong point; **— *adv.*** very, much, hard

Stärke *f.* strength, force, power; intensity; largeness; violence; thickness; number, quantity; forte, strong point; starch; **–grad** *m.* degree of strength, intensity; **–mehl** *neu.* cornstarch; **–zucker** *m.* glucose

stärke: –haltig *adj.* containing starch, starchy; **–en** *v.* to strengthen, to invigorate; to starch; **sich –en** to take refreshments; **–end** *adj.* restorative, strengthening; tonic

Starkstrom *m.* (elec.) high tension; **–leitung** *f.* power line, power circuit

Stärkungsmittel *neu.* restorative

starr *adj.* stiff, rigid; staring; unbending; **— vor Entsetzen** terror-stricken; **— vor Erstaunen** (*or* **Überraschung**) flabbergasted, thunderstruck; **–en** *v.* to stare; to gape; **–köpfig** *adj.* headstrong, obstinate

Starr: –heit *f.* stiffness, rigidity; inflexibility; **–krampf** *m.* tetanus

Start *m.* start; take-off; **–bahn** *f.* (avi.) runway; **–er** *m.* starter; **–ordnung** *f.* starting order; **–rakete** *f.* booster rocket; **–zählung** *f.* countdown

starten *v.* to start; (avi.) to take off

startklar *adj.* (avi.) ready for the take off

Statik *f.* statics

Station *f.* station; stop; (hospital) ward; **freie —** free board and lodging; **–svors-**

teher *m.* stationmaster

stationieren *v.* to station

Statist *m.* (film, theat.) extra, supernumerary; **–ik** *f.* statistics; **–iker** *m.* statistician

statistisch *adj.* statistic(al)

Stativ *neu.* stand, support; tripod

Statt *f.* place, stead; **an Eides —** in lieu of an oath; **an Kindes —** annehmen to adopt a child; **–halter** *m.* governor

statt *prep.* and *conj.* instead of, in lieu of; **— meiner** in my place; **–finden, –haben** *v.* to take place, to happen; **–geben** *v.* to permit, to grant; **–haft** *adj.* admissible, allowable; legal; **–lich** *adj.* stately; imposing; considerable; grand

Stätte *f.* place, room

Statue *f.* statue

statuieren *v.* to establish; **ein Exempel —** to make an example of; to set up as a warning

Statur *f.* stature; figure, height; size

Status *m.* state of affairs

Statut *neu.* statute, regulations

Staub *m.* dust; powder; pollen; **in den —** ziehen to drag through the mire; **sich aus dem — machen** to escape, to abscond; **viel — aufwirbeln** to cause a stir; **–beutel** *m.* (bot.) anther; **–blatt** *neu.*, **–gefäss** *neu.* (bot.) stamen; **–faden** *m.* (bot.) stamen, filament; **–fleck** *m.* dust speck; **–geborene** *m.* (bibl.) mortal man; **–kamm** *m.* fine-tooth comb; **–korn** *neu.* dust particle; **–lappen** *m.*, **–tuch** *neu.* dustcloth; **–mantel** *m.* dust coat; **–sauger** *m.* vacuum cleaner; **–wedel** *m.* feather duster; **–zucker** *m.* powdered sugar

stäuben *v.* to dust; to raise dust; to spray

staubig *adj.* dusty, powdery

Staude *f.* shrub, bush, tall plant

stauen *f.* to stow (goods); to dam (water); **sich —** to block; to bank up; to rise

staunen *v.* to be astonished, to be amazed; to marvel; **–enswert** *adj.* astonishing, amazing

Stearinkerze *f.* tallow (*oder* paraffin) candle

Stech: –apfel *m.* thorn, apple; **–becken** *neu.* bedpan; **–eisen** *neu.* punch; piercer; **–er** *m.* engraver; (gun) hair trigger; **–fliege** *f.* gadfly; **–ginster** *m.* juniper; **–mücke** *f.* gnat; **–palme** *f.* holly, ilex; **–schritt** *m.* goose step

stechen *v.* to prick; to sting; to pierce; to stab; (flea) to bite; to engrave; to cut; (cards) to trump; to tap (smelting furnace); (sun) to burn; to stick (pig); **durch und durch —** to transfix; **ihn sticht der Hafer** he is in high spirits;

in die Augen — to take one's fancy; **in See —** to put to sea

Steck: –brief *m.* warrant of arrest; **–dose** *f.* (elec.) wall plug; **–en** *m.* stick, staff; **–enpferd** *neu.* fad, hobby; **–er** *m.* (elec.) plug; **–kissen** *neu.* cushion for carrying a baby; **–kontakt** *m.* (elec.) plug; **–ling** *m.* (bot.) cutting; seedling; **–nadel** *f.* pin; **–rübe** *f.* turnip; **–schlüssel** *m.* box wrench

stecken *v.* to stick; to put, to set, to plant; to fix; to pin up; to be attached, to be stuck; to be hidden; to be involved; **Geld in ein Geschäft —** to invest money in a business; **im Elend —** to be in great misery; **in Brand —** to set on fire; **jemand in den Sack —** to outdo someone; **unter einer Decke —** to have a secret understanding; to be an accomplice; **— bleiben** *v.* to be stuck; to break down; **— lassen** to leave (key in door, etc.)

Stefan *m.* Stephen

Steg *m.* path; footbridge; (mus.) bridge; (trouser) strap; (typ.) stick; **–reif** *m.* extempore; **aus dem –reif sprechen** to extemporize

Steh: –bierhalle *f.* tavern; **–kragen** *m.* stand-up collar; **–lampe** *f.* floor lamp, **–leiter** *f.* stepladder; **–platz** *m.* standing place

stehen *v.* to stand; to stop; to be erect; to be; to suit, to become; (dog) to point; **an der Spitze —** to be at the head; **es steht bei Dir** its up to you; **für jemand gut —** to vouch for someone; **geschrieben —** to be written; **mir steht der Verstand still** I am at my wit's end; **Modell —** to serve as a model; **unter Waffen —** to be under arms; **wie steht's mit dir?** what about you? **zu Diensten —** to be at one's service; **— bleiben** to stop; **–d** *adj.* standing; allein **–d** isolated; lonely; **–den Fusses** on the spot; **–des Kapital** fixed capital; **–des Wasser** stagnant water; **— lassen** to let alone, to leave

stehlen *v.* to steal, to rob, to pilfer; **dem lieben Gott die Zeit —** to idle away one's time; **sich davon —** to sneak away

steif *adj.* stiff, rigid; benumbed; formal; **halt die Ohren —!** be brave! **— und fest behaupten** to assert obstinately; **–en** *v.* to stiffen

steigen *v.* to climb, to ascend; to mount; to increase; **herunter —** to descend; **ins Bett —** to go to bed; **— lassen** to fly (a kite)

steigern *v.* to raise, to increase; to heighten; to intensify; (auction) to bid;

(gram.) to compare

steil *adj.* steep, precipitous

Stein *m.* stone, rock; monument; gravestone; kernel; gem; (checkers) piece; **einen — im Brett haben** to be in favor with someone; **es fiel mir ein — vom Herzen** that's a load off my mind; — **des Anstosses** stumbling block; — **und Bein frieren** to freeze hard; — **und Bein schwören** to swear on a stack of bibles; **über Stock und — laufen** to run at full speed; **–adler** *m.* golden eagle; **–block** *m.* boulder; **–brecher** *m.* quarryman; stone crusher; **–bruch** *m.* quarry; **–damm** *m.* pier, mole; paved road; **–druck** *m.* lithography; **–eiche** *f.* holm oak; **–garten** *m.* rock garden; **–geröll(e)** *neu.* rubble, shingle; **–gut** *neu.* earthenware, crockery; **–hauer** *m.*, **–metz** *m.* stone mason; **–kohle** *f.* (pit)coal; **–pflaster** *neu.* stone pavement; **–pilz** *m.* edible mushroom; **–salz** *neu.* rock salt; **–schleifer** *m.* stone polisher; **–schneider** *m.* lapidary; **–setzer** *m.* paver; **–wand** *f.* stone wall; **–wurf** *m.* stone's throw; **–zeit** *f.* Stone Age

stein: –alt *adj.* as old as the hills; **–ern** *adj.*, **–ig** *adj.* rocky, stony; **–igen** *v.* to stone; **–reich** *adj.* full of stones; immensely rich

Steiss *m.* buttocks; rump; **–bein** *neu.* coccyx

Stell: –age *f.* stand; shelf; **–dichein** *neu.* rendezvous; tryst; **–e** *f.* place, spot, stand; position, situation; (book) passage; **an jemandes –e treten** to replace someone; **an Ort und –e sein** to be in place; **an –e von** instead of; **auf der –e** immediately; **offene –e** vacancy; **von der –e kommen** to make progress; **zur –e schaffen** to deliver; **zur –e sein** to be present; **–enjäger** *m.* job hunter; **–ennachweis** *m.*, **–envermittlung** *f.* employment agency; **–macher** *m.* cartwright, wheelwright; **–motor** *m.* servomotor; **–ung** *f.* position; posture; attitude; situation; (mil.) line; **seine –ung nehmen** to express one's opinion; **–ungnahme** *f.* comment; **–ungsgesuch** *neu.* application; **–vertreter** *m.* representative; deputy; substitute; proxy; **–wagen** *m.* omnibus for outings; **–werk** *neu.* signal box

stell: –bar *adj.* adjustable, movable; **–en** *v.* to put, to place; to set; to regulate; to furnish, to provide; to corner, to arrest; **auf sich selbst gestellt sein** to be independent; **einen Antrag –en** to propose; (pol.) to move; **einen Bürgen –en** to find bail; **gut gestellt sein** to be

well off; **in Frage –en** to question; **in Zweifel –en** to doubt; **nach dem Leben –en** to make an attempt on (someone's) life; **sich feindlich –en** to oppose; **sich –en** to (take a) stand; to feign, to pretend; to give oneself up; **sich –en auf** to cost; **sich –en zu** to behave towards; **vor Augen –en** to expose to view; **zur Diskussion –en** to invite a discussion upon; **zur Rede –en** to call to account; **zur Schau –en** to exhibit; **Zeugen –en** to produce witnesses; **–vertretend** *adj.* vicarious, supplementary; delegated

Stelz: –bein *neu.*, **–fuss** *m.* wooden leg; **–e** *f.* stilt; **–vogel** *m.* (orn.) wader

Stemmeisen *neu.* chisel

stemmen *v.* to prop, to support; to stem; to lift (weight); **sich — to** resist; to oppose

Stempel *m.* stamp; die, puncheon; postmark; brand; (bot.) pistil; (mech.) piston; **–gebühr** *f.* stamping fee; **–kissen** *neu.* ink pad; **–schneider** *m.* stamp cutter; die sinker

stempeln *v.* to stamp, to mark; **— gehen** to be on the dole

Stengel *m.* stalk, stem

Steno: –gramm *neu.* shorthand notes; **–graph** *m.* stenographer; **–graphie** *f.* stenography, shorthand; **–typist** *m.*, **–typistin** *f.* stenographer and typist

stenographieren *v.* to write (*oder* take down) shorthand

stenographisch *adj.* stenographic; shorthand

Stepp: –decke *f.* quilt; **–stich** *m.* backstitch

steppen *v.* to quilt

Sterbe: –bett *neu.*, **–lager** *neu.* deathbed; **–fall** *m.* death; **–hemd** *neu.* shroud; **–kasse** *f.* burial fund; **–liste** *f.* register of deaths; **–sakramente** *neu. pl.* last sacraments

sterben *v.* to die; **im — liegen** to be dying; **vor Langeweile — to** be bored to death; **–skrank** *adj.* fatally ill; **–smüde** *adj.* dead-tired

sterblich *adj.* mortal

Sterblichkeitsziffer *f.* death rate

Stereo: –metrie *f.* stereometry; **–skop** *neu.* stereoscope; **–typ** *m.* stereotype

stereotyp *adj.* stereotype(d)

steril *adj.* sterile; **–ilisieren** *v.* to sterilize

Stern *m.* star; (typ.) asterisk; **–bild** *neu.* constellation; **–deuter** *m.* astrologer; **–enbanner** *neu.* Star-Spangled Banner; **–kunde** *f.* astronomy; **–schnuppe** *f.* shooting star; **–warte** *f.* astronomical observatory

stet(ig) *adj.* steady, constant, continual

stets *adv.* always; constantly, continually

Steuer *neu.* helm, rudder; **–bord** *neu.* starboard; **–knüppel** *m.* (avi.) control stick; **–mann** *m.* helmsman; deck officer; **–mannskunst** *f.* art of navigation; **–rad** *neu.* steering wheel; **–ruder** *neu.* rudder, helm; **–ung** *f.* steering (gear); **–vorrichtung** *f.* steering apparatus (*oder* gear)

Steuer *f.* tax; **–amt** *neu.* revenue office; **–anschlag** *m.* assessment; **–beamte** *m.* revenue officer; **–einnehmer** *m.* tax collector; **–erklärung** *f.* income tax return; **–hinterziehung** *f.* tax fraud; **–politik** *f.* fiscal policy; **–satz** *m.* tax rate; **–zahler** *m* taxpayer; **–zuschlag** *m.* surtax

steuerfrei *adj.* tax-exempt

steuern *v.* to steer, to navigate, to drive; to pilot; **einer Sache —** to repress something; **— zu** to contribute to

steuerpflichtig *adj.* subject to taxation

Stich *m.* sting, bite, prick; stitch, puncture; stab; engraving; (cards) trick; (fencing) thrust; (mil.) hitch, knot; (spade) cut; (fig.) gibe, taunt; **einen — haben** to turn sour; (coll.) to have a screw loose; **im — lassen** to forsake, to desert; **— halten** to stand the test; **–blatt** *neu.* (sword) guard; trump card; **–el** *m.* engraving tool; graver; **–elei** *f.* (coll.) needlework; gibe, sneer, taunt; **–ler** *m.* taunter; giber, sneerer; **–ling** *m.* stickleback; **–probe** *f.* sample taken at random; **–tag** *m.* fixed day; **–waffe** *f.* pointed weapon; **–wahl** *f.* final ballot; **–wort** *neu.* catchword; cue; **–wortverzeichnis** *neu.* list of subjects; index; **–wunde** *f.* stab

stich: **–elhaarig** *adj.* wire-haired; **–eln** *v.* to stitch; to taunt, to gibe, to sneer; **–fest**, **–haltig** *adj.* standing the test; valid; sound, plausible

Stick: **–erei** *f.* embroidery; **–garn** *neu.* embroidery cotton; **–gaze** *f.* needle-point canvas; **–husten** *m.* hooping cough; **–luft** *f.* stuffy air; **–muster** *neu.* embroidery pattern; **–rahmen** *m.* embroidery hoop; **–stoff** *m.* nitrogen; **–zeug** *neu.* embroidery materials

stick: **–ig** *adj.* stuffy, close; suffocating; **–stoffhaltig** *adj.* nitrogenous

sticken *v.* to embroider

stieben *v.* to disperse, to scatter; to fly about; to spray; to give off (dust, etc.)

Stief: **–bruder** *m.* stepbrother; **–eltern** *pl.* stepparents; **–kind** *neu.* stepchild; **–mutter** *f.* stepmother; **–mütterchen** *neu.* pansy; **–sohn** *m.* stepson; **–vater** *m.* stepfather

Stiefel *m.* boot; **–anzieher** *m.* shoehorn; **–knecht** *m.* bootjack; **–putzer** *m.* boot-

black; **–schaft** *m.* (boot) leg; **–wichse** *f.* shoe polish

Stiege *f.* staircase, stairs; score (20)

Stieglitz *m.* goldfinch, thistle finch

Stiel *m.* handle, stick; stem, stalk; **mit Stumpf und —** with root and branch; **–stich** *m.* hemstitch

Stier *m.* bull; Taurus; **–kampf** *m.* bullfight; **–kämpfer** *m.* bullfighter, matador

Stift *m.* peg, pin; pencil, crayon; (coll.) apprentice; **—** *neu.* charitable foundation; convent, chapter; **–er** *m.* founder; donor; **–sherr** *m.* canon, prebendary; **–shütte** *f.* (bibl.) Tabernacle; **–skirche** *f.* collegiate church; **–ungsfest** *neu.* founder's (*oder* commemoration) day

stiften *v.* to found, to establish; to donate

stigmatisieren *v.* to stigmatize

Stil *m.* style; manner, usage, kind; **–blüte** *f.* pun; **–istik** *f.* style of composition

still *adj.* still; silent, quiet; calm; motionless; tacïturn, peaceful; **–e Messe** Low Mass; **–e Neigung** unexpressed love; **–e Woche** Holy Week; **–e Zeit** (com.) dull season; **–er Gesellschafter** (com.) silent partner; **–er Vorbehalt** mental reservation; **–bleiben** *v.* to keep quiet; **–(l)egen** *v.* to shut down; **–en** *v.* to calm; to stanch; to quench; to appease; to nurse, to suckle; **–halten** *v.* to keep still, to stop; **–(l)iegen** *v.* to lie quietly; to stand still; **–schweigen** *v.* to be silent; **–schweigen** *v.* to take no notice (of); **–schweigend** *adj.* silent; tacit, implied; **–sitzen** *v.* to sit quietly; **nicht –sitzen können** to be fidgety; **–stehen** *v.* to stand still, to stop; **stillgestanden!** (mil.) attention! **–stehend** *adj.* stationary, stagnant; **–vergnügt** *adj.* quietly enjoying, inwardly serene

Still: **–e** *f.* silence; calmness; peace; **in aller –e** in secret, privately; silently; **–eben** *neu.* (art.) still life; **–(l)egung** *f.* shutdown; **–schweigen** *neu.* silence; **–stand** *m.* standstill, stoppage; deadlock; (wirtschaftlich) *m.* recession

der Stille Ozean *m.* the Pacific Ocean

Stimm: **–abgabe** *f.* voting, vote; **–band** *neu.* vocal cord; **–bruch** *m.* breaking of the voice; **–e** *f.* voice; vote; comment; (mus.) part; **gut bei –e sein** to be in good voice; **–enfang** *m.* canvassing; **–engleichheit** *f.* voting parity; **–enmehrheit** *f.* majority of votes; **–enminderheit** *f.* minority of votes; **–er** *m.* tuner; **–gabel** *f.* tuning fork; **–lage** *f.* register, pitch; **–recht** *neu.* suffrage; **–umfang** *m.* range of a voice; **–ung** *f.* tuning; pitch, key; frame of mind; mood; atmosphere; impression; **–ung**

machen to canvass, to cheer up; **-ungs-mensch** m. moody person; **-vieh** neu. (coll.) mass of voters; henchmen; **-wechsel** m. breaking of the voice; **-zettel** m. ballot

stimm: -berechtigt adj. entitled to vote; **-en** v. to tune; to vote; to prejudice; to put in a good (oder bad) humor; to suit; to be correct, to correspond (to); **-haft** adj. voiced; **-los** adj. voiceless

stink: -en v. to stink; **-end** adj., **-ig** adj. stinking; rancid; **-faul** adj. very lazy

Stinkbombe f. stinkpot, stink bomb

Stinktier neu. skunk

Stipendiat m. holder of a scholarship

Stipendium neu. scholarship

stippen v. to dip, to steep

Stirn f. forehead; (fig.) impudence; face; **die — bieten** to defy; to face; **-binde** f. headband; **-locke** f. forelock; **-riemen** m. (horse) frontlet; **-runzeln** neu. frowning; **-seite** f. front

stöbern v. to hunt; to rummage; to drift

stochern v. to poke, to stir; **in den Zähnen — to pick one's teeth**

Stock m. stick, staff, cane; rod; stem; trunk; floor, story; (bee) hive; (mus.) baton; (printing) block; **über — und Stein** up hill and down dale; **-engländer** m. typical Englishman; **-fisch** m. dried cod; (fig.) blockhead; **-fleck** m. mildew; **-haus** neu. (dial.) jail; **-makler** m. stockbroker; **-rose** f. hollyhock; **-werk** neu. floor, story

stock: -blind adj. stone-blind; **-dumm** adj. utterly stupid; **-en** v. to stop, to stagnate; to pause, to hesitate; to falter, to flag; to coagulate; to curdle, to turn mouldy; **-finster** adj. pitch-dark; **-ig** adj. decayed; **-steif** adj. stiff as a poker; **-taub** adj. stone-deaf

Stoff m. stuff, material; matter, substance; subject; fabric; **-wechsel** m. metabolism

stöhnen v. to groan, to moan

Stoiker m. stoic

stoisch adj. stoic(al)

Stola f. stole

Stolle f., **-n** m. loaf-shaped Christmas cake; **-n** m. post; deep dugout; (min.) gallery

stolpern v. to stumble, to trip; to blunder

stolz adj. proud; haughty; arrogant; majestic; **-ieren** v. to strut, to stalk, to flaunt

Stolz m. pride, haughtiness, arrogance

Stopf: -en m. (dial.) cork, stopper; **-er** m. stuffer; darner; **-garn** neu. darning cotton; **-mittel** neu. astringent; **-nadel** f. darning needle

stopfen v. to stuff, to cram; to plug, to stop up; to darn; **jemand den Mund — to silence someone; -d** adj. constipating; astringent

Stopp: -licht neu. stop light; **-uhr** f. stop watch

Stoppel f. stubble

stoppeln v. to glean; to patch

stoppen v. to stop, to interrupt

Stör m. sturgeon

Stör: -enfried m. intruder; mischief-maker; marplot; **-ung** f. disturbance; (rad.) jamming, statics; **geistige -ung** mental disorder

Storch m. stork; **-schnabel** m. stork's bill; cranesbill; pantograph

stören v. to disturb; to trouble; to intrude; (rad.) to jam, to interfere

störr: -ig adj., **-isch** adj. intractable; headstrong; restive

Stoss m. push, thrust; blow, knock; punch; kick; jolt; recoil, shock; stroke; impact; heap, pile; **-dämpfer** m. shock absorber, bumper; **-degen** m. foil, rapier; **-kraft** f. impetus; impact; **-kurs (Rakete)** m. collision course; **-seufzer** m. deep sigh; **-stange** f. bumper, push rod; **-truppen** f. pl. shock troops; **-verkehr** m. rush-hour traffic; **-welle** f. shock wave; **-zahn** m. tusk

stossen v. to push, to shove, to bump; to thrust; to kick; to nudge; to pound, to crush; to punch, to knock, to strike; **auf Hindernisse — to encounter obstacles; in die Trompete — to sound the trumpet; sich an etwas — to be shocked by something; — an to knock against; to border on; — aus to expel; über den Haufen — to overthrow; von Land — to put to sea; von sich — to cast off, to repudiate; vor den Kopf — to affront; to offend; zu jemand — to join someone**

stottern v. to stutter, to stammer

stracks adv. directly, straight ahead

Straf: -anstalt f. penitentiary; **-e** f. punishment; fine; penalty; **bei -e von on penalty of; eine -e absitzen to serve time (in prison); -erlass** m. (law) pardon; amnesty; **-fälligkeit** f. culpability; **-gefangene** m. convict; **-gericht** neu. criminal court; (bibl.) judgment; **-gesetz** neu. penal law; **-losigkeit** f. impunity; **-mandat** neu. penalty; **-porto** neu. postage fine; **-prozess** m., criminal case; **-recht** neu. criminal law; **-rechtswissenschaft** f. penology; **-richter** m. criminal judge; **-verfahren** neu. criminal procedure; **-vollzug** m. execution of a sentence

straf: **-bar** *adj.* criminal; punishable, culpable; **-en** *v.* to punish, to chastise; to fine; **-ender** Blick reproachful look; **-fällig** *adj.* punishable; **-frei** *adj.*, **-los** *adj.* exempt from punishment; unpunished; **-mündig** *adj.* of responsible age; **-rechtlich** *adj.* criminal, penal; **-würdig** *adj.* deserving punishment

straff *adj.* tight, stretched; taut; rigid; strict; **-en** *v.* to tighten, to stretch

sträflich *adj.* punishable; unpardonable

Sträfling *m.* convict, prisoner

Strahl *m.* beam, ray; jet; flash; (geom.) radius; **-enbrechung** *f.* refraction; **-enkranz** *m.*, **-enkrone** *f.* halo; aureole; nimbus; **-enlehre** *f.* radiology; **-ung** *f.* radiation

strahl: **-en** *v.* to beam, to radiate; **-enbrechend** *adj.* refractive; **-end** *adj.* radiant; **-ig** *adj.* radial, radiating

Strähne *f.* strand (of hair); skein (of yarn)

stramm *adj.* stretched, tight, taut; robust; strapping; **— stehen** (mil.) to stand at attention

strampeln *v.* to fidget, to struggle; **sich bloss —** to kick the bedclothes off

Strand *m.* beach, strand; seashore; **auf — laufen** to strand; **-bad** *neu.* seaside resort; **-gut** *neu.* flotsam, jetsam; **-hafer** *m.* (bot.) bent grass; **-hütte** *f.* cabana; **-korb** *m.* beach chair; **-läufer** *m.* sandpiper; **-räuber** *m.* wrecker; **-recht** *neu.* right of salvage; **-schuhe** *m. pl.* beach slippers; **-wächter** *m.* coast guardsman

stranden *v.* to strand, to run ashore

Strang *m.* rope, cord, trace; strand (of hair); skein (of yarn); (rail.) track; **am gleichen — ziehen** to act in unison; **über die Stränge schlagen** to kick over the traces; **wenn alle Stränge reissen** if worst comes to worst; **zum — verurteilen** to condemn to the gallows

strangulieren *v.* to strangle

Strapaze *f.* exertion, strain, hardship

strapazieren *v.* to overexert, to strain; to wear out

Strasse *f.* street; highway, road; strait(s); **an der —** by the wayside; **jemand auf die — setzen** to turn someone out; **-narbeiter** *m.* roadman; **-nbahn** *f.* streetcar; **-nbau** *m.* road construction; **-ndamm** *m.* roadway; **-ndirne** *f.* streetwalker; **-nfeger** *m.*, **-nkehrer** *m.* street cleaner; **-nhändler** *m.* street vendor; **-njunge** *m.* street arab; **-nlaterne** *f.* street lamp; **-nräuber** *m.* highwayman; **-nrennen** *neu.* road race; **-nschild** *neu.* street sign; **-nüberführung** *f.* overpass;

Stratosphäre *f.* stratosphere; **-nflugzeug** *neu.* stratocruiser

sträuben *v.* to ruffle, to bristle; **das Haar sträubt sich** the hair stands on end; **sich — gegen** to struggle against; to resist

Strauch *m.* shrub, brush; **-dieb** *m.* footpad; **-werk** *neu.* shrubbery, brushwood

straucheln *v.* to stumble; (fig.) to sin, to err

Strauss *m.* ostrich; struggle, combat, fight; bouquet, bunch (of flowers)

streb: **-en** *v.* to strive, to aspire; to struggle (for); to endeavor; **zum Mittelpunkt -ende Kraft** centripetal force; **-erhaft** *adj.*, **-erisch** *adj.* ambitious; **-sam** *adj.* industrious, zealous

Strecke *f.* stretch; extent, tract; distance; (geom.) straight line; (hunt.) bag; (min.) gallery; (rail.) line; **zur — bringen** to shoot down, to bag; **-narbeiter** *m.* track worker; platelayer; **-nwärter** *m.* trackwalker

streck: **-bar** *adj.* extensible, ductile, malleable; **-en** *v.* to stretch, to extend; **to eke; die Waffen -en** to lay down arms, to surrender; **in gestrecktem Lauf** at full speed; **zu Boden -en** to knock down; **-enweise** *adv.* in some parts; here and there

Streich *m.* stroke, blow; prank, trick; **auf einen —** at one blow; **jemand einen — spielen** to play a trick on somebody; **-holz** *neu.*, **-hölzchen** *neu.* match; **-instrument** *neu.* (mus.) stringed instrument; **-quartett** *neu.* string quartet; **-riemen** *m.* razor strop

streicheln *v.* to caress, to stroke gently

streichen *v.* to stroke; to paint; to rush (past); to sweep (over); to stroll; to mitigate; to spread (butter); to strop; to strike (match); to lower (sails, flag); to play (violin); to cancel, to obliterate; **frisch gestrichen!** wet paint! **gestrichen voll** full to the brim; **vor jemand die Segel —** to submit to someone

Streif: **-e** *f.* patrol; raid; **-en** *m.* stripe, band; streak, strip; **-jagd** *f.* shooting expedition; **-kolonne** *f.*, **-kommando** *neu.* raiding party; **-licht** *neu.* side light; **-zug** *m.* expedition; scouting raid

streifen *v.* to stripe, to streak; to strip; to touch slightly; to graze, to scrape; to ramble, to roam; (mil.) *v.* to buzz; to strafe; **die Ärmel in die Höhe —** to turn up the sleeves

Streik *m.* strike; **in den — treten** to go on strike; **-brecher** *m.* strikebreaker; scab; **-kasse** *f.* strike fund; **-posten** *m.* picket

streiken *v.* to (be on) strike

Streit *m.* quarrel, fight; dispute, competition; **-axt** *f.* battle-ax; **-er** *m.* combatant, fighter; disputant; –fall *m.* controversy, quarrel; –frage *f.* matter in dispute; question at issue; –hammel *m.* (coll.) brawler, squabbler; –igkeit *f.* difference; quarrel; –kräfte *f. pl.* (mil.) forces; –punkt *m.* point of controversy; –sache *f.* controversial matter; –schrift *f.* polemical pamphlet

streit: –bar *adj.* pugnacious, warlike; valiant; –en *v.* to quarrel, to fight, to dispute; –ig *adj.* debatable; doubtful; –ig machen to contest; –lustig *adj.* pugnacious; –süchtig *adj.* contentious; quarrelsome

streng *adj.* severe, rigorous, stern, harsh; strict; austere; stringent; sharp; –er Arrest close confinement; –er Kritiker carping critic; –genommen *adv.* strictly speaking; –gläubig *adj.* orthodox

Strenge *f.* rigor, sternness, harshness; severity, austerity; strictness, sharpness

Streu *f.* litter; bed of straw; –büchse *f.*, –er *m.* shaker; dredger; –zucker *m.* powdered sugar

streuen *v.* to strew, to scatter; to spread; to litter

Strich *m.* dash, stroke, line; (compass) point; district, region, zone; (birds) flight; migration; (fabric) grain; auf den — gehen (coll.) to walk the streets; es geht mir gegen den — it goes against the grain; jemand auf den — haben (coll.) to bear a grudge against someone; nach — und Faden thoroughly; –einteilung *f.* graduation; –regen *m.* local shower

strichweise *adv.* locally; by zones; in flights

Strick *m.* cord, rope; (coll.) rascal; wenn alle –e reissen if worst comes to worst; –arbeit *f.*, –erei *f.* knitting; –leiter *f.* rope ladder; –nadel *f.* knitting needle

stricken *v.* to knit

Striegel *m.* currycomb

striegeln *v.* to currycomb; to handle roughly

Strieme *f.*, Striemen *m.* stripe, streak

striemig *adj.* covered with wales; streaked

strittig *adj.* debatable, disputed; doubtful

Stroboskop *neu.* stroboscope

Stroh *neu.* straw, thatch; leeres — dreschen to waste one's words; –dach *neu.* thatched roof; –halm *m.* blade of straw; –kopf *m.* simpleton; –mann *m.* scarecrow; dummy; –sack *m.* straw mattress; –witwe *f.* grass widow; –witwer *m.* grass widower

stroh: –farben *adj.*, –gelb *adj.* straw-colored; –ig *adj.* strawy

Strolch *m.* loafer, tramp, vagabond, bum

Strom *m.* stream; torrent; flow; current; –erzeuger *m.* dynamo; –kreis *m.* (elec.) circuit; –schnelle *f. pl.* rapids; –spannung *f.* voltage; –unterbrecher *m.* (elec.) circuit breaker, cutout; –zähler *m.* electricity meter

strom: –ab(wärts) *adv.* downstream; –auf(wärts) *adv.* upstream; –linienförmig *adj.* streamlined; –weise *adv.* in floods

strömen *v.* to stream, to flow, to gush, to pour; to flock, to crowd

Stromer *m.* tramp, loafer

Strömung *f.* current, flow, drift; tendency

Strontium *neu.* strontium

Strophe *f.* stanza, verse

strotzen *v.* to be puffed up; to exuberate; –d *adj.* crammed full; robust, vigorous; vor Gesundheit –d in the pink of health

Strudel *m.* whirlpool, eddy; rush; strudel

Strumpf *m.* stocking, hose; (gas) mantle; sich auf die Strümpfe machen to make off; –band *neu.* garter; –halter *m.* suspender; –waren *f. pl.* hosiery

struppig *adj.* bristle, shaggy; unkempt, rough

Stube *f.* room, apartment, chamber; gute — living room, parlor; –narrest *m.* confinement to one's room; –nfliege *f.* common fly; –ngelehrte *m.* (fig.) bookworm; –ngenosse *m.* roommate; –nhocker *m.* stay-at-home; –nluft *f.* close air; –nmädchen *neu.* housemaid, chambermaid; –nmaler *m.* house painter

stubenrein *adj.* housebroken (pets)

Stuck *m.* stucco; –decke *f.* stuccoed ceiling

Stück *neu.* piece, bit; fragment; lump; (cattle) head; passage; play; aus freien –en of one's own accord; ein starkes — a bit thick; grosse –e halten auf to think much of; in vielen –en in many respects; sich grosse –e einbilden to be very conceited; –arbeiter *m.* pieceworker; –enzucker *m.* lump sugar; –giesserei *f.* cannon foundry; –güter *neu. pl.* piece goods; –lohn *m.* piece-work rates; –werk *neu.* imperfect work, patchwork

stück: –eln *v.* to cut into pieces; to piece; –en to piece, to patch; –weise *adv.* in pieces, piece by piece

Student *m.* student, undergraduate; –enblume *f.* marigold; –enjahre *neu. pl.* college days; –enschaft *f.* student body

Studi: –e *f.* study, sketch, essay; –endirektor *m.* headmaster (high school); –engang *m.* course of study; –erstube *f.*, –o *neu.* study; –osus *m.* (coll.) student; **-um** *neu.* study, education

studieren *v.* to study, to go to college; **to** investigate, to do research on

Stufe *f.* step, stair, rung; shade, stage; degree; **auf gleicher — mit** on a level with; **-nfolge** *f.* gradation, succession; **-nleiter** *f.* scale, gradation

stufen *v.* to graduate, to scale; **-artig** *adj.* steplike; graduated; **-weise** *adv.* by degrees, gradually

Stuhl *m.* chair; seat; stool; pew; **der Heilige — the** Holy See; **jemand den — vor die Tür setzen** to turn someone out; **-bein** *neu.* leg of a chair; **-gang** *m.* evacuation of the bowels; **-lehne** *f.* chair back

Stulle *f.* (coll.) slice of bread and butter

stülpen *v.* to turn up; to clap (*oder* put) on

stumm *adj.* dumb, mute; mum, silent, speechless

Stummel *m.* stump, end; butt

Stumpen *m.* stump; (hat) rough body; Swiss cigar

Stümper *m.* blunderer, bungler; **-ei** *f.* bungling

stumpf *adj.* blunt; obtuse; dull; **-sinnig** *adj.* dull-witted, stupid

Stunde *f.* hour; lesson, period; **zur — at** the present moment, immediately; **-nbuch** *neu.* prayer book; **-ngeld** *neu.* fee for lessons; **-nglas** *neu.* hourglass; **-nlohn** *m.* hourly wage rate; **-nplan** *m.* schedule

stunden *v.* to grant a respite, to allow time; **-lang** *adj.* for hours; **-weise** *adv.* by the hour

stündlich *adj.* hourly; every hour

Stundung *f.* respite, short grace; delay in payment; **-sfrist** *f.* grace (for payment due)

Stupsnase *f.* snub nose; turned-up nose

Sturm *m.* storm; tempest; assault; fury, turmoil; **ein — im Wasserglas** a tempest in a teapot; **im — nehmen** to take by storm; **— laufen** to assault, to storm; **— läuten** to ring the alarm; **-bataillon** *neu.* shock battalion; **-glocke** *f.* alarm bell, tocsin; **-leiter** *f.* scaling ladder; **-riemen** *m.* chin strap; **-schritt** *m.* double quickstep; **-wind** *m.* hurricane, heavy gale; **-zentrum** *neu.* cell

stürmen *v.* to (take by) storm; to dash, to rush along; to rage; to be stormy

Stürmer *m.* stormer, assaulter; (sport) forward

stürmisch *adj.* stormy, tempestuous; (fig.) impetuous, turbulent; passionate

Sturz *m.* fall, tumble; plunge, crash; overthrow; ruin; **zum — bringen** to overthrow; **-acker** *m.* newly plowed field;

-bach *m.* torrent; **-flug** *m.* nose dive; **-helm** *m.* crash helmet; **-kampfflieger** *m.* dive bomber

stürzen *v.* to fall, to tumble, to plunge; to (over)throw; to rush, to dash; to stream; (avi.) to dive, to crash; **ins Verderben — to** ruin; **sich in Kosten — to** incur heavy expenses; **vom Thron — to** dethrone

Stuss *m.* (coll.) nonsense, foolish talk

Stute *f.* mare; **-nfüllen** *neu.* filly; foal

Stütz: -balken *m.* supporting beam, joist; **-e** *f.* prop, stay, support; help; **-mauer** *f.* buttress, retaining wall; **-pfeiler** *m.* pillar, support; (fig.) base; strong point; fulcrum

Stutz: -bart *m.* trimmed beard; **-en** *m.* short rifle, carbine; nozzle; **-er** *m.* dandy, fop; **-flügel** *m.* baby grand piano; **-ohr** *neu.* cropped ear; **-uhr** *f.* mantelpiece clock

stutz: -en *v.* to curtail, to crop, to dock, to trim, to lop; to clip; to be startled, to hesitate; to become suspicious; **-erhaft** *adj.* dandified, foppish; **-ig** *adj.* startled, taken aback; flabbergasted, perplexed

Sub: -jekt *neu.* subject; fellow; **-jektivität** *f.* subjectivity; **-limat** *neu.* sublimity; **-skribent** *m.* subscriber; **-stantiv** *neu.* substantive, noun; **-stanz** *f.* substance, matter; **-strat** *neu.* substratum; **-vention** *f.* subsidy

subtil *adj.* subtle, fine, delicate

Suche *f.* search, quest, tracking; **auf der — nach** in search for; **-er** *m.* seeker; spotlight; searchlight; (phot.) viewfinder

suchen *v.* to search, to look for; to seek; to try (to do); to be at a loss (for); **das Weite —** to run away; **hier haben Sie nichts zu —!** you have no business here!

Sucht *f.* mania, passion, rage; disease

süchtig *adj.* having a mania for; addicted to

Sud *m.* boiling, decoction; **-elei** *f.* dirty (*oder* slovenly) work; daubing; scribbling; **-ler** *m.* bungler; dauber; scribbler; quack

Süd, Süden *m.* south; **-früchte** *f. pl.* tropical fruits; **-länder** *m.* southerner

sudeln *v.* to bungle, to botch; to daub

südlich *adj.* southern; **— adv.** southerly **das Südliche Eismeer** *neu.* Antarctic Ocean

Südpol *m.* South Pole

süffig *adj.* tasty; delicious; pleasant **to** drink

suggerieren *v.* to suggest; to influence

Sühn: -e *f.*, **-ung** *f.* atonement; reconciliation; **–opfer** *neu.* expiatory sacrifice

sühnen *v.* to expiate, to atone for

Sulz *m.*, **Sülze** *f.* jelly; meat jelly; brawn

summarisch *adj.* summary

Summe *f.* sum, total; amount; **die —
ziehen** to sum up; **höchste —** maximum

summen *v.* to buzz, to hum; to tingle

Summer *m.* buzzer

summieren *v.* to add up; **sich — to** run up

Sumpf *m.* swamp, bog, marsh, fen; morass; (min.) sump; **einen — austrocknen** to drain a marsh; **–fieber** *neu.*
swamp fever; malaria; **–huhn** *neu.* coot;
(coll.) boozer; **–lache** *f.* slough; **–vögel**
m. pl. wading birds

sumpfig *adj.* boggy, swampy, marshy

Sund *m.* sound, strait(s)

Sünd: –e *f.* sin, trespass, misdeed; **–enbock** *m.* scapegoat; **–enfall** *m.* (bibl.)
fall of man; **–engeld** new. ill-gotten
money; enormous sum; **–entilgung** *f.*
propitiation; **–envergebung** *f.* absolution; **–er** *m.* sinner, transgressor; **armer
–er** culprit; poor wretch; **–flut** *f.* the
Deluge

sünd: –ig *adj.*, **–haft** *adj.* sinful, culpable;
–igen *v.* to sin, to transgress

superklug *adj.* overwise; too clever, pert

superlativisch *adj.* superlative

Suppe *f.* soup, broth; **die — auslöffeln
müssen** to have to take the rap;
jemand die — versalzen (coll.) to spoil
someone's pleasure; **–nkräuter** *neu. pl.*
potherbs; **–nlöffel** *m.* tablespoon;
–nschüssel *f.* soup tureen; **–nwürfel** *m.*
soup cube; **–nwürze** *f.* seasoning

suppig *adj.* soupy; souplike, liquid

Supremat *neu.* supremacy

surren *v.* to hum, to whir, to whiz, to buzz

Surrogat *neu.* substitute

suspendieren *v.* to suspend

süss *adj.* sweet; lovely; **–en** *v.* to sweeten;
–lich *adj.* sweetish; saccharine

Süss: –e *f.* sweetness; **–holz** *neu.* licorice;
–holz raspeln to spoon; to flirt; **–igkeit**
f. sweetness; suavity; **–igkeiten** *pl.*
sweets; **–(s)peise** *f.* dessert; **–(s)toff** *m.*
saccharine; **–wasser** *neu.* fresh water

Symbol *neu.* symbol; **–ik** *f.* symbolism

symbolisch *adj.* symbolic(al)

Symmetrie *f.* symmetry

symmetrisch *adj.* symmetric(al)

Sympathie *f.* sympathy; **–streik** *m.* sympathetic strike

sympathisch *adj.* sympathetic; congenial,
pleasant

Symphonie *f.* symphony

symptomatisch *adj.* symptomatic(al)

Synagoge *f.* synagogue

Syndik: –at *neu.* syndicate, cartel; **–us**
m. magistrate

Synode *f.* synod

synonym *adj.* synonymous

Synthese *f.* synthesis

synthetisch *adj.* synthetic(al)

Syphilis *f.* syphilis

syphilitisch *adj.* syphilitic

Syrien *neu.* Syria

Syringe *f.* lilac

systematisch *adj.* systematic

Szen: –arium *neu.* scenario; **–e** *f.* stage,
scene; **in –e setzen** (theat.) to rehearse,
to stage; **sich in –e setzen** to show off;
–erie *f.* scenery; landscape

Szepter *neu.* scepter

T

Tabak *m.* tobacco; **–bau** *m.* cultivation of
tobacco; **–sbeutel** *m.* tobacco pouch;
–sdose *f.* snuff box

tabellarisch *adj.* tabular, tabulated

Tabelle *f.* table; index; schedule

Tabernakel *neu.* tabernacle

Tablett *neu.* tray, salver; **–e** *f.* lozenge

tabu *adj.* taboo

Taburett *neu.* taboret, stool

Tachometer *m.* speedometer

Tadel *m.* reprimand, blame; fault; **ohne
—** blameless, faultless; **über allen —**
erhaben beyond reproach

tadel: –los *adj.* faultless, irreproachable;
–n *v.* to blame, to find fault with; to
reprimand; **–nswert** *adj.* blamable, objectionable; **–süchtig** *adj.* censorious,
faultfinding

Tafel *f.* table, tablet; blackboard, slate;
plate, slab; (chocolate) bar; dinner;
chart, index, diagram; **die — aufheben**
to rise from the table; **–aufsatz** *m.*
centerpiece; **–berg** *m.* plateau; **–besteck**
neu. knife, fork and spoon; **–butter** *f.*
best butter; **–geschirr** *neu.* dinner service; **–glas** *neu.* plate glass; **–musik** *f.*
dinner music; **–obst** *neu.* dessert (fruit);
–runde *f.* guests; round table; **–tuch**
neu. tablecloth; **–zeug** *neu.* table linen
and plateware

tafeln *v.* to dine, to banquet, to feast

täfeln *v.* to inlay, to wainscot, to panel

Taf(fe)t *m.* taffeta

Tag *m.* day; daylight; lifetime; **an den
bringen** to bring to light; **auf seine alten –e** in his old age; **dieser –e** one
of these days; **einen — um den anderen**
every other day; **er hat seinen guten —**
he is in a good mood; **es ist heller —**
it is broad daylight; **es wird — day is**
breaking; **in den — hineinleben** to live

from day to day; **–s darauf** the next day; **unter –e arbeiten** (min.) to work underground; **vor Jahr und — a long time ago**; **–ebau** m. strip mining; **–eblatt** neu. daily newspaper; **–ebuch** neu. diary; daybook; **–edieb** m. idler; **–egeld** neu. daily allowance; **–elöhner** m. day laborer; **–esanbruch** m. daybreak; **–esangabe** f. date; **–esbefehl** m. (mil.) order of the day; **–eskasse** f. (theat.) daytime box office; **–eskurs** m. (com.) daily quotation; **–esordnung** f. agenda; **–espresse** f. daily press; **–esstempel** m. date stamp; **–eszeitung** f. daily newspaper; **–ewerk** neu. day's work; **–schicht** f. day shift; **–undnachtgleiche** f. equinox; **–ung** f. meeting, session

tag: –elang adj. for days; **–en** v. to dawn; to meet, to sit, to confer; **–süber** adv. during the day; **–täglich** adj. daily, every day

täglich adj. daily; every day

Taifun m. typhoon

Taille f. waist, bodice; (cards) round

Takel neu. (naut.) tackle; **–age** f., **–ung** f., **–werk** neu. rigging

Takt m. tact; (mus.) measure, time; **den — angeben** (or schlagen) to beat time; **den — halten** to keep time; **–gefühl** neu. tactfulness; **–stock** m. (mus.) baton; **–strich** m. (mus.) bar

takt: –fest adj. keeping good time; sound; firm; **–ieren** v. (mus.) to beat time, to conduct; **–los** adj. tactless, indiscreet; **–mässig** adj. well-timed, rhythmical

Taktik f. tactics

taktisch adj. tactical

Tal neu. valley; dale, glen; **–fahrt** f. descent; trip downstream; **–kessel** m. basin; **–mulde** f., **–senke** f. depression of a valley; **–sohle** f. bed of a valley; **–sperre** f. dam

Talar m. judge's gown, robe

Talent neu. talent, ability

Talg m. tallow; suet; **–licht** neu., **–kerze** f. tallow candle

Talk m. talc(um); **–erde** f. magnesia

Tam: –bour m. drummer; **–bourmajor** m. drum major; **–burin** neu. tambourine; **–tam** neu. tom-tom; **–tam schlagen** to make a great fuss

Tand m. bauble, gew-gaw; trifle; toy

tändeln v. to dally, to trifle; to flirt

Tank m. tank; **–anlage** f. fuel tank; **–stelle** f. filling station; **–wagen** m. tank car; **–wart** m., **–wärter** m. gas station attendant

tanken v. to tank; (auto.) to fill up

Tann m. (poet.) pine forest; **–e** f. fir; **–en-**

zapfen m. fir cone

Tante f. aunt

Tanz m. dance; **das –bein schwingen** (coll.) to dance; **–bär** m. dancing bear; **–boden** m., **–saal** m. dance hall; ballroom; **–erei** f. dance, hop

tänzeln v. to trip, to mince; **to amble**

Tänzer m., **Tänzerin** f. dancer

Tapet neu. carpet; **etwas aufs — bringen** to broach a subject; **–e** f. wallpaper

tapezieren v. to (hang) wallpaper

Tapezierer m. paper hanger; upholsterer

ta–'er adj. brave, fearless, valiant

Tapisseriewaren f. pl. tapestry goods

tappen v. to walk heavily; to grope; **to fumble**

täppisch, tapsig adj. awkward, clumsy

Tarantel f. tarantula

Tarif m. tariff; (rail.) rates; list of charges; wage scale; **–lohn** m. standard wages; **–vertrag** m. wage agreement

tarnen v. to camouflage, to disguise, to screen

Tarnkappe f. magic hood

Tasche f. pocket; bag, pouch; purse; **jemand in die — stecken** (coll.) to be superior to someone; **–nausgabe** f. pocket edition; **–ndieb** m. pickpocket; **–nfeuerzeug** neu. pocket lighter; **–ngeld** neu. allowance; **–nkrebs** m. common crab; **–nlampe** f. flashlight; **–nspieler** m. juggler; **–ntuch** neu. handkerchief

Tasse f. cup (and saucer); **–nkopf** m. cup

Tast: –atur f. keyboard; **–e** f. (piano, typewriter) key; **–sinn** m. sense of touch, feeling; **–werkzeug** neu. organ of touch, feeler

tasten v. to touch, to feel; to grope; **to fumble**

Tat f. deed, act, action; **auf frischer — ertappen** to catch red-handed; **in der — indeed**; as a matter of fact; **–bestand** m. facts (of a case); **–einheit** f. (law) coincidence; **–kraft** f. energy; **–sache** f. fact

tat: –enlos adj. inactive, idle; **–kräftig** adj. energetic; **–sächlich** adj. factual, real; **–sächlich** adv. in fact

Tät: –er m. perpetrator, culprit; **–erschaft** f. guilt, perpetration; **–igkeit** f. activity, action; occupation; **–igkeitswort** neu. verb; **–lichkeit** f. (law) assault and battery

tät: –ig adj. active, busy, employed; **–igen** v. to do, to settle; **–lich** adj. violent; **–lich werden** to assault

Tatze f. paw; claw

Tau neu. cable, rope; **— m. dew**; **–werk** neu. cordage, rigging; **–wetter** neu. thaw; **–ziehen** neu. tug of war

'aub *adj.* deaf; dead; empty, hollow; numb; **-stumm** *adj.* deaf-mute

Taub: **-e** *f.* pigeon, dove; **-enschlag** *m.* dovecot; **-enzüchter** *m.* pigeon fancier; **-er** *m.*, **Täuberich** *m.* male pigeon; **-stumme** *m.* deaf-mute

Tauch: **-batterie** *f.* plunge battery; **-er** *m.* diver; **-erglocke** *f.* diving bell; **-erkolben** *m.* (mech.) plunger

tauchen *v.* to plunge; to dive, to submerge

tauen *v.* to thaw; to melt; (naut.) to tow

Tauf: **-becken** *neu.*, **-stein** *m.* baptismal font; **-buch** *neu.* parish register; **-e** *f.* baptism, christening; **aus der -e heben** to be godfather (*oder* godmother); to initiate, to originate; **-kapelle** *f.* baptistry; **-name** *m.* Christian (*oder* given) name; **-pate** *m.* godfather; **-schein** *m.* certificate of baptism

taufen *v.* to baptize, to christen; **Wein —** to water (*oder* adulterate) wine

Täufling *m.* child (*oder* person) to be baptized

taugen *v.* to be fit (*oder* good for); to be of use (*oder* value); **nichts —** to be worthless

Taugenichts *m.* good-for-nothing

tauglich *adj.* fit, good; adapted; useful, able

Taumel *m.* giddiness, ecstasy, frenzy

taumeln *v.* to reel, to stagger; to be giddy

Tausch *m.* exchange, barter; **-geschäft** *neu.*, **-handel** *m.* barter

tauschen *v.* to exchange, to barter

täuschen *v.* to deceive, to delude, to cheat; to trick; **sich —** to be mistaken; **-d** *adj.* delusive, illusory; **-de Ähnlichkeit** striking resemblance; **-d nachgemacht** copied perfectly

tausend *adj.* thousand; **-fach** *adj.*, **-fältig** *adj.* thousandfold; **-jährig** *adj.* millenial; **-mal** *adv.* a thousand times

Tausend *neu.* thousand; **vom —** per thousand; **-er** *m.* thousand; 1,000 banknote; **-künstler** *m.* jack-of-all-trades; conjurer; **-schön(chen)** *neu.* daisy; **-stel** *neu.* a thousandth

Tax: **-ameter** *m.* taximeter; **-ator** *m.* appraiser

Taxe *f.* valuation; tax, fee, charge, rate; taxicab

taxieren *v.* to evaluate, to assess; to tax

Technik *f.* technics; industry; technology; technique, skill; **-er** *m.* technician, engineer; **-um** *neu.* technical school

technisch *adj.* technical

Teckel *m.* dachshund

Tee *m.* tea; **-brett** *neu.* tea tray; **-kanne** *f.* teapot; **-kessel** *m.* teakettle; **-löffel** *m.* teaspoon; **-rose** *f.* tea rose; **-sieb**

neu. tea strainer; **-strauch** *m.* tea plant

Teer *m.* tar; **-farben** *f. pl.* aniline dyes; **-jacke** *f.* (coll.) sailor

teeren *v.* to tar

Teich *m.* pond; **-binse** *f.* bulrush; **-kolben** *m.* cattail; **-rose** *f.* water lily; **-wirtschaft** *f.* fish culture (in ponds)

Teig *m.* dough, paste; **-waren** *f. pl.* noodle products

teigig *adj.* doughy

Teil *m.* part; portion; share; party, side; **edle -e** vital parts; **ein grosser — a great deal; ich für mein —** so far as I am concerned; **sich seinen — denken** to have one's own ideas; **zum —** partly, to some extent; **-chen** *neu.* particle; **-er** *m.* divider; divisor; **-haber** *m.* partner, joint proprietor; participant; **-nahme** *f.* participation; interest, sympathy; **-nehmer** *m.* participant; subscriber; **-strecke** *f.* section; **-ung** *f.* division, partition; **-zahlung** *f.* part-payment, instalment

teil: **-bar** *adj.* divisible; **-en** *v.* to divide; to distribute; to share; **sich -en** to share in; to branch off; **geteilte Gefühle** mixed feelings; **geteilter Meinung sein** to be of different opinions; **-haben** *v.* to participate (*oder* share) in; **-nahmslos** *adj.* unconcerned; indifferent, apathetic; **-nehmen** *v.* to participate; to sympathize; **-s** *adv.* partly; **-weise** *adj.* partial; **-weise** *adv.* partly, to some extent

Teint *m.* complexion

Tele: **-fon** *neu.* telephone; **-fonanruf** *m.* telephone call; **-fonanschluss** *m.* telephone connection (*oder* extension); **-fonist** *m.*, **-fonistin** *f.* telephone operator; **-fonzelle** *f.* telephone booth; **-fonzentrale** *f.* telephone exchange; **-gramm** *neu.* telegram; **-graf** *m.* telegraph; **-grafie** *f.* telegraphy; **-grafist** *m.* telegrapher; **-skop** *neu.* telescope

tele: **-fonieren** *v.* to telephone; **-fonisch** *adj.* telephonic; **-grafieren** *v.* to telegraph; **-grafisch** *adj.* telegraphic(al); **-skopisch** *adj.* telescopic(al)

Teller *m.* plate; **-eisen** *neu.* double-jawed trap; **-mütze** *f.* flat cap; **-tuch** *neu.* dish towel

Temp: **-el** *m.* temple; **-elherr** *m.*, **-ler** *m.* Knight Templar; **-elraub** *m.*, **-elschändung** *f.* sacrilege

temper: **-amentslos** *adj.* spiritless; **-amentsvoll** *adj.* high-spirited, passionate; **-erieren** *v.* to temper; **to** moderate, to assuage

Tempera *f.* (art.) tempera, distemper

Temperatur *f.* temperature

Temperenzler *m.* teetotaler

Tempo *neu.* tempo; measure, time; pace; rate

Tendenz *f.* tendency; **–stück** *neu.* play with a purpose

tendenziös *adj.* tendentious, biased

Tenne *f.* threshing floor

Tennis *neu.* tennis; **–platz** *m.* tennis court; **–schläger** *m.* tennis racket

Tenor *m.* tenor; substance, topic

Teppich *m.* carpet, rug; **–kehrmaschine** *f.* carpet sweeper; **–nagel** *m.* tack

Termin *m.* term, time; fixed day; (law) summons; deadline; **–geschäft** *neu.* (com.) futures; **–grenze** *f.* deadline; **–ologie** *f.* terminology; **–us technicus** *m.* technical term

Terpentin *m.* and *neu.* turpentine

Terr: –ain *neu.* ground, terrain; **–asse** *f.* terrace; **–itorium** *neu.* territory

terrorisieren *v.* to terrorize

Tertia *f.* fourth class of an undergraduate college; **–ner** *m.* student of a Tertia

Testament *neu.* testament, will; **ohne —** **sterben** to die intestate; **–svollstrecker** *m.* executor

testamentarisch *adj.* testamentary; **—** *adv.* by will

teuer *adj.* costly, expensive; dear; beloved; cherished; **wie — ist es?** what does it cost?

Teu(e)rung *f.* dearth; scarcity; high cost of living; **–zuschlag** *m.* cost-of-living increase

Teufel *m.* devil; demon; fiend; **das weiss der — nobody** knows that; **den — an die Wand malen** talk of the devil and he will appear; **in –s Küche geraten** (*or* **kommen**) to get into an awful mess; **jemand zum —** **jagen** to send someone packing; **pfui —!** how disgusting! **zum — gehen** to go to rack and ruin; **zum — noch einmal!** the deuce! **–ei** *f.* deviltry; **–sbraten** *m.* (coll.) rake, scamp; **–sbrut** *f.* hellish crew

teuflisch *adj.* devilish, diabolical; inhuman

Text *m.* text; libretto; **aus dem — kommen** (fig.) to lose the thread; **jemand den — lesen** to reprimand someone; **–band** *neu.* teleprompter; **–buch** *neu.* text, libretto; **–ilien** *f. pl.* textiles

Theater *neu.* theater; stage; **–besuch** *m.* playgoing; **–besucher** *m.* playgoer; **–direktor** *m.* theater manager; **–kasse** *f.* box office; **–stück** *neu.* drama, play; **–vorstellung** *f.* theatrical performance; **–zettel** *m.* playbill; program

theatralisch *adj.* theatrical

Theke *f.* (restaurant) counter, bar

Thema *neu.* topic, subject, theme

Theo: –loge *m.* theologian; **–logie** *f.* theology; **–rie** *f.* theory; **–soph** *m.* theosophist; **–sophie** *f.* theosophy

theoretisch *adj.* theoretical

Theorie *f.* theory

Thermodynamik *f.* thermodynamics

Thermoionik *f.* thermionics

These *f.* thesis

Thron *m.* throne; **–besteigung** *f.* accession to the throne; **–folge** *f.* succession to the throne; **–himmel** *m.* canopy; **–rede** *f.* (sovereign's) address to the people

thronen *v.* to be enthroned; to reign

Thun(fisch) *m.* tunny, tuna

Thymian *m.* thyme

ticken *v.* to tick

tief *adj.* deep; low; far; dark; profound; innermost; utmost; **das lässt — blicken** that tells a tale; **–er stimmen** to lower the pitch; **zu — singen** to sing flat; **–gehend** *adj.* profound; (naut.) deep-drawing; **–greifend** *adj.* far-reaching, radical; **–gründig** *adj.* deep, profound; **–liegend** *adj.* low-lying, deep-seated; (eyes) sunken; **–schürfend** *adj.* thorough, profound; **–sinnig** *adj.* pensive; melancholy

Tief *neu.* depression; **–angriff** *m.* low-flying attack; **–bau** *m.* underground building (*oder* engineering); **–blick** *m.* penetration; **–druck** *m.* low pressure; copperplate printing; **–e** *f.* depth, profundity; **–ebene** *f.* lowland, plain; **–enboot** *neu.* bathyscaphe; **–enmessung** *f.* bathymetry; **–gang** *m.* (naut.) draft; **–schlag** *m.* hit below the belt, low blow

Tiegel *m.* saucepan; crucible

Tier *neu.* animal; beast; **ein grosses —** (coll.) a big shot; **–art** *f.* species of animal; **–arzneikunde** *f.* veterinary science; **–arzt** *m.* veterinarian; **–bändiger** *m.* tamer of wild animals; **–garten** *m.* zoological garden; **–kreis** *m.* zodiac; **–kunde** *f.* zoology; **–quälerei** *f.* cruelty to animals; **–reich** *neu.* animal kingdom; **–schutzverein** *m.* society for the prevention of cruelty to animals

tierärztlich *adj.* veterinary

tierisch *adj.* animal; bestial, brutal

Tiger *m.* tiger; **–in** *f.* tigress

tilgen *v.* to extinguish; to blot out; to annul; to amortize; (typ.) to delete

Tilgung *f.* cancellation; amortization; (typ.) deletion; redemption; **–sfond(s)** *m.* sinking fund

Tinktur *f.* tincture

Tinte *f.* ink; **in der — sitzen** (coll.) to be in the soup; **–nfass** *neu.* inkwell; **–nfisch**

m. cuttlefish; –nklecks *m.* ink blot; –nstift *m.* indelible pencil; –nwischer *m.* pen wiper

tippeln *v.* to tiptoe; to tramp, to hike

tippen *v.* to tap, to touch lightly; to type-(write); — auf to suspect; to set on

Tippfräulein *neu.*, **Tipse** *f.* (coll.) female typist

Tirol *neu.* Tyrol

Tisch *m.* table; board; meal; **am grünen** — at the conference table; **reinen** — **machen** to make a clean sweep; **unter den** — **fallen** not to come under consideration; **vor** — before a meal; **zu** — **bitten** (*or* **laden**) to invite to dinner; –dame *f.*, –herr *m.* dinner partner; –decke *f.*, –tuch *neu.* tablecloth; –gebet *neu.* grace at meals; –gesellschaft *f.* dinner party; –karte *f.* place card; –lade *f.* table drawer; –leindeckdich *neu.* magic table; –ler *m.* carpenter; –lerei *f.* carpentry, carpenter's shop; –platte *f.* table top; –rede *f.* after-dinner speech; toast; –rücken *neu.* table turning; –tennis *neu.* ping-pong; –zeit *f.* dinner time

Titan(e) *m.* Titan; — *neu.* titanium

Titel *m.* title; head(ing); claim; –bild *neu.* frontispiece; –blatt *neu.* title page; –halter *m.*, –verteidiger *m.* title holder

Titulatur *f.* titles

titulieren *v.* to title, to style, to call

Toast *m.* toast, health; toasted bread

toben *v.* to rage, to rave; to roar; to romp

Tobsucht *f.* frenzy, raving madness

Tochter *f.* daughter; –haus *neu.* (com.) branch; –kirche *f.* branch church; –land *neu.*, –staat *m.* colony; –sprache *f.* derivative language

Töchterschule *f.* girls' school; **Höhere** — girl's college

Tod *m.* death; decease; **auf den** — **liegen** to be mortally ill; **der weisse** — avalanche; death by freezing; **des –es sein** to be doomed; **Kampf auf Leben und** — mortal combat; –esangst *f.* agony; mortal fear; –esanzeige *f.* death notice; –esart *f.* manner of death; –esfall *m.* (case of) death; casualty; –esgefahr *f.* deadly peril; –eskampf *m.* death struggle, last agony; –eskandidat *m.* dying (*oder* doomed) person; –esstoss *m.* death blow; –esstrafe *f.* capital punishment; –estag *m.* anniversary of someone's death; –esurteil *neu.* death sentence; –feind *m.* mortal enemy; –sünde *f.* deadly sin

tod: –bringend *adj.* deadly, fatal; –krank *adj.* deathly sick, mortally ill; –müde *adj.* dead tired; –wund *adj.* mortally wounded

tödlich *adj.* deadly; fatal, mortal, murderous

Toilette *f.* dress; dressing table; toilet; — **machen** to dress; to spruce up; –ngarnitur *f.* toilet set; –npapier *neu.* toilet paper

Toleranz *f.* tolerance, toleration

toll *adj.* mad, raving; frantic; excessive; extravagant; –en *v.* to fool about; to frolic; to romp

Toll: –e *f.* (coll.) tuft; topknot; –haus *neu.* lunatic asylum; –häusler *m.* madman; –kirsche *f.* deadly nightshade, belladonna; –kopf *m.* madcap; –wut *f.* hydrophobia, rabies

Tolpatsch, **Tölpel** *m.* awkward (*oder* clumsy) person

Tomate *f.* tomato

Ton *m.* clay; tone, note; accent, stress; tint; fashion; –art *f.* (mus.) key; –bandgerät *neu.* tape recorder; –dichtung *f.* musical composition; –fall *m.* cadence; intonation, modulation; –fanatiker *m.* audiophile; –farbe *f.* timbre; –film *m.* sound film; –folge *f.* (mus.) scale; melody; –führung *f.* melody; –gefäss *neu.* earthen vessel; –höhe *f.* pitch; –ika *f.* (mus.) tonic; –kunst *f.* musical art; –künstler *m.* musician; –lage *f.* (mus.) range, pitch; –leiter *f.* (mus.) scale; gamut; –mass *neu.* metrical quantity; –papier *neu.* tinted paper; –setzer *m.* composer; –silbe *f.* accented syllable; –stufe *f.* pitch; –taube *f.* clay pigeon; –waren *f. pl.* pottery

tönen *v.* to (re)sound; to ring; to shade; to tint, to tone

tönern *adj.* of clay, earthen

Tonne *f.* tun, butt; barrel, cask; (naut.) ton (1,000 kilograms, 2,205 pounds); –ngehalt *m.* tannage; –ngewölbe *neu.* barrel vault

Tonsur *f.* tonsure

Topas *m.* topaz

Topf *m.* pot, crock, jar; **alles in einen** — **werfen** to treat all alike; –gucker *m.* meddlesome person; –lappen *m.* potholder

Töpfer *m.* potter; –ei *f.* potter's workshop (*oder* trade); –scheibe *f.* potter's wheel; –waren *f. pl.* crockery, pottery, earthenware

topp! *interj.* agreed! all right!

Tor *neu.* gate(way); (sports) goal; –hüter *m.* gatekeeper; porter; goalkeeper; –latte *f.*, –pfosten *m.* goal post; –schluss *m.* closing of the gates; **kurz vor** –esschluss just before the end; –schütze *m.* (sports) scorer; –stoss *m.*

goal kick; **–wart** m. goalkeeper

Tor m. fool, simpleton; **–heit** f. folly, silliness

Torf m. peat; **–moor** neu. peat bog

töricht adj. foolish, stupid, silly

Tornister m. knapsack, schoolbag; (mil.) pack

torpedieren v. to torpedo

Torpedo m. torpedo; **–bootzerstörer** m. (torpedo boat) destroyer

Torte f. fancy (oder layer) cake; tart; **–nbäcker** m. pastry cook; **–nheber** m. cake server

Tortur f. torture

tosen v. to rage, to roar

tot adj. dead; lifeless; desolate; dull; stagnant; (sports) out of play; **–e Hand** (law) mortmain; **–er Punkt** dead center; deadlock; **–es Fleisch** (med.) proud flesh; **–es Rennen** dead heat; **–enblass** adj., **–enbleich** adj. deathly pale; **–geboren** adj. stillborn; **–lachen** v., sich **–lachen** to split one's sides with laughter; **–schlagen** v. to kill; to waste (time); **–schweigen** v. to hush up; **–sicher** adj. cocksure; **–stellen** v., sich **–stellen** to feign death

Tot: **–e** m. dead person; corpse; **–enacker** m. cemetery; **–enamt** neu. burial service; **–enbahre** f. bier; **–enbett** neu. deathbed; **–enfeier** f. obsequies; **–engeläut(e)** neu. knell; **–engeleit** neu. funeral procession; **–engerippe** neu. skeleton; **–engräber** m. gravedigger; **–engruft** f. vault; **–enhemd** neu. shroud; **–enkopf** m. skull; **–enliste** f. death roll; casualty list; **–enmarsch** m. funeral march; **–enmaske** f. death mask; **–enmesse** f. mass for the dead, requiem; **–enschau** f. coroner's inquest; **–enschein** m. certificate of death; **–enstarre** f. rigor mortis; **–enstille** f. dead silence; **–entanz** m. dance macabre; **–enwagen** m. hearse; **–geburt** f. stillborn child; **–schlag** m. manslaughter; **–schläger** m. murderer; loaded cane

totalitär adj. totalitarian

das Tote Meer neu. the Dead Sea

töten v. to kill, to slay; to deaden; to mortify; sich — to commit suicide

Tour f. journey, trip; round; (dance) figure; (mech.) revolution, turn; **in einer** — without stopping; **–enrad** neu. roadster; **–enwagen** m. station wagon; **–enzahl** f. number of revolutions; **–enzähler** m. speed indicator; **–ist** m. tourist; **–nee** f. (theat.) tour(ing)

Trab m. trot; im — at a trot; on the run; jemand auf den — bringen (coll.) to make someone speed up; **–er** m. trotter;

–rennbahn f. trotting course

Trabant m. satellite

traben v. to trot; (coll.) to hurry

Tracht f. dress, costume; fashion; load; eine — Prügel a sound thrashing

trachten v. — nach to desire, to strive for; to seek after; to aspire to; **jemand nach dem Leben** — to make an attempt on someone's life

traditionell adj. traditional

Trag: **–bahre** f., **–e** f. litter, stretcher; **–balken** m. beam, girder; **–band** neu. brace, strap, suspender; **–fähigkeit** f. carrying capacity; (naut.) tonnage; (soil) productiveness; **–fläche** f. (avi.) wing; **–himmel** m. canopy; **–riemen** m. strap; **–sessel** m. sedan chair; **–weite** f. range; import(ance); consequence; **–zeit** f. (zool.) period of gestation

trag: **–bar** adj. portable; endurable; **–en** v. to carry, to bear; to wear; to support; to yield; to produce; to endure; to be pregnant; **bei sich –en** to have about one; **sich gut –en** to wear well; **sich –en mit** to plan, to work on; **Sorge –en um** to be anxious about; **–fähig** adj. capable of bearing

Träg: **–er** m. carrier, porter; holder, bearer, wearer; prop, support, girder; **–heit** f. slowness; **–heitsgesetz** neu. law of inertia; **–heitssteuerung** (Rakete) f. inertial guidance

träge adj. lazy, indolent; sluggish; inert

Tragik f. tragic art; calamity

tragisch adj. tragic(al); calamitous, sad

Tragöd: **–e** m. tragic actor; **–ie** f. tragedy; **–in** f. tragic actress

Train m. (mil.) train; army service corps; **–er** m. trainer; **–ing** neu. training; coaching; **–ingsanzug** m. training suit; **–kolonne** f. transport column

trainieren v. to train, to coach

Traktat m. and neu. treatise; tract; **treaty**

traktieren v. to treat, to entertain

Tramp: **–el** m. and neu. awkward (oder clumsy) person; **–tier** neu. dromedary; **–olin** m. and neu. trampoline; springboard

Tran m. train oil; (whale) blubber; **im** — **sein** (coll.) to be drunk (oder sleepy); **–chierbesteck** neu. carving set

tranchieren v. to carve, to cut up

Träne f. tear; **–ngas** neu. tear gas

tränen v. to run with tears; (eyes) to water

Trank m. drink, draught, beverage; potion

Tränke f. watering place; horse pond

tränken v. to give to drink; to water; to drench; to soak, to saturate, to impregnate

Trans: –**formator** m. (elec.) transformer; –**mission** f. transmission; –**missionsapparat** m. transmitter; –**missionswelle** f. connecting shaft; –**parent** neu. transparency; –**piration** f. perspiration; –**port** m. transportation, carriage, shipment; –**porteur** m. transporter, carrier; (geom.) protractor; –**portschiff** neu. troop ship, transport

trans: –**ferieren** v. to transfer; –**pirieren** v. to perspire; –**ponieren** v. transpose; –**portabel** adj. transportable, movable; –**portieren** v. to transport, to convey, to ship; –**zendent(al)** adj. transcendent(al), beyond conception

trappe(l)n v. to patter, to trot, to trip

trassieren v. to draw (a draft on)

Tratsch m. (coll.) gossip; tittle-tattle

Tratte f. (com.) draft

Trau: –**altar** m. marriage altar; –**handlung** f. marriage ceremony; –**rede** f. clergyman's address to the bridal pair; –**ring** m. wedding ring; –**schein** m. marriage certificate; –**ung** f. marriage ceremony; wedding; –**zeuge** m. witness to a wedding

Traube f. grape; bunch of grapes; cluster, raceme; –**nblut** neu. (poet.) wine; –**ngeländer** neu. vine trellis; –**nlese** f. vintage; –**nmost** m. grape juice, new wine, must; –**npresse** f. wine press; –**nzucker** m. grape sugar

trauen v. to trust, to confide; to marry

Trauer f. grief, sorrow; affliction; mourning; –**anzeige** f. announcement of a death; –**botschaft** f. sad news; –**fall** m. death; –**flor** m. crape; –**gefolge** neu., –**zug** m. funeral procession; –**gottesdienst** m. funeral service; –**haus** neu. house of mourning; –**marsch** m. funeral march; –**rand** m. black edge; –**schleier** m. mourning veil; –**spiel** neu. tragedy; –**weide** f. weeping willow; –**zeit** f. time of mourning

trauern v. to grieve; to be in mourning

Traufe f. gutter, eaves; **vom Regen in die —** from the frying pan into the fire

traulich adj. intimate, familiar; cozy, snug

Traum m. dream, fancy, illusion; **quälender —** nightmare; –**bild** neu., –**gesicht** neu. vision; –**deuter** m. interpreter of dreams; –**spiel** neu. phantasmagoria; –**welt** f. realm of dreams

träumen v. to dream, to daydream; to imagine

Träumer m. dreamer; –**erei** f. dreaming; daydream; fancy, reverie, musing

traumhaft adj. dreamlike, fairylike, unreal

traurig adj. sad, sorrowful, mournful; dreary

traut adj. beloved, dear; cozy, snug, homey

travestieren v. to travesty

Treber pl. husks of grapes; brewer's grains

Trecker m. tractor

Treff neu. (cards) club(s); (coll.) meeting place; –**en** neu. meeting, encounter; battle; –**er** m. hit; prize, winning ticket; luck; –**punkt** m. rendezvous; (mil.) point of impact

treff: –**en** v. to hit, to strike; to affect; to find, to meet, to encounter; to join; to befall, to concern; to take (measures); to make (preparations); (art and phot.) to achieve likeness; **das Los traf ihn** the lot fell on him; **das trifft sich gut** that's lucky; **empfindlich —** (fig.) to cut to the quick; **sich getroffen fühlen** to feel hurt; –**end** adj. wellaimed, striking; appropriate; –**lich** adj. excellent, exquisite; –**sicher** adj. accurate, sure of one's aim

Treib: –**eis** neu. drift ice; –**er** m. driver, drover, beater; –**haus** neu. hothouse, conservatory; –**holz** neu. driftwood; –**jagd** f. battue; –**riemen** m. drivebelt; –**sand** m. quicksand; –**stoff** m. fuel, propellant

treiben v. to drive, to propel; to float, to drift; (bot.) to germinate; to chase (metal); to impel, to urge; to expel; to pursue; to practice; to study, to cultivate; **etwas auf die Spitze —** to push something to extremes; **in die Ecke —** to corner; **jemand aus dem Haus —** to eject somebody; **vor sich her —** (sports) to dribble; **Wild —** to beat up game

trennbar adj. separable, divisible

trennen v. to separate, to sever; to interrupt, to disconnect; to divide; to undo, to rip (seam); **sich —** to part, to separate; to branch off

Trennung f. separation, severance; dissolution; division; –**slinie** f. demarcation line; (mil.) formation boundary; –**sstrich** m. hyphen

trepp: –**ab** adv. downstairs; –**auf** adv. upstairs; –**enförmig** adj. rising like steps

Treppe f. staircase, stairs; **eine — hoch wohnen** to live on the second floor; –**nabsatz** m. landing; –**ngeländer** neu. banisters; railing; –**nhaus** neu. well of a staircase; –**nläufer** m. stair carpet; –**witz** m. afterwit; bad joke

Tresse f. lace; (mil.) stripe

treten v. to tread, to step, to walk; to pedal, to treadle; **auf der Stelle —** (mil.) to mark time; **ins Haus —** to enter the house; **in Verbindung —** to make connections; **jemand unter die**

Augen — to face someone; jemand zu **nahe** — to offend (oder hurt) someone; **über die Ufer** — to overflow the banks; **zutage** — to come to light

treu adj. faithful, true; loyal; accurate; retentive (memory); **−brüchig** adj. faithless, perfidious; **−herzig** adj. candid, guileless; simple-minded; **−lich** adj. faithfully, truly; **−los** adj. faithless, perfidious

Treu f. **auf — und Glauben** in good faith; **−bruch** m. breach of faith, perfidy; **−e** f. faithfulness, fidelity, loyalty, accuracy; **−händer** m. trustee; **−handgesellschaft** f. trust company

Triangel m. triangle

Tribun m. tribune; **−al** neu. tribunal

Tribüne f. platform, grandstand; gallery

Tribut m. tribute

tributpflichtig adj. tributary

Trichine f. trichina

Trichter m. funnel; crater

Trick m. trick, dodge; **−film** m. stunt (oder animated) film

Trieb m. shoot, sprout; driving; impetus; instinct; inclination; **−feder** f. main spring; motive; **−kraft** f. motive power **−rad** neu. driving wheel; **−sand** m. quicksand; **−stange** f. connecting rod; **−wagen** m. rail car; **−werk** neu. gear; mechanism; driving unit

Trift f. drift, floating; pastur(ag)e

triftig adj. cogent, plausible, good, weighty

Trigonometrie f. trigonometry

Trikot m. and neu. tricot; tights; **−agen** f. pl. knitted goods; hosiery

Triller m. (mus.) trill, quaver; warble

Trink: −er m. drinker; drunkard; **−gelage** neu. drinking bout, carousal; **−geld** neu. tip, gratuity; **−glas** neu. drinking glass; **−halle** f. pump room; **−spruch** m. toast; **−wasser** neu. drinking water

trinken v. to drink; to imbibe, to absorb; **— auf** to drink to, to toast

Trio neu. trio; **−le** f. (mus.) triplet

trippeln v. to trip

Tritt m. pace, step; tread(ing), kick; footfall, footprint; treadle; footboard; footstool; **— halten** to keep in step; **−brett** neu. running board; **−leiter** f. stepladder

Triumph m. triumph; **−ator** m. victor; conquering hero; **−bogen** m. triumphal arch

triumphieren v. to triumph

trocken adj. dry, arid; boring, dull, tedious; **noch nicht — hinter den Ohren to be green; −legen** v. to drain, to dry up

Trocken: −apparat m. dehydrator; **−batterie** f. dry cell battery; **−boden** m. drying loft; **−dock** neu. dry dock; **auf dem −en sitzen** to be high and dry (oder without money); **sein Schäfchen im −en haben** to have one's share secure; **−eis** neu. dry ice; **−milch** f. powdered milk

Trockenrasierer m. electric razor

trocknen v. to dry, to drain, to dehydrate

Tröd: −el m. secondhand goods; rubbish, junk; **−elei** f. dawdling, loafing; **−elgeschäft** neu., **−elladen** m. secondhand store; **−elmarkt** m. old clothes market; **−ler** m. secondhand dealer; dawdler

trödeln v. to dawdle, to loiter, to hesitate, to be slow

Trog m. trough

Troja neu. Troy

Trommel f. drum; (anat.) tympanum; (mech.) tumbler, cylinder; **−fell** neu. drumhead; tympanic membrane; **−feuer** neu. drumfire; **−schlag** m. drumbeat; **−schlegel** m. drumstick; **−wirbel** m. roll of drums

trommeln v. to (beat the) drum; **mit den Fingern —** to beat the devil's tattoo

Trommler m. drummer

Trompete f. trumpet; **−ngeschmetter** neu. blare of trumpets; **−nschall** m. sound of trumpets; **−nstoss** m. flourish of trumpets

Tropen pl. tropics; **−helm** m. sun (oder pith) helmet; **−koller** m. tropical frenzy

Tropf m. simpleton; **armer —** poor wretch; **−en** m. drop; (perspiration) bead; **−enfänger** m. drip catcher; **−stein** m. stalactite

tropf: −en v. to drop, to drip, to trickle; **−nass** adj. dripping wet; **−enweise** adv. by drops, drop by drop

tröpfeln v. to drop, to drip, to trickle

Trophäe f. trophy

tropisch adj. tropic(al)

Tross m. (mil.) supply train; baggage; followers; crowd

Trost m. consolation, comfort, solace; **nicht (recht) bei −e sein** not to be in one's right mind; **−preis** m. consolation prize

trost: −bringend adj., **−reich** adj. comforting, consolatory; cheering; **−los** adj. disconsolate, hopeless; cheerless, desolate

trösten v. to console, to comfort, to solace

Tröster m. comforter, consoler

Trott m. trot; **−el** m. dunce, idiot, fool; **−oir** neu. sidewalk, pavement

trotten v. to trot

Trotz m. obstinacy, defiance, insolence; **— bieten** to defy; **zum — in** defiance (oder in spite) of; **−kopf** m. stubborn (oder bullheaded) person

trotz *prep.* in spite of, notwithstanding; **–dem** *adv.* and *conj.* nevertheless, in spite of that; (al)though; **–en** *v.* to defy; to be obstinate (*oder* stubborn); to sulk; **–ig** *adj.*, **–köpfig** *adj.* defiant, obstinate, refractory, sulky, sullen

trüb *adj.* muddy, turbid; dim, dull, gloomy, cloudy; sad; dreary; **–en** *v.* to make muddy; to dull, to darken; to spoil, to sadden; **der Himmel trübt sich** the sky is overcast; **er sieht aus, als ob er kein Wässerchen –en könnte** he is the picture of innocence; **–selig** *adj.* sad, wretched; **–sinnig** *adj.* melancholy

Trüb: im –en fischen to fish in troubled waters; **–sal** *f.* affliction, distress, misery; **–sal blasen** (coll.) to be in the dumps; **–sinn** *m.* melancholy, gloom

Trubel *m.* turmoil, confusion; commotion, bustle

trudeln *v.* to trundle; (avi.) to spin

Trug *m.* deception, fraud; delusion, illusion; **–bild** *neu.* phantom, optical illusion; **–schluss** *m.* false conclusion, fallacy

trügen *v.* to deceive, to delude, to mislead

trügerisch *adj.* deceitful, deceptive, delusive

Truhe *f.* chest, trunk

Trümmer *pl.* ruins, debris, remains; fragments

Trumpf *m.* trump, trump card; **seine Trümpfe ausspielen** to use every advantage

trumpfen *v.* to trump

Trunk *m.* draught, drink(ing); **dem — ergeben** addicted to drink; **sich dem — ergeben** to take to the bottle; **–enbold** *m.* drunkard; **–sucht** *f.* dipsomania; **–süchtige** *m.* dipsomaniac

trunken *adj.* drunk, tipsy; elated; exuberant

trunksüchtig *adj.* dipsomaniacal, drink-craving

Trupp *m.* troop, band, gang, squad; **–e** *f.* troupe, company; (mil.) troop, body, unit; **–en** *pl.* forces; **–enaushebung** *f.* levy of troops; **–engattung** *f.* branch of the service; **–enschau** *f.* military review; **–enteil** *m.* military unit; **–enübungsplatz** *m.* maneuver grounds; **–enverband** *m.* (mil.) formation, unit; **–enverbandplatz** *m.* regimental first-aid post

Truthahn *m.* tom turkey

Truthenne *f.* turkey hen

Trutz *m.* defiance, resistance, offensive

die Tschechoslowakei *f.* Czechoslovakia

Tube *f.* tube

Tuberk: –el *f.* tubercle; **–elbildung** *f.*

tuberculation; **–ulose** *f.* tuberculosis

tuberkulös *adj.* tuberculous

Tuch *neu.* cloth, fabric; scarf, shawl; **–fabrik** *f.* textile mill; **–fühlung** *f.* close touch; **–händler** *m.* clothier, draper; **–waren** *f. pl.* clothing, drapery

tüchtig *adj.* qualified, capable, efficient; thorough; good; **— adv.** very much, thoroughly

Tücke *f.* malice, trick, spite; whim

tückisch *adj.* malicious, deceitful, spiteful; (med.) malignant; (animals) vicious

tüfteln *v.* to puzzle (over), to split hairs

Tugend *f.* virtue; **–bold** *m.* self-righteous person; paragon of virtue; sham moralist; **–richter** *m.* moralist, censor

tugend: –haft *adj.*, **–sam** *adj.*, **–reich** *adj.* virtuous

Tüll *m.* tulle; **–spitze** *f.* net lace

Tulpe *f.* tulip; **–nzwiebel** *f.* tulip bulb

tummeln *v.* to put in motion; to exercise; **sich —** to bustle about, to hurry

Tummelplatz *m.* playground; scene of activity

Tümpel *m.* pool, puddle

Tumult *m.* tumult, riot; **–uant** *m.* rioter

tun *v.* to do, to execute; to perform, to act; to work, to be busy; to put; to affect, to pretend; **das tut nichts that doesn't matter, des Guten zuviel —** to overdo something; **es ist ihm nur um das Geld zu —** he cares only about the money; **es ist mir sehr darum zu —** I am anxious about it; **es mit jemand zu — bekommen** to get into trouble with someone; **es tut mir leid** I am sorry; **nichts mit jemand zu —** haben to have no business with someone; **schön — to** flirt; **so — als ob** to pretend to; **weh —** to grieve, to hurt; **–lich** *adj.* feasible, practicable, advisable; **–lichst** *adj.* utmost; **–lichst** *adv.* if possible

Tun *neu.* doing(s), action, conduct; **–ichtgut** *m.* ne'er-do-well

Tünche *f.* whitewash; (fig.) varnish, veneer

tünchen *v.* to whitewash; (fig.) to varnish

Tunke *f.* sauce, gravy

tunken *v.* to dip, to soak, to steep, to dunk

Tunnel *m.* tunnel

Tüpfel *m.* and *neu.* dot, spot, tittle, jot; **etwas bis aufs –chen wissen** to know something in minute detail

tüpfeln *v.* to dot, to spot, to stipple

tupfen *v.* to touch lightly, to dab; to dot

Tür *f.* door; jemand **die — weisen,** jemand **den Stuhl vor die — setzen** to turn somebody out; **mit der — ins Haus fallen** to blurt out; **offene –en**

einrennen to belabor the obvious; **vor der — stehen** to be imminent; **zwischen — und Angel** on the point of leaving; in a dilemma; **–angel** f. door hinge; **–flügel** m. door wing; **–füllung** f. door panel; **–griff** m. door handle; **–hüter** m., **–steher** m. doorkeeper, porter, janitor; **–klinke** f. door latch; **–schild** neu. doorplate; **–schwelle** f. threshold

Turbine f. turbine; **–nanlage** f. turbine plant; **–nluftstrahlmotor** m. turbojet

die Türkei f. Turkey

Türkis m. turquoise

Turm m. tower, steeple; turret; (chess) castle, rook; **–fahne** f. vane; **–falke** m. kestrel; sparrow hawk; **–lukendeckel** m. (mil.) turret door (oder hatch); **–schwalbe** f. (orn.) swift; **–spitze** f. spire; **–uhr** f. church clock; tower clock

türmen v. to pile up; (coll.) to scamper off; **sich — to +ower**, to rise high

Türmer m. watchman (oder warder) of a tower

Turn–: –en neu., **–erei** f. gymnastics; **–er** m. gymnast; **–erschaft** f., **–verein** m. gymnastic club; **–gerät** neu. gymnastic apparatus; **–halle** f. gym(nasium); **–hosen** f. pl. gym bloomers

turnen v. to practice gymnastics

Turnier neu. tournament; tilting; **–platz** m. tiltyard; **–schranken** f. pl. lists

Turteltaube f. turtledove

Tusch m. (mus.) flourish; **–e** f. India ink; **–farbe** f. water color; **–kasten** m. paint box

tuscheln v. to whisper

tuschen v. to draw with India ink

Tüt: –e f. paper bag; cone (for ice cream); **–tel** m., **–telchen** neu. dot; jot

Typ m., **–us** m., **–e** f. type; **–hus** m. typhoid fever; **–ograf** m. typographer; **–opografie** f. typography

Tyrann m. tyrant; **–ei** f. tyranny; **–enmord** m., **–enmörder** m. tyrannicide

tyrannisch adj. tyrannic(al)

U

übel adj. bad, evil; ill, sick; **dabei kann einem — werden** it is enough to make one sick; **es sieht — mit ihm aus** he is in a bad way; **mir ist — I** feel sick; **nicht — not** bad; **— (auf)nehmen** to take amiss; **wohl oder — willing** or not; **–gelaunt** adj. ill-humored; cross, sulky; **–nehmerisch** adj. easily offended; touchy; **–wollend** aaj. malevolent

Übel neu. evil; ailment, illness; **–befinden**

neu. indisposition; **–keit** f. nausea, sickness; **–stand** m. inconvenience; drawback, abuse; **–tat** f. misdeed; **–täter** m. evil-doer

üben v. to exercise, to practice; to drill, to train; **Geduld — to** have patience; **geübt sein** to be skilled; **Gewalt — to** use violence; **Rache — to** take revenge

über prep. above, over; exceeding, higher than; beyond; across; (up)on; more than; during; about, concerning; — adv. over, in excess; completely; thoroughly; **die ganze Zeit — all** the while; **etwas — haben** to be tired of something; **heute — acht Tage** a week from today; **jemand — sein** to surpass someone; **— alle Massen** exceedingly, indescribably; **— kurz oder lang** sooner or later; **–s Jahr** next year; **wir sind noch nicht — den Berg** we are not out of the woods yet

überall adv. everywhere; all over; throughout

überaltert adj. overaged

überanstrengen v. to overexert, to overstrain

überantworten v. to deliver up; to surrender; (law) to extradite

überarbeiten v. to revise, to retouch; **sich — to** overwork oneself

überaus adv. exceedingly, extremely

Überbau m. superstructure

Überbein neu. ganglion

überbelichten v. (phot.) to overexpose

überbieten v. to outbid; to excel, to surpass

Überbleibsel neu. remainder, residue, leftover

Überblick m. survey, view; summary, synopsis

Überbrettl neu. special kind of cabaret

überbringen v. to deliver, to bring to

Überbringer m. bearer, carrier

überbrücken v. to bridge (over); to span

überdachen v. to roof, to shelter

überdenken v. to think over, to reconsider

überdies adv. moreover

Überdruck m. excess pressure; overprint; compression; **–kombination** f. space suit

Überdruss m. disgust; repletion, satiety

überdrüssig adj. tired of; satiated

übereignen v. to assign, to convey

übereilen v. to precipitate; to scamp (work)

überein adv. conformably; in accordance; **–ander** adv. one above the other; **die Beine –ander schlagen** to cross one's legs; **–kommen** v. to come to an agreement; **–stimmen** v. to agree; to correspond; **–stimmend** adj. corresponding

Überein: −kommen *neu.*, **−kunft** *f.* agreement, arrangement; **−stimmung** *f.* harmony, conformity

überessen *v.* **sich —** to overeat

überfahren *v.* to pass (*oder* run) over; to drive across, to cross

Überfahrt *v.* passage, crossing

Überfall *m.* sudden attack, raid; surprise; **−kommando** *neu.* (police) flying squad

überfallen *v.* to attack suddenly; to raid; to overtake; to surprise

überfällig *adj.* overdue

überflügeln *v.* (mil.) to outflank; to surpass

Überfluss *m.* abundance, plenty; redundancy; **im —** abundantly; **zum —** needlessly

überflüssig *adj.* superfluous; redundant

überfluten *v.* to overflow, to inundate

überfordern *v.* to overcharge; overweight

überführen *v.* to convey; to convict; to convince; (chem.) to convert, to transform

Überführung *f.* conveying, transfer; conviction; (chem.) conversion, transformation; overpass

überfüllen *v.* to overfill, to overload; to overcrowd; to overstock

Übergabe *f.* delivery; surrender; handing over

Übergang *m.* crossing; transition; change; **−smantel** *m.* light topcoat; **−szeit** *f.* transition period; **−szustand** *m.* transitional state ·

übergeben *v.* to deliver, to hand over, to surrender; **sich —** to vomit

übergeh(e)n *v.* to go (*oder* pass) over; to change into (*oder* over); to ignore, to omit

Übergewicht *neu.* overweight; preponderance, superiority; **das — bekommen** to become top-heavy; to get the upper hand

Übergriff *m.* encroachment, infringement

Überhandnahme *f.* increase, spread, prevalence

überhandnehmen *v.* to increase, to spread; to become prevalent (*oder* too numerous)

überhäufen *v.* to overburden; to overwhelm

überhaupt *adv.* in general, on the whole; altogether; **— nicht** not at all

überheben *v.* to spare, to exempt from; **sich —** to injure oneself (by overlifting); to be overbearing (*oder* presumptuous)

überheblich *adj.* arrogant, overbearing

überhitzen *v.* to overheat; to superheat

überholen *v.* to haul over; to outdistance; to outstrip, to surpass; to overhaul, to check

überholt *adj.* out of date, antiquated

überhören *v.* to fail to hear; to ignore; to hear someone's homework (or lessons)

überirdisch *adj.* supernatural, unearthly

überkippen *v.* to tip over, to keel

Überkleid *neu.* upper garment

überkochen *v.* to boil over; to fret and fume

überladen *v.* to **overload;** to overdo; **den Magen —** to overeat; **—** *adj.* overdone, too profuse

Überlandflug *m.* (avi.) cross-country flight

überlassen *v.* to leave, to give up; to cede, to transfer; to abandon; to give way

überlaufen *v.* to run over, to overflow; (mil.) to desert; to pester, to importune; **es überläuft mich** I am overcome (by a feeling)

Überläufer *m.* deserter; renegade

überleb: −en *v.* to outlive, to survive; **−engross** *adj.* bigger than life-size; **−t** *adj.* out of date, antiquated, old-fashioned

Überlebende *m.* survivor

überlegen *v.* to lay over, to cover; (coll.) to whip; to consider, to reflect upon; **—** *adj.* superior; **er ist ihm —** he excels him

Überlegenheit *f.* superiority, preponderance

Überlegung *f.* reflection, consideration, deliberation; **mit — verübtes Verbrechen** premeditated crime; **ohne —** thoughtlessly

überleiten *v.* to lead over (*oder* across); to form a transition

überlesen *v.* to reread; to skim; to peruse; to overlook

überliefern *v.* to deliver, to hand over; to transmit, to pass (on); to surrender

Überlieferung *f.* delivery; tradition; surrender

überlisten *v.* to outwit, to dupe, to deceive

übermachen *v.* to transmit; to bequeath

Übermacht *f.* superior power; predominance

übermächtig *adj.* too powerful; overwhelming

übermangansauer *adj.* permanganic

übermannen *v.* to overcome, to overpower

Übermass *neu.* excess; **im —** excessively

übermässig *adj.* excessive, exorbitant

Übermensch *m.* superman

übermenschlich *adj.* superhuman

übermitteln *v.* to send, to convey; to transmit

übermorgen *adj.* the day after tomorrow

übermüdet *adj.* overtired, overfatigued

Übermut *m.* high spirits, wantonness; insolence

übermütig *adj.* high-spirited, frolicsome; presumptuous, insolent

übernachten *v.* to stay over night

Übernahme *f.* taking over; undertaking; –bedingungen *f. pl.* conditions of acceptance

übernatürlich *adj.* supernatural

übernehmen *v.* to take over (*oder* in hand); to undertake; to assume responsibility; sich — to overwork oneself; to overeat

überquer *adv.* crossways, across; –en to cross

überragen *v.* to overtop; to excel, to surpass

überraschen *v.* to surprise

überreden *v.* to persuade

überreich *adj.* too rich; abounding in, –en to hand over, to present; –lich *adj.* superabundant

überreif *adj.* overripe

Überrest *m.* remainder, rest; remains; residue

Überrock *m.* overcoat, topcoat

überrumpeln *v.* to (take by) surprise

Überrumpelung *f.* surprisal; sudden attack

übersatt *adj.* satiated; glutted, surfeited

überschallgeschwindigkeit *f.* supersonic speed; ultrasonic speed

überschätzen *v.* to overestimate, to overrate

überschauen *v.* to overview; to survey

überschäumen *v.* to foam over; to exuberate

Überschicht *f.* extra shift; overtime

überschiessen *v.* to overshoot; to fall forward; to overflow; to exceed; –de Summe surplus

Überschlag *m.* estimate, rough calculation; somersault; (dress) facing

überschlagen *v.* to estimate; to skip; sich — to tumble over, to turn a somersault; (avi.) to loop the loop; die Stimme überschlägt sich the voice breaks

überschnappen *v.* to go crazy; mit der Stimme — to squeak, to shrill

überschneiden *v.* to intersect, to overlap

überschreiben *v.* to transfer; to superscribe; to head, to title; to carry over

überschreien *v.* to cry down; sich — to overstrain one's voice

überschreiten *v.* to cross over; to exceed; to transgress; to infringe; (com.) to overdraw

Überschrift *f.* superscription; heading, title

Überschuh *m.* overshoe, galosh

überschuldet *adj.* involved in debts

Überschuss *m.* surplus, excess, profit

überschüssig *adj.* surplus, excess, leftover

überschütten *v.* to cover; to overwhelm

Überschwang *m.* exuberance, rapture

überschwemmen *v.* to flood, to inundate

überschwenglich *adj.* exuberant, rapturous

überseeisch *adj.* oversea(s), transoceanic

übersehen *v.* to survey; to overlook

übersenden *v.* to send, to transmit, to consign

Übersender *m.* sender, consignor; remitter

übersetzen *v.* to pass (*oder* carry) over, to cross; to translate

Übersetzung *f.* translation; (mech.) gear

Übersicht *f.* survey; view; summary, synopsis, abstract; –skarte *f.* general plan

übersichtlich *adj.* clear, lucid; easily seen

übersiedeln *v.* to move; to emigrate

übersinnlich *adj.* transcendental; metaphysical

überspannen *v.* to stretch over; to carpet, to cover with; to overstrain; to exaggerate

überspannt *adj.* overstrained; eccentric

überspringen *v.* to overleap; to skip, to omit

überstechen *v.* (cards) to overtrump

überstehen *v.* to stand over; to project; to endure; to get over; to survive

übersteigen *v.* to step (*oder* climb) over; to surmount, to exceed

übersteigern *v.* to overbid, to outbid

überstimmen *v.* to tune too high; to outvote

Überstunde *f.*, –n *pl.* overtime

überstürzen *v.* to topple; to hurry; to precipitate; sich — to act rashly

übertönen *v.* to drown out; to deafen

übertragbar *adj.* transferable; contagious

übertragen *v.* to carry over; to transfer; to give up to, to entrust with; to transmit; to transcribe; to infect with; –e Bedeutung figurative sense

übertreffen *v.* to excel, to surpass; to beat

übertreiben *v.* to exaggerate, to overdo

übertreten *v.* to go (*oder* step) over; to change sides; to violate, to transgress, to trespass; to sprain (ankle)

übertrieben *adj.* exaggerated, excessive; extravagant; extreme; exorbitant

Übertritt *m.* going over; (rel.) conversion

übertrumpfen *v.* to overtrump; to outwit

übertünchen *v.* to whitewash; to gloss over

übervölkert *adj.* overpopulated

übervorteilen v. to overreach; to defraud

überwachen v. to supervise; to control; to shadow

überwältigen v. to overcome, to overpower; to overwhelm; to subdue; **-d** adj. imposing

überweisen v. to assign, to transfer; to remit

Überweisungsscheck m. transfer check

überwiegen v. to outweigh; to predominate; **-d** adj. predominant; **-d** adv. mainly, chiefly

überwinden v. to overcome; to conquer; to get over, to surmount; ein überwundener Standpunkt an outmoded viewpoint

überwintern v. to winter; to hibernate

überwuchern v. to overgrow; to overrun

Überwurf m. loose gown, cloak; wrap, shawl

Überzahl f. surplus; odds; majority

überzählig adj. supernumerary, superfluous

überzeugen v. to convince, to persuade

Überzeugung f. conviction, belief

überziehen v. to put on; to pull over; (com.) to overdraw; Bett — to change bed linen; einen Sessel — to upholster a chair; sich — to become overcast

Überzieher m. overcoat, topcoat

überzuckern v. to sugar coat; to candy, to frost, to ice

Überzug m. cover, coat(ing); crust; slip

üblich adj. usual, customary, prevailing

übrig adj. left over, remaining; die —en the others, the rest; ein -es tun to do more than is necessary; etwas für jemand — haben to care for someone; im -en for the rest, in other respects; nichts zu wünschen — lassen to leave nothing to be desired; -ens adv. by the way, after all; besides, moreover

Ufer neu. bank, beach, shore; coast; **-damm** m. embankment; **-seite** f. riverside

uferlos adj. boundless; extravagant

Uhr f. clock, watch; hour, time; es ist ein — it's one o'clock; wieviel — ist's? what's the time? **-werk** neu. clockwork; **-zeiger** m. hand of a clock (oder watch)

Uhu m. great horned owl

Ulan m. (mil.) uhlan, lancer

Ulk m. fun, joke, merry prank

ulken v. to have fun, to joke, to tease

ulkig adj. funny, amusing, comical

Ulme f. elm

Ultimo m. (com.) last day of the month

Ultra-Hochfrequenz f. ultrahigh frequency

um prep. about; round; at; because of,

for; by; einen Tag — den anderen day after day; every other day; rechts —! right face! — die Hälfte mehr half as much again; — drei Uhr at three o'clock; — ein Jahr älter a year older; -s Leben kommen to die; — so besser! so much the better! — sein to be over; to expire; — adv. about; — und — from (oder on) all sides; — conj. — zu in order to

umadressieren v. to redirect (mail)

umändern v. to alter, to change; to transform

umarbeiten v. to recast, to remodel; to rework

umarmen v. to embrace, to hug

Umbau m. reconstruction, alterations

umbauen v. to rebuild, to reconstruct

umbehalten v. to keep on (wrap, etc.)

umbiegen v. to bend, to turn back (oder down)

umbilden v. to recast, to remodel, to transform; to reconstruct; to reform

umbinden v. to tie round; to put on; to rebind

umblasen v. to blow down (oder over)

umblättern v. to turn over (leaf of book)

umblicken v. to look around; to glance back

umbrechen v. to break down (oder up); (typ.) to make up, to page

umbringen v. to kill, to murder; to make away with; sich — to commit suicide

Umbruch m. radical change, revolution; (typ.) paging; page proof

umdrehen v. to turn over (oder around); den Hals — to wring somebody's neck; den Spiess — to turn the tables on someone; sich — to rotate, to revolve, to turn round

umdüstert adj. dark, gloomy

umeinander adv. round (oder for) each other

umfahren v. to run over; to drive (oder sail) around; to circumnavigate

umfallen v. to fall down; to upset

Umfang m. circumference, periphery; extent, size; compass, range; bulk, volume

umfangen v. to embrace; to surround

umfangreich adj. extensive, voluminous; wide

umfassen v. to embrace, to encircle; to include; (mil.) to outflank; mit einem Blick — to take in at a glance; **-d** adj. comprehensive, extensive

umflort adj. veiled; muffled; (eyes) dim

umformen v. to transform; to remodel; to reform, to convert

Umformer m. transformer, converter; reformer

Umfrage *f.* inquiry, poll, canvass

Umfriedung *f.* enclosure, fence

Umgang *m.* (going) round, circuit; procession; social intercourse, association; (arch.) circular gallery; **–sformen** *f. pl.* manners; **–ssprache** *f.* colloquial language

umgänglich *adj.* sociable, companionable

umgarnen *v.* to ensnare, to trap; to enmesh

umgaukeln *v.* to flit (*oder* hover) around; to wrap in (illusions)

umgeben *v.* to surround; to enclose; to fence in

Umgebung *f.* surroundings, neighborhood; associates, company; background, environment

Umgegend *f.* neighborhood, vicinity, environs

umgeh(e)n *v.* to go around; to circulate; (mil.) to outflank; to avoid, to evade; (ghost) to haunt; **mit etwas —** to be occupied with something, to plan to do something; **mit jemand —** to associate with someone; **–d** *adj.* **mit –der Post** by return mail; **–d** *adv.* immediately

umgekehrt *adj.* contrary, opposite, reverse; **—** *adv.* on the contrary, vice versa

umgestalten *v.* to alter, to transform, to reorganize; to metamorphose

umgraben *v.* (soil) to dig (*oder* break) up

umgrenzen *v.* to encircle; to circumscribe, to limit; to fence

umhaben *v.* to have around one (*oder* on)

umhalsen *v.* to embrace, to hug

Umhang *m.* cape, shawl, wrap

Umhängetasche *f.* shoulder bag

umhauen *v.* to cut down, to fell

umher *adv.* around; about; here and there

umhin *adv.* **ich kann nicht —** I can't help it

umhüllen *v.* to wrap, to encase, to protect; to veil, to cover

Umkehr *f.* turning back; return; conversion; **–ung** *f.* reversal, subversion, inversion

umkehren *v.* to turn back (*oder* about, round, over); to return; to reverse; to invert; to convert; to overthrow, to subvert

umkippen *v.* to overturn; to tip over

umklammern *v.* to clasp; to clutch; to encircle

umklappen *v.* to turn down (collar)

umkleiden *v.* to clothe; to cover; **sich —** to change one's dress

Umkleideraum *m.* dressing room

umkommen *v.* to die, to perish; to be wasted

Umkreis *m.* circumference, circuit; radius

umkreisen *v.* to turn (*oder* circle, revolve) round; to encircle; to rotate; **(die Erde)** *v.* to orbit

umlagern *v.* to surround; to besiege

Umlauf *m.* circulation; rotation; revolving, revolution, turn; circular; **in —** **setzen** to circulate; to spread (rumors)

umlaufen *v.* to run down; to revolve, to circulate

umlegen *v.* to lay down; to put on; to shift, to relay; to lay around (someone or something); (sl.) to kill

umleiten *v.* to conduct in another direction; to divert

umlenken *v.* to turn round (*oder* back)

umlernen *v.* to readjust one's views

umliegend *adj.* surrounding, neighboring

ummauern *v.* to wall in, to fortify

umnachtet *adj.* wrapped in darkness; deranged

umnebeln *v.* to wrap in fog; to becloud

umpacken *v.* to repack

umpflanzen *v.* to transplant; to plant around

umpflügen *v.* to plow up

umquartieren *v.* to remove to other quarters

umranken *v.* to twine around

umrechnen *v.* (com.) to change, to convert

Umrechnungskurs *m.* rate of exchange

umreissen *v.* to pull down; to outline

umringen *v.* to encircle, to encompass

Umriss *m.* outline, contour, sketch

umrühren *v.* to stir up (*oder* around)

umsatteln *v.* to resaddle; to change one's occupation; (pol.) to change sides

Umsatz *m.* sales, turnover, returns

umsäumen *v.* to hem; to surround

umschalten *v.* to switch (*oder* change) over

Umschalter *m.* switch, commutator; (typewriter) shift key

Umschau *f.* look(ing) round; **— halten to** look around; to reconnoiter, to scout

umschauen *v.* **sich —** to look around

umschichtig *adv.* by turns, alternately

umschiffen *v.* to circumnavigate; **to** double (a cape)

Umschlag *m.* cover, wrapper; envelope; (book) jacket; hem, cuff; (com.) transfer, reshipment; (med.) compress; change, turn; **–papier** *neu.* wrapping paper; **–shafen** *m.* port of reshipment; **–tuch** *neu.* wrap, shawl

umschlagen *v.* to topple; to overturn, to knock down; to shift; (naut.) to capsize; (voice) to break; to turn (a hem) up (*oder* down); to turn over (a page); to change, to degenerate

umschliessen v. to enclose, to surround

umschlingen v. to embrace; to clasp around

umschmelzen v. to recast, to remelt

umschreiben v. to rewrite; to transcribe; to circumscribe; to reindorse, to transfer

Umschreibung f. transcription; paraphrase

umschütten v. to spill; to decant; to transfuse

umschwärmen v. to swarm round; to adore

Umschweif m. digression; circumlocution; -e machen to digress; ohne -e bluntly, plainly

umschwenken v. to wheel around; to change one's mind

Umschwung m. change; revulsion; revolution; (gym.) swing round the bar

umsehen v. sich — to look back (oder around); to go sightseeing

Umsehen neu. im — in a twinkling

umsetzen v. to transpose; to transplant; to sell, to turn over; to convert

Umsichgreifen neu. spread(ing)

Umsicht f. circumspection, prudence, caution

umsichtig adj. circumspect, prudent, cautious

umsonst adv. for nothing, gratis; in vain

umspannen v. to change (horses); to enclose, to encompass; (elec.) to transform

umspringen v. to jump around; to change, to veer; — mit to treat, to manage

Umstand m. circumstance, fact; -skleid neu. maternity dress; -swort neu. adverb

Umstände m. pl. particulars; ceremonies, formalities; fuss, trouble, ado; grosse — machen to raise great difficulties; in anderen -n sein to be pregnant; mildernde — (law) extenuating circumstances; ohne — without ceremony; unter allen -n in any case, at all events; unter keinen -n on no account; unter solchen -n as matters stand; unter -n circumstances permitting

umständlich adj. circumstantial, involved; ceremonious, formal; fussy

umstehen v. to stand round (oder about); to surround; -d adj. on the next page

Umsteige: -billet neu., -(fahr)karte f., -fahrschein m., -r m. transfer ticket

umsteigen v. to change (trains), to transfer

umstellen v. to arrange differently; to shift, to transpose; to invert; to con-

vert; to surround, to beset; sich — to adapt oneself

umstimmen v. to tune to another pitch; jemand — to change someone's mind

umstossen v. to knock down; to upset, to overturn; to annul, to invalidate

umstricken v. to ensnare, to entangle

umstritten adj. controversial, disputed

umstülpen v. to tip over; to turn upside down

Umsturz m. overthrow; subversion; revolution

Umstürzler m. anarchist, revolutionist

umtaufen v. to rebaptize; to give a new name

Umtausch m. exchange

umtauschen v. to exchange

Umtriebe m. pl. intrigues, machinations

umtun v. to put on; sich — to look for

umwälzen v. to roll round; to revolutionize

Umwälzung f. radical change; revolution

umwandeln v. to change, to transform, to convert

Umwandlungsprozess m. metamorphosis

umwechseln v. to exchange; to change (money)

Umweg m. roundabout way, detour; bypass; auf -en indirectly; -e machen to bypass

Umwelt f. environment, milieu

umwenden v. to turn over; sich — to turn around, to look back

umwerben v. to court, to woo

umwerfen v. to overturn, to upset; to throw round (oder over); to put on (coat)

umwerten v. to revaluate

umwühlen v. to uproot, to rummage all around

umzäunen v. to fence in, to enclose

umziehen v. to change (clothes); to move (to); to surround; to cover all around; to become overcast; to walk round

umzingeln v. to encircle, to surround

Umzug m. moving; procession, demonstration

unab: -änderlich adj. unalterable, irrevocable; -hängig adj. independent; -kömmlich adj. indispensable, reserved; -lässig adj. incessant; -sehbar adj. unbounded, immeasurable, immense; -sichtlich adj. unintentional; accidental; -weisbar adj., -weislich adj. imperative; unavoidable; -wendbar adj. inevitable

Unabhängigkeit f. independence; -serklärung f. Declaration of Independence

unähnlich adj. unlike, dissimilar

unan: -fechtbar adj. incontestable, indisputable; **–gebracht** *adj.* out of place, unsuitable; **–gefochten** *adj.* undisputed; unhindered; **–gemessen** *adj.* inadequate, unsuitable; improper; **–greifbar** *adj.* unassailable; incontestable; **–nehmbar** *adj.* unacceptable; **–sehnlich** *adj.* poor-looking, plain; insignificant; **–tastbar** *adj.* inviolable, unassailable; unimpeachable

Unannehmlichkeit *f.* inconvenience, annoyance

Unart *f.* bad habit (*oder* behavior)

unartig *adj.* badly behaved, naughty, rude

unauf: –findbar *adj.* undiscoverable; **–geschlossen** *adj.* unexploited, undeveloped; **–haltbar** *adj.*, **–haltsam** *adj.* irresistible; incessant; **–hörlich** *adj.* incessant, constant; **–lösbar** *adj.*, **–löslich** *adj.* indissoluble, inexplicable; **–schiebbar** *adj.*, **–schieblich** *adj.* pressing, urgent

unaus: –bleiblich *adj.* inevitable, certain; **–führbar** *adj.* impracticable, unfeasible; **–gesetzt** *adj.* uninterrupted, incessant; **–löschbar** *adj.*, **–löschlich** *adj.* inextinguishable, indelible; **–sprechlich** *adj.* inexpressible, indescribable; immense; **–stehlich** *adj.* unbearable, intolerable; **–weichbar** *adj.*, **–weichlich** *adj.* unavoidable; inevitable

unbändig *adj.* unruly, intractable; tremendous

unbarmherzig *adj.* unmerciful, pitiless; cruel

unbeabsichtigt *adj.* unintentional

unbeachtet *adj.* unnoticed, disregarded

unbeanstandet *adj.* unopposed; unobjectionable

unbebaut *adj.* uncultivated

unbedacht(sam) *adj.* inconsiderate, thoughtless

unbedenklich *adj.* unobjectionable, harmless; — *adv.* unhesitatingly, without scruples

unbedeutend *adj.* insignificant, trifling

unbedingt *adj.* unconditional, absolute, implicit

unbeeinflusst *adj.* unprejudiced, unbiased

unbeeinträchtigt *adj.* uninjured, unhindered

unbefahrbar *adj.* impassable, impracticable

unbefangen *adj.* impartial, unprejudiced, natural

unbefleckt *adj.* unsullied, spotless; immaculate

unbefriedigt *adj.* unsatisfied; disappointed

unbefugt *adj.* unauthorized, incompetent

unbegreiflich *adj.* incomprehensible, inconceivable; mysterious

unbegrenzt *adj.* unlimited, unbounded

unbegründet *adj.* unfounded; baseless

Unbehagen *neu.* uneasiness, discomfort

unbehaglich *adj.* uncomfortable, uneasy

unbehelligt *adj.* undisturbed, unmolested

unbeholfen *adj.* awkward, clumsy; ungainly

unbeirrbar, unbeirrt *adj.* imperturable

unbekannt *adj.* unknown; unacquainted (with); ignorant (of)

unbekümmert *adj.* unconcerned; carefree

unbelästigt *adj.* unmolested

unbelebt *adj.* inanimate, lifeless; dull, empty

unbemerkt *adj.* unnoticed, unperceived

unbemittelt *adj.* impecunious, poor

unbenutzt *adj.* unused, unemployed; uninvested

unberechenbar *adj.* incalculable; unreliable

unberechtigt *adj.* unauthorized; unfounded; unjustified; unlawful

unberücksichtigt *adj.* unconsidered; disregarded

unberufen *adj.* unbidden, unauthorized; —I knock on wood! — *adv.* intrusively

unberührt *adj.* untouched; intact; virgin

unbeschädigt *adj.* uninjured, undamaged

unbescheiden *adj.* immodest; arrogant; insolent

unbescholten *adj.* blameless, irreproachable; (law) without previous conviction

unbeschränkt *adj.* unrestricted; absolute

unbeschreiblich *adj.* indescribable; — *adv.* exceedingly, extremely

unbeschwert *adj.* unburdened, light

unbeseelt *adj.* soulless, inanimate

unbesehen *adv.* without examination (*oder* inspection); without hesitation

unbesetzt *adj.* unoccupied; vacant; plain

unbesiegbar, unbesieglich *adj.* invincible

unbesonnen *adj.* thoughtless, heedless; rash

unbesorgt *adj.* unconcerned, carefree; sei —I don't worry!

Unbestand *m.*, **Unbeständigkeit** *f.* inconstancy; changeableness; unsteadiness

unbeständig *adj.* unstable; inconstant

unbestechbar, unbestechlich *adj.* incorruptible

unbestellbar *adj.* not deliverable

unbestimmbar *adj.* indeterminable, nondescript

unbestimmt *adj.* undetermined, undecided; uncertain; indistinct; indefinite

unbestreitbar *adj.* incontestable, indisputable

unbestritten *adj.* uncontested, undisputed

unbeteiligt *adj.* not concerned; indifferent

unbetont *adj.* unaccented, unstressed
unbeträchtlich *adj.* inconsiderable, trifling
unbeugsam *adj.* inflexible; stubborn, obstinate
unbewacht *adj.* unwatched, unguarded
unbewaffnet *adj.* unarmed; naked (eye)
unbewandert *adj.* inexperienced; unskilled
unbeweglich *adj.* immovable; -es Gut real estate
unbewohnbar *adj.* uninhabitable
unbewohnt *adj.* uninhabited; vacant; desolated
unbewusst *adj.* unconscious; involuntary
unbezahlbar *adj.* invaluable; priceless
unbezahlt *adj.* unpaid; outstanding
unbezähmbar *adj.* untamable, indomitable
unbezwingbar, unbezwinglich *adj.* invincible; unconquerable; unsurmountable; indomitable
unbiegsam *adj.* unbending, inflexible; rigid
Unbill *f.* injury, injustice; wrong; inclemency
unbillig *adj.* unfair, unjust, unreasonable
unbotmässig *adj.* insubordinate, rebellious
unbrauchbar *adj.* useless; unserviceable; unfit
und *conj.* and; na —? well? nothing more?
Undank *m.*, **Undankbarkeit** *f.* ingratitude
undenkbar *adj.* unthinkable, inconceivable
undenklich *adj.* immemorial
Unding *neu.* absurdity, impossibility; nonsense
undurchführbar *adj.* impracticable, unfeasible
undurchlässig *adj.* impermeable, impervious (to)
undurchsichtig *adj.* not transparent, opaque
uneben *adj.* uneven; rough; hilly; unsuitable; nicht — not bad, rather good; -bürtig *adj.* of inferior rank; inferior
unecht *adj.* not genuine, false; artificial; (colors) not fast; (math.) improper
unehelich *adj.* illegitimate
unehr: -enhaft *adj.* dishonorable; -erbietig *adj.* disrespectful; -lich *adj.* dishonest, insincere; underhanded; false
uneigennützig *adj.* disinterested, unselfish
uneigentlich *adj.* not literal, figurative
unein: -bringlich *adj.* irretrievable; -gedenk *adj.* regardless of; -geschränkt *adj.* unrestricted; -ig *adj.* disagreeing, discordant; -s *adv.* -s sein to disagree
unempfänglich *adj.* unsusceptible, unreceptive
unempfindlich *adj.* insensible (to), insensitive; indifferent, callous
unendlich *adj.* infinite, endless; vast
unent: -behrlich *adj.* indispensable; -geltlich *adj.* gratuitous, free; -schieden *adj.* undecided; (game) drawn; irresolute; -schiedene Frage open question; -schlossen *adj.* irresolute, hesitating; -schuldbar *adj.* inexcusable; -wegt *adj.* undeviating, steadfast, persistent; -wirrbar *adj.* inextricable; -zifferbar *adj.* undecipherable
uner: -achtet *prep.* notwithstanding, in spite of; -bittlich *adj.* inexorable, pitiless; -fahren *adj.* inexperienced; -findlich *adj.* undiscoverable, incomprehensible; -forschlich *adj.* inscrutable; -forscht *adj.* unexplored; -freulich *adj.* unpleasant, annoying; -füllbar *adj.* unrealizable; -giebig *adj.* unproductive; -gründlich *adj.* unfathomable; impenetrable; -heblich *adj.* insignificant, irrelevant; -hört *adj.* unheard (of); shocking; exorbitant; -kannt *adj.* unrecognized; -klärlich *adj.* inexplicable, perplexing; -lässlich *adj.* indispensable; -laubt *adj.* unlawful, prohibited; -ledigt *adj.* unfinished, unsettled; -messlich *adj.* immeasurable, immense; -müdlich *adj.* untiring; indefatigable; -quicklich *adj.* unpleasant; uncomfortable; -reichbar *adj.* unattainable; -reicht *adj.* unequalled; (sports) record; -sättlich *adj.* insatiable; -schlossen *adj.* undeveloped; -schöpflich *adj.* inexhaustible; -schrocken *adj.* intrepid, fearless; -schütterlich *adj.* imperturbable, firm; -schwinglich *adj.* beyond one's means; unattainable; -setzlich *adj.* irreplaceable; irreparable; -spriesslich *adj.* unprofitable; unpleasant; -träglich *adj.* intolerable; -wartet *adj.* unexpected; -weislich *adj.* undemonstrable; -widert *adj.* unanswered; unrequited; -wünscht *adj.* undesirable; unwelcome; -zogen *adj.* uneducated; ill-bred
unfähig *adj.* incapable; unable; disabled
Unfall *m.* accident; -station *f.* first-aid station; -versicherung *f.* accident insurance
unfassbar, unfasslich *adj.* inconceivable, incomprehensible. unintelligible
unfehlbar *adj.* infallible; — *adv.* certainly
unfein *adj.* coarse, indelicate, unmannerly
unfern *adv.* not far off, near(by); — *prep.* not far from, near
unfertig *adj.* unfinished, unready; immature

Unflat *m.* dirt, filth, nasty mess
unflätig *adj.* dirty, filthy; obscene
unförmig *adj.* deformed, misshapen; monstrous
unfrankiert *adj.* (mail) not prepaid; unfranked
unfreiwillig *adj.* involuntary, compulsory
Unfriede *m.* discord, dissension
unfruchtbar *adj.* unfruitful; barren, sterile
Unfug *m.* mischief, nuisance; misbehavior; **grober —** (law) disturbance of the peace
ungeachtet *adj.·* not esteemed; **—** *prep.* notwithstanding, despite; **—** *conj.* although
ungeahndet *adj.* unpunished
ungeahnt *adj.* not anticipated, unexpected
ungebärdig *adj.* unruly, wild; unmannerly
ungebeten *adj.* unbidden, uninvited
ungebräuchlich *adj.* unusual; obsolete
Ungebühr *f.* indecency, impropriety; injustice
ungebührlich *adj.* indecent, improper; undue
ungebunden *adj.* unbound; unrestrained, free, loose; dissolute; **-e Rede** prose
ungedeckt *adj.* uncovered, unsheltered; (com.) dishonored; (table) not yet set
Ungeduld *f.* impatience
ungefähr *adj.* approximate; **—** *adv.* about, nearly; **von —** by chance, accidentally; **-det** *adj.* safe; not endangered; **-lich** *adj.* harmless
ungegliedert *adj.* unjointed, inarticulate
ungehalten *adj.* unkept; indignant; impatient
ungeheissen *adj.* unbidden; **—** *adv.* voluntarily
ungeheuchelt *adj.* unfeigned, sincere
Ungeheuer *neu.* monster; **-lichkeit** *f.* atrocity
ungeheuer *adj.* monstrous; colossal, enormous; **—** *adv.* exceedingly; **-lich** *adj.* monstrous
ungehobelt *adj.* unplaned; unmannered, rude
ungehörig *adj.* undue, unbecoming, improper
Ungehorsam *m.* disobedience; insubordination
ungekünstelt *adj.* artless; unaffected, natural
ungeladen *adj.* (gun) unloaded; uninvited
ungeläufig *adj.* unfamiliar; not fluent
ungelegen *adj.* inconvenient, inopportune
Ungelegenheit *f.* inconvenience, annoyance
ungelenk(ig) *adj.* awkward, clumsy, stiff
ungelernt *adj.* unskilled, untaught
ungelöscht *adj.* unquenched; unslaked

(lime)
Ungemach *neu.* misfortune, hardship, adversity
ungemein *adj.* uncommon, extraordinary
ungemütlich *adj.* uncomfortable; unpleasant
ungenannt *adj.* unnamed; anonymous
ungenau *adj.* inaccurate, inexact
ungeniert *adj.* unceremonious; free and easy
ungeniessbar *adj.* uneatable, unpalatable
ungenügend *adj.* insufficient; unsatisfactory
ungenügsam *adj.* insatiable
ungeordnet *adj.* unarranged, unsettled
ungepflegt *adj.* untended; untidy, neglected
ungerade *adj.* not straight; uneven; odd
ungeraten *adj.* spoilt; undutiful; abortive
ungerecht *adj.* unjust, unfair; **-fertigt** *adj.* unjustified, unwarranted
ungereimt *adj.* rhymeless; absurd
ungern *adv.* unwillingly, reluctantly
ungesäuert *adj.* unleavened
ungesäumt *adj.* seamless, unhemmed; immediate, prompt; **—** *adv.* without delay, at once
ungeschehen *adj.* undone
Ungeschick *neu.* misfortune
ungeschickt *adj.* inept, unskillful; awkward
ungeschlacht *adj.* uncouth; coarse; clumsy
ungeschliffen *adj.* unpolished; rude, uncouth
ungeschoren *adj.* unshorn, unshaven; unmolested; **— lassen** to leave alone; not to bother
ungesehen *adj.* unseen, unnoticed
ungesetzlich *adj.* illegal, unlawful
ungestalt(et) *adj.* deformed, misshapen
ungestört *adj.* undisturbed, uninterrupted
ungestraft *adj.* unpunished; **—** *adv.* with impunity
ungestüm *adj.* impetuous, violent, raging
Ungestüm *m. and neu.* impetuosity, violence
ungeteilt *adj.* undivided; unanimous; entire
Ungetüm *neu.* monster
ungewiss *adj.* uncertain, doubtful
Ungewissheit *f.* uncertainty; **in — lassen** to keep in suspense
Ungewitter *neu.* thunderstorm; **violent** storm
ungewöhnlich *adj.* uncommon, unusual; strange
ungewohnt *adj.* unaccustomed, unfamiliar
ungezählt *adj.* uncounted; innumerable
Ungeziefer *neu.* vermin

ungeziemend *adj.* unseemly; improper

ungezogen *adj.* naughty; ill-bred; uncivil

ungezwungen *adj.* unforced; unaffected, easy

Unglaube *m.* disbelief, unbelief

ungläubig *adj.* incredulous, unbelieving

unglaublich *adj.* incredible

ungleich *adj.* unequal; uneven; odd; unlike, dissimilar; different; — *adv.* incomparably, much; **–artig** *adj.* dissimilar, heterogeneous; **–förmig** *adj.* unequal; irregular; **–mässig** *adj.* disproportionate, unsymmetrical

Unglimpf *m.* harshness; affront; insult; wrong

Unglück *neu.* misfortune; bad luck; accident; calamity, disaster; **–sbotschaft** *f.* evil tidings; **–sfall** *m.* accident, mishap; casualty; **–srabe** *m.* hoodoo; **–sstunde** *f.* fatal hour; **–svogel** *m.* bird of ill omen; unlucky person

unglück: **–lich** *adj.* unhappy; fatal, unrequited; **–licherweise** *adv.* unfortunately, by mischance; **–selig** *adj.* unfortunate, disastrous

Ungnade *f.* disgrace, disfavor; **in — fallen** to be disgraced; to incur displeasure

ungnädig *adj.* ungracious, unkind, ill-humored

ungültig *adj.* invalid; not available; not current; **für — erklären,** **— machen** to invalidate, to void; to annul, to cancel

Ungunst *f.* disfavor; inclemency; unkindness

ungünstig *adj.* unfavorable, disadvantageous

ungut *adj.* unkind; **nichts für —!** no harm meant! don't be offended!

unhaltbar *adj.* not durable; untenable

unharmonisch *adj.* inharmonious, discordant

Unheil *neu.* evil, harm; disaster, calamity; **–stifter** *m.* mischief-maker

unheil: **–bar** *adj.* incurable; **–bringend** *adj.* disastrous, ruinous; **–schwanger** *adj.* fraught with disaster; **–voll** *adj.* calamitous

unheimlich *adj.* gruesome, sinister; **ihm wurde — zumute** he began to feel alarmed (*oder* uneasy); **— adv.** tremendously

unhöflich *adj.* impolite, uncivil, disrespectful

Unhold *m.* fiend, demon, monster

unhörbar *adj.* inaudible

unhygienisch *adj.* unsanitary

Uni: –form *f.* uniform; **–kum** *neu.* unique example (*oder* person); **–versalerbe** *m.* sole heir; **–versalmittel** *neu.* universal remedy, panacea; **–versität** *f.* university; **–versum** *neu.* universe

uni: –formiert *adj.* uniformed, uniform; **–versal** *adj.,* **–versell** *adj.* universal

Unke *f.* toad; (coll.) croaker

unkenntlich *adj.* unrecognizable

Unkenntnis *f.* ignorance

unkeusch *adj.* unchaste; impure, lewd

unklar *adj.* indistinct; unintelligible, obscure

unklug *adj.* imprudent, unwise

unkörperlich *adj.* incorporeal, immaterial

Unkosten *pl.* costs, charges, expenses

Unkraut *neu.* weed(s); **— vergeht nicht** evil doesn't perish

unkündbar *adj.* unredeemable; consolidated; permanent (position)

unkundig *adj.* unacquainted (with); ignorant

unlängst *adv.* not long ago, recently, lately

unlauter *adj.* impure; insincere, unfair

unleugbar *adj.* undeniable; incontestable

unlieb *adj.* disagreeable; **–enswürdig** *adj.* unfriendly; **–sam** *adj.* disagreeable, unpleasant

unliniert *adj.* unruled, without lines

unlogisch *adj.* illogical

unlösbar, unlöslich *adj.* insoluble

Unlust *f.* dislike, disinclination; aversion

unlustig *adj.* listless; disinclined, reluctant

unmännlich *adj.* unmanly

Unmass *neu.,* **Unmasse** *f.* vast quantity, immense number

unmassgeblich *adj.* unauthoritative; **nach meiner –en Meinung** in my humble opinion

unmässig *adj.* immoderate; excessive

Unmenge *f.* vast quantity (*oder* number)

Unmensch *m.* monster, brute

unmenschlich *adj.* inhuman, brutal; monstrous; barbarous; **–e Kraft** enormous strength

unmerklich *adj.* imperceptible

unmittelbar *adj.* immediate, direct

unmöbliert *adj.* unfurnished

unmodern *adj.* unfashionable; out-of-date

unmöglich *adj.* impossible; out of the question; **sich — machen** to compromise oneself

unmoralisch *adj.* immoral

unmündig *adj.* minor; under age

Unmut *m.* displeasure, ill humor, peevishness

unnachahmlich *adj.* inimitable

unnachgiebig *adj.* unyielding, relentless

unnahbar *adj.* unapproachable, inaccessible

unnatürlich *adj.* unnatural, affected

unnötig *adj.* unnecessary, superfluous; **–erweise** *adv.* unnecessarily, needlessly

unnütz adj. useless, unprofitable; idle, vain; (coll.) fresh, naughty

Unordnung f. disorder, untidiness; confusion; **in — bringen** to throw into confusion; **to disarrange; in — sein to be in a mess**

unparteiisch adj. impartial, unbiased

Unparteiische m. referee, umpire

unpassend adj. unfit, unsuitable; improper; unbecoming; inopportune; **sie benahm sich sehr — she behaved in an unladylike way**

unpässlich adj. indisposed; ailing

unpolitisch adj. unpolitic; undiplomatic

unpraktisch adj. impracticable; unskillful

unqualifiziert adj. unqualified

Unrat m. dirt, garbage, refuse; **excrements; — wittern to smell a rat**

unrätlich, unratsam adj. inadvisable

Unrecht neu. injustice; wrong; error; **an den –en kommen to meet one's match; im — sein, — haben to be mistaken (oder wrong); jemand — geben to decide against someone; jemand — tun to wrong someone**

unrecht adj. wrong; unfair, unjust; improper, inopportune; **am –en Ort sein to be out of place; –mässig** adj. unlawful, illegal

unregelmässig adj. irregular; abnormal

unrein adj. unclean, impure; **–er Diamant clouded (oder flawed) diamond; –er Ton (mus.) discord; ins –e schreiben to make a rough copy; –lich** adj. dirty, filthy

unrentabel adj. unremunerative

unrettbar adj. past help, irrecoverable; **— verloren irretrievably lost**

unrichtig adj. incorrect, wrong; erroneous

Unruh f. (watch) balance; **–e** f. uneasiness; commotion, disturbance; riot; **–estifter** m. agitator, disturber of the peace

unruhig adj. restless, unquiet; uneasy; agitated; turbulent; **–e See rough sea; –es Pferd restive horse; –e Zeiten troubled times**

uns pron. (to) us; ourselves; **ein Freund von — a friend of ours; unter — between ourselves; wir sehen — nie we never see each other; –er** pron. our, ours; of us; **erbarme dich –er have mercy upon us; –(e)rige** adj. ours; our people; **–ereiner** pron., **–ereins** pron. one of us, such as we; **–erseits** adv. for our part, as for us; **–ersgleichen** adj. people like us; **–erthalben** adv., **–ertwegen** adv., **–ertwillen** adv. on our account; for our sakes

unsachlich adj. not to the point; subjective

unsagbar, unsäglich adj. inexpressible; unutterable; immense

unsanft adj. ungentle, harsh

unsauber adj. unclean, dirty; filthy; unfair

unschädlich adj. harmless, innocuous; **— machen to render harmless; to disarm; to neutralize**

unschätzbar adj. invaluable; priceless

unscheinbar adj. unpretentious; plain

unschicklich adj. improper, unseemly; indecent

unschlüssig adj. irresolute; undecided

unschön adj. unlovely, unsightly; **unfair**

Unschuld f. innocence

unschuldig adj. innocent, guiltless; harmless

unschwer adj. not difficult, easy

unselbständig adj. dependent (on others)

unselig adj. unfortunate; fatal, accursed

unsicher adj. insecure, unsafe; unsteady; uncertain; irresolute; precarious

unsichtbar adj. invisible

Unsinn m. nonsense, absurdity

unsinnig adj. nonsensical, unreasonable; absurd

Unsitte f. bad habit; abuse

unsittlich adj. immoral; indecent

unstatthaft adj. inadmissible, illicit; illegal

unsterblich adj. immortal; **— machen to immortalize**

Unstern m. unlucky star; disaster, misfortune

unstet adj. unsteady; inconstant; restless

unstillbar adj. unappeasable, unquenchable

unsträflich adj. irreproachable; blameless

unstreitig adj. incontestable, indisputable; **— adv. undoubtedly**

unsympathisch adj. unpleasant, disagreeable; **er ist mir — I don't like him**

untadelhaft, untadelig adj. blameless; irreproachable

Untat f. crime, outrage

untätig adj. inactive, idle

untauglich adj. unfit; useless; disabled

unteilbar adj. indivisible

unten adv. below; downstairs; at the bottom; **nach — downward; — durch sein (coll.) to be despised; von oben bis — from top to bottom; von — auf dienen to rise from the ranks; –an** adv. at the lower end

unter prep. under; below, beneath, underneath; among(st); by; during; **nicht — drei Pfund not less than three pounds; — der Hand privately; — dieser Bedingung on this condition; — freiem**

Himmel in the open air; — seiner Regierung in his reign; — Tage (min.) underground; — uns among ourselves; between us; — *adj.* under, lower, inferior

Unter *m.* (cards) jack, knave

Unterabteilung *f.* subdivision; subunit

Unterarm *m.* forearm

Unterbau *m.* substructure, foundation

unterbauen *v.* to build a substructure; to lay a foundation; to undergird

Unterbeamte *m.* subordinate official

unterbelichten *v.* (phot.) to underexpose

Unterbett *neu.* underbedding, feather bed

Unterbewusstsein *neu.* (the) subconscious

unterbieten *v.* to underbid, to undercut, to undersell; (sports) to lower (record)

Unterbilanz *f.* (com.) deficit

unterbleiben *v.* to be left undone; not to take place; to cease, to be discontinued

unterbrechen *v.* to interrupt; to cut short; to stop; to intercept; to break (circuit)

Unterbrechung *f.* interruption; intermission; break, stop; disturbance

unterbreiten *v.* to spread underneath; jemand — to lay (*oder* submit to) someone

unterbringen *v.* to place; to accomodate; to shelter; to settle; to billet (troops)

unter der Hand *adv.* secretly

underdes(sen) *adv.* meanwhile, in the meantime

Unterdruckkammer *f.* altitude chamber

unterdrücken *v.* to oppress; to repress; to suppress; to crush, to quell

untereinander *adv.* each other; among themselves; mutually, reciprocally

unterernährt *adj.* undernourished, underfed

unterfangen *v.* to dare; to undertake

Unterfangen *neu.* undertaking, venture

Unterfertigte *m.* (the) undersigned

Unterführung *f.* subway; underpass

Untergang *m.* setting; sinking; decline; destruction, ruin, fall

Untergebene *m.* subordinate, menial; inferior

unterge(h)en *v.* to sink, to founder; (ast.) to set; to decline, to perish

untergeordnet *adj.* subordinate; –e Rolle minor part; von –er Bedeutung of secondary importance

Untergeschoss *neu.* basement

Untergestell *neu.* undercarriage, chassis

Untergewicht *neu.* underweight

untergraben *v.* to undermine, to sap

Untergrund *m.* subsoil; substructure; background; underground; –bahn *f.* (rail.) subway

unterhalb *prep.* below, under, at the lower end

Unterhalt *m.* maintenance, support, livelihood; –ung *f.* conversation; amusement, entertainment; maintenance; –ungslektüre *f.*, –ungsliteratur *f.* light reading

unterhalt: –en *v.* to support, to maintain, to keep up; to entertain, to amuse; sich –en to converse (with); to enjoy oneself; –end *adj.*, –sam *adj.* amusing, entertaining

unterhandeln *v.* to negotiate, to parley

Unterhändler *m.* negotiator, mediator; agent; (coll.) go-between

Unterhandlung *f.* negotiation; in –en stehen to carry on negotiations

Unterhaus *neu.* Lower House, House of Commons; House of Representatives

Unterhemd *neu.* undershirt

unterhöhlen *v.* to undermine; to tunnel

Unterholz *neu.* underwood, underbrush

Unterhosen *f. pl.* underpants, drawers

unterirdisch *adj.* underground; subterranean

unterjochen *v.* to subdue, to subjugate

Unterkiefer *m.* lower jaw

Unterkleid *neu.* slip; –ung *f.* underwear

unterkommen *v.* to find accommodations (*oder* lodging); to get employment

Unterkommen *neu.* accommodation, lodging, shelter; employment

Unterkörper *m.* underbody

unterkriegen *v.* to get the better of; sich nicht — lassen to hold one's own (ground)

Unterkunft *f.* accommodation, lodging, shelter

Unterlage *f.* foundation, basis; support; document, evidence, record; blotting pad; (geol.) substratum

Unterlass *m.* ohne — without intermission; incessantly

unterlassen *v.* to neglect, to omit; to fail to do; to abstain (from)

unterlaufen *v.* to slip in; to occur; es können leicht Fehler — mistakes can easily be made; mit Blut — suffused with blood, bloodshot

unterlegen *v.* to lay (*oder* put) underneath; to attach (meaning to); to set (words to music)

Unterleib *m.* abdomen; bowels

unterliegen *v.* to succumb; to be defeated (*oder* overcome); es unterliegt keinem Zweifel there is not doubt about it

Unterlippe *f.* underlip; lower lip

untermengen, untermischen *v.* to intermix; to mix up; to intermingle

unterminieren *v.* to undermine; –d *adj.* (mil.) subversive

unternehmen v. to undertake; to attempt; **-d** adj. enterprising, lively; bold, daring

Unternehmer m. contractor; entrepreneur; employer; **-verband** m. syndicate, pool

Unternehmung f. enterprise; operation

Unteroffizier m. (mil.) noncommissioned officer; corporal; (naut.) petty officer

unterordnen v. to subordinate; **von untergeordneter Bedeutung** of secondary importance

Unterpfand neu. pledge, security

Unterprima f. lower division of the highest grade of a German Junior college

unterreden v. **sich —** to converse, to confer

Unterricht m. teaching, training; instruction, lesson; **-sbriefe** m. pl. instruction by correspondence; **-sfach** neu. branch of instruction, educational subject; **-swesen** neu. public instruction, educational matters

unterrichten v. to instruct, to teach; to educate, to train; to inform; **sich von etwas —** to inform oneself

Unterrock m. petticoat

untersagen v. to forbid, to prohibit; to interdict

Untersatz m. basis; stand; pedestal; saucer; (phil.) minor proposition

unterschätzen v. to underestimate, to underrate

unterscheiden v. to distinguish; to differentiate; to discern; **sich — von** to differ from

Unterscheidungsmerkmal neu. distinctive mark

Unterschenkel m. (anat.) shank

unterschieben v. to push (oder shove) under; to substitute; to foist upon; to insinuate

Unterschied m. difference, distinction; **ohne —** indiscriminately

unterschied: **-en** adj., **-lich** adj. different, distinct; **-slos** adv. indiscriminately, without distinction (oder exception)

unterschlagen v. to embezzle; to intercept; to suppress; to defraud

Unterschleif m. embezzlement, fraud

Unterschlupf m. refuge, shelter

unterschreiben v. to sign; to subscribe to

Unterschrift f. signature; caption

Unterseeboot neu. submarine

unterseeisch adj. submarine

Untersekunda f. lower division of the second grade of a German secondary school

untersetzt adj. thick-set, stocky, dumpy

Unterstaatssekretär m. Undersecretary of State

Unterstand m. cover, shelter; (mil.) dugout

unterstehen v. to stand under; to take shelter; to be subordinate to; **sich —** to dare, to venture

unterstreichen v. to underline; to emphasize

Unterstufe f. (school) lower grade

unterstützen v. to aid, to assist, to support; to second; to patronize, to subsidize

Unterstützungsfonds m. relief fund

untersuchen v. to inquire (oder search) into; to examine; to scrutinize; to explore; to analyze; to investigate; to probe

Untersuchung f. investigation; **-sgefangene** m. prisoner under trial; **-shaft** f. detention before trial; **-srichter** m. examining judge

Untertan m. subject; serf, vassal

untertänig adj. humble, submissive, subject

Untertasse f. saucer

untertauchen v. to dive, to dip; to submerge

Unterteil m. lower part; base, bottom

Untertitel m. subtitle, subheading

Unterton m. undertone; (phys.) accessory sound

unterwärts adj. downwards; underneath

Unterwäsche f. underwear

Unterwasserbombe f. depth charge

unterwegs adv. on the way; **immer —** always on the move

unterweisen v. to instruct, to teach

Unterwelt f. underworld, lower regions; Hades

unterwerfen v. to subjugate, to subdue; to subject; **sich —** to submit, to be resigned

unterwinden v. **sich —** to venture upon; to undertake; to attempt

unterwühlen v. to undermine

unterwürfig adj. submissive; servile

Unterzeichn: **-er** m. signatory; **-ete** m. undersigned; **-ung** f. signing; ratification

Unterzeug neu. underwear

unterziehen v. to draw under; to put on underneath; **sich einer Operation —** to submit to (oder undergo) an operation; **sich einer Sache —** to undertake something

Untiefe f. shallow place, sandbank; (fig.) bottomless depth, abyss

Untier neu. monster; savage animal

untilgbar adj. indelible; irredeemable

untrennbar adj. inseparable

untreu adj. unfaithful, disloyal; **einer**

Sache — werden to desert a cause
Untreue *f.* unfaithfulness, disloyalty; —
im Amt breach of trust
untröstlich *adj.* disconsolate, inconsolable
untrüglich *adj.* infallible, unmistakable
untüchtig *adj.* incapable, unfit; incompetent
Untugend *f.* bad habit, vice
unüber: **–legt** *adj.* inconsiderate, rash;
–sehbar *adj.* incalculable; immense,
vast; **–setzbar** *adj.* untranslatable;
–steigbar *adj.* insurmountable; **–tragbar** *adj.* not transferable; unassignable;
–treffbar *adj.*, **–trefflich** *adj.* unsurpassable, unequalled; **–troffen** *adj.* unexcelled, unsurpassed; **–windlich** *adj.*
invincible, unconquerable; insurmountable
unum: **–gänglich** *adj.* indispensable; inevitable; **–schränkt** *adj.* unlimited;
absolute; **–stösslich** *adj.* irrefutable,
irrevocable; **–wunden** *adj.* unreserved;
candid, frank, plain
ununterbrochen *adj.* uninterrupted; incessant
unveränderlich *adj.* unchangeable; invariable; **–e Weltall** steady-state universe
unverantwortlich *adj.* irresponsible; inexcusable
unverbesserlich *adj.* incorrigible
unverbindlich *adj.* disobliging, unkind
unverblümt *adj.* blunt, plain; unadorned
unverbrennbar *adj.* incombustible
unverbürgt *adj.* unwarranted; unconfirmed
unverdaulich *adj.* indigestible
unverderbt, unverdorben *adj.* uncorrupted, unspoiled; unblemished; pure,
spotless
unverdient *adj.* undeserved, unmerited;
unjust; **–ermassen** *adv.* undeservingly,
unjustly
unverdrossen *adj.* indefatigable, untiring
unverdünnt *adj.* undiluted
unverehelicht *adj.* unmarried; single
unvereinbar *adj.* incompatible, irreconcilable
unverfälscht *adj.* unadulterated; genuine,
pure
unverfänglich *adj.* not captious, harmless
unverfroren *adj.* unabashed, audacious;
impudent
unvergänglich *adj.* imperishable; immortal
unvergesslich *adj.* unforgettable
unvergleichlich *adj.* incomparable; unique
unverhältnismässig *adj.* disproportionate;
excessive
unverheiratet *adj.* unmarried
unverhofft *adj.* unexpected; unforeseen;

–es Glück windfall
unverhohlen *adj.* unconcealed; frank,
open
unverkäuflich *adj.* unsaleable, unmarketable; **–e Ware** dead stock
unverkennbar *adj.* unmistakable; evident
unverkürzt *adj.* uncurtailed; unabridged
unverletzbar *adj.* invulnerable; inviolable
unverletzt *adj.* unhurt, uninjured; undamaged
unvermählt *adj.* unmarried
unvermeidbar, unvermeidlich *adj.* unavoidable; inevitable; fatal
unvermerkt *adj.* unperceived; unnoticed
unvermischt *adj.* unmixed; unadulterated; unalloyed; pure
unvermittelt *adj.* abrupt, sudden
Unvermögen *neu.* incapacity; impotence
unvermögend *adj.* incapable; impotent;
powerless; penniless, poor
unvermutet *adj.* unexpected, unforeseen
unvernehmlich *adj.* inaudible; unintelligible
Unvernunft *f.* unreasonableness; folly
unvernünftig *adj.* unreasonable; irrational
unverrichtet *adj.* unperformed, not carried out
unverrückt *adv.* immovably; fixedly; —
ansehen to gaze steadily at
unverschämt *adj.* shameless, impudent;
–e Preise exhorbitant prices
unverschuldet *adj.* undeserved, unmerited; not in debt; unencumbered;
–erweise *adv.* undeservedly; innocently
unversehens *adv.* unawares, unexpectedly
unversehrt *adj.* uninjured; intact, safe
unversichert *adj.* uninsured
unversiegbar, unversieglich *adj.* inexhaustible
unversöhnlich *adj.* irreconcilable; implacable
unversorgt *adj.* unprovided for, destitute
Unverstand *m.* want of judgment (*oder*
sense); lack of intelligence; folly,
stupidity
unverständig *adj.* imprudent; foolish, unwise
unverständlich *adj.* unintelligible; incomprehensible; **die Sache ist mir ganz —**
I cannot make head or tail of the affair
unversteuerbar *adj.* untaxable
unversucht *adj.* unattempted, untried;
nichts — lassen to leave no stone unturned
unvertilgbar *adj.* indelible, indestructible
unverträglich *adj.* unsociable, incompatible; intolerant, quarrelsome
unverwandt *adj.* unmoved, steadfast,
fixed
unverweilt *adv.* without delay, immedi-

ately
unverweslich *adj.* incorruptible, undecaying
unverwundbar *adj.* invulnerable
unverwüstlich *adj.* indestructible; inexhaustible; everlasting; irrepressible (humor)
unverzagt *adj.* undismayed, undaunted, bold
unverzeihlich *adj.* unpardonable, inexcusable
unverzinsbar, unverzinslich *adj.* paying no interest
unverzüglich *adj.* immediate, instant, prompt
unvoll: **-endet** *adj.* uncompleted, unfinished; **-kommen** *adj.* imperfect, defective; **-ständig** *adj.* incomplete
unvor: **-bereitet** *adj.* unprepared; extempore; **-denklich** *adj.* immemorial; **-hergesehen** *adj.* unforeseen, unexpected; **-sätzlich** *adj.* unpremeditated, unintentional; **-sichtig** *adj.* incautious; imprudent; **-teilhaft** *adj.* unprofitable, disadvantageous; unbecoming; **-teilhaft aussehen** not to look one's best
unwahr *adj.* untrue, false; **-haftig** *adj.* untruthful, insincere; **-scheinlich** *adj.* improbable, unlikely
unwandelbar *adj.* immutable, unchangeable
unwegsam *adj.* impassable, impracticable
unweit *adv.* not far off, near(by); — *prep.* not far from, close to, near
unwert *adj.* unworthy
Unwesen *neu.* disorder; annoyance, nuisance; **sein — treiben** to be up to one's tricks; to haunt (a place)
unwesentlich *adj.* unessential, immaterial; unimportant; **das ist — that** doesn't matter
Unwetter *neu.* bad weather; thunderstorm
unwichtig *adj.* unimportant, insignificant
unwider: **-legbar** *adj.*, **-leglich** *adj.* irrefutable; **-ruflich** *adj.* irrevocable; **-stehlich** *adj.* irresistible
unwill: **-ig** *adj.* unwilling; reluctant; indignant; **-kommen** *adj.* unwelcome; unpleasant; **-kürlich** *adj.* involuntary, instinctive
Unwille *m.* indignation; wrath, reluctance
unwirklich *adj.* unreal
unwirksam *adj.* ineffectual, inoperative; void
unwirsch *adj.* cross, rude, uncouth
unwirtschaftlich *adj.* uneconomic
unwissen: **-d** *adj.* ignorant; **-schaftlich** *adj.* unscientific; **-tlich** *adv.* unknowingly

unwohl *adj.* unwell, indisposed
Unwohlsein *neu.* indisposition; menstruation
unwohnlich *adj.* uninhabitable; uncomfortable
unwürdig *adj.* unworthy
Unzahl *f.* immense number
unzählbar, unzählig *adj.* innumerable, countless
Unze *f.* ounce
Unzeit *f.* wrong time; **zur — inopportunely**
unzeitgemäss *adj.* behind the times, inopportune
unzeitig *adj.* untimely, ill-timed; premature
unzerbrechlich *adj.* unbreakable, infrangible
unzerreissbar *adj.* untearable, solid
unzerstörbar *adj.* indestructible, imperishable
unzertrennlich *adj.* inseparable; inherent
unziemend, unziemlich *adj.* unbecoming, improper
unzivilisiert *adj.* uncivilized; barbarous
Unzucht *f.* unchastity; prostitution
unzüchtig *adj.* unchaste; lewd; obscene
unzufrieden *adj.* dissatisfied, discontented
unzu: **-gänglich** *adj.* inaccessible; reserved; **-länglich** *adj.* inadequate, insufficient; **-lässig** *adj.* inadmissible; **-rechnungsfähig** *adj.* irresponsible; imbecile; **-reichend** *adj.* insufficient; **-sammenhängend** *adj.* disconnected; incoherent; **-ständig** *adj.* incompetent; **-träglich** *adj.* disadvantageous; unwholesome; **-treffend** *adj.* incorrect; **-verlässig** *adj.* unreliable, uncertain
unzweckmässig *adj.* inexpedient, unsuitable
unzweideutig *adj.* unequivocal, unambiguous
unzweifelhaft *adj.* undoubted, indubitable
üppig *adj.* luxuriant; exuberant; voluptuous; abundant; well-developed (shape)
Urahn *m.* great-grandfather; ancestor; **-e** *f.* great-grandmother; ancestress
uralt *adj.* old as the hills; ancient, primeval
Uran *neu.* uranium
Uraufführung *f.* first performance
urbar *adj.* arable; cultivated; **— machen** to bring under cultivation, to cultivate
Urbewohner *m. pl.* aborigines
Urbild *neu.* original, prototype, archetype
Urchristentum *neu.* primitive Christianity; the early Church
Ureinwohner *m. pl.* native inhabitants
Ureltern *pl.* first parents; ancestors
Urenkel *m.* great-grandchild; great-

grandson; –in f. great-granddaughter

Urgross: –eltern pl. great-grandparents; –mutter f. great-grandmother; –vater m. great-grandfather

Urheber m. author, originator, creator; –recht neu. copyright; –schaft f. authorship

Urin m. urine

urinieren v. to urinate

Urkunde f. document; record; charter; evidence

Urlaub m. leave; furlough; vacation; –er m. soldier on furlough

Urmensch m. primitive man

Urne f. urn; ballot box; zur — gehen to vote

urplötzlich adj. very sudden

Urquell m. primary source; origin

Ursache f. cause, reason, motive; keine — don't mention it

ursächlich adj. causal; causative

Urschrift f. original text; first draft

Ursprache f. primitive (oder original) language

Ursprung m. source; origin; beginning, cause

ursprünglich adj. original, primitive, primary

Urstoff m. primary matter; element

Urteil neu. judgment, opinion; sentence, verdict; –seröffnung f. publication of a judgment; –skraft f., –svermögen neu. power of judgment; –sspruch m. sentence, verdict

urteil: –en v. to express one's opinion; to judge; to pass sentence; –sfähig adj. competent to judge, judicious; –slos adj. without judgment, injudicious

Urtext m. original text

Urtier neu. protozoan, primitive animal

Urureltern pl. progenitors, early ancestors

Urvater m. first progenitor

Urvolk neu. primitive people; aborigines

Urwahl f. primary election

Urwald m. primeval forest

urwüchsig adj. native, original; rough, blunt

Urzeit f. primeval period

Usurpator m. usurper

usurpieren v. to usurp

Utensilien f. pl. utensils, tools, implements

Utopie f. Utopian scheme, chimera

utopisch adj. utopian

uzen v. (coll.) to tease, to fool

V

vag adj. vague; –abundieren v. to tramp, to roam, to stroll about

Vagabund m. vagabond, tramp, bum; –entum neu. vagrancy

Vakanz f. vacancy

Valuta f. rate (of exchange); currency

Vampir m. vampire

Van Allens Radiationsgürtel m. Van Allen Radiation Belt

Vanille f. vanilla; –nschote f. vanilla bean

Var: –iante f. variant; –iation f. variation; –ieté neu. variety theater

variieren v. to vary; to compose variations

Vas: –all m. vassal; –allenstaat m. satellite

Vase f. vase

Vaselin neu., **Vaseline** f. Vaseline

Vater m. father; –haus neu. parental house; –land neu. native country; –landsliebe f. patriotism; –mörder m. parricide; (coll.) high stiff collar; –schaft f. paternity, fatherhood; –sname m. surname; –stadt f. native city; –stelle f., –stelle vertreten to be a father to; to father; –teil neu. patrimony; –unser neu. Lord's Prayer

vater: –ländisch adj. national, patriotic; –landsliebend adj. patriotic; –los adj. fatherless

väterlich adj. fatherly, paternal; –erseits adv. on the father's side

vege: –tarisch adj. vegetarian; –tativ adj. vegetative; vegetable; –tieren to vegetate

Vegetarier m. vegetarian

Vehemenz f. vehemence

Veilchen neu. violet; –wurzel f. orris root

Veitstanz m. St. Vitus' dance

Vene f. vein; –nentzündung f. phlebitis

venerisch adj. venereal

Ventil neu. valve; –ator m. ventilator; fan

verab: –folgen v. to deliver, to hand over; to remit; –reden v. to agree upon; sich –reden to make an appointment (oder a date); –redetermassen adv. as agreed upon; –reichen v. to give, to hand over; –säumen to neglect, to omit; –scheuen v. to abhor, to detest; –scheuenswert adj., –scheuenswürdig adj. abominable, detestable; –schieden v. to discharge, to dismiss; to disband; ein Gesetz –schieden to pass a bill; sich –schieden to take leave of, to bid farewell

verachten v. to despise, to disdain

verächtlich adj. contemptuous; contemptible

verallgemeinern v. to generalize

veraltet adj. antiquated, obsolete

veran: –kern v. to anchor, to moor; to establish firmly; –lagen v. to assess; –lagt adj. gifted, talented; –lassen v. to cause, to occasion; to induce;

-schaulichen v. to illustrate; to make clear; **-schlagen** v. to estimate, to rate; **-stalten** v. to arrange, to organize

Veran: -lagung f. assessment; talent, disposition; **-staltung** f. arrangement; (sport) event; performance

Veranda f. veranda, porch

veränderlich adj. changeable, variable; unstable; unsettled; fluctuating

verändern v. to alter, to change; to vary; to transform; **sich —** to become changed; (coll.) to take another position

verantwort: -en v. to answer (oder account) for; **sich -en** to justify oneself; **-lich** adj. responsible; **-ungslos** adj. irresponsible; **-ungsvoll** adj. imposing responsibility

Verantwortung f. responsibility; justification; **auf seine —** at his own risk; **zur — ziehen** to call to account

verar: -beiten v. to work up; to manufacture; to assimilate; to digest; to wear out; **-gen** v. to take amiss, to misconstrue; **-men** v. to become impoverished; **-zten** v. (coll.) to doctor

verauktionieren v. to (sell at) auction

verausgaben v. to spend; **sich —** to run short of money

veräusserlich adj. alienable; saleable

veräussern v. to alienate; to dispose of

verballhornen v. to edit ridiculously

Verband m. union; formation, unit; (med.) bandage, dressing; **-flug** m. formation; **-päckchen** neu. (mil.) field dressing; **-platz** m. first-aid station; **-smitglied** neu. member of a society; **-stoff** m., **-zeug** neu. bandaging material

verbannen v. to banish, to exile; to outlaw

verbarrikadieren v. to barricade, to block

verbauen v. to build (oder block) up; to obstruct; to spend in building, to build badly

verbergen v. to conceal, to hide

verbessern v. to correct; to improve

verbeugen v. **sich —** to (make a) bow

verbiegen v. to bend, to twist, to warp

verbieten v. to forbid, to prohibit

verbilligen v. to reduce in price, to cheapen

verbinden v. to bind (up); to bandage, to dress (wound); to join, to unite; to combine; (tel.) to connect; **ich bin Ihnen sehr verbunden** I am very much obliged to you

verbindlich adj. binding, obligatory; obliging

Verbindlichkeit f. obligation; liability; obligingness, courtesy

Verbindung f. combination, union; asso-

ciation, society, contact; communication, connection; blending (of colors); amalgamation; compound; **sich in — setzen** to get into touch, to contact; **-sbahn** f. (rail.) branch line; **-sgang** m. connecting passage; **-smann** m. mediator; **-soffizier** m. liaison officer; **-sstück** neu. joint; coupling, tie

verbissen adj. obstinate; crabbed, dogged

verbitten v. not to permit; **das verbitte ich mir** I won't stand that

verbittern v. to embitter

verblassen v. to fade, to (turn) pale

verblättern v. to lose one's place (in book)

Verbleib m. whereabouts

verbleichen v. to (turn) pale; to fade

verblenden v. to blind; to screen; to mask; to face (wall); to delude, to infatuate

verblichen adj. faded; deceased

Verblichene m. deceased

verblüffen v. to bewilder, to dumbfound

verblühen v. to fade, to wither

verblümt adj. veiled; figurative, allusive

verbluten v. **sich —** to bleed to death

verbohrt adj. obstinate, stubborn; mad

verborgen v. to lend; **—** adj. concealed, hidden, secret; **-erweise** adv. stealthily

Verbot neu. prohibition, veto

verboten adj. forbidden, prohibited; illicit; **-er Eingang!** no admission!

Verbrauch m. consumption; expenditure; **-er** m. consumer; **-ssteuer** f. excise tax

verbrauchen v. to consume, to use; to wear out

Verbrech: -en neu. crime; **-er** m. criminal, felon; **-erkolonie** f. penal colony; **-tum**

verbrechen v. to commit (a crime)

verbrecherisch adj. criminal

verbreiten v. to spread, to diffuse; to disseminate; to circulate; **sich — über** to enlarge upon (a theme); to expatiate on

verbrennbar adj. combustible

verbrennen v. to burn; to scorch; to cremate

Verbrennung f. burn(ing); combustion; cremation; **— 2. Grades** second-degree burn; **-smotor** m. combustion engine; **-sofen** m. crematory, incinerator

verbriefen v. to guarantee by documents

verbringen v. to pass (time); to spend

verbrüdern v. **sich —** to fraternize

verbrühen v. to scald

verbuchen v. to book

Verb(um) neu. verb; **-alinjurie** f. (law) libel

verbummeln v. to trifle (oder idle) away; (coll.) to forget, to neglect

verbunden adj. united, connected; obliged

verbünden v. **sich — mit** to ally (oder unite) oneself with

Verbündete m. ally, confederate

verbürgen v. to guarantee; **sich — für** to vouch (*oder* answer) for

verbüssen v. to suffer the consequences; to serve time; to complete a sentence

Verdacht m. suspicion; distrust

verdächtig adj. suspicious; doubtful

verdächtigen v. to cast suspicion on; to distrust; to accuse, to incriminate

Verdächtigung f. insinuation; false charge

verdamm: -en v. to condemn; to damn; **-enswert** adj. damnable; **-t!** interj. damn it!

Verdammnis f. damnation, perdition

Verdammung f. condemnation; damnation

verdampfen v. to evaporate; to vaporize

verdanken v. to owe to; to be obliged to

Verdau: -lichkeit f. digestibleness; **-ung** f. digestion; **-ungsbeschwerden** f. pl., **-ungsstörung** f. indigestion

verdauen v. to digest

Verdeck neu. (mech.) top, hood; (naut.) deck

verdecken v. to cover; to conceal; to veil

verdenken v. to take amiss; to blame

Verderb m. ruin; decay; waste; **-en** neu. corruption; destruction; ruin; **-er** m. corrupter; destroyer

verderb: -en v. to spoil; to destroy, to ruin; to corrupt; to perish; **es mit jemand -en** to lose someone's favor; **sich den Magen -en** to upset one's stomach; **-lich** adj. perishable, pernicious; fatal; **-t** adj. corrupted; depraved

verdeutlichen v. to elucidate; to make plain

verdeutschen v. to translate into German

verdichten v. to condense, to compress; to solidify; to consolidate

verdicken v. to thicken, to condense

verdien: -en v. to earn; to deserve; to merit; **er hat sich um sein Land -t gemacht** he has served his country well; **habe ich das um Sie -t?** have I deserved that from you? **-stlich** adj., **-stvoll** adj., **-t** adj. deserving; meritorious; **-termassen** adv., **-terweise** adv. deservedly; according to one's merit

Verdienst m. earnings; gain, profit; — neu. merit; **-spanne** f. margin of profit

verdingen v. to hire out; **sich —** to take a position

verdolmetschen v. to interpret

verdonnern v. (coll.) to condemn, to punish

verdoppeln v. to double; to redouble

verdorben adj. spoiled, tainted; depraved

verdorren v. to dry up, to wither

verdrängen v. to push aside; to displace; to repress, to supplant; to inhibit

verdrehen v. to twist; to sprain; (eyes) to roll; to distort, to misrepresent; **jemand den Kopf —** to turn someone's head

verdreht adj. distorted, twisted; cracked, crazy, mad; misrepresented

verdreifachen v. to treble, to triple

verdriessen v. to annoy, to grieve; **es sich nicht — lassen** not to be discouraged by; **sich keine Mühe — lassen** to spare no pains

verdriesslich adj. annoyed, cross, peevish; ill-humored; annoying, irksome, unpleasant

verdrossen adj. sulky, listless, cross

verdrucken v. to misprint

Verdruss m. annoyance, vexation, trouble

verduften v. to evaporate; (coll.) to slip away, to vanish

verdummen v. to make (*oder* become) stupid

verdunkeln v. to darken, to cloud; to black out; to eclipse; to obscure

Verdunk(e)lung f. darkening; black-out; eclipse; dimming; **-sgefahr** f. (law) danger of prejudicing the course of justice

verdünnen v. to thin; to dilute; to rarefy

verdunsten v. to evaporate

verdursten v. to die of thirst

verdüstern v. to darken, to cloud; to obscure

verdutzen v. to bewilder, to disconcert

verdutzt adj. dumbfounded, startled

veredeln v. to ennoble; to improve, to refine; (bot.) to graft

vereh(e)lichen v. to marry

verehr: -en v. to respect; to revere; to adore, to worship; **jemand etwas -en** to give someone a present; **-lich** adj., **-t** adj. esteemed, honored; **-ungswert** adj., **-ungswürdig** adj. estimable, admirable, respected

Verehrer m. admirer, worshiper, lover

vereid(ig)en v. to swear in, to put under oath

Verein m. association, club, society; **im — mit** in conjunction with; **-igung** f. union; combination; junction; unification; alliance, coalition; fusion; **-zelung** f. isolation; detachment

verein: -bar adj. combinable, compatible; consistent; **-baren** v. to agree upon; to arrange; **-(ig)en** v. to unite, to combine, to join; **sich -(ig)en** to associate, to ally, to reconcile; **-fachen** v. to simplify; **-heitlichen** v. to unify; to standardize; **-nahmen** v. to take in (money); **-samen** v. to become isolated (*oder* lonely); **-zelt** adj. isolated; sporadic; solitary

die Vereinigten Staaten (von Amerika) *pl.* the United States (of America)

vereisen *v.* to turn to ice; to freeze; to glaciate

vereiteln *v.* to frustrate, to baffle

verelenden *v.* to become wretched, to pauperize

verenden *v.* to die, to perish

verenge(r)n *v.* to narrow; to contract; to tighten, to constrict

vererben *v.* to bequeath, to leave; to transmit; **sich —** to be hereditary; **sich — auf** to devolve on

Vererbung *f.* (act of) bequeathing; hereditary transmission; **-sforschung** *f.* genetics; **-sgesetz** *neu.* genetic code

verewigen *v.* to perpetuate; to immortalize

verewigt *adj.* deceased; late; immortalized

verfahren *v.* to deal with, to treat; to proceed; to spend money (*oder* time) in driving; to muddle; **sich —** to miss one's way; to be on the wrong track; **—** *adj.* bungled; muddled; hopeless

Verfahren *neu.* proceeding(s); procedure; process; method, dealing

Verfall *m.* decay, decline; deterioration; degeneracy; (com.) maturity; foreclosure

verfälschen *v.* to falsify, to forge; to adulterate; to counterfeit

verfänglich *adj.* insidious; embarrassing; risky

verfärben *v.* to use (*oder* spoil) in dyeing; **sich —** to change color; to turn pale, to fade

verfass: -en *v.* to compose, to write; eine Urkunde -en to draft (*oder* draw up) a document; **-ungsmässig** *adj.* constitutional; **-ungswidrig** *adj.* unconstitutional

Verfass: -er *m.* author; **-erin** *f.* authoress

Verfassung *f.* condition, state; disposition, mood; constitution

verfaulen *v.* to rot, to putrefy; to decay

verfechten *v.* to fight for, to defend; to advocate, to champion

verfehlen *v.* to miss; to fail to do

verfehlt *adj.* unsuccessful; spoiled; bungled

Verfehlung *f.* mistake, failure; lapse; offense

verfeinden *v.* **sich — mit** to fall out with; to make an enemy of

verfeinern *v.* to refine; to improve, to polish

verfemen *v.* to outlaw

verfertigen *v.* to make, to manufacture

Verfettung *f.* fatty degeneration

verfeuern *v.* to burn, to blaze away; to waste

verfilmen *v.* to film, to picture, to screen

verfinstern *v.* to darken; to eclipse

verfitzen *v.* to entangle

verflachen *v.* to become flat (*oder* shallow); to decline (intellectually)

verflechten *v.* to interlace; to implicate

verfliegen *v.* to fly away; to evaporate; to vanish; to pass quickly; **sich —** (avi.) to lose one's way

verfliessen *v.* to flow away; to elapse

verflixt! *interj.* (coll.) confound it!

verflossen *adj.* past; late

verfluchen *v.* to curse, to damn

verflucht *adj.* accursed, damned; **—!** *interj.* darn it! **—** *adv.* (coll.) very

verflüchtigen *v.* to volatilize; **sich — to** evaporate

Verfolg *m.* course, progress; **-er** *m.* pursuer; prosecutor; **-ung** *f.* pursuit; prosecution; **-ungswahn** *m.* persecution complex

verfolgen *v.* to pursue; to persecute

verfrachten *v.* to load, to ship; to charter

verfressen *adj.* (coll.) voracious

verfrüht *adj.* premature

verfügbar *adj.* available

verfügen *v.* to decree, to order, to ordain; **sich —** to betake oneself; **— über** to dispose of; to have control of, to be master of

Verfügung *f.* decree; order; disposal

verführen *v.* to entice, to tempt; to seduce

verführerisch *adj.* enticing; seductive

vergaloppieren *v.* **sich —** (coll.) to blunder

vergangen *adj.* past, bygone, last

Vergangenheit *f.* past; (gram.) past tense

vergänglich *adj.* transitory, transient; perishable

Vergaser *m.* carburetor

vergeb: -en *v.* to give away, to dispose of; to bestow, to confer; (cards) to misdeal; to forgive, to pardon; **sich etwas -en** to degrade oneself; **-en sein** to be engaged; to be filled (position); **-ens** *adv.* in vain; **-lich** *adj.* futile, unavailing; idle

vergegenwärtigen *v.* to represent; **sich —** to realize, to imagine

vergeh(e)n *v.* to pass; to fade; to perish; to elapse; **sich — gegen** to offend (against), to injure; to assault, to violate; **— vor** to die of; **vor jemand —** to feel inferior

vergeistigen *v.* to spiritualize; to alcoholize

vergelten *v.* to repay; to retaliate; to return

vergessen *v.* to forget; to neglect

Vergessenheit *f.* oblivion

vergesslich *adj.* forgetful

vergeuden v. to squander, to waste; to lavish, to dissipate

vergewaltigen v. to violate; to rape

vergewissern v. sich — to make sure of; to ascertain

vergiessen v. to shed, to spill

vergiften v. to poison; to contaminate

vergilbt adj. yellowed

Vergissmeinnicht neu. forget-me-not

vergittern v. to enclose with latticework

Vergleich m. comparison; agreement; compromise

vergleich: **-bar** adj. comparable; **-en** v. to compare; to collate; to settle; sich **-en mit** to come to terms with; to compromise; **-sweise** adv. by way of agreement

verglimmen v. to cease glimmering; to burn out; to die away

Vergnüg: **-en** neu. amusement; pleasure; fun; **-ung** f. entertainment, pleasure; **-ungsreise** f. pleasure trip

vergnügen v. to amuse, to divert; sich — to enjoy (oder amuse) oneself

vergnügt adj. gay, cheerful; delighted, glad

vergolden v. to gild

vergönnen v. to permit; to grant; not to begrudge

vergöttern v. to deify; to idolize, to adore

vergraben v. to hide in the ground; to bury

vergrämt adj. grief-stricken, woebegone

vergreifen v. sich — to seize by mistake; (mus.) to touch the wrong key; sich — **an** to lay hands on; to violate; to steal

vergrössern v. to enlarge; to extend; to increase; to magnify; to exaggerate

Vergrösserung f. enlargement; **-sapparat** m. enlarging camera; **-sglas** neu. magnifying glass

Vergünstigung f. favor; privilege, concession; (com.) rebate

vergüten v. to reimburse, to compensate; to indemnify; to refund, to restore

verhaften v. to arrest; to take into custody

Verhaftung f. arrest; **-sbefehl** m. arrest warrant

verhallen v. (sounds) to die (oder fade) away

verhalten v. to suppress, to restrain; sich — to behave, to conduct (oneself); sich — **zu** to be in proportion to (oder the ratio of)

Verhalten neu. behavior, conduct, attitude

Verhältnis neu. relation; proportion, ratio; love affair; **-se** pl. circumstances, situation; **-wort** neu. preposition

verhältnismässig adj. proportional, rela-

tive

verhältniswidrig adj. disproportionate

Verhaltungsmassregeln f. pl. rules of conduct; instructions

verhandeln v. to negotiate, to parley; (law) to plead; to debate

Verhandlung f. negotiation, parley; trial; **-ssystem** neu. parliamentary system

verhängen v. to hang over, to veil; eine Strafe — to inflict punishment

Verhängnis neu. destiny, fate; disaster

verhängnisvoll adj. fatal, fateful; unfortunate, disastrous

verharren v. to remain, to persevere

verhärten v. to harden, to grow hard

verhaspeln v. to tangle up; sich — to become confused; to break down (in speech)

verhasst adj. hated, odious

verhätscheln v. to coddle, to pamper, to spoil

verhauen v. (coll.) to thrash; sich — (coll.) to blunder

verheeren v. to devastate, to ravage; **-d** adj. devastating; catastrophic; (coll.) awful

verhehlen v. to conceal, to hide

verheimlichen v. to keep secret; to disguise

verheiraten v. to marry; to get married

verheissen v. to promise

verheissungsvoll adj. promising

verhelfen v. jemand zu etwas — to help a person obtain something

verherrlichen v. to glorify, to extol

verhetzen v. to instigate, to stir up

verhexen v. to bewitch, to enchant

verhindern v. to hinder, to prevent

verhöhnen v. to deride; to sneer

Verhör neu. trial; examination, interrogation

verhören v. to interrogate, to examine, to hear; sich — to misunderstand

verhüllen v. to cover, to veil; to disguise

verhundertfachen v. to multiply a hundredfold

verhungern v. to die of hunger; to starve

verhunzen v. to bungle, to spoil

verhüten v. to prevent, to avert; **-d** adj. preventive, preservative; prophylactic

verirren v. sich — to go astray, to err

Verirrung f. straying, aberration; mistake

verjagen v. to drive away, to expel

verjähren v. to become superannuated, to grow obsolete

verjährt adj. superannuated; **-es Recht** prescriptive right

verjüngen v. to rejuvenate; (art and geom.) to reduce; **es verjüngt sich** it tapers off

verkalken v. to calcify; to calcine
verkalkulieren v. sich — to miscalculate
verkappt adj. disgusted; secret
verkatert adj. (coll.) suffering from a hangover
Verkauf m. sale; **–spreis** m. selling price
verkaufen v. to sell; to dispose of
Verkäufer m. seller; retailer; salesman
verkäuflich adj. saleable; for sale; venal
Verkehr m. traffic; commerce, trade; intercourse; communication; **aus dem —ziehen** to withdraw from service (oder circulation); **–sader** f. traffic artery; **–sampel** f. traffic light; **–sandrang** m. traffic rush; **–sordnung** f. traffic regulations; **–sstockung** f., **–sstörung** f. traffic block; bottleneck; breakdown; **–swesen** neu. traffic; train service
verkehren v. to turn (the wrong way); to invert; to convert; to transform; to pervert; to frequent, to visit, to have intercourse (with); **sich — in to change into**
verkehrt adj. inverted, reversed; upside down; incorrect, wrong; absurd
verkennen v. to misjudge; to underrate
verketten v. to chain (oder link) together
Verkettung f. concatenation; coincidence
verketzern v. to charge with heresy; to caluminate; to slander
verkitten v. to cement; to putty up
verklagen v. to accuse; to sue
Verklagte m. accused; defendant
verklären v. to glorify; to transfigure
verklausulieren v. to stipulate; to limit by provisos; to guard by clauses
verkleben v. to paste (oder glue, gum) up
verkleiden v. to disguise; to mask; to line, to face, to wainscot
verkleinern v. to diminish; to reduce; to belittle; to disparage
Verkleinerung f. miniaturization; **–swort** neu. (gram.) diminutive
verklingen v. (mus.) to die (oder fade) away
Verknappung f. scarcity, shortage
verknittern v. to crumple, to crease
verknöchern v. to ossify; to grow pedantic
verknoten v. to knot; to entangle
verknüpfen v. to knot (oder tie) together; to link; to combine; to entail, to involve
verkochen v. to boil away, to use in cooking
verkohlen v. to carbonize; (coll.) to hoax
verkommen v. to deteriorate, to decay; to degenerate; — adj. ruined; degenerate; depraved
verkorken v. to cork (up)
verkörpern v. to embody; to personify
verkrachen v. (coll.) to become bankrupt; sich — mit (coll.) to fall out with

verkramen v. (coll.) to disarrange, to mislay
verkriechen v. sich — to hide; to creep away
verkrümmt adj. bent, crooked; misshapen
verkrüppelt adj. crippled; deformed; maimed
verkrustet adj. incrusted
verkühlen v. sich — to catch cold
verkümmern v. to become stunted; to atrophy; to pine away; to embitter, to curtail
verkünd(ig)en v. to announce, to make known; to proclaim; **das Evangelium — to preach the gospel; ein Urteil — to pronounce sentence**
verkuppeln v. to couple; to procure, to pander
verkürzen v. to shorten; to abridge; to curtail; to diminish; to contract; **sich die Zeit — to pass away the time**
verlachen v. to deride, to ridicule
verladen v. to load, to ship, to entrain
Verlag m. publishing house; **–sartikel** m. publication; **–sbuchhändler** m. publisher; **–srecht** neu. copyright; **–szeichen** neu. colophon
verlangen v. to demand; to require; to desire; — nach to long for, to crave for
Verlangen neu. demand; request; desire; longing; **auf — by request, on demand**
verlängern v. to lengthen; to extend, to prolong
verlangsamen v. to slow down, to retard
Verlass m. auf ihn ist kein — he cannot be relied on
verlassen v. to leave, to quit; to abandon, to forsake, to desert; **sich — auf to rely on; — adj. forsaken, abandoned; lonely**
verlässlich adj. reliable, trustworthy
Verlaub m. mit — with your permission
Verlauf m. course; expiration; progress; **einen schlimmen — nehmen to take a bad turn; nach — von after the lapse of**
verlaufen v. to pass, to expire; to take its course; to proceed; to turn out; **sich — to lose one's way; to disperse, to scatter; — adj. stray, lost; forlorn**
verlautbaren v. to make known; to divulge
verlauten v. to become known; **— lassen to give to understand, to hint; wie verlautet as reported**
verleben v. to spend, to pass
verlebt adj. past, spent; worn out, decrepit
verlegen v. to shift, to transfer, to remove; to misplace; to block, to obstruct; to defer, to postpone; to publish; **sich auf**

etwas — to take up (*oder* go in for) something; — *adj.* confused, embarrassed; um etwas — sein to be at a loss for something

Verlegenheit *f.* dilemma, embarrassment

Verleger *m.* publisher

Verlegung *f.* shifting, transfer; postponement, misplacement; publishing

verleiden *v.* to disgust (with); to spoil

verleihen *v.* to lend out, to loan; to bestow, to confer (on); to grant; seinen Gefühlen Ausdruck — to express one's feelings

verleiten *v.* to mislead; to induce; to seduce

verlernen *v.* to unlearn; to forget (how to do)

verlesen *v.* to read aloud; to call (the roll); to pick (vegetables); sich — to misread

verletz: –bar *adj.*, –lich *adj.* damageable; vulnerable, susceptible, touchy; –en *v.* to damage; to hurt, to injure, to wound; to violate; –end *adj.* offensive, insulting

verleugnen *v.* to deny; to disavow; to renounce; sich — lassen to pretend not to be at home

verleumden *v.* to slander, to defame

verlieben *v.* sich — to fall in love

verlieren *v.* to lose; to shed; to waste; sich — to get lost; to disperse; to disappear

Verlies *neu.* dungeon

Verlob: –te *m.* fiancé; –te *f.* fiancée; –ung *f.*, Verlöbnis *neu.* betrothal, engagement

verloben *v.* sich — to become engaged (to)

verlocken *v.* to allure, to entice; to seduce; –d *adj.* enticing, tempting

verlogen *adj.* mendacious, lying, untruthful

verlohnen *v.* es verlohnt sich nicht der Mühe it is not worth while, it doesn't pay

verloren *adj.* lost, forlorn, stray; lonely; fruitless; der –e Sohn the Prodigal Son; –e Eier poached eggs; — geben to give up for lost; –geh(e)n to be lost

verlöschen *v.* to extinguish; to efface, to obliterate; to go (*oder* burn) out

verlosen *v.* to dispose of by lot; to raffle

verlöten *v.* to solder up

verlottern, verludern, verlumpen *v.* to waste, to squander, to ruin; to go to the dogs

Verlust *m.* loss, privation; bereavement; leak, waste; bei — von under pain of, with forfeiture of; –e *pl.* (mil.) casualties

verlustig *adj.* einer Sache — gehen to

lose (*oder* forfeit) something

vermachen *v.* to bequeath

Vermächtnis *neu.* bequest, legacy

vermählen *v.* to marry; to give in marriage

vermaledeien *v.* to curse, to execrate

vermauern *v.* to wall in (*oder* up)

vermehren *v.* to increase, to augment; to multiply; to enlarge; to propagate

vermeid: –bar *adj.*, –lich *adj.* avoidable; –en *v.* to avoid; to evade; to shun; to elude

vermeinen *v.* to believe, to think, to suppose

vermeintlich *adj.* alleged, supposed, pretended

vermelden *v.* to announce, to notify

vermengen *v.* to blend, to mingle, to confound

Vermerk *m.* note, comment, entry

vermerken *v.* to note down, to record; to observe; to remark; übel — to take amiss

vermessen *v.* to measure; to survey; sich — to measure incorrectly; to dare (*oder* presume) to; — *adj.* bold, audacious

Vermessenheit *f.* boldness; presumption

vermieten *v.* to rent, to lease, to hire out

Vermieter *m.* landlord; lessor

vermindern *v.* to decrease, to diminish; to abate, to impair; to reduce

vermischen *v.* to mix; to mingle; to blend

vermissen *v.* to miss; to deplore, to regret

vermitteln *v.* to mediate, to negotiate, to bring about; to intercede, to interpose

vermittels(t) *prep.* by means of, through

Vermittler *m.* mediator, arbitrator; agent, go-between; matchmaker

Vermittlung *f.* mediation, negotiation; agency; (tel.) exchange, operator

vermodern *v.* to mould; to decay, to rot

vermöge *prep.* by virtue of, through; –n *v.* to be able (*oder* in a position) to do; to have influence (over); to prevail upon; –nd *adj.* wealthy, rich

Vermögen *neu.* ability, power; capacity, faculty; means, property, wealth; –sabgabe *f.* capital levy; –sverhältnisse *neu. pl.* pecuniary circumstances

vermummen *v.* to muffle up, to mask

vermuten *v.* to presume, to surmise, to suspect

vermutlich *adj.* presumable, likely, probable

vernachlässigen *v.* to neglect, to slight

vernageln *v.* to nail up

vernähen *v.* to sew up

vernarben *v.* to cicatrize, to heal up

vernarren *v.* sich — in to become infatuated with, to dote on

Vernehm: –en *neu.* dem –en nach from what we hear, according to report; –ung *f.* examination; hearing; interrogation; trial

vernehmen *v.* to perceive; to hear, to understand; (law) to interrogate, to examine; **sich — lassen** to speak, to intimate

vernehmlich *adj.* distinct, intelligible

verneigen *v.* **sich —** to curtsy, to bow

verneinen *v.* to answer in the negative; to deny, to disavow; –d *adj.* negative

vernichten *v.* to annihilate, to destroy

vernickeln *v.* to (plate with) nickel

vernieten *v.* to rivet

Vernunft *f.* reason; intelligence; judgment; sense; **die gesunde —** common sense; **jemand zur — bringen** to bring someone to his senses; **— annehmen** to listen to reason

vernünftig *adj.* sensible; logical, reasonable; rational; wise, judicious

veröden *v.* to become desolate; to devastate

Verödung *f.* desolation, devastation; depopulation, stagnation; (med.) obliteration

veröffentlichen *v.* to make public, to publish; **ein Gesetz —** to promulgate a law

verordnen *v.* to order; to decree; to prescribe

verpachten *v.* to lease; to farm out

verpacken *v.* to pack (*oder* wrap) up

Verpackungsgewicht *neu.* tare (weight)

verpassen *v.* to let slip; to miss, to lose

verpesten *v.* to infect; to poison

verpfänden *v.* to pawn, to pledge, to mortgage

verpflanzen *v.* to transplant

verpflegen *v.* to board, to feed, to cater for

Verpflegung *f.* feeding, board; food, diet; maintenance; provision(ing)

verpflichten *v.* to oblige, to engage; **sich zu etwas —** to pledge oneself to do something; **zu Dank —** to put under obligation

Verpflichtung *f.* obligation; duty; commitment, engagement; **gemeinsame –en** joint liabilities

verpfuschen *v.* to bungle, to botch, to scamp

verplappern, verplaudern *v.* to waste in gossip; **sich —** to blab, to give oneself away

verplempern *v.* to spend foolishly; to fritter

verpönt *adj.* prohibited, taboo

verprassen *v.* to dissipate, to waste

verproviantieren *v.* to provision, to supply

verprügeln *v.* to thrash soundly

verpulvern *v.* to pulverize; (coll.) to squander

verpuppen *v.* **sich —** to change into a pupa

verpusten *v.* **sich —** (coll.) to recover one's breath; to rest

verputzen *v.* to roughcast, to plaster; (coll.) to eat, to polish off

verqualmt *adj.* filled with smoke

verquicken *v.* to amalgamate; to combine, to mix

verquollen *adj.* bloated, swollen, warped (wood)

verrammeln *v.* to bar, to block, to barricade

Verrat *m.* treason, treachery; betrayal

verraten *v.* to betray; to disclose, to show

Verräter *m.* betrayer, traitor; informer; –ei *f.* treachery; treasonable conduct

verräterisch *adj.* treacherous; perfidious

verräuchern *v.* to blacken (*oder* fill) with smoke; to burn up incense

verrauschen *v.* to die (*oder* rush, pass) away

verrechnen *v.* to reckon up, to charge; **sich —** to miscalculate, to be mistaken

Verrechnung *f.* reckoning; balancing (of account); –sscheck *m.* (com.) counter check; –sstelle *f.* (com.) clearinghouse

verregnen *v.* to be spoiled by rain

verreiben *v.* to grind well, to rub away

verreisen *v.* to go on a trip, to travel

verreissen *v.* to tear to pieces; to criticize sharply

verrenken *v.* to dislocate, to sprain

verrennen *v.* **sich —** to adhere stubbornly (to); to run the wrong way; to get stuck

verrichten *v.* to accomplish, to perform, to do

verriegeln *v.* to bolt; to bar, to barricade

verringern *v.* to diminish, to lessen, to reduce

verrinnen *v.* to run off (*oder* away); to elapse

verrohen *v.* to become brutal

verrosten *v.* to rust

verrucht *adj.* infamous, vile; wicked

verrücken *v.* to remove, to shift; to displace

verrückt *adj.* crazy, mad, cracked; **er macht mich —** he drives me mad

Verrückte *m.* lunatic, madman, insane person

Verruf *m.* **in — kommen** to fall into discredit

verrufen *v.* to condemn, to decry; — *adj.* infamous, disreputable, notorious

Vers *m.* verse; stanza, strophe; **ich kann mir keinen — daraus** (*or* **darauf**)

machen I can't make head or tail of it

versagen v. to deny, to refuse; to fail, to break down; (gun) to misfire; **versagt sein** to be engaged; to have a prior appointment

Versager m. failure; misfire

versalzen v. to oversalt; to spoil

versammeln v. to assemble, to bring together; to convene; **sich** — to meet, to assemble

Versammlung f. assembly, meeting, convention

Versand m. dispatch; shipment; export(ation); **–geschäft** neu. export business; mail-order house

versanden v. to become choked up with sand; (fig.) to stick

Versatz m. pawn(ing), pledge; **–amt** neu. pawnshop; **–stück** neu. (theat.) movable scenery

versauern v. to turn sour; to become morose

versaufen v. (coll.) to waste in drinking

versäumen v. to miss, to neglect, to omit

Versäumnis neu. neglect, omission; delay; loss of time

verschachern v. to barter away

verschaffen v. to procure, to provide; **jemand Recht** — to obtain justice for someone; **sich Recht** — to take the law into one's own hands

verschämt adj. ashamed, bashful

verschanzen v. to entrench, to fortify; **sich** — **hinter** to take shelter behind

verschärfen v. to sharpen; to aggravate; to intensify; to make worse; **die Gegensätze** — **sich** the contrasts become more pronounced

verscharren v. to bury (without ceremony)

verscheiden v. to die, to expire, to pass away

verschenken v. to give away, to make a present; to donate; to pour out (beverages)

verscherzen v. to trifle away, to lose (by folly)

verscheuchen v. to scare away; to banish

verschicken v. to send away; to dispatch, to forward; to deport (criminals)

Verschiebebahnhof m. (rail.) switchyard

verschieben v. to shift, to displace; (rail.) to shunt; to postpone; to black-market

verschieden adj. different; dissimilar; diverse; **–e Artikel** sundries; **zu –en Malen** on various occasions; **–artig** adj. various, heterogeneous; **–erlei** adj. of various kinds, divers; **–farbig** adj. variegated; **–tlich** adv. repeatedly, differently

verschiessen v. to use up (ammunition); to fade, to lose color

verschiffen v. to ship, to export

verschimmeln v. to become moldy

verschlafen v. to miss by sleeping; to spend sleeping; to sleep off; to oversleep; — adj. sleepy, drowsy

Verschlag m. wooden partition; box, shed

verschlagen v. to board up; to nail up; to partition off; to spoil by beating; to lose one's place (in books); **das verschlägt einem dem Atem** that takes away one's breath; — **werden** to be driven out of one's course; — adj. lukewarm; cunning, sly

verschlammen v. to silt up, to get muddied

verschlechtern v. to make worse, to impair; **sich** — to become worse, to deteriorate

verschleiern v. to veil, to screen; to conceal

verschleiert adj. veiled; clouded, hazy; **mit –er Stimme** with a husky voice

verschleifen v. to ruin in grinding; to slur

verschleimen v. to choke up with mucus

verschleissen v. to wear out, to be used up

verschleppen v. to carry off; to misplace; to delay, to protract; to spread (disease)

verschleudern v. to hurl away; to dissipate; to squander; to sell at a loss, to dump

verschliessen v. to close, to shut, to lock up; **sein Herz** — to harden one's heart; **sich einer Sache** — to shut one's eyes to something

verschlimmern v. to make worse; to aggravate; **sich** — to grow worse

verschlingen v. to devour, to swallow; to intertwine; to twist, to entangle

verschlossen adj. closed, locked; reserved

verschlucken v. to swallow; **sich** — **to** swallow the wrong way

Verschluss m. lock(ing), fastener, zipper; clasp, plug, zeal; (phot.) shutter; **unter** — under lock and key; **–laut** m. (gram.) explosive consonant; **–stück** neu. plug, stopper

verschmachten v. to languish, to pine away

verschmähen v. to disdain, to despise, to scorn

verschmelzen v. to melt (together); to fuse; to blend; to coalesce, to amalgamate

verschmerzen v. to get over (the loss of)

verschmieren v. to smear; to daub; to use up in greasing; to waste (paper) in scribbling

verschmitzt *adj.* cunning, sly, crafty

verschmutzt *adj.* dirty, filthy, soiled

verschnappen *v.* sich — to let the cat out of the bag; to give oneself away

verschnaufen *v.* sich — to recover one's breath; to rest

verschneiden *v.* to cut away (*oder* badly); to trim, to prune, to clip; to blend, to adulterate (wine); to castrate

verschneit *adj.* snowed in, covered with snow

verschnörkelt *adj.* adorned with flourishes

verschnupft *adj.* stuffed up with a cold; annoyed, piqued, vexed, miffed

verschnüren *v.* to tie up, to cord, to lace

verschollen *adj.* lost, missing; long past

verschonen *v.* to spare; to exempt

verschönern *v.* to beautify, to embellish, to adorn; to improve

verschossen *adj.* discolored, faded; **er ist mächtig in sie —** (coll.) he is madly in love with her

verschrauben *v.* to screw on; to overscrew

verschreiben *v.* to use up in writing; to order, to write for; to prescribe; to assign; (law) to make over; to write incorrectly; **sich —** to make a slip (in writing); to sell oneself (to); to set one's heart upon

verschrien *adj.* in bad repute, decried

verschroben *adj.* eccentric, odd, queer

verschrumpelt *adj.* shrivelled, wrinkled

verschüchtern *v.* to intimidate

verschulden *v.* to be guilty (*oder* the cause) of; to become involved in debts

verschuldet *adj.* indebted; encumbered

verschütten *v.* to spill; to fill up, to bury

verschwägert *adj.* related by marriage

verschwatzen, verschwätzen *v.* to spend in chatting (*oder* gossiping)

verschweigen *v.* to keep secret; to conceal

verschwenden *v.* to lavish, to squander

Verschwender *m.* spendthrift, squanderer, prodigal

verschwenderisch *adj.* wasteful, prodigal

verschwiegen *adj.* discreet; reticent

verschwinden *v.* to disappear, to vanish

verschwistert *adj.* brother and sister; closely united

verschwitzen *v.* to soil (*oder* exhale, get rid of) by perspiration; (coll.) to forget

verschwommen *adj.* indistinct, hazy, vague

verschwören *v.* to forswear, to abjure; **sich — mit** to conspire (*oder* plot) with

versehen *v.* to equip with, to provide; to perform, to administer; to keep; **ehe man sich versieht** unexpectedly; suddenly; **sich —** to overlook; to make a mistake; **-tlich** *adv.* inadvertently, by mistake

Versehen *neu.* oversight, mistake, slip

versehren *v.* to hurt, to injure, to damage

versenden *v.* to send, to dispatch, to forward

versengen *v.* to singe, to scorch, to parch

versenken *v.* to sink; to submerge; to lower; **sich —** to become absorbed in

Versenkung *f.* sinking; (theat.) trap door

versessen *v.* **— auf** to be eager for; to bent on; to be mad about, to be obsessed by

versetzen *v.* to displace, to transfer, to shift; to promote; to transpose; to transplant; to pawn, to pledge; to mix; to alloy; to give, to deal; to put into; to reply

versichern *v.* to assure, to affirm; to insure; **sich —** to make sure of, to ascertain

Versicherung *f.* assurance, affirmation; insurance; **-schein** *m.* insurance policy

versiegeln *v.* to seal (up)

versilbern *v.* to silver, to plate; (coll.) to turn into money

versinken *v.* to sink, to become submerged; to be absorbed (in)

versinnbildlichen *v.* to symbolize, to allegorize

versinnlichen *v.* to make perceptible; to grow (*oder* make) sensual; to materialize

versoffen *adj.* (coll.) drunk(en)

versohlen *v.* (coll.) to thrash

versöhnen *v.* to appease; **sich — mit** to reconcile oneself with (*oder* to)

versöhnlich *adj.* conciliatory, forgiving

versorgen *v.* to furnish (with), to provide, to supply; to maintain; to care for

Versorger *m.* breadwinner, supporter

versorgt *adj.* worried; provided for

verspäten *v.* to delay, to retard; **sich —** to be (*oder* come) too late

Verspätung *f.* delay, lateness; **der Zug hat eine Stunde —** the train is an hour overdue

verspeisen *v.* to eat up; to consume

versperren *v.* to bar, to block; to obstruct, to close, to lock up

verspielen *v.* to lose (in gambling); **es bei jemand —** to lose a person's favor

verspotten *v.* to deride, to ridicule

versprechen *v.* to promise; **sich etwas — von** to expect much of; **sich —** to make a slip of the tongue

versprengen *v.* to disperse, to scatter

verspritzen *v.* to squirt, to shed, to spill

verspüren *v.* to feel, to perceive; to be aware

verstaatlichen v. to nationalize

Verstand m. intelligence, intellect; comprehension; judgment; **da steht mir der — still I'm at my wit's end; das geht über meinen —** that's past my comprehension; **den — verlieren** to go out of one's mind; **gesunder —** common sense; **–esmensch** m. matter-of-fact person; **–esschärfe** f. mental acumen, sagacity

verständ: –ig adj. intelligent; reasonable; sensible; judicious; **–igen** v. to inform; **sich –igen mit** to come to terms with; **–lich** adj. comprehensible, intelligible; clear; **sich –lich machen** to make oneself understood; **–nislos** adj. devoid of understanding; unappreciative; imbecile; **–nisvoll** adj. understanding; appreciative; intelligent

Verständ: –igkeit f. prudence; good sense; **–igung** f. understanding; agreement; (tel.) reception; **–nis** neu. comprehension; sympathy

verstärken v. to strengthen, to reinforce; to amplify; to intensify; to increase

Verstärker m. amplifier; intensifier

verstatten v. to allow, to permit, to grant

verstauben v. to become dusty

verstäuben v. to spray

verstauchen v. to sprain

Versteck neu. hiding place, retreat; ambush; **–spiel** neu. hide-and-seek (game)

verstecken v. to conceal, to hide

versteckt adj. concealed, hidden; underhanded, veiled, secret; **–e Absicht** ulterior motive

verstehen v. to understand, to comprehend; to know; **es versteht sich von selbst** it goes without saying; **etwas zu — geben** to hint, to intimate; **falsch — to misunderstand, to misconstrue; sich — auf** to be skilled at; **sich zu etwas — to agree to; was — Sie darunter?** what do you mean by it?

versteifen v. to stiffen, to prop; **sich — auf** to insist upon, to make a point of

versteigern v. to (sell by) auction

versteinern v. to turn to stone, to petrify

verstellbar adj. adjustable

verstellen v. to shift; to misplace; to block, to obstruct; to disguise; **sich — to feign**

versteuern v. to pay tax on

verstimmen v. to put out of tune; to annoy, to upset

verstimmt adj. out of tune; cross, upset

verstockt adj. obdurate; impenitent; stubborn

verstohlen adj. stealthy, furtive, secret

verstopfen v. to stop up; to block; to constipate

verstorben adj. deceased, late

verstört adj. disconcerted, bewildered; upset, troubled; disordered (mind); haggard

Verstoss m. offense, fault; infraction, violation; **–ene** m. outcast, outlaw

verstossen v. to transgress; to violate; to cast out, to repudiate; to banish; to expel

verstreichen v. to pass, to slip by, to elapse; to use up in smearing (oder painting)

verstreuen v. to disperse, to scatter; to litter

verstricken v. to use up in knitting; to ensnare; **sich — to** become involved

verstümmeln v. to maim, to mutilate, to cripple

verstummen v. to become silent (oder speechless); to be struck dumb

Versuch m. experiment; trial; test; attempt; **–er** m. tempter, seducer; **–sanstalt** f. research institute; **–sballon** m. research balloon; (fig.) kite; **–skaninchen** neu. guinea pig; victim (of experiments)

versuchen v. to try, to attempt; to test; to taste; to sample; to tempt, to entice

versuchsweise adv. by way of experiment; tentatively; **— annehmen** to accept on approval

versumpfen v. to become marshy; to become corrupt; to grow dissolute

versündigen v. sich **— to** sin (against); to offend, to trespass

versunken adj. sunk; (fig.) lost, absorbed

versüssen v. to sweeten

vertagen v. to adjourn; to put off

vertändeln v. to idle (oder trifle) away

vertauschen v. to exchange; to mistake; to permute, to substitute

verteidigen v. to defend; to advocate

Verteidiger m. defender; defense counsel; (sports) back

verteilen v. to distribute; to apportion; to allot; to dispense; to assign

verteuern v. to raise the price of

verteufelt adj. devilish, infernal; **— adv.** awfully

vertiefen v. to deepen, to make deeper; **sich — in** to become absorbed in; to plunge into

Vertieftsein neu. preoccupation

Vertiefung f. deepening; cavity, hollow; absorption, engrossment

vertiert adj. bestial, brutal, brutish

vertilgen v. to exterminate, to eradicate; to destroy; to consume

vertonen v. to set to music, to compose

Vertrag *m.* agreement. contract; treaty; **–sbruch** *m.* breach of contract

vertrag: –en *v.* to carry away; to bear, to endure; to wear out; **es verträgt sich nicht** it is incompatible; **ich kann diese Speise nicht –en** this food doesn't agree with me; **sich –en mit** to agree (*oder* get on well) with; **sich wieder –en** to settle differences, to make it up; **–lich** *adj.* contractual; **–lich** *adv.* as stipulated, as agreed upon; **–smässig** *adv.* in accordance with an agreement; **–sschliessend** *adj.* contracting; **–swidrig** *adj.* contrary to an agreement

verträglich *adj.* compatible, sociable

vertrau: –en *v.* to rely upon, to trust; **–ensselig** *adj.* too trusting; **–ensvoll** *adj.* full of confidence; **–enswürdig** *adj.* trustworthy, reliable; **–lich** *adj.* confidential, private, intimate; **–t** *adj.* intimate, familiar; **–t mit** conversant with; versed in

Vertrauen *neu.* confidence, reliance, trust; **im —** between ourselves; **jemand sein — schenken** to place confidence in someone; **–smann** *n.* trustworthy person, confidant; **–sseligkeit** *f.* blind confidence; **–sstellung** *f.* position of trust; **–svotum** *neu.* vote of confidence

vertrauern *v.* to mourn (*oder* grieve) away

verträumen *v.* to dream away

vertreiben *v.* to drive away; to expel; to turn out; to banish; to sell, to distribute; **sich die Zeit —** to pass away the time

vertreten *v.* to substitute for; to represent; to answer for, to plead for; **jemand den Weg —** to block (*oder* stand in) someone's way; **sich den Fuss — to sprain one's foot; sich die Beine — to stretch one's legs

Vertreter *m.* proxy, substitute; representative, deputy; advocate; (com.) agent

Vertretung *f.* representation; replacement; **in —** acting (*oder* signed) for

Vertrieb *m.* sale, distribution

vertrinken *v.* to spend on drink

vertrocknen *v.* to dry up, to wither

vertrödeln *v.* to fritter (*oder* idle) away

vertrösten *v.* to give hope to, to console; to put off

vertrusten *v.* (com.) to pool, to monopolize

vertun *v.* to squander, to waste

vertuschen *v.* to hush up; to hide, to conceal

verübeln *v.* to blame for; to take amiss

verüben *v.* to commit, to perpetrate

verulken *v.* to make fun of, to tease

verun: –ehren *v.* to disgrace. to dishonor;

–einigen *v.* to disunite; **sich –einigen** to fall out, to quarrel; **–glimpfen** *v.* to slander, to revile; **–glücken** *v.* to meet with an accident; to fail; to die, to perish; **–reinigen** *v.* to soil; to defile, to pollute; **–stalten** *v.* to disfigure, to deface; **–treuen** *v.* to embezzle, to misappropriate; **–zieren** *v.* to disfigure, to mar

verursachen *v.* to cause, to give rise to; to bring about; to originate; to provoke

verurteilen *v.* to condemn, to sentence

vervielfachen, vervielfältigen *v.* to multiply; to duplicate, to copy; to reproduce

Vervielfältigungsmaschine *f.* duplicator; mimeograph

vervollkommnen *v.* to perfect, to improve

vervollständigen *v.* to complete, to replenish

verwachsen *v.* to grow together; to heal up; to be engrossed in; **—** *adj.* grown together; deformed

verwahr: –en *v.* to guard, to keep; **jemand zu –en geben** to entrust to someone's care; **sich –en** to protest (against), to resist; **–losen** *v.* to neglect; to be neglected; **–lost** *adj.* neglected; abandoned, uncared for

Verwahrung *f.* custody, guard(ing); keeping, care; **— einlegen** to enter a protest (against)

verwaist *adj.* orphaned; deserted

verwalten *v.* to administer, to manage; to supervise; to govern, to hold (office)

Verwaltung *f.* administration; management, supervision; **–sdienst** *m.* civil service; **–srat** *m.* board of management

verwandeln *v.* to convert; to transform, to metamorphose; to turn into

Verwandlung *f.* conversion; transformation; metamorphosis; (theat.) shifting of scenes; **–skünstler** *m.* quick-change artist

verwandt *adj.* kindred, related; similar, cognate; **–schaftlich** *adj.* kindred, as (among) relatives

Verwandt: –e *m.* and *f.* relative, kinsman; **–schaft** *f.* kinship, relationship; relatives; congeniality, affinity

verwarnen *v.* to warn, to caution; to admonish

verwaschen *v.* to wash out, to use up in washing; **—** *adj.* hazy, vague, indistinct; faded

verweben *v.* to interweave

verwechseln *v.* to (mis)take for; **to exchange; to confuse, to confound

verwegen *adj.* bold, daring, audacious

verwehen *v.* to blow away; to be scattered; to cover (by drifting)

verweichlichen v. to coddle, to become effeminate (oder weak, delicate); to enervate

verweigern v. to deny, to refuse

verweilen v. to stay, to linger, to stop; — bei to dwell on

verweint adj. tear-stained, tearful

Verweis m. rebuke, reprimand, reproof; reference; —ung f. banishment, exile; unter —ung auf with reference to

verweisen v. to rebuke, to reprimand, to reprove; des Landes — to banish, to exile; — auf to refer to

verwelken v. to fade, to wither

verweltlichen v. to make (oder become) worldly; to secularize

verwenden v. to use, to utilize; to employ; to apply; to spend; sich — für to intercede for

Verwendung f. use; utilization; —sfähigkeit f. usability; (mil.) accessibility

verwerfen v. to reject; to disapprove; (cards) to play the wrong card; (law) to dismiss (case); to quash (verdict); (zool.) to miscarry

verwerflich adj. objectionable; blamable

verwerten v. to utilize, to turn to account

verwesen v. to rot, to decompose, to putrefy; (poet.) to administer, to supervise

verwichen adj. bygone, former, last, past

verwickeln v. to entangle, to embroil, to involve; to complicate

verwildern v. to grow wild; to become unmanageable (oder depraved); to be neglected

verwinden v. to get over, to overcome; to distort; (avi.) to twist, to warp

verwirken v. to forfeit, to incure, to lose

verwirklichen v. to realize, to materialize

verwirren v. to entangle, to confuse, to perplex; to bewilder, to embarrass

verwischen v. to wipe out, to efface

verwittert adj. weather-beaten; dilapidated

verwitwet adj. widowed

verwöhnen v. to coddle, to pamper, to spoil

verworfen adj. depraved; infamous, abandoned

verworren adj. confused, intricate

verwund: —bar adj. vulnerable; touchy; —en v. to wound; to hurt, to injure; —erlich adj. astonishing; —ern v. to astonish; sich —ern to be amazed (oder surprised); to wonder

verwunschen adj. enchanted, bewitched

verwünschen v. to bewitch; to curse; to cast a spell (on); to execrate

verwünscht adj. cursed, confounded; —!

interj. damn it! hang it!

verwurzeln v. to become firmly rooted

verwüsten v. to lay waste, to devastate

verzagen v. to lose heart, to grow despondent

verzählen v. sich — to miscount, to miscalculate

verzapfen v. to draw from a tap; to join by mortise

verzärteln v. to coddle, to pet, to pamper

verzaubern v. to bewitch, to charm, to enchant

verzehren v. to eat (up); to consume

verzeichnen v. to misdraw; to record, to list, to register

Verzeichnis neu. list, register, roll; inventory; catalogue; index; specification

verzeihen v. to pardon, to forgive; — Sie! excuse me! I beg your pardon

verzerren v. to distort; to twist; to grimace

verzetteln v. to scatter; to fritter away

Verzicht m. renunciation; resignation; — leisten to renounce

verzichten v. to renounce, to forgo, to waive

verziehen v. to remove; to stay; to distort; to be slow, to delay; to spoil (child); keine Miene — not to move a muscle; sich — to warp; to disappear, to disperse, to vanish

verzieren v. to adorn, to trim, to embellish

Verzierung f. adornment, ornament, flourish

verzögern v. to delay, to retard; sich — to be late (oder deferred)

verzollen v. to pay duty on; Haben Sie etwas zu —? Do you have anything to declare?

verzücken v. to enrapture, to entrance

verzuckern v. to sweeten, to ice, to sugarcoat

Verzug m. delay; Gefahr im —! danger ahead! ohne — immediately; —stage m. pl. days of grace; —szinsen m. pl. interest on back payments

Verzweiflung f. despair; despondency; aus reiner — out of sheer desperation; zur — bringen to drive mad

verzweigen v. to branch out, to ramify

verzwickt adj. complicated, intricate; queer

Vesper f. vespers; —zeit f. afternoon snack

Veteran m. veteran (soldier)

Veterinär m. veterinarian

Veto neu. veto; ein — einlegen to veto something

Vettel f. hag, slut, witch

Vetter m. male cousin; —nwirtschaft f. nepotism

Vexier: –bild *neu.* picture puzzle; –schloss *neu.* combination lock; –spiegel *m.* distorting mirror

Vibraphon *neu.* (mus.) vibraphone

vibrieren *v.* to vibrate

Vieh *neu.* cattle; beast; **–bestand** *m.* livestock; **–hof** *m.* stockyard; farmyard; **–seuche** *f.* cattle plague; foot-and-mouth disease; **–zucht** *f.* cattle breeding

viehisch *adj.* bestial, brutish, brutal

viel *adj.* and *adv.* much; numerous; often; das **–e** Geld all that money; ein bisschen — a little too much; in **–em** in many respects; **mehr als zu** — more than enough; **noch einmal so** — as much again; **recht** —, **sehr** — plenty of, a great deal; **um –es besser** better by far; **–e** many; **–artig** *adj.* manifold, various; **–bändig** *adj.* many-volumed; **–beschäftigt** *adj.* very busy; **–deutig** *adj.* ambiguous, equivocal; **–erlei** *adj.* of many kinds, divers; **–fach** *adj.* multifarious, repeated; **–fach** *adv.* in many cases, frequently; **–fältig** *adj.* various; manifold; **–gestaltig** *adj.* multiform; **–jährig** *adj.* of many years, of long standing; **–köpfig** *adj.* many-headed, numerous; **–leicht** *adv.* perhaps; **–malig** *adj.* often repeated; frequent; **–mals** *adv.* many times, often, frequently; **–mehr** *adv.* rather, much more; **–mehr** *conj.* rather; on the contrary; **–sagend** *adj.* expressive, significant; **–seitig** *adj.* many-sided; versatile; **–silbig** *adj.* polysyllabic; **–sprachig** *adj.* polyglot; **–stimmig** *adj.* polyphonic; **–verheissend** *adj.*, **–versprechend** *adj.* most promising; **–zellig** *adj.* multicellular

Viel: **–eck** *neu.* polygon; **–frass** *m.* glutton; wolverine; **–götterei** *f.* polytheism; **–heit** *f.* multiplicity, multitude; **–liebchen** *neu.* darling; **–stufenrakete** *f.* multistage rocket; **–weiberei** *f.* polygamy

vier *adj.* four; **auf allen –en** on all fours; **unter — Augen** privately; **zu –en** by fours; **–blätt(e)rig** *adj.* four-leafed; **–eckig** *adj.* quadrangular, square; **–erlei** *adj.* of four kinds; **–fach** *adj.*, **–fältig** *adj.* fourfold, quadruple; **–füssig** *adj.* four-footed, quadruped; **–gestrichen** *adj.* (mus.) four-times accented; **–händig** *adj.* four-handed; **–händig spielen** to play a duet; **–jährig** *adj.* of (*oder* lasting) four years; **–mal** *adv.* four times; **–malig** *adj.* occurring four times; **–schrötig** *adj.* square-built, clumsy; **–seitig** *adj.* four-sided, quadrilateral; **–spännig** *adj.* drawn by four horses; **–stellig** *adj.* of four digits; **–stimmig**

adj. for four voices; **–stöckig** *adj.* four storied; **–tägig** *adj.* of four days; **–te** *adj.* fourth; **–teilen** to quarter; **–teilig** *adj.* in (*oder* of) four parts; **–teljährlich** *adj.* quarterly; **–telstündig** *adj.* lasting a quarter of an hour; **–telstündlich** *adj.* every quarter of an hour; **–tens** *adv.* fourthly; **–zehn** *adj.* fourteen; **–zehnte** *adj.* fourteenth; **–zeilig** *adj.* four-lined; **–zig** *adj.* forty; **–zigste** *adj.* fortieth

Vier *f.* four; **–eck** *neu.* square, quadrangle; **–er** *m.* four; four-oared boat; **–füss(l)er** *m.* quadruped; **–gespann** *neu.* team of four horses; quadriga; **–ling** *m.* quadruplet; **–radbremse** *f.* four-wheel brake; **–spänner** *m.* four-in-hand (coach); **–taktmotor** *m.* four-stroke engine; **–tel** *neu.* fourth part, quarter; district; **–telnote** *f.* quarter note; **–ung** *f.* (arch.) crossing; **–vierteltakt** *m.* (mus.) common measure; **–ziger** *m.* person forty (*oder* more) years old; **–zigstel** *neu.* fortieth part

Vierwaldstättersee *m.* Lake Lucerne

Vikar *m.* vicar, curate

Viktor-Viktor! (avi. Verstanden!) Roger!

Viktualien *pl.* victuals, provisions

Villenkolonie *f.* garden city

Viol: **–a** *f.* (mus.) viola; **–e** *f.* (bot.) viola, violet; **–ine** *f.* violin; **–in(en)schlüssel** *m.* treble clef; **–oncell(o)** *neu.* (violin) cello

violett *adj.* violet

virtuos *adj.* artistic, masterly, brilliant

Virtuos: **–e** *m.*, **–in** *f.* virtuoso, artist; **–ität** *f.* virtuosity, mastery

visieren *v.* to adjust, to gauge; to aim at; to visa, to endorse, to examine (passport)

Vision *f.* vision, phantom; **–är** *m.* visionary

Visitation *f.* search; inspection

Visite *f.* visit, call; **–nkarte** *f.* calling card

visitieren *v.* to search, to inspect

Visum *neu.* visa

vivat! *interj.* long live! hurrah!

Vize: **–admiral** *m.* vice-admiral; **–kanzler** *m.* vice-chancellor; **–könig** *m.* viceroy

Vlies *neu.* fleece

Vogel *m.* bird; **den — abschiessen** to carry off the prize; **einen — haben** to be cracked; **komischer — queer fellow; **–bauer** *m.* bird cage; **–beerbaum** *m.* mountain ash, rowan; **–fänger** *m.*, **–steller** *m.* bird catcher, fowler; **–futter** *neu.* birdseed; **–haus** *neu.* aviary; **–hecke** *f.* breeding cage; **–herd** *m.* fowling place, decoy; **–kenner** *m.* ornithologist; **–kunde** *f.* ornithology; **–leim** *m.* birdlime; **–perspektive** *f.* bird's eye view; **–scheuche** *f.* scarecrow; **–stange** *f.* perch, roost; **–strich** *m.*, **–zug** *m.* migration of birds; **–warte** *f.* ornithological station

vogelfrei *adj.* free as a bird; outlawed

Vogesen *pl.* Vosges Mountains

Vogt *m.* overseer, steward; bailiff; governor

Vokabel *f.* word

Vokabular(ium) *neu.* vocabulary, stock of words

Vokal *m.* vowel; **–musik** *f.* vocal music

Volk *neu.* people; nation; tribe; crowd; lower classes; (bees) swarm; (partridges) covey; **der Mann aus dem —** the man in the street; **–sabstimmung** *f.*, **–sentscheid** *m.* plebiscite; **–saufruhr** *m.*, **–saufstand** *m.* general uprising; **–sausgabe** *f.* popular edition; **–sbewegung** *f.* national movement; **–sbibliothek** *f.* public library; **–sbildung** *f.* national education; **–sdichte** *f.* density of population; **–sdichter** *m.* popular (*oder* national) poet; **–sfest** *neu.* national festival; **–sgenosse** *m.* fellow countryman; **–sgunst** *f.* popularity; **–shaufe(n)** *m.* crowd; mob; **–sjustiz** *f.* lynch law; **–sküche** *f.* soup kitchen; **–slied** *neu.* folk song; **–smärchen** *neu.* popular fairy tale; **–sredner** *m.* popular speaker; stump orator; **–sschlag** *m.* race; **–sschule** *f.* primary school; **–ssitte** *f.* national custom; **–ssprache** *f.* national speech; popular language; **–sstamm** *m.* tribe, race; **–stracht** *f.* national costume; **–stum** *neu.* nationality; national characteristics; **–sversammlung** *f.* public meeting; **–svertreter** *m.* representative of the people; **–swirt** *m.* political economist; **–swirtschaft** *f.* political economics; **–swirtschaftslehre** *f.* political economy; **–swohlfahrt** *f.* national welfare; **–szählung** *f.* census

Völker: –bund *m.* League of Nations; **–kunde** *f.* ethnology; **–recht** *neu.* international law; **–schlacht** *f.* battle of nations; armageddon; **–wanderung** *f.* migration of nations

völkisch *adj.* national, racial

volkreich *adj.* populous

volkstümlich *adj.* national, popular

voll *adj.* full, filled; replete; complete, entire; whole; rounded; (coll.) drunk; **aus dem –en schöpfen** to draw freely from one's store (of ideas, information, wealth); **aus –em Herzen** from the bottom of one's heart; **aus –er Brust** heartily; **aus –er Kehle** at the top of one's voice; **den Mund — nehmen** to brag, to boast; **die Uhr hat — geschla-**

gen the clock has struck the full hour; **in –er Arbeit** in the midst of work; **in –er Fahrt** at full speed; **mit –em Recht** with perfect right; **nicht für — nehmen** (coll.) not to take seriously; **sich –essen** to eat one's fill; **–auf** *adv.* abundantly, plentifully; **–blütig** *adj.* full-blooded, plethoric; **–bringen** to accomplish; **–enden** *v.* to finish, to complete; **–ends** *adv.* completely; finally; altogether; quite; **–er** *adj.* full of; **–führen** *v.* to carry out, to execute; **–gepfropft** *adj.*, **–gestopft** *adj.* crammed (full); **–gültig** *adj.* of full value, valid; **–jährig** *adj.* of (full) age; **–kommen** *adj.* perfect; complete; **–(l)eibig** *adj.* corpulent; **–machen** *v.* (coll.) to fill up, to complete; to dirty; **–spurig** *adj.* (rail.) standard-gauged; **–ständig** *adj.* complete, entire; **–ständig** *adv.* quite perfectly; **–strekken** *v.* to execute; **–tönend** *adj.* sonorous; stereophonic; **–wertig** *adj.* of high quality, of full value; **–zählig** *adj.* complete; **–ziehen** *v.* to accomplish, to execute; to take place

Voll: –bad *neu.* complete bath; **–bart** *m.* full beard; **–besitz** *m.* full possession; **–blut** *neu.* thoroughbred (horse); **–blütigkeit** *f.* plethora; **–dampf** *m.* full steam; **–gefühl** *neu.* full consciousness; **–gummi** *m.* solid rubber; **–jährigkeit** *f.* full age; majority; **–kraft** *f.* full vigor; prime; **–macht** *f.* full power; power of attorney; warrant, authority; **–matrose** *m.* able-bodied seaman; **–milch** *f.* whole milk; **–schiff** *neu.* full-rigged ship; **–spurbahn** *f.* standard gauge railroad; **–strecker** *m.* executor; **–streckungsbeamte** *m.* executive officer; **–streckungsbefehl** *m.* writ of execution; **–treffer** *m.* direct hit; **–versammlung** *f.* General Assembly; plenary session; plenum; **–ziehung** *f.*, **–zug** *m.* accomplishment, execution

völlig *adj.* full, entire, complete, thorough; **–er Ablass** plenary indulgence; **— adv.** quite, entirely, completely; **— wach** wide awake

Volontär *m.* volunteer; unsalaried clerk

Volt *neu.* (elec.) volt; **–e** *f.* (sports) vault; volt; (cards) sleight of hand; **eine –e schlagen** (cards) to make a pass; **–messer** *m.* voltmeter

Volumen *neu.* volume; capacity, content

von *prep.* from; about, by; of; in; on; **einer — vielen** one out of many; **— mir aus** as far as I am concerned; if you like it; **— Rechts wegen by right(s); — Sinnen kommen** to lose one's head; **–einander** *adv.* apart, separate; from (*oder* of) each other; **–nöten** *adv.* necessary; **–statten** *adv.* **–statten gehen** to proceed; to progress

vor *prep.* before, previous; in front of; ahead of; in the presence of; with, for, of; from, against; **fünf Minuten — drei Uhr** five minutes to three; **nach wie —** now as before; as usual; **— acht Tagen** a week ago; **— allem** above all; **— der Tür sein** to be at the door; **— der Zeit** prematurely; **— sich gehen** to take place, to occur; **–sich hin** to oneself

Vorabend *m.* eve

vorahnen *v.* to have a foreboding

Vorahnung *f.* propensity

voran *adv.* before, at the head; in front; on(wards); first; **—!** go ahead (*oder* on)!; **–geh(e)n** *v.* to take the lead; to precede; **mit gutem Beispiel –geh(e)n** to set a good example; **–kommen** *v.* to advance, to progress; **–stellen** *v.* to place in front of; to prefer

Voranschlag *m.* rough calculation, estimate

Voranzeige *f.* preliminary announcement

Vorarbeit *f.* preliminary (*oder* preparatory) work; **–er** *m.* foreman; **–erin** *f.* forewoman

vorarbeiten *v.* to prepare one's work (*oder* the ground) to show how to work

voraus *adv.* ahead of, in front; **etwas — haben** to have an advantage over; **im — in advance, beforehand, in anticipation; –bedingen** *v.* to stipulate in advance; **–bezahlen** *v.* to prepay; **–gehen** *v.* to lead the way, to precede; **–nehmen** *v.* to anticipate, to forestall; **–sagen** *v.* to forecast, to predict; **–sehen** *v.* to foresee; **–setzen** *v.* to assume, to presume; to (pre)suppose; **als bekannt –setzen** to take for granted; **–sichtlich** *adj.* probable, presumable, prospective

Voraus: **–setzung** *f.* assumption; supposition; hypothesis; **–sicht** *f.* foresight, prudence; **–truppe** *f.* vanguard; advance guard

Vorbau *m.* front building; projecting structure

vorbauen *v.* to build out (*oder* in front of); to take precautions against; to prevent

Vorbedacht *m.* forethought, premeditation; **mit — deliberately, on purpose

Vorbedeutung *f.* foreboding, omen, portent

vorbedingen *v.* to stipulate beforehand

Vorbehalt *m.* reservation, proviso; **ohne — unconditionally; unter — aller Rechte** all rights reserved

vorbehalt: –en *v.* **sich –en** to reserve to oneself; **–lich** *prep.* with reservations;

on condition that; –slos *adj.* unconditional

vorbei *adv.* along, by; over, past; done, gone; **–geh(e)n** *v.* to go (*oder* pass) by; to miss the mark; **–lassen** *v.* to let pass; **–reden** *v.* to be at cross purposes; **–schiessen** *v.* to miss (target)

Vorbeimarsch *m.* march(ing) past, review

Vorbemerkung *f.* preliminary remark; preamble

vorbereiten *v.* to prepare; **–d** *adj.* preparatory

Vorbesprechung *f.* preliminary discussion

vorbeugen *v.* to obviate, to prevent; **sich — to bend forward; –d** *adj.* precautionary, preventive, prophylactic

Vorbild *neu.* model; prototype, original; **–ung** *f.* preparatory training

vorbildlich *adj.* exemplary, ideal; typical

vorbinden *v.* to put (*oder* tie) on

Vorbote *m.* forerunner; harbinger, precursor

vorbringen *v.* to bring forward; to produce; to state, to advance, to propose; to utter

Vorbühne *f.* proscenium

vorchristlich *adj.* pre-Christian

vordatieren *v.* to antedate

vordem *adv.* formerly, of old

Vorder: –achse *f.* front axle; **–ansicht** *f.* front view; **–fuss** *m.* forefoot; **–grund** *m.* foreground; **–hand** *f.* forehand; (cards) lead; **–lader** *m.* muzzle loader; **–lauf** *m.* (zool.) foreleg; **–mann** *m.* previous endorser; front rank man; **–radantrieb** *m.* front-wheel drive; **–reihe** *f.* front rank; **–seite** *f.* front (side); face (of coin); **–steven** *m.* (naut.) stem; **–teil** *m.* and *neu.* front; forepart; (naut.) prow; **–treffen** *neu.* (mil.) front line

vordrängen *v.* to push (*oder* press) forward

vordringen *v.* to advance; to gain ground

vordringlich *adj.* urgent; intrusive

Vordruck *m.* (printed) form

vorehelich *adj.* prenuptial

voreilig *adj.* overhasty, precipitate, rash

voreingenommen *adj.* biased, prejudiced

Voreltern *pl.* forefathers, ancestors

vorenthalten *v.* to keep back, to withhold

Vorfahr *m.* ancestor, progenitor

vorfahren *v.* to drive up (to); to stop at; to drive in advance of; to pass in driving

Vorfahrtsrecht *neu.* right-of-way (in traffic)

Vorfall *m.* incident, occurrence; event; case; (med.) prolapse

vorfallen *v.* to happen, to occur

Vorfeier *f.* preliminary celebration

vorfinden v. to find, to meet, to come upon
vorflunkern v. jemand etwas — to tell someone a fib
Vorfreude f. joy of anticipation
Vorfrühling m. early (oder premature) spring
vorführen v. to bring forward; to demonstrate, to present, to produce; (horse) to trot out
Vorgabe f. (sports) points given, handicap
Vorgang m. event, incident; precedent
Vorgänger m. predecessor
Vorgarten m. front garden
vorgeben v. to pretend, to allege; (sports) to give (oder allow) points
Vorgebirge neu. promontory, cape; foothills
vorgeblich adj. pretended, so-called
vorgefasst adj. preconceived (opinion)
vorgeh(e)n v. to advance; to go first, to proceed; to occur; to take (oder have) precedence; (watch) to be fast
Vorgeh(e)n neu. advance, proceedings; precedence; **gemeinschaftliches** — concerted action
Vorgeschichte f. prehistory; antecedents
vorgeschichtlich adj. prehistoric(al)
Vorgeschmack m. foretaste
Vorgesetzte m. superior, chief, principal
vorgestern adv. the day before yesterday
vorhaben v. to have on, to wear; to be busy with; to intend, to have in mind
Vorhalle f. entrance hall, vestibule, lobby
Vorhand f. (cards) lead; (com.) precedence; (tennis) forehand
vorhanden adj. on hand, in stock; existent; existing; present, available
Vorhang m. curtain
Vorhängeschloss neu. padlock
Vorhaut f. foreskin, prepuce
Vorhemd neu. dicky; shirt front
vorher adv. before(hand); in advance, previously; **-bestimmen** v. to predetermine, to predestine; **-geh(e)n** v. to precede; **-gehend** adj. preceding, foregoing; **-ig** adj. previous, preceding, former; **-sagen** v. to foretell, to predict; **-sehen** v. to foresee, to anticipate
vorherrschen v. to predominate, to prevail; **-d** adj. predominant, prevailing, prevalent
vorheucheln v. to feign, to pretend
vorhin adv. a little while ago; **erst** — only just now
Vorhof m. forecourt; front yard; vestibule; (heart) auricle
Vorhut f. (mil.) vanguard
vorig adj. former, preceding; last, past
Vorinstanz f. (law) lower court
vorjährig adj. of last year, last year's

Vorkammer f. anteroom; (heart) auricle
Vorkämpfer m. champion, pioneer
Vorkaufsrecht neu. right of pre-emption, option
Vorkehrung f. precaution; arrangement; **-en treffen** to take precautions; **-smassregeln** f. pl. preventive measures
Vorkenntnisse f. pl. preliminary (oder basic) knowledge; rudiments (of a subject)
vorkommen v. to come forward; to occur, to take place; to be found; to appear, to seem
Vorkommnis neu. event, occurrence
Vorkriegszeit f. prewar days (oder period)
vorladen v. (law) to cite, to summon
Vorlage f. model, pattern; (pol.) bill
vorlängst adv. long ago
vorlassen v. to give precedence; to admit
Vorlauf m. start; elimination race
Vorläufer m. forerunner, precursor; pioneer
vorläufig adj. provisional, temporary; — adv. for the present, in the meantime
vorlaut adj. forward, immodest; pert
Vorleg: **-ebesteck** neu. carvers; **-er** m. mat, rug; **-eschloss** neu. padlock
vorlegen v. to put before (oder on); (meal) to help (to); to produce, to submit; to display, to show; **sich** — to lean forward
vorlesen v. to read aloud to; to gather the first ripe grapes
Vorlesung f. lecture, recital
vorletzt adj. last but one, penultimate
Vorliebe f. predilection; preference
vorliebnehmen v. to be satisfied (with)
vorliegen v. to lie before; to be under consideration; to exist, to be; **-d** adj. present, in question, in hand
vorlügen v. to tell lies (to)
vormachen v. to put on (oder before), to show how to do; to impose upon, to deceive
Vormacht f. leading power; supremacy
vormalig adj. former
vormals adv. formerly, once upon a time
Vormann m. foreman; front rank man; previous endorser
Vormarsch m. advance, march onward
Vormittag m. forenoon; morning
vormittags adv. in the forenoon
Vormund m. guardian, trustee; **-schaft** f. guardianship, tutelage
vorn adv. in (oder on the) front; before; **nach** — forward; **nach** — **heraus wohnen** to have front rooms; **von** **-(e)** opposite, facing; **von** — **anfangen** to begin anew (oder at the beginning); **von -herein** from the first, to begin

with; **−an** *adv.* in front; **−ehin** *adv.* to the front; **−(e)weg** *adv.* from the start; to begin with; **−über** *adv.* (bent) forward

Vorname *m.* first (*oder* Christian) name

vornehm *adj.* of high rank; distinguished; noble; **— tun** to put on airs: **−en** *v.* to put on (apron); jemand **−en** to take someone to task, to reprimand someone; sich **−en** to make up; to intend, to resolve; **−lich** *adv.* especially, chiefly; **−st** *adj.* foremost; die **−ste Pflicht** the first (*oder* principal) duty

Vorort *m.* suburb; **−sbewohner** *m.* suburbanite; **−sverkehr** *m.* suburban traffic

Vorposten *m.* outpost

Vorrang *m.* precedence, priority; preeminence

Vorrat *m.* stock, store(s); provisions, supply; **−shaus** *neu.* storehouse, warehouse; **−skammer** *f.* storeroom, pantry; **−sverzeichnis** *neu.* inventory; **−swagen** *m.* (rail.) tender

vorrätig *adj.* in stock, on hand, available; nicht mehr **—** out of stock

vorrechnen *v.* to reckon up (for someone); to give an account of

Vorrecht *neu.* privilege, prerogative; älteres **—** priority, seniority

Vorrede *f.* introduction; preamble, preface; prologue

vorreden *v.* to tell a plausible tale; to talk (someone) into

Vorredner *m.* previous speaker

vorreiten *v.* to ride in front of; to put (a horse) through (its) paces; jemand etwas **—** (fig.) to parade something before someone

vorrichten *v.* to prepare, to make ready

Vorrichtung *f.* preparation, arrangement; apparatus, appliance; device, mechanism

vorrücken *v.* to move forward; to advance, to progress; (watch) to set ahead

Vorsaal *m.* entrance hall; lobby

vorsagen *v.* to tell, to recite; to prompt

Vorsänger *m.* leader of a choir, precentor

Vorsatz *m.* intention, plan, purpose; resolution; mit **—** intentionally, on purpose; deliberately

vorsätzlich *adj.* intentional, deliberate; (law) with malice aforethought

Vorschein *m.* zum **— bringen** to bring forward; to produce; zum **— kommen** to come to light

vorschieben *v.* to push (*oder* shove) forward; to use as pretext; to pretend; einen Riegel **—** to slip a bolt

vorschiessen *v.* to shoot (*oder* rush) forth; to show how to shoot; to advance

(money)

Vorschlag *m.* proposal, proposition; offer; (mus.) grace (note); (pol.) motion; ein **— zur Güte** conciliatory suggestion

vorschlagen *v.* to propose, to suggest, to offer; (mus.) to beat time; (pol.) to move

Vorschlussrunde *f.* (sports) semifinal

Vorschneidebrett *neu.* carving board

vorschneiden *v.* to carve (at table)

vorschreiben *v.* to write beforehand (*oder* in front of); to direct, to order; ich lasse mir nichts **—** I won't be dictated to

Vorschrift *f.* instruction, regulation, order, prescription

vorschriftsmässig *adj.* according to direction

Vorschub *m.* aid, support; (mech.) feed, advance; **— leisten** to further, to favor

Vorschule *f.* preparatory school

Vorschuss *m.* payment in advance

vorschützen *v.* to plead, to pretend

vorschwindeln *v.* jemand etwas **—** to humbug (*oder* bamboozle) someone, to tell someone lies

vorsehen *v.* to provide for; sich **—** to take care of, to be cautious; to beware of

Vorsehung *f.* providence

vorsetzen *v.* to place (*oder* put) before; to offer, to serve (food); to set over (someone); sich **—** to intend, to purpose

Vorsicht *f.* foresight, caution, prudence; providence; **—!** beware! look out! take care! **−smassregel** *f.* precaution(ary measure)

vorsichtig *adj.* cautious, prudent, careful

Vorsilbe *f.* prefix

vorsingen *v.* to sing to; to lead (a choir)

vorsintflutlich *adj.* antediluvian

Vorsitz *m.* chairmanship, presidency; den **— führen** to be in the chair, to preside; den **— übernehmen** to take the chair; **−er** *m.*, **−ende** *m.* chairman, presiding officer

Vorsommer *m.* early summer

Vorsorge *f.* precaution, foresight

vorsorglich *adj.* provident, cautious; **—** *adv.* as a precaution

vorspannen *v.* to put (horses) to; to span before, to stretch in front of

Vorspeise *f.* hors d'oeuvre, appetizer, relish

vorspiegeln *v.* to deceive, to delude

Vorspiegelung *f.* pretense; delusion; **—** falscher Tatsachen misrepresentation of facts

Vorspiel *neu.* prelude, overture; curtain raiser

vorspielen *v.* to play to (*oder* before)

vorsprechen v. to pronounce to; to teach how to pronounce; to recite; to call on, to visit

vorspringen v. to leap forward; to project, to jut out; **-d** adj. projecting; prominent

Vorsprung m. projection; advantage, lead

Vorstadt f. suburb

Vorstädter m., **-in** f. suburbanite

vorstädtisch adj. suburban

Vorstand m. board of directors; governing committee; chairman, president

vorstechen v. to be conspicuous (oder prominent); to predominate; to prepare holes by pricking

Vorstecknadel f. scarf pin

Vorsteh: -er m. chief, head; director, manager, superintendent; (church) elder; **-erdrüse** f. prostate gland; **-hund** m. pointer, setter

vorsteh(e)n v. to jut out, to project; to administer, to direct, to manage

vorstellen v. to put forward; to set ahead (watch); to introduce, to present; to represent; to mean, to signify; to point out; to remonstrate, to protest; **sich etwas —** to conceive, to imagine, to fancy; **das kann man sich nicht —** that's inconceivable

Vorstellung f. introduction, presentation; performance; remonstrance; notion, idea; **-svermögen** neu. imagination, imaginative faculty

Vorstoss m. advance, thrust; forward push

vorstrecken v. to stretch forward; to stick out; **Geld —** to advance money

Vorstufe f. first step(s); preliminary stage; introduction, first elements

Vortänzer m. leader of a dance

vortäuschen v. to feign, to pretend

Vorteil m. advantage; benefit, profit

vorteilhaft adj. advantageous, favorable; profitable; **— aussehen** to look one's best

Vortrag m. lecture; delivery, elocution; performance, recitation; discourse, report; (com.) balance carried forward; recital; **-ende** m. lecturer, speaker, performer; **-skünstler** m. elocutionist, recitalist; performer

vortragen v. to lecture; to recite; to report; to perform; to carry forward; to express

vortrefflich adj. excellent; splendid

vortreten v. to come (oder step) forward; to project, to protrude

Vortritt m. precedence; **unter — preceded by**

Vortrupp m. outpost, vanguard

vorüber adv. over, past, by, along; gone; **-gehen** v. to pass by (oder over, away); **-gehend** adj. transitory; passing; temporary

Vorübergehende m. passer-by

Vorübung f. preparatory exercise, previous practice

Voruntersuchung f. preliminary examination

Vorurteil neu. prejudice; bias, prepossession

Vorverkauf m. advance sale (oder booking)

vorvor: -gestern adv. three days ago; **-ig** adj. penultimate; **-letzt** adj. third last

Vorwand m. pretext, pretense; excuse

vorwärts adv. forward(s); onward; **—!** interj. go ahead! move on! start! **-geh(e)n** v. to advance; to progress, to improve; **-kommen** v. to make headway, to get on, to prosper; **-treiben** v. to drive forward; to propel

vorweg adv. beforehand; **-nehmen** v. to anticipate

vorweisen v. to exhibit, to show, to produce

Vorwelt f. former ages; prehistoric world

vorwerfen v. to throw before (oder forward); **jemand etwas —** to reproach someone with something

vorwiegen v. to outweigh; to predominate; to prevail; **-d** adj. predominant, prevalent; **-d** adv. mostly, chiefly, principally

Vorwissen neu. previous knowledge; **ohne mein —** without my knowledge, unknown to me

Vorwitz m. curiosity; inquisitiveness; forwardness; impertinence, pertness

Vorwort neu. foreword, preface

Vorwurf m. reproach, blame; subject, motif

vorwurfs: -frei adj., **-los** adj. irreproachable, unimpeachable; **-voll** adj. reproachful

vorzählen v. to count before (oder over); to enumerate

Vorzeichen neu. omen; sign; (mus.) signature

vorzeichnen v. to sketch, to trace out, to mark, to indicate

vorzeigen v. to produce, to show, to display; **einen Wechsel —** to present a draft

Vorzeit f. antiquity; prehistoric times; **die graue —** the dawn of history

vorziehen v. to draw (forth); to prefer

Vorzimmer neu. antechamber; waiting room

Vorzug m. preference; priority, superiority; advantage; merit; excellence; −spreis *m.* special (*oder* exceptional) price

vorzüglich *adj.* excellent, choice; first-class; — *adv.* especially

vorzugsweise *adv.* by preference, chiefly

Vulkan *m.* volcano; −fiber *f.* vulcanized fiber

vulkanisch *adj.* volcanic

vulkanisieren *v.* to vulcanize, to retread

Vulkanisierung *f.* retread

W

Waage *f.* balance, scales; weighing machine; (ast.) Scales, Libra; (gym.) horizontal position; **jemand die — halten** to be a match for someone; **sich die — halten** to counterbalance; −schale *f.* scale(s), balance

waagerecht *adj.* horizontal, level

wab: −b(e)lig *adj.* wobbly; −beln *v.* to wobble; −bern *v.* to flicker

Wabe *f.* honeycomb

wach *adj.* awake, brisk, alert; **ganz — wide awake; — werden to awake;** −ehabend *adj.* on duty; −en *v.* to be (*oder* keep) awake; to watch, to guard; −sam *adj.* watchful, vigilant

Wach: −e *f.* guard, sentry; watch(man); guard room; police station; **auf −e ziehen** to mount guard; **die −e ablösen** to relieve the guard; −e **stehen** to be on guard; −traum *m.* daydream

Wacholder *m.* juniper; gin

Wachs *neu.* wax; −abdruck *m.* wax impression; −figurenkabinett *neu.* wax-works; −leinwand *f.*, −tuch *neu.* oilcloth; −stock *m.* wax taper; −zieher *m.* wax goods manufacturer

wachsen *v.* to grow, to increase; to thrive; to wax; **er ist ihm ans Herz gewachsen** he has become very fond of him; **jemand gewachsen sein** to be a match for someone

wächsern *adj.* waxen; of wax; pale (as wax)

Wachstum *neu.* growth; increase

Wacht *f.* guard, watch; −dienst *m.* guard duty; −meister *m.* sergeant-major (of cavalry); −posten *m.* sentry; −stube *f.* guard-room; −turm *m.* watchtower

Wachtel *f.* quail; −hund *m.* spaniel; −schlag *m.* call of the quail

Wächter *m.* watchman; warden; lookout man

wack: −(e)lig *adj.* shaky, tottering, rickety; (tooth) loose; −eln *v.* to shake, to rock; to totter; to be loose

wacker *adj.* brave, upright; — *adv.*

bravely; heartily; soundly

Wade *f.* calf (of leg); −nbein *neu.* fibula

Waffe *f.* weapon, arm(s); **die −n ergreifen** to take up arms; **unter −n stehen** to be under arms; −ndienst *m.* military service; −ngang *m.* armed conflict; −ngattung *f.* (mil.) branch of service; −nrock *m.* (mil.) uniform coat; −nruhe *f.* cease-fire; truce; −nschein *m.* gun license; −nschmied *m.* armorer; −nstillstand *m.* armistice, truce

Waffel *f.* waffle

waffnen *v.* to arm

Wag: −ehals *m.* daredevil; −emut *m.* daring; −estück *neu.* daring enterprise; −halsigkeit *f.* foolhardiness; −nis *neu.* risk, hazard

wagen *v.* to venture, to dare; to hazard, to risk; to attempt

Wagen *m.* carriage, coach; vehicle; car, van, wagon; **der grosse —** (ast.) the Big Dipper; −burg *f.* barricade of wagons; −decke *f.* tarpaulin cover; −heber *m.* jack; −lenker *m.* driver; −macher *m.* cartwright; −schlag *m.* carriage door; −schmiere *f.* lubricant

wägen *v.* to weigh; to consider

Waggon *m.* (rail.) car; truck

Wahl *f.* choice, selection; option; election, poll(ing); **seine — treffen** to make one's choice; **vor die — stellen** to let one choose; **zur — vorschlagen** to nominate; −bericht *m.* election return; −bezirk *m.* electoral district; constituency; ward; −fach *neu.* optional subject; −fähigkeit *f.* eligibility; franchise; −handlung *f.* election; −heimat *f.* country of one's choice; −kreis *m.* ward, constituency; −kugel *f.* ballot; −liste *f.* register of electors; −lokal *neu.* polling place; −programm *neu.* (pol.) platform; −recht *neu.* right to vote, franchise; **allgemeines −recht** *neu.* universal suffrage; −spruch *m.* motto, device; maxim; −stimme *f.* vote; −urne *f.* ballot box; −versammlung *f.* election meeting; caucus; −verwandtschaft *f.* elective affinity; congeniality; −zelle *f.* polling booth; −zettel *m.* ballot

wähl: −bar *adj.* eligible; −en *v.* to choose, to pick out, to select; to elect, to vote; (tel.) to dial; −erisch *adj.* choosy; fastidious

Wähler *m.* voter; −schaft *f.* body of voters; constituency; −scheibe *f.* (tel.) dial

Wahn *m.* delusion, illusion; hallucination; fancy, folly; −bild *neu.* phantom, chimera; −sinn *m.* insanity, madness; −sinnige *m.* lunatic, madman; −witz *m.*

frenzy, absurdity

wähnen *v.* to imagine, to presume, to fancy

wahnsinnig *adj.* insane, mad; frantic; (coll.) terrific

wahnwitzig *adj.* absurd, senseless, foolish

wahr *adj.* true; genuine; real, proper, veritable; **er will es nicht — haben** he won't admit it; **nicht —! isn't it! sein Wort — machen** to keep one's promise; **so — mir Gott helfe!** so help me God! **— werden** to come true; **–en** *v.* to keep (up); to watch over; to preserve; **–haft(ig)** *adj.* sincere, truthful; genuine; real, actual, **–heitsgemäss** *adj.*, **–heitsgetreu** *adj.*, **–heitsliebend** *adj.* true, truthful; **–lich** *adv.* truly, certainly; (bibl.) verily; **–nehmbar** *adj.* perceivable, noticeable; **–nehmen** *v.* to notice, to perceive; to make use of; to look after; **–sagen** to tell fortunes; to prophesy; **–scheinlich** *adj.* probable, likely

Wahr: –heit *f.* truth; **jemand die –heit sagen** to speak bluntly; **–nehmung** *f.* perception; observation; care (of); **–nehmungsvermögen** *neu.* perceptive faculty; **–sager** *m.* fortuneteller, soothsayer; **–sagung** *f.* fortunetelling, prophecy; **–scheinlichkeitsrechnung** *f.* theory of probabilities; **–spruch** *m.* (law) verdict; **–zeichen** *neu.* landmark; token, sign, omen

währen *v.* to continue, to last; **–d** *prep.* during; **–d** *conj.* while, whilst; **–ddem** *adv.*, **–ddessen** *adv.* in the meantime, meanwhile

Währung *f.* currency, monetary standard

Waise *f.* orphan; **–nhaus** *neu.* orphanage; **–nknabe** *m.* orphan boy; **er ist der reinste –nknabe** he doesn't know a thing

Wal, Walfisch *m.* whale; **–fischfahrer** *m.* whaler; **–fischfang** *m.* whaling; **–fischtran** *m.* train oil; **–ross** *neu.* walrus

Wald *m.* wood, forest; **–brand** *m.* forest fire; **–einsamkeit** *f.* woodland retreat; **–erdbeere** *m.* wild strawberry; **–esdunkel** *neu.* forest gloom; **–essaum** *m.* forest edge; **–esel** *m.* wild ass; **–eule** *f.* brown owl; **–gegend** *f.* woodland; **–gehege** *neu.* forest preserve; **–geist** *m.* faun, satyr; **–horn** *neu.* French horn; **–hüter** *m.* forest ranger; **–läufer** *m.* forester; **–meister** *m.* (bot.) woodruff; **–nymphe** *f.* dryad; **–schnepfe** *f.* woodcock; **–schrat** *m.* forest sprite; **–ung** *f.* wood(land); **–wiese** *f.* glade; **–wirtschaft** *f.* forestry

Wäldchen *neu.* bush, grove; shrubbery; thicket

waldig *adj.* wooded, woody; forested

walken *v.* to full (cloth)

Walküre *f.* Valkyrie

Wall *m.* rampart; embankment; **–graben** *m.* moat

wallen *v.* to bubble, to simmer, to boil; to undulate; to float, to flutter; to become agitated; (poet.) to wander, to roam

wallfahren *v.* to go on a pilgrimage

Wallfahrer *m.* pilgrim

Wallfahrt *f.* pilgrimage

Walnuss *f.* walnut; **weisser –baum** hickory

Walpurgisnacht *f.* Witches' Sabbath

walten *v.* to govern, to rule; to carry out, to execute; **das walte Gott!** God grant it! **Gnade — lassen** to show mercy

walzen *v.* to roll (out); to waltz

wälzen *v.* to roll; **Bücher — to consult many weighty books; die Schuld auf jemand anderen** — to lay the blame on somebody else; **Gedanken — to ponder; sich — to roll; to wallow, to welter**

Wams *neu.* jacket; doublet; jerkin

Wand *f.* wall; partition; side; (med.) coat; **jemand an die — drücken** to shove someone aside; **spanische — folding screen; –bekleidung** *f.* wainscot(ing); **–gemälde** *neu.*, **–malerei** *f.* fresco; mural painting; **–karte** *f.* wall map; **–leuchter** *m.* bracket (for lighting); **–schirm** *m.* screen; **–spiegel** *m.* pier glass; **–tafel** *f.* blackboard; **–teppich** *m.* tapestry; **–ung** *f.* wall, partition

Wandel *m.* change, alteration; behavior, conduct; **Handel und — trade and** traffic; **–gang** *m.*, **–halle** *f.* foyer, lobby; **–stern** *m.* planet

wandelbar *adj.* changeable, variable; fickle

Wander: –bühne *f.* traveling theater; **–bursche** *m.* traveling journeyman; **–er** *m.* wanderer, hiker; **–heuschrecke** *f.* migratory locust; **–niere** *f.* floating kidney; **–prediger** *m.* itinerant preacher; **–preis** *m.* challenge cup (*oder* trophy); **–ratte** *f.* brown (*oder* sewer) rat; **–raupe** *f.* larvae of processionary moth; **–schaft** *f.* travels, hiking; migration; **–smann** *m.* wanderer, wayfarer; traveler; **–stab** *m.* walking stick; **zum –stab greifen** to set out on travels; **–trieb** *m.* roving spirit; migratory instinct; **–truppe** *f.* (theat.) strolling players; **–ung** *f.* walking tour; hike; excursion; migration; **–vögel** *m. pl.* birds of passage; members of a German hiking movement; **–volk** *neu.* nomadic people

wandern *v.* to wander, to travel; to hike

Wandlung *f.* change; transformation; (rel.) transsubstantiation

Wange *f.* cheek

wankelmütig *adj.* inconstant, fickle

wanken *v.* to stagger, to totter; to waver

wann *adv.* when; **dann und — now and then**; sometimes; **seit — ist er hier?** how long has he been here?

Wanne *f.* tub; bath; (agr.) winnowing fan

Wappen *neu.* coat of arms; escutcheon; **-kunde** *f.* heraldry; **-schild** *neu.* escutcheon; **-schmuck** *m.* emblazonry; **-spruch** *m.* heraldic motto; **-tier** *neu.* heraldic animal

wappnen *v.* to arm

Ware *f.* ware, article; **-n** *pl.* goods, merchandise; **-nbestand** *m.* stock on hand; **-nhaus** *neu.* department store; **-nlager** *neu.* stock in trade; warehouse; **-nniederlage** *f.* magazine, warehouse; **-nprobe** *f.* sample; **-nzeichen** *neu.* trade-mark

warm *adj.* warm, hot; **jemand den Kopf — machen** to excite someone; **sich jemand — halten** to keep someone in good humor; **Speisen — stellen** to keep food hot; **-blütig** *adj.* warm blooded

Warm: -bier *neu.* hot ale; **-wasserheizung** *f.* hot water (*oder* central) heating; **-wasserversorgung** *f.* hot-water supply

Wärm: -e *f.* warmth; heat; ardor; **-eabgabe** *f.* loss of heat; **-eeinheit** *f.* thermal unit; **-egrad** *m.* degree of heat, temperature; **-elehre** *f.* science of heat; **-eleiter** *m.* conductor of heat; **-emesser** *m.* calorimeter, thermometer; **-flasche** *f.* hot-water bottle

wärmen *v.* to warm, to heat; **sich — to** warm oneself; to bask

Warn: -er *m.* warner; **-ungssignal** *neu.* danger signal; **-nungstafel** *f.* warning signboard

warnen *v.* to warn, to admonish, to caution

warten *v.* to wait, to stay; to attend to, to nurse, to look after; **da können sie lange — they** may wait till doomsday; **er lässt immer auf sich — he** is never on time; **— auf to wait for; — lassen** to keep waiting

Wärter *m.* attendant, keeper; care-taker; warder; (male) nurse; **-in** *f.* nurse

warum *adv.* why, for what reason

Warze *f.* wart; nipple, teat

was *pron.* what; that which, that, which; something; **— auch immer, — nur** what(so)ever; no matter what; **— für (ein)?** what kind (*oder* sort) of?

Wasch: -anstalt *f.* laundry; **-automat** (öffentlich) *m.* laundromat; **-bär** *m.*

raccoon; **-becken** *neu.* wash basin; **-frau** *f.* laundress, washerwoman; **-geschirr** *neu.* washstand set; **-kessel** *m.* wash boiler; **-küche** *f.* laundry; **-lappen** *m.* wash cloth; (coll.) weakling; **-leder** *neu.* chamois; **-mittel** *neu.* lotion; **-raum** *m.* washroom; lavatory; **-tisch** *m.*, **-toilette** *f.* washstand; **-zettel** *m.* laundry list; publisher's blurb

Wäsche *f.* wash(ing); linen; **heute ist grosse — today is wash day; in die — geben** to send to the laundry; **-beutel** *m.* laundry bag; **-geschäft** *neu.* lingerie, underclothing business; **-klammer** *f.* clothespin; **-leine** *f.* clothesline; **-mangel** *f.*, **-rolle** *f.* mangle; **-rei** *f.* laundry; **-rin** *f.* laundress; **-schrank** *m.* linen cupboard

waschecht *adj.* (color-)fast; (coll.) genuine

waschen *v.* to wash; **jemand den Kopf — (coll.)** to scold someone; **mit allen Wassern gewaschen sein** to be sly (*oder* crafty)

Wasser *neu.* water; luster (of stones); (poet.) watercourse, sea; **ins — fallen** (coll.) to come to naught; **jemand nicht das — reichen können** to be inferior to someone; **Kölnisches — eau de Cologne; mit allen -n gewaschen sein** (coll.) to be cunning; **sich über — halten** (coll.) to keep one's head above water; **unter — setzen** to inundate, to flood; **— abschlagen** (*or* **lassen**) to urinate; **— ziehen** to leak; **zu — werden** to melt away; **zu — und zu Lande** by land and sea; **-armut** *f.* drouth; **-ball** *m.* water polo; **-baukunst** *f.* hydraulics; **-behälter** *m.* cistern, reservoir, water tank; **-blase** *f.* bubble; vesicle; **-bombe** *f.* depth charge; **-druck** *m.* hydrostatic pressure; **-fall** *m.* waterfall; **-farbe** *f.* water color, distemper; **-fläche** *f.* water level (*oder* surface); **-flugzeug** *neu.* seaplane; **-graben** *m.* ditch, drain; moat; **-hahn** *m.* faucet, tap; **-heilanstalt** *f.* water cure establishment; **-hose** *f.* waterspout; **-huhn** *neu.* coot; **-jungfer** *f.* naiad, nymph; mermaid; dragonfly; **-karte** *f.* hydrographic chart; **-kopf** *m.* hydrocephalus; **-kraft** *f.* water power; **-krug** *m.* pitcher; **-kunst** *f.* artificial fountain; hydraulics; **-lache** *f.* pool; **-lauf** *m.* water-course; **-leitung** *f.* water pipes; aqueduct; **-linse** *f.* duckweed; **-mann** *m.* water sprite; (ast.) Aquarius; **-messer** *m.* hydrometer; **-pest** *f.* pondweed; **-pflanze** *f.* aquatic plant; **-ratte** *f.* water rat; old sailor, sea dog; good swimmer; **-rinne** *f.*

gutter; **–scheide** *f.* watershed; **–rutschbahn** *f.* water chute; **–scheu** *f.* hydrophobia; **–schlange** *f.* water snake; (ast.) Hydra; **–schlauch** *m.* water hose; **–schraube** *f.* hydraulic screw; **–snot** *f.* flood; **–speier** *m.* gargoyle; **–skilaufen** *neu.* water-skiing; **–spiegel** *m.* water surface; water level (*oder* table); **–sport** *m.* aquatics; **–stand** *m.* water level; tide level; **–standsmesser** *m.* water gauge; **–stiefel** *m. pl.* rubber boots; **–stoff** *m.* hydrogen; **–stoffsuperroxyd** *neu.* hydrogen peroxide; **–strahl** *m.* jet of water; **–strasse** *f.* waterway, navigable river; **–sucht** *f.* dropsy; **–suppe** *f.* thin gruel; **–tier** *neu.* aquatic

wasser: –arm *adj.* arid; **–dicht** *adj.* waterproof; watertight; **–frei** *adj.* anhydrous; **–haltig** *adj.* containing water, hydrated; **–reich** *adj.* abounding in water resources; **–scheu** *adj.* hydrophobic; **–süchtig** *adj.* dropsical

wässerig *adj.* watery; insipid animal; **–tiefenmessung** *f.* bathymetry; **–verdrängung** *f.* (naut.) water displacement; **–vögel** *m. pl.* waterfowl; **–waage** *f.* water level; **–werk** *neu.* waterworks; **–zeichen** *neu.* watermark

wässern *v.* to water, to irrigate; to soak, to steep; (phot.) to wash

waten *v.* to wade

Watt *neu.* (elec.) watt; sand banks (covered at high tide), muddy shallows

Watte *f.* wadding; (med.) cotton; **–ebausch** *m.* cotton ball

wattieren *v.* to pad, to wad, to quilt

Wauwau *m.* (child's) doggie; (coll.) bugbear

Web: –e(r)baum *m.* weaver's beam; warp beam; **–ekante** *f.* selvage; **–er** *m.* weaver; **–erei** *f.* weaving (mill); texture; **–erknecht** *m.* (ent.) daddy longlegs; **–erschiffchen** *neu.* shuttle; **–stuhl** *m.* loom; **–waren** *f. pl.* textiles

weben *v.* to weave; (poet.) to float

Wechsel *m.* change, alteration; turn, rotation; fluctuation; exchange; relay; bill of exchange; (hunting) runway; eigener — note of hand; gezogener — draft; offener — credit letter; **–balg** *m.* changeling; **–bewegung** *f.* reciprocal movement; **–beziehung** *f.* correlation; **–fälle** *m. pl.* ups and downs, vicissitudes; **–fieber** *neu.* intermittent fever; **–folge** *f.* alternation; **–geld** *neu.* change, small coin(s); **–gesang** *m.* antiphony; **–gespräch** *neu.* dialogue; **–getriebe** *neu.* change gear; **–jahre** *neu. pl.* (med.) climacteric; **–kurs** *m.* rate of exchange; **–reiter** *m.* speculator in drafts; **–schal**

tung *f.* change-over switch; **–seitigkeit** *f.* reciprocity; **–strom** *m.* (elec.) alternating current; **–stube** *f.* exchange office; **–winkel** *m.* adjacent angle; **–wirkung** *f.* reciprocal action; **–wirtschaft** *f.* rotation of crops

wechseln *v.* to change, to alternate; to exchange; (hunting) to pass; to shift (scene); die Zähne — to cut new teeth; den Aufenthaltsort — to move elsewhere

Wechselseitiger Verkehr *m.* intercom

Wechsler *m.* money changer, banker

wecken *v.* to wake, to awaken; to rouse, to call

Wecker *m.* alarm clock; awakener

Wedel *m.* fan; duster; frond, palm leaf; (zool.) brush, tail

weder *conj.* neither

Weg *m.* way, course, path; road, passage, route; trip, errand, walk; method, means; am **–e** by the roadside; auf halbem **–e** halfway; auf gütlichem **–e** amicably; aus dem **–(e)** geh(e)n to get out of the way; to evade; aus dem **–(e)** räumen to remove; ein tüchtiges Stück **–es** a good distance; in die **–e** leiten to prepare; kürzester — short cut; nicht über den — trauen not to trust; verbotener **–!** no trespassing! **–bereiter** *m.* forerunner, pioneer; **–ebau** *m.* road making; **–edorn** *m.* buckthorn; **–elag(e)rer** *m.* highwayman; **–enge** *f.* defile; **–erich** *m.* plantain; **–(e)geld** *neu.* (turnpike) toll; **–scheide** *f.* crossroads, road fork; **–strecke** *f.* length of the way; distance; **–stunde** *f.* distance per hour; **–warte** *f.* chicory; **–weiser** *m.* guide(book); signpost; **–zehrung** *f.* provisions (for a trip); **–zug** *m.* departure; removal

weg *adv.* away; off; gone, lost, disappeared; er hat einen — (coll.) he is tipsy; ganz — sein (coll.) to be enraptured (about); — da! be off there! **–bar** *adj.*, **–sam** *adj.* passable, accessible; **–begeben** *v.*, sich **–begeben** to go away; to withdraw; **–bekommen** *v.* to get off; (fig.) to grasp; **–bleiben** *v.* to stay away; to be omitted; **–bringen** *v.* to carry away, to remove; (spot) to take out; **–dürfen** *v.* to be allowed to go away; **–en** *prep.* on account of, because of; in consideration of; for the sake of; in consequence of; owing to; von Rechts **–en** by right; **–fahren** *v.* to cart away; to drive off; **–fallen** *v.* not to take place; to be omitted; **–haben** *v.* to have received; to be well up in; **–helfen** *v.* to help to get away; **–holen** *v.* to fetch away; to catch (cold); **–jagen** v. to drive away; to gallop off; **–kommen** v. to get away (oder lost); **–können** v. to be able to get away; **–lassen** v. to let go; to omit; **sich –machen** to make off; **–müssen** v. to be obliged to go away; **–nehmen** v. to take away; to confiscate; to occupy (space); **–räumen** v. to clear away, to remove; **–reisen** v. to depart; **–rücken** v. to move away; to withdraw; **–schaffen** v. to clear away, to remove; **–scheren** v. to shear off; **sich –scheren** to be off; **–sehen** v. to look away; to shut one's eyes to; **–setzen** v. to put aside; to jump (over); **–treten** v. to step aside; (mil.) to break ranks; **–wenden** v. to turn away; **–werfen** v. to throw away; **sich –werfen** to degrade oneself; **–werfend** adj. contemptuous, disdainful; **–ziehen** v. to draw away; to move; to migrate

Weh neu. pain; woe; grief; **–e** f. drift; **–en** pl. labor pains; **–mutter** f. midwife

Wehr f. defense, resistance; weapon, arm; bulwark; — neu. weir, spillway; **–bezirk** m. military district; **–dienst** m. (mil.) service; **–gang** m. battlement, parapet; **–gehänge** neu., **–gehenk** neu. sword belt; **–gesetz** neu. military service law; **–kraft** f. armed forces; **–macht** f. Armed Forces; **–pflicht** f. compulsory military service; **–stand** m. military profession; **–vorlage** f. military service bill

wehr: –en v. to restrain, to hinder, to forbid; **sich (seiner Haut) –en** to defend oneself, to resist; **–fähig** adj., **–haft** adj. able to bear arms; strong; **–los** adj. defenseless; unarmed; **–los machen** to disarm; **–pflichtig** adj. subject to military service

Weib neu. female; woman; wife; **–chen** neu. little woman; (zool.) female; **–erart** f. woman's way(s); **–erfeind** m. woman hater; misogynist; **–erheld** m. ladies' man; **–erherrschaft** f. petticoat government; **–sbild** neu. female; (coll.) hussy, wench; **–svolk** neu. womankind, womanfolk

weiblich adj. feminine; female

weich adj. soft, tender; weak; mellow; smooth; **–es Ei** soft-boiled egg; **–werden** to soften; to be moved; **–en** v. to give way (oder in); to withdraw; to yield; to soften, to soak; (prices) to decline; **nicht von der Stelle –en** not to budge an inch; **von jemand –en** to abandon someone; **zum –en bringen** to push back, to repel; **–gestimmt** adj. in a gentle mood; **–herzig** adj. tender-

hearted; **–lich** adj. soft; flabby; sloppy; effeminate; weak, indolent

Weich: –bild neu. precincts (of city); **–e** f. softness; (anat.) flank, groin; (rail.) switch; **–ensteller** m. switchman

Weichsel f. Vistula

weid: –en v. to graze, to pasture; **sich –en an** to feast on, to delight in; **–en** adj. willow; **–gerecht** adj., **–männisch** adj. huntsmanlike; sportsmanlike; **–lich** adv. thoroughly, very much; **–wund** adj. shot in the intestines; death wound

Weid: –e f. pasture; willow, osier; **–engeflecht** neu. wickerwork; **–enkätzchen** neu. willow catkin; **–mann** m. hunter, sportsman; **–mannsheil** neu. hunter's greeting; **–messer** neu. hunting knife; **–werk** neu. chase, hunting

weigern v. to decline, to refuse; **sich —** to refuse (to do)

Weih m., **–e** f. (orn.) kite; **–bischof** m. suffragan bishop; **–e** f. consecration; ordination; inauguration; solemnity; **–gabe** f. votive offering; **–nacht** f., **–nachten** pl. Christmas; **–nachtsabend** m. Christmas Eve; **–nachstbescherung** f. distribution of Christmas gifts; **–slied** neu. Christmas carol; **–smann** m. Santa Claus; **–rauch** m. incense; **–rauchfass** neu. censer; **–wasser** neu. holy water; **–wasserbecken** neu. font; holy-water vessel; **–(wasser)wedel** m. holy-water sprinkler

weihen v. to consecrate; to dedicate, to ordain

Weiher m. pond

weihevoll adj. solemn, hallowed

weil conj. because, since; (poet.) as long as; **–and** adv. (poet.) formerly, of old; deceased; **–en** v. to stay; to linger; to delay

Weile f. while; (space of) time; leisure; **damit hat es gute — there's no hurry about that; Eile mit — make haste** slowly

Weiler m. hamlet

Wein m. wine; vine; grapes; **jemand reinen — einschenken** to tell someone the whole truth; **wilder —** Virginia creeper; **–bau** m. wine growing, viticulture; **–beere** f. grape; **–berg** m. vineyard; **–bergschnecke** f. edible snail; **–brand** m. cognac, brandy; **–ernte** f. vintage; **–fass** neu. wine cask; **–gegend** f. wine district; **–geist** m. ethyl alcohol; **–händler** m. wine merchant; **–hefe** f. dregs of wine; **–karte** f. wine list; **–kelter** f. winepress; **–kenner** m. connoisseur of wine; **–küfer** m. wine cooper; **–laub** neu. vine leaves; **–laube**

f. vine arbor; **–lese** *f.* vintage; **–probe** *f.* sample (*oder* tasting) of wine; **–rebe** *f.,* **–stock** *m.* grapevine; **–säure** *f.* acidity of wine; tartaric acid; **–schank** *m.* retail(ing) of wine; **–schenk** *m.* cupbearer; **–schenke** *f.* wine tavern; **–stein** *m.* tartar; **–traube** *f.* (bunch of) grape(s); **–trester** *pl.* husks of pressed grapes; **–zwang** *m.* obligation to order wine (with meal)

weinen *v.* to weep, to cry, to shed tears

weis: –e *adj.* wise; prudent; **–en** *v.* to point out (*oder* at); to show; to direct; to refer (to); **von sich** (*or* **der Hand**) **–en** to reject, to decline; **–en aus** to expel; **–lich** *adv.* wisely; prudently; **–machen** *v.* to make (one) believe a thing; to hoax; **–sagen** *v.* to predict, to prophesy

Weis: –e *m.* wise man, sage; **–e** *f.* way, manner; custom, habit; melody, tune; **auf diese –e** in this way; **auf keine –e** by no means; **–el** *m.* queen bee; **–er** *m.* indicator, pointer; **–ung** *f.* order, instruction

Weisheit *f.* wisdom; prudence; **mit seiner –heit am Ende sein** to be at one's wits' end; **–sager** *m.* prophet, fortuneteller; **–sagung** *f.* prophecy

weiss *adj.* white; clean, blank; hoary; **eine –e Weste haben** to be innocent; **jemand — waschen** to whitewash someone; **–er Sonntag** Sunday after Easter; **–e Blutkörperchen** leucocyte; **–en** to whiten; to whitewash; **–glühend** *adj.* white-hot, incandescent

weit *adj.* wide, extensive, spacious; capacious; distant, far, remote; immense, vast; loose; **bei –em** by far; **bei –em nicht** not at all; **das geht zu —** that's going too far; **es — bringen** (coll.) to get on in the world; **im –esten Sinne des Wortes** in the broadest sense of the word; **nicht — her sein** (coll.) to be of little value; **so — ist es also gekommen!** things have come to such a point! **Treib es nicht zu —!** Don't overdo it! **— gefehlt!** quite wrong! **wenn alles so — ist** when everything is ready; **–ab** *adv.* far away; **–aus** *adv.* by far; much; **–blickend** *adj.* farsighted; **–en** *v.* to widen, to expand; to stretch; **–gehend** *adj.* extensive, vast; **–greifend** *adj.* far-reaching; **–her** *adv.* from afar; **–hergeholt** *adj.* far-fetched; **–herzig** *adj.* broad-minded; magnanimous; tolerant; **–hin** *adv.* far away (*oder* off); **–läufig** *adj.* distant; spacious; detailed, circumstantial; **–maschig** *adj.* widemeshed; **–reichend** *adj.* far-reaching;

–schweifig *adj.* long-winded; prolix; tedious; **–sichtig** *adj.* farsighted; longsighted; **–spurig** *adj.* (rail.) broadgauge; **–tragend** *adj.* far-reaching; of long range; **–verbreitet** *adj.* widespread, prevalent, general

Weit: –blick *m.* farsightedness; **–e** *f.* width; extensiveness; distance; size; capacity; range; **das — suchen** to take to one's heels; **–sprung** *m.* broad jump

weiter *adj.* wider; farther, further; **—** *adv.* farther, further; more, else; on, forward; **bis auf –es** until further notice; **for the present; nur —!** go on! **ohne –es** without more ado, immediately; **und so — and so on; — niemand** no one else; **–befördern** *v.* to forward; **–bestehen** *v.* to continue to exist; **–bringen** *v.* to help on; **es –bringen** to make progress; **–führen** *v.* to carry on; **–geben** *v.* to pass on (to); **–geh(e)n** *v.* to walk on; to continue; **–hin** *adv.* in future, after that; **–kommen** *v.* to get on; **–können** *v.* to be able to go on; **–leiten** *v.* to transmit, to forward; **–lesen** *v.* to go on reading; **–sagen** *v.* to tell (others)

Weizen *m.* wheat; **sein — blüht** he seems to be in clover (*oder* doing well)

welch *pron.* and *adj.* what, which, who, that; some, any; **–er auch immer** whosoever; **–erart** *adv.*, **–ergestalt** *adv.* in what way, by what means, how; **–erlei** *adv.* of what kind

welk *adj.* withered, faded, flabby, limp; **–en** *v.* to wither, to fade; to droop

Well: –blech *neu.* corrugated sheet iron; **–e** *f.* wave; billow; breaker; (mech.) shaft, spindle; axle; (brushwood) bundle; **–enbad** *neu.* swimming pool with artificial waves; **–enbereich** *m.* (rad.) wave range; **–enberg** *m.* mountainous wave; **–enbewegung** *f.* undulation; **–enbrecher** *m.* breakwater; **–enkamm** *m.* crest of wave; **–enlänge** *f.* wave length; **–enlinie** *f.* wavy line; **–enreiter** *m.* surf rider; **–enschlag** *m.* dashing of waves; **–ensittich** *m.* parakeet; **–ental** *neu.* wave trough; **–entheorie** *f.* theory; **–fleisch** *neu.* freshly slaughtered boiled pork; **–pappe** *f.* corrugated cardboard

wellen *v.* to wave, to corrugate; to simmer

welsch *adj.* Italian, French; outlandish

Welt *f.* world; universe; people; **auf der — on earth; aus der — schaffen** to put out of the way; **in die — setzen, zur — bringen** to give birth to; **das Licht der — erblicken** to be born; **–all** *neu.* universe; macrocosm; **–alter** *neu.* age; period of history; **–anschauung** *f.* philosophical conception of the world (oder history); **–ausstellung** f. world fair; **–beschreibung** f. cosmography; **–bildung** f. good breeding; **–bürger** m. cosmopolite; **–entstehungslehre** f. cosmogony; **–enbummler** m. globe-trotter; **–ereignis** neu. event of world-wide importance; **–erfahrung** f. experience in worldly affairs; **–friede(n)** m. universal peace; **–gebäude** neu. cosmic system; **–geistliche** m. secular priest; **–gericht** neu. Last Judgment; **–handel** m. international trade; **–kind** neu. worldling; **–körper** m. celestial body, sphere; **–kugel** f. globe; **–lage** f. general political situation; **–lauf** m. course of the world; **–macht** f. world power; **–meer** neu. ocean; **–meister** m. world champion; **–ordnung** f. cosmic system; natural laws; **–postverein** m. International Postal Union; **–raum** m. space; **–raumfahrer** m. astronaut; **–raummedizin** f. space medicine; **–raumnavigation** f. astronavigation; **–raumschiff** neu. space capsule; **–sprache** f. universal language; **–stadt** f. metropolis; **–untergang** m. end of the world; **–wende** f. turning point in world history

welt: –bekannt adj., **–berühmt** adj. world-famous; **–entrückt** adj. isolated; **–erfahren** adj., **–klug** adj. worldly-wise; **–erschütternd** adj. world-shaking; **–fremd** adj. ignorant of the world; solitary; **–lich** adj. worldly; secular; profane; temporal; **–männisch** adj. well-bred, gentlemanly; **–umspannend** adj. world-embracing; universal

Wemfall m. dative case

Wend: –e f. turn(ing); change, new epoch; **–ehals** m. (orn.) wryneck; **–ekreis** m. tropic; **–eltreppe** f. spiral staircase; **–epunkt** m. turning point; crisis; solstice; **–ung** f. turn(ing); change; crisis; (mil.) wheeling; phrase, saying

wenden v. to turn (round); (avi.) to yaw; **bitte —!** please turn to (page)! **Geld — an** to spend money on; **sich — an** to turn (oder apply) to

wenig adj. little; few; **das –ste** the least; **die –sten** only a few; **ein — a** little; somewhat; **fünf –er drei** five minus three; **nichts –er als** anything but; **nicht –er als** no less than; **nicht zum –sten** last but not least; **so — auch** however few; **–er** less; fewer; **–er werden** to decrease, to diminish; **zwei Dollar zu —** two dollars short; **–stens** adv. at least

Wenigkeit f. small quantity; trifle; **meine — my humble self

wenn conj. when; if, in case; **— auch** however, even if; **— auch noch** howsoever; **— doch** if only; **— etwa** if by chance; **— nur** provided that; **–gleich** conj., **–schon** conj. (al)though, even if

wer pron. who; which; (coll.) someone; **— auch immer** whoever; **— da?** who goes there?

Werb: –eabteilung f. advertising department; **–enummer** f. complimentary copy; **–eoffizier** m. recruiting officer; **–er** m. suitor, wooer; recruiting officer; **–etrommel** f., **die –etrommel rühren** to make propaganda; to publicize clamorously; **–ung** f. courting, courtship; recruiting; canvassing; advertising, publicity, propaganda; **–ungskosten** pl. advertising expenses

werben v. to recruit, to enlist; to court, to woo; to sue (for); to propagandize, **to** publicize; to advertise; to canvass

Werdegang m. development; process; evolution; career

werden v. to become, to grow; to turn out; **aus ihm wird nichts — he will** never amount to anything; **es muss anders — there must be a change;** **geliebt — to be loved; — zu to turn** into; **–de Mutter** mother-to-be

werfen v. to throw; to fling, to hurl, **to** pitch; to cast; to project; to bring forth (young); **aufs Papier — to jot down on** paper; **durcheinander — to muddle up;** **sich — to warp; sich — auf to apply** oneself to; **über den Haufen — to over-** throw; to upset

Werft f. shipyard, wharf; (avi.) work-shops

Werk neu. work; labor; act(ion), deed; creation; works; production; factory, workshops; mechanism; **ans — geh(e)n, Hand ans — legen** to set to work; **ins — setzen** to set going; **zu –e gehen** to proceed; **–meister** m. foreman; **–leute** pl. workmen, hands; **–spionage** f. industrial spying; **–statt** f., **–stätte** f. workshop; **–stoff** m. material; **–student** m. working student; **–tag** m. working day; weekday; **–zeug** neu. tool, implement; (fig.) organ

Wermut m. wormwood; vermouth; bitterness

wert adj. worth(y); valuable; dear, esteemed; **–beständig** adj. stable, of fixed value; **–en** v. to evaluate, to estimate, to appraise; **–geschätzt** adj. esteemed; **–los** adj. worthless; **–schätzen** v. to esteem highly; to appreciate; to value; **–voll** adj. precious, valuable

Wert m. worth, value; price, rate; importance, use; stress; merit; **fester —** (math.) fixed quantity; **gleicher —** equivalent; **im —e von** at a price of; **— legen auf** to attach great importance to; **—angabe** *f.* declaration of value; **—bestimmung** *f.* evaluation; **—brief** *m.* registered letter; **—gegenstände** *m. pl.*, **—sachen** *f. pl.* valuables; **—igkeit** *f.* (chem.) valence; **—messer** *m.* standard of value; **—paket** *neu.* registered parcel; **—papiere** *neu. pl.* securities; **—sendung** *f.* shipment of declared valuables; **—urteil** *neu.* value judgment; **—zeichen** *neu.* paper money; stamp

wes *pron.*, **—sen** *pron.* whose; **—halb** *adv.* and *conj.*, **—wegen** *adj.* and *conj.* why, wherefore, on account of which, therefore, so

Wesen *neu.* being, creature; essence; nature, character; manners, way, conduct; system, organization; fuss, ado; **sein — treiben** to go about; to haunt; **viel —s machen** to make a fuss about; **—seinheit** *f.* consubstantiality; **—szug** *m.* characteristic feature

wesen—los *adj.* unsubstantial, unreal; shadowy; **—seigen** *adj.* characteristic; **—sgleich** *adj.* homogeneous; **—tlich** *adj.* essential, substantial; basic material; intrinsic

Wespe *f.* wasp; **—nstich** *m.* wasp's sting

West *m.* west; (poet.) west wind; **—en** *m.* (the) West, Occident; **—mächte** *f. pl.* Western Powers

Weste *f.* vest; **eine reine (or weisse) —e haben** to be unimpeachable

Westfalen *neu.* Westphalia

Westpreussen *neu.* West Prussia

westwärts *adv.* westward

wett *adj.* equal, even; **—eifern** to rival, to emulate, to compete; **—en** *v.* to bet, to wager; **—machen** *v.* to make up for; **—rüsten** *v.* to compete in armament

Wett—bewerb *m.* competition; (sports) event; **—bewerber** *m.* competitor, rival; **—e** *f.* bet, wager; **eine —e eingehen** to lay a bet; **um die —e laufen** to race; **Was gilt die —e?** What do you bet? **—eifer** *m.* emulation, rivalry; **—fahrt** *f.* (boat, car, etc.) race; **—flug** *m.* air race; **—kampf** *m.* contest, match; prize fight; **—lauf** *m.* footrace; **—rennen** *neu.* race; **—rudern** *neu.* rowing match; **—spiel** *neu.* match, tournament; **—streit** *m.* competition, contest, match

Wetter *neu.* weather; storm, tempest; **alle —!** good gracious! **schlagendes —** firedamp; **—bericht** *m.* meteorological report; **—dienst** *m.* weather bureau; meteorological service; **—fahne** *f.*

weather vane; **—häuschen** *neu.* weather box (barometer); **—karte** *f.* weather map; **—kunde** *f.* meteorology; **—lage** *f.* atmospheric conditions; **—leuchten** *neu.* sheet lightning; **—sturz** *m.* sudden fall in temperature; **—umschlag** *m.* change of weather; **—voraussage** *f.* weather forecast; **—warte** *f.* meteorological station; **—zeichen** *neu.* storm signal

wetter—fest *adj.* weatherproof; **—leuchten** *v.* to lighten (without thunder); **—n** *v.* to lighten and thunder; to be stormy; to curse and swear; **—wendisch** *adj.* changeable, fickle

wetzen *v.* to whet, to sharpen, to hone

Wetzstein *m.* whetstone, hone

Wichs *m.* (coll.) full dress; **—bürste** *f.* polishing brush; **—e** *f.* polish; (coll.) thrashing

wichsen *v.* to polish; (coll.) to thrash

Wicht *m.* creature; chit; imp; **—elmann** *m.* brownie, goblin; **—igtuer** *m.* pompous person

wichtig *adj.* important, momentous; **sich — machen, — tun** to assume an air of importance

Wickel *m.* wrapping; curler; **beim — kriegen** (*oder* **nehmen**) to collar; **—band** *neu.* swaddling band; **—kind** *neu.* baby

wickeln *v.* to wind (round); to roll (up); to wrap; to swaddle; (hair) to curl

Widder *m.* ram; (ast.) Aries

wider *prep.* against, contrary (*oder* in opposition) to; versus; **—borstig** *adj.* obstinate; **—fahren** *v.* to happen to, to befall; to meet with; **—hallen** *v.* to echo, to resound; **—legen** *v.* to refute; **—lich** *adj.* repugnant, repulsive, disgusting; **—n** *v.* to disgust; **—natürlich** *adj.* unnatural; **—raten** *v.* to dissuade (from); **—rechtlich** *adj.* illegal, unlawful; **—rufen** *v.* to recant, to retract, to revoke; to withdraw; **—ruflich** *adj.* revocable; **—scheinen** *v.* to reflect; **—setzen** *v.*, **sich —setzen** to oppose, to resist; **—setzlich** *adj.* insubordinate, refractory; **—sinnig** *adj.* nonsensical, absurd; contradictory; **—spenstig** *adj.* obstinate, refractory; unruly; intractable; **—spiegeln** *v.* to reflect, to mirror; **—sprechen** *v.* to contradict; to oppose; **—sprechend** *adj.* contradictory; **—steh(e)n** *v.* to resist, to withstand; **—streben** *v.* to struggle against, to resist; **—strebend** *adj.* reluctant; **—streiten** *v.* to conflict; to be contrary to; **—wärtig** *adj.* disgusting, annoying; **—willig** *adj.* reluctant, unwilling

Wider—haken *m.* barbed hook; **—hall** *m.* echo, reverberation; response; **—part** *m.* opponent, adversary; opposition; **—rede**

f. contradiction; **–rist** *m.* withers; **–ruf** *m.* recantation; disavowal; (law) disclaimer; **bis auf –ruf** until recalled; **–sacher** *m.* adversary; **–schein** *m.* reflection; **–sinn** *m.* absurdity; nonsense; **–spruch** *m.* contradiction; **–stand** *m.* resistance; (elec.) rheostat; **–streit** *m.* conflict; opposition; contest; **–wille** *m.* aversion; dislike, disgust; reluctance; antipathy

widmen *v.* to dedicate; **sich einer Sache — to devote** oneself to something

Widmung *f.* dedication; **–sexemplar** *neu.* presentation copy

widrig *adj.* contrary, adverse; disgusting; repugnant; **–enfalls** *adv.* failing which

wie *adv.* how; — *conj.* as, like, such; — **auch immer** however; — **bitte?** beg your pardon? — **dem auch sei** be that as it may be; — **du mir so ich dir** tit for tat; **–so** *adv.* why; **–viel** *adv.* how much (*oder* many); **der –vielte ist heute?** what day of the month is it? **–wohl** *conj.* although

wieder *adv.* again; anew; back, in return; **hin und — now and then; immer — again and again; — zu sich kommen** to recover; **–anknüpfen** *v.* to renew (acquaintance); **–anstellen** *v.* to reinstall; **–aufbauen** *v.* to reconstruct; **–aufkommen** *v.* to come into fashion again; to recover; **–aufleben** *v.* to revive; **–aufnehmen** *v.* to resume; **–bekommen** *v.* to get back; to recover; **–beleben** *v.* to reanimate; to revive; **–bringen** *v.* to return, to restore; **–einsetzen** to replace; to reinstate; **–erkennen** *v.* to recognize; **–ersetzen** *v.*, **–erstatten** *v.* to restore, to refund; **–finden** *v.* to find; to recover; **–geben** *v.* to return; to reproduce; **–gutmachen** *v.* to compensate; **–herstellen** *v.* to re-establish, to repair; to restore; **–holen** *v.* to fetch back; to repeat, to reiterate; **–holt** *adv.* repeatedly, often; **–käuen** *v.* to ruminate; **–kehren** *v.* to return, to come back; to recur; **–um** *adv.* again, anew

Wiederbelebung (durch künstliche Atmung) *f.* resuscitation

Wiedereintritt (in die Erdatmosphäre) *m.* re-entry

Wiege *f.* cradle; **–messer** *neu.* mincing knife; **–nlied** *neu.* lullaby

wiegen *v.* to weigh; to rock; to mince

wiehern *v.* to neigh; **–des Gelächter** horse-laugh

Wien *neu.* Vienna

Wiese *f.* meadow; **–l** *neu.* weasel; **–ngrund** *m.* grassy valley; meadow land; **–nschaumkraut** *neu.* (bot.) lady's smock, cuckooflower

Wiking *m.* Viking

wild *adj.* wild, savage; fierce, ferocious, unruly; enraged, turbulent; untidy; **–e Ehe** common-law marriage; **–e Flucht** headlong flight; rout; **–er Wein** Virginia creeper; **–er Streik** wildcat strike; **–es Fleisch** (med.) proud flesh; **–es Haar** dishevelled hair; **— machen** to exasperate; **— werden** to become furious; (horse) to shy; **–ern** *v.* to poach; **–fremd** *adj.* quite strange; **–ledern** *adj.* buckskin

Wild *neu.* game, deer, venison; **–bach** *m.* torrent; **–bad** *neu.* thermal springs (*oder* baths); **–bahn** *f.* hunting ground; **–bret** *neu.* game, venison; **–dieb** *m.*, **–erer** *m.* poacher; **–e** *m.* savage; **–fang** *m.* unruly child; tomboy; **–gehege** *neu.*, **–park** *m.* game preserve; **–hüter** *m.* gamekeeper; **–leder** *neu.* suede; **–ling** *m.* wild tree (*oder* animal, etc.); **–nis** *f.* wilderness; **–schaden** *m.* damage caused by game; **–schütz(e)** *m.* poacher; **–schwein** *neu.* wild boar; **–stand** *m.* stock of game; **–wasser** *neu.* torrent

Wilhelm *m.* William

Will: –e *m.* will; volition; determination; intention; **aus freiem –en** of one's own accord; voluntarily; **böser –e** malice; **jemand zu –en sein** to comply with someone's wishes; **mit –en** on purpose, intentionally; **–ens sein** to be ready (to do something); **wider –en** unwillingly; unintentionally; **–enskraft** *f.* will power; **–komm** *m.*, **–kommen** *neu.* welcome; **–kür** *f.* arbitrary action; despotism; **er ist ihrer –kür preisgegeben** he is at their mercy

will: –enlos *adj.* lacking will power; irresolute; **–entlich** *adj.* intentional; **–fahren** *v.* to comply with; to grant; **–fährig** *adj.* compliant, accomodating; **–ig** *adj.* willing, ready; **–kommen** *adj.* welcome; opportune; acceptable; **–kürlich** *adj.* arbitrary, despotic, unlimited

wimmeln *v.* to swarm (*oder* be crowded) with

wimmern *v.* to whimper, to moan

Wimpel *m.* pennant, pennon

Wimper *f.* eyelash; **ohne mit der — zu zucken** without turning a hair

Wind *m.* wind, breeze; (med.) flatulence; **bei — und Wetter** in storm and rain; **den Mantel nach dem — hängen** to trim one's sails to the wind; **in den — reden** to speak in vain; **in den — schlagen** to disregard; **vor dem — segeln** to run before the wind; **— bekommen von** to get scent of; **— machen**

to boast, to brag; **–beutel** *m.* cream puff; (coll.) windbag; **–beutelei** *f.* bragging, humbug; **–bruch** *m.* windfall; **–e** *f.* winch; windlass; reel; (bot.) bindweed; **–ei** *neu.* addled egg; **–el** *f.* diaper; **–eln** *pl.* swaddling clothes; **–eseile** *f.* (fig.) lightning speed; **–fahne** *f.* weather vane; **–fang** *m.* windbreak; **–harfe** *f.* Aeolian harp; **–hose** *f.* whirlwind; **–hund** *m.* greyhound; (coll.) windbag; **–jacke** *f.* weatherproof jacket; **–licht** *neu.* hurricane lamp; **–messer** *m.* anemometer; **–mühle** *f.* windmill; **–mühlenflugzeug** *neu.* helicopter; **–pocken** *f.* chicken pox; **–röschen** *neu.* anemone; **–rose** *f.* compass card; **–sack** *m.* wind cone; **–sbraut** *f.* gale, hurricane; **–(schutz)scheibe** *f.* windshield; **–stille** *f.* calm; **–stoss** *m.* gust of wind; **–ung** *f.* winding, turn; sinuosity; coil, whorl; worm (of screw); **–zug** *m.* draft, current of air

wind: **–elweich** *adj.* compliant; **–elweich schlagen** to beat to a pulp; **–en** to wind, to reel; to hoist; to bind (wreath); **sich –en** to wind, to twine (round); to meander; to writhe; **–ig** *adj.* windy; (coll.) unreliable; **–schief** *adj.* warped; **–still** *adj.* calm; **–wärts** *adv.* windward

Windel *f.* diaper; **–n** *pl.* swaddling clothes

Windung *f.* winding, turn; sinuosity; coil, whorl; worm (of screw)

Wink *m.* wink; hint, tip; insinuation; **–er** *m.* signaler; **–zeichen** *neu.* semaphore

Winkel *m.* angle; corner, nook; (mil.) chevron; **–advokat** *m.* shyster lawyer; **–blatt** *neu.* oscure local newspaper; **–eisen** *neu.* steel square (*oder* rule); **–haken** *m.* try square, rule; (typ.) composing stick; **–mass** *neu.* square; **–messer** *m.* protractor; goniometer; **–poet** *m.* obscure poet; **–zug** *m.* trick, dodge; subterfuge

winkelrecht *adj.* at right angles

winken *v.* to wink, to wave, to make a sign; to semaphore; **mit dem Laternenpfahl** (*or* **Zaunpfahl, Scheunentor**) **—** to give a broad hint

winseln *v.* to whimper, to whine, to wail

Winter *m.* winter; **–aufenthalt** *m.* winter resort; **–frucht** *f.*, **–getreide** *neu.*, **–korn** *neu.* winter grain; **–garten** *m.* conservatory; **–schlaf** *m.* hibernation; **–schlussverkauf** *m.* winter clearance sale; **–überzieher** *m.* winter overcoat

Winzer *m.* vinegrower; vintager

winzig *adj.* diminutive, minute; **tiny**

Wipfel *m.* treetop

Wippe *f.* seesaw

wir *pron.* we; **— alle** all of us

Wirbel *m.* whirl(pool); eddy; vertebra; (drum) roll; (hair) whorl; (violin) peg; **–kasten** *m.* (violin) neck for pegs; **–knochen** *m.* vertebra; **–säule** *f.* spine; **–sturm** *m.* cyclone, tornado, hurricane; **–tier** *neu.* vertebrate; **–wind** *m.* whirlwind

wirk: **–en** *v.* to work, to effect, to produce; to knit (hosiery); to knead (dough); **–en auf** to affect, to influence, to impress; **–lich** *adj.* real, actual; true, genuine; **–sam** *adj.* effective, efficacious, efficient

Wirk: **–ung** *f.* effect, result; **–ungskreis** *m.* sphere of activity (*oder* influence); province; **–waren** *f. pl.* knitwear

wirr *adj.* confused, dishevelled; chaotic

Wirr: **–en** *f. pl.* disorders, troubles; **–kopf** *m.* muddlehead; **–nis** *f.*, **–sal** *neu.* confusion, disorder; **–warr** *m.* medley; jumble, muddle; chaos

Wirsingkohl *m.* savoy (cabbage)

Wirt *m.* host; innkeeper; landlord; **–in** *f.* hostess; innkeeper; landlady; **–schaft** *f.* housekeeping; household; inn; economics, economy; doings; (coll.) mess; **–schafter** *m.*, **–schafterin** *f.* housekeeper; manager; steward(ess); **–schaftler** *m.* teacher of economics; industrial leader; **–schaftsgebäude** *neu. pl.* farm buildings; **–schaftsgeld** *neu.* housekeeping money; **–schaftsgruppe** *f.* trust, corporation; **–schaftsjahr** *neu.* fiscal year; **–schaftspolitik** *f.* economics; **–schaftsprüfer** *m.* auditor; **–shaus** *neu.* tavern; inn; **–sleute** *pl.* host and hostess

wirt: **–lich** *adj.* hospitable, habitable; **–schaften** to keep house; to manage; **to** economize; (coll.) to rummage; **–schaftlich** *adj.* economic(al); profitable; thrifty

Wisch *m.* (paper) scrap; (straw) wisp; **–er** *m.* wiper; (drawing) stump; (coll.) rebuke; **–lappen** *m.* dust cloth, wiping rag

wischen *v.* to wipe; (drawing) to stump

Wismut *m.* and *neu.* bismuth

wispern *v.* to whisper

Wissbegierde *f.* thirst for learning, curiosity

wissen *v.* to know, to be acquainted with; **er will alles besser —** he's a know-it-all; **jemand Dank —** to be grateful; **sie will ihn glücklich —** she wishes him to be happy; **sie will nichts von ihm —** she wants to have nothing to do with him; **weder aus noch ein —** not to know which way to turn; **–schaftlich** *adj.* scientific, scholarly; **–tlich** *adj.*

knowing; deliberate; **–tlich** *adv.* on purpose

Wissen *neu.* knowledge; learning; **meines –s** as far as I know; **nach bestem — und Gewissen** most conscientiously; **wider besseres —** against one's better judgment; **–schaft** *f.* science, knowledge; **–schaftler** *m.* scientist, scholar; **–sdrang** *m.*, **–sdurst** *m.* thirst for knowledge

wittern *v.* to scent, to perceive, to suspect

Witterung *f.* weather; scent; **–sumschlag** *m.* change of weather; **–sverhältnisse** *neu. pl.* atmospheric conditions

Witwe *f.* widow; dowager; **–nschaft** *f.*, **–nstand** *m.* widowhood; **–ntracht** *f.* widow's weeds; **–r** *m.* widower

Witz *m.* wit(tiness); joke; witticism; **–e machen** to crack jokes; **–blatt** *neu.* comic paper; **–bold** *m.* joker; **–elei** *f.* joking, banter

witzeln *v.* to ridicule; to joke

wo *adv.* where, when; in which; **— auch immer** wherever; **— nicht** if not, unless; **–anders** *adv.* somewhere else, elsewhere; **–bei** *adv.* where(at); whereby; in (*oder* through) which; **–durch** *adv.* by what (*oder* which) means; **–fern** *adv.* so far as; provided that; if; **–fern nicht** unless; **–für** *adv.* for which; what for; **–gegen** *adv.* against what (*oder* which); in return for what (*oder* which); **–gegen** *conj.* whilst, whereas, on the other hand; **–her** *adv.* wherefrom; from what place; **–her weiss er das?** how does he know that? **–hin** *adv.* whither; where to, to what (*oder* which) place; **–hinaus** *adv.* which way, to what place; **–mit** *adv.* by what (means), wherewith; **–möglich** *adv.* perhaps, possibly; **–nach** *adv.* after what (*oder* which); whereafter, whereupon; **–ran** *adv.* whereon; at (*oder* by, of) what; **–rauf** *adv.* whereupon; **–raus** *adv.* out of what; from which; **–rein** *adv.* into what (*oder* which); **–rin** *adv.* in what (*oder* which); wherein; **–rüber** *adv.* over which; of (*oder* about) what; whereat; **–rum** *adv.* about what (*oder* which); **–runter** *adv.* beneath what; among which; **–selbst** *adv.* where; **–von** *adv.* whereof; about what; of which; **–vor** *adv.* before what, of which; **–zu** *adv.* for which; what for; why

Woche *f.* week; **–n** *f. pl.*, **–nbett** *neu.* childbed; **–nblatt** *neu.* weekly paper; **–nende** *neu.* weekend; **–nlohn** *m.* weekly wages; **–nschau** *f.* weekly review; newsreel; **–ntag** *m.* weekday

wochen: –lang *adj.* for weeks; **–tags** *adv.*

on weekdays; **–weise** *adj.* by the week

wöchentlich *adj.* weekly; every (*oder* **a, by** the) week

Wöchnerin *f.* woman in childbed

Woge *f.* wave, billow

wogen *v.* to surge, to wave, to heave; **hin und her —** to fluctuate, to undulate

wohl *adv.* well; probably, presumably, very likely; **— prep.** about; **er wird — reich** sein he is rich, I suppose; **leben Sie —!** good-bye! **sich — sein lassen** to enjoy oneself; **— bekomm's!** your health! here's to you! **— dem, der** happy he who; **— oder übel** whether one likes it or not; **–an!** *interj.* now then! come on! **–auf** *adv.* well, in good health; **–bedacht** *adj.* well-considered; **–behalten** *adj.* safe and sound; **–bekannt** *adj.* well-known, familiar; **–beleibt** *adj.* corpulent; **–erzogen** *adj.* well-bred; **–feil** *adj.* cheap; **–geartet** *adj.* well-disposed, well-bred; **–gefällig** *adj.* pleasant; complacent; **–gelitten** *adj.* well liked, popular; **–gemeint** *adj.* well-meant; **–gemut** *adj.* cheerful, gay; **–genährt** *adj.* well-fed; **–geneigt** *adj.* well-affected; **–gestaltet** *adj.* well-shaped; **–habend** *adj.* wealthy; **–ig** *adj.* comfortable, happy; **–klingend** *adj.* harmonious, melodious; **–meinend** *adj.* well-meaning, benevolent; **–riechend** *adj.* fragrant, sweet-scented; **–schmeckend** *adj.* tasty, savory; **–tätig** *adj.* beneficent, charitable; **–tuend** *adj.* comforting, pleasant; **–tun** *v.* to do good; to be pleasant; **–überlegt** *adj.* well-considered; **–unterrichtet** *adj.* well-informed; **–verdient** *adj.* well-deserved; **–versorgt** *adj.* well-provided; **–verstanden** *adj.* well-understood; **–weislich** *adv.* prudently, wisely; **–wollend** *adj.* kindly, benevolent

Wohl *neu.* well-being, welfare, prosperity; **auf Ihr —!** your health! good luck! **–befinden** *neu.* good health, well-being; **–behagen** *neu.* (feeling of) comfort, ease; **–ergeh(e)n** *neu.* welfare, prosperity; **–fahrt** *f.* welfare; **–fahrtspflege** *f.* welfare work; **–gefallen** *neu.* pleasure, satisfaction; **sich in –gefallen auflösen** (coll.) to end peacefully; to come to naught; **–geruch** *m.* fragrance, perfume; **–geschmack** *m.* pleasant flavor; **–habenheit** *f.* opulence, wealth; **–klang** *m.*, **–laut** *m.* melodious sound; harmony; **–leben** *neu.* luxurious living; life of pleasure; **–sein** *neu.* well-being; good health; **–stand** *m.* prosperity; **–tat** *f.* comfort, blessing; charity; **–täter** *m.* benefactor; **–wollen** *neu.* good will, benevolence

wohn: **-en** *v.* to live, to dwell, to reside, to stay; **-haft** *adj.* living, resident; **-lich** *adj.* cosy, snug, comfortable

Wohn: **-gebäude** *neu.*, **-haus** *neu.* dwelling (*oder* apartment) house; **-küche** *f.* room with kitchenette; **-ort** *m.*, **-sitz** *m.* domicile, legal residence; **-stube** *f.*, **-zimmer** *neu.* living room; **-ung** *f.* dwelling, habitation; rooms, apartment; flat; **-ungsnachweis** *m.* housing agency; **-ungsnot** *f.* housing shortage; **-ungswechsel** *m.* change of residence; **-viertel** *neu.* residential section; **-wagen** *m.* trailer

Wölbung *f.* vault(ing); arch, dome; curvature

Wolf *m.* wolf; (med.) abrasion; **-seisen** *neu.* wolf trap; **-shunger** *m.* ravenous hunger; **-smilch** *f.* (bot.) spurge; **-ram** *neu.* tungsten

Wolke *f.* cloud; **aus allen -n fallen** to be thunderstruck; **-nbruch** *m.* cloudburst; **-nhöhe** *f.* ceiling; **-nkratzer** *m.* skyscraper; **-nkuckucksheim** *neu.* dreamland, Utopia; **-nschicht** *f.* stratum (of clouds); **-nwand** *f.* cloudbank; overcast

wolkig *adj.* clouded, cloudy

Woll: **-decke** *f.* woolen blanket; **-e** *f.* wool; fleece; **in die -e geraten** (coll.) to start a fight; **-stoff** *m.* woolen material

Woll: **-en** *neu.* will(ingness), volition; **-ust** *f.* voluptuousness, lust; **-üstling** *m.* voluptuary

woll: **-en** *v.* to want, to wish; to be willing; to intend; to be about to; **das will etwas heissen!** that's something! **das will ich meinen** I should say so; **dem mag sein wie es -e** be that as it may be; **er mag -en oder nicht** whether he likes it or not; **er will dagewesen sein** he claims to have been there; **hoch hinaus -en** to have lofty ideas; **ich -te lieber** I would rather; I prefer; **wir -en gehen** let us go

wollen *adj.* woolen, worsted

Wonne *f.* delight, bliss; **-monat** *m.*, **-mond** *m.* month of May

wonne: **-sam** *adj.* delightful; **-trunken** *adj.* enraptured

worfeln *v.* to winnow

Wort *neu.* word; expression, term; saying; promise; **aufs — gehorchen** to obey implicitly; **das grosse — führen** to brag; **das — ergreifen** to begin to speak; **das — erteilen** to give permission to speak; **einer Sache das — reden** to speak for something; **ein — gibt das andere** one word leads to another; **es ist kein wahres — daran** there isn't a grain of truth in it; **ins — fallen** to in-terrupt; **jemand zu -e kommen lassen** to let a person have his say; **kein — mehr!** not another word! **um nicht viele -e zu machen** to cut a long story short; **— halten** to keep (one's) word; **-e verschwenden** to waste (one's) breath; **-ableitung** *f.* derivation of words; etymology; **-aufwand** *m.* verbosity; **-bildung** *f.* word formation; **-bruch** *m.* breach of promise; **-emacher** *m.* verbose speaker; **-fechter** *m.* stickler for words; **-folge** *f.* word order; **-fügungslehre** *f.* syntax; **-führer** *m.* speaker; spokesman; **-gefecht** *neu.* dispute; **-klauber** *m.* hairsplitter, quibbler; **-laut** *m.* text, wording; **-schatz** *m.* vocabulary; **-schwall** *m.* bombast, verbosity; **-spiel** *neu.* pun; **-wechsel** *m.* dispute, altercation

Wörterbuch *neu.* dictionary

wörtlich *adj.* verbal, verbatim; literal

Wrack *neu.* wreck

wringen *v.* to wring

Wucher *m.* usury; profiteering; **-er** *m.* usurer, profiteer; **-gewinn** *m.* inordinate profit; **-ung** *f.* exuberance; growth, tumor; **-zins** *m.* usurious interest

wuchern *v.* to grow luxuriantly; to practice usury, to profiteer; to make the most of; **mit seinem Pfunde — to** utilize one's talent

Wuchs *m.* growth; stature, development; figure

Wucht *f.* burden, weight; force, impetus

wuchtig *adj.* heavy, weighty

Wühl: **-arbeit** *f.* subversive activity; **-er** *m.* agitator; **-erei** *f.* agitation; **-maus** *f.* vole

wühlen *v.* to dig; to root; to burrow; to rummage; to stir up, to agitate; **im Gelde — to** be rolling in money

Wulst *m.* and *f.* swelling; roll, pad; protuberance; **-lippen** *f. pl.* blubber lips

Wund: **-arzt** *m.* surgeon; **-e** *f.* wound; **-mal** *neu.* scar; **-male** *pl.* stigmata; **-schorf** *m.* scab

Wunder *neu.* miracle; marvel, wonder; **es grenzt an ein — it** borders on the supernatural; **sein blaues — erleben** (coll.) to be amazed; **-bild** *neu.* miracleworking image; **-ding** *neu.* marvellous thing; marvel; **-doktor** *m.* quack; **-glaube** *m.* belief in miracles; **-horn** *neu.* magic horn; **-kind** *neu.* infant prodigy; **-land** *neu.* fairyland; **-täter** *m.* miracle worker; **-tier** *neu.* monster; prodigy; **-welt** *f.* enchanted world; **-zeichen** *neu.* miraculous sign

wunder das nimmt mich — I am surprised; **sich — was einbilden** (coll.)

to be very cocky; **–bar** *adj.* wonderful, marvelous; amazing; **–barerweise** *adv.* strange to say; **–hübsch** *adj.* exceedingly pretty; **–lich** *adj.* strange, odd; moody; **sich –n** *v.* über to wonder at, to be surprised at; **–sam** *adj.* wonderful, strange; **–schön** *adj.* very beautiful, exquisite; **–tätig** *adj.* wonder-working; miraculous; **–voll** *adj.* wonderful, marvelous; admirable

Wunsch *m.* wish, desire; **auf — by** request; **mit den besten Wünschen zum Fest** with the compliments of the season; **nach —** as desired; **–bild** *neu.* ideal; **–form** *f.* (gram.) optative form; **–zettel** *m.* list of things desired; letter to Santa Claus

Wünschelrute *f.* divining rod

wünschen *v.* to wish, to desire; **Glück —** to congratulate; **–swert** *adj.* desirable

Würd: –e *f.* dignity; honor; rank, title; **akademische –e** academic degree; **unter aller –e** beneath contempt; **–enträger** *m.* dignitary

würd: –elos *adj.* undignified; **–evoll** *adj.* dignified; **–ig** *adj.* worthy; deserving of; dignified, respectable; **–igen** *v.* to appreciate; to evaluate; to honor; **nicht eines Wortes –igen** not to grant a word (to)

Wurf *m.* cast, throw(ing); brood, litter; **alles auf einen — setzen** to stake all on one throw; **zum — ausholen** to get ready to throw; **–bahn** *f.* trajectory; **–geschoss** *neu.* projectile; **–scheibe** *f.* discus; **–sendung** *f.* direct mail advertising; **–speer** *m.*, **–spiess** *m.* javelin; **–weite** *f.* range of throw

Würfel *m.* die; cube; **der — ist gefallen** the die is cast; **–becher** *m.* dice box; **–bude** *f.* booth for dice throwing; **–muster** *neu.* checkered pattern; **–spiel** *neu.* dice game; **–zucker** *m.* lump sugar

würfel: –förmig *adj.* cubic form; **–ig** *adj.* cubical; checkered; **–n** *v.* to play at dice; to checker

würgen *v.* to choke; to retch, to strangle; to throttle

Würger *m.* strangler; murderer; butcher-bird

Wurm *m.* worm; grub, maggot; (poet.) dragon; **— neu.** (coll.) poor little thing; **–fortsatz** *m.* vermiform appendix; **–frass** *m.* damage done by worms; **–mehl** *neu.* worm cast; **–stich** *m.*, **–loch** *neu.* wormhole

Wurst *f.* sausage; **das ist mir —** (coll.) I don't care; **— wider —** (coll.) tit for tat; **–blatt** *neu.* (coll.) small obscure newspaper; **–waren** *f. pl.* sausages

Württemberg *neu.* Wurtemberg

Würze *f.* seasoning, flavor, spice; zest, piquancy; **in der Kürze liegt die —** brevity is the soul of wit

Wurzel *f.* root; **— fassen** (*or* **schlagen**) to take root; **–behandlung** *f.* (dent.) root treatment; **–faser** *f.* root fiber, rootlet; **–gemüse** *neu.* edible roots; **–keim** *m.* radicle; **–knolle** *f.*, **–knollen** *m.* bulb, tuber; **–schössling** *m.* layer, runner, sucker; **–werk** *neu.* root system; **–zeichen** *neu.* radical sign; **–ziehen** *neu.* extraction of roots

würzen *v.* to season, to spice, to flavor

Wust *m.* confusion; chaos; mess

wüst *adj.* waste, desolate; desert(ed); confused; unruly, disorderly; vulgar, rude; dissolute; **–en** *v.* to spoil; to live profligately

Wüst: –e *f.* desert, wilderness; **–enei** *f.* desolate region; **–enschiff** *neu.* (poet.) camel; **–ling** *m.* debauchee, dissolute person

Wut *f.* fury, rage; frenzy; **in — geraten** to fly into a rage; **–anfall** *m.* fit of rage; paroxysm

wut: –entbrannt *adj.* infuriated, enraged; **–schnaubend** *adj.*, **–schäumend** *adj.* foaming with rage; frenzied, rabid

wüt: –en *v.* to rage, to be furious; **–end** *adj.*, **–ig** *adj.* furious, enraged; mad

Wüterich *m.* ruthless (*oder* frantic) fellow

X

X *neu.*, **man kann ihm kein — für ein U machen** he is not easily taken in

X-Beine *neu. pl.* knock-knees

x-beinig *adj.* knock-kneed

x-beliebig *adj.* any, whatever; whoever

Xenie *f.* (satirical) epigram

x-mal *adv.* many times; ever so often

X-Strahlen *m. pl.* X-rays

xte *adj.* nth; **zum –n Male** for the umpteenth time

Xylophon *neu.* xylophone

Y

yankeehaft *adj.* Yankee-like

Ypsilon *neu.* the letter Y

Ysop *m.* hyssop

Z

Zacke *f.*, **Zacken** *m.* peak, point; (fork) prong; (mountain) crag; (saw) dent, tooth; (wall) crenel, spike; (wheel) cog; scallop

zackig *adj.* indented, notched; pointed;

scalloped; serrate.l, crenate; pinked
zaghaft *adj.* faint-hearted, timid; hesitant
zäh(e) *adj.* tough, tenacious; viscous
Zähegrad *m.* viscosity
Zahl *f.* number; figure, cipher; **gerade** — even number; **ungerade** — odd number; **–er** *m.* payer; **–karte** *f.* money order blank; **–kellner** *m.* headwaiter; **–meister** *m.* paymaster; **–stelle** *f.* cashier's office; **–tag** *m.* payday; due date; **–ung** *f.* payment; **–ungsfähigkeit** *f.* solvency; **–ungsfrist** *f.*, **–ungsbedingung** *f.* term of payment; **–ungsmittel** *neu.* (legal) tender; **–ungsschwierigkeiten** *f.* *pl.* pecuniary difficulties; **–wort** *neu.* numeral
zahl: –bar *adj.* payable; **–en** *v.* to pay; **–enmässig** *adj.* numerical; **–los** *adj.* innumerable, countless; **–reich** *adj.* numerous; **–ungsfähig** *adj.* solvent; **–ungsunfähig** *adj.* insolvent
Zähl: –er *m.* counter, meter, numerator; **–ung** *f.* counting; census; computation; **–werk** *neu.* meter, counter, register
zählen *v.* to count, to enumerate; to reckon, to score; — **auf** to rely upon; — **zu** to belong to, to count with
zahm *adj.* tame, domestic, tractable
zähmen *v.* to tame, to domesticate, to break in; to subdue, to restrain, to curb
Zahn *m.* tooth; fang, tusk; cog; jemand **auf den** — **fühlen** (coll.) to sound out someone; **–arzt** *m.* dentist; **–bein** *neu.* dentine; **–bürste** *f.* toothbrush; **–ersatz** *m.* artificial teeth; **–fäule** *f.* caries, tooth decay; **–fleisch** *neu.* *pl.* gums; **–entzündung** *f.* gingivitis; **–geschwür** *neu.* gumboil; **–heilkunde** *f.* dentistry; **–höhle** *f.* (tooth) socket; **–lücke** *f.* gap between teeth; **–pasta** *f.* tooth paste; **–rad** *neu.* cogwheel; **–radbahn** *f.* rack railroad; **–reissen** *neu.*, **–schmerz** *m.* toothache; **–schmelz** *m.* (tooth) enamel; **–stein** *m.* tartar, scale; **–stocher** *m.* toothpick; **–wasser** *neu.* mouthwash; **–wechsel** *m.* second dentition
zahn: –en *v.* to teethe; **–förmig** *adj.* dentiform; **–los** *adj* toothless
Zähne: –fletschen *neu.* showing one's teeth; **–klappern** *neu.* chattering of teeth; **–knirschen** *neu.* gnashing of teeth
Zange *f.* pliers; pincers; tongs; tweezers; forceps; forcipated claw
Zank *m.* quarrel; altercation, wrangle; **–apfel** *m.* bone of contention; **–teufel** *m.* shrew
zank: –en *v.* to quarrel, to wrangle; **–haft** *adj.*, **–süchtig** *adj.* quarrelsome, contentious

Zänker *m.* quarrelsome person; wrangler
Zapf: –en *m.* plug, peg, pin; bung, tap; tenon, pivot, trunnion; (bot.) cone; **–enloch** *neu.* mortise; **–enstreich** *m.* (mil.) tattoo; **–er** *m.* tapster, barman
Zäpfchen *neu.* small plug; uvula
zapfen *v.* to tap
zappeln *v.* to fidget, to struggle; **jemand** — **lassen** to keep someone in suspense
zart *adj.* tender; delicate, frail, fragile; young; **–besaitet** *adj.* sensitive; **–fühlend** *adj.* tactful, sensitive; tender-hearted
zärtlich *adj.* affectionate, fond; tender
Zauber *m.* magic, spell, charm, enchantment; **–buch** *neu.* conjuring book; **–ei** *f.* magic, sorcery; **–er** *m.* magician, conjurer; charmer; **–formel** *f.* magic formula, incantation; **–in** *f.* sorceress, witch; **–kunst** *f.* black magic; **–künstler** *m.* illusionist; conjurer; **–kunststück** *neu.* conjuring trick; **–posse** *f.* fairy play; **–spruch** *m.* incantation; **–trank** *m.* magic potion
zauber: –haft *adj.*, **–isch** *adj.* magical, fascinating; **–kräftig** *adj.* magical; **–n** *v.* to practice magic; to conjure; to produce by magic
zaudern *v.* to delay, to hesitate; to tarry
Zaum *m.* bridle; **im** — **halten** to keep a tight rein on, to restrain; to check, to curb
zäumen *v.* to bridle; to restrain, to check
Zaun *m.* fence; einen Streit vom **–e brechen** to pick a quarrel; **–gast** *m.* nonpaying spectator; **–könig** *m.* wren; **–pfahl** *m.* fence post; mit dem **–pfahl winken** to give a broad hint
zausen *v.* to tug (*oder* pull) about; to tousle
Zech: –bruder *m.* tippler, boozer; **–e** *f.* bill, reckoning; die **–e bezahlen** to pay the bill; **–er** *m.* tippler, carouser; **–gelage** *neu.* carousal, drinking bout; **–prellerei** *f.* evading payment of bill
zechen *v.* to carouse, to tipple; to drink
Zeder *f.* cedar
Zehe *f.* toe; **–nspitze** *f.* tiptoe
zehn *adj.* ten; **–erlei** *adj.* of ten kinds; **–fach** *adj.*, **–fältig** *adj.* tenfold; **–te** *adj.* tenth; **–tens** *adv.* tenthly, in the tenth place
Zehn *f.*, **–er** *m.* ten; **–eck** *neu.* decagon; **–ender** *m.* stag with ten antlers; **–erreihe** *f.* column of tens; **–te** *m.* tithe; tenth; **–tel** *neu.* tenth part
Zehrung *f.* consumption; waste; expenses; provisions; letzte — extreme unction
Zeichen *neu.* sign, signal; mark, token; brand, stamp; badge, indication, symp-

tom; omen; seines —s ein Tischler sein to be a carpenter by trade; –brett *neu.* drawing board; –buch *neu.* sketch book; –kunst *f.* (art of) drawing; –lehrer *m.* drawing instructor; –setzung *f.* punctuation; –sprache *f.* sign language; –stift *m.* crayon, drawing pencil; –vorlage *f.* drawing copy

zeichnen *v.* to draw, to sketch, to design; to mark; to sign; to subscribe

Zeichner *m.* draftsman; designer; subscriber

Zeige: –finger *m.* forefinger, index; –r *m.* (clock) hand; –stab *m.*, –stock *m.* pointer

zeigen *v.* to show, to point; to display, to manifest; to exhibit; to prove, to demonstrate; **sich —** to appear; to turn out

Zeile *f.* line; row; –ngussmaschine *f.* linotype

Zeisig *m.* siskin; **lockerer —** (sl.) fast fellow

Zeit *f.* time, term; epoch, period, age; season; tense; **auf —** on credit; **damit hat es —** there is no hurry; **die ganze — über** ever since; **du liebe —!** Good heavens! **mit der — fortschreiten** to keep pace with the times; **nach geraumer —** after a considerable period; **vor der —** prematurely; **während der —** in the meantime; **— seines Lebens** during his lifetime; **zu gleicher —** simultaneously; **zur —** at present; in time; in the time of; **zu –en** now and then; –abschnitt *m.* epoch, period; –alter *neu.* age, generation; –angabe *f.* time, date; –aufnahme *f.* time exposure; –aufwand *m.* time spent; –einheit *f.* unit(y) of time; –einteilung *f.* timing, timetable; –folge *f.* chronological order; –form *f.* tense; –funk *m.* (rad.) topical talk; –genosse *m.* contemporary; –geschäft *neu.* installment business; –geschichte *f.* contemporary history; –karte *f.* season ticket; –karteninhaber *m.* commuter; –lage *f.* juncture, state of affairs; –lauf *m.* course of events, period; –lupe *f.* slow motion; –mass *neu.* (mus.) time; (poet.) quantity; –messer *m.* chronometer, metronome; –nehmer *m.* timekeeper; –ordnung *f.* chronological order; –punkt *m.* moment; –raffer *m.* (film) quick motion; –raum *m.* period, interval; –rechnung *f.* chronology; **christliche –rechnung** Christian era; –schrift *f.* journal, periodical, magazine; –tafel *f.* chronological table; –umstände *m. pl.* circumstances; junctures; –vertreib *m.*

pastime, amusement; –wort *neu.* verb; –zeichen *neu.* time signal; –zünder *m.* time fuse

zeit: –gemäss *adj.* timely, opportune; up-to-date; seasonable; –genössisch *adj.* contemporary; –ig *adj.* early, timely; mature; –igen *v.* to mature; to effect; –lebens *adv.* for (*oder* during) life; –lich *adj.* temporal; –weilig *adj.* temporary, provisional; –weise *adv.* for a time, from time to time

Zeitung *f.* newspaper; –sausschnitt *m.* press clipping; –sbeilage *f.* supplement; –sente *f.* canard, newspaper hoax; –sexpedition *f.* newspaper office; –sjunge *m.* paper boy; –skiosk *m.* newsstand; –snotiz *f.* press item; –swesen *neu.* journalism, the (daily) press

zelebrieren *v.* to celebrate; to read (Mass)

Zell: –e *f.* cell; –gewebe *neu.* cellular tissue; –stoff *m.*, –ulose *f.* cellulose

Zelot *m.* zealot

Zelt *neu.* tent; –bahn *f.* tarpaulin; –lager *neu.* camp; –platz *m.* tourist court

Zement *m.* cement; –stahl *m.* reinforced concrete

zementieren *v.* to cement

Zenit *m.* zenith

zensieren *v.* to censor, to give grades

Zensor *m.* censor

Zensur *f.* censoring, censorship; school marks

Zent: –enarfeier *f.* centenary; –imeter *m.* and *neu.* centimeter; –ner *m.* hundredweight; fifty kilograms; –nerlast *f.* (fig.) heavy burden

zentnerschwer *adj.* very heavy

Zentral: –e *f.* central office; telephone exchange; –heizung *f.* central heating

zentralisieren *v.* to centralize

zentrisch *adj.* centric(al)

Zentrum *neu.* center (party); bull's eye

Zepter *neu.* scepter

zerbeissen *v.* to bite into pieces; to crunch

zerbersten *v.* to burst, to split in pieces

zerbrechen *v.* to break up, to smash, to shatter; **sich den Kopf —** to rack one's brains

zerbrechlich *adj.* breakable, fragile, brittle

zerdrücken *v.* to crush, to squash; to crumple

Zeremonie *f.* ceremony

Zeremonienmeister *m.* master-of-ceremonies (M.C.)

zeremoniell *adj.* ceremonial

zerfahren *v.* to crush (*oder* ruin) by driving over; **—** *adj.* absent-minded, scatter-brained

zerfallen *v.* to fall to pieces; to decay; to disintegrate; to be divided (into); —

sein mit to be on bad terms with
zerfetzen *v.* to shred; to mutilate, to slash
zerfleischen *v.* to lacerate, to mangle
zerfliessen *v.* to flow (*oder* melt) away; to dissolve; to disperse
zerfressen *v.* to gnaw away; to corrode
zergeh(e)n *v.* to dissolve, to melt; to dwindle
zergliedern *v.* to dismember; to dissect; to analyze; to decompose
zerhacken *v.* to chop to pieces; to mince
zerhauen *v.* to cut up
zerkauen *v.* to chew well
zerkleinern *v.* to reduce to bits; to chop up
zerklopfen *v.* to pound to pieces
zerknautschen, zerknittern, zerknüllen *v.* to crush, to crumble
zerknirscht *adj.* contrite
zerkratzen *v.* to mar with scratches, to scratch
zerlegbar *adj.* separable, divisible, collapsible
zerlegen *v.* to divide, to part; to cut up; to carve (roast); to dissect; to analyze
zerlumpt *adj.* ragged, tattered
zermahlen *v.* to grind up, to pulverize
zermalmen *v.* to crush, to crunch, to pulverize
zernagen *v.* to gnaw through; to corrode
zerplatzen *v.* to burst apart
zerquetschen *v.* to crush, to squash; to bruise
Zerrbild *neu.* caricature
zerreiben *v.* to rub away, to grind down
zerreissen *v.* to tear up; to lacerate; to wear out; **die Ohren —** to grate on the ears
zerren *v.* to drag; to pull; to strain (muscle)
zerrinnen *v.* to melt away; to vanish
Zerrissenheit *f.* tattered (*oder* torn) condition; raggedness; disunion; mental conflict
zerrütten *v.* to disorganize; to ruin; to undermine (health); to derange
zerschiessen *v.* to shoot to pieces
zerschlagen *v.* to batter, to shatter; to destroy; **ganz — sein** to be completely exhausted; **sich — to** come to naught; **— adj.** battered, broken
zerschmettern *v.* to shatter, to smash
zerschneiden *v.* to cut into pieces; to sever
zersetzen *v.* to decompose; to undermine, to demoralize; to dissolve
zerspalten *v.* to cleave, to split
zersprengen *v.* to blast, to burst open
zerspringen *v.* to burst, to break; to crack
zerstampfen *v.* to crush; to trample down
zerstäuben *v.* to pulverize; to spray

Zerstäuber *m.* atomizer; sprayer
zerstören *v.* to destroy, to demolish, to ruin; to disorganize; to devastate
zerstreuen *v.* to disperse; to dissipate, to dispel; to divert
zerstreut *adj.* scattered, dispersed; diffused; absent-minded, preoccupied
Zerstreutheit *f.* absent-mindedness
Zerstreuung *f.* dispersion; diversion
zerteilen *v.* to divide; to cut up; to disperse
zertreten *v.* to crush (*oder* trample) down
zertrümmern *v.* to lay in ruins; to demolish, to wreck, to smash; to split (atoms)
Zerwürfnis *neu.* dissension, discord
zerzausen *v.* to pull to pieces; to dishevel
Zetergeschrei *neu.* cry of murder; outcry
Zettel *m.* scrap (*oder* slip) of paper; label; bill; poster; **-kasten** *m.* filing cabinet
Zeug *neu.* stuff, material; fabric, cloth; matter; implements, tools; trash; **arbeiten, was das — hält** to work with might and main; **das — haben zu** to have the ability to do; **dummes — nonsense; jemand am -e flicken** to slander someone; **sich ins — legen** to put one's shoulder to the wheel; **-haus** *neu.* armory, arsenal
Zeuge *m.* witness; **-naussage** *f.* testimony; deposition
Zeugnis *neu.* evidence, testimony; attestation; testimonial; school report
zeugen *v.* to testify, to give evidence (of); to beget, to procreate, to generate; to produce
Zibetkatze *f.* civet cat
Zichorie *f.* chicory
Zicke *f.*, **Zicklein** *neu.* kid
Zickzack *m.* zigzag; **-bergbahn** *f.* switchback
Ziege *f.* (she-)goat; doe; **-nbart** *m.* goatee; **-nbock** *m.* he-goat; buck; **-nleder** *neu.* kid leather; **-npeter** *m.* mumps
Ziegel *m.* brick; tile; **-brenner** *m.* brickmaker; **-(brenner)ei** *f.* brickyard; **-dach** *neu.* tiled roof; **-ofen** *m.* brick kiln; **-stein** *m.* brick
Zieh:-brunnen *m.* draw well; **-harmonika** *f.* accordion; **-kind** *neu.* foster child; **-tag** *m.* moving day; **-ung** *f.* (lottery) drawing; **-ungsliste** *f.* (lottery) list of prize-winners
ziehen *v.* to pull, to draw; to haul, to tow; to extract; to cultivate; to breed; to move; to march along; to be drafty, to ache; to attract; to weigh; to make (comparison); to take off (hat); to build (wall); to dig (trench); **auf Fäden**

— to string; **auf Flaschen** — to bottle; **den kürzeren** — to get the short end of it; **die Bilanz** — (com.) to strike balance; **ein Geschützrohr** — to rifle **a gun; in die Fremde** — to go abroad; **in die Länge** — to draw out, to protract; **in Erwägung** — to take into consideration; **nach sich** — to have consequences; **sich** — to warp, to extend; **Wasser** — to leak, to absorb water

Ziel *neu.* aim, object; destination; goal, target, winning post; term, limit; **sich ein** — **setzen** to aim at; **–band** *neu.* (sport) tape; **–fernrohr** *neu.* telescopic sight; **–findung** *f.* (avi.) homing; **–gerät** *neu.* gunsight; **–scheibe** *f.* target

ziel: –bewusst *adj.* steadily pursuing one's aim; resolute; **–en** *v.* to aim; to allude; **–los** *adj.* aimless; **–sicher** *adj.* sure of one's aim

ziemen *v.* to be seemly (*oder* suitable)

ziemlich *adj.* suitable, fit; becoming; — *adv.* fairly, very; tolerably, rather; — **dasselbe** almost alike; — oft pretty often

Zier *f.*, **–at** *m.*, **–de** *f.* decoration, ornament; embellishment; **–affe** *m.* (coll.) dandy, fop; **–erei** *f.* affectation; **–garten** *m.* flower (*oder* ornamental) garden; **–leiste** *f.* ornamental border; **–puppe** *f.* (coll.) clotheshorse

zieren *v.* to adorn; to decorate; to embellish; to honor; **sich** — to be affected (*oder* coy)

zierlich *adj.* graceful; delicate; pretty

Ziffer *f.* figure, number, numeral; digit, cipher; **–blatt** *neu.* (watch) dial, face

ziffernmässig *adj.* numerical; — *adv.* by figures

Zigarette *f.* cigarette; **–netui** *neu.* cigarette case; **–nspitze** *f.* cigarette holder

Zigarre *f.* cigar; **–ndeckblatt** *neu.* wrapper; **–nkiste** *f.* cigar box; **–nspitze** *f.* cigar tip; cigar holder

Zigeuner *m.* gipsy

Zimbel *f.* cymbal

Zimmer *neu.* room; apartment; **–antenne** *f.* indoor aerial; **–arbeit** *f.* carpentry; **–decke** *f.* ceiling; **–einrichtung** *f.* furniture; (act of) furnishing; **–flucht** *f.* suite of rooms; **–geselle** *m.* journeyman carpenter; **–herr** *m.* lodger; **–mädchen** *neu.* housemaid; **–mann** *m.* carpenter; **–pflanze** *f.* indoor plant; **–vermieterin** *f.* landlady

zimmern *v.* to carpenter; to timber; to make

zimperlich *adj.* prim, prudish; supersensitive

Zimt *m.* cinnamon

Zink *neu.* and *m.* zinc

Zinke *f.* prong; tooth; tennon; cornet; secret mark (on cards)

Zinn *neu.* tin; pewter; **–kraut** horsetail

Zinne *f.* battlement; pinnacle

zinnenförmig *adj.* crenelated

zinnern *adj.* (of) tin, pewter

zinnoberrot *adj.* vermillion

Zins *m.* rent, tax; (bibl.) tribute; **–en** *pl.* interest; **mit** — **und –eszins** in full measure; **–fuss** *m.*, **–satz** *m.* rate of interest; **–schein** *m.* coupon; dividend warrant

zins: –bar *adj.*, **–pflichtig** *adj.* tributary; **–(en)bringend** *adj.* interest-bearing; **–(en)bringend anlegen** to put out at interest

Zipfel *m.* point, tip, corner; lappet; **–mütze** *f.* tasseled cap; nightcap

zipf(e)lig *adj.* peaked, pointed

Zipperlein *neu.* (coll.) gout

Zirk: –el *m.* circle; compasses; **–ular** *neu.* circular, pamphlet; **–us** *m.* circus

zirkulieren *v.* to circulate

zirpen *v.* to chirp, to stridulate

zischeln *v.* to whisper

zischen *v.* to hiss; to whiz; to fizzle

Zischlaut *m.* hissing sound; (gram.) sibilant

Zisterne *f.* cistern

Zisterzienser *m.* Cistercian monk

Zitadelle *f.* citadel

Zitat *neu.* citation, quotation

zitieren *v.* to cite, to quote; to summon, to call up; **falsch** — to misquote

Zitron: –at *neu.* candied lemon peel; citron; **–e** *f.* lemon; **–enfalter** *m.* brimstone butterfly; **–ensäure** *f.* citric acid

zitterig *adj.* trembling, tremulous; shaky

zittern *v.* to shake, to tremble; to shiver

Zitze *f.* nipple, teat, dug

zivil *adj.* civil; moderate, reasonable; **–isatorisch** *adj.* civilizing; **–isieren** to civilize; **–rechtlich** *adj.* according to civil law

Zivil *neu.* civilians; **in** — in civilian dress; **–bevölkerung** *f.* civilian population; **–isation** *f.* civilization; **–ist** *m.* civilian; **–prozess** *m.* (law) civil suit; **–prozessordnung** *f.* civil procedure code

Zofe *f.* lady's maid

zögern *v.* to delay, to hesitate; to linger

Zögling *m.* pupil; boarder

Zölibat *neu.* celibacy

Zoll *m.* inch; duty, tariff; customs; tribute; **–abfertigung** *f.* customs clearance; **–amt** *neu.* customhouse; **–angabe** *f.* customs declaration; **–revision** *f.* customs examination; **–schein** *m.* clearance paper; **–speicher** *m.* bonded warehouse; **–stock** *m.* yardstick; **–verband** *m.*, **–verein** *m.* customs union; **–vergünstigungen** *f. pl.* preferential tariff; **–verschluss** *m.* customs seal, bond

zoll: –en *v.* to pay duty (*oder* respect); **–frei** *adj.* duty-free; **–pflichtig** *adj.* dutiable

Zöllner *m.* customs collector; (bibl.) publican

Zoo *m.* zoo; **–loge** *m.* zoologist; **–logie** *f.* zoology

zoologisch *adj.* zoologic(al)

Zopf *m.* pigtail; plait, tress; (coll.) pedantry, red tape; **falscher —** (hair) switch

Zorn *m.* anger, rage, wrath

zornig *adj.* angry, enraged, wrathful

Zote *f.* obscenity, smutty joke; **–nreisser** *m.* obscene talker

zottig *adj.* matted, shaggy

zu *prep.* in, at; by, on; (up) to; as; for; with; **—** *adv.* too; towards; closed; **ab und —** now and then; **mach —!** close it! (coll.) hurry up! **nur —!** go on! **— Fuss** on foot; **–m Beispiel** for instance; **–m Glück** fortunately; **–m Teil** partially; **–r See** at sea; **— zweien** by (*oder* in) twos

zuallererst *adv.* first of all

zuallerletzt *adv.* last of all

Zubehör *neu.* and *m.* accessories, appurtenances; conveniences; trimmings

zubeissen *v.* to bite, to snap at; to eat away

zubekommen *v.* to get in addition, to get closed

Zuber *m.* tub

zubereiten *v.* to prepare; to cook, to mix

zubilligen *v.* to grant, to concede

zubinden *v.* to bind (*oder* tie) up; **die Augen —** to blindfold

zubleiben *v.* to remain closed (*oder* locked)

zublinzeln *v.* to wink at

zubringen *v.* to bring to; to prompt; **die Zeit —** to pass (*oder* spend) time

Zucht *f.* breed(ing); rearing; cultivation; growing; training, drill; discipline; decency; **in — halten** to keep strict discipline; **–buch** *neu.* studbook; **–haus** *neu.* penitentiary; **–häusler** *m.* convict; **–hausstrafe** *f.* penal servitude; **–hengst** *m.* stallion; **–meister** *m.* disciplinarian, taskmaster; **–mittel** *neu.* means of correction; **–rute** *f.* rod, scourge; **–sau** *f.* brood sow; **–schaf** *neu.* breeding ewe; **–stute** *f.* brood mare; **–vieh** *neu.* breeding cattle; **–wahl** *f.* natural selection

zücht: –en *v.* to breed, to grow, to cultivate; to propagate; **–ig** *adj.* chaste,

decent; **–igen** *v.* to chastise, to scourge, to flog; to punish

zuchtlos *adj.* insubordinate, undisciplined; dissolute, loose

zucken *v.* to twitch, to jerk, to wince; (lightning) to flash; **mit den Schultern** (*or* **Achseln**) **—** to shrug one's shoulders

zücken *v.* to draw

Zucker *m.* sugar; **–bäcker** *m.* confectioner; **–dose** *f.* sugar bowl; **–erbse** *f.* sweet pea; **–guss** *m.* icing; **–hut** *m.* sugar loaf; **–krankheit** *f.* diabetes; **–mäulchen** *neu.* (coll.) sweet tooth; **–melone** *f.* honeydew melon; **–rohr** *neu.* sugar cane; **–rübe** *f.* sugar beet; **–syrup** *m.* molasses; **–werk** *neu.* confectionery, sweets

Zuckung *f.* convulsion, twitch

zudecken *v.* to cover up; to conceal

zudem *adv.* besides, moreover, in addition

zudenken *v.* to intend (as a present) for

zudiktieren *v.* to decree; to inflict

Zudrang *m.* rush (to), run (on)

zudrehen *v.* to turn off; **jemand den Rücken —** to turn one's back on someone

zudringlich *adj.* obtrusive, importunate

zudrücken *v.* to close, to shut; **ein Auge —** to overlook, to connive at

zueignen *v.* to dedicate; **sich widerrechtlich —** to usurp; **sich —** to appropriate

zueilen *v.* to hasten (*oder* run, rush) towards

zueinander *adv.* to each other

zuerkennen *v.* to award, to adjudge, to sentence to

zuerst *adv.* firstly, first of all; first

zuerteilen *v.* to allow, to apportion; to bestow

zufahren *v.* to drive (*oder* go) on; to rush upon

Zufahrt *f.* driveway; **–sstrasse** *f.* approach road

Zufall *m.* chance, accident; occurrence; **durch —** accidentally; **–streffer** *m.* chance hit

zufallen *v.* to fall to, to close; to devolve on

zufällig *adj.* accidental, casual, fortuitous

Zufälligkeit *f.* chance; contingency

zufassen *v.* to lend a hand; to catch hold of

zufliessen *v.* to flow towards (*oder* into); (words) to come readily

Zuflucht *f.* refuge, shelter; recourse

zuflüstern *v.* to whisper to; to prompt

zufolge *prep.* according to, in consequence of

zufrieden *adj.* content, satisfied; **lass ihn —!** let him alone! **sich — geben** to acquiesce in; **–stellen** *v.* to content, to satisfy; **-stellend** *adj.* satisfactory

zufrieren *v.* to freeze up (*oder* over)

zufügen *v.* to add; to do, to cause; **Schaden** — to inflict harm

Zufuhr *f.* supply(ing); provisions

zuführen *v.* to bring (*oder* lead) to; (mech.) to feed; to supply; to convey

Zug *m.* drawing, pull(ing); draft; current; procession; expedition; train; (birds) flight, migration; (chess) move; (cloud) drift; (mil.) platoon, squad, troop; (mountain) range; (pen) stroke, dash; (fig.) characteristic, feature; inclination; **dem — des Herzens folgen** to obey the inner voice; **den — erreichen** to catch the train; **er ist am -e** it's his move; **im rechten — sein** to be in full swing; **in den letzten Zügen liegen** to breathe one's last; **in einem —** uninterruptedly; **in vollen Zügen** deeply, very thoroughly; **— um —** without delay, move for move; **durchgehender — through** train; **-abteil** *neu.* (rail.) compartment; **-brücke** *f.* drawbridge; **-führer** *m.* (rail.) conductor; platoon (*oder* squad) leader; **-kraft** *f.* tractive power; attraction; **-leine** *f.* towrope; **-luft** *f.* draft, current of air; **-mittel** *neu.* attraction; **-netz** *neu.* dragnet; **-pflaster** *neu.* blister, vesicatory; **-stück** *neu.* popular play, attraction; **-tier** *neu.* draft animal; **-verkehr** *m.* railroad traffic; **-vogel** *m.* bird of passage

Zugabe *f.* addition, extra; (theat.) encore

Zugang *m.* access, admittance; entrance; increase; approach, way to

zugänglich *adj.* accessible; approachable

zugeben *v.* to add, to give into the bargain; to allow; to confess, to admit

zugegen *adj.* present

zugeh(e)n *v.* to close, to shut; to move on; to walk faster; to happen; **jemandem — to** come to one's hand; **— lassen to** forward

zugehören *v.* to belong to, to be part of

Zugehörigkeit *f.* membership; relationship

zugeknöpft *adj.* (fig.) uncommunicative, reserved

Zügel *m.* bridle, rein; (fig.) check, curb; **die — schiessen lassen** to give full rein to; to let loose (one's passions, etc.)

zügellos *adj.* unbridled; unrestrained, unruly

zugeritten *adj.* broken in (for riding)

zugesellen *v.* to associate with, to join

zugestandenermassen *adv.* admittedly

Zugeständnis *neu.* concession, admission

zugestehen *v.* to concede, to grant; to admit

zugetan *adj.* attached (*oder* devoted) to

zugiessen *v.* to add (by pouring); to fill up

zugig *adj.* drafty

zugleich *adv.* simultaneously; also; together

zugreifen *v.* to grasp at; to help oneself (at table); to lend a hand; to take (opportunity)

zugrunde *adv.*, **— gehen** to perish; to become ruined; **-legen** *v.* to base upon; **— liegen** to be based upon; **— richten** to destroy; to ruin

zugunsten *adv.* in favor of; for the benefit of

zugute *adv.*, **— halten** to allow for; to pardon; **— kommen** to be for the benefit of; **jemand etwas -kommen lassen** to give a person the benefit of something; **-tun, sich etwas -tun** to indulge in something; to be proud (of)

zuguterletzt *adv.* finally, last of all

zuhalten *v.* to keep closed

Zuhälter *m.* pimp, procurer

zuhängen *v.* to hang (*oder* cover) with

Zuhause *neu.* home

zuheilen *v.* to heal up

Zuhilfenahme *f.* unter — von with the aid of

zuhinterst *adv.* at the very end, last of all

Zuhörer *m.* listener; **-schaft** *f.* audience

zujauchzen, zujubeln *v.* to cheer, to hail

zukehren *v.* to turn to(wards); **das Gesicht — to** face; **den Rücken — to** turn one's back to

zuklappen *v.* to slam, to bang; to close

zukleben *v.* to paste (*oder* glue) up; to gum

zuklinken *v.* to latch

zuknöpfen *v.* to button up

zukommen *v.* to be due to; to fall to the share of; to befit; **das kommt ihr nicht zu** she has no right to that; **— auf to** approach

zukorken *v.* to cork up

Zukunft *f.* future; time to come; future tense

zukünftig *adj.* future; **— adv.** in future

zulächeln *v.* to smile at

Zulage *f.* increase, addition; extra pay, bonus

zulande *adv.*, **bei uns — in** my country

zulangen *v.* to hand (to); to help oneself (at table)

zulänglich *adv.* sufficient, adequate

zulassen *v.* to leave closed; to admit; to allow

zulässig *adj.* admissible; permissible; **das ist nicht — that** is not allowed

Zulauf *m.* crowd, rush; **grossen — haben** to draw crowds; to be much run after

zulaufen *v.* to run to (*oder* towards, on,

faster); **spitz** — to taper off

zuleide *adv.* — **tun** to hurt, to (do) harm

Zuleitung *f.* conducting; lead, supply

zuletzt *adv.* finally, ultimately; last

zuliebe *adv.* for the sake of

zumachen *v.* to close, to shut; to stop up; to button

zumal *adv.* chiefly, especially, particularly

zumauern *v.* to wall (*oder* brick) up

zumeist *adv.* mostly, for the most part

zumessen *v.* to mete out; to allot, to apportion

zumindest *adv.* at least

zumute *adv.* in the mood of; **mir ist nicht wohl** — I feel out of sorts; **-n** *v.* to expect of; **sich zuviel -n** to attempt too much

Zumutung *f.* unreasonable demand; **eine starke** — an impudent demand, imputation

zunächst *prep.* next (*oder* close) to; — *adv.* first; above all; to begin with

zunageln *v.* to nail down (*oder* up)

zunähen *v.* to sew up (*oder* together)

Zunahme *f.* increase, growth

Zuname *m.* surname; family name

Zünd: -er *m.* fuse, igniter; **-holz** *neu.*, **-hölzchen** *neu.* match; **-hütchen** *neu.* percussion cap; **-kabel** *neu.* ignition cord; **-kapsel** *f.* detonator; **-kerze** *f.* spark plug; **-loch** *neu.* (gun) vent; touchhole; **-nadelgewehr** *neu.* needle gun; **-schnur** *f.* fuse; **-stoff** *m.* combustible (*oder* inflammable) material; fuel; **-ung** *f.* ignition, priming

zünden *v.* to catch fire; to kindle, to ignite; to inflame; **-d** *adj.* inflammatory; inciting

Zunder *m.* tinder, punk

zunehmen *v.* to increase; **-de Jahre** advancing years; **-der Mond** waxing moon

zuneigen *v.*, **sich** — to bend toward; to incline to; **sich dem Ende** — to draw to a close

Zuneigung *f.* affection; sympathy; inclination; — **fassen zu** to take a liking to

Zunft *f.* corporation, guild; **-genosse** *m.* guild member; fellow craftsman

zünftig *adj.* according to the rules of a guild; skilled, expert; (coll.) proper, thorough

Zunge *f.* tongue; language; (ichth.) sole; (mus.) reed; **belegte** — furred tongue; **eine feine** — **haben** to be a gourmet; **eine schwere** — **haben** to speak thickly; **er trägt das Herz auf der** — he wears his heart on his sleeve; **es schwebt mir auf der** — I have it on the tip of my tongue; **-ndrescher** *m.*

babbler; **-nlaut** *m.* lingual sound

zunichte *adv.* ruined; **-machen** *v.* to annihilate; to destroy, to frustrate; **-werden** *v.* to come to nothing

zunicken *v.* to nod to

zunutze *adv.* **sich** — **machen** to profit by, to utilize; to turn to account

zuoberst *adv.* at the top; uppermost

zupacken *v.* to grasp at; to set to work

zupfen *v.* to pick, to pluck; to pull, to tug

Zupfgeige *f.* (coll.) guitar

zuraten *v.* to advise, to recommend

zurechnen *v.* to add; to attribute to, to impute

zurechnungsfähig *adj.* accountable; responsible, of sound mind

zurecht *adv.* right(ly); in (good) time; with reason; **-bringen** *v.* to accomplish; **-finden** *v.* **sich -finden** to find one's way; to begin to know; **-kommen** *v.* to arrive in time; to get on well; **-legen** *v.* to lay out; **sich etwas -legen** to figure out something; **-machen** *v.* to prepare; **sich -machen** to make up, to dress; **-rücken** *v.* to put right; **-setzen** *v.* **jemand den Kopf -setzen** to set someone straight; **-weisen** *v.* to show the way; to reprimand

Zurechtweisung *f.* instruction; reprimand

zureden *v.* to urge on, to encourage

zureichen *v.* to hand to, to suffice; **-d** *adj.* sufficient, adequate

zurichten *v.* to prepare, to make ready; to dress; to cook; **übel** — to maltreat

zuriegeln *v.* to bolt (up)

zürnen *v.* to be angry (with)

Zurschaustellung *f.* display, exhibition

zurück *adv.* back(wards); behind; in arrears; late; **—!** *interj.* stand back! **-beben** *v.* to shrink back; to recoil; **-begeben** *v.* to return; **-behalten** *v.* to keep back; to detain; **-bekommen** *v.* to get back; to retrieve; **-berufen** *v.* to recall; **-bleiben** *v.* to stay behind; **-bringen** *v.* to bring back; to retard; to recall; **-datieren** *v.* to antedate; **-drängen** *v.* to push back; to repress; **-eilen** *v.* to hurry back; **-erinnern** *v.* to recollect; to remind; **-erobern** *v.* to reconquer; **-fahren** *v.* to drive back; to start back; **-fallen** *v.* to fall back; to relapse; **-fordern** *v.* to reclaim; **-führen** *v.* to lead (*oder* trace) back; to attribute (*oder* reduce) to; **-geben** *v.* to give back; **-geh(e)n** *v.* to go back, to retreat; to decrease, to decline; to fall off; **-gehen auf** to originate in; **-greifen** *v.* to go back (to), to refer (to); **-gezogen** *adj.* retired, secluded; **-halten** *v.* to hold back; to restrain; to curb, to repress;

to delay; to conceal; to refrain from; to reserve; **–haltend** *adj.* reserved; **–kehren** *v.*, **–kommen** *v.* to go back, to return; **–legen** *v.* to lay back (*oder* aside); to spare; to clear (distance); to attain (age); to go through (course); to lie back; **–liegen** *v.* to belong to the past; **–nehmen** *v.* to take back, to withdraw; to revoke; **–prallen** *v.* to rebound, to recoil; **–rufen** *v.* to recall; ins Leben **–rufen** to revive; **–schlagen** *v.* to strike back; to repel, to repulse; to throw off (quilt); to throw open (coat); to return (ball); **–schrecken** *v.* to frighten away; to shrink (from); **–sehnen** *v.* to long to return; **–sein** *v.* to be back(ward); to be behind the times; **–setzen** *v.* to put back; to reduce; to neglect, to slight; **–springen** *v.* to jump back; to rebound; (arch.) to recede; **–stehen** *v.* to stand back; to be inferior to; **–stellen** *v.* to put back (*oder* aside); (mil.) to defer; **–stossen** *v.* to push back; to repel; **–stossend** *adj.* repulsive; **–strahlen** *v.* to reflect; **–treten** *v.* to step back; to recede; to retire, to resign; **–versetzen** *v.* to put back; to restore; **–verweisen** *v.* to refer back; **–weichen** *v.* to fall back; to retreat; to yield; to recede; to shrink back (from); **–weisen** *v.* to send back; to reject; to repel; to refer back; **–werfen** *v.* to throw (*oder* drive) back; to reflect; to repulse; **–wirken** *v.* to react (upon); **–zahlen** *v.* to repay, to refund; **–ziehen** *v.* to draw back; to withdraw, to retract; sich **–ziehen** to retreat, to move (*oder* march) back; to retire

Zurück: –gabe *f.* giving back, restitution; **–kunft** *f.* return; **–nahme** *f.* taking back; withdrawal; retraction; revocation; recantation; **–setzung** *f.* disregard, slight, snub

Zuruf *m.* acclamation; call, shout

zurufen *v.* to call (*oder* shout) to

zurüsten *v.* to prepare; to fit out, to equip

Zusage *f.* promise, assent

zusagen *v.* to promise; to agree, to please, to suit; jemand auf den Kopf — to tell to someone's face; **–d** *adj.* suitable

zusammen *adv.* (all) together; in all; **–ballen** *v.* to clench (fist); to concentrate; to conglomerate; (clouds) to gather, to draw near; **–beissen** *v.* to grit one's teeth; **–berufen** *v.* to convoke; **–brechen** *v.* to break down, to collapse; **–bringen** *v.* to amass; to assemble, to collect; **–drängen** *v.* to compress; to concentrate, to condense; **–drehen** *v.* to twist together; **–drücken** *v.* to compress;

–fahren *v.* to collide; to start, to wince; **–fallen** *v.* to collapse; to coincide; **–falten** *v.* to fold up; **–fassen** *v.* to summarize; to combine, to concentrate; **–flicken** *v.* to patch together; **–fliessen** *v.* to flow together, to meet; **–fügen** *v.* to join together; to unite; **–führen** *v.* to bring together; **–geben** *v.* to marry; **–geh(e)n** *v.* to go together; to match, to agree well; to shrink; **–gehörig** *adj.* homogeneous; correlated; **–geraten** *v.* to collide; to quarrel; **–gesetzt** *adj.* composite; compound; complex; **–gewürfelt** *adj.* motley; **–halten** *v.* to keep (*oder* stick) together; to compare; **–hängen** *v.* to be connected (with); to cohere; **–hangslos** *adj.* disconnected, incoherent; **–hauen** *v.* to cut to pieces; to thrash soundly; **–häufen** *v.* to accumulate, to amass; **–klappbar** *adj.* collapsible, folding; **–klappen** *v.* to fold up; (coll.) to collapse; **–klingen** *v.* to harmonize; **–kommen** *v.* to come together, to meet; **–laufen** *v.* to run together; to shrink; to curdle; **–legen** *v.* to lay (*oder* club) together; to fold up; to fuse; **–nehmen** *v.* to gather (up); sich **–nehmen** to collect oneself; to be on one's good behavior; **–passen** *v.* to adjust, to fit, to match; **–pferchen** *v.* to squeeze together, to crowd; to pen up (cattle); **–raffen** *v.* to snatch up; sich **–raffen** to pull oneself together; **–rechnen** *v.* to add up; **–reimen** *v.* to understand; sich **–reimen** to fit in, to make sense; **–rotten** *v.* to assemble a gang; sich **–rotten** to flock together, to conspire; **–rücken** *v.* to draw nearer; **–rufen** *v.* to convoke; **–schiessen** *v.* to shoot down; to contribute; **–schlagen** *v.* to strike together; to smash; to clap (hands); to click (heels); (water) to close over; **–schliessen** *v.* to join, to amalgamate; to close (ranks); **–schmelzen** *v.* to melt away (*oder* together); **–schnüren** *v.* to tie together (*oder* up); to wring (heart); **–schrecken** *v.* to startle; **–schrumpfen** *v.* to shrivel up, to shrink; **–schweissen** *v.* to weld together; **–setzen** *v.* to combine, to compound, to compose; sich **–setzen** to sit down together; to consist of; **–sinken** to sink down; **–stecken** *v.* to pin (*oder* put) together; to conspire; **–stellen** *v.* to put together; to collate; to compile; **–stoppeln** *v.* (coll.) to bungle; **–stossen** *v.* to collide, to clash; to clink (glasses); to conflict; to adjoin; **–stückeln** *v.* to patch up, to piece together; **–stürzen** *v.* to collapse; **–tragen** *v.* to carry together;

to compile; –treffen v. to encounter; to coincide; –treten v. to meet; to convene; –wirken to co-operate; –zählen v. to add up; –ziehen v. to draw together; to concentrate, to contract

Zusammen: –arbeit f. co-operation; –bruch m. breakdown, collapse; –fluss m. confluence; junction; –halt m. coherence, cohesion; –hang m. connection; cohesion; –klang m. consonance; harmony, accord; –kunft f. assembly, meeting; conference, convention; interview; –schluss m. federation, union; amalgamation, –setzung f. combination, synthesis; structure; compound; –spiel neu. teamwork; –stoss m. collision; conflict; encounter; –treffen neu. meeting, simultaneity

Zusatz m. addition; appendix, supplement; postscript; codicil; alloy; (pol.) rider

zuschanden adv. frustrated; — machen to destroy, to foil, to thwart, to frustrate; — werden to be ruined; to come to naught

zuscharren v. to fill up (hole)

zuschauen v. to look on, to watch

Zuschauer m. spectator, onlooker; — pl. audience; –raum m. seats, auditorium

zuschicken v. to forward to; to remit

zuschieben v. to push towards; to close by pushing; **die Schuld** — to put the blame on

Zuschlag m. addition, increase; extra charge; surtax; bonus; (auction) knocking down; (min.) flux; –karte f. additional ticket

zuschlagen v. to strike; to bang, to slam; (auction) to knock down; to add as a flux

zuschliessen v. to lock up; to close

zuschmeissen v. to slam; to throw to

zuschnallen v. to buckle; to strap up

zuschnappen v. to snap at

zuschneiden v. to cut up (oder out)

Zuschnitt m. cut; style; structure

zuschreiben v. to attribute (oder ascribe, owe) to; to credit with; to accept an invitation (by letter)

zuschreiten v. to step up to; to walk briskly

Zuschrift f. communication, letter

zuschütten v. to add to; to fill up

zusehen v. to look on, to watch; to take care of, to see to

zusetzen v. to add to; to lose (time, money, health); to put on (fire)

zusichern v. to assure of, to promise

Zuspeise f. side dish

zusperren v. to bar, to close, to lock

zuspitzen v. to point, to sharpen; **sich** — to taper; to become critical

Zusprache f. kindly encouragement; consolation

zusprechen v. **dem Essen** — **to eat** heartily; **jemand etwas** — to adjudge something to a person; **Mut** — **to** encourage; **Trost** — to comfort

Zuspruch m. encouragement, consolation; customers; approval, praise

Zustand m. condition, state; **in gutem** — in good order (oder repair); **Zustände** pl. nervous attack, hysterical fit

zustande adv. –bringen to bring about, to accomplish; –kommen to take place, to come about; **nicht** –**kommen** not to come off

zuständig adj. pertaining (oder belonging) to; authorized, competent, responsible

zustatten adv. — **kommen** to be useful to

zustecken v. to pin up; **jemand etwas** — to slip something to a person

zusteh(e)n v. to belong (oder be due) to; **es steht ihr nicht zu** she has no right to it

zustellen v. to deliver (oder forward, ship) to; to block up, to obstruct

Zustellungsurkunde f. writ of summons

zustimmen v. to agree to; –d adj. affirmative

zustopfen v. to stop up; to mend, to darn

zustossen v. to push to; to shut; to thrust forward; to befall, to happen to

zustreben v. to stream to; to flow into

Zustrom m. influx; crowd, multitude; flow

zustürzen v. to rush upon

zustutzen v. to trim, to fit, to adapt

zutage adv. — **bringen,** — **fördern to** bring to light; to uncover; — **liegen to** be evident; — **treten** to come to light; to crop out

Zutat f. ingredient, seasoning; trimming

zuteil adv. — werden to fall to one's share; **jemand etwas** — werden lassen to allot (oder grant) something to a person; –en v. to allot, to assign; to apportion; to adjudge; to bestow

Zuteilung f. allotment

zutragen v. to carry to; to report; **sich** — to happen, to take place

Zuträger m. gossip, scandalmonger; informer; –ei f. talebearing, slandering

zuträglich adj. advantageous; useful, beneficial; wholesome; **schwere Speisen sind ihm nicht** — rich food does **not** agree with him

zutrauen v. jemand etwas — to give one credit for something; **jemand nicht viel** — to have no high opinion of someone

Zutrauen *neu.* confidence, trust

zutraulich *adj.* confiding, trusting; sociable

zutreffen *v.* to come true, to prove correct; **-d** *adj.* correct, right, true; to the point

zutrinken *v.* to drink to

Zutritt *m.* access, admission; entrance; **überall — haben** to be welcome everywhere

Zutun *neu.* help, assistance; interference

zuunterst *adv.* at the very bottom

zuverlässig *adj.* dependable, reliable, certain; **von -er Seite** on good authority

Zuversicht *f.* confidence, trust

zuviel *adv.* too much; **des Guten — tun** to go too far; **mehr als —** more than enough

zuvor *adv.* before, previously; first (of all); **-kommen** to anticipate; to forestall; **-kommend** *adj.* obliging, complaisant; **-tun, es jemand -tun** to surpass someone

Zuwachs *m.* increase, growth, enlargement; **auf — berechnet** allowing for growth

zuwachsen *v.* to grow together; to become overgrown; to heal up; to fall to one's share

zuwege *adv.* **— bringen** to bring about; to accomplish, to effect

zuweilen *adv.* sometimes, at times, occasionally

zuweisen *v.* to allot (*oder* assign) to

zuwenden *v.* to turn to(wards); to bestow on, to devote to

zuwerfen *v.* to throw to(wards); to slam (door); to cast (glances); to fill (with earth)

zuwider *adj.* repugnant, distasteful; **—** *prep.* against, contrary to; **-handeln** to contravene; **-laufen** to run counter to, to be contrary to; **-sein** to be repugnant to; to displease

zuwinken *v.* to wave (*oder* nod) to

zuzahlen *v.* to pay extra

zuzeiten *adv.* at times, sometimes

zuziehen *v.* to draw together; to tighten; to call in, to consult; to move in; to immigrate; **sich —** to incur; to catch (disease)

Zuzug *m.* immigration; reinforcements

zwacken *v.* (dial.) to pinch; to torment

Zwang *m.* compulsion; constraint, restraint; force; **sich keinen — antun** (*or* **auferlegen**) to be free and easy; **sich — antun** to restrain oneself; **-sanleihe** *f.* forced loan; **-sarbeit** *f.* compulsory labor; **-sbeitreibung** *f.* forced collection; **-sgestellung** *f.* arrest; **-sjacke** *f.* strait jacket; **-slage** *f.* embarrassing position; **-smassregel** *f.* coercive measure; **-sversteigerung** *f.* forced sale; **-svollstreckung** *f.* (law) distress; **-svorstellung** *f.* hallucination; **-swirtschaft** *f.* government control

zwanzig *adj.* twenty; **-erlei** *adj.* of twenty kinds; **-fach** *adj.*, **-fältig** *adj.* twentyfold; **-ste** *adj.* twentieth

Zwanzig *f.* twenty; **-er** *m.* twenty; **man of twenty**; **-stel** *neu.* twentieth part

zwar *adv.* indeed; no doubt; although; **und —** namely, that is

Zweck *m.* purpose, aim, design, goal; **das hat wenig —** that's of no use; **der — heiligt die Mittel** the end justifies the means

zweck: -dienlich *adj.*, **-entsprechend** *adj.*, **-mässig** *adj.* serviceable, expedient, appropriate; **-en to peg, to tack**; **-los** *adj.* aimless, useless; **-s** *prep.* for the purpose of; **-widrig** *adj.* unsuitable; inexpedient; inappropriate

zwei *adj.* two; **zu -en** in pairs; **two by two**; **-beinig** *adj.* two-legged; **-bettig** *adj.* with two beds; **-deutig** *adj.* ambiguous, doubtful; obscene; **-erlei** *adj.* of two kinds; different; **-fach** *adj.*, **-fältig** *adj.* double, twofold; **in -facher Ausführung** in duplicate; **-geschlechtig** *adj.* hermaphrodite; bisexual; **-gestrichen** *adj.* (mus.) twice accented; **-gleisig** *adj.* double-tracked; **-gliedrig** *adj.* in two ranks; (math.) binomial; **-händig** *adj.* two-handed; for two hands; **-jährig** *adj.* two years old; biennial; **-jährlich** *adj.* occurring every two years; **-mal** *adv.* twice; **-malig** *adj.* (done) twice; **-motorig** *adj.* twinengined; **-reihig** *adj.* having two rows; (coat) double-breasted; **-schläfrig** *adj.* for two sleepers; **-schneidig** *adj.* double-edged; ambiguous; **-silbig** *adj.* disyllabic; **-spännig** *adj.* drawn by two horses; **-sprachig** *adj.* bilingual; **-stimmig** *adj.* for two voices; **-stündig** *adj.* of (*oder* lasting) two hours; **-stündlich** *adj.* occurring every two hours; **-te** *adj.* second; another; **aus -ter Hand** secondhand; **-teilig** *adj.* two-piece; bipartite; **-tens** *adv.* secondly, in the second place; **-tletzte** *adj.* penultimate; **-wertig** *adj.* bivalent; **-zackig** *adj.* two-pronged; **-zeilig** *adj.* of (*oder* in) two lines; **-züngig** *adj.* double-tongued; doubledealing, hypocritical

Zwei *f.* two; deuce; **-decker** *m.* biplane; **-er** *m.* two; **-gespann** *neu.* two-horse team; **-händer** *m.* two-handed sword; **-heit** *f.* duality; **-hufer** *m.* clovenfooted animal; **-kampf** *m.* duel; **-röhrenapparat** *m.* two-tube (radio) set;

–sitzer *m.* two-seater; –taktmotor *m.* two-stroke engine; –unddreissigstelnote *f.* (mus.) demisemiquaver; –vierteltakt *m.* (mus.) two-four time; –zeiler *m.* couplet, distich

Zweifel *m.* doubt, suspicion; ohne — undoubtedly; certainly; –sfall *m.* doubtful case; –sucht *f.* skepticism

zweifel: –haft *adj.* doubtful, dubious; suspicious; –los *adj.* doubtless, certain; –n to doubt; to question; to suspect

Zweifler *m.* doubter, skeptic

Zweig *m.* branch; bough, twig; line, section; er wird nie auf einen grünen — kommen (coll.) he will never prosper; –bahn *f.* (rail.) branch line; –geschäft *neu.*, –niederlassung *f.* subsidiary firm; –stelle *f.* branch office

Zwerchfell *neu.* (anat.) diaphragm

Zwerg *m.* dwarf, midget; pygmy; brownie

Zwick: –el *m.* gusset; gore; (arch.) spandrel; clock (of stocking); –er *m.* eye glasses; pince-nez

zwicken *v.* to pinch, to nip; to twitch

Zwie: –gespräch *neu.* dialogue, conversation, colloquy; –licht *neu.* twilight; –spalt *m.*, –tracht *f.* dissension, discord; schism; –sprache *f.* conversation, dialogue

zwie: –fach *adj.*, –fältig *adj.* double, twofold; –spältig *adj.*, –trächtig *adj.* discordant, disunited, conflicting

Zwieback *m.* zwieback, biscuit, rusk

Zwiebel *f.* onion; bulb; (coll.) pocket watch; –fische *m.* *pl.* jumbled type

Zwil(li)ch *m.* ticking (fabric)

Zwilling *m.* twin; –e *pl.* (ast.) Gemini

Zwing: –burg *f.* stronghold; –e *f.* vise, clamp; ferrule; –er *m.* cage; dungeon; kennel; arena; –herr *m.* despot, tyrant

zwingen *v.* to compel, to force; to subdue; to accomplish; –d *adj.* urgent; forcible, cogent

zwinkern *v.* to blink, to wink, to twinkle

Zwirn *m.* thread, twine, twisted yarn

zwischen *prep.* between, among(st); –durch *adv.* in between, at times; through, in the midst; –her *adv.* meanwhile; –planetarisch *adj.* interplanetary; –staatlich *adj.* international

Zwischen: –akt *m.* interlude, entr'acte; –oemerkung *f.* interpolated remark; –deck *neu.* lower deck, steerage;

–ergebnis *neu.* preliminary result; –fall *m.* incident; episode; –flügel *m.* (avi.) flap; –frage *f.* question; –gericht *neu.* intermediate dish; –glied *neu.* connecting link; –handel *m.* wholesale; transportation business; jobbing; –händler *m.* wholesaler; agent; jobber; –handlung *f.* episode; –lage *f.* interposition; –landung *f.* intermediate landing; Flug ohne –landung non-stop flight; –mauer *f.* partition wall; –pause *f.* interval, interlude; break; –raum *m.* intervening space, interstice; interval; –rede *f.* interruption; –redner *m.* interlocutor; –regierung *f.* interregnum; –ruf *m.* loud interruption; exclamation; –satz *m.* insertion; parenthesis; –spiel *neu.* intermezzo, interlude; –stecker *m.* adapter (plug); –stock *m.* intermediate story; mezzanine; –stück *neu.* inset; –stufe *f.* intermediate grade (*oder* stage); –träger *m.* scandalmonger, talebearer; –vorhang *m.* drop curtain; –zeit *f.* intervening time, interval; in der –zeit in the meantime; –zünder *m.* booster

Zwist *m.* dissension, discord, quarrel

zwitschern *v.* to chirp, to twitter

zwitterhaft *adj.* mongrel, hybrid

zwölf *adj.* twelve; –eckig *adj.* dodecagonal; –erlei *adj.* of twelve kinds; –fach *adj.*, –fältig *adj.* twelvefold; –flächig *adj.* dodecahedral; –jährig *adj.* twelveyear-old; –malig *adj.* occurring twelve times; –stündig *adj.* of twelve hours; –te *adj.* twelfth; –tens *adv.* twelfthly

Zwölf *f.* twelve; –eck *neu.* dodecagon; –fingerdarmgeschwür *neu.* (med.) duodenal ulcer; –te *m.* twelfth; –tel *neu.* twelfth part

Zyklon *m.* cyclone; –e *f.* (weather) low pressure area

Zyklop *m.* Cyclops; –en *pl.* Cyclopes

Zyklotron *neu.* cyclotron, Elektronenbeschleuniger

Zylinder *m.* cylinder; lamp chimney; silk (*oder* top) hat; –presse *f.* roller press

Zyniker *m.* Cynic; cynic

Zypern *neu.* Cyprus

Zypresse *f.* cypress

Zyste *f.* cyst

ENGLISH—GERMAN

ENGLISCH—DEUTSCH

ABBREVIATIONS

abbr.	abbreviation	lit.	literature
adj.	adjective	*m.*	masculine
adv.	adverb	math.	mathematics
avi.	aviation	mech.	mechanics
agr.	agriculture	med.	medicine
Am.	American	mil.	military
anat.	anatomy	min.	mining, minerals
arch.	architecture	mus.	music
art.	article	*n.*	noun
ast.	astronomy	naut.	nautical
auto.	automobile	*neu.*	neuter
bibl.	biblical	opt.	optical
biol.	biology	orn.	ornithology
bot.	botany	phil.	philosophy
chem.	chemistry	phot.	photography
coll.	colloquial	phy.	physics
com.	commerce	physiol.	physiology
conj.	conjunction	*pl.*	plural
dent.	dentistry	poet.	poetry
dial.	dialectal	pol.	politics
eccl.	ecclesiastic	*p.p.*	past participle
educ.	education	*prep.*	preposition
elec.	electricity	*pron.*	pronoun
ent.	entomology	rad.	radio
f.	feminine	rail.	railway
fig.	figurative(ly)	rel.	religion
geog.	geography	rhet.	rhetoric
geol.	geology	*sing.*	singular
geom.	geometry	sl.	slang
gram.	grammar	theat.	theater
hort.	horticulture	TV	television
ichth.	ichthyology	typ.	typography
interj.	interjection	*v.*	verb
interr.	interrogative	zool.	zoology

ENGLISH — GERMAN

A

a *art.* ein

abandon *v.* aufgeben, verlassen; überlassen; **-ed** *adj.* verworfen; aufgegeben, verlassen

abase *v.* erniedrigen, demütigen

abate *v.* ermässigen, verringern, nachlassen; (law) aufheben

abbey *n.* Abtei

abbot *n.* Abt

abbreviate *v.* abkürzen, reduzieren

abbreviation *n.* Abkürzung

abdicate *v.* abdanken; aufgeben, entsagen

abdication *n.* Abdankung; Verzicht

abdomen *n.* Unterleib; Bauch

abduct *v.* entführen, wegführen; (med.) abziehen; **-ion** *n.* Entführung

aberration *n.* Abweichung; Abirrung

abet *v.* aufhetzen, anstiften; Vorschub leisten

abeyance *n.* Unentschiedenheit; in — herrenlos; unentschieden, in der Schwebe

abhor *v.* verabscheuen; **-rence** *n.* Abscheu

abide *v.* bleiben, warten; wohnen; — by verharren bei; standhalten; I cannot — him ich kann ihn nicht ausstehen

ability *n.* Fähigkeit; *pl.* geistige Anlagen; to the best of one's — nach besten Kräften

able *adj.* fähig, tüchtig, geschickt; be — to imstande sein zu, können

able-bodied *adj.* dienstfähig, tauglich; kräftig

abnormal *adj.* abnorm, regelwidrig

aboard *adv.* an Bord; all —! an Bord! (rail.) einsteigen!

abolish *v.* abschaffen

abolition *n.* Abschaffung

abominable *adj.* abscheulich, widerwärtig

aborigine *n.* Ureinwohner

abort *n.* (mech.) Fehler; (avi.) unvollständiger Fliegereinsatz

abortion *n.* Fehlgeburt; Abtreibung

about *prep.* um, herum; über; etwa; **send someone — his business** jemandem heimleuchten; **what —?** was soll das heissen? — *adv.* etwa, ungefähr; herum, umher; **all** — überall; **be — to do something** im Begriff sein etwas zu tun; **set** — in Angriff nehmen

about-face *n.* Kehrtwendung

above *prep.* über, mehr als; — *adv.* oben, darüber; — all vor allem; **be — erhaben sein über**; — *adj.* obig

aboveboard *adj.* offen, ehrlich

above-mentioned *adj.* oben erwähnt

abrasion *n.* Abschürfung, Abnutzung

abrasive *adj.* abschabend, abschleifend; — *n.* Schmirgelpapier, Politur

abreast *adv.* nebeneinander; **be — of the times** mit der Zeit Schritt halten

abridge *v.* verkürzen; beschränken

abroad *adv.* im (ins) Ausland; im Freien; **get — bekannt werden**

abrupt *adj.* plötzlich; schroff

abscess *n.* Geschwür

absence *n.* Abwesenheit; Mangel; **leave of — Urlaub**

absent *adj.* abwesend, fehlend; **-ee** *n.* Abwesende

absent-minded *adj.* geistesabwesend, zerstreut

absolute *adj.* unbedingt; absolut; unabhängig; unbeschränkt; vollkommen; **-ly** *adv.* durchaus; unbeschränkt

absolution *n.* Lossprechung, Absolution

absolve v. freisprechen, entbinden
absorb v. aufsaugen, absorbieren; ganz in Anspruch nehmen
absorption n. Aufsaugung; Vertieftsein
abstain v. sich enthalten
abstinence n. Enthaltsamkeit
abstract n. Abriss, Auszug; Inbegriff; — v. abstrahieren; abziehen; ablenken; — adj. abstrakt; schwer verständlich; **–ion** n. Abstraktion; Absonderung; **–ionism** n. (art) abstrakte Kunstrichtung
absurd adj. absurd; albern, sinnwidrig; **-ity** n. Sinnwidrigkeit, Ungereimtheit
abtruse adj. schwer verständlich, dunkel
abundance n. Überfluss, Fülle; Überschwang; **in** — in Hülle und Fülle
abundant adj. reich an; überschüssig
abuse n. Missbrauch; Beschimpfung; — v. missbrauchen; misshandeln
abusive adj. missbräuchlich; verletzend
academic adj. akademisch; **— freedom** akademische Freiheit
academy n. Akademie, Hochschule
accede v. zustimmen; beitreten; antreten
accelerate v. beschleunigen
acceleration n. Beschleunigung
accelerator n. Gashebel, Gaspedal
accelerometer n. Beschleunigungsmesser
accent n. Akzent; Betonung; Aussprache; — v., **-uate** v. akzentuieren; betonen
accept v. annehmen; akzeptieren; gelten lassen; **-able** adj. annehmbar; akzeptabel; angenehm; **-ance** n. Annahme, Aufnahme
access n. Zutritt, Zugang; Anfall; **-ible** adj. erreichbar, zugänglich; **-ibility** n. (mil. avi.) Verwendungsfähigkeit
accessory n. (law) Mitschuldige; — pl. Zubehör; — adj. zugehörig
accident n. Zufall; Unfall; **-al** adj. zufällig; unwesentlich
acclamation n. Beifall, Zuruf; Jubel
accommodate v. anpassen; unterbringen; versehen, versorgen; schlichten
accommodating adj. gefällig, entgegenkommend
accommodation n. Anpassung; Aushilfe; Bequemlichkeit; Unterkunft
accompaniment n. Begleitung
accompany v. begleiten
accomplice n. Mitschuldige, Komplice
accomplish v. ausführen, vollenden; **-ed** adj. ausgebildet; **-ment** n. Vollendung, Ausführung; Bildung, Talent; **-ments** n. pl. Fähigkeiten, Kenntnisse
accord n. Übereinstimmung; Einklang; **of one's own** — freiwillig, aus eigenem Antrieb; **with one** — einstimmig, einmütig; — v. übereinstimmen; gewähren, gestatten; **-ance** n. Übereinstim-

mung; **in –ance with** gemäss, übereinstimmend mit; **-ing** prep. **-ing to** entsprechend, nach; **-ingly** adv. demgemäss
account n. Rechnung, Konto; Bericht, Darstellung; **be of no** — unbedeutend sein; nichts taugen; **call (someone) to** — von (jemandem) Rechenschaft verlangen; **give an** — Rechenschaft ablegen; berichten; **keep an** — ein Konto (or Guthaben) halten (or haben); **on** — of wegen; **on no** — auf keinen Fall, um keinen Preis; **take into** — berücksichtigen; — v. **— for** erklären, Rechenschaft ablegen; **-able** adj. erklärlich, rechenschaftspflichtig; verantwortlich; **-ant** n. Rechnungsführer; Buchhalter; Bücherrevisor; **-ing** n. Buchhaltung; Erklärung; Rechtfertigung
acculturation n. (demography) kulturelle Anpassung
accumulate v. anhäufen, aufhäufen; ansammeln; (coll.) aufstapeln
accuracy n. Richtigkeit; Genauigkeit; Sorgfalt; Pünktlichkeit
accurate adj. richtig; genau; sorgfältig
accusation n. Anklage, Beschuldigung
accuse v. anklagen, beschuldigen; vorwerfen; **-d** n. Angeklagte, Beschuldigte
accustom v. gewöhnen; **become –ed to** sich gewöhnen an; **-ed** adj. gewöhnt
ace n. (cards) As; (sports) Meister, Kanone
acerbic acid n. Resinsäure
acetate n. Azetat; essigsaures Salz
acetone n. Azeton
acetylene n. Azetylen
ache n. Schmerz, Weh; — v. weh tun, schmerzen
achieve v. vollbringen; zustandebringen; erlangen, gewinnen; **-ment** n. Ausführung; Gewinn, Werk
aching adj. schmerzhaft, schmerzend
acid n. Säure; **— test** Säureprobe; (fig.) Feuerprobe; — adj. sauer; herb; **-ity** n. Säure; Herbheit, Schärfe
acknowledge v. anerkennen; zugestehen; (com.) bestätigen, erkenntlich sein für
acknowledgment n. Anerkennung; Eingeständnis; Bestätigung
acme n. Gipfel, Höhe; Höhepunkt
acne n. Akne, Hautfinne, Pickel
acorn n. Eichel
acoustics n. Akustik, Schallehre
acquaint v. bekanntmachen, vertraut machen; mitteilen, berichten; **be –ed with bekannt sein mit, kennen; become –ed with** kennenlernen, bekanntwerden mit; **-ance** n. Bekanntschaft, Kenntnis;

Bekannte

acquire *v.* erwerben, erlangen; erreichen, gewinnen; erlernen

acquisition *n.* Erwerb; Errungenschaft

acre *n.* Acker, *pl.* Ländereien; **–age** *n.* Flächeninhalt, Umfang

acrobat *n.* Akrobat; **–ics** *n.* Akrobatik

across *adv.* hinüber, herüber; — *prep.* über, quer (über); (mitten) durch; — **the** street auf der anderen Strassenseite

acrylic acid *n.* Resinsäure

act *n.* Tat, Handlung; Werk; Schritt; Akte; Beschluss, Gesetz; Akt, Aufzug; **in the** — im Begriff, auf frischer Tat; **put on an** — sich aufspielen; **Acts** (rel.) Apostelgeschichte; — *v.* wirken, tätig (*or* aktiv) sein, handeln; funktionieren; (theat.) darstellen, spielen; — **on** handeln; **–ing** *n.* Tat, Handeln; Spiel(en), Schauspielkunst; **–ing** *adj.* handelnd, tätig; **–or** *n.* Schauspieler, Darsteller; **–ress** *n.* Schauspielerin, Darstellerin

action *n.* Handlung, Wirkung, Tätigkeit; Tat; (law) Klage, Prozess; (mech.) Gang, Werk; (mil.) Gefecht, Schlacht; **be killed in** — fallen; **bring an** — **against** verklagen; **in full** — auf Hochtouren, in vollem Gange; **take** — vorgehen

activate *v.* ins Leben rufen; aktivieren; (mil.) aufstellen

activation *n.* Aktivierung

active *adj.* tätig, aktiv; geschäftig, lebhaft; wirksam

activity *n.* Tätigkeit, Betriebsamkeit

actual *adj.* tatsächlich, wirklich, eigentlich; gegenwärtig, aktuell; **–ity** *n.* Wirklichkeit

acute *adj.* scharf, brennend; akut; spitz; betont; schrill; (med.) hitzig; (fig.) scharfsinnig; — **angle** spitzer Winkel

ad *n.* Annonce, Anzeige

A.D. *abbr.* Anno Domini, im Jahre des Herrn

adapt *v.* anpassen, zurechtmachen; bearbeiten; **–able** *adj.* anpassungsfähig; **–ability** *n.* Anpassungsfähigkeit

add *v.* hinzufügen, beifügen; addieren; vermehren; — **up** zusammenzählen, summieren; **–ing** *adj.* addierend; **–ing** machine Additionsmaschine; **–ition** *n.* Zusatz, Beifügung; Addition; Vermehrung; **in –ition** ausserdem, übrigens, noch dazu; **in –ition to** ausser, neben; **–itional** *adj.* zusätzlich, hinzukommend, Zusatz-

adder *n.* Natter, Otter

addict *n.* Rauschgiftsüchtige; **–ed** *adj.* zugetan, ergeben; verfallen

address *n.* Adresse, Anschrift; (fig.)

Anrede, Ansprache; — *v.* adressieren; (fig.) anreden, sich wenden (*or* richten); **–ee** *n.* Empfänger, Adressat

adenoid *n.* Adenoide, Drüsenschwellung

adept *adj.* eingeweiht, erfahren, geschickt

adequate *adj.* angemessen, entsprechend; hinreichend, genügend, zulänglich

adhere *v.* ankleben; anhaften, festhalten; zugetan sein

adhesive *adj.* anhaftend, anklebend; (fig.) anhänglich; — **plaster** Leukoplast, Heftpflaster; — **tape** Klebestreifen

adjacent *adj.* anliegend, anstossend, benachbart

adjective *n.* Adjektiv, Eigenschaftswort; — *adj.* adjektivisch

adjoin *v.* angrenzen an; **–ing** *adj.* benachbart, angrenzend

adjourn *v.* vertagen, aufschieben; **–ment** *n.* Vertagung, Aufschub

adjust *v.* anpassen, berichtigen, einstellen; (ad)justieren, eichen; (fig.) schlichten; **–able** *adj.* anpassbar, verstellbar; **–ment** *n.* Anordnung; Berichtigung, Ausgleichung; Justierung; Schlichtung

adjutant *n.* Adjutant; — **general** *n.* Generaladjutant

ad-lib *n.* dem Interpreten überlassen, nach Belieben; Extempore; — *v.* improvisieren, extemporieren

administer *v.* verwalten, handhaben; darreichen, spenden, austeilen

administration *n.* Verwaltung; Ausgabe, Verteilung; Darreichung; (law) Handhabung

administrative *adj.* verwaltend, Verwaltungs-

admirable *adj.* vortrefflich, bewundernswert

admiral *n.* Admiral; **rear** — Konteradmiral

admiration *n.* Bewunderung, Verehrung

admire *v.* bewundern, verehren; **–r** *n.* Bewunderer, Verehrer, Anbeter

admiringly *adv.* bewunderungsvoll, verehrungsvoll

admission *n.* Eintritt, Zutritt; Zulassung, Aufnahme; (fig.) Bekenntnis, Zugeständnis; — **charge** Eintrittsgeld

admit *v.* zulassen, Zutritt gewähren; (her)einlassen; gestatten; (fig.) zugeben, gestehen; **–tance** *n.* Zulassung, Zutritt; Einlass

admonish *v.* ermahnen; warnen, verwarnen

ado *n.* Wesen, Getue, Aufheben, Lärm; Mühe

adolescence *n.* Jugendzeit; Jünglingsalter

adolescent *adj.* jugendlich; (fig.) unreif

adopt *v.* annehmen, adoptieren; (fig.) sich

aneignen; **–ed** *adj.* angenommen; **–ion** *n.* Annahme; Adoption

adorable *adj.* anbetungswürdig

adoration *n.* Anbetung, Verehrung

adore *v.* anbeten, verehren; leidenschaftlich lieben

adorn *v.* schmücken, zieren, verschönern

adrenalin *n.* Adrenalin

adrift *adj.* treibend; (fig.) ratlos

adult *n.* Erwachsene; — *adj.* erwachsen, reif

adulterate *v.* verfälschen, verderben

adultery *n.* Ehebruch; **commit** — ehebrechen

advance *n.* Vorwärtsgehen, Vorrücken, Vormarsch; Beförderung; Fortschritt; Antrag; Vorschuss, Auslage; Aufschlag, Preiserhöhung; (mil.) Angriff; **in** — im voraus, als Vorschuss; — *v.* hervortreten, vorwärtsgehen, vordringen, vorrücken, vorschreiten; befördern; vorausbezahlen, vorschiessen, auslegen; steigen; (mil.) angreifen; **–ment** *n.* Beförderung, Förderung, Fortschritt

advantage *n.* Vorteil, Vorzug; Überlegenheit; (com.) Nutzen, Gewinn; **have the** — übertreffen; **take** — of einen Vorteil (*or* Gewinn) ziehen aus, benutzen, ausnutzen; **–ous** *adj.* vorteilhaft, günstig

advent *n.* Ankunft, Herannahen; **Advent** Advent(szeit)

adventure *n.* Abenteurer, Wagestück; — *v.* wagen, riskieren; **–r** *n.* Abenteurer

adverb *n.* Adverb, Umstandswort

adversary *n.* Gegner, Widersacher, Feind

advertise *v.* anzeigen, annoncieren, inserieren; **–ment** *n.* Anzeige, Annonce, Inserat; Reklame, Ankündigung; **–r** *n.* Anzeiger; Inserent; Anzeigeblatt

advertising *n.* Reklame; Werbung

advice *n.* Rat(schlag); Gutachten; (com.) Bericht; **ask** — of sich Rat holen bei

advisable *adj.* ratsam, rätlich

advise *v.* belehren, (be)raten; melden, benachrichtigen; — **against** abraten von; **–r** (*oder* **advisor**) *n.* Ratgeber, Berater

advisory *adj.* ratgebend, beratend

advocate *n.* Fürsprecher, Anwalt

aerial *n.* (rad.) Antenne; — *adj.* luftig

aeroballistics *n.* Luftschiesslehre

aerodynamics *n.* Fluglehre, Aerodynamik

aeroembolism *n.* Höhenkrankheit

aeromedicine *n.* Luftfahrtmedizin

aerospace *n.* Luft- und Raumfahrt

aesthetic *adj.* ästhetisch; **–s** *n. pl.* Ästhetik

affair *n.* Sache, Angelegenheit, Affäre; (com.) Geschäft, Handel; **foreign –s** auswärtige Angelegenheiten

affect *v.* (be)rühren, betreffen, einwirken;

angreifen; (er)heucheln; **–ation** *n.* Affektiertheit, Ziererei; Verstellung; **–ed** *adj.* affektiert, erkünstelt; **–ing** *adj.* rührend, ergreifend

affection *n.* Anhänglichkeit, Zuneigung, Liebe; **–ate** *adj.* liebevoll, zärtlich; herzlich, gütig; **your –ate** dein dich liebender

affidavit *n.* schriftliche Eideserklärung

affiliation *n.* Angliederung, Aufnahme

affinity *n.* Verwandtschaft

affirm *v.* behaupten, bejahen; bekräftigen; beteuern; (law) bestätigen; **–ation** *n.* Behauptung, Bejahung, Versicherung; Bekräftigung; (law) Bestätigung; **–ative** *adj.* bejahend; **–ative** *n.* Jawort; Bejahung

affix *n.* Anhang, Beilage; — *v.* anheften, befestigen; anhängen, beifügen; aufdrücken

afflict *v.* betrüben, kränken; peinigen, quälen, heimsuchen; **–ed with** heimgesucht von; **–ion** *n.* Betrübnis, Schmerz, Elend, Not, Pein

affluence *n.* Überfluss, Reichtum

afford *v.* sich leisten, erschwingen; gewähren, bieten

affront *n.* Beleidigung, Schimpf; — *v.* beschimpfen, beleidigen

afghan *n.* gestrickte (*or* gehäkelte) Decke

afield *adv.* vom rechten Wege ab; (von Hause) weg; ins Feld; im Felde

afire *adj.* brennend; in Flammen

aflame *adj.* in Flammen; brennend, lodernd

afloat *adj.* flott, schwimmend; umlaufend, im Gange

afoot *adv.* zu Fuss; in Bewegung, im Gange

aforesaid *adj.* vorher erwähnt, vorerwähnt

afraid *adj.* ängstlich, erschrocken; besorgt, bange; **be** — of sich fürchten (*or* Angst haben) vor

after *prep.* nach; hinter; gemäss; — **all** nach alledem; schliesslich; eben doch; — **that** nachher, danach, daraufhin; — **this** in Zukunft; **day** — **day** Tag für Tag; **day** — **tomorrow** übermorgen; **look** — sich kümmern um; **one** — **the other** hintereinander; **take** — ähneln; — *conj.* nachdem; — *adv.* darauf, nachher, hinterher; **–ward(s)** *adv.* nachher, danach, hierauf, später

aftereffect *n.* Nachwirkung

afterglow *n.* Nachglanz, Abglanz; Abendrot

afterlife *n.* späteres (*or* zukünftiges) Leben

aftermath *n.* Folgen, Nachwirkungen;

Nachernte

afternoon *n.* Nachmittag; **this — heute nachmittag**

afterthought *n.* nachträglicher Einfall

again *adv.* wieder(um), von neuem, nochmals; zurück; ausserdem, dagegen;— **and — immer wieder**

against *prep.* gegen, wider; vor, an, bei

age *n.* Alter, Lebenszeit; Zeit(alter), Epoche; Geschlecht; **in —s seit einer Ewigkeit; of — mündig, volljährig; old — hohes Alter, Greisenalter; under — unmündig; — *v.* altern, alt werden; -ed** *adj.* alt, bejahrt

agency *n.* Agentur, Vermittlung

agenda *n.* Agenda, Tagesordnung

agent *n.* Vertreter, Agent; Geschäftsträger; (chem.) wirkende Kraft, Agens

aggravate *v.* erschweren, verstärken, verschlimmern; (fig.) reizen, ärgern

aggravating *adj.* erschwerend, verschärfend; (fig.) ärgerlich, unangenehm; verdriesslich

aggravation *n.* Erschwerung, Verschlimmerung; Verärgerung

aggregate *n.* Aggregat, Anhäufung; Masse, Summe; **in the — insgesamt, im ganzen**

aggression *n.* Angriff, Anfall

aggressive *adj.* angreifend streitlustig

aggressor *n.* Angreifer, Aggressor

aggrieve *v.* betrüben, kränken; bedrücken

aghast *adj.* bestürzt, entsetzt

agile *adj.* flink, behend, gewandt, agil

agility *n.* Behendigkeit, Beweglichkeit

agitate *v.* bewegen, schütteln; agitieren, werben; aufregen, beunruhigen

agitation *n.* Unruhe, Aufregung; Agitation

agitator *n.* Agitator, Aufwiegler, Hetzer

aglow *adv.* and *adj.* (er)glühend; gerötet

agnostic *n.* Agnostiker; — *adj.* agnostisch

ago *adv.* vergangen, vorüber; vor; **long — vor langer Zeit; not long — vor kurzem**

agonize *v.* (mit dem Tode) ringen; quälen

agonizing *adj.* qualvoll, schmerzlich

agony *n.* Qual, Seelenangst

agrarian *adj.* agrarisch, landwirtschaftlich

agree *v.* einverstanden sein; übereinstimmen; **— on sich einigen über; — with übereinstimmen mit; zuträglich sein, zusagen; -able** *adj.* angenehm, gefällig; **-ment** *n.* Übereinkommen, Vereinbarung; Abkommen, Vertrag, Abmachung; **be in —ment** (sich) einig sein; **by —ment laut Übereinkommen, im Einverständnis**

agricultural *adj.* landwirtschaftlich

agriculture *n.* Landwirtschaft, Ackerbau

agrobiology *n.* Pflanzenernährungskunde

aground *adv.* gestrandet, aufgelaufen

ague *n.* Schüttelfrost, Wechselfieber

ahead *adv.* nach vorn, voraus, vorwärts; **get — vorwärtskommen; go — weitermachen; vorwärts streben; vorangehen; straight — geradeaus**

aid *n.* Hilfe, Beistand; Hilfsmittel; — *v.* helfen, beistehen

aide(-de-camp) *n.* Adjutant

ail *v.* unpässlich sein; **what —s you? was fehlt dir? -ing** *adj.* leidend, kränklich, unpässlich; **-ment** *n.* Krankheit, Leiden

aileron *n.* Quersteuer

aim *n.* Ziel, Zweck, Absicht; — *v.* zielen; trachten, beabsichtigen; (mil.) visieren; **-less** *adj.* ziellos, zwecklos

air *n.* Luft; Miene, Gebärde; Melodie, Lied; (fig.) Öffentlichkeit; **give oneself —s, put on —s sich grosstun (*or* aufspielen); in the open — im Freien, unter freiem Himmel; — base Luftstützpunkt; Flughafen; — blast Windstoss; — brake Luftdruckbremse; — chamber Luftkammer; Windkammer; — corps Luftwaffe; — cushion Luftkissen; — force Luftwaffe; — gun Luftgewehr; — hole Luftloch; — lift Luftbrücke; — mail Luftpost, Flugpost; — passage Luftkanal; — power Luftmacht; — pump Luftpumpe; — raid Luftangriff, Fliegerangriff; — shaft Luftschacht, Wetterschacht; — valve Luftventil; — *v.* (aus)lüften; abkühlen, trocknen; (fig.) veröffentlichen; -ing** *n.* Lüftung; (fig.) Spaziergang; **-y** *adj.* luftig; leicht, dünn; (fig.) munter, leichtsinnig

airborne *adj.* auf dem Luftwege transportiert

airbrush *n.* pneumatischer Zerstäuber

air-condition *v.* mit einer Klimaanlage versehen; **-ing** *n.* Klimaanlage

air-cool *v.* luftkühlen

aircraft *n.* Flugzeug; **— carrier Flugzeugträger, Flugzeugmutterschiff**

airfield *n.* Flugplatz, Flugfeld

air-launch *n.* Raketenabschuss vom Flugzeug

airline *n.* Luftverkehrslinie; **-r** *n.* Verkehrsflugzeug

air lock *n.* Eintrittsschleuse

air meet *n.* Luftkampf; Luftschau

airplane *n.* Flugzeug

air pocket *n.* Luftloch

airport *n.* Flughafen

airship *n.* Luftschiff

airtight *adj.* hermetisch, luftdicht

airway *n.* Wetterschacht; Luftweg, Fluglinie; (rad.) Welle

aisle *n.* Gang; Seitenschiff

ajar *adj.* angelehnt, halb offen

alacrity *n.* Bereitwilligkeit, Lebhaftigkeit

alarm n. Alarm: Lärm; (mil.) Warnruf; (fig.) Furcht, Besorgnis; **fire** — Feueralarm; **sound the** — (mil.) Alarm schlagen (or blasen); — adj. — **clock** Wecker; — v. alarmieren, lärmen; beunruhigen, erschrecken; **-ing** adj. beunruhigend, erschreckend; **-ist** n. Miesmacher, Bangemacher

alas! interj. ach! o weh! leider!

album n. Stammbuch; Gästebuch; Album

albumen n. Albumin, Fiweisstoff, Eiweiss

alcohol n. Alkohol; **rubbing** — Alkohol zum Einreiben; **-ic** n. Alkoholiker; **-ic** adj. alkoholisch

alderman n. Stadtverordnete, Ratsherr; Aldermann

alert adj. wachsam, aufgeweckt; flink; munter; **be on the** — sich bereithalten, auf der Hut sein; **-ness** n. Wachsamkeit, Flinkheit; Munterkeit

alga n. Alge

algebra n. Algebra

alias n. angenommener Name, Pseudonym, Künstlername; — adj. sogenannt, alias

alibi n. Alibi

alien n. Fremde, Ausländer; — adj. fremd, ausländisch; andersartig; **-ate** v. entfremden, abspenstig machen

alight v. absteigen, aussteigen, absitzen; sich niederlassen, landen

align v. ausrichten; in Linie bringen; **-ment** n. Ausrichten; Richtung

alike adj. ähnlich, gleich; — adv. ebenso, in gleicher Weise; gleichmässig

alimentary adj. nährend, nahrhaft; — **canal** Verdauungskanal

alimony n. Unterhaltsbeitrag; pl. Alimente

alive adj. lebendig; lebhaft, munter; (fig.) empfänglich; **be** — leben, am Leben sein; **be** — **with** belebt sein von; wimmeln von; **keep** — am Leben bleiben; über Wasser halten

alkali n. Alkali, Laugensalz; **-ne** adj. alkalisch, laugenhaft

all adj. ganz; alle; — **kinds** (oder **sorts**) **of** allerlei; — **the world** die ganze Welt, jedermann; — **year** (**round**) das ganze Jahr (hindurch); **by** — **means** gewiss; auf jeden Fall; **for** — **that** trotzdem; **for** — **the world** durchaus, gerade; **on** — **fours** auf allen Vieren; **one and** — alle insgesamt; **that is** — punktum, genug; **with** — **my heart** aus vollem Herzen; — adv. ganz, gänzlich, völlig; **above** — vor allem, vor allen Dingen; **after** — schliesslich, letzten Endes; **along** (schon) immer, die ganze Zeit über; — **around** ringsumher; — **at once**

auf einmal, plötzlich; — **clear** die Luft ist rein; Fntwarnung; — **gone fort,** hin, alle; — **in ganz** kaputt, hin; (—) **in** — im ganzen, alles in allem; — **of a sudden** mit einem Mal, ganz plötzlich; — **out** ganz dafür, unbedingt; — **over** überall; — **right** schön, gut; in Ordnung; — **the better** um so besser; — **the same** trotzdem; ganz gleich; — **told** alles in allem, im ganzen genommen; **at** — überhaupt, durchaus; **for** — I **know** soviel ich weiss; **not at** — überhaupt nicht, keineswegs, gar nicht; **nothing at** — gar nichts; **once and for** — ein für allemal

allege v. behaupten, anführen; **-ed** adj. angeblich

allegiance n. Treue, Gehorsam

allegory n. Allegorie, Sinnbild

allergic adj. allergisch, überempfindlich

allergy n. Allergie

alleviate v. erleichtern, mildern, lindern

alley n. Gasse, Durchgang, Gang; Allee

alliance n. Allianz, Bündnis; (fig.) Verwandtschaft

allied adj. verbündet, alliiert; (fig.) verwandt, verbunden

alligator n. Alligator, Krokodil

alliteration n. Alliteration, Stabreim

allocate v. zuteilen, anweisen

allocation n. Zuteilung, Anweisung

allot v. zuteilen; austeilen

all-out adj. vollkommen, mit voller Kraft; erschöpft

allow v. erlauben, gestatten; anrechnen, ansetzen; — **oneself** sich gönnen; **-able** adj. zulässig, erlaubt; **-ance** n. Taschengeld; (com.) Abzug, Rabatt; (fig.) Rücksicht, Nachsicht; **make -ance for** zugute halten

alloy n. Legierung, Mischung; — v. legieren, (ver)mischen

all-round adj. vieseitig, in allen Sätteln gerecht

allspice n. Piment

all-time adj. allzeitig

allude v. hinweisen, anspielen

alluring adj. verlockend, reizend

allusion n. Hinweis, Anspielung

ally n. Verbündete, Alliierte, Bundesgenosse; — v. verbünden, vereinigen; verbinden

almanac n. Almanach, Kalender

almighty adj. allmächtig

almond n. Mandel; — **brittle** Mandelnougatstücke; — **tree** Mandelbaum

almost adv. fast, beinahe

alms n. Almosen

alone adj. allein, einzeln, einzig; — adv. einfach, nur; **let** (oder **leave**) — in Ruhe

(or Frieden) lassen
along adv. entlang, dahin, weiter; längs:
all — schon immer; **get** — **with aus-**
kommen mit; **take** — mitnehmen; —
prep. entlang, längs
alongside adv. längsseits, Seite an Seite
aloof adv. fern, von ferne; weitab
aloud adv. laut, hörbar
alphabet n. Alphabet; **-ic(al)** adj. alphabetisch
already adv. bereits, schon
also adv. auch, ebenfalls; ausserdem
altar n. Altar
alternate n. Stellvertreter; — v. abwechseln; — adj. abwechselnd, wechselseitig; **on** — **days** einen Tag um den
anderen
alternating adj. wechselnd; — **current**
Wechselstrom
alternative n. Alternative, Auswahl; —
adj. alternativ, abwechselnd
altimeter n. Höhenmesser
although conj. obgleich, wenn auch,
obwohl
altitude n. Höhe; — **chamber** n. Unterdruckkammer
alto n. Alt(stimme)
altogether adv. insgesamt; durchaus
altruism n. Altruismus; Nächstenliebe,
Uneigennützigkeit
alum n. Alaun
aluminum n. Aluminium
always adv. immer, stets, jederzeit
a.m., A.M. abbr. am Vormittag, vormittags
amalgamate v. (sich) verschmelzen
amass v. anhäufen, ansammeln
amateur n. Amateur, Liebhaber; Dilettant; **-ish** adj. dilettantisch
amaze v. in Erstaunen setzen, verblüffen;
-ment n. Erstaunen, Verwunderung
amazing adj. erstaunlich, wunderbar,
verblüffend
ambassador n. Gesandte, Botschafter
amber n. Bernstein; Bernsteingelb; —
adj. bernsteinfarben, bernsteinen;
Bernstein-
ambiguity n. Zweideutigkeit, Doppelsinn
ambiguous adj. zweideutig; zweifelhaft;
ambition n. Ehrgeiz, Streben
ambitious adj. ehrgeizig, begierig
ambivalent adj. zweiwertig, doppelwertig
ambivert adj. zweigesichtig; einen ge-
spaltenen Charakter habend
amble v. im Passgang gehen (or reiten)
ambulance n. Anbulanz, Krankenwagen
ambush n. Hinterhalt, Versteck, Lauer;
— v. auflauern; überfallen
amen n. Amen; — adv. amen, so soll es
sein; so ist es

amenable adj. zugänglich, willfährig
amend v. berichtigen, abändern; verbessern; **-ment** n. Frgänzung, Änderung;
(pol.) Verbesserungsantrag
amends n. Ersatz, Genugtuung; (law)
Vergütung, Frstattung; **make** — ersetzen, wiedergutmachen
amenity n. Annehmlichkeit
America n. Amerika; **-n** n. (male) Ameri-
kaner; (female) Amerikanerin; **-n** adj.
amerikanisch
americanize v. amerikanisieren
amethyst n. Amethyst
amiable adj. freundlich, liebenswürdig
amicable adj. freundschaftlich, friedlich
amid(st) prep. inmitten, mitten unter
ammonia n. Ammoniak; **liquid** — Sal-
miakgeist
ammunition n. Munition, Schiessbedarf
amnesia n. Amnesie, Gedächtnisverlust
amnesty n. Amnestie, Straferlass, Begnadigung
amoeba n. Amöbe
amoebic dysentery n. Amöbenruhr
among(st) prep. unter, zwischen; — **other**
things unter anderem; **from** — **aus**
. . . hervor
amorous adj. amorös; verliebt; Liebes-
amount n. Summe, Anzahl, Betrag; — v.
sich belaufen, betragen, ausmachen; —
to sich belaufen auf; **he** **-ed to very**
little er war nicht viel wert
ampere n. Ampere
amphibious adj. amphibisch
amphitheater n. Amphitheater
ample adj. weit; geräumig; genügend,
reichlich
amplification n. Erweiterung, Vergrösserung; Verstärkung
amplifier n. Verstärker
amplify v. erweitern, vergrössern, ausdehnen; ausführlich darstellen; (rad.)
verstärken
amplitude n. Weite, Umfang; —**modulation**
(rad.) Wellenschwingungsweite
amputate v. amputieren, abnehmen
amputation n. Amputation
amputee n. Amputierte
amuse v. unterhalten, amüsieren; — oneself sich die Zeit vertreiben; **-ment** n.
Unterhaltung, Amüsement; Zeitvertreib; Vergnügen; **-ment park** Vergnü-
gungspark
amusing adj. amüsant, unterhaltend
analysis n. Analyse, Zergliederung, Zer-
legung
analytical adj. analytisch
analyze v. analysieren, zergliedern, zerlegen
anarchy n. Anarchie, Gesetzlosigkeit

anatomical adj. anatomisch
anatomy n. Anatomie
ancestor n. Vorfahr, Ahnherr, Stammvater; pl. Ahnen
ancestral adj. angestammt, vererbt
ancestry n. Geschlecht, Geburt; Abstammung, Vorfahren
anchor n. Anker; (fig.) Zuflucht; lie (oder ride) at — vor Anker liegen; weigh — den Anker lichten; — v. (ver)ankern, vor Anker gehen; -age n. Ankerplatz
ancient adj. (ur)alt, ehrwürdig; ehemalig
and conj. und; — so on und so weiter
andiron n. Kaminbock
androsterone n. Androsteron (männliches Hormon)
anecdote n. Anekdote, Witz
anemometer n. Luftströmungsmesser, Anemometer
anemic adj. blutarm, anämisch
anesthesia n. Anästhesie; Unempfindlichkeit
anesthetic n. Betäubungsmittel
anew adv. wieder(um); noch einmal, von neuem
angel n. Engel; — food cake Mürbeteigkuchen; -ic(al) adj. engelhaft, engelgleich
anger n. Zorn, Wut, Unwille; — v. ärgern, erzürnen, verdriessen
angina n. Angina; — pectoris Angina Pektoris, Herzbräune
angiocardiogram n. Herzgefässbild(kurve)
angle n. Winkel, Ecke; — iron Angelhaken; from all -s von allen Seiten; — v. angeln; zu fangen suchen; -r n. Angler
angry adj. wütend, zornig, ärgerlich, böse; become — wütend werden, sich ärgern
anguish n. Angst, Pein, Qual; Seelenschmerz
angular adj. winkelig, eckig; ungelenk
animal n. Tier; — adj. tierisch, animalisch; Tier-; (fig.) sinnlich
animate v. beleben, beseelen; anregen, aufmuntern; -d adj. belebt, lebendig, lebhaft; beseelt
animation n. Belebung, Beseelung; (film) Trickzeichnung; (fig.) Lebhaftigkeit
anise n. Anis
ankle n. Fussknöchel, Fussgelenk, Enkel
annex n. Anhang, Zusatz; Nachtrag; (arch.) Anbau, Nebengebäude; — v. sich aneignen, annektieren, anhängen, beifügen; -ation n. Aneignung, Einverleibung, Annektierung; Anfügung, Beifügung
annihilate v. vernichten, zerstören; abschaffen
annihilation n. Vernichtung

anniversary n. Jahrestag, Jahresfeier
annotation n. Anmerkung, Note, Glosse
announce v. melden, anzeigen, ankündigen; -ment n. Anzeige, Ankündigung; -r n. Ansager
annoy v. belästigen, plagen, verdriessen; -ance n. Belästigung, Plage, Störung; -ing adj. lästig, ärgerlich
annual adj. jährlich, alljährlich; einjährig; — n. Jahrbuch; (bot.) einjährige Pflanze
annuity n. Jahresrente; Jahreszahlung; life — Lebensrente
annul v. aufheben, abschaffen; annullieren, für ungültig erklären; -ment n. Aufhebung, Abschaffung
anode n. Anode
anodize v. eloxieren, anodisieren
anoint v. salben, einbalsamieren
anomaly n. Anomalie, Abweichung
anon adv. sogleich, sofort; bald
anonymous adj. anonym, ungenannt
another adj. ein anderer (or zweiter); noch ein; one — einander, sich gegenseitig
anoxemia n. Sauerstoffmangel im Blut
anoxia n. Sauerstoffmangel
answer n. Antwort, Beantwortung; Resultat, Lösung; — v. (be)antworten, erwidern, entgegnen; -able adj. verantwortlich
ant n. Ameise
antagonism n. Antagonismus, Widerstand, Feindschaft
antagonist n. Antagonist, Widersacher, Gegner; -ic adj. antagonistisch, widerstreitend
antagonize v. vor den Kopf stossen
antartic adj. antarktisch
antecedent n. Vorausgehende; pl. frühere Ereignisse (or Umstände); Vorleben; — adj. früher; vorausgehend
antedate v. zurückdatieren; vorwegnehmen
antelope n. Antilope
antenna n. (rad.) Antenne; (zool.) Fühler
anteroom n. Vorzimmer
anthem n. Hymne
anthology n. Anthologie, Gedichtsammlung
anthracite n. Anthrazit
anthropology n. Anthropologie, Menschenkunde
antiaircraft adj. Flugabwehr-, Fliegerabwehr-, Flak-
antibiotic adj. antibiotisch; — n. Antibiotikum, keimtötende Bakterie
antibody n. Antikörper, Schutzstoff
anticipate v. vorwegnehmen, zuvorkommen; voraussehen
anticipation n. Erwartung, Vorgefühl

anticlimax n. Antiklimax, Niedergang
antidote n. Gegengift
anti-electron n. Gegenelektron
antifreeze n. Frostschutzmittel
antihistamine n. Antihistamin
antimissile n. Abwehrgeschoss
antimissile missile n. Raketenabwehr-
geschoss
antipathy n. Antipathie, Widerwille, Abneigung
antiproton n. Gegenelektrizitätsatom
antiquated adj. altmodisch, veraltet
antique n. Antike; — **dealer** Antiquitä-
tenhändler; — adj. antik
antiquity n. Altertum, Antiquität
anti-Semitic adj. antisemitisch
antiseptic adj. antiseptisch
antisocial adj. ungesellig, unsozial
antisubmarine adj. U-bootabwehr-
antitank adj. Panzerabwehr-
antithesis n. Gegensatz
antitoxin n. Gegengift
antitrust adj. gegen Kartelle gerichtet
antler n. Geweihsprosse; pl. Geweih
antonym n. Antonym, Gegenbegriff
anvil n. Amboss
anxiety n. Angst, Besorgnis; Beklemmung
anxious adj. ängstlich, bang; besorgt;
gespannt; **be — to do** begierig sein zu
tun
any adj. irgendein, irgendwelcher; jeder;
— **more** mehr; **not** — kein
anybody pron. irgendeiner; (irgend)je-
mand; jeder(mann)
anyhow adv. trotzdem; irgendwie
anyone pron. irgendeiner, (irgend)je-
mand; jeder(mann)
anything pron. (irgend)etwas; alles; —
but nichts weniger als; — **else** sonst
etwas; **not for** — um keinen Preis
anyway adv. jedenfalls, trotzdem; irgendwie
anywhere adv. irgendwo(hin)
apart adv. getrennt; auseinander; für sich,
beiseite; — **from** abgesehen von; **take**
— **auseinandernehmen; tell** — unterscheiden
apartment n. Wohnung; — **house** Mietshaus
apathetic adj. apathisch
apathy n. Apathie, Gleichgültigkeit
ape n. Affe; — v. nachahmen, nachäffen
apex n. Spitze, Gipfel
apiary n. Bienenhaus, Bienenstand
apiece adv. je, für das Stück
apogee n. Erdferne; höchster Punkt der
Flugbahn (Rakete)
apologize v. sich entschuldigen, um Entschuldigung bitten, Abbitte tun
apology n. Entschuldigung, Abbitte

apoplexy n. Schlag(anfall), Schlagfluss
apostle n. Apostel, Jünger
apothecary n. Apotheker
apparatus n. Apparat, Gerät, Vorrichtung
apparent adj. augenscheinlich, scheinbar,
offenbar; **-ly** adv. scheinbar, anscheinend
apparition n. Gespenst, Erscheinung
appeal n. dringende Bitte; Reiz, Anziehungskraft; (law) Berufung, Aufruf;
— v. ersuchen, dringend bitten; wirken,
gefallen; (law) Berufung einlegen,
appellieren; **-ing** adj. flehend; reizend
appear v. erscheinen, sich zeigen; scheinen; (law) sich stellen; (theat.) auftreten; **it** **-s that** es stellt sich heraus,
dass; **-ance** n. Erscheinen, Auftreten;
Erscheinung, Aussehen; Schein; **to all**
-ances allem Anschein nach
appease v. befriedigen, beruhigen, stillen,
mildern; beilegen; **-ment** n. Befriedigung, Beruhigung
append v. beifügen, anhängen; hinzufügen; **-age** n. Anhang, Anhängsel
appendectomy n. (med.) Blinddarmopera-
tion
appendicitis n. Blinddarmentzündung
appendix n. Blinddarm; (lit.) Anhang,
Zusatz
appetite n. Appetit
appetizer n. Vorspeise, Appetitanreger
appetizing adj. appetitlich
applaud v. Beifall spenden; loben, beklatschen
applause n. Beifall, Applaus
apple n. Apfel; — adj. — **pie** Apfelkuchen
applesauce n. Apfelmus
appliance n. Gerät, Vorrichtung
applicable adj. anwendbar, passend
applicant n. Antragsteller, Bewerber
application n. Bewerbung, Gesuch; Anwendung, Anlegung; Gebrauch; Fleiss;
(med.) Verband, Umschlag; — **blank**
Bewerbungsformular
applied arts n. pl. angewandte Künste;
Kunstgewerbe
apply v. anwenden, gebrauchen; sich
wenden; auflegen; — **for** sich bewerben
um; — **to** gelten für, sich beziehen auf
appoint v. ernennen; festsetzen, bestimmen; **-ment** n. Ernennung, Festsetzung, Bestimmung; Verabredung;
make an -ment sich berabreden; sich
anmelden
apposition n. **in** — beigefügt
appraisal n. Abschätzung, Taxierung
appraise v. abschätzen, taxieren; **-r** n.
Taxator
appreciable adj. merklich, schätzbar
appreciate v. würdigen; schätzen; wahr-

nehmen; aufwerten; — it für etwas dankbar sein

appreciation n. Dank, Anerkennung; Verständnis; Preissteigerung, Wertzunahme

appreciative adj. dankbar, anerkennend

apprehend v. ergreifen, verhaften; (fig.) erfassen, verstehen, befürchten

apprehension n. Besorgnis, Angst; Verhaftung, Fassungskraft

apprehensive adj. furchtsam, besorgt; **become** — argwöhnisch werden

apprentice n. Lehrling; — v. in die Lehre geben; **–ship** n. Lehre

approach n. Annäherung, Herannahen; Zugang, Auffahrt; (mil.) Laufgraben; **use the right** — richtig an die Sache herangehen; — v. näher kommen, sich nähern; sich wenden an; herantreten an

approbation n. Billigung, Genehmigung; Beifall

appropriate adj. angebracht, passend; — v. sich aneignen; bewilligen, aussetzen

appropriation n. Geldbewilligung; Aneignung; Verwendung

approval n. Billigung, Beifall; **on** — auf Probe, zur Ansicht

approve v. billigen, gutheissen

approximate v. (sich) nähern, nahe (or näher) bringen; — adj., **–ly** adv. annähernd

approximation n. Annäherung

apricot n. Aprikose, Marille

April n. April; — **shower** Aprilwetter

apron n. Schürze, Schurz; — **string** Schürzenband; **be tied to one's mother's** — **strings** ein Muttersöhnchen (or Mutterkind) sein

apropos adv. apropos; — **of** bezüglich; — adj. passend; —! interj. ja so! was ich noch sagen wollte! apropos!

apt adj. tüchtig, fähig; passend; geneigt

aptitude n. Fähigkeit, Tauglichkeit, Eignung; Geneigtheit

aquamarine n. Aquamarine; Meergrün

aquaplane n. Gleitbrett, Wellenreiter

aquarium n. Aquarium

aquatic adj. im Wasser lebend, Wasser-

aqueduct n. Aquädukt, Wasserleitung

aquiline adj. adlerartig, Adler-

arable adj. pflügbar, bestellbar, urbar

arbiter n. Schiedsrichter, Unparteiische; Gebieter

arbitrary adj. willkürlich, eigenwillig

arbitrate v. entscheiden, schlichten

arbitration n. Schiedsspruch, Entscheidung

arbor n. Laube

arc n. Bogen; (elec.) Lichtbogen

arcade n. Arkade, Bogengang

arch n. Bogen, Gewölbe; **fallen –es** Senkfüsse; — v. (sich) wölben; bogenförmig machen; — adj. schlau; schelmisch; **–ed** adj. gewölbt, bogenförmig; **–er** n. Bogenschütze; **–ery** n. Bogenschiessen, Kunst des Bogenschiessens

archaeology n. Archäologie, Altertumskunde

archaic adj. archaisch, altertümlich

archbishop n. Erzbischof

archduke n. Grossherzog; (Austrian) Erzherzog; (Russian) Grossfürst

architect n. Architekt, Baumeister; **–ural** adj. architektonisch, baulich; **–ure** n. Baukunst, Baustil; Architektur

archway n. Bogengang, überwölbter Torweg

arctic adj. arktisch

ardent adj. glühend, feurig; leidenschaftlich

ardor n. Eifer, Inbrunst; Glut

area n. Fläche; Flächeninhalt; Ausdehnung; Gebiet, Gegend, Areal

arena n. Kampfplatz, Arena

Argentine n. Argentinien

argue v. (sich) streiten, erörtern; behaupten; bestreiten

argument n. Argument; Auseinandersetzung, Erörterung, Wortwechsel; **–ation** n. Beweisführung

aria n. Arie

arise v. aufstehen, sich erheben; entstehen, aufkommen, auftauchen

aristocracy n. Aristokratie, Adel

aristocrat n. Aristokrat; **–ic** adj. aristokratisch, vornehm

arithmetic n. Arithmetik, Rechenkunst; **–al** adj. arithmetisch

ark n. Arche

arm n. Arm; Armstütze, Seitenlehne; (bot.) Ast, Zweig; (geog.) Abzweigung; pl. Waffen; Wappen; **be under** — unter Waffen stehen; **bear** — als Soldat dienen; **by force of** — mit bewaffneter Hand; **small** — Handfeuerwaffen; **up in** — in vollem Aufruhr, empört; — v. bewaffnen, rüsten

armament n. Aufrüstung; Kriegsausrüstung; Kriegsmacht; Bewaffnung

armature n. Rüstung, Waffen; Armature

armchair n. Lehnstuhl, Armsessel

armhole n. Armloch

armistice n. Waffenstillstand

armor n. Rüstung; Panzer; Panzerung; — **plate** Panzerplatte; — v. panzern

armory n. Arsenal, Zeughaus

armpit n. Achselhöhle

army n. Armee, Heer

aroma n. Aroma; **–tic** adj. aromatisch, würzig, wohlriechend

around *prep.* um . . . herum; — *adv.*
(rund)herum; ringsherum; umher; im
Kreise; von Ort zu Ort; nahebei, dabei,
in der Nähe; ungefähr

arouse *v.* aufwecken; erwecken, erregen

arrange *v.* einrichten, ordnen; ausmachen,
beilegen; (mus.) bearbeiten; **-ment** *n.*
Einrichtung, Ordnung, Anordnung;
(mus.) Bearbeitung; **make -ments**
Vorbereitungen treffen

arrears *n.* **in** — rückständig

arrest *n.* Arrest, Verhaftung; **under** — **in**
Arrest, verhaftet; — *v.* verhaften

arrival *n.* Ankunft, Auftreten; Ankömmling

arrive *v.* (an)kommen, erscheinen; — **at**
erreichen, erlangen; ankommen in

arrogance *n.* Arroganz, Anmassung

arrogant *adj.* arrogant, anmassend, hochmütig

arrow *n.* Pfeil

arrowhead *n.* Pfeilspitze

arsenal *n.* Arsenal, Zeughaus

arsenic *n.* Arsen

arson *n.* Brandstiftung

art *n.* Kunst; Geschicklichkeit; List,
Verschlagenheit; Kniff; *pl.* **the fine** —
die schönen Künste; **-ful** *adj.* listig,
schlau, verschlagen; **-isan** *n.* Handwerker, Kunsthandwerker; **-ist** *n.*
Künstler; **-istic** *adj.* künstlerisch; **-less**
adj. einfach, schlicht, kunstlos

arteriosclerosis *n.* Arterienverkalkung

artery *n.* Arterie, Pulsader

arthritis *n.* Gelenkentzündung, Gicht

artichoke *n.* Artischoke

article *n.* Gegenstand, Sache; Artikel,
Ware, Posten; (lit.) Aufsatz

articulate *adj.* artikuliert, deutlich, vernehmbar; — *v.* artikulieren, deutlich
aussprechen

artifact, artefact *n.* Kunsterzeugnis;
(archäologisch) primitiver Gebrauchsgegenstand

artifice *n.* Kunstgriff; Schlauheit, List

artificial *adj.* künstlich

artillery *n.* Artillerie

as *conj.* and *adv.* wie, (eben)so wie; so,
als; da, denn, weil; wenn, während;
was; — **far** — bis (zu); soweit; soviel;
— **far** — **I am concerned** was mich
betrifft, von mir aus; — **good** — so gut
wie; — **if** als ob (*or* wenn); — **soon** —
sobald, sowie; — **yet** bis jetzt, bisher

asbestos *n.* Asbest

ascend *v.* (hin)aufsteigen, besteigen;
hinauffahren; (time) hinaufreichen;
-ancy *n.* Überlegenheit, Einfluss

ascension *n.* Auffahrt, Aufsteigen; (rel.)
Himmelfahrt

ascent *n.* Aufstieg, Hinaufsteigen

ascertain *v.* ermitteln, feststellen; sich
vergewissern

ascetic *n.* Asket; — *adj.* asketisch

ascribe *v.* zuschreiben, beilegen, beimessen

ash *n.* Esche; *pl.* Asche, sterbliche Überreste; — **tray** Aschbecher; **Ash
Wednesday** Aschermittwoch; **-en** *adj.*
eschen; aschgrau, aschfarben

ashamed *adj.* beschämt, verschämt, **be**
— sich schämen

ashore *adv.* gelandet, gestrandet; am (*or*
ans) Ufer

Asia *n.* Asien

Asia Minor *n.* Kleinasien

aside *adv.* beiseite, abseits; getrennt;
seitwärts; — **from** abgesehen von; put
(*oder* set) — beiseitelegen; zurücklegen;
stand — zur Seite gehen (*or* treten)

asinine *adj.* eselhaft, dumm; Esels-

ask *v.* fragen, sich erkundigen; verlangen,
fordern; bitten, ersuchen; einladen,
auffordern; — **a question** eine Frage
stellen; — **for** fragen (*or* verlangen)
nach

askance *adv.* schief, quer; (coll.) scheel

askew *adv.* schief, von der Seite

asleep *adj.* and *adv.* schlafend; **be** —
schlafen, eingeschlafen sein; **fall** —
einschlafen

asparagus *n.* Spargel

aspect *n.* Anblick; Aussehen; Aussicht,
Lage; Gesichtspunkt, Vorzeichen

aspen *n.* Espe, Zitterpappel

aspersion *n.* Verleumdung, Schmähung

asphalt *n.* Asphalt

asphyxia *n.* Pulsstockung, Scheintod,
Erstickungstod; **-te** *v.* ersticken

asphyxiation *n.* Erstickung

aspiration *n.* Streben, Trachten, Sehnen

aspire *v.* streben, trachten

ass *n.* Esel; (fig.) Dummkopf

assail *v.* angreifen, überfallen, bestürmen;
-ant *n.* Angreifer

assassin *n.* Attentäter, Meuchelmörder;
-ate *v.* (meuchlerisch) ermorden; **-ation**
n. Ermordung, Attentat, Meuchelmord

assault *n.* Angriff, Anfall; Sturm, Bestürmung; (law) tätliche Beleidigung; —
and battery tätlicher Angriff; — *v.*
angreifen, bestürmen; (law) tätlich
beleidigen

assay *v.* proben, probieren, prüfen

assemblage *n.* Versammlung; Verbindung

assemble *v.* (sich) versammeln, zusammenrufen; zusammensetzen; (mech.)
montieren

assembly *n.* Versammlung, Gesellschaft;
(mech.) Montage, Montierung; (mil.)

Sammelsignal; (pol.) Repräsentantenhaus, Unterhaus; — line laufendes
Band; Fliessband

assert v. behaupten, erklären; verteidigen;
–ion n. Behauptung, Erklärung; Verteidigung

assess v. beteuern; (ab)schätzen, taxie-
ren; **–ment** n. Einschätzung; Steuer,
Abgabe; **-or** n. Assessor; **-or of taxes**
Steuereinschätzer, Taxator

asset n. Guthaben, Aktiva, Aktivbestand

assign v. erteilen, zuteilen, zuweisen;
auferlegen; ernennen, bestimmen; (law)
übertragen; (fig.) angeben; **–ment** n.
Aufgabe, Hausarbeit; Auftrag; Zuteilung, Zuweisung

assimilate v. (sich) assimilieren, einverleiben, anpassen

assimilation n. Assimilierung, Einverleibung, Anpassung

assist v. helfen, mitwirken, beistehen;
–ance n. Hilfe, Mitwirkung, Beistand;
–ant n. Gehilfe, Beistand, Assistent

associate n. Teilhaber, Kompagnon, Gesellschafter, Partner; Kollege, Genosse;
— v. verkehren, (sich) verbinden; —
adj. verbunden, assoziiert, verbündet;
begleitend

association n. Vereinigung, Verein, Verband, Gesellschaft; Verbindung

assort v. sortieren, ordnen; **–ed** adj. gemischt; **–ment** n. Auswahl, Sortiment

assume v. annehmen, voraussetzen; übernehmen; sich anmassen; **–d** adj. angenommen

assumption n. Annahme, Voraussetzung;
Übernehmen

assurance n. Versicherung, Zusicherung,
Gewähr; Selbstvertrauen

assure v. sichern; versichern; **–d** adj.
selbstbewusst; **–dly** adv. sicherlich,
gewiss

asterisk n. (typ.) Sternchen

asthma n. Asthma, Atemnot

astigmatism n. Sehstörungen

astonish v. in Erstaunen setzen, staunen;
–ing adj. erstaunlich, wunderbar;
–ment n. Erstaunen, Überraschung,
Verwunderung

astound v. in Staunen (or Schrecken)
versetzen, verblüffen

astray adv. irre, vom rechten Wege ab;
go — irregehen, fehlgehen; lead —
irreführen; verführen

astrobiology n. Astrobiologie

astrology n. Astrologie, Sterndeuterei

astronaut n. Weltraumfahrer, Astronaut

astronavigation n. Weltraumnavigation

astronomer n. Astronom, Sternenforscher

astronomy n. Astronomie, Sternenkunde

astrophysics n. Astrophysik

asunder adj. getrennt, auseinander

asylum n. Asyl; (fig.) Zufluchtsort;
insane (oder lunatic) — Irrenhaus

at prep. an, aus, bei, durch, für, in, mit,
nach, über, um; von, vor, zu; — **all**
überhaupt; — **all costs** um jeden Preis;
— **all events** auf jeden Fall, jedenfalls;
— **best** bestenfalls; — **first** zuerst; —
home daheim, zuhause; — **large in**
Freiheit, frei; — **last** endlich; — **least**
wenigstens, mindestens; — **length**
schliesslich; — **most** höchstens; —
noon mittags; — **once** sofort; auf
einmal; — **peace** im Frieden; — **pleas-**
ure nach Belieben; — **your** (oder **our**)
house bei dir (or uns); — **sea** auf See;
(fig.) ratlos, ungewiss; — **stake** auf dem
Spiel(e); — **that** dabei; — **times** zuweilen; — **war** im Krieg(e); — **will** nach
Belieben; — **work** bei der Arbeit; —
your service zu Ihren (or deinen)
Diensten

atheism n. Atheismus, Gottesleugnung

atheist n. Atheist, Gottesleugner

athlete n. Athlet; **—'s foot** ringförmige
Fussflechte

athletic adj. athletisch; kräftig, stark; —
n. (pl.) Athletik

atlas n. Atlas, Kartenwerk

atmosphere n. Atmosphäre

atoll n. Atoll, Koralleninsel

atom n. Atom; — **bomb** (A-bomb) Atom-
bombe; **–ic** adj. atomisch; **–ic energy**
Atomenergie, Atomkraft; **–ic pile**
Atomsäule

atomizer n. Zerstäuber

atone v. büssen, sühnen; **–ment** n. Busse,
Sühne; Genugtuung; (rel.) Versöhnung,
Sühneopfer; **Day of Atonement** Ver-
söhnungstag

atrocious adj. abscheulich, grässlich,
grausam

atrocity n. Greueltat, Abscheulichkeit,
Barbarei

attach v. befestigen, verknüpfen, anhängen, anheften; zuteilen; pfänden lassen;
— **importance** Bedeutung beilegen; **–ed**
adj. be **–ed to** hängen an, gehören zu;
–ment n. Zuneigung, Anhänglichkeit

attaché n. Attaché, Gesandtschaftsrat

attack n. Angriff; (med.) Anfall; — v.
angreifen, anpacken; (med.) befallen

attain v. erreichen, erlangen, gewinnen;
–able adj. erreichbar; **–ment** n. Erreich-
ung, Erlangung; Gewinn; **–ment** pl.
Kenntnisse, Fertigkeiten

attempt n. Versuch, Anschlag; Attentat;
— v. versuchen, wagen

attend v. beiwohnen, anwesend sein,

besuchen; (med.) behandeln, pflegen; aufwarten; — to erledigen; –ance n. Bedienung; Anwesenheit, Besuch, Zuhörerschaft; –ant n. Wärter, Diener; –ant adj. begleitend, anwesend; diensttuend

attention n. Aufmerksamkeit, Achtung; call — to hinweisen (or Aufmerksamkeit lenken) auf; give — to aufmerksam sein; pay — aufpassen; pay — to beachten, achtgeben auf; (fig.) den Hof machen; pay no — ignorieren; stand at — strammstehen

attentive adj. aufmerksam, achtsam; be — aufmerksam sein; (fig.) den Hof machen

attest v. bezeugen, beglaubigen, bescheinigen

attic n. Dachstube, Boden; pl. Dachgeschoss

attire n. Kleidung, Tracht; — v. (an)kleiden, schmücken

attitude n. Haltung, Stellung, Lage

attorney n. Anwalt; — at law Rechtsanwalt; **Attorney General** Justizminister; power of — schriftliche Vollmacht

attract v. anziehen, reizen, fesseln; — attention Aufmerksamkeit erregen; without –ing attention unauffällig; –ion n. Anziehung(skraft), Reiz; (theat.) Glanznummer, Attraktion; –ive adj. anziehend, vorteilhaft, verlockend; attraktiv

attribute n. Eigenschaft; Merkmal, Attribut; Eigenschaftswort; — v. zuschreiben, beimessen, beilegen

auburn n. Rotbraun, Kastanienbraun; — adj. rotbraun, kastanienbraun

auction n. Auktion, Versteigerung; — v. (ver)auktionieren, versteigern; –eer n. Auktionator, Versteigerer

audacity n. Kühnheit, Unverschämtheit, Frechheit

audible adj. hörbar, vernehmbar, vernehmlich

audience n. Publikum; Zuhörer(schaft); Zuschauer; Audienz, Empfang

audiophile n. Tonfanatiker, Audiophile

audit n. Rechnungsprüfung; — v. Rechnungen (or Bücher) prüfen; (educ.) als Gasthörer studieren; –or Bücherrevisor, Rechnungsprüfer; Zuhörer

audition n. Vorsprechen, Vorsingen

auditorium n. Auditorium, Hörsaal

auditory adj. Gehör; — nerve Gehörnerv

auger n. Bohrer; (avi.) abtrudeln

aught n. Etwas; (math.) Null; — adv. etwas, irgendetwas, irgendwie

augment v. zunehmen, vermehren, vergrössern

august adj. erhaben, herrlich, hehr

August n. August

aunt n. Tante

aura n. Hauch, Duft

aureomycin n. Aureomyzin

auspices n. pl. Auspizien, Vorbedeutungen; under the — of unter dem Schutz(e) von

auspicious adj. günstig, glücklich

austere adj. streng, ernst, hart; herb; mässig, enthaltsam

austerity n. Strenge, Ernst, Härte; Mässigkeit, Enthaltsamkeit

Austria n. Österreich

authentic adj. zuverlässig, glaubwürdig, verbürgt; echt; –ate v. verbürgen, als echt erweisen; –ity n. Glaubwürdigkeit, Echtheit

author n. Autor, Verfasser; Schriftsteller

authoritative adj. autorisiert, bevollmächtigt

authorities n. pl. Behörde

authority n. Autorität; Befugnis, Gewalt; Ansehen; Glaubwürdigkeit; Quelle; on one's own — auf eigene Verantwortung; without — umberechtigt

authorization n. Ermächtigung, Bevollmächtigung

authorize v. berechtigen, ermächtigen, autorisieren

autobiography n. Autobiographie

autocracy n. Autokratie

autocrat n. Autokrat; –ic adj. autokratisch

autogiro n. Hubschrauber, Windmühlenflugzeug

autograph n. Autogramm; Originalhandschrift; Urschrift; — v. eigenhändig unterschreiben

automatic n. Selbstladepistole; — adj. automatisch; –ally adv. mechanisch

automation n. Automation, Automatisierung

automaton n. Automat; Robot(er)

automobile n. Automobil, Wagen

automotive adj. mit Selbstantrieb; Automobil-

autonomy n. Selbstverwaltung, Autonomie

autopsy n. Autopsie, Leichenschau

autumn n. Herbst; –al adj. herbstlich

auxiliary n. Helfer, Beistand; Verbündete; — adj. helfend, Hilfs-; — forces Hilfstruppen; — verb Hilfszeitwort

avail n. Nutzen, Vorteil; — v. nützen, helfen; — oneself of Gebrauch machen von, benutzen; –able adj. verfügbar, erhältlich, zugänglich

avalanche n. Lawine

avenge v. rächen, ahnden; –r n. Rächer

avenue *n.* Strasse, Chaussee, Allee, Promenade

average *n.* Durchschnitt; **on the —** durchschnittlich; — *adj.* durchschnittlich; — *v.* im Durchschnitt rechnen; durchschnittlich betragen (*or* arbeiten, zahlen)

averse *adj.* abgeneigt, widerwillig

aversion *n.* Abneigung, Widerwille(n), Aversion, Abscheu

avert *v.* ablenken, abwenden, verhüten

aviary *n.* Vogelhaus

aviation *n.* Flugwesen, Fliegerei; Aviatik

aviator *n.* Flieger; Aviatiker

avocado *n.* Avokado (Birne)

avocation *n.* Steckenpferd, Zeitvertreib; Nebenbeschäftigung

avoid *v.* (ver)meiden, scheuen, entgehen; **–able** *adj.* vermeidlich, vermeidbar; **–ance** *n.* Vermeidung, Meiden

await *v.* erwarten, entgegensehen

awake *v.* (er)wecken; erwachen; — *adj.* wach, munter; aufgeweckt; **–n** *v.* (er)wecken

award *n.* Preis; Urteil, Entscheidung; — *v.* zuerkennen, zusprechen; gewähren

aware *adj.* bewusst; **be — of** Kenntnis haben von, sich bewusst sein

away *adv.* (hin)weg, ab, fort; abwesend; auswärts, entfernt; — **from** entfernt (*or* abwesend) von; — **from home von** Hause fort; **far —** weit entfernt

awe *n.* Ehrfurcht, Furcht, Scheu

awe-struck *adj.* von Ehrfurcht (*or* Scheu) ergriffen

awful *adj.* furchtbar, schrecklich, entsetzlich

awhile *adv.* eine Weile (*or* Zeitlang)

awkward *adj.* ungeschickt, linkisch; plump; (fig.) peinlich, unangenehm

awl *n.* Ahle, Pfriem

awning *n.* Markise, Sonnensegel

ax(e) *n.* Axt, Beil

axiom *n.* Axiom, Grundsatz; **–atic** *adj.* grundsätzlich, unumstösslich

axis *n.* Achse, Mittellinie; Staatenbund

axle *n.* Achse

aye *adv.* ja

B

babble *n.* Geschwätz, Gewäsch; Murmeln; — *v.* schwatzen, plappern; stammeln; murmeln

babe *n.* Säugling, kleines Kind

babushka *n.* farbiges (*or* gemustertes) Kopftuch

baby *n.* Baby; Nesthäkchen; **— boy** Bübchen; **— buggy** Kinderwagen; **— carriage** Kinderwagen; **— girl** kleines

Mädchen; **— v.** verhätscheln, wie ein Baby behandeln; **— oneself sich verpimpeln; –hood** *n.* erste (*or* frühe) Kindheit, Säuglingsalter; **–ish** *adj.* kindisch, kindlich; einfältig

bachelor *n.* Junggeselle; (educ.) Bakkalaureus

bacillus *n.* Bazillus, Bazille, Mikrobe

back *n.* Rücken, Kreuz; Rückseite; Kehrseite; Lehne; (sports) Verteidiger; — **to —** Rücken an Rücken; **behind one's —** hinter jemandes Rücken; heimlich; **flat on one's —** bettlägrig; **his — is up** er ist aufgebracht; **turn one's —** den Rücken kehren; im Stich lassen; — *adj.* letzt, hinter; entlegen; rückständig; **— door** Hintertür; **— number alte** Nummer, frühere Ausgabe; **— payment** rückständige Zahlung; **— seat** Rücksitz; (fig.) untergeordnete Stellung; **— stairs** Hintertreppe; **— street** Hintergasse; **— talk** Widerspruch; — *adv.* zurück; wieder; vorher, früher; **— and forth** auf und ab, hin und her; (in) — of hinter; **come —** zurückkommen; **go —** zurückgehen, sich zurückziehen; **stand —!** zurück! **step —** zurücktreten; **— v.** beistehen, unterstützen; favorisieren; hinter (jemandem) stehen; rückwärtsfahren; zurückgehen, zurücktreten; **— up** zurückgehen, zurückfahren, rückwärtsfahren; **–er** *n.* Unterstützende, Beistand; (theat.) Geldgeber; **–ing** *n.* Unterstützung; (theat.) Finanzierung

backbone *n.* Rückgrat; (fig.) Willenskraft

backdrop *n.* Prospekt

backfire *n.* Frühzündung, Rückzündung

backgammon *n.* Puffspiel

background *n.* Hintergrund; (fig.) Vorbildung

backlog *n.* nicht ausgeführte Bestellungen (*or* Arbeiten)

backslide *v.* abfallen; rückfällig werden

backspin *n.* (sports) Rückwärtsdrehung; **put a — on a ball** dem Ball eine Rückwärtsdrehung geben

backstage *adv.* (theat.) hinter den Kulissen

backstop *n.* Ballfänger

backstroke *n.* Rückenschwimmen

backward *adj.* rückwärts gerichtet; langsam, träge; rückständig; zurückgeblieben; schüchtern; **–s** *adv.* rückwärts, zurück; nach hinten; verkehrt; **— and forward** hin und her

backwoodsman *n.* Hinterwäldler

bacon *n.* Speck

bacteria *n. pl.* Bakterien; **–l** *adj.* bakteriell

bacteriology *n.* Bakteriologie

bad *adj.* schlecht, schlimm; arg, böse; übel, lasterhaft; ungesund; minderwertig; — **debt** uneinbringliche Schuld; **from** — **to worse** aus dem Regen in die Traufe, immer schlimmer; **have a** — **cold** stark erkältet sein; **too** — **zu** schade; **-ly** *adv.* schlecht; ernstlich, dringend, sehr; **he is -ly off** es geht ihm sehr schlecht; **I want this -ly** ich brauche dies sehr

badge *n.* Abzeichen, Dienstzeichen, Amtszeichen; (fig.) Kennzeichen, Merkmal

badger *n.* Dachs; — *v.* hetzen, plagen

badminton *n.* ein Federballspiel

baffle *v.* verspotten, vereiteln, verwirren; durchkreuzen

bag *n.* Sack, Tüte, Beutel, Tasche; Koffer; — **and baggage** Sack und Pack; **sleeping** — Schlafsack; **to be left holding the** — die Suppe auslöffeln müssen; — *v.* fangen, schiessen; (coll.) einstekken; **-gy** *adj.* bauschig, beutelig

baggage *n.* Gepäck; **excess** — Zusatzgepäck, Übergewicht; — **car** Gepäckwagen; — **check** Gepäckschein; — **master** Gepäckmeister; — **office** Gepäckaufgabe, Gepäckausgabe

bagpipe *n.* Dudelsack(pfeife)

bail *n.* Bürgschaft, Kaution; **be out on** — durch Kautionsstellung freikommen; **put up** — Kaution stellen; — *v.* ausschöpfen; — **out** Bürgschaft leisten für (avi.) mit dem Fallschirm abspringen

bailiff *n.* Gerichtsdiener

bait *n.* Köder, Lockspeise; (fig.) Lockung; — *v.* ködern, anlocken; (fig.) quälen, hetzen; — **one's hook with** an die Angel stecken

bake *v.* backen; braten; brennen; **-r** *n.* Bäcker; **-r's dozen** Bäcker Dutzend (13); **-ry** *n.* Bäckerei

baking *n.* Backen; Braten; Brennen; — *adj.* — **powder** Backpulver; — **soda** Speisesoda, Natron

balance *n.* Waage; Gleichgewicht; (com.) Bilanz, Rechnungsabschluss, Saldo, Bestand; Rest; **amount of** — Saldobetrag; — **of power** politisches Gleichgewicht, Kräfteausgleich; — **of trade** Handelsbilanz; — **sheet** Bilanzbogen; **his life hung in the** — er schwebte zwischen Tod und Leben; **strike a** — Bilanz ziehen; — *v.* (aus)balancieren; (com.) ausgleichen, Bilanz ziehen, saldieren

balcony *n.* Balkon; (theat.) Rang

bald *adj.* kahl, kahlköpfig; (fig.) nackt, unverhüllt; — **spot** kahle Stelle, Glatze; **-ness** *n.* Kahlheit; (fig.) Nacktheit

bale *n.* Ballen, Bündel; — *v.* in Ballen (*or* Bündel) packen; ballen, bündeln

balk *v.* aufhalten, durchkreuzen, verhindern

ball *n.* Kugel, Ball; Knäuel; **keep the** — **rolling** im Gang erhalten; —**bearing** Kugellager

ballad *n.* Ballade

ballast *n.* Ballast; (rail.) Schotter

ballerina *n.* Ballerina, Ballettänzerin

ballet *n.* Ballett; — **dancer** Ballettänzer

ballistic missile *n.* ferngelenktes Raketengeschoss

ballistics *n.* Schiesslehre; Wurflehre

balloon *n.* Ballon, Luftballon

ballot *n.* Stimmzettel; Wahlkugel; Wahl (durch Abgabe von Kugeln), Abstimmung; — **box** Wahlurne; **secret** — geheime Wahl; — *v.* abstimmen, wählen

ballplayer *n.* Ballspieler

ball-point pen *n.* Kugelschreiber

ballroom *n.* Tanzsaal, Ballsaal

ballyhoo *n.* Marktschreierei

balm *n.* Balsam, Linderung, Trost; **-y** *adj.* balsamisch, duftend, lindernd; (coll.) verrückt

balsam *n.* Balsam

Baltic Sea *n.* Ostsee

balustrade *n.* Balustrade, Geländer

bamboo *n.* Bambus, Bambusrohr

bamboozle *v.* betrügen, beschwindeln

ban *n.* Bann, Verbannung; — *v.* bannen, ächten; verbieten

banana *n.* Banane

band *n.* Band, Schnur; Gürtel; Borte, Streifen; (mus.) Kapelle; (fig.) Schar, Bande; — **leader** Kapellmeister; — **wagon** (pol. coll.) Triumpfwagen; — *v.* — **together** sich vereinigen

bandage *n.* Verband, Binde, Bandage; — *v.* verbinden, bandagieren

bandbox *n.* Hutschachtel, Putzschachtel

bandit *n.* Bandit

bandstand *n.* Musikpavillon

bang *n.* Schlag, Hieb, Knall; Ponyfrisur; — *v.* (zu)schlagen; knallen, krachen; — **around** (**up**) misshandeln; —! *interj.* bums! krach!

banish *v.* verbannen; **-ment** *n.* Verbannung

banister *n.* Geländer

bank *n.* Bank; Spielbank; Ufer, Strand; Erhöhung; Damm, Böschung; — **account** Bankkonto; — **bill** Bankwechsel; — **note** Banknote; **savings** — Sparkasse; — *v.* auf die Bank bringen, hinterlegen; eindämmen; (fire) unterhalten; — **an airplane** mit dem Flugzeug zur Kurve ansetzen; — **on** bauen auf;

-er *n.* Bankier; Bankhalter; -ing *n.* Bankgeschäft; — house Bankhaus

bankbook *n.* Bankbuch

bankrupt *adj.* bankrott; zahlungsunfähig; — *n.* Bankrotteur, Gemeinschuldner; -cy *n.* Konkurs, Bankrott

banner *n.* Fahne, Flagge, Banner

banns *n. pl.* Aufgebot; **publish the —** aufbieten

banquet *n.* Bankett, Festmahl, Festessen; — *v.* bankettieren, festlich bewirten, schmausen

Bantam *n.* Bantamhuhn, Zwerghuhn

baptism *n.* Taufe; — **of fire** Feuertaufe

baptize *v.* taufen

bar *n.* Bar; Stange, Barre, Stab; Tafel; Büfett, Theke; (gymn.) Barren, Reck; (law) Schranke, Advokatur; (mus.) Takt, Taktstrich; (fig.) Hindernis, Querstrich; **be admitted to the — als** Rechtsanwalt zugelassen sein; **prisoner at the —** Gefangener vor Gericht; — *v.* verriegeln; vesperren; ausschliessen; -(ring) *prep.* ausser, ausgenommen -red *adj.* gestreift

barb *n.* Widerhaken, Stachel; -ed *adj.* mit Widerhaken versehen; -ed wire Stacheldraht

barbarian *n.* Barbar, Unmensch, Rohling; — *adj.* barbarisch, roh

barbarity *n.* Grausamkeit, Roheit; Barbarei

barbarous *adj.* barbarisch, roh

barbecue *n.* grosser Bratrost; im Ganzen gebratenes Tier; — *v.* im Ganzen braten

barber *n.* Friseur, Barbier; — shop Friseurladen

barbiturate *n.* Barbitursäure

bare *adj.* bar, nackt, unbekleidet; offen; leer; rein; kahl, entlaubt; — *v.* entblössen, enthüllen; -ly *adv.* kaum, knapp

barefaced *adj.* unverschämt, schamlos, frech

barefoot(ed) *adj.* barfuss, barfüssig

bareheaded *adj.* barhäuptig, mit blossem Kopf

barelegged *adj.* nacktbeinig, mit blossen Beinen

bargain *n.* Vertrag; Handel, Kauf, Geschäft; Gelegenheitskauf; — counter Ladentisch für herabgesetzte waren; **into the —** in den Kauf, obendrein; **it's a —!** abgemacht! — *v.* handeln, feilschen

barge *n.* Barke; Hausboot; Lastkahn

baritone *n.* Bariton

bark *n.* (bot.) Rinde, Borke; (dog) Bellen, Kläffen, Gebell; (naut.) Barke; **his — is worse than his bite** Hunde, die bellen, beissen nicht; — *v.* bellen, kläffen;

abstossen, abschürfen; — **at** anbellen; — **up the wrong tree** auf falscher Fährte sein

barley *n.* Gerste

barmaid *n.* Kellnerin, Bardame

barn *n.* Scheune, Scheuer

barnacle *n.* Entenmuschel; (fig.) Klette

barnyard *n.* Scheunenhof, Scheunenplatz

barometer *n.* Barometer

baron *n.* Baron, Freiherr; (fig.) Industriemagnat; -ess *n.* Baronin, Baronesse, Freifrau; -et *n.* Baronet

baroque *adj.* barock; (fig.) seltsam

barrack *n.* Baracke, Hütte. (agr.) Schober; *pl.* Kaserne; (coll.) Mietskaserne

barracuda *n.* Pfeilhecht

barrage *n.* Sperrfeuer; — balloon Sperrballon

barrel *n.* Tonne, Fass

barren *adj.* unfruchtbar; steril; kahl; trokken, unproduktiv; -ness *n.* Unfruchtbarkeit, Dürre, Dürftigkeit; Leere, Geistesarmut

barricade *n.* Barrikade, Sperre, Hindernis; — *v.* verbarrikadieren, versperren

barrier *n.* Schranke; Barriere; (mil.) Verschanzung; (rail.) Schlagbaum; (fig.) Hindernis

barroom *n.* Barraum, Schenkstube

bartender *n.* Barkellner

barter *n.* Tausch, Tauschhandel; — *v.* eintauschen, vertauschen; (coll.) verschachern

basal metabolism *n.* Stoffwechselbasis

base *n.* (arch.) Sockel; Fundament, Grundfläche; (avi., mil., naut.) Stützpunkt; (chem.) Base, Lauge; (geom.) Grundlinie; (sports) Mal; (fig.) Grundlage; — **hit** Treffer; — *v.* basieren, stützen, gründen, begründen; **be -d on** beruhen auf; — *adj.* klein, niedrig; gemein; (fig.) verächtlich; -less *adj.* grundlos; -ment *n.* Keller; -ness *n.* Niederträchtigkeit; Gemeinheit

baseball *n.* Baseball (amerikanisches Schlagballspiel)

baseboard *n.* untere Wandtäfelung, Wandsockel

bashful *adj.* scheu, schüchtern; -ness *n.* Scheu, Schüchternheit

basic *adj.* fundamental, grundlegend; (chem.) basisch

basin *n.* Becken, Bassin; (geol.) Flussbecken, Stromgebiet

basis *n.* Grundlage, Basis; Grund

bask *v.* sich wärmen (*or* sonnen)

basket *n.* Korb; -ful *n.* Korbvoll

basketball *n.* Korbball(spiel)

basket case *n.* (med.) Arm- und Beinamputierte

bas-relief *n.* Flachrelief
bass *n.* (ichth.) Barsch; (mus.) Bass, Bassist; — **clef** F-Schlüssel, Bassschlüssel; — **drum** Riesentrommel; — **horn** Tuba; — **viol** Violincello; — *adj.* niedrig, tief
bassoon *n.* Fagott
bastard *n.* Bastard, uneheliches Kind; — *adj.* unehelich; (fig.) falsch, unecht
baste *v.* (cooking) mit Fett übergiessen; (sewing) heften
bat *n.* (baseball) Schläger, Schlagholz; (zool.) Fledermaus; **be at** — am Schlagen (*or* an der Reihe) sein; **go to** — **for** unterstützen; — *v.* schlagen, treffen; **without** —**ting an eye** ohne mit der Wimper zu zucken; —**ter** *n.* (baseball) Schläger; (cooking) Teig; —**ter** *v.* zerschlagen, zertrümmern; klopfen, schlagen, stossen; —**ter down** einschlagen; —**ting** *n.* Schlagen (des Balles)
batch *n.* Schub; Menge; Trupp, Schicht
bath *n.* Bad; — **towel** Badetuch; —**e** *v.* baden; **be** —**ed in** umgeben sein von; **be** —**ed in tears** in Tränen schwimmen; —**ing** *n.* Bad, Baden; —**ing beach** Badestrand; —**ing cap** Badekappe; —**ing suit** Badeanzug, Schwimmanzug; —**ing trunks** Badehosen, Schwimmhosen
bathhouse *n.* Badeanstalt
bathrobe *n.* Bademantel
bathroom *n.* Badezimmer
bathtub *n.* Wanne, Badewanne
bathymetry *n.* Wassertiefenmessung
bathyscaphe *n.* Tiefenboot
baton *n.* Taktstock, Dirigentenstab; Stab
battery *n.* Batterie; (law) tätlicher Angriff; — **cell** Batterieelement; **dry** — Trockenelement; **the** — **is dead** die Batterie ist ausgebrannt (*or* tot)
battle *n.* Kampf, Schlacht, Gefecht; — **cry** Schlachtruf, Feldruf; — **front** Schlachtfront; — **royal** allgemeine Rauferei; **that's half the** — das heisst halb gewonnen; — *v.* kämpfen, streiten, fechten; — **it out** es austragen
battlefield *n.* Schlachtfeld
battleground *n.* Kriegsschauplatz
battleship *n.* Schlachtschiff
Bavaria *n.* Bayern
bawl *v.* schreien, brüllen, plärren; ausrufen, — **out** ausschimpfen
bay *n.* (arch.) Nische, Erker; (bot.) Lorbeer; (geog.) Bucht, Bai, Meerbusen; (horse) Fuchs; — **rum** Bairum, Pimentrum; — **window** Erkerfenster, Fensternische; **hold** (*oder* **keep**) **at** — in Schach halten, stellen; **stand at** — sich widersetzen. sich zur Wehr setzen; — *v.* bellen

bayonet *n.* Seitengewehr, Bajonett; — *v.* mit dem Bajonett niederstossen (*or* treiben)
bayou *n.* Nebenarm, Nebenfluss
bazaar *n.* Basar, Verkaufshalle
bazooka *n.* Panzerabwehrgeschütz, **Pak**
be *v.* sein, werden; existieren; — **ill** krank sein; — **in a hurry** es eilig haben; — **off** sich fortmachen; — **right** recht haben; — **well** sich wohl befinden (*or* fühlen), gesund sein; **that is to** — zukünftig; —**ing** *n.* Sein, Dasein, Existenz; (poet.) Wesen; **for the time** —**ing** einstweilen, augenblicklich
beach *n.* Strand, Ufer; — *v.* auf den Strand ziehen (*or* setzen, laufen lassen)
beachcomber *n.* Vagabund
beachhead *n.* Landungskopf
beacon *n.* Leuchtfeuer, Signalfeuer; Leuchtturm; (avi.) Kontroll- (*or* Warn-)station (Funk *or* Radar)
bead *n.* Glasperle, Perle; Kügelchen; Tropfen; *pl.* Halsband; Rosenkranz; —**work** *n.* Perlstickerei
beagle *n.* Vorstehhund, Spürhund
beak *n.* Schnabel; Tülle; —**er** *n.* Becher
beam *n.* (arch.) Baum; Balken; Schwelle; (naut.) Breite; (opt.) Strahl, Lichtstrahl; (rad.) Signal; (fig.) Glanz; — *v.* strahlen, glänzen; —**ing** *adj.* glänzend, strahlend, leuchtend
bean *n.* Bohne; **kidney** — Feuerbohne; **string** — grüne Bohne; **wax** — Wachsbohne
bear *n.* (zool.) Bär; (com.) Baissier; **grizzly** — Grizzlybär, Graubär; — *v.* tragen, ertragen; gebären; aushalten, leiden; überbringen; — **a grudge** nachtragen; — **down** überwinden; niederdrücken; — **in mind** nicht vergessen; — **oneself** sich benehmen; — **witness** Zeugnis ablegen; —**able** *adj.* ertragbar, erträglich; —**er** *n.* Träger, Überbringer; (com.) Wechselinhaber; —**ing** *n.* Haltung; (mech.) Lager; Beziehung, Verhältnis; **get one's** —**ings** sich orientieren, **have** —**ing on** zu tun haben mit; **lose one's** —**ings** seinen Halt verlieren
beard *n.* Bart; — *v.* Trotz bieten, entgegentreten; —**ed** *adj.* bärtig; —**less** *adj.* bartlos; (fig.) jugendlich
beast *n.* Tier, Vieh; Bestie; (fig.) roher (*or* brutaler) Mensch; — **of burden** Lasttier; —**liness** *n.* Bestialität; Roheit, Ekelhaftigkeit; —**ly** *adj.* bestialisch, viehisch; brutal, ekelhaft
beat *n.* Schlag; (mus.) Takt, Taktschlag; Runde, Rundgang, Revier; (coll.) Sphäre, Bereich; **dead** — Schmarotzer; — *v.* schlagen, prügeln; klopfen; rüh-

ren; besiegen; gewinnen; — **a path** einen Weg bahnen; — **around the bush** Umschweife machen; — **into shape** in richtige Form bringen; — **someone's brain out** jemandem den Schädel einschlagen; — **time** Takt schlagen; — **to it** zuvorkommen; — **up** verhauen, verprügeln; **that –s everything** das übertrifft alles; **that –s me** das geht über meinen Horizont; **–en** *adj.* geschlagen, besiegt; gebahnt, ausgetreten; **–en track** herkömmliche Art und Weise; **–er** *n.* Schläger, Schlegel, Stössel; (hunting) Treiber; **egg –er** Schneeschläger; **–ing** *n.* Schlagen, Prügeln; **give a good –ing** eine tüchtige Tracht Prügel verabreichen

beatify *v.* seligsprechen, seligmachen

Beatitudes *n. pl.* Seligpreisungen

beatnik *n.* Halbstarke, Neunik

beau *n.* Liebhaber, Anbeter

beautiful *adj.* schön, prächtig; (fig.) ausgezeichnet

beautify *v.* verschönern

beauty *n.* Schönheit; schöne Frau, Schöne; Pracht; — **parlor**, — **shop** Schönheitssalon; — **sleep** Schönheitsschlaf; — **spot** Schönheitspflästerchen

beaver *n.* Biber

because *conj.* weil, denn da; — **of** wegen

beck *n.* **be at one's** — **and call** jemandem vollständig zur Verfügung stehen

beckon *v.* zunicken, auffordern

become *v.* werden; wohl anstehen, sich schicken, sich eignen; gut kleiden; **what has** — **of him?** was ist aus ihm geworden? wo ist er hingekommen?

becoming *adj.* passend, kleidsam, schikklich

bed *n.* Bett, Lager; (agr.) Beet; (geol.) Lagerung; — **and bedding** Bett und Bettzeug; — **of thorns** Schmerzenslager; — **sheet** Leintuch, Bettuch; **get out of** — aufstehen; **go to** — zu Bett gehen, schlafengehen; **make the** — das Bett machen; **put to** — zu Bett bringen; **river** — Flussbett; **stay in** — im Bett bleiben; **take to** — bettlägerig werden; **–ding** *n.* Bettzeug

bedbug *n.* Bettwanze

bedclothes *n. pl.* Bettbezüge

bedcover *n.* Bettüberzug, Bettbezug

bedeck *v.* zieren, schmücken

bedfellow *n.* Bettgenosse

bedpan *n.* Stechbecken

bedquilt *n.* Steppdecke

bedridden *adj.* bettlägerig

bedrock *n.* festes Gebirge; Grundlage

bedroom *n.* Schlafzimmer

bedside *n.* Bettseite; — **manner** Kran-

kenzimmermanieren

bedspread *n.* Bettdecke

bedspring *n.* Sprungfeder (im Bett)

bedstead *n.* Bettstelle

bedtime *n.* Schlafenszeit

bee *n.* Biene; spelling — Buchstabierwettbewerb

beech *n.* Buche

beechnut *n.* Buchecker

beef *n.* Rindfleisch; (coll.) Rindvieh; — **tea** Kraftbrühe; **chipped** — getrocknete Rindfleischstreifen; **corned** — geräuchertes (*or* gesalzenes) Rindfleisch, Pökelfleisch; Büchsenfleisch; **roast** — Roastbeef, Rostbraten; **–y** *adj.* fleischig

beefsteak *n.* Beefsteak

beehive *n.* Bienenkorb, Bienenstock

beeline *n.* Luftlinie

beer *n.* Bier; — **barrel** Bierfass, Biertonne

beeswax *n.* Bienenwachs

beet *n.* (rote) Rübe, Runkelrübe; — **greens** Runkelrübenkraut; — **sugar** Rübenzucker

beetle *n.* Käfer; Schabe

before *adv.* vorn, voran; vorher, zuvor, vormals, eher, ehemals; früher, bereits, schon; **an hour** — eine Stunde früher; **the day** — am vorigen Tag; **never** — noch nie; — *prep.* vor; — **long** bald; **es dauert nicht mehr lang; the day** — **yesterday** vorgestern; — *conj.* ehe, bevor, eher als; lieber als

beforehand *adv.* zuvor, im voraus; vorher

befriend *v.* sich anfreunden; begünstigen, beistehen

beg *v.* bitten, ersuchen; flehen; betteln, erbetteln; — **leave** um Erlaubnis bitten; **I** — **your pardon** ich bitte um Verzeihung, entschuldigen Sie; wie bitte? **I** — **to be excused** ich bitte um Entschuldigung; ich bitte, gehen zu dürfen; **–ging** *n.* Betteln, Bettelei; **–ging** *adj.* bettelnd, bittend

beget *v.* erzeugen, hervorbringen

beggar *n.* Bettler; Arme, Elende; **–ly** *adj.* bettelhaft; armselig, verächtlich

begin *v.* beginnen, anfangen; entstehen; **to** — **with** anfänglich, erstens; **–ner** *n.* Anfänger, Neuling; **–ning** *n.* Anfang, Beginn; Ursprung; **–nings** *n.* Anfangsgründe, Grundelemente; **at the** — **ning** im Anfang; **from the** —**ning** von Anfang an; **from** —**ning to end** von Anfang bis zu Ende, von A bis Zet

begrudge *v.* misgönnen, nicht gönnen; beneiden

behalf *n.* **in** (*oder* **on**) — **of** zugunsten von; im Namen von

behave *v.* sich betragen (*or* benehmen); — **yourself** benimm dich anständig

behavior *n.* Betragen, Benehmen; Verhalten, Aufführung; **be on one's good — sich gut benehmen**; sich zusammennehmen; **-ism** *n.* Psychologie des guten Betragens

behead *v.* enthaupten, köpfen

behind *prep.* hinter; **be — the eight ball** in der Patsche sitzen; **—** *adv.* hinten, dahinter, hinterher, nach hinten; zurück; rückständig; **be — nachgehen**; stecken hinter; rückständig sein; **fall — zurückbleiben**

behold *v.* anblicken, erblicken; betrachten; **—!** *interj.* siehe da!

beige *n.* Beige, Gelbgrau

belated *adj.* verspätet

belch *n.* Aufstossen, Rülpsen; **—** *v.* aufstossen, rülpsen; **— forth** ausspeien

belfry *n.* Kirchturm, Glockenturm

Belgium *n.* Belgien

belie *v.* verleumden; **Lügen strafen;** widersprechen, täuschen

belief *n.* Glaube; Vertrauen; Meinung, Überzeugung; (rel.) Glaubensbekenntnis; **to the best of my — meiner innersten** Überzeugung nach

believable *adj.* glaublich, glaubhaft

believe *v.* glauben, meinen, vertrauen; **— in** glauben an; **-r** *n.* Gläubige, Glaubende

belittle *v.* verkleinern, herabsetzen

bell *n.* Glocke, Klingel, Schelle; (naut.) Stunde

bellboy *n.* Hotelpage

belle *n.* Schönheit; **— of the ball** Ballkönigin

bellhop *n.* Hotelpage

belligerence *n.* Kampflust

belligerent *n.* kriegführende Partei; **—** *adj.* kriegführend; kriegsliebend

bellows *n.* Blasebalg, Gebläse

bell-shaped *adj.* glocl enförmig, glockenartig

belly *n.* Bauch, Wanst; **—** *v.* (an)schwellen

belong *v.* gehören, angehören; betreffen; **-ings** *n. pl.* Eigentum, Besitztum, Habe

beloved *adj* geliebt, teuer

below *adv.* unten, nach unten; hinunter, herunter; unter, niedriger, tiefer; **—** *prep.* unter(halb)

belt *n.* Gürtel, Gurt, Koppel; (geog.) Region, Meerenge; (mech.) Treibriemen; **transmission — Transmissionsriemen; hit below the — gemein sein; tighten one's — den** Gürtel enger schnallen, hungern

bemoan *v.* beklagen, betrauern

bench *n.* Bank; (law) Gerichtshof, Richterbank; (mech.) Werkbank, Arbeits-

tisch; (pol.) Sitz, Reihe

bend *n.* Biegung, Krümmung; **—** *v.* beugen, biegen, krümmen; neigen; (fig.) bezwingen, unterwerfen; **— down,** **— over** sich neigen, sich bücken

beneath *adv.* unten; **—** *prep.* unter, unterhalb

benediction *n.* Segen

benefactor *n.* Wohltäter

beneficent *adj.* wohltätig

beneficial *adj.* nützlich, vorteilhaft, zuträglich; (law) nutzniessend

beneficiary *n.* Almosenempfänger, Erbe

benefit *n.* Nutzen, Vorteil, Wohltat; (theat.) Benefiz; **for the — of** zum Nutzen (or Vorteil) von; **he always gives me the — of the doubt** im Zweifelsfalle entscheidet er immer zu meinen Gunsten; **—** *v.* nützen, begünstigen, fördern; **— by** Vorteil ziehen aus

benevolence *n.* Wohlwollen, Güte; Wohltat

benevolent *adj.* wohlwollend, gütig; wohltätig; **— society** Wohltätigkeitsverein

benighted *adj.* umnachtet

benign *adj.* gütig, liebreich; günstig, wohltuend; mild; (med.) gutartig

bent *n.* Richtung, Neigung; **—** *adj.* gebogen, krumm; geneigt; **— on** erpicht auf, entschlossen zu

Benzedrine *n.* Benzedrin

benzine *n.* Benzin

bequeath *v.* vermachen, hinterlassen

bequest *n.* Vermächtnis, Legat

bereave *v.* berauben; **-ed** *adj.* leidtragend, hinterblieben; **-ment** *n.* Beraubung; schmerzlicher Verlust

beret *n.* Barett

Bering Strait *n.* Beringstrasse

berry *n.* Beere

berserk *adj.* wütend

berth *n.* Bett, Koje; Ankergrund; **give a wide — to** weit aus dem Wege gehen

beseech *v.* bitten, beschwören, flehen

besetting *adj.* **— sin** Gewohnheitssünde

beside *prep.* neben, bei; ausser; **— oneself,** ausser sich; **that is — the question** (*oder* point) das hat nichts damit zu tun; **—** *adv.* ausserdem; **-s** *adv.* ausserdem; übrigens; **-s** *prep.* ausser, neben

besiege *v.* belagern, bestürmen

bespeak *v.* (vorher) bestellen

best *adj.* beste; **— girl** Schatz, Geliebte; **— man** Brautführer; **— seller** Erfolgswerk; **put one's — foot forward** sein Bestes tun; **—** *adv.* am besten, aufs beste; **—** *n.* Beste; **at — bestenfalls;** **do one's — sein** Möglichstes tun; **for the — zum** Besten; **get the — of** übervorteilen; **make the —** of sich abfinden mit; gute Miene zum bösen Spiel machen; **to the — of my knowledge** soviel ich weiss; **to the — of one's ability** nach besten Kräften; **— v.** übertreffen

bestow *v.* erteilen, schenken; gebrauchen; **— (up)on** verleihen

bet *n.* Wette, Einsatz; **— v.** wetten, setzen; **-ter** (*oder* **-tor**) *n.* Wettende

betray *v.* verraten; missbrauchen; verführen; **-al** *n.* Verrat

better *adj.* besser; **— half** bessere Hälfte, Ehehälfte; **for the —** zum Vorteil; **get the — of** übertreffen; **— adv.** besser; mehr; **all the —** umso besser; **be — off** besser dran sein; **— and —** immer mehr (*or* besser); **so much the —** umso (*or* desto) besser; **think — of it** sich eines Besseren besinnen; **we'd — go** es ist besser, wir gehen; wir sollten lieber gehen; **-s** *n. pl.* Vorgesetzten; **— v.** (ver)bessern; übertreffen; befördern

between *prep.* zwischen, unter; **few and far —** selten; **— you and me** unter uns, unter vier Augen; **— adv.** dazwischen

betweentimes *adv.* dann und wann, bisweilen

bevel *n.* Schrägung, Schrägmass; **— v.** abschrägen

beverage *n.* Getränk, Trank; **cold —** Erfrischung

bevy *n.* Trupp, Rudel, Schar, Schwarm

beware *v.* sich in acht nehmen, sich hüten; achtgeben; **—!** *interj.* gib acht! hüte dich!

bewilder *v.* verwirren, bestürzen; irreführen; **-ed** *adj.* verwirrt, **-ment** *n.* Verwirrung, Bestürzung

bewitch *v.* behexen, bezaubern; **-ing** *adj.* bezaubernd, reizend

beyond *prep.* jenseits, über, ausser, auf der anderen Seite, nach; **— belief** unglaublich; **— hope** hoffnungslos; **— one's reach** unerreichbar; **— recovery** unheilbar; **it is — me** es übersteigt meine Kräfte, das verstehe ich nicht; **— adv.** darüber hinaus, ausserhalb, jenseits; **— n.** Jenseits

biannual *adj.* zweimal jährlich

bias *n.* Vorurteil, Neigung; **free from —** vorurteilsfrei; **on the —** schräg; **— v.** beeinflussen; **-ed** *adj.* beeinflusst, voreingenommen

bib *n.* Schürzenlatz, Kinderlätzchen

Bible *n.* Bibel, Heilige Schrift

Biblical *adj.* biblisch

bibliography *n.* Bibliographie

bicarbonate of soda *n.* doppelkohlensaures Natron

biceps *n.* Bizeps

bicker *v.* zanken, streiten

bicycle *n.* Fahrrad; **ride a —** radfahren, radeln

bicyclist *n.* Radfahrer

bid *n.* Gebot, Angebot; (cards) Ansage; **— v.** bieten, gebieten, befehlen; (cards) melden, ansagen; **— adieu** Lebewohl sagen; **-der** *n.* Bieter, Bietende; **-ding** *n.* Bieten; Gebot, Befehl

bide *v.* erwarten, abwarten

biennial *adj.* zweijährig, zweijährlich

bier *n.* Bahre, Totenbahre

bifocals *n. pl.* Bifokalgläser

big *adj.* gross, dick; (fig.) hoch, vornehm; **Big Dipper** Grosser Wagen (*or* Bär); **— game** Grosswild; **— talk** Prahlerei; **-ness** *n.* Grösse, Dicke; Umfang

bigamist *n.* Bigamist

bigamy *n.* Bigamie, Mehrehe

bighearted *adj.* grossherzig, grosszügig

bigot *n.* Frömmler; **-ed** *adj.* bigott; **-ry** *n.* Bigotterie, Frömmelei

bike *n.* Fahrrad

bilateral *adj.* zweiseitig, bilateral

bile *n.* Galle; (fig.) Bitterkeit

bilingual *adj.* zweisprachig

bill *n.* Schnabel; Schein, Note; Zettel; (com.) Rechnung; (pol.) Gesetz, Gesetzesentwurf, Gesetzesvorlage; **— of exchange** Wechsel, Kurszettel; **— of fare** Speisekarte; **— of health** Gesundheitsattest; **— of lading** Frachtbrief; **Bill of Rights** Freiheitsurkunde; **— of sale** Kaufvertrag; **hand —** Reklamezettel; **— v.** berechnen; **— for** in Rechnung stellen; **— payable** *n.* fällige Rechnung; **— receivable** unbezahlte Rechnung

billboard *n.* Anschlagebrett

billet *n.* Billett, Zettel; (mil.) Quartier; **— v.** einquartieren

billfold *n.* Brieftasche

billiard ball *n.* Billardkugel

billiards *n.* Billard(spiel)

billion *n.* (USA) Milliarde (1.000.000.000); Billion (1.000.000.000.000); **-aire** *n.* (USA) Milliardär; Billionär

billow *n.* Woge, Sturzwelle; **-y** *adj.* wogend, schwellend, wogig

bimonthly *adj.* zweimonatig, zweimonatlich

bin *n.* Kasten, Kiste; Behälter

binary *adj.* binär, aus zwei Einheiten bestehend; **— digit, bit** Büromaschinen-Bit, Binärziffer; **— stars** (ast.) Doppelsterne (um ein Zentrum)

bind *v.* binden, zwingen, verpflichten; (med.) verbinden; **— off** abketten; **-er** *n.* Binder; Buchbinder; **-ery** *n.* Buchbinderei; **-ing** n. Einband; cloth **-ing** Leineneinband; **paper -ing** Pappeinband; **-ing** adj. verbindlich

bingo n. Bingo, Lotteriespiel

binoculars n. pl. Ferngläser; Operngläser

binomial adj. binomisch, zweigliedrig; — **theorem** binomischer Lehrsatz

biochemistry n. Biochemie

biogenesis n. Biogenese, Entwicklungsgeschichte; biogenetisches Grundgesetz; Rekapitulationstheorie

biographer n. Biograph

biographical adj. biographisch

biography n. Biographie

biological adj. biologisch; — **warfare** Bakterienkrieg

biology n. Biologie

biometry n. Biometrie

bipartisan adj. beide Parteien vertretend

biplane n. Doppeldecker

birch n. Birke

bird n. Vogel; — **cage** Vogelkäfig; — **dog** Hühnerhund; — **watcher** Vogelbeobachter; — of **prey** Raubvogel

birdie n. (golf) ein Schlag unter par

bird's-eye view n. Vogelperspektive

birth n. Geburt; Abstammung, Herkunft; Entstehung, Veranlassung; — **certificate** Geburtsschein; — **control** Geburtenbeschränkung; — **rate** Geburtenziffer; give — gebären, ins Leben rufen

birthday n. Geburtstag, Wiegenfest

birthmark n. Muttermal

birthplace n. Geburtsort

biscuit n. Keks, Biskuit ‡

bisect v. in zwei Teile zerschneiden, halbieren

bishop n. Bischof; (chess) Läufer

bison n. Bison, Büffel, Auerochs, Wisent

bit n. Kleinigkeit; Gebiss; (mech.) Bohrspitze; pl. Trümmer; **a** — **ein** wenig, etwas; — **by** — allmählich; **every** — ganz und gar; **not a** — nicht im geringsten

bitch n. (zool.) Hündin; (sl.) Weibsbild

bite n. Biss, Stich; (ichth.) Anbeissen; — v. beissen, anbeissen; schneiden, stechen; — **the dust** ins Gras beissen

biting adj. beissend, schneidend, scharf

bitter adj. bitter, herb, schmerzhaft; **-ness** n. Bitterkeit, Verbitterung

bittern n. Rohrdommel

bituminous adj. bituminös, erdpechartig; — **coal** bituminöse Kohle

biweekly adj. zweiwöchentlich; — adv. alle vierzehn Tage

bizarre adj. bizarr, seltsam

black adj. schwarz; dunkel; (fig.) finster, düster; — **list** schwarze Liste; — **magic** schwarze Magie (or Kunst); — **market**

Schwarzmarkt, Schleichhandel; — **sheep** schwarzes Schaf, Taugenichts; — **widow** amerikanische Riesenspinne; — n. Schwarz, Schwärze; Neger; — v. wichsen; **-en** v. schwarz (or dunkel) werden; schwärzen; (fig.) anschwärzen, verleumden; **-ness** n. Schwärze, Dunkelheit

blackberry n. Brombeere

blackbird n. Amsel

blackboard n. Wandtafel, Tafel, schwarzes Brett

Black Forest n. Schwarzwald

blackhead n. Mitesser, Talkdrüsenverstopfung

black-list v. auf die schwarze Liste setzen

blackmail n. Erpressung; — v. erpressen

blackout n. Verdunkelung; (med.) Ohnmacht

blacksmith n. Schmied

bladder n. Blase, Harnblase

blade n. (bot.) Blatt, Halm; (mech.) Klinge; — of **a propeller** Propellerflügel

blade dispenser n. Klingenspender

blame n. Tadel; Schuld; Verantwortung; — v. tadeln, schelten, rügen; **-less** adj. untadelhaft, unschuldig

blanch v. bleichen, weissen; (cooking) abrühen

bland adj. sanft, mild

blank n. Formular; Weisse; leerer Raum, Lücke; unbeschriebenes Blatt, Blanko; (fig.) Nichts, Niete; — adj. weiss, blanko, leer; — **cartridge** Platzpatrone; — **check** Blankoscheck; — **verse** Blankvers

blanket n. Decke; — **instructions** Blankovollmacht; Blankobefehl; (mil.) künstliche Vernebelung; — v. bedecken

blare v. schmettern; brüllen

blaspheme v. lästern, fluchen

blasphemous adj. lästernd

blasphemy n. Gotteslästerung, Blasphemie

blast n. Sturm, Windstoss; Blasen; Explosion; Gebläse; Luftdruck; — **furnace** Hochofen; — v. sprengen, vernichten; (fig.) verderben, vereiteln; **-ing** n. Sprengung

blast-off n. Raketenabschuss

blaze n. Flamme, Glut; Lichtschein, Strahl; Brand; — v. flammen; lodern; leuchten

blazing adj. prall

bleach v. bleichen, weiss machen; **-ing** n. Bleiche; Bleichen

bleachers n. pl. offene Tribüne

bleak adj. kahl, öde; kalt, frostig; (fig.) freudlos

bleed v. bluten; (med.) zur Ader lassen; **-ing** n. Blutung; Aderlass; **-ing** adj.

blutend; -ing heart Goldlack

blemish n. Makel, Fehler; Gebrechen; (fig.) Schandfleck; — v. beflecken

blend n. Mischung, Zusammenstellung; — v. (ver)mischen, verschmelzen; zusammenpassen

bless v. segnen; beglücken; -ed adj. selig, gesegnet, glücklich; -ing n. Segen, Wohltat; Tischgebet

blight n. Mehltau, Brand; Rost; Frostschaden; Gifthauch

blimp n. Luftschiff

blind adj. blind; — alley Sackgasse; fly — blind (or nur mit Hilfe der Instrumente) fliegen; — man Blinde; — spot Punkt des mangelnden Verständnisses; — v. blenden; (fig.) verblenden; — n. Blende; (sports) Versteck; (fig.) Vorwand; Venetian —s Jalousien, Rouleaus, Rolläden; -ly adv. blind, unbesonnen; -ness n. Blindheit

blindfold n. Augenbinde; — v. die Augen verbinden; — adj. mit verbundenen Augen; (fig.) verwegen

blindman's buff n. Blindekuh(spiel)

blink n. blinken, blinzeln; schimmern; (fig.) nicht sehen wollen; — n. Blinken; Schimmer; -er n. Blinkfeuer; -ers n. pl. Scheuklappen

bliss n. Wonne; Freude; Entzücken; -ful adj. wonnevoll, selig

blister n. Blase, Pustel; (mech.) Luftblase; — v. Blasen bilden (or ziehen)

blizzard n. Blizzard, Schneesturm

bloat v. aufblasen, aufblähen

bloc n. Zweckverband, Zweckvereinigung

block n. Block, Klotz; Häuserblock; (mech.) Kloben, Rolle, Hutform; (fig.) Sperrung, Stockung; — and tackle Flaschenzug; — system Blocksystem, Absperrsystem; — v. hindern, hemmen, blockieren; (ver)sperren; (art) skizzieren; (hats) pressen

blockade n. Blockade; run a — Blockade brechen; -ade v. blockieren

blockhouse n. Blockhaus

blond(e) n. Blonde, Blondine; peroxide — Wasserstoffblondine; — adj. blond, hell

blood n. Blut; Abstammung, Menschenschlag; — bank Blutbank; — count Zählung der Blutkörper; — donor Blutspender; — group Blutgruppe; — plasma Blutplasma; — poisoning Blutvergiftung; — pressure Blutdruck; — test Blutprobe; — transfusion Blutübertragung; — vessel Blutgefäss, Ader; in cold — kaltblütig; -y adj. blutig, blutbefleckt

bloodhound n. Bluthund, Schweisshund;

(fig.) Verfolger

bloodshed n. Blutvergiessen, Mord

bloodshot adj. blutunterlaufen

bloodstain n. Blutfleck; -ed adj. blutbefleckt

bloodsucker n. Blutsauger; (fig.) Erpresser

bloodthirsty adj. blutdürstig, blutrünstig

bloom n. Blüte; Blume; Flaum; (fig.) Blütezeit, Jugendfrische; — v. blühen, erblühen; florieren

bloomers n. pl. Reformhosen für Frauen

blossom n. Blüte; — v. blühen, Blüten treiben

blot n. Klecks, Fleck; — v. löschen; beklecksen, beflecken; — out versperren, ausstreichen; -ter n. Löscher, Löschpapier

blotch n. Pustel; Klecks

blouse n. Bluse

blow n. Schlag, Streich, Hieb; (fig.) Unglücksfall; — v. blasen, wehen; — away wegwehen; — one's brains out sich eine Kugel durch den Kopf jagen; — one's nose sich die Nase putzen; — out ausblasen; platzen; — over vorübergehen; — the horn hupen; — up sprengen, explodieren; aufblasen

blower n. Gebläse

blowout n. Reifenpanne, Platzen

blowpipe n. Blasrohr; Lötrohr

blowtorch n. Lötlampe

blubber n. Tran; — v. flennen, plärren, weinen

blue n. Blau; (fig.) Himmel, Meer; — jay Blauhäher; — adj. blau, bläulich; (fig.) schwermütig, traurig; — v. blau färben, blauen; n. pl. Schwermut, Melancholie

blueberry n. Blaubeere

bluebird n. Blaukehlchen

blue-blooded adj. blaublütig, aristokratisch

blue-eyed adj. blauäugig

blueprint n. Blaupause, Blaudruck; Heliographie

bluff n. Abhang; Bluff, Irreführung; — adj. schroff, steil; rauh, barsch; — v. bluffen, verblüffen

bluing, blueing n. Waschblau

bluish adj. bläulich

blunder n. Fehler, Missgriff, Schnitzer; — v. Fehler (or Schnitzer) machen; (sports) stolpern

blunt adj. stumpf, grob, plump; — v. abstumpfen; (fig.) unterdrücken

blur n. Flecken, Klecks; (fig.) Makel; Undeutlichkeit; — v. beflecken, verwischen, auslöschen

blurt r. — out herausplatzen

blush n. Erröten, Schamröte; — v. erröten; (fig.) verwirrt sein, sich schämen

boa n. Boa, Riesenschlange; — constric-tor Abgottschlange; Boa Constrictor

boar n. Eber, Keiler; wild — Wildschwein

board n. Brett; Tafel, Tisch; (naut.) Board; (fig.) Kost, Pension; — and lodging Kost und Logis; — of educa-tion Unterrichtsamt; — of examination Prüfungskommission; — of health Ge-sundheitsamt; — of trade Handelsamt, Börsenkommission; — of trustees Direktorium, Verwaltungsrat; free on — (f.o.b.) frei Schiff; on — an Bord; **school** — Schulbehörde; — v. an Bord gehen, einsteigen, beköstigen; in Pen-sion; — up belegen; **-er** n. Kostgänger, Pensionär

boarding house n. Pension

boarding school n. Internat, Pensionat

boast n. Prahlerei, Rühmen; — v. prahlen, grosstun; — about (oder of) sich rüh-men, herausstreichen, stolz sein auf; **-ful** adj. prahlerisch

boat n. Boot, Kahn, Barke; Schiff, Fahr-zeug; be in the same — in der gleichen Lage sein; **-ing** n. Bootfahren, Ruders-port; Wasserfahrt

boathouse n. Bootshaus

boatman n. Bootsgast, Bootsführer

bob n. Stoss, Ruck; Bubikopf; (mech.) Pendelgewicht; Flott; — v. rücken; baumeln; stutzen; kurz schneiden

bobbin n. Spule, Klöppel

bobby pin n. Haarspange

bobby sox (oder socks) n. Söckchen

bobby soxer n. Halbwüchsige, ausgelas-sener Backfisch

bobcat n. Luchs

bobolink n. amerikanischer Reisstar

bobsled n. Bob(sleigh)

bodily adj. leiblich, körperlich; (fig.) ge-waltätig

body n. Körper, Leib; Rumpf, Stamm; Leiche, Leichnam; Körperschaft, Ge-sellschaft; (mil.) Abteilung

bodyguard n. Leibwache; (mil.) Leibgarde

bog n. Sumpf, Moor; — v. versinken, versenken

bogus adj. nachgemacht, unecht

Bohemia n. Böhmen

Bohemian adj. Bohemien-, aussergewöhn-lich

boil n. Kochen, Sieden; (med.) Furunkel, Geschwür; — v. kochen, sieden, wallen; **-er** n. Kessel; (mech.) Dampfkessel; **-ing** adj. kochend, siedend; (fig.) auf-wallend, erregt; **-ing point** Siedepunkt

boisterous adj. rauh, stürmisch, unge-stüm; (fig.) lärmend, geräuschvoll

bold adj. unverschämt; kühn, mutig;

unerschrocken; hervortretend; **-ness** n. Kühnheit, Verwegenheit; Unver-schämtheit

boldface n. (typ.) Fettdruck

bold-faced adj. unverschämt, frech; (typ.) fett

boll n. Samenkapsel; — weevil Baum-wollkäfer; **cotton** — Baumwollsamen

boloney n. Jagdwurst; (sl.) Wertlosigkeit, Nichtswürdigkeit

bolster n. Polster, Kissen; — v. (aus)-polstern; — up unterstützen

bolt n. Riegel; Schraube; Bolzen; (cloth) Ballen, Rolle; — out of the blue Blitz aus heiterem Himmel; — v. verriegeln, zuriegeln; durchgehen; (pol.) verlassen, nicht unterstützen

bomb n. Bombe; (fig.) Überraschung; — shelter Luftschutzkeller; — v. bombar-dieren, bomben; **-er** n. Bomber, Bom-benflugzeug

bombard v. bombardieren, beschiessen; **-ier** n. Offizier, der das Bombardement leitet; **-ment** n. Bombardement, Be-schiessung

bombproof adj. bombenfest, bomben-sicher

bombshell n. Bombe; (fig.) Überraschung

bombsight n. Bombenzielgerät

bonbon n. Bonbon, Zuckerwerk

bond n. Band; (com.) Obligation, Schuld-verschreibung; **government** **-s** Staats-papiere; — v. sicher anordnen (or einteilen, festlegen); (com.) Sicherheit anbieten; **-age** n. Gefangenschaft; Knechtschaft, Sklaverei

bondholder n. Wertpapierbesitzer, Obli-gationsinhaber

bondsman n. Bürge; Leibeigene

bone n. Knochen, Bein; (ichth.) Gräte, Fischbein; — china Steingut; — v. Knochen (or Gräten) entfernen, entgrä-ten; (sewing) Fischbein einsetzen; **-less** adj. knochenlos, grätenlos; (fig.) haltlos

bonfire n. Freudenfeuer

bonnet n. Damenhut; Haube

bonus n. Vergütung, Prämie, Gratifika-tion, Bonus; (com.) Gewinnanteil, Dividendenerhöhung

bony adj. beinern, knöchern

booby n. Tölpel; — trap Falle

book n. Buch; (mus.) Textbuch, Libretto; (com.) Geschäftsbuch, Kassenbuch; — end Buchstütze; — review Buchbespre-chung, Buchkritik; — value Bilanz-überschuss, Buchwert; — v. buchen, eintragen; anschreiben, aufschreiben; bestellen; **-ie** n. Winkelbuchmacher; **-ing** n. Buchung, Eintragung; Platz-bestellung; **-ing office** Billettschalter,

Fahrkartenschalter; (theat.) Tageskasse; **-let** n. Broschüre; Büchlein
bookbinder n. Buchbinder
bookcase n. Bücherschrank, Bücherkiste
bookkeeper n. Buchhalter, Buchführer
bookkeeping n. Buchführung, Buchhaltung; **double entry** — doppelte Buchführung; **single entry** — einfache Buchführung
bookmaker n. Buchmacher
bookmark n. Lesezeichen, Buchzeichen
bookplate n. Exlibris, Eigentumszeichen
bookseller n. Buchhändler
bookshelf n. Bücherbrett
bookstand n. Büchergestell, Buchladen
bookstore, bookshop n. Buchhandlung
boom n. Dröhnen, Donnern; (com.) Hochkonjunktur, Aufschwung, Hausse; (naut.) Spiere; **sonic** — Schallexplosion; — **town** emporschiessende Stadt; — v. dröhnen, donnern; (fig.) florieren
boomerang n. Bumerang
boon n. Wohltat, Gnade, Gabe
boondoggle v. frivole Dinge tun
boor n. Lümmel; **-ish** adj. lümmelhaft, grob
boost n. Schub, Stoss; — v. Reklame (or Lärm) machen für; herauftreiben, ankurbeln; **-er** n. (com.) Preissteigerer; (elec.) Hilfsmotor; Puffersatz; Zwischenzünder; (pol.) Anhänger; **-er rocket** n. Startrakete, Antriebsrakete
boot n. Stiefel; **riding** — Reitstiefel; **to** — **obendrein; -ee** n., **-ie** n. Kinderschuh
booth n. Bude; **telephone** — Telefonzelle
bootleg v. Alkohol schmuggeln; **-ger** n. Alkoholschmuggler
booty n. Beute, Raub
booze n. Trank, Getränk; — v. trinken
border n. Grenze, Rand; Einfassung, Saum, Borte; — **line** Grenzlinie; — v. einfassen, besetzen; grenzen, begrenzen; — **on** angrenzen, anstossen
borderland n. Grenzland, Nachbarland
borderline case n. Grenzfall
bore n. Bohrung, Bohrloch; Kaliber; langweiliger Mensch; — v. bohren; langweilen, belästigen
boric adj. Bor-; — **acid** Borsäure
boring adj. langweilig
born adj. geboren, bestimmt; **be** — **to** bestimmt sein zu
borrow v. leihen, borgen, entlehnen; **-er** n. Borger, Entleiher
bosom n. Busen, Brust; (fig.) Schoss, Tiefe; — **of a shirt** Hemdbrust; — adj. — **friend** Busenfreund
boss n. Chef, Herr, Vorgesetzte; — v. treiben; (coll.) herumkommandieren;

-y adj. herrisch, gebieterisch
botanical adj. botanisch
botany n. Botanik
botch n. Pfuscharbeit; — v. pfuschen, stümpern
both pron. and adj. beide, beides; — conj. sowohl
bother v. belästigen, plagen; sich bemühen; — n. Belästigung, Plage; Mühe
bottle n. Flasche, Karaffe; — v. auf Flaschen ziehen
bottleneck n. Flaschenhals; Engpass; Strassenverengung; Verkehrsstockung
bottom n. Boden, Grund; Unterteil, Grundfläche, Basis; (fig.) Ursache; Tiefe; **at** — im Grunde; **be at the** — of die Triebfeder (or Seele) einer Sache sein; zugrunde liegen; **false** — Doppelboden; **from top to** — von oben bis unten; — adj. unter; unterst, niedrigst, letzt; — **drawer** unterste Schublade; — **land** reiche Flussebene; **-less** adj. bodenlose, grundlos; (fig.) unergründlich
bough n. Zweig, Ast
bouillon n. Bouillon, Fleischbrühe
boulder n. Geröll, Felsblock
bounce v. aufspringen (lassen); hinauswerfen; — n. Sprung; **-er** n. Rausschmeisser
bound n. Grenze, Schranke; Grenzstein, Markstein; Sprung; **beyond all -s** alle Grenzen überschreitend; **keep within -s** sich in Schranken halten; **out of -s** ausserhalb des Erlaubten; **within -s** mässig; innerhalb des Erlaubten; — v. beschränken; begrenzen; springen; — adj. gebunden; verpflichtet; entschlossen; (naut.) unterwegs; — **for** auf der Reise nach; **it is** — **to es muss**; **-ary** n. Grenze, Grenzlinie; **-less** adj. unbeschränkt, grenzenlos, unbegrenzt
bounteous, bountiful adj. gütig, freigebig; reichlich
bounty n. Güte, Freigebigkeit; Belohnung
bouquet n. Blumenstrauss, Bukett; (wine) Blume
bout n. Streit, Kampf; (med.) Anfall; (sports) Wettkampf; **drinking** — Trinkgelage
bow n. (courtesy) Verbeugung, Verneigung; (fashion) Schleife; (naut.) Bug; (sports) Bogen; — v. sich verbeugen, neigen; sich unterwerfen; den Bogen führen; einen Bogen machen
bowels n. pl. Eingeweide; — **of the earth** Erdinnere
bower n. Laube, Landsitz
bowl n. Schale, Schüssel; Bowle, Humpen; (sports) Kugel, Ball; Sportplatz; — v.

rollen, schieben, kugeln; (sports) kegeln; –er n. Kegler; –ing n. Kegeln; –ing alley Kegelbahn; –ing pin Kegel

bowlegged adj. krummbeinig; (coll.) o-beinig

box n. Schachtel, Karton, Kiste; Behälter, Büchse; Stand, Bude; (bot.) Buchsbaum; (law) Geschworenenbank; (mail) Briefkasten; (theat.) Loge; — on the ear Ohrfeige; hot — (rail.) heissgelaufenes Getriebe; (prisoner's) — Anklagebank; — elder Eschenahorn; — office Theaterkasse; — seat Logenplatz; — v. boxen; in Schachteln (or Kartons, Kisten) packen; –er n. Boxer; –ing n. Boxen; –ing glove Boxhandschuh

boxcar n. Güterwagen

boy n. Knabe, Junge, Bube, Bursche; Bediente; — scout Pfadfinder; –hood n. Knabenalter; –ish adj. knabenhaft

boycott n. Boykott; — v. boykottieren

boysenberry n. Brombeere mit Himbeergeschmack

bra, brassiere n. Büha, Büstenhalter

brace n. Band, Gurt; Paar: (arch.) Winkelband, Stützbalken; (med.) Spange, Klammer; (mech.) Drillbohrer; — v. absteifen, abspreizen; stemmen; gürten, klammern; (fig.) anspannen; — up sich zusammennehmen

bracelet n. Armband

bracing adj. stärkend, erfrischend

bracket n. Klammer; (arch.) Konsole; (fig.) Klasse; — v. einklammern

brag v. prahlen; aufschneiden; –gart n. Prahler, Aufschneider

braid n. Zopf; Borte, Litze, Schnur; — v. flechten

braille n. Braille, Blindenschrift

brain n. Gehirn; pl. Verstand, Kopf; (coll.) Hirn; blow one's –s out sich eine Kugel durch den Kopf jagen; rack one's –s sich den Kopf zerbrechen; — storm Gedankenblitz; — trust Ratgebergruppe; — v. den Schädel einschlagen; — wash v. das Gehirn waschen; –y adj. geistreich, gescheit

brake n. (bot.) Breche; (mech.) Bremse, Bremsvorrichtung; — band Bremsband; four-wheel — Vierradbremse; put on (oder apply) the –s bremsen; release the –s die Bremse loslassen; — v. bremsen

brakeman n. Bremser

bramble n. Brombeerstrauch, Dorngebüsch

bran n. Kleie

branch n. Zweig, Ast; (com.) Filiale, Zweigniederlassung; (geol.) Flussarm;

(zool.) Geweihsprosse; (fig.) Abzweigung; Abschnitt; — of (art, science, trade, etc.) Fach; — of the sea Meeresarm; — line Zweigbahn; — v. — off abstammen, abzweigen; — out sich verzweigen, grösser werden

brand n. Marke, Sorte; Brand; (fig.) Schandfleck; — v. einbrennen; (fig.) brandmarken

brandish v. schwingen, schwenken

brand-new adj. (funkel)nagelneu

brandy n. Kognak, Weinbrand

brass n. Messing; (mil. sl.) hohes Tier; — band Blasorchester; (mil.) Trompeterkorps; — adj. messingartig

brassie n. messingbeschlagener Golfstock

bravado n. Drohung, Herausforderung

brave adj. brav, tapfer, mutig; kühn, unerschrocken; (fig.) stattlich, glänzend; — v. herausfordern, trotzen; mutig begegnen; — n. Krieger; –ry n. Mut, Tapferkeit, Unerschrockenheit

brawn n. Muskelkraft

brazier n. Kohlenpfanne

Brazil n. Brasilien

breach n. Bruch, Riss, Sprung; (law) Übertretung, Verletzung; (mil.) Bresche, Durchbruch; (fig.) Uneinigkeit, Zwist; — of faith Treubruch; — of promise Wortbruch

bread n. Brot; (slice of) — and butter Butterbrot; (fig.) Lebensunterhalt; — -and-butter letter Dankbrief für Gastfreundschaft

breadbasket n. Brotkorb; (fig.) Kornkammer; (sl.) Magen

breadth n. Breite, Fülle, Weite; (fig.) Hochherzigkeit

breadwinner n. Brotverdiener; Ernährer

break n. Bruch; Pause; Chance; (law) Fluchtversuch; bad — Pech; — of day Tagesanbruch; — v. brechen; zerschlagen; einschlagen; auflösen; beibringen; ruinieren; kassieren; dressieren; — down zusammenbrechen; stecken bleiben; — in anlernen; — into einbrechen; — of (a habit) abgewöhnen; — off abbrechen, aufhören; — one's neck sich das Genick brechen; — open aufbrechen, erbrechen; — out ausbrechen; — the bank die Bank sprengen; — the ice das Eis brechen; — through durchbrechen; — to pieces zerbrechen; — up (sich) auflösen; –able adj. zerbrechlich; –age n. Brechen, Zerbrechen; Bruch; –er n. Brecher, Sturzsee; –ing adj. (zer)brechend; –ing point Festigkeitsgrenze

breakdown n. Zusammenbruch; Panne; Betriebsstörung; Misslingen; **nervous**

— Nervenzusammenbruch

breakfast n. Frühstück; — v. frühstücken

breast n. Brust; (fig.) Busen; Gewissen; (arch.) Brüstung; — **stroke** Brustschwimmen; **make a clean** — **of** alles eingestehen; — v. sich entgegenstemmen; trotzen, die Stirn bieten

breath n. Atem; Hauch; (fig.) Augenblick, Moment; — **of air** Lüftchen; **catch one's** — Atem holen (or schöpfen); **out of** — atemlos; **-e** v. atmen, einatmen, ausatmen; leise äussern, (fig.) leben; **-ing** n. Atmen, Hauchen; **-less** adj. atemlos, ausser Atem

breath-taking adj. atemraubend

breech n. Steiss; — **of a gun** Kanonenverschluss; **-es** n. pl. Sporthosen, Reithosen, Breeches

breed n. Brut, Art, Rasse, Zucht; (fig.) Herkunft, Schlag; — v. züchten, aufziehen; gebären, erzeugen, sich vermehren; **-er** n. Züchter; **-ing** n. Züchten; (fig.) Bildung, Herkunft, Lebensart

breeze n. Brise, Wind; — v. stürmen

bremsstrahlung n. Bremsstrahlung

brethren n. pl. Brüder

brew n. Gebräu; — v. brauen, mischen; (fig.) anstiften, anzetteln; **-er** n. Brauer; **-ery** n. Brauerei

briar, brier n. Dornstrauch, Hagebuttenstrauch; Bruyèrepfeife

bribe n. Bestechung, Bestechungsgeld; — v. bestechen; **-ry** n. Bestechung

bric-a-brac n. Antiquitäten; Nippsachen, Nippes; Krimskrams

brick n. Ziegel, Backstein; — adj. ziegelartig, ziegelförmig

brickbat n. Ziegelstück, Ziegelbrocken

bricklayer n. Maurer

brickwork n. Rohbau (aus Ziegeln); Backsteinbau

brickyard n. Ziegelei, Ziegellager

bridal adj. bräutlich, hochzeitlich

bride n. Braut; (fig.) junge Frau, Neuvermählte

bridegroom n. Bräutigam; Neuvermählte

bridesmaid n. Brautjungfer

bridge n. Brücke; (cards) Bridge; (mus.) Steg; — v. eine Brücke schlagen; überbrücken

bridgehead n. Brückenkopf

bridgework n. Brückenbau; (dent.) Zahnbrücke

bridle n. Zügel, Zaum; — adj. — **path** Reitweg; — v. zügeln, (auf)zäumen; (fig.) den Kopf zurückwerfen

brief n. kurze Darstellung des Klagepunktes; Klagebeantwortung; — **case** Aktentasche; **hold a** — **for** befürworten;

in — mit kurzen Worten, kurz gesagt; — adj. kurz, bündig; flüchtig, knapp; **-ing** n. Einsatzbesprechung; Befehlsausgabe; Lagebesprechung

brigade n. Brigade

brigadier general n. Brigadegeneral

brigand n. Räuber

bright adj. hell, glänzend, heiter; (fig.) geistreich, fröhlich; gescheit, aufgeweckt, lebhaft; — **and early in aller Frühe; -en** v. erleuchten, erhellen; polieren; wieder Mut fassen; **-ness** n. Glanz, Helle, Klarheit; Heiterkeit

Bright's disease n. Bright'sche Krankheit, Nierenkrankheit

brilliance n. Glanz; Scharfsinn

brilliant adj. glänzend, brillant, strahlend, leuchtend; (fig.) geistreich; ausgezeichnet; — n. Brillant

brim n. Rand, Krempe; — v. bis zum Rand füllen, übervoll sein; **-ful** adj. bis zum Rande voll

brimstone n. Schwefel

brine n. Salzwasser, Sole

bring v. bringen, mitbringen, herbringen; (law) erheben, einbringen; — **about** bewerkstelligen, herbeiführen; — **along** mitbringen; — **down** herunterbringen; — **forth** hervorbringen; — **out** herausbringen, aufdecken; — **to** wieder zu sich bringen; — **to bear** geltend machen; — **up** erziehen; heraufbringen; vorbringen

brink n. Rand, Kante; steiles Ufer

brisk adj. lebhaft, rasch; flink; frisch; **-ness** n. Lebhaftigkeit

bristle n. Borste, Stachel; — v. sträuben, starren

Britain n. Britannien

Brittany n. Bretagne

brittle adj. spröde, brüchig; zerbrechlich; (fig.) schwach, leicht zerstörbar

broad adj. breit, weit; gross; liberal, deutlich; (coll.) dreist; — **jump** Weitsprung; **in** — **daylight** am hellen Tage; **-en** v. ausweiten, ausbreiten; erweitern, verbreitern

broadcast n. Sendung, Rundfunksendung; — v. senden; **-ing** n. Rundfunk; **-ing station** Sender, Rundfunkstation

broadcloth n. feines Baumwolltuch

broad-minded adj. weitherzig, duldsam; **-ness** n. Weitherzigkeit, Duldsamkeit

broadside n. Breitseite

brocade n. Brokat

brochure n. Broschüre

brogue n. (gebrochene) Mundart

broil v. unter der Flamme braten; schmoren; **-er** n. Bratrost; Brathuhn

broke (sl.) adj. ruiniert; **-n** adj. gebro-

chen, zerbrochen; **be** — kaputt sein;
— English gebrochenes (or gerade-
brechtes) Englisch
broker n. Makler, Agent; Zwischenhändler; insurance — Versicherungsagent;
-age n. Maklergeschäft; Maklergebühr
bromide n. Brom; Gemeinplatz
bronchial adj. bronchial; — tube Bron-
chie, Luftröhre
bronchitis n. Bronchitis
bronchopneumonia n. bronchiale Lungenentzündung
bronco n. ungezähmtes Pferd
bronze n. Bronze, Bronzefarbe; **Bronze
Age** Bronzezeit; — v. bronzieren
brooch n. Brosche, Spange
brood n. Brut; — v. (aus)brüten, ersinnen
brook n. Bach; — v, ertragen, erdulden,
aushalten
broom n. Besen; (bot.) Ginster
broomstick n. Besenstiel
broth n. Suppe, Fleischbrühe
brother n. Bruder; — hood n. Brüderschaft;
Brüderlichkeit; **-ly** adj. brüderlich
brother-in-law n. Schwager
brow n. Stirn; Augenbraue; (geol.) Abhang
brown n. Braun; — adj. braun, brünett,
bräunlich; — **paper** braunes Papier,
Packpapier; — **sugar** brauner Zucker,
Rohzucker; **dark** — dunkelbraun; — v.
(sich) bräunen, braun machen (or
werden)
Bruges n. Brügge
bruise n. Quetschung; — v. zermalmen,
zerquetschen; (coll.) braun und blau
schlagen
brunch n. zweites Frühstück
brunet(te) n. Brünett(e); — adj. brünett
Brunswick n. Braunschweig
brunt n. Stoss, Heftigkeit; Gewalt
brush n. Bürste; (art) Pinsel; (bot.)
Gebüsch, Gestrüpp, Unterholz; (elec.)
Strahlenbündel; (mil.) Scharmützel;
Lunte; (zool.) Rute; — v. fegen, bürsten; kehren, wischen; — **against**
anstreifen; — **aside** beiseiteschieben;
— **off** abbürsten; (fig.) abweisen; —
one's teeth sich die Zähne putzen
brushwood n. Gestrüpp, Reisig
brutal adj. roh, brutal; **-ity** n. Roheit,
Brutalität
brute n. Rohling; Tier; (coll.) Scheusal;
— adj. tierisch, viehisch
BTU (British Thermal Unit) n. britische
Wärmeeinheit (Hitzemenge erforderlich um 1 Pfd. Wasser 1° zu erwärmen)
bubble n. Blase; Tand, Bagatelle;
(coll.) Schwindel; — v. sieden, sprudeln, Blasen werfen; (fig.) gurgeln,

murmeln; — **over** überschäumen,
übersprudeln
bubonic plague n. Beulenpest
buccaneer n. Seeräuber, Freibeuter
bucket n. Eimer, Kübel
buckle n. Schnalle; — v. schnallen, zuschnallen; sich werfen; — **down** to sich
ins Zeug legen, um
buckram n. Steifleinen
buckshot n. Rehposten
buckwheat n. Buchweizen
bud n. Knospe, Auge; Keim, Sprosse;
(sl.) Debütantin; **nip in the** — im
Keime ersticken; — v. knospen, keimen, sprossen; sich entwickeln; okulieren, veredeln; **-ding** adj. knospend;
(fig.) angehend
buddy (coll.) n. Gefährte, Genosse,
Kamerad
budge v. sich regen (or rühren); von der
Stelle gehen
budget n. Budget, Haushaltsplan, Etat;
— v. einteilen
buff n. Lederfarbe, Braungelb; — adj.
lederfarben, braungelb; — v. (ab)le-
dern, polieren; **-er** n. Polierinstrument,
Nagelpolierer
buffalo n. Büffel
buffer n. Puffer; — **state** Pufferstaat
buffet n. Büffet, Anrichte, Kredenz;
Geschirrschrank; Schenktisch; — v.
puffen
bug n. Käfer; Wanze
bugbear n. Popanz, Schreckbild
buggy n. Einspänner; **baby** — Kinderwagen
bugle n. Signalhorn, Waldhorn; — **call**
Hornsignal; **-r** n. Hornbläser, Hornist
build v. bauen, erbauen, aufbauen; (fig.)
bilden, gründen; — **up** aufbauen; **-er**
n. Erbauer; Baumeister; Konstrukteur;
(fig.) Schöpfer; **-ing** n. Gebäude,
Bau(werk); Erbauen, Konstruktion
bulb n. (bot.) Zwiebel, Knolle; (elec.)
Birne
bulge n. Anschwellung, Wulst; (arch.)
Ausbauchung; — v. hervorragen, aus-
bauchen
bulk n. Masse, Menge, Umfang, Volumen; **in** — in Bausch und Bogen; **-y**
adj. gross, dick; unhandlich, sperrig
bulkhead n. (mil.) luftdrucksichere Pan-
zertür; (naut.) Schott; (avi.) Rumpf-
versteifung
bull n. Stier, Bulle; (com.) Haussier
bulldog n. Bulldogge
bulldoze v. einschüchtern, ins Bockshorn
jagen; **-r** n. Planierungsraupenfahrzeug
bullet n. Kugel, Geschoss
bulletin n. Bulletin, Tagesbericht; kurze

Bekanntmachung; — **board** Anschlagebrett

bulletproof *adj.* kugelfest, kugelsicher

bullfight *n.* Stierkampf, Stiergefecht; **-er** *n.* Stierkämpfer, Torero

bullfrog *n.* Ochsenfrosch

bullion *n.* Goldbarren, Silberbarren

bull's-eye *n.* Zentrum einer Schiessscheibe; Schuss ins Zentrum

bulrush *n.* Teichbinse, Sumpfbinse

bulwark *n.* Bollwerk, Bastei; (fig.) Schutz

bum *n.* Taugenichts, Landstreicher

bumblebee *n.* Hummel

bump *n.* Beule; Schlag, Stoss; — *v.* stossen, schlagen; — **into** stossen gegen; (fig.) sehen; **-er** *n.* (auto.) Stosstange; **-er** *adj.* riesengross; höchst, best; **-y** *adj.* holperig

bun *n.* Brötchen, Semmel

bunch *n.* Bund; Bündel, Büschel; Menge; (coll.) Bande; — **of flowers** Blumenstrauss; — **of grapes** Weintraube; — *v.* zu einem Bündel zusammenstellen

bundle *n.* Bund, Bündel; Paket; Rolle; **small** — Päckchen; — *v.* bündeln, einpacken, zusammenrollen; — **up** bündeln; warm einwickeln

bungalow *n.* einstöckiges Sommerhaus; Bungalow

bungle *v.* stümpern, pfuschen

bunion *n.* Schwellung am Ballen (*or* grossen Zeh)

bunk *n.* Koje; Wandbett; (sl.) Geschwätz, leeres Gerede

bunker *n.* Bunker; Behälter; (golf) Hindernis vor dem Golfloch

bunkhouse *n.* Herberge

buoy *n.* Boje, Ankerboje; — *v.* — **up** flott erhalten; (fig.) aufrechterhalten; **-ant** *adj.* schwimmend; (fig.) heiter

burden *n.* Last, Bürde; — *v.* beladen, belasten; (fig.) beschweren

bureau *n.* Büro; Amtszimmer, Geschäftszimmer; Kommode; **-crat** *n.* Bürokrat

bureaucracy *n.* Bürokratie; (fig.) Amtsschimmel

burglar *n.* Einbrecher; — **alarm** Einbruchsalarm; **-y** *n.* Einbruch

burial *n.* Beerdigung, Begräbnis; — **ground** Begräbnisplatz; Friedhof

burlap *n.* grobe Leinwand

burlesque *n.* Burleske, Posse, Satire; — *v.* lächerlich machen, travestieren

burn *n.* Brandmal, Brandwunde; — *v.* brennen, verbrennen; anbrennen; bräunen; — **down** niederbrennen; **-ing hot** glühend heiss; — **one's bridges behind one** alle Brücken hinter sich abbrechen; — **up** verbrennen; **money to** — Geld wie Heu; **-er** *n.* Brenner

burnish *v.* polieren, glätten

burrow *n.* Bau, Loch; — *v.* Löcher graben, sich eingraben; (fig.) sich verkriechen

burst *n.* Bersten, Platzen; Explosion; (fig.) Ausbruch; — *v.* bersten, platzen; zerspringen, aufspringen; explodieren; — **in**(**to**) hereinplatzen; — **into tears** in Tränen ausbrechen; — **out laughing** in lautes Gelächter ausbrechen

bury *v.* begraben, beerdigen; vergraben; (fig.) verbergen; — **the hatchet** die Streitaxt begraben, Frieden schliessen

bus *n.* Bus, Omnibus; — **boy** Pikkolo

bush *n.* Busch, Strauch; Dickicht, Gebüsch; **-y** *adj.* buschig

bushel *n.* Scheffel; (fig.) grosse Menge, Haufen

bushing *n.* (elec.) Durchführungsisolator

busily *adv.* fleissig, geschäftig; rastlos

business *n.* Geschäft, Handel; Beschäftigung, Beruf; Arbeit, Tätigkeit; (fig.) Angelegenheit, Sache; — **before pleasure** erst kommt die Arbeit, dann das Vergnügen; **do** — **with** Geschäfte machen mit; **mind your own** — kümmere dich um deine eigenen Angelegenheiten; **on** — geschäftlich; **that's none of your** — das geht dich nichts an

businesslike *adj.* geschäftsmässig, kaufmännisch; (fig.) praktisch

businessman *n.* Kaufmann, Geschäftsmann

bust *n.* Büste; Brust, Busen

bustle *n.* Lärm, Getöse; Geschäftigkeit; (clothing) Tornüre; — *v.* sich tummeln (*or* rühren)

busy *adj.* beschäftigt, rührig, tätig, eifrig; **the number is** — die Nummer ist besetzt; — *v.* beschäftigen

busybody *n.* Zudringliche; einer, der seine Nase in fremde Angelegenheiten steckt

but *conj.* aber, jedoch; sondern; ausser dass; — *prep.* ausser; **all** — fast; **bis auf**; — *adv.* nur

butcher *n.* Fleischer, Metzger, Schlächter; (fig.) Mörder; — **shop** Fleischerei; — *v.* (ab)schlachten; (fig.) morden; **-y** *n.* Metzelei

butler *n.* Haushofmeister; Kellermeister; —**'s pantry** Speisekammer

butt *n.* Kolben; Stummel; Zielscheibe; — *v.* stossen, anstossen; — **in** sich einmischen

butter *n.* Butter; — **dish** Butterdose; — **knife** Buttermesser; — *v.* buttern, mit Butter bestreichen; — **up** (sich) einschmeicheln

buttercup *n.* Butterblume

butterfingered *adj.* mit ungeschickten Händen

butterfly n. Schmetterling; (fig.) Unbeständige

buttermilk n. Buttermilch

butterscotch n. Butterkaramelle

button n. Knopf; — v. anknöpfen, zuknöpfen

buttonhole n. Knopfloch

buttress n. (arch.) Strebe(pfeiler); (fig.) Stütze; **flying** — Strebebogen; — v. stützen

buy v. kaufen; einkaufen; (fig.) erkaufen, bestechen; — **for cash** gegen Barzahlung kaufen; — **off** abfinden; — **on credit** auf Kredit kaufen; — **out** den Anteil abkaufen von; — **secondhand** gebrauchte Sachen kaufen; — **up** aufkaufen; **-er** n. Käufer, Einkäufer

buzz v. (mil.) schwirren; streifen

by prep. an, bei, neben; über; auf; bis zu; gegen, um; innerhalb, während; für, nach, durch, mit, von; vermittels, vermöge; gemäss, zufolge; — **far** weitaus, bei weitem; — **oneself** allein; — **that** damit, darunter; — **the way** apropos; — adv. nahe, dabei, zugegen; ab, beiseite, nebenbei, weg; vorbei; vorüber; — **and** — nach und nach

bygone adj. vergangen, veraltet; früher; **-s** n. pl. vergangene Dinge, alte Sachen

bylaw n. Satzung, Statut; Nebengesetz

bypass n. Umgehungsstrasse, Entlastungsstrasse; Nebenweg; — v. umgehen, einen Umweg machen; entlasten

bypath, byway n. Nebenweg

by-product n. Nebenprodukt

bystander n. Umstehende, Zuschauer

byword n. Sprichwort

C

cab n. Taxi; (rail., truck) Führerstand

cabana n. Strandhütte; Wohnlaube

cabaret n. Kabarett; (coll.) Musikkaffeehaus

cabbage n. Kohl, Kraut; (sl.) Geld

cabin n. Hütte, Häuschen; (naut.) Kabine, Kajüte, Koje; — **boy** Schiffsjunge

cabinet n. Kabinett, Ministerium; Stube; Schrank

cabinetmaker n. Kunsttischler

cable n. Kabel, Seil; Ankertau, Trosse; Kabeldepesche; — **address** Telegrammadresse; — **car** Drahtseilbahnwagen; — v. kabeln

cablegram n. Kabel(depesche)

caboodle n. **the whole** — (coll.) der ganze Klimbim, die ganze Gesellschaft

caboose n. Personenwagen an einem Güterzug

cabstand n. Taxistand, Taxihalteplatz

cackle n. Gegacker, Geschnatter; — v. gakkern, schnattern

cactus n. Kaktus

cad n. Prolet, ungebildeter Mensch

cadaver n. Kadaver; **-ous** adj. leichenhaft, leichenblass

caddie, caddy n. Golfstockträger, Golfjunge

cadence n. Kadenz; Tonfall; Takt

cadenza n. Kadenz

cadet n. Kadett

Caesarean adj. cäsarisch; — **(section)** Kaiserschnitt

café n. Kaffeehaus, Café; Kaffeerestaurant

cafeteria n. Restaurant mit Selbstbedienung

caffeine n. Koffein

cage n. Käfig; (mech.) Förderkorb; (coll.) Gefängnis; — v. einsperren

cake n. Kuchen, Torte; (fig.) Stuck; — **of soap** Seifenstück; — v. hart werden (or machen)

calamity n. Kalamität, Unglück, Elend

calcify v. verkalken

calcimine n. Kalkmilch

calcium n. Kalzium; — **carbonate** Kalziumkarbonat; (coll.) kohlensaurer Kalk

calculate v. kalkulieren, berechnen; (fig.) abwägen, vermuten; beabsichtigen

calculating adj. kalkulierend, berechnend; — **machine** Rechenmaschine

calculation n. Kalkulation, Berechnung

calculator n. Kalkulator, Berechner; Rechenmaschine

calculus n. Rechnung; **differential** — Differentialrechnung; **integral** — Integralrechnung

caldron n. Kessel

calendar n. Kalender; (law) Liste der Gerichtsfälle; — v. registrieren

calf n. Kalb; Kalbleder; (anat.) Wade

calfskin n. Kalbfell, Kalbleder

caliber n. Kaliber; (fig.) geistige Befähigung, Wert

calibrate v. kalibrieren, richtige Weite (or Grade, Masse) finden

calibration n. Eichung; Gradeinteilung

calico n. Kaliko

caliper n. Kaliberzirkel

calisthenics n. Freiübungen

call n. Ruf, Schrei; Anspruch, Forderung; kurzer Besuch; (com.) Nachfrage; (mil.) Appell; (orn.) Lockruf; (tel.) Anruf, Gespräch; **long distance** — Ferngespräch; **on** — bereit, verfügbar; — v. rufen, ausrufen; schreien; herbeirufen; wecken; Besuch machen; nennen, benennen; (cards) ansagen; (law) vorladen; — **down** ausschelten; — **for** abholen, fordern; — **off** absagen, abberufen; — **on** besuchen; — **together** berufen, zusammenrufen; — **the roll** die Namensliste verlesen; — **to order** zur Ordnung rufen; — **up** anrufen; (mil.) aufrufen; –**er** n. Besucher; Rufer; –**ing** n. Beruf; Berufung; –**ing card** Visitenkarte

calligraphy n. Kalligrafie, Schönschreibekunst

calm n. Ruhe, Stille; (naut.) Windstille; — adj. ruhig, still; gelassen; **keep** — **die** Ruhe bewahren; — v. beruhigen; — **down** sich beruhigen; sich legen, nachlassen; –**ness** n Ruhe, Stille

caloric adj. Wärme-, Heissluft-

calorie n. Kalorie; Wärmeeinheit

calorimeter n. Wärmeeinheitenmesser

calumny n. Verleumdung

Calvinism n. Kalvinismus

calyx n. Kelch

cam n. Nocken

camaraderie n. Kameradschaft

cambric n. Battist

camel n. Kamel; –**'s hair** Kamelhaar

camellia n. Kamelie

cameo n. Kamee

camera n. Kamera, Fotoapparat; **candid** — Geheimkamera; **motion picture** — Filmkamera

camouflage n. Tarnung; — v. tarnen

camp n. Lager; Feldlager; **army** — Heerlager; — v. lagern, kampieren; –**er** n. Lagerbewohner, Kampierende

campaign n. Feldzug, Kampagne; — v. an einem Feldzug (or einer Kampagne) teilnehmen

campfire n. Lagerfeuer

campground n. Lagerplatz

campus n. Gebäude und Grundbesitz einer Hochschule; Sportplatz

camshaft n. Nockenwelle

can n. Büchse, Dose; — **opener** Büchsenöffner; — v. können; (coll.) dürfen; konservieren, einmachen, einkochen; –**ned** adj. konserviert, in Konservendosen eingemacht; –**ned goods** Konservendosen; –**nery** n. Konservenfabrik

canal n. Kanal

canary n. Kanarienvogel

canasta n. Canasta, Kanasta

cancel v. aufheben, ungültig machen; durchstreichen; absagen; (stamps) abstempeln, entwerten; –**lation** n. Annulierung, Aufhebung; Ausstreichen; Abbestellung, Abstemplung

cancer n. Krebs; –**ous** adj. krebsartig

candelabrum n. Kandelaber, Armleuchter

candid adj. aufrichtig, offen

candidate n. Kandidat, Bewerber

candle n. Kerze, Licht; **burn the** — **at both ends** seine Kräfte (or Mittel) verschwenden; **he can't hold a** — **to her** er kann ihr das Wasser nicht reichen; — **power** Kerze, Lichtstärke

candlelight n. Kerzenlicht

candlestick n. Leuchter

candy n. Süssigkeit(en), Bonbon(s), Zuckerwerk; — v. kandieren, verzukkern

cane n. Rohr; Spazierstock; — **sugar** Rohrzucker

canine adj. hündisch, Hunde-

canker n. Krebs; (bot.) Brand; (fig.) Krebsschaden

cannibal n. Kannibale, Menschenfresser; — adj. kannibalisch; –**ism** n. Kannibalismus

cannon n. Kanone, Geschütz; (billiards) Karambolage; — **ball** Kanonenkugel; — v. beschiessen; (billiards) karambolieren; –**ade** n. Kanonade; Beschiessung (coll.) Karombolage

canny adj. schlau; vorsichtig; sparsam

canoe n. Kanu, Paddelboot; Einbaum

canon n. Regal, Richtschnur; (rel. and mus.) Kanon; — **law** kanonisches Recht, Kirchenrecht; –**ize** v. heiligsprechen; (fig.) verherrlichen

canopy n. Baldachin; (avi.) Glaskuppel der Pilotenkanzel

cantaloupe n. Zuckermelone

cantata n. Kantate

canteen n. Kantine; Feldflasche

canton n. Bezirk, Kanton, Kreis; –**ment** n. Kantonnement; Einquartierung

canvas n. (art) Leinwand, Ölgemälde; (camping) Zeltleinwand; (naut.) Segeltuch, Segel

canvass n. Sichtung, Prüfung; Bewerbung; (pol.) Wahlprüfung; — v. sichten, prüfen; bewerben; (pol.) **Wahlreden halten, Stimmen fangen**

canyon n. Felsenschlucht

cap n. Mütze, Kappe; (dent.) Krone; (mech.) Deckel, Verschluss, Haube; — **and gown** Barett und Talar, akademische Tracht; — v. bedecken, mit einer Kappe versehen; (fig.) übertreffen; — **the climax** das Äusserste erreichen

capability n. Fähigkeit; Vermögen

capable adj. tüchtig, fähig, imstande, geeignet

capacious adj. geräumig, umfassend, weit

capacity n. Gehalt, Rauminhalt, Aufnahmefähigkeit; Kapazität; Befähigung, Fähigkeit; Eigenschaft, Funktion

cape n. (geog.) Kap, Vorgebirge; (clothing) Kape, Kragenmantel

Cape of Good Hope *n.* Kap der guten Hoffnung

caper *n.* Kapriole, Luftsprung; (bot.) Kaper; (fig.) toller Streich; **cut -s** Kapriolen machen; — *v.* hüpfen, springen

capillary *n.* Kapillargefäss, Haargefäss; — *adj.* Kapillar-; haarfein, haarförmig; — **attraction** Kapillarität

capital *n.* Hauptstadt; (arch.) Kapitell, Säulenkopf; (com.) Kapital, Stammvermögen; (typ.) grosser Buchstabe; **make — of** Nutzen ziehen aus; — *adj.* Kapital-, Haupt-; besonders, überragend; vortrefflich; (law) peinlich, Todes-; — **crime** Kapitalverbrechen; — **goods** Produktionsgüter; — **letters** grosse Buchstaben; — **punishment** Todesstrafe; — **stock** Aktienkapital; **-ism** *n.* Kapitalismus; **-ist** *n.* Kapitalist; **-ize** *v.* gross schreiben; kapitalisieren; (fig.) gewinnen

capitol *n.* Kapitol, Regierungsgebäude

capitulate *v.* kapitulieren

capitulation *n.* Kapitulation

capon *n.* Kapaun, Kapphahn

caprice *n.* Kaprize, Einfall, Laune

capricious *adj.* kapriziös, launenhaft

capsize *v.* kentern, umschlagen

capsule *n.* Kapsel, Hülle, Hülse; (chem.) Probiertiegel

captain *n.* (mil.) Hauptmann, Rittmeister; (naut. and sports) Kapitän; (fig.) Anführer

caption *n.* (film) Untertitel; (typ.) Titelzeile, Überschrift

captivate *v.* bestricken, bezaubern, fesseln

captivating *adj.* fesselnd, reizend

captive *n.* Gefangene; (fig.) Bezauberte; — *adj.* gefangen; (fig.) bestrickt, bezaubert, gefesselt

captivity *n.* Gefangenschaft, Knechtschaft

captor *n.* Erbeuter, Fänger; (naut.) Kaperer

capture *n.* Einnahme, Gefangennahme; (law) Verhaftung; (naut.) Kapern, Prise; — *v.* einnehmen, fangen; erbeuten; (law) verhaften; (naut.) kapern

car *n.* Wagen, Auto; (avi.) Gondel; (rail.) Waggon; **armored —** Panzerwagen; — **pool** Fahrbereitschaft; Interessengemeinschaft von Wagenbesitzern; — **port** Autoschuppen

caramel *n.* Karamel(le)

caravan *n.* Karawane

caraway *n.* Kümmel

carbide *n.* Karbid

carbolic *adj.* karbolsauer; — **acid** Karbolsäure, Phenol

carbon *n.* Kohlenstoff; (elec.) Kohlestift; — **copy** Durchschlag; — **dioxide** Kohlendioxyd; — **monoxide** Kohlenmonoxyd; — **paper** Kohlepapier, Blaupapier

carbonic *adj.* Kohlen-; — **acid** Kohlensäure

carborundum *n.* Siliziumkarbid, Karborundum

carbuncle *n.* Karbunkel, Furunkel

carburetor *n.* Vergaser

carcass *n.* Aas, Kadaver

carcinogen *n.* Krebserreger, krebserregende Substanz

carcinoma *n.* (med.) Krebsgeschwür

card *n.* Karte; Mitteilung, Geschäftsanzeige; it's in the **-s** es steht in den Karten; — **index** Kartei; — **table** Spieltisch; — *v.* krempeln, rauhen

cardboard *n.* Pappe, Pappdeckel

cardiac *adj.* (med.) Herz-; (pharm.) herzstärkend

cardinal *n.* (eccl.) Kardinal; (orn.) Rotfink; — *adj.* Kardinal-, Haupt-; vorzüglich; — **number** Grundzahl

cardiogram *n.* Kardiogramm

cardiology *n.* Kardiologie

cardiovascular *adj.* herzmuskulär

care *n.* Sorge, Vorsicht, Pflege; Behandlung; Aufsicht, Wartung; — **of** per Adresse; **take —! *interj.* Achtung! Vorsicht! take —! not** to sich hüten zu; **take — of** sich kümmern um, sorgen für; erledigen; aufbewahren; schonen; **take — of** oneself sich pflegen; **take —** to dafür sorgen, dass; — *v.* sorgen, sich kümmern; pflegen; beaufsichtigen; — **for** mögen, geneigt sein; sich kümmern um, pflegen; **-d for** versorgt; **for all I —** meinetwegen; **I don't —** es ist mir gleich (or einerlei); **I don't — much for** it ich mache mir nicht viel daraus; **what do I —!** Was geht's mich an! **who -s?** Wen interessiert das? **-ful** *adj.* vorsichtig, sorgfältig; **-fulness** *n.* Vorsicht, Sorgfalt; **-less** *adj.* sorglos, unbekümmert; unachtsam, nachlässig; leichtsinnig; **-lessness** *n.* Unachtsamkeit, Nachlässigkeit

career *n.* Laufbahn, Beruf; Karriere; — *v.* eilen, rasen, rennen

carefree *adj.* sorglos

caress *n.* Liebkosung; — *v.* liebkosen, streicheln; schmeicheln

caretaker *n.* Wärter, Wächter

careworn *adj.* abgehärmt, gramerfüllt

carfare *n.* Fahrgeld, Fahrpreis

cargo *n.* Kargo, Fracht, Schiffsladung

caribou *n.* amerikanisches Renntier, Ren

caricature *n.* Karikatur; — *v.* karikieren

carload n. Wagenladung
carnal adj. fleischlich, sinnlich
carnation n. Nelke
carnival n. Karneval, Fasching
carnivorous adj. fleischfressend
carol n. Lobgesang, Jubellied; — v. singen; lobpreisen, jubilieren
carouse v. saufen, zechen; -l n. Karussell
carp n. Karpfen; — v. bekritteln, verspotten; -ing adj. tadelsüchtig
carpenter n. Zimmermann, Tischler
carpentry n. Zimmerhandwerk, Tischlerarbeit
carpet n. Teppich; — sweeper Teppichkehrmaschine; — v. mit Teppichen belegen
carpetbagger n. politischer Abenteurer; Nutzniesser
carpool n. Mitfahrerzentrale
carriage n. Wagen, Fuhrwerk; Haltung, Benehmen; (avi. and mech.) Gestell, Lafette.
carrier n. Träger, Bote, Überbringer, Spediteur (med.) Bazillenträger; — pigeon Brieftaube
carrot n. Karotte, Mohrrübe, Möhre
carry v. tragen, fahren, führen, befördern, bringen, transportieren, übertragen; fortsetzen; (mil.) einnehmen, erobern; durchsetzen, gewinnen; — a motion einen Antrag durchbringen; — away fortreissen, fortschaffen; — on weiterführen; — oneself sich betragen (or benehmen); — out (oder through) erfüllen, ausführen, durchführen; — weight Gewicht haben; -ing adj. -ing charge Transportspesen
cart n. Karre(n); Wagen; put the — before the horse das Pferd am Schwanz aufzäumen; turn — wheels radschlagen; — v. karren; — away wegschaffen; -age n. Fuhrlohn, Transportkosten
Carthage n. Karthago
cartilage n. Knorpel
cartography n. Kartografie
carton n. Karton
cartoon n. Karikatur(enserie); Musterzeichnung; (film) Zeichenfilm, Trickfilm; -ist n. Karikaturenzeichner
cartridge n. Kartusche, Patrone
carve v. (meat) zerlegen, tranchieren, vorschneiden; (metal) gravieren; (stone) aushauen, meisseln; (wood) schnitzen; -r n. (meat) Tranchierer, Vorschneider; (stone) Bildhauer, Steinmetz; (wood) Schnitzer
carving knife n. Tranchiermesser, Schnitzmesser
carving set n. Tranchierbesteck
cascade n. Kaskade, Wasserfall; (fig.)

Feuerwerk
case n. Behälter, Etui, Futteral; Gehäuse, Kasten, Kiste; Fach; Besteck; Hülle; Fall, Lage, Sache; (gram.) Fall; (law) Prozess; (typ.) Schriftart, Setzkasten; in any — auf jeden Fall; in — falls, im Falle dass; in — of bei, im Falle von
casemate n. bombensicheres Arsenal; Kasematte
casement n. Fensterflügel, Verschalung
cash n. Bargeld, Barschaft; — and carry Barverkauf (zum Mitnehmen); — in advance Vorauszahlung; — on delivery Lieferung per Nachnahme; — on hand Bargeld; in — bar; — register Registrierkasse; — v. einkassieren, einlösen; — in on verdienen bei; -ier n. Kassierer; -ier's check voll gedeckter Bankscheck
cashbook n. Kassabuch; Kassenbuch
cashbox n. Geldkassette
cashew n. Cachou, brasilianische Akazie
cashmere n. Kaschmir
casing n. Überzug, Verkleidung; Futteral, Gehäuse
casino n. Kasino; Klubhaus
cask n. Tonne, Fass
casket n. Kästchen; Sarg
Caspian Sea n. das Kaspische Meer
casserole n. Kasserole, Tiegel
cassock n. Soutane, Priesterrock
cast n. Werfen; Wurf; Wurfweite; (art) Färbung, Schattierung; (mech.) Guss, Gussform, Gusstück; (med.) Gipsverband; (naut.) Auswerfen; (theat.) Besetzung; (fig.) Art, Form, Gattung; Äussere; — adj. — iron Gusseisen; — v. werfen; auswerfen; (mech.) formen, giessen; (theat.) besetzen; — aside fortwerfen; — a vote abstimmen, wählen; — lots auslosen; — on anschlagen; the die is — der Würfel ist gefallen; -er n. Laufrolle; -ing n. (mech.) Giessen, Gussform; (theat.) Rollenverteilung; -ing adj. ausschlaggebend, entscheidend
castanet n. Kastagnette
castaway n. Verworfene; (naut.) Schiffbrüchige
castdown adj. gedemütigt, entmutigt
caste n. Kaste, Klasse; lose — seine Stellung in der Gesellschaft verlieren
castle n. Schloss, Burg, Kastell; (chess) Turm; — in the air (oder in Spain) Luftschloss; — v. rochieren
castoff adj. weggeworfen; abgelegt; wertlos
castor oil n. Rizinusöl
castrate v. kastrieren
casual adj. zufällig; gelegentlich; —

acquaintance flüchtige Bekannte; **–ty** *n.* Unfall, Todesfall; (mil.) Verlust

cat *n.* Katze; **let the — out of the bag** die Katze aus dem Sack lassen; **— nap** Nickerchen; **–ty** *adj.* tückisch, hinterlistig

catabolism *n.* (med.) Katabolismus, zerlegender Stoffwechsel

catacombs *n. pl.* Katakomben

catafighter *n.* Katapultflugzeug

catalogue *n.* Katalog, Verzeichnis; **—** *v.* katalogisieren

catapult *n.* Katapult

cataract *n.* Katarakt, Wasserfall, Wolkenbruch; (med.) grauer Star

catarrh *n.* Katarrh

catastrophe *n.* Katastrophe

catch *n.* Fang; Beute; Vorteil; Griff, Verschluss, Haken; Klinke; Stockung; (sports) Auffangen; **a good — ein guter Fang; eine gute Partie; — of a door** Türklinke, Schliesshaken; **play —** Ball spielen; **—** *v.* fangen; erreichen, bekommen, erwischen; überfallen; (er)fassen; treffen; (mech.) ineinandergreifen; (med.) sich holen, angesteckt werden; (sports) auffangen; **— a train** einen Zug erreichen; **— cold** sich erkälten; **— fire** Feuer fangen, in Brand geraten; **— hold of** ergreifen, habhaft werden; **—** (coll.) kapieren; **— on** hängen bleiben; (coll.) kapieren; **— one's eye** ins Auge fallen; **— up** nachkommen; **— up with** einholen; **— basin** Abflussbassin, Bewässerungsbecken; **–er** *n.* Fänger; **–ing** *adj.* ansteckend; **–ing tune** einschmeichelnde Melodie; **–y** *adj.* anziehend, einnehmend, packend; verfänglich

catchall *n.* Sammelkasten

catchword *n.* Schlagwort, Stichwort; Losungswort; (pol.) Parteiparole

catechism *n.* Katechismus

category *n.* Kategorie

cater *v.* mit Nahrungsmittelversorgen; für die Tafel (*or* Unterhaltung, Bedürfnisse) sorgen; **—** *n.* Lebensmittellieferant, Proviantmeister; Versorger

cater-cornered *adj.* diagonal

caterpillar *n.* Raupe; **— tractor** Raupenschlepper

caterwaul *n.* Katzenmusik; **—** *v.* miauen

catgut *n.* Darmsaite

cathedral *n.* Dom, Kathedrale, Münster

cathode *n.* Kathode; **— rays** Kathodenstrahlen

Catholic *n.* Katholik; **—** *adj.* katholisch; **–ism** *n.* Katholizismus

catnip *n.* Katzenminze

cat's paw *n.* Gefoppte, Willenlose

catsup *n.* Ketchup, pikante Tomaten-sauce

cattle *n.* Vieh, Rinder; **— breeding** Viehzucht; **— car** Viehwagen; **— ranch** Viehweide, Rinderfarm; **— show** Viehausstellung

cattleman *n.* Viehzüchter

caucus *n.* Vorversammlung

cauliflower *n.* Blumenkohl

causal *adj.* kausal, ursächlich

cause *n.* Grund, Ursache; (fig.) Angelegenheit, Sache; **show — Rechtsgründe** angeben; **—** *v.* veranlassen, verursachen; erregen; bewirken; **–less** *adj.* grundlos, unbegründet

caustic *adj.* kaustisch, ätzend; (fig.) satirisch, beissend

cauterize *v.* ausbrennen, beizen

caution *n.* Vorsicht, Behutsamkeit; Warnung, Verwarnung; **—** *v.* warnen, verwarnen

cautious *adj.* vorsichtig, behutsam

cavalcade *n.* Kavalkade

cavalier *n.* Kavalier; **—** *adj.* hochmütig, verächtlich

cavalry *n.* Kavallerie

cavalryman *n.* Kavallerist

cave *n.* Höhle, Grube; **— dweller** Höhlenbewohner, Troglodyt; **— man** Höhlenmensch, Troglodyt; **—** *v.* **in** einstürzen

cavern *n.* Höhle, Kaverne

caviar *n.* Kaviar

cavil *v.* bekritteln, nörgeln

cavity *n.* Höhlung, Vertiefung; Höhle

caw *v.* krächzen

cease *v.* aufhören, ablassen; abstehen, einstellen; (fig.) ruhen; **— fire** das Feuer einstellen; **–less** *adj.* unaufhörlich

cedar *n.* Zeder; **—** *adj.* zedern, aus Zedernholz

cede *v.* abtreten, überlassen

ceiling *n.* Decke; (avi.) Flughöhe, Steighöhe; **— price** Höchstpreis; **— zero** Flughöhe Null

celebrate *v.* feiern; preisen, verherrlichen; (rel.) lesen; **–d** *adj.* berühmt, gefeiert

celebration *n.* Feier, Fest; (fig.) Verherrlichung

celebrity *n.* Berühmtheit

celery *n.* Sellerie

celestial *adj.* himmlisch, göttlich

cell *n.* (biol.) Zelle; (elec.) galvanisches Element; Sturmzentrum; **— of a party** (pol.) Parteikern

cellar *n.* Keller

cello *n.* Cello

cellophane *n.* Zellophan

cellular *adj.* zellig, zellförmig

celluloid *n.* Zelluloid

cellulose *n.* Zellulose

cement n. Zement; Kitt, Mörtel; rubber — flüssiger Klebstoff; — v. zementieren; (fig.) fest verbinden

cemetery n. Friedhof, Kirchhof

censor n. Zensor; — v. der Zensur unterwerfen, (über)prüfen, zensieren; -ship n. Zensur, Zensoramt

censure n. Tadel, Rüge, Verweis; — v. tadeln, kritisieren

census n. Volkszählung, Zensus

cent n. Cent; Pfennig; Hundert

centenary n. Jahrhundertfeier, hundertjähriges Jubiläum; — adj. hundertjährig

centennial n. Hundertjahrfeier; — adj. hundertjährig

center n. Mitte, Mittelpunkt Zentrum; — of gravity Schwerpunkt; — v. konzentrieren; in den Mittelpunkt stellen

centerboard n. (naut.) Schwert

centerpiece n. Tafelaufsatz

centigrade adj. hundertgradig, hundertteilig

centimeter n. Zentimeter

central adj. zentral; — heating Zentralheizung; -ization n. Zentralisierung; Zentralisation; -ize v. zentralisieren

Central Alps n. Mittelalpen

centrifugal adj. zentrifugal, vom Mittelpunkt wegstrebend; — force Zentrifugalkraft

centripetal adj. zentripetal, zum Mittelpunkt strebend; — force Zentripetalkraft

century n. Jahrhundert

ceramics n. pl. Keramik; Töpferkunst

cereal n. Getreide(pflanze)

cerebral palsy n. (med.) Gehirnlähmung

ceremonial n. Zeremoniell; — adj. zeremoniell, feierlich, förmlich

ceremonious adj. zeremoniell, förmlich

ceremony n. Umstand, Zeremonie; Feier; without — ohne Umstände

certain adj. gewiss, sicher, unzweifelhaft; unfehlbar, unvermeidlich; -ly adv. bestimmt, zuverlässig, allerdings, sicherlich; -ty n. Gewissheit, Sicherheit, Bestimmtheit; with -ty mit Zuverlässigkeit (or Bestimmtheit)

certificate n. Attest, Zeugnis, Schein

certification n. Beglaubigung, Bescheinigung

certified adj. beglaubigt, bescheinigt; — check beglaubigter Scheck; — public accountant amtlicher Rechnungsführer

certify v. bezeugen, beglaubigen, bescheinigen

certitude n. Gewissheit, Sicherheit

cessation n. Aufhören, Einstellen; Schluss; — of hostilities Einstellung der Feindseligkeiten

cession n. Abtretung

cesspool n. Senkgrube

chafe v. reiben, frottieren; (med.) wundreiben, sich scheuern; (fig.) aufregen, erzürnen

chaff n. Häcksel, Spreu; (fig.) Neckerei; (auch window avi.) Staniolstreifen zur Störung von Radar; — v. aufziehen, necken

chagrin n. Ärger, Verdruss; — v. ärgern

chain n. Kette, Fessel; Reihe; pl. Sklavenketten, Gefangenschaft; — gang Abteilung zusammengeketteter Verbrecher; — reaction Kettenreaktion; — smoker Kettenraucher; — stitch Kettenstich; — store Kettenladen, Zweiggeschäft (eines Warenkonzerns); — v. fesseln, (an)ketten

chair n. Stuhl, Sessel; Sitz; Professur; (pol.) Präsidium; Vorsitzende; address the — sich an den Vorsitzenden wenden; take the — den Vorsitz übernehmen; — car Salonwagen

chairman n. Vorsitzende

chalice n. Kelch

chalk n. Kreide; — v. mit Kreide zeichnen (or schreiben, mischen); — up to auf Konto schreiben

challenge n. Aufforderung, Herausforderung; (law) Verwerfung; (mil.) Anruf; — v. auffordern, herausfordern; (law) verwerfen; (mil.) anrufen

chamber n. Kammer, Zimmer; (law) Gerichtszimmer; — of commerce Handelskammer; — music Kammermusik; -lain n. Kammerherr; Kämmerer

chambermaid n. Kammermädchen, Zimmermädchen

chamois n. Gemse; Gemsenleder, Sämischleder

champagne n. Champagner, Sekt

champion n. Meister, Champion; (fig.) Verfechter; — v. verteidigen; beschützen; -ship n. Meisterschaft; (fig.) Verteidigung

chance n. Gelegenheit, Chance, Möglichkeit; Wahrscheinlichkeit; Los, Zufall; by — zufällig; not a — keine Spur; on the — mit der Hoffnung; stand a — Aussicht haben; take a — das Glück versuchen, es darauf ankommen lassen; — v. sich begeben, geschehen, wagen, es ankommen lassen auf; — adj. zufällig, gelegentlich

chancel n. Altarplatz, Hochchor

chancellor n. Kanzler

chandelier n. Kronleuchter, Lüster; Kandelaber, Armleuchter

change n. Änderung, Veränderung; Wechsel, Abwechselung, Übergang; Kleingeld; (mus.) Modulation, Variation; — of heart Gefühlsveränderung; for a — zur Abwechslung; give — for herausgeben auf; make — in Kleingeld umwechseln; — v. (sich) (ver)ändern; tauschen; wechseln; (baby) trockenlegen; (rail.) umsteigen; — clothes sich umziehen; — for the better sich verbessern; — for the worse sich verschlechtern (or verschlimmern); — hands den Besitzer wechseln; — one's mind sich anders besinnen, anderen Sinnes werden; –able adj. veränderlich, unbeständig; (color) schillernd; –less adj. unveränderlich, beständig

channel n. Kanal; Flussbett; Rinne, Gosse; (naut.) Fahrwasser; (pol.) Dienstweg, Amtsweg; (rad.) Sender; — v. kanalisieren, aushöhlen, furchen

chant n. Gesang, Melodie, Weise; — v. singen, besingen; (coll.) herunterleiern

chanticleer n. Hahn

chaos n. Chaos; Wirrwarr

chaotic adj. chaotisch; verworren

chap n. (coll.) Bursche, Kerl; pl. Lederüberkleid; — v. aufspringen, rissig werden; spalten; –ped adj. aufgesprungen, rissig

chapel n. Kapelle

chaperon n. Anstandsdame; — v. (als Anstandsdame) begleiten

chaplain n. Kaplan; army — Feldprediger; navy — Schiffsgeistliche

chapter n. Kapitel, Abschnitt

char v. verkohlen

character n. Charakter; Art; Rang; Person, Figur; Festigkeit; Buchstabe; (theat.) Rolle; (fig.) Original; Zeugnis; act out of — aus der Rolle fallen; in — dem Charakter gemäss; –istic n. Eigenschaft; Kennzeichen; –istic adj. eigentümlich, charakteristisch; –ize v. charakterisieren

charade n. Scharade

charcoal n. Holzkohle; — burner Köhler

charge n. Preis, Forderung; Last, Belastung; Anweisung, Auftrag; Ladung; Aufsicht, Verwahrung; Mündel, Pflegling; (law) Anklage, Beschuldigung; Rechtsbelehrung; (mil.) Angriff; be in — of leiten; in Verwahrung haben; extra — Nebenkosten, Aufschlag; free of — unentgeltlich, gratis; in — of die Aufsicht über; take — of sich annehmen, die Leitung übernehmen; — account Spesenkonto; — v. anrechnen, berechnen; belasten; anweisen, beauftragen; (elec.) laden; (law) anklagen, beschuldigen; (mil.) angreifen; — for

verlangen, fordern; — to one's account auf die Rechnung setzen, das Konto belasten; — with beschuldigen; –r n. Dienstpferd; Schlachtross

chariot n. Triumpfwagen; Staatswagen; –eer n. Wagenlenker

charitable adj. wohltätig, barmherzig, mildtätig; (fig.) gütig, nachsichtig

charity n. Wohltätigkeit, Barmherzigkeit, Mildtätigkeit; Güte, Nachsicht; (fig.) Liebeswerk, Stiftung; Almosen

charm n. Charme; Reiz, Zauber; Anmut; (fig.) Amulett, Zauber(mittel); — v. (be)zaubern; fesseln, entzücken; (fig.) behexen; –ing adj. charmant, reizend, entzückend

chart n. Tabelle; (naut.) Karte, Seekarte; — v. auf einer Karte verzeichnen; –er n. Stiftungsurkunde; Privilegium; (fig.) Vorrecht; –er member Stiftungsmitglied; –er v. durch Urkunde festsetzen; privilegieren; (naut.) chartern; befrachten, verfrachten; (fig.) bevorrechten

charwoman n. Scheuerfrau, Reinemachefrau

chase n. Jagd, Verfolgung; give — nachjagen, nachsetzen; — v. jagen, hetzen; nachsetzen, verfolgen; –r n. (coll.) leichtes Getränk (neben alkoholischen Getränken)

chassis n. Fahrgestell, Rahmen; (mil.) Lafette

chaste adj. keusch, züchtig; (fig.) edel, rein; –n v. strafen; reinigen; (ver)bessern; (fig.) demütigen

chastise v. züchtigen; (rel.) kasteien; –ment n. Strafe, Züchtigung

chastity n. Keuschheit, Reinheit

chat n. Geplauder, Plauderei; Unterhaltung; — v. plaudern, schwatzen; –ter n. Geplauder, Geplapper, Geschwätz; Klappern; (orn.) Geschnatter, Gezwitscher; –ter v. plappern, schwatzen; klappern; schnattern, zwitschern; his teeth –ter with cold er klappert vor Kälte mit den Zähnen; –ting n. Klappern; (orn.) Gezwitscher; Geschnatter; (fig.) Tratsch; –ty adj. geschwätzig, schwatzhaft

chattel n. bewegliche Gut, Habe; goods and –s Hab und Gut

chatterbox n. Plaudertasche, Schwätzer(in)

chauffeur n. Chauffeur, Fahrer

cheap n. billig, wohlfeil; gering, gemein, ordinär; feel — sich gering (or klein) fühlen; get off — mit blauem Auge davonkommen; –en v. herabsetzen, verbilligen; –ness n. Billigkeit, Wohlfeilheit; (fig.) Gemeinheit

cheat *n.* Betrüger, Schwindler; — *v.* betrügen, (be)schwindeln, mogeln; — out of betrügen um; **-er** *n.* Betrüger, Schwindler, Gauner

check *n.* Scheck; Hemmnis, Hindernis, Einhalt, Unterbrechung; Marke, Schein; Kontrolle; (chess) Schach; (fabrik) Karo, karierte Muster; (mil.) Schlappe; (fig.) Dämpfer, Zügel; Unfall; **coat** (*oder* **hat**) — Garderobenmarke; **hold** (*oder* **keep**) **in** — in Schach halten; **traveler's** — Reisescheck; — **list** Kontrollverzeichnis; — *v.* hemmen, hindern; einhalten, unterbrechen; kontrollieren, nachsehen; abgeben, zur Aufbewahrung geben; bezeichnen, markieren; (chess) Schach bieten; (fig.) dämpfen, zügeln; — **in** eintragen; — **off** abhaken, abstreichen; — **up on** kontrollieren, sich erkundigen über; — **with** übereinstimmen mit

checker *v.* karieren; **-ed** *adj.* kariert

checkerboard *n.* Damebrett

checkers *n.* Damespiel

checking account *n.* Bankkonto

checkmate *n.* Schachmatt; — *v.* schachmatt setzen

check point *n.* Kontrollstelle

checkup *n.* gründliche Untersuchung

cheek *n.* Wange, Backe; (coll.) Dreistigkeit, Stirn; — **by jowl** dicht beieinander, in vertraulicher Gemeinschaft; **with one's tongue in one's** — schalkhaft

checkbone *n.* Backenknochen

cheer *n.* Heiterkeit; Stimmung; Ermutigung, Trost; Beifallsruf, Zujauchsen; *pl.* Beifall, Applaus, Hochlebenlassen; **be of good** — guter Dinge sein; — *v.* ermutigen, trösten; aufmuntern; (zu)jubeln, Beifall spenden, mit Beifall begrüssen; — **up** aufheitern; sich trösten; **-ful** *adj.* froh, heiter, munter; **-fulness** *n.* Heiterkeit, Frohsinn; **-ing** *adj.* tröstend, trostreich; **-ing** *n.* Beifallrufen; **-less** *adj.* freudlos, trostlos

cheese *n.* Käse

cheesecloth *n.* Wachstuch

chef *n.* Küchenchef

chemical *adj.* chemisch; — **engineering** Chemotechnik; — **warfare** chemischer Krieg; **-s** *n. pl.* Chemikalien

chemist *n.* Chemiker; **-ry** *n.* Chemie

chemosphere *n.* Luftschicht ca 32–80 Km. über der Erde

cherish *v.* mit Liebe behandeln, hegen, pflegen; festhalten an; — **the hope** die Hoffnung aufrechterhalten (*or* hegen)

cherry *n.* Kirsche; — *adj.* kirschrot; Kirschenholz-; — **brandy** Kirschbrannt-wein; **-stone** Kirschkern

cherub *n.* Cherub

chess *n.* Schach(spiel)

chessboard *n.* Schachbrett

chessman *n.* Schachfigur

chest *n.* Kiste, Kasten, Koffer; Lade, Truhe; Kommode; (anat.) Brust(kasten); — **of drawers** Kommode

chestnut *n.* Kastanie; — *adj.* kastanienbraun; — **tree** Kastanienbaum

chevron *n.* Wappensparren; (mil.) Winkel, Tresse

chew *v.* kauen; (coll.) grübeln; **-ing** *adj.* **-ing gum** Kaugummi

chic *n.* Schick; (fig.) Geschmack; — *adj.* schick, geschmackvoll, stilgerecht

Chicago *n.* Chicago

chicanery *n.* Schikane, Rechtsverdrehung; Haarspalterei

chick *n.* Küken; **-en** *n.* Huhn, Hühnchen, Küken, Küchlein; **-en** *adj.* **-en pox** Windpocken

chicken-hearted *adj.* furchtsam, feige

chick-pea *n.* Kichererbse

chickweed *n.* Vogelmiere, rotes Sandkraut

chicory *n.* Zichorie, Wegwarte

chide *v.* schmähen, tadeln; keifen, schelten

chief *n.* Chef, Haupt, Oberhaupt; Anführer, Häuptling; — **of staff** Generalstabschef; — *adj.* erst, höchst, oberst; hauptsächlich, vorzüglichst; Ober-, Haupt-; — **clerk** Hauptbuchhalter; Chefsekretär; — **justice** Richter am Obersten Gerichtshof

chieftain *n.* Stammeshäuptling, Hauptmann

chiffon *n.* Chiffon; **-iere** *n.* Kommode; Kästchen

chilblain *n.* Frostbeule

child *n.* Kind; **ever since I was a** — von Kindheit an; **with** — in anderen Umständen, schwanger; **-ish** *adj.* kindisch; **-like** *adj.* kindlich

childbirth *n.* Geburt, Niederkunft

childhood *n.* Kindheit; **second** — zweite Kindheit, Kindischwerden im Alter

chili *n.* spanischer Pfeffer; — **sauce** gepfefferte Tomatensauce

chill *adj.* eisig, frostig, kalt; (fig.) entmutigend, niederdrückend; — *n.* Frost, Kälte, Schauer; (med.) Frösteln, Schüttelfrost; (fig.) Entmutigung; — *v.* erkälten, erstarren; abkühlen; (metal) abschrecken; (fig.) dämpfen, entmutigen; niederschlagen; **-y** *adj.* frostig, kühl; **I feel -y** mich fröstelt

chime *n.* Glockenspiel, Geläute; (fig.) Einklang, Harmonie; — *v.* ertönen

lassen, zusammenklingen; (fig.) übereinstimmen harmonieren
chimera *n.* Chimäre, Schimäre; Hirnges-
pinst, Schreckbild
chimerical *adj.* schimärisch, phantastisch
chimney *n.* Kamin, Schornstein, Esse;
(lamp) Zylinder; — **sweep** Schornsteinfeger
chimpanzee *n.* Schimpanse
chin *n.* Kinn; — **up!** Kopf hoch!
china(ware) *n.* Porzellan
chinchilla *n.* Chinchilla
chink *n.* Riss, Ritze; Spalt, Spalte; — *v.*
— **up** ausfüllen
chintz *n.* Möbelkattun
chip *n.* Splitter, Span; Spielmarke; **a** —
off the old block aus demselben Holz
geschnitzt; — *v.* bearbeiten, behauen;
abschleifen; — **in** beitragen zu
chipmunk *n.* gestreiftes Erdhörnchen
chiropodist *n.* Pedikürer; Fussspezialist
chiropractor *n.* Chiropraktiker, Handauf-
leger
chirp *n.* Zirpen, Zwitschern; — *v.* zirpen,
zwitschern; piepen, pfeifen
chisel *n.* Meissel, Stemmeisen; Stichel;
— *v.* meisseln; (sl.) betrügen; **-er** *n.*
Betrüger, Gauner
chitchat *n.* Schnickschnack, Geschwätz
chivalrous *adj.* chevaleresk, ritterlich,
galant
chivalry *n.* Ritterlichkeit; Rittertum
chives *n. pl.* Schnittlauch
chloremia *n.* (med.) Bleichsucht
chlorine *n.* Chlor
chloroform *n.* Chloroform; **administer** —
mit Chloroform betäuben; — *v.* chloroformieren
chloromycetin *n.* Chloromycetine
chlorophyll *n.* Chlorophyll, Blattgrün
chock-full *adj.* gedrängt voll, übervoll
chocolate *n.* Schokolade; Praliné
choice *n.* Wahl, Auswahl; Ausgewähltes;
Sortiment, Vorrat; — *adj.* (aus)erlesen,
ausgesucht, vorzüglich
choir *n.* Chor
choirmaster *n.* Chorleiter
choke *n.* Würgung; Erstickungsanfall;
(auto) Drosselklappe; — *v.* ersticken,
würgen; (mech.) verstopfen; drosseln;
— **back** herunterschlucken; **-r** *n.*
Halsbinde, Krawatte; Stehkragen
cholera *n.* Cholera
choleric *adj.* cholerisch, jähzornig; hitzig
cholesterol *n.* Cholesterin, Gallenfett
choose *v.* wählen, auswählen; belieben;
mögen, vorziehen, wollen
choosy *adj.* wählerisch
chop *n.* Hieb, Schlag; Kotelett(e); Rippenstück; Scheibe, Schnitte, Stück; *pl.*

Kinnbacken; **breaded** — **paniertes**
Kotelett; **lick one's -s** sich das Maul
lecken; — *v.* zerhauen, zerhacken;
schlagen; — **down** fällen, niederhauen;
— **off** abhacken; **-ped meat** Hack-
fleisch; — **up** zerhacken; **-per** *n.*
Hackmesser; **-py** *adj.* stürmisch; abge-
brochen; plötzlich umschlagend; unbeständig, unstet
choral *adj.* chorartig; Chor-; **-e** *n.* **Choral**
chord *n.* Akkord, Zusammenklang
chore *n.* leichte Arbeit, Auftrag; *pl.* **Farm-**
arbeiten, Hausarbeiten
choreography *n.* Choreographie
chorister *n.* Chorist, Chorsänger; **Chor-**
leiter
chorus *n.* Chor; Refrain; Kehrreim
chosen *adj.* erwählt, auserlesen; — **few**
die wenigen Auserwählten
chowder *n.* dicke Suppe, Milchsuppe
Christ *n.* Christus; **-endom** *n.* **Christen-**
tum, Christenheit
christen *v.* taufen; **-ing** *n.* Taufe
Christian *n.* Christ; — *adj.* christlich; —
name Taufname, Vorname; **-ity** —
Christentum; **-ize** *v.* zum Christentum
bekehren
Christmas *n.* Weihnacht(en), Christfest,
Weihnachtsfest; **Merry** —! Fröhliche
Weihnachten; — *adj.* — **carol** Weih-
nachtslied; — **Day** Weihnachtstag; —
Eve Weihnachtsabend, Heilige Abend;
— **present** Weihnachtsgeschenk; —
tree Weihnachtsbaum, Christbaum
chromium *n.* Chrom
Chromosome *n.* Chromosom
chronic *adj.* chronisch
chronicle *n.* Chronik; — *v.* in eine Chronik
aufnehmen, aufzeichnen
chronological *adj.* chronologisch; **in** —
order in der richtigen Zeitfolge
chronology *n.* Chronologie, Zeitfolge;
Zeitrechnung
chrysalis *n.* Puppe
chrysanthemum *n.* Chrysantheme, Chrysanthemum
chubby *adj.* plump, rundlich
chuckle *n.* Kichern; Kakeln; — *v.* kichern,
in sich hineinlachen; gackern, kakeln
chum *n.* Freund, Kamerad; **school** —
Schulkamerad; **-my** *adj.* intim
chunk *n.* Klumpen; kurzes, dickes Stück
church *n.* Kirche; — *adj.* kirchlich; **Kirch-**
churchgoer *n.* Kirchgänger
churchman *n.* Geistliche; Klerikale
churchyard *n.* Kirchhof; Friedhof
churlish *adj.* grob, plump, roh; (fig.)
geizig; schwierig
churn *n.* Butterfass; — *v.* buttern; (fig.)
erschüttern, schütteln; schäumen

chute *n.* Abwurfschacht; Gleitbahn; Stromschnelle

cicada *n.* Zikade; Baumgrille

cider *n.* Zider, Apfelwein

cigar *n.* Zigarre; — **butt** Zigarrenstummel; — **box** Zigarrenkiste; — **case** Zigarrenetui; — **holder** Zigarrenspitze

cigarette *n.* Zigarette; — **butt** Zigarettenstummel; — **case** Zigarettenetui; — **holder** Zigarettenhalter, Zigarettenspitze; — **lighter** Feuerzeug

cinch *n.* Sattelgurt; (fig.) Gewissheit; (sl.) eine sichere Sache; Kleinigkeit, Kinderspiel

cinder *n.* Schlacke; Kohlenstäubchen; burnt to a — verkohlt

Cinderella *n.* Aschenbrödel, Aschenputtel

cinnamon *n.* Zimt

cipher *n.* Chiffre, Geheimschrift; Null; Nummer, Zahl, Ziffer; — *v.* chiffrieren; (aus)rechnen

circle *n.* Kreis, Zirkel; Umfang, Umkreis; Ring; **dress** — erster Rang; **family** — Familienkreis; **vicious** — Zirkelschluss; — *v.* (um)kreisen, zirkeln

circuit *n.* Kreis, Umkreis; Kreislauf; (elec.) Stromkreis, Leitung, Schaltung; (law) Gerichtsbezirk; (fig.) Ausdehnung, Fläche; **short** — Kurzschluss; — **breaker** Stromunterbrecher; — **court** Bezirksgericht; **-ous** *adj.* weitläufig, weitschweifig

circular *n.* Rundschreiben; — *adj.* kreisförmig, Kreis-; **-ize** *v.* zirkulieren; Rundschreiben versenden

circulate *v.* zirkulieren; in Umlauf setzen; umlaufen

circulating *adj.* zirkulierend, umlaufend; (math.) periodisch; — **librar**y Leihbibliothek

circulation *n.* Zirkulation, Umlauf, Kreislauf; Verbreitung; Auflage; — (of the blood) Blutkreislauf; **put into** — in Umlauf bringen

circumcise *v.* beschneiden

circumcision *n.* Beschneidung

circumference *n.* Umfang, Kreisumfang

circumflex *n.* Zirkumflex; — *adj.* gebogen, gekrümmt

circumlocution *n.* Umschreibung

circumnavigate *v.* umschiffen, **umsegeln;** die Erde umgehen

circumscribe *v.* umschreiben; umgrenzen, begrenzen, beschränken

circumspect *adj.* umsichtig, behutsam, vorsichtig

circumstance *n.* Umstand; Zufall; Sachlage, Zustand; *pl.* Verhältnisse, Einzelheiten

circumstantial *adj.* umständlich, einge-

hend; (fig.) unwesentlich, zufällig; — **evidence** Indizienbeweis

circumvent *v.* umgehen, überlisten; um-stellen; **-tion** *n.* Überlistung

circus *n.* Zirkus

cirrhosis *n.* Schrumpfung

cistern *n.* Zisterne, Wasserreservoir

citation *n.* Erwähnung; (law) Vorladung; Zitierung; (lit.) Zitat, Aufführung

cite *v.* erwähnen, nennen; (law) zitieren, vorladen; (lit.) anführen

cither *n.* Zither

citified *adj.* städtisch; bürgerlich; eingebürgert

citizen *n.* Bürger, Städter; Staatsbürger; Zivilist; **fellow** — Mitbürger; **-ry** *n.* Bürgerschaft; **-ship** *n.* Staatsangehörigkeit; Bürgerrecht

citric *adj.* zitronensauer; Zitronen-; — **acid** Zitronsäure

citron *n.* Zitrone

citrus *adj.* citrusartig; — **fruit** Citrusfrucht

city *n.* Stadt, — *adj.* städtisch; Stadt-; — **hall** Rathaus; — **manager** Stadtverwalter; — **planning** Stadtplanung

civet (**cat**) *n.* Zibetkatze

civic *adj.* bürgerlich; Bürger-; **-s** *n.* Bürgerkunde; Zivilrecht

civil *adj.* bürgerlich, zivil; Bürger-; höflich, gesittet; (law) zivilrechtlich, gesetzlich; — **engineer** Zivilingenieur; — **law** bürgerliches Recht; — **liberty** bürgerliche Freiheit; — **right** bürgerliches Ehrenrecht; — **servant** Staatsbeamt; — **service** Zivilverwaltung; — **war** Bürgerkrieg; **-ian** *n.* Zivilist; **-ian** *adj.* **-ian clothes** Zivilkleider, Zivil; **-ian life** Zivilleben; **-ity** *n.* Höflichkeit, Artigkeit; **-ization** *n.* Kultur; Gesittung, Zivilisation; **-ize** *v.* zivilisieren

clad *adj.* bekleidet, gekleidet

claim *n.* Anspruch, Anrecht; (law) Rechtsanspruch; (min.) Grubenanteil; **lay** — **to** Anspruch erheben auf; — *v.* beanspruchen, fordern, verlangen

clairvoyance *n.* Hellsehen, Vorausschauen; (fig.) Scharfsinn

clam *n.* Muschel

clambake *n.* Muschelbacken, Muschelkochen

clamber *v.* klimmen, klettern

clammy *adj.* feucht, kalt, klebrig, klamm

clamor *n.* Geschrei, Lärm; Getöse, Tumult; — *v.* schreien, verlangen; **-ous** *adj.* lärmend, schreiend

clamp *n.* Krampe, Klampe, Klammer; — *v.* klammern, klemmen

clan *n.* clan, Sippe, Stamm; (pol.) Clique; (sl.) Sippschaft; **-ish** *adj.* Sippen-; zu einer Clique angehörend; annänglich

clandestine n. Untergrundbewegung

clank n. Geklirr, Gerassel; — v. klirren rasseln

clansman n. Stammesmitglied

clap n. Klaps, Schlag; Beifallsklatschen; — of thunder Donnerschlag; — v. klappen, klatschen, klopfen; schlagen; Beifall klatschen; — hands in die Hände klatschen; — into jail ins Gefängnis werfen; -per n. Klöppel; -ping n. Applaus

claptrap n. Effekthascherei; Unsinn, Windbeutelei

clarification n. Aufklärung; Läuterung

clarify v. (auf)klären; läutern

clarinet n. Klarinette; — player Klarinettist

clarity n. Klarheit, Glanz

clash n. Geklirr, Geschmetter; Schlag, Stoss; Zusammenstoss; (fig.) Widerstreit, Widerspruch; — v. klirren, schmettern; schlagen, (zusammen)stossen; (fig.) widerstreiten

clasp n. Haken, Klammer, Spange; Schloss; (fig.) Umarmung, Umklammerung; hand — Händedruck; — adj. — knife Klappmesser, Taschenmesser; — v. einhaken, schliessen; ergreifen, festhalten; (fig.) umarmen, umklammern; — hands sich die Hände schütteln; -ed adj. (hands) gefaltet

class n. Klasse; Stunde, Vorlesung, Kurs; Stand, Gesellschaftsklasse; Kategorie; Jahrgang; — v. ordnen, klassifizieren; -ification n. Klassifizierung; -ify v. klassifizieren, einordnen

classic(al) adj. klassisch; mustergültig; -ism n. Klassizismus

classmate n. Klassenkamerad

classroom n. Klassenzimmer, Schulraum

clatter n. Gerassel, Geklapper; (fig.) Geschwätz; — v. rasseln, klappern; (fig.) schwatzen

clause n. Klausel; Redeteil; Satzteil

claustrophobia n. Platzangst

clavicle n. Schlüsselbein

claw n. Klaue, Kralle; Pfote, Tatze; — v. klauen, krallen, (zer)kratzen

clay n. Ton, Lehm; (fig.) Asche, Staub; — pigeon Tontaube; — pit Lehmgrube

clean adj. rein, sauber, blank, unbeschrieben; unvermischt; fehlerfrei; glatt; geschickt; gänzlich, völlig; — v. reinigen, säubern, saubermachen, aufräumen; putzen, polieren; — house Grossreinemachen; — out ausräumen; — up sich waschen; -er n. Reiniger, Putzer; Reinigungsmittel; -ers n. Reinigungsanstalt; -ing n. Reinigung, Aufräu-

men, Säuberung; -ing adj. -ing rag Putztuch, Wischtusch; -ing woman Putzfrau; -liness n. Reinlichkeit, Sauberkeit; (fig.) Reinheit; -se v. reinigen, säubern, putzen, scheuern; ausfegen, auskehren; spülen, waschen; (fig.) befreien, lossprechen; -ser n. Putzmittel, Scheuerpulver

clean-cut adj. genau begrenzt (or bestimmt, bezeichnet)

clear adj. klar; hell, rein; deutlich, unzweifelhaft; vollständig, unbedingt; frei, offen; (com.) netto; (weather) heiter; (fig.) fleckenlos, unschuldig; — profit Nettogewinn; in the — von aller Schuld rein; — v. klären, aufklären; aufheitern; leeren, räumen; vorbeigehen, Hindernisse nehmen; entlasten; (com.) bar einnehmen; freimachen; verzollen; (law) rechtfertigen; (naut.) klar machen; lossprechen; — away wegräumen; — one's throat sich räuspern; — out ausräumen; ausreissen, sich aus dem Staube machen; — the way den Weg freimachen; — the table den Tisch abräumen; — up aufklären; sich aufhellen; -ance n. Freimachung, Räumung; Zwischenraum; (com.) Ausverkauf; Verzollung; (naut.) Klarmachen; -ing n. Abholzen; Lichtung; (com.) Abrechnung; -ing in the forest Waldlichtung; -ly adv. deutlich, genau; augenscheinlich, offenbar; -ness n. Klarheit, Deutlichkeit, Helligkeit; Freiheit

clear-cut adj. gedrängt, kurz; abgesondert, unterschieden

clear-headed adj. verständig, einsichtig

clearing-house n. Abrechnungsstelle

clear-sighted adj. klarsehend

cleave v. (sich) spalten; zerreissen; eindringen; haften, kleben; aufspringen, bersten; -r n. Hackmesser

cleft n. Kluft, Riss, Ritze; Spalt, Spalte; — adj. — palate Gaumenspalte

clemency n. Gnade, Milde, Nachsicht

clement adj. gnädig, mild, nachsichtig

clench v. festhalten, ergreifen; packen; — one's fist die Faust ballen; — one's teeth die Zähne zusammenbeissen

clergy n. Geistlichkeit

clergyman n. Geistliche

clerical adj. klerikal, geistlich; schriftlich, Schreib-; — error Schreibfehler; — work Büroarbeit, schriftliche Arbeit

clerk n. Büroangestellte; Schreiber; Sekretär; town — Stadtsekretär; — v. als Angestellter arbeiten

clever adj. geschickt, gewandt, tüchtig; klug, gescheit; — fellow geriebener

Bursche; **-ness** *n.* Geschicklichkeit, Gewandtheit, Tüchtigkeit

cliché *n.* Klischee

click *n.* Ticken, Knipsen, Knistern; Einschnappen; Knacken; (mech.) Sperrhaken, Klinke; — *v.* ticken, knipsen, knistern, knacken; (sl.) klappen; einschlagen; — **one's heels** die Hacken zusammenschlagen

client *n.* Klient; Kunde; **-ele** *n.* Klientel, Kundschaft

cliff *n.* Abhang, Klippe; — **dweller** Felsenbewohner, Vorfahre der Püebloindianer

climate *n.* Klima

climax *n.* Klimax, Höhepunkt

climb *v.* besteigen; (er)klettern; steigen; — **indicator** *n.* Aufstiegmessgerät

clinch *n.* (mech.) Klinke, Niet, Vernietung; (sports) Clinch; (fig.) Halt, Umklammerung; — *v.* (mech.) vernieten; festmachen; (fig.) abschliessen, endgültig erledigen; **-er** *n.* (mech.) Klammer, Klampe; (fig.) treffende Antwort; Trumpf; **that's a -er** das trifft den Nagel auf den Kopf

cling *v.* anhaften; sich klammern, festhalten; (clothes) eng anliegen; **-ing** *adj.* **-ing vine** Ranke

clinic *n.* Klinik; **-al** *adj.* klinisch

clink *n.* Klingen, Geklirr; — *v.* klingen, klirren; — **glasses together** mit den Gläsern anstossen; **-er** *n.* Klinker, Backstein

clip *n.* Klipp, Spange; Klammer; Schlag; rascher Gang; (mil.) Patronenrahmen; **paper** — Büroklammer, Klammer; — *v.* (ab)schneiden, beschneiden, ausschneiden; scheren, stutzen; — **together** zusammenklammern; **-per** *n.* (avi.) Transozeanflugzeug; (mech.) Schere, Haarschneidemaschine; (naut.) Klipper, Schnellsegler; **-ping** *n.* Ausschnitt

clique *n.* Clique, Sippschaft

cloak *n.* Mantel; (fig.) Deckmantel, Vorwand; — *v.* einhüllen; (fig.) bemänteln, verbergen

cloakroom *n.* Garderobe, Kleiderablage

clock *n.* Uhr; Tageszeit; (hosiery) Zwikkel; **punch the** — die Zeit(karte) stempeln; **round the** — zwölf volle Stunden; — *v.* abstoppen, mit der Stoppuhr messen

clockwise *adv.* wie die Uhrzeiger laufend

clockwork *n.* Uhrwerk; **like** — pünktlich wie ein Uhrwerk

:lod *n.* Klumpen; Erdscholle; (fig.) Tölpel

:lodhopper *n.* Bauernlümmel

:log *n.* Holzschuh; Beschwerde; (fig.) Fessel, Hindernis; — *v.* hemmen; vers-

topfen; stocken

cloister *n.* Kloster; (arch.) Kreuzgang; **-ed** *adj.* einsam, abgeschieden

close *n.* Abschluss, Ende, Schluss; — *v.* (zu-)schliessen, zumachen; abschliessen, beendigen; verschliessen, sperren; — **in on** hereinbrechen über, umzingeln; — **off** abschliessen, sperren; — **up** verschliessen; (mil.) die Reihen schliessen; — *adj.* nah(e), dicht, eng; geizig; genau; verschwiegen; (weather) drückend, schwül, dumpf; — **call** knappes Entkommen; — **fight** gleichwertiger Kampf; — **quarters** Handgemenge, Nahkampf; **pay** — **attention** gut aufpassen; — *adv.* nahe, dicht, eng; genau; — **by** dicht bei, nahe, in der Nähe; — **to** nahe bei; — **to the wind** dicht am Winde; **from** — **up** in (*or* von) der Nähe; **-ed** *adj.* verschlossen, versperrt; **-ed shop** Betrieb unter Gewerkschaftszwang; **-ness** *n.* Enge, Knappheit; Kargheit; Schwüle; Sparsamkeit; Genauigkeit; Festigkeit; **-ing** *n.* Schliessen, Schluss

closed-circuit *n.* (rad. and TV) Regionalprogramm

closefisted *adj.* filzig

closet *n.* Wandschrank; Kabinett; Klosett; — *adj.* geheim, privat; (fig.) unpraktisch; — *v.* in einen Wandschrank schliessen; beiseitenehmen

close-up *n.* Grossaufnahme

clot *n.* Klümpchen; — *v.* gerinnen, verdichten

cloth *n.* Stoff, Tuch, Zeug, Gewebe; Leinwand, Lappen; **make up out of whole** — aus der Luft greifen; **-e** *v.* kleiden, bekleiden, einkleiden; *pl.* Kleider, Kleidung, Wäsche; **suit of -es** Anzug; **-es closet** Kleiderschrank; **-es dryer**, **-es hanger** Kleiderbügel; **-es hook** Kleiderhaken; **-es rack**, **-es tree** Kleiderständer; **-ing** *n.* Kleider, Kleidung; **article of -ing** Kleidungsstück

clothesbasket *n.* Wäschekorb

clothesbrush *n.* Kleiderbürste

clothesline *n.* Wäscheleine

clothespin *n.* Wäscheklammer, Klammer

cloture *n.* Abschluss; (pol.) Diskussionsschluss

cloud *n.* Wolke; Trübung; — *v.* umwölken, bewölken; bedecken, verdunkeln; — **up** sich bewölken; **-iness** *n.* Bewölkung, Umwölkung; Unklarheit; Trübe; **-y** *adj.* bewölkt, wolkig; düster, trübe; (fig.) traurig, unklar

cloudburst *n.* Wolkenbruch

clout *n.* Knuff, Schlag; — *v.* schlagen

clove *n.* Gewürznelke

cloven-footed adj. spaltfüssig, zweihufig
clover n. Klee; live in — wie die Made im Speck leben; **–leaf** (auto.) Kleeblattkreuzung
clown n. Clown; Hanswurst, Possenreisser
club n. Verein, Klub; Keule, Schlegel, Stock; (cards) Treff, Kreuz; (sports) Schläger, Schlagholz; — **car** Klubwagen; — **sandwich** mehrschichtiger Sandwich; — v. niederschlagen; beisteuern, zusammenlegen; sich vereinigen
clubfoot n. Klumpfuss
clubhouse n. Klubhaus
clubroom n. Klubzimmer
cluck v. gluck(s)en
clue n. Anhaltspunkt, Leitfaden, Schlüssel
clump n. Klumpen, Klotz; (fig.) Gruppe; — v. trampeln; schwerfällig gehen
clumsiness n. Plumpheit, Ungeschicklichkeit
clumsy adj. plump, ungeschickt
cluster n. Büschel, Traube; Schwarm, Haufen; — v. sich sammeln; (bee) schwärmen; (fig.) sich häufen
clutch n. Griff, Festhalten; Haken; (auto.) Kuppelung; pl. Klauen; **release the —** die Kuppelung loslassen; **step on the —** auf die Kuppelung treten; **throw in the —** die Kuppelung einschalten; **throw out the —** auskuppeln; — **pedal** Kuppelungspedal; — v. greifen, packen, festhalten
clutter n. Unordnung, Wirrwarr; — v. durcheinanderwerfen, in Verwirrung (or Unordnung) bringen; — **up** verwirren
coach n. Kutsche, Wagen; Personenwagen; Privatlehrer; Repetitor; (sports) Trainer; — v. einpauken; (sports) trainieren
coachman n. Kutscher
coagulate v. koagulieren, gerinnen (machen)
coal n. Kohle, Steinkohle; — **car** Tender; — **field** Kohlenflöz, Kohlenrevier; — **gas** Leuchtgas, Steinkohlengas; — **mine** Kohlenbergwerk; — **oil** Rohpetroleum; — **tar** Kohlenteer
coalbin n. Kohlenbehälter, Kohlenkasten
coalesce v. sich verbinden (or verschmelzen, vereinigen)
coalition n. Koalition, Verbindung, Bund
coarse adj. gemein, grob, rauh, roh; — **language** anstössige Sprache; **–n** v. grob werden (or machen); **–ness** n. Gemeinheit, Grobheit, Rauheit; Roheit; (grain) Grobkörnigkeit
coarse-grained adj. grobkörnig, grobfaserig

coast n. Küste, Strand, Ufer; **the — is clear** die Bahn ist frei, die Luft ist rein; — **guard** Küstenwache; Strandwächter; — **line** Uferlinie; — v. hinunterfahren; abwärtsgleiten; **–er** n. (naut.) Küstenfahrer; **–er** adj. **–er brake** Rückbremse
coaster n. Gläseruntersatz
coat n. Mantel, Rock, Überzieher; Jacke; (zool.) Fell, Pelz; — **of arms** Wappenschild; — **of mail** Panzerhemd; — **of paint** Anstrich; — **hanger** Kleiderbügel; — v. bekleiden, belegen; überstreichen; überziehen; **–ing** n. Bedeckung, Bekleidung; Anstrich, Überzug
coatroom n. Garderobenraum
coauthor n. Mitautor, Mitarbeiter
coax v. beschwatzen, erschmeicheln; (fig.) bereden, überreden
coaxial cable n. Achsenkabel
cob n. kleines, kräftiges Pferd; Klumpen; männlicher Schwan; Maiskolben
cobalt n. Kobalt
cobble v. flicken; **–r** n. Flickschuster; (fig.) Pfuscher; (cooking) Obsttörtchen
cobblestone n. Kieselstein, Feldstein, Kopfstein
cobra n. Kobra, Brillenschlange
cobweb n. Spinngewebe
cocaine n. Kokain
cock n. Hahn; — v. (gun) spannen; — **the ears** die Ohren spitzen; — **the head** den Kopf hochtragen; **–er** n. Kampfhahnzüchter; **–y** adj. eingebildet
cockade n. Kokarde
cockatoo n. Kakadu
cockcrow n. Hahnenschrei; (fig.) Tagesanbruch
cockeyed adj. schielend; (sl.) schief; besoffen
cockfight(ing) n. Hahnenkampf
cockle n. (bot.) Kornrade; (zool.) Herzmuschel
cockney n. Cockney, waschechter Londoner; Londoner Dialekt
cockpit n. Hahnenkampfarena; (avi.) offene Kanzel; (naut.) Raumdeck; Schiffsverbandplatz
cockroach n. Küchenschabe, Kakerlake
cocksure adj. bombensicher, ganz sicher
cocktail n. Cocktail; Vorspeise
cocoa n. Kakao; Kakaopulver, Kakaotrank; Kokospalme
coconut n. Kokosnuss; — **milk** Kokosmilch; — **tree** Kokospalme
cocoon n. Kokon
cod n. Dorsch, Kabeljau
c.o.d. abr. per Nachnahme
coddle v. dämpfen; verhätscheln, verwöhnen

code n. (law) Gesetzbuch; (naut.) Signal-
buch; (fig.) Chiffre, Geheimschrift; —
v. chiffrieren
codeine n. Kodein; Methylmorphin
codfish n. Dorsch, Kabeljau
cod-liver oil n. Lebertran
coed n. Schülerin in einer Schule für
Gemeinschaftserziehung
coeducation n. Gemeinschaftserziehung;
-al adj. gemeinschaftlich erzogen
coefficient n. Koeffizient
coerce v. einschränken; anhalten, zwingen
coercion n. Einschränkung; Zwang
coexist v. koexistieren, gleichzeitig vorhanden sein; -ence n. Koexistenz,
Gleichzeitigkeit
coffee n. Kaffee; — bean Kaffeebohne; —
break Kaffeepause; — color Kaffee-
braun; — cup Kaffeetasse; — grounds
Kaffeesatz; — plantation Kaffeeplan-
tage; — shop Kaffeehaus, Café
coffeepot n. Kaffeekanne
coffer n. Koffer, Schmuckkasten; Geld-
kasten
coffin n. Sarg
cog n. Radzahn; — railway Zahnradbahn
cognac n. Kognak
cognition n. Kenntnis, Kunde; Erkennen
cogwheel n. Zahnrad
cohabit v. zusammenleben
cohere v. zusammenhängen; übereinstimmen; -nce n. Zusammenhang, Übereinstimmung; -nt adj. kohärent,
zusammenhängend; übereinstimmend
cohesion n. Kohäsion, gegenseitige Anziehungskraft
coiffure n. Coiffure, Haartracht
coil n. (elec.) Spule; (mech.) Rolle, Winde,
Windung; — of rope Taurolle; — v.
aufrollen, aufwickeln; — up zusammenrollen
coincide v. zusammentreffen, übereinstimmen; -nce n. Zusammentreffen,
Übereinstimmung
coke n. Koks
colander n. Durchschlag
cold n. Kälte, Frost; (med.) Erkältung,
Schnupfen; catch — sich erkälten; —
adj. kalt, frostig; (fig.) gleichgültig;
keusch; leidenschaftslos; teilnahmlos;
— cream Cold-Cream, Hautcreme; —
cuts Aufschnitt; — feet Angst; — front
Kaltluftfront; — snap plötzlicher
Kälteumschwung; — sore Schnupfen-
ausschlag; — storage Kühlraumlage-
rung; Kühlhaus; — war kalter Krieg;
— wave Kältewelle; I am — mir ist
kalt, mich friert; turn a — shoulder to
über die Achsel ansehen; -ness f. Kälte
cold-blooded adj. gefühllos, kaltblütig

coleslaw n. Krautsalat
colic n. Kolik
coliseum n. Kolosseum
collaborate v. zusammenarbeiten
collaborator n. Mitarbeiter
collage n. Kollage, Klebebild
collapse n. Kollaps, Zusammenbruch;
Einsturz; Verfall; — v. zusammenbrechen, einfallen
collapsible adj. zusammenklappbar; —
boat Faltboot
collar n. Kragen; Halsband, Halsring;
(horse) Kummet; (mech.) Ring, Reifen;
— v. mit einem Kragen versehen; beim
Kragen packen; (coll.) kontrollieren
collarbone n. Schlüsselbein
collateral adj. gleichlaufend, gleichzeitig;
seitlich; indirekt; parallel; Seiten-,
Neben-; — note Schuldschein mit zu-
sätzlicher Deckung; — n. zusätzliche
Deckung
colleague n. Kollege
collect v. (sich) sammeln, einsammeln;
einkassieren; (taxes) erheben, eintreiben; send — unter Nachnahme senden;
-ed adj. gesammelt, gefasst; -ion n.
Sammlung; (taxes) Erhebung, Eintreibung; (mail) Leerung; -ive adj. gesammelt, vereinigt; kollektiv, gemeinschaftlich; Sammel-; -ive bargaining
Tarifabkommen; -ive noun Kollekti-
vum, Sammelwort; -ive security Kol-
lektivsicherheit; -or n. Sammler; Kassierer, Kollektor; -or (elec.) Stromab-
nehmer; (taxes) Steuereinnehmer;
ticket -or Fahrkartenkontrolleur
college n. höhere Schule; Hoschule,
Universität; Kollegium, Fakultät
collegiate adj. kollegial; akademisch
collide v. zusammenstossen, kollidieren;
(fig.) widerstreiten
collie n. schottischer Schäferhund; Collie
collision n. Zusammenstoss; — course
(Rakete) Kollisionskurs; Stosskurs
colloquial adj. Umgangs-, Gesprächs-,
familiär; -ism n. Ausdruck der Um-
gangssprache
collusion n. heimliches Einverständnis,
Durchstecherei
Cologne n. Köln
colon n. (anat.) Dickdarm; (gram.) Dop-
pelpunkt
colonel n. Oberst; lieutenant — Oberstleutnant
colonial adj. kolonial
colonist n. Kolonist
colonize v. kolonisieren
colony n. Kolonie
color n. Farbe, Färbung; Anstrich; (mil.)
Fahne, Flagge; (fig.) Anschein; Eigen-

art; Ausdruck; Deckmantel, Vorwand; local — Lokalfarbe; lose — abfärben, verfärben, verblassen; show one's true –s sein wahres Gesicht zeigen, die Maske abwerfen; under false –s unter falscher Flagge; with flying –s mit fliegenden Fahnen; — v. färben; anmalen, anstreichen; erröten, beschönigen; -ation n. Färbung, Kolorit; Farbengebung; -ed adj. bunt, farbig, gefärbt; dunkelhäutig; -ed man Neger; -ful adj. farbenreich, farbenprächtig; -ing n. Färbung; Kolorit, Farbengebung; Gesichtsfarbe; -less adj. farblos

color-blind adj. farbenblind; -ness Farbenblindheit

colossal adj. kolossal

colt n. Füllen, Fohlen; (fig.) Wildfang, Neuling

column n. (arch.) Säule; (math. and typ.) Rubrik, Spalte; (mil.) Kolonne; **spinal** — Rückgrat; -ist n. Autor für eine bestimmte Zeitungsrubrik

coma n. Schlafsucht; Koma

comb n. Kamm; Striegel; (bee) Wabe; **pocket** — Taschenkamm; — v. kämmen; striegeln; (mech.) hecheln, krempeln; (fig.) durchsuchen; — **one's hair** sich kämmen; -er n. Schaumwelle

combat n. Kampf, Gefecht; **single** — Einzelkampf, Zweikampf; — v. (be)kämpfen, bestreiten; -ant n. Kämpfer, Kriegsteilnehmer; (fig.) Verfechter; -ant adj. kämpfend, streitend; (mil.) aktiv

combination n. Kombination, Verbindung, Vereinigung; Bündnis; Zusammenstellung; (fig.) Komplott

combine n. Geschäftsverband; Kartell; (agr.) Mähdrescher; — v. (sich) verbinden, (sich) vereinigen

combustion n. Verbrennung, Entzündung; **spontaneous** — Selbstentzündung; — **chamber** n. Brennkammer; — **engine** Brennkraftmotor

come v. kommen; fallen; — **about** sich ereignen, zustande kommen; — **across** stossen auf, zufällig treffen; — **after** (nach)folgen; abholen kommen; — **again** wiederkommen; — **along** mitkommen; gehen; — **apart** entzwei (or in Stücke) gehen; — **around** herumkommen, sich bekehren; — **back** zurückkommen; — **before** vortreten; vorgehen; — **between** dazwischentreten; — **by** vorbeikommen; zufällig erlangen; — **down** herunterkommen; (price) herabsetzen; — **down with** sich ins Bett legen mit; — **forward** vortreten; — **from** herkommen, herstammen;

— **home** (to) heimkommen, nahegehen; — **in** hereinkommen, eintreten; — **in!** herein!; — **near** nahekommen; beinahe; — **now!** komm doch!; — **of** entstehen; — **off** abkommen, loskommen; — **on** herankommen; wachsen; — **on!** nur zu!; — **out** herauskommen; sich zeigen; sich erklären; — **over** herüberkommen; — **to** wieder zu sich kommen; kommen auf (or zu); — **to nothing** zu Wasser werden; — **to pass** geschehen; — **true** in Erfüllung gehen; — **under** fallen unter; — **up** (her)aufkommen; aufgehen; — **up to** einholen; entsprechen; — **upon** stossen auf; -r n. Kommende, Ankommende; (fig.) Bewerber

comeback n. Rückkehr, Wiederkehr; Wiederherstellung; (theat.) Wiederauftreten; (coll.) Erwiderung

comedian n. Komiker; Komödiant

comedy n. Komödie, Lustspiel

comet n. Komet

comfort n. Bequemlichkeit, Behaglichkeit; Trost; — v. trösten, erquicken; -able n. Steppdecke; -able adj. bequem; -er n. Steppdecke; Tröster; -ing adj. tröstend, tröstlich, ermutigend

comic adj. komisch; — **opera** komische Oper; — n. Komiker; Karikatur(enreihe); -al adj. komisch

comma n. Komma, Beistrich

command n. Befehl, Gebot; (mil.) Kommando; (fig.) Herrschaft; **be in** — befehlen, gebieten; **by your** — auf Ihren Befehl; **have a** — **of** beherrschen; — adj. — **performance** Auftreten von Künstlern bei Hof; — v. befehlen, kommandieren; beherrschen; -ant n. Kommandant; -eer v. (mil.) zum Militärdienst zwingen; requirieren; in Beschlag nehmen; -er n. (mil.) Kommandeur, Befehlshaber; (naut.) Kapitän; -er in chief Oberbefehlshaber; lieutenant -er Kapitänleutnant, Fregattenleutnant; -ing adj. gebietend, befehlshaberisch, beherrschend; (mil.) kommandierend; -ment n. (bibl.) Gebot; (fig.) Vorschrift; -o n. Sturmtrupp, Stosstrupp; Sturmsoldat

commemorate v. gedenken, das Andenken feiern, erinnern an

commemoration n. Gedächtnisfeier; Erinnerung

commence v. anfangen, beginnen; -ment n. Anfang, Beginn; (educ.) Promotion

commend v. loben, rühmen; empfehlen; -able adj. lobenswert, empfehlenswert; -ation n. Lob, Empfehlung

comment n. Bemerkung, Anmerkung, Erläuterung; — v. kommentieren, erläutern, sich auslassen über; **–ary** n. Kommentar, Abhandlung; (fig.) Denkwürdigkeit; **–ator** n. Kommentator, Erklärer

commerce n. Handel, Verkehr

commercial adj. kaufmännisch, kommerziell; Handels-, Geschäfts-; **—** plane Verkehrsflugzeug; **—** n. Werbeprogramm; (rad.) Werbefunk; **–ize** v. in den Handel bringen

commiserate v. bedauern, bemitleiden

commissary n. Kommissar; Ausrüstungsgeschäft

commission n. Kommission, .Auftrag, Vollmacht; (com.) Provision; (mil. and naut.) Offizierspatent; **in** — in Dienst gestellt; **on** — auf (or unter) Provision; **out of** — ausser Dienst; **—** v. beauftragen, bevollmächtigen; abordnen, ernennen; **–er** n. Kommissar, Beauftragte

commit v. übergeben, anvertrauen; (law) begehen, verüben; überweisen; **—** oneself sich binden; (coll.) sich eine Blösse geben; **— to memory** sich einprägen; **— to prison** ins Gefängnis stecken; **— to writing** zu Papier bringen; **–ment** n. Anvertrauen; Überweisung; Verpflichtung; Begehung; (law) Verhaftungsbefehl

committee n. Ausschuss, Komitee, Kommission

commode n. Kommode

commodity n. Artikel, Ware

common adj. gemein, gemeinsam, allgemein, alltäglich, gewöhnlich; häufig, üblich; bürgerlich; niedrig; **— carrier** öffentliches Verkehrsunternehmen; **— law** Gewohnheitsrecht; **— people** gewöhnliches Volk; **— sense** gesunder Menschenverstand; **— stock** Stammaktie, Aktienstock; **have in —** gemein haben; **in —** gemeinsam, gemeinschaftlich; **–er** n. Bürger; Gemeine

commonplace adj. abgedroschen, gewöhnlich; **—** n. Gemeinplatz

commonwealth n. bürgerliche Gesellschaft (or Verfassung); Gemeinwesen; (pol.) Staat, Staatenverbindung

commotion n. Aufruhr, Tumult; Bewegung

communal adj. kommunal, Gemeinde-

commune n. Kommune; **—** v. sich besprechen (or unterhalten); (rel.) kommunizieren

communicant n. Kommunikant

communicate v. mitteilen; benachrichtigen; teilen; (rel.) das Abendmahl nehmen

communication n. Mitteilung, Nachricht, Verbindung; (fig.) Gedankenaustausch; **lines of** — Verbindungswege

communion n. Gemeinschaft; (rel.) Kommunion, Abendmahl; **take** — das Abendmahl empfangen

communism n. Kommunismus

communist n. Kommunist

community n. Gemeinde; Gemeinschaft; **—** adj. kommunal; **— center** öffentlicher Versammlungsort; **— chest** gemeinschaftlicher Wohltätigkeitsfonds

commutation n. Veränderung, Vertauschung; (law) Strafmilderung; **— ticket** Zeitkarte, Monatskarte, Wochenkarte

commutator n. Stromwender, Umschalter

commute v. verändern, ablösen; umwandeln; (rail.) regelmässig auf einer Strecke verkehren; (law) die Strafe mildern; **–r** n. Zeitkarteninhaber

compact n. Vertrag, Pakt; Puderdose; **—** adj. bündig, kompakt; dicht, fest; kurz; (auto.) n. Kleinwagen; **—** v. verbinden, verdichten; **–ness** n. Dichtigkeit, Festigkeit; (fig.) Gedrungenheit

companion n. Genosse, Gefährte, Kompagnon; Gegenstück, Seitenstück; **–able** adj. gesellig; **–ship** n. Gesellschaft; Genossenschaft

companionate marriage n. Kameradschaftsehe

company n. Gesellschaft, Firma; (mil.) Kompagnie; (fig.) Umgang, Verkehr; **— union** Betriebsgewerkschaft; **keep —** Gesellschaft leisten; **keep — with** vertraulich verkehren mit; **part —** auseinandergehen

comparable adj. vergleichbar

comparative n. Komparativ; **—** adj. vergleichend; verhältnismässig; relativ; **— degree** Komparativform

compare v. (sich) vergleichen, gleichstellen; (gram.) steigern; **beyond —** unvergleichlich

comparison n. Vergleich, Vergleichung; Steigerung; Gleichnis, Verhältnis; **beyond —** ohne Frage; **by way of —** vergleichsweise; **in — with** im Vergleich mit

compartment n. Abteilung, Fach; (rail.) Abteil; **smoking —** Raucherabteil

compass n. Kompass; Umfang, Umkreis; Bereich, Bezirk; (mech.) Zirkel; (mus.) Stimmumfang; **— card** Windrose; **—** v. umgeben; umgehen; vollenden; anstiften

compassion n. Erbarmen, Mitleid

compassionate adj. mitleidig

compatibility n. Verträglichkeit, Vereinbarkeit

compatible adj. verträglich, schicklich

compel v. zwingen, nötigen

compendium n. Abriss, Auszug; Handbuch

compensate v. kompensieren; ausgleichen, ersetzen; entschädigen

compensation n. Ersatz, Vergütung; Entschädigung; (com.) Lohn

compete v. konkurrieren; mitbewerben, wetteifern; sich messen

competent adj. kompetent, fähig; fachkundig, zuständig; berechtigt

competition n. Konkurrenz; Wettbewerb

competitive adj. konkurrenzfähig, wettbewerbsfähig; Konkurrenz-

competitor n. Konkurrent, Mitbewerber

compile v. zusammentragen; sammeln

complacency n. Behagen, Wohlgefallen; Selbstzufriedenheit, Selbstgefälligkeit

complain v. klagen; sich beklagen (or beschweren); (law) Klage führen; -ant n. Kläger; -t n. Klage; (med.) Krankheit, Übel

complement n. Ergänzung, Komplement; Gesamtzahl, Vollständigkeit; (gram.) Prädikatsnomen; -ary adj. ergänzend, Ergänzungs-

complete adj. ganz, vollständig, komplett; — v. vervollständigen, vollenden, komplettieren; (fig.) erfüllen

completion n. Ergänzung; Vollendung, Erfüllung

complex n. Komplex; inferiority — Minderwertigkeitskomplex; — adj. kompliziert, verwickelt; zusammengesetzt; -ity n. Verwicklung, Schwierigkeit

complexion n. Gesichtsfarbe, Hautfarbe, Teint; (fig.) Aussehen, Gemütsart; Natur, Temperament

compliance n. Einwilligung, Willfährigkeit; in — with gemäss

complicate v. komplizieren, verwickeln; -d adj. kompliziert, verwickelt

complication n. Verwicklung, Komplikation

complicity n. Mitschuld

compliment n. Kompliment, Artigkeit, Schmeichelei; — v. komplimentieren; beglückwünschen; -ary adj. artig, höflich; -ary copy Freiexemplar

comply v. einwilligen, nachgeben, sich fügen

component n. Komponente, Bestandteil; — adj. einen Teil ausmachend, Bestand-

compose v. zusammensetzen, zusammenstellen; (art.) entwerfen; (lit.) verfassen, dichten; (mus.) komponieren; (typ.) setzen; (fig.) beruhigen, beilegen, schlichten; — oneself sich beruhigen (or fassen); -d adj. gefasst, ruhig; be

-d of bestehen aus; -r n. (lit.) Dichter, Verfasser; (mus.) Komponist

composing room n. Setzersaal

composition n. Zusammensetzung, Zusammenstellung; (art) Anordnung, Entwurf, Stil; (chem.) Mischung, Verbindung; (lit.) Aufsatz; (mus.) Komposition; (typ.) Schriftsatz, Setzkunst

compositor n. Schriftsetzer

composure n. Gemütsruhe, Fassung

compound n. Gemisch, Masse, Zusammensetzung; (chem.) Verbindung; (gram.) Kompositum, zusammengesetztes Wort; (fig.) Umzäunung; — v. zusammensetzen; mengen; mischen; ausgleichen, tilgen; ablösen, belegen; sich vertragen (or vergleichen); — adj. zusammengesetzt; — interest Zinseszins

comprehend v. einschliessen, enthalten; (fig.) verstehen, begreifen

comprehension n. Inbegriff, Umfang, Umfassung; Einbeziehung; (fig.) Begriffsvermögen, Fassungskraft

comprehensive adj. umfassend; bündig, kurz; (fig.) verständig

compress n. Kompresse, Umschlag; — v. zusammendrücken, zusammenpressen; (fig.) kondensieren; -ed adj. -ed air Druckluft, Pressluft; -ion n. Zusammendrücken; Druck; -or n. Kompressor

comprise v. einschliessen, in sich fassen, bestehen aus, enthalten

compromise n. Kompromiss; — v. einen Kompromiss schliessen; sich vergleichen; kompromittieren, blossstellen

comptometer n. Rechenmaschine, Komptometer

comptroller n. Kontrolleur

compulsion n. Nötigung, Zwang

compulsory adj. zwangsweise, zwingend; Zwangs-

computation n. Rechnen, Rechnung, Berechnung; Überschlag

compute v. berechnen, rechnen; -er n. Kalkulator

comrade n. Kamerad, Gefährte, Genosse

con adv. dagegen, wider; pro and — für und wider; — n. Kontra, Gegengründe; the pros and -s Gründe und Gegengründe; — v. prüfen

concave adj. konkav

conceal v. verbergen, verstecken, verhehlen; verheimlichen, verschweigen; -ment n. Verborgenheit, Versteck; (fig.) Geheimhaltung, Verheimlichung

concede v. bewilligen, einräumen, zugestehen; (fig.) anerkennen, zugeben

conceit n. Einbildung; Einfall; günstige

Meinung; Eitelkeit; **-ed** *adj.* eingebildet, dünkelhaft

conceivable *adj.* begreiflich, denkbar

conceive *v.* sich denken (*or* vorstellen); begreifen, erfassen; ausdrücken, fassen; (med.) empfangen; (zool.) trächtig werden

concentrate *v.* (sich) konzentrieren

concentration *n.* Konzentration, Konzentrierung; — *adj.* — **camp** Konzentrationslager

concept *n.* Konzept; Begriff; **-ion** *n.* Konzeption, Vorstellung, Begriff; Entwurf; Empfängnis; **Immaculate Conception** Unbefleckte Empfängnis

concern *n.* Firma, Geschäft; Konzern; Sache, Angelegenheit; Anteil, Interesse; Bedeutung, Beziehung; Sorge, Kummer, Teilnahme; — *v.* angehen, betreffen, interessieren; **-ed** *adj.* beteiligt, interessiert; betreten, betroffen; besorgt; **as far as he's -ed** was ihn betrifft; **be -ed about** besorgt sein um; **be -ed with** zu tun haben mit; **the parties -ed** die Beteiligten; **-ing** *prep.* in Bezug auf, hinsichtlich, betreffs

concert *n.* (mus.) Konzert; (fig.) Einvernehmen, Verabredung; **-ed** *adj.* gemeinschaftlich

concertina *n.* Konzertina

concertmaster *n.* Konzertmeister, erster Geiger

concession *n.* Konzession; Zugeständnis; **-aire** *n.* Konzessionierte

conciliate *v.* aussöhnen, versöhnen; gewinnen

conciliation *n.* Versöhnung, Aussöhnung

conclave *n.* Konklave; geheime Versammlung

conclude *v.* (be)schliessen, entscheiden

conclusion *n.* Schluss, Beschluss; Folgerung; **in** — schliesslich, zum Schluss

conclusive *adj.* entscheidend, abschliessend, endgültig; — **evidence** schlagender Beweis

concoct *v.* zubereiten; (fig.) aussinnen, planen; **-ion** *n.* Zubereitung; Gebräu; (fig.) Anstiftung, Ausbrütung

concomitant *adj.* begleitend, mitwirkend, mitverbunden; — *n.* Begleitumstand

concord *n.* Einigkeit, Einklang, Eintracht; Übereinstimmung, Harmonie

concrete *n.* Beton; Steinmörtel; **reinforced** — Eisenbeton; — *adj.* konkret; gegenständlich, greifbar; dicht, fest; — **mixer** Betonmischmaschine

concubine *n.* Konkubine

concussion *n.* Erschütterung

condemn *v.* missbilligen; verdammen, ver-

werfen; (law) verurteilen; **-ation** *n.* Missbilligung; Verdammung, Verwerfung; (law) Verurteilung

condensation *n.* Kondensierung, Verdichtung; (fig.) Abkürzung

condense *v.* kondensieren, eindicken, verdichten; (fig.) (ab)kürzen; **-d** *adj.* **-d milk** kondensierte Milch, Büchsenmilch; **-r** *n.* Kondensator

condescension *n.* Herablassung

condiment *n.* Würze

condition *n.* Bedingung; Beschaffenheit; Rang, Stand; Umstände, Verhältnisse; **on** — **that** unter der Bedingung, dass; **on no** — unter keinen Umständen; **-al** *adj.* bedingt; abhängig; eingeschränkt; Bedingungs-; **-al clause** Bedingungssatz; **-al** *n.* Konditional, Bedingungsform; **-ed** *adj.* bedingt, beschaffen, geartet; **-ed reflex** konditioneller Reflex

condole *v.* kondolieren, Beileid bezeigen; **-nce** *n.* Kondolenz, Beileid

condone *v.* verzeihen, nachsehen

conducive *adj.* dienlich, förderlich, beitragend

conduct *n.* Führung; (com.) Verwaltung; (elec.) Leitung; (fig.) Benehmen, Betragen; **safe** — freies (*or* sicheres) Geleit; — *v.* führen; (elec.) leiten; (mil.) bedecken, geleiten; (mus.) dirigieren; — **oneself** sich benehmen (*or* betragen); **-ion** *n.* Leitung, Leitungsfähigkeit; **-or** *n.* Anführer; (mus.) Dirigent, Kapellmeister; (phy.) Leiter, Konduktor; Blitzableiter; (rail.) Schaffner, Kondukteur

conduit *n.* Leitung; Röhre; Abzug, Kanal

cone *n.* Kegel; (bot.) Zapfen; **ice-cream** — Eiskremtüte

confab *n.* Geplauder, Gespräch

confection *n.* Mischung, Zubereitung; Konfekt; (fashion) Konfektionsartikel; **-ery** *n.* Konfekt; Konditorei

confederacy *n.* Bund, Bündnis; Bundesgenossenschaft; Konföderation

confederate *n.* Verbündete, Bundesgenosse; Mitschuldige; — *adj.* verbündet; — *v.* sich verbünden

confederation *n.* Bund, Bündnis; Staatenbund

confer *v.* sich besprechen, konferieren; erteilen, übertragen, verleihen; **-ence** *n.* Beratung, Besprechung, Konferenz, Tagung

confess *v.* bekennen, einräumen, (zu)gestehen; (eccl.) beichten; **-ion** *n.* Bekenntnis, Geständnis; (eccl.) Beichte; **-ional** *n.* Beichtstuhl; **-ional** *adj.* konfessionell; **-or** *n.* Beichtvater

confetti *n.* Konfetti, Papierschnitzel

confidant *n.* Mitwisser, Vertraute
confide *v.* anvertrauen; vertrauen, sich verlassen; **-nce** *n.* Vertrauen, Zuversicht; Eröffnung; **in strictest -nce** im vollsten Vertrauen; **-nce man** Bauernfänger; **-nt** *adj.* vertrauend, vertrauensvoll, zuversichtlich; **-ntial** *adj.* vertraulich, vertraut; geheim; **speaking -ntially** unter uns gesagt
confiding *adj.* vertrauensselig, vertrauend
confine *n.* Grenze, Schranke; — *v.* (be)grenzen, beschränken, einengen, einschliessen; **be -ed** niederkommen, in den Wochen liegen; **be -ed to bed** das Bett hüten müssen; **-ment** *n.* Beschränkung; (law) Gefangenschaft, Haft; (med.) Bettlägerigkeit; Entbindung, Niederkunft
confirm *v.* bestätigen, bekräftigen, bestärken; (eccl.) konfirmieren, einsegnen, firme(l)n; **-ation** *n.* Bestätigung, Bekräftigung, Bestärkung; (eccl.) Konfirmation, Einsegnung, Firm(el)ung; **-ed** *adj.* bestimmt, fest; (med.) chronisch, unheilbar; (fig.) unverbesserlich
confiscate *v.* beschlagnahmen, einziehen, konfiszieren
conflagration *n.* Brand, Feuersbrunst
conflict *n.* Zusammenstoss; Kampf; Konflikt, Streit; — *v.* sich widersprechen, widerstreiten; **-ing** *adj.* **-ing views** entgegengesetzte Ansichten
conform *v.* anpassen, sich fügen (*or* richten); **-ation** *n.* Bildung, Gestalt, Gestaltung; Bau, Zusammensetzung, Anpassung; **-ity** *n.* Übereinstimmung; Ähnlichkeit; Fügsamkeit
confound *v.* verwirren, verwechseln; — **him!** der Teufel soll ihn holen! — **it!** verdammt! **-ed** *adj.* verflucht, verwünscht; verwirrt; scheusslich
confront *v.* konfrontieren, gegenüberstellen; entgegentreten
confuse *n.* verwirren, verwechseln; bestürzen, aus der Fassung bringen; **-d** *adj.* verwirrt, verworren, unklar, konfus; bestürzt
confusion *n.* Verwirrung, Konfusion; Verwechslung; Durcheinander; Bestürzung
congeal *n.* erstarren; gefrieren; gerinnen
congenial *adj.* geistesverwandt, kongenial; (fig.) sympathisch
congenital *adj.* angeboren
conger eel *n.* Seeaal
congested *adj.* angesammelt, überfüllt
congestion *n.* Anhäufung, Ansammlung; (med.) Kongestion, Blutandrang
conglomeration *n.* Konglomerat, Anhäufung, Ansammlung
congratulate *v.* gratulieren, beglückwün-schen

congratulation *n.* Glückwunsch, Gratulation
congregate *v.* (sich) versammeln, zusammenkommen
congregation *n.* Gemeinde, Versammlung; **-al** *adj.* Gemeinde-, Kirchengemeinde; unabhängig
congress *n.* Kongress; **-ional** *adj.* Kongress-
congressman *n.* Kongressabgeordnete
congruity *n.* Kongruenz, Folgerichtigkeit, Übereinstimmung
conic(al) *adj.* konisch, kegelförmig; — **section** Kegelschnitt
conjecture *n.* Vermutung, Konjektur, Mutmassung; — *v.* mutmassen, vermuten
conjugal *adj.* ehelich, Ehe-
conjugation *n.* Konjugation, Abwandlung
conjunction *n.* Binderwort, Verbindung
conjunctive *n.* Konjunktiv, Möglichkeitsform; — *adj.* konjunktivisch; abhängig, bedingt; verbindend
conjure *v.* beschwören, behexen, bezaubern; **-r** *n.* Beschwörer, Hexenmeister, Zauberer
connect *v.* (sich) verbinden, verknüpfen; zusammenfügen; anschliessen; (elec. and mech.) koppeln, schalten; **-ed** *adj.* verbunden, verknüpft; zusammengefügt, zusammenhängend; (fig.) verwandt; **-ing** *adj.* **-ing rod** *n.* Pleuelstange; **-ion** *n.* Beziehung; Zusammenhang, Verbindung; (elec.) Schaltung; (rail.) Anschluss
conniption (fit) *n.* Wahnsinnsanfall
connivance *n.* Duldung, Nachsicht; (law) stillschweigendes Einverständnis
connoisseur *v.* Kenner, Kunstliebhaber
conquer *v.* besiegen, bezwingen, erobern; erringen, überwinden; **-or** *n.* Sieger, Eroberer
conquest *n.* Eroberung, Sieg, Besitzergreifung
conscience *n.* Gewissen; (fig.) Bewusstsein, Vernunft
conscience-stricken *adj.* von Gewissensbissen gepeinigt
conscientious *adj.* gewissenhaft; — **objector** Kriegsdienstverweigerer; **-ness** *n.* Gewissenhaftigkeit
conscious *adj.* bei Bewusstsein; bewusst; (fig.) kundig, unterrichtet; **-ness** *n.* Bewusstsein; (fig.) Kenntnis
conscript *n.* ausgehobener Rekrut, Dienstpflichtige(xix); — *v.* zwangsweise ausheben
conscription *n.* Zwangsaushebung, allgemeine Wehrpflicht

consecrate v. einsegnen, heiligen; weihen, widmen

consecration n. Einsegnung, Heiligung; Weihe, Weihung, Widmung

consecutive adj. folgend, konsekutiv, folgerichtig; aufeinanderfolgend; — **clause** Folgesatz; — **narrative** zusammenhängende Erzählung

consensus n. Übereinstimmung, Zustimmung

consent n. Zustimmung, Einwilligung, Genehmigung; — v. zustimmen, einwilligen, genehmigen

consequence n. Konsequenz; Folge, Ergebnis; Wirkung, Einfluss, Bedeutung; (phil.) Schlusssatz; **as a** (oder **in**) — folglich, infolgedessen; **that's of no** — das ist ohne Bedeutung

consequential adj. konsequent, folgerichtig; (er)folgend, notwendig; (fig.) eingebildet, hochtrabend

consequently adv. folglich, infolgedessen, daher

conservation n. Erhaltung, Konservierung, Aufbewahrung

conservative n. Konservative; — adj. konservativ; (fig.) vorsichtig

conservatory n. Treibhaus, Gewächshaus; (mus.) Konservatorium

consider v. betrachten; bedenken, erwägen, überlegen; berücksichtigen; halten für; **-able** adj. beträchtlich, ansehnlich; **-ate** adj. aufmerksam; bedächtig, rücksichtsvoll; **-ation** n. Betrachtung, Erwägung, Überlegung; Bedeutung, Wichtigkeit; Rücksicht; Entschädigung; Vergütung; (law) Gegenleistung; **be under -ation** erwogen werden, noch nicht entschieden sein; **take into -ation** in Erwägung ziehen, berücksichtigen; **-ing** prep. in Anbetracht

consign v. überweisen, übergeben, übersenden, übertragen; anvertrauen; richten an; hinterlegen; **-ee** n. Warenempfänger; **-ment** n. Übersendung, Versendung, Zustellung; **on -ment** in Kommission

consist v. bestehen; **-ency** n. Dichtigkeit, Festigkeit; Folgerichtigkeit, Übereinstimmung; **-ent** adj. konsequent; übereinstimmend

consolation n. Trost, Tröstung

console n. Konsole; (arch.) Kragstein; — v. trösten

consolidate v. konsolidieren, festigen; (fig.) vereinigen, zusammenziehen

consolidation n. Konsolidierung; Festigung, Verdichtung; Vereinigung

consoling adj. tröstend, trostreich

consommé n. Consommé, klare Fleischbrühe

consort n. Konsorte, Gemahl; **Prince** — Prinzgemahl; — v. sich gesellen; (fig.) übereinstimmen

conspicuous adj. auffallend, sichtbar; deutlich; hervorragend; **be** — hervorragen

conspiracy n. Verschwörung, Konspiration; (fig.) Zusammenwirken

conspirator n. Verschworene, Verschwörer

conspire v. sich verschwören, konspirieren; (fig.) zusammenwirken

constable n. Polizist, Schutzmann; Konstabel

constabulary n. Polizei, Schutzmannschaft

Constance, Lake of n. Bodensee

constancy n. Beständigkeit, Beharrlichkeit; Bestand, Dauer; Standhaftigkeit; Treue

constant adj. beständig, beharrlich; unverändert, ständig; treu; fortwährend, dauernd

constellation n. Konstellation, Sternbild

consternation n. Konsternation, Bestürzung

constipate v. verstopfen

constipation n. Verstopfung

constituency n. Wählerschaft; Wahlbezirk

constituent n. Wähler; Bestandteil; — adj. konstituierend, wählend; verfassunggebend; Grund-, Bestand-

constitute v. ausmachen; konstituieren, errichten; bestellen, ernennen; beauftragen, einsetzen, bevollmächtigen; festsetzen, herbeiführen

constitution n. Verfassung, Konstitution; Beschaffenheit, Bildung; Anordnung, Festsetzung; Körperbau, Körperbeschaffenehit; **-al** n. Verdauungsspaziergang; **-al** adj. konstitutionell, verfassungsgemäss; (fig.) begründet; natürlich, temperamentsgemäss; **-ality** n. Verfassungsmässigkeit

constrain v. zwingen, nötigen; (fig.) einsperren, fesseln; **-t** n. Zwang, Nötigung; Befangenheit; Haft, Einschränkung; **under -t** unter Zwang

construct v. bauen, aufstellen, errichten, konstruieren; zusammenfügen, zusammensetzen; entwerfen; bilden, erdenken, gestalten; **-ion** n. Konstruktion, Bau, Aufführung, Errichtung; Zusammenfügung, Zusammensetzung; (arch.) Bauart, Bauwerk; (gram.) Satzbau; (fig.) Auslegung, Bildung, Gestaltung; **-ive** adj. konstruktiv, bildend, ordnend; aufbauend; **-or** n. Konstrukteur, Erbauer; Erfinder, Urheber

construe *v.* konstruieren; (fig.) auslegen, deuten

consul *n.* Konsul; **-ar** *adj.* konsularisch; **-ate** *n.* Konsulat

consult *v.* sich beraten, konsultieren; um Rat fragen; (fig.) nachschlagen; **-ant** *n.* Berater; **-ation** *n.* Konsultation; Beratung

consume *v.* verbrauchen, konsumieren; **-r** *n.* Abnehmer Konsument, Verbraucher; **-rs' goods** Verbrauchsgüter

consummation *n.* Vollendung, Vollziehung; (fig.) Ende

consumption *n.* Verbrauch; (med.) Auszehrung, Schwindsucht

consumptive *adj.* schwindsüchtig, verzehrend

contact *n.* Berührung, Kontakt, Verbindung; (elec.) Stromschluss; (mil.) Fühlung; **— lens** Kontaktlinse; **—** *v.* sich in Verbindung setzen mit, in Verbindung treten mit

contagion *n.* Ansteckung; Seuche

contagious *adj.* ansteckend

contain *v.* enthalten, fassen; bestehen aus; (fig.) (sich) zurückhalten; **-er** *n.* Behälter

contaminate *v.* verunreinigen; beflecken, vergiften

contemplate *v.* beabsichtigen; beschauen, betrachten; nachsinnen

contemplation *n.* Betrachtung; Nachdenken, Nachsinnen; Vorhaben

contemplative *adj.* nachdenklich

contemporary *adj.* gleichzeitig, zeitgenössisch; **—** *n.* Zeitgenosse

contempt *n.* Verachtung, Geringschätzung; **— of court** Missachtung des Gerichtshofes; **-ible** *adj.* unwürdig, verachtenswert; verächtlich; **-uous** *adj.* verächtlich, geringschätzig; hochmütig

contend *v.* kämpfen, ringen, streiten; sich bewerben; (fig.) behaupten, streben

content *n.* Zufriedenheit; Gehalt; *pl.* Inhalt; **table of —s** Inhaltsverzeichnis; **to one's heart's —** zur völligen Zufriedenheit; **—** *adj.* zufrieden; geneigt, willens; **—** *v.* befriedigen, zufriedenstellen; **-ed** *adj.* genügsam, zufrieden; **-ment** *n.* Genügsamkeit, Zufriedenheit

contention *n.* Streit, Hader; Beweisführung, Streitpunkt; **bone of -ion** Zankapfel

contentious *adj.* streitsüchtig, zänkisch

contest *n.* Kampf, Streit; Wettbewerb; **—** *v.* bestreiten, anfechten; streben; **-ant** *n.* Kampfteilnehmer; Wettkämpfer; Mitbewerber; (pol.) Wahlkandidat

context *n.* Zusammenhang

contiguous *adj.* anstossend, angrenzend

continence *n.* Enthaltsamkeit, Mässigung; (fig.) Keuschheit

continent *n.* Kontinent; **—** *adj.* enthaltsam, mässig; (fig.) keusch; **-al** *adj.* kontinental

contingency *n.* Zufall, Zufälligkeit; (fig.) Möglichkeit

contingent *n.* Zufall; Anteil, Beitrag; (mil.) Kontingent, Truppenteil; **—** *adj.* zufällig; (fig.) möglich; **— on** abhängig von

continual *adj.* beständig, fortwährend; unaufhörlich, ununterbrochen; (coll.) ewig

continuance *n.* Fortdauer; (law) Aufschub

continuation *n.* Fortsetzung, Weiterführung, Prolongation, Übertragung

continue *v.* dauern, fortsetzen, weiterführen; beibehalten; behalten, erhalten; verlängern; anhalten, beharren; fortfahren; **to be -d** Fortsetzung folgt

continuity *n.* Stetigkeit, Fortdauer; (film) Drehbuch; (rad.) Manuskript

continuous *adj.* fortdauernd, fortlaufend; stetig, ununterbrochen

contort *v.* krümmen, winden; (fig.) verdrehen, verzerren; **-ion** *n.* Drehung, Krümmung; **-ionist** *n.* Schlangenmensch

contour *n.* Kontur, Umriss

contraband *n.* Konterbande, Schmuggelware, Schmuggel(ei); **—** *adj.* gesetzlich verboten

contract *n.* Vertrag, Kontrakt; **—** *v.* einen Vertrag schliessen; sich vertraglich verpflichten; kontrahieren; (sich) zusammenziehen; (fig.) sich aneignen; (gram. and math.) abkürzen, verkürzen; **— a debt** Schulden machen; **— a disease** sich eine Krankheit zuziehen; **-ion** *n.* Zusammenziehung; (gram. and math.) Abkürzung, Verkürzung; (med.) Schrumpfung; **-or** *n.* Unternehmer,

contradict *v.* widersprechen; **-ion** *n.* Widerspruch; **-ory** *adj.* widersprechend

contrail *n.* (avi.) Kondensstreifen

contralto *n.* Kontra-Alt; Kontra-Altistin

contraption *n.* (coll.) Maschine, Vorrichtung

contrary *adj.* konträr, entgegengesetzt; verkehrt; ungünstig, widrig, widerspenstig; **— to** gegen, zuwider; **—** *n.* Gegenteil, Gegensatz; **on the —** im Gegenteil; **to the —** dagegen

contrast *n.* Gegensatz; Kontrast; **—** *v.* vergleichen, gegenüberstellen; kontrastieren; **— with** sich abheben von, abstechen von

contribute *v.* beitragen, beisteuern, spenden; mitwirken

contribution n. Beitrag, Spende, Kontribution; Mitwirkung

contributor n. Beisteuernde, Beitragende, Mitwirkende; Mitarbeiter

contrite adj. reuevoll; bereuend, zerknirscht

contrition n. Reue, Zerknirschung

contrivance n. Erfindung; Vorrichtung; Entwurf; Kniff; (fig.) Erfindungsgabe, Findigkeit

contrive v. erfinden, ersinnen; entwerfen; ausdenken; veranstalten

control n. Kontrolle, Aufsicht, Prüfung, Überwachung; Herrschaft, Beherrschung; Einhalt, Hemmung; pl. Steuerung; under — in der Gewalt; — tower Kontrollturm; — v. kontrollieren; beaufsichtigen, prüfen, überwachen; beschränken, einschränken; (avi. and mech.) lenken, steuern; — oneself sich beherrschen; -er n. Kontrolleur, Leiter, Aufseher, Überwacher; Regulator

controversial adj. strittig, Streit-

controversy n. Streit, Kontroverse

conundrum n. Scherzrätsel; kaum lösbare Frage

convalesce v. genesen; -nce n. Genesung, Konvaleszenz; -nt adj. genesend; Genesungs-

convene v. (sich) versammeln, zusammenberufen

convenience n. Bequemlichkeit; Angemessenheit, Schicklichkeit; Komfort; at your earliest — baldmöglichst, umgehend; at your own — ganz nach Ihrem Belieben

convenient adj. bequem; passend, schicklich; gelegen, günstig

convent n. Kloster, Konvent

convention n. Versammlung, Zusammenkunft, Tagung; Übereinkunft, Vertrag; (fig.) Konvention, Brauch, Herkommen; -al adj. konventionell; -ality n. Haften am Hergebrachten, Konventionalismus

conversation n. Gespräch, Unterhaltung, Konversation; -alist n. gewandter Gesellschafter, guter Unterhalter

converse n. Umkehrung, Gegensatz; — adj. umgekehrt, entgegengesetzt; — v. reden, sich unterhalten

conversion n. Umtausch, Umwandlung; (pol.) Meinungswechsel, Übertritt; (rel.) Bekehrung

convert n. Bekehrte, Konvertit; — v. umwandeln, umkehren, umstellen; (rel.) bekehren; -er n. (elec.) Umformer; (rel.) Bekehrer; -ibility n. Umwandelbarkeit; (rel.) Bekehrbarkeit; -ible n. Kabriolett; -ible adj. umwandelbar,

umsetzbar; vertauschbar

convex adj. konvex; erhaben, gewölbt

convict n. Sträfling, Zuchthäusler; — v. überführen; (law) schuldig erklären; -ion n. Überzeugung; (law) Überführung, Schuldigerklärung

convince v. überzeugen

convincing adj. überzeugend; — proof schlagender Beweis

convivial adj. festlich; gesellig; gastlich; (fig.) lustig; Fest-

convocation n. Einberufung; Versammlung

convoy n. (mil.) Bedeckung, Eskorte; (naut.) Geleitzug

convulse v. in Zuckungen versetzen; (fig.) erschüttern; be -d with laughter sich vor Lachen ausschütten

convulsion n. Krampf, Zuckung

cook n. Koch, Köchin; — v. Kochen; — a person's goose jemand den Garaus machen; — up ausdenken; -ery n. Kochkunst; -ing n. Kochen; Küche; -ing adj. kochend; -ing utensils Küchengeräte

cookbook n. Kochbuch

cookie, **cooky** n. Kleingebäck, Keks

cool n. Frische, Kühle; — adj. kühl, frisch; kalt, gleichgültig, teilnahmslos; gelassen; (coll.) unverfroren; bar, rund; keep — ruhig bleiben; — v. (ab)kühlen, sich erfrischen; — off abkühlen; (sich) beruhigen; — one's heels lange warten; -er n. Kühler; Kühlmittel; (sl.) Gefängnis; -ness n. Kühle; (fig.) Kälte, Kaltblütigkeit; Gleichgültigkeit, Lauheit; (coll.) Frechheit

cool-headed adj. besonnen

coolie n. Kuli

coon n. Waschbär

coop n. Hühnerkäfig; (sl.) Gefängnis; fly the — ausbrechen; — v. — up einsperren

cooper n. Böttcher, Fassbinder; Küfer; -age n. Böttcherei, Fassbinderei

co-op n. Kooperative, Genossenschaft; Konsumgeschäft; Genossenschaftsmiethaus; -erate v. mitwirken, zusammenwirken; -eration n. Mitwirkung, (genossenschaftliche) Zusammenarbeit; -erative n. Konsumverein, Kooperative; Konsumgeschäft; -erative adj. kooperativ, mitwirkend

co-ordinate v. koordinieren, zusammenfassen; gleichschalten; — adj. gleichgestellt; — n. Koordinate

co-ordination n. Koordination; Gleichschaltung; (physiol.) Zusammenwirkung

coot n. Wasserhuhn; –ie n. Laus

cop n. Polizist; — v. fangen; stehlen

copal n. Kopal

copartner n. Beteiligte, Teilhaber

cope v. kämpfen; I can't — with it ich kann damit nicht fertig werden

coping n. Mauerkappe

copious adj. reich(lich); übervoll; weitläufig, wortreich

copilot n. zweiter Pilot

copper n. Kupfer; Kupfermünze; Kupferfarbe; (sl.) Polizist; — adj. kupfern, kupferrot

copperhead n. Mokassingschlange

copperplate n. Kupferplatte; Kupferstich

coppersmith n. Kupferschmied

copra n. Kopra

copulate v. sich verbinden (or paaren)

copulation n. Verbindung; Paarung, Begattung

copy n. Abschrift, Kopie; Muster, Medell; Nachahmung, Nachbildung; Exemplar, Abdruck; Nummer; Manuskript; — **desk** Redaktion für Aktuelles und Schlagzeilen; — v. abschreiben, kopieren; nachahmen, nachbilden; nachmachen; abzeichnen

copybook n. Schreibheft; Kopierbuch

copycat n. Nachäffer

copyright n. Copyright, Urheberrecht, Verlagsrecht; — v. ein Copyright anmelden (or erwerben)

coquet v. kokettieren; –ry n. Koketterie, Gefallsucht; –te n. Kokette; -tish adj. kokett, gefallssüchtig

coral n. Koralle; — adj. korallen; korallenrot; — diver Korallenfischer; — reef Korallenriff

cord n. Schnur, Bindfaden, Kordel; Leine; (anat.) Strang, Band; (wood) Klafter; — v. (auf)klaftern

cordage n. Tauwerk

cordial adj. herzlich, freundlich; — n. Magenlikör; –ity n. Herzlichkeit, Wärme

corduroy n. Kord, gerippter Baumwollstoff; — road Knüppeldamm

core n. Kern, Herz, Mark; (bot.) Kerngehäuse

corespondent n. mitangeklagter Ehebrecher

cork n. Kork, Stöpsel, Pfropfen; (bot.) Korkeiche, Korkrinde; — v. verkorken, zustöpseln; -age n. Pfropfengeld

corkscrew n. Korkenzieher

corn n. Mais; Korn, Getreide; (med.) Hühnerauge; — borer Kornkäferlarve; Maisbohrer; — popper Maisröster; — v. einsalzen, einpökeln; –y adj. hornig; (med.) mit Hühneraugen übersät;

(coll.) abgedroschen

corncob n. Maiskolben

corncrib n. Maisspeicher

corner n. Ecke, Winkel; (com.) Aufkaufen; turn the — um die Ecke gehen; (fig.) über den Berg kommen; — shelf Eckgestell; — v. in die Ecke (or Enge) treiben; aufkaufen; -ed adj. winkelig, eckig; (coll.) in der Klemme sein

corner stone n. Eckstein; Gedenkstein

cornet n. Kornett, Horn

cornfield n. Maisfeld

cornflower n. Kornblume

cornice n. Kranzleiste, Gesims

cornstalk n. Maisstengel

cornstarch n. Maisstärke

corollary n. Folgesatz

coronation n. Krönung

coroner n. Leichenbeschauer

coronet n. kleine Krone; (poet.) Kranz

corporal n. Korporal, Obergefreite; — adj. körperlich, leiblich

corporation n. Körperschaft, Korporation

corps n. Korps

corpse n. Leiche, Leichnam

corpulent adj. stark, fleischig, beleibt, korpulent

corpuscle n. Blutkörperchen, Zelle

correct v. verbessern, berichtigen, korrigieren; zurechtweisen; — adj. richtig, korrekt; –ion n. Verbesserung, Berichtigung, Korrektur; house of –ion Besserungsanstalt, Zuchthaus; –ive adj. bessernd, berichtigend; –ive n. Besserungsmittel

correlation n. Wechselbeziehung

correspond v. in Briefwechsel stehen, korrespondieren; entsprechen; -ence n. Korrespondenz; Übereinstimmung; carry on a –ence in Briefwechsel stehen; -ence adj. -ence school Schule für Fernunterricht; –ent n. Korrespondent, Berichterstatter; Briefschreiber; –ing adj. entsprechend, passend

corridor n. Gang, Flur, Korridor

corroborate v. bestärken, bestätigen

corrode v. zerfressen, zernagen, ätzen

corrosive adj. zerfressend, ätzend

corrupt v. verderben, verführen; korrumpieren; — adj. verderbt, korrupt; –ible adj. korrumpiert, bestechlich, verderbbar; –ion n. Verdorbenheit, Korruption, Fäulnis

corsage n. Ansteckblume

corset n. Korsett

cortisone n. Nebennierensubstanz, Kortison

cosmetic n. Kosmetik, Schönheitsmittel; — adj. kosmetisch, verschönernd; Schönheits-

cosmic *adj.* kosmisch; — **rays** Höhenstrahlen
cosmology *n.* Kosmologie
cosmonaut *n.* Kosmonaut
cosmopolitan *n.* Weltbürger
cost *n.* Preis, Aufwand; Kosten; **at all** -'s, **at any** — um jeden Preis; **at less than** — unter Einkaufspreis; — **of living** Lebenshaltungskosten; — **accounting** Unkostenverrechnung; — *v.* kosten; -**ly** *adj.* teuer, kostspielig
costume *n.* Tracht, Kostüm, Kleid
cot *n.* Feldbett
cottage *n.* Landhaus; Hütte, Häuschen; — **cheese** Quark, weisser Käse, Topfen
cotton *n.* Baumwolle; Kattun; (med.) Watte; — **flannel** Kattunflanell; — **gin** Entkernmaschine; — **goods** Baumwollwaren; — **mill** Baumwollspinnerei; — **thread** Baumwollgarn; — *v.* — **to** liebgewinnen
couch *n.* Sofa, Couch, Chaiselongue; — *v.* ausdrücken, erfassen
cough *n.* Husten; — **drop** Hustenbonbon; — *v.* husten
council *n.* Ratsversammlung; Beratung; **city** — Stadtrat; -(l)**or** *n.* Ratsmitglied, Stadtverordnete, Ratsherr, Stadtrat
counsel *n.* Rat; Beratung; (law) Rechtsanwalt; — *v.* raten; beraten; -(l)**or** *n.* Ratgeber, Berater, Sach(ver)walter
count *n.* Summe, Zahlung; Graf; (law) Anklagepunkt; — *v.* zählen, rechnen; — **on** rechnen mit, sich verlassen auf; -**er** *n.* Zahltisch, Theke; (cards) Spielmarke; **Geiger** -**er** Geigerzähler; -**less** *adj.* zahllos, unzählig
countdown *n.* Startzählung
countenance *n.* Gesicht, Miene; Fassung; Gunst; — *v.* begünstigen, zulassen
counter *n.* Ladentisch; — *adv.* entgegen, zuwider; — *adj.* entgegengesetzt, Gegen-; — *v.* einen Gegenschlag führen
counteract *v.* entgegenwirken, zuwiderhandeln
counterattack *n.* Gegenangriff
counterbalance *n.* Gegengewicht; — *v.* ausgleichen, aufwiegen
counterclockwise *adv.* in entgegengesetzter Richtung des Uhrzeigers laufend
counterfeit *n.* Unechte, Fälschung; Falschgeld; — *v.* fälschen, verfälschen, nachmachen; erheucheln; — *adj.* gefälscht, verfälscht; nachgemacht, unecht; erheuchelt; -**er** *n.* Fälscher; Falschmünzer; Heuchler
counterintelligence *n.* Gegenspionage, Spionageabwehrdienst
counteroffensive *n.* Gegenoffensive
counterpoint *n.* Kontrapunkt

countersign *n.* Gegenzeichnung; (mil.) Losungswort; — *v.* gegenzeichnen, mitunterschreiben
counterweight *n.* Gleichgewicht; Gegengewicht
countess *n.* Gräfin
country *n.* Land; Vaterland, Heimat; Gegend; **out of the** — im Ausland; Land-; — **club** Geselligkeitsverein; — **house** Villa, Landhaus
countryman *n.* Landsmann; Landmann, Bauer
countryside *n.* Landstrich, Land
county *n.* Kreis, Provinz; — **seat** Kreisstadt
coup *n.* Schlag, Streich; (sports) Meisterschaft; — **d'état** Staatsstreich; — **de grace** Gnadenstoss
coupe *n.* Coupé; Wagen (mit zwei Türen)
couple *n.* Paar; Ehepaar; **a** — **of** ein paar; — *v.* koppeln, (sich) paaren; sich ehelich verbinden; -**t** *n.* Reimpaar
coupling *n.* Kuppelung
coupon *n.* Coupon, Abschnitt
courage *n.* Mut, Tapferkeit, Courage; **take** — beherzt sein; -**ous** *adj.* brav, tapfer, mutig
courier *n.* Kurier, Eilbote
course *n.* Lauf, Verlauf, Kurs; Gang; Reihe, Kursus; Wettrennen; **as a matter of** — ganz selbstverständlich; **in due** — zu seiner Zeit, zur rechten Zeit; **in the** — im Laufe; **in the** — **of time** mit der Zeit; **of** — natürlich, gewiss, selbstverständlich
court *n.* Hof; Kur; (law) Gericht, Gerichtshof; (sports) Platz, Spielplatz; — *v.* den Hof machen; sich bewerben; -**eous** *adj.* höflich, gefällig, -**esy** *n.* Höflichkeit; -**ier** *n.* Höfling; -**ly** *adj.* **and** *adv.* höflich, artig; schmeichlerisch; Hof-; -**ship** *n.* Werben
courthouse *n.* Gerichtsgebäude
court-martial *n.* Kriegsgericht; — *v.* vor ein Kriegsgericht stellen
courtroom *n.* Gerichtssaal
courtyard *n.* Hof
cousin *n.* Vetter, Cousin; Base, Kusine; **first** — leiblicher Vetter, Geschwisterkind
cove *n.* kleine Bucht; Obdach
covenant *n.* Vertrag, Kontrakt; (rel.) Bund; — *v.* einswerden, übereinkommen
cover *n.* Deckel, Decke; Überzug, Umschlag; Deckung; Kuvert, Gedeck; (fig.) Deckmantel; **under separate** — mit derselben Post; — **charge** Bedienung; — *v.* (be)decken; überziehen, einwickeln, einschlagen; verbergen;

schützen; zurücklegen; (gun) bestreichen; (newspaper sl.) berichten; -ing
n. Decke, Bekleidung, Hülle; -let n.
Bettdecke

cow n. Kuh; Weibchen; — v. entmutigen,
einschüchtern

coward n. Feigling, Memme; Hasenfuss;
–ice n. Feigheit; -ly adj. and adv. feige

cowboy n. Cowboy, Rinderhirt, Kuhhirt

cower v. kauern, hocken

cowherd n. Rinderhirt, Kuhhirt

cowhide n. Rinderhaut, Kuhhaut; Rinds-
leder

cowl n. Kappe, Kapuze

co-worker n. Mitarbeiter

cowpuncher n. Cowboy

coy adj. schüchtern, spröde; zimperlich

coyote n. Steppenwolf, Präriewolf, Ko-
yote

cozy adj. gemütlich, behaglich; — n.
Teewärmer, Kaffeewärmer

crab n. (ast.) Krebs; (zool.) Krabbe,
Taschenkrebs; (sl.) Sauertopf; catch a
— den Streich verfehlen, krebsen; —
apple Holzapfel; — v. sich beklagen,
nörgeln; -bed adj., -by adj. verärgert,
mürrisch, sauertöpfisch

crack n. Sprung, Riss, Spalt(e); Krach,
Knall; — of dawn Morgengrauen; — v.
springen, platzen; reissen, spalten,
knallen; knacken, aufbrechen; zerbrechen; — a joke einen Witz reissen; —
down niederschlagen; -ed gesprungen;
(coll.) verrückt; -er n. knuspriger
Biskuit; -le v. knistern, knattern; -ling
n. Geknister; (cooking) Grieben;
Kruste

crackpot n. harmlos Verrückter

crack-up n. Absturz

cradle n. Wiege; — v. wiegen, einwiegen

craft n. Geschick(lichkeit), Fertigkeit;
Gewerbe; List; (naut.) Schiff, Boot; —
union Zunft, Gewerkschaft; -iness n.
Schlauheit, Verschlagenheit; -y adj.
listig, verschlagen

craftsman n. Handwerker

cram v. (ver)stopfen, anfüllen; nudeln;
(sl.) ochsen, pauken

cramp n. Krampf; — v. beengen, einschränken

cranberry n. Preiselbeere

crane n. (mech. and naut.) Kran; (zool.)
Kranich; — v. sich den Hals ausrecken;
zaudern

cranium n. Schädel, Hirnschale

crank n. Windung; (mech.) Kurbel; (sl.)
Verschrobene; — v. ankurbeln; -y adj.
reizbar, launenhaft

crankcase n. Kurbelgehäuse, Kurbelka-
sten

crankshaft n. Kurbelwelle

crape n. Flor, Krepp; Trauerflor

craps(hooting) n. amerikanisches Wür-
felspiel

crash n. Krach, Lärm; Zusammenstoss;
(avi.) Absturz; — v. krachen, knirschen; (ein)stürzen; (avi.) abstürzen;
–land v. (avi.) bruchlanden

crash landing n. Bruchlandung

crate n. Lattenkiste; Packkorb

crater n. Krater, Erdtrichter

crave v. verlangen, sehen, flehen

craving n. Begierde, Sehnsucht

crawl v. kriechen; be —ing with wimmeln
von; — n. Kraulen

crayfish n. Krebs

crayon n. Zeichenstift, Farbstift

crazy adj. toll, verrückt; — bone Ellbogenknochen, Musikantenknochen; —
quilt Flickendecke

cream n. Sahne, Rahm; Creme, Krem;
(fig.) Beste; — of tartar Weinsteinpul-
ver; — of the crop Beste; whipped —
Schlagsahne; — cheese Sahnenkäse; —
puff Krapfen; — separator Entsahner;
— v. abrahmen, entsahnen; schlagen;
mit Sahne vermischen; (fig.) das Beste
nehmen; -ery n. Molkerei; -y adj.
sahnig, cremefarben

crease n. Falte, Kniff; — v. falten, kniffen,
umbiegen, zerknittern

create v. (er)schaffen; verursachen; ernennen

creation n. Schöpfung; (fashion) Kreation

creative adj. schaffend, schöpferisch

creator n. Schöpfer

creature n. Geschöpf, Tier, Kreatur

credentials n. pl. Empfehlungsschreiben;
Beglaubigungsschreiben

credible adj. glaubwürdig, glaublich

credit n. Kredit, Haben; Glaubwürdigkeit; Ansehen; be a — to Ehre machen;
give — for anrechnen; zutrauen; letter
of — Kreditbrief; on — auf Kredit;
— balance Kreditbestand; — slip
Gutschein; — v. kreditieren, gutschrei-
ben; glauben, trauen; — with gutschrei-
ben; -able adj. kreditfähig; achtbar,
ehrenvoll; -or n. Gläubiger

credulous adj. leichtgläubig

creed n. Kredo, Glaubensbekenntnis

creek n. Bach; Unterschlupf

creep v. kriechen, schleichen; -er n.
Kriecher, Schleicher; (bot.) Schling-
pflanze; -y adj. gruselig

cremate v. (Leichen) verbrennen

creole n. Kreole; — adj. kreolisch

creosote n. Kreosot

crepe n. Krepp; — de Chine Crepe de
Chine; — paper Kreppapier

crescendo *n.* Krescendo; *adj.* and *adv.* crescendo, anschwellend

crescent *n.* Halbmond, Mondsichel; — *adj.* halbmondförmig; zunehmend

crest *n.* Wappen; Schopf; Kamm; Rükken, Gipfel

crestfallen *adj.* niedergeschlagen, mutlos

crevice *n.* Riss, Spalte

crew *n.* Mannschaft, Besatzung, Bemannung

crib *n.* Kinderbett, Krippe

cricket *n.* (ent.) Grille, Heimchen; (sports) Kricket

Crimea *n.* die Krim

crime *n.* Verbrechen, Frevel

criminal *n.* Verbrecher; — *adj.* kriminell, verbrecherisch; Kriminal-, Straf-

criminology *n.* Kriminalistik

crimson *n.* Karmesin, Karmin; — *adj.* karmesinrot, karminrot; — *v.* erröten

crinoline *n.* Krinoline, Reifrock

cripple *n.* Krüppel; — *v.* lähmen, verkrüppeln; entkräften

crisis *n.* Krise, Krisis, Höhepunkt, Wendepunkt

crisp *adj.* knusperig; kraus, frisch

crisscross *adj.* kreuz und quer laufend; — *v.* kreuz und quer laufen, durchkreuzen

critic *n.* Kritiker; art — Kunstrichter; -al *adj.* kritisch, prüfend; entscheidend; bedenklich; -ism *n.* Kritik, Beurteilung, Besprechung; -ize *v.* kritisieren, prüfen; tadeln, bekritteln; rezensieren

croak *v.* quaken, krächzen; (sl.) sterben; — *n.* Quaken, Gekrächze

crochet *n.* Häkelei, Häkelarbeit; — *v.* häkeln

crock *n.* Steinguttopf; -ery *n.* Steingut, Töpferware

crocodile *n.* Krokodil; — tears Krokodilstränen

crone *n.* altes Weib

crony *n.* Busenfreund, alter Bekannte

crook *n.* Haken, Krümmung; (sl.) Schwindler; — *v.* krümmen, beugen; -ed *adj.* schräg, schief, krumm; unehrlich, lasterhaft

croon *v.* wimmern; leise singen

crop *n.* Ernte; Kropf; — *v.* abschneiden, stutzen; pflücken, ernten; abfressen; — up auftauchen

cross *n.* Kreuz; Kruzifix; Kreuzung; — *adj.* kreuzweise, quer; kreuzend; Kreuz-, Quer-; böse, ärgerlich; entgegengesetzt; be at — purposes sich unabsichtlich bekämpfen; — reference Hinweis von Buchabschnitt zu Buchabschnitt; — section Querschnitt; — *v.* übergehen, hinübergehen, kreuzen; ent-

gegentreten; in den Weg kommen; bekreuzen; — one's fingers die Daumen halten; — out durchstreichen; it -es my mind mir kam der Gedanke; -ing *n.* Übergang, Kreuzung; Kreuzweg; Überfahrt; Rassenkreuzung; street — Strassenübergang

crossbreed *n.* Mischling; Mischrasse; — *v.* kreuzen; durch Kreuzung züchten

cross-country *adj.* querfeldein

crosscut *adj.* quer durchschneidend; — saw Kreuzsäge; — *n.* Kreuzhieb, Querschlag

cross-examination *n.* Kreuzverhör

cross-examine *v.* ins Kreuzverhör nehmen

cross-eyed *adj.* schielend

cross-question *v.* ein Kreuzverhör anstellen mit; hin und her fragen

crossroad *n.* Querstrasse, Kreuzweg; *pl.* Scheidewege

crosswise *adj.* kreuzweise, schief

crossword puzzle *n.* Kreuzworträtsel

crotch *n.* Gabelung, Haken

crouch *v.* sich schmiegen (*or* kauern), hocken

croup *n.* (horse) Kruppe; (med.) Kehlkopfbräune

crow *n.* Krähe; Krähen; — *v.* krähen; prahlen

crowbar *n.* Brecheisen

crowd *n.* Menge, Masse, Haufen; Gedränge; — of people Menschenmenge; — *v.* (sich) drängen, pressen; schwärmen, wimmeln; -ed *adj.* gedrängt, zusammengepresst, überfüllt

crown *n.* Krone, Kranz; Spitze, Gipfel; Scheitel; — prince Kronprinz; — *v.* krönen, ehren, auszeichnen

crucible *n.* Schmelztiegel; Feuerprobe; — steel Schmelztiegelstahl

crucifix *n.* Kruzifix; -ion *n.* Kreuzigung

crucify *v.* kreuzigen

crude *adj.* roh, unreif, unbearbeitet, Roh-

cruel *adj.* grausam, unmenschlich, hart; -ty *n.* Grausamkeit

cruise *v.* Kreuzen, Seefahrt; — *v.* kreuzen; -r *n.* Kreuzer

crumb *n.* Krume, Brocken; — *v.* zerkrümeln; panieren; -le *v.* zerkrümeln, zerbröckeln

crumple *v.* zerdrücken, zerknüllen

crusade *n.* Kreuzzug; -r *n.* Kreuzfahrer

crush *v.* zerquetschen; unterdrücker; — *n.* Gedränge; (sl.) Zuneigung

crust *n.* Kruste, Rinde, Schale; -y *adj.* krustig, rindig, schalig; grämlich

crutch *n.* Krücke

cry *n.* Ruf, Geschrei, Schrei; Ausrufen; a far — from weit entfernt von; — *v.* rufen, schreien; ausrufen; weinen; -ing

n. Weinen, Gejammer
crybaby *n.* Jammerlappen
crystal *n.* Kristall; — *adj.* kristallen;
kristallklar; — gazing Kristallseherei;
–line *adj.* kristallen; Kristall-; **–lize** *v.*
kristallisieren
cub *n.* Junge, Junges; — *adj.* — reporter
junger Reporter
cubbyhole *n.* Versteck; kleiner Raum
cube *n.* Würfel, Kubus
cubic(al) *adj.* kubisch, Kubik-,
cubism *n.* Kubismus
cuckoo *n.* Kuckuck; — *adj.* verrückt
cucumber *n.* Gurke
cud *n.* chew one's — wiederkauen
cuddle *v.* herzen, liebkosen
cudgel *n.* Knüttel, Keule; — *v.* durchprügeln; — one's brains sich den Kopf
zerbrechen
cue *n.* Stichwort; (billiards) Queue
cuff *n.* Manschette; Umschlag; Faust-
schlag; — links Manschettenknöpfe;
— *v.* schlagen, puffen, knuffen
culinary *adj.* kulinarisch; Küchen-, Koch-
culminate *v.* kulminieren, gipfeln; den
Gipfel erreichen
culprit *n.* Beklagte, Schuldige, Verbrecher
cult *n.* Kult, Kultus, Verehrung
cultivate *v.* bearbeiten, kultivieren; pflegen; ausbilden
cultivation *n.* Kultivierung; Ackerbau;
Bildung; Gesittung; Ausbildung,
Pflege, Zucht; Übung
cultivator *n.* Pfleger, Züchter; Bodenbear-
beitungsgerät
culture *n.* Kultur, Pflege, Geistesbildung;
–ed *adj.* kultiviert, gebildet
culvert *n.* Abzugskanal
cunning *n.* Kenntnis, Wissen; List,
Schlauheit; — *adj.* schlau, verschmitzt;
reizend, entzückend
cup *n.* Tasse, Becher; (fig. and bot.)
Kelch; (sports) Cup, Pokal; **–ful** *n.*
Bechervoll
cupboard *n.* Küchenschrank, Silber-
schrank
cupcake *n.* Törtchen
cupola *n.* Kuppel, Kuppelgewölbe
cur *n.* Köter; Halunke
curable *adj.* heilbar
curate *n.* Hilfspfarrer
curative *adj.* heilsam; — *n.* Heilmittel
curator *n.* Kurator, Verwalter; Vormund
curb *n.* Beschränkung, Einschränkung;
steinerne Einfassung; Kinnkette; — *v.*
beschränken, einschränken; im Zaum
halten, zügeln
curbstone *n.* Rinnstein, Bordschwelle
curd *n.* Quark, dicke Milch; **–le** *v.* gerinnen (lassen); erstarren (lassen)

cure *n.* Kur; Heilmittel; — *v.* heilen,
kurieren; pökeln, räuchern; (skins)
beizen, gerben
cure-all *n.* Allheilmittel, Wundermittel
curfew *n.* Abendglocke; abendliches Aus-
gehverbot, Polizeistunde
curio *n.* Rarität, Seltenheit, Kuriosität;
–sity *n.* Neugier(de), Kuriosität; Rarität; **–us** *adj.* kurios, seltsam, sonderlich;
neugierig
curl *n.* Locke; Kräuselung; Windung; —
v. (sich) kräuseln, sich winden; sich
locken; — up aufrollen; **–ing** *adj.* **–ing**
iron Brennschere; **–y** *adj.* lockig, kraus
currant *n.* Johannesbeere; Korinthe
currency *n.* Währung, Zahlungsmittel;
Verbreitung, Umlauf
current *n.* Strömung, Strom; Lauf, Gang;
— *adj.* laufend, strömend; heutig;
geläufig; allgemein (bekannt); kursie-
rend; the — issue die letzte Ausgabe
curriculum *n.* Kurrikulum, Lehrplan
curse *n.* Fluch, Verwünschung; — *v.*
(ver)fluchen, schwören; verdammen
curtail *v.* beschränken; (ab)kürzen,
stutzen
curtain *n.* Vorhang; Gardine, Schleier;
— call Hervorruf; — raiser Vorspiel;
— rod Vorhangstange, Gardinenstange;
— *v.* umhüllen, verhängen, verschleiern
curvature *n.* Krümmung
curve *n.* Kurve, Bogen; — *v.* (sich) biegen, (sich) krümmen
cushion *n.* Kissen, Polster; (billiard)
Bande
custard *n.* Eierrahm
custodian *n.* Kustos, Verwahrer, Hüter;
Vormund
custody *n.* Verwahrung, Aufsicht; Haft,
Gewahrsam; Verhaftung
custom *n.* Sitte, Gebrauch, Gewohnheit;
(law) Gewohnheitsrecht; *pl.* Zoll; **–ary**
adj. gewöhnlich, üblich, gebräuchlich;
–er *n.* Kunde, Käufer; (sl.) Kerl
custom-built, custom-made *adj.* nach
Mass gemacht, Mass-
customhouse *n.* Zollamt
cut *n.* Schnitt, Hieb; Scheibe, Schnitte,
Stück; (art) Stich; Holzschnitt; (cards)
Abheben; Stechen; (price) Herabsetzung; (salary) Abzug, Kürzung; — *v.*
schneiden, verwunden; (cards) abheben; stechen; (class) schwänzen; (cloth)
scheren, abschneiden; (gem) schleifen;
(grass) mähen; schneiden; (hair) stutzen; (meat) vorschneiden; (price) herabsetzen, drücken; (salary) kürzen;
(teeth) durchbrechen; (tree) fällen; —
across querüber gehen; — down fällen;
vermindern; — off abschneiden; (elec.)

unterbrechen; — **out** ausschneiden; zuschneiden; — **short** abkürzen; ins Wort fallen; — **up** zerschneiden; — *adj.* beschnitten, gespalten, zersägt; verwundet; — **and dried** fix und fertig; — **glass** geschliffenes Glas; **–lery** *n.* Messerschmiedware; Essbestecke; **–let** *n.* Kotelett; **–ter** *n.* Schneidende; Schneider, Zuschneider; Schnitzer; (naut.) Kutter; **–ting** *n.* Schneiden; (bot.) Ableger, Steckling; (paper) Abschnitt, Ausschnitt, Schnitzel; **–ing** *adj.* scharf, schneidend, beissend

cutback *n.* Herabsetzung, Verminderung; (film) Rückblende

cute *adj.* hübsch, lieblich

cuticle *n.* Oberhaut; Nagelhaut

cutoff *n.* Abkürzung; Absperrung, Unterbrechung

cutout *n.* Umschalter; (elec.) Sicherung; Ausschalter

cut-rate *adj.* Rabatt-

cutthroat *n.* Halsabschneider, Meuchelmörder; — *adj.* mörderisch, halsabschneiderisch

cyanide *n.* Zyan(id)

cycle *n.* Zyklus, Periode; Kreis, Zirkel; Fahrrad

cyclist *n.* Radfahrer

cyclone *n.* Zyklon, Wirbelsturm

cyclotron *n.* Zyklotron, Elektronenbeschleuniger

cylinder *n.* Zylinder, Walze, Rolle; — **head** Zylinderhut, Zylinderrolle

cylindric(al) *adj.* zylindrisch, walzenförmig

cypress *n.* Zypresse

Cyprus *n.* Cypern

cyst *n.* Zyste, Eitersack

czar *n.* Zar

Czechoslovakia *n.* die Tschechoslowakei

D

dab *n.* Klecks, Fleck; Klaps; Betupfen; — *v.* tappen, tippen; beschmieren, abklatschen

dabble *v.* bespritzen, plätschern; stümpern, pfuschen; — **in** hinein pfuschen in

dachshund *n.* Dackel

dacron *n.* Dakron

dad(dy) *n.* Papa(chen), Vati

daffodil *n.* gelbe Narzisse

dagger *n.* Dolch, Stilett

dahlia *n.* Dahlie

daily *adj.* täglich; — (paper) Tageszeitung

daintiness *n.* Feinheit, Zartheit; Niedlichkeit

dainty *adj.* elegant, fein; nett, zierlich; — *n.* Leckerbissen, Naschwerk

dairy *n.* Molkerei, Milchgeschäft; — **farm** Meierei, Milchwirtschaft

daisy *n.* Gänseblümchen, Massliebchen

dale *n.* Tal

dally *v.* tändeln, schäkern; vertändeln

dam *n.* Damm, Deich, Talsperre; (zool.) Muttertier; — *v.* dämmen, stauen

damage *n.* Schaden, Nachteil, Verlust; *pl.* Schadenersatz; — *v.* schaden, beschädigen

damask *n.* Damast; — *adj.* damasten, damastartig

dame *n.* Dame, vornehme Frau

damn *v.* verdammen, verfluchen, verwünschen; — *interj.* verflucht!; — **it!** verdammt! **–able** *adj.* verdammenswert; schändlich; **–ation** *n.* Verdammung, Verfluchung; (bibl.) Verdammnis; **–ed** *adj.* verdammt; abscheulich, scheusslich

damp *n.* Feuchtigkeit; (min.) Schwaden; — *adj.* feucht, dunstig; dumpf; **–en** *v.* anfeuchten, befeuchten; dämpfen; (fig.) niederschlagen; **–ness** *n.* Feuchtigkeit

damper *n.* Dämpfer; Klappe, Schieber

damsel *n.* Jungfrau, Fräulein, junges Mädchen

dance *n.* Tanz; Ball; — **hall** Tanzhalle; — *v.* tanzen; **–er** *n.* Tänzer

dandelion *n.* Löwenzahn

dandruff *n.* Schuppen, Schinn, Kopfschorf

dandy *n.* Dandy, Geck; — *adj.* vortrefflich

danger *n.* Gefahr; — **zone** Gefahrenzone; **–ous** *adj.* gefährlich

dangle *v.* baumeln, schwanken

dank *adj.* feucht, nasskalt, dunstig

Danube *n.* Donau

dapper *adj.* nett, niedlich, schmuck

dare *n.* Herausforderung; — *v.* wagen, herausfordern; sich unterstehen (*or* erkühnen)

daredevil *n.* Wagehals

daring *n.* Kühnheit, Dreistigkeit, Tollkühnheit; — *adj.* kühn, verwegen, dreist

dark *adj.* dunkel, finster, trübe; schwarz, schwärzlich; böse, verbrecherisch; geheimnisvoll; **Dark Ages** Mittelalter; **Dark Continent** schwarzer Kontinent, Afrika; — **horse** unbekannter Bewerber; — *n.* Dunkel(heit); Verborgenheit, Ungewissheit; Undeutlichkeit; Unwissenheit; **in the** — im Dunkeln; **leave in the** — im Ungewissen lassen; **–en** *v.* verdunkeln, verfinstern; schwärzen; (fig.) verdüstern, verwirren; **–ness** *n.* Dunkelheit, Finsternis

darkroom *n.* Dunkelkammer

darling *n.* Liebling, Herzblatt; — *adj.*

teuer, lieb, wert

darn *n.* stopfen, ausbessern; — *n.* gestopfte Stelle; — it! *interj.* verwünscht! **-ing** *n.* Stopferei; **-ing needle** Stopfnadel

dash *n.* Schlag, Stoss, Streich; Sturz, Sprung; Prise; (typ.) Gedankenstrich; — *v.* schlagen, stossen, schleudern; besprengen, bespritzen; zerstören, vernichten; stürzen; — **off** wegstürzen; skizzieren, flüchtig entwerfen; **-ing** *adj.* flott, schneidig, kühn

dashboard *n.* Armaturenbrett

data *n. pl.* Daten; Angaben, Tatsachen

date *n.* Datum, Zeitangabe; Zeitraum, Zeitpunkt; Verabredung; (bot.) Dattel; **up to** — bis heute; zeitgemäss, modern; **auf dem Laufenden; what is the** —? welches Datum (*or* den wievielten) haben wir heute? — **line** Datumsgrenze, Nullmeridian; Zeitungsdatum; — *v.* datieren, ansetzen; ausgehen mit, verabredet sein mit; — **from** zurückgehen auf; **-d** *adj.* veraltet, altmodisch

daub *n.* Klecks, Schmiererei; (art) Geschmiere; — *v.* (be)schmieren, beschmutzen, besudeln

daughter *n.* Tochter

daughter-in-law *n.* Schwiegertochter

dauntless *adj.* furchtlos, verwegen, unerschrocken

davenport *n.* Sofa, Schlafsofa

dawn *n.* Morgendämmerung, Tagesanbruch; (fig.) Anfang, Erwachen; — *v.* ...gen, dämmern; (fig.) sich entfalten

day *n.* Tag; Tageslicht; **a** — täglich, pro Tag; **by the** — tageweise, täglich; **carry the** — die Schlacht gewinnen; — **after** — von einem Tag zum anderen, Tag für Tag; — **after tomorrow** übermorgen; — **before yesterday** vorgestern; — **by** — von Tag zu Tag, täglich; **-s of grace** Verzugstage; **every** — jeden Tag; **every other** — jeden zweiten Tag; **from** — **to** — von Tag zu Tag; **on the following** — am nächsten Tage; **one** — eines Tages, einst; **the other** — neulich; **these** **-s** heutzutage; — **laborer** Tagelöhner, tageweise Beschäftigte; — **letter** verbilligtes Telegramm (ausserhalb der Geschäftsstunden); — **nursery** Spielschule; — **school** Externat; — **shift** Tagesschicht

daybreak *n.* Tagesanbruch

daylight *n.* Tageslicht

daylight-saving time *n.* Sommerzeit

daze *n.* Betäubung, Verwirrung; — *v.* betäuben, verwirren

dazzle *v.* blenden; verblenden, verwirren

deacon *n.* Diakon(us)

deactivate *v.* unwirksam machen; (Radiumaktivität) neutralisieren

dead *adj.* tot, gestorben, leblos; erloschen; unempfindlich; (bot.) verdorrt, verwelkt; (law) bürgerlich tot; (mus.) tonlos, verlöschend; (window) blind; — **body** Leichnam; — **calm** vollkommene Windstille; — **center** unbeweglicher Mittelpunkt; — **end** Sackgasse; — **heat** unentschiedener Wettkampf; — **letter** unbestellbarer Brief; — **reckoning** Berechnung des zurückgelegten Weges; — **shot** Scharfschütze; — **silence** Totenstille; — **weight** unnütze (*or* schwere, drückende) Last; — *n.* Tote; Tiefe, Stille; — *adj.* vollkommen, völlig, unbedingt; **-en** *v.* (er)töten; dämpfen, abschwächen, abstumpfen; **-ly** *adj.* tötlich; gefährlich; **-ly sin** Todsünde

deadline *n.* Termin; Redaktionsschluss

deadlock *n.* Stillstand, Stockung

Dead Sea *n.* das Tote Meer

deaf *adj.* taub, schwerhörig; — **and dumb** taubstumm; **fall on** — **ears** kein Gehör finden, tauben Ohren predigen; **-en** *v.* taub machen, betäuben; **-ness** *n.* Taubheit, Schwerhörigkeit

deaf-mute *n.* Taubstumme

deal *n.* Teil, Menge; (cards) Kartengeben; (com.) Handel, Geschäft; **a good** — ziemlich viel; **a great** — sehr viel; — *v.* teilen, austeilen, verteilen; handeln, vermitteln; (cards) geben; — **with** sich befassen mit, behandeln; **-er** *n.* (cards) Kartengeber; (com.) Händler; **-ings** *n. pl.* Handlungsweise; Umgang, Verkehr

dean *n.* (educ.) Dekan; (rel.) Dechant

dear *adj.* lieb, wert; teuer, kostspielig; **Dear Sir** Sehr geehrter Herr; — *n.* Liebling; Lieber

dearth *n.* Teuerung; Mangel

death *n.* Tod; Todesfall; **put to** — hinrichten; — **penalty** Todesstrafe; — **rate** Sterblichkeitsziffer; — **warrant** Todesurteil; **-less** *adj.* unsterblich; **-like** *adj.* totenähnlich; **-ly** *adj.* tödlich, verderblich

deathbed *n.* Sterbebett

debase *v.* verringern, verschlechtern; entwerten

debatable *adj.* streitig, bestreitbar

debate *n.* Erörterung, Debatte; Wortstreit; — *v.* erörtern, verhandeln, debattieren; — **with oneself** sich überlegen, erwägen

debauch *v.* verführen, verderben, verleiten; **-ery** *n.* Schwelgerei, Ausschweifung

debit *n.* Debet, Soll; Schuld; — **balance**

Schuldabrechnung; — v. belasten, zu Lasten schreiben

debrief v. Flugbericht erstatten (nach Landung); **-ing** n. Flugbericht

debris n. Überbleibsel, Ruinen; (geol.) Trümmer

debt n. Schuld(en); **bad** — nicht einzutreibende Schuld; **be in** — verschuldet sein; **floating** — schwebende Schuld; **public** — öffentliche Schuld; **run into** — sich in Schulden stürzen; **-or** n. Schuldner, Debitor

debut n. Debüt, erstes Auftreten; **make one's** — zum ersten Mal auftreten; **-ante** n. Debütantin

decade n. Jahrzehnt; Zehnerreihe

decadence n. Dekadenz, Verfall

decadent adj. dekadent, verfallen

decamp v. das Lager abbrechen, aufbrechen; ausreissen

decapitate v. enthaupten

decay n. Verfall, Verwesung; (bot.) Verblühen; (med.) Abnahme; — v. verfallen, abnehmen; verwelken

deceased adj. verstorben, abgestorben; — n. Verstorbene

deceit n. Betrug, Täuschung, Falschheit; **-ful** adj. (be)trügerisch, täuschend, listig

deceive v. (be)trügen, täuschen, irreleiten

December n. Dezember

decency n. Anstand, Schicklichkeit

decent adj. anständig, schicklich; leidlich, ziemlich gut

deception n. Betrug; Irreführung, Täuschung

deceptive adj. (be)trügerisch, täuschend

decibel n. Lautstärkemesser

decide v. entscheiden, beschliessen, bestimmen; sich entschliessen; **-dly** adv. entschieden, bestimmt

decimal adj. dezimal; — **point** Komma; — n. Dezimalbruch

decipher v. entziffern, enträtseln

decision n. Entscheidung, Entschluss; Entschlossenheit

decisive adj. entschlossen; entscheidend

deck n. Deck, Verdeck; (cards) Kartenpaket; — **chair** Liegestuhl; — **hand** Matrose; — v. (be)decken; bekleiden; schmücken

declaim v. deklamieren; eifern (gegen)

declaration n. Erklärung; (cards) Ansage; (law) Klageführung

declare v. erklären; angeben, deklarieren; behaupten

declination n. Neigung; Abweichung: (ast. and phy.) Deklination

decline v. ablehnen, verweigern; abnehmen, verfallen; (sich) neigen; (gram.)

deklinieren, abwandeln; — n. Sinken, Abnahme; (med.) Verfall; **be on the** — zu Ende gehen, verfallen

decode v. entziffern

decompose v. (sich) zersetzen, verwesen; zerlegen

decontaminate v. entgiften, reinigen

decorate v. schmücken, verzieren, dekorieren

decoration n. Verzierung; Dekoration; Orden, Auszeichnung

decorator n. Dekorateur, Dekorationsmaler

decorous adj. schicklich, geziemend, anständig

decoy n. Köder; Lockvogel; — v. ködern, kirren, (ver)locken

decrease v. abnehmen, (sich) vermindern

decree n. Erlass, Verordnung, Dekret; Rechtsbeschluss; Bescheid; — v. verordnen, beschliessen

decrepit adj. abgelebt, gebrochen, altersschwach

dedicate v. widmen, weihen, dedizieren

dedication n. Widmung, Weihung, Zueignung

deduct v. abziehen, abrechnen; **-ion** n. Abzug, Abziehen; Herleitung, Schlussfolgerung

deed n. Tat, Handlung; Urkunde, Dokument; — v. überschreiben, übertragen

deep n. Tiefe Abgrund; — adj. tief; vertieft; gründlich, versteckt; scharfsinnig; (color) dunkel; **-en** v. (sich) vertiefen; dunkler werden (or machen); vergrössern; (sich) steigern

deep-freezer n. Tiefgefriermaschine

deep-rooted, deep-seated adj. tief eingewurzelt

deer n. Hirsch, Rotwild

defame v. verunglimpfen, defamieren

defeat n. Niederlage; Vernichtung; — v. vernichten, schlagen; vereiteln; ablehnen; **-ist** n. Defaitist, Flaumacher

defend v. (sich) verteidigen, beschützen, bewahren; **-ant** n. Beklagte, Verklagte; **-er** n. Verteidiger

defense n. Verteidigung, Rechtfertigung; Schutz; **-less** adj. wehrlos, schutzlos

defensive n. Defensive, Verteidigung; — adj. defensiv, verteidigend; Schutz-, Verteidigungs-

defer v. aufschieben, verschieben; zögern; — **to** überlassen, sich fügen; **-ence** n. Nachgiebigkeit, Rücksichtnahme; Ehrerbietung; **in -ence to** aus Rücksicht gegen; **-ential** adj. ehrerbietig, rücksichtsvoll; **-ment** n. Aufschub, Verschiebung

defiance n. Herausforderung; Trotz,

Hohn; **in** — **of** zum Hohn (*or* Trotz)
deficiency *n.* Fehler, Mangel(haftigkeit);
Unzulänglichkeit
deficient *adj.* mangelhaft, unzulänglich
deficit *n.* Defizit, Fehlbetrag, Manko
defile *n.* Engpass, Hohlweg; Defilee; — *v.*
defilieren; beschmutzen, verderben
define *v.* definieren, erklären, bestimmen;
umgrenzen, festsetzen
definite *adj.* bestimmt, deutlich, genau
definition *n.* Definition, Begriffsbestim-
mung, Erklärung
definitive *adj.* bestimmt, definitiv, endgültig, entschieden, ausdrücklich
deflate *v.* Luft (*or* Gas) herauslassen, entleeren
deflect *v.* ablenken, abbiegen, abwenden,
abweichen
deform *v.* entstellen, verunstalten; **-ed**
adj. entstellt, verunstaltet; verwachsen;
-ity *n.* Verunstaltung, Ungestaltheit;
Missgestalt; Hässlichkeit
defraud *v.* betrügen, unterschlagen
defray *v.* bezahlen, bestreiten
defrost *v.* enteisen, auftauen; **-er** *n.* Ent-
eiser; Frostschutzmittel
defunct *adj.* verstorben; nicht mehr vorhanden
defy *v.* herausfordern, trotzen
degenerate *v.* ausarten, entarten, degene-
rieren; — *adj.* entartet, degeneriert
degeneration *n.* Entartung, Degeneration
degrade *v.* erniedrigen; degradieren
degree *n.* Grad, Rang; Stufe; **by -s** allmählich, stufenweise
dehumidify *v.* die Feuchtigkeit entziehen
dehydrate *v.* dehydrieren, Wasserstoff
entziehen
deify *v.* vergöttlichen, vergöttern
deity *n.* Gottheit, Gott
dejected *adj.* entmutigt, mutlos, niedergeschlagen
dejection *n.* Niedergeschlagenheit,
Schwermut
delay *n.* Verschiebung, Verzögerung, Aufschub; **without** — unverzüglich; — *v.*
aufhalten; (ver)zögern; aufschieben
delectable *adj.* ergötzlich, köstlich
delegate *n.* Delegierte, Abgeordnete; —
v. delegieren, abordnen; übertragen
delegation *n.* Abordnung, Delegation
delete *v.* auslöschen, streichen, tilgen
deliberate *v.* erwägen, überlegen; nachdenken; — *adj.* absichtlich, bewusst;
bedächtig
deliberation *n.* Erwägung, Überlegung,
Vorsicht
delicacy *n.* Feinheit, Zartheit, Zartgefühl;
Delikatesse; Wohlgeschmack
delicate *adj.* zart, fein, empfindlich; deli-

kat, wohlschmeckend, schmackhaft;
heikel, wählerisch
delicatessen *n.* Feinkost, Delikatessen
delicious *adj.* köstlich, delikat
delight *n.* Vergnügen, Freude, Lust; **take**
— **in** Freude haben an; — *v.* entzücken;
(sich) erfreuen, (sich) ergötzen; **-ed**
adj. entzückt, erfreut; **-ful** *adj.* entzückend, köstlich, reizend
delineate *v.* entwerfen, skizzieren; beschreiben
delineation *n.* Entwurf, Skizze; Beschreibung
delinquency *n.* Pflichtvergessenheit; Vergehen, Verbrechen, Kriminalität
delinquent *n.* Delinquent, Verbrecher,
Missetäter
delirious *adj.* wahnsinnig, rasend; irre;
be — wahnsinnig sein; irre reden,
phantasieren
delirium *n.* Delirium, Wahnsinn; Verzückung; — **tremens** Delirium tremens,
Säuferwahnsinn
deliver *v.* befreien, erlösen; (com.) (ab)-
liefern, abgeben, übergeben; einreichen;
(lecture) halten, vortragen; (med.) entbinden; (message) ausrichten; (opinion)
äussern; **-ance** *n.* Befreiung, Erlösung;
Ausführung; **-y** *n.* Übergabe; (com.)
Lieferung, Ablieferung; Zustellung;
(lecture) Vortrag; (med.) Niederkunft;
general -y Ausgabestelle für post-
lagernde Briefe
delta *n.* Delta
delude *v.* betrügen, täuschen, anführen
deluge *n.* Überschwemmung; (bibl.) Sintflut; — *v.* überschwemmen, überfluten
delusion *n.* Täuschung, Wahn, Trug,
Blendwerk
de luxe *adj.* luxuriös, kostbar, kostspielig
delve *v.* graben; ergründen, erforschen
demagogue *n.* Demagoge, Aufwiegler
demand *n.* Verlangen; Forderung, Anspruch; Bedarf; Nachfrage; **in** — be-
gehrt; **on** — auf Verlangen; bei Sicht;
— *v.* verlangen, fordern; erfordern, beanspruchen
demeanor *n.* Betragen, Benehmen
demented *adj.* wahnsinnig, verrückt
demerit *n.* Fehler, Schuld; Unwürdigkeit;
(educ.) Tadel
demilitarize *v.* entmilitarisieren
demise *n.* Ableben, Verscheiden
demitasse *n.* Mokkaschale
demobilize *v.* demobilisieren, abrüsten
democracy *n.* Demokratie
democrat *n.* Demokrat; **-ic** *adj.* demo-
kratisch
demolish *v.* demolieren, abbrechen; abtragen, zerstören

demolition n. Niederreissen, Abtragung, Zerstörung; — **bomb** Sprengbombe

demon n. Dämon, böser Geist, Teufel

demonstrate v. beweisen, demonstrieren

demonstration n. Beweis; Demonstration, Massenkundgebung

demonstrative adj. beweisend, demonstrativ, darlegend; ausdrucksvoll

demonstrator n. Beweisführer, Demonstrator, Erklärer

demoralize v. demoralisieren

demote v. degradieren, erniedrigen

demotion n. Degradierung, Erniedrigung

demur n. Bedenken, Zweifel, Einwand; — v. bedenken, zweifeln, zögern; Einwendungen erheben

den n. Höhle, Grube; Bude

denature v. vergällen, ungeniessbar machen; -d adj. -d alcohol verunreinigter Alkohol

denazification n. Entnazifizierung

deniable adj. verneinbar, abzuleugnen

denial n. Leugnen, Verleugnung; Verneinung; Absage

denim n. Drill(ich), grobes Kattungewebe

Denmark n. Dänemark

denomination n. Benennung; Anzeige; Klasse; Konfession

denominator n. Nenner; **common —** Hauptnenner

denote v. bezeichnen, bedeuten

denounce v. anzeigen, angeben, denunzieren; anklagen

dense adj. dicht, fest; beschränkt

density n. Dichte, Dichtheit

dent n. Beule, Eindruck; — v. eindrücken, verbeulen

dental adj. die Zähne betreffend, Zahn-

dentifrice n. Zahnpasta, Zahnpulver

dentine n. Dentin, Zahnbein

dentist n. Zahnarzt, Dentist

denture n. künstliches Gebiss

denture n. künstliches Gebiss

denunciation n. Anzeige, Denunziation

deny v. leugnen, bestreiten, verneinen; verleugnen; abschlagen

deodorant n. geruchtilgendes Mittel

depart v. abreisen, wegfahren; sich trennen, scheiden; abweichen; sterben, verscheiden; -ment n. Abteilung, Bezirk; Fach, Branche; Ministerium; -ment store Warenhaus, Kaufhaus; -ure n. Abreise; Trennung; Abweichung; Tod

depend v. abhängen; hängen, schweben; sich verlassen (auf) it -s es kommt darauf an; -able adj. zuverlässig, verlässlich; -ence n. Abhängigkeit, Zusammenhang; Vertrauen, Zuversicht; -ency n. Zubehör; abhängiges Gebiet, Kolonie; -ent n. Abhängige, Anhänger;

-ent adj. abhängig, angewiesen; in der Schwebe; -ent upon berufend auf

depict v. abmalen, schildern, beschreiben

depilatory adj. enthaarend; — n. Enthaarungsmittel

depletion allowance n. Abnutzungsvergütung, Ausbeutungsvergütung

deplorable adj. bejammernswert; erbärmlich, kläglich

deplore v. beklagen, betrauern, bejammern

deport v. deportieren, fortschaffen; verbannen; -ation n. Verbannung, Ausweisung; -ment n. Haltung, Benehmen, Betragen

depose v. absetzen, entthronen; (law) bezeugen, erhärten

deposit n. Einzahlung; Anzahlung; Hinterlegung, Depositum; (geol. and phy.) Lager, Ablagerung; — v. deponieren, hinterlegen; einzahlen; -ion n. Aussage; Ablagerung; -or n. Deponent; Einzahler; -ory n. Aufbewahrungsort, Lager

depot n. Bahnhof, Depot; Niederlage

deprave v. verführen, verderben, verschlechtern

deprecate v. missbilligen, tadeln

depreciate v. herabsetzen, geringschätzen; im Werte sinken

depreciation n. Herabsetzung; Geringschätzung; (com.) Entwertung, Fallen

depress v. niederdrücken, niederschlagen, deprimieren; bedrücken, entmutigen; -ion n. Depression, Niedergang; Niedergeschlagenheit

deprive v. entziehen, berauben

depth n. Tiefe; — **bomb,** — **charge** Unterwasserbombe

deputation n. Deputation, Abordnung

deputy n. Deputierte, Abgeordnete, Stellvertreter

derail v. entgleisen, zum Entgleisen bringen

deranged adj. verrückt, verwirrt; (geistig) gestört, derangiert

derby n. steifer, runder Filzhut (mit schmaler Krempe)

derelict n. herrenloses Gut; Wrack; — adj. verlassen, herrenlos; -ion n. Vernachlässigung; Pflichtvergessenheit; Aufgeben, Verlassen

deride v. verlachen, verhöhnen, verspotten

derision n. Verspottung; Spott, Hohn

derivation n. Ableitung

derivative n. Ableitung

derive v. ableiten, herleiten

dermatology n. Dermatologie, Hautlehre

derogatory adj. beeinträchtigend, nachteilig, herabwürdigend

derrick *n.* Ladebaum; (oil) Vorturm

descend *v.* hinabsteigen; sich senken; (min.) einfahren; (fig.) sich herablassen; **be –ed** abstammen; **–ant** *n.* Nachkomme, Abkömmling

descent *n.* Niedergang, Abstieg; Abhang; (min.) Einfahrt; (fig.) Abstammung

describe *v.* beschreiben, schildern, darstellen

description *n.* Schilderung, Beschreibung; Art

descriptive *adj.* beschreibend, schildernd

desecrate *v.* entweihen, profanieren

desegregation *n.* Rassenrehabilitierung

desert *n.* Wüste, Einöde; *pl.* Verdienst; **— *v.*** desertieren, fahnenflüchtig werden; verlassen; **–er** *n.* Deserteur, Fahnenflüchtige; Ausreisser; **–ion** *n.* Fahnenflucht; Abfall

deserve *v.* verdienen; sich verdient machen

deserving *adj.* verdient, verdienstvoll, würdig

design *n.* Entwurf, Plan; Muster; **— *v.*** entwerfen, ersinnen; planen, beabsichtigen; **–ate** *v.* bezeichnen, ernennen, bestimmen; **–ation** *n.* Bestimmung, Bezeichnung; Ernennung; **–er** *n.* Entwerfer; Zeichner; **–ing** *adj.* verschlagen, hinterlistig

desirability *n.* Erwünschtheit, Wünschenswerte

desirable *adj.* wünschenswert, begehrenswert

desire *n.* Wunsch; Begierde; Lust; **— *v.*** verlangen, wünschen, begehren; (er)bitten

desirous *adj.* begierig, lüstern

desk *n.* Schreibtisch, Pult; Katheder; Schultisch

desolate *v.* verheeren, verwüsten; **— *adj.*** einsam, öde; trostlos

desolation *n.* Verheerung, Verwüstung; Öde; Schwermut

despair *n.* Verzweiflung, Hoffnungslosigkeit; **— *v.*** verzweifeln; **–ing** *adj.* verzweifelnd, verzweifelt

despatch see dispatch

desperate *adj.* verzweifelt, hoffnungslos; verwegen

desperation *n.* Verzweiflung

despise *v.* verachten, verabscheuen

despite *prep.* trotz, ungeachtet

despondent *adj.* mutlos, verzweifelnd, verzagt

despot *n.* Despot, Gewaltherrscher; **–ic** *adj.* despotisch, unumschränkt; **–ism** *n.* Despotismus, Gewaltherrschaft

dessert *n.* Nachtisch, Dessert

destination *n.* Bestimmung(sort)

destiny *n.* Bestimmung, Schicksal, Geschick

destitute *adj.* hilflos, verlassen; mittellos

destitution *n.* Mangel, Entbehrung; Verlassenheit

destroy *v.* zerstören, vernichten; ausrotten; **–er** *n.* Zerstörer, Vernichter

destruction *n.* Zerstörung, Vernichtung, Untergang

destructive *adj.* zerstörend, vernichtend

detach *v.* ablösen, trennen; (mil.) abkommandieren; (fig.) abspenstig machen; **–ment** *n.* Abteilung, Sonderkommando; Gleichgültigkeit

detail *v.* eingehend darstellen, detaillieren; (mil.) abkommandieren; **— *n.*** Einzelheit, Detail; (mil.) Abkommandierung, Abkommandierte, Sonderkommando; **go into —** auf Einzelheiten eingehen; **in —** ausführlich, umständlich

detain *v.* aufhalten, hindern, zurückhalten; (law) in Haft behalten

detect *v.* entdecken, ermitteln, ertappen; **–ion** *n.* Entdeckung; **–ive** *n.* Detektiv, Geheimpolizist; **–ive** *adj.* Detektiv-; **–or** *n.* Detektor

detention *n.* Vorenthaltung; Verzug; Haft

detergent *n.* Reinigungsmittel

deteriorate *v.* (sich) verschlechtern, an Wert verlieren; entarten

deterioration *n.* Verschlechterung, Entartung

determination *n.* Entschlossenheit, Bestimmtheit; Entschluss, Beschluss

determine *v.* bestimmen, beschliessen

deterrence *n.* Hindernis; Hürde; Verzögerung; (mil.) Abschreckung

detest *v.* verabscheuen; **–able** *adj.* abscheulich

dethrone *v.* enthronen

detonate *v.* detonieren, explodieren (lassen); verpuffen

detonation *n.* Detonation, Explosion, Knall; Verpuffung

detour *n.* Umweg, Umleitung; **— *v.*** umleiten

detract *v.* abziehen, beeinträchtigen, schmälern

detriment *n.* Nachteil, Schaden, Abbruch; **–al** *adj.* nachteilig, schädlich

deuce *n.* (cards and dice) Zwei; (tennis) Gleichstand; (sl.) Teufel

devaluate *v.* entwerten

devaluation *n.* Entwertung

devastate *v.* verwüsten, verheeren

devastation *n.* Verwüstung

develop *v.* entwickeln, entfalten, erschliessen; **–ment** *n.* Entwicklung, Entfaltung; Ereignis

deviate *v.* abweichen; ableiten

deviation *n.* Abweichung; Ableitung; **–ist** *n.* Abtrünnige; Titoist, nicht linientreuer Kommunist

device *n.* Vorrichtung, Entwurf, Plan; List, Kunstgriff; Devise, Wahlspruch

devil *n.* Teufel; between the — and the deep blue sea in der Klemme; — *v.* plagen; stark würzen; **–ed** *adj.* stark gewürzt; **–ed eggs** russische Eier; **–ish** *adj.* teuflisch; verteufelt; **–try** *n.* Teufelei; Verwegenheit

devious *adj.* abweichend, abwegig; irrig

devitalize *v.* der Lebenskraft berauben

devoid *adj.* ermangelnd, leer; — of ohne

devote *v.* weihen, widmen; ergeben

devotion *n.* Hingabe; Ergebenheit; Weihe, Widmung

devour *v.* verzehren, verschlingen

devout *adj.* fromm, inbrünstig, andächtig; aufrichtig

dew *n.* Tau; **–y** *adj.* tauig; betaut

dewdrop *n.* Tautropfen

dextrose *n.* Dextrose, Traubenzucker

diabetes *n.* Diabetes, Zuckerkrankheit

diabetic *adj.* diabetisch, zuckerkrank

diabolic(al) *adj.* diabolisch, teuflisch; boshaft

diadem *n.* Diadem

diagnose *v.* diagnostizieren, eine Diagnose stellen

diagnosis *n.* Diagnose

diagonal *n.* Diagonale, Querlinie; — *adj.* diagonal, schräg

diagram *n.* Diagramm, Figur, graphische Darstellung, Schaubild

dial *n.* (clock) Zifferblatt; Sonnenuhr; (mech.) Anzeigetafel; (tel.) Wählerscheibe, Nummernscheibe; — telephone Selbstanschlusstelefon, Wählerfernsprecher; — *v.* wählen

dialect *n.* Dialekt, Mundart

dialog(ue) *n.* Dialog, Zwiegespräch

diameter *n.* Durchmesser

diamond *n.* Diamant; (cards) Karo; (geom.) Rhombus, Raute; (sports) Baseballfeld; — cutter Diamantenschleifer

diaper *n.* Windel

diaphragm *n.* (med.) Zwerchfell; (opt.) Blende; (tel.) Membran(e)

diarrhea *n.* Diarrhöe, Durchfall

diary *n.* Tagebuch

diathermy *n.* Diathermie, Bestrahlung

dice *n. pl.* Würfel

dichotomy *n.* Dichotomie, Zweiteilung

dicker *v.* feilschen, handeln

dictaphone *n.* Diktafon

dictate *n.* Diktieren; Vorschrift, Regel, Gebot; — *v.* diktieren, vorschreiben

dictation *n.* Diktat; Vorschrift

dictator *n.* Diktator, unumschränkter Machthaber; **–ial** *adj.* diktatorisch, unumschränkt, gebieterisch; **–ship** *n.* Diktatur, Gewaltherrschaft

diction *n.* Diktion, Ausdruck, Redeweise, Stil; **–ary** *n.* Wörterbuch, Lexikon

die *n.* Würfel; Zufall, Los; (mech.) Stempel; Prägestock

die *v.* sterben, umkommen; vergehen; — away verhallen, ersterben; — down ausgehen, verlöschen; — out aussterben; never say —! verzweifle nie!

diesel engine *n.* Dieselmotor

diet *n.* Diät; Speise, Nahrung; Reichstag; — *v.* diät leben, Diät halten; **–etics** *n.* Ernährungslehre; **–ician** *n.* Diätfachmann

differ *v.* abweichen, sich unterscheiden; anderer Meinung sein; **–ence** *n.* Unterschied, Verschiedenheit; Differenz, Streit; **–ent** *adj.* anders, verschieden; **–ential** *n.* Differential, **–entiate** *v.* differenzieren, unterscheiden

difficult *adj.* schwer, schwierig, mühsam; eigensinnig; **–y** *n.* Schwierigkeit, Hindernis

dig *v.* (um)graben; wühlen; — up ausgraben; **–ger** *n.* Grabende, Gräber, Erdarbeiter; **–gings** *n. pl.* Minenbezirk, Minengebiet; (coll.) Wohnung

digest *n.* Übersicht, Auszug, Abriss; — *v.* verdauen, verarbeiten; **–ible** *adj.* verdaulich; **–ion** *n.* Verdauung; Digestion; **–ive** *adj.* verdauungsfördernd

digit *n.* Fingerbreite; (math.) Ziffer (unter zehn), Stelle

dignified *adj.* würdevoll, stattlich, erhaben

dignify *v.* ehren, auszeichnen

dignitary *n.* Würdenträger, Prälat

dignity *n.* Würde, Erhabenheit

dike *n.* Deich, Damm

dilapidate *v.* zerstören, verfallen (lassen)

dilemma *n.* Dilemma, Verlegenheit, Klemme

diligence *n.* Fleiss, Eifer

diligent *adj.* fleissig, eifrig

dilute *v.* verdünnen, (ab)schwächen, verwässern; — *adj.* verdünnt; kraftlos, schwach

dim *adj.* unklar, matt, trübe; dunkel; — *v.* (sich) verdunkeln, trüben; — lights abblenden; **–ness** *n.* Unklarheit; Dunkel; Trübheit, Mattheit

dime *n.* Zehncentstück; — novel Schundroman

dimension *n.* Dimension, Ausdehnung, Umfang

diminish *v.* verringern, (sich) vermindern, abnehmen; **–ing** *adj.* verringert, vermindert

diminutive *adj.* klein, winzig; verkleinernd

dimple *n.* Grübchen

din *n.* Lärm, Getöse; — *v.* betäuben

dine *v.* speisen, dinieren; **-r** *n.* Speisende; Speisewagen; **-tte** *n.* Essnische

dingy *adj.* schmutzig, schwärzlich

dining *adj.* Speise-; — car Speisewagen; — room Esszimmer, Speisezimmer, Speisesaal

dinner *n.* Essen, Mittagessen, Abendessen, Festessen; — jacket Smoking

dinosaur *n.* Dinosaurier

dint *n.* by — of durch, mittels, kraft, vermöge

diocese *n.* Diözese, Bischofssprengel

diorama *n.* Diorama, Reliefbild

dioxide *n.* Dioxyd

dip *v.* (ein)tauchen; färben; untersinken; (sich) senken; — *n.* Eintauchen, kurzes Bad; Abhang, Senkung; **-per** *n.* Kochlöffel, Schöpflöffel; **Big** (*or* **Great**) **Dipper** grosser Bär, grosser Wagen

diphtheria *n.* Diphterie, Halsbräune

diphthong *n.* Diphthong, Doppellaut

diploma *n.* Diplom, Urkunde; **-cy** *n.* Diplomatie; **-t** *n.* Diplomat; **-tic** *adj.* diplomatisch, taktvoll

direct *adj.* gerade, direkt; klar, deutlich; offen; — current Gleichstrom; — hit Volltreffer; — object direktes Objekt; — *adv.* geradeswegs; unmittelbar; — *v.* richten, lenken, leiten, führen, anweisen, anordnen; hinweisen, zeigen; adressieren; **-ion** *n.* Richtung; Leitung, Führung; Anweisung, Anordnung, Direktion; **-ions** *pl.* Gebrauchsanweisung; **-tion finder** Peilvorrichtung; **-ive** *n.* Direktive, Richtschnur, Weisung; **-or** *n.* Direktor, Leiter; **board of -ors** Vorstand, Direktion; **-ory** *n.* Adressbuch, Einwohnerverzeichnis; Telefonbuch

dirndl *n.* Dirndl

dirt *n.* Schmutz, Dreck; Erde, Erdboden; — road Feldweg; **-y** *adj.* schmutzig, unsauber; gemein, schändlich; **-y trick** Schurkenstreich; — *v.* beschmutzen, besudeln

dirt-cheap *adj.* spottbillig

disability *n.* Unvermögen, Unfähigkeit; Rechtsunfähigkeit

disable *v.* unfähig (*or* unbrauchbar, kampfunfähig) machen; ausserstand setzen; **-d** *adj.* untauglich, dienstunfähig

disadvantage *n.* Nachteil, Schaden

disagree *v.* nicht übereinstimmen, nicht einverstanden sein; (food) nicht zuträglich sein; **-able** *adj.* unangenehm, verdriesslich; **-ment** *n.* Verschieden-

heit; Meinungsverschiedenheit, Streit

disappear *v.* verschwinden; **-ance** *n.* Verschwinden

disappoint *v.* enttäuschen, täuschen; vereiteln; **-ed** *adj.* enttäuscht; **-ment** *n.* Enttäuschung; Misslingen, Fehlschlag

disapproval *n.* Missbilligung

disapprove *v.* misbilligen, tadeln, verwerfen

disarm *v.* entwaffnen, unschädlich machen; abrüsten; **-ament** *n.* Entwaffnung, Abrüstung

disaster *n.* Unfall, Katastrophe, Unheil

disastrous *adj.* unheilvoll, verhängnisvoll

disband *v.* entlassen, (sich) auflösen

disburse *v.* auszahlen; vorschiessen; **-ment** *n.* Auszahlung; Vorschuss

disc *n.* Scheibe

discard *v.* verwerfen, weglegen; entlassen; (cards) ablegen; — *n.* Verwerfen; Abwerfen; abgeworfene Karte; abgelegte Sache

discern *v.* unterscheiden; erkennen, wahrnehmen; beurteilen; **-ible** *adj.* unterscheidbar, erkennbar, sichtbar; **-ing** *adj.* unterscheidend, einsichtsvoll; **-ment** *n.* Unterscheidung, Einsicht

discharge *n.* Entlassung; (com.) Erfüllung, Bezahlung; (elec.) Entladung; (gun) Abschuss, Abfeuern; (med.) Eiter(ung), Ausfluss; — *v.* entlassen; abladen, löschen, entladen; feuern; eitern

disciple *n.* Jünger, Schüler

disciplinary *adj.* disziplinarisch

discipline *n.* Disziplin, Zucht; Züchtigung; — *v.* bestrafen, züchtigen; erziehen

disclose *v.* eröffnen, offenbaren, enthüllen

disclosure *n.* Eröffnung, Offenbarung, Enthüllung

discolor *v.* (sich) verfärben; (fig.) entstellen; **-ation** *n.* Verfärbung; (fig.) Entstellung

discomfort *n.* Unbehagen, Missvergnügen

disconcert *v.* vereiteln, verwirren, ausser Fassung bringen

disconnect *v.* trennen; auskuppeln; (elec.) ausschalten

discontent *n.* Unzufriedenheit, Missvergnügen; — *v.* unzufrieden (*or* missvergnügt) machen; **-ed** *adj.* unzufrieden, missvergnügt

discontinue *v.* unterbrechen, aufgeben; aufhören

discord(ance) *n.* Zwietracht, Uneinigkeit; (mus.) Dissonanz, Disharmonie, Missklang

discotheque *n.* Nachtlokal mit Schallplattenmusik

discount *n.* Diskonto, Abzug, Rabatt; —

v. diskontieren, abrechnen, abziehen; (fig.) mit Vorsicht aufnehmen, nicht für voll nehmen

discourage *n.* entmutigen, abschrecken; **-ment** *n.* Entmutigung, Abschreckung

discourse *n.* Rede, Diskurs, Unterhaltung; — *v.* reden, sprechen, unterhalten

discourteous *adj.* unhöflich, unartig; grob

discourtesy *n.* Unhöflichkeit; Roheit

discover *v.* entdecken, aufdecken; erspähen; ausfindig machen; **-y** *n.* Entdeckung, Auffindung; Enthüllung; Fund

discredit *n.* schlechter Ruf, Diskredit; — *v.* nicht glauben; beschimpfen, verunglimpfen

discreet *adj.* diskret, verschwiegen; vorsichtig

discretion *n.* Diskretion, Verschwiegenheit; Umsicht, Besonnenheit; Takt

discriminate *v.* unterscheiden

discriminating *adj.* unterscheidend; scharfsinnig, einsichtsvoll

discrimination *n.* Unterscheidung; Scharfsinn

discus *n.* Diskus, Wurfscheibe

discuss *v.* besprechen, erörtern, verhandeln

discussion *n.* Verhandlung, Diskussion

disease *n.* Krankheit; **-d** *adj.* krank, leidend

disembark *v.* landen, ausschiffen, aussteigen

disfavor *n.* Ungnade, Missfallen

disfigure *v.* entstellen, verunstalten; **-ment** *n.* Entstellung, Verunstaltung

disgrace *n.* Schande; Ungnade; — *v.* entehren, schänden; in Ungnade fallen; **-ful** *adj.* entehrend, schimpflich

disguise *n.* Verkleidung, Maske, Vorwand; — *v.* verhehlen, verkleiden

disgust *n.* Widerwille, Abscheu, Ekel; Abneigung; **cause** — Widerwillen erregen; — *v.* anekeln; verleiden; **be -ed** sich ärgern; **-ing** *adj.* eklig, ekelhaft, widerwärtig

dish *n.* Schüssel; Gericht, Platte, Speise; **set of -es** Tafelgeschirr; — *v.* — **up** anrichten, auftragen, auftischen

dishcloth, dishrag *n.* Tischtuch; Geschirrtuch

dishearten *v.* entmutigen, verzagen

dishonest *adj.* unredlich, unehrlich; **-y** *n.* Unredlichkeit, Unehrlichkeit

dishonor *n.* Schande, Unehre; Nichtbezahlung; — *v.* entehren; nicht bezahlen; **-able** *adj.* entehrend, schimpflich; ehrlos, gewissenlos

dishpan *n.* Abwaschschüssel

dishwasher *n.* Tellerwäscher; Geschirr-

waschmaschine

dishwater *n.* Abwaschwasser, Spülwasser

disillusion *n.* Enttäuschung; Ernüchterung; — *v.* enttäuschen, ernüchtern

disinclined *adj.* abgeneigt

disinfect *v.* disinfizieren; **-ant** *n.* Desinfektionsmittel

disinherit *v.* enterben

disintegrate *v.* zerfallen, (sich in seine Bestandteile) auflösen

disintegration *n.* Verwitterung; Auflösung

disinterested *adj.* uneigennützig; unparteiisch

disk *n.* Scheibe; — **jockey** Schallplattenjongleur; Tonoperateur

dislike *n.* Abneigung, Missfallen; Widerwillen; — *v.* missbilligen, nicht mögen, nicht leiden können

dislocate *v.* verrenken, ausrenken; (fig.) verwirren

dislodge *v.* ausquartieren, verlegen; (hunting) verjagen

disloyal *adj.* treulos, verräterisch; **-ty** *n.* Treulosigkeit, Untreue

dismal *adj.* düster, trübselig, traurig, schrecklich; schaurig, öde

dismantle *v.* entkleiden, entblössen; (mil.) demontieren; schleifen; (naut.) abtakeln

dismay *n.* Bestürzung; Schrecken, Furcht; — *v.* bestürzen; erschrecken

dismember *v.* zergliedern, zerstückeln

dismiss *v.* entlassen, verabschieden; abweisen; **-al** *n.*, **-ion** *n.* Entlassung; Abdankung, Abschied; Abweisung

dismount *v.* absteigen, absitzen; abmontieren

disobedience *n.* Ungehorsam, Widerspenstigkeit

disobedient *adj.* ungehorsam, widerspenstig

disobey *v.* nicht gehorchen, ungehorsam sein; missachten

disorder *n.* Unordnung, Verwirrung; Aufruhr; (med.) Krankheit; Störung; — *v.* in Unordnung bringen, verwirren; zerrütten; **-ly** *adj.* unordentlich, verwirrt; ordnungswidrig; liederlich

disorganization *n.* Auflösung, Zerrüttung

disorganize *v.* desorganisieren, zerrütten; in Unordnung bringen

disown *v.* verleugnen, verstossen, nicht anerkennen

disparage *v.* herabsetzen, verunglimpfen; **-ment** *n.* Verkleinerung, Herabsetzung

dispatch *n.* Absendung; Erledigung; Abfertigung; Depesche, Eilbrief; Eile; — *v.* absenden, expedieren; erledigen; eilen; beseitigen

dispel *v.* vertreiben, verjagen; verbannen

dispensary n. Apotheke; Klinik

dispensation n. Dispens(ation), Austeilung, Verteilung; Vergebung, Verzeihung

dispense v. austeilen, verteilen; verwalten; verzichten, erlassen; entbinden; (med.) bereiten

disperse v. zerstreuen, vertreiben, zerteilen

displace v. versetzen, verlegen, verrücken; **–d person** Heimatvertriebene, Zwangsverschleppte; **–ment** n. Verrückung, Versetzung, Verschiebung; (naut.) Wasserverdrängung

display n. Entfaltung, Aufwand; (com.) Ausstellung, Schau; Auslage; — v. zur Schau stellen, ausstellen; entfalten, zeigen

displease v. missfallen; beleidigen, verletzen

displeasure n. Missfallen, Missvergnügen; Unwille, Verdruss

disposal n. Einrichtung, Anordnung; **I'm at your** — ich stehe zu Ihrer Verfügung

dispose v. (an)ordnen, einrichten; unterbringen; verfügen; abschaffen, loswerden; **–ed** adj. gesinnt, gestimmt, geneigt

disposition n. Einrichtung, Ordnung; Temperament, Gemütsart; Gesinnung

dispossess v. vertreiben, berauben; enteignen

disproportion n. Missverhältnis; **–ate** adj. unverhältnismässig, unproportioniert

disprove v. widerlegen

disputable adj. bestreitbar, streitig

dispute n. Auseinandersetzung, Wortwechsel; Disput, Debatte; — v. bestreiten, streitig machen, abstreiten; debattieren, erörtern

disregard v. missachten; ignorieren, übersehen; — n. Missachtung; Vernachlässigung, Nicht(be)achtung

disrepair n. schlechter Zustand

disreputable adj. verrufen; schimpflich

disrepute n. Verruf, Schande

disrespect n. Unehrerbietigkeit; Missachtung; Unhöflichkeit, Grobheit; **–ful** adj. unehrerbietig; unhöflich, unartig

disrobe v. entkleiden

disrupt v. zerreissen, spalten; **–ion** n. Zerreissen; Bruch, Spaltung

dissatisfaction n. Unzufriedenheit, Missvergnügen

dissatisfied adj. unzufrieden, missvergnügt

dissatisfy v. nicht befriedigen; unzufrieden machen

dissect v. zerschneiden, zerlegen; (anat.) sezieren; (fig.) zergliedern; **–ion** n. Zer-

gliederung; (anat.) Sektion, Sezieren, Obduktion

dissemble v. verhehlen, verbergen; heucheln, schmeicheln

disseminate v. aussäen; aussprengen, verbreiten

dissension n. Zwietracht, Zwist, Streit

dissent n. Meinungsverschiedenheit; Abweichung; — v. anderer Meinung sein; abweichen, nicht übereinstimmen; **–er** n. Andersdenkende, Dissident

dissertation n. Dissertation, Abhandlung, Auseinandersetzung

dissimilar adj. ungleichartig, unähnlich

dissipate v. verschwenden; ausschweifen; zerstreuen

dissipation n. Verschwendung; Ausschweifung; Zerstreuung

dissolute adj. liederlich, wüst, ausschweifend

dissolution n. Auflösung, Zersetzung

dissolve v. (sich) auflösen, trennen; schmelzen; vergehen

dissonant adj. abweichend; (mus.) misstönend

dissuade v. abraten

distaff n. Rocken; — **side** weibliche Linie

distance n. Entfernung, Strecke, Ferne, Abstand; **at a** — von weitem; **in the** — in der Ferne; **keep at a** — fern halten; **keep one's** — sich fern halten

distant adj. fern, entfernt; zurückhaltend; **very** — weit entfernt

distaste n. Widerwillen, Ekel, Abneigung; **–ful** adj. ekelhaft, ekelerregend; widerwärtig

distemper n. (color) Leimfarbe, Temperafarbe; (dog) Staupe

distil(l) v. destillieren; herabtröpfeln (lassen); **–lation** n. Destillierung; **–lery** n. Branntweinbrennerei

distinct adj. klar, deutlich; unterschieden, verschieden; getrennt; **–ion** n. Unterscheidung, Unterschied; Vorzug, Würde; Auszeichnung; **–ive** adj. unterscheidend, eigentümlich; besondere; **–ness** n. Deutlichkeit; Bestimmtheit

distinguish v. unterscheiden; auszeichnen

distort v. verzerren, verdrehen, verziehen; **–ion** n. Verzerrung, Verdrehung

distract v. zerstreuen; abziehen, ablenken; beunruhigen; **–ed** adj. bestürzt, verrückt; **–ion** n. Zerstreuung; Ablenkung; Zerstreutheit

distress n. Not, Elend; Pein, Qual, Kummer; — v. quälen, peinigen; erschöpfen, überanstrengen

distribute v. verteilen, austeilen, verbreiten

distribution n. Verteilung, Austeilung,

Verbreitung

distributor n. Verteiler, Austeiler

district n. Bezirk, Kreis; Gebiet, Zone; — **attorney** Staatsanwalt

distrust n. Misstrauen, Zweifel; — v. misstrauen, zweifeln; -**ful** adj. misstrauisch, argwöhnisch

disturb v. stören; in Unordnung bringen; aufrühren; beunruhigen; -**ance** n. Störung; Aufruhr

ditch n. Graben; **fight to the last** — bis zum letzten Blutstropfen kämpfen; — v. in einen Graben fahren (or werfen); (sl.) im Stich lassen

ditto n. Gleiche, Erwähnte; — adv. dito, desgleichen; — adj. — **marks** Anführungszeichen

ditty n. Liedchen

divan n. Diwan, Sofa

dive n. (sports) Tauchen; Kopfsprung; Sturzflug; (coll.) Spelunke; — v. (unter)tauchen; einen Sturzflug machen; — **bomber** Sturzkampfflugzeug; -**er** n. Taucher

diverge v. divergieren, auseinanderlaufen, abweichen; -**nce** n. Divergieren, Auseinanderlaufen, Abweichen; -**nt** adj. divergierend, abweichend

divers adj. diverse, etliche, verschiedene; -**e** adj. verschieden, mannigfaltig; -**ify** v. verschieden machen; Abwechslung bringen in; -**ity** n. Verschiedenheit, Mannigfaltigkeit

diversion n. Ablenkung, Zerstreuung, Zeitvertreib

divert v. abwenden, ablenken; zerstreuen, belustigen

divide v. teilen, dividieren; scheiden, trennen; sich spalten, sich entzweien; — **by two** durch zwei teilen (or dividieren); — n. Wasserscheide; -**nd** n. Dividende, Gewinnanteil; (math.) Dividend

divine n. Theologe, Geistliche, Priester; — adj. göttlich, heilig; — v. weissagen; ahnen

diving n. Tauchen; Kunstspringen; (avi.) Sturzfliegen; tauchend; — **bell** Taucherglocke; — **suit** Taucheranzug

divinity n. Gottheit, Göttlichkeit; Theologie

divisible adj. teilbar

division n. Division; Teilung; Abteilung; (pol.) Wahlkreis, Bezirk

divisor n. Divisor, Teiler

divorce n. Scheidung, Trennung; **get a** — sich scheiden lassen; — v. scheiden, trennen; wegnehmen

divorcé n. Geschiedene

divulge v. verbreiten, ausplaudern

dizziness n. Schwindel

dizzy adj. schwindlig, schwindelnd; (coll.) duselig; **I feel** — mir ist schwindelig

do v. tun, machen, ausführen, verrichten; passen, gehen; genügen; — **away with** abschaffen, beseitigen; — **without** entbehren müssen; **how** — **you** —? Wie geht es Ihnen? -**er** n. Täter, Vollbringer; -**ing** n. Werk; -**ings** Taten, Begebenheiten; Treiben; -**ne** adj. getan, geschehen; beendigt, fertig; (food) gar, gut

docile adj. gelehrig, lenksam, fügsam

dock n. (bot.) Ampfer; (law) Anklagebank; (naut.) Dock; (zool.) Schwanzstummel; **dry** — Trockendock; — v. stutzen, verkürzen; abziehen; (naut.) docken

doctor n. Doktor, Arzt; -**'s office** Sprechzimmer; — v. ärztlich behandeln, kurieren; (sl.) doktern, fälschen, zustutzen

doctrine n. Lehre, Doktrin

document n. Dokument, Urkunde; Beleg; — v. dokumentieren, beurkunden, belegen; -**ary** adj. dokumentarisch, urkundlich

dodge n. Seitensprung; Kniff, Schlich, Winkelzug; — v. ausweichen, vermeiden, Ausflüchte gebrauchen

doe n. Reh, Hindin; Häsin

doff v. ausziehen, ablegen

dog n. Hund; Rüde, Bock; (coll.) Kerl, Bursche; — **in the manger** Neidhammel; **go to the** -**s** auf den Hund kommen; — **days** Hundstage; — **fancier** Hundeliebhaber; **Dog Star** Hundsstern, Sirius; — v. hetzen, sich an jemandes Fersen heften; -**ged** adj. störrisch, starrköpfig, verbissen

dogcart n. leichter Jagdwagen

dogfight n. Luftzweikampf

doghouse n. Hundehütte; **be in the** — (ehelichen) Verdruss haben

dogma n. Dogma, Grundsatz; Glaubenslehre; -**tic** adj. dogmatisch; gebieterisch

dogsear n. Eselsohr

dogwood n. Kornelkirsche

doily n. Spitzendeckchen, Dessertserviette

dole n. Austeilung, Verteilung; Anteil; — v. verteilen; — **out** austeilen, herausrücken; -**ful** adj. kummervoll, kläglich, trübselig

doll n. Puppe; Zierpuppe

dollar n. Dollar; **silver** — Silberdollar

dolphin n. Delphin

domain n. Gebiet, Domäne; Gut, Herrschaft

dome n. Kuppel, Dom

domestic adj. häuslich; einheimisch, inländisch; gezähmt; Haus-, Privat-; — **animal** Haustier; **-ate** v. zähmen; heimisch werden

dominance n. Herrschen; Macht, Gewalt

dominate v. (be)herrschen, vorherrschen

domination n. Herrschaft

domineer v. beherrschen, dominieren; **-ing** adj. gebieterisch, herrisch; übermütig

dominion n. Herrschaft, Gebiet; Dominion

domino n. Domino; pl Domino(spiel)

don v. anziehen, anlegen

donate v. schenken, geben, widmen

donation n. Schenkung, Widmung

donkey n. Esel; — **engine** Hilfsmaschine

donor n. Geber, Spender; **blood** — Blutspender

doodle v. kritzeln, bekritzeln; — n. Kritzelei; **-r** n. Kritzler, Bekritzler

doom n. Schicksal, Los; Urteil; — v. verurteilen; bestimmen

doomsday n. Jüngster Tag; Weltuntergang

door n. Tür, Pforte, Tor; **out of** **-s** draussen; — **mat** Fussabtreter, Fussmatte

doorbell n. Klingel

doorkeeper, doorman n. Pförtner, Portier

doorknob n. Türknopf

doorpost n. Torpfosten, Türpfosten

doorstep n. Stufe vor der Haustür

doorway n. Torweg, Hauseingang, Tür

dope n. Rauschgift, Betäubungsmittel; (sl.) Dummkopf; vertrauliche Auskunft; — **fiend** Rauschgiftsüchtige; — v. betäuben; dopen

dormant adj. schlafend; ungebraucht, unbenutzt

dormer (window) n. Bodenfenster, Dachfenster

dormitory n. Schlafsaal

dose n. Dosis, Arzneimenge; Pille; — v. dosieren. Arznei verordnen

dot n. Punkt, Pünktchen; Tüpfel; **on the** — pünktlich; auf die Minute; — v. punktieren, tüpfeln

dote v. vernarrt sein; faseln

double n. Doppelte; Doppelgänger; (theat. and film) Double; pl. (sports) Doppel; — adj. doppelt; zweideutig; — **bass** Kontrabass; — **bed** zweischläfriges Bett; — **chin** Doppelkinn; — **cross** Doppelverrat, Hintergehen; — **entry** doppelte Buchführung; — **feature** Doppelvorstellung; — v. (sich) verdoppeln; zusammenlegen, falten; (cards) Kontra ansagen; — **up** sich krümmen; zusammen-

krümmen

double-breasted adj. zweireihig

double-cross v. hintergehen

double-dealing n. Falschheit, Doppelzüngigkeit

double-feature n. (theat.) zwei Hauptfilme

double-quick adj. schnell, im Geschwindschritt

doubt n. Zweifel, Bedenken; **no** — zweifellos, sicherlich; **without** — ohne Zweifel, zweifellos; — v. (be)zweifeln; argwöhnen; **-er** n. Zweifler; **-ful** adj. bedenklich, zweifelnd; zweifelhaft, fraglich; verdächtig; **-less** adj. zweifellos, gewiss

dough n. Teig; (sl.) Geld

doughnut n. Pfannkuchen, Krapfen, Spritzkuchen

douse v. tauchen, ins Wasser stürzen; (naut.) laufen lassen; (sl.) auslöschen

dove n. Taube; **ring** — Ringeltaube

dovetail v. genau ineinanderpassen

dowager n. Frau (or Witwe) von Stand

dowel n. Dübel; Holzpflock

down n. Daune, Flaum; Düne, Hügel, Hügelland; **ups and** **-s** Wechselfälle; — prep. and adv. nieder, unten; herab, hinab; herunter; hinunter; (nom.) bezahlt; **five dollars** — fünf Dollar als Anzahlung; **up and** — auf und ab; — adj. niedrig, wenig; (com.) billig; **(sun)** untergegangen; **be** — **and out** auf den Hund gekommen sein; — **payment** Anzahlung; — interj. nieder! (hin)ab! kusch dich! — v. niederwerfen; abschiessen; hinunterstürzen, (hin)abstürzen; **-y** adj. flaumig, sanft, weich

downcast adj. niedergeschlagen

downfall n. Sturz, Niedergang, Untergang, Fall

downhearted adj. verzagt, niedergeschlagen, gedrückt

downpour n. Platzregen, Wolkenbruch, Guss

downright adv. gerade heraus, völlig, durchaus; — adj. offenherzig, ausgesprochen; völlig

downstairs n. pl. unteres Stockwerk; — adv. (nach) unten, die Treppe hinunter

downtown adv. in die (or der) Stadt; — adj. in der Innenstadt liegend

downward adj. (sich) senkend, abschüssig; **-s** adv. abwärts, niederwärts; hinab

dowry n. Mitgift, Ausstattung

doze n. Schlummer, Schläfchen; — v. schlummern, duseln; — **off** einnicken

dozen n. Dutzend; **by the** — dutzendweise

drab adj. mausgrau; eintönig; trüb(e)

draft, draught n. Zug; (art and lit.) Entwurf; (com.) Tratte, Wechsel, Scheck:

(drink) Trunk, Schluck; Trank; (mil.) Musterung; Sonderkommando; Ersatz, Nachschub; (naut.) Tiefgang; **honor a** — einen Wechsel einlösen; **on** — vom Fass; **rough** — Rohentwurf; **sight** — Sichtwechsel; — **board** Musterungskommission; — **horse** Zugpferd; — *v.* entwerfen, skizzieren; mustern, auswählen, einziehen; **-ee** *n.* Rekrut, Militärdienstfähige; **-ing** *adj.* **-ing board** Zeichenbrett; **-y** *adj.* zugig

draftsman *n.* Zeichner; Entwerfer

drag *v.* schleppen; eggen; mit einem Schleppnetz fischen; — *n.* (coll.) Einfluss; — **chute** Bremsfallschirm

dragnet *n.* Schleppnetz

dragon *n.* Drache

dragonfly *n.* Libelle, Wasserjungfer

drain *n.* Abfluss, Abzugsgraben, Ableitung; (fig.) Belastung; — *v.* (ent)-leeren; ableiten; entwässern, trockenlegen; ablaufen; (fig.) berauben; **-age** *n.* Entwässerung, Trokkenlegung

drainpipe *n.* Abzugsrohr, Abflussrohr

drake *n.* Enterich

dram *n.* Drachme; Trunk, Schluck

drama *n.* Drama; **-tic** *adj.* dramatisch; **-tics** *n.* Dramatik, dramatische Kunst; **-tist** *n.* Dramatiker; **-tization** *n.* Dramatisierung; **-tize** *v.* dramatisieren

drape *v.* drapieren, behängen; umhüllen; in Falten legen; schmücken; — *n.* Vorhang; **-ry** *n.* Vorhang; Drapierung, Faltenwurf; Stoff, Gewebe, Tuchwaren

drastic *adj.* drastisch, kräftig

draw *n.* Ziehung; Lotterie; Los; (fishing) Zug, Fang; (sports) Unentschieden; (theat.) Zugstück; **in a** — unentschieden; — *v.* ziehen, in die Länge ziehen; (air) einatmen; (art) zeichnen, skizzieren; (bow) spannen; (curtain) aufziehen, zuziehen; (fluids) abziehen; (meat) ausnehmen, ausweiden; (theat.) anziehen, erregen; (teeth) (aus)ziehen; — **blood** Blut vergiessen, schröpfen; — **lines** Linien ziehen; — **lots** Nummern ziehen; — **near** (*or* nigh) sich nähern; — **off** abziehen; — **on** anlocken; — **out** herausnehmen; ausforschen; — **the line** eine Grenze ziehen; — **up** abfassen; aufstellen; **-er** *n.* Schublade; **-ers** Unterhose; **-ing** *n.* Ziehen, Ziehung; Zeichnung; **-ing** *adj.* **-ing account** offenes Konto; **-ing card** Zugstück; **-ing room** Empfangszimmer, Salon; Zeichensaal

drawback *n.* Schattenseite, Kehrseite; Nachteil, Hindernis

drawbridge *n.* Zugbrücke

drayman *n.* Rollkutscher

dread *n.* Furcht, Entsetzen; Ehrfurcht; Scheu; — *adj.* furchtbar, schrecklich; erhaben; — *v.* (sich) fürchten, ein Grauen empfinden; **-ful** *adj.* furchtbar, schrecklich; entsetzlich

dream *n.* Traum, Träumerei; — *v.* träumen, ahnen; **-er** *n.* Träumer; **-y** *adj.* träumerisch, traumhaft

dreariness *n.* Düsterkeit, Traurigkeit, Öde

dreary *adj.* traurig, trübselig, trostlos; düster, öde

dredge *n.* Bagger; Schleppnetz; — *v.* (aus)baggern, mit dem Schleppnetz fischen

dredging machine *n.* Bagger

drench *v.* durchnässen

dress *n.* Kleid, Anzug; Kleidung; **in full** — in vollem Staat; — **rehearsal** Kostümprobe; — **suit** Gesellschaftsanzug; — *v.* (sich) anziehen, kleiden; (hair) frisieren; (med.) verbinden; (mil.) sich ausrichten, in Linie aufstellen; — **up** sich zurechtmachen (*or* herasuputzen); **get -ed** sich anziehen; **-er** *n.* Kommode; **-ing** *n.* Ankleiden, Zurichten; Behandlung; (cooking) Zutat; (med.) Verband; **salad -ing** Salatsauce; **-ing gown** Schlafrock, Morgenrock; **-ing table** Frisiertoilette; **-y** *adj.* sich geschmackvoll kleidend; putzsüchtig; modisch

dressmaker *n.* Damenschneider(in)

dribble *v.* tröpfeln, träufeln; geifern, sabbern; (sports) dribbeln, treiben

drift *n.* Trieb(kraft), Antrieb; Treiben; (geol.) Geschiebe; (naut.) Abtrift; (phil.) Tendenz, Absicht; — *v.* dahintreiben; schwimmen; sich anhäufen

driftwood *n.* Treibholz

drill *n.* Bohrer, Drillbohrer; (mil.) Drill, Exerzieren; — *v.* bohren, drillen; (mil.) exerzieren

drink *n.* Getränk; Trank, Trunk, Schluck; — *v.* trinken, saufen, zechen; — **to** trinken auf; **-er** *n.* Trinker, Säufer; **-ing fountain** Trinkbrunnen

drip *n.* Tropfen; Tröpfeln; Traufe; — *v.* tröpfeln, tropfen, triefen; träufeln; **-ings** *n. pl.* Bratenfett

drive *n.* Fahrweg; Ausfahrt, Ausfahren, Fahren; Spazierfahrt; Kampagne; Schwung; Treiben; (hunting) Treiben, Hetzen; (mech.) Antrieb; **four-wheel** — Vierradantrieb; **go for a** — eine Autofahrt machen; — *v.* treiben, fahren, ausfahren, lenken; (com.) betreiben, leiten; (engine) fahren; (hit)

schlagen; (hunting) jagen, hetzen; (nails) einschlagen; — **a bargain** ein gutes Geschäft abschliessen; — **at** hinauswollen auf; — **away** vertreiben; fortfahren; — **back** zurücktreiben; zurückfahren; — **crazy** (*oder* **mad**) verrückt machen; — **off** wegjagen, abweisen; — **on** zufahren; — **out** forttreiben, hinausfahren; — **to** despair zur Verzweiflung bringen; — **up** auftreiben; **-r** *n*. Fahrer, Chauffeur; **-r's license** Führerschein
drive-in *n*. Autobahngaststätte mit Bedienung am Wagen; Freilichtkino
driveway *n*. Fahrweg
drizzle *n*. Sprühregen; — *v*. sprühen, nieseln, fein regnen
drogue *n*. Bremsfallschirm
drone *n*. Drohne; Müssiggänger; Summen, Brummen; (avi.) ferngelenkte, unbemannte Rakete; — *v*. faulenzen
droop *v*. zusammenfallen; sinken lassen; verwelken; den Kopf hängen lassen
drop *n*. Tropfen; Fall, Sinken; *pl*. **drops**, Bonbons; **lemon** — Zitronendrops; **letter** — Briefeinwurf, Briefschlitz; **curtain** — Zwischen(akts)vorhang; — **hammer** elektrischer Schmiedehammer; — **leaf** Klappbrett, zusammenklappbare Tischplatte; — *v*. tröpfeln; lecken; fallen (lassen); absetzen, aufgeben; senden; sinken; (bombs) (ab) werfen; — **asleep** einschlafen; — **in** zufällig vorsprechen; — **off** abfallen; abgeben; einschlafen; — **out** ausscheiden
dropsy *n*. Wassersucht
drought, drouth *n*. Trockenheit, Dürre
drove *n*. Herde, Trieb, Trift; Getümmel, Auflauf
drown *v*. ertrinken, ertränken; übertönen; überfluten
drowsiness *n*. Schläfrigkeit
drudge *n*. Packesel, Schwerarbeitende; — *v*. sich abplacken (*or* abplagen); **-ry** *n*. Plakkerei
drug *n*. Droge, Arzneiware; Rauschgift; — *v*. Schlafmittel nehmen (*or* geben); **-gist** *n*. Apotheker, Drogist
drugstore *n*. Drogerie
drum *n*. Trommel; (anat.) Trommelhöhle; — **major** Tambourmajor; — *v*. trommeln; — **into** einpauken; — **up** (zusammen)trommeln; **-mer** *n*. Trommler, Tambour; Handlungsreisende
drumstick *n*. Trommelschlegel; (cooking) Keule
drunk *adj*. (be)trunken; **get** — sich betrinken; — *n*. Betrunkene, Besoffene; **-ard** *n*. Trunkenbold; **-en** *adj*. (be)trunken; **-en revel** Ausschweifung, Orgie; **-enness** *n*. Trunkenheit; Trunk-

sucht
dry *adj*. trocken, dürr; geräuchert; **gedörrt**; nüchtern; langweilig; herb; — **battery** Trockenbatterie; — **cell** Trockenelement; — **cleaner** chemische Reinigung(sanstalt); — **cleaning** chemische Reinigung; — **dock** Trockendock; — **goods** *n*. *pl*. Kurzwaren, Schnittwaren, Baumwollwaren; — **ice** Trockeneis; — **measure** Trockenmass; — **rot** Schwamm, Trockenfäule; — *v*. (ab)trocknen, austrocknen; dörren, rösten; **-er** *n*. Trockner; **-ness** *n*. Trockenheit, Dürre
dry-clean *v*. chemisch reinigen
dual *adj*. zwei bezeichnend, **zwiefach**, doppelt; — **control** Doppelkontrolle
dub *v*. nachsynchronisieren; nachträglich einsetzen
dubious *adj*. zweifelhaft; schwankend, unschlüssig
duchess *n*. Herzogin
duck *n*. Ente; — *v*. (unter)tauchen, sich ducken (or bücken); neigen
duct *n*. Gang; Röhre, Rohr; Kanal; **-less** *adj*. (anat. and bot.) röhrenlos
dud *n*. Blindgänger
dude *n*. Geck, Stutzer; — **ranch** Ranch mit Fremdenverkehr
due *adj*. schuldig, zustehend; gebührend; fällig, zahlbar; **become** (*oder* **fall**) — fällig werden; — **bill** Schuldschein; — **to** durch; wegen; **in** — **time** zur richtigen Zeit; — *n*. Gebühr, Schuld, Recht; Anspruch; Lohn; *pl*. Abgaben, Gebühren; **give someone his -s** jemandem das Seinige geben; — *adv*. gerade; genau nach
dugout *n*. Unterstand
duke *n*. Herzog; **-dom** *n*. Herzogtum
dull *adj*. dumm, albern; träge, schwerfällig; stumpf; dumpf; düster; (color) matt, dunkel; (com.) flau, still; — *v*. abstumpfen; (sich) trüben; **-ness** *n*. Dummheit, Stumpfsinn; Trägheit, Mattigkeit; Langweiligkeit; Teilnahmslosigkeit; Flaute, Stille
duly *adv*. angemessen, pflichtgemäss
dumb *adj*. dumm, töricht; stumm, sprachlos
dumbbell *n*. Hantel
dumb-waiter *n*. Speiseaufzug
dum(b)found *v*. zum Schweigen bringen, verblüffen
dummy *n*. Kleiderpuppe, Attrappe; (cards and fig.) Strohmann
dump *n*. Schuttabladeplatz, Abfallhaufen; **be** (**down**) **in the -s** schwermütig sein, vor sich hinstarren; — **truck** Kippwagen; — *v*. auskippen; abladen, ab-

werfen; auf den Markt werfen; **-ling**
n. Kloss, Knödel
dumping ground n. Schuttabladeplatz
dunce n. Dummkopf, Einfaltspinsel
dune n. Düne, Sandhügel
dung n. Mist, Dünger; — v. düngen
dungeon n. Verliess, Kerker
dunghill n. Dunghaufen, Misthaufen
duodenal ulcer n. (med.) Zwölffinger-
darmgeschwür
dupe n. Angeführte, Betrogene, Gimpel;
— v. täuschen, anführen
duplex n. Zweifamilienwohnung; Zwei-
familienhaus; — adj. doppelt, **zweifach**
duplicate n. Duplikat, Kopie; — v. verdoppeln; wiederholen; abschreiben; —
adj. doppelt, zweifach
duplicity n. Zweideutigkeit, Falschheit;
Doppelzüngigkeit
durability n. Dauerhaftigkeit
durable adj. dauerhaft, dauernd
duration n. Dauer, Fortdauer
duress n. Bedrückung, Zwang
during prep. während
dusk n. Dämmerung, Halbdunkel, Zwielicht; **-y** adj. dämmerig, dunkel; trübe,
düster
dust n. Staub; Kehricht, Müll; Asche;
house — Wohnungsstaub; — **bowl**
Ursprung (or Quelle) des Sandsturms;
— **storm** Sandsturm; — v. abstauben,
ausstauben; abbürsten, abwischen; bestäuben; **-y** adj. staubig, bestäubt;
staubartig
dustpan n. Kehrrichtschaufel, Müll-
schaufel
dutiable adj. steuerpflichtig, zollpflichtig;
— **goods** zollpflichtige Waren
dutiful adj. pflichtgetreu; gehorsam;
ehrerbietig
duty n. Pflicht, Verpflichtung, Schuldigkeit; Aufgabe; (mil. and naut.) Dienst;
(tax, etc.) Zoll, Abgabe, Steuer; **be off**
— dienstfrei sein; **be on** — im Dienst
sein, Dienst haben
dwarf n. Zwerg; — v. verkrüppeln, verkleinern; zusammenschrumpfen; in den
Schatten stellen; in der Entwicklung
hindern; — adj. Zwerg-; niedrig, klein,
winzig
dwell v. wohnen; — (up)on verweilen bei,
sich aufhalten bei; **-er** n. Einwohner,
Bewohner, **-ing** n. Wohnung, Behausung
dwindle v. sich vermindern, abnehmen;
schwinden
dye n. Farbe, Färbung; Farbstoff; — v.
färben; **-ing** n. Färben
dynamic adj. dynamisch; **-s** n. pl. Dyna-
mik

dynamite n. Dynamit
dynamo n. Dynamo
dynasty n. Dynastie
dyspepsia n. Verdauungsstörung

E

each adj. jeder, jede, jedes; — **and every**
one jeder einzelne; — **one** (ein)jeder;
— **other** einander, sich; — pron. (ein)-
jeder
eager adj. eifrig, begierig; brennend;
-ness n. Begierde, Eifer
eagle n. Adler
eagle-eyed adj. adleräugig, scharfsichtig
ear n. Ohr; Gehör; (bot.) Ähre, Kolben;
by — nach dem Gehör; — **of corn**
Maiskolben; — **muff** Ohrenschützer;
— **specialist** Ohrenspezialist; — **trum-**
pet Hörrohr
earache n. Ohrenschmerzen
eardrum n. Trommelfell
earl n. Graf
early adj. früh, (früh)zeitig; — **bird**
Frühaufsteher; — **life** Jugendzeit
earmark n. Kennzeichen; — v. kennzeichnen, vormerken
earn v. verdienen, erwerben, gewinnen;
-ings n. pl. Lohn, Verdienst, Einkommen
earnest adj. ernst(haft); eifrig, begierig;
— **money** Handgeld; — n. Ernst; **I am**
in — es ist mein voller Ernst; **-ness n.**
Eifer, Sorgfalt; Ernst(haftigkeit)
earphone n. Kopfhörer
earring n. Ohrring
earshot n. Hörweite
earth n. Erde, Boden; Land; Welt; **-en**
adj. irdisch; tönern, irden; **-ly** adj.
irdisch, weltlich; körperlich, sinnlich;
no **-ly reason** kein erdenklicher Grund,
nicht der geringste Grund; **-y** adj.
erdig; erdfarben, erdfahl
earthenware n. Steingut, Töpferware
earthquake n. Erdbeben
earwax n. Ohrenschmalz
ease n. Ruhe; Behaglichkeit, Ungezwungenheit; Behagen; Leichtigkeit; Linderung; **at** — frei, ungezwungen; rührt
euch! — v. lindern, mildern, beruhigen;
— **up** nachlassen
easel n. Staffelei, Gestell
easiness n. Leichtigkeit, Gemächlichkeit
east n. Osten, Ost; Orient, Morgenland;
— adj. and adv. Ost-, östlich; — **of**
östlich von; **-erly** adj. östlich, Ost-;
-erly wind Ostwind; **-erly** adv. ostwärts, nach Osten; **-ern** adj. östlich;
orientalisch, morgenländisch
Easter n. Ostern, Osterfest; Oster-; — **egg**

Osterei

eastward *adj.* östlich; — *adv.* ostwärts, nach Osten

easy *adj.* leicht; bequem, behaglich, gemächlich; — chair Lehnstuhl; live on — street im Wohlstand leben; take it —! nur ruhig! sachte!

easygoing *adj.* gemütlich, bequem; gutmütig; leichtsinnig

eat *v.* essen, verzehren; (chem.) zerfressen, eindringen; (zool.) fressen; — up aufessen

eaves *n. pl.* Dachrinne, Traufe

eavesdrop *v.* lauschen; -per *n.* Lauscher, Horcher

ebb *n.* Ebbe; Abnahme, Neige; — and flow Ebbe und Flut; — *adj.* — tide Ebbe: — *v.* ebben; ablaufen, abnehmen

ebony *n.* Ebenholz

eccentric *adj.* exzentrisch, überspannt; -ity *n.* Überspanntheit

ecclesiastic *n.* Geistliche; — *adj.* geistlich, kirchlich

echelon *n.* Staffel(aufstellung)

echo *n.* Echo, Widerhall; — *v.* widerhallen, echoen; wiederholen

eclipse *n.* Finsternis, Verfinsterung; — *v.* verfinstern, verdunkeln

ecliptic *n.* Sonnenbahn, Ekliptik

economic *adj.* volkswirtschaftlich, ökonomisch; -al *adj.* sparsam, haushälterisch; wirtschaftlich; -s *n. pl.* Volkswirtschaftslehre; Haushaltungskunst

economist *v.* Nationalökonom, Volkswirtschaftslehrer; Volkswirt; Haushälter; Sparer

economize *v.* (er)sparen; sparsam anwenden

economy *n.* Wirtschaft; Haushalt(ung); Ersparnis, Ökonomie

ecstasy *n.* Ekstase, Verzückung

ecstatic *adj.* ekstatisch, verzückt, schwärmerisch

ecumenical *adj.* ökumenisch

eczema *n.* Ekzem, Hautflechte, Hautausschlag

edge *n.* Schärfe, Schneide; Rand, Kante; on — gespannt, gereizt; — *v.* einfassen, säumen; sich seitwärts bewegen; vorrücken, vordringen; — away vorsichtig wegrücken

edible *adj.* essbar

edict *n.* Edikt, Verordnung, Erlass

edifice *n.* Gebäude, grösser Bau

edify *v.* belehren, überreden; erbauen

edit *v.* herausgeben, redigieren; -ion *n.* Ausgabe, Auflage; -or *n.* Redakteur, Herausgeber; -or in chief Chefredakteur; -orial *n.* Leitartikel; -orial *adj.*

redaktionell; Redaktions-

educate *v.* erziehen, unterrichten, (aus)-bilden; -d *adj.* gebildet, erzogen

education *n.* Erziehung, Unterricht, Ausbildung; Bildung; -al *adj.* erzieherisch, pädagogisch; Erziehungs-

educator *n.* Erzieher

eel *n.* Aal

efface *v.* auslöschen, ausstreichen; verwischen, tilgen; in den Schatten stellen; — oneself in den Hintergrund treten

effect *n.* Wirkung, Effekt; Eindruck; *pl.* Effekten, Habseligkeiten; for — um Eindruck zu machen; go into — in Kraft treten; have an — wirken; in — in der Tat; put into — in Kraft setzen; take — wirken; — *v.* bewirken, ausführen; -ive *adj.* wirksam, kräftig

effeminate *adj.* weibisch, verweichlicht

effervescent *adj.* aufbrausend

efficacious *adj.* wirksam, kräftig

efficacy *n.* Wirksamkeit, wirkende Kraft

efficiency *n.* Wirksamkeit, Tüchtigkeit, Leistungsfähigkeit

efficient *adj.* wirkend, wirksam, tüchtig, ausgebildet; leistungsfähig

efflorescence *n.* Blüte, Entfaltung; (fig.) Blütezeit;(chem.)Auswittern,Beschlag; (med.) Hautausschlag; (min.) Anflug

effort *n.* Anstrengung, Bestrebung, Bemühung; make an — sich bemühen (or anstrengen)

effusive *adj.* übertrieben; verschwenderisch; überschwenglich

egg *n.* Ei; fried — Spiegelei; hard-boiled — hart(gekocht)es Ei; poached — verlorenes Ei; scrambled — Rührei; soft-boiled — weich(gekocht)es Ei; — cell Eizelle; — cup Eierbecher; — white Eiweiss; — yolk Eidotter, Eigelb

eggnog *n.* Eierlikör

eggshell *n.* Eierschale

ego *n.* Ich, Ego; -tism *n.* Egoismus, Selbstsucht; Selbstüberhebung; -tistic(al) *adj.* egoistisch, selbstsüchtig

Egypt *n.* Ägypten

eiderdown *n.* Eiderdaune

eight *adj.* acht; — ball Billiardkugel No. 8; behind the — ball im Schlamassel sein; — *n.* Acht(er); -een *adj.* achtzehn; -een *n.* Achtzehn; Achtzehner; -eenth *adj.* achtzehnt; — *n.* Achtzehnte; Achtzehntel; -fold *adj.* achtfach; -h *adj.* acht; -h *n.* Achte; Achtel; -ieth *adj.* achtzigst; -ieth *n.* Achtzigste; Achtzigstel; -y *adj.* achtzig; -y *n.* Achtzig; Achtziger

either *pron.* and *adj.* einer, jeder; beide; not — keiner; — *conj.* entweder; — . . . or entweder . . . oder

ejaculation n. Ausruf; Stossgebet

eject v. vertreiben, verjagen; ausstossen; **–ion** n. Vertreibung; (med.) Auswurf; **–ion seat** (avi.) Schleudersitz

El abbr. Hochbahn

elaborate v. ausarbeiten; — upon etwas genauer beschreiben; — adj. ausgearbeitet, ausgefeilt; detailliert

elapse v. verstreichen, vergehen, verfliessen

elastic adj. elastisch, federnd, dehnbar; — n. Gummiband; **–ity** n. Elastizität, Dehnbarkeit; Spannkraft

elate v. ermutigen, aufblähen; **–d** adj. erhaben, stolz

elbow n. Ellbogen; Krümmung, Biegung; (mech.) Knie, Winkel; — v. mit dem Ellbogen (weg-)stossen

elbowroom n. Ellbogenfreiheit, Bewegungsfreiheit, Spielraum

elder n. Ältere, Senior; Kirchenälteste; (bot.) Holunder; — adj. älter; **–ly** adj. ältlich, älter

eldest adj. ältest-

elect v. (er)wählen, auswählen; — adj. ausgewählt, (aus)erwählt; **–ion** n. Wahl, Abstimmung; **–ioneering** n. Wahlpropaganda; **–ive** adj. wählend; Wahl-; **–ive** n. Wahlfach; **–or** n. Wähler; **–oral** adj. die Wahl betreffend, Wahl-; Wähler-; **–oral college** Wahlausschuss; **–orate** n. Wähler(schaft)

electric adj. elektrisch; — bulb Glühbirne; — cable elektrisches Kabel; — chair elektischer Stuhl; — charge elektrische Ladung; — eye Elektronenauge; Selenzelle; — fixtures elektrische Installation; — meter Stromzähler; — motor Elektromotor; — plant Elektrizitätswerk; — railroad elektrischer Zug; — shock elektrischer Schlag; — welding elektrisches Schweissen; **–al** adj. elektrisch; **–al engineer** Elektrotechniker; **–al engineering** Elektrotechnik; **–ian** n. Elektriker; **–ity** n. Elektrizität; — razor Trockenrasier-Apparat

electrify v. elektrisieren

electrocardiogram n. EKG, Elektrokardiogramm

electrocute v. elektrisch hinrichten (or töten)

electrocution n. elektrisches Hinrichten (or Töten)

electrode n. Elektrode

electrolysis n. Elektrolyse

electrolyte n. Elektrolyt

electromagnet n. Elektromagnet; **–ic** adj. elektromagnetisch; **–ic field** elektromagnetisches Feld

electromotive adj. elektromotorisch; — force elektromotorische Kraft

electron n. Elektron; **–ics** n. Elektronik, Elektronenlehre

electroplate v. galvanisieren; galvanisch versilbern (or vergolden, etc.)

electrotherapie n. elektrische Heilbehandlung

elegance n. Feinheit, Eleganz, Vornehmheit

elegant adj. elegant, fein; geschmackvoll; vornehm

elegy n. Elegie, Klagelied

element n. Element, Bestandteil; Urstoff, Grundstoff; pl. Elemente, Anfangsgründe; Naturgewalten; **–al** adj. elementar, naturgewaltig, wesentlich; **–ary** adj. elementar, einfach; Natur-; Anfangs-; **–ary school** Volksschule, Grundschule

elephant n. Elefant

elevate v. hochheben, erhöhen, erheben; **–d** adj. erhoben, hoch; erhaben; **–d railroad** Hochbahn; **–d train** Hochbahnzug

elevation n. Erhebung, Erhöhung; Höhe

elevator n. Fahrstuhl, Aufzug; (avi.) Höhensteuer; grain — Getreidespeicher

eleven adj. elf; — n. Elf(er); **–th** adj. elfte; **–th** n. Elfte; Elftel

elf n. Kobold, Elf; **–in** adj. elfisch, elfengleich; Elfen-

eligible adj. wählbar; wünschenswert, passend; heiratsfähig

eliminate v. ausmerzen, beseitigen; absondern, ausscheiden

elk n. Elch, Elen

ellipse n. Ellipse

elliptic(al) adj. elliptisch; unvollständig

elm n. Ulme, Rüster

elocution n. Aussprache, Vortragskunst

elope v. entlaufen, durchgehen; entführen; sich entführen lassen; **–ment** n. Entlaufen, Entführung; Fortlaufen

eloquence n. Beredsamkeit

eloquent adj. beredt, beredsam

else adj. and adv. anders, weiter, sonst; nothing — sonst nichts; or — sonst; somewhere — irgendwo anders, anderswo; what —? was sonst? — conj. sonst, wo nicht

elsewhere adv. anderswo, sonstwo, woanders

elucidate v. aufklären, erläutern

elude v. ausweichen, geschickt umgehen

emaciate v. abzehren, abmagern, ausmergeln

emanate v. ausfliessen, ausstrahlen; herrühren

emancipate v. emanzipieren, befreien

emancipation n. Emanzipation, Befreiung

emancipator *n*. Befreier

embalm *v*. einbalsamieren; **–ment** *n*. Einbalsamierung

embargo *n*. Hafensperre; Handelsverbot; — *v*. (den Hafen, Handel) sperren; (ship) beschlagnahmen

embark *v*. (sich) einschiffen; sich einlassen; **–ation** *n*. Einschiffung, Verladung

embarrass *v*. in Verlegenheit setzen, verwirren; **–ed** *adj*. verlegen; **–ing** *adj*. peinlich; **–ment** *n*. Verlegenheit; Verwicklung, Verwirrung

embassy *n*. Gesandtschaft, Botschaft

embellish *v*. verschönern, ausschmücken

ember *v*. glühende Kohle (*or* Asche)

embezzle *v*. veruntreuen, unterschlagen; **–ment** *n*. Veruntreuung, Unterschlagung; **–r** *n*. Veruntreuer, Unterschlagende

embitter *v*. verbittern, erbittern

emblem *n*. Emblem, Sinnbild, Kennzeichen

embody *v*. verkörpern; einverleiben; umfassen, enthalten

embrace *n*. Umarmung; — *v*. (sich) umarmen, umfassen; enthalten; annehmen

embroider *v*. sticken; verschönern, ausschmücken; **–y** *n*. Stickerei; **–y frame** Stickrahmen; **–y needle** Sticknadel

embryo *n*. Embryo, Leibesfrucht; (fig.) Keim

emerald *n*. Smaragd; — *adj*. smaragdfarben

emerge *v*. auftauchen, emporkommen; entstehen; **–ncy** *n*. dringende Not, schwierige Lage; unerwartetes Ereignis; **–ncy brake** Notbremse; **–ncy exit** Notausgang; **–ncy landing** Notlandung; **–ncy landing field** provisorisches Landefeld

emeritus *adj*. emeritiert, in den Ruhestand versetzt

emery *n*. Schmirgel, Korund

emigrant *n*. Auswanderer, Emigrant

emigrate *v*. auswandern, emigrieren

emigration *n*. Auswanderung, Emigration

eminence *n*. Erhöhung, Anhöhe; hoher Rang, Auszeichnung; (eccl.) Eminenz; (fig.) Gipfel

eminent *adj*. hervorragend, eminent; vorzüglich; — **domain** staatliches Vorrecht, Staatsgebiet

emotion *n*. Rührung, Gefühl(sregung); Erregung; **–al** *adj*. gefühlsmässig; gefühlvoll; leicht erregbar

empennage *n*. Flugzeugschwanzflosse

emperor *n*. Kaiser

emphasis *n*. Nachdruck, Betonung

emphasize *v*. ausdrücklich betonen

emphatic *adj*. emphatisch, nachdrücklich, eindringlich

emphysema *n*. Emphysem

empire *n*. Reich; Kaiserreich

empiric(al) *adj*. erfahrungsmässig

employ *n*. Beschäftigung, Dienst; **Anstellung**; — *v*. anwenden, (ge)brauchen; beschäftigen, anstellen; **–ee** *n*. Angestellte, Arbeitnehmer; **–er** *n*. Arbeitgeber; **–ment** *n*. Beschäftigung, Arbeit, Tätigkeit; **–ment agency** Arbeitsamt, Arbeitsvermittlung, Arbeitsnachweis

emporium *n*. Handelsplatz, Stapelplatz

empower *v*. ermächtigen, bevollmächtigen

empress *n*. Kaiserin

emptiness *n*. Leere, Nichtigkeit

empty *adj*. leer; hungrig; (fig.) hohl, eitel; — *v*. (ent)leeren, ausräumen; sich entleeren, (*or* ergiessen)

empty-handed *adj*. mit leeren Händen

emulate *v*. wetteifern mit, nacheifern

emulsion *n*. Emulsion

enable *v*. ermöglichen, befähigen; ermächtigen

enact *v*. erlassen, verfügen, verordnen; (theat.) darstellen

enamel *n*. Email(le), Schmelz, Glasur; — *v*. emaillieren, glasieren

enamored *adj*. verliebt

encampment *n*. Lager, Feldlager

enchant *v*. fesseln, entzücken, bezaubern; **–ing** *adj*. fesselnd, entzückend, bezaubernd; **–ment** *n*. Bezauberung; Zauberei, Zauber

encircle *v*. umringen, umfassen

enclose *v*. einschliessen, umgeben; (letter) beifügen, einlegen; enthalten; (field, etc.) einzäunen, einfrieden

enclosure *n*. Einschliessung; (letter) Beilage, Einlage; (field, etc.) Einzäunung; Gehege; Einfriedung; Zaun, Hecke

encompass *v*. umschliessen, einschliessen

encore *n*. Dacaporuf, Wiederholung; Zugabe; —! *interj*. noch einmal! da capo!; — *v*. noch einmal verlangen

encounter *n*. Zusammentreffen, Begegnung; (mil.) Gefecht, Treffen; Zusammenstoss; — *v*. (zusammen)treffen; sich begegnen, stossen auf

encourage *v*. ermutigen, ermuntern; fordern, unterstützen; **–ment** *n*. Ermutigung, Ermunterung; Förderung, Unterstützung

encouraging *adj*. ermutigend, aufmunternd

encroach *v*. Eingriffe tun; — **upon** eingreifen in, stören; — **upon someone's kindness** jemandes Güte missbrauchen

encumbrance *n*. Bürde; Belastung; Hindernis

encyclopedia *n.* Enzyklopädie, Konversationslexikon

end *n.* Ende; Absicht, Zweck; Ziel; Tod, Vernichtung; **be at an — am Ende sein, aus sein; bring to an — zu Ende führen; — to — der Länge nach; his hair stood on — seine Haare standen zu Berge; in the — auf die Dauer, schliesslich; make both —s meet aus- kommen, sich nach der Decke strecken; no — unendlich, endlos; on — aufrecht; ununterbrochen; hintereinander; put an — to ein Ende machen mit; the — justifies the means der Zweck heiligt die Mittel; to the bitter — bis zum bitteren Ende; bis zum äussersten; without — unendlich; — *v.* (be)enden, vollenden; (fig.) vernichten; sterben; all's well that —s well Ende gut, alles gut; —ing** *n.* Ende, Schluss; (gram.) Endung; **—less** *adj.* unendlich, endlos

endanger *v.* gefährden

endeavor *n.* Bemühung, Bestreben; — *v.* sich bemühen, sich bestreben

endorse *v.* übertragen, überschreiben, indossieren, girieren; (fig.) unterstüt- zen, bestätigen, beipflichten; **—ment** *n.* Indossament; (fig.) Bestätigung, Un- terstützung

endow *v.* ausstatten, aussteuern, (eccl.) dotieren; **—ment** *n.* Ausstattung, Aus- steuer, Dotation; Stiftung; (fig.) Talent

endurable *adj.* erträglich, leidlich

endurance *n.* Ausdauer, Geduld; Erdul- den, Ertragen; Dauer

endure *v.* dulden, aushalten, ertragen; dauern

endways, endwise *adv.* gerade, aufrecht

enema *n.* Klistier, Einlauf

enemy *n.* Feind, Gegner

energetic *adj.* energisch, kraftvoll, tat- kräftig

energy *n.* Energie, Tatkraft; Nachdruck, Wirksamkeit

enervate *v.* entnerven, schwächen

enforce *v.* erzwingen, durchsetzen; durch- führen; **—ment** *n.* Erzwingung, Durch- setzung; Durchführung

engage *v.* verpflichten, engagieren, anstel- len, beschäftigen; (mil.) angreifen; — **in betreiben, sich einlassen auf; —ed** *adj.* verlobt; beschäftigt; verpflichtet; **—ment** *n.* Verlobung; Verabredung; (mil.) Angriff

engaging *adj.* einnehmend, gewinnend, reizend

engender *v.* (er)zeugen

engine *n.* Maschine; Motor; Lokomotive; Mittel; **— room Maschinenraum; —er**

n. Ingenieur, Techniker, Maschinen- bauer; Lokomotivführer; (mil.) Pio- nier; (naut.) Maschinist; **—er** *v.* durch- setzen, einrichten, bauen; **—ering** *n.* Ingenieurwesen, Maschinenbaukunst

England *n.* England

English Channel *n.* der Ärmelkanal

engraft *v.* veredeln, aufsetzen, pfropfen, okulieren

engrave *v.* gravieren, stechen, eingraben; (fig.) einprägen

engraving *n.* Gravierung, Gravieren; (metal) Stich; (wood) Schnitt

engross *v.* ganz in Anspruch nehmen; **an sich ziehen; —ed** *adj.* vertieft

enhance *v.* erhöhen, steigern; übertreiben; (fig.) vergrössern

enigma *n.* Rätsel; **—tic** *adj.* rätselhaft, dunkel

enjoin *v.* befehlen, auferlegen; einschär- fen, vorschreiben; verbieten

enjoy *v.* geniessen; sich erfreuen; besitzen; **— oneself sich (gut) unterhalten, sich amüsieren; —able** *adj.* angenehm, er- freulich, genussreich; **—ment** *n.* Genuss; Vergnügen, Freude

enlarge *v.* zunehmen, weiten; ausdehnen; erweitern; (phot.) vergrössern; (fig.) sich verbreiten; **—ment** *n.* Zunahme; Erweiterung; (phot.) Vergrösserung

enlighten *v.* erleuchten, erhellen; aufklä- ren, belehren; **—ment** *n.* Erleuchtung; Aufklärung

enlist *v.* sich anwerben lassen; (an)wer- ben; gewinnen (für); **—ment** *n.* Anwer- bung

enliven *v.* beleben, ermuntern

enmity *n.* Feindschaft, Feindseligkeit

enormity *n.* Ungeheuerlichkeit

enormous *adj.* enorm, ungeheuer

enough *adj.* and *adv.* genug, genügend; **be — genügen; (aus)reichen, langen; be good — to so gut sein und; — *n.* Genüge

enquire *v.* see **inquire**

enrage *v.* wütend machen, aufbringen; **—d** *adj.* wütend, aufgebracht

enroll *v.* eintragen, einschreiben, anmel- den; (mil.) anwerben; (naut.) anmu- stern; **—ment** *n.* Eintragung, Einschrei- ben, Anmeldung

enshrine *v.* einschliessen, als Heiligtum verwahren

ensign *n.* Abzeichen, Fahne, Flagge; (naut.) Fähnrich

enslave *v.* knechten, unterjochen

ensue *v.* folgen; sich ergeben; sich ereig- nen, nachfolgen

ensure *v.* sichern, versichern, verbürgen

entail *n.* Vererben; Erbfolge; — *v.* vererben; zur Folge haben, erfordern

entangle v. verwirren, verwickeln, verstricken

enter v. eintreten, betreten; eingehen; eintragen, einschreiben; (sports) melden, nennen

enteritis n. (med.) Darmverschluss

enterprise n. Unternehmen, Unternehmung; free — Gewerbefreiheit

enterprising adj. unternehmend; verwegen, kühn

entertain v. unterhalten, bewirten; hegen; -er n. Wirt; Unterhalter, Unterhaltende; -ment n. Unterhaltung, Zerstreuung; Bewirtung; Schaustellung, Aufführung

enthrone v. einsetzen; auf den Thron setzen

enthusiasm n. Begeisterung, Enthusiasmus

enthusiast n. Schwärmer, Enthusiast; -ic adj. schwärmend, begeistert, enthusiastisch

entice v. (ver)locken, reizen; -ment n. Verlockung, Reiz

entire adj. ganz, gesamt, vollkommen, unversehrt, ungeschmälert, vollständig, ungeteilt; -ly adv. gänzlich, durchaus, völlig; herzlich; entschieden; lediglich; -ty n. Ganzheit, Gesamtheit; Vollständigkeit, Unversehrtheit

entitle v. betiteln, benennen; berechtigen

entity n. Sein; Wesen(heit)

entomology n. Entomologie, Insektenkunde

entrance n. Eingang; Einfahrt; Einlass, Eintritt, Eintreten; (theat.) Auftreten; — v. entzücken, hinreissen

entreat v. bitten, ersuchen, erflehen; -y n. Bitte, Gesuch

entrée n. Entree, Eintritt, Zutritt; (cooking) Hauptgericht

entrench v. see intrench

entry n. Eingang; Eintritt; (com.) Eintragung, Buchung; (sports) Nennung, Meldung; (theat.) Auftritt

entwine v. (um)winden, verflechten

enumerate v. aufzählen, zählen

enunciate v. ausdrücken, aussprechen; aufstellen

enunciation n. Aussprache, Vortrag; Aufstellung

envelop v. einhüllen, einwickeln, umgeben; -e n. Umschlag, Hülle; Briefumschlag

enviable adj. beneidenswert

envious adj. neidisch, missgünstig

environment n. Umgebung

envoy n. Gesandte

envy n. Neid, Missgunst; — v. beneiden,

missgönnen

enzyme n. Enzym, Ferment

epaulet n. Epaulette, Achselstück

epic n. Epos, Heldengedicht; — adj. episch

epidemic n. Epidemie, Seuche; — adj. epidemisch, seuchenartig

epidermis n. Epidermis, Oberhaut

epigram n. Epigramm, Sinngedicht, Spottgedicht

epilepsy n. Epilepsie, Fallsucht

epileptic adj. epileptisch, fallsüchtig; — n. Epileptiker, Fallsüchtige(r)

epilogue n. Epilog, Nachwort

episcopalian n. Mitglied einer Bischofskirche; — adj. bischöflich

episode n. Episode

epistle n. Brief, Epistel, Sendschreiben

epitaph n. Epitaph, Grabschrift

epithet n. Attribut, Beiwort; Benennung

epitome n. Auszug, Abriss

epoch n. Epoche, Zeitabschnitt, Zeitpunkt

equable adj. gleichförmig, gleichmässig, gleichmütig

equal n. Gleiche; — adj. gleich, gleichmässig; be — to gewachsen sein; — v. gleichen, gleichkommen; -ity n. Gleichheit, Gleichmässigkeit; -ize v. gleichmachen, ausgleichen

equanimity n. Gleichmut

equation n. Gleichung

equator n. Äquator; -ial adj. äquatorial

equestrian n. Kunstreiter; — adj. reitend; Reit-, Reiter-

equidistant adj. parallel, gleichweit entfernt

equilateral adj. gleichseitig

equilibrium n. Gleichgewicht

equinox n. Tag- und Nachtgleiche

equip v. ausstatten, ausrüsten; -age n. Ausrüstung; Equipage, Kutsche; -ment n. Ausstattung, Ausrüstung; standard -ment Normalausrüstung

equitable adj. billig, gerecht; unparteiisch

equity n. Billigkeit, Gerechtigkeit, Unparteilichkeit; (law) Billigkeitsrecht

equivalent n. Gegenwert, Gleichwertigkeit, Äquivalent; — adj. gleichwertig, gleichbedeutend

equivocal adj. zweideutig, doppelsinnig; zweifelhaft, unbestimmt

era n. Ära, Zeit(rechnung); Periode, Zeitalter

eradicate v. ausrotten, entwurzeln

eradication n. Ausrottung, Entwurzelung

erase v. ausradieren, auslöschen; verwischen; -r n. Radiergummi; Wischer

erasure n. Rasur, Ausradieren, Ausradierung, Streichung

ere *prep.* vor; — *conj.* ehe, bevor

erect *v.* aufstellen, errichten, aufrichten; — *adj.* aufrecht, gerade; **-ion** *n.* Errichtung, Aufrichtung

ermine *n.* Hermelin, Hermelinpelz

erode *v.* anfressen, zerfressen; benagen

erosion *n.* Auswaschung, Zerfressung

err *v.* sich irren; fehlen, sündigen; **-atic** *adj.* wandernd; seltsam, exzentrisch; **-oneous** *adj.* irrig, falsch; unrichtig; **-or** *n.* Irrtum, Fehler, Schnitzer

errand *n.* Auftrag, Botengang; Bestellung; **run an** — einen Auftrag ausführen; — **boy** Laufbursche

erudition *n.* Gelehrsamkeit

erupt *v.* ausbrechen, hervorbrechen; **-ion** *n.* Ausbruch; Ausschlag; Eruption

escalate *v.* (mil.) ausbreiten, grössere Kreise ziehen, ausarten

escalator *n.* Rolltreppe

escapade *n.* Eskapade, Seitensprung

escape *n.* Flucht; Entrinnen, Entweichen; **have a narrow** — mit knapper Not davonkommen; **make one's** — sich aus dem Staube machen; — **capsule** Notkapsel (bemannte Rakete); — **hatch** Notausstieg (bemannte Rakete); — *v.* entgehen, entfliehen, entweichen; (fig.) entfallen

escort *n.* Gefolge, Begleitung; Geleit, Eskorte; — *v.* begleiten, geleiten, eskortieren

escutcheon *n.* Wappenschild; Namensschild

esophagus *n.* Speiseröhre

especial *adj.* besonder, hauptsächlich, speziell; vorzüglich

espionage *n.* Spionage; Spionieren

esquire *n.* Wohlgeboren, Hochwohlgeboren

essay *n.* Essay, kurze Abhandlung, Aufsatz; Versuch; — *v.* versuchen, erproben

essence *n.* Essenz, Extrakt; Wesen(heit), Geist

essential *adj.* wesentlich; wichtig; — *n.* Hauptsache, Wesentliche, Wichtigste

establish *v.* feststellen, festsetzen; errichten, einrichten; (be)gründen; — **oneself** eine Position erringen, sich niederlassen; **-ment** *n.* Gründung, Errichtung; Festsetzung; Organisation, Haushalt; Bestand

estate *n.* Gut, Besitz, Vermögen; Nachlass; Konkursmasse; Stand, Zustand

esteem *n.* Hochachtung, Würdigung; Ansehen; — *v.* abschätzen; hochachten; **-ed** *adj.* geachtet, hochgeschätzt

esthetic *adj.* ästhetisch, schöngeistig; **-s** *n. pl.* Ästhetik, Schönheitslehre

Esthonia *n.* Estland

estimable *adj.* achtungswert; schätzbar.

estimate *n.* Schätzung, Voranschlag, Kosten(vor)anschlag; *v.* berechnen, abschätzen

estimation *n.* Schätzung, Überschlag; Voranschlag; Meinung, Achtung

estrange *v.* entfremden, fernhalten

estrogen *n.* Estrogen (weibliches Hormon)

etc. *abbr.* usw. (und so weiter)

etch *v.* ätzen, radieren; **-ing** *n.* Ätzung, Radierung

eternal *adj.* ewig, immerwährend

eternity *n.* Ewigkeit

ether *n.* Äther; **-eal** *adj.* ätherisch, himmlisch

ethical *adj.* ethisch, moralisch, sittlich

ethics *n.* Ethik, Sittenlehre, Moral

ethnology *n.* Völkerkunde

ethyl *n.* Äthyl; Kohlenwasserstoff

etiquette *n.* Etikette, gute Sitte

etymology *n.* Etymologie, Wortursprungslehre

eucalyptus *n.* Eukalyptus

Eucharist *n.* Abendmahl(sfeier); **-ic** *adj.* eucharistisch; Abendmahls-

eugenics *n.* Rassenhygiene

eulogize *v.* loben

eulogy *n.* Lobpreisung, Lobrede

euphonious *adj.* wohllautend; euphonisch

Europe *n.* Europa; **-an** *n.* Europäer; **-an** *adj.* europäisch

euthanasia *n.* Euthanasie; schmerzloses Töten unheilbarer Kranker

evacuate *v.* evakuieren, räumen; entleeren, wegschaffen

evacuee *n.* Evakuierte; Ausgewiesene

evade *v.* ausweichen, umgehen, sich drücken vor

evaluate *v.* (ab)schätzen, einschätzen

evaluation *n.* Abschätzung, Wertbestimmung

evangelical *adj.* evangelisch

evangelist *n.* Evangelist; Wanderprediger

evaporate *v.* verdampfen (lassen), verdunsten; (fig.) verduften; **-d** *adj.* **-d milk** kondensierte Milch

evaporation *n.* Verdampfung, Verdunstung

evasion *n.* Entweichen; Ausflucht, Umgehung

eve *n.* Abend; Vorabend

even *adj.* gerade, eben, gleich; glatt; gleichförmig, gleichmässig; gelassen, ausgeglichen; rund, genau; **break** — auf seine Kosten kommen; — **number** gerade Zahl; — **sum** runde Summe; **get** — heimzahlen; **odd or** — gerade oder ungerade; **on** — **terms** in gutem Einvernehmen; **we are** — wir sind quitt; — *adv.* selbst, sogar; — if wenn auch, selbst wenn; — more noch mehr; — now selbst jetzt, auch jetzt; — so trotzdem; — though wenn auch, obwohl; not — nicht einmal; — *v.* ebnen; glätten, gleichstellen; -ness *n.* Gleichheit, Gleichförmigkeit; Ebenheit; Seelenruhe

evening *n.* Abend; good — guten Abend; in the — abends, am Abend; this — heute abend; — *adj.* Abend-; — clothes Abendkleider, Gesellschaftskleider; — star Abendstern, Venus

event *n.* Ereignis, Begebenheit, Vorfall; (sports) Veranstaltung; at all —s, in any — auf alle Fälle, jedenfalls; in the — im Falle; -ful *adj.* ereignisreich; wichtig, merkwürdig; -ual *adj.* eventuell, möglich; etwaig, schliesslich

ever *adv.* immer, stets, beständig; je, jemals; — since von der Zeit an; — so long eine Ewigkeit; — so much soviel wie irgend möglich; for — and — immer und ewig, immerfort; auf ewig; hardly — fast nie

evergreen *n.* Immergrün; — *adj.* immergrün

everlasting *adj.* ewig, unaufhörlich, unverwüstlich

evermore *adv.* immerfort, stets; je wieder

every *adj.* alle; jeder; jede, jedes; alle möglichen; — now and then, — once in a while dann und wann, ab und zu; — one jeder; — time jedesmal; — two years alle zwei Jahre

everybody *pron.* jedermann, jeder, jede, jedes; alle; — else alle anderen

everyday *adj.* alltäglich, allgemein; Alltags-

everyone *pron.* jedermann, jeder, jede, jedes; alle; — else alle anderen

everything *pron.* alles

everywhere *adv.* überall

evidence *n.* Beweis; (law) Beweismaterial, Beweismittel; Zeuge, Zeugnis; give — Zeugnis ablegen; — *v.* augenscheinlich machen, dartun; beweisen, zeugen

evident *adj.* offenbar, augenscheinlich, klar

evil *n.* Übel, Böse, Bosheit; — *adj.* übel, böse, schlecht, schlimm

evildoer *n.* Übeltäter

evil-minded *adj.* übelgesinnt

evoke *v.* hervorrufen, wachrufen; (herauf)beschwören

evolution *n.* Entwicklung, Entfaltung

evolve *v.* entwickeln, (sich) entfalten

exact *adj.* genau, exakt, sorgfältig; pünktlich; — *v.* erpressen, fordern, eintreiben; -ing *adj.* streng, anspruchsvoll; genau;

-ion *n.* Erpressung; ungebührliche Forderung; Eintreibung; -itude *n.*, -ness *n.* Exaktheit, Genauigkeit, Pünktlichkeit

exaggerate *v.* übertreiben, vergrössern

exalt *v.* erheben, erhöhen; -ation *n.* Erhebung, Erhöhung; Begeisterung, Verzücktheit

examination *n.* Prüfung, Examen; Untersuchung; (law) Verhör; medical — ärztliche Untersuchung

examine *v.* prüfen, untersuchen; betrachten; (law) verhören, vernehmen; -r *n.* Prüfer, Untersuchende; (law) Verhörende, Vernehmende

example *n.* Beispiel, Vorbild; Exempel, Warnung, Lehre; Exemplar, Muster; for — zum Beispiel; make an — ein Beispiel statuieren, exemplarisch bestrafen; set a good — mit gutem Beispiel vorangehen; set an — ein Beispiel geben

exasperate *v.* reizen, erbittern, ärgern

exasperation *n.* Erbitterung, Reizung

excavate *v.* aushöhlen, ausgraben

excavation *n.* Ausgrabung, Aushöhlung; Höhle

exceed *v.* überschreiten, übersteigen; übertreffen; -ingly *adv.* ausserordentlich, äusserst, überaus

excel *v.* übertreffen, überragen; hervorragen, sich hervortun; -lence *n.* Vortrefflichkeit, Vollkommenheit, Feinheit; -lency *n.* Excellenz; -lent *adj.* ausgezeichnet, vorzüglich, (vor)trefflich

except *conj.* ausser, es sei denn, dass; — *prep.* ausser, ausgenommen; — for bis auf, abgesehen von; — *v.* ausschliessen, ausnehmen; -ing *prep.* mit Ausnahme von; -ion *n.* Ausnahme; Einwendung, Einwand; -ional *adj.* aussergewöhnlich, ungewöhnlich

excess *n.* Überschuss; Übermass, Unmässigkeit; be in — of übersteigen; to — im Übermass; — *adj.* überschüssig; — baggage Überfracht; -ive *adj.* übermässig, übertrieben

exchange *n.* Austausch, Tausch; Wechsel; in — for im Austausch für; money — Wechselstube; rate of — Kurs, Wechselkurs; (stock) — Börse; telephone — Fernsprechamt, Telefonzentrale; — *v.* (aus)tauschen, vertauschen, umtauschen, eintauschen; wechseln; -able *adj.* auswechselbar, austauschbar; Tausch-

excise *n.* Warensteuer, Verbrauchssteuer

excitable *adj.* reizbar, erregbar

excite *v.* aufregen, wachrufen; erregen, anregen, reizen; get -d sich aufregen;

-dly *adv.* aufgeregt; -ment *n.* Aufregung, Anregung; Erregung, Reizung

exciting *adj.* aufregend; erregend

exclaim *v.* schreien, ausrufen

exclamation *n.* Geschrei, Ausruf(ung); — mark, — point Ausrufungszeichen

exclude *v.* ausschliessen

exclusion *n.* Ausschluss,. Ausschliessung

exclusive *adj.* ausschliesslich, alleinig, exklusiv

excommunicate *v.* exkommunizieren

excretion *n.* Auswurf, Aussonderung

excursion *n.* Ausflug, Abstecher

excusable *adj.* entschuldbar; verzeihlich

excuse *n.* Entschuldigung; Ausflucht, Vorwand; — *v.* entschuldigen, verzeihen

execute *v.* ausführen, vollziehen; (law) hinrichten; (mus.) vorspielen

execution *n.* Ausführung, Durchführung; (law) Hinrichtung; (mus. and theat.) Vortrag, Spiel, Technik; -er *n.* Henker, Scharfrichter

executive *n.* Exekutive, Staatsgewalt; Direktor; — *adj.* exekutiv, ausübend, vollziehend

executor *n.* Testamentsvollstrecker

exemplary *adj.* musterhaft, nachahmenswert; exemplarisch; Muster-

exemplify *v.* erläutern, (durch Beispiele) belegen

exempt *adj.* befreit, verschont; — *v.* befreien, verschonen; -ion *n.* Befreiung, Freisein, Ausnahme

exercise *n.* Übung, Praxis; Ausübung, Anwendung; (gymn.) Leibesübung; (mil.) Exerzieren; — *v.* üben; sich Bewegung machen; ausüben; gebrauchen, anwenden; exerzieren; (horse) zureiten

exert *v.* anstrengen; geltend machen; — oneself sich bemühen; -ion *n.* Anstrengung, Bemühung; Äusserung, Anwendung

exhale *v.* ausatmen, aushauchen; verdunsten

exhaust *v.* erschöpfen, entleeren; — *n.* Auspuff; — fan Aussenventilator; — gas Abgas; — manifold Sammelleerung; — pipe Auspuffrohr; — steam Abdampf; — valve Auslassventil; -ed *adj.* (com.) vergriffen; -ible *adj.* erschöpfbar; -ing *adj.* ermüdend; -ion *n.* Erschöpfung; -ive *adj.* erschöpfend

exhibit *n.* Ausstellung, Schau; Ausstellungsstück; Schaustellung; Warenauslage; (law) Beweisschrift; on — zur Besichtigung, zur Schau gestellt; — *v.* ausstellen, zeigen; aufweisen; darlegen; -ion *n.* Ausstellung, Schau; Darstel-

lung, Darlegung; -or *n.* Aussteller

exhilaration *n.* Erheiterung, Heiterkeit

exhort *v.* ermahnen, zureden; raten, warnen; -ation *n.* Ermahnung, Zureden; Mahnrede

exhume *v.* exhumieren, wieder ausgraben

exigency *n.* Dringlichkeit, Erfordernis, Bedarf; kritische Lage

exile *n.* Verbannte; Verbannung, Exil; — *v.* verbannen

exist *v.* vorhanden sein, existieren; leben; bestehen; -ence *n.* Existenz, Dasein; Leben; Bestehen; -ent *adj.* vorhanden, bestehend

exit *n.* Ausgang; (theat.) Abtreten, Abgang

exodus *n.* Auszug, Abwanderung; **Exodus** zweites Buch Mosis

exonerate *v.* freisprechen, reinigen; rechtfertigen; entlasten

exorbitant *adj.* übermässig, übertrieben

exotic fuel *n.* hochenergetischer Treibstoff

expand *v.* (sich) ausdehnen, (sich)ausbreiten; (sich) erweitern; (bot.) aufblühen

expansion *n.* Ausdehnung, Ausbreitung; Weite

expansive *adj.* ausdehnungsfähig; ausgedehnt; (fig.) gefühlvoll, mitfühlend; mitteilsam

expatriate *v.* aus dem Heimatland verbannen; — *n.* Vaterlandslose, Heimatlose

expect *v.* erwarten, warten; zumuten, vermuten, annehmen, glauben; she is -ing sie ist guter Hoffnung; -ant *adj.* erwartend; Anwartschaft habend; werdend; -ation *n.* Erwartung; Vermutung, Hoffnung; Aussicht

expediency *n.* Schicklichkeit, Ratsamkeit, Zweckmässigkeit; Nützlichkeitsprinzip

expedient *adj.* schicklich, passend; ratsam; zweckmässig, nützlich; — *n.* Ausweg, Notbehelf, Mittel

expedition *n.* Eile, Schnelligkeit; Ausführung; Forschungsreise; Expedition; (mil.) Feldzug, Kriegszug

expel *v.* vertreiben, ausstossen; (educ.) relegieren, ausschliessen

expend *v.* ausgeben, auslegen; verbrauchen, verzehren; -able *adj.* entbehrlich; -iture *n.* Ausgabe, Ausgeben; Aufwand, Verbrauch

expense *n.* Ausgabe, Auslage; *pl.* Unkosten, Kosten, Spesen; at the — of auf Kosten von

expensive *adj.* teuer, kostspielig

experience *n.* Erfahrung, Erlebnis; — *v.*

erfahren, erleben, erleiden; **-d** *adj.* erfahren, erprobt; geschickt

experiment *n.* Versuch, Experiment; — *v.* versuchen, experimentieren; **-al** *adj.* erfahrungsgemäss, experimentell; Experimental-

expert *n.* Sachverständige, Fachmann; — *adj.* beschlagen, erfahren, geschickt

expiate *v.* sühnen, büssen

expiration *n.* Ablauf, Verlauf; Ende, Schluss; (fig.) letzter Atemzug, Tod; Ausatmen

expire *v.* sterben; verscheiden; verfliessen; ausatmen, aushauchen; ablaufen, verfallen, fällig werden, erlöschen

explain *v.* erklären, erläutern; auseinandersetzen

explanation *n.* Erklärung, Aufklärung, Auslegung; Auseinandersetzung

explicit *adj.* deutlich, klar, ausdrücklich; rückhaltlos, bestimmt

explode *v.* explodieren, platzen; sprengen, bersten

exploration *n.* Erforschung, Untersuchung

explore *v.* untersuchen, erforschen; **-r** *n.* Forscher, Erforscher; Forschungsreisende

explosion *n.* Explosion, Sprengung, Bersten; (fig.) Ausbruch

explosive *adj.* explosiv; Knall-, Spreng-; — *n.* Sprengstoff

exponent *n.* Erläuterer, Erklärer; Vertreter; (math.) Exponent, Potenzzahl

export *v.* exportieren, ausführen; — *n.* Export, Ausfuhr; Ausführware; **-er** *n.* Exporteur

expose *v.* aussetzen; ausstellen; aufdecken; blozstellen, enthüllen; (phot.) belichten

exposé *n.* Exposé, Darstellung; Aufdeckung

exposition *n.* Erklärung, Auslegung; Ausstellung; Darstellung

expostulate *v.* ernste Vorstellungen machen; — **with** Vorhaltungen machen, zur Rede stellen

exposure *n.* Enthüllung; Blozstellung; Ausgesetztsein; (arch.) Lage; (phot.) Belichtung

expound *v.* erklären, auslegen

express *v.* äussern, ausdrücken, darstellen; — *adj.* schnell; Express-, Eil-; ausdrücklich, bestimmt, deutlich; (by) — per Express, per Eilgut; durch Eilboten; — **company** Paketpostgesellschaft; — **train** D-Zug; Schnellzug; — *n.* Express; Eilbote; Schnellzug, Expresszug; **-ion** *n.* Ausdruck, Äusserung; **-ive** *adj.* ausdrückend, ausdrucksvoll; **-ly** *adv.* eigens, absichtlich, ausdrück-

lich

expressman *n.* Paketpostangestellte

expressway *n.* Schnellstrasse

expropriate *v.* enteignen

expulsion *n.* Vertreibung, Austreibung; (educ.) Relegierung; (med.) Abführen

extemporaneous, extemporary *adj.* extemporiert, unvorbereitet, improvisiert, aus dem Stegreif

extemporize *v.* extemporieren, unvorbereitet sprechen (*or* schreiben, spielen)

extend *v.* reichen, (sich) ausdehnen; verlängern, strecken; erweitern, vergrössern; erweisen, gewähren

extension *n.* Ausdehnung, Erweiterung; (arch.) Anbau; (tel.) Nebenanschluss, Apparat; — **cord** Verlängerungsschnur

extensive *adj.* ausgedehnt, umfassend

extent *n.* Weite, Grösse, Umfang; Grad, Ausdehnung; **to a certain** — gewissermassen, bis zu einem gewissen Grade; **to the** — **of** bis zum Betrage von

extenuate *v.* verdünnen, entkräften, schwächen, mildern

extenuating circumstances *n.* mildernde Umstände

exterior *n.* Äussere, Aussenseite; — *adj.* äusserlich

exterminate *v.* vertilgen, ausrotten, zerstören

extermination *n.* Vertilgung, Ausrottung

external *adj.* äusserlich, äusserst; *pl.* Äussere, äussere Form; Äusserlichkeiten; — *adv.* ausserhalb

extinct *adj.* erloschen, aufgehoben; ausgestorben, untergegangen; **-ion** *n.* Erlöschen; Tilgung; Aussterben, Untergang, Vernichtung

extinguish *v.* auslöschen, ersticken; verdunkeln; vernichten; abschaffen, tilgen; **-er** *n.* Löscher; **fire -er** Feuerlöscher

extra *n.* Aussergewöhnliche; Sonderleistung, Sonderarbeit; (film) Chargenspieler, Statist; (newspaper) Extrablatt; — *adj.* extra, ungewöhnlich, ausserordentlich; übrig; Extra-; Neben-, Sonder-; — **charges** Nebenkosten; — **pay** Zulage; — **work** Mehrarbeit, Nebenarbeit; — *adv.* besonders, ausserdem, extra

extract *n.* Auszug, Extrakt, Zitat; — *v.* ausziehen, ausschneiden; ableiten; herauslocken; **-ion** *n.* Ausziehen, Auszug; Abkunft, Herkunft

extracurricular *adj.* Nebenstudien betreffend, Neben-

extradition *n.* Auslieferung

extraordinary *adj.* ausserordentlich, aussergewöhnlich, besonder, Extra-

extravagance *n.* Extravaganz, Übertreibung, Übermass; Verschwendung

extravagant *adj.* extravagant, übertrieben, übermässig; verschwenderisch

extreme *n.* Äusserste, Extrem; höchsten Grad; äusserste Massnahme; Übertreibung; **carry** (*oder* go) **to —s** auf die Spitze treiben; — *adj.* äusserst, übermässig, extrem

extremist *n.* Anhänger extremer Anschauungen; (pol.) Ultraradikale

extremity *n.* Äusserste, äusserste Not (*or* Verlegenheit); höchster Grad; *pl.* Extremitäten, Gliedmassen

extricate *v.* herausreissen, herauswinden, losmachen; (chem.) entwickeln

exuberance *n.* Überfluss, Fülle, Üppigkeit, Überschwenglichkeit

exuberant *adj.* üppig, überschwenglich, übermässig

exult *v.* frohlocken, jauchzen; **-ant** *adj.* frohlockend; **-ation** *n.* Frohlocken, Jubel

eye *n.* Auge; (fig.) Blick, Gesicht(skreis); (sewing) Öhr, Öse; **an — for an —** Auge um Auge; **black —** blaues Auge; **catch someone's —** jemandes Aufmerksamkeit fesseln; **evil —** böser Blick; **have an — for** Sinn haben für; **hooks and —s** Haken und Ösen; **in the —s of the law** vom Standpunkte des Gesetzes; **in the twinkling of an —** im Augenblick, im Nu; **keep an — on** ein wachsames Auge haben auf; **see — to —** im gleichen Lichte sehen; — *v.* anschauen, ansehen, betrachten; angucken, blicken auf

eyeball *n.* Augapfel

eyebrow *n.* Augenbraue

eyecup *n.* Augenglas

eyelash *n.* Augenwimper

eyelet *n.* Schnürloch; Guckloch; Öse

eyelid *n.* Augenlid

eyeshade *n.* Augenschirm

eyesight *n.* Augenlicht, Gesicht; Sehkraft

eyesore *n.* Gerstenkorn; **be an —** ein Dorn im Auge sein

eyestrain *n.* Augen(über)anstrengung

eyetooth *n.* Augenzahn

eyewash *n.* Augenwasser, Augenbad; (coll.) Schwindel, Mumpitz

eyewitness *n.* Augenzeuge

F

fable *n.* Fabel, Sage, Märchen; Lüge; **-d** *adj.* fabelhaft, erdichtet

fabric *n.* Stoff, Gewebe; Gefüge; **-ate** *v.* fabrizieren, verfertigen, herstellen; erdichten, erfinden; bauen, errichten;

fälschen; **-ation** *n.* Fabrikation, Herstellung; Erdichtung; Fälschung

fabulous *adj.* fabelhaft

face *n.* Gesicht, Angesicht; Ausdruck, Miene; (arch., furniture) Front, Vorderseite, Fassade, Aussenseite; Oberfläche; (clock) Zifferblatt; (coin) Bildseite; (geom.) Fläche; (typ.) Bildtype; (fig.) Dreistigkeit, Unverschämtheit; **at — value** für bare Münze; — **card** Bildkarte; — **lifting** Hebung der Wangenhaut; — **to —** von Angesicht zu Angesicht; persönlich; — **to —** with angesichts, gegenüber; — **value** Nennwert; **in the — of** in Gegenwart von. (fig.) trotz; **in the — of heavy odds** trotz widriger Umstände; **lose — an** Ansehen verlieren; **make a — Grimassen** (*or* Gesichter) schneiden; **on the — of it** allem Anschein nach, augenscheinlich; **put the best — on things** gute Miene zum bösen Spiel machen; **save (one's) —** den Anschein wahren; **show one's —** sich sehen (*or* blicken) lassen; — *v.* ins Gesicht sehen, ansehen; gegenüber liegen, gegenüberstehen; entgegentreten, trotzen; (arch.) bedecken, bekleiden; hinausgehen **auf**; (sewing) aufschlagen, besetzen, einfassen; — **on** gehen (*or* gerichtet sein) auf; — **the music** die Folgen auf sich nehmen

facetious *adj.* witzig, drolling; **scherzhaft**, lustig

facial *adj.* das Gesicht betreffend; Gesichts-; — *n.* Gesichtskosmetik

facile *adj.* leicht; leutselig, umgänglich; nachgiebig, gefällig; flink, geschickt

facilitate *v.* erleichtern, fördern

facility *n.* Leichtigkeit, Gewandtheit, Geschicklichkeit; Schwäche, Nachgiebigkeit; Leutseligkeit

facing *n.* Besatz, Einfassung, Aufschlag; (arch.) Verkleidung

fact *n.* Tatsache; Wirklichkeit; Tat; *pl.* Tatbestand; **as a matter of —** zwar, tatsächlich; **in — in** der Tat, wirklich; *pl.* — **are —** Tatsache bleibt Tatsache; **the — of the case** der Sachverhalt; **-ual** *adj.* faktisch, tatsächlich

faction *n.* Partei; Fraktion

factor *n.* Faktor; (fig.) Umstand

factory *n.* Fabrik

faculty *n.* Fakultät; Lehrerkollegium; Fähigkeit, Befähigung, Gabe

fad *n.* Grille, Liebhaberei; Steckenpferd, Modetorheit

fade *v.* verblassen, verschiessen; (bot.) verwelken; (mus.) verklingen, abklingen; **-less** *adj.* lichtecht, farbecht

fade-out *n.* Abblenden, langsames Verschwinden

fag *v.* sich abarbeiten, ermüden, erschöpfen

Fahrenheit *adj.* Fahrenheit-

fail *v.* scheitern, fehlschlagen, misslingen; fehlen, mangeln; stocken, versagen, nachlassen; (agr.) missraten; (com.) Bankrott machen; (educ.) durchfallen; (med.) verfallen, abnehmen; — *n.* without — unfehlbar, ganz gewiss; –ing *n.* Fehler, Schwäche; –ing *prep.* mangels; –ure *n.* Misslingen, Versagen, Fehlschlag(en), Misserfolg; Versager, Zusammenbruch; (com.) Zahlungseinstellung, Bankrott; (med.) Sinken, Verfall; **be a –ure** keinen Erfolg haben; **heart –ure** Herzschlag

faint *n.* Ohnmacht; — *adj.* schwach, matt; ohnmächtig, kraftlos; — *v.* ohnmächtig werden, in Ohnmacht fallen; **–ness** *n.* Schwäche, Mattigkeit; Undeutlichkeit

fair *n.* Jahrmarkt, Markt; Messe; — *adj.* gerecht, unparteiisch, ehrlich; schön, hübsch; sauber, leserlich; (hair) blond; (complexion) hell; (sport) fair; (fig.) gewöhnlich, Mittel-; — **copy** Reinschrift; — **play** ehrliches Spiel; — **trade** gegenseitige Handelsbeziehung; — **weather** günstiges (*or* schönes) Wetter; **–ly** *adv.* schön, ehrlich, billig; leidlich, ziemlich; **–ly well** ziemlich gut; **–ness** *n.* Aufrichtigkeit, Ehrlichkeit; Unbescholtenheit, Redlichkeit; Billigkeit; Unparteilichkeit; Hellfarbigkeit Blondheit

fair-minded *adj.* vorurteilsfrei

fair-trade agreement *n.* gegenseitiges Handelsabkommen

fair-weather friend *n.* Freund im Glück

fairy *n.* Fee, Elfe; — *adj.* feenhaft, zauberisch; Feen-; — **tale** Märchen

fairyland *n.* Märchenland, Feenreich

faith *n.* Glauben(sbekenntnis), Religion; Vertrauen; Treue; **in good** — auf Treu und Glauben; **–ful** *n.* Gläubige; **–ful** *adj.* treu, getreu; gläubig; ehrlich; gewissenhaft; **–fully yours** hochachtungsvoll, Ihr sehr ergebener; **–less** *adj.* ungetreu, treulos

fake *n.* Schwindel, Fälschung, betrügerische Nachahmung; Schwindler; — *adj.* betrügerisch, gefälscht; — *v.* nachahmen, nachmachen, zurechtmachen, fälschen; **–r** *n.* Betrüger, Fälscher

falcon *n.* Falke

fall *n.* Fall(en), Sturz; Untergang, Zusammenbruch; Fällen; (com.) Sinken, Fallen; (season) Herbst; *pl.* Fälle, Gefälle; — *v.* fallen, hinfallen, umfallen;

fällen; (arch.) einfallen, einstürzen; (bot.) abfallen, herunterfallen; (com.) sinken; (wind) sich legen; (zool.) krepieren; — **apart** (*oder* to pieces) zerfallen; — **asleep** einschlafen; — **away** abfallen, abmagern; — **back** zurückfallen; sein Wort nicht halten; — **back again** wieder zurückweichen; — **back on** zurückgreifen auf; — **behind** zurückbleiben; im Rückstand bleiben; — **for** (person) sich verlieben in; — **for** (thing) hereinfallen auf; — **in** einfallen; (mil.) antreten; — **in love** sich verlieben; — **off** herunterfallen; zurückgehen; — **on** überfallen; — **out** ausfallen, sich überwerfen; (mil.) austreten; — **short** nicht hinreichen (*or* ausreichen); — **sick** krank werden; — **through** durchfallen, misslingen; — **upon** befallen, plötzlich angreifen; **–en** *adj.* gefallen; **–en arches** Senkfuss

fallacious *adj.* trügerisch, irreleitend

fallacy *n.* Täuschung; Irrtum

fallout *n.* radioaktiver Niederschlag

false *adj.* falsch; unrichtig; unecht; unwahr, treulos; — **alarm** blinder Alarm; — **bottom** Doppelboden; — **pretense** Vorspieglung falscher Tatsachen; — **step** Fehltritt; — **teeth** falsche Zähne; **–hood** *n.* Lüge, Falschheit, Unwahrheit; Heuchelei, Unredlichkeit

falsetto *n.* Falsett, Fistelstimme; Kopfstimme

falsies *n. pl.* falscher Busen, Schaumgummibusen

falsify *v.* (ver)fälschen

falter *v.* schwanken, zögern, wanken; stolpern, straucheln; stottern, stammeln

fame *n.* Ruhm, Ruf; **–d** *adj.* berühmt

familiar *adj.* vertraut, vertraulich, intim; wohlbekannt; alltäglich; gewöhnlich; — **with** vertraut mit; **–ity** *n.* Vertraulichkeit, Vertrautheit; **–ize** *v.* vertraut machen

family *n.* Familie; Geschlecht; (bot. and zool.) Gattung; — **doctor** Hausarzt; — **tree** Stammbaum

famine *n.* Hungersnot; Teuerung, Mangel

famous *adj.* berühmt, famos, ausgezeichnet

fan *n.* Fächer; (mech.) Ventilator; Gebläse; (sl.) Anhänger; Liebhaber, Fex; — *v.* fächeln; anfachen; (fig.) entflammen; — **oneself** sich Luft zufächeln

fanatic *n.* Fanatiker, Schwärmer; **–(al)** *adj.* fanatisch, schwärmerisch; **–ism** *n.* Fanatismus

fanciful *adj.* phantastisch, schwärmerisch,

wunderlich; launenhaft

fancy *n.* Phantasie, Einbildungskraft, Einbildung; Grille; Geschmack; Lust; Liebhaberei; — *v.* sich vorstellen, sich einbilden; wähnen; — *adj.* elegant, bunt, phantastisch, übertrieben; — **goods** Modeartikel, Luxusartikeln, Galanteriewaren

fancywork *n.* feine(weibliche)Handarbeit

fanfare *n.* Fanfare, Tusch

fang *n.* Fang(zahn), Giftzahn

fantastic *adj.* phantastisch, eingebildet; seltsam, wunderlich

fantasy *n.* Phantasie, Phantasie

far *adj.* fern, weit, entfernt; — **away** weit entfernt; — **be it from me** das sei fern von mir; — **cry** weite Entfernung, grosser Gegensatz; — **from** keineswegs; — **off** entlegen; weit entfernt; **on the** — **side** auf der anderen Seite; — *adv.* fern, weit; sehr, ganz; **as** — **as** bis zu, bis an; soweit; soviel; **by** —, — **and away** bei weitem, um vieles; — **and near**, — **and wide** weit und breit; **so** — bis jetzt; **so** — **as** soviel

farce *n.* Posse, Schwank

fare *n.* Fahrgeld, Fahrpreis; Fahrgast; Speise, Kost; — *v.* fahren, ergehen; sich befinden; — **ill** schlimm daransein; — **well** gut wegkommen

farewell *n.* Lebewohl, Abschied; —! *interj.* lebe wohl! auf Wiedersehen!

farfetched *adj.* weit hergeholt, gesucht, gezwungen

farm *n.* Gut, Bauernhof, Meierei, Farm; Pachtgut; — **hand** Tagelöhner, Landarbeiter; — *v.* bearbeiten, bebauen; (ver)pachten; **-er** *n.* Bauer, Landwirt, Landmann; **small** **-er** Kleinbauer, Häusler; **-ing** *n.* Ackerbau, Landbau

farmhouse *n.* Bauernhaus, Gutshaus, Farmhaus

farmyard *n.* Wirtschaftshof, Gutshof, Bauernhof

far-off *adj.* weit entfernt

far-reaching *adj.* weitreichend, weittragend

farsighted *adj.* (med.) weitsichtig; (fig.) umsichtig, vorsichtig

farther *adj.* and *adv.* weiter, ferner, entfernter

farthermost *adj.* weitest, fernst

farthest *adj.* weitest, fernst, entferntest; — *adv.* am fernsten, am weitesten

fascinate *v.* bezaubern, verzaubern, fesseln

fascinating *adj.* bezaubernd, reizend, spannend, fesselnd

fascination *n.* Bezauberung, Zauber, Reiz; Faszination

fascism *n.* Faschismus

fascist *n.* Faschist

fashion *n.* Mode; Form, Gestalt, Art; Schnitt; **in** — nach der Mode; **latest** — neueste Mode; **out of** — unmodern; **-able** *adj.* elegant, modisch, modern

fast *n.* Fasten; — **day** Fasttag; — *v.* fasten; — *adj.* fest, tief; unbeweglich; schnell, rasch; waschecht, lichtecht; leichtlebig, flott; **the clock is** — die Uhr geht vor; **-ing** *n.* Fasten, Enthaltsamkeit; **-ness** *n.* Festigkeit, Sicherheit; Stärke; Schnelligkeit; (mil.) Feste

fasten *v.* befestigen, festmachen, verschliessen; heften; sich halten an; **-er** *n.* Befestiger, Befestigungsmittel; **patent -er** Druckknopf; **-ing** *n.* Befestigungsmittel; Schloss, Riegel, Haken

fat *n.* Fett, Schmalz; — *adj.* dick, fett, feist, plump; **become** — dick werden; mästen; **-ness** *n.* Fettigkeit, Wohlbeleibtheit; **-ten** *v.* fett machen, fett werden; mästen; (agr.) fruchtbar machen, düngen; **-ty** *adj.* fettig; **-ty** *n.* Dickerchen

fatal *adj.* verhängnisvoll, tödlich, fatal; **-ism** *n.* Fatalismus; **-ity** *n.* Verhängnis; Unglück(sfall); (mil.) Verlust

fate *n.* Schicksal, Verhängnis, Geschick; **-ful** *adj.* verhängnisvoll

father *n.* Vater; (eccl.) Pater; **-hood** *n.* Vaterschaft; **-less** *adj.* vaterlos; **-ly** *adj.* väterlich

father-in-law *n.* Schwiegervater

fatherland *n.* Vaterland

fathom *n.* (naut.) Faden; — *v.* sondieren, abmessen; (fig.) ergründen, eindringen; **-less** *adj.* unergründlich, bodenlos

fatigue *n.* Ermüdung, Müdigkeit, Ermattung; Strapaze; — *v.* ermüden, ermatten

faucet *n.* Hahn, Zapfen

fault *n.* Fehler; Verfehlung, Vergehen; Irrtum; Schuld; **be at** — schuld daran sein; **find** — etwas auszusetzen haben; **-less** *adj.* fehlerlos, tadellos; **-y** *adj.* fehlerhaft, mangelhaft; tadelnswert

faultfinder *n.* Tadler, Krittler, Nörgler, Mäkler

faultfinding *adj.* tadelsüchtig, nörgelnd, krittelnd, mäkelnd

faun *n.* Faun, Waldgott

favor *n.* Gunst, Gefallen; Gnade, Milde; **balance in your** — Saldo zu Ihren Gunsten; **be in** — in Gunst stehen; **be in** — **of** für etwas sein, dafür sein; **in** — **of** zu Gunsten von; — *v.* begünstigen; — **us with a song** erfreuen Sie uns mit einem Lied; — **us with your visit** beehren Sie uns mit Ihrem Besuch; **he -s his father** er ähnelt dem

Vater; **-able** *adj.* günstig. geneigt, gewogen; dienlich, zustimmend; freundlich; **-ite** *n.* Günstling, Liebling; Favorit; **-ite** *adj.* begünstigt; Lieblings-; **-itism** *n.* Günstlingswirtschaft; Favorisieren

fear *n.* Furcht, Angst; Besorgnis; **for —** **of** aus Angst vor; **—** *v.* (be)fürchten; sich fürchten, besorgen; **-ful** *adj.* furchtsam, bange; furchtbar, schrecklich; **-less** *adj.* furchtlos, unerschrocken; **-some** *adj.* fürchterlich; furchtsam

feasible *adj.* ausführbar, möglich

feast *n.* Fest; Festtag; Festessen, Schmaus; (fig.) Leckerbissen; **—** *v.* speisen, festlich bewirten; schmausen, sich gütlich tun

feat *n.* Heldentat, Leistung, Tat; Kunststück

feather *n.* Feder; *pl.* Geflügel; **— bed** Federbett; **light as a —** federleicht; **that's a —** **in his cap** darauf kann er sich etwas einbilden; **—** *v.* befiedern, schmücken; **-ed** *adj.* federig, befiedert, gefiedert; **-y** *adj.* federartig, federig, federleicht

featherbedding *n.* durch Gewerkschaftsvertrag bedingte Anstellung unnötiger Arbeiter

featherweight *n.* Federgewicht

feature *n.* Hauptzug, Merkmal; Hauptfilm; *pl.* Züge, Gesichtszüge; **—** *v.* ausgestalten; in der Hauptrolle darstellen; (fig.) gross aufmachen

February *n.* Februar

federal *adj.* Bundes-; föderativ, verbündet; föderalistisch

federate *adj.* verbündet, föderiert; **—** *v.* (sich) verbünden, zu einem Staatenbund zusammenschliessen

federation *n.* Staatenbund, Verband, Föderation

fee *n.* Gebühr; Honorar, Lohn; Trinkgeld; Eintrittsgeld; Beitrag

feeble *adj.* schwach, matt

feeble-minded *adj.* schwachköpfig, geistesschwach

feed *n.* Futter, Nahrung; (mech.) Zuleitung, Vorsorgung; **—** *v.* füttern, speisen, nähren; essen; sich nähren; vorsorgen, versehen; **-er** *n.* (agr.) Fütterer, Viehmäster; (mech.) Futterapparat; (mech.) Zuführung, Zuleitung

feedback *n.* (recording machine) Rückkoppelung

feel *n.* Fühlen, Gefühl(ssinn); Empfindung; **—** *v.* fühlen, empfinden, spüren; sich fühlen; **— about** halten von; **— like** Lust haben auf (*or* zu); **— one's way** sich durchtasten; **-er** *n.*

Fühler, Fühlhorn; **put out a —er das** Gelände sondieren, einen Fühler ausstrecken; **-ing** *n.* Gefühl, Fühlen; Empfindung, Mitgefühl; **-ing** *adj.* fühlend, gefühlvoll; tief empfunden; mitleidig

feign *v.* heucheln, sich verstellen; erdichten; simulieren; **— to do** vorgeben zu tun

feint *n.* Verstellung, Finte; (mil.) Scheinangriff

felicitation *n.* Gratulation, Glückwunsch

felicity *n.* Glück(seligkeit)

feline *adj.* katzenartig

fell *v.* fällen, umhauen

fellow *n.* Gefährte, Genosse; Kollege, Kamerad; Kerl, Bursche; Mitglied; **— citizen** Mitbürger; **— countryman** Landsmann; **— creature** Mitmensch, Mitgeschöpf; **— member** Vereinsmitglied; **— student** Studiengenosse; **— traveler** Reisegefährte; (pol.) Mitläufer; Anhänger (aber nicht Mitglied einer Partei; **-ship** *n.* Gemeinschaft, Kameradschaft; Mitgliedschaft; (educ.) Stipendium

felly *n.* Felge

felon *n.* Verbrecher; **-y** *n.* Kapitalverbrechen

felt *n.* Filz; **—** *v.* (sich) verfilzen

female *n.* Weib, Weibchen; **—** *adj.* weiblich

feminine *adj.* weiblich, weibisch; feminin

fence *n.* Zaun, Umzäunung, Einfriedung; (law) Hehler; **—** *v.* einzäunen; (sports) fechten, parieren; (fig.) abwehren; **-r** *n.* Fechter; Fechtmeister

fencing *n.* Fechten, Fechtkunst

ferment *n.* Gärung, Erregung; Ferment; **—** *v.* gären, in Gärung geraten; **-ation** *n.* Gärung; Fermentierung

fern *n.* Farn(kraut)

ferocious *adj.* wild, raubgierig; grimmig, grausam

ferocity *n.* Wildheit, Grausamkeit

ferret *n.* Frettchen; **—** *v.* **— out** herausbringen, vertreiben; aufspüren

ferrous *adj.* eisenhaltig

ferry *n.* Fähre; **—** *v.* überführen, übersetzen

ferryboat *n.* Fähre, Fährboot

fertile *adj.* fruchtbar, ergiebig; (fig.) erfinderisch, schöpferisch

fertility *n.* Fruchtbarkeit

fertilization *n.* Fruchtbarmachung, Befruchtung

fertilize *v.* befruchten; fruchtbar machen, düngen; **-r** *n.* Dünger, Düngemittel

fervent *adj.* heiss, glühend, inbrünstig

fervid *adj.* brennend, siedend; hitzig

fervor *n.* Eifer; Hitze, Glut

fester *v.* eitern, schwären, faulen

festival *n.* Fest; — *adj.* festlich, Fest-

festivity *n.* Festlichkeit, Lustbarkeit

fetch *v.* (ab)holen, einholen, einbringen

fête *n.* Fest; — *v.* feiern

fetter *v.* fesseln; *pl.* Fesseln, Ketten

feud *n.* Leh(e)n; **-al** *adj.* feudal, lehnbar, Lehns-; **-alism** *n.* Lehnswesen

feud *n.* Fehde, Streit

fever *n.* Fieber; yellow — gelbes Fieber; **-ish** *adj.* fieberhaft; fieberkrank

few *adj.* wenige; einige; **a** — ein paar, einige wenige; **quite a** — ziemlich viel; **-er** *adv.* weniger

fiancé *n.* Verlobte, Bräutigam; **-e** *n.* Verlobte, Braut

fib *n.* Notlüge, Schwindelei, Finte; — *v.* flunkern, lügen

fiber, fibre *n.* Faser, Fiber

fickle *adj.* unbeständig, veränderlich, wankelmütig

fiction *n.* Dichtung, Erdichtung, Fiktion; Prosaliteratur, Romanliteratur

fictitious *adj.* fingiert, nachgemacht; erdichtet, eingebildet; unecht

fiddle *n.* Geige, Violine; Fiedel; **play second** — eine untergeordnete Rolle spielen; — *v.* fiedeln, geigen; tändeln; **-r** *n.* Geiger; Fiedler, Spielmann

fidelity *n.* Wahrhaftigkeit, Ehrlichkeit, Treue; **high** — höchste Tongenauigkeit (*or* Pflichttreue, Wahrhaftigkeit, Redlichkeit); Raumton

fidget *v.* unruhig sein, umher zappeln; nervös machen

field *n.* Feld; Acker, Weide; Grund; Schlachtfeld; (sports) Spielfeld, Sportplatz; (fig.) Bereich; — **artillery** Feldartillerie; — **day** Felddienstübung; (fig.) grosser Tag; — **glass** Feldglas, Feldstecher; — **hospital** Feldlazarett; — **kitchen** Feldküche, Gulaschkanone; — **marshal** Feldmarschall; — **mouse** Feldmaus; — **officer** Stabsoffizier; **-er** *n.* Spieler im Feld, Fänger

fierce *adj.* wild, hitzig, wütend; grimmig, ungestüm; **-ness** *n.* Wildheit, Ungestüm, Grimmigkeit

fife *n.* Pfeife, Querpfeife; **-r** *n.* Pfeifer

fifteen *n.* Fünfzehn(er); — *adj.* fünfzehn; **-th** *n.* Fünfzehnte, Fünfzehntel; **-th** *adj.* fünfzehnt

fifth *n.* Fünfte, Fünftel; — *adj.* fünft; — **column** fünfte Kolonne, Spionage- und Sabotageorganisation im Hinterland; — **columnist** Mitglied der fünften Kolonne; — **wheel** fünftes Rad am Wagen

fiftieth *n.* Fünfzigste, Fünfzigstel; — *adj.*

fünfzigst

fifty *n.* Fünfzig; — *adj.* fünfzig; **in his fifties** in den Fünfzigern

fifty-fifty *adj.* halb und halb, zu gleichen Teilen

fig *n.* Feige; (coll.) Kleinigkeit, Pfifferling; — **tree** Feigenbaum

fight *n.* Kampf, Streit; (mil.) Gefecht, Treffen; (sports) Ringkampf, Boxkampf; — *v.* kämpfen, streiten; bekämpfen; boxen, ringen, raufen; fechten; duellieren; **-er** *n.* Kämpfer, Streiter; Fechter, Boxer, Schläger; **-er** (plane) Kampfflugzeug, Jagdflugzeug; **-ing** *n.* Kampf

figment *n.* Erdichtung

figure *n.* Figur, Form, Gestalt; Abbildung; (math.) Zahl, Ziffer, Nummer; — **of speech** Redewendung; — **skater** Eiskunstläufer; — **skating** Eiskunstlauf; — *v.* formen, gestalten; abbilden, darstellen; sich zeigen; rechnen; (theat.) eine Rolle spielen; (coll.) sich vorstellen; — **on** rechnen auf; — **out** lösen, berechnen; **-d** *adj.* gemustert

figurehead *n.* Galionsbild, Bugfigur; nomineller Leiter

filament *n.* Fäserchen; Staubfaden; (elec.) Glühfaden

file *n.* Aktendeckel, Aktenordner; Aktenbündel; Kartei, Kartothek; (mech.) Feile; (mil.) Reihe; (sewing) Aufreihfaden; **on** — in den Akten; **single** — Gänsemarsch; — **clerk** Registraturangestellte; — **leader** Vordermann, Flügelmann; — *v.* (ein)ordnen, ablegen, registrieren; einbringen; (mech.) feilen; — **by** defilieren, vorbeiziehen

filibuster *n.* Freibeuter; (pol.) Dauerredner (um Gesetzesanträge oder Gesetzesannahme zu verhindern); Quertreiber

filing *n.* Registratur; Ordnung, Einordnung; *pl.* Feilspäne; — **card** Karteikarte; — **case** Karteischrank, Kartothekkasten

fill *n.* Fülle; Genüge; Füllung; **eat one's** — sich satt essen; — *v.* (an)füllen, ausfüllen; erfüllen, vollbringen; innehaben, besetzen; (voll)stopfen; — **an order** einen Auftrag erledigen (*or* ausführen); — **a tooth** einen Zahn plombieren (*or* füllen); — **in** eintragen, einsetzen, ausfülen; — **out** ausfüllen; — **the bill** allen Anforderungen genügen; — **up** voll machen, auffüllen; sich füllen; **-er** *n.* Füller; Trichter; Einlage; (fig.) Lückenbüsser; **-ing** *n.* Füllung; (dent.) Plombe; — **station** Tankstelle

filet *n.* Stirnband; (cooking) Filet, Lendenstück

filly n. Stutenfüllen

film n. Schicht; Schleier; (med.) Membrane, Häutchen; (phot.) Film; — strip Filmstreifen, Bildstreifen, Bildband; roll of — Rollfilm; — v. filmen

filter n. Filter; — v. filtern, filtrieren, durchseihen

filter-tip adj. mit Filter, Filter-

filth, filthiness n. Schmutz, Unrat; Schmutzigkeit; -y adj. schmutzig, unrein; trübe; (fig.) gemein, unflätig

fin n. Finne; Flosse; (sl.) Fünfdollarnote

final adj. letzt, endlich; definitiv, endgültig; End-, Schluss-; n. pl. (sports) Endrunde, Schlussrunde; (educ.) Schlussprüfungen; -ist n. Teilnehmer an der Schlussrunde; -ity n. Endgültigkeit, Endzustand; Endlichkeit

finance n. Finanzwesen; pl. Finanzen, Einkünfte; — v. finanzieren, finanziell unterstützen

financial adj. finanziell, wirtschaftlich

financier n. Geldmann, Finanzmann

finch n. Fink

find n. Fund; — v. finden, treffen; auffinden, ausfindig machen; entdecken, ermitteln; (law) erklären, erkennen, befinden; — fault with tadeln; — out ermitteln, herausbringen; -er n. Finder, Entdecker; (phot.) Sucher; -ing n. Fund, Entdeckung; Erkenntnis; (law) Resultat, Ausspruch, Urteil

fine n. Geldstrafe, Busse; — v, zu einer Geldstrafe verurteilen, mit einer Geldstrafe belegen; — adj. fein, zart, dünn; spitz; schön, herrlich, vortrefflich; verfeinert; feingebildet; vornehm, elegant; the — arts die schönen Künste; — v. zu einer Geldstrafe verurteilen, mit einer Geldstrafe belegen; -ness n. Feinheit, Eleganz; Vortrefflichkeit; (min.) Feingehalt, Reinheit

finery n. Staat, Glanz, Putz

finespun adj. feingesponnen

finger n. Finger; finger wave (ohne Wickler gelegte) Kaltwelle; have a — in the pie die Hand mit im Spiele haben; keep one's -s crossed den Daumen halten; — v. betasten, befühlen; (mus.) mit Fingersatz versehen, spielen, üben; -ing n. Fingern, Betasten; (mus.) Fingersatz

fingernail n. Fingernagel; — polish Nagellack

fingerprint n. Fingerabdruck

finicky adj. affektiert, geziert; wählerisch

finish n. Ende, Schluss; Vollendung, Fertigstellung; Lack, Politur; (sports) Endkampf; — v. (be)enden, beendigen; aufhören; vollenden, fertigmachen;

(sports sl.) den Rest geben; — (drinking) austrinken; — (eating) aufessen; — (talking) ausreden, zuende reden; -ed adj. beendet, fertig; vollendet

finite adj. endlich, begrenzt

fir n. Tanne, Fichte, Föhre

fire n. Feuer, Flamme; Brand, Feuersbrunst; Licht, Glanz, Leidenschaft; (mil.) Geschützfeuer; — alarm Feuermelder; — department Feuerwehr; — engine Feuerspritze; — escape Rettungsleiter; Nottreppe; — extinguisher Feuerlöscher, Löschapparat; — insurance Feuerversicherung; — screen Ofenschirm; Kamingitter; — ship Feuerschiff; be on — brennen, in Brand stehen; build (oder make) a — ein Feuer machen (or anzünden); open — das Feuer eröffnen; set on — anzünden; set — to in Brand setzen; — v. schiessen, feuern; entlassen, hinausschmeissen; anzünden, heizen

firearms n. pl. Feuerwaffen

firebrand n. Feuerbrand; Aufwiegler

firecracker n. Schwärmer, Knallkapsel, Knallbonbon, Knallfrosch

firefly n. Glühwürmchen, Leuchtkäfer

fireman n. Feuerwehrmann; (rail.) Heizer

fireplace n. Herd; Kamin

fireplug n. Hydrant

firepower n. Feuerstärke

fireproof adj. feuerfest, feuersicher

fireside n. Herd; Kamin; (fig.) Häuslichkeit; by the — am Kamin; im häuslichen Kreise

firetrap n. Feuerfalle; leicht entzündbares Gebäude

firewarden n. Branddirektor

fireworks n. pl. Feuerwerk, Feuerwerkskörper

firing n. Anzünden; Heizung, Feuerung; (mil.) Abfeuern; (coll.) Entlassung; — line Feuerzone, Frontlinie; — pin Zündnadel

firm n. Firma, Geschäftshaus; — adj. fest, sicher; beständig, standhaft; -ness n. Festigkeit, Entschlossenheit

first adj. erste, vorderste, vorzüglichste; — aid erste Hilfe; — mate Obersteuermann; — name Vorname; — night Première; — nighter Premièrenbesucher; in the — place an erster Stelle; — adv. zuerst, erstens; eher; at — zuerst; — come — served wer zuerst kommt, mahlt zuerst; — of all vor allen Dingen; to go — vorangehen; — n. Erste

first-aid adj. erste Hilfe leistend; — kit Erstehilfekasten

first-class adj. erstklassig; private — Gefreite

firsthand *adj.* aus erster Hand

first-rate *adj.* ersten Ranges, ausgezeichnet

fiscal *adj.* fiskalisch; Finanz-

fish *n.* Fisch; — **bowl** Goldfischglas; — **market** Fischmarkt; — **story** Anglerlatein; — *v.* fischen, angeln; (fig.) erhaschen; **-ery** *n.* Fischerei; **-ing** *n.* Fischen, Fischfang; **-ing boat** Fischerboot; **-ing line** Angelschnur; **-ing rod** Angelrute; **-ing smack** Fischereikutter; **-ing tackle** Angelgerät; **-y** *adj.* fisch-(art)ig; fischreich; (coll.) verdächtig, faul

fisherman *n.* Fischer

fishhook *n.* Angelhaken

fishpond *n.* Fischteich

fission *n.* Spaltung; **nuclear** — Kernspaltung; **-able** *adj.* spaltbar

fist *n.* Faust

fit *n.* Anfall, Ausbruch; Einfall, Laune; — *adj.* fähig, geeignet, passend, tauglich; angemessen, schicklich; (sports) in guter Form; — *v.* passen; anpassen; (mech.) montieren, aufstellen; **be** — **for** taugen zu; — **in**(to) hineinpassen; übereinstimmen; — **out** ausrüsten, einrichten; **-ful** *adj.* veränderlich, launenhaft, unstet; krampfartig; **-ness** *n.* Eignung, Tauglichkeit; Schicklichkeit; **-ter** *n.* Zubereiter, Zurichter; Einrichter; Monteur; Installateur; **-ting** *n.* Anprobe, Probe; Zurechtmachen, Anpassen; Montieren, Montierung; Ausrüstung; Installation; **-tings** *pl.* Zubehör; Ausrüstungsgegenstände; **-ting** *adj.* passend, geeignet

five *n.* Fünf(er); — *adj.* fünf

fix *n.* üble Lage, Klemme; — *v.* herrichten, instandsetzen, reparieren; festmachen, befestigen; heften, richten auf; bestimmen; sich niederlassen, sich festsetzen; — **up** ordnen, einrichten; **-ation** *n.* Festhalten, Festmachen, Fixierung; **-ed** *adj.* fest, feststehend; bestimmt; starr; (chem.) feuerfest; nicht flüchtig; **-ture** *n.* Feststehend; Einrichtung; Inventarstück

fizz *n.* Zischen, Sprühen, Sprudeln; (fig.) Sodawasser; — *v.* zischen, sprühen, sprudeln; **-le** *n.* misslungenes Unternehmen; Abfallen, Steckenbleiben; **-le** *v.* stecken bleiben; zischen

flabbergast *v.* verblüffen

flabby *adj.* schlaff, welk; (fig.) kraftlos, gehaltlos

flag *n.* Fahne, Flagge; (bot.) Kalmus, Schwertlilie; — **officer** Flaggoffizier; — **of truce** Friedensfahne, Parlamentär-

fahne; — *v.* ermatten, erschlaffen, nachlassen; Flaggensignale geben; — **a train** einen Zug durch Flaggensignale zum Halten bringen; **-ging** *adj.* schlaff werdend

flagpole *n.* Fahnenstange

flagrant *adj.* abscheulich, berüchtigt; offenkundig

flagship *n.* Flaggschiff

flagstaff *n.* Fahnenstange

flagstone *n.* Fliese, Platte

flail *n.* Dreschflegel; — *v.* dreschen

flair *n.* Spürsinn, Witterung; Sinn, feine Nase

flake *n.* Flocke; Schicht, Schuppe; — *v.* — **off** abschuppen; (sich) abblättern

flaky *adj.* flockig, schuppig; geschichtet

flamboyant *adj.* auffallend, flammend; (arch.) im flämischen Stil gehalten

flame *n.* Flamme; Feuer, Hitze; Heftigkeit; Leidenschaft; (coll.) Flamme; — **thrower** Flammenwerfer; — *v.* flammen, lodern; auffahren

flaming *adj.* flammend; feurig; glühend

flamingo *n.* Flamingo

flammable *adj.* entzündbar, entflammbar

flank *n.* Flanke, Seite; (mil.) Flügel; — *v.* flankieren, umgehen

flannel *n.* Flanell; **-ette** *n.* Baumwollflanell

flap *n.* Klappe; (anat.) Lappen; (avi.) Bremsklappe am Flugzeug; Zwischenflügel; (coat) Schoss; (hat) Krempe; (wing) Schlag; — *v.* klappen; klapsen schlagen; lose herabhängen; flattern

flapjack *n.* Pfannkuchen

flare *n.* Leuchtsignal; Leuchtpatrone; (fig.) Prahlerei; — *v.* flackern, lodern; flimmern, schimmern; — **up** aufbrausen

flare-up *n.* Aufflackern, Aufbrausen; plötzlicher Streit

flash *n.* Blitz; **in a** — im Augenblick (*or* Nu); — **back** Rückblende; — **bulb** Blitzlichtlampe; — **of lightning** Blitzstrahl; — *v.* blitzen; aufflammen, ausbrechen; aufleuchten; auflodern; **-ing** *n.* Blitzen; Flutung; **-y** *adj.* schimmernd; auffallend, sensationell; oberflächlich, geschmacklos

flashlight *n.* Taschenlampe

flask *n.* Flakon, Fläschchen

flat *n.* Ebene, Fläche, Niederung; Wohnung; (mus.) Flauheit, Tiefe; (naut.) Untiefe, Sandbank; (theat.) Hintergrund; — *adj.* flach, platt; abgestanden, geschmacklos, fade, schal; unbedingt, absolut; (color) matt; (com.) flau; (mus.) moll, tief; — **tire** geplatzter Reifen, Plattfuss; — **silver** Essbesteck, Tafelsilber; **-ness** *n.* Flachheit, Plattheit; Flauheit; (mus.) Erniedrigung; −ten v. (sich) abflachen, verflachen; ebnen; niederdrücken, entmutigen; (mus.) dämpfen, erniedrigen

flat-bottomed adj. flachbödig

flat-chested adj. flachbrüstig

flatfoot n. Plattfuss

flat-footed adj. plattfüssig; (sl.) entschieden, entschlossen

flatiron n. Plätteisen, Bügeleisen

flatter v. schmeicheln; entzücken; −er n. Schmeichler; −ing adj. schmeichelhaft, schmeichlerisch; −y n. Schmeichelei

flaunt v. prunket mit, sich aufblähen

flavor n. Geschmack; Wohlgeruch, Aroma; (wine) Blume, Bouquet; (fig.) Beigeschmack; — v. würzen; −ing n. Aroma; Würzen

flaw n. Sprung, Riss, Bruch; Fehler; Flecken; −less adj. fehlerlos, makellos

flax n. Flachs, Lein; −en adj. flachsen, flachsartig; Flachs-; blond

flaxseed n. Leinsamen

flea n. Floh

flea-bitten adj. vom Floh gestochen; gesprenkelt

flee v. fliehen, verlassen; meiden

fleece n. Schaffell; Vlies; — v. scheren; (fig.) rupfen, prellen

fleecy adj. wollig, wollreich; flockig

fleet n. Flotte; — adj. flink, schnell; flüchtig; −ing adj. flüchtig, vergänglich

flesh n. Fleisch; Körper; Fleischeslust; Fleisch-; — color Fleischfarbe; −y adj. fleischig, fett

flesh-colored adj. fleischfarben

flexibility n. Biegsamkeit; Lenksamkeit

flexible adj. biegsam, lenksam

flight n. Flucht, Entrinnen; (arch.) Treppe; (avi.) Flug; Fliegen; Kette; (orn.) Schwarm; — deck Abflugdeck; — mechanic Bordmechaniker; — of stairs Treppe(nstufen); — pattern Flugordnung über Flugplatz; Flugschema; — strip Flugstreifen, Einflugschneise; −y adj. leichtsinnig, zerstreut, unbeständig; lebhaft

flimsy adj. dünn, schwach; nichtig

flinch v. zurückweichen, zurückschrecken

fling n. Wurf, Schlag; Freiheit, Ausbruch; Stichelei; — v. werfen, schleudern; eilen, fliegen; sticheln

flint n. Kiesel; Feuerstein

flip n. Klaps; Ruck; (drink) Flip; — v. schnipsen, schnellen; klapsen

flippant adj. vorlaut; wegwerfend; leichtfertig, frivol

flirt n. Kokette; Hofmacher; — v. flirten, schäkern, liebäugeln, kokettieren; −ation n. Flirt, Liebelei

float n. Floss; Schwimmer; Flott; (naut.) Rettungsboje; — v. schwimmen, schweben, fluten; (naut.) flott sein; in Gang bringen; treiben, flössen; (coll.) flottmachen; überschwemmen; — a loan eine Anleihe auflegen; −ing adj. schwimmend, treibend; schwankend, unbestimmt; −ing dock Schwimmdock

flock n. Herde; (eccl.) Gemeinde; (orn.) Schwarm; (fig.) Haufen, Menge; — v. zusammenströmen; sich scharen

flog v. (aus)peitschen, züchtigen; schlagen, prügeln

flood n. Flut, Überschwemmung; — tide Flut, Gezeit; — v. überfluten, überschwemmen

floodgate n. Fluttor; Schleusentor

floodlight n. Scheinwerferlicht

floor n. Boden, Fussboden; (arch.) Stockwerk, Etage; (pol.) Sitzungssaal; Recht zum Wort; — leader Parteiführer; — plan Grundriss; — show Varietévorführung; — ground — Erdgeschoss; — v. dielen, mit Dielen belegen; niederschlagen, überwinden; −ing n. Fussboden(belag)

floorwalker n. Verkaufsabteilungschef

flop n. Durchfall; — v. (hin)plumpsen; misslingen

flora n. Flora; Pflanzenwelt; −l adj. Blüten-; Blumen-

florid adj. blühend, blumenreich; frisch; (arch.) verziert, überladen

florist n. Blumenhändler

floss (silk) n. Florettseide; (bot.) Samenwolle

flounce n. Volant, Falbel; Krause, Faltenbesatz; hastige Bewegung; — v. plätschern, planschen; sich hastig bewegen; mit Volants besetzen

flour n. Mehl; — v. mit Mehl bestreuen; −ish n. Blüte, Verzierung, Schnörkel; (mus.) Fanfare, Tusch; −ish v. gedeihen, blühen, florieren; schwingen, schwenken

flow n. Fluss, Strom; Zufluss, Erguss, Schwall, Überfluss; — v. fliessen, strömen; überfliessen, sich ergiessen

flower n. Blume, Blüte; (fig.) Zierde, Beste, Feinste; — girl Blumenmädchen; Brautjungfer; — v. blühen, −ed adj. geblümt; −ing adj. blumig, blühend; −y adj. blumig, blumenreich, geblümt

flowerpot n. Blumentopf

flu n. Grippe, Influenza

fluctuate v. schwanken, unschlüssig sein; fluktuieren

fluctuation n. Schwankung, Schwanken

flue n. Rauchfang, Kaminrohr; (mech.) Heizkanal

fluency *n.* Geläufigkeit; Fluss

fluent *adj.* fliessend, geläufig

fluff *n.* Staubflocke, Flaum; flaumartiger Überzug, flockige Schicht; — *v.* verpuffen; **-y** *adj.* flaumig, flockig

fluid *n.* Flüssigkeit; — *adj.* flüssig

flunk *v.* versagen, durchfallen

flunkey *n.* Lakai, Bediente; Speichellecker

fluorescent *adj.* fluoreszierend, schillernd

fluorine *n.* Fluorin

fluoroscope *n.* Durchleuchtungsapparat

flurry *n.* Verwirrung, Aufregung; Windstoss, Brise; **snow —** Schneegestöber; — *v.* aufregen, verwirren; beunruhigen, bestürzen

flush *n.* Erröten, Glut; Aufwallung; (fig.) Frische, Blüte; (cards) Flöte; **royal —** grosse (*or* volle) Flöte; — *v.* erröten; strömen, schiessen; — **the toilet** die Toilette (aus)spülen; — *adj.* frisch, blühend; reif; übervoll; glatt, gleich; **be — gut bei Kasse sein**

fluster *v.* verwirren, aufregen

flute *n.* Flöte; Kannelierung; — *v.* flöten, auf der Flöte spielen; **-d** *adj.* gerillt, geriefelt

flutist *n.* Flötist, Flötenspieler

flutter *n.* Geflatter; Verwirrung; Erregung, Unruhe; — *v.* flattern, zittern; erregt sein; in Aufregung bringen

fly *n.* Fliege; (baseball) Flugball; (fishing) künstliche Fliege; — *v.* fliegen; eilen, fliehen; — **into a passion** in Zorn geraten; **-er** *n.*, **flier** *n.* Flieger; **-ing** *n.* Fliegen; **-ing** *adj.* fliegend, eilig, schnell; **Flug-**; **-ing boat** Flugboot; **-ing field** Flugfeld; **-ing squirrel** Flughörnchen; **-ing** *adj.* fliegend, eilig, schnell; **-ing colors** fliegende Fahnen; **-ing fish** fliegender Fisch; **-ing fortress** fliegende Festung, **-ing saucer** fliegende Untertasse

flyleaf *n.* Vorsatzblatt

flypaper *n.* Fliegenfänger

flyweight *n.* Fliegengewicht

flywheel *n.* Schwungrad

foal *n.* Fohlen, Füllen; — *v.* fohlen, werfen

foam *n.* Schaum; — *v.* schäumen, geifern; **-y** *adj.* schaumig, schaumbedeckt

fob *n.* Uhranhänger

focal *adj.* im Brennpunkt stehend

focus *n.* Brennpunkt, Fokus; — *v.* in einem Brennpunkt vereinigen; (phot.) einstellen

fodder *n.* Futter; Fütterung

foe *n.* Feind, Gegner

fog *n.* Nebel; Umnebelung; (fig.) Unsicherheit; — *v.* umnebeln, verdüstern; verwirren; **-gy** *adj.* neblig, dunstig; (fig.) benebelt

foghorn *n.* Nebelhorn

foil *n.* Folie; (mirror) Belag; (sports) Florett, Rapier; — *v.* vereiteln, täuschen; überwinden, übertreffen

fold *n.* Falte, Falz, Kniff; — *v.* falten, falzen; zusammenlegen; **-er** *n.* Umschlag; Heft, Broschüre; **-ing** *adj.* zusammenlegbar; Falt-, Klapp-; **-ing bed** Feldbett, Klappbett; **-ing boat** Faltboot; **-ing chair** Klappstuhl

foliage *n.* Laub(werk)

folk *n.* Volk; Leute; **common —** einfache Leute; Volks-; — **dance** Volkstanz; — **music** Volksmusik; — **song** Volkslied; — **tale** Volksmärchen

folklore *n.* Volkskunde; Volkssagen

follow *v.* folgen, nachgehen; nachfolgen; befolgen; (com.) sich widmen; (phil.) zur Richtschnur nehmen; **as -s wie** folgt, folgendermassen; — **suit** Farbe bekennen; bedienen; — **up** verfolgen; **-er** *n.* Anhänger; Verehrer; **-ers** *pl.* Gefolge, Anhang; **-ing** *n.* Gefolge, Gefolgschaft, Anhängerschaft; **-ing** *adj.* folgend, kommend

follow-up *adj.* verfolgend, nachlaufend

folly *n.* Torheit, Narrheit; Unsinn

foment *v.* erregen, anstiften

fond *adj.* zärtlich, vernarrt; **be — of** gern haben, lieben; **-ness** *n.* Zärtlichkeit; Liebhaberei; Vorliebe

font *n.* Taufbecken

food *n.* Speise, Nahrung, Lebensmittel; (mil.) Proviant, Verpflegung; (zool.) Futter; *pl.* Nahrungsmittel

foodstuff *n.* Nahrungsmittel

fool *n.* Narr, Tor; Hanswurst; **to make a — out of someone** jemanden zum besten haben; — *v.* betrügen, prellen; **Spass machen; -ish** *adj.* töricht; närrisch, albern, eitel, läppisch; **-ishness** *n.* Narrheit, Dummheit, Torheit; Unsinn

foolhardy *adj.* tollkühn; dummdreist

foolproof *adj.* kinderleicht; betriebssicher

foot *n.* Fuss; Fussende; (lit.) Versfuss; (mil.) Fussvolk; — **by —** Schritt für Schritt; — **soldier** Infanterist; **on —**, **by —** zu Fuss; **square —** Quadratfuss; — *v.* — **the bill** aufkommen für; **-ing** *n.* Basis, Grund; Standpunkt, Stellung

foot-and-mouth disease *n.* Maul- und Klauenseuche

football *n.* Fussball (spiel)

footboard *n.* Trittbrett

footbridge *n.* Laufbrücke, Steg

footgear *n.* Schuhwerk

foothill *n.* Vorgebirge

foothold *n.* fester Standpunkt; Tritt; Halt, Stütze

footlights *n. pl.* Rampenlicht; **before the — auf der Bühne**

footman *n.* Bediente, Lakai

footnote *n.* Fussnote, Anmerkung

footpath *n.* Fusspfad, Fussweg

footprint *n.* Fussabdruck, Fuzspur, Fuzstapfe

footrace *n.* Wettlauf

footrest *n.* Fussbank, Schemel

footsore *adj.* fusskrank, wundgelaufen

footstep *n.* Tritt, Schritt; Spur

footstool *n.* Fussbank, Schemel

footwork *n.* (sports) Fussbewegungen, Fussarbeit

for *prep.* für, zu, wegen; während, seit; als; nach; gegen; zum besten, zugunsten; (an)statt vor, um; **— all that** trotzdem; **— example, — instance** zum Beispiel; **what —? wofür? wozu? warum? — conj.** denn

forbear *v.* sich enthalten, unterlassen, abstehen; **-ance** *n.* Geduld, Nachsicht; Unterlassung, Enthaltung

forbid *v.* verbieten, untersagen; **God —!** Gott behüte! **-den** *adj.* verboten, unerlaubt; **-ding** *adj.* abstossend, widerwärtig, abschreckend

force *n.* Kraft, Gewalt; Macht, Stärke; Nachdruck; (law) Gesetzeskraft, Gültigkeit; *pl.* Streitkräfte, Truppen; **come into —** in Kraft treten; **from — of habit** aus alter Gewohnheit, die Macht der Gewohnheit; **in —** in Kraft; **police — Polizei(truppe); — v.** zwingen, nötigen; erzwingen, durchsetzen; **— back** zurücktreiben; **— one's way** sich hineindrängen (*or* einen Weg bahnen); **— open** aufbrechen; **-d** *adj.* gezwungen, erzwungen; erkünstelt; **— landing** Notlandung; **— march** Eilmarsch; **-ful** *adj.* kräftig, stark; wirkungsvoll

forceps *n.* (med.) Zange, Geburtenzange

forcible *adj.* gewaltsam, wirksam; eindringlich; zwingend, ungestüm

ford *n.* Furt; **— v.** durchwaten

forearm *n.* Vorderarm; **— v.** im Voraus bewaffnen

forebear *n.* Vorfahr, Ahn

forebode *v.* ahnen, voraussehen

foreboding *n.* Ahnung, Voraussage; Vorzeichen

forecast *n.* Voraussage, Vorhersage; **weather — Wetterbericht, Wettervorhersage; — v.** voraussagen

foreclose *v.* ausschliessen, abweisen; **— a mortgage** eine Hypothek für verfallen erklären

foreclosure *n.* Abweisung; Sperre

forefather *n.* Vorfahr, Ahn

forefinger *n.* Zeigefinger

forego *v.* verzichten auf, aufgeben; **-ing** *adj.* vorhergehend; vorig, früher; **-ne** *adj.* vorausgegangen; **-ne conclusion** vorgefasste Schlussfolgerung; Selbstverständlichkeit

foreground *n.* Vordergrund

forehead *n.* Stirn

foreign *adj.* ausländisch, fremd, auswärtig; **-er** *n.* Fremde, Ausländer

foreign-born *adj.* im Ausland geboren

foreleg *n.* Vorderbein, Vorderfuss

forelock *n.* Stirnhaar

foreman *n.* Vormann, Vorarbeiter; Aufseher, Werkmeister; (jury) Obmann

foremost *adj.* vorderst, erst; vornehmst; **— adv.** zuerst, voran, voraus; **first and — zu allererst**

forenoon *n.* Vormittag

forensic *adj.* gerichtlich, redegewandt

foreordain *v.* vorher verordnen (*or* bestimmen)

forepaw *n.* Vorderpfote

forequarter *n.* Vorderviertel

forerunner *n.* Vorläufer, Vorbote

foresail *n.* (naut.) Focksegel

foresee *v.* voraussehen, vorherwissen

foreshadow *v.* vorher andeuten, ahnen

foresight *n.* Voraussicht, Vorsicht; **-ed** *adj.* voraussehend, vorsichtig

forest *n.* Wald, Waldung; Forst; **-er** *n.* Förster, Waldheger; **-ry** *n.* Forstkultur

foretaste *n.* Vorgeschmack; **— v.** vorausnehmen; im Voraus geniessen

foretell *v.* voraussagen, weissagen; vorbedeuten

forethought *n.* Vorbedacht, Vorsorge

forever *adv.* auf immer, zu aller Zeit

forevermore *adv.* auf immer und ewig

forewarn *v.* vorher warnen (*or* ankünden)

foreword *n.* Vorwort

forfeit *n.* Verwirkung; Strafe, Geldbusse; **— v.** verwirken, verlieren; verscherzen

forge *n.* Schmiede, Esse; **— v.** schmieden; fälschen, nachmachen; erdichten; **-r** *n.* Schmied; Fälscher, Falschmünzer; **-ry** *n.* Fälschung; Erfindung, Lüge

forget *v.* vergessen; vernachlässigen; **-ful** *adj.* vergesslich; achtlos, nachlässig; **-fulness** *n.* Vergesslichkeit; Vergessenheit; Vernachlässigung

forget-me-not *n.* Vergissmeinnicht

forgive *v.* verzeihen, vergeben; **-ness** *n.* Vergebung, Verzeihung

forgiving *adj.* versöhnlich, nachsichtig; mild

fork *n.* Gabel; (geog.) Gabelung; Wegarm; Flussarm; **— v.** (sich) gabeln; **-ed** *adj.* gegabelt; gabelförmig; zickzackförmig; Gabel-

forlorn *adj.* verloren, verlassen, einsam; hoffnungslos

form *n.* Form, Gestalt; Formalität, Brauch; Formular, Fragebogen; Bank, Klasse; — **letter** schematisierter Brief; **in good** — in guter Verfassung; **matter of** — Formalität, Formsache; — *v.* formen; (sich) bilden, (sich) gestalten; ausbilden; erdenken; (mil.) (sich) formieren; — **an alliance** ein Bündnis schliessen; — **an idea** (*or* **opinion**) sich eine Meinung bilden; — **a plan** einen Plan entwerfen; **-less** *adj.* formlos, ungestaltet

formal *adj.* förmlich, formell; **-ity** *n.* Formsache, Formalität; Förmlichkeit

format *n.* Entwurf; Matrize

formation *n.* Bildung, Gestaltung; (avi.) Verband; — **flying** *n.* Verbandfliegen

former *adj.* vorig; ehemalig, früher; vorerwähnt; **the** — **der erstere;** **-ly** *adv.* ehemals, früher, vormals; sonst

formic acid *n.* Ameisensäure

formula *n.* Formel; Regel; (med.) Rezept; **-te** *v.* formulieren; **-tion** *n.* Formulierung

forsake *v.* verlassen, aufgeben, entsagen

fort *n.* Festung(swerk); Fort; **-ification** *n.* Befestigung, Festungsbau; **-ify** *v.* befestigen; verstärken; **-ress** *n.* Festung

fortitude *n.* Geistesstärke, Standhaftigkeit, Mut

forth *adv.* hervor; vorwärts, weiter; heraus, hinaus; **and so** — und so weiter; **from this day** — von heute an

forthcoming *adj.* bevorstehend, bereit; erscheinend, herauskommend

forthright *adj.* geradeaus, aufrichtig

forthwith *adv.* sofort, sogleich

fortieth *adj.* vierzigst; — *n.* Vierzigste; Vierzigstel

fortnight *n.* vierzehn Tage, zwei Wochen; **-ly** *adj.* and *adv.* vierzehntägig

fortunate *adj.* glücklich; **-ly** *adv.* glücklicherweise

fortune *n.* Glück; Vermögen; Schicksal, Zufall; — **hunter** Mitgiftjäger; Glücksjäger; **tell a** — wahrsagen

fortune teller *n.* Wahrsager

forty *adj.* vierzig; — *n.* Vierzig(er)

forward *adj.* vorder; zeitig vorgeschritten, frühreif; voreilig, näseweis, keck, vorlaut; bereit, eifrig; — **pass** Vorbeigang; — *adv.* vorwärts, voran; weiter, fort; — *n.* Stürmer; — *v.* absenden, versenden, befördern; nachsenden; beschleunigen; **—(s)** *adv.* vorwärts, voran

fossil *n.* Fossil; — *adj.* fossil, versteinert

foster *v.* ernähren, pflegen; hegen, nähren; (be)fördern, begünstigen; — *adj.*

Pflege-; — **brother** Pflegebruder; — **child** Pflegekind; — **father** Pflegevater; — **mother** Pflegemutter

foul *n.* Zusammenstoss; unerlaubter Hieb (or Schlag); — *adj.* widerwärtig, ekelhaft; schmutzig, unrein; faul(ig), stinkend; verdorben; unehrlich, unerlaubt; Schimpf-; (law) ungesetzlich, verboten; (naut.) unklar; — **ball** ins Aus; — **play** regelwidriges (or unehrliches) Spiel, Schwindel

found *v.* (be)gründen, stiften; **-ation** *n.* Gründung, Errichtung; Stiftung; (arch.) Fundament, Grund, Grundmauer; (fig.) Grundlage; **-er** *n.* Gründer, Stifter; Erbauer

foundry *n.* Giesserei, Schmelzhütte

fountain *n.* Quelle, Fontäne, Springbrunnen; — **pen** Füllfeder(halter)

fountainhead *n.* Urquell; (fig.) Ursprung

four *adj.* vier; — *n.* Vier(er) **on all -s** auf allen Vieren; **-some** *n.* Vierer; **-teen** *adj.* vierzehn; **-teen** *n.* Vierzehn(er); **-teenth** *adj.* vierzehnt; **-teenth** *n.* Vierzehnte, Vierzehntel; **-th** *adj.* viert; **-th** *n.* Vierte, Viertel; (mus.) Quarte

four-footed *adj.* vierfüssig

four-wheel brake *n.* Vierradbremse

fowl *n.* Vogel; Huhn; Geflügel, Federvieh

fox *n.* Fuchs; (fig.) Schlaukopf; — **terrier** Foxterrier; **-y** *adj.* fuchs(art)ig; schlau, verschmitzt

foxglove *n.* Fingerhut

foyer *n.* Foyer, Vorhalle, Wandelhalle

fraction *n.* Bruchstück; (math.) Bruch; **-al** *adj.* Bruch-; gebrochen; (fig.) unbedeutend

fracture *n.* Bruch; (med.) Knochenbruch; — *v.* (zer)brechen

fragile *adj.* zerbrechlich; gebrechlich, hinfällig, schwach

fragment *n.* Fragment, Bruchstück; **-ary** *adj.* bruchstückartig, lückenhaft; **-arily** *adv.* stückweise

fragrance *n.* Duft, Wohlgeruch; **Aroma**

fragrant *adj.* duftig, wohlriechend

frail *adj.* zerbrechlich; zart; schwach; **-ty** *n.* Schwäche, Schwachheit; Gebrechlichkeit

frame *n.* Rahmen, Einfassung; Gefüge, Bau, Gebälk, Zimmerwerk; (mech.) Gestell, Gerüst; (naut.) Spant; (fig.) Körper, Form; Stimmung; — **of mind** Gemütsverfassung; — *v.* (ein)rahmen, einfassen; bilden, bauen, zusammenfassen; (fig.) formen; (lit.) **entwerfen**, erfinden

framework *n.* Bau, System

France *n.* Frankreich

franchise *n.* Freiheit; (law) Vorrecht;

(pol.) Wahlrecht
Franconia n. Franken
frank n. Portofreiheit; — adj. frei, offen, aufrichtig; franko, portofrei; — v. portofrei versenden; frankieren; **-ness** n. Offenheit, Aufrichtigkeit
frankfurter n. Frankfurter (Würstchen)
frantic adj. wild, toll, rasend; wahnsinnig; **-ally** adv. rasend, wahnsinnig
fraternal adj. brüderlich
fraternity n. Brüderlichkeit; Bruderschaft, Orden, Zunft; (educ.) Verbindung
fraternize v. sich verbrüdern, fraternisieren
fraud n. Betrug, Schwindel; **-ulent** adj. betrügerisch
fraught adj. beladen, befrachtet; angefüllt
freak n. Missbildung, Sehenswürdigkeit; **-ish** adj. grillenhaft, launisch; wunderlich
freckle n. Sommersprosse; **-d** adj. sommersprossig
free adj. frei, unabhängig; kostenlos, unentgeltlich, gratis; freigebig; offen(herzig); öffentlich; — **and easy** zwanglos, ungezwungen, leicht; — **on board** (f.o.b.) frei an Bord; — **port** Freihafen; — **sample** Gratisprobe; — **speech** Redefreiheit; — **trade** Freihandel; — **verse** Blankvers; — **will** freier Wille, Willensfreiheit; — v. befreien, freilassen; freimachen; **-dom** n. Freiheit, Unabhängigkeit; Freimütigkeit, Vertraulichkeit, Ungezwungenheit; Leichtigkeit; **-dom of speech** Redefreiheit
freeborn adj. freigeboren
freebooter n. Freibeuter
free fall n. (avi.) Freifall
free-for-all n. allgemeine Schlägerei
freehand adj. freihändig
free-lance adj. unabhängig, freischaffend
freeman n. freier Mann, Vollbürger
Freemason n. Freimaurer
free-spoken adj. freimütig, offen
freethinker n. Freidenker, Freigeist
freeway n. Autobahn
freewheel n. Freilauf
freeze v. (er)frieren, gefrieren (lassen); (fig.) erstarren; **-r** n. Gefrierapparat; **deep** — Tiefgefriermaschine
freezing adj. gefrierend, eisig; Gefrier-, Kälte-; — **point** Gefrierpunkt
freight n. Fracht, Ladung; Frachtlohn; Frachtgeld; — **car** Güterwagen; — **elevator** Güteraufzug; — **train** Güterzug; **by** — per Fracht, als Frachtgut; — v. befrachten, beladen; verladen; **-er** n. Frachter, Frachtdampfer

French adj. französisch; — **door** Flügeltür; — **dressing** Salatsauce; — **fried potatoes** pommes frites; — **horn** Waldhorn; — **leave** ohne Abschied verschwinden; — **windows** Flügelfenster; Balkontür, Verandatür
frenzy n. Wahnsinn, Tobsucht, Raserei
frequency n. Häufigkeit; (elec.) Frequenz; — **modulation** Frequenzmodulation; **high** — Hochfrequenz
frequent adj. häufig; — v. häufig besuchen; frequentieren
fresco n. Fresko, Wandmalerei; Wandgemälde
fresh adj. frisch; gesund; neu, unerfahren; erfrischt, munter; (butter) ungesalzen; (eggs) frischgelegt; (water) süss; (coll.) frech, angeheitert; — **water** Süsswasser; **-en** v. erfrischen, erneuern; auffrischen; zunehmen; **-ness** n. Frische, Neuheit; Gesundheit; (wind) Kühle; (fig.) Unerfahrenheit, Unverdorbenheit; (sl.) Frechheit
freshman n. Neuling, Anfänger; (coll.) Fuchs
fret v. (sich) ärgern; (sich) grämen; (sich) aufreiben; **-ful** adj. ärgerlich, mürrisch
fret saw n. Laubsäge
Freudian adj. nach Sigmund Freud
friar n. Mönch
friction n. Reibung; — **tape** Isolierband
Friday n. Freitag; **Good** — Karfreitag
fried adj. gebraten; Brat-; — **chicken** Brathuhn; — **eggs** Spiegeleier, Setzeier; — **fish** Bratfisch; — **potatoes** Bratkartoffeln
friend n. Freund; Bekannte; (rel.) Quäker; **be close -s** nahe befreundet sein; **make -s** Freundschaften schliessen; **-less** adj. freundlos, verlassen; **-liness** n. freundschaftliche Gesinnung, Wohlwollen; **-ly** adj. freundlich, freundschaftlich, befreundet; wohlwollend; **-ship** n. Freundschaft
fright n. Schrecken, Furcht, Entsetzen; **-en** v. erschrecken; **be -ened** erschrecken, bange sein vor; **-en away** verscheuchen; **-ful** adj. schrecklich, entsetzlich
frigid adj. kalt, eisig; frostig; (fig.) herzlos, frigid
fringe n. Franse, Besatz; Rand, Saum; — v. mit Fransen besetzen; (um)säumen
frisk v. hüpfen, springen; (fig.) abtasten, filzen; **-y** adj. hüpfend, tanzend; fröhlich, munter, lustig
fritter n. Fetzen, Stückchen; (cooking) Krapfen; — v. — **away** vergeuden, vertändeln, vertrödeln

frivolity *n.* Leichtsinn, Leichtfertigkeit; Frivolität

frivolous *adj.* leichtsinnig, leichtfertig; frivol; wertlos, nichtig

fro *adv.* to and — auf und ab, hin und her

frock *n.* Kleid; Kinderkleid; Kittel

frog *n.* Frosch; (dress) Schnurverschluss; (rail.) Kreuzungsstück; **–man** Froschmensch

from *prep.* von, aus; seit; vor, gegen; wegen, nach; entfernt von; infolge von; — first to last von A bis Z; — morning till night von früh bis spät; — now on von jetzt an; — top to bottom von oben bis unten

front *n.* Front; Vorderseite; Stirn; **in** — of vor, gegenüber von; **shirt** — Vorhemd; Chemisett; — *adj.* vorder, erst; Vorder- — **door** Haustür; — **line** Front(linie); — **row** erste Reihe; — **seat** Vordersitz; — *v.* — **on** gegenüberstehen; gegenübertreten; gerichtet sein nach; **–al** *adj.* frontal; Stirn-, Front-; **–age** *n.* Vorderfront

frontier *n.* Grenze, Grenzgebiet, Grenzland

frost *n.* Frost, Reif; (fig.) Frostigkeit; — *v.* mit Zuckerguss versehen, glasieren; **–ed** *adj.* bereift; glasiert, mit Zuckerguss versehen; **–ed glass** Milchglas; **–ing** *n.* Zuckerglasur; **–y** *adj.* frostig, eisig; eiskalt; (fig.) eisgrau, ergraut

frostbitten *adj.* erfroren

frown *n.* Stirnrunzeln; — *v.* die Stirn runzelnd, finster blicken; — **on** missbilligen

frozen *adj.* gefroren, erstarrt

frugal *adj.* mässig, einfach, frugal; genügsam, sparsam

fruit *n.* Frucht, Obst; Folge, Erfolg, Gewinn; — **fly** Blütenstecher; — **grower** Obstzüchter; — **knife** Obstmesser; — **salad** Obstsalat; — **stand** Obststand; — **store** Obstladen; — **sugar** Fruchtzucker; — **tree** Obstbaum; **candied –s** kandierte Früchte; **–ful** *adj.* fruchtbar; ergiebig, gewinnbringend; **–less** *adj.* unfruchtbar; unnütz, vergeblich, fruchtlos

fruitcake *n.* Fruchttorte, Obstkuchen

frustration *n.* Vereitelung; (fig.) Querstrich

fry *n.* Laich; — *v.* braten; **–ing** *adj.* bratend; **–ing pan** *n.* Bratpfanne

fudge *n.* Schokoladenmasse

fuel *n.* Heizmaterial; Feuerung; Treibstoff, Kraftstoff; — **gauge** Benzinmesser; — **oil** Heizöl; — **tank** Benzintank

fugitive *n.* Flüchtling; — *adj.* flüchtig

fulcrum *n.* Stützpunkt

fulfil(1) *v.* erfüllen, vollziehen; **–ment** *n.* Erfüllung, Vollziehung

full *adj.* voll ganz, völlig; vollständig, vollkommen; satt; weit; besetzt; reichlich; **at** — length in voller Länge; (fig.) ausführlich; **at** — **speed** mit höchster (or in voller) Geschwindigkeit; — **description** ausführliche Beschreibung; — **dress** Gesellschaftsanzug; — **moon** Vollmond; — of voll von, voller; — **power** unumschränkte Vollmacht; — **steam ahead!** Volldampf voraus! — **time** ganztägig, Voll-; **in** — vollständig; **in** — **swing** in freiem Lauf; — *adv.* völlig, ganz, genau; gerade; recht, sehr; **–ness** *n.* Vollsein, Fülle; **in its –ness** in vollem Umfange; **the –ness of time** die festgesetzte Zeit

fullback *n.* Verteidiger

full-grown *adj.* völlig erwachsen, ausgewachsen; (bot.) hochstämmig

full-length *adj.* lebensgross

fumble *n.* Tölpelei; — *v.* umhertappen, umhergreifen

fume *n.* Dampf, Rauch, Dunst; — *v.* rauchen, räuchern; dampfen, dunsten; (fig.) rasen, aufgebracht sein

fumigate *v.* (aus)räuchern

fuming *adj.* rauchend; (fig.) aufgebracht

fun *n.* Spass, Scherz; **for** — zum Spass; **have** — Spass haben, sich unterhalten; **make** — of spotten (or sich lustig machen) über; **–ny** *adj.* komisch, spasshaft; seltsam; **–ny bone** Ellbogenknochen, Musikantenknochen; **strike as –ny** komisch vorkommen

function *n.* Funktion, Tätigkeit, Verrichtung; — *v.* funktionieren, tätig sein; **–al** *adj.* funktionell; amtlich; **–ary** *n.* Funktionär; Beamte, Amtsträger

fund *n.* Fonds, Kapital; Vorrat; *pl.* Gelder; Staatspapiere; Staatsschulden; — *v.* fundieren; (money) anlegen

fundamental *adj.* Grund-; wesentlich; **–s** *n. pl.* Grundlage; Hauptsache; Grundpfeiler

funeral *n.* Begräbnis, Leichenbegängnis; — **director** Begräbnisleiter; — **parlor** Begräbnishalle

fungus *n.* Pilz, Schwamm

funnel *n.* Rauchfang, Schornstein; Trichter

fur *n.* Pelz; Fell; (med.) Belag; — **coat** Pelzmantel; **–red** *adj.* pelzig, haarig; (med.) belegt; **–rier** *n.* Pelzhändler; Kürschner; **–ry** *adj.* pelzartig

furious *adj.* wütend, rasend; heftig, ungestüm

furlough *n.* Urlaub; — *v.* beurlauben

furnace *n.* Ofen; Schmelzofen; blast —
Hochofen; open-hearth — Siemens-
Martin Ofen

furnish *v.* versehen, versorgen; verschaffen, liefern; ausstatten, möblieren; —
a house ein•Haus einrichten; -ed *adj.*
möbliert; -ings *n. pl.* Wohnungsein-
richtung, Ausrüstungsgegenstände;
Mobiliar

furniture *n.* Möbel; Hausrat, Mobiliar;
piece of — Möbelstück; set of —
Möbelgarnitur

furor *n.* Wut, Raserei

furrow *n.* Furche; (anat.) Runzel; — *v.*
furchen, durchfurchen

further *adj.* weiter, ferner, entfernt; anderweitig; jenseitig; — particulars nähere Umstände; until — notice bis auf
weiteres; — *adv.* weiter, ferner; überdies, noch dazu; — *v.* (be)fördern

furthermore *adv.* ausserdem, ferner, überdies

furthest *adj.* fernst, weitest; — *adv.* am
fernsten, am weitesten; at the —
spätestens

furtive *adj.* verstohlen, heimlich

furuncle *n.* Furunkel

fury *n.* Wut, Raserei; Heftigkeit; blind —
blinde Wut

fuse *n.* Zünder, Zündschnur; (elec.) Sicherung; — box Sicherungsgehäuse; — *v.*
schmelzen, verschmelzen; -e *n.* Wind-
streichhölzchen

fuselage *n.* Flugzeugrumpf

fusion *n.* Schmelzen, Schmelzung; (fig.)
Fusion, Verschmelzung

fuss *n.* Störung, Aufruhr; (coll.) Wesen,
Getue; — *v.* viel Aufhebens machen;
-y *adj.* übertrieben umständlich, geschäftig; viel Aufhebens machend

futile *adj.* nutzlos, unnütz; wertlos,
nichtig

future *adj.* künftig, zukünftig; — *n.*
Zukunft; (gram.) Futurum; in the —
in Zukunft, zukünftig

fuzz *n.* Flaum, Fäserchen; -y *adj.* flockig,
faserig; flaumig; (coll.) angeduselt

G

gab *n.* Geschwätz, Geplauder; gift of —
ein gutes Mundwerk; — *v.* schwatzen,
schnattern

gabardine *n.* Gabardin

gable *n.* Giebel

gadfly *n.* Pferdebremse

gadget *n.* Vorrichtung, Einrichtung;
Kniff, Pfiff

gag *n.* Knebel; (theat.) improvisierter
Witz; (fig.) Knebel; — *v.* knebeln;

mundtot machen

gaiety *n.* Munterkeit, Fröhlichkeit

gain *n.* Gewinn, Vorteil, Nutzen; — *v.*
gewinnen, erwerben, erlangen; (clock)
vorgehen; — weight zunehmen; -ful
adj. gewinnbringend, einträglich

gait *n.* Gang, Gangart; Haltung

gala *adj.* feierlich, prunkhaft; Gala-; -xy
n. Milchstrasse; (fig.) glänzende Versammlung; -xy of stars Sternenmeer

gale *n.* steife Brise

gall *n.* Galle; (fig.) Bitterkeit, Unverschämtheit; — bladder Gallenblase; —
v. belästigen, quälen; reizen, ärgern

gallant *adj.* brav, tapfer; höflich, galant;
stattlich; — *n.* Galan, Liebhaber; -ry
n. Tapferkeit; Galanterie, Artigkeit

gallery *n.* Galerie; Säulenhalle; Korridor;
(min.) Stollen

galley *n.* (naut.) Galeere, Kombüse;
Schiffsküche; (typ.) Setzschiff; —
proof Korrekturabzug

gallivant *v.* umherziehen

gallon *n.* Gallone

gallop *n.* Galopp; — *v.* galoppieren (lassen); (fig.) schnell laufen

gallows *n.* Galgen

gallstone *n.* Gallenstein

galosh *n.* Galosche, Überschuh

galvanize *v.* galvanisieren

gamble *v.* spielen, wetten; — away verspielen; — *n.* Glücksspiel; -r *n.* Spieler,
Hasardeur

gambling *n.* Spiel, Glücksspiel; — house
Spielkasino, Spielhölle

game *n.* Spiel, Belustigung; Partie; (hunting) Wild; — license Jagdschein; —
warden Wildhüter; big — Grosswild;
adj. spielbereit, mutig; (hunting) jagd-
bar; Wild-; — leg lahmes Bein

gamecock *n.* Kampfhahn

gamekeeper *n.* Wildheger, Wildhüter

gamesmanship *n.* Sportlichkeit, Zünftigkeit

gamma *n.* Gamma; — globulin Gamma-
globulin; — rays Gammastrahlen

gang *n.* Abteilung, Truppe; Schar, Bande,
Rotte; -ster *n.* Gangster, Verbrecher

ganglion *n.* Überbein, Nervenknoten;
(fig.) Knoten

gangplank *n.* Laufplanke, Laufsteg

gangrene *n.* Wundbrand

gangway *n.* Durchgang, Mittelgang;
(naut.) Fallreep, Laufplanke

gantry *n.* Polarkran; Gerüstkran; —
tower Krangerüstturm; (rocket) Bedienungsturm

gap *n.* Lücke, Bresche; Kluft, Riss; -e *v.*
gähnen, klaffen; gaffen; -er *n.* Gaffer

garage *n.* Garage, Autoschuppen

garb n. Tracht, Kleidung, Gewand

garbage n. Abfall, Auswurf; Schund; — **can** Abfallbehälter, Mülleimer; — **pail** Abfalleimer, Mistkübel

garble v. verstümmeln, entstellen

garden n. Garten; — v. Gartenbau betreiben; als Garten anlegen; -er n. Gärtner; -ing n. Gärtnerei; Gartenarbeit

gargle n. Gurgelwasser, Mundwasser; — v. gurgeln

garland n. Kranz, Girlande; (arch.) Laubgehänge; (fig.) Blumenlese; — v. bekränzen

garlic n. Knoblauch

garment n. Kleid, Kleidung; Gewand

garner v. aufspeichern

garnet n. Granat

garnish n. Garnierung, Schmuck, Zierrat; — v. garnieren, schmücken, verzieren

garnishee v. gerichtlich mit Beschlag belegen

garret n. Bodengeschoss, Dachstube

garrison n. Besatzung; Garnison; Fort; — v. mit einer Besatzung versehen, in Garnison legen

garter n. Strumpfband, Sockenhalter; — **snake** amerikanische Gürtelschlange; Order of the — Hosenbandorden

gas n. Gas, Leuchtgas; Benzin; — **attack** Gasangriff; — **cooker** Gaskocher; — **fitter** Gasinstallateur, Gasrohrleger; — **jet** Gasflamme; — **main** Gashauptleitung; — **mask** Gasmaske; — **meter** Gasmesser, Gasuhr; — **pipe** Gasrohr; — **station** Tankstelle; — **tank** Benzintank; -eous adj. gasartig, gasförmig; -oline n. Benzin; Gasolin; -oline tank Benzintank; -oline station Tankstelle

gash n. Schmarre, klaffende Wunde; — v. tief verwunden, aufschlitzen

gasket n. (mech.) Dichtung; (naut.) kurzes Tau

gasp n. Keuchen, Luftschnappen, schweres Atmen; — v. keuchen, schwer atmen; — **for breath** nach Luft schnappen; — **out** ausatmen, aushauchen

gastrorectomy n. operative Magenentfernung

gasworks n. pl. Gaswerke

gate n. Tor, Pforte; (rail.) Schranke

gatekeeper n. Portier; (rail.) Schrankenwärter

gateway n. Torweg, Einfahrt

gather v. sammeln, pflücken; sich (ver)sammeln; folgern, schliessen; zusammenziehen; -ing n. Versammlung

gaudy adj. bunt, prunkend, geputzt

gauge, gage n. Mass(stab), Eichmass; (arch.) Messlatte; (rail.) Spurweite; — v. abmessen, ausmessen; eichen; abschätzen

gauntlet n. Panzerhandschuh; Stulphandschuh; (fig.) Fehdehandschuh; **run the** — Spiessruten laufen

gauze n. Gaze, Flor

gavel n. Hammer (des Vorsitzenden)

gawk v. gaffen; -y adj. tölpelhaft, linkisch

gay adj. lustig, fröhlich; bunt, glänzend; lebhaft, flott; (fig.) liederlich

gaze n. Anstarren, Anstaunen; — v. starren; anstaunen; — **at** anstaunen

gazette n. Zeitung; Amtsblatt, Staatsanzeiger

gear n. Stoff, Zeug; Kleidung, Tracht; (mech.) Triebrad, Zahnrad; Getriebe, Gang; out of — ausgeschaltet; put in — in Gang setzen; shift into second — den zweiten Gang einschalten; shift — umschalten; throw out of — (den Mechanismus) ausschalten

gearshift n. (auto.) Schaltung

Geiger counter n. Geigerzähler

gelatin(e) n. Gelatine, Gallerte

gem n. Edelstein; Gemme; (fig.) Juwel, Glanzstück

gender n. Geschlecht

gene n. Gen

genealogy n. Genealogie, Geschlechterkunde; Stammbaum

general n. General, Feldherr; — **staff** (mil.) Generalstab; — adj. allgemein, gewöhnlich; Haupt-, General-; — **delivery** hauptpostlagernd; — **election** allgemeine Wahlen; in — im allgemeinen; -ity n. Allgemeinheit; -ization n. Verallgemeinerung; -ize v. verallgemeinern

generate v. erzeugen, entwickeln

generation n. Erzeugung; Entwicklung; Generation, Menschenalter, Zeitalter

generator n. Generator; Erzeuger

generic adj. Gattungs-; generisch

generosity n. Freigebigkeit; Edelmut, Grossmut

generous adj. freigebig, grosszügig; reichlich; grossmütig

genesis n. Zeugung, Werden; Genesis, Genesis, erstes Buch Mosis

genetic code n. Vererbungsgesetz

genetics n. Genetik, Vererbungslehre

Geneva n. Genf

genial adj. freundlich; belebend, anregend, munter, lustig; -ity n. Freundlichkeit, Munterkeit, Lustigkeit

genitals n. pl. Geschlechtsteile, Genitalien

genius n. Genius, Genie; Schutzgeist; Schöpfungskraft

gentian n. Enzian

gentile n. Nichtjude; Heide; — adj. nichtjüdisch; heidnisch

gentility n. Vornehmheit, Lebensart

gentle *adj.* mild, sanft; lind; zahm; vornehm, edel; **–ness** *n.* Milde, Güte; Sanftmut

gentleman *n.* Herr; Ehrenmann, Gentleman;.**–'s agreement** freundschaftliches Übereinkommen

gently *adv.* mild, sanft; leise

genuflection, genuflexion *n.* Knien, Kniebeuge

genuine *adj.* echt, rein; wahr, natürlich; unverfälscht; **–ness** *n.* Echtheit, Wahrheit

genus *n.* Geschlecht, Gattung

geographer *n.* Geograph

geographic(al) *adj.* geographisch

geography *n.* Geographie, Erdkunde

geological *adj.* geologisch, erdgeschichtlich

geologist *n.* Geologe

geology *n.* Geologie

geometric(al) *adj.* geometrisch; **— progression** geometrische Progression

geometry *n.* Geometrie, Raumlehre; **plane —** Planimetrie; **solid —** Stereometrie

geophysics *n.* Geophysik

geophysical *adj.* geophysikalisch

geopolitics *n.* Geopolitik

geranium Geranium, Storchschnabel

germ *n.* Keim; Erreger; **— cell** Keimzelle; **— plasm** Keimplasma; **–icide** *n.* keimtötendes Mittel; **–inate** *v.* keimen (lassen); spriessen; **–ination** *n.* Keimen, Spriessen

German *adj.* deutsch; **— measles** *n. pl.* Röteln; **–y** *n.* Deutschland

gestation *n.* Schwangerschaft; (zool.) Trächtigkeit

gesticulate *v.* gestikulieren, Gesten machen

gesture *n.* Gebärde, Geste; **— v.** gestikulieren

get *v.* werden; bekommen, erhalten, erlangen; besorgen, holen, sich verschaffen; finden; kommen; machen; bewegen; gewinnen; **— about** herumkommen; **— along** vorwärtskommen; auskommen; **— around** herumkommen (um); **— at** erreichen, anlangen; **— away** sich davon machen; wegbringen; **— away with** durchkommen mit; **— back** zurückerhalten; zurückkommen; **— behind** zurückbleiben; **— by** auskommen; **— done** machen lassen; fertig werden; **— down** herunterkommen; hinunterbringen, hinunterschlucken; **— even with** sich rächen an; **— in** einsteigen; hereinkommen; hineinbringen; ankommen; **— into** hinein geraten; einsteigen; **— off** aussteigen; davon-

kommen; (clothes) ausziehen; **— on** einsteigen; weiterkommen; (clothes) anziehen; **— out** aussteigen; herausbekommen; herausbringen; **— over** überwinden; **— rid of** loswerden; **— the better of** übertölpeln; **— through** durchkommen; durchbringen; **— to** ankommen; **— together** zusammenkommen; sich vereinigen; **— up** aufstehen; wecken; **— well** wieder gesund werden

getaway *n.* Entweichen, Flucht

getup *n.* Ausstattung, Aufmachung

geyser *n.* Geiser, heisser Springbrunnen

G-force *n.* Gravitationskraft der Erde; Fliehkraft

ghastly *adj.* grausig, grässlich; geisterhaft

ghetto *n.* G(h)etto, Judenviertel

ghost *n.* Gespenst, Geist; **— writer** Berufschriftsteller, der für einen anderen schreibt; **have not the — of a chance** nicht die geringste Aussicht auf Erfolg haben; **–ly** *adj.* gespensterhaft, geisterhaft

giant *n.* Riese; Gigant; **— adj.** riesenhaft, riesig; gigantisch

giddy *adj.* schwindlich; schwindelerregend; (fig.) leichtsinnig

gift *n.* Gabe; Geschenk; (law) Schenkung; (fig.) Talent; **–ed** *adj.* begabt

gigantic *adj.* riesenhaft, riesig; gigantisch

giggle *n.* Kichern, Gekicher; **— v.** kichern

gild *v.* vergolden; **–ing** *n.* Vergolden, Vergoldung

gill *n.* (hen) Kehllappen; (ichth.) Kiemen; (measure) Viertelpinte

gilt *n.* Vergoldung; **— adj.** vergoldet

gilt-edged *adj.* mit Goldschnitt versehen; (coll.) hochfein, prima

gimmick *n.* sinnreiche Vorrichtung; Trick, Kniff

gin *n.* Gin; Entkörnungsmaschine; **— rummy** Ginrummy; **— v.** entkörnen

ginger *n.* Ingwer; **— ale** Ingwerbier; **— adj.** gelblichbraun; **–ly** *adv.* and *adj.* zimperlich; bedächtig, sorgfältig

gingerbread *n.* Pfefferkuchen, Lebuchen

gingersnap *n.* Ingwerkeks

gingivitis *n.* (med.) Zahnfleischentzündung

~~gird~~ *v.* gürten, umgürten; **–le** *n.* Gurt, Gürtel; **–le** *v.* umgeben, umschliessen; umgürten

girder *n.* Träger, Tragbalken

girl *n.* Mädchen; (coll.) Dienstmädchen, Magd; **— scout** Pfadfinderin; **–hood** *n.* Mädchentum; Mädchenjahre; **–ish** *adj.* mädchenhaft

girth *n.* Umfang; Sattelgurt

gist *n.* Hauptpunkt, Kern; Wesen

give *v.* geben, schenken; übergeben, darbieten; verursachen; vortragen, mitteilen; gestatten, erlauben; aussprechen, ausstossen; angeben, nachgeben; — **a lift** unter die Arme greifen; — **account** Rechenschaft ablegen; — **away** verschenken; (sich) verraten; — **away the bride** Brautvater sein; die Braut (dem Bräutigam) geben; — **away the show** die Katze aus dem Sack lassen; — **birth** gebären, das Leben schenken, zur Welt bringen; — **credit** zutrauen, anerkennen; — **evidence** Zeugnis ablegen; — **in** nachgeben; — **off** von sich geben; — **out** ausgeben, austeilen; — **over** überlassen, abtreten; — **up** aufgeben, verzichten; — **way** Raum geben, nachgeben; **-n** *adj.* gegeben, festgesetzt, bestimmt; geneigt; — **name** Taufname; — **time** bestimmte Zeit; **-r** *n.* Geber, Schenkende(r)

give-and-take *n.* Gedankenaustausch; Ausgleich

gizzard *n.* Kropf, Magen; (fig.) Stimmung

glacier *n.* Gletscher, Firn

glad *adj.* heiter, froh; erfreulich, angenehm; **I am — to see you** es freut mich Sie zu sehen; **-den** *v.* erfreuen, erheitern; **-ness** *n.* Freude, Frölichkeit

glade *n.* Lichtung

gladiolus *n.* Gladiole

glamor, glamour *n.* Reiz, Zauber; Blendwerk; **-ous** *adj.* zauberhaft, reizend

glance *n.* flüchtiger Blick; **at first** — auf den ersten Blick, sofort; — *v.* flüchtig blicken; streifen, berühren

gland *n.* Drüse; **-ular** *adj.* drüsenartig

glare *n.* Blenden; Schimmer; durchdringender Blick; — *v.* scheinen, strahlen, funkeln, glänzen; blenden; hervorstechen; wild starren

glass *n.* Glas; Trinkglas; Fenster; Spiegel; — **blower** Glasbläser; — **case** Glaskasten; — **cutter** Glasschleifer; — **eye** Glasauge; *pl.* Augengläser; — *adj.* glasartig, gläsern; Glas-; **-sy** *adj.* glasig, gläsern; glatt; starr

glasshouse *n.* Treibhaus

glassware *n.* Glasgeschirr, Glaswaren

glasswork *n.* Glasarbeit; Glashütte

glaucoma *n.* grüner Star; Glaukom

glaze *v.* verglasen; glasieren, lasieren; polieren, glätten; **-d** *adj.* verglast; glasiert; poliert

gleam *n.* Schein, Schimmer; Strahl, Lichtstrahl; Blitzstrahl; — *v.* strahlen, glänzen, schimmern, scheinen

glean *v.* (ein)sammeln; nachlesen, abernten

glee *n.* Lustbarkeit, Heiterkeit, Frölichkeit; (mus.) Rundgesang, Wechselgesang; — **club** Gesangverein, Liedertafel; **gleeful** *adj.* lustig, fröhlich

glen *n.* Bergschlucht, Talenge

glib *adj.* fliessend, glatt; schwatzhaft, zungenfertig

glide *n.* Gleiten; Schleifen; — *v.* gleiten, schleifen; (avi.) segelfliegen; **-r** *n.* (avi.) Segelflugzeug, Gleitflugzeug; Segelflieger

glimmer *n.* Schimmer, Glimmer; — *v.* schimmern, glimmern

glimpse *n.* flüchtiger Blick; Flimmer; — *v.* flüchtig sehen; **catch a — of** einen Augenblick flüchtig zu sehen bekommen

glint *n.* Lichtschein, Glanz; — *v.* glitzern, glänzen, blitzen

gloat *v.* — **over** sich weiden an

global *adj.* global, weltumfassend

globe *n.* Kugel; Globus, Erdkugel, Erde, Erdball

globe-trotter *n.* Globetrotter, Weltenbummler

gloom *n.* Dunkel(heit); Trübsinn, Schwermut; **-y** *adj.* düster, trüb; schwermütig; traurig, verdriesslich

glorification *n.* Verherrlichung; (rel.) Verklärung

glorify *v.* verherrlichen; (rel.) verklären

glorious *adj.* glorreich, ruhmreich; herrlich, köstlich, prächtig

glory *n.* Herrlichkeit, Glorie; Ruhm, Glanz, Stolz; (rel.) Heiligenschein; — *v.* frohlocken, sich freuen; sich rühmen

gloss *n.* Glosse, Randbemerkung; Glanz, Politur; — *v.* Randbemerkungen (*or* Glossen) machen; — **over** beschönigen; **-y** *adj.* glatt, glänzend

glossary *n.* Glossar, Wörterbuch

glove *n.* Handschuh; (sports) Boxhandschuh; — *v.* behandschuhen

glow *n.* Glut, Glühen; — *v.* glühen, erglühen; **-er** *v.* finster blicken, anstarren

glucose *n.* Glykose, Traubenzucker

glue *n.* Leim, Klebstoff, Bindemittel; — *v.* leimen, kleben; vereinigen

glum *adj.* mürrisch, verdriesslich

glutton *n.* Schlemmer, Schwelger; Fresser, Vielfrass; **-ous** *adj.* gefrässig; **-y** *n.* Gefrässigkeit; Völlerei

glycerin(e) *n.* Glyzerin

gnarled *adj.* knorrig

gnash *v.* knirschen; — **one's teeth** mit den Zähnen knirschen

gnat *n.* Mücke, Stechmücke

gnaw *v.* (zer)nagen, zerfressen; — **one's lips** sich auf die Lippen beissen

gnome *n.* Gnom, Erdgeist

go *v.* gehen, fahren; weggehen, wegfahren; reisen, laufen; werden; arbeiten; um-

laufen; reichen, sich erstrecken; —
against widerstreiten; — **ahead** vorangehen, vorwärtsgehen; — **astray** sich
verirren; sündigen; — **at** losgehen auf;
angreifen; — **away** weggehen, abreisen;
— **back on** zurücknehmen; — **by** vorbeigehen; sich richten nach; führen; —
down (hin)untergehen; fallen; — **far**
weit gehen; viel gelten; — **for** holen;
losgehen auf; — **in for** sich interessieren
für; — **into** hineingehen; eingehen auf,
untersuchen; — **off** losgehen; (sich)
verlaufen; — **on** vorwärtskommen, vorwärtsgehen; — **out** ausgehen; — **over**
übergehen; prüfen; — **through** durchgehen; durchmachen; (fig.) vergeuden;
— **to it!** geh zu! drauf los! — **under**
untergehen; unterliegen; führen; —
with begleiten; passen zu; — **without**
entbehren; **I am** –ing **to** ich werde; **it's**
no — so geht's nicht; **let** — **of** loslassen;
let someone — jemanden laufen lassen;
on the — in steter Bewegung; –ing *n.*
Gehen, Gang; Abreise; (fig.) Wandel;
–ing *adj.* gehend, vorkommend, vorhanden; –ing, –ing, –ne zum ersten,
zum zweiten, zum dritten (*or* letzten);
–ne *adj.* weg, fort; hin; (fig.) tot,
gestorben

goal *n.* Ziel, Pfahl; Mal; (sports) Tor; —
line Torlinie; — **post** Torpfosten

goalkeeper *n.* Torhüter

goat *n.* Ziege, Geiss

gobble *v.* gierig verschlingen, **an sich**
reissen; kollern; –**r** *n.* Truthahn

gobbledygook *n.* Kauderwelsch

go-between *n.* Vermittler, Unterhändler;
Zwischenträger

goblet *n.* Becher

goblin *n.* Kobold; Elf

God *n.* Gott; Gottheit; Göttlichkeit; **act**
of — Naturereignis; — **willing** so Gott
will; **thank** — Gott sei Dank

god *n.* Abgott, Götze; Gott; –**ess** *n.*
Göttin; –**less** *adj.* gottlos; –**like** *adj.*
göttlich, gottähnlich; –**ly** *adj.* gottselig,
gottesfürchtig

godchild *n.* Patenkind

godfather *n.* Pate; Taufzeuge, Gevatter

godmother *n.* Patin; Gevatterin

godsend *n.* Gottesgabe, unerwarteter
Gewinn

goggle *v.* glotzen; –**s** *n. pl.* Schutzbrille

goiter, goitre *n.* Kropf

gold *n.* Gold; (fig.) Reichtum, Geld;
Goldgelb; — **brick** Schwindel; wertvolle
Ware, die nach Bezahlung in wertloses
Gut umgetauscht wird; — **digger**
Goldgräber; (fig.) Glücksjägerin; —
dust Goldstaub; — **leaf** Blattgold; —

mine Goldgrube; — **rush** Jagd nach
Gold, Goldrausch; — **standard** Goldwährung; –**en** *adj.* golden; goldgelb;
(fig.) kostbar, glücklich; –**en mean**
goldener Mittelweg; –**en rule** goldene
Regel; –**en wedding** goldene Hochzeit

goldenrod *n.* Goldrute, Goldregen

goldsmith *n.* Goldschmied

golf *n.* Golf(spiel); — **club** Golfstock;
Golfklub; — **course** Golfplatz; — **links**
Golffeld; –**er** *n.* Golfspieler

good *adj.* gut; heilsam, dienlich; recht;
gütig; gerecht, echt, gültig; günstig;
(child) artig, brav; **as** — **as gold** kreuz-
brav; **for** — für (*or* auf) immer; **gone**
for — fort auf Nimmerwiedersehen; —
at geschickt zu; — **breeding** Wohlerzo-
genheit; — **for** gut gegen (*or* für); —
health Wohlbefinden; gute Gesundheit; — **humor** gute Laune; **Good**
Neighbor Policy gute Nachbarpolitik;
— **news** frohe Botschaft; — **sense**
gesunder Menschenverstand; — **turn**
Gefallen; — **will** guter Wille; Wohlwollen; **have a** — **time** sich amüsieren;
in — **time** rechtzeitig; **it's no** — es
nützt nichts; es ist nicht zu gebrauchen;
make — Erfolg haben; zurückzahlen;
gutmachen; **too** — **zu schade;** —! gut!
fein! schön! — *n.* Gute; *pl.* Vermögen,
Besitz; Waren, Güter; Effekten; **house-**
hold –**s** Hausgerät, bewegliche Habe;
–**ly** *adj.* schön, anmutig, reizend; angenehm; ansehnlich; –**ness** *n.* Güte;
Freundlichkeit; **for** –**ness sake** um
Himmels willen, meine Güte; **my** –**ness**
du meine Güte

good-by(e) *n.* Lebewohl; —! *interj.* lebe
wohl! adieu! **say** — sich verabschieden

good-for-nothing *n.* Nichtsnutz, Taugenichts; — *adj.* untauglich, unbrauchbar

goodhearted *adj.* gutherzig

good-looking *adj.* schön, hübsch

good-natured *adj.* gutmütig

goon *n.* Schläger (im Dienst von Gang-
stern, Streikenden, Streikbrechern,
etc.)

goose *n.* Gans; Gänsebraten; — **flesh,**
— **pimples** Gänsehaut; — **step** Parade-
schritt

gooseberry *n.* Stachelbeere

gopher *n.* Erdhörnchen

gorge *n.* Schlucht; Gurgel, Kehle,
Schlund; — *v.* fressen, vollstopfen,
verschlingen, verschlucken

gorgeous *adj.* prächtig, prachtvoll

gorilla *n.* Gorilla

gormandize *v.* schlemmen; fressen

gospel *n.* Evangelium

gossamer *n.* Sommerfaden, Altweibersommer; feine Gaze; — *adj.* leicht, dünn; (fig.) flüchtig

gossip *n.* Klatsch, Geschwätz; Schwätzer, Klatschbase; — *v.* klatschen, schwatzen

gouge *n.* Hohleisen, Hohlmeissel; — *v.* ausmeisseln, aushöhlen; (fig.) prellen

goulash *n.* Gulasch

gout *n.* Gicht, Podagra

govern *v.* regieren, (be)herrschen; lenken, leiten; **-ess** *n.* Gouvernante, Erzieherin; **-ment** *n.* Regierung; Leitung, Führung; Herrschaft; Regierungsform; **-ment bonds** Staatspapiere; **municipal -ment** Magistrat; **-mental** *adj.* Regierungs-; **-or** *n.* Statthalter, Gouverneur; Herrscher; (mech.) Regulator

gown *n.* Kleid; Gewand, Überwurf; Robe, Talar, Amtskleidung

grab *n.* Griff, Erschnappen; — *v.* ergreifen, packen, schnappen

grace *n.* Gnade, Gunst; Anmut, Grazie; Tischgebet; **say** — das Tischgebet sprechen; — *v.* schmücken, zieren; auszeichnen; **-ful** *adj.* anmutig; zierlich; graziös; günstig; **-less** *adj.* reizlos; verdorben, unverschämt

gracious *adj.* angenehm, reizend; gnädig, gütig; — **God!** gütiger Himmel! mein Gott! meine Güte! ach du liebe Zeit!

gradation *n.* Abstufung, Steigerung; (fig.) Grad, Stufe

grade *n.* Grad, Stufe, Rang; Qualität; (educ.) Note, Zensur; Klasse; **— crossing** Neigungskreuzung; **— school** Volksschule; **passing —** die Note "Bestanden"; — *v.* abstufen, ordnen; ebnen, planieren

gradient *n.* Steigung; Neigung

gradual *adj.* allmählich, stufenweise

graduate *n.* Graduierte, Absolvent, Promovierte; — *v.* abstufen, in Grade einteilen; absolvieren, promovieren; **be -d** einen Grad erreicht haben, promoviert haben

graduation *n.* Gradeinteilung; Promotion, Promovierung

graft *n.* Schiebung, Schwindel, Betrug; Erpressung, Bestechung; (agr.) Pfropfreis; (med.) Einimpfung, Verpflanzung; — *v.* erpressen, erschwindeln; pfropfen; verpflanzen, übertragen

grain *n.* Getreide; Korn; Gran, Faser; Faserung, Körnung; (wood) Struktur, Maserung; **— alcohol** Getreidealkohol, Äthylalkohol; **— merchant** Getreidehändler; **against the —** gegen den Strich, widersinnig; **mixed —** Mischkorn; **-y** *adj.* körnig, gekörnt

gram *n.* Gramm

grammar *n.* Grammatik, Sprachlehre; **—**

school Volksschule

grammatical *adj.* grammat(ikal)isch

gramophone *n.* Grammofon

granary *n.* Kornspeicher, Kornboden, Getreidekammer

grand *adj.* gross, grossartig; wichtig, bedeutend; oberst; Haupt-, Gross-; — *n.* (sl.) tausend Dollar; Tausenddollarnote; **-eur** *n.* Grösse, Grossartigkeit; Hoheit, Erhabenheit; **-iose** *adj.* grandios, grossartig; pomphaft

grandchild *n.* Enkel(kind)

granddaughter *n.* Enkelin

grandfather *n.* Grossvater

grandmother *n.* Grossmutter

grandparents *n. pl.* Grosseltern

grandson *n.* Enkel

grandstand *n.* Haupttribüne

granite *n.* Granit

grant *n.* Gewährung, Bewilligung, Erlaubnis; (law) Schenkungsurkunde; — *v.* bewilligen, gestatten, gewähren, erlauben; zugeben; **-ing that** zugestanden; **take for -ed** als erwiesen (*or* selbstverständlich) annehmen

granular *adj.* granuliert, körnig, gekörnt

granule *n.* Körnchen

grape *n.* Traube, Weinbeere; **bunch of -s** Weintraube

grapefruit *n.* Pompelmuse, Grapefruit

grapevine *n.* Weinstock, Weinrebe; **to learn something by the —** etwas läuten hören

graph *n.* Diagramm, graphische Darstellung

graphic *adj.* graphisch, anschaulich, beschreibend

graphite *n.* Graphit, Reissblei

grasp *n.* Griff, Greifen; Händedruck; Erfassen; — *v.* fassen, ergreifen; begreifen; **-ing** *adj.* habgierig, geizig

grass *n.* Gras, Rasen, Wiese, Weide; (agr. coll.) Grünfutter; **-y** *adj.* grasig, grasartig; grasreich; grasgrün

grasshopper *n.* Heuschrecke; Grashüpfer

grate *n.* Gitter, Gatter; Rost; — *v.* kratzen, knirschen; (zer)reiben, raspeln; **— on my nerves** an meinen Nerven reissen, mir auf die Nerven fallen; **-r** *n.* Reibeisen, Reibe

grateful *adj.* dankbar, erkenntlich

gratification *n.* Befriedigung, Annehmlichkeit; Belohnung

gratify *v.* befriedigen, erfreuen

grating *n.* Gitter, Gatter; Kratzen, Knirschen; Reiben; — *adj.* schrill; kratzend, knirschend; reibend; peinlich, unangenehm

gratitude *n.* Dankbarkeit, Erkenntlichkeit

grave n. Grab
grave adj. ernst, feierlich; ernsthaft; gewichtig; (mus.) tief; -ly adv. schwer
gravedigger n. Totengräber
gravel n. Kies, Sand
graveyard n. Friedhof, Kirchhof
gravitate v. zuneigen
ravitation n. Gravitation, Schwerkraft; Hang
gravity n. Gewicht, Schwere; (fig.) Ernst, Feierlichkeit, Bedeutung; center of — Schwerpunkt; force of — Schwerkraft, Anziehungskraft; specific — spezifisches Gewicht
gravy n. Tunke, Sauce, Bratensosse; — boat Sauciere, Sossenschüssel
gray, grey n. Grau; — adj. grau; (fig.) altersgrau; — v. grau machen, ergrauen; grauen, dämmern; -ish adj. gräulich
graze v. weiden, grasen, abgrasen; streifen, schrammen
grease n. Fett; Schmiere; — v. schmieren, einfetten, ölen
greasy adj. fettig, schmierig, ölig
great adj. gross; grossmütig; grossartig; beträchtlich, ansehnlich; berühmt; hervorragend; -ly adv. sehr, bedeutend; -ness n. Grösse, Bedeutung, Wichtigkeit; Macht, Stärke; Pracht, Erhabenheit, Herrlichkeit
Great Britain n. Grossbritannien
great-grandchild n. Urenkelkind
great-grandparents n. pl. Urgrosseltern
Greece n. Hellas
greed, greediness n. Gier, Habgier; Begier, Heisshunger; -y adj. gierig, gefrässig; begierig
green n. Grün; Laubgrün; (golf) Golfgrün; pl. Suppengrün, Gemüse; — adj. grün; frisch, neu; jung, unreif, unerfahren; kränklich; -ish adj. grünlich
greenback n. amerikanische Banknote
green-eyed adj. grünäugig
greenhorn n. Grünschnabel, Neuling
greenhouse n. Gewächshaus, Treibhaus
Greenland n. Grönland
greet v. grüssen, begrüssen; -ing n. Gruss, Begrüssung
grenade n. Granate
greyhound n. Windhund, Windspiel
grid n. Bratrost; Gitter; (elec.) Netzplatte; Zentralelektrode; Elektrofilter
griddle n. Kuchenblech
griddlecake n. Pfannkuchen
gridiron n. Bratrost; (sports) Fussballfeld, Fussballspiel
grief n. Kummer, Gram, Schmerz; Beschwerde
grievance n. Klagegrund, Übelstand; Ver-

driesslichkeit
grieve v. kränken, betrüben; ärgern; bekümmern; trauern, sich grämen
grievous adj. schmerzlich, verdriesslich; kränkend; schwer, drückend
grill n. Grill, Bratrost; — v. grillen, rösten
grille n. Gitter; Gitterfenster
grim adj. grimmig; finster; abstossend; scheusslich; -ness n. Grimmigkeit
grimace n. Grimasse, Fratze
grime n. Schmutz, Russ
grimy adj. schmutzig, russig
grin n. Grinsen; — v. grinsen
grind v. mahlen, zerreiben, schroten; wetzen, schleifen; (educ. sl.) einpauken, büffeln; (organ) drehen, spielen; — one's teeth mit den Zähnen knirschen; — n. Mahlen; (coll.) Plackerei, Büffler; -er n. Mühle
grindstone n. Schleifstein, Mühlstein, Drehscheibe
grip n. Griff, Handdruck; Fassungskraft; (coll.) Reisetasche; — v. fassen, packen; erfassen; -ping adj. ergreifend, festhaltend
gripe n. Klage, Übel; — v. peinigen; sich beklagen; sich nicht wohl fühlen
grippe n. Grippe
grisly adj. grässlich, gräulich, grausig, scheusslich
gristle n. Knorpel
grit n. Griess, Kies, grober Sand; (fig.) Mut; pl. Schrot, Kleie, Grütze; -ty adj. sandig, kiesig
grizzly, grizzled adj. ergraut, gräulich; grau gesprenkelt; grauhaarig; — bear Grizzlybär, grauer Bär
groan n. Seufzen, Stöhnen, Murren, Ächzen; — v. stöhnen, seufzen, murren, ächzen
grocer n. Kolonialwarenhändler, Lebensmittelhändler; -y n. Grünkramladen, Kolonialwarenhandlung, Lebensmittelgeschäft; -ies n. pl. Lebensmittel, Kolonialwaren, Grünkram
groggy adj. unsicher gehend, schwankend; (sl.) betrunken, taumelnd, betäubt
groin n. Schamleiste, Leistengegend
groom n. Bräutigam; Stalljunge, Reitknecht; — v. pflegen, besorgen; vorbereiten
groove n. Grube, Rinne, Furche, Rille; Schallrille; Führungsrille; (mech.) Nut; — v. aushöhlen, furchen; (mech.) nuten, fugen, riefeln
grope v. tasten, betasten; (umher)tappen
gross n. Hauptmasse, Hauptteil; Gros; — amount Gesamtsumme; — Bruttobetrag; — profit Bruttogewinn; — weight Bruttogewicht; — adj. gross, dick, fett;

grob, roh; unanständig; schwerfällig; dumm; brutto; **-ly** *adv.* höchst, sehr, in hohem Grade

grotesque *adj.* grotesk, seltsam

ground *n.* Grund, Boden, Erde; Erdboden; Land, Gegend; Grundlage; (art.) Grundierung; (mil.) Gelände; Anlagen; — **control** Boden-Radarpeilung; — **control approach (GCA)** Anflug mit Hilfe von Bondenradargeräten; — **floor** Erdgeschoss; — **hog** Murmeltier; — **squirrel** Erdhörnchen; — **swell** Grundsee; — **wire** Erdleitung; **above** — oberirdisch; **below** — unterirdisch; **down to the** — vollständig; **on the** — that weil, wegen; **stand one's** — sich behaupten; — *v.* niederlegen, (be)gründen; (avi.) Flugverbot erlassen; (elec., rad.) erden; (naut.) auf Grund laufen, auflaufen; **-less** *adj.* grundlos, unbegründet

groundbreaking *n.* Spatenstich

groundwork *n.* (arch.) Fundament, Grundmauer, Unterbau; Erdarbeit; (fig.) Grundlage

group *n.* Gruppe; (mil.) Geschwader; — *v.* (sich) gruppieren, zusammenstellen

grouse *n.* Waldhuhn, Birkhuhn

grove *n.* Gehölz, Hain

grow *v.* wachsen; werden; zunehmen; entstehen; aufziehen, anbauen, züchten; — **from** entstehen; — **old** altern; — **together** verwachsen, zusammenwachsen; — **up** heranwachsen; **-er** *n.* Pflanzer, Züchter; **-th** *n.* Wachstum, Wuchs; (med.) Gewächs; (fig.) Gedeihen, Zunahme

growl *n.* Knurren, Brummen; — *v.* knurren, brummen

grownup *n.* Erwachsene

grown-up *adj.* erwachsen

grub *n.* Larve, Raupe, Made; (coll.) Essen, Nahrung; Prolet; — *v.* graben, wühlen; sich placken

grudge *n.* Widerwillen, Abneigung, Groll; **bear a** — übelwollen, grollen; — *v.* widerstreben; (be)neiden, missgönnen; vorenthalten

grudgingly *adv.* murrend, widerwillig, ungern

gruel *n.* Grütze, Haferschleim

gruesome *adj.* grausig, entsetzlich

gruff *adj.* rauh, schroff, barsch; mürrisch

grumble *v.* murren, brummen, knurren

grumpy *adj.* mürrisch, böse; knurrig, brummig

grunt *v.* grunzen; — *n.* Grunzen

guarantee *n.* Garantie, Bürgschaft; Bürge; — *v.* bürgen für, garantieren, sichern; sich verbürgen

guarantor *n.* Bürge, Gewährsmann, Garant

guaranty *n.* Garantie, Bürgschaft, Gewähr(leistung)

guard *n.* Wache, Bewachung; Wacht, Hut, Schutz; Wächter, Hüter; (mech.) Schutzblech, Sicherheitskette; (mil.) Wachtposten, Wachmannschaft, Schildwache, Garde; (rail.) Schrankenwärter, Bahnwärter; (sports) Verteidigung, Auslage, Parade; **advance** — Vorhut; **on** — auf Wache; auf der Hut; **under** — unter Schutz; — *v.* (be)hüten, schützen; bewachen; begleiten, geleiten; (cards) decken; — **against** sich hüten vor; sich in acht nehmen vor; **-ed** *adj.* behutsam, vorsichtig; **-ian** *n.* Wächter, Hüter; (law) Vormund, Pfleger; **-ian angel** Schutzengel; **-ianship** *n.* Vormundschaft, Obhut

guardhouse *n.* Wachthaus, Wachtlokal; Lagergefängnis

guer(r)illa *n.* Guerillakämpfer, Partisan

guess *n.* Mutmassung, Vermutung; — *v.* (er)raten; mutmassen, vermuten; **I** — ich denke

guesswork *n.* Vermutung; Raterei

guest *n.* Gast

guidance *n.* Führung, Leitung; — **beam** (avi.) Führungsstrahl; Fahrstrahl

guide *n.* Führer, Leiter, Lenker; Führung, Leitung, Lenkung; Reiseführer; — *v.* führen, leiten, lenken; **-d** *adj.* lenkbar; **-d missile** ferngesteuertes (*or* lenkbares) Geschoss

guidebook *n.* Reisehandbuch, Reiseführer

guidepost *n.* Wegweiser

guild *n.* Gilde, Zunft, Innung

guile *n.* Arglist, Betrug; Kunstgriff; **-less** *adj.* arglos, offen, aufrichtig

guillotine *n.* Guillotine, Fallbeil

guilt *n.* Schuld; Strafbarkeit; **-less** *adj.* schuldlos, unschuldig; harmlos; **-y** *adj.* schuldig; strafbar, verbrecherisch; lasterhaft; **plead -y** sein Verbrechen eingestehen; **plead not -y** sein Verbrechen ableugnen

guinea *n.* Guinee; — **pig** Meerschweinchen; (fig.) Versuchskaninchen

guitar *n.* Gitarre; **small** — Zupfgeige

gulch *n.* tiefe Schlucht

gulf *n.* Meerbusen, Golf; Abgrund, Schlund; Strudel

Gulf Stream *n.* Golfstrom

gull *n.* Möwe

gullet *n.* Gurgel, Schlund, Speiseröhre

gullible *adj.* leichtgläubig, leicht **zu** täuschen

gully *n.* Giessbachschlucht; Abzugsgraben

gulp *n.* Schluck; — *v.* (gierig) schlucken,

würgen
gum *n.* Gummi, Gummierung; Schleim; (anat.) Gaumen; **chewing** — Kaugummi; — **tree** Gummibaum; — *v.* gummieren, kleben; **-my** *adj.* gummiartig; gummiert; klebrig
gumdrop *n.* Gummibonbon
gumption *n.* Verstand, Mutterwitz
gumwood *n.* Eukalyptusbaum
gun *n.* Gewehr, Feuerwaffe; Kanone, Geschütz; — **barrel** Gewehrlauf, Geschützrohr; — **metal** Kanonenmetall, Rotguss; **-ner** *n.* Schütze; (mil.) Artillerist, Kanonier, ◦Feuerwerker; (naut.) Stückmeister
gunboat *n.* Kanonenboot
gunfire *n.* Geschützfeuer, Kannonade
gunny *n.* Jute(leinewand); — **sack** Jutesack
gunpowder *n.* Schiesspulver
gunshot *n.* Schuss; Schussweite
gunsight *n.* Zielgerät
gunwale *n.* Schan(z) deck, Dollbord
gurgle *n.* Gurgeln; — *v.* gurgeln, glucksen
gush *n.* Guss, Erguss; (fig.) Hervorbrechen; Herzenserguss; — *v.* (sich) ergiessen, stürzen, hervorströmen; (fig.) schwärmen; **-er** *n.* Erdöldurchbruch
gust *n.* Bö, Windstoss; (fig.) Ausbruch; — **load** (avi.) Luftwiderstand
gusto *n.* Gusto, Geschmack, Genuss
gut *n.* Darm; Magen, Bauch; *pl.* Eingeweide, Gedärm; **I haven't the -s** (sl.) Ich habe nicht den Mut; — *v.* ausweiden, ausnehmen; **-ter** *n.* Gosse, Rinnstein; Dachrinne; **-tural** *adj.* kehlig, guttural; Kehl-
guy *n.* Bursche, Kerl
gym(nasium) *n.* Turnhalle
gymnastic *adj.* gymnastisch; Turn-; **-s** *n pl.* Gymnastik, Leibesübungen
gynecologist *n.* Gynäkologe, Frauenarzt
gyp *n.* Schwindel; — *v.* betrügen, beschwindeln
Gypsum *n.* Gips
gypsy, gipsy *n.* Zigeuner; — *adj.* zigeunerhaft
gyroscope *n.* Kreiselachse; Gyroskop

H

habeas corpus *n.* Habeaskorpus; **writ of** — Freilassungsbefehl
haberdasher *n.* Kurzwarenhändler, Herrenmodegeschäftsinhaber; **-y** *n.* Kurzwaren, Herrenmodeartikel; Kurzwarenhandlung; Herrenmodegeschäft
habit *n.* Gewohnheit, Lebensweise; Amtstracht, Kleidung; **break oneself of the** — **of** sich abgewöhnen zu; **get into the**

— **of** sich angewöhnen zu; **-able** *adj.* bewohnbar, wohnlich; **-at** *n.* Fundort, Heimat; **-ation** *n.* Wohnung, Wohnsitz; **-ual** *adj.* gewöhnlich, gewohnheitsmässig; gewohnt; Gewohnheits-; **-uate** *v.* (an)gewöhnen
hack *n.* Taxi; Miet(s)wagen; (coll.) Skribent; Klepper; — *v.* (zer)hacken; kurz (*or* trocken) husten
haddock *n.* Schellfisch
hag *n.* Hexe, Furie, hässliche Alte
haggard *adj.* hager, abgehärmt
the Hague *n.* der Haag
hail *n.* Hagel; Gruss, Grüssen; — *v.* (nieder) hageln; anrufen; grüssen; — **from** stammen, kommen aus; —! *interj.* Heil! Glückauf!
hailstorm *n.* Hagelsturm, Hagelwetter
hair *n.* Haar; **by a** — um ein Haar; **comb one's** — sich die Haare kämmen; **cut one's** — sich die Haare (ab)schneiden; — *adj.* — **dryer** Föhn; — **ribbon** Haarband; — **trigger** Gewehrabzug; **-less** *adj.* haarlos; kahl, glatzköpfig; **-y** *adj.* haarig, behaart
hairbrush *n.* Haarbürste
haircut *n.* Haarschnitt
hairdo *n.* Haartracht, Frisur
hairdresser *n.* Friseur; **-'s (shop)** Frisiersalon
hairpin *n.* Haarnadel
hair-raising *adj.* haarsträubend
hairsplitting *n.* Haarspalterei
hale *adj.* gesund, kräftig, rüstig, frisch
half *n.* Hälfte; — *adj.* halb; Halb-; — **blood** Halbblut; — **brother** Halbbruder; — **pay** Halblohn; — **sister** Halbschwester; — **sole** Halbsohle; — **(time)** Halbzeit; — **tone** Halbton; — **year** Halbjahr; **one and a** — anderthalb, eineinhalb
halfback *n.* Läufer; Deckungsspieler
half-blooded *adj.* halbblütig
half-breed *n.* Mischling; — *adj.* halbbürtig
half-caste *n.* Mischling, Halbblut·
halfhearted *adj.* lau, gleichgültig
half-hour *n.* halbe Stunde; — *adj.* halbstündig
half-moon *n.* Halbmond
half-track *n.* Panzerwagen
half-witted *adj.* albern, töricht, einfältig
half-year *adj.* halbjährlich
halibut *n.* Heilbutt
halitosis *n.* Mundfäule
hall *n.* Saal, Halle; Gang, Korridor, Vorhalle; Markthalle; Gerichtssaal; (educ.) Aula, Kollegium; (entrance) — Diele, Vorzimmer
hallmark *n.* Feingehaltszeichen, Echt-

heitsstempel
hallow v. heiligen; weihen
Halloween n. Abend vor Allerheiligen;
  (fig.) Hexensabbat
hallucination n. Halluzination, Sinnestäuschung
hallway n. Flur, Korridor
halo n. Heiligenschein; (ast.) Hof
halt n. Halt; Halten; Haltestelle; — v.
  halten, haltmachen; anhalten; —!
  interj. Halt! — adj. lahm, hinkend
halter n. Halfter; Leibchen
halve v. halbieren
ham n. Schinken; (anat.) Schenkel; (sl.)
  pathetischer Schauspieler, Komödiant
hamburger n. Beefsteak, Bratklops
hamlet n. Dörfchen, Flecken
hammer n. Hammer; Schalghammer;
  (gun) Hahn; — v. hämmern, schmieden
hammock n. Hängematte
hamper n. Esskorb; (clothes) — Schmutz-
  wäschekorb; — v. hemmen, belästigen
hand n. Hand; Handbreite; (aid) Hilfe;
  (cards) Karten (in der Hand); (labor)
  Mann, Arbeiter; Handfertigkeit;
  (naut.) Matrose; (side) Seite; (watch)
  Zeiger; (writing) Handschrift; (fig.)
  Kunst; **at** — zur Hand, bei der Hand;
  at first — aus erster Hand; **be on** —
  da sein, zur Hand sein; **by** — mit der
  Hand; **change —s** den Besitzer wechseln; **from — to** — von einer Hand in
  die andere; **get out of** — ausser Rand
  und Band geraten; **—s down** ohne
  Schwierigkeit; **—s off!** interj. Hände
  weg! **—s up!** interj. Hände hoch! **in** —
  im Gange; **in the —s of** in der Gewalt
  von; **lay one's —s on** ergreifen; **lend a
  (helping)** — behilflich sein; **of one's —s**
  aus den Händen; **on** — vorrätig, auf
  Lager; **on the one** — einerseits; **on the
  other** — andererseits; **shake —s** sich die
  Hände schütteln; **take the law in one's
  own —s** sich selbst Recht verschaffen;
  upper — Oberhand; **wash one's —s of**
  sich die Hände in Unschuld waschen
  wegen; **with one's own** — eigenhändig;
  — v. übergeben, überreichen; **— down**
  herunterreichen; **— in** einreichen; **—
  out** austeilen, ausgeben; **— over** überliefern; **— up** heraufreichen; **-iness** n.
  Handlichkeit; **-le** n. Heft, Griff; Hen-
  kel; (fig.) Handhabe; **-le bar** Lenkstange; **-le** v. handhaben, gebrauchen;
  anfassen, befühlen; leiten, führen; (fig.)
  behandeln; **-y** adj. geschickt, gewandt;
  handlich, bequem; nützlich; **-y man**
  Handlanger
handbag n. Handtasche
handbill n. Plakat; Reklamezettel

handbook n. Handbuch; (sl.) Geschäftsbuch eines Winkelbuchmachers
handclasp n. Händedruck
handcuff n. Handschelle, Handfessel; —
  v. Handschellen (or Handfesseln) anlegen
handful n. Handvoll
handicap n. Handikap, Vorgabe; — v.
  hemmen; (extra) belasten
handicraft n. Handarbeit, Handfertigkeit;
  Handwerk
handiwork n. Handarbeit
handkerchief n. Taschentuch
handmade adj. handgemacht
handout n. Aushilfe; Werbebroschüre;
  (sl.) Almosen, milde Gabe
hand-picked adj. persönlich ausgesucht,
  eigenhändig ausgewählt
handrail n. Geländerstange
handsaw n. Handsäge, Stichsäge
handshake n. Händedruck
handsome adj. schön, hübsch; ansehnlich,
  beträchtlich; freigebig
hand-to-hand adj. Hand-; — fight Handgemenge
handwriting n. Handschrift
hang v. (auf)hängen; einhängen, umhän-
  gen; schweben; — on sich anklammern;
  — up aufhängen; — n. Hang; Abhang,
  Neigung; get the — of vertraut werden
  mit, erfassen; **-er** n. Kleiderbügel;
  -er-on n. Anhänger; (coll.) Schmarotzer; **-ing** n. Hängen, Erhängen; **-ings**
  pl. Behang, Vorhänge; Tapeten
hangar n. Hangar, Flugzeughalle
hangman n. Henker
hangnail n. Niednagel, Neidnagel
hangout n. Stammplatz
hang-over n. Kater, Katzenjammer
hanker v. sich sehnen, verlangen
hankering n. Sehnsucht, Verlangen
Hanover n. Hannover
haphazard n. Zufall, Geratewohl; — adj.
  zufällig
hapless adj. unglücklich
happen v. geschehen, sich ereignen (or
  zutragen); passieren; **I** — to be ich bin
  zufällig; **-ing** n. Vorkommen, Vorfall,
  Ereignis
happily adv. glücklicherweise, auf ge-
  schickte Art; glücklich
happiness n. Glück; Glückseligkeit,
  Freude
happy adj. glücklich, glückselig; zufrieden; günstig, geschickt
happy-go-lucky adj. unbekümmert, sorglos; leichtsinnig
harass v. ermüden, erschöpfen; ärgern,
  quälen; belästigen, beunruhigen
harbor n. Hafen; Zuflucht; Unterkunft,

Obdach; — *v.* beherbergen, hegen, schützen

hard *adj.* hart; schwer, schwierig, mühsam; fest; zäh; streng; heftig. scharf; tüchtig, fleissig; **drive a — bargain** bis zum Äussersten feilschen; **— and fast** bindend, unabänderlich; **— cash** klingende Münze, Bargeld; **— cider** (alkoholisierter) Apfelwein; **— coal** Anthrazit; **— labor** Zwangsarbeit; **— of hearing** schwerhörig; **— to believe** schwer zu glauben; **— to digest** schwerverdaulich; **— up** knapp; **try —** sich sehr bemühen; — *adv.* schwierig, mit Schwierigkeiten, mit Mühe; heftig; **-en** *v.* härten, stählen; abhärten; (sich) verhärten; gewöhnen; unempfindlich werden; **-ly** *adv.* kaum, schwerlich; **-ly ever** fast nie; **-ness** *n.* Härte, Festigkeit; Schwierigkeit; Grausamkeit; Not; **-ship** *n.* Unglück, Ungemach, Bedrükkung, Mühsal; **-y** *adj.* kräftig, stark; kühn, mutig, tapfer; (bot.) winterhart

hard-boiled *adj.* hart(gekocht); (fig.) hartgesotten

hardhearted *adj.* hartherzig, unbarmherzig

hardtop *n.* Stahlverdeck; — *adj.* mit Stahlverdeck versehen

hardware *n.* Metallwaren; **— store** Metallwarengeschäft

hardwood *n.* Hartholz

hard-working *adj.* fleissig, arbeitsam

hare *n.* Hase

harelip *n.* Hasenscharte

harem *n.* Harem

hark *v.* horchen, lauschen; **—!** *interj.* horch! hört!

harlot *n.* Hure, Dirne

harm *n.* Schaden, Verletzung; Harm, Unrecht; — *v.* schaden, schädigen, ein Leid zufügen, verletzen; **-ful** *adj.* schädlich, nachteilig; verderblich, böse; **-less** *adj.* harmlos, unschädlich; schuldlos

harmonic *adj.* harmonisch, übereinstimmend; **-a** *n.* Harmonika

harmonious *adj.* harmonisch; zusammenstimmend, wohlklingend; symmetrisch; (fig.) einträchtig, friedlich

harmonize *v.* harmonieren, übereinstimmen; einig sein; in Einklang bringen

harmony *n.* Harmonie, Einklang; Ebenmass; (fig.) Eintracht

harness *n.* Geschirr; — *v.* anschirren

harp *n.* Harfe; — *v.* Harfe spielen; — **on** herumreiten auf; **-ist** *n.* Harfner, Harfenist; **-sichord** *n.* Spinett

harpoon *n.* Harpune; — *v.* harpunieren

harrow *n.* Egge; — *v.* eggen; (fig.) quälen, plagen; **-ing** *adj.* herzzerreissend, schrecklich

harsh *adj.* streng; rauh, barsch; herb, hart; grell; **-ness** *n.* Rauheit, Herbheit, Härte; Barschheit

hart *n.* Hirsch

harum-scarum *adj.* flüchtig, leichtsinnig, wild

harvest *n.* Ernte; Ertrag, Gewinn; — *v.* ernten, einbringen; **-er** *n.* Mähmaschine

hash *n.* Haschee, Gehacktes; **make — of** verderben, verpfuschen; — *v.* haschieren, zerhacken

hassock *n.* gepolsterte Fussbank; Kniekissen

haste *n.* Eile, Schnelligkeit; Hast; **be in —** Eile haben; **— makes waste** Eile mit Weile; **-n** *v.* (sich) eilen, beeilen, beschleunigen

hasty *adj.* eilig, schnell, hastig; hitzig, eifrig; übereilt, voreilig

hat *n.* Hut; **-s off!** *interj.* Hut ab! **-ter** *n.* Hutmacher; Hutverkäufer

hatband *n.* Hutband, Hutschnur

hatch *n.* Halbtür; (naut.) Luke; — *v.* aushekken, ausbrüten; schräffieren; **-ing** *n.* Schraffieren, Schraffierung

hatchet *n.* Axt, Beil

hate *n.* Hass, Abscheu; — *v.* hassen, verabscheuen; **-ful** *adj.* verhasst, hasserfüllt, gehässig

hatpin *n.* Hutnadel

hatrack *n.* Hutrechen

hatred *n.* Hass, Groll

haughty *adj.* hochmütig, stolz; anmassend

haul *n.* Ziehen, Schleppen; Zug, Fang, Fischzug; (sl.) Diebesbeute; — *v.* ziehen, holen; schleppen; (min.) fördern; (naut.) den Kurs ändern

haunch *n.* Hüfte; Hinterhand; Keule

haunt *n.* Stammplatz; — *v.* häufig besuchen; heimsuchen; spuken; **-ed** *adj.* behext, verwunschen; heimgesucht, verfolgt

have *v.* haben, besitzen; erhalten, bekommen; verstehen; gestatten; (meal) einnehmen; **— about one** bei sich haben; **— on** anhaben; **— done** tun lassen; **— made** machen lassen; **— to** müssen; **I had better** go es wäre besser, wenn ich ginge; **I had my hair cut** ich liess mir das Haar schneiden; **I had rather** go ich möchte lieber gehen

haven *n.* Hafen, Freistatt, Freistätte

havoc *n.* Verwüstung, Verheerung

hawk *n.* Habicht, Falke; — *v.* hökern, hausieren; **-er** *n.* Höker, Hausierer

hawk-eyed *adj.* falkenäugig; (fig.) scharfsichtig

hawthorn *n.* Weissdorn, Hagedorn

hay n. Heu; — **fever** Heuschnupfen, Heufieber

hayfield n. Heufeld

hayloft n. Heuboden

haymaker n. Heumacher, Heuwender; (sports sl.) ziellos kreisender Boxhieb

haystack n. Heuschober

haze n. Dunst, Nebel; Höhenrauch

hazel n. Haselbusch, Haselstrauch; nussbraun, hellbraun

hazy adj. neblig, dunstig; dunkel, nebelhaft, verschwommen

he pron. er

head n. Kopf, Haupt; Führer, Leiter; Chef, Vorstand; Stück; Kopfende, Oberteil; Quelle; Spitze, Vorderseite, Vorderteil; Titel(kopf); Überschrift; Vorgebirge, Landspitze; at the — oben; am oberen Ende; an der Spitze; by a — um Kopfeslänge; come to a — sich zuspitzen, zur Krise kommen; from — to foot von Kopf bis Fuss, von oben bis unten; go to one's — zu Kopfe steigen; — first Kopf voran; — of hair Haarwuchs; — over heels Hals über Kopf; —s or tails Kopf oder Wappen (or Adler); I can't make — or tail of it ich kann daraus nicht klug werden; keep one's — die Fassung bewahren; lose one's — den Kopf verlieren; out of one's — verrückt; put —s together die Köpfe zusammenstecken, sich beraten; take it into one's — sich in den Kopf setzen; — adj. erst, vorderst, vornehmst, hauptsächlich; — wind Gegenwind; — v. leiten, anführen, befehligen; an der Spitze stehen, der Erste sein; vorangehen; be —ed gehen; — for auf dem Wege sein nach; zusteuern auf; — off verhüten; —ing n. Titel, Überschrift; —less adj. kopflos; (fig.) ohne Oberhaupt; —y adj. übereilt, ungestüm; berauschend

headache n. Kopfschmerz(en)

headdress n. Kopfbedeckung; Kopfputz; Frisur

headgear n. Kopfschmuck; Kopfputz

headlight n. Scheinwerfer

headline n. Kopfzeile, Titelzeile

headlong adj. kopfüber; ungestüm, unbesonnen

headmaster n. Klassenlehrer

head-on adv. gerade entgegen

headpiece n. Kopfstück; (typ.) Kopfleiste; Zierleiste

headquarters n. Hauptquartier, Stabsquartier; police — Polizeidirektion

headset n. Kopfhörer

headstone n. Grabstein

headstrong adj. halsstarrig, hartnäckig

be — eigensinnig sein

headwaiter n. Oberkellner

headway n. Fortschritt, Erfolg; (naut.) Volldampf voraus; make — vorwärtskommen

heal v. heilen, wiederherstellen; genesen; versöhnen

health n. Gesundheit, Wohlbefinden; be in good — sich wohl befinden; be in poor — sich nicht wohl befinden, kränklich sein; -ful adj. gesund, wohl; heilsam, der Gesundheit zuträglich; -y adj. gesund, wohl

heap n. Haufe(n), Menge; Masse; — v. (an)häufen, aufhäufen; auftürmen, ansammeln, beladen

hear v. hören, erfahren; anhören, zuhören; hinhören, achtgeben; (law) verhören, gerichtlich untersuchen; -er n. Hörer; Zuhörer; -ing n. Gehör(sinn); Schallweite, Hörweite; (law) Verhör, Untersuchung; out of -ing ausser Hörweite

hearken v. horchen, lauschen, zuhören

hearsay n. Hörensagen, Gerücht, Gerede; by — vom Hörensagen

hearse n. Leichenwagen, Totenbahre

heart n. Herz; (fig.) Gemüt; Kern, Mitte, Mittelpunkt, Wesentliche; at — im Grunde (genommen); by — auswendig; get to the — of auf den Grund kommen; have the — es übers Herz bringen; — and soul mit Leib und Seele; lose — den Mut verlieren; my — fails me mein Mut sinkt; sick at — gemütskrank; take — Mut fassen; take to — beherzigen; to one's -'s content zur vollsten Zufriedenheit; with all my — von ganzem Herzen; — trouble Herzkrankheit, Herzbeschwerden; -iness n. Herzlichkeit, Aufrichtigkeit; Herzhaftigkeit; -less adj. herzlos, hartherzig, grausam, gefühllos; -y adj. herzlich, innig; aufrichtig; herzhaft; nahrhaft, kräftig

heartache n. Kummer, Herzensangst

heartbeat n. Herzschlag

heartbreak n. Herzenskummer, Herzeleid

heartbroken adj. tief bekümmert

heartburn n. Sodbrennen

heartfelt adj. innig, tief empfunden, aufrichtig

hearth n. Herd; (fig.) Heim, Familienkreis

hearthstone n. Herdstein; (fig.) Heim

heartsick adj. herzkrank; gemütskrank

heart-to-heart adj. freimütig, offen

heat n. Hitze, Glut; (sports) Einzelrennen; (zool.) Brunst, Läufigkeit; (fig.) Eifer, Erregung; dead — totes (or unentschiedenes) Rennen; in — brün-

stig, läufig; **prickly** — Hautausschlag;
— **shield** hitzefestes Panzerschild (bemannte Rakete); — **wave** Hitzewelle;
— v. (sich) erhitzen, erwärmen, heizen;
-er n. Heizvorrichtung, Ofen, Wärme-
apparat; **-ing** n. Heizung, Erwärmung;
central — Zentralheizung; **-ing pad**
Heizkissen
heath n. Heide
heathen n. Heide, Götzendiener
heat-resistant adj. feuerfest, hitzebe-
ständig
heave n. Heben, Aufheben; Wogen,
Schwellen; Keuchen, Seufzen; pl.
Engbrüstigkeit; — v. (sich) heben,
erheben; wogen, schwellen; ausstossen;
keuchen; (mech.) aufwinden, emporheben; (naut.) hieven, winden
heaven n. Himmel, Firmament; **-s!** interj.
(gerechter) Himmel! **-ly** adj. himmlisch; erhaben, heilig
heavily adv. schwer; träge, langsam; (fig.)
traurig
heaviness n. Schwere, Gewicht, Druck;
(fig.) Schwerfälligkeit, Langsamkeit;
Kummer
heavy adj. schwer, drückend; fett; schwerfällig; heftig, stark; (fig.) drückend,
lästig; **be** — fett sein; — **sea** hohe See
heavyweight n. Schwergewicht
heckle v. hecheln, frotzeln, necken; **-r** n.
Hechler, Frotzler; Stichler
hectic adj. hektisch
hedge n. Hecke, Zaun; — **sparrow** Gras-
mücke; — v. einzäunen, einhegen
hedgehog n. Igel
heed n. Aufmerksamkeit, Acht(ung); —
v. achtgeben auf, sorgfältig beachten;
-less adj. achtlos, unbekümmert
heel n. Ferse; (shoe) Absatz; (sl.) Schuft;
rubber — Gummiabsatz; **take to one's**
-s das Hasenpanier ergreifen, ausreissen; — v. — **over** sich auf die Seite
neigen; überholen
heifer n. Färse, junge Kuh, Sterke
height n. Höhe, Höhepunkt; Anhöhe,
Gipfel; **-en** v. erhöhen, vergrössern,
verstärken, steigern, vermehren
heir n. Erbe; — **apparent** rechtmässiger
Erbe; **-dom** n. Erbschaft; Erbanspruch,
Erbfolge; **-ess** n. Erbin; **-loom** n.
Erbstück
helibus n. Hubschrauber-Nahverkehr
helicopter n. Hubschrauber
hell n. Hölle; **-ish** adj. höllisch, abscheulich
hello! interj. Hallo!
helm n. Steuerruder; Helm
helmet n. Helm
help n. Hilfe, Beistand; Hilfsmittel;

Gehilfe, Arbeiter; (med.) Heilmittel,
Kur; — v. helfen, beistehen; behilflich
sein; verhelfen; reichen; bedienen;
abhelfen, vermeiden; — **oneself** sich
(selbst) bedienen; — **out** aushelfen, aus
der Not helfen; — **to** verhelfen zu;
— **yourself** langen Sie nur zu; **how can**
I — **it?** was kann ich dafür? **I cannot** —
it ich kann es nicht ändern; **-er** n.
Gehilfe, Helfer; Beistand; **-ful** adj.
hilfreich, behilflich; nützlich; **-ing** n.
Portion; **-less** adj. hilflos, ratlos
helpmate n. Gefährte, Gehilfe; Gatte,
Gattin
helter-skelter adv. holterdiepolter; **Hals**
über Kopf
hem n. Saum, Rand, Einfassung; — v.
säumen; räuspern, stottern; — **in**
umsäumen, einschliessen
hemisphere n. Halbkugel, Hemisphäre
hemlock n. Hemlocktanne, Schierlings-
tanne; Schierling
hemorrhage n. Blutsturz
hemorrhoids n. pl. Hämorrhoiden
hemp n. Hanf
hemstitch v. mit Hohlsaum verzieren
hen n. Henne, Huhn
hence adv. daher, deshalb; von hier, von
hinnen; fort, weg; von jetzt an, von
nun an
henceforth adv. von nun an, fort an,
hinfort
henchman n. feiler Anhänger
hencoop n. Hühnerstall; Hühnerkorb
henhouse n. Hühnerhaus
henpecked adj. unter dem Pantoffel
stehend
her pron. sie, ihr; **-s** pron. ihrer; der (or
die, das) ihrige; **a friend of -s** eine ihrer
Freundinnen
herald n. Herold; Bote, Ausrufer; **-ic** adj.
heraldisch; **-ry** n. Wappenkunde,
Heraldik
herb n. Kraut; **-age** n. Futterkräuter
Herculean adj. herkulisch
herd n. Herde, Rudel, Trupp; — v. in
Herden gehen, sich gesellen; **zu** einer
Herde vereinigen; **-er** n. Hirt
herdsman n. Hirt
here adv. hier, her; hierher, hierin; — **and**
there hier und dort; — **below** hienie-
den; **-'s to you!** auf dein Wohl! **that's**
neither — **nor there** das gehört nicht
zur Sache; **-'** adj. hiesig
hereabout(s) adv. hier herum, in dieser
Gegend
hereafter n. Zukunft, zukünftige Zustand; Jenseits; — **adv.** hiernach, in
Zukunft, künftig
hereat adv. hierbei, hierüber

hereby adv. hierdurch
hereditary adj. erblich; vererbbar; ererbt
heredity n. Vererbung; Erblichkeit
hereinafter adv. hierin nachstehend
heresy n. Ketzerei
heretic n. Ketzer; **-al** adj. ketzerisch
heretofore adv. vorhin; vordem, ehemals
hereupon adv. darauf, darauf hin
heritage n. Erbschaft, Erbe
hermetically adv. hermetisch. luftdicht
hermit n. Einsiedler, Eremit, Klausner;
  -age n. Einsiedelei, Klause
hernia n. Bruch
hero n. Held; Halbgott, Heros; **-ic** adj.
  heroisch, heldenmütig, tapfer; **-ics**
  n. pl. Heldenhafte; Hochtrabende,
  Übertriebene; **-ine** n. Heldin; **-ism** n.
  Heldenmut, Heroismus
herring n. Hering; **smoked — Bückling**
herringbone n. Fischgrätenmuster, Grä-
  tenstich
herself pron. (sie, ihr) selbst; sich; **by —**
  von selbst, allein; **she is not — sie fühlt
  sich nicht wohl**
hesitant adj. zögernd, zaudernd; unschlüssig; stockend
hesitate v. zögern, zaudern; unschlüssig
  sein; stocken
hesitation n. Zögern, Zaudern; Unschlüssigkeit; Stocken
heterogeneous adj. heterogen, ungleich,
  verschieden, fremdartig
heterosexual adj. heterosexuell, vom anderen Geschlecht angezogen
hew v. hacken
hexagon n. Sechseck
hexameter n. Hexameter, Sechsfuss
heyday n. Höhepunkt, Hochflut; Munterkeit
hiccup, hiccough n. Schlucken, Schluck-
  auf; **—** v. schlucken, den Schlucken
  haben
hidden adj. verborgen, geheim
hide n. Haut, Fell; **—** v. verbergen, verstecken; (fig.) verheimlichen
hide-and-seek n. Versteckspiel
hideous adj. scheusslich, schrecklich,
  grässlich, fürchterlich
hide-out n. Versteck, Schlupfwinkel
hiding n. Verbergen, Verborgenheit; **—**
  adj. verbergend; **— place Versteck,**
  Schlupfwinkel
hierarchy n. Hierarchie; Rangordnung
high adj. hoch, gross; erhaben, vornehm;
  stark; hochstrebend; (sl.) angetrunken;
  **— and dry auf dem Trockenen; — and
  low auf und ab; weit und breit; (fig.)**
  überall; **— frequency Hochfrequenz;
  High German Hochdeutsch; — light
  Hochpunkt, Höhepunkt; — school**

Mittelschule, höhere Schule; **— sea(s)**
offenes Meer; hochgehende See; **—
spirits gehobene Stimmung; — tension**
Hochspannung; **— tide Flut; — time**
höchste Zeit; **— treason Hochverrat;
— voltage Starkstrom; — water Hoch-**
wasser; **— wind starker Wind; — n.**
Hohe, Höhe; (auto.) Höchstgeschwindigkeit; höchster Gang; **-ly** adv. hoch,
sehr; höchst, höchlich; **-ness** n. Hoheit;
Höhe; Erhabenheit
highball n. Highball; Cocktail mit Eis
high-brow adj. hyperintellektuell; die
  geistige Überlegenheit fühlen lassend
highfalutin(g) adj. prahlend, schwülstig
high-flown adj. hochfliegend, aufgeblasen
high-grade adj. hochgradig
highhanded adj. anmassend, hochfahrend
highlight v. betonen. Nachdruck legen auf
high-minded adj. hochherzig, hochgesinnt
high-pitched adj. hoch; schrill, gellend
high-powered adj. **(an Pferdekräften)**
  stark (h.p.)
high-pressure adj. **Hochdruck-; auf-**
  dringlich
high-priced adj. sehr teuer
highroad n. Landstrasse
high-sounding adj. hochtönend, **hochtra-**
  bend
high-spirited adj. hochsinnig; trotzig,
  reizbar
high-strung adj. hochgespannt; übermütig
high-test adj. best erprobt
high-water mark n. Hochwassermarke
highway n. Landstrasse, Chaussee; **—
  robbery Strassenraub; (fig.) Betrug**
highwayman n. Strassenräuber
hike n. Fussmarsch, Wanderung; **— v.**
  wandern
hill n. Hügel, kleiner Berg; Haufen; **-y**
  adj. hügelig
hillside n. Bergabhang
hilltop n. Bergspitze
him pron. ihn, ihm
himself pron. (er, or ohn, ihm, sich) **selbst**
hinder v. (ver)hindern; aufhalten
hindmost adj. hinterst, letzt
hindquarter n. Hinterviertel, Hinterteil
hindrance n. Hindernis, Verhinderung;
  Schaden, Nachteil
hinge n. Angel, Scharnier; (fig.) Angel-
  punkt, Hauptpunkt; **— v. — on ab-**
  hängen von; sich drehen um
hint n. Wink, Fingerzeig; Andeutung,
  Anspielung; **take a — sich gesagt sein**
  lassen; **— v. andeuten, zu verstehen**
  geben; **— at anspielen auf**
hip n. Hüfte; (bot.) Hagebutte; **— roof**
  Walmdach, Satteldach

hipbone n. Hüftbein, Hüftknochen

hippopotamus n. Flusspferd, Nilpferd

hire n. Miete; Lohn, Arbeitslohn; **for —** zu vermieten; **—** v. mieten, pachten; dingen; (naut.) heuern; **-ling** n. Mietling

his pron. sein, seiner; der (or die, das) seinige

hiss v. zischen; pfeifen; auszischen; **-ing** n. Zischen, Gezische

historian n. Historiker, Geschichtsschreiber

historic(al) adj. historisch, geschichtlich

history n. Geschichte

hit n. Schlag, Stoss, Streich; Glücksfall; (mus.) Schlager; (sports) Treffer; (theat.) Erfolg(sschlager); **—** v. schlagen, stossen; treffen, erraten

hitch n. Ruck, Zuck; Haken, Schwierigkeit; **—** v. anbinden, festmachen; (naut.) festknoten

hitchhike v. trampen, als Anhalter reisen

hive n. Bienenstock, Bienernkorb; Bienenschwarm; pl. Hautausschlag, Nesselfieber

hoard n. Schatz, Vorrat, Hort; **—** v. aufhäufen, horten, hamstern

hoarfrost n. Rauhreif

hoarse adj. heiser, rauh; misstönend; **-ness** n. Heiserkeit, Rauheit

hoary adj. eisgrau, altersgrau; weisslich; ehrwürdig

hoax n. Täuschung, Finte, Fopperei; (newspaper sl.) Ente; **—** v. foppen, täuschen

hobble v. hinken, humpeln; (an den Füssen) fesseln

hobby n. Steckenpferd, Liebhaberei

hobbyhorse n. Steckenpferd

hobnail n. Sohlennagel

hobnob v. auf vertrautem Fuss stehen; zusammen zechen

hobo n. Landstreicher, Vagabund

hockey n. Hockey

hodgepodge n. Mischmasch; Eintopfgericht

hoe n. Hacke, Haue; **—** v. hacken, behacken; anhäufeln

hog n. Schwein; (fig.) Schmutzfink; **-gish** adj. schweinisch, schmutzig; gierig, gefrässig

hogshead n. Oxhoft; Packfass

hoist n. Kran, Aufzug; **—** v. hochziehen, aufziehen, aufwinden; (naut.) hissen; **— a drink** einen kippen

hold n. Halt; Griff; Macht, Gewalt; Haft; (mil.) Festung; (naut.) Laderaum; **get — of** ergreifen; **take — of** anfassen; **—** v. halten, fassen, greifen; besitzen, festhalten; anhalten; einhalten; veranstalten, abhalten; gelten; (mus.) anhalten; **— forth** zu ausführlich vortragen (or darbieten); **— good** gelten, sich bewähren; **— no water** nicht Stich halten; **— off** abhalten; **— office** ein Amt bekleiden; **— on** anhalten, fortsetzen; **— one's own** sich behaupten, standhalten; **— one's tongue** schweigen, den Mund halten; **— out against** sich widersetzen; **— over** verbleiben; **— true** sich als wahr bestätigen; **— up** aufhalten; stützen; überfallen; **-er** n. Halter, Behälter; Inhaber, Besitzer; **cigar —** Zigarrenspitze; **-ing** n. Halten; Besitz; **-ing** adj. haltend; **-ing company** Dachgesellschaft (von Konzernen)

holdup n. Raubüberfall; Aufschub

hole n. Loch, Höhle, Grube; (coll.) Klemme, Patsche

holiday n. Feiertag, Festtag; freier Tag; **half —** Halbfeiertag; pl. Ferien, Urlaubszeit

holiness n. Heiligkeit; Frömmigkeit

hollow n. Höhle, Höhlung; Loch, Grube; (mech.) Nut, Rinne; **—** adj. hohl, leer; (fig.) falsch, wertlos; **—** v. aushöhlen, hohl machen

hollyhock n. Stockrose

holster n. Halfter

holy adj. heilig; fromm, tugendhaft; **— water** Weihwasser; **Holy Week** Karwoche

home n. Heim; Haus, Haus, Wohnung, Wohnort, Geburtsort; (sports) Ziel; **at —** zu Hause, daheim; **charity begins at —** jeder ist sich selbst der Nächste; **—** adj. heimisch, einheimisch; inländisch; häuslich; derb, tüchtig; (sports) nahe dem Ziel, das Ziel erreichend; **— economics** Hauswirtschaftslehre; **— plate** Ausgangsbasis, Zielbasis; **— rule** Selbst-regierung; **— run** Vierbasisrunde; **— town** Vaterstadt, Heimatstadt; **—** adv. nach Hause, heim; zurück; daheim; **— strike** den Nagel auf den Kopf treffen; **-less** adj. heimatlos; obdachlos; **-like** adj. heimisch, gemütlich; wie zu Hause; **-liness** n. Einfachheit, Schlichtheit; **-ly** adj. einfach, schlicht; hausbacken; hässlich

homeland n. Heimat(land)

homemade adj. zu Hause (or selbst) gemacht

homemaker n. Hausweib, Hausfrau

homeopathy n. Homöopathie

homesick adj. Heimweh habend; **-ness** n. Heimweh

homespun n. Homespun, rauhhaariges Wollgewebe; **—** adj. zu Hause (or selbst) gesponnen homestead *n.* Heimstätte; Grundeigentum; Gehöft

homestretch *n.* Zielgerade

homeward(s) *adv.* heimwärts, nach Hause

homework *n.* Heimarbeit, Hausarbeit

homicide *n.* Mord, Totschlag

homily *n.* Kanzelrede, Lehrpredigt

homing *n.* (avi.) Zielfindung; Eigenpeilung

homing pigeon *n.* Brieftaube

hominy *n.* (grob gemahlener) Mais, Maisbrei

homogeneous *adj.* homogen, gleichartig

homogenized *adj.* homogenisiert; neutralisiert (Fettgehalt in Milchprodukten)

homosexual *adj.* homosexuell

honest *adj.* ehrlich, redlich; aufrichtig; –y *n.* Ehrlichkeit, Redlichkeit, Aufrichtigkeit

honey *n.* Honig; (fig.) Süssigkeit, Lieblichkeit; (coll.) Herzchen, Täubchen; –ed *adj.* mit Honig bedeckt; (fig.) süss, lieblich

honeybee *n.* Honigbiene

honeycomb *n.* Honigwabe, Honigzelle

honeydew melon *n.* weisse Zuckermelone

honeymoon *n.* Flitterwochen

honeysuckle *n.* Geissblatt, Jelängerjelieber

honk *n.* Hupe; — *v.* hupen, tuten; — the horn hupen

honor *n.* Ehre; Achtung, Hochachtung; Rechtschaffenheit; Keuschheit; Auszeichnung, Ehrenzeichen; *pl.* Honneurs, Ehrenbezeigungen; in his — ihm zu Ehren; point of — Ehrenpunkt; word of — Ehrenwort; Your Honor Euer Ehrwürden; — *v.* ehren, achten; verehren, hochachten; auszeichnen; (com.) honorieren, anerkennen; –able *adj.* ehrenvoll, rühmlich; ehrenhaft; rechtschaffen, redlich; ehrbar; –ary *adj.* ehrend; –ary degree akademischer Ehrengrad; –ary doctor Ehrendoktor, Doktor ehrenhalber (Dr. h.c.)

honorarium *n.* Honorar; Gebühren

hood *n.* Kapuze, Kappe; (mech.) Haube, Deckel; — *v.* verkappen

hoodlum *n.* Strolch, Raufbold

hoodoo *n.* Unheilbringer; — *v.* Unheil bringen

hoodwink *v.* täuschen

hoof *n.* Huf, Klaue; —-and-mouth disease Maul und Klauenseuche

hook *n.* Haken; Türangel; (agr.) Sichel; by — or by crook es mag biegen oder brechen; so oder so; –s and eyes Haken und Ösen; — *v.* anhaken, festhaken, einhaken, zuhaken; angeln; stehlen, klemmen; (sports) Haken schlagen; — on anhaken; — up einstellen; anhaken;

anspannen; –ed *adj.* krumm, hakenförmig, hakig; –ed rug handgeknüpfter Teppich

hookup *n.* (rad.) Ringsendung

hookworm *n.* Hakenwurm

hoop *n.* Tonnenband, Fassreifen; Ring; — skirt Reifrock

hoot *n.* Geschrei, Geheul; — *v.* schreien, heulen, auszischen

hop *n.* Hupf, Sprung; *pl.* Hopfen; — *v.* hopsen, hüpfen, springen; Hopfen ernten

hope *n.* Hoffnung, Vertrauen, Zuversicht; he is past all — es ist aus mit ihm, für ihn ist nichts mehr zu hoffen; — against — verzweifelt hoffen; — *v.* hoffen, vertrauen; — for the best das Beste hoffen; — *adj.* — chest Ausstattungstruhe; –ful *adj.* hoffnungsvoll, vielversprechend; –ful *n.* vielversprechender Junge; –less *adj.* hoffnungslos, verzweifelt

hopper *n.* Trichterkasten; Spülkasten

horde *n.* Horde, Bande

horizon *n.* Horizont, Gesichtskreis

horizontal *adj.* waagerecht, horizontal

hormone *n.* Hormon, Drüsensekret

horn *n.* Horn; Geweih; (ast.) Mondsichel; (auto.) Hupe; –ed *adj.* gehörnt; gekrümmt; –ed owl Ohreule, Uhu; –y *adj.* hörnern, hornig; Horn-

hornet *n.* Hornisse

hornpipe *n.* Hornpfeife; Matrosentanz

horoscope *n.* Horoskop; Gestirnstand

horrible *adj.* schrecklich, fürchterlich; entsetzlich, grässlich

horrid *adj.* scheusslich, abscheulich

horrify *v.* erschrecken, entsetzen; erschauern lassen

horror *n.* Greuel, Schrecken; Schauder, Grausen

horror-stricken *adj.* von Entsetzen ergriffen; von Schreck erfasst

hors d'oeuvre *n.* Hors d'oeuvre, Vorspeise, Nebengericht

horse *n.* Pferd, Ross, Gaul; (mech.) Gestell, Gerüst, Bock; black — Rappe; bay — Fuchs; get on one's high — sich aufs hohe Pferd setzen; white — Schimmel; — chestnut Rosskastanie; — race Pferderennen

horseback *n.* on — zu Pferde

horsefly *n.* Pferdebremse

horsehair *n.* Rosshaar, Pferdehaar

horsehide *n.* Pferdehaut

horselaugh *n.* wieherndes Lachen; Gewieher

horseman *n.* Reiter; –ship *n.* Reitkunst

horseplay *n.* derber Spass, grober Witz

horsepower *n.* Pferdekraft, Pferdestärke

horse-radish n. Meerrettich

horseshoe n. Hufeisen

hose n. Strumpf; Schlauch; — v. mit einem Schlauch bespritzen

hosiery n. Strumpfwaren

hospitable adj. gastlich, fastfreundlich, gastfrei

hospital n. Krankenhaus; Hospital, Spital; (mil.) Lazarett; — ward Krankenhausabteilung; —ity n. Gastfreundschaft, Gastfreiheit; —ization n. Krankenhausunterbringung; —ization insurance Krankenkasse, Kranken-(haus)versicherung

host n. Wirt, Gastgeber; Menge, Schwarm; (rel.) Messopfer, Hostie; —age n. Geisel, Bürge; —ess n. Wirtin; Gastgeberin

hostel n. Gasthof, Herberge; Studentenheim

hostile adj. feindlich, feindselig

hot adj. heiss; hitzig, heftig; eifrig; scharf, stark gewürzt; noch frisch; be in — water in der Patsche stecken; — air Heissluft; (coll.) blauer Dunst; — dog heisse Frankfurter (Würstchen); grow — erhitzen

hotbed n. Mistbeet, Pflanzstätte; (fig.) Brutstätte

hot-blooded adj. heissblütig

hotbox n. (rail.) heissgelaufener Getriebekasten

hotel n. Hotel, Gasthof

hothouse n. Treibhaus

hot-rod n. Amateurrennwagen

hot-tempered adj. heissblütig, jähzornig

hot-water bottle n. Wärmflasche

hound n. Jagdhund, Hetzhund, Spürhund; (coll.) Hund; — v. jagen, hetzen, verfolgen

hour n. Stunde; Zeit; Uhr; pl. Dienststunden; Horen, Stundengebete; for —s stundenlang; — hand Stundenzeiger; —ly adv. stündlich; häufig, fortwährend; —ly adj. stündlich, häufig

house n. Haus; Wohnhaus; Wohnung, Wohnsitz; Haushalt; Geschlecht, Familie; (com.) Handelshaus, Firma; (pol.) Kammer, Parlament; (theat.) Publikum; — of cards Kartenhaus; — of correction Besserungsanstalt; House of Representatives Repräsentantenhaus; Abgeordnetenhaus; — party Hausgesellschaft; keep — den Haushalt führen; — v. hausen, wohnen

houseboat n. Hausboot

housefly n. Stubenfliege

household n. Haushalt(ung); — goods Hauseinrichtung; Haushaltungsgegenstände; — management Hauswirt-

schaft; -er n. Haushaltungsvorstand, Familienoberhaupt, Hausvater; Hausherr

housekeeper n. Haushälterin, Wirtschafterin

housekeeping n. Haushaltung; — money Wirtschaftsgeld

housemaid n. Hausmädchen

housemate n. Hausgenosse

housetop n. Dach

housewarming n. Einzugsfeier

housewife n. Hausfrau

housework n. Haushaltsarbeit

housing n. Obdach; Wohnung; (mech.) Gehäuse; — shortage Wohnungsnot

hovel n. Schuppen; Hütte

hover v. schweben; verweilen, zögern

how adv. and interr. wie, auf welche Weise, warum; — are you? wie geht es Ihnen? — come? wieso? wie kommt das? — do you do? guten Tag! — goes it? wie steht's? — is it? wie kommt es? — many? wieviele? how much? wieviel?

however adv. jedoch, dennoch; wie auch immer, jedenfalls; nichtsdestoweniger

howitzer n. Haubitze

howl n. Geheul; — v. heulen; wehklagen

howsoever adv. wie sehr auch immer; gleichwohl

hub n. Nabe; (fig.) Mittelpunkt

hubbub n. Lärm, Tumult

huckleberry n. Heidelbeerenart

huckster n. Höker, Hausierer

huddle n. Zusammenkauern; (football) Beratung (während des Zusammenkauerns); — v. sich schieben (or drängen); — together sich zusammendrängen

hue n. Färbung, Farbe; Schrei, Geschrei; — and cry Zetergeschrei; Verbrecherjagd

hug n. Umarmung; — v. umarmen, umfassen, liebkosen, hätscheln; (naut.) dicht anfahren

huge adj. riesig, kolossal, ungeheuer; unermesslich

hull n. (bot.) Hülse, Hülle, Schale; (naut.) Schiffsrumpf, Unterschiff; — v. schälen, enthülsen

hullabaloo n. Wirrwarr, Tumult, Tohuwabohu

hum n. Summen, Gesumme; Gebrumme, Gemurmel; — v. summen, brummen; (fig.) in Erregung sein

human n. Mensch; — adj. menschlich; — being Mensch; -e adj. human, menschenfreundlich; gutmütig, leutselig; humanistisch, philologisch; -ism n. Humanismus; Menschlichkeit; -itarian n. Menschenfreund; (phil. and rel.)

Leugner der Gottheit Christi; **-itarian** *adj.* menschenfreundlich; **-ity** *n.* Menschheit; Humanität, Milde; Menschlichkeit, Menschenliebe; **-ize** *v.* vermenschlichen; Menschenliebe einflössen; menschlich werden (*or* machen), gesittet werden (*or* machen)

humankind *n.* Menschengeschlecht

humble *adj.* bescheiden, anspruchslos, demütig; niedrig, nieder, gering; — *v.* erniedrigen, demütigen; unterwerfen; **-ness** *n.* Demut, Bescheidenheit

humbug *n.* Humbug, Unsinn

humdrum *adj.* eintönig, uninteressant, langweilig

humid *adj.* nass, feucht; **-ify** *v.* (be)nässen, anfeuchten; **-ity** *n.* Nässe, Feuchtigkeit; *or n.* Einrichtung zur Aufrechterhaltung der Luftfeuchtigkeit

humiliate *v.* demütigen, erniedrigen

humiliation *n.* Demütigung, Erniedrigung

humility *n.* Demut, Bescheidenheit; Unterwürfigkeit

hummingbird *n.* Kolibri

humor *n.* Humor; Stimmung, Laune; **bad** — schlechte Laune; — *v.* willfahren, sich anpassen; gefällig sein; den Willen lassen; **-ist** *n.* Humorist, Spassvogel; **-ous** *adj.* humoristisch, launig, spasshaft

hump *n.* Buckel, Höcker

humpbacked *adj.* bucklig, höckerig

humus *n.* Humus

hunch *n.* Buckel, Höcker; (coll.) Ahnung; — *v.* krümmen

hunchback *n.* Buckel; Bucklige; **-ed** *adj.* bucklig, höckerig

hundred *n.* Hundert(er); — *adj.* hundert; **-fold** *adj.* hundertfach; **-th** *n.* Hundertste; Hundertstel; **-th** *adj.* hundertst

hundredweight *n.* Zentner

hunger *n.* Hunger; heftiges Verlangen; — *adj.* — **strike** Hungerstreik; — *v.* hungern, darben; verlangen (nach)

hungry *adj.* hungrig; verhungert; (fig.) begierig; **be** — Hunger haben

hunk *n.* grosses (*or* dickes) Stück

hunt *n.* Jagd; (fig.) Nachsetzen, Verfolgen, Suchen; — *v.* jagen, hetzen; abjagen, durchjagen; nachsetzen, verfolgen; — **for** suchen; **-er** *n.* Jäger; **-ing** *n.* Jagd; **-ing license** Jagdschein

hurdle *n.* Hürde; *pl.* Hürden, Hindernisse; Hindernisrennen

hurdy-gurdy *n.* Leierkasten, Drehorgel

hurl *v.* werfen, schleudern; (fig.) ausstossen, heftig äussern

hurly-burly *n.* Tumult, Tohuwabohu

hurrah! *interj.* hurra! — *n.* Hurra

hurricane *n.* Hurrikan, Orkan, Wirbel-

sturm

hurried *adj.* übereilt, schnell

hurry *n.* Eile, Hast; Übereilung; Unruhe; **be in a** — es eilig haben; — *v.* sich beeilen; beschleunigen, übereilen; hasten; — **away** entführen; — **back** eilig zurückkommen; — **on** antreiben; — **over** schnell hinweggehen über; — up eilen, sich beeilen

hurt *n.* Verwundung, Verletzung; Schaden, Nachteil; Übel; — *v.* verletzen; weh tun, schmerzen; schädigen, schaden; — *adj.* verletzt, verwundet

husband *n.* Mann, Gatte; — *v.* sparsam umgehen mit; **-ry** *n.* Landwirtschaft

hush *n.* Ruhe; Stille; — **money** Schweigegeld; —! *interj.* still! st! pst! — *v.* zum Schweigen bringen; (fig.) besänftigen; — up vertuschen

husk *n.* Schale, Hülse, Schote; — *v.* schälen, enthülsen

huskiness *n.* Heiserkeit, Rauheit (der Stimme)

husky *n.* Eskimohund; — *adj.* rauh, heiser, trocken; (coll.) kräftig

hustle *v.* stossen, drängen; sich drängen

hut *n.* Hütte; (mil.) Baracke

hybrid *n.* Bastard, Mischling; Kreuzung, Hybride; — *adj.* hybrid

hydraulic *adj.* hydraulisch; — **engineering** Wasserbau; **-s** *n.* Hydraulik

hydrochloric *adj.* salzsauer; — **acid** Chlorwasserstoff, Salzsäure

hydroelectric *adj.* hydroelektrisch

hydrogen *n.* Wasserstoff; — **bomb** Wasserstoffbombe; — **peroxide** Wasserstoffsuperoxyd

hydromatic *adj.* (system) automatisches hydraulisches System

hydronics *n.* Lehre vom Erhitzen and kühlen von Flüssigkeiten

hydroplane *n.* Wasserflugzeug; Rennboot

hyena *n.* Hyäne

hygiene *n.* Hygiene, Gesundheitslehre

hygienic *adj.* hygienisch

hymn *n.* Choral; **-al** *n.* Gesangbuch

hypergolic (self-igniting fuel) *n.* selbstzündender Treibstoff; — **ignition** *n.* Selbstzündung

hypersensitive *adj.* überempfindlich

hypersonic (5 Mach or more) *adj.* schneller als die 5malige Schallgeschwindigkeit

hypertension *n.* Überspannung, Überanspannung

hyphen *n.* Bindestrich; **-ate** *v.* mit Bindestrich schreiben (*or* verbinden)

hypnosis *n.* Hypnose

hypnotism *n.* Hypnotismus

hypnotist *n.* Hypnotiseur

hypnotize *v.* hypnotisieren; einschläfern

hypocrisy *n.* Heuchelei
hypocrite *n.* Heuchler, Scheinheilige; Hypokrit
hypocritical *adj.* heuchlerisch, scheinheilig
hypodermic *adj.* unter der Haut liegend; — **injection** Einspritzung unter die Haut; — **syringe** hypodermische Spritze
hypothesis *n.* Hypothese
hypothetical *adj.* hypothetisch
hysteria *n.* Hysterie
hysteric(al) *adj.* hysterisch; (fig.) launisch
hysterics *n. pl.* hysterischer Anfall; hysterischer Lachkrampf

I

I *pron.* ich
iambic *adj.* jambisch
ICBM (intercontinental ballistic missile) *n.* interkontinentales Fernlenkgeschoss
ice *n.* Eis; Gefrorenes; — **age** Eiszeit; — **bag** Eisbeutel; — **cream** Speiseeis, Gefrorenes; — **hockey** Eishockey; — **pack** Packeis, Treibeis; (med.) Eisbeutel; — **pick** Eispickel; — **skate** Schlittschuh; Schlittschuhlaufen; — **water** Eiswasser; — *v.* glasieren, mit Zuckerguss versehen, überzuckern; gefrieren, mit Eis bedecken
iceberg *n.* Eisberg
iceboat *n.* Segelschlitten
icebound *adj.* Eis umschlossen, zugefroren
icebox *n.* Eisschrank, Eiskiste
icebreaker *n.* Eisbrecher
icehouse *n.* Gefrierhaus, Eiskeller
Iceland *n.* Island
iceman *n.* Eishändler; Eisarbeiter
ichthyology *n.* Fischkunde
icicle *n.* Eiszapfen
icing *n.* Zuckerguss, Zuckerglasur
Iconoscope *n.* Ikonoskop, Elektronenstrahlabtaster
icy *adj.* eisig; (fig.) kühl, kalt
idea *n.* Idee, Begriff, Vorstellung; Ahnung, Einfall; (mus.) Thema; **clever** — guter Einfall; **he has no** — er hat keine Ahnung; **the** — **of such a thing!** stell sich einer das vor!
ideal *n.* Ideal, Vorbild, Muster; — *adj.* ideal, vorbildlich, mustergültig; ideell; eingebildet; **-ism** *n.* Idealismus; **-ist** *n.* Idealist; **-istic** *adj.* idealistisch; **-ize** *v.* idealisieren
identical *adj.* identisch, gleichbedeutend
identification *n.* Identifikation, Identifizierung; — **card** Personalausweis; — **papers** Personalpapiere
identify *v.* identifizieren; — **oneself** sich ausweisen
identity *n.* Identität; Persönlichkeit; Eigenart
ideology *n.* Ideologie, Begriffslehre
idiocy *n.* Idiotie, Verstandesschwäche, Blödsinn
idiom *n.* Idiom, Mundart, Dialekt; Spracheigentümlichkeit; **-atic(al)** *adj.* idiomatisch, mundartlich
idiot *n.* Idiot, Schwachsinnige; **-ic** *adj.* idiotisch, schwachsinnig
idle *adj.* unbeschäftigt, untätig, müssig; faul, arbeitsscheu; eitel, leer; — *v.* faulenzen, müssig gehen; vertändeln; (mech.) leerlaufen; **-ness** *n.* Müssiggang, Musse; Trägheit, Faulheit; **-r** *n.* Müssiggänger, Faulenzer
idol *n.* Idol, Abgott; Götzenbild; Trugbild; **-atry** *n.* Abgötterei, Götzendienst; **-ize** *v.* vergöttern
idyl(l) *n.* Idyll(e); **-lic** *adj.* idyllisch
if *conj.* wenn, falls, wofern; ob, wiewohl, obschon; — **not** wo nicht, wenn nicht; — **so** in diesem Fall
igloo *n.* Iglu, Eskimohütte
ignite *v.* anzünden, entzünden; (chem.) erhitzen
ignition *n.* Zündung; Entzündung, Verbrennung; Erhitzung; — **spark** Zündfunke; — **switch** Zündhebel, Zündungsschalter
ignoble *adj.* gering, wertlos; unedel, unwürdig, niedrig
ignoramus *n.* Ignorant, Nichtswisser
ignorance *n.* Unwissenheit, Ignoranz, Unkenntniss; (fig.) Einfältigkeit
ignorant *adj.* unwissend, unkundig, ignorant
ignore *v.* keine Notiz nehmen, nicht beachten, ignorieren; nicht wissen (*or* kennen)
ill *n.* Übel; Laster, Bosheit; Unglück; — *adj.* krank; übel, schlecht; **become** — erkranken; — **at ease** unruhig, unbehaglich; — *adv.* schwerlich, kaum; **-ness** *n.* Krankheit, Unpässlichkeit
ill-advised *adj.* schlecht beraten
ill-bred *adj.* schlecht erzogen; ungebildet
ill-disposed *adj.* schlecht gelaunt; übelgesinnt
illegal *adj.* illegal, ungesetzlich, widerrechtlich
illegible *adj.* unleserlich
illegitimate *adj.* unehelich, illegitim; unrechtmässig
ill-gotten *adj.* unrechtmässig (*or* unehrlich) erworben
ill-health *n.* Unwohlsein, Unpässlichkeit
ill-humored *adj.* schlecht gelaunt
illicit *adj.* unerlaubt, verboten; unzulässig

illimitable *adj.* unbegrenzbar, grenzenlos

illiteracy *n.* Analphabetentum; Unwissenheit, Ungelehrtheit

illiterate *adj.* des Schreibens und Lesens unkundig; unwissend, ungebildet

ill-mannered *adj.* schlecht gesittet, taktlos

ill-natured *adj.* bosartig, boshaft; verdriesslich

illogical *adj.* unlogisch

ill-pleased *adj.* unzufrieden, missvergnügt

ill-starred *adj.* zum Unglück bestimmt, unglücklich

ill-tempered *adj.* verdriesslich, mürrisch

ill-timed *adj.* ungelegen

illuminate *v.* illuminieren, erhellen, beleuchten; (fig.) aufklären

illumination *n.* Illumination, Erhellung, Beleuchtung; (fig.) Aufklärung

illumine *v.* erleuchten; erläutern

illusion *n.* Illusion, Blendwerk, Wahnbild; (physiol.) Sinnestäuschung

illustrate *v.* illustrieren, erklären; bebildern; -d *adj.* illustriert; erklärt; bebildert

illustration *n.* Illustration; Illustrierung, Erklärung; Bebilderung

illustrative *adj.* erläuternd, erklärend

illustrator *n.* Illustrator, Illustrierende

illustrious *adj.* berühmt, glänzend, ausgezeichnet

image *n.* Bild(nis), Abbild, Ebenbild; -ry *n.* Bildwerk; bildliche Rede, lebhafte Schilderung

imaginable *adj.* denkbar, erdenklich

imaginary *adj.* eingebildet, imaginär

imagination *n.* Einbildung(skraft)

imaginative *adj.* erfinderisch; Einbildungs-

imagine *v.* sich einbilden, sich vorstellen; ersinnen, (er)denken; meinen; just —I denk nur!

imbecile *n.* Schwachsinnige; — *adj.* geistesschwach, schwachsinnig

imbibe *v.* einsaugen, einziehen; schlürfen

imbue *v.* einweichen, durchnetzen; tränken; tief färben

imitate *v.* nachahmen, nachmachen, imitieren

imitation *n.* Nachahmung, Imitation; — leather Kunstleder

imitator *n.* Nachahmer, Imitator

immaculate *adj.* unbefleckt, rein

immature *adj.* unreif; vorzeitig, verfrüht

immeasurable *adj.* unmessbar, unermesslich

immediate *adj.* unmittelbar, direkt; sofortig, unverzüglich; -ly *adv.* sogleich, augenblicklich, sofort

immense *adj.* unermesslich, ungeheuer

immensity *n.* Unermesslichkeit

immerse *v.* eintauchen, versenken; (fig.) vertiefen

immersion *n.* Eintauchen, Versenkung; (fig.) Vertiefung

immigrant *n.* Immigrant, Einwanderer

immigrate *v.* einwandern

immigration *n.* Einwanderung

immoderate *adj.* übermässig, unmässig, masslos

immodest *adj.* unbescheiden, anmassend; unanständig

immoral *adj.* unmoralisch, unsittlich; -ity *n.* Unmoral, Unsittlichkeit

immortal *adj.* unsterblich, unvergänglich; -ity *n.* Unsterblichkeit; -ize *v.* unsterblich machen (or werden); verewigen

immovable *adj.* unbeweglich; unabänderlich; (fig.) unerschütterlich; -s *n. pl.* Immobilien, Liegenschaften

immune *adj.* immun, unempfindlich; geschützt

immunity *n.* Befreiung, Freiheit; (med.) Unempfänglichkeit, Immunität

immunize *v.* immunisieren

imp *n.* Kobold; Schelm; -ish *adj.* koboldartig, teuflisch

impact *n.* Stoss, Aufschlag; — velocity Aufschlag (Anschlag) Geschwindigkeit

impair *v.* verschlechtern, verschlimmern; beinträchtigen

impale *v.* pfählen, aufspiessen, festnageln

impalpable *adj.* unfühlbar; (fig.) unfassbar

impart *v.* mitteilen; erteilen, verleihen, geben

impartial *adj.* unparteiisch; gerecht; -ity *n.* Unparteilichkeit, Objektivität

impassable *adj.* ungangbar, unwegsam

impassioned *adj.* erregt, leidenschaftlich

impassive *adj.* unempfindlich, gefühllos; unbeweglich

impatience *n.* Ungeduld; Unduldsamkeit

impatient *adj.* ungeduldig, unduldsam

impeach *v.* in Frage stellen, anfechten, anzweifeln; zur Verantwortung ziehen, beschuldigen, anklagen

impede *v.* verhindern, erschweren

impediment *n.* Hindernis

impel *v.* antreiben, vorwärtstreiben; drängen

impend *v.* (über)hängen, schweben; (fig.) bevorstehen, drohen

impenetrable *adj.* undurchdringlich; (fig.) unerforschlich, unergründlich

impenitent *adj.* unbussfertig, vorstockt

imperative *adj.* befehlend, gebietend; notwendig, dringend; — *n.* Imperativ, Befehlsform

imperceptible *adj.* unmerklich; verschwindend klein

imperfect *adj.* unvollkommen, unvollständig; mangelhaft; — *n.* Imperfekt(um); **-ion** *n.* Unvollkommenheit; Mangelhaftigkeit; Gebrechen

imperial *adj.* kaiserlich; grossartig; Reichs-; **-ism** *n.* Kaisertum; (fig.) Imperialismus, Weltherrschaftspolitik; **-ist** *n.* Kaisertreue; (fig.) Imperialist, Anhänger der Weltherrschaftspolitik

imperil *v.* gefährden

imperious *adj.* herrisch, herrschsüchtig, gebieterisch; herrschend; dringend

imperishable *adj.* unvergänglich, unzerstörbar

impersonal *adj.* unpersönlich

impersonate *v.* verkörpern; (theat.) darstellen

impersonation *n.* Personifikation, Verkörperung; (theat.) Darstellung

impertinence *n.* Frechheit, Unverschämtheit; Impertinenz

impertinent *adj.* frech, unverschämt

impervious *adj.* unzugänglich, undurchdringlich, undurchlässig

impetuous *adj.* ungestüm, heftig

impetus *n.* Antrieb

impious *adj.* ruchlos, gottlos, ehrfurchtslos

implacable *adj.* unerbittlich, unversöhnlich; unbarmherzig

implant *v.* einpflanzen, einimpfen

implement *n.* Werkzeug, Gerät; Hilfsmittel, Zubehör; — *v.* ausführen, erfüllen

implicate *v.* verwickeln, hineinziehen

implication *n.* Verwicklung; Teilnahme; Folgerung

implicit *adj.* verwickelt, stillschweigend; (fig.) unbedingt, blind

implied *adj.* miteinbegriffen, gefolgert

implore *v.* (an)flehen; erbitten, erflehen

imply *v.* umfassen, bedeuten; andeuten

impolite *adj.* unhöflich, ungesittet

import *n.* Import, Einfuhr; Bedeutung, Wichtigkeit; Tragweite; — duties Einfuhrzoll; — *v.* importieren, einführen; (fig.) bedeuten, besagen; **-ance** *n.* Wichtigkeit; Bedeutsamkeit, Einfluss; Gewicht, Anmassung; **-ant** *adj.* wichtig, bedeutsam; anmassend; **-ation** *n.* Import, Wareneinfuhr; Einfuhr(artikel); Zufuhr; **-er** *n.* Importeur

impose *v.* auferlegen, aufbürden; — upon ausnutzen, missbrauchen; täuschen

imposing *adj.* eindrucksvoll, achtunggebietend; imposant, grossartig

imposition *n.* Auferlegung, Auflage, Steuer; Bürde, Zumutung; Betrug, Täuschung

impossibility *n.* Unmöglichkeit

impossible *adj.* unmöglich

impost *n.* Auflage, Abgabe; Steuer, Zoll

impostor *n.* Betrüger

imposture *n.* Betrug, Betrügerei

impotence *n.* Unvermögen, Unfähigkeit; (med.) Impotenz, Zeugungsunfähigkeit

impotent *adj.* unfähig, hinfällig; (med.) zeugungsunfähig, impotent

impound *v.* einpferchen, einschliessen; (law) in Verwahrung nehmen

impracticable *adj.* unausführbar; unbrauchbar; ungangbar

impractical *adj.* unpraktisch

impregnable *adj.* uneinnehmbar, unüberwindlich

impregnate *v.* schwängern, befruchten; (chem.) imprägnieren, durchtränken

impress *n.* Eindruck, Merkmal; Abdruck, Aufdruck; — *v.* Eindruck machen, beeindrucken; eindrücken; **-ion** *n.* Eindruck; Gepräge, Stempel; (typ.) Abdruck, Abzug, Auflage; give the **-ion** den Eindruck machen; **-ionable** *adj.* empfänglich, leicht zu beeinflussen; **-ive** *adj.* eindrucksvoll; nachdrucksvoll, ergreifend

imprint *n.* Aufdruck, Druckvermerk; printer's — Druckereiangabe; publisher's — Verlagsangabe; — *v.* aufdrücken, abdrucken, (ein)prägen

imprison *v.* ins Gefängnis setzen, einkerkern, einsperren; **-ment** *n.* Haft, Gefangenschaft; Einkerkerung; false **-ment** ungesetzliche Haft

improbable *adj.* unwahrscheinlich

improper *adj.* ungehörig, unpassend, ungeeignet; — fraction unechter Bruch

impropriety *n.* Ungehörigkeit; Untauglichkeit; Ungenauigkeit

improve *v.* verbessern; sich bessern, besser werden; **-ment** *n.* Verbesserung, Besserung; Fortschritt

improvident *adj.* unvorsichtig; sorglos, leichtsinnig

improvisation *n.* Improvisation, Stegreifdichtung; Improvisieren

improvise *v.* improvisieren

imprudence *n.* Unvorsichtigkeit, Unklugheit

imprudent *adj.* unvorsichtig, unklug

impudent *adj.* unverschämt, dreist, frech

impulse *n.* Trieb, Antrieb; Impuls

impulsive *adj.* impulsiv, antreibend

impure *adj.* unrein, unsauber; (fig.) unkeusch, unzüchtig

impurity *n.* Unreinheit, Unsauberkeit; (fig.) Unlauterkeit

impute *v.* zuschreiben; anrechnen, beimessen

in *prep.* in, innerhalb; an, auf; bei, zu; von, unter; nach; binnen, während; —

adv. darin, herein, hinein; da, hier, zu Hause; — itself an und für sich; there is nothing — it da ist nichts Wahres daran

inability *n.* Unfähigkeit, Unvermögen; — to pay Zahlungsunfähigkeit

inaccessibility *n.* Unzugänglichkeit, Unerreichbarkeit

inaccessible *adj.* unzugänglich, unerreichbar

inaccuracy *n.* Ungenauigkeit, Unrichtigkeit

inaccurate *adj.* ungenau, unrichtig

inactive *adj.* untätig, müssig, träge; ausser Dienst

inactivity *n.* Untätigkeit, Beschäftigungslosigkeit

inadequacy *n.* Unzulänglichkeit, Unangemessenheit

inadequate *adj.* unzulänglich, unangemessen

inadvertent *adj.* unbeabsichtigt; unachtsam, versehentlich

inalienable *adj.* unveräusserlich

inane *adj.* leer; geistlos, nichtig; albern, fade

inanimate *adj.* unbeseelt, unbelebt; leblos

inapt *adj.* ungeeignet; ungeschickt

inarticulate *adj.* (zool.) gliederlos; (fig.) sinnlos, sprachlos; ungegliedert

inasmuch *adv.* insofern; insoweit

inaudible *adj.* unhörbar

inaugural *adj.* Antritts-, Einweihungs-

inaugurate *v.* feierlich einführen; einweihen; ins Leben rufen

inauguration *n.* Einweihung; Einsetzung, Einführung

inborn *adj.* angeboren, natürlich; eingeboren, ererbt

incalculable *adj.* unberechenbar, unmessbar

incandescent *adj.* erglühend, weissglühend; — light Glühlicht

incantation *n.* Beschwörung; Zauberformel; Entzücken

incapable *adj.* unfähig, ungeeignet

incapacitate *v.* unfähig machen, ausser Gefecht setzen

incarcerate *v.* einkerkern, einsperren

incarnation *n.* Fleischwerdung

incase *v.* einschliessen, umschliessen

incendiary *n.* Brandstifter; Aufwiegler, Aufhetzer; — bomb Brandbombe; — *adj.* brandstiftend: aufreizend

incense *n.* Weihrauch; — *v.* erregen, erzürnen, aufbringen; beweihräuchern, durchduften

incentive *n.* Ansporn, Antrieb; — *adj.* anfeuernd, antreibend

inception *n.* Beginn

incessant *adj.* unaufhörlich, unablässig; beständig

incest *n.* Inzest, Blutschande

inch *n.* Zoll; (fig.) Kleinigkeit; every — jeder Zoll, durch und durch; — *v.* zollweise vorrücken (*or* zurückweichen)

incident *n.* Ereignis, Vorfall; — *adj.* zufällig, beiläufig; vorkommend; abhängig; einfallend; –al *adj.* gelegentlich, nebensächlich; –ally *adv.* nebenbei; übrigens

incinerate *v.* einäschern

incinerator *n.* Verbrennungsofen

incipient *adj.* anfangend, beginnend; einleitend

incision *n.* Einschnitt, Schnitt

incisive *adj.* (ein)schneidend, scharf

incisor *n.* Schneidezahn

incite *v.* anspornen, anstacheln, anregen

inclement *adj.* unfreundlich, rauh

inclination *n.* Neigung; (fig.) Hang, Lust

incline *n.* Abhang, Abdachung; — *v.* (sich) neigen; geneigt sein; –ed *adj.* geneigt, aufgelegt; –ed plane schiefe Ebene

inclose *v.* einschliessen, umgeben; (letter) beifügen

inclosure *n.* Einzäunung; Einschliessung; (letter) Einlage, Beilage

include *v.* einschliessen, umfassen, enthalten; –d *adj.* eingeschlossen, einschliesslich

inclusion *n.* Einschliessung

inclusive *adj.* einschliessend, umschliessend; einschliesslich

incognito *n.* Inkognito; — *adj.* inkognito, unbekannt, unerkannt

incoherent *adj.* zusammenhanglos; unzusammenhängend; inkonsequent; locker, lose

incombustible *adj.* unverbrennlich, nicht entflammbar

income *n.* Einkommen, Ertrag; — tax Einkommensteuer

incoming *adj.* neu eintretend; ankommend, eintreffend

incommensurable *adj.* unmessbar, unvergleichbar

incommutable *adj.* unvertauschbar

incomparable *adj.* unvergleichlich

incompatible *adj.* unvereinbar; unverträglich

incompetence *n.* Unfähigkeit, Untauglichkeit; Unzulänglichkeit; Unzuständigkeit

incompetent *adj.* unbefugt, unzuständig; unfähig; unzulänglich

incomplete *adj.* unvollständig, unvollendet, unvollkommen

incomprehensible *adj.* unbegreiflich, unverständlich

inconceivable adj. unfassbar, unbegreiflich

incongruous adj. unangemessen, unpassend; widersinnig

inconsequential adj. inkonsequent, folgewidrig

inconsiderate adj. unbedacht, unbedachtsam, unüberlegt; rücksichtslos

inconsistent adj. inkonsequent, unvereinbar, widersprechend; ungereimt, absurd

inconspicuous adj. unauffällig, unmerklich

inconstant adj. unbeständig, wechselnd

inconvenience n. Unbequemlichkeit, Ungelegenheit; — v. belästigen, lästig fallen

inconvenient adj. unbequem, lästig, störend; **at a most** — **time** zu sehr ungelegener Zeit

incorporate v. vereinigen, vermischen; verkörpern, einverleiben; — adj. verkörpert, einverleibt

incorporation n. Vereinigung, Vermischung; Einverleibung

incorrect adj. unrichtig, ungenau, falsch

incorrigible adj unverbesserlich

incorruptible adj. unbestechlich

increase n. Zunahme, Wachstum; Vergrösserung, Vermehrung, Steigerung, Zuwachs; — v. wachsen, vermehren; zunehmen; vergrössern

increasing adv. mehr und mehr, in zunehmendem Masse

incredible adj. unglaublich

incredulity n. Ungläubigkeit, Unglaube, Skeptizismus

incredulous adj. ungläubig, skeptisch

incriminate v. beschuldigen, belasten

incubation n. Brüten; (med.) Inkubation

incubator n. Brutofen, Brutapparat

incumbent n. Amtsinhaber, Beamte; — adj. aufliegend; obliegend; **be** — **on** obliegen

incur v. sich zuziehen, auf sich laden; — **debts** Schulden machen

incurable adj. unheilbar

indebted adj. verschuldet, verpflichtet; **I'm** — **to you for everything** ich verdanke Ihnen alles; **-ness** n. Verschuldung, Verpflichtung

indecency n. Unziemlichkeit, Unschicklichkeit, Unanständigkeit

indecent adj. unziemlich, unschicklich; unanständig, obszön

indecision n. Unentschlossenheit, Unschlüssigkeit

indecisive adj. unentschlossen, schwankend; ungewiss, unentschieden

indeed adv. wirklich, allerdings; **zwar;**

freilich; **yes** —! ja gewiss!

indefinite adj. unbestimmt, unentschieden; unbeschränkt, unbegrenzt

indelible adj. unauslöschlich, unvertilgbar

indemnity n. Sicherstellung; Entschädigung; (pol.) nachträgliche Genehmigung; — **bond** sichergestellte Schuldverschreibung

indent v. auszacken, einkerben; (law) einen Vertrag abschliessen; **-ation** n. Auszackung, Einschnitt; **-ure** n. Vertrag, Kontrakt

independence n. Unabhängigkeit; **Independence Day** Tag der Unabhängigkeitserklärung

independent adj. unabhängig, ungebunden, selbständig

indescribable adj. unbeschreiblich, unbeschreibbar

indestructible adj. unzerstörbar

indeterminable adj. unbestimmbar

index n. Index, Register, Verzeichnis; (math.) Exponent; — **finger** Zeigefinger; — v. registrieren, einordnen, mit einem Inhaltsverzeichnis versehen

India n. Indien

indicate v. anzeigen, andeuten

indication n. Anzeige, Angabe; Anzeichen, Merkmal

indicative adj. anzeigend, andeutend; — n. Indikativ

indicator n. Anzeiger; (elec.) Indikator; (mech.) Anzeigevorrichtung

indict v. verklagen, belangen, anklagen; **-ment** n. Anklage

indifference n. Gleichgültigkeit; Gleichmut

indifferent adj. gleichgültig, indifferent; mittelmässig; schlecht; unwesentlich

indigenous adj. eingeboren, einheimisch

indigent adj. bedürftig, arm

indigestible adj. unverdaulich

indigestion n. Verdauungsschwäche, Verdauungsstörung; Unverdaulichkeit

indignant adj. unwillig, indigniert, entrüstet

indignation n. Unwille, Entrüstung, Indignation

indignity n. Unwürdigkeit; Beleidigung, Beschimpfung

indirect adj. indirekt, mittelbar

indiscreet adj. indiskret, taktlos

indiscretion n. Indiskretion, Vertrauensbruch, Taktlosigkeit

indiscriminate adj. unterschiedslos, wahllos

indispensable adj. unerlässlich, unentbehrlich

indisposed adj. unpässlich, indisponiert;

abgeneigt

indisposition *n.* Unpässlichkeit, Indisposition

indisputable *adj.* unbestreitbar

indistinct *adj.* undeutlich; verworren, unklar

indistinguishable *adj.* ununterscheidbar, ohne Rangunterschied

individual *n.* Individuum, Einzelwesen; — *adj.* individuell, persönlich, eigentümlich; **-ism** *n.* Individualismus; Selbstsucht; **-ity** *n.* Individualität, Eigentümlichkeit

indivisible *adj.* unteilbar, unzertrennlich

indoctrinate *v.* unterrichten, unterweisen

indolence *n.* Trägheit, Lässigkeit

indolent *adj.* indolent, träge, lässig; schlaff

indomitable *adj.* unbezwingbar, standhaft, unbezähmbar

indoor *adv.* drinnen; **-s** im Hause, zu Hause; Haus-, Zimmer-

indorse *v.* indossieren, girieren, begeben; bestätigen, annehmen; **-ment** *n.* Indossament, Giro, Übertragung; Genehmigung; **-r** *n.* Indossant, Girant

indubitable *adj.* unzweifelhaft, zweifellos

induce *v.* veranlassen, bestimmen; überreden; (elec. and phil.) induzieren; **-ment** *n.* Veranlassung, Anlass; Beweggrund; Reizmittel

induct *v.* einführen, einweihen, einsetzen; **-ion** *n.* Einführung, Einsetzung; (elec. and phil.) Induktion; **-ion coil** Induktionsrolle; **-ive** *adj.* bewegend, verleitend; erzeugend, veranlassend; (elec. and phil.) induktiv, Induktions-

indulge *v.* nachsichtig sein, schonend behandeln; gewähren; — **in something** sich einer Sache hingeben, einer Sache frönen; **-nce** *n.* Nachsicht, Schonung; Nachgiebigkeit; Sichgehenlassen, Zügellosigkeit; (rel.) Ablass; **-nt** *adj.* nachsichtig, schonend; mild

industrial *adj.* industriell, gewerbetreibend, Gewerbe-; **-ism** *n.* Gewerbetätigkeit; Industrialismus; **-ist** *n.* Industrielle

industrious *adj.* fleissig, betriebsam

industry *n.* Industrie; Fleiss, Betriebsamkeit; Gewerbe

ineffable *adj.* unaussprechlich

ineffective *adj.* unwirksam, fruchtlos; unfähig

inefficiency *n.* Unwirksamkeit, Untüchtigkeit

inefficient *adj.* untüchtig, unwirksam

ineligible *adj.* unwählbar; dienstuntauglich

inept *adj.* abgeschmackt, albern, unpas-

send; **-itude** *n.* Abgeschmacktheit, Albernheit

inequality *n.* Ungleichheit; Missverhältnis

inequitable *adj.* ungerecht, unbillig

inertial guidance *n.* Trägheitssteuerung

inescapable *adj.* unentrinnbar

inevitable *adj.* unvermeidlich

inexact *adj.* ungenau

inexcusable *adj.* unentschuldbar, **unverzeihlich**; unverantwortlich

inexhaustible *adj.* unerschöpflich

inexpedient *adj.* unzweckmässig, **unpassend**

inexpensive *adj.* billig, wohlfeil

inexperienced *adj.* unerfahren

inexplicable *adj.* unerklärlich, **unverständlich**

infallible *adj.* unfehlbar, untrüglich, sicher, zuverlässig

infamous *adj.* ehrlos, entehrend; verrufen, berüchtigt; infam

infamy *n.* Ehrlosigkeit, Schande; **In-famie**, Schändlichkeit, Niedertracht

infancy *n.* Kindheit, Kindesalter; **(law)** Unmündigkeit, Minderjährigkeit

infant *n.* Kind; Säugling; (law) Unmündige; — *adj.* kindlich, jugendlich, jung; unentwickelt; **-icide** *n.* Kindesmord, Kindermord; Kindermörder; **-ile** *adj.* kindlich, infantil; **-ile paralysis** Kinderlähmung

infantry *n.* Infanterie, Fussvolk

infatuation *n.* Betörung, Verblendung; Vernarrtheit

infect *v.* infizieren, anstecken; **-ion** *n.* Infektion, Infizierung, Ansteckung; **-ious** *adj.* ansteckend; Ansteckungs-

infer *v.* folgern, schliessen; **-ence** *n.* Folgerung, Schluss

inferior *adj.* untergeordnet, niedriger, minderwertig; of — **quality** von minderwertiger Beschaffenheit, von geringer Qualität; **-ity** *n.* geringerer Wert; Minderwertigkeit, Inferiorität; **-ity complex** Minderwertigkeitskomplex

infernal *adj.* höllisch, teuflisch, infernalisch; Höllen-

infest *v.* überschwemmen; plagen, heimsuchen

infidel *n.* Ungläubige, Heide; — *adj.* ungläubig; **-ity** *n.* Treulosigkeit, Treubruch, Untreue; Unglaube, Ungläubigkeit

infield *n.* Innenfeld; **-er** *n.* Innenspieler

infiltrate *v.* eindringen; durchsickern; durchdringen

infiltration *n.* Infiltration; Durchsickern; Eindringen

infinite *n.* Unendlichkeit; — *adj.* unendlich, unbegrenzt; zahllos, ungeheuer

infinitesimal *adj.* unendlich klein; — **calculus** Infinitesimalrechnung, Differential und Integralrechnung

infinitive *n.* Infinitiv, Nennform

infinity *n.* Endlosigkeit, Unendlichkeit, Unbegrenztheit; unendliche Grösse (*or* Menge)

infirm *adj.* schwach, unsicher; (med.) gebrechlich, kraftlos; **-ary** *n.* Krankenstube; Krankenhaus, Hospital; **-ity** *n.* Schwäche, Schwachheit; Gebrechen; Gebrechlichkeit

inflame *v.* (sich) entflammen; (med.) (sich) entzünden

inflammable *adj.* entzündlich, feuergefährlich

inflammation *n.* Entzündung

inflammatory *adj.* erhitzend, aufregend; entflammend; aufrührerisch, hetzerisch; Hetz-; (med.) entzündlich

inflate *v.* aufblasen, aufblähen; künstlich steigern

inflation *n.* Aufblähung; Aufgeblasenheit; (money) Inflation

inflection *n.* Biegung, Krümmung; (gram.) Beugung; (voice) Modulation

inflexible *adj.* unbiegsam, unveränderlich, unbeugsam

inflict *v.* auferlegen, verhängen; zufügen; **-ion** *n.* Auferlegung, Verhängung; Zufügung; Strafe, Plage

influence *n.* Einfluss, Einwirkung; — *v.* einwirken auf, beeinflussen

influential *adj.* einflussreich

influenza *n.* Grippe, Influenza

influx *n.* Zufliessen, Einströmen; Zufluss, Zustrom; Zufuhr

infold *v.* einhüllen, umschliessen

inform *v.* benachrichtigen, informieren, unterrichten, in Kenntnis setzen; — **against** denunzieren, angeben; **-ant** *n.* Benachrichtiger, Berichterstatter; Gewährsmann; **-ation** *n.* Auskunft, Benachrichtigung; Unterweisung; **-ation bureau** Auskunftsbüro; **-ation desk** Auskunft(sstand); **-ed** *adj.* benachrichtigt, informiert, belehrt; **-er** *n.* Denunziant, Angeber

informal *adj.* unzeremoniell; formlos; regelwidrig; **-ality** *n.* Formlosigkeit; Regelwidrigkeit

infraction *n.* Brechen, Bruch; Verletzung, Übertretung

infrared *adj.* infrarot

infrequent *adj.* ungewöhnlich, selten

infringe *v.* eingreifen, übergreifen; übertreten, verletzen; **-ment** *n.* Bruch, Verletzung; Übertretung

infuriate *v.* wütend machen

infusion *n.* Einflössung; Aufguss

ingenious *adj.* genial, begabt, erfinderisch; geistreich, sinnreich

ingenuity *n.* Scharfsinn, Genie, Geist, Begabung

ingenuous *adj.* freimütig, offenherzig, aufrichtig; unbefangen

ingot *n.* Barren, Block, Stange

ingrained *adj.* eingewurzelt, eingefleischt

ingrate *n.* Undankbare

ingratitude *n.* Undank(barkeit)

ingredient *n.* Bestandteil

ingrown *adj.* einwärts (*or* nach innen) wachsend; — **nail** eingewachsener Nagel

inhabit *v.* (be)wohnen; **-able** *adj.* bewohnbar; **-ant** *n.* Bewohner, Einwohner

inhalation *n.* Einatmung; (med.) Inhalation

inhale *v.* einatmen; (med.) inhalieren

inherent *adj.* anhaftend, angeboren, eigen; innewohnend

inherit *v.* (be)erben; **-ance** *n.* Erbschaft, Erbe, Erbgut, Erbteil; (fig.) Vererbung; **-ance tax** Erbschaftssteuer

inhibit *v.* zurückhalten, hemmen, hindern, Einhalt gebieten, verbieten; **-ion** *n.* Verhinderung, Hemmung, Verbot

inhospitable *adj.* ungastlich, unwirtlich

inhuman *adj.* unmenschlich; **-ity** *n.* Unmenschlichkeit

inimitable *adj.* unnachahmbar, unnachahmlich

iniquity *n.* Unbilligkeit, Ungerechtigkeit; Schlechtigkeit; Missetat

initial *n.* Anfangsbuchstabe, Initiale; — *adj.* anfänglich, beginnend; Anfangs-; — *v.* mit den Anfangsbuchstaben (eines Namens) versehen

initiate *v.* einführen, einweihen; anfangen, beginnen

initiation *n.* Einführung, Einweihung; Einleitung, Beginn

initiative *n.* Initiative; einleitende Handlung; **take the** — den ersten Schritt tun; — *adj.* einleitend, einführend

inject *v.* injizieren, einspritzen; einwerfen, eingiessen; **-ion** *n.* Injektion, Einspritzung; — **pump** *n.* Einspritzpumpe

injunction *n.* Einschärfung, Vorschrift; (law) gerichtliche Aufforderung, Verbot

injure *v.* schaden, beschädigen, verletzen; beleidigen

injurious *adj.* schädlich, nachteilig

injury *n.* Schaden, Beschädigung, Verletzung; Unrecht; Beleidigung

injustice *n.* Ungerechtigkeit, Unrecht

ink *n.* Tinte; — **blot** Tintenkleks; **India** — Tusche; **printer's** — Druckerschwärze;

— *v.* mit Tinte beschmieren, beflecken; **-y** *adj.* tint(enart)ig; Tinten; (fig.) dunkel

inkling *n.* Andeutung, Gemunkel; Ahnung

inkpad *n.* Stempelkissen

inkstand, inkwell *n.* Tintenfass; Schreibzeug

inlaid *adj.* eingelegt, getäfelt

inlay *n.* Furnierholz; Einlegearbeit; gold — Goldeinlegearbeit; — *v.* einlegen, furnieren, täfeln, Parkett legen

inmate *n.* Insasse, Mitbewohner; Hausgenosse

inmost *adj.* innerst; geheimst, verborgenst

inn *n.* Gasthof, Wirtshaus, Herberge

innate *adj.* angeboren, natürlich; eigen

inner *adj.* inner, inwendig; innerlich; — tube Luftschlauch

innermost *adj.* innerst

inning *n.* Spielabschnitt; Dransein

innkeeper *n.* Gastwirt

innocence *n.* Unschuld, Schuldlosigkeit; Harmlosigkeit; Einfalt

innocent *adj.* unschuldig, schuldlos; unschädlich, harmlos

innovation *n.* Neuerung

innumerable *adj.* unzählbar, unzählig; zahllos

inoculate *v.* (hort.) okulieren, propfen; (med.) (ein)impfen

inoculation *n.* (hort.) Okulieren; (med.) Impfen, Impfung; (fig.) Einimpfung

inoffensive *adj.* unschädlich, arglos, harmlos

inopportune *adj.* ungelegen, unzeitig

inorganic *adj.* unorganisch, unbelebt

inquest *n.* gerichtliche Untersuchung; amtliche Leichenschau

inquire *v.* (nach)fragen, sich erkundigen; erfragen, erforschen; **-r** *n.* Untersuchende, Nachfragende

inquiry *n.* Untersuchung; Anfrage, Nachfrage, Erkundigung; Forschung

inquisitive *adj.* neugierig, wissbegierig; nachspürend; **-ness** *n.* Neugier, Wissbegierde

inquisitor *n.* Inquisitor; Untersuchende; (law) Untersuchungsrichter

inroad *n.* Einfall, Beutezug, Streifzug; (fig.) Übergriff, Anmassung

insane *adj.* wahnsinnig, irre, verrückt; — asylum Irrenhaus, Irrenanstalt

insanity *n.* Wahnsinn, Geistesstörung, Irrsinn, Verrücktheit

inscribe *v.* einschreiben, aufschreiben; eintragen, aufzeichnen

inscription *n.* Inschrift, Aufschrift; Einschreibung, Eintragung; Widmung

insect *n.* Insekt, Kerbtier; Ungeziefer; — poison Insektengift; — powder In-

sektenpulver; **-icide** *n.* Insektenvertilgungsmittel

insecure *adj.* unsicher, ungewiss

insecurity *n.* Unsicherheit, Ungewissheit

insensibility *n.* Gefühllosigkeit, Empfindungslosigkeit; Unempfindlichkeit, Bewusstlosigkeit; Gleichgültigkeit

insensible *adj.* gefühllos, empfindungslos; unempfindlich; unmerklich; bewusstlos

inseparable *adj.* unzertrennlich, untrennbar

insert *v.* einlegen, einfügen, einsetzen; einrücken; inserieren; **-ion** *n.* Inserat, Anzeige; Einfügung, Einschaltung, Eintragung

inset *n.* Einsatz; Einlage, Beilage

inside *n.* Innere; Innenseite; (fig.) Innerste, Wesentlichste; — out nach aussen gekehrt; verkehrt; *pl.* Inneres, Eingeweide; **on the** — drinnen; **toward the** — nach innen gerichtet; — *adj.* inner, inwendig; — *adv.* innen, drinnen; — *prep.* innerhalb; **-r** *n.* Eingeweihte

insight *n.* Einblick, Einsicht; Scharfsinn

insignia *n.* Insignien, Abzeichen; Kennzeichen

insignificance *n.* Bedeutungslosigkeit; Geringfügigkeit; Verächtlichkeit

insignificant *adj.* unbedeutend, geringfügig, unwichtig; bedeutungslos

insincere *adj.* unaufrichtig, falsch; täuschend

insincerity *n.* Unaufrichtigkeit; Falschheit; Täuschung

insinuate *v.* zu verstehen geben, andeuten sich einschmeicheln

insinuation *n.* Einflüsterung, Einschmeichlung; Anspielung, Andeutung;

insipid *adj.* geschmacklos, unschmackhaft

insist *v.* bestehen, beharren; hervorheben, betonen; **-ence** *n.* Bestehen, Beharrlichkeit; Betonung, Hervorhebung; **-ent** *adj.* hartnäckig, beharrend, beharrlich; eindringlich

insole *n.* Brandsohle, Einlegesohle

insolence *n.* Frechheit, Unverschämtheit, Anmassung

insolent *adj.* frech, unverschämt, anmassend

insoluble *adj.* unauflöslich

insolvent *adj.* zahlungsunfähig

insomnia *n.* Schlaflosigkeit

insomuch *adv.* dergestalt, dermassen; so sehr

inspect *v.* inspizieren, besichtigen; beaufsichtigen; untersuchen; **-ion** *n.* Inspektion; Beaufsichtigung; Untersuchung, Prüfung; tour of — Inspektionsreise; **-or** *n.* Inspektor, Inspekteur, Aufseher

inspiration *n.* Inspiration, Eingebung; Begeisterung; (med.) Einatmung

inspire v. inspirieren, begeistern; inhalieren, einatmen; einhauchen

instability n. Unbeständigkeit, Wankelmütigkeit

install v. einrichten, einbauen, installieren; bestallen, einsetzen, einführen; **-ation** n. Installation, Einrichtung; Bestallung, Einsetzung, Einführung

instal(l)ment n. Rate, Teilzahlung; Fortsetzung

instance n. Beispiel, Fall; Instanz; for — zum Beispiel

instant n. Augenblick, Moment, Nu; — adj. gegenwärtig, unmittelbar; augenblicklich, momentan; dringend, laufend; on the 20th — am 20. des laufenden Monats; **-ly** adv. sogleich, augenblicklich; **-aneous** adj. augenblicklich, unverzüglich, im Nu geschehend

instead adv. stattdessen, dafür; — of (an)statt

instep n. Spann, Rist

instigate v. aufreizen, antreiben; anstiften, hetzen

instigation n. Anstiftung, Aufhetzung; Antrieb

instil(l) v. eintröpfeln, einträufeln; (fig.) einflössen, einprägen

instinct n. Instinkt, Naturtrieb; — adj. angeregt, belebt; erfüllt; **-ive** adj. unwillkürlich, instinktiv

institute n. Institute, Anstalt; — v. einrichten, errichten, einsetzen; verordnen

institution n. Anstalt, Institut, Institution; Einrichtung; Anordnung

instruct v. lehren, unterrichten, erziehen, unterweisen; **-ion** n. Unterricht, Belehrung, Instruktion; Anweisung, Gebrauchsanweisung; **-ive** adj. lehrreich, belehrend, instruktiv; **-or** n. Lehrer, Unterweiser, Instrukteur

instrument n. Instrument; Werkzeug; Gerät, apparat, Vorrichtung; (law) Urkunde, Dokument; — **approach** (avi.) Anpeilung zur Landung, Blindanflug; — **board** Armaturenbrett; — **flight** Blindflug; — v. instrumentieren; **-al** adj. dienlich, förderlich, behilflich

insubordinate adj. ungehorsam

insubordination n. Ungehorsam

insufferable adj. unerträglich, unleidlich

insufficient adj. ungenügend, unzulänglich; untauglich; — **evidence** unzulänglicher Beweis

insular adj. insular, inselartig, Insel-; isoliert, alleinstehend; unduldsam

insulate v. isolieren, absondern

insulation n. Isolierung, Absonderung, Vereinzelung

insulator n. Isolator, Nichtleiter

insulin n. Insulin

insult n. Beleidigung, Beschimpfung; — v. beschimpfen, beleidigen

insupportable adj. unerträglich, unausstehlich

insurance n. Versicherung; — **agent** Versicherungsagent; — **broker** Versicherungsmakler; — **policy** Versicherungspolice; — **premium** Versicherungsprämie; **accident** — Unfallversicherung; **burglary** — Einbruchversicherung; **fire** — Feuerversicherung; **life** — Lebensversicherung

insure v. versichern, verbürgen

insurgent n. Aufständische, Aufrührer, Insurgent; — adj. aufrührerisch

insurrection n. Aufstand, Aufruhr; Empörung

intact adj. unberührt, unversehrt, unverletzt, intakt

intake n. Einmündung, Einlass; Einlauf; Einnahme

intangible adj. unberührbar; unfühlbar; unfassbar

integer n. Ganze; ganze Zahl

integrate v. vervollständigen, ergänzen; (math.) integrieren, ergänzen

integrity n. Ganzheit, Vollständigkeit; (fig.) Redlichkeit, Unbescholtenheit

intellect n. Intellekt, Verstand, Urteilskraft; **-ual** n. Intellektuelle; **-ual** adj. intellektuell, vernünftig, urteilsfähig; Verstandes-

intelligence n. Intelligenz, Verstand; Einsicht; (mil.) Nachricht, Auskunft; — **test** Intelligenztest, Intelligenzprüfung

intelligent adj. intelligent, verständig, gescheit, einsichtsvoll; **-sia** n. Intelligenzia

intelligible adj. verständlich, fasslich; deutlich

intemperate adj. masslos, unmässig; ausschweifend

intend v. beabsichtigen, vorhaben; wollen; **-ant** n. Verwalter, Vorsteher; (theat.) Intendant

intense adj. intensiv, heftig, stark; angestrengt, angespannt

intensify v. (sich) verstärken, steigern, intensiver werden

intensity n. Stärke, Grad; Heftigkeit; Intensität, Spannung

intensive adj. intensiv. heftig, stark; verstärkend; angespannt

intent adj. gespannt, aufmerksam; eifrig, bedacht, erpicht; — n. Absicht, Vorhaben, Plan; **-ion** n. Absicht. Intention, Vorsatz; Zweck; **-ional** adj. absichtlich, vorsätzlich

inter v. beerdigen, begraben

intercede v. vermitteln, sich verwenden, Fürsprache einlegen

intercept v. abfangen, auffangen; hindern, aufhalten, unterbrechen; (rad.) abhören, mithören; **-or** n. Auffänger; **-or missile** n. Abwehrrakete; **-or plane** Jagdflugzeug

intercession n. Dazwischentreten, Vermittlung, Fürbitte

interchange n. Austausch, Abwechslung; Tauschhandel; — v. austauschen, vertauschen; abwechseln; **-able** adj. austauschbar, auswechselbar

intercollegiate adj. zwischen den Hochschulen

intercom n. Wechselseitiger Verkehr

intercourse n. Verkehr, Umgang; Verbindung

interdenominational adj. zwischen den Religionen

interdepartmental adj. zwischen den Abteilungen

interdependence n. gegenseitige Abhängigkeit

interdict v. verbieten, untersagen

interest n. Interesse, Anteilnahme; Zins; Vorteil, Nutzen; Anrecht, Anteil; compound — Zinseszins; rate of — Zinsfuss; — v. interessieren; be **-ed** in sich interessieren für, Anteil nehmen an; **-ing** adj. interessant, anziehend, fesselnd

interfere v. sich einmischen; dazwischenkommen; dazwischentreten, einschreiten; **-nce** n. Einmischung, Einspruch; Dazwischentreten; (phys.) Interferenz; (rad.) Störung

interhemispheric adj. zwischen östlicher und westlicher Hemisphäre

interim n. Interimszeit, Zwischenzeit

interior n. Innere, Inwendige; Inland; Binnenland; — adj. inner, innerlich; inländisch, binnenländisch

interject v. dazwischenwerfen, einschieben, einschalten; **-ion** n. (gram.) Ausruf; (fig.) Dazwischenwerfen, Einschieben

interlace v. durchflechten, durchweben; sich kreuzen

interlock v. ineinanderschliessen, ineinandergreifen; verschränken

interloper n. Eindringling

interlude n. Zwischenspiel; Unterbrechung

intermarriage n. Mischehe

intermarry v. untereinander heiraten

intermeddle v. sich einmischen

intermediary n. Vermittler, Zwischenhändler; — adj. vermittelnd

intermediate n. Vermittelnde; — adj. vermittelnd, Zwischen-, Mittel-

interment n. Beerdigung, Bestattung

interminable adj. grenzenlos, unendlich

intermingle v. (sich) vermischen

intermission n. Pause; Unterbrechung, Aussetzen

intermittent adj. zeitweilig aussetzend, ruckweise

intern v. internieren; **-ment** n. Internierung

intern(e) n. Hospitant, Assistenzarzt; **-ship** n. Hospitantenschaft, Hospitieren (in Krankenhäusern)

internal adj. inner, innerlich

international adj. international

interplanetary adj. zwischenplanetarisch; interplanetar

interpolate v. einschalten; einschieben

interpret v. deuten, interpretieren, auslegen; verdolmetschen, übersetzen; **-ation** n. Auslegung, Erklärung, Interpretation; (art) Auffassung; (theat.) Rollenwiedergabe; **-er** n. Dolmetscher

interrelated adj. gegenseitig verknüpft

interrogate v. verhören, förmlich befragen

interrogation n. Verhör, Fragen, Befragen; — point Fragezeichen

interrupt v. unterbrechen, stören; **-ion** n. Unterbrechung, Störung; Hemmung, Pause

interscholastic adj. zwischen den Schulen

intersect v. sich schneiden (or kreuzen); **-ion** n. Durchschneiden, Schnitt; (math.) Schnittpunkt; (rail.) Kreuzung

interspace n. Zwischenraum

intersperse v. dazwischensetzen, einstreuen, einmengen; untermengen

interstate adj. zwischenstaatlich

intertwine v. (sich) verflechten, ineinanderschlingen

interurban adj. zwischen den Städten

interval n. Zwischenraum, Abstand, Intervall; at **-s** in Abständen

intervene v. dazwischenkommen, intervenieren; einschreiten; vermitteln

intervention n. Dazwischenkunft, Einmischung; Vermittlung

interview n. Interview, Unterredung, Befragung; Zusammenkunft; **-er** n. Interviewer, Befrager

interwoven adj. durchflochten, ineinandergewebt

intestinal adj. die Eingeweide betreffend; Eingeweide-, Darm-

intestines n. pl. Eingeweide

intimacy n. Vertraulichkeit, Innigkeit

intimate n. Vertraute, Busenfreund; — adj. innig, vertraut, intim, eng; — v. andeuten, zu verstehen geben

intimation n. Andeutung, Fingerzeig

intimidate *v.* einschüchtern, furchtsam machen

intimidation *n.* Einschüchterung

into *prep.* in, auf, zu

intolerable *adj.* unerträglich, unausstehlich

intolerant *adj.* intolerant, unduldsam

intonation *n.* Intonation, Tongebung; Modulation; Ausdruck, Tonfall, Betonung

intoxicant *n.* Rauschmittel

intoxicate *v.* betrunken machen, berauschen

intoxication *n.* Rausch, Berauschung; Trunkenheit

intramural *adj.* innerhalb der Mauern befindlich; (anat.) innerorganisch

intransitive *adj.* intransitiv

intrench *v.* eingraben, verschanzen

intrepid *adj.* unerschrocken, beherzt

intricate *adj.* verwickelt, schwierig

intrigue *n.* Intrige, Truggewebe, Arglist, Ränke; — *v.* intrigieren, Ränke schmieden

introduce *v.* vorstellen, einführen, bekanntmachen; einleiten

introduction *n.* Einführung, Einleitung; Vorstellung, Bekanntmachen

introductory *adj.* einleitend

introvert *n.* Introvert, Nachinnengekehrte; — *adj.* introvertiert

intrude *v.* (sich) eindrängen, (sich) aufdrängen; stören; **-r** *n.* Eindringling, Zudringliche; Störenfried; ungebetener Gast

intrusion *n.* Eindrängen, Aufdrängen; Zudringlichkeit; (law) Besitzentziehung

intrust *v.* anvertrauen, betrauen

intuition *n.* Intuition, Anschauung, unmittelbare Erkenntnis

intuitive *adj.* intuitiv, unmittelbar erkennend

inundate *v.* überschwemmen

inundation *n.* Überschwemmung

invade *v.* einfallen, überfallen; **-r** *n.* Eindringling, Angreifer

invalid *n.* Invalide, Kranke; — *adj.* kränklich; invalide, dienstunfähig; ungültig; **-ate** *v.* ungültig machen; (ab)schwächen, entkräften

invaluable *adj.* unschätzbar

invariable *adj.* unveränderlich, beständig

invasion *n.* Invasion, Einfall, Angriff, Eingriff; (med.) Anfall

inveigh *v.* schimpfen, schmähen

inveigle *v.* verleiten, verlocken, verführen

invent *v.* erfinden, erdenken, erdichten; **-ion** *n.* Erfindung; Erdichtung, Lüge; **-ive** *adj.* erfindungsreich, erfinderisch; sinnreich; **-or** *n.* Erfinder, Urheber; Erdichter

inventory *n.* Inventar; Bestand; Verzeichnis; — *v.* Inventur aufnehmen

inverse *adj.* umgekehrt, entgegengesetzt

invert *v.* umkehren, umwenden; (gram. and mus.) umkehren; **-er** *n.* Gleichstrom-Wechselstrom Transformator

invest *v.* anlegen, investieren; **bekleiden; -ment** *n.* Anlage, Investierung

investigate *v.* erforschen, untersuchen, nachforschen

investigation *n.* Untersuchung; Forschung

investigator *n.* Untersuchende; Forscher

inveterate *adj.* eingewurzelt, hartnäckig

invigorate *v.* kräftigen, stärken, beleben

invincible *adj.* unbesiegbar, unüberwindlich

invisible *adj.* unsichtbar

invitation *n.* Einladung; Aufforderung; (fig.) Lockung

invite *v.* einladen, auffordern; herbeilocken; herausfordern

inviting *adj.* einladend, lockend, anziehend

invoice *n.* Rechnung; Frachtbrief; — **book** Rechnungsbuch; **pro forma** — fingierte Rechnung; — *v.* in Rechnung stellen

invoke *v.* anrufen, anflehen; beschwören; (law) aufrufen

involuntary *adj.* unwillkürlich, unfreiwillig

involve *v.* verwickeln, einwickeln; in sich schliessen, enthalten; (fig.) verwirren; (math.) potenzieren

invulnerable *adj.* unverwundbar, unanfechtbar

inward *adj.* inner(lich); — *adv.* einwärts, nach innen

iodine *n.* Jod

ion *n.* Ion; **-ization** *n.* Ionisierung; **-osphere** *n.* Ionosphäre

iota *n.* Jota, Iota

irascible *adj.* reizbar, jähzornig

irate *adj.* zornig, wütend; gereizt

IRBM (intermediate range ballistic missile) *n.* Fernlenkgeschoss mittlerer Reichweite

ire *n.* Zorn

Ireland *n.* Irland

iris *n.* Regenbogen; (anat.) Iris, Regenbogenhaut; (bot.) Schwertlilie

irk *v.* ermüden, verdriessen; schmerzen; **-some** *adj.* ermüdend, beschwerlich

iron *n.* Eisen; Bügeleisen; **-s** *pl.* Fesseln; — **age** Eisenzeit; **angle** — Winkelband, Winkeleisen; **black** — Schwarzblech; **cast** — Gusseisen; **galvanized sheet** — verzinktes Eisenblech; — **lung** eiserne Lunge; **pig** — Roheisen; **white** — Weissblech; **wrought** — Schmiedeeisen; —

adj. eisern; (fig.) unerschütterlich, hart; — curtain eiserne Vorhang; — lung eiserne Lunge; — ration eiserne Ration; — *v.* bügeln, plätten; — out in Ordnung bringen; –ing *n.* Plätten, Bügeln; –ing board Plättbrett, Bügelbrett

ironclad *adj.* gepanzert; (fig.) festgefügt

ironic(al) *adj.* ironisch, spöttisch

ironware *n.* Eisenwaren

ironworks *n. pl.* Eisenhütte, Eisengiesserei

irony *n.* Ironie, Spöttelei; Spottrede

irradiate *v.* bestrahlen, bescheinen, beleuchten; (fig.) erleuchten; strahlen machen

irrational *adj.* irrational, unberechenbar; unvernünftig, unsinnig

irreconcilable *adj.* unversöhnlich; unvereinbar

irrecoverable *adj.* unersetzlich, unwiederbringlich (verloren)

irredeemable *adj.* nicht tilgbar, nicht kündbar; nicht einlösbar; unverbesserlich

irregular *adj.* unregelmässig, regelwidrig; unrichtig; –ity *n.* Unregelmässigkeit, Regelwidrigkeit; Unrichtigkeit

irrelevant *adj.* unerheblich, belanglos; (law) nicht zur Sache gehörend

irremovable *adj.* nicht entfernbar; unabsetzbar

irreparable *adj.* unersetzlich; nicht wieder gutzumachen

irrepressible *adj.* unbezähmbar, ununterdrückbar

irreproachable *adj.* tadellos, unsträflich, vorwurfsfrei

irresistible *adj.* unwiderstehlich

irresolute *adj.* unentschlossen, unschlüssig, schwankend

irrespective *prep.* — of ohne Rücksicht auf, rücksichtslos gegen; unabhängig von

irresponsible *adj.* unverantwortlich

irreverent *adj.* unehrerbietig

irrigate *v.* bewässern, befeuchten; berieseln

irrigation *n.* Bewässerung, Berieselung; — canal Berieselungskanal

irritable *adj.* reizbar, erregbar

irritant *n.* Reizmittel

irritate *v.* reizen, aufbringen; irritieren; (med.) entzünden

irritation *n.* Aufregung, Erregung; (med.) Reizung, Entzündung

irruption *n.* Einbruch, Einfall

isinglas *n.* Fischleim, Hausenblase

island *n.* Insel, Eiland; –er *n.* Insulaner, Inselbewohner

isle *n.* Insel, Eiland

isobar *n.* Linie gleichen Luftdruckes

isolate *v.* absondern, isolieren

isolation *n.* Abgesondertheit; Isolierung; –ist *n.* Isolationist

isosceles *adj.* gleichschenklig

isothermal *adj.* gleichtemperiert; gleichwarm

issuance *n.* Ausgabe

issue *n.* Nummer, Ausgabe; Folge, Resultat, Ergebnis; (law) Streitfrage; Nachkommenschaft; avoid the — der Frage ausweichen; that's not the — darum handelt es sich nicht; — *v.* (her)ausgeben

it *pron.* es

Italy *n.* Italien

itch *n.* Jucken; (med.) Krätze; (fig.) Verlangen, Begierde; — *v.* jucken; (fig.) darauf brennen; –y *adj.* juckend; krätzig

item *n.* Einzelheit, Punkt, Gegenstand, Posten; –ize *v.* einzeln aufzählen (*or* notieren)

itinerant *adj.* umherreisend, umherwandernd, umherziehend

itinerary *n.* Reisebeschreibung, Reisehandbuch; Reiseplan

its *pron.* sein(er); dessen, deren

itself *pron.* (es) selbst, sich; by — für sich allein, besonders; in — an sich

ivory *n.* Elfenbein; Elfenbeinfarbe; — *adj.* elfenbeinern, elfenbeinartig

ivy *n.* Efeu

J

jab *n.* Stich, Stoss, Schlag; (boxing) gerader Linke; — *v.* stechen, stossen, schlagen; (boxing) gerade (links) schlagen

jabber *n.* Geschnatter, Geplapper; — *v.* plappern, schnattern

jack *n.* (cards) Bube, Unter; (mech.) Wagenheber; Winde, Flaschenzug; (naut.) Matrose, Teerjacke; — pot Haupttreffer; — rabbit rammler; — *v.* — up aufschrauben; aufwinden

jackal *n.* Schakal

jackass *n.* Esel(shengst); (fig.) Esel

jackdaw *n.* Dohle

jacket *n.* Jacke, Jackett, Wams, Rock; Mantel; (potato) Schale; book — Buchumschlag

jack-in-the-box *n.* Schachtelmännchen

jackknife *n.* Klappmesser, Taschenmesser

jack-of-all-trades *n.* Hans Dampf in allen Gassen; be a — sich mit allen möglichen Dingen beschäftigen

jack-o'-lantern *n.* Kürbislaterne; Irrlicht

jag *n.* Kerbe, Zacke, Scharte; Ladung.

Last; Portion; — v. kerben; (aus)-zacken; -ged adj. gekerbt, gezähnt, schartig

jaguar n. Jaguar

jail n. Gefängnis, Kerker; — v. einkerkern; -er n. Gefängniswärter, Kerkermeister

jailbird n. Galgenvogel, Zuchthäusler

jalopy n. alter Kasten

jam n. Marmelade; (coll.) Gedränge; Patsche, Klemme; — v. drücken, pressen; verklemmen, festsitzen; (rad.) stören

jamboree n. Pfadfindertreffen; laute Lustbarkeit

jangle n. Missklang, Gerassel; Lärm, Zänkerei; — v. zanken; misstönen, rasseln, schrillen

janitor n. Pförtner, Türsteher; Hausmeister

January n. Januar

jar n. Krug; Glas; Knarren; Misston, Misshelligkeit; — v. erzittern machen; misstönend berühren; in scharfem Gegensatz stehen

jargon n. Jargon, Kauderwelsch

jasmine n. Jasmin

jato (jet assisted take-off) n. Raketenstart

jaundice n. Gelbsucht

jaunt n. Wanderung, Ausflug

javelin n. Wurfspiess, Speer

jaw n. Kiefer, Kinnbacken

jawbone n. Kiefernknochen, Kinnlade

jay n. Eichelhäher

jaywalk n. Fussgängerverkehssünde

jazz n. Jazz; — band Jazzorchester, Jazzkapelle

jealous adj. eifersüchtig; neidisch; misstrauisch; be — of eifersüchtig (or argwöhnisch) sein auf; -y n. Eifersucht, Neid; Misstrauen, Argwohn

jeans n. pl. Hosen aus blauem Baumwollköper

jeep n. Jeep

jeer n. Hohn, Spott; — v. (ver)höhnen, (ver)spotten

jelly n. Gelee; Gallert, Sülze

jellyfish n. Meduse, Qualle; (fig.) Schlappschwanz

jeopardize v. gefährden, aufs Spiel setzen

jerk n. Stoss, Ruck; (sl.) Kerl; — v. zucken; reissen; schnellen; -y adj. stossweise, sprungartig, krampfhaft

jersey n. Jersey; Wolljacke; feingekämmter Wollstoff

jest n. Witz; Scherz, Spass; — v. scherzen, spassen; -er n. Spassvogel, Possenreisser; (court) -er Hofnarr

Jesus Christ n. Jesus Christus

jet n. Wurf, Strahl; Röhre, Düse; **gas** —

Gasflamme; Gashahn; — plane Düsenflugzeug; -propulsion Düsenantrieb; — stream Düsenstrahl

jet-propelled adj. mit Düsenantrieb

jettison v. über Bord werfen

Jew n. Jude; **Wandering** — ewige Jude; -ish adj. jüdisch

jewel n. Edelstein, Juwel, Kleinod; pl. Geschmeide, Schmuck; -er n. Juwelier; -ry n. Schmuck, Juwelen, Juwelierarbeit

jibe v. umlegen, überholen; übergehen; (coll.) übereinstimmen

jiffy n. Augenblick, Nu

jig n. lustiger Tanz; — saw Wippsäge

jiggle v. hüpfen, wackeln; umherhüpfen

jigsaw puzzle n. Puzzlespiel

jilt v. täuschen; sitzen lassen

jingle n. Geklingel; — v. klingen, klingeln; klimpern; klirren

jingoist n. Chauvinist

jinx n. Unheilbringer; — v. Unheil bringen

jitterbug n. Jitterbug; Anhänger der Swingmusik

jitters n. Nervosität, Angst

jive n. Spelunke

job n. Arbeit, Stellung; Auftrag, Geschäft, Aufgabe; — lot Ramschware; — work Akkordarbeit; -ber n. Akkordarbeiter; Makler; -less adj. stellungslos, arbeitslos

jockey n. Jockey, Berufsreiter; — v. prellen, (be)gaunern; geschickt zu Werke gehen

jocular adj. scherzhaft

jocund adj. froh, heiter, lustig, munter

join v. verbinden, zusammenfügen; sich verbinden (or vereinigen, anschliessen), eintreten in; angrenzen, anstossen; -er n. Tischler, Zimmermann

joint n. (anat.) Gelenk; (geol.) Riss, Spalte; (meat) Lendenstück, Keule; (mech.) Scharnier, Fuge; (sl.) Spelunke; **throw out of** — sich verrenken; — adj. verbunden, vereinigt, gemeinsam; — account gemeinschaftliche Rechnung; — heir Miterbe; -ly adv. gemeinschaftlich

joke n. Witz, Scherz, Spass; **in** — scherzweise; **play a** — einen Witz reissen; **play a** — **on someone** jemandem einen Schabernack spielen; — v. scherzen, spassen; schäkern, necken; -r n. Spassmacher, Spassvogel; (cards) Joker

jollity n. Lustigkeit; Lustbarkeit

jolly adj. lustig, munter, fidel

jolt n. Stoss, Gerüttel; — v. stossen, schütteln, rütteln

jonquil n. Narzissenart, Osterglocke

jostle v. anstossen; wegstossen, fortstossen, verdrängen

jot *n.* Jota; Pünktchen, Kleinigkeit; **not a** — nicht das Geringste; — *v.* — **down** schnell niederschrieben, kurz vermerken

journal *n.* Tagebuch; Journal; Tageblatt, Tagezeitung; (mech.) Zapfen; **–ism** *n.* Journalismus, Zeitungswesen; **–ist** *n.* Journalist, Zeitungsschreiber

journey *n.* Reise; — *v.* reisen, wandern

journeyman *n.* Geselle, Gehilfe

jovial *adj.* jovial, aufgeräumt; frohsinnig

joy *n.* Freude, Entzücken; **give** — Freude bereiten; **wish** — Glück wünschen; — **rider** Schwarzfahrer; **–ful** *adj.*, **–ous** *adj.* freudig, fröhlich, froh; erfreulich

jubilant *adj.* jubelnd, frohlockend

jubilee *n.* Jubiläum, Jubelfeier; Freudenfest

Judaism *n.* Judentum

judge *n.* Richter, Schiedsrichter; Sachverständige; — *v.* richten, urteilen; beurteilen, Recht sprechen

judgment *n.* Urteil; Urteilsspruch; Beurteilung, Meinung, Ansicht; Urteilsvermögen; **pass** — Urteil fällen; — **day** jüngster Tag

judicial *adj.* richterlich, gerichtlich; Gerichts-; kritisch, unterscheidend; — **murder** Justizmord

judiciary *n.* Richterstand, Richtertum; — *adj.* richterlich, gerichtlich

jug *n.* Krug; (sl.) Gefängnis

juggle *v.* jonglieren, Taschenspielerkunststücke machen; gaukeln, täuschen; betrügen; **–r** *n.* Jongleur, Taschenspieler; Gaukler; Betrüger

jugular *adj.* die Kehle betreffend; Hals-; — **vein** Halsschlagader

juice *n.* Saft; Kraft, Gehalt; (coll.) Strom

juicy *adj.* saftig, kraftvoll; (coll.) pikant

jujitsu *n.* Jiu-Jitsu

jukebox *n.* Musikautomat

July *n.* Juli

jumble *n.* Verwirrung, Wirrwarr, Durcheinander; — *v.* vermengen, verwirren; durcheinander werfen

jumbo *adj.* übergross; plump, dick; elefantenartig

jump *n.* Sprung, Absprung, Salta; — *v.* springen, abspringen; auffahren; überspringen; **–er** *n.* Jumper; Springer, Abspringende; Hüpfende; **–ing** *n.* Springen, Hüpfen; **–ing** *adj.* springend, hüpfend; **–ing jack** Hampelmann; **–y** *adj.* nervös, sprunghaft

junction *n.* Verbindung, Vereinigung; (geom.) Berührung(spunkt); (rail.) Knotenpunkt, Kreuzung

juncture *n.* Verbindungspunkt, Verbindungsstelle; Krisis, Konjunktur

June *n.* Juni; — **bug** Junikäfer

jungle *n.* Dschungel

junior *n.* Jüngere, Junior; Gehilfe; — **college** Juniorenhochschule; — **school** Vorstufe der Mittelschule; — **adj.** jüngere; Unter-

juniper *n.* Wacholder

junk *n.* Abfall, Kehrricht; (naut.) Dschonke

junket *n.* Rahm; Näscherei; (fig.) Lustbarkeit; — *v.* schmausen

junkman *n.* Mistbauer

jurisdiction *n.* Rechtsprechung; Gerichtsbarkeit, Jurisdiktion; Gerichtsbezirk

jurisprudence *n.* Juristerei, Rechtswissenschaft

jurist *n.* Jurist, Rechtskundige

juror *n.* Geschworene; Preisrichter

jury *n.* Schwurgericht, Geschworenengericht; Preisgericht, Jury

juryman *n.* Geschworene

just *adj.* gerecht, ehrlich, ordentlich, rechtschaffen; — *adv.* gerade, genau; eben nur; richtig; — **as gerade wie**; eben als; — **as well ebensogut**, — **now** eben jetzt, soeben; **–ice** *n.* Gerechtigkeit, Justiz; Richter; **do –ice** Gerechtigkeit widerfahren lassen; **Justice of Peace** Friedensrichter; **–ifiable** *adj.* rechtfertigend, rechtmässig; **–ification** *n.* Rechtfertigung; Verteidigung; **–ify** *v.* rechtfertigen; **be –ified recht haben**

jut *v.* hervorragen, hervorstehen

jute *n.* Jute

juvenile *adj.* jugendlich, jung; Kinder-, Jugend-; — **court Jugendgericht**; — **delinquency Jugendkriminalität**; — **delinquent jugendlicher Verbrecher**

K

kaleidoscope *n.* Kaleidoskop

kangaroo *n.* Känguruh

keel *n.* Kiel; — *v.* umschlagen, **auf dem Rücken liegen**

keen *adj.* eifrig, begierig, erpicht; scharf; energisch, lebhaft; **–ness** *n.* Schärfe; Heftigkeit, Eifer; Scharfsinn, Feinheit

keep *n.* Obhut, Unterhalt; Burgverliess; — *v.* behalten, bewahren, erhalten; halten, führen; bleiben, sich aufhalten; feiern, befolgen; — **a secret ein Geheimnis bewahren**; — **away (sich) fernhalten**; — **books Buch führen**; — **down** unterdrücken; — **from hindern an**, abhalten von, sich enthalten; — **in mind im Gedächtnis behalten**; — **off** abhalten; fernbleiben; — **on fortfahren**, dabei bleiben; — **one's temper sich** beherrschen; — **out (sich) fernhalten**; — **quiet still sein** (or **bleiben**); — **time**

Takt (*or* Schritt) halten, die Zeit einhalten; — **track** of sich merken; — **up** fortfahren; — **up with** Schritt halten mit, nachkommen; — **your shirt on!** bewahre ruhig Blut! **-er** *n.* Aufseher; Bewahrer, Verwahrer; Wärter; Hüter, Kustos; **-ing** *n.* Aufsicht; Verwahrung, Bewahrung; Pflege, Obhut; Gewahrsam, Haft; Einklang, Übereinstimmung

keepsake *n.* Andenken, Erinnerungsgabe

keg *n.* Fässchen

kennel *n.* Hundezwinger; Hundehütte

kernel *n.* Kern; (fig.) Hauptsache

kerosene *n.* Kerosin, Leuchtpetroleum

kettle *n.* Kessel

key *n.* Schlüssel; (mech.) Keil, Splint; (mus.) Taste, Klappe; Ton; Musikschlüssel; (typewriter) Taste; — **ring** Schlüsselring, Schlüsselbund; — **man** Mann in Schlüsselstellung; **master** — Hauptschlüssel

keyboard *n.* Tastatur, Klaviatur

keyhole *n.* Schlüsselloch

keynote *n.* Grundton, Tonart; — **speech** Einleitungsrede

keystone *n.* Schlusstein; Grundstein; (fig.) Grundlage

kibitzer *n.* Kibitz

kick *n.* Tritt, Stoss; Fusstritt; Hufschlag; Rückschlag, Rückstoss; (coll.) Spass; — *v.* (mit dem Fuss) stossen, schlagen, treten, einen Fusstritt geben; — **the bucket,** — **off** ins Gras beissen; — **out** hinauswerfen; — **over the traces** über die Stränge schlagen

kickoff *n.* Abstoss

kid *n.* Zicklein, Kitze; (coll.) Kind, Junge; — *v.* zum besten haben, necken

kidnap *v.* Kinder (*or* Menschen) rauben, entführen; **-er** *n.* Kinderräuber, Menschenräuber; **-ing** *n.* Kinderraub, Menschenraub

kidney *n.* Niere

kidskin *n.* Ziegenfell, Ziegenleder

kill *v.* töten, erschlagen, umbringen; schlachten; — **time** die Zeit totschlagen (*or* vertreiben); **-er** *n.* Totschläger; Schlächter; **-ing** *n.* Töten; Schlachten

kill-joy *n.* Störenfried; Spassverderber

kiln *n.* Brennofen, Röstofen; Darre; **brick** — Kachelofen

kilocycle *n.* Kilozyklus; 1,000 Zyklen

kilogram *n.* Kilogramm; 1,000 Gramm

kilometer *n.* Kilometer; 1,000 Meter

kilowatt *n.* Kilowatt; — **hour** Kilowattstunde

kilt *n.* Kilt; kurzer, schottischer Rock

kimono *n.* Kimono

kin *n.* Verwandten; **next of** — die nächsten Verwandten

kind *n.* Art, Gattung, Geschlecht; Sorte; **all.-s of** allerlei; **human** — Menschengeschlecht; **in** — in Waren; **nothing of the** —! mitnichten! **of that** — derartig; **of the** — dergleichen; **the same** — **of** gleichartig; **what** — **of** was für ein; — *adj.* freundlich, gütig, liebenswürdig; **would you be so** — **to** würden Sie so freundlich sein zu; **-liness** *n.* Güte, Freundlichkeit; **-ly** *adj.* gütig, mild; freundlich, liebenswürdig; angenehm, wohltätig; **-ness** *n.* Güte, Freundlichkeit, Gefälligkeit; **have the -ness to** sei so freundlich zu

kindergarten *n.* Kindergarten

kindhearted *adj.* gutherzig, gütig, wohlwollend

kindle *v.* anzünden, entzünden; (fig.) entflammen, sich entzünden

kindling *n.* — **wood** Holz zum Anzünden

kindred *n.* Verwandtschaft; Verwandten; — *adj.* verwandt, gleichartig, ähnlich

Kinescope *n.* Kinoskop, Kathodenröhre mit Bildschirm

kinetic *adj.* kinetisch, bewegend, motorisch; **-s** *n. pl.* Kinetik, Bewegungslehre

king *n.* König; (cards, chess) König; (checkers) Dame; **-dom** *n.* Königreich, Königtum; (zool.) Reich; **-dom of God** Reich Gottes; **-ly** *adj.* königlich

kingfisher *n.* Eisvogel

kingpin *n.* Kegelkönig, Hauptkegel

king size *adj.* (cigarette) Grossformat

kink *n.* Schleife; (coll.) Schrulle, Sparren; **-y** *adj.* mit Schleifen besetzt; kraus

kinsfolk *n.* Verwandten, Verwandtschaft

kinsman *n.* Verwandte

kipper *n.* Lachs, Räucherhering; — *v.* einsalzen und leicht räuchern

kiss *n.* Kuss; — *v.* (sich) küssen

kiss-proof *adj.* kussecht

kit *n.* Ausrüstung, Ausstattung; **first-aid** — Ersthilfe-Ausrüstung

kitchen *n.* Küche; — **police** Küchendienst; — **range,** — **stove** Küchenherd; — **utensils** Küchengeräte; **-ette** *n.* Kleinküche

kite *n.* Drache; (orn.) Gabelweih; roter Milan; **fly a** — einen Drachen steigen lassen

kitten *n.* Kätzchen, junge Katze

kitty *n.* Kätzchen; Spieleinsatz, Sparbüchse

knack *n.* Kniff, Kunstgriff; Fertigkeit

knapsack *n.* Tornister, Ranzen

knave *n.* Schurke, Schelm; (cards) Bube, Unter; **-ry** *n.* Büberei, Schurkenstreich; Schelmerei

knead *v.* kneten; massieren; zusammenkneten

knee *n.* Knie

kneecap *n.* Kniescheibe; Kniekappe

knee-deep *adj.* knietief

kneel *v.* knien, auf den Knien liegen; — down auf die Knie fallen

kneepad *n.* Kniekissen

knell *n.* Geläute; (fig.) Grabgeläute; — *v.* tönen, klingen; durch Geläut verkünden

knickerbockers, knickers *n. pl.* Knickerbocker, halblange Pumphosen

knife *n.* Messer; — *v.* stechen, schneiden; (coll.) hinterlistig zu Fall bringen

knight *n.* Ritter; (chess) Springer, Pferd; (fig.) Kämpe; — *v.* zum Ritter schlagen; -hood *n.* Ritterschaft, Rittertum, Ritterwürde

knit *v.* stricken; (bone) verknüpfen, vereinigen; — one's brows die Stirne runzeln; -ting *n.* Stricken, Strickerei, Strickarbeit; -ting needle Stricknadel

knob *n.* Knopf, Knauf, Griff; Kuppe

knock *n.* Schlag, Stoss; Klopfen, Pochen; — *v.* klopfen, pochen; schlagen, stossen; prallen; — down niederschlagen; -er *n.* Klopfer, Schläger

knock-kneed *adj.* x-beinig; hinkend

knockout *n.* Knockout, Niederschlag

knoll *n.* Hügel, Bergspitze, Kuppe

knot *n.* Knoten; Knorren; Ast; — *v.* knoten, verknüpfen; (fig.) verwirren, verflechten; -ted *adj.* knotig, knorrig; (fig.) verworren, verschlungen; -ty *adj.* knotig, knorrig; (fig.) verwickelt

knothole *n.* Astloch

know *v.* wissen, kennen; verstehen; he -s a thing or two er ist durchtrieben; I — positively ich weiss es bestimmt; I — what's what ich weiss, was ich weiss; — a thing perfectly eine Sache vollkommen beherrschen; -ing *adj.* verständig; bewusst, wissentlich; geschickt, schlau; -ingly *adv.* wissentlich; -ledge *n.* Kenntnis(se), Wissen; Erkenntnis; Wissenschaft; to my -ledge soviel ich weiss; -n *adj.* gewusst; bekannt

know-how *n.* Spezialkenntnis; Könner

knuckle *n.* Knöchel; (meat) Kniestück; Eisbein, Dickbein, Dünnbein; — *v.* — down, — under sich unterwerfen

Kodak *n.* Kodak

kosher *adj.* koscher, rein

L

label *n.* Etikette, Zettel; Aufschrift; — *v.* etikettieren, mit einer Aufschrift versehen; auszeichnen

labor *n.* Arbeit; Mühe, Anstrengung; (med.) Geburtswehen; Labor Day Arbeiterfeiertag; — union Arbeitergewerkschaft; be in — in den Wehen liegen; hard — Zwangsarbeit; — *v.* arbeiten; sich abmühen (or anstrengen); ausarbeiten; — under a mistake sich im Irrtum befinden; -er *n.* Arbeiter; day -er Tagelöhner; kurzfristig Beschäftigte; -ious *adj.* mühselig, mühsam, mühevoll; arbeitsam, fleissig, emsig

laboratory *n.* Laboratorium

laborsaving *adj.* Arbeit ersparend; Handarbeit ersetzend

labyrinth *n.* Labyrinth, Irrgang; (fig.) Verwicklung

lace *n.* Spitze; Litze, Schnur, Borte, Tresse; — *v.* schnüren; besetzen

lacework *n.* Spitzenarbeit, Posamentierarbeit

lack *n.* Mangel, Bedürfnis; — *v.* fehlen, mangeln; entbehren, bedürfen; be -ing es fehlen lassen an; there is something -ing in him er hat seine Mängel (or Schwächen)

lackadaisical *adj.* gleichgültig, schlaff, träge

lackey *n.* Lakai, Bediente

lacquer *n.* Lack, Firnis; Lackarbeit; — *v.* lackieren, firnissen

lad *n.* Junge, Bursche; Gefährte

ladder *n.* Leiter, Stufenleiter; (naut.) Strickleiter, Schiffstreppe

laden *adj.* beladen, befrachtet

lading *n.* Ladung, Fracht; bill of — Frachtbrief

ladle *n.* Schöpflöffel; — *v.* (aus)schöpfen, auslöffeln

lady *n.* Dame; Edelfrau, Freifrau; (coll.) Liebste; Ladies and Gentlemen Meine Damen und Herren; ladies' room Damentoilette; young — Fräulein, junges Mädchen

ladybird, ladybug *n.* Marienkäfer

ladyfinger *n.* Biskuit

lady-killer *n.* Herzenbrecher, Frauenheld

ladylike *adj.* damenhaft, wohlerzogen

ladylove *n.* Geliebte

lag *v.* zaudern, zögern; zurückbleiben, zuletzt kommen

laggard *adj.* langsam, saumselig, lässig, träge; — *n.* Saumselige, Zauderer, Träge, Langsame

lagoon *n.* Lagune

laity *n.* Laien

lake *n.* See; — dwelling Pfahlbau

lamb *n.* Lamm; (meat) Lammfleisch; Lamb of God Lamm Gottes; — chop Lammkotelett

lambskin *n.* Lammfell, Lammleder

lame *adj.* lahm, verkrüppelt; hinkend;

(fig.) unvollkommen, mangelhaft; — **excuse** faule Ausrede; — *v.* lähmen, zum Krüppel machen; -**ness** *n.* Lahmheit, Lähmung; (fig.) Schwäche

lament *n.* Wehklage, Jammer; — *v.* (be)klagen, jammern, trauern; -**able** *adj.* beklagenswert; jämmerlich, kläglich; -**ation** *n.* Jammer, Wehklage

lamp *n.* Lampe; Leuchte, Licht; — **shade** Lampenschirm; **electric** — elektrische Lampe

lampoon *n.* Schmähschrift; — *v.* schmähen

lamplight *n.* Lampenlicht

lamppost *n.* Laternenpfahl

lance *n.* Lanze, Speer, Wurfspiess; — *v.* durchbohren; (med.) aufschneiden; -**t** *n.* Lanzette

land *n.* Land; Grund, Boden, Erde; Grundstück; — *v.* landen; an Land bringen, ausladen, löschen; (fig.) in Sicherheit bringen; -**ing** *n.* Landung, Landen; (stairs) Treppenabsatz; -**ing place** Landeplatz, Flugfeld; **emergency** -**ing** Notlandung; **emergency** -**ing field** Notlandeplatz

landholder *n.* Landeigentümer, Grundbesitzer, Gutsbesitzer

landlady *n.* Hauswirtin; — **of an inn** Gastwirtin

landlord *n.* Hausbesitzer; — **of an inn** Gastwirt

landlubber *n.* Landratte

landmark *n.* Landmarke, Grenzstein; Markstein

landowner *n.* Grundbesitzer, Gutsbesitzer

landscape *n.* Landschaft; (art) Landschaftsbild; — **gardener** Gartenarchitekt; — **gardening** Landschaftsgärtnerei

landslide *n.* Erdrutsch, Bergsturz; (pol.) Wahlsieg (mit überwiegender Mehrheit)

landsman *n.* Landsmann, Landbewohner; (naut.) Landratte

lane *n.* Weg, Gasse; Doppelreihe, Spalier; **traffic** — Fahrbahn

language *n.* Sprache; Ausdrucksweise, Stil; **German** — deutsche Sprache

languid *adj.* schlaff, matt, schwach; langsam, schleichend, träge; flau

languish *v.* schmachten; ermatten, erschlaffen; dahinschwinden; -**ing** *adj.* schmachtend; ermattend, erschlaffend; matt, schlaff, flau

lank *adj.* dünn, schlank; schlicht; -**y** *adj.* schmächtig, dürr

lanolin(e) *n.* Lanolin

lantern *n.* Laterne

lap *n.* Schoss; Vorstoss; (sports) Runde;

— *v.* bespülen; falten, legen, einhüllen, umschlagen; umschliessen; — **up** auflecken

lapel *n.* Aufschlag, Taschenklappe

lapse *n.* Fall, Gleiten; Verlauf, Verfall; Fehler, Fehltritt, Versehen; — *v.* verlaufen, verfliessen; verfallen; (ab)fallen

lard *n.* Schweinefett, Schmalz; — *v.* spicken, einfetten, schmieren

larder *n.* Speisekammer, Speiseschrank

large *adj.* gross, breit, dick, stark; weit; beträchtlich; **at** — frei, ungehindert

lariat *n.* Lasso; Bindeseil, Wurfschlinge

lark *n.* Lerche; (coll.) Schabernack

larva *n.* Larve, Puppe

laryngitis *n.* Kehlkopfentzündung

larynx *n.* Kehlkopf

laser *n.* (abbr.) (light amplification by stimulated emission of radiation) Laser (Lichtverstärkung durch Strahlungsanregung unter Verwendung einer fremden Strahlungsquelle)

lash *n.* Schnur; Schlag, Hieb; Peitsche; Wimper; — *v.* peitschen; (fig.) geisseln

lass *n.* Mädchen, junge Frau

lassitude *n.* Müdigkeit, Abgespanntheit, Mattigkeit

lasso *n.* Lasso, Wurfschlinge

last *adj.* letzt; vorig; **be on one's** — **legs** sich nicht mehr zu helfen wissen; — **judgment** Jüngstes Gericht; — **night** gestern abend; — **supper** letztes Abendmahl; **next to** — vorletzt; — *n.* Letzte; Ende; (shoe) Leisten; **breathe one's** — in den letzten Zügen liegen; **to the very** — bis zum Ende; — *adv.* zuletzt; **at** — endlich; — **of all** zuletzt, am Ende; — *v.* dauern, bestehen, bleiben, währen; ausreichen; -**ing** *adj.* dauerhaft, dauernd, beständig; -**ly** *adv.* zuletzt, endlich, schliesslich

latch *n.* Klinke, Drücker; Sicherheitsschloss; — *v.* einklinken, zuklinken

late *adj.* spät, verspätet; verstorben, selig; vorig, jüngst; **be (too)** — sich verspäten; **of** — kürzlich, jüngst; — *adv.* spät; -**ly** *adv.* kürzlich, neulich, unlängst, vor kurzem; -**ness** *n.* Zuspätkommen, Verspätung; Späte; Neuheit; -**r** *adj.* and *adv.* später; -**r on** späterhin; -**st** *adj.* spätest, neuest; -**st fashion** neu(e)ste Mode; **at the** -**st** spätestens

latent *adj.* latent, verborgen, geheim, versteckt; (phys.) gebunden

lath *n.* Latte; — *v.* mit Latten versehen

lathe *n.* Drehbank

lather *n.* Seifenschaum; — *v.* einseifen, schäumen

Latin *n.* Latein; Lateiner; — *adj.* lateinisch

Latin-American n. Südamerikaner; — adj. südamerikanisch

latitude n. Breite; (fig.) Spielraum

latter adj. letzter, später; **the —** dieser

lattice n. Gitter(werk); Lattenwerk

Latvia n. Lettland

laud n. Lob, Preis; Lobgesang; — v. loben, preisen; **–able** adj. löblich, lobenswert; **–atory** adj. lobend, preisend

laugh n. Lache(n), Gelächter; — v. lachen; **— at** auslachen; **— in one's sleeve** sich ins Fäustchen lachen; **— off** sich lachend hinwegsetzen über; **–able** adj. lächerlich; **–ing** adj. lachend; **–ing gas** Lachgas; **it is no –ing matter** es ist nicht zum Lachen; **–ter** n. Gelächter; **hearty –er** herzliches Lachen

laughingstock n. Gegenstand des Spottes, Zielscheibe des Gelächters

launch n. Stapellauf; **–ing** n. Abschuss; **–ing pad** Raketenabschussbasis; **–ing rail** Raketenabschussführungsschiene; **–ing tube** Raketenabschussführungsrohr; — v. vom Stapel lassen; schleudern; (fig.) in Gang setzen

launder v. waschen und rollen (or plätten)

laundromat n. öffentlicher Waschautomat

laundry n. Wäscherei, Wäsche

laundryman n. Wäschemann

laurel n. Lorbeer; (fig.) Lorbeerkranz, Ehre, Ruhm

lavatory n. Waschraum, Toilette, Abort

lavish adj. verschwenderisch, freigebig; — v. verschwenden, vergeuden

law n. Gesetz, Recht; Rechtswissenschaft; Prozess, Gerichtsverfahren; **according to —** gesetzmässig, rechtmässig; **at —** gerichtlich; **by —** gesetzlich; **take the — into one's own hands** sich selbst Recht verschaffen; **–ful** adj. gesetzlich, gerichtlich; rechtmässig; gültig; **–less** adj. gesetzlos, ungesetzlich; (fig.) zügellos; **–lessness** n. Gesetzlosigkeit, Ungesetzlichkeit; (fig.) Zügellosigkeit; **–yer** n. Rechtsanwalt, Advokat; Jurist, Rechtsgelehrte

law-abiding adj. die Gesetze einhaltend

lawbreaker n. Gesetzes Übertreter; (fig.) Verbrecher

lawgiver n. Gesetzgeber

lawmaker n. Verfasser von Gesetzen

lawn n. Rasen(platz); (cloth) Batist; **— mower** Rasenmähmaschine, Rasenmäher

lawsuit n. Prozess, Rechtshandel

lax adj. schlaff, locker, lose; lax, lässig; **–ity** n. Schlaffheit, Lockerheit; Laxheit

laxative n. Abführmittel; — adj. abführend

lay v. legen, stellen, setzen; wetten; **—**

away aufheben, beiseite legen; **— claim to** Anspruch erheben auf; **— off** abbauen, entlassen; — n. Lage; Lied, Gesang; — adj. weltlich, Laien–; **— brother** Laienbruder; **–er** n. Schicht, Lage; (bot.) Ableger; (zool.) Legehenne; **–er cake** Schichttorte

layette n. Babyausstattung

layman n. Laie

layoff n. zeitweilige Entlassung

laziness n. Faulheit, Trägheit, Lässigkeit

lazy adj. faul, träge, müssig, langsam

lead n. Leitung, Führung; Vorsprung; (cards) Vorhand; (elec.) Leitung, Leiter; (theat.) Hauptrolle; **take the —** die Leitung (or den Vorsitz) übernehmen; — v. führen, leiten; vorangehen; anführen, befehligen; (cards) anspielen, ausspielen; (mus.) dirigieren; vorsingen; **— a dance** vortanzen; **— astray** irreführen; **— off** ableiten; eröffnen; **— the field** die Führung haben; **— the way** vorangehen; **— up to** hinauswollen auf; **–er** n. Führer, Leiter; Anführer, Rädelsführer; (mus.) Dirigent, Kapellmeister; **–ership** n. Führerschaft; Leitung, Aufsicht; **–ing** adj. leitend, lenkend, führend; hervorragend; erste, vornehmste; **–ing article** Leitartikel; Hauptartikel; **–ing axle** Vorderachse; **–ing horse** Spitzenpferd; **–ing lady** erste Liebhaberin (or Heldin); **–ing man** erster Liebhaber (or Held); **–ing note** grosse Septime; **–ing question** Suggestivfrage

lead n. (min.) Blei; (naut.) Lot, Senkblei; (typ.) Durchschuss; **— pencil** Bleistift; **— adj.** bleiern; **–en** adj. bleiern; bleifarben; (fig.) düster; schwerfällig, glanzlos

leaf n. Blatt; (door) Flügel; (table) Klappe; **turn over a new —** ein neues Leben beginnen; — v. **— through** durchblättern, herumblättern in; **–less** adj. blattlos, entblättert; **–let** n. Blättchen, Zettel; Prospekt, Flugschrift; **–y** adj. belaubt, laubreich

league n. Bund, Liga; Bündnis; (naut.) Seemeile; — v. (sich) verbünden

leak n. Leck, Ritze; **spring a —** leck werden; — v. lecken, leck sein; **— out** auslaufen, austropfen; (fig.) bekannt werden, durchsickern; **–age** n. Leckwerden; Undichtheit, Auslaufen; (elec.) Ableitung; (gas) Verlust; (news) Durchsickern; **–y** adj. leck, undicht, durchlässig

leakproof adj. undurchlässig, undurchlöcherbar

lean v. (sich) lehnen, anlehnen, auflehnen; sich neigen, schief stehen; sich stützen (*or* aufstützen); — **against** (sich) lehnen gegen; — **forward** sich vorlehnen; — **on** sich stützen auf; (fig.) sich verlassen auf; -**ing** *n.* Neigung

lean, leanness *n.* Magere, mageres Fleisch; — *adj.* mager, dürr, dünn

leap *n.* Sprung, Satz, Salto; **by** -**s** sprungweise; — **year** Schaltjahr; — *v.* springen, hüpfen

leapfrog *n.* Bockspringen; — *v.* bockspringen

learn *v.* (er)lernen; hören, erfahren; -**ed** *adj.* gelehrt, wissenschaftlich gebildet; -**edly** *adv.* erfahren, bewandert, in gelehrter Weise, als Gelehrter; -**ing** *n.* Lernen; Gelehrsamkeit, Wissen

lease *n.* Vermietung, Verpachtung; Miete, Pacht; Mietvertrag; Mietzeit; — *v.* vermieten, verpachten

leash *n.* Leine, Koppel; — *v.* koppeln, an der Leine führen

least *adj.* kleinste, geringste; mindeste, wenigste; — *adv.* am wenigsten; **at** — wenigstens, mindestens; — **of all** am allerwenigsten; **not in the** — nicht im geringsten, keineswegs; **the** — **possible** am wenigsten möglich; — *n.* Kleinste, Geringste

leather *n.* Leder; — *adj.* ledern, Leder-; -**ette** *n.* Ledertuch; Kunstleder; -**y** *adj.* ledern, lederartig

leave *n.* Urlaub; Abschied; Erlaubnis; — **of absence** Urlaub; **take** — Abschied nehmen; **take** — **of one's senses** den Verstand verlieren; — *v.* lassen; verlassen; übriglassen, dalassen, zurücklassen; aufgeben; vermachen, hinterlassen; abreisen, abfahren, fortgehen, weggehen; — **alone** in Ruhe (*or* Frieden) lassen; — **home** das Haus (*or* Zuhause) verlassen; — **open** offen (*or* unentschieden) lassen; — **word** Bescheid hinterlassen; **she** -**s** it to you sie überlässt es Ihnen

leaven *n.* Sauerteig, Hefe; — *v.* säuern, gären; (fig.) beeinflussen

leave-taking *n.* Abschiednehmen, Lebewohl

leavings *n. pl.* Überbleibsel, Reste

lectern *n.* Lesepult, Chorpult

lecture *n.* Vortrag, Vorlesung, Kolleg; Verweis, Strafpredigt; — *v.* vorlesen, vortragen; zurechtweisen, abkanzeln; -**r** *n.* Vortragende; (college) Dozent, Professor

ledge *n.* Sims, Leiste, Rand; (min.) Schicht, Lager

ledger *n.* (arch.) Querbalken, Schwelle; (com.) Hauptbuch; — **line** Hilfsnotenlinie

lee *n.* Schutz; (naut.) Lee(seite); — *adj.* lee

leech *n.* Blutegel; (fig.) Blutsauger

leer *n.* Seitenblick. lüsterner Blick; — *v.* schielen, lüstern blicken

lees *n. pl.* Bodensatz, Hefe

leeway *n.* Abtrift; **give** — gewähren lassen

left *adj.* linke; —' *adv.* links; — *n.* Linke; (pol.) Linkspartei(en); **at the** — **of** links von; **on the** — zur Linken, auf der Linken; **to the** — (nach) links; -**ist** *n.* Linke, Anhänger einer Linkspartei

left-handed *adj.* linkshändig; (fig.) linkisch

leftover *n.* Überbleibsel, Rest

leg *n.* Bein; Schenkel; (boot) Schaft; (meat) Keule, Schlegel; **he hasn't a** — **to stand on** er hat keinen Grund unter den Füssen; — **of a compass** Kompasschenkel; **pull someone's** — jemanden zum besten haben; **wooden** — Holzbein, Stelzfuss

legacy *n.* Vermächtnis, Legat

legal *adj.* gesetzlich, gesetzmässig, legal; rechtskräftig, rechtsgültig; Rechts-; — **tender** gesetzlich anerkanntes Zahlungsmittel; -**ity** *n.* Gesetzlichkeit, Gesetzmässigkeit; Legalität; -**ize** *v.* rechtskräftig machen, gerichtlich bestätigen, für rechtmässig erklären

legation *n.* Legation, Gesandtschaft

legend *n.* Sage, Legende; Inschrift; Umschrift; -**ary** *adj.* sagenhaft, legendär

legging *n.* Gamasche

legibility *n.* Leserlichkeit, Lesbarkeit

legible *adj.* leserlich, lesbar; (fig.) erkennbar, deutlich

legislate *v.* Gesetze geben; durch Gesetze bewirken

legislation *n.* Gesetzgebung

legislative *adj.* gesetzgebend, gesetzlich, — **body** gesetzgebende Gewalt

legislator *n.* Gesetzgeber

legislature *n.* Gesetzgebung; gesetzgebender Körper

legitimate *adj.* ehelich, legitim; rechtmässig, gesetzlich

leisure *n.* Musse, Freizeit; Bequemlichkeit; **at** — in Musse; **at one's** — nach seiner Bequemlichkeit, bei passender Gelegenheit; — *adj.* frei, müssig, unbeschäftigt; — **hours** Mussestunden; -**ly** *adj.* mit Musse

lemon *n.* Zitrone, Limone; Zitronenbaum; — **drop** Zitronenbonbon; — **squeezer** Zitronenpresse; -**ade** *n.* Limonade

lend *v.* (aus)leihen, verleihen, verborgen; (fig.) geben, gewähren, leisten; -**er** *n.* Leihende, Leiher, Verleiher

length n. Länge; Dauer; Strecke, Ausdehnung; **at full** — in voller Länge; (art) in Lebensgrösse; **at great** — sehr ausführlich; **at** — vollständig, zuletzt; **-en** v. verlängern; dehnen; **-y** adj. ausgedehnt; weitschweifig, langweilig

lengthwise adv. der Länge nach; — adj. der Länge nach gehend

leniency n. Milde, Sanftmut

lenient adj. mild, nachsichtig

lens n. Linse; **burning** — Brennglas

Lent n. Fasten(zeit)

lentil n. Linse

leopard n. Leopard

leper n. Leprakranke, Aussätzige

leprosy n. Lepra, Aussatz

less adj. and adv. kleiner, geringer; weniger; — prep. abzüglich; **-en** v. abnehmen, sich vermindern; verkleinern, verringern

lessee n. Mieter, Pächter

lesson n. Aufgabe; Lektion, Übungsstück; Lehrstunde, Lehre

lessor n. Vermieter, Verpächter

lest conj. damit nicht; aus Furcht, dass

let v. lassen, erlauben, gestatten; vermieten, verpachten; verdingen

letdown n. Herablassung; Enttäuschung

letter n. Brief, Schreiben; Buchstabe, Type; (fig.) buchstäblicher Sinn; pl. Literatur, Wissenschaft; **capital** — Grossbuchstabe; — **box** Briefkasten; — **carrier** Briefträger; — **drop** Briefeinwurf; — **opener** Brieföffner; — **of credit** Kreditbrief; — **of introduction** Enfürungsschreiben; **capital** — Grossbuchstabe; **lower-case** — kleiner Buchstabe; **registered** — eingeschriebener Brief; **unclaimed** — unbestellbarer Brief; — v. mit Buchstaben versehen

letterhead n. Briefkopf

lettuce n. Salat, Kopfsalat, Blattsalat

leucocyte n. Leukozyt, weisses Blutkörperchen

leukemia n. Leukämie

levee n. Uferdamm

level n. Höhe, Niveau; Ebene, Fläche; Wasserwage; Richtscheit; — adj. waagerecht; eben, glatt, flach, gerade; — v. ebnen, planieren; einebnen, gleichmachen; richten

levelheaded adj. verständig, mit gesundem Urteil begabt

lever n. Hebel, Hebebaum; Schwengel; **-age** n. Hebelwirkung; Hebelkraft

levity n. Leichtheit, Leichtigkeit; (fig.) Leichtsinn, Leichtfertigkeit

lewd adj. unzüchtig, schlüpfrig, liederlich

lexicon n. Lexikon, Wörterbuch

liability n. Verbindlichkeit, Verpflichtung;

Haftpflicht; Verantwortlichkeit; pl. Passiva, Schulden

liable adj. haftbar, haftpflichtig; verantwortlich; ausgesetzt, unterworfen

liar n. Lügner

libel n. Schmähschrift, Verleumdung; — v. schmähen, verleumden; **-(l)er** n. Schmäher, Lästerer, Verleumder; **-(l)ous** adj. schmähend, lästernd; verleumdend

liberal adj. liberal, freigesinnt; grossmütig, vorurteilslos; freigebig; — n. Liberale; **-ism** n. Liberalismus; **-ity** n. Grossherzigkeit, Freisinnigkeit, Freigebigkeit; **-ly** adv. frei gewährt, reichlich; zügellos

liberate v. befreien; freigeben, freilassen

liberation n. Befreiung

liberator n. Befreier

liberty n. Freiheit; **be at** — frei sein; **freie Hand haben**; **set at** — befreien, in Freiheit setzen; **take liberties with sich** Freiheiten herausnehmen; **take the** — of sich die Freiheit nehmen zu

librarian n. Bibliothekar

library n. Bibliothek

license n. Konzession, Erlaubnis, Genehmigung, Lizenz, Gewerbeschein; — **number** Lizenznummer; — **plate** Nummernschild; — v. konzessionieren, behördlich bewilligen, berechtigen

licentious adj. übertrieben, unbändig; ausgelassen, ausschweifend, zügellos

lick n. Lecken; Schlag, Streich; Salzlecke; — v. (be)lecken; schlagen, prügeln; übertreffen, besiegen; — **up** auflecken

licorice n. Süssholz, Lakritze

lid n. Deckel, Klappe; (eye) Lid

lie n. Lüge, Erdichtung, Fabel; **Lage**; **give the** — **to** Lügen strafen; **tell -s** lügen; **white** — Notlüge; — v. liegen, ruhen; lügen, fabeln

Liége n. Lüttich

lien n. Pfandrecht

lieu n. **in** — **of** anstatt

lieutenant n. (mil.) Leutnant; (pol.) Stellvertreter; — **colonel** Oberstleutnant; — **commander** Korvettenkapitän; — **general** Generalleutnant; **first** — Oberleutnant

life n. Leben; Lebensdauer; Person, Menschenleben; Lebensart; Wesen, Lebewesen; Lebhaftigkeit; Lebensbeschreibung; Lebensgrösse; — **annuity** Lebensrente; — **belt** Rettungsgürtel; — **buoy** Rettungsboje; — **insurance** Lebensversicherung; — **preserver** Schwimmgürtel; Totschläger; — **raft** Rettungsfloss; **come to** — zur Welt kommen; **early** — Jugend; **for** — fürs

Leben, auf Lebenszeit; **from —** nach dem Leben, nach der Natur; **in the prime of —** in der Blüte des Lebens; **married — Fheleben; matter of —** and **death** Angelegenheit auf Leben und Tod;·**way of —** Lebensweise; **-less** adj. leblos, unbelebt; tot; (fig.) kraftlos; **-like** adj. lebensgetreu, naturgetreu

lifeboat n. Rettungsboot

lifeguard n. Rettungsschwimmer, Bademeister

lifelong adj. lebenslang, lebenslänglich

lifesaver n. Lebensretter

life-size adj. lebensgross

lifetime n. Lebenszeit, Lebensdauer; **once in a —** einmal im Leben; **—** adj. lebenslänglich

lifework n. Lebenswerk

lift n. Heben, Aufheben; Erhebung, Aufschwung; (mech.) Hub; Aufzug; **give someone a —** jemandem helfen (or im Auto mitnehmen); **—** r. (er)heben, aufheben, lüften; sich heben, aufsteigen; (coll.) wegnehmen, stehlen

ligament n. Band, Fessel; (anat.) Sehne, Flechse

light n. Licht, Tageslicht; Helligkeit; **in the —** of wie; **—** v. leuchten, anzünden, entzünden; beleuchten, erhalten; hell sein, sich entzünden; **— up** (er)leuchten, aufleuchten; **—** adj. hell, licht; leicht; unbeladen; gering; mässig; schwach; **-en** v. lichter (or heller) werden; leuchten, blitzen; erleuchten; (fig.) erleichtern; **-ing** n. Beleuchtung; **-ly** adv. leicht(fertig), geringschätzig, verächtlich; **-ness** n. Leichtigkeit; Helligkeit; Leichtheit, Gewandtheit

lighter n. (naut.) Leichter; Leuchtschiff; (cigarette) Feuerzeug

lightning n. Blitz; **heat —** Wetterleuchten; **— bug** Leuchtkäfer; **— rod** Blitzableiter

lighthearted adj. leichten Herzens, heiter; sorglos, lustig

lighthouse n. Leuchtturm

lightweight n. Leichtgewicht

like n. Gleiche, Ähnliche; pl. Neigungen; **—** adj. gleich, ähnlich, gleichartig; **—** adv. ebenso, gleich(sam), ähnlich; prep. wie, gleich; **be —** ähneln; **— father — son** der Apfel fällt nicht weit vom Stamm; **—** v. gern haben, mögen; **be -d** beliebt sein; **-able** adj. angenehm, reizend, liebenswürdig; **-lihood** n. Wahrscheinlichkeit, Anschein; **-ly** adj. wahrscheinlich; geeignet; **not -ly** wohl schwerlich, kaum; **-n** v. vergleichen; **-ness** n. Ähnlichkeit, Gleichheit; Ebenbild

likewise adv. ebenso, gleichfalls

liking n. Neigung, Wohlgefallen

lilac n. Flieder; Lila; **—** adj. lila(farben)

lilt n. rhythmischer Schwung; Tanzen; **—** v. trällern, lustig singen

lily n. Lilie; **— of the valley** Maiglöckchen, Maiblume; **—** adj. lilienhaft, lilienweiss; rein, keusch

limb n. (anat.) Glied; (ast.) Rand; (bot.) Ast, Arm; Rand; (geol.) Ausläufer; (fig.) Stück, Teil

limber adj. biegsam, geschmeidig; (fig.) nachgiebig; **—** v. aufprotzen

lime n. Vogelleim; (bot.) Lindenbaum; Zitronenbaum; (min.) Kalk, Mörtel

limelight n. Scheinwerferlicht; Mittelpunkt des öffentlichen Interesses

limestone n. Kalkstein

limit n. Grenze, Schranke, Ziel; Frist; Gebiet, Bezirk; **there is a — to everything** alles hat seine Grenzen; **to the —** bis aufs Äusserste; **—** v. beschränken, einschränken, begrenzen; **-ation** n. Beschränkung, Einschränkung; Abgrenzung; (law) Verjährungsfrist; **-ed** adj. begrenzt, eingeschränkt; **-ed in time** befristet; **-less** adj. unbegrenzt, unbeschränkt, grenzenlos

limousine n. Limousine

limp n. Lahmen, Hinken, Humpeln; **—** v. lahmen, hinken, humpeln; **—** adj. schlaff, schlapp

linden n. Linde

line n. Linie, Reihe; Leine, Schnur; (com.) Zweig, Fach; (genealogy) Stamm, Geschlecht; (lit.) Vers, Zeile; (rail.) Linie, Bahn, Spur, Geleise; (tel.) Leitung; (typ.) Zeile; (fig.) Richtung; **keep in —** im Glied bleiben, in Zaum halten; **— of argument** Beweisführung; **stand in —** Schlange stehen; **—** v. (ab)füttern, ausfüttern, polstern; Spalier bilden, umsäumen; lin(i)ieren, Linien ziehen; **— up** (sich) in Linie (or Reihen) aufstellen; **-age** n. Geschlecht, Familie; Stammbaum; **-al** adj. gerade, direkt; g(e)radlinig, Längen-; ererbt, angestammt; direkt abstammend; **-ar** adj. linear; g(e)radlinie; (bot.) fadenförmig, linienförmig

lineman n. (football) Stürmer; (tel.) Streckenarbeiter

linen n. Leinen, Linnen, Leinewand, Leinenzeug; Wäsche, Bettwäsche; **dirty —** Schmutzwäsche; **—** adj. leinen, aus Leinwand

line-up n. Formation; (baseball) Spielerliste; (football) Aufstellung; (police) Reihe vorgeführter Personen

linger v. sich aufhalten, zaudern, zögern;

säumen; -ing *adj.* langsam, schleichend, zögernd

lingerie *n.* Damenwäsche

linguist *n.* Sprachforscher

liniment *n.* Salbe, Einreibung

lining *n.* Futter, Besatz, Ausfütterung; (arch.) Wandbekleidung; silver — Silberverbrämung

link *n.* Glied, Gelenk, Schleife, Band; (fig.) Bindeglied; — *v.* (sich) verketten, (sich) verbinden

linnet *n.* Hänfling

linoleum *n.* Linoleum

Linotype *n.* Linotype, Setzmaschine

linseed *n.* Leinsamen

lint *n.* Scharpie

lintel *n.* Oberbalken, Oberschwelle, Fenstersturz

lion *n.* Löwe; (lit.) Leu; (fig.) Held des Tages; —'s share Löwenanteil; -ess *n.* Löwin

lip *n.* Lippe; (edge) Rand; (coll.) Unverschämtheit

lipstick *n.* Lippenstift

liquefy *v.* schmelzen, flüssig machen (*or* werden); auflösen

liqueur *n.* Likör

liquid *n.* Flüssigkeit; — *adj.* flüssig, fliessend; (mus.) sanft tönend, schmelzend; — air flüssige Luft; — measure Flüssigkeitsmass; -ate *v.* liquidieren; -ation *n.* Liquidation, Abwicklung, Auflösung; Bezahlung, Abtragung

liquor *n.* Alkohol, alkoholisches Getränk; — dealer Spirituosenhändler

lisp *n.* Lispeln; — *v.* lispeln

list *n.* Liste, Verzeichnis; Leiste, Streifen; Rand, Saum; (naut.) Schlagseite; *pl.* Schranken; — price Katalogpreis; — *v.* registrieren, katalogisieren, in eine Liste eintragen, verzeichnen; (naut.) Schlagseite haben

listen *v.* anhören, zuhören; horchen, lauschen; -er *n.* Hörer, Zuhörer; Horcher, Lauscher

litany *n.* Litanei, Bittgebet

liter *n.* Liter

literacy *n.* wissenschaftliche Bildung, Belesenheit

literal *adj.* wörtlich, buchstäblich; Buchstaben

literary *adj.* literarisch, gelehrt, schriftstellerisch

literate *adj.* gebildet, literarisch

literature *n.* Literatur, Schrifttum

lithograph *n.* Lithographie, Steindruck; — *v.* lithographieren; -y *n.* Lithographie, Steindruckkunst

litigation *n.* Prozess, Rechtsstreit

litter *n.* Tragbahre; Brut, Wurf; Streu,

Strohmatte; (fig.) Unordnung; — *v.* umherwerfen, verstreuen, in Unordnung bringen

litterbug *n.* Schmutzfink, Strassenbeschmutzer

little *n.* Kleine, Wenige; Kleinigkeit; — *adj.* klein; kurz; gering(fügig), wenig; etwas; — one Kleines; very — sehr wenig; — *adv.* wenig; kaum; a — ein wenig, etwas; — by — nach und nach

liturgy *n.* Liturgie

live *v.* leben; wohnen; sich nähren; — on leben von; — up to erfüllen; -er *n.* Lebende; Wohnende, Bewohner

live *adj.* lebend, lebendig; lebhaft, frisch; (bullet) scharf; (coal) glühend; (elec.) geladen; -lihood *n.* Lebensunterhalt, Auskommen; -liness *n.* Lebhaftigkeit, Munterkeit; -ly *adj.* lebhaft, munter, lebendig, heiter

livelong *adj.* langanhaltend; the — day den lieben, langen Tag

liver *n.* Leber

liverwurst *n.* Leberwurst

livery *n.* Livree, Uniform

livestock *n.* Vieh(stand)

living *n.* Leben; Lebensunterhalt; *pl.* Lebendigen; make a — sein Auskommen haben; — *adj.* lebend(ig); glühend; (fig.) tätig, belebend; — room Wohnzimmer; — wage angemessenes Gehalt

Livonia *n.* Livland

lizard *n.* Eidechse

llama *n.* Lama

load *n.* Last, Bürde; Ladung; (mech.) Belastung; — *v.* laden; beladen, befrachten; beschweren, belasten

loaf *n.* Laib; Brot; — *v.* müssig gehen, bummeln, herumlungern; -er *n.* Müssiggänger, Bummler

loam *n.* Lehm

loan *n.* Darlehen, Anleihe; — *v.* (aus)leihen

loathe *v.* sich ekeln; hassen; verabscheuen

loathing *n.* Widerwille, Ekel, Abscheu

lobby *n.* Vorhalle, Vorsaal, Korridor; (pol.) Wandelgang; Gruppe, die Abgeordnete zu beeinflussen sucht; (theat.) Foyer; — *v.* (pol.) beeinflussen; -ist *n.* (pol.) Beeinflusser

lobe *n.* Lappen; Keule (radar) Radarauffanggerät; — of the ear Ohrläppchen; — of the lungs Lungenflügel

local *n.* Lokal; Ortsbewohner; Lokalnachricht; (rail.) Ortszug; — *adj.* lokal, örtlich, räumlich; hiesig; -e *n.* Örtlichkeit; -ity *n.* Ort; -ize *v.* lokalisieren

locate *v.* abgrenzen; ausfindig machen; (die Grenzen) bestimmen; (mil.) erkunden; be -d gelegen sein; (fig.) liegen, wohnen

location *n.* Lage; Unterbringung; Vermietung; Landvermessung; (film) Ort der Aussenaufnahme

lock *n.* Schloss; Schleuse; Locke, Flocke; — **stitch** Steppstich; —, **stock and barrel** die ganze Geschichte; **air** — pneumatische Schleuse; **under** — **and key** hinter Schloss und Riegel; — *v.* schliessen, verschliessen, sich abschliessen; (mech.) verkuppeln; — **in** einschliessen, einsperren; — **out** ausschliessen, aussperren; — **up** abschliessen, absperren; **-er** *n.* verschliessbarer Kasten (*or* Schrank); Schliessfach; Kühlanlage; **-er room** Garderobe

locket *n.* Medaillon

lockjaw *n.* Kinnbackenkrampf

lockout *n.* Aussperrung

locksmith *n.* Schlosser

locomotion *n.* Ortsveränderung

locomotive *n.* Lokomotive

locust *n.* Heuschrecke, Zikade; (bot.) unechte Akazie

lodestar *n.* Leitstern, Polarstern

lodge *n.* Hütte, Häuschen; Loge; — *v.* wohnen, beherbergen; unterbringen, übernachten; hinterlegen, lagern; **-r** *n.* Mieter, Hausbewohner

lodging *n.* Wohnung, Logis; *pl.* Mietswohnung

loft *n.* Dachgeschoss, Dachkammer; Boden, Speicher

loftiness *n.* Höhe, Erhabenheit; (fig.) Stolz, Grösse

lofty *adj.* hoch; erhaben, stattlich

log *n.* Klotz, Block; (naut.) Log; — **cabin** Blockhaus; **-ging** *n.* Holzfällen, Holzflössen

logbook *n.* Logbuch, Schiffsjournal

logic *n.* Logik; **-al** *adj.* logisch, folgerichtig

logistics *n.* Einquartierung

logrolling *n.* Holzflössen; (pol.) gegenseitige Unterstützung (*or* Begünstigung)

loin *n.* Lende; Lendenstück, Nierenbraten

loiter *v.* sich aufhalten, zögern, trödeln, bummeln; **-er** *n.* Zauderer, Müssiggänger, Faulenzer, Bummler

lone *adj.* einsam, einzeln, weltabgeschieden; ledig; **-liness** *n.* Einsamkeit, Verlassenheit; **-ly** *adj.* einsam, verlassen; **-some** *adj.* einsam, vereinsamt

long *adj.* lang; langwierig, weitläufig; weitgehend; **a** — **time** lange; **as** — **as** solange; **in the** — **run** am Ende, zuletzt; — **ago** vor langer Zeit; — **odds** hoher Einsatz; — *adv.* lange, über, hindurch; **all day** — den ganzen Tag lang; — *n.* Länge; — *v.* verlangen, sich sehnen; **-ing** *n.* Sehnsucht, Verlangen; **-ing** *adj.*

sehnsüchtig, verlangend

long-distance *adj.* weit entfernt; — **call** Ferngespräch

long-haired *adj.* langhaarig; (coll.) übercultiviert

longhand *n.* Handschrift

longitude *n.* Länge

longitudinal *adj.* der Länge nach, Längen-

long-lived *adj.* langlebig, sich lange haltend

long-playing *adj.* langspielend; **Langspiel-**

long-term *adj.* langfristig

long-winded *adj.* langatmig

look *n.* Blick; Anblick; Ansehen, Aussehen, Miene; — *v.* blicken, sehen, schauen; scheinen; aussehen; — **after** aufpassen auf; — **around** umschauen; — **at** ansehen, betrachten; — **down** (verächtlich) herabsehen; — **for** suchen; — **forward to** sich freuen auf; — **into** untersuchen; — **on** betrachten; zuschauen; — **out** achtgeben; Achtung! — **over** (*oder* **through**) durchsehen; — **up** aufblicken; aufsuchen, nachschlagen; **that's how it -s to me** so kommt es mir vor; **-ing** *adj.* **-ing glass** Spiegel

lookout *n.* (mil.) Ausschau, Ausblick; Wache; (naut.) Ausguck, Auslug; (fig.) Aussicht

loom *n.* Webstuhl; — *v.* sichtbar werden; undeutlich erscheinen

loop *n.* Schleife, Schlinge; Biegung, Krümmung; Öse; (avi.) Looping; (sich) winden; (avi.) einen Looping fliegen

loophole *n.* Guckloch, Luke; (mil.) Schiessscharte; (coll.) Schlupfloch; (fig.) Ausflucht, Vorwand

loose *adj.* los(e), frei, locker; einzeln; unzusammenhängend; **be at** — **ends** nicht recht wissen, was zu tun; **get** — loskommen; **set** — **in** Freiheit setzen; — *v.* lösen, befreien; **-n** *v.* lose (*or* locker) machen; lösen, auflösen; losmachen, losbinden; ablösen, freimachen; (fig.) trennen; **-ness** *n.* Lockerheit; (fig.) Liederlichkeit

loose-jointed *adj.* gelenkig

loose-leaf *adj.* mit losen Blättern

loot *n.* Beute, Raubgut; — *v.* plündern, erbeuten

lop *v.* schlaff hängen; beschneiden, stutzen

lope *n.* Trott, langer Schritt; — *v.* trotten

lop-eared *adj.* mit Hängeohren

lopsided *adj.* schief, einseitig

loquacious *adj.* geschwätzig, redselig

lord *n.* Herr, Gebieter; Lord; **Lord Herr, Gott, Herrgott; Almighty Lord** Allmächtiger Gott; **good Lord!** grosser Gott! **Lord's Prayer** Vaterunser; **Lord's Supper** Heiliges Abendmahl; — *v.* — **it**

den grossen Herrn spielen; — it over herrschen (or gebieten) über; -ly adj. herrenmässig; vornehm, stattlich; stolz, hochmütig; -ship n. Herrschaft; (title) Lordschaft

lore n. Kenntnis, Wissenschaft, Lehre, Kunde

Lorraine n. Lothringen

lose v. verlieren, einbüssen; verspielen; den Kürzeren ziehen; versäumen, verpassen; (watch) nachgehen; — color abfärben, sich verfärben; — ground Einfluss verlieren; — heart (or courage) den Mut verlieren; — one's senses den Verstand verlieren; — one's temper ärgerlich werden; — one's way sich verirren; — out vollständig verlieren; — sight of aus den Augen verlieren; -r n. Verlierer, Verspieler; good -r guter Verlierer

loss n. Verlust, Einbusse; Nachteil, Schaden; be at a — verlegen sein

lost adj. be — verloren gehen; give up for — verloren geben

lot n. Los, Geschick; Teil, Anteil; Posten; Partie, Bande, Gesellschaft, Menge; Parzelle; Kabel; a —, -s eine Menge, ein Haufen; **building** — Bauplatz; **draw** -s Lose ziehen

lotion n. Scheinheitswasser; **eye** — Augenwasser

lottery n. Lotterie

loud adj. laut, geräuschvoll; grell, auffallend; -ness n. Lautheit, Lautstärke; Geschrei, Lärm

loudspeaker n. Lautsprecher

lounge n. Foyer, Wandelgang; Sofa, Chaiselongue; — v. müssiggehen, schlendern; faulenzen

louse n. Laus; **plant** — Blattlaus

lousy adj. lausig; (fig.) gemein, filzig

Louvain n. Löwen

lovable adj. liebenswürdig

love n. Liebe; Liebchen, Liebste; Vorliebe, Liebschaft; (tennis) Null; be in — verliebt sein; **fall in** — sich verlieben; **make** — den Hof machen; — v. lieben, liebhaben; -liness n. Lieblichkeit, Liebenswürdigkeit; -ly adj. lieblich, liebenswürdig; allerliebst, wunderschön; -r n. Liebhaber, Liebende

lovebird n. Wellensittich, Sperlingspapagei

love-making n. Hofmachen, Courschneiden

lovesick adj. liebeskrank

loving adj. liebend

low n. Niedrige; — adj. niedrig, tief; gering, mässig; seicht, billig, wohlfeil; (med.) schwach; (mus.) dunkel, leise;

(fig.) niedergeschlagen; — v. brüllen, muhen; -er adj. niedriger, tiefer; niedere, untere; -er berth untere Bett; -er case Kleinbuchstabe; -er v. herunterlassen, herablassen; senken, sinken; herabsetzen; schwächen; erniedrigen; -liness n. Erniedrigung; -ly adj. demütig, bescheiden; gering, gewöhnlich

lox (liquid oxygen) n. flüssiger Sauerstoff; — v. mit flüssigem Sauerstoff füllen

loyal adj. loyal, treu ergeben; (ge)treu, beständig, zuverlässig; -ist n. Loyale, Treugesinnte; -ty n. Treue, Loyalität

lozenge n. Rhombus; Pastille, Bonbon

lube n. ölen, Schmieren

lubricant n. Schmiermittel; — adj. schlüpfrig; schmierend

lubricate v. ölen, schmieren

lubrication n. Ölen, Schmieren

Lucerne, Lake of n. Vierwaldstättersee

lucid adj. licht, leuchtend; hell, glänzend; klar, durchsichtig

luck n. Glück(sfall); Zufall; **bad** — Unglück, Pech; **by** — glücklicherweise; **good** — Glück, Chance; -ily adv. zum Glück, glücklicherweise; -less adj. unglücklich, erfolglos; ungünstig; -y adj. glücklich, erfolgreich; günstig; **be** -y Glück haben; -y **chance** günstige Gelegenheit

lucrative adj. gewinnbringend, einträglich; lukrativ

lug v. ziehen, zerren, schleppen

luggage n. Gepäck, Reisegepäck; — **rack** Gepäcknetz, Gepäckständer

lukewarm adj. lauwarm; (fig.) gleichgültig

lull n. Einlullen; Windpause, Windstille; — v. einlullen; (fig.) beruhigen, stillen

lullaby n. Schlummerlied, Wiegenlied

lumber n. Bauholz; — **dealer** Bauholzhändler

lumberjack n. Holzfäller, Holzarbeiter

lumberman n. Holzhändler; Holzfäller

lumberyard n. Holzplatz

luminous adj. leuchtend, glänzend; lichtvoll; Licht-, Leucht-

lump n. Klumpen, Stück; Masse, Ganze, Menge, Haufen; Beule, Schlag; — **sugar** Würfelzucker, Stückzucker; — **sum** runde Summe, Gesamtsumme; — v. vereinigen, zusammenwerfen

lunacy n. (med.) Mondsucht; (fig.) Irrsinn, Wahnsinn, Verrücktheit

lunatic adj. (med.) mondsüchtig; (fig.) irrsinnig, wahnsinnig, verrückt; — **asylum** Irrenhaus; — n. Irrsinnige, Wahnsinnige

'unch n. Imbiss; Gabelfrühstück; — v. frühstücken; -eon n. formelles Essen,

Mittagessen
lung *n.* Lunge, Lungenflügel; **iron —** eiserne Lunge
lunge *n.* Ausfall, Stoss; Bewegung, Ruck; **— v.** stossen, ausfallen; losstürzen
lurch *n.* Taumeln, Ruck; (naut.) Überholen; **leave in the —** im Stich lassen; **— v.** taumeln, wanken; (naut.) überholen
lure *n.* (fishing) Köder; (fig.) Lockmittel; **— v.** ködern, (an)locken, reizen
luscious *adj.* köstlich, schmackhaft; saftig, süss; lieblich; (fig.) übersüss, widerlich
lush *adj.* frisch, saftig, üppig
lust *n.* Begierde, Wollust; Lust, Gier; Hang, Sucht; **— v.** begehren, gelüsten; sich sehnen; **-y** *adj.* munter, lebhaft; lustig, fröhlich; kräftig, tüchtig, rüstig
luster, *n.* Glanz, Schimmer
lute *n.* Laute
Lutheran *n.* Lutheraner; **— adj.** lutherisch
luxuriant *adj.* üppig, wuchernd
luxurious *adj.* luxuriös, verschwenderisch, schwelgerisch
luxury *n.* Luxus, Verschwendung; Üppigkeit, Wohlleben
lyceum *n.* Lyzeum
lye *n.* Lauge
lying *n.* Lüge, Unwahrheit; **— adj.** lügnerisch, lügend
lymph *n.* Lymphe; (med.) Impfstoff; **-atic** *adj.* lymphatisch; (fig.) schlaff
lynch *n.* Volksjustiz; Lynchen; **— v.** lynchen, Volksjustiz ausüben
lyre *n.* Leier
lyric(al) *adj.* lyrisch
lysol *n.* Lysol

M

macabre *adj.* todesdüster
macadam *n.* Schotter(strasse); Asphalt
Mach *n.* Geschwindigkeitsmasseinheit-1-mal die Schallgeschwindigkeit (nach Ernst Mach, Physiker)
machination *n.* Anstiftung, *pl.* Ränke
machine *n.* Maschine; Triebwerk, Getriebe; (pol.) Organisation; **— gun** Maschinengewehr; **— tool** Werkzeugmaschine; **— v.** mit Maschinen arbeiten, maschinell herstellen; **-ry** *n.* Maschinerie, Mechanismus
machinist *n.* Maschinist; Maschinenarbeiter, Maschinenmeister; Maschinenbauer, Maschinenbauingenieur
mackerel *n.* Makrele
mackintosh *n.* Regenmantel
macrocosm *n.* Makrokosmos, Weltall
mad *adj.* toll, verrückt, wahnsinnig; böse

zornig; **go — verrückt werden; it's enough to drive one —** man könnte aus der Haut fahren; **— dog** toller Hund; **-den v.** toll (*or* rasend, böse, wütend) machen; rasend werden; **-ness** *n.* Tollheit, Verrücktheit, Wahnsinn; Tollwut; Wut, Zorn; (fig.) Begeisterung
madam *n.* gnädige Frau; Hausfrau
made *adj.* gemacht, angefertigt, hergestellt; ausgebildet
made-to-order *adj.* auf Bestellung gemacht
made-up *adj.* ausgedacht, zurechtgemacht; geschminkt
madhouse *n.* Tollhaus, Irrenhaus
madman *n.* Wahnsinnige, Verrückte
magazine *n.* Zeitschrift; Magazin; Lagerhaus, Speicher; (naut.) Pulverkammer
magic *n.* Zauber; Magie, Zauberei, Zauberkunst; **— adj.** magisch, zauberhaft; bezaubernd; **-ian** *n.* Magier, Zauberer, Zauberkünstler
magistrate *n.* Beamte, Gerichtsbeamte; Polizeirichter
magnanimity *n.* Grossherzigkeit, Grossmut
magnanimous *adj.* grossherzig, grossmütig
magnesium *n.* Magnesium; **— sulphate** Bittersalz
magnet *n.* Magnet; **-ic** *adj.* magnetisch; **-ism** *n.* Magnetismus, magnetische Kraft
magneto *n.* Zündapparat; Magnetzündung
magnificence *n.* Pracht, Herrlichkeit, Grossartigkeit
magnificent *adj.* prachtvoll, herrlich, grossartig
magnify *v.* vergrössern
magnifying glass *n.* Vergrösserungsglas, Lupe
magnitude *n.* Grösse, Umfang; (fig.) Wichtigkeit
magpie *n.* Elster
mahogany *n.* Mahagonibaum, Mahagoniholz; **— adj.** mahagonifarben
maid *n.* Mädchen, Jungfrau; **Maid, Magd; old — alte Jungfer; -en n.** Mädchen, Jungfrau; **-en** *adj.* mädchenhaft, jungfräulich; unverheiratet; (fig.) neu, frisch; **-en speech** Jungfernrede; **-en voyage** Jungfernfahrt
mail *n.* Post(sendung); Panzer, Rüstung; **by — per Post; by registered —** eingeschrieben; **by return —** postwendend, mit umgehender Post
mailbag *n.* Briefbeutel
mailbox *n.* Briefkasten
mailman *n.* Briefträger, Postbote

mail-order house n. Postversandgeschäft

maim v. verstümmeln, verkrüppeln

main n. Hauptrohr; Gewalt, Macht, Stärke; Hauptteil, überhaupt; **in the —** zum grössten Teil, überhaupt; **—** adj. hauptsächlich, wichtigst, Haupt-; gewaltig, mächtig; ganz, voll; **by —** strength, **by —** force mit voller Kraft; **—** office Zentralbüro; **rising —** Steigleitung

mainland n. Festland

mainspring n. Haupt(trieb)feder

mainstay n. (naut.) Grosstag; (fig.) Hauptstütze

maintain v. (aufrecht)erhalten, weiterführen, unterhalten; behaupten

maintenance n. Erhaltung; Aufrechterhaltung; Unterhalt; Behauptung

maize n. Mais

majestic adj. majestätisch

majesty n. Majestät; (fig.) Hoheit, Erhabenheit, Würde

major n. (educ.) Hauptstudienfach; (law) Mündige, Grossjährige; (mil.) Major; (phil.) Hauptsatz; **— general** Generalmajor; **—** adj. grossjährig, majorenn, mündig; grösser, wichtiger; weiter, breiter; **— part** grössten Teil; **-ity** n. Mehrzahl, Mehrheit; (law) Mündigkeit; (mil.) Majorsrang

make n. Fabrikat, Marke, Erzeugnis; Bau, Form, Gestalt; Stil, Schnitt; **—** v. machen, anfertigen, fabrizieren, schaffen, herstellen; zwingen; verdienen, gewinnen; ergeben; **— a choice** eine Wahl treffen; **— a speech** eine Rede halten; **— contact** den Stromkreis schliessen, anschliessen; in Kontakt treten, den Kontakt aufnehmen; **— fun of** sich lustig machen über; **— good** Wort halten; erfüllen; rechtfertigen; vergüten; **— money** Geld verdienen, reich werden; **— off** durchbrennen; **— out** entziffern; ausfertigen, ausfüllen; gelingen; **— over** umarbeiten; überweisen; **— peace** Frieden schliessen; **— sure** sich vergewissern; **— up** zusammenstellen; bilden, erfinden; sich versöhnen; sich schminken; nachholen; **— up for** wieder gutmachen; **— up one's mind** einen Entschluss fassen; **— use of** Nutzen ziehen aus; **— war** Krieg führen; **-r** n. Fabrikant; Verfertiger; **the Maker** der Schöpfer

make-believe n. Vorwand, Schein, Spiegelfechterei; **—** adj. vorgeblich, scheinbar

makeshift n. Notbehelf, Lückenbüsser; **—** adj. behelfsmässig; interimistisch

make-up n. Beschaffenheit, Natur;

(theat.) Schminke(n), Maske, Ausstaffierung, Verkleidung, Ausstattung; (typ.) Umbruch

making n. Machen; **he has the –s of er** hat das Zeug zu; **in the —** im Werden

maladjustment n. schlechtes Anpassungsvermögen

malady n. Unpässlichkeit, Krankheit

malaprop(ism) n. Wortverdrehung

malaria n. Malaria, Sumpffieber, Wechselfieber

male n. Mann; (zool.) Männchen; **—** adj. männlich

malefactor n. Übeltäter, Missetäter

malevolent adj. böswillig, feindselig

malice n. Bosheit, Arglist; (law) böse Absicht

malicious adj. boshaft, arglistig, heimtückisch; (law) böswillig

malign adj. unheilvoll, nachteilig, schädlich; **—** v. beschimpfen, verleumden, lästern; **-ant** adj. boshaft; (med.) bösartig

mallard n. Enterich, Erpel

malleable adj. hämmerbar; (fig.) schmiegsam, biegsam

mallet n. Hammer, Schlegel

malnutrition n. Unterernährung

malpractice n. Quacksalberei

malt n. Malz; (coll.) Eisgetränk

maltreat v. schlecht (or unfreundlich) behandeln

ma(m)ma n. Mama

mammal n. Säugetier

mammoth n. Mammut; **—** adj. mammutartig, riesig

man n. Mann, Mensch; Diener, Arbeiter; Soldat, Matrose; (chess) Figur, Stein; **— overboard!** Mann über Bord! **men's room** Herrentoilette; **—** v. bemannen; **-ful** adj. männlich, mannhaft, tapfer; **-hood** n. Männlichkeit, Mannhaftigkeit; Mannesalter; Menschentum; **-ikin** n. Mannequin, Probiermamsell; Gliederpuppe; **-kind** n. Menschheit, Menschengeschlecht; **-like** adj. menschlich, menschenähnlich; männlich; **-liness** n. Männlichkeit, Mannhaftigkeit; **-ly** adj. männlich, mannhaft, tapfer

manage v. verwalten, leiten; handhaben, behandeln, gebrauchen; bändigen; sich behelfen, schonen; **-able** adj. handlich, lenksam, fügsam; **-ment** n. Leitung, Verwaltung, Direktion, Geschäftsführung; Handhabung, Behandlung; (rail.) Betriebsplan; **-r** n. Vorsteher, Leiter, Direktor, Geschäftsführer; Verwalter; Haushalter

mandate n. Mandat; Befehl, Erlass; (law)

Vollmacht, Auftrag
mandolin n. Mandoline
mane n. Mähne
maneuver n. Manöver; — v. manövrieren
manganese n. Mangan
mange n. Räude
manger n. Krippe, Futtertrog
mangle n. Mangel, Rolle; — v. zerhacken, zerfetzen; verstümmeln
manhole n. Einsteigloch
manicure n. Handpflege, Maniküre; — v. maniküren
manifest n. Kundgebung; Manifest; — adj. augenscheinlich, offenbar; — v. offenbaren, zeigen, kundtun; –ation n. Offenbarung; Kundgebung; –o n. Bekanntmachung, Proklamation, Manifest
manifold adj. mannigfaltig, mannigfach
manila paper n. Manilapapier
manipulate v. handhaben, behandeln, manipulieren
manipulation n. Handhabung, Verfahren; Kunstgriff, Manipulation
mannequin n. Mannequin, Probiermamsell
manner n. Art, Weise; (lit.) Manier, Stil; pl. Manieren, Benehmen, Sitte, Lebensart; in such a — so dass; in this — auf diese Weise; –ism n. Manieriertheit, Künstelei; –ly adj. manierlich, gesittet, höflich
manor n. Landgut, Gutsbesitz
manpower n. (verfügbares) Menschenmaterial
mansion n. (herrschaftliches) Wohnhaus
manslaughter n. Totschlag
mantel n. Kaminmantel, Mauermantel
mantle n. Mantel; (fig.) Deckmantel, Schleier, Überzug
manual n. Handbuch, Leitfaden; Manual; — adj. manuell; Hand-; — training handwerklicher Unterricht, Handarbeitsunterricht
manufacture n. Fabrikation, Anfertigung; — v. fabrizieren, verarbeiten, anfertigen; –r n. Fabrikant
manufacturing n. Fabrikation, Anfertigung
manure n. Dünger, Dung, Mist
manuscript n. Manuskript, Handschrift, Original
many adj. manch, macherlei; viel, vielerlei, zahlreich; a great — sehr viele; in — ways auf vielerlei Art; — a mancher, manch ein; — a time sehr oft
map n. Karte, Landkarte, Himmelskarte; — maker Kartograph, Landkartenzeichner; road — Strassenkarte, Autokarte; — v. aufzeichnen, kartographie-

ren; — out planen, darstellen
maple n. Ahorn
mar v. entstellen; beschädigen; verderben; (fig.) stören
marauder n. Marodeur, Plünderer
marble n. Marmor; (art) Marmorbildwerk, Marmorstatue; (game) Murmel; — adj. marmorn, marmoriert; — v. marmorieren
march n. Marsch; Gang, Schritt; (fig.) Fortschritt; March n. März; — v. marschieren, ziehen, gehen, schreiten
mare n. Mähre, Stute
margarine n. Margarine, Kunstbutter
margin n. Rand; (fig.) Grenzé, Spielraum; (com.) Gewinnspanne; –al adj. am Rande, Rand-; (com.) äusserst
marigold n. Ringelblume, Dotterblume
marijuana, marihuana n. Marihuana
marina n. Bootsanlegestelle; Bootshafen
marine n. Seesoldat; Marine, Seewesen; — adj. Marine-, See-, Schiffs-; –r n. Seemann, Matrose
marionette n. Marionette, Drahtpuppe
marital adj. ehelich
maritime adj. an der See liegend (or lebend); See-, Küsten-, Schiffahrts-
mark n. Zeichen, Merkmal, Marke; Strieme, Narbe; Fleck, Mal; Stempel; Spur; Ziel; (educ.) Note; hit the — das Ziel treffen; miss the — das Ziel verfehlen; — v. (be)zeichnen, markieren, kennzeichnen; zensieren; sich merken; — down notieren; (price) herabsetzen; — my words! merken Sie sich das! — time auf der Stelle treten
market n. Markt, Messe, Jahrmarkt; Absatz; Nachfrage; Marktpreis; Handelsplatz; — place Marktplatz; meat — Fleischmarkt; open — öffentlicher Markt; — v. einkaufen; auf den Markt bringen, verkaufen; –able adj. verkäuflich, gangbar
marksman n. Scharfschütze
markup n. Verdienstaufschlag
marmalade n. Marmelade
marmot n. Murmeltier
marriage n. Ehe; Heirat, Hochzeit; (fig.) enge Verbindung; by — angeheiratet; civil — Ziviltrauung; give away in — zur Frau geben, verheiraten; –able adj. heiratsfähig, mannbar
married adj. verheiratet, verehelicht; ehelich; be — verheiratet sein; get — sich verheiraten, heiraten, verheiratet werden; newly — neuvermählt
marrow n. Knochenmark; (fig.) Kern, Beste
marry v. heiraten; verheiraten, trauen, vermählen

marsh *n.* Marsch(land), Sumpf, Morast; **—y** *adj.* morastig, sumpfig

marshal *n.* Marschall; field **—** Feldmarschall, Generalfeldmarschall

marshmallow *n.* Süssigkeit (aus geschlagenem Zucker)

mart *n.* Markt, Messe

martin *n.* Mauerschwalbe

martyr *n.* Märtyrer, Glaubenszeuge; **—dom** *n.* Märtyrertum; (fig.) Marterqualen

marvel *n.* Wunder; Verwunderung, Bewunderung; **—** *v.* sich (ver)wundern; **—(l)ous** *adj.* wunderbar, herrlich; erstaunlich, unglaublich

mascara *n.* Wimperntusche

mascot *n.* Talisman, Maskotte, Glücksbringer

masculine *adj.* männlich; mannhaft, kühn

mash *n.* Maische, Mischfutter; **—** *v.* zerdrücken, zerquetschen; **—ed** *adj.* zerstampft; **—ed** potatoes Kartoffelbrei, Kartoffelpüree, Quetschkartoffel, Stampfkartoffel

mask *n.* Maske; Maskierung, Tarnung; **—** *v.* maskieren, verkleiden; tarnen

mason *n.* Maurer, Steinmetz; **—ry** *n.* Maurerhandwerk; Mauerwerk; **stone —ry** Steinmetzarbeit

masquerade *n.* Maskerade

mass *n.* Masse, Menge, Haufe(n); (min.) Mittel; (eccl.) Messe; **—** production Massenproduktion; **—** *v.* (sich) anhäufen, (sich) ansammeln; **—ive** *adj.* massiv, schwer, fest; gediegen; derb

massacre *n.* Blutbad, Gemetzel; **—** *v.* niedermetzeln, massakrieren

massage *n.* Massage; **—** *v.* massieren

mast *n.* Mast; Mastbaum

master *n.* Meister, Herr, Gebieter; (educ.) Lehrer; **—** key Hauptschlüssel; **—** mind hervorragender Geist; bedeutender Mensch; **—** stroke, **—** touch Meisterstreich, Meisterstück; **—ful** *adj.* herrisch, gebieterisch; meisterhaft; **—ly** *adj.* meisterhaft; **—y** *n.* Meisterschaft, Gewandtheit; Beherrschung, Herrschaft, Macht; Obhand, Vorrang

masthead *n.* Zeitungskopf; (naut.) Mastspitze

masticate *v.* (zer)kauen

mastoid *adj.* zitzenförmig, warzenförmig

mat *n.* Matte, Decke; **—** *v.* mit Matten bedecken, belegen; verflechten; mattieren; **—** *adj.* matt

match *n.* Streichholz, Zündholz; Gleiche, Ähnliche, Passende; Heirat; Wette, Übereinkunft; (sports) Wettkampf, Spiel, Partie, Match; **be a —** for someone jemandem gewachsen sein; **—** *v.*

zusammenpassen, entsprechen; anpassen; paaren; **—less** *adj.* unvergleichlich, ohnegleichen

matchbook *n.* Streichholzheft

matchbox *n.* Streichholzschachtel

matchmaker *n.* Heiratsvermittler

mate *n.* Gatte, Gattin; Genosse, Gefährte, Kamerad; Gehilfe, Geselle; (chess) Matt; (naut.) Maat; **first —** Obermaat; (zool.) Männchen, Weibchen; **—** *v.* (sich) vereinigen, verbinden; verheiraten, vermählen; paaren, gatten; (chess) matt setzen

material *n.* Material, Stoff, Bestandteil; **—** *adj.* materiell, körperlich; wesentlich, wichtig; **—ism** *n.* Materialismus, materialistische Weltanschauung; **—istic** *adj.* materialistisch; **—ize** *v.* materialisieren, realisieren; (sich) verwirklichen

maternal *adj.* mütterlich; mütterlicherseits

maternity *n.* Mutterschaft; Mütterlichkeit; **—** hospital Entbindungsheim

mathematical *adj.* mathematisch; (fig.) exakt, beweisbar

mathematician *n.* Mathematiker

mathematics *n.* Mathematik

matinee *n.* Matinee

mating *n.* Paarung; **—** time Paarungszeit

matriarchy *n.* Mutterherrschaft

matriculate *v.* immatrikulieren, (sich) einschreiben

matriculation *n.* Immatrikulation

matrimonial *adj.* ehelich

matrimony *n.* Ehe, Ehestand

matrix *n.* (bot. and geol.) Mutterboden; (mech.) Matrize, Gussform; (fig.) Nährboden

matron *n.* Matrone; Hausmutter, Oberin, Vorsteherin

matter *n.* Sache, Angelegenheit; Stoff; Geschäft; (phy. and phil.) Materie, Substanz; (fig.) Wichtigkeit, Bedeutung; **as a —** of fact tatsächlich, wirklich; **for that —** was dies betrifft; **— of** course Selbstverständlichkeit, ausgemachte Tatsache; **— of form** eine blosse Formsache; **no —** es macht nichts (aus), es hat nichts zu sagen, gleichviel; **the —** in hand die vorliegende Angelegenheit; **what is the —?** um was handelt es sich? was ist los? **what is the — with him?** was fehlt ihm? **—** *v.* ausmachen, darauf ankommen, von Bedeutung sein

matter-of-course *adj.* selbstverständlich

matter-of-fact *adj.* tatsächlich, wirklich

mattress *n.* Matratze; **air —** Luftmatratze; **spring —** Sprungfedermatratze

mature *adj.* reif; fällig; reiflich; **—** *v.*

reifen, zeitigen; fällig werden
maturity n. Reife; Fälligkeit, Verfallszeit
maul v. zerschlagen; misshandeln
mausoleum n. Mausoleum, Grabmal
maxim n. Maxime, Grundsatz; Denkspruch
maximum n. Maximum, Höchstmass; — adj. höchste, grösste
may v. mag, kann, darf; **May** n. Mai; **May Day** ersten Mai
maybe adv. vielleicht, möglicherweise
Mayence n. Mainz
mayonnaise n. Mayonnaise
mayor n. Bürgermeister
maze n. Bestürzung, Verwirrung; Labyrinth, Irrgang
M.C. (master-of-ceremonies) n. Conferencier, Zeremonienmeister
me pron. mir, mich
meadow n. Wiese, Anger
meager, meagre adj. mager, dünn, dürr; dürftig, arm; unfruchtbar
meal n. Mahl(zeit); Mehl, Maismehl; **-y** adj. mehlig; (fig.) blass
mean v. meinen, denken; bedeuten, heissen; wollen, beabsichtigen; bestimmen, sagen; gedenken, willens sein; **I — business** ich rede im Ernst; **you don't — it** das meinst du doch nicht wirklich; **—** n. Mitte; Mittel; Mittelmässigkeit, Durchschnitt; pl. Mittel, Werkzeug; Vermögen, Einkommen; **by all -s** durchaus, jedenfalls; **by -s of** mittels; **by no -s** keineswegs; **live within one's -s** den Verhältnissen entsprechend leben; **ways and -s** das Mittel zum Zweck, Mittel und Wege; **—** adj. gemein, niedrig; gering; niederträchtig; filzig; mittel(mässig); **-ing** n. Bedeutung, Sinn; Meinung, Absicht; **-ness** n. Gemeinheit, Niedrigkeit; Niederträchtigkeit; Armseligkeit
meantime adv. inzwischen, unterdessen; **—** n. Zwischenzeit; **in the —** inzwischen
meanwhile adv. inzwischen, unterdessen; **—** n. **in the —** mittlerweile
measles n. pl. Masern
measure n. Mass(einheit); Massnahme, Massregel; (lit.) Silbenmass; (mus.) Zeitmass, Takt, Rhythmus; **beyond —** ausserordentlich; **in some —** gewissermassen; **—** v. (ab)messen, ausmessen; ermessen; Mass nehmen; **-ment** n. Mass; Messung, Vermessung, Abmessung
meat n. Fleisch; **broiled —** unter der Flamme gebratenes Fleisch; **dark —** dunkles (or trockenes) Fleisch; **fried —** Braten, Schmorbraten; **light —** weisses (or zartes) Fleisch; **roast —** Braten;

what is one man's — is another man's poison des Einen Tod ist des anderen Brot; eines schickt sich nicht für alle
mechanic n. Mechaniker, Maschinenarbeiter; **-al** adj. mechanisch; (fig.) unbewusst, unwillkürlich; **-al engineering** Maschinenbau; **-al man** Roboter, Maschinenmensch; **-s** n. Mechanik, Maschinenlehre
mechanism n. Mechanismus, Getriebe; Triebwerk; **defense —** Verteidigungsmaschinerie
medal n. Medaille, Denkmünze, Schaumünze; **-lion** n. Medaillon
meddle v. sich mischen (or vermengen); sich einmischen (or einlassen); **-r** n. Eindringling, Lästige, Unberufene
meddlesome adj. zudringlich, vorwitzig, lästig
mediate v. vermitteln
mediator n. Vermittler, Unterhändler
medical adj. medizinisch, ärztlich; **examination** ärztliche Untersuchung
medicinal adj. medizinisch, heilkräftig, heilsam
medicine n. Medizin, Heilkunde; **Arznei**
medieval adj. mittelalterlich
mediocre adj. mittelmässig
mediocrity n. Mittelmässigkeit; **kleiner Geist**
meditate v. nachsinnen, grübeln; meditieren
meditation n. Nachdenken; Betrachtung; Meditation
Mediterranean Sea n. Mittelmeer
medium n. Mittel, Hilfsmittel; Mitte; Medium; **—** adj. mittel(mässig); Mittel-, Durchschnitts-
medium-sized adj. mittelgross
medley n. Gemisch, Mischmasch; (mus.) Potpourri
meek adj. demütig, bescheiden; mild, sanf(tmütig); **-ness** n. Demut, Bescheidenheit; Milde, Mildheit, Sanftmut
meet v. treffen, begegnen, stossen auf; entgegenkommen; nachkommen, erfüllen; sich treffen (or versammeln); **go to — entgegengehen, entgegenkommen; make both ends — mit seinen Einkünften auskommen; till we — again** bis wir uns wiedersehen; **-ing** n. Versammlung, Zusammentreffen, Zusammenkunft; Sitzung, Beratung; (sports) Renntag, Wettkampf
megaphone n. Megaphon, Sprachrohr
melancholy n. Schwermut, Melancholie; **—** adj. schwermütig, melancholisch
mellow adj. reif; weich, mürbe; sanft, angenehm; (mus.) voll, rund; (fig.) zart, freundlich; **—** v. reifen; weich (or

mürbe) machen; weich (*or* mürbe, sanft) werden; sich mildern

melodious *adj.* melodisch, wohlklingend

melody *n.* Melodie, Singweise

melon *n.* Melone

melt *v.* schmelzen, (sich) auflösen, zergehen, zerfliessen; **–ing** *adj.* schmelzend; **–ing point** Schmelzpunkt; **–ing pot** Schmelztiegel

member *n.* Mitglied, Glied; — **of congress** Abgeordnete; **–ship** *n.* Mitgliedschaft; Mitgliederzahl

membrane *n.* Membrane, Häutchen

memento *n.* Erinnerungszeichen, Andenken, Memento

memo *abbr.* Notiz, Bemerkung

memoir *n.* Bericht, Denkschrift; — *pl.* Memoiren, Biographie

memorable *adj.* denkwürdig, merkwürdig

memorandum *n.* Memorandum, Denkschrift, Note; — **book** Merkbuch

memorial *n.* Denkmal; — *adj.* dem Andenken (*or* Gedächtnis) dienend; **Memorial Day** 30. Mai, Heldengedenktag

memorize *v.* auswendig lernen, memorieren

memory *n.* Gedächtnis, Erinnerung(svermögen); Andenken; **in — of zum** Andenken an

menace *n.* Drohung; — *v.* (be)drohen

menagerie *n.* Menagerie

mend *n.* Besserung; Ausbesserung; — *v.* ausbessern, flicken; (ver)bessern; besser werden

mendicant *n.* Bettler; — *adj.* bettelnd, bettelarm; Bettel-

menial *adj.* knechtisch, niedrig

meningitis *n.* Hirnhautentzündung

menstruation *n.* Menstruation, Monatskrankheit

mental *adj.* geistig, innerlich; Geistes-, Kopf-; — **hospital** Nervenheilanstalt, Irrenhaus; **–ity** *n.* Geisteskraft; Mentalität

mention *n.* Erwähnung, Meldung; — *v.* erwähnen, anführen, melden; **don't — it** es ist nicht der Rede wert; **not to —** geschweige denn, abgesehen von

menu *n.* Menü, Speisekarte

mercantile *adj.* merkantil, kaufmännisch, Handels-

mercenary *n.* Mietling, Söldner; — *adj.* gedungen, feil, käuflich; gewinnsüchtig

mercerize *v.* merzerisieren, Seidenglanz geben

merchandise *n.* Ware(n)

merchant *n.* Kaufmann; Händler, Krämer; — **marine** Handelsflotte

merciful *adj.* gnädig, barmherzig

merciless *adj.* unbarmherzig, mitleidlos; grausam

Mercurochrome *n.* Quecksilberchrom, Desinfektionsmittel

mercury *n.* Quecksilber; (ast.) Merkur

mercy *n.* Gnade, Barmherzigkeit, Mitleid; **be at someone's —** in jemandes **Gewalt** (*or* jemandem preisgegeben) sein

mere *adj.* bloss, allein; rein, lauter; **–ly** *adv.* nur, bloss

merge *v.* einverleiben, verschmelzen; aufgehen; **–r** *n.* Fusion, Verschmelzung, Einverleibung

meridian *n.* Meridian, Mittagslinie; (fig.) Gipfel, Höhepunkt

merit *n.* Verdienst; Lohn, Wert; (law) Hauptpunkt; — *v.* verdienen; sich verdient machen; **–orious** *adj.* verdienstlich

mermaid *n.* Seejungfer, Meermädchen, Nixe

merriment *n.* Fröhlichkeit, Munterkeit

merry *adj.* fröhlich, munter, lustig, ergötzlich

merry-go-round *n.* Karussell, Ringelspiel

mesh *n.* Masche, Netz; — *v.* (sich) verstricken, ineinandergreifen

mess *n.* Unordnung, Verwirrung; (cooking) Gericht, Schüssel; (mil.) Messe; (naut.) Back; — *v.* verpfuschen, **in** Unordnung bringen

message *n.* Botschaft, Mitteilung

messenger *n.* Bote, Kurier, Laufjunge

metabolism *n.* Stoffwechsel, Grundumsatz

metal *n.* Metall; **–lic** *adj.* metallisch, metallen; **–lurgy** *n.* Metallurgie, Hüttenkunde

metaphor *n.* Metapher

metaphysical *adj.* metaphysisch

metaphysics *n.* Metaphysik

mete *v.* abmessen

meteor *n.* Meteor; **–ite** *n.* Meteorstein; **–ology** *n.* Meteorologie

meter, metre *n.* Meter; Vermass, Metrik; Messer; (elec.) Zähler; (gas) Gasuhr

method *n.* Methode, System, Lehrweise; **–ic(al)** *adj.* methodisch

Methodist *n.* Methodist

methylene *n.* Methylen

metric *adj.* metrisch, Vers-; messend, Mass-; — **system** Dezimalsystem

metropolis *n.* Hauptstadt, Metropole

metropolitan *n.* Grozstädter; — *adj.* grossstädtisch; Grozstadt-, Stadt-

mettle *n.* Grundstoff, Temperament

mezzanine *n.* Zwischenstock

mica *n.* Glimmer

microbe *n.* Mikrobe, Bakterie

microbiology *n.* Mikrobiologie

microfilm *n.* Mikrofilm

microgroove n. Schallplattenrille

micron n. Mikromillimeter; Mikron

microphone n. Mikrofon

microscope n. Mikroskop

microwave n. Ultrakurzwelle; Mikrowelle

mid adj. mitten; **-dle** n. Mitte; Taille; in the **-dle** of mitten in (or auf); **-dle** adj. mittel, mittler; **Middle Ages** Mittelalter; **-dle class** Mittelstand; **-st** n. Mitte; **in the -st** of mitten in (or (auf); **-st** prep. inmitten

midday n. Mittag

middle-aged adj. von mittlerem Alter

middleman n. Mittelsmann, Makler, Zwischenhändler

middleweight n. Mittelgewicht; Mittelgewichtler

middy (blouse) n. Matrosenbluse

midget n. Zwerg, Knirps

midnight n. Mitternacht

midshipman n. Seekadett

midsummer n. Hochsommer; Sommersonnenwende

midway n. Mittelweg; — adv. auf halbem Wege, unterwegs; — adj. in der Mitte befindlich

midwife n. Hebamme, Geburtshelferin

mien n. Miene, Haltung

might n. Macht, Gewalt; Kraft, Stärke; **-y** adj. mächtig, gewaltig; kräftig; gross, bedeutend, wichtig

migraine n. Migräne

migrant n. (orn.) Zugvogel; (zool.) Wandertier; — adj. wandernd

migrate v. auswandern, fortziehen

migration n. Auswanderung, Fortziehen; (orn. and zool.) Wanderung

migratory adj. wandern, nomadisch, umherziehend; Zug-

Milan n. Mailand

mild adj. mild, gelinde, sanft; leicht; schwach; nachsichtig, freundlich; **-ness** n. Milde, Sanftheit

mildew n. Mehltau; Brand; Moder, Schimmel; — v. brandig werden, mit Mehltau überziehen

mile n. Meile; **-age** n. Meilenlänge, Meilenzahl

milestone n. Meilenstein

militant adj. streitend, kriegführend; streitbar

militarism n. Militarismus

military n. Militär; Soldaten, Truppen; — adj. militärisch, Kriegs-; **compulsory — service** Wehrpflicht; — **police** Militärpolizei

militia n. Miliz, Bürgerwehr, Landwehr

milk n. Milch; — **of magnesia** Magnesiumhydroxyd; — v. melken; **-ing** adj. Melk-; **-ing machine** Melkapparat; **-y**

adj. milchig; **Milky Way** Milchstrasse

milkmaid n. Kuhmagd, Melkerin

milkman n. Milchmann

milksop n. Milchbart, Grünling

milkweed n. Wolfsmilch

mill n. Mühle; Fabrik; — v. mahlen, zerreiben; (coin) prägen, rändeln; **-er** n. Müller

millet n. Hirse

millennium n. Jahrtausend; tausendjähriges Reich

milligram n. Milligramm

millimeter n. Millimeter

milliner n. Putzmacherin; Modistin; **-y** n. Modeware, Putzware; **-y shop** Putzwarengeschäft

million n. Million; **-aire** n. Millionär

millstone n. Mühlstein

Mimeograph n. Abzugsmaschine, Mimeograph

mimic n. Nachäffer; Mime, Schauspieler; — v. nachahmen, nachäffen; **-ry** n. Nachahmung, Nachäffung; (zool.) Angleichung, Mimikry

mince v. zerhacken, zerstückeln; beschönigen; sich zieren, stolzieren

mincemeat n. Gehacktes, Schabefleisch; Fleischpastetenfüllung; — **pie** Fleischpastete

mind n. Geist, Verstand; Gesinnung, Meinung, Ansicht, Urteil; Sinn, Gemüt; **make up one's —** einen Entschluss fassen; **of sound —** bei vollem Verstande; — **reader** Gedankenleser; — v. merken, achten; bemerken, beachten; achthaben, aufpassen, sich kümmern um; **I don't —** es ist mir gleich, ich habe nichts dagegen; **-ful** adj. achtsam, aufmerksam

mine pron. mein; der (or die, das) meinige

mine n. Grube, Bergwerk; (mil.) Mine; (fig.) Fundgrube; — **field** Minenfeld; — **sweeper** Minensuchboot; **-r** n. Bergmann, Bergarbeiter, Grubenarbeiter; Minenleger, Minierer

mineral n. Mineral; — **oil** Mineralöl; — **water** Mineralwasser; — adj. mineralisch

mingle v. mischen, vermengen

miniature n. Miniatur(gemälde); — adj. in Miniatur

miniaturization n. Verkleinerung

minimize v. aufs kleinste Mass zurückführen; verkleinern, verringern

minimum n. Minimum, Kleinste, Geringste; Mindestmass; — adj. minimal; — **wage** Mindestlohn

mining n. Bergbau

minister n. (eccl.) Geistliche, Priester,

Pastor; (pol.) Minister, Gesandte
ministry *n.* Geistlichkeit; geistliches Amt; Ministerium
mink *n.* Nerz
minor *n.* Minderjährige; — *adj.* minderjährig; kleiner, geringer; unbedeutend; (mus.) moll; –ity *n.* Minderheit; (law) Minderjährigkeit
minstrel *n.* Spielmann, fahrende Sänger; (coll.) Negersänger
mint *n.* Münzstätte; (bot.) Pfefferminz; — *v.* prägen, münzen
minuet *n.* Menuett
minus *n.* Minuszeichen; — *adj.* negativ; —amount Fehlbetrag; — *prep.* ohne, weniger
minute *n.* Minute; Augenblick; *pl.* Protokoll; — hand Minutenzeiger; — *adj.* klein, winzig; genau
miocardium *n.* Herzmuskel
miracle *n.* Wunder
miraculous *adj.* wunderbar, übernatürlich
mirage *n.* Luftspiegelung, Fata Morgana; (fig.) Täuschung
mire *n.* Kot, Schlamm
mirror *n.* Spiegel; (fig.) Vorbild
mirth *n.* Frohsinn, Freude; Fröhlichkeit; –ful *adj.* fröhlich, lustig
misadventure *n.* Unfall, Unglück; Missgeschick
misapprehension *n.* Missverständnis
misbehave *v.* sich schlecht (*or* unpassend) benehmen
misbelief *n.* Irrglaube
miscalculate *v.* falsch berechnen (*or* abschätzen); sich verrechnen
miscarriage *n.* Fehlgeburt, Frühgeburt; (fig.) Fehlschlag, Misslingen
miscarry *v.* zu früh gebären; misslingen, missglücken; fehlschlagen
miscellaneous *adj.* gemischt; vermischt; vielseitig
mischance *n.* Missgeschick, Unfall
mischief *n.* Unheil, Unglück; Unfug, Unrecht; Schaden, Nachteil
mischievous *adj.* mutwillig, nachteilig, verderblich; boshaft
misconduct *n.* schlechtes Benehmen; schlechte Verwaltung
misconstrue *v.* missdeuten
misdeal *v.* sich vergeben, falsch austeilen
misdeed *n.* Missetat
misdemeanor *n.* Fehltritt; (law) Vergehen
misdirect *v.* irreleiten; falsch adressieren
miser *n.* Geizhals; –ly *adj.* geizig, filzig
miserable *adj.* elend, unglücklich, erbärmlich
misery *n.* Elend, Not
misfire *n.* Versager, Fehlzündung
misfit *n.* Nichtpassen, Fehlerhaftigkeit;

Ungeeignete
misfortune *n.* Unglück(sfall), Missgeschick
misgiving *n.* Besorgnis, Befürchtung, böse Ahnung
mishap *n.* Unfall, Unglück
misinform *v.* falsch berichten (*or* belehren, unterrichten)
misinterpret *v.* missdeuten, falsch auslegen
misjudge *v.* falsch beurteilen, verkennen
mislay *v.* verlegen
mislead *v.* irreführen; (fig.) verführen, verleiten; –ing *adj.* irreführend
mismanagement *n.* schlechte Verwaltung (*or* Führung)
misnomer *n.* falsche Benennung; (law) Namensirrtum
misogynist *n.* Weiberfeind
misplace *v.* falsch stellen, verlegen; (fig.) übel anbringen
misprint *n.* Druckfehler; — *v.* verdrucken
mispronounce *v.* falsch aussprechen
misrepresent *v.* falsch (*or* ungenau) darstellen, verdrehen; –ation *n.* falsche Darstellung, Verdrehung
misrule *n.* schlechte Regierung; ungerechte Leitung
miss *n.* Fräulein
miss *n.* Fehlschuss, Fehlstoss, Fehlwurf; — *v.* verfehlen, versäumen, vermissen; auslassen, übergehen; missen, entbehren; — one's mark fehlschiessen; –ing *adj.* fehlend, ausbleibend; vermisst, verschollen; fort, abwesend
missal *n.* Messbuch
misshapen *adj.* verunstaltet, entstellt, ungestalt
missile *n.* Wurfgeschoss; Projektil, Geschoss
mission *n.* Mission; Missionshaus; Sendung, Auftrag, Botschaft; Lebensziel; –ary *n.* Missionar
misspell *v.* falsch buchstabieren (*or* schreiben)
misstatement *n.* falsche Angabe
misstep *n.* Fehltritt; Missgriff
mist *n.* Nebel; –y *adj.* neblig, wolkig, feucht; (fig.) unklar, dunkel
mistake *n.* Irrtum, Versehen; Missgriff, Missverständnis; Fehler; by — aus Versehen; — *v.* verkennen, verwechseln; missverstehen; –n *adj.* falsch, irrig; be –n sich irren
Mister *n.* Herr
mistletoe *n.* Mistel
mistreat *v.* misshandeln; missbrauchen; –ment *n.* Misshandlung; Missbrauch
mistress *n.* Herrin, Gebieterin; Lehrerin; Geliebte

mistrial n. ergebnisloses Strafverfahren
mistrust n. Misstrauen, Argwohn; — v. misstrauen argwöhnen
misunderstand v. missverstehen, falsch auslegen; **-ing** n. Missverständnis, Irrtum
misuse v. missbrauchen; misshandeln
mite n. Milbe; (fig.) Kleinigkeit
miter, mitre n. Mitra, Bischofsmütze
mitigate v. lindern, mildern, abschwächen, besänftigen
mitt(en) n. Fausthandschuh
mix v. mischen, mengen; (sich) vermischen, vermengen; **-ed** adj. vermischt, vermengt; gemischt, Misch-; **-ed up** verwirrt, verwickelt; **-er** n. Mixer; Mischer; concrete **-er** Betonmischmaschine; electric **-er** Elektromix; **-ture** n. Mischung, Gemisch; Vermischung; Mixtur
moan n. Stöhnen, Ächzen; — v. stöhnen, ächzen
mob n. Mob, Pöbel; Gesindel, Rotte; (coll.) Bande; — v. anfallen; anpöbeln
mobile adj. beweglich, mobil
mobility n. Beweglichkeit
mobilization n. Mobilmachung, Kriegsrüstung, Kriegsbereitschaft
mobilize v. mobil machen, rüsten, mobilisieren; (fig.) beweglich machen
mock v. (ver)spotten, verhöhnen; nachahmen, täuschen; — adj. falsch, unecht, nachgemacht; Schein-; — orange Pfeifenstrauch; **-ery** n. Spott, Spötterei; Blendwerk; **-ingly** adv. spotten, spöttisch nachahmend
mockingbird n. Spottdrossel
mock-up n. Attrappe; Flugzeugmodell
mode n. Mode, Sitte, Gebrauch; Art und Weise, Form, Modus; (mech.) Verfahren; (mus.) Tonart
model n. Modell; Muster, Schablone; (fig.) Vorbild; — adj. musterhaft, vorbildlich; — v. modellieren; (ab)formen, gestalten; (coll.) modeln
moderate v. mässigen, mildern, lindern, beruhigen; einschränken; — adj. mässig; gemässigt; mild; mittelmässig
moderation n. Mässigung, Mässigkeit; Gleichmut
moderator n. Mittelmann; Examinator
modern adj. modern, jetzig, neu; **-ism** n. Neuerungssucht; **-istic** adj. neuerungssüchtig; **-ize** v. modernisieren, erneuern
modest adj. bescheiden, anspruchslos, mässig; sittsam; **-y** n. Bescheidenheit, Anspruchslosigkeit; Sittsamkeit
modification n. Abänderung, Veränderung
modify v. abändern, einschränken, mildern; (gram.) näher bestimmen

modulate v. modulieren, anpassen
modulator n. (rad.) Tonblende
mohair n. Mohär, Kamelhaar; Angorahaar
moist adj. feucht, nass; **-en** v. befeuchten, anfeuchten; benetzen, nässen; **-ure** n. Feuchtigkeit, Nässe
molar adj. zermalmend, zermahlend; — tooth Backenzahn
molasses n. Melasse, Sirup
mold n. Form; Gussform, Schablone; (agr.) Gartenerde, Blumenerde; (chem.) Schimmel; (fig.) Bildung, Körperbau; — v. formen, bilden; schimmeln; **-er** v. zerfallen, vermodern, verwittern; zerbröckeln; **-ing** n. Formen; (arch.) Ornament; Gesims, Fries; **-y** adj. schimmelig, modrig, dumpfig
mole n. Leberfleck, Mal, Muttermal; (zool.) Maulwurf
molecule n. Molekül
molest v. belästigen
mollify v. besänftigen; lindern, mildern
mollusk n. Molluske, Weichtier
molt v. (sich) mausern, haaren, häuten
molten adj. geschmolzen, gegossen
moment n. Augenblick, Moment; Wichtigkeit; **at the** — im Augenblick, gerade jetzt; **in a** — gleich, sofort; **the very** — gerade als; **-ary** adj. momentan, augenblicklich; verübergehend, flüchtig; **-ous** adj. wichtig, bedeutend, folgenschwer
momentum n. Moment, Triebkraft
monarch n. Monarch, Alleinherrscher; **-ist** n. Monarchist; **-y** n. Monarchie
monastery n. Mönchskloster, Kloster
Monday n. Montag
money n. Geld; Münze, Zahlungsmittel; (fig.) Reichtum, Vermögen; — order Geldanweisung, Postanweisung; **-ed** adj. reich, vermögend
mongrel n. Mischling, Bastard; — adj. gemischt, Bastard-
monitor n. Klassenordner; (rad.) Monitor; — v. rückkoppeln
monk n. Mönch
monkey n. Affe; (fig.) Maulaffe; Range; — wrench Schraubenschlüssel, Engländer
monogamy n. Monogamie, Einehe
monogram n. Monogramm
monolith n. Monolith
monolog(ue) n. Monolog, Selbstgespräch
monoplane n. Eindecker
monopolize v. monopolisieren; (fig.) an sich reissen
monopoly n. Monopol, Alleinhandel
monorail n. Einschienenbahn
monotonous adj. eintönig, einförmig monoton; langweilig

Monotype Monotypsetzmaschine; Setzen an der Monotypmaschine

monoxide *n.* Monoxyd

monsoon *n.* Monsun, Passatwind

monster *n.* Ungeheuer, Scheusal; Missgeburt

monstrosity *n.* Ungeheuerlichkeit, Widernatürlichkeit

monstrous *adj.* ungeheuer, monströs; unnatürlich

month *n.* Monat; –s allowance Monatszuschuss, monatliches Taschengeld; –'s pay Monatsgehalt, Monatslohn; next — nächtster Monat; this — dieser Monat; –ly *adj.* monatlich

Montreal *n.* Montreal

monument *n.* Denkmal, Monument; –al *adj.* monumental, riesig; Denkmal-, Gedächtnis-, Gedenk-

mood *n.* Stimmung, Laune; (gram.) Modus; –y *adj.* launisch; mürrisch, verdriesslich, verstimmt

moon *n.* Mond

moonbeam *n.* Mondstrahl

moonlight *n.* Mondlicht, Mondschein

moonshine *n.* Mondschein; (fig.) Faselei; (sl.) heimlich destillierter Alkohol

moor *n.* Moor, Morast; Moor *n.* Maure, Mohr; — *v.* vertäuen; –ing *n.* Vertäuung

moose *n.* Elch, Elen

moot *adj.* streitig, diskutierbar

mop *n.* Scheuerbesen, Mop; — *v.* (auf)-wischen

mope *v.* schwermütig (*or* niedergeschlagen, träumerisch) sein

moral *n.* Moral, Sittlichkeit; Ethik, Sittenlehre; Nutzanwendung; — *adj.* moralisch, sittlich; –ist *n.* Moralist, Tugendrichter, Sittenlehrer; –ity *n.* Sittenlehre; Sittlichkeit; –ize *v.* moralisieren

morale *n.* Mut; Geisteszucht

morass *n.* Morast, Sumpf

Moravia *n.* Mähren

morbid *adj.* krankhaft

more *n.* Mehr, Grössere; — *adj.* mehr; ferner, andere; weiter, grösser; — *adv.* mehr, wieder(um), dazu; — and — immer mehr; — or less mehr oder weniger; no — nicht(s) mehr; no — than ebensowenig wie; once — noch einmal; one — noch eines; some — noch etwas; the — the better je mehr desto besser

moreover *adv.* ausserdem, überdies; auch, weiter, ferner

morgue *n.* Leichenschauhaus

morning *n.* Morgen; Vormittag; good — guten Morgen; in the — am Morgen

(*or* Vormittag); morgens; this — heute morgen; — *adj.* früh, morgendlich, Morgen-

morning-glory *n.* Aurikelart

morocco (leather) *n.* Maroquin, Saffianleder

moron *n.* Schwachsinnige

morphine *n.* Morphium

morrow *n.* Morgen, folgender **Tag**

Morse code *n.* Morsealphabet

morsel *n.* Bissen, Bisschen, Stückchen

mortal *n.* Sterbliche, Mensch; — *adj.* sterblich, tödlich, todbringend; Todes-; menschlich; fürchterlich; –ity *n.* Sterblichkeit(sziffer)

mortar *n.* (arch.) Mörtel; (mil.) Mörser; — and pestle Mörser and Schlegel

mortgage *n.* Hypothek, Pfandgut; Verpfändung; — *v.* verpfänden, mit Hypotheken belasten

mortification *n.* Kasteiung, Ertötung; Beleidigung, Demütigung; (med.) Absterben, Brand

mortify *v.* kasteien, ertöten; beleidigen, demütigen; (med.) absterben, den Brand bekommen

mortise *n.* Zapfenloch; — *v.* verzapfen

mortuary *n.* Leichenhalle; Begräbniskapelle; — *adj.* Toten-, Leichen-

mosque *n.* Moschee

mosquito *n.* Moskito

moss *n.* Moos; Torf; Moor; –y *adj.* moosig, bemoost

most *n.* Meiste, Höchste, Äusserste; — *adj.* meiste; grösste, höchste; — *adv.* meist(ens), sehr; at — höchstens, im besten Falle; — of all am meisten; –ly *adv.* meisten(teil)s

motel *n.* Autohotel, Motel

moth *n.* Motte, Nachtfalter; — **ball** Mottenkugel; in — balls eingekampfert, eingemottet

mother *n.* Mutter; — tongue Muttersprache; — *v.* bemuttern; –hood *n.* Mutterschaft; –less *adj.* mutterlos; –ly *adj.* mütterlich

mother-in-law *n.* Schwiegermutter

mother-of-pearl *n.* Perlmutter

motif *n.* Leitmotiv

motion *n.* Bewegung, Gang; Antrieb, Regung; (pol.) Antrag, Vorschlag; make a — einen Antrag stellen; — picture Film; — *v.* ein Zeichen geben, zuwinken; –less *adj.* bewegungslos, regungslos

motivate *v.* motivieren, begründen

motive *n.* Motiv, Beweggrund; Antrieb; — *adj.* motiviert; bewegend; — power Triebkraft

motley *adj.* bunt(scheckig); buntgekleidet

motor *n.* Motor; — **court** Autoplatz; — **launch** Motorbarkasse; — *v.* im Wagen (*or* Auto) fahren; — *adj.* motorisch, bewegend; **-ist** *n.* Kraftfahrer

motorboat *n.* Motorboot

motorbus *n.* Autobus

motorcar *n.* Auto(mobil), **Kraftwagen,** Wagen

motorcycle *n.* Motorrad, Kraftfahrrad

motorman *n.* Motorführer

motto *n.* Motto, Sinnspruch, Devise

mound *n.* Erdhügel, Erdwall

mount *n.* Berg, Hügel; Reitpferd; Karton, Bilderrahmen; '— *v.* (hinauf)steigen; aufsitzen, besteigen; montieren, errichten; aufziehen; (mil.) in Stellung bringen; **-ed** *adj.* beritten; **-ing** *n.* Aufziehen; Einfassung; Garnitur, Ausrüstung

mountain *n.* Berg, Gebirge; **range of —** *pl.* Bergkette, Gebirgszug; — *adj.* gewaltig, berghoch; Berg-, Gebirgs-; **-eer** *n.* Bergsteiger; Bergbewohner; **-ous** *adj.* gebirgig, bergig

mourn *v.* (be)trauern; (be)klagen; **-er** *n.* Trauernde, Leidtragende; **-ful** *adj.* trauervoll, kummervoll, traurig; Trauer-; **-ing** *n.* Trauer, Trauern, Trauerkleidung

mouse *n.* Maus; — **trap** Mausefalle

mouth *n.* Mund; Mündung, Öffnung; Loch, Mundloch; (zool.) Maul; **by word of —** mündlich; **make one's — water** den Mund wässerig machen; — **organ** Mundharmonika; — *v.* in den Mund nehmen; laut (*or* affektiert) sprechen; **-ful** *n.* Mundvoll, Bissen

mouthpiece *n.* Mundstück; (coll.) Wortführer, Verteidiger, Sprachrohr

move *n.* Bewegung; Ausziehen, Umzug; Zug; (fig.) Schritt, Massregel; — *v.* bewegen, rühren; sich fortbewegen (*or* rühren); (aus)ziehen, umziehen; (pol.) beantragen; **-ment** *n.* Bewegung; Handlung, Gang; Schwung; (mus.) Satz; (watch) Werk, Gehwerk; **-r** *n.* Bewegende, Anstifter, Urheber; Spediteur

mov(e)able *adj.* beweglich, veränderlich, lose; — *n. pl.* Mobilien, Mobiliar; bewegliche Habe

movie *n.* Film; *pl.* Kino

moving *adj.* bewegend, beweglich; rührend; — **picture** Film(bild), Kinostück

mow *v.* (ab)mähen, schneiden; **-er** *n.* Mäher, Schnitter; Mähmaschine; **-ing** *adj.* mähend; **-ing machine** Mähmaschine

much *adj.* viel; — *adv.* weit, bei weitem, sehr; **he is too — for me** ich bin ihm nicht gewachsen; **very —** sehr

mucilage *n.* Gummilösung

muck *n.* Dünger, Kompost, Mist; **Unrat,** Schmutz

mucous *adj.* schleimig, schlüpfrig

mucus *n.* Schleim

mud *n.* Schlamm, Kot; Schlick; **Lehm;** **-dle** *n.* Wirrwarr, Verwirrung, Konfusion; **-dle** *v.* trüben, benebeln; konfus (*or* verwirrt, schlammig, betrunken) machen; **-dy** *adj.* schlammig, trübe; schmutzig, beschmutzt; verworren, konfus; irdisch

mudguard *n.* Kotflügel, Schutzblech

muff *n.* Muff(e); — *v.* verderben, verpfuschen

muffin *n.* Teegebäck

muffle *v.* einhüllen, verhüllen; dämpfen; **-r** *n.* Halstuch, Wollbinde; (auto) Schalldämpfer, Auspufftopf

mug *n.* Krug, Becher

muggy *adj.* schwül

mulberry *n.* Maulbeere

mulch *n.* Streu

mule *n.* Maulesel, Maultier

Multigraph *n.* Verfielfältigungsmaschine

multiplication *n.* Vervielfältigung; Multiplikation; — **table** Einmaleins

multiplier *n.* Multiplikator, Vermehrer

multiply *v.* multiplizieren; (sich) vermehren; vervielfältigen

multi-stage rocket *n.* Vielstufenrakete

multitude *n.* Vielzahl, Mehrheit; Menge

multitudinous *adj.* zahlreich, vielfältig; unermesslich

mum! *interj.* st! still! — *adj.* stumm, still; **keep —** den Mund halten

mumble *n.* Murmeln, Gemurmel; — *v.* murmeln, mummeln; muffeln; knabbern

mummy *n.* Mumie

mumps *n. pl.* Mumps, Ziegenpeter

munch *v.* bedächtig (*or* geräuschvoll) kauen, schmatzen

mundane *adj.* weltlich, irdisch

Munich *n.* München

municipal *adj.* städtisch; Stadt-, Gemeinde-; — **government** Magistrat; **-ity** *n.* Stadtbezirk

munition *n.* Munition; *pl.* Kriegsvorräte

mural *adj.* mauerähnlich, mauerartig; Mauer-, Wand-; — *n.* Wandgemälde

murder *n.* Mord; — *v.* (er)morden; **-er** *n.* Mörder; **-ous** *adj.* mörderisch; blutgierig, grausam

murmur *n.* Gemurmel; Murmeln; Gemurr; Gerücht; (med.) Geräusch; — *v.* murmeln, plätschern; rauschen; murren

muscle *n.* Muskel; (fig.) Muskelkraft

muscle-bound *adj.* übertrainiert

muscular *adj.* muskulös; — **dystrophy** *n.* (med.) Muskelschwund

muse *v.* nachdenken, nachsinnen

museum *n.* Museum

mush *n.* Maisbrei, Mehlbrei

mushroom *n.* Pilz; — *v.* plötzlich emporschiessen

music *n.* Musik; Tonkunst, Tonstück Noten; — **box** Spieldose; **-al** *adj.* musikalisch; (fig.) wohlklingend, harmonisch; Musik-; **-al comedy** musikalische Komödie, Singspiel; **-ian** *n.* Musiker, Musikant; Tonkünstler

musing *n.* Nachdenken, Sinnen; — *adj.* nachdenklich, sinnend

musk *n.* Moschus, Bisam

musket *n.* Muskete, Flinte; **-eer** *n.* Musketier

muskrat *n.* Bisamratte

muslin *n.* Musselin, Nesseltuch

muss *n.* Unordnung; — *v.* verwirren

mussel *n.* Miesmuschel

must *v.* muss; I — not ich darf nicht; — *n.* Muss; Most

mustache *n.* Schnurrbart

mustard *n.* Senf, Mostrich; — **gas** Gelbkreuzgas, Senfgas

muster *n.* Musterung, Heerschau, Parade; — *v.* mustern: aufbringen, auftreiben

musty *adj.* dumpfig, schimmelig, moderig, muffig; abgestanden, schal

mutation *n.* Änderung, Veränderung, Wechsel; (med.) Mutieren, Mutation

mute *n.* Stumme; — *adj.* stumm; lautlos

mutilate *v.* verstümmeln

mutilation *n.* Verstümmelung

mutineer *n.* Meuterer, Aufwiegler

mutinous *adj.* meuterisch, rebellisch, aufrührerisch

mutiny *n.* Meuterei, Auflehnung; Aufruhr; — *v.* meutern

mutter *n.* Gemurmel, Gemurr; — *v.* murmeln, murren; munkeln

mutton *n.* Hammelfleisch

mutual *adj.* gegenseitig, beiderseitig; gemeinsam; by — consent in gegenseitigem Einvernehmen

muzzle *n.* Maulkorb; (gun) Mündung; (coll.) Maul, Schnauze; — *v.* mit einem Maulkorb versehen, den Mund stopfen, knebeln; schnüffeln

my *pron.* mein; **-self** *pron.* mich, mir; ich selbst (or selber)

myriad *n.* Myriade; — *adj.* zahllos, unzählig

mysterious *adj.* geheimnisvoll, rätselhaft, mysteriös

mystery *n.* Geheimnis, Rätsel; Mysterium; — **story** Kriminalgeschichte

mystic *adj.* mystisch, geheimnisvoll; — *n.*

Mystiker; **-al** *adj.* mystisch; **-ism** *n.* Mystizismus

myth *n.* Mythus, Mythe; Sage, Fabel; **-ical** *adj.* mythisch, sagenhaft, fabelhaft; **-ology** *n.* Mythologie, Götterlehre

N

nab *v.* erwischen, ergreifen

nacelle *n.* Ballonkorb; Flugzeugrumpf

nag *n.* Pferd, Mähre, Klepper; — *v.* ärgern, nörgeln; quälen, zusetzen

nail *n.* Nagel; — **file** Nagelfeile; — *v.* (an)nageln, festnageln; beim Wort nehmen

naive *adj.* naiv natürlich; unbefangen

naked *adj.* nackt. bloss, entblösst; (bot.) kahl; (fig.) unverhüllt, einfach; **entirely — splitterfasernackt**; **-ness** *n.* Nacktheit, Blösse; (fig.) Offenheit, Unverhülltheit

name *n.* Name, Benennung, Titel; by — dem Namen nach; in — only nur dem Namen nach; **what is your** —? wie heissen Sie? — *v.* (be-)nennen; bezeichnen, erwähnen; ernennen, bestimmen; be **-d** heissen; **-less** *adj.* namenlos, unbenannt; (fig.) unsäglich; **-ly** *adv.* nämlich; **-sake** *n.* Namensvetter

nap *n.* Schläfchen, Nickerchen; — *v.* schlummern

nape *n.* Nacken, Genick

naphtha *n.* Naphtha

napkin *n.* Serviette, Mundtuch

narcissus *n.* Narzisse

narcotic *n.* Betäubungsmittel, Narkotikum; — *adj.* narkotisch

narration *n.* Erzählung, Schilderung

narrative *n.* Bericht, Geschichte; — *adj.* erzählend, schildernd

narrator *n.* Erzähler, Schilderer

narrow *n.* Engpass, Meerenge; — *adj.* eng, schmal, beschränkt; have a — escape mit knapper Not entrinnen; — *v.* (sich) verengen; schmälern, verkleinern, beschränken; **-ness** *n.* Enge, Schmalheit; Beschränktheit

narrow-gauge *adj.* schmalspurig

narrow-minded *adj.* kleindenkend, engherzig

nasal *adj.* Nasal; Nasen-; näselnd

nasturtium *n.* Kresse

nasty *adj.* garstig, schlimm, schlecht; übel

nation *n.* Nation; Volk; **-al** *adj.* national, Volks-, Staats-; **-alism** *n.* Nationalismus; **-alist** *n.* Nationalist; **-ality** *n.* Nationalität, Staatsangehörigkeit; **-alize** *v.* nationalisieren, verstaatlichen

nation-wide *adj.* weit verbreitet, von Grenze zu Grenze

native *n.* Eingeborene, Einheimische; **a —**

of gebürtig aus, geboren in; — *adj.*
(ein)heimisch, eingeboren, angeboren;
— **land** Geburtsland

nativity *n.* Geburt; Nativität

natural *adj.* natürlich, naturgemäss;
angeboren; unehelich; (art) naturgetreu, lebenswahr; — **gas** Naturgas; —
history Naturgeschichte; — **resources**
Bodenschätze; — **science** Naturkunde;
— *n.* (mus.) Auflösungszeichen; —**ly** *adv.*
natürlich, von Natur aus; —**ism** *n.*
Naturalismus, Naturzustand; —**ist** *n.*
Naturalist, Naturforscher; —**ization** *n.*
Naturalisierung, Einbürgerung; —**ize** *v.*
naturalisieren, einbürgern

nature *n.* Natur; Wesen, Naturell; **good**
— Gutartigkeit

naught *n.* Null, Nichts; Wertlose

naughty *adj.* unartig, ungezogen

nausea *n.* Übelkeit; —**te** *v.* verabscheuen;
be —**ted** sich ekeln

nautical *adj.* nautisch; See-, Schiffs-,
Marine-

naval *adj.* See-, Schiffs-, Flotten-, Marine-

navel *n.* Nabel

navigable *adj.* schiffbar, befahrbar; lenkbar, steuerbar

navigate *v.* navigieren, schiffen, befahren;
lenken, steuern

navigation *n.* Navigation

navigator *n.* Schiffer, Seefahrer; Steuermann

navy *n.* Marine; Flotte, Seemacht; —
blue Marineblau

nay *adv.* nein; **the yeas and** —**s** die Ja- und
Nein-Stimmen, das Für und Wider

near *prep.* nahe, dicht; — *adj.* nahe-
(liegend), in der Nähe; vertraut, nahe
verwandt (*or* befreundet); — *adv.* nahe,
dicht heran; beinahe, nahezu, fast; —
v. sich nähern, näherkommen; —**ly** *adv.*
fast, beinahe; —**ness** *n.* Nähe

nearby *adj.* nahe(liegend); — *adv.* in der
Nähe

nearsighted *adj.* kurzsichtig; — **person**
Kurzsichtige

neat *adj.*. ordentlich, sauber, rein; nett,
niedlich, zierlich

nebulous *adj.* neb(e)lig, wolkig; nebelhaft

necessary *adj.* notwendig, nötig; erforderlich

necessitate *v.* nötigen, zwingen; erfordern,
notwendig machen

necessity *n.* Notwendigkeit, Bedarf;
Zwang

neck *n.* Hals, Nacken; Genick; — **of land**
Landenge

neckerchief *n.* Halstuch

necklace *n.* Halskette, Halsband

necktie *n.* Krawatte, Schlips; Halsbinde

neckwear *n.* Krawatten, Schlipse

need *n.* Not, Mangel; Bedarf; Bedürfnis;
— *v.* brauchen, bedürfen, nötig haben;
—**ful** *adj.* notwendig, nötig; —**less** *adj.*
unnötig, vergeblich; —**y** *adj.* (hilfs)-
bedürftig; arm(selig)

needle *n.* Nadel; **be on pins and** — *pl.*
wie auf Nadeln sitzen; **darning** —
Stopfnadel; **hypodermic** — Injektionsnadel

needlework *n.* Nadelarbeit, Handarbeit;
Stickerei

negation *n.* Verneinung

negative *n.* Verneinung; (phot.) Negativ;
— *adj.* negativ, verneint; verneinend

neglect *n.* Vernachlässigung, Nachlässigkeit; — *v.* vernachlässigen; versäumen

negligee *n.* Negligé

negligence *n.* Unachtsamkeit, Sorglosig-
keit; (law) Fahrlässigkeit

negligent *adj.* unachtsam, sorglos; nachlässig; (law) fahrlässig

negligible *adj.* unwesentlich, nicht
beachtenswert

negotiable *adj.* umsetzbar, verkäuflich

negotiate *v.* verhandeln, unterhandeln

negotiation *n.* Verhandlung, Vermittlung;
Unterhandeln; Abschluss

Negress *n.* Negerin

Negro *n* Neger

neigh *n.* Wiehern; — *v.* wiehern

neighbor *n.* Nachbar; Nächste; —**hood** *n.*
Nachbarschaft; —**ing** *adj.* benachbart;
—**ly** *adj.* nachbarlich

neither *conj.* weder; — *adj.* and *pron.*
keiner

neomycin *n.* Neomycin.

neon *n.* Neon; — **light** Neonlicht

nephew *n.* Neffe

nephritis *n.* (med.) Nierenentzündung

nerve *n.* Nerv; (fig.) Mut; (coll.) Stirn;
—**less** *adj.* entnervt, kraftlos

nervous *adj.* nervös, reizbar; nerven-
schwach; nervig, nachdrücklich, Ner-
ven-; —**ness** *n.* Nervosität

nest *n.* Nest, Brutstätte; — **egg** Nestei;
—**le** *v.* nisten; sich einnisten (*or* einschmeicheln)

net *n.* Netz; Schlinge, Falle, Fallstrick;
— *adj.* netto, rein; — **balance** Netto-
bilanz; — **cost** Nettokosten; — **proceeds** Nettoertrag; — **profit** Reingewinn; — *v.* netto einnehmen

Netherlands *n.* Niederlande

nettle *n.* Nessel; — *v.* ärgern, necheln

network *n.* Rundfunknetz

neuralgia *n.* Nervenschmerz, Neuralgie

neuritis *n.* Nervenentzündung

neuron *n.* Nervenzelle

neurosis *n.* Neurose

neurotic *adj.* neurotisch

neutral *adj.* neutral, unparteiisch; -ity *n.* Neutralität; -ize *v.* neutralisieren, unwirksam machen; für neutral erklären

neutron *n.* Neutron

never *adv.* nie(mals), durchaus nicht, gar nicht; — mind! das hat nichts zu sagen! macht nichts!

nevertheless *adv.* nichtsdestoweniger, dessenungeachtet, dennoch

new *adj.* neu, frisch; unerfahren; New Year Neujahr; New Year's Eve Silvester(abend); — *adv.* neulich, soeben, seit kurzem; -ness *n.* Neuheit, Neuerung; (fig.) Unerfahrenheit; -sy *adj.* voller Neuigkeiten

newborn *n.* Neugeborene; — *adj.* neugeboren

newcomer *n.* Ankömmling, Neuling

newfangled *adj.* neumodisch

new-found *adj.* neu erfunden (*or* gefunden)

Newfoundland *n.* Neufundland

newlywed *n.* Neuvermählte; — *adj.* neuvermählt; jungverheiratet

news *n.* Nachricht, Neuigkeit; Nachrichten, Neuigkeiten

newsboy *n.* Zeitungsjunge

newscast *n.* Nachrichtensendung

newsletter *n.* Presserundschreiben

newspaper *n.* Zeitung; — clipping Zeitungsausschnitt

newsprint *n.* Zeitungspapier

newsreel *n.* Wochenschau

newsstand *n.* Zeitungsstand, Zeitungskiosk

next *adj.* nächst, folgend; — door nebenan; — time ein anderes Mal; the — day am nächsten Tag; — *adv.* zunächst, gleich darauf; dann; — to neben; — to nothing fast gar nichts; — *prep.* nächst, bei, an

nib *n.* Nadelspitze

nibble *v.* (be)nagen, (be)knabbern

nice *adj.* nett, hübsch; fein, zart, zierlich; empfindlich, sorgfältig; -ly *adv.* nett, lieblich, sanft; genau, richtig; -ty *n.* Feinheit, Zartheit, Zierlichkeit

niche *n.* Nische; (fig.) Versteck

nick *n.* Kerbe, Einschnitt; in the — of time zur rechten Zeit; wie gerufen; — *v.* (ein)kerben, einschneiden

nickel *n.* Nickel, Fünfcentstück

nickel-plated *adj.* vernickelt

nickname *n.* Spitzname, Kosename; — *v.* mit Spitznamen (*or* Kosenamen) rufen

nicotine *n.* Nikotin

niece *n.* Nichte

night *n.* Nacht; Abend; by — nachts, bei Nacht; — club Nachtklub, Nachtlokal;

— letter verbilligtes Brieftelegramm (ausserhalb der Geschäftsstunden); — school Abendschule, Fortbildungsschule; -ly *adj.* nächtlich, Nacht-; -ly *adv.* jede Nacht, allnächtlich

nightcap *n.* Schlafmütze; (coll.) Schlaftrunk

nightfall *n.* Einbruch der Nacht

nightgown *n.* Schlafrock; Nachthemd, Nachtgewand

nightingale *n.* Nachtigall

nightmare *n.* Alp(drücken), Nachtmahr

nightshade *n.* Nachtschatten

nightshirt *n.* Nachthemd

nihilism *n.* Nihilismus

nimble *adj.* flink, hurtig; gewandt, behend

nine *adj.* neun; — *n.* Neun(er); -fold *adj.* neunfach; -teen *adj.* neunzehn; -teen *n.* Neunzehn(er); -teenth *adj.* neunzehnt; -teenth *n.* Neunzehnte; Neunzehntel; -tieth *adj.* neunzigst; -tieth *n.* Neunzigste; Neunzigstel; -ty *adj.* neunzig; -ty *n.* Neunzig(er)

ninny *n.* Tropf, Dummkopf

ninth *adj.* neunt; — *n.* Neunte; Neuntel

nip *n.* Schlückchen; — *v.* nippen; kneifen, zwicken; (cold) schneiden; — in the bud im Keime ersticken; -ping *adj.* scharf, streng; beissend, schneidend

nipple *n.* Brustwarze, Zitze; Sauger, Nuckel

niter, nitre *n.* Salpeter

nitrate *n.* Nitrat, salpetersaures Salz

nitrogen *n.* Stickstoff; Nitrogen

no *adv.* nein, nicht; — *adj.* kein; by — means durchaus nicht; in — way keineswegs; — man's land Niemandsland; — one niemand, kein; there is — such thing nichts dergleichen, so etwas gibt es nicht; — *n.* Nein; Absage

nobility *n.* Adel(stand)

noble *n.* Adlige; — *adj.* edel, vornehm, grossmütig; -ness *n.* Adel, Würde; Edelmut

nobleman *n.* Edelman

nobody *pron.* niemand; — *n.* unbedeutende Person

nocturnal *adj.* nächtlich, Nacht-

nod *n.* Nicken, Wink; — *v.* nicken, winken; (fig.) schlafen, träumen

noise *n.* Lärm, Geräusch; make — lärmen, Aufsehen machen; -less *adj.* geräuschlos, still

noisy *adj.* lärmend, geräuschvoll; aufdringlich

nomad *n.* Nomade; -ic *adj.* nomadisch; unstet

nominal *adj.* nominell, namentlich; Namen-; angeblich

nominate *v.* aufstellen, zur Wahl vor-

schlagen; ernennen; nominieren
nomination *n.* Aufstellung, Ernennung
nominative *n.* Nominativ, Nennfall
nominee *n.* Vorgeschlagene
nonacceptance *n.* Nichtannahme, Annahmeverweigerung
nonaggression *n.* Nichtangriff
nonalcoholic *adj.* alkoholfrei
nonchalant *adj.* nonchalant, nachlässig
noncombatant *n.* Nichtkämpfer, Zivilist
noncommissioned *adj.* nicht bevollmächtigt; — officer Unteroffizier
noncommittal *adj.* (sich) nicht bindend; reserviert
nonconformist *n.* Dissident
none *pron.* kein, niemand; — *adv.* nichts, keineswegs
nonentity *n.* Null, Nichts; Unding, Erdichtung
nonessential *adj.* unwesentlich
nonobservance *n.* Nichtbeobachtung
nonpartisan *n.* ,Parteilose; — *adj.* unparteiisch, parteilos
nonpayment *n.* Nicht(be)zahlung
nonproductive *adj.* unproduktiv, nichts erzeugend
nonsectarian *adj.* nicht sektiererisch
nonsense *n.* Unsinn
nonsensical *adj.* unsinnig, sinnlos, albern
nonskid *adj.* nicht rutschend; Gleitschutz-
nonstop *adj.* ununterbrochen, ohne Pause; Nonstop-
noodle *n.* Nudel
nook *n.* Ecke, Winkel; Schlupfwinkel
noon *n.* Mittag
noonday *n.* Mittag(szeit)
noontide *n.* Mittagszeit
noose *n.* Schleife, Schlinge; Fallstrick, Falle
nor *conj.* noch; auch nicht; **neither** . . . — weder . . . noch
norm *n.* Norm, Regel, Muster; **-al** *adj.* normal, regelrecht, vorschriftsmässig; **-al school** Berufsschule; Lehrerseminar; **-alize** *v.* normalisieren
north *n.* Nord(en); Nordstaaten; — **Pole** Nordpol; — *adj.* and *adv.* nördlich; **-ern** *adj.* nördlich, Nord-; **-erly** *adj.* and *adv.* nördlich; **-ward** *adj.* nördlich; **-wards** *adv.* nordwärts, nach (*or* von) Norden
northeast *n.* Nordosten; — *adj.* and *adv.* nordöstlich; **-ern** *adj.* nordöstlich
north-northeast *n.* Nordnordost; — *adj.* and *adv.* nordnordöstlich
north-northwest *n.* Nordnordwest; — *adj.* and *adv.* nordnordwestlich
North Pole *n.* Nordpol
northwest *n.* Nordwesten; — *adj.* and *adv.* nordwestlich; **-ern** *adj.* nord-

westlich
Norway *n.* Norwegen
nose *n.* Nase; Schnauze; **blow one's** — sich die Nase schnauben; **bridge of the** — Nasenrücken; **lead by the** — nasführen, an der Nase herumführen; **pay through the** — übermässig bezahlen; — **dive** Sturzflug
nosebag *n.* Futterbeutel
nosebleed *n.* Nasenbluten
nostalgia *n.* Heimweh; Nostalgie
nostril *n.* Nasenloch; Nüster
not *adv.* nicht; — **any gar** kein; — **(as) yet** noch nicht; — **at all** keineswegs; — **even** nicht einmal
notable *n.* Standesperson; — *adj.* merkwürdig, bemerkenswert; ansehnlich, beträchtlich
notary *n.* Notar
notation *n.* Aufzeichnung; (math. and mus.) Bezeichnung
notch *n.* Kerbe, Einschnitt, Scharte; Kimme; (geol.) Engpass; — *v.* kerben, einschneiden
note *n.* Notiz, Anmerkung; Note; Ruf, Ansehen; Nachricht, Kunde; (com.) Rechnung, Schuldschein; (mus.) Note, Ton; **take** — *pl.* sich Aufzeichnungen machen; — *v.* notieren, anzeigen, bezeichnen; beachten; **-d** *adj.* berühmt, bekannt; berüchtigt
notebook *n.* Notizbuch
noteworthy *adj.* beachtenswert, merkwürdig
nothing *n.* Nichts, Null; Unbedeutenheit, Nichtigkeit; **for** — umsonst; **next to** — fast nichts; — **but** nichts als; — *adv.* durchaus nicht
notice *n.* Notiz. Nachricht, Anzeige; Ankündigung, Bekanntmachung; Beachtung, Aufmerksamkeit; Kündigung; **at a moment's** — jeden Augenblick; **at short** — kurzfristig; **give** — **(to)** kündigen; **until further** — bis auf weiteres; — *v.* bemerken, beachten; **-able** *adj.* wahrnehmbar, bemerkbar; bemerkenswert, beachtlich
notification *n.* Anzeige, Bekanntmachung; Vorladung
notify *v.* anzeigen; vorladen
notion *n.* Begriff. Idee; Ahnung; Absicht; *pl.* Kleinigkeiten, Kindereien, Luftschlösser; Kurzwaren
notoriety *n.* Offenkundigkeit
notorious *adj.* berüchtigt, offenkundig
notwithstanding *conj.* obgleich, trotzdem; — *prep.* ungeachtet, trotz; — *adv.* nichtsdestoweniger, dennoch, trotzdem
nought *n.* Null, Nichts
noun *n.* Hauptwort, Substantiv

nourish *v.* (er)nähren; erhalten, hegen, pflegen, unterhalten; nahrhaft sein; **–ment** *n.* Nahrung(smittel)

novel *n.* Roman; — *adj.* neu, ungewöhnlich, überraschend; **–ist** *n.* Romanschriftsteller; **–ty** *n.* Neuheit; Ungewöhnlichkeit

Novocain *n.* Novokain

now *adv.* nun, jetzt; eben, kürzlich; bald, dann; **by** — schon jetzt; **just** — soeben; — **and then** dann und wann, hier und da; **till** — bis jetzt; — *interj.* nun aber! jetzt! — *conj.* nun da

nowadays *adv.* heutzutage

nowhere *adv.* nirgend(wo)

nozzle *n.* Düse; Mundstück, Tülle; (zool.) Schnauze, Rüssel

nuclear *adj.* kernförmig; Kern-; — **fission** Kernspaltung; — **war** Kernwaffenkrieg

nucleic acid *n.* (phys.) Kernsäure

nucleus *n.* Kern

nude *n.* Nackte; — *adj.* nackt, bloss

nudge *n.* leichtes Anstossen, Rippenstoss; — *v.* leicht (*or* heimlich) anstossen

nudist *n.* Nudist, Anhänger der Nacktkultur

nudity *n.* Nacktheit, Blösse

nugget *n.* Goldklumpen

nuisance *n.* Plage, Schaden; Unfug, Verdruss, Ärgernis

null *adj.* nichtig, ungültig; null; fehlend; **–ify** *v.* ungültig machen (*or* erklären)

numb *adj.* starr, erstarrt; betäubt; — *v.* erstarren, betäuben

number *n.* Zahl; Nummer, Ziffer; Menge, Anzahl; (gram.) Zahl; **back** — alte Ausgabe; **round** — runde Summe; — *v.* numerieren, zählen, rechnen; **–less** *adj.* zahllos, unzählig

numeral *n.* Zahl(zeichen), Ziffer; (gram.) Zahlwort; — *adj.* Zahl-

numerator *n.* Zähler

numerous *adj.* zahlreich, sehr viele

numismatics *n.* Münzkunde

nun *n.* Nonne; **–nery** *n.* Nonnenkloster

nuptial *adj.* hochzeitlich, ehelich; Hochzeits-, Ehe-, Braut-; — *n. pl.* Hochzeit, Trauung

Nuremberg *n.* Nürnberg

nurse *n* Schwester, Krankenschwester, Pflegerin; Kindermädchen; **male** — Pfleger, Wärter; **wet** — Amme; — *v.* pflegen; grossziehen; nähren, stillen; **–ry** *n.* Kinderstube; (agr.) Baumschule, Pflanzschule, Schonung; **–ry school** Kindergarten; **–ry rhymes** Kinderlieder

nursemaid *n.* Kindermädchen

nursing *n.* Krankenpflege; Kinderpflege; — **bottle** Milchflasche, Saugflasche

nut *n.* Nuss; (mech.) Schraubenmutter;

(coll.) **be –s** verrückt sein

nutcracker *n.* Nussknacker

nutmeg *n.* Muskatnuss

nutriment *n.* Nahrung; Futter

nutrition *n.* Ernährung, Nahrung; Nährwert

nutritious, nutritive *adj.* nährend, nahrhaft; Ernährungs-

nutshell *n.* Nusschale; (fig.) Kleinigkeit; **in a** — kurz und bündig, in wenigen Worten, in aller Kürze

nylon *n.* Nylon

nymph *n.* Nymphe

O

oaf *n.* Dummkopf, Einfaltspinsel, Tölpel

oak *n.* Eiche; Eichenholz; **–en** *adj.* eichen

oar *n.* Ruder, Riemen

oarsman *n.* Ruderer

oasis *n.* Oase

oat *n.* Hafer

oath *n.* Eid, Schwur; Verwünschung, Fluch

oatmeal *n.* Haferflocken, Hafermehl; Haferschleim

obdurate *adj.* verhärtet, verstockt; hartherzig; halsstarrig

obedience *n.* Gehorsam, Unterwerfung

obedient *adj.* gehorsam, unterwürfig

obese *adj.* feist, fett(leibig)

obesity *n.* Fettleibigkeit, Feistheit

obey *v.* gehorchen, befolgen

obituary *n.* Todesanzeige; Totenliste; Nachruf, Nekrolog

object *n.* Gegenstand, Objekt; Ziel, Zweck; **–ive** *n.* (gram.) Objektsfall; (mil.) Operationsziel; (phot.) Objektiv; (fig.) Endziel; **–ive** *adj.* objektiv, gegenständlich, sachlich; **–ivity** *n.* Objektivität, Sachlichkeit

object *v.* Einspruch erheben, einwenden; entgegenstellen, vorhalten; **–ion** *n.* Einwand, Einspruch, Einwurf; **raise an –ion** einen Einwand erheben; **–ionable** *adj.* anrüchig, nicht einwandfrei

obligation *n.* Verpflichtung; Verbindlichkeit; (com.) Schuldschein; **be under** — verpflichtet (*or* verbunden) sein

obligatory *adj.* verbindlich, bindend, verpflichtend, obligatorisch

oblige *v.* zwingen; verpflichten, bewegen, nötigen

obliging *adj.* gefällig, verbindlich

oblique *adj.* schräg, schief; indirekt, mittelbar; unaufrichtig

oblivion *n.* Vergessenheit; Vergesslichkeit

oblivious *adj.* vergesslich, vergessend

oblong *adj.* länglich; — *n.* Rechteck

obnoxious *adj.* anstössig, widerwärtig, abstossend

oboe *n.* Oboe

obscene *adj.* unanständig, zotig

obscenity *n.* Unanständigkeit; Schlüpfrigkeit, Zote

obscure *adj.* dunkel, unbekannt; unklar obskur; — *v.* verdunkeln, verkleinern

obscurity *n.* Dunkelheit, Unbekannte, Unklarheit, Obskurität

obsequious *adj.* kriechend, unterwürfig, servil, willfährig

observance *n.* Befolgung, Innehaltung; Brauch; (eccl.) Observanz

observant *adj.* beobachtend, befolgend; achtsam

observation *n.* Beobachtung; Befolgung; Bemerkung; — car Aussichtswagen

observatory *n.* Sternwarte, Observatorium

observe *v.* beobachten, wahrnehmen; bemerken; beachten, halten; —r *n.* Beobachter; Zuschauer; Befolger

observing *adj.* aufmerksam, sorgfältig

obstacle *n.* Hindernis

obstetrician *n.* Geburtshelfer

obstetrics *n.* Geburtshilfe

obstinacy *n.* Hartnäckigkeit, Halsstarrigkeit, Eigensinn

obstinate *adj.* hartnäckig, halsstarrig, eigensinnig

obstruct *v.* verstopfen, versperren; hemmen, verzögern; —ion *n.* Verstopfung; Hindernis, Hemmung; Verzögerung

obtain *v.* bekommen, erhalten, erlangen; —able *adj.* erhältlich, erreichbar

obvious *adj.* klar, deutlich; augenscheinlich, unverkennbar

occasion *n.* Gelegenheit, Anlass, Veranlassung; — *v.* veranlassen, verursachen, bewirken; —al *adj.* gelegentlich, zufällig; Gelegenheits-

occident *n.* Westen, Abendland; Okzident; —al *adj.* westlich, abendländisch

occult *adj.* okkult, verborgen, geheim; —ism *n.* Okkultismus, Geheimwissenschaft

occupant *n.* Besitzer, Inhaber; Bewohner

occupation *n.* Beruf, Beschäftigung; Besetzung; — army Besatzungstruppen

occupy *v.* besitzen, innehaben, einnehmen; bewohnen; in Besitz nehmen, besetzen; beschäftigen; be occupied with arbeiten an

occur *v.* geschehen, vorkommen, sich ereignen; einfallen; —rence *n.* Ereignis, Vorkommnis; Vorfall

ocean *n.* Ozean, Weltmeer; —arium Museum für Meereskunde; —ography Meereskunde; —ic *adj.* Meeres-, See-

o'clock *adv.* pünktlich; genau; **two —** genau zwei Uhr

octagon *n.* Achteck; Oktagon

octane *n.* Oktan; — rating Oktanzahl

octave *n.* Oktave

octopus *n.* Achtfüssler; Polyp, **Krake**

ocular *adj.* okular; Augen-

oculist *n.* Augenarzt

odd *adj.* seltsam, sonderbar; **ungerade;** einzeln; etwaig; —ity *n.* Seltsamkeit, Sonderbarkeit; **—s** *n.* (pl.) Vorgabe, Vorteil; Unterschied; Wahrscheinlichkeit; ungleiche Wette (or Partie); **—s and ends** Reste, Überbleibsel, Abfälle

ode *n.* Ode

odo(u)r *n.* Geruch; Duft, Wohlgeruch

of *prep.* von, aus, unter, über, an, bei, in, nach, vor, durch

off *adv.* ab, weg, fort, davon, herunter; entlegen, entfernt, weit, fern; aus dahin; verloren, zu Ende; flott, frei; **— and on** ab und an, ab und zu, hin und her; — *prep.* von . . . weg; von . . . her; fort von; (naut.) auf der Höhe von; — *adj.* entferntest; Seiten-, Neben-; —! *interj.* weg! fort! **hands —!** Hände weg!

off-color *adj.* schlüpfrig, unanständig; verfärbt

offend *v.* beleidigen, ärgern; sich vergehen, verstossen; —er *n.* Beleidiger, Verletzer; Missetäter

offense *n.* Beleidigung, Verstoss; Übertretung; (law) Vergehen; **take —** übelnehmen

offensive *n.* Angriff, Offensive; — *adj.* offensiv, angreifend; Angriffs-; beleidigend, anstössig

offer *n.* Angebot; Offerte; Anerbieten; — *v.* offerieren, (an)bieten; sich darbieten (or zeigen); — **one's service** seine Dienste anbieten; —ing *n.* Anerbieten; Opfer(ung)

offertory *n.* Kollekte, Opfergabe

offhand *adj.* and *adv.* auf der Stelle, aus dem Stegreif; ungezwungen, frei

office *n.* Amt, Büro, Geschäft, Lokal; Dienst, Funktion, Pflicht; — **boy** Laufbursche; — **hours** Geschäftsstunden, Dienststunden; — **supplies** Büroartikel; —r *n.* Beamte; Offizier; Polizist

official *n.* Beamte; — *adj.* offiziell, amtlich, Amts-

officiate *v.* amtieren; (eccl.) den Gottesdienst leiten

offset *n.* (bot. and zool.) Sprössling, Ableger, Seitenzweig; (com.) Gegenforderung, Gegenrechnung; (typ.) Offsetdruck; — *v.* ausgleichen, kompensieren

offshoot *n.* Ausläufer, Spross; (fig.) Abzweigung

offshore *adv.* von der Küste ab (*or* her); vom Lande entfernt

offside *adj.* abseitig; — *adv.* abseits

offspring *n.* Nachkömmling, Abkömmling; Spross

oft(en) *adv.* oft, öfters, oftmals; häufig, wiederholt

ogle *v.* beäugeln, liebäugeln

ogre *n.* Menschenfresser, Ungeheuer

oil *n.* Öl; Petroleum; **crude** — Rohpetroleum; **drying** — rasch trocknendes Öl; **heavy** — Schweröl; **mineral** — Mineralöl; **vegetable** — Pflanzenöl; — **color** Ölfarbe; — **field** Ölfeld; — **painting** Ölgemälde; — **well** Petroleumquelle; — *v.* (ein)ölen, einfetten, (ein)schmieren; **-y** *adj.* ölig, ölhaltig; (fig.) glatt, geschmeidig; salbungsvoll

oilcan *n.* Ölkanne

oilcloth *n.* Wachstuch

oilskin *n.* Ölzeug

ointment *n.* Salbe

okay, o.k. *n.* Zustimmung, Bestätigung; — *adj.* richtig, billigend; — *v.* billigen, zustimmen; —! *interj.* stimmt! richtig! in Ordnung!

okra *n.* Eibisch

old *adj.* alt, altbekannt, altbewährt; verbraucht, abgenutzt; veraltet, altmodisch; **become** (*or* **grow**) — alt werden, altern; **of** — von jeher, ehemals; — **age** hohes Alter, Greisenalter; — **hand** alter Praktikus; — **maid** alte Jungfer; — **timer** Alte; Altmodische; **Old World** alte Welt, östliche Hemisphäre

old-age pension *n.* Altersrente

old-fashioned *adj.* altmodisch

old-time *adj.* aus alter Zeit

oleomargarine *n.* Margarine, Kunstbutter

olfactory *adj.* Geruchs-

olive *n.* Olive; Olivengrün; — **branch** Olivenzweig, Ölzweig; — **drab** Graugrün; — **grove** Olivenhain, Olivenpflanzung; — **oil** Olivenöl; — **tree** Olivenbaum, Ölbaum; — *adj.* olivengrün

omelet(te) *n.* Omelett(e), Eierkuchen

omen *n.* Vorzeichen, Omen

ominous *adj.* unhe lvoll; ominös

omission *n.* Auslassung, Weglassung, Unterlassung

omit *v.* auslassen, unterlassen; übersehen; versäumen

omnibus *.n.* Omnibus; Sammelband, Sammlung; (lit.) Allumfassend

omnipotent *adj.* allmächtig

omniscience *n.* Allwissenheit

on *prep.* auf, an, zu, in, über; von, unter; vor, hinter; bei, mit, nach; — *adv.* darauf, fort, vorwärts, weiter; ferner; **and so** — und so weiter; — **and** — immer weiter; —! *interj.* vorwärts!

once *adv.* einmal, einst; vormals, dereinst; **at** — (so)gleich, auf einmal; **for** — diesmal; — **(and) for all** ein für allemal; — **more** noch einmal, wieder; — **upon a time** es war einmal; — *conj.* sobald

one *adj.* ein; einzig; — **and the same** einerlei; — **day** eines Tages; — *pron.* ein; man; — **and all** alle und jeder; — **another** einander, sich; — **by** — einer nach dem anderen, einzeln; — *n.* Eins, Einser

oneself *pron.* (man) selbst, sich; **by** — aus eigenem Antriebe, von selbst; **with** — mit sich selbst

one-sided *adj.* einseitig

onetime *adj.* einstmalig, einmalig

one-track *adj.* eingleisig; — **mind** beschränkter Verstand

one-way *adj.* einbahnig; — **street** Einbahnstrasse; — **trip** einfache Fahrt; — **ticket** Fahrkarte für den Hinweg

onion *n.* Zwiebel

onionskin *n.* seidig-glänzendes Durchschlagpapier

onlooker *n.* Zuschauer

only *adj.* einzig; — **yesterday** erst gestern; — *adv.* nur, bloss; allein; erst

onset *n.* Angriff, Sturm; Anfang, Beginn

onto *prep.* nach . . . hin; auf

onward *adv.* nach vorne, vorwärts; weiter fort; — *adj.* fortschreitend; vorgeschritten; vorgerückt; **-s** *adv.* nach vorne, vorwärts

onyx *n.* Onyx

opal *n.* Opal

open *adj.* offen, auf; frei, geöffnet, öffentlich; offenbar, aufrichtig, offenherzig, freigebig; unentschieden; **in the** — **air** unter freiem Himmel, im Freien; — **house** offenes Haus; — **letter** offener Brief; — **question** offene (*or* offenstehende) Frage; — **season** Jagdzeit; — **secret** offenes Geheimnis; — **shop** Unternehmen für organisierte und unorganisierte Arbeiter; — *v.* öffnen, aufmachen; aufgehen; aufschlagen; freimachen, entfalten; eröffnen, beginnen; aufschliessen; **-ing** *n.* Öffnung; Eröffnung; freier Platz, offene Stelle; Anfang, Beginn; **-ing** *adj.* eröffnend, beginnend; Eröffnungs-

open-air *adj.* im Freien befindlich; Freilicht-

openhanded *adj.* freigebig, mildtätig

openhearted *adj.* offenherzig, aufrichtig

open-minded *adj.* offenherzig, aufrichtig; vorurteilslos, unbefangen

openmouthed *adj.* mit offenem Munde; gaffend

opera *n.* Oper; — **glass(es)** Opernglas; — **hat** Klapphut; — **house** Opernhaus; **-tic** *adj.* zur Oper gehörig, opernhaft

operate *v.* (ein)wirken, tätig sein; (com.) leiten, betreiben; (mech.) in Gang setzen; (med.) operieren

operation *n.* Wirkung; Verfahren, Verrichtung; (com.) Leitung, Unternehmen; (mech.) Betrieb; Bewegung, Gang; (med. and mil.) Operation; **have an —** operiert werden

operator *n.* Wirkende, Bewirkende; Maschinenarbeiter; (com.) Betriebsleiter, Geschäftsleiter; (med.) Operateur; (tel.) Telefonist(in); (coll.) Spekulant

operetta *n.* Operette

ophthalmologist *n.* Augenarzt, Augenspezialist

ophthalmoscope *n.* Augenspiegel

opiate *n.* Schlafmittel, Opiat

opinion *n.* Meinung, Ansicht; Gutachten; (law) Gerichtsbeschluss; **give an —** seine Meinung sagen, ein Gutachten abgeben; **in my —** meiner Meinung nach; **public —** öffentliche Meinung

opossum *n.* Beutelratte, Opossum

opponent *n.* Gegner, Opponent

opportune *adj.* gelegen, passend, günstig

opportunity *n.* (günstige) Gelegenheit

oppose *v.* entgegensetzen, entgegenstellen; opponieren; (sich) widersetzen

opposite *n.* Gegenteil, Gegensatz; Gegner, Satzung, Gesetz; — *adj.* gegenüberliegend, gegenüberstehend; entgegengesetzt; **take the — side** für die andere (or gegnerische) Seite ergreifen; — *adv.* and *prep.* gegenüber

opposition *n.* Gegenseite; Widerstand, Widerspruch; Opposition

oppress *n.* bedrücken, unterdrücken; überwältigen; **-ion** *n.* Druck, Unterdrückung; Überwältigung; **-ive** *adj.* (be)drückend, tyrannisch; **-or** *n.* Bedrücker, Unterdrücker; Tyrann

optic *adj.* Augen-, Seh-; **-al** *adj.* optisch; **-ian** *n.* Optiker; **-s** *n.* Optik

optimism *n.* Optimismus

optimist *n.* Optimist; **-ic** *adj.* optimistisch

option *n.* Wahl, Wahlrecht; **-al** *adj.* freigestellt, unverbindlich

optometrist *n.* Augenfachmann, Optiker

optometry *n.* Messung der Sehschärfe

or *conj.* oder; oder . . . **—** entweder . . . oder; — **else** sonst, andrenfalls

oral *adj.* mündlich, Mund-

orange *n.* Apfelsine, Orange; — **juice** Orangensaft; — **tree** Orangenbaum; — *adj.* orangenfarben

oration *n.* Rede, Standrede

orator *n.* Redner, Sprecher; **-y** *n.* Redekunst, Beredsamkeit

orb *n.* Himmelskörper; (med.) Augapfel

orbit *n.* Augenhöhle; Bahn; Kreisbahn; Erdkreisbahn; — *v.* die Erde umkreisen

orbital decay *n.* allmähliche Verkleinerung der Eklipse durch Luftwiderstand

orchard *n.* Obstgarten

orchestra *n.* Orchester; **-te** *v.* orchestrieren

ordain *v.* anordnen, verordnen; ordinieren, die Priesterweihe geben (or nehmen)

ordeal *n.* Gottesurteil; (fig.) Feuerprobe

order *n.* Befehl, Verordnung, Verfügung; Ordnung; Orden(szeichen); Klasse, Rang; (com.) Auftrag, Bestellung, Order; (math.) Grad, Reihe; *pl.* Weihegrade; **by —** of im Auftrag von; **in —** in Ordnung; angebracht; **in — to** um . . . zu, damit; **make to —** nach Mass machen; **on —** in Auftrag; — **of battle** Schlachtordnung; **out of —** in Unordnung; nicht bei der Sache; **rush —** Eilauftrag; **standing —** Geschäftsordnung; — *v.* befehlen; verordnen; (an)ordnen; (com.) bestellen; — **around** herumkommandieren; **-ly** *n.* Ordonnanz, Offizier vom Dienst; Lazarettgehilfe, Wärter; **-ly** *adj.* ordentlich, wohlgeordnet, regelmässig; fügsam, gesittet; Ordonnanz-

ordinance *n.* Verordnung, Verfügung; Satzung, Gesetz

ordinary *adj.* gewöhnlich, üblich, gebräuchlich; gemein, niedrig

ordnance *n.* Artillerie, schweres Geschütz

ore *n.* Erz, Metall; — **deposit** Erzlager

organ *n.* Organ, Stimme; Werkzeug; (mus.) Orgel, Harmonium; — **stop** Orgelregister; **internal —** (*pl.*) innere Organe; **-ic** *adj.* organisch; **-ism** *n.* Organismus; **-ist** *n.* Organist

organdy *n.* Organdy

organ-grinder *n.* Leierkastenmann

organization *n.* Organisation, Organisierung; Bildung, Errichtung

organize *v.* organisieren

orgy *n.* Orgie

orient *n.* Orient, Morgenland, Osten; — *v.* orientieren; **-al** *adj.* orientalisch, morgenländisch; östlich; **-ation** *n.* Orientierung

orifice *n.* Öffnung, Mündung

origin *n.* Ursprung; Herkunft, Abstammung; **-al** *n.* Original, Urbild, Urschrift; **-al** *adj.* ursprünglich, originell; **-ality** *n.* Originalität; **-ate** *v.* entsprin-

gen; erzeugen, hervorbringen
oriole n. Pirol, Goldamsel
ornament n. Verzierung, Ornament; — v. verzieren, (aus)schmücken; -al adj. ornamental, ornamentartig; zierend
ornithologist n. Ornithologe, Vogelkenner
orphan n. Waise; — adj. verwaist; -age n. Waisenhaus
orthodontics n. Orthodontie, Zahnkorrektur
orthodox adj. orthodox, strenggläubig, rechtgläubig
orthography n. Orthographie, Rechtschreibung
orthopedics n. Orthopädie
oscillate v. schwingen, pendeln; schwanken
oscillator n. (elec.) Schwingungserreger; (rad.) Frequenzgenerator
osmosis n. Osmose, Durchtritt
ossify v. verknöchern
ostensible adj. scheinbar, angeblich
ostentation n. Gepränge, Prahlerei
ostentatious adj. prangend, prahlerisch
osteopathy n. Knochenheilkunde; Osteopathie
ostrich n. Strauss
other adj. ander; each — einander; every — day einen Tag um den anderen; the — day dieser Tage, neulich; — pron. andere
otherwise adv. anders, sonst
otter n. Otter, Fischotter
ought v. sollte, müsste
ounce n. Unze
our pron. unser; -s pron. unsere
ourselves pron. pl. selbst, uns (selbst)
oust v. verdrängen, vertreiben; entheben
out adv. aus; draussen; heraus, hinaus; nicht zu Hause; fort, weg; offenkundig, bekannt, entdeckt; ausser Amt, nicht im Dienst; erschöpft, verbraucht; (sports) aus, nicht mehr im Spiel; — prep. aus, draussen, ausser; —! interj. heraus! hinaus! fort! weg! — n. Aus; -er adj. äusser; äusserst, fernst, Aussen-; -ing n. Spaziergang, Ausflug; Landpartie
out-and-out adj. durch und durch, völlig
outbid v. überbieten
outbreak n. Ausbruch, Aufruhr
outbuilding n. Nebengebäude
outburst n. Ausbruch, Explosion
outcast n. Ausgestossene, Verbannte; — adj. ausgestossen; verbannt
outcome n. Ergebnis, Resultat
outcry n. Aufschrei; Geschrei
outdated adj. veraltet, überholt
outdo v. übertreffen, zuvortun
outdoor adj. ausser dem Haus; Aussen-;

— exercise Freiübungen; -s adv. draussen, im Freien; nicht im Hause
outermost adj. äusserst
outfield n. Aussenfeld; -er n. Aussenspieler
outfit n. Ausstattung, Ausrüstung
outgrow v. herauswachsen, überwuchern; verwachsen; -th n. Auswuchs, Sprössling
outhouse n. Nebengebäude, Hinterhaus
outlandish adj. ausländisch, fremd(artig), seltsam
outlast v. überdauern
outlaw n. Geächtete, Vogelfreie; Verbrecher; — v. ächten, für vogelfrei erklären
outlay n. Auslage, Ausgabe; Betriebskosten
outlet n. Ausfluss, Abfluss; Ausweg; Absatzgebiet
outline n. Umriss, Skizze; — v. entwerfen, skizzieren, umreissen
outlive v. überleben, überdauern
outlook n. Ausblick, Aussicht; Ausguck
outlying adj. auswärtig; ausserhalb (or entfernt, abseits) liegend
outmoded adj. unmodern, aus der Mode gekommen
outmost adj. äusserst
outnumber v. zahlenmässig übertreffen
out-of-date adj. unzeitgemäss, veraltet
out-of-door(s) adj. ausserhalb des Hauses; im Freien stattfindend (or wachsend)
out-of-the-way adj. abgelegen, abgesondert; versteckt
outpatient n. Patient in ambulanter Behandlung
outpost n. Vorposten
output n. Ausbeute, Ertrag; (com.) Produktion; (min.) Förderung
outrage n. Ausschreitung, Gewalttätigkeit; Frevel; — v. beleidigen, schändlich behandeln; -ous adj. zügellos, gewalttätig; schimpflich; übermässig
outrank v. den höheren Rang haben; rangieren über
outright adj. and adv. gerade heraus; offen, ohne Vorbehalt; völlig
outset n. Anfang, Beginn
outside n. Aussenseite; Äussere; — adj. äusser, äusserst; Aussen-; — adv. (dr)aussen; — prep. — (of) ausserhalb; -r n. Aussenseiter
outskirts n. pl. Grenze, Saum, Peripherie
outspoken adj. ausgesprochen; ehrlich, freimütig; offen
outstanding adj. hervorragend; — debts Aussenstände
outstretch v. ausstrecken; weit öffnen
outward adj. äusser; äusserlich; nach

aussen; — *adv.* auswärts, nach (dr)aussen; –ly *adv.* äusserlich

outweigh *v.* das Übergewicht haben; überwiegen

outwit *v.* an Einsicht übertreffen; überlisten

outworn *adj.* abgenutzt, verbraucht; abgetragen

oval *n.* Oval; — *adj.* oval

ovary *n.* Eierstock; (bot.) Fruchtknoten

ovation *n.* Ovation

oven *n.* Ofen

over *prep.* über; jenseits; an, auf; bei, vor; — *adv.* hinüber, herüber; darüber; übrig; vorbei, vorüber; wieder, nochmals; übermässig, zu sehr; all — überall, ganz fertig; — again noch einmal; — and above ausserdem, über und über; — and — (again) immer wieder; — there da (*or* dort) drüben; — *adj.* ober

overage *adj.* zu alt, veraltet

over-all *adj.* überall, allgemein

overalls *n. pl.* Overalls, arbeitsanzug

overbearing *adj.* anmassend, hochfahrend

overboard *adv.* über Bord

overburden *v.* überladen, überlasten

overcharge *n.* Überteuerung; — *v.* überteuern, überfordern; überladen

overcoat *n.* Überrock, Überzieher

overcome *v.* überwinden, überwältigen; be — hingerissen sein

overcooked *adj.* ausgekocht, zu lange gekocht

overcrowd *v.* überfüllen

overdo *v.* übertreiben, überanstrengen; zu stark (*or* weit) treiben; zu viel tun; –ne *adj.* übertrieben; überanstrengt; zu stark gekocht

overdose *n.* Überdosis

overdrive *n.* Geschwindigkeitsregler

overdue *adj.* überfällig; verfallen; verspätet

overeat *v.* sich überessen

overestimate *v.* überschätzen

overexposure *n.* Überbelichtung

overflow *n.* Überschwemmung; Überfluss; — *v.* überfluten, überschwemmen; überfliessen

overgrown *adj.* übermässig gross; überwachsen

overhaul *v.* überholen, einholen; völlig ausbessern; gründlich nachsehen

overhead *n.* Unkosten, Geschäftskosten; — *adv.* ober; (dr.)oben; im oberen Stock

overhear *v.* belauschen

overheat *v.* überhitzen, überheizen; (mech.) heiss laufen lassen

overjoyed *adj.* übermässig entzückt (*or* erfreut)

overland *adj.* zu Lande; Überland-; — *adv.* auf dem Lande, über Land

overlap *v.* überragen; überschneiden, übereinandergreifen, übereinanderliegen; überlappen

overload *n.* Über(be)lastung; — *v.* überladen, überlasten

overlook *v.* übersehen, überblicken, überschauen; hinabblicken auf; hervorragen; überlesen

overlord *n.* Ober(lehens)herr

overnight *adj.* and *adv.* über Nacht

overpass *n.* Übergang, Überführung

overpower *v.* überwältigen, unterdrücken

overproduction *n.* Produktionsüberschuss

overrate *v.* überschätzen; zu hoch veranschlagen (*or* veranlagen)

overrule *v.* verwerfen, zurückweisen; überstimmen

overrun *v.* überholen, übertreffen; überlaufen, überrennen; überwachsen

oversea *adj.* überseeisch; –s *adv.* über See

oversee *v.* beaufsichtigen, überwachen; –r *n.* Aufseher, Inspektor

overshadow *v.* überschatten, beschatten, verdunkeln

overshoe *n.* Überschuh

oversight *n.* Versehen, Auslassung

oversleep *v.* verschlafen

overstep *v.* überschreiten

overstuffed *adj.* völlig (aus)gepolstert

oversupply *n.* Überangebot, Überfluss; überreiche Versorgung (*or* Zufuhr)

overtake *v.* einholen, überholen; überraschen, überfallen

overtax *v.* zu hoch besteuern; überschätzen

overthrow *n.* Umsturz, Niederwerfung; — *v.* umstürzen, umwerfen, umstossen

overtime *n.* Überstunden

overture *n.* Vorschlag, Angebot; (mus.) Ouvertüre

overturn *v.* umwerfen, umkehren, umschlagen

overview *n.* Überblick, Übersicht; Inspektion

overweight *n.* Übergewicht; — *adj.* überladen

overwhelm *v.* überwältigen, zerschmettern; überschütten; –ing *adj.* überwältigend, erdrückend

overwork *n.* Überarbeitung; — *v.* (sich) überarbeiten (*or* übermüden)

ovum *n.* Ei

owe *v.* schuldig sein, schulden, verdanken

owl *n.* Eule; Kauz

own *adj.* eigen; einzig; my — self ich

selbst; of one's — für sich allein; of one's — accord aus eigenem Antrieb, von selbst; — v. besitzen; -er n. Besitzer, Inhaber; Eigentümer; -ership n. Eigentum(srecht); Besitz

ox n. Ochse

oxalic acid n. Oxalsäure, Kleesäure

oxide n. Oxyd

oxidize v. oxydieren

oxygen n. Sauerstoff; — tent Sauerstoffzelt

oyster n. Auster

P

pace n. Schritt, Tritt; Gang; (mus.) Tempo, Geschwindigkeit; keep — Schritt halten; — v. (einher)schreiten, gehen; (sports) Schrittmacher sein; — off abschreiten

Pacific Ocean n. Stiller Ozean

pacifist n. Pazifist

pacify v. beruhigen, besänftigen, befriedigen

pack n. Pack, Paket; Bündel; Menge, Fülle; Last, Bürde; Meute, Rotte, Rudel; Bande; (cards) Spiel; — animal Packesel, Lasttier; — train Lastzug; — v. (zusammen) packen, bepacken, zusammendrängen; parteiisch zusammensetzen; — up einpacken; -age n. Paket, Ballen; Verpackung; -er n. Packer, Verpacker; Packmaschine; -et n. Paket; -ing n. Packen, Verpacken; Verpackung, Packmaterial; (mech.) Dichtung; -ing house Fleischkonservenfabrik; Packhaus

pact n. Vertrag, Pakt

pad n. Kissen, Polster; Wulst, Bausch; Block; (zool.) Ballen; Fährte; — of paper Papierblock; — v. auspolstern; wattieren; -ding n. Polsterung, Wattierung; Polstermaterial

paddle v. paddeln; (coll.) tätscheln; — wheel Schaufelrad; — n. Paddel

padlock n. Vorhängeschloss; — v. mit einem Vorhängeschloss versehen (or verschliessen)

pagan n. Heide; — adj. heidnisch; -ism n. Heidentum

page n. Page; Botenjunge, Amtsdiener; Blatt, Seite; — v. paginieren, mit Seitenzahlen versehen; durch Namensaufruf herausfinden

pageant n. Festspiel, Aufzug; Schaustück; -ry n. Schaugepränge, Prunkaufzug

pail n. Eimer, Kübel

pain n. Schmerz, Pein, Qual; Sorge, Kummer; pl. Mühe, Leiden; Wehen; — v.

quälen, peinigen; Schmerz verursachen; -ful adj. schmerzhaft, schmerzlich; peinlich, quälend; -less adj. schmerzlos

painstaking adj. arbeitsam, gewissenhaft; peinlich, sorgfältig

paint n. Farbe; Anstrich; Schminke; — v. malen; anstreichen; (sich) schminken; -er n. Maler; Anstreicher; -ing n. Gemälde; Malen, Malerei

paintbrush n. Malerpinsel; Antreicherpinsel

pair n. Paar; — v. (sich) paaren, vereinigen; sich verbinden

pajamas n. pl. Pyjama, Schlafanzug

pal n. Gefährte, Kamerad

palace n. Palast

palatable adj. schmackhaft, wohlschmeckend

palate n. Gaumen; (fig.) Geschmack

palatial adj. palastartig

Palatinate n. Pfalz

pale v. (er)bleichen, erblassen; — adj. bleich, blass; (fig.) matt; -ness n. Blässe, Farblosigkeit

paleface n. Bleichgesicht

palette n. Palette

palisade n. Palisade

pall n. Bahrtuch, Leichentuch; — v. langweilen, schal werden, den Reiz verlieren

pallbearer n. Bahrtuchhalter

pallet n. Strohlager, Strohsack

palm n. Handfläche, Handteller; (bot.) Palme, Palmbaum; (fig.) Sieg; Palm Sunday Palmsonntag; — v. in der Handfläche verbergen; — off a thing on someone jemandem etwas andrehen; -etto n. Palmetto

palpitate v. klopfen, schlagen; zittern, zucken

palpitation n. Klopfen, Schlag(en); Herzklopfen

palsied adj. gelähmt, gichtbrüchig, wackelig

palsy n. Lähmung; (fig.) Ohnmacht

pamper v. verzärteln

pamphlet n. Broschüre, Prospekt, Flugschrift, Pamphlet

pan n. Pfanne, Tiegel

panacea n. Allheilmittel, Wundermittel

Panama hat n. Panamahut

pancake n. Pfannkuchen, Eierkuchen

pancreas n. Bauchspeicheldrüse

panda n. Panda, Katzenbär; giant — Riesenpanda, Bambusbär

pandemonium n. Höllenlärm

pane n. Scheibe, Platte; Fach, Füllung

panel n. (arch.) Füllung, Fach; Tafel; (law) Geschworenenliste, Geschworenenbank; (fig.) Sachverständigengruppe; — discussion Sachverständigengespräch

pang n. plötzlicher Schmerz, Stich; Angst, Qual

panhandler n. Bettler

panic n. Panik, panischer Schrecken; — adj. panisch; **-ky** adj. beunruhigt; beunruhigend

panic-stricken adj. von Schrecken ergriffen (or gelähmt)

panorama n. Panorama

pansy n. Stiefmütterchen

pant n. Keuchen, Herzklopfen; pl. Hosen, Unterhosen; — v. keuchen, nach Luft schnappen; (heart) pochen; (fig.) verlangen, streben; **-aloons** n. pl. Beinkleider; **-ies** n. pl. Schlüpfer

pantheism n. Pantheismus

panther n. Panther

pantomime n. Pantomime, Gebärdenspiel

pantry n. Speisekammer, Vorratskammer

papa n. Papa

papacy n. Papsttum

papal adj. päpstlich

pa(w)paw n. Papaya

paper n. Papier; Zeitung; Blatt, Zettel; Tapete; Vortrag, Vorlesung; (educ.) schriftliche Arbeit, Fragebogen; pl. Briefschaften, Dokumente, Akten; **blotting** — Löschpapier; **carbon** — Kohlepapier; **toilet** — Toilettenpapier; papieren; — **bag** Papiertüte; — **boy** Zeitungsjunge; — **chase** Schnitzeljagd; — **clip** Büroklammer, Heftklammer; — **cutter** Papierschneider, Papierschneidemaschine; — **knife** Papiermesser; — **money** Papiergeld; — v. tapezieren

paperweight n. Briefbeschwerer

par n. Gleichheit, gleicher Wert; Pari; **at** — auf Pari, gleich an Wert; — adj. — **value** Gleichwertigkeit, Pariwert; — prep. — **excellence** par excellence, vorzugsweise

parable n. Parabel, Gleichnis

parachute n. Fallschirm

parade n. Parade; Prunk(aufzug), Gepränge; — v. paradieren; in Parade aufmarschieren; prunken; (mil.) defilieren, vorbeiziehen

paradise n. Paradies

paraffin n. Paraffin

paragon n. Vorbild, Muster

paragraph n. Paragraph, Absatz, Abschnitt

parakeet n. Wellensittich, Sittich

parallel n. Parallele, Parallellinie; (geog.) Parallelkreis; — adj. parallel, gleichlaufend; — v. parallel machen (or laufen)

paralysis n. Lähmung, Paralyse; **infantile** — Kinderlähmung

paralyze v. lähmen, lahmlegen

paramedics n. (mil.) Fallschirm-Sanitätspersonal

paramilitary n. pseudomilitärisch, halbmilitärisch

paramount adj. höchst, unumschränkt

paraphernalia n. Ausstaffierung

paraphrase n. Umschreibung, Paraphrase; — v. umschreiben, paraphrasieren

parasite n. Parasit, Schmarotzer

paratroops n. pl. Fallschirmtruppen

parboil v. ankochen; braten, schmoren

parcel n. Paket, Ballen; Teil, Stück; Parzelle; Menge, Masse; **small** — Päckchen; — **post** Paketpost; — v. parzellieren, abteilen

parch v. austrocknen, verdorren; rösten, dörren

parchment n. Pergament

pardon n. Verzeihung, Vergebung; Pardon; (law) Begnadigung; — v. entschuldigen, verzeihen, vergeben; begnadigen; **-able** adj. verzeihlich

pare v. schälen; (ab)schneiden, beschneiden

parent n. Vater, Mutter; pl. Eltern; **-age** n. Familie, Abstammung, Herkunft; Elternschaft; (fig.) Urheberschaft; **-al** adj. elterlich; väterlich, mütterlich; **-hood** n. Elternschaft

parenthesis n. Parenthese, Einschaltung; (typ.) Klammer

paring knife n. Schälmesser

parings n. pl. Schale, Späne, Abfall

Paris green n. Pariser Grün

parish n. Gemeinde, Kirchspiel; **-ioner** n. Gemeindemitglied, Pfarrkind

parity n. Gleichheit, Gleichstellung, Gleichberechtigung; (agr.) Preisabkommen

park n. Park, Anlage(n); Garten; — v. parken; **-ing** n. Parken; **-ing place** Parkplatz

parkway n. Parkstrasse; schöngelegene Autostrasse; Allee

parley n. Unterhandlung, Unterredung; — v. unterhandeln

parliament n. Parlament; **-ary** adj. parlamentarisch

parlor n. Salon, Empfangszimmer; Gastzimmer; **funeral** — Begräbnishalle; — **car** Salonwagen

parochial adj. Pfarr-, Gemeinde-

parole n. Parole, Losungswort; Ehrenwort; **on** — auf Ehrenwort (entlassen); — v. bedingt entlassen

paroxysm n. Paroxysmus, Anfall

parquet n. Parkett

parrot n. Papagei; (fig.) Nachschwätzer; — v. nachplappern

parsley *n.* Petersilie
parsnip *n.* Pastinakwurzel
parson *n.* Pfarrer, Pastor; **-age** *n.* Pfarr-haus
part *n.* Teil, Anteil; Bestandteil, Stück, Glied; Stadtteil, Gegend; Lieferung; Seite, Partei; Pflicht; (hair) Scheitel; (mus.) Stimme, Partie; (theat.) Rolle; *pl.* Anlagen, Talente, Fähigkeiten; **do one's —** seine Schuldigkeit tun; **for my —** meinerseits; **for the most —** grösstenteils; **in — teilweise; — of speech** Redeteil; **take — in** teilnehmen an; **take someone's —** für jemand Partei ergreifen; **— payment** Teilzahlung; **—** *v.* (sich) trennen, aufgeben, scheiden; (hair) scheiteln; **-ing** *n.* Trennung, Abschied; Teilung, Scheidung; Scheiteln; **-ly** *adv.* teils, zum Teil; in gewissem Grade
partake *v.* teilhaben, teilnehmen; mitessen
partial *adj.* teilweise, Teil-; parteiisch, einseitig, eingenommen; **-ity** *n.* Parteilichkeit, Vorliebe
participant *n.* Teilnehmer; **—** *adj.* teilnehmend
participate *v.* teilnehmen, teilhaben
participation *n.* Teilnahme
participle *n.* Partizip, Mittelwort
particle *n.* Stückchen, Teilchen; (gram.) unbeugbares Wort (Verhältnis-, Binde- oder Umstandswort); (phys.) Partikelchen
particular *adj.* besonder, einzeln; wählerisch; sonderbar; **—** *n.* Einzelheit; **in —** insbesondere, besonders
partisan *n.* Partisan, Parteigänger; Partisane; **-ship** *n.* Parteigängertum, Parteigeist
partition *n.* Einteilung, Teilung; (arch.) Scheidewand; **—** *v.* (ein)teilen, verteilen
partner *n.* Partner, Teilhaber, Teilnehmer; Gefährte, Gesellschafter; Tänzer, Mitspieler; **silent —** stiller Teilhaber; **-ship** *n.* Teilhaberschaft, Gemeinschaft; Handelsgesellschaft; **general -ship** Gesellschaft mit unbeschränkter Haftung; **limited -ship** Gesellschaft mit beschränkter Haftung; **silent -ship** stille Teilhaberschaft
partridge *n.* Rebhuhn
part-time job *n.* Nebenbeschäftigung
party *n.* Partei; Gesellschaft; Partie; Teilhaber, Teilnehmer; Interessent; Beteiligte; (mil.) Abteilung; **— line** Gemeinschaftstelefon
pass *n.* Pass, Engpass; Zugang, Durchfahrt; Reisepass, Passierschein; (mil.) Urlaubsschein; (sports) Zuspielen, Aus-

fall; (theat.) Freikarte; **—** *v.* (vorüber) gehen; einholen, überholen; passieren; genehmigen; (über)reichen; bestehen, annehmen; (cards) passen; **come to —** geschehen; **— away** sterben; **— by** vorübergehen; **— for** gelten für; **— judgment** (*oder* **sentence**) ein Urteil fällen; **— off** ausgeben; **— on** weitersagen; weitergeben; **— out** ohnmächtig werden; **— over** übersehen, übergehen; **-able** *adj.* gangbar, leidlich; passierbar; **-age** *n.* Korridor, Gang; Passage; Durchreise, Überfahrt; (book) Absatz, Abschnitt; (mus.) Lauf; (pol.) Annahme; **-é** *adj.* passé, veraltet, altmodisch; **-enger** *n.* Reisende, Fahrgast, Passagier; **-ing** *n.* Vorbeigehen, Hinübergehen; Durchgang; (pol.) Durchbringen; **in -ing** im Vorbeigehen; nebenher; **-ing** *adj.* vorübergehend; gegenwärtig, jeweilig; dahineilend, flüchtig; **-ing grade** (educ.) Versetzungsnote to make a — *v.* Avancen machen; (avi.) den Flugplatz anfliegen
passer-by *n.* Vorübergehende
passion *n.* Leidenschaft, Liebe, Verlangen; Wut, Ärger, Zorn; Passion; **-ate** *adj.* leidenschaftlich, begeistert, passioniert
passive *adj.* passiv, leidend, untätig
passkey *n.* Hauptschlüssel, Drücker
Passover *n.* Passah(fest)
passport *n.* Pass, Reisepass; (mil.) Passierschein, Geleitbrief
password *n.* Parole, Losung(swort)
past *n.* Vergangenheit, Vergangene; **—** *adj.* vergangen, verflossen; vorbei, ehemalig; vorüber, hin; vorig, früher; **— master** Altmeister; **— participle** Partizip der Vergangenheit; **— perfect** Plusquamperfekt; **— tense** Zeitform der Vergangenheit; **—** *prep.* vorbei an; über; nach; **a quarter — nine** viertel Zehn, Viertel nach Neun; **at half — seven** um halb acht; **— all belief** unglaublich; **— comparison** unvergleichlich; **—** *adv.* vorbei, vorüber
paste *n.* Paste, Teig; Kleister, Klebstoff; Pappe; **—** *v.* pappen, kleistern; (auf)kleben
pasteboard *n.* Pappdeckel, Pappe
pasteurize *v.* pasteurisieren, keimfrei machen
pastime *n.* Zeitvertreib, Kurzweil
pastor *n.* Pastor
pastoral *adj.* pastoral, seelsorgerisch; Hirten-
pastry *n.* Gebäck; Pastete, Torte; **Konditorware; — shop** Konditorei
pasture *n.* Weide, Weideland, Futter; **—**

v. (ab)weiden, grasen: auf die Weide treiben

pasty *adj.* teig(art)ig; bleich

pat *n.* Schlag, Klaps; — *adv.* and *adj.* eben recht, passend; bequem, treffend; **stand — seinen Standpunkt verteidigen;** — *v.* tappen, patschen, tätsche.n; — **on the back** beglückwünschen

patch *n.* Fleck, Flicken, Lappen; — *v.* flicken, ausbessern; — **up** flicken, zusammenstoppeln

patchwork *n.* Flickwerk, Flickerei

patent *n.* Patent, Privilegien, Freibrief; — *adj.* offen(bar); — **fastener** Druckknopf; — **leather** Lackleder; — **medicine** Markenmedizin; — *v.* patentieren

paternal *adj.* väterlich

paternity *n.* Vaterschaft

path *n.* Pfad, Weg; **-less** *adj.* pfadlos, unwegsam

pathetic *adj.* rührend, pathetisch

pathfinder *n.* Pfadfinder

pathological *adj.* pathologisch

pathology *n.* Pathologie, Krankheitslehre

pathos *n.* Pathos

pathway *n.* Pfad, Weg, Fussteig

patience *n.* Geduld, Ausdauer; (cards) Patience

patient *n.* Patient, Kranke; — *adj.* geduldig; ausdauernd, beharrlich

patio *n.* Patio, spanischer Innenhof

patriarch *n.* Patriarch

patriot *n.* Patriot; **-ic** *adj.* patriotisch; **-ism** *n.* Patriotismus, Vaterlandsliebe

patrol *n.* Patrouille, Runde; — *v.* patrouillieren

patrolman *n.* Schutzmann auf Streife

patron *n.* Patron, Schutzherr; Gönner; Kunde; — **saint** Schutzheilige; **-age** *n.* Protektion, Gönnerschaft; Schutz; **-ize** *v.* beschützen, begünstigen; gönnerhaft behandeln; besuchen

patter *n.* Klapper, Platschen; Getrappe; — *v.* klappern, plappern, trappeln

pattern *n.* Muster, Modell, Probe; Vorbild

patty *n.* Pastetchen

paunch *n.* Bauch, Wanst

pauper *n.* Arme, Almosenempfänger

pause *n.* Pause, Unterbrechung; (mus.) Fermate; — *v.* pausieren, innehalten, verweilen

pave *v.* pflastern; (fig.) bedecken; — **the way** den Weg bahnen (*or* ebnen); **-ment** *n.* Pflaster(ung), Pflastermaterial

pavilion *n.* Pavillon, Lusthaus; Zelt

paving *n.* Pflaster

paw *n.* Pfote, Klaue, Tatze; — *v.* mit den Pfoten stossen (*or* schlagen, stampfen, scharren); (be)patschen

pawn *n.* Pfand; (chess) Bauer; — *v.* ver-

pfänden, versetzen

pawnbroker *n.* Pfandleiher

pawnshop *n.* Pfandleihe, Leihhaus

pay *n.* Zahlung, Bezahlung, Auszahlung; Lohn, Gehalt; **half — Halbsold; in the — of** im Dienste von; — **roll** Gehaltsliste; — *v.* (be)zahlen, auszahlen; belohnen, vergelten; erweisen, entrichten; — **a visit** einen Besuch abstatten; — **attention** achtgeben; — **back** zurückzahlen; — **no attention** keine Aufmerksamkeit schenken; — **off** abzahlen; — **one's way** seinen Verbindlichkeiten nachkommen; — **up** vollständig auszahlen; **-able** *adj.* zahlbar; schuldig, fällig; **-ing** *adj.* zahlend; **-ing teller** Kassierer (am Auszahlungsschalter); **-ment** *n.* Zahlung, Bezahlung; Lohn, Belohnung; **cash -ment** Barzahlung; **deferred -ment** verspätete (*or* aufgeschobene) Zahlung; **-ment in advance** Vorauszahlung; **-ment in full** volle Auszahlung; **-ment in part** Teilzahlung; **-ment on account** (*oder* **by installment**) Ab(schlags)zahlung; **stop -ment** die Zahlungen einstellen; **terms of -ment** Zahlungsbedingungen

payday *n.* Zahltag

payload *n.* Nutzlast

paymaster *n.* Auszahler; (mil. and naut.) Zahlmeister

payoff *n.* Ergebnis; Auszahlung

pea *n.* Erbse; — **green** Erbsengrün

peace *n.* Friede(n), Sicherheit, Ruhe, Eintracht; **-able** *adj.* friedfertig, friedliebend; **-ful** *adj.* friedlich; ungestört

peacemaker *n.* Friedenstifter

peach *n.* Pfirsich; — **tree** Pfirsichbaum

peacock *n.* Pfau

peak *n.* Spitze, Gipfel; — *adj.* — **performance** Spitzenleistung; **-ed** *adj.* spitz; kränklich aussehend

peal *n.* Geläute, Glockenspiel; Gekrach, Schall, Schlag, Geschmetter; — *v.* läuten; schallen, schmettern; krachen, dröhnen

peanut *n.* Erdnuss; — **brittle** Erdnussnougatstücken; — **butter** Erdnussbutter

pear *n.* Birne; — **tree** Birn(en)baum

pearl *n.* Perle; **-y** *adj.* perlartig, perlmutterartig; perlenfarben; perlenreich

peasant *n.* Bauer, Landmann

peat *n.* Torf

pebble *n.* Kiesel(stein)

pecan *n.* Hickorynuss; — **tree** Hickorybaum

peck *n.* Doppelgallone, Viertelscheffel; Schnabelschlag, Schnappen; — *v.* picken, hacken peculiar *adj.* eigentümlich, besonders, seltsam; -ity *n.* Eigentümlichkeit, Besonderheit; Seltsamkeit

pecuniary *adj.* geldlich, pekuniär; Geld-; — difficulties Zahlungsschwierigkeiten

pedal *n.* Pedal; Fusshebel; *v.* treten

peddle *v.* hausieren; -r *n.* Hausierer

pedestal *n.* Fussgestell; Piedestal, Säulenfuss; large — Postament

pedestrian *n.* Fussgänger

pediatrician *n.* Kinderarzt

pedigree *n.* Stammbaum; Herkunft; -d *adj.* mit Stammbaum versehen

peek *n.* Blick, Blinzeln; — *v.* spähen, blinzeln

peel *n.* Schale, Rinde, Haut; — *v.* (ab)schälen, abhäuten; sich schälen

peep *n.* heimlicher (*or* verstohlener) Blick; — *v.* neugierig (*or* heimlich, verstohlen) blicken

peephole *n.* Guckloch

peer *n.* Pair; Ebenbürtige, Gleiche; — *v.* schauen, spähen, lugen; -less *adj.* unvergleichlich, einzig

peevish *adj.* launisch, verdriesslich, mürrisch

peg *n.* Pflock, Holznagel; Dübel, Spund; Klammer; Haken; (mus.) Wirbel; — *v.* festpflöcken, abstecken

pelican *n.* Pelikan

pellagra *n.* Hautflechte

pellet *n.* Kügelchen; Schrotkorn

pell-mell *adv.* durcheinander, ganz verworren; blindlings

pelt *n.* Pelz, Fell; — *v.* bewerfen; niederstürzen, niederprasseln

pelvis *n.* Becken

pen *n.* Feder; Schreibfeder; Hürde, Verschlag; stroke of the — Federzug; — name Schriftstellername; — *v.* schreiben, abfassen; einpferchen

penal *adj.* Straf-, strafbar, sträflich; -ize *v.* mit Strafe belegen; strafen; -ty *n.* Strafe, Busse; Strafpunkt

penance *n.* Busse, Büssung

pencil *n.* Bleistift, Zeichenstift; — of rays Strahlenbündel; — protector Bleistifthülse; — sharpener Bleistiftanspitzer; — *v.* zeichnen, entwerfen; (eyebrow) nachziehen

pendant *n.* Anhänger; Gehänge; Gegenstück, Pendant

pending *adj.* schwebend, noch anhängig, unentschieden

pendulum *n.* Pendel, Perpendikel

penetrate *v.* durchdringen

penetration *n.* Durchdringung, Eindringen; Scharfsinn

penguin *n.* Pinguin

penholder *n.* Federhalter

penicillin *n.* Penicillin

peninsula *n.* Halbinsel

penis *n.* Penis, männliches Glied

penitence *n.* Busse, Reue, Zerknirschung

penitent *adj.* bussfertig, reuig; zerknirscht; -iary *n.* Zuchthaus; Besserungsanstalt

penknife *n.* Federmesser

penmanship *n.* Schreibkunst; Schrift

pennant *n.* Wimpel, Fähnchen

penniless *adj.* ohne Geld, dürftig, arm

penny *n.* Pfennig

penology *n.* Kriminal-, Strafrechtswissenschaft

pension *n.* Pension, Rente, Ruhegehalt; widow's — Witwenrente; — *v.* pensionieren; -er *n.* Pensionär, Rentenempfänger

pentagon *n.* Fünfeck, Pentagon

pentameter *n.* Pentameter, fünffüssiger Vers

penthouse *n.* Luxuswohnung im obersten Stock; Schutzdach

pent-up *adj.* beschränkt, verhalten

penurious *adj.* karg, geizig

peony *n.* Päonie, Pfingstrose

people *n.* Volk, Nation; Leute, Menschen; Verwandte; — *v.* bevölkern

pep *n.* Energie, Initiative, Mut; — talk anfeuernde Rede

pepper *n.* Pfeffer; green — grüne Paprikaschote; red — roter (*or* spanischer) Pfeffer; Paprika, Piment; — *v.* pfeffern; -y *adj.* gepfeffert; (fig.) lebhaft, schlagfertig

pepper-and-salt *adj.* pfeffer- und salzfarben; grau meliert

peppermint *n.* Pfefferminz(e); — drops Pfefferminzplätzchen

pepsin *n.* Pepsin

peptic *adj.* Verdauungs-

per *prep.* per, durch, für, mit, laut; — annum pro Jahr, jährlich; — capita pro Kopf; — cent Prozent; — diem pro Tag, täglich; Diäten

perambulator *n.* Kinderwagen

percale *n.* Perkal, feinfädiger Baumwollstoff

perceive *v.* (be)merken, wahrnehmen; erlangen, empfinden

percentage *n.* Prozentsatz

perceptible *adj.* wahrnehmbar, bemerkbar; vernehmlich

perception *n.* Wahrnehmung, Empfindung(svermögen); Anschauung, Vorstellung

perch *n.* Stange; (ichth.) Barsch; — *v.* sitzen; sich setzen

perchance *adv.* vielleicht; von ungefähr

percolator *n.* Perkolator, Kaffeemaschine

percussion *n.* Erschütterung, Stoss; —

cap Zündhütchen; — **instrument** Schlaginstrument

perdition *n.* Verdammnis, Verderben

perfect *adj.* vollkommen, vollendet, perfekt; gültig; — *n.* Perfekt; — *v.* vervollkommen, vollenden, ausbilden; –ion *n.* Vollkommenheit, Vervollkommnung; Vollendung; Perfektion

perfidious *adj.* treulos, verräterisch, perfid

perforate *v.* durchbohren, durchlöchern, perforieren

perforation *n.* Perforation, Lochung

perforce *adj.* gewaltsam; notgedrungen

perform *v.* vollziehen, ausführen; erfüllen, verrichten; (mus. and theat.) spielen, vortragen; aufführen, darstellen; –ance *n.* Ausführung, Verrichtung, Vollendung, Erfüllung; (mus. and theat.) Spiel, Vortrag; Aufführung; Vorstellung; Darstellung; first –ance Erstaufführung; –er *n.* Ausführende, Vollbringer; (mus. and theat.) Künstler, Vortragende; Schauspieler, Darsteller

perfume *n.* Parfüm; Duft, Wohlgeruch; — bottle Parfümflasche; — *v.* parfümieren

perfunctory *adj.* gewohnheitsmässig, mechanisch; oberflächlich, gedankenlos

perhaps *adv.* vielleicht, etwa; möglicherweise

pericardium *n.* Herzbeutel

perigee *n.* (ast.) Erdnähe

peril *n.* Gefahr; –ous *adj.* gefährlich, gefahrvoll

perimeter *n.* Umfang; Umkreis

period *n.* Periode, Zeitraum, Zeitpunkt; Ziel, Ende; (typ.) Punkt; — of grace letzte Frist, -ic *adj.* periodisch; –ical *n.* Zeitschrift, Revue; –ical *adj.* periodisch, wiederkehrend

periscope *n.* Sehrohr, Periskop

perish *v.* umkommen, zugrundegehen; –able *adj.* vergänglich, verderblich

peritonitis *n.* Bauchfellentzündung

perjure *v.* — oneself falsch schwören, einen Meineid leisten

perjury *n.* Meineid

perk *v.* — up sich aufmuntern (or herausputzen, recken, aufrichten); — up one's ears die Ohren spitzen; –y *adj.* schick; keck, übermütig, selbstbewusst

permanence *n.* Fortdauer; Beständigkeit

permanent *adj.* ständig, dauernd, anhaltend; — wave Dauerwelle

permissible *adj.* zulässig

permission *n.* Erlaubnis

permit *n.* Erlaubnis; Erlaubnisschein, Passierschein; — *v.* erlauben, gestatten

pernicious *adj.* verderblich, schädlich; gefährlich, nachteilig

peroxide *n.* Superoxyd; — blonde Wasserstoffblondine

perpendicular *adj.* senkrecht; aufrecht, steil; — *n.* Senkrechte; Perpendikel

perpetrate *v.* begehen, verüben, verbrechen

perpetual *adj.* beständig, fortwährend, ewig

perplex *v.* verwirren, bestürzen; –ity *n.* Verwirrung, Bestürzung; Verworrenheit

persecute *v.* verfolgen; quälen, drangsalieren

persecution *n.* Verfolgung, Belästigung

perseverance *n.* Beharrlichkeit, Standhaftigkeit; Ausdauer

persevere *v.* beharren, ausdauern

persimmon *n.* Dattelpflaume

persist *v.* beharren, verharren; hartnäckig bestehen; –ence *n.*, –ency *n.* Beharrlichkeit; Hartnäckigkeit, Eigensinn; Dauer; –ent *adj.* beharrlich, hartnäckig, eigensinnig

person *n.* Person, Mensch; (theat.) Rolle; in — selbst, in eigener Person; –able *adj.* hübsch, ansehnlich, wohlgebildet; –age *n.* Persönlichkeit, Standesperson; –al *adj.* persönlich; (fig.) anzüglich; –al property persönlicher Besitz, persönliches Vermögen; –ality *n.* Persönlichkeit; (fig.) Anzüglichkeit; –ification *n.* Verkörperung, Personifizierung; –ify *v.* verkörpern, personifizieren; –nel *n.* Personal, Belegschaft

perspective *n.* Perspektive, Ausblick; — *adj.* perspektivisch

perspiration *n.* Schweiss, Ausdünstung

perspire *v.* (aus)schwitzen

persuade *v.* überzeugen, überreden; einreden

persuasion *n.* Überzeugung, Überredung; Meinung

persuasive *adj.* überredend, überzeugend

pert *adj.* keck, vorlaut; naseweis; unverschämt

pertain *v.* (an)gehören; gebühren, betreffen

pertinence *n.* Angemessenheit, Schicklichkeit; Geeignetheit

pertinent *adj.* angemessen, schicklich, passend; zweckdienlich

perusal *n.* Durchlesen, Durchsicht

pervade *v.* durchdringen; durchziehen

perverse *adj.* widernatürlich, pervers; verkehrt; (fig.) verdreht

perversion *n.* Verdrehung, Abkehr

pervert *v.* verdrehen, verkehren, umkehren; fälschen; verführen

pessimism *n.* Pessimismus

pessimist *n.* Pessimist, Schwarzseher; –ic

adj. pessimistisch

pest n. Pest, Seuche; (fig.) Plage; **-er** v. belästigen, beunruhigen, plagen; **-ilence** n. Seuche, Pestilenz

pet n. Liebling, Lieblingstier; Schosskind, Schosstier; Schoss-, Lieblings-; zahm; **— name** Kosename; **—** v. (ver)hätscheln; **-ting** n. Verzärteln, Liebkosen

petal n. Blumenblatt, Blütenblatt

petition n. Bitte, Bittschrift, Gesuch; (pol.) Protest; **make a —** ein Gesuch einreichen; **—** v. bitten, ersuchen

petrel n. Sturmvogel

petrify v. versteinern

petrol n. Benzin; **-eum** n. Petroleum, Erdöl; **-eum** adj. **-eum jelly** Vaseline

petticoat n. Unterrock

pettiness n. Geringfügigkeit, Unbedeutenheit; Kleinlichkeit

petty adj. klein, geringfügig, unbedeutend; kleinlich; **— cash** Portokasse; **— larceny** (kleiner) Diebstahl; **— officer** Obermaat; **— thief** kleiner Dieb

petulant adj. übellaunig, verdriesslich; launenhaft, empfindlich

petunia n. Petunie

pew n. Kirchenstuhl, Kirchenbank

pewter n. Zinn

phantom n. Phantom; Gespenst

pharmaceutic(al) adj. pharmazeutisch

pharmacist n. Apotheker, Pharmazeut

pharmacy n. Apotheke

pharynx n. Rachenhöhle

phase n. Phase, Wandlung, Stadium

pheasant n. Fasan

phenobarbital n. Karbolbarbitursäure, Phenobarbital

phenol n. Phenol, Karbolsäure

phenomenal adj. phänomenal, erstaunlich

phenomenon n. Phänomen, Wunder

philander v. schäkern; **-er** n. Schwerenöter

philanthropist n. Philantrop, Menschenfreund

philanthropy n. Philanthropie, Menschenliebe

philatelist n. Philatelist, Briefmarkensammler

philharmonic adj. philharmonisch

philology n. Philologie, Sprachwissenschaft

philosopher n. Philosoph

philosophic(al) adj. philosophisch

philosophize v. philosophieren

philosophy n. Philosophie

phlegm n. Schleim; Phlegma; **-atic** adj. phlegmatisch

phobia n. Phobie, krankhafte Angst

phone n. Telefon; **-tic** adj. phonetisch; **-tics** n. Phonetik, Lautbildungslehre

phonograph n. Grammofon

phosphate n. Phosphat

phosphorescent adj. phosphoreszierend

phosphorus n. Phosphor

photo n. Foto; **— finish** Sieg durch Zielfotografie; **-genic** adj. fotogen

photoelectric adj. fotoelektrisch

photoengraving n. Hochdruckätzung

photograph n. Fotografie; **—** v. fotografieren; **be -ed** fotografiert werden (or sein) **-er** n. Fotograf; **-ic** adj. fotografisch; **-y** n. Fotografie

photogravure n. Lichtkupferätzung

photoplay n. Filmdrama

photostat n. Fotostat, Fotokopiermaschine

phrase n. Phrase, Redensart, Ausdruck; Satz; **—** v. ausdrücken, phrasieren; **-ology** n. Ausdrucksweise, Phraseologie

physic n. Arznei, Heilmittel; Abführmittel; **-al** n. Körperübung; Untersuchung; **-al** adj. physisch, körperlich; **-al education** körperliche Ausbildung; **-al geography** physikalische Geographie; **-al sciences** Naturwissenschaften; **-ian** n. Arzt; **attending -ian** behandelnder Arzt; **-ist** n. Physiker, Naturforscher; **-s** n. Physik, Naturlehre

physiognomy n. Gesichtsbildung; Physiognomie

physiological adj. physiologisch

physiology n. Physiologie

physique n. Figur, Körperbau

pianist n. Pianist

piano n. Klavier, Piano; **grand —** Flügel; **player —** Pianola

piazza n. Platz; (arch.) Säulengang, Veranda

pica type n. Ciceroschrift

piccalili n. scharf gewürztes Gemüse

piccolo n. Piccoloflöte, Oktavflöte

pick n. Picke, Haue, Spitzhacke; (fig.) Auswahl, Beste; **—** v. picken, hacken; aussuchen, auswählen; lesen, pflücken; **— a pocket** einen Taschendiebstahl begehen; **— out** auswählen; **— up** aufheben, aufnehmen; (auf)picken, aufgabeln

pickaninny n. kleines Kind (or Negerkind)

pickax(e) n. Picke; Hacke

pickerel n. Hecht(art)

picket n. Pfahl, Pflock; (mil.) Pikett, Vorposten; Streikposten; **— fence** Pfahlzaun; **—** v. einpfählen

pickle n. Eingepökelte; Essiggurke; **—** v. (ein)pökeln, in Essig einmachen

pickpocket n. Taschendieb, Langfinger

pickup n. Beschleunigung; (phonograph) Tonarm, Tonabnehmer; (coll.) Aufgabeln; (—truck) offener Lieferwagen

picnic n. Picknick; **—** v. picknicken

pictorial *adj.* malerisch; illustriert; Maler-
picture *n.* Bild(nis), Gemälde, Zeichnung,
Fotografie; Schilderung, Beschreibung;
— **puzzle** Vexierbild; — **window** Bild-
fenster, Fenster mit schönem Ausblick;
— *v.* malen, abbilden; schildern; vorstellen; **-sque** *adj.* malerisch
pie *n.* Pastete
piece *n.* Stück; (chess) Figur; (mil.) Geschütz; **give someone a** — **of one's
mind** jemand die Meinung sagen; **go
to** **-s** entzwei gehen; — *v.* stücke(l)n,
flicken. ausbessern. ansetzen
piecemeal *adv.* stückweise; — *adj.* einzeln
piecework *n.* Akkordarbeit, Stückarbeit
pier *n.* Landungsplatz, Hafendamm,
Mole; (arch.) Pfeiler
pierce *v.* durchstechen, durchbohren, eindringen; (fig.) durchblicken, durchschauen
piercing *adj.* durchdringend; schneidend;
scharf; (fig.) rührend
piety *n.* Frömmigkeit; Pietät
pig *n.* Schwein, Ferkel; (min.) Mulde;
-gish *adj.* schweinisch, unflätig
pigeon *n.* Taube; **clay** — Tontaube; **cock**
— Täuberich; **homing** — Brieftaube
pigeonhole *n.* kleiner Taubenschlag; (fig.)
kleines Schreibtischfach
piggyback *n.* Huckepack
pigpen, pigsty *n.* Schweinekoben,
Schweinestall
pike *n.* (ichth.) Hecht; (mil.) Pike
pile *n.* Haufen; Pfahl; (elec.) galvanische
Säule; (fabric) Flor; *pl.* Hämorrhoiden;
— **driver** Ramme; — *v.* aufschichten,
aufhäufen. aufstapeln
pilgrim *n.* Pilger, Wallfahrer; **-age** *n.*
Wallfahrt, Pilgerfahrt
pill *n.* Pille
pillar *n.* Pfeiler, Träger, Säule; Stütze
pillory *n.* Pranger; — *v.* an den Pranger
stellen
pillow *n.* Kopfkissen, Kissen, Polster
pillowcase, pillowslip *n.* Kissenüberzug,
Polsterüberzug
pilot *n.* (avi.) Pilot, Flieger; (naut.)
Lotse, Steuermann; (fig.) Führer; —
burner Sparbrenner; — **light** Kontroll-
lampe; — *v.* (avi.) fliegen; (naut.)
lotsen, steuern; (fig.) führen
pim(i)ento *n.* Jamaikapfeffer
pimpel *n.* Pickel, Pustel
pin *n.* Nadel; Anstecknadel; (bowling)
Kegel; (mech.) Stift, Pflock, Nagel;
(mus.) Wirbel; (fig.) Kleinigkeit; (sl.)
Bein; **safet.** — Sicherheitsnadel; — *v.*
anstecken, anheften
pinafore *n.* Lätzchen, Kinderschürze
pincers *n. pl.* Kneifzange, Beisszange;

(zool.) Scheren
pinch *n.* Kneifen; Kniff; Prise; (coll.)
Klemme; — *v.* kneifen, zwicken, klemmen
pine *n.* Kiefer, Föhre; — *v.* **sich abhärmen;** schmachten; — **for sich seh-**
nen nach
pineapple *n.* Ananas
pinfeather *n.* Stoppelfeder
pingpong *n.* Pingpong, Tischtennis
pink *n.* Rosa; (bot.) Nelke; (fig.) Gipfel;
in the — **of condition** in bester Verfassung; — *adj.* blassrot, rosa
pinpoint *v.* präzise angreifen (*or* festlegen)
pint *n.* Pinte (0,57 Liter)
pin-up *n.* Schönheitsfotografie; — *adj.*
Schönheits-
pioneer *n.* Pionier; (fig.) Bahnbrecher
pious *adj.* fromm, gottesfürchtig
pipe *n.* Rohr; Röhre, Röhrenleitung; Ta-
bakspfeife; (mus.) Pfeife; — *v.* pfeifen,
Flöte spielen; durch Röhren leiten; **-r**
n. Pfeifer
pipeline *n.* Rohrnetz; Leitungsnetz
piping *n.* Pfeifen, Pfiff; Röhrensystem;
(dress) Paspel; — *adj.* pfeifend; siedend; (fig.) sanft, ruhevoll
piquant *adj.* pikant
pique *n.* Groll, Pikiertheit; — *v.* beleidigen, kränken, reizen
piracy *n.* Seeräuberei; (fig.) Raub geist-
igen Eigentums; unbefugtes Nachdrucken; Plagiat
pirate *n.* Pirat, Seeräuber; (fig.) Plagiator;
— *v.* Seeräuberei treiben; unbefugt
nachdrucken; (rad.) schwarzhören
pistil *n.* Stempel, Griffel
pistol *n.* Pistole
piston *n.* (mech.) Kolben; (mus.) Klappe,
Ventil; — **engine** Kolbenmotor; — **rod**
Kolbenstange
pit *n.* Grube; Höhle; (agr.) Miete; (bot.)
Stein; (com.) Börse; (med.) Narbe;
(theat.) Parterre; (fig.) Grab; — *v.* in
einer Grube fangen (*or* vergraben); **ge-
geneinander hetzen; entgegenstellen**
pitch *n.* Wurf; Grad, Höhe, Neigung;
(chem.) Pech; (mech.) Zahneinteilung,
Schraubenganghöhe; (mus.) Tonlage;
(naut.) Stampfen; — *v.* werfen; aufstellen, aufschlagen; verpichen; (mus.)
den Grundton angeben, stimmen;
(naut.) stampfen; **-er** *n.* Krug; (baseball) Werfer; **-ing** *n.* (naut.) Stampfen
pitchfork *n.* Heugabel
pitfall *n.* Fallgrube; (fig.) Falle
pith *n.* (bot.) Mark; (fig.) Kern, **Kraft,**
Energie; **-y** *adj.* mark(art)ig; kernig,
kräftig
pitiful *adj.* mitleiderregend; erbärmlich,

jämmerlich
pitiless *adj.* mitleidslos, unbarmherzig
pituitary *adj.* schleimig, Schleim; — **gland** Hirnanhang
pity *n.* Mitleid, Erbarmen; — *v.* bemitleiden, bedauern
pivot *n.* Zapfen, Angel; (fig.) Drehpunkt
placard *n.* Plakat, Anschlagzettel
place *n.* Platz; Stätte, Ort, Stelle; Ortschaft, Stadt; Wohnort, Wohnsitz; Stellung, Rang, Amt; (theat.) Sitz; — *v.* stellen, setzen, legen; herrichten; einordnen, unterbringen; **-ment** *n.* Unterbringung
plagiarize *v.* plagiieren, abschreiben, ausschreiben
plague *n.* Pest, Seuche; Plage; — *v.* heimsuchen, plagen
plain *adj.* einfach, schlicht; deutlich, klar, verständlich; offenbar; unumwunden, offen, redlich, aufrichtig; ungekünstelt; unansehnlich; ungemustert, einfarbig; — *n.* Ebene, Prärie; **-ness** *n.* Einfachheit, Schlichtheit; Klarheit, Deutlichkeit, Verständlichkeit; Unansehnlichkeit
plain-clothes man *n.* Geheimpolizist, Detektiv
plaint *n.* Beschwerde, Einspruch; Klage(schrift); (poet.) Wehklage; **-iff** *n.* Kläger; **-ive** *adj.* jammernd, kläglich
plait *n.* Falte; Flechte; Zopf; — *v.* falten, (ver)flechten
plan *n.* Plan, Entwurf; Grundriss; Projekt; — *v.* planen, beabsichtigen; entwerfen
plane *n.* Ebene, Fläche; (mech.) Hobel; Flugzeug, Tragfläche; — *v.* hobeln; ebnen, glätten; — *adj.* flach, eben; — tree Platane
planet *n.* Planet; **-arium** *n.* Planetarium
plank *n.* Planke, Bohle; (pol.) Programmpunkt; — *v.* dielen, verschalen
plant *n.* Pflanze, Gewächs; Setzling, Steckling; (com.) Betriebsanlage, Fabrik; (coll.) Kniff, Schwindel; Irreführung, Falle; — *v.* (an)pflanzen, einpflanzen; anlegen, ansiedeln; aufpflanzen; aufstellen, errichten; **-er** *n.* Pflanzer; Plantagenbesitzer
plantation *n.* Pflanzung; Plantage
plaque *n.* Plakette
plasma *n.* (phys.) Plasma
plaster *n.* Gips, Stuck; Bewurf, Tünche; (med.) Pflaster; — *v.* bewerfen, tünchen; überkleben; (med.) bepflastern; (fig.) bedecken; **sticking** — Heftpflaster; — **cast** Gipsverband; **-er** *n.* Stukkateur; Gipsarbeiter; **-ing** *n.* Stuck; Bewerfen mit Mörtel; Tünchen

plastic *adj.* plastisch; bildend, formend; bildungsfähig, formbar; Kunststoff-; **-s** *n.* Plastik; Kunststoff
plate *n.* Platte, Tafel; Teller; Tafelgeschirr, Tafelsilber; — *v.* plattieren, versilbern; — **glass** Tafelglas, Spiegelglas
plateau *n.* Hochebene, Plateau
platform *n.* Tribüne; (pol.) Parteiprogramm; (rail.) Bahnsteig
platinum *n.* Platin
platitude *n.* Plattheit
platonic *adj.* platonisch
platoon *n.* Zug
platter *n.* grosse, flache Schüssel
plausible *adj.* plausibel, glaubwürdig, einleuchtend, überzeugend
play *n.* Spiel(erei); Spielraum; Handlungsweise; (mech.) Gang; (theat.) Schauspiel; Vorstellung, Aufführung; **keep in** — in Gang halten; — *v.* spielen; tändeln; (cards) ausspielen; (mus.) aufspielen; (theat.) aufführen; darstellen; — **a joke** einen Streich spielen; — **up to** sich aufspielen; **-er** *n.* Spieler; (theat.) Schauspieler; **-er piano** Pianola; **-ful** *adj.* spielend, spielerisch; scherzhaft, lustig; **-ing** *adj.* spielend; **-ing card** Spielkarte
playboy *n.* Lebemann
playfellow, playmate *n.* Spielkamerad, Gefährte
playground *n.* Spielplatz, Tummelplatz; Schulhof
playhouse *n.* Schauspielhaus, Theater
playpen *n.* Laufstall
plaything *n.* Spielzeug
playwright *n.* Schauspielauthor
plea *n.* Beweisgrund; Rechtfertigung, Verteidigung; Entschuldigung, Vorwand, Ausrede; **put in a** — einen Einwand vorbringen; **-d** *v.* plädieren, vor Gericht reden; sich entschuldigen (or rechtfertigen); als Beweis anführen; einwenden; **-d guilty** sich schuldig bekennen; **-ding** *n.* Plädieren; Schriftsatz; **-dings** *n. pl.* Prozessakten; Gerichtsverhandlungen
pleasant *adj.* angenehm; munter, vergnügt, heiter; **-ry** *n.* Munterkeit, Fröhlichkeit; Scherz, Witz
please *v.* belieben, geruhen; vergnügen, ergötzen; (jemandem) gefallen, angenehm sein, befriedigen; **do as you** — tu, was Dir gefällt, mach, was du willst; **if you** — bitte; — **be seated** bitte, nehmen Sie Platz; **-d to meet you** ich bin erfreut, Sie kennenzulernen
pleasing *adj.* gefällig, angenehm
pleasure *n.* Vergnügen, Gefallen; Freude.

Lust; at — nach Belieben

pleat n. Falte; Flechte; — v. falten; flechten; –ing n. Falten; Flechten

plebiscite n. Volksentscheid, Plebiszit

pledge n. Pfand, Unterpfand; Bürgschaft, Sicherheit; Gelübde; — v. verpfänden, sich verpflichten, versichern

plenteous, plentiful adj. voll, reichlich; ergiebig, fruchtbar

plenty n. Fülle, Überfluss; Menge; — adj. reichlich

plenum n. (pol.) Plenum, Gesamtheit; — **chamber** Sitzungssaal

pleurisy n. Rippenfellentzündung, Brustfellentzündung

pliable, pliant adj. biegsam, geschmeidig; nachgiebig; passend

pliers n. pl. Drahtzange, Flachzange

plight n. Zwangslage; Zustand; — v. versprechen, verpfänden

plod v. mühsam (or schwerfällig) gehen; schuften, sich mühen (or plagen); (educ.) büffeln; –der n. angestrengt Arbeitender; (educ.) Büffler

plot n. Parzelle, Flecken; Entwurf, Grundriss, Plan; Anschlag, Komplott, Verschwörung; (lit.) Handlung, Knoten; — v. entwerfen, planen; anzetteln; sich verschwören; –ter n. Entwerfer, Urheber; Anstifter, Verschwörer

plow, plough n. Pflug; Pflügen, Ackerbau; — v. pflügen, ackern; durchfurchen; (naut.) durchschiffen; **gang** — Mehrscharpflug; **rotary** — Wendepflug, Kippflug; –ing n. Pflügen

plowboy n. Ackerknecht

plowman n. Pflüger, Landmann

plowshare n. Pflugschar

pluck n. Zupfen, Ruck; Mut, Schneid; — v. pflücken, zupfen; rupfen; –y adj. mutig, tollkühn; (phot.) scharf, klar

plug n. Pflock, Pfropfen; Zapfen, Stöpsel, Verschlusstück; (elec.) Stecker; Steckdose; **spark** — Zündkerze; — v. verstopfen, zustopfen; (ein)stöpseln

plum n. Pflaume, Zwetschge; — **pudding** Rosinenpudding; — **tart** Zwetschgentorte; — **tree** Pflaumenbaum

plumage n. Gefieder, Federkleid

plumb n. Lot, Senkblei; — adj. lotrecht, senkrecht, gerade; (coll.) vollkommen; — **line** Lotleine, Senkschnur; senkrechte Linie; — v. richten, loten; löten; –er n. Klempner, Rohrleger, Installateur; Bleigiesser; –ing n. Rohrlegerarbeit, Installationsarbeit; Bleigiesserei

plump adj. plump, drall, feist; derb, grob; — v. aufschwellen, dick werden; plumpsen; herausplatzen; — adv. geradezu, glatt, offen; rundweg; plötzlich, mit einem Ruck; —! interj. plumps!

plunder n. Raub, Diebstahl; Beute; — v. berauben, (aus)plündern

plunge n. Untertauchen, Bad; Sturz, Sprung; (coll.) Patsche; — v. (unter)tauchen; fallen, stürzen, sinken; spekulieren; –r n. Taucher; (mech.) Kolben; Tauchkolben; (coll.) Spekulant

plural n. Plural, Mehrzahl; — adj. mehr(fach); –ity n. Mehrheit, Vielheit, Mehrzahl; (pol.) Majorität

plus prep. plus, mehr

plush n. Plüsch

plutocrat n. Plutokrat

plutonium n. Plutonium

ply n. Falte; Flechte; Windung; — v. falten, biegen; winden; betreiben; bedrängen, zusetzen; (naut.) lavieren, regelmässig fahren

plywood n. Sperrholz

pneumatic adj. pneumatisch; — **brake** Luftdruckbremse

pneumonia n. Lungenentzündung

poach v. zertreten; matschig sein (or werden); (hunting) wildern; –ed adj. –ed eggs verlorene Eier; –er n. Wilddieb, Wilderer

pock n. Pocke, Blatter

pocket n. Tasche, Beutel, Sack; (billiards) Loch; (min.) Erznest; — v. einstecken, heimlich nehmen; — **money** Taschengeld; — **veto** die Annahme eines Gesetzesentwurfes durch Nichtunterschreiben verzögern

pocketbook n. Taschenbuch; Brieftasche

pocketful n. Taschevoll

pocketknife n. Taschenmesser

pock-marked adj. pockennarbig

pod n. Hülse, Schale, Schote; (zool.) Herde, Schwarm, Zug

poem n. Gedicht, Dichtung

poet n. Poet, Dichter; –ic(al) adj. poetisch, dichterisch; –ic **license** dichterische Freiheit; –ry n. Poesie, Dichtkunst; **pastoral** –ry Hirtengedicht, Idylle; **write** –ry dichten, Verse schreiben

poinsettia n. Poinsettia

point n. Punkt; Spitze; Strich, Kante; Frage, Sache; Pointe; Schärfe; Hinsicht, Rücksicht; (art) Graviernadel, Radiernadel; (cards) Auge; (geol.) Vorgebirge, Landspitze; (hunting) Geweihsprosse; Stehen, Anzeigen; (law) Streitpunkt; (lit.) Hauptpunkt, Nachdruck; (mil.) Anweisung, Befehl; (naut.) Kompasstrich; Besteck; (sports) Punkt, Treffer; (time) Zeitpunkt, Augenblick; pl. Weichen; (gram.) Vokalzeichen; **at all** –s **ganz**

und gar; boiling — Siedepunkt; **bring to a** — zu Ende bringen; **come to the** — zur Sache kommen; **decimal** — Komma; Dezimalstelle; **freezing** — Gefrierpunkt; **gain one's** — sein Ziel erreichen; **get the** — die Sache verstehen (or begreifen); **in** — of in Hinsicht auf; **main** — Hauptpunkt, Hauptsache; **make a** — of auf etwas bestehen (or drängen); — of **honor** Ehrenpunkt, Ehrensache; — of **order** Punkt der Geschäftsordnung; — of **view** Gesichtspunkt; **speak to the** — zur Sache sprechen; **strain a** — eine Ausnahme machen, es nicht genau nehmen; **that's the** — das ist es, darum geht es; **that's not the** — das gehört nicht hierher; **to the** — genau, gänzlich; **turning** — Wendepunkt; — v. punktieren; spitzen, schärfen; zeigen, hinweisen; (hunting) stehen; (mil.) anlegen, richten, zielen; **-ed** adj. spitz; zugespitzt; punktiert; (fig.) anzüglich, scharf; **-er** n. Zeiger, Weiser; Zeigestock; (hunting) Hühnerhund, Vorstehhund; **-less** adj. stumpf; (fig.) witzlos

point-blank adv. (schnur)gerade; unverhohlen; — adj. unumwunden, rundweg, offen

poise n. Gewicht, Gleichgewicht; Haltung; — v. (ab)wägen, balanzieren; im Gleichgewicht halten

poison n. Gift; Gifttrank; — v. vergiften; (fig.) verführen; — adj. — **gas** Giftgas; —**ivy** giftiger Efeu; **-ing** n. Vergiftung; **-ous** adj. giftig; (fig.) verderblich, schädlich

poke n. Schlag, Stoss; — v. stossen; stochern, stöbern; fühlen, tasten; — **fun at** sich lustig machen über; — **one's nose into other people's affairs** seine Nase in andrer Leute Angelegenheiten stecken; **-r** n. Feuerhaken, Schüreisen; (cards) Poker(spiel)

polar adj. Polar-; — **bear** Eisbär; **-ity** n. Polarität; **-ize** v. polarisieren

pole n. Pfahl, Pfosten, Stange; (ast., phys. and fig.) Pol; — **vault** Stabhochsprung

polestar n. Polarstern; (fig.) Leitstern

police n. Polizei; — **court** Polizeigericht; — **dog** Polizeihund; — **headquarters** Polizeipräsidium; Polizeidirektion; — **state** Polizeistaat; — **trap** Autofalle; — v. überwachen

policeman n. Polizist, Schutzmann, Wachmann

policewoman n. Polizistin, Polizeiagentin

policy n. Politik; Police; **insurance** — Versicherungspolice

policyholder n. Policeninhaber

polio(myelitis) n. Poliomyelitis, spinale Kinderlähmung

polish n. Politur; Polieren; (fig.) Glätte, Schliff; — v. polieren, glätten; (fig.) verfeinern; **-ed** adj. poliert, glänzend, glatt; (fig.) gesittet

polite adj. höflich, gefällig; **-ness** n. Höflichkeit, Gefälligkeit

political adj. politisch; — **economy** Volkswirtschaft; — **group** Interessenverband; — **science** Staatswissenschaft

politician n. Staatsmann, Politiker

politics n. (pl.) Politik

polka n. Polka; — adj. — **dot** Punktmuster

poll n. Wahl, Abstimmung; Stimmenzählung; (fig.) Kopf, Schädel; pl. Wahllisten; Wahllokal; — **tax** Kopfsteuer; — v. kappen, stutzen; abschneiden; registrieren, eintragen; abstimmen, seine Stimme abgeben; (Wähler) befragen; (sports) besiegen; **-ing** n. Wählen, Abstimmen; Wahlakt, Wahlbeteiligung; **-ing** adj. **-ing booth** Wahlbude; **-ing place** Wahllokal

pollen n. Pollen, Blütenstaub

pollinate v. bestäuben

pollination n. Bestäubung

pollute v. beflecken, entweihen; **schänden**

pollution n. Befleckung, Verunreinigung;

polo n. Polo

polygamist n. Polygamist

polygamy n. Polygamie, Vielweiberei

polygraph n. Lügendetektor, Polygraph

polymerization n. Polymerisierung

Pomerania n. Pommern

pommel n. Knopf, Knauf

pomp n. Pomp, Pracht, Gepränge; **-ous** adj. pompös, prunkvoll, hochtrabend

pompadour n. hochgekämmtes Haar

pond n. Teich, Weiher

ponder v. erwägen, überlegen; nachsinnen; **-ous** adj. schwer, gewichtig; schwerfällig

pontiff n. Pontifex, Papst; Hohepriester

pontoon n. Ponton, Brückenkahn; — **bridge** Pontonbrücke

pony n. Pony; (educ.) Eselsbrücke

poodle n. Pudel

pool n. Pfuhl, Teich, Lache; (billiards) Poule(spiel); (cards) Spieleinsatz; (com.) Ring, Trust, Kartell; gemeinsame Kasse; (race) Totalisator; — v. einen Ring (or Konzern, Interessengemeinschaft) bilden; sich zusammenschliessen

poolroom n. Wettlokal; Billardzimmer

poor adj. arm, (be)dürftig; ärmlich, armselig; schlecht; (agr.) mager, dürr, unfruchtbar; — **farm** Armenkolonie; — **health** schwache Gesundheit; — **law** Armenrecht

poorhouse n. Armenhaus

poor-spirited adj. bösartig, gemein, feige

pop n. Knall, Klatsch; Sekt; — v. knallen, puffen; (coll.) anhalten; — in hineinplatzen; — off entwischen; — the question einen Heiratsantrag machen; —I interj. paff! puff! — goes the weasel! weg war es! -per n. Maisröster

popcorn n. Puffmais, gerösteter Mais

pope n. Papst

poplar n. Pappel

poppy n. Mohn

populace n. Pöbel, gemeines Volk

popular adj. populär, volkstümlich, Volks-; -ity n. Popularität, Volkstümlichkeit; -ize v. popularisieren, volkstümlich machen; gemeinverständlich darstellen

population n. Bevölkerung

populous adj. volkreich, stark bevölkert

porcelain n. Porzellan

porch n. Vorhalle; Veranda, Vorbau

porcupine n. Stachelschwein

pore n. Pore; (bot.) Staubbeutel

pork n. Schweinefleisch; — chop Schweinekotelett; — sausage Bratwurst (aus Schweinefleisch)

porous adj. porös, löcherig

porpoise n. Tümmler, Meerschwein

porridge n. Hafergrütze, Haferschleim

port n. Hafen, Ankerplatz; Backbord; Tor, Pforte; Luke, Öffnung; Haltung, Anstand; Portwein

portable adj. tragbar; — typewriter Reiseschreibmaschine

portage n. Tragen, Transport; Ladung, Fracht, Gepäck; Trägerlohn, Zustellungsgebühr

portal n. Portal, Haupttor; — vein Pfortader

portend v. vorbedeuten, verkünd(ig)en

porter n. Portier, Pförtner; Träger, Dienstmann; Porter(bier)

porterhouse steak n. Ochsenrostbraten

portfolio n. Mappe; (pol.) Portefeuille

porthole n. Luke, Öffnung; (mil.) Schiezscharte

portiere n. Portiere, Türvorhang

portion n. Portion, Anteil; Erbteil, Heiratsgut; Ration; (fig.) Schicksal; — v. (ver)teilen, austeilen; ausstatten

portly adj. stattlich, ansehnlich; (coll.) beleibt

portrait n. Porträt, Bild(nis)

portray v. porträtieren, (ab)malen, schildern

pose n. Pose, Positur; — v. posieren, in

Positur stellen, aufstellen, aufwerfen

position n. Position, Haltung; Stellung, Stand, Lage; Grundsatz, Behauptung

positive adj. positiv; bestimmt, ausdrücklich; — n. (gram. and phot.) Positiv

posse n. Aufgebot, bewaffnete Macht; (coll.) Schar, Haufen, Masse

possess v. besitzen; beherrschen; — oneself of in Besitz nehmen, sich einer Sache bemächtigen; -ion n. Besitz; be in -ion of innehaben; get -ion of sich bemächtigen; take -ion of Besitz ergreifen von; -ive adj. besitzanzeigend; -or n. Besitzer, Eigentümer

possibility n. Möglichkeit

possible adj. möglich

possibly adv. möglicherweise, vielleicht

post n. Post; Botschaft; (arch.) Pfosten, Pfahl; (com.) Stelle, Amt, Posten; Stellung; (mil.) Posten; — card Postkarte; — office Postamt, Postverwaltung; — v. postieren; anschlagen; eintragen; ernennen; zur Post geben, einstecken; — no bills! Plakate ankleben verboten! -age n. Porto; -age stamp Briefmarke; -al adj. postalisch; -al order Postanweisung; -er n. Kurier, Eilbote; Plakat

post: -erior adj. nachkommend, später, nachherig; hinter, Hinter-; -erity n. Nachkommenschaft; Nachwelt; -pone v. aufschieben, verschieben; vernachlässigen; unterordnen; -ponement n. Aufschub, Verzug; Unterordnung; -humous nachgeboren, nachgelassen, hinterlassen; posthum; -ure n. Stellung; Gestalt, Haltung; Zustand

postgraduate n. (nach Erlangung eines Grades) Weiterstudierende; — adj. (nach Erlangung eines Grades) weiterstudierend

postman n. Briefträger, Postbote; rural — Landbriefträger

postmark n. Poststempel

postmaster n. Postmeister, Postdirektor

post-mortem n. Leichenschau; — adj. nach dem Tode geschehend

post-office box n. Postfach

postpaid adj. frankiert; portofrei, franko

postscript n. Nachschrift, Nachtrag

postwar adj. Nachkriegs-

posy n. Motto, Denkspruch; Blumenstrauss

pot n. Topf, Tiegel; Krug, Kanne; (cards) Einsatz; (mech.) Schmelztiegel; — v. im Topf aufbewahren, einkochen, einmachen; eintopfen; — roast Schmorfleisch; -ter n. Töpfer; -tery n. Tongeschirr, Steingut; Töpferei

potato n. Kartoffel, Erdapfel; baked -es

überbackene Kartoffeln; fried –es Bratkartoffeln; mashed –es Quetschkartoffel, Kartoffelpüree; sweet — Batate,
süsse Kartoffel; — beetle, — bug
Kartoffelkäfer; — blight Kartoffel-
mehltau

potbellied adj. dickbäuchig

potboiler n. Brotverdienst

potency n. Kraft, Macht, Stärke; Potenz;
potent adj. mächtig, vermögend, stark;
potent; –ate n. Machthaber, Potentat;
–ial adj. möglich; potentiell, mächtig;
–ial mood Möglichkeitsform; –iality n.
Möglichkeit, Wirkungsvermögen; Po-
tenzial; (elec.) Spannung

potherbs n. Küchenkräuter, Suppengrün

pothole n. (geol.) Gletscherloch; (mech.)
Schlagloch

potion n. Arzneitrank

potluck n. take — fürlieb nehmen mit
dem, was die Küche gibt

pouch n. Beutel, Tasche; (mil.) Patronen-
tasche; (orn.) Kropf; (coll.) Dick-
bauch; — v. einstecken; beschenken

poultice n. Breiumschlag

poultry n. Geflügel, Federvieh; — yard
Geflügelhof

pounce n. Stoss, Sprung; (art.) Pause;
(orn.) Klaue, Kralle; — v. durchlöchern,
durchbohren; krallen, klauen; pausen;
herabstossen, sich stürzen auf

pound n. Pfund; Einzäunung; Fischsam-
melbecken; — sterling englisches Pfund
(20 shillings); — v. pfänden; einsperren;
zerstampfen, zerstossen

pour v. giessen, schütten; strömen, rinnen;
sich ergiessen

pout n. Schmollen; — v. schmollen,
(Lippen) aufwerfen

poverty n. Armut, Mangel

poverty-stricken adj. verarmt, dürftig

powder n. Pulver, Puder, Staub; (mil.)
Schiesspulver; — case Puderdose; —
magazine Pulvermagazin; — puff Puderquaste; — v. pulverisieren; (sich)
pudern, bepudern; bestäuben, bestreuen; (fig.) übersäen; –ed adj. pul-
verisiert; gepudert, bestreut; fein gemustert

power n. Kraft, Stärke, Macht; Vermögen; (law) Vollmacht; Zurechnungs-
fähigkeit; (math.) Potenz; (mech.)
Kraft, Last; (mil.) Heeresmacht;
(naut.) Seemacht; (pol.) Autorität,
Regierung, Staat; Gewalt; horse —
Pferdestärke; in — an der Macht; —
of attorney Anwaltsvollmacht; the –s
that be die höheren Mächte; reasoning
–s Urteilskraft; — dive (avi.) Sturzflug; — drill Kraftbohrer; — plant

Kraftwerk, Kraftanlage; –ful adj. kräftig, mächtig; einflussreich; –less adj.
kraftlos, machtlos, ohnmächtig

powerhouse n. Kraftwerk; (sports) spiel-
starke Mannschaft

powwow n. laute politische Versammlung; Indianerversammlung; lärmende
Krankheitsbeschwörung, Kriegstanz;
— v. laute (politische) Versammlungen
abhalten

pox n. Syphilis; chicken — Windpocken;
cow — Kuhpocken; small — Pocken,
Blattern

practicability n. Ausführbarkeit

practicable adj. ausführbar, gangbar,
brauchbar; fahrbar

practical adj. praktisch, tatsächlich, wirklich; geschickt; — joke handgreiflicher
Spass; — nurse ausgebildete Kranken-
pflegerin

practice n. Praxis, Ausübung; Anwendung, Ausführung; Brauch, Gewohnheit; Übung, Training; pl. Kunstgriffe,
Schliche, Kniffe; —, practise v. prak-
tizieren, ausüben; anwenden, ausführen, betreiben; üben, trainieren

practitioner n. Praktiker, geschickter
Mensch; Gesundbeter; general —
praktischer Arzt

pragmatic(al) adj. pragmatisch; gemeinnützig; geschäftig, wichtigtuerisch

Prague n. Prag

prairie n. Prärie; — chicken Präriehuhn;
— dog Präriehund

praise n. Preis, Lob; Anerkennung, Danksagung; — v. preisen, loben; anerkennen, rühmen, verherrlichen

praiseworthy adj. preiswürdig, lobenswert

prance v. paradieren, einherstolzieren;
(horse) sich bäumen

prank n. Possen, Streich; Schelmerei,
Schabernack

prattle n. Geplapper; — v. schwatzen,
plappern

pray v. beten; (er)bitten, ersuchen; –er n.
Gebet, Andacht; Bitte, Gesuch; the
Lord's Prayer das Vaterunser; –er book
Gebetbuch; –er meeting Betstunde;
Gebetsversammlung; –er wheel Gebets-
mühle

preach v. predigen; lehren, verkünden; –er
n. Prediger; –ing n. Predigen, Predigt;
Lehre; (coll.) Strafpredigt

preamble n. Vorrede, Einleitung; Präam-
bel

prearrange v. vorher anordnen, vorbereiten

precarious adj. widerruflich, kündbar;
prekär, zweifelhaft, unsicher

precaution n. Vorsicht(smassregel); Be-

hutsamkeit; **-ary** *adj.* vorsichtig, vorbeugend; Vorsichts-, Warnungs-
precede *v.* vor(an)gehen, vorausgehen;
den Vorrang haben; einführen; **-nce** *n.*
Vorausgehen; Vorrang, Vortritt, Vorzug; **-nt** *n.* Präzedenzfall, Rechtsbei-
spiel; **-nt** *adj.* vor(an)gehend, vorausgehend; früher
preceding *adj.* vorhergehend
precept *n.* Vorschrift, Regel; Gebot, Unterweisung; (law) Vorladung, Verordnung
precinct *n.* Distrikt, Bezirk, Bereich, Gebiet; Grenze; Gehege
precious *adj.* kostbar, teuer; geziert; —
stone Edelstein
precipice *n.* Klippe, Abgrund
precipitate *v.* (herab)stürzen; (chem.)
fällen; (fig.) überstürzen, beschleunigen; — *adj.* überstürzt, übereilt;
voreilig, vorschnell; plötzlich; — *n.*
(chem.) Niederschlag
precipitation *n.* Sturz; Hast; (chem.)
Niederschlag
precise *adj.* präzis; bestimmt, genau; (fig.)
pedantisch
precision *n.* Präzision, Genauigkeit
predecessor *n.* Vorgänger
predestination *n.* Prädestination, Vorher-
bestimmung
predicament *n.* Kategorie, Ordnung; Verlegenheit, kritische Lage
predicate *n.* Prädikat, Aussage; — *v.*
behaupten, aussagen; begründen
predict *v.* vorhersagen, verkünd(ig)en;
prophezeien; **-ion** *n.* Prophezeiung,
Weissagung
predisposed *adj.* vorbereitend; geneigt (*or*
empfänglich) machend
predominant *adj.* vorherrschend, über-
wiegend
predominate *v.* vorherrschen; beherrschen,
die Oberhand haben
pre-eminence *n.* Hervorragen, Hervorstechen; Vorrang, Vorzug
pre-eminent *adj.* hervorragend, hervor-
stechend; ausgezeichnet
preexistence *n.* früheres Dasein
prefabricate *v.* Bauteile (zur späteren
Zusammensetzung) herstellen
preface *n.* Vorrede, Vorwort; Einleitung;
— *v.* einleiten
prefect *n.* Präfekt
prefer *v.* vorziehen; vorbringen, einen
Antrag stellen; **-able** *adj.* vorzuziehend,
vorzüglicher (als); **-ence** *n.* Vorziehen;
Bevorzugung; Vorliebe; Präferenz, Vor-
zugsrecht; **-ential** *adj.* Vorzugs-, bevorzugt; **-red** *adj.* bevorzugt; **-red stock**
Prioritätsaktien, Vorzugsaktien

prefix *n.* Vorsilbe; — *v.* vor(an)setzen
pregnancy *n.* Schwangerschaft; (zool.)
Trächtigkeit; (fig.) Fruchtbarkeit
pregnant *adj.* schwanger; (zool.) trächtig;
(fig.) fruchtbar, inhaltvoll
preheat *v.* vorwärmen, vorheizen
prehistoric *adj.* prähistorisch
prejudice *n.* Voreingenommenheit, Vorurteil; Schaden; — *v.* vorher einnehmen, Abbruch tun
prelate *n.* Prälat
preliminary *adj.* vorläufig; einleitend, Vor-
prelude *n.* Einleitung, Vorspiel; — *v.*
präludieren; einleiten
premature *adj.* frühreif; vorzeitig; (fig.)
übereilt, vorschnell
premedical *adj.* vormedizinisch
premeditate *v.* vorher bedenken (*or* überlegen); **-d** *adj.* **-d murder** vorbedachter
(*or* geplanter) Mord
premier *n.* Ministerpräsident, Premier-
minister
première *n.* Première, Uraufführung,
Erstaufführung; Debüt
premise *n.* Voraussetzung; *pl.* vorerwähn-
te Punkte; Grundstück, Haus und
Nebengebäude; — *v.* vorausschicken
premium *n.* Prämie, Preis; Zinsen; Belohnung; **at a** — pari, sehr gesucht
premonition *n.* Warnung; Vorahnung
preoccupation *n.* Vorwegnahme; Voreingenommenheit, Vorurteil
prepaid *adj.* vorher bezahlt, frankiert
preparation *n.* Vorbereitung, Zubereitung;
(chem.) Präparat
preparatory *adj.* präpariert, vorbereitet,
zubereitet; vorbereitend
prepare *v.* vorbereiten, zubereiten; prä-
parieren
prepay *v.* voraus bezahlen; frankieren,
freimachen; **-ment** *n.* Vorausbezah-
lung; Frankieren
preponderance *n.* Übergewicht
preposition *n.* Präposition, Verhältniswort
preposterous *adj.* verkehrt, widersinnig;
unnatürlich, albern
prerequisite *n.* Vorbedingung; — *adj.* vorher erforderlich, zuerst nötig
prerogative *n.* Vorrecht; — *adj.* vorge-
hend, bevorrechtigt
prescribe *v.* vorschreiben, befehlen; (law)
verjähren; (med.) verordnen, verschreiben
prescription *n.* Vorschrift, Verordnung;
(law) Verjährung; (med.) Rezept
presence *n.* Gegenwart, Anwesenheit,
Vorhandensein; Erscheinung, Ge-
spenst; **in** — gegenwärtig; **in** — **of** im
Beisein (*or* in Gegenwart) von, angesichts; — **of mind** Geistesgegenwart

present n. Geschenk; (gram.) Gegenwart, Präsens; pl. Dokumente, Schriftstücke; at — gegenwärtig; be — at beiwohnen; by the — hierdurch, beigefügt; for the — vorläufig, im Augenblick; — adj. gegenwärtig, anwesend, vorhanden; laufend, sofort, augenblicklich; fertig, bereit; all — alle Anwesenden; in the — case im vorliegenden Falle; — company excepted die Anwesenden ausgeschlossen; — crisis gegenwärtige Krise; — money bares Geld; — participle Partizip des Präsens; — value Gegenwartswert; this — jetzt; — v. präsentieren, vorstellen, vorführen, zeigen; anbieten, schenken, geben; (theat.) darstellen, darbieten; — a draft einen Wechsel vorzeigen; — arms das Gewehr präsentieren; — itself es zeigt sich von selbst; — oneself sich selbst vorstellen; — oneself to view persönlich erscheinen; -able adj. vorstellbar, präsentierbar; -ation n. Darstellung, Vorstellung; Vorlage

present-day adj. heutig

presentiment n. Vorgefühl, Ahnung

preservation n. Bewahrung, Erhaltung; Konservierung

preserve n. Konserve, Eingemachte; Wildpark, Gehege; pl. Eingemachte; Schutzbrille; — v. bewahren, erhalten, retten, schützen, hegen, konservieren, einmachen; — timber Holz imprägnieren

preside v. präsidieren, den Vorsitz (or die Aufsicht) führen; -ncy n. Präsidium, Präsidentenschaft; -nt n. Präsident; Vorsitzende, Vorsteher; -ntial adj. präsidial; Präsidenten-

press n. Pressen, Druck; Gedränge, Andrang; Dringlichkeit; Bedrängnis, Verlegenheit; Presse, Kelter; Zeitungswesen, Journalismus; Druckgewerbe; — v. pressen, drücken; auspressen, keltern; (be)drängen, treiben, nötigen, beschleunigen; aufzwingen; be -ed for in Verlegenheit (or Bedrängnis) sein wegen; -ing adj. pressend, drängend, dringend; -ure n. Druck, Spannung; -ure cooker Dampfkochtopf; -ure -gauge Druckmesser; -ure suit n. Druckkombination; -urize v. (avi.) den Luftdruck regulieren; -urized cabin n. Druckkabine

presswork n. Druckarbeit

prestige n. Prestige, Nimbus, Ansehen

presume v. annehmen, vermuten

presuppose v. voraussetzen

pretend v. vorgeben, heucheln; -er n. Heuchler

pretense, pretence n. Vorwand, Scheingrund; Anspruch; false — Vorspiegelung falscher Tatsachen

pretentious adj. anspruchsvoll, anmassend

pretext n. Vorwand; on — unter dem Vorwand

prettiness n. Niedlichkeit, Nettigkeit; Geziertheit

pretty adj. hübsch, niedlich; artig, nett; fein, sauber

pretzel n. Bre(t)zel

prevail v. überhandnehmen; vorherrschen; die Oberhand gewinnen (or haben); -ing adj. vorherrschend; allgemein geltend; häufig

prevalent adj. vorherrschend, geltend, weit verbreitet; mächtig, überlegen

prevent v. zuvorkommen, verhüten, verhindern; vorbeugen, vorbauen; -able adj. verhütbar; -ion n. Vorbeugung, Verhütung; Verhinderung; -ive adj. vorbeugend, Schutz-; -ive n. Präservativ

preview n. Vorschau

previous adj. vorhergehend; vorläufig; — payment Vorschusszahlung

prewar adj. Vorkriegs-

prey n. Raub, Beute; beast of — Raubtier; bird of — Raubvogel; — v. rauben, plündern; erbeuten; (fig.) nagen

price n. Preis; Lohn, Belohnung; (fig.) Wert; above — unschätzbar; at any — um jeden Preis; best — günstigster Preis; cost — Einkaufspreis; fall in -s Preissturz; fixed — fester Preis; high -s hohe Preise; lowest — niedrigster Preis; sale — Verkaufspreis; trade — Engrospreis, Handelspreis; — control Preiskontrolle; — list Preisliste, Kursliste; — mark Preisangabe; — v. den Preis festsetzen, auszeichnen; -less adj. unschätzbar, unbezahlbar

prick n. Stachel, Dorn, Spitze; Ahle, Pfrieme; Stich, Biss; Punkt, Ziel; -s of conscience Gewissensbisse; — v. (durch)stechen; anspornen, anstacheln, antreiben; punktieren, foltern; prikkeln; — a card eine Spielkarte markieren; — up one's ears die Ohren spitzen; -ly adj. stachelig, dornig, juckend, stechend; prickelnd; -ly heat Hitzepickel; -ly pear Feigenkaktus

pride n. Stolz; Hochmut, Überhebung; (fig.) Pracht, Gepränge; — will have a fall Hochmut kommt vor dem Fall; in the — of his years in der Blüte seiner Jahre; take — in auf etwas stolz sein; — v. stolz sein, sich gross tun; — oneself on sich brüsten mit

priest n. Priester, Geistliche; **–hood** n. Priesteramt, Priesterwürde; Priesterschaft

prim adj. schmuck, sauber, fein; geziert, gekünstelt, steif

primacy n. Vorrang, Vortritt

primarily adv. zuerst, ursprünglich, anfänglich; insbesonders

primary n. Hauptsache; (ast.) Hauptplanet; (pol.) Vorwahl; — adj. primär; erst, hauptsächlich, höchst; ursprünglich, primitiv; Ur-, Anfangs-, Grund-, Haupt-, Elementar-; — **accent** Hauptbetonung; — **coil** Hauptspule; — **colors** Grundfarben; — **education** Volksschulbildung; — **election** Urwahl; — **school** Elementarschule, Volksschule, Grundschule

prime n. Anfang, Ursprung; Erste, Beste; Kern, Blüte; (com.) beste Qualität; (math.) Primzahl; (mus.) Grundton, Prime; (fig.) Frühling, Jugend; Lebenskraft; — adj. erst, vorzüglichst, vornehmst; (math.) unteilbar, einfach; (fig.) jugendlich, blühend; ursprünglich; — **creation** Urschöpfung; — **minister** Ministerpräsident; — v. grundieren; vorbereiten; anstiften; **–r** n. Fibel, Abcbuch; Elementarbuch; Zündapparat; **–val** adj. ursprünglich, urzeitlich

priming n. Grundierung; (mil.) Zündung; — adj. — **coat** Grundanstrich

primitive n. (gram.) Stammwort; — adj. primitiv, ursprünglich, anfänglich; einfach, roh; Stamm-, Grund-; — **rock** Urgestein

primrose n. Primel, Schlüsselblume; (color) Rötlichgelb

prince n. Prinz, Fürst; — **consort** Prinzgemahl; **–ly** adj. prinzlich, fürstlich; **–ss** n. Prinzessin, Fürstin

principal n. Hauptperson; Chef, Prinzipal, Lehrherr; Rektor, Direktor; — adj. vornehmst, hauptsächlich, Haupt-; **–ity** n. Fürstentum, Fürstenwürde; **–ly** adv. vornehmlich, besonders

principle n. Prinzip, Grundsatz; (chem.) Grundbestandteil

print n. Druck; Abdruck, Kopie; Kupferstich, Holzstich; Druckschrift; (phot.) Abzug; (fig.) Eindruck, Mal, Form; **in** — im Druck, gedruckt; **out of** — vergriffen; — v. (ab)drucken, bedrucken; kopieren; mustern; (phot.) **abziehen**; (fig.) einprägen; **–ed** adj. gedruckt, bedruckt; **–ed cotton** bedruckter Baumwollstoff; **–ed matter** Drucksache; **–er** n. Drucker, Buchdrucker; **–er's devil** Druckfehlerteufel; **–er's ink**

Druckerschwärze; **–ing** n. Drucken, Bedrucken; **art of –ing** Buchdruckerkunst; **–ing office** Druckerei; **–ing press** Druckmaschine, Druckerpresse

printshop n. Druckerei

prior n. Prior; — adj. früher, älter; — adv. — **to** vor; **–ity** n. Priorität; Vorrang, Vorzug(srecht)

prism n. Prisma

prison n. Gefängnis, Kerker; — v. einkerkern; **–er** n. Gefangene; — **of war** Kriegsgefangene

privacy n. Abgeschiedenheit, Zurückgezogenheit, Stille; Heimlichkeit

private n. (mil.) Gemeine; **in** — unter vier Augen; — adj. privat, Privat-; geheim, heimlich, verborgen; vertraulich; nicht amtlich (or öffentlich); eigen, persönlich

privation n. Entbehrung, Entblössung, Mangel

privilege n. Privileg, Vorrecht, Sonderrecht; — v. privilegieren, bevorrechten

prize n. Preis, Prämie, Lohn, Belohnung; Vorteil, Gewinn; (naut.) Prise; — **fight** Boxkampf, Ringkampf; — **question** Preisfrage; — **ring** Ring für Preiskämpfe; — v. gewinnen; belohnen; schätzen, taxieren; wegnehmen; (naut.) aufbringen

prizefighter n. Berufsboxer, Berufsringer

pro prep. pro, für; — adv. vor(wärts); anstatt; — n. (pol.) Jasager; (sports) Berufsspieler; **the –s and cons** das Für und Wider, die Ja- und Neinstimmen

probability n. Wahrscheinlichkeit

probable adj. wahrscheinlich, mutmasslich

probation n. Beweisführung, Prüfung; (eccl.) Noviziat; (law) bedingte Freisprechung, Bewährungsfrist; Probezeit; **–er** n. Prüfling; (eccl.) Novize; (law) unter Bewährungsfrist Stehende

probe n. Sonde; — v. sondieren, gründlich untersuchen

problem n. Problem, Aufgabe

procedure n. Prozedur, Verfahren; Handlungsweise

proceed v. vor(wärts)gehen, fortschreiten, fortfahren; hervorkommen, vonstatten gehen; (law) gerichtlich belangen, einschreiten; **–ing** n. Verfahren; **–ings** pl. Rechtsgang, Rechtsverfahren; Akten, Protokolle; Verhandlungen; **–s** n. pl. Ertrag, Gewinn; **gross –s** Bruttoertrag; **net –s** Reinertrag, Nettogewinn

process n. Prozess; Fortschreiten, Fortschritt; Verlauf, Vorgang; (anat. and bot.) Fortsatz, Verlängerung; (chem. and law) Verfahren; (phot.) Entwicklung; — *v.* prozessieren, vorladen, belangen; behandeln; reproduzieren, entwickeln; –ion *n.* Prozession, Umzug

proclaim *v.* proklamieren, bekanntgeben, verkünden

proclamation *n.* Proklamation, Bekanntmachung

procrastinate *v.* verschieben, aufschieben; (ver)zögern, zaudern

procure *v.* anschaffen, besorgen, verschaffen; erhalten, erlangen; erwerben; bewirken

prod *n.* Stachelstock; Ahle; Stich; — *v.* stechen; anspornen

prodigal *n.* Verschwender; — *adj.* verschwenderisch; **the — son** (bibl.) der verlorene Sohn

prodigy *n.* Wunder; Monstrum, Missgeburt

produce *n.* Erzeugnis, Produkt; Ertrag; — *v.* produzieren, erzeugen; einbringen, hervorbringen; (theat.) inszenieren; –r *n.* Produzent, Erzeuger, Hersteller; (theat.) Produzent

product *n.* Produkt, Werk; Schöpfung; Frucht; –ion *n.* Produktion, Erzeugung; Beibringung, Vorlegung; (theat.) Regie; –ion cost Gestehungskosten; –ive *adj.* produktiv, schöpferisch; ertragreich, fruchtbar

profane *adj.* profan, weltlich; gottlos, lästerlich; — *v.* profanieren, entweihen

profanity *n.* Ruchlosigkeit, Gottlosigkeit; Entweihung, Profanierung

profess *v.* bekennen, gestehen; behaupten, ausüben, betreiben; –edly *adv.* ausgesprochen, unverhohlen; unleugbar; –ion *n.* Beruf, Handwerk; Bekenntnis; –ional *adj.* berufsmässig, professionell, Berufs–; –or *n.* Professor

proficiency *n.* Tüchtigkeit, Fertigkeit

proficient *adj.* tüchtig, geschickt; bewandert

profile *n.* Profil, Seitenansicht

profit *n.* Profit, Gewinn, Nutzen, Ertrag; **net — Reingewinn; — and loss** Verdienst und Verlust; **— sharing** Gewinnbeteiligung; — *v.* profitieren, gewinnen; **— by** Nutzen ziehen aus; –able *adj.* einträglich, vorteilhaft, gewinnbringend; –eer *n.* Profitmacher, Schieber; –eer *v.* Profite machen, schieben, Schiebergeschäfte betreiben

profligate *adj.* liederlich, verschwenderisch

profound *adj.* tief(gehend), gründlich; scharfsinnig, tiefgründig

profuse *adj.* übervoll, übermässig; verschwenderisch

profusion *n.* Überfluss; Verschwendung

progenitor *n.* Vorfahr, Ahn

prognosis *n.* Prognose

prognostication *n.* Voraussage; (med.) Prognose

program(me) *n.* Programm

progress *n.* Fortschritt; Fortschreiten; — *v.* Fortschritte machen, fortschreiten; –ive *adj.* progressiv, forschreitend, zunehmend; fortschrittlich

prohibit *v.* verbieten, untersagen; verhindern; –ion *n.* Prohibition; Verhinderung, Verbot, Einhalt

project *n.* Projekt, Plan, Entwurf; — *v.* vorspringen; entwerfen, planen, vorhaben; –ile *n.* Geschoss, Projektil; –ion *n.* Entwurf; Vorsprung; (film) Projektion; –or *n.* Erfinder, Entwerfer; (film) Projektionsapparat

proletarian *n.* Proletarier; — *adj.* proletarisch

proletariat *n.* Proletariat

prologue *n.* Prolog; Einleitung, Vorwort

prolong *v.* verlängern, dehnen; prolongieren

promenade *n.* Promenade; Spaziergang; — *v.* prominieren, spazierengehen

prominence *n.* Prominenz, Berühmtheit; Vorsprung

prominent *adj.* prominent, hervorragend; **be — berühmt** (*or* bekannt) sein

promiscuous *adj.* vermengt, vermischt; verworren; unterschiedslos

promise *n.* Versprechen, Zusage; (fig.) Erwartung; — *v.* versprechen

promising *adj.* viel versprechend, verheissungsvoll

promissory *adj.* versprechend; — **note** Eigenwechsel, Promesse

promote *v.* (be)fördern; gründen; –r *n.* Förderer, Gönner; Gründer; Anstifter

promotion *n.* Förderung, Begünstigung; Beförderung

prompt *adj.* prompt, unverzüglich, sofortig; pünktlich; bereit; — *v.* antreiben, veranlassen; (theat.) soufflieren

prone *adj.* geneigt, gesenkt; hingestreckt

prong *n.* Spitze; Zacke, Zinke

pronoun *n.* Fürwort, Pronomen

pronounce *v.* aussprechen, betonen; verkünden, erklären; entscheiden; –d *adj.* ausgesprochen, entschieden; –ment *n.* Erklärung, Äusserung

pronunciation *n.* Aussprache

proof *n.* Beweis, Probe; — *adj.* standhaft, undurchdringlich, fest; bewährt

proofread *v.* Korrektur lesen; –er *n.* Korrektor, Korrekturleser

prop *n.* Stütze, Strebe; — *v.* stützen, tragen

propaganda *n.* Propaganda

propagate v. propagieren, verbreiten

propel v. vorwärtstreiben; fortbewegen; **-ler** n. Propeller; **-ler blade** Propellerflügel

propensity n. Vorahnung

proper adj. eigen, eigentlich, eigentümlich; geeignet; proper, anständig, sauber, nett; gründlich; — **name** Eigenname; — **fraction** (math.) echter Bruch; **in** — **form** in passender Form; **-ly** adv. eigentlich, richtig

property n. Eigentum, Vermögen; Eigenschaft; Grundstück, Grundbesitz

prophecy n. Prophezeiung, Weissagung

prophesy v. prophezeien, weissagen

prophet n. Prophet; **-ic** adj. prophetisch

prophylactic adj. prophylaktisch, vorbeugend; — n. Vorbeugungsmittel, Gegenmittel

propitious adj. geneigt, gnädig; günstig; gütig; glücklich

proportion n. Proportion, Verhältnis; Gleichmass; Anteil; (math.) Proportionale; — v. in ein Verhältnis bringen; **-al** adj. proportional, verhältnismässig; gleichmässig; **-ate** adj. angemessen, im richtigen Verhältnis stehend; **-ed** adj. proportioniert, im richtigen Verhältnis stehend

proposal n. Vorschlag; — **of marriage** Heiratsantrag

propose v. vorschlagen, beantragen; beabsichtigen; anhalten

proposition n. Vorschlag, Antrag; (gram., math. and phil.) Behauptung; Lehrsatz

proprietor n. Eigentümer, Inhaber, Besitzer

propriety n. Genauigkeit, Richtigkeit; Schicklichkeit

propulsion n. Antrieb, Fortbewegung

prorate v. gleichmässig verteilen

prosaic adj. prosaisch, alltäglich

prose n. Prosa; — **writer** Prosaschriftsteller, Prosaiker

prosecute v. verfolgen; fortsetzen, betreiben; (law) anklagen, einklagen

prosecution n. Verfolgung, Durchführung; (law) Anklage, gerichtliche Verfolgung

prosecutor n. Verfolger, Durchführende; (law) Kläger, Ankläger; Staatsanwalt

prospect n. Ansicht; Aussicht, Erwartung; **-ive** adj. zukünftig, voraussichtlich; vorausblickend; **-or** n. Schürfer, Goldgräber; (fig.) Spekulant; **-us** n. Prospekt; Ankündigung, Voranzeige

prosper v. gedeihen, gelingen; **-ity** n. Wohlstand; Gedeihen, Wohlfahrt; **-ous** adj. glücklich, günstig

prostitute n. Prostituierte; — v. prostituieren; preisgeben, entwürdigen

prostitution n. Prostitution

prostration n. Niederwerfung, Demütigung; Erschöpfung; Fussfall

prosy adj. langweilig, prosaisch

protect v. (be)schützen, sichern; (chess) decken; **-ion** n. Schutz; **-ive** adj. schützend, Schutz-; **-ive coloring** Schutzfärbung; **-or** n. Schützer; **-orate** n. Protektorat

protégé n. Schützling

protein n. Protein, Eiweissstoff

protest n. Protest, Einspruch, Widerspruch; — v. protestieren, sich verwahren, Einspruch erheben

Protestant n. Protestant

protocol n. Protokoll; — v. protokollieren

proton n. Proton

protoplasm n. Protoplasma, Urgebilde

prototype n. Urbild, Vorbild, Muster

protract v. aufschieben, verzögern, in die Länge ziehen

protrude v. (her)vortreten; hervorstehen, überhängen; ausstrecken

proud adj. stolz, trotzig; hochmütig; froh; — **flesh** wildes Fleisch

prove v. prüfen, beweisen, dartun; probieren, erproben; sich ergeben (or erweisen); (law) beglaubigen

proverb n. Sprichwort; **-ial** adj. sprichwörtlich

provide v. anschaffen, verschaffen; besorgen; bereithalten; versehen, versorgen; (law) vorsehen, festsetzen; **-ed** conj. **-ed that** vorausgesetzt, dass; wofern nur, wenn anders; **-ed** adj. angeschafft, verschafft; besorgt, versorgt, unterhalten; bereithaltend; **-nce** n. Vorsehung; Vor(aus)sicht, Vorsorge; **-nt** adj. fürsorglich; vorsichtig; haushälterisch; **-ntial** adj. durch die Vorsehung bestimmt; glücklich, gelegen; **-r** n. Fürsorgende, Versorger; Lieferant

province n. Provinz; Bezirk, Gebiet; (fig.) Wirkungskreis

provincial n. Provinzler, Provinzbewohner; — adj. provinziell, kleinstädtisch

provision n. Beschaffung, Fürsorge; Vorrat; Provision, Maklerlohn; pl. Proviant, Vorrat; Nahrungsmittel, Lebensmittel; Mundvorrat; **-al** adj. provisorisch, vorläufig

provocation n. Provokation, Herausforderung

provocative n. Reizmittel, Reizung; — adj. provokatorisch, aufreizend, herausfordernd

provoke v. provozieren, herausfordern; aufreizen

provoking adj. herausfordernd, empörend; erbitternd, ärgerlich

prowess *n.* Tapferkeit, Heldenmut
prowl *v.* herumstöbern, umherstreichen; **-er** *n.* Plünderer, Räuber; Einbrecher; Bummler
proximity *n.* Nähe, Nachbarschaft
proxy *n.* Stellvertretung; Stellvertreter, Bevollmächtigte; Vollmacht
prude *n.* Prüde, Spröde; **-ry** *n.* Prüderie, Zimperlichkeit
prudence *n.* Klugheit, Vorsicht, Bedachtsamkeit
prudent *adj.* klug, vorsichtig; bedachtsam; sparsam
prudish *adj.* prüde, spröde; zimperlich; steif
prune *n.* Backpflaume; — *v.* stutzen, beschneiden
pruning *n.* Beschneiden, Stutzen; *pl.* Reisigholz; — **hook** Gartensichel; — **knife** Gartenmesser; — **shears** Baumschere
pry *v.* spähen, gucken; (coll.) die Nase hineinstecken
psalm *n.* Psalm
pseudonym *n.* Pseudonym, Deckname
psychiatrist *n.* Psychiater
psychiatry *n.* Psychiatrie
psychic *adj.* psychisch, seelisch
psychoanalysis *n.* Psychoanalyse
psychologic(al) *adj.* psychologisch
psychologist *n.* Psychologe
psychopathic *adj.* psychopathisch, geistig
psychrometer *n.* Feuchtemesser für Atmosphären
ptomain(e) *n.* Ptomain, Leichenalkaloid; — **poison** Leichengift; — **poisoning** Leichenvergiftung
public *n.* Publikum; Offentlichkeit; Gemeinwohl; **in** — vor aller Welt; **make** — öffentlich bekanntmachen; — *adj.* öffentlich; publik; offenkundig; gemeinnützig; Staats-; — **appointment** Staatsstellung; — **auction** öffentliche Versteigerung; — **debt** Staatsschuld; — **enemy** Staatsfeind; — **function** öffentliches Amt; — **library** Volksbücherei; — **official** Staatsbeamte; — **opinion** öffentliche Meinung; — **property** Staatseigentum; — **relations** Meinungsforschung; Propagandaabteilung; — **spirit** Gemeinsinn; — **utilities** öffentl che Betriebe (Elektrizität, Gas, Wasser; Verkehrswesen); — **works** öffentliche Bauten; **-ation** *n.* Herausgabe; Bekanntmachung, Veröffentlichung; **-ist** *n.* Publizist; **-ity** *n.* Offentlichkeit; Reklame, Propaganda; **-ize** *v.* veröffentlichen, publizieren
publish *v.* veröffentlichen; verlegen, herausgeben; **-er** *n.* Verleger, Herausgeber;

-ing *n.* Verlegen, Herausgeben; **-ing company** Verlag(sgesellschaft); **-ing house** Verlag(shaus)
puck *n.* Elf, Kobold, Puck
pucker *n.* Falte, Bausch; — *v.* (sich) falten, runzeln; zusammenziehen
pudding *n.* Pudding
puddle *n.* Pfuhl, Pfütze, Lache; — *v.* verschlämmen, besudeln; plantschen
pudgy *adj.* fleischig; untersetzt
puff *n.* Hauch, Windstoss; Paff; (baking) Windbeutel; (coll.) Lobhudelei; Schwindelreklame; **powder** — Puderquaste; — *v.* blasen; rauchen, paffen; aufblasen, aufbauschen; anpreisen; **-y** *adj.* aufgeblasen, geschwollen; bauschig; (naut.) böig; (fig.) schwülstig
pug *n.* Mops; Knetlehm; — *v.* (Lehm) kneten; (mit Lehm) verschmieren; — *adj.* — **nose** Stupsnase
pugilism *n.* Boxkunst
pugilist *n.* Faustkämpfer, Boxer
pull *n.* Ziehen, Reissen; Zug, Ruck; (pol.) Einfluss; (sl.) Vorteil; — *v.* ziehen, reissen, zerren; rupfen, zupfen; (naut.) rudern; — **off** aufbrechen, abreissen; — **out** ausziehen, ausreissen; — **through** durchbringen; durchkommen; — **up** weggehen; heraufziehen, ausrotten; anziehen; anhalten; **-er** *n.* Reisser, Raufer; **nail -er** Kistenöffner
pulley *n.* Rolle, Scheibe; Treibrad; Flaschenzug
pulmonary, pulmonic *adj.* Lungen-
pulmotor *n.* Atemgerät, Sauerstoffapparat
pulp *n.* Fruchtmark, Fruchtfleisch; (mech.) Lumpenbrei; — *adj.* — **magazine** Sensationsblatt
pulpit *n.* Kanzel, Katheder
pulpwood *n.* Holz zur Papierbereitung
pulsate *v.* pulsieren; pochen, schlagen
pulse *n.* Puls(schlag)
pulsejet *n.* Antriebsrakete; — **engine** Raketenmotor
pulverize *v.* pulverisieren; zu Staub werden (*or* machen)
puma *n.* Puma, Kuguar, Berglöwe
pump *n.* Pumpe; **air** — Luftpumpe; **feed** — Speisepumpe; — **room** Trinkhalle; — *v.* (aus)pumpen; aufblasen; (coll.) ausforschen, ausfragen; **-er** *n.* Pumper; Petroleumbrunnen; (sports) Niederlage
pumpkin *n.* Kürbis
pun *n.* Wortspiel, Wortwitz; — *v.* witzeln, mit Worten spielen
punch *n.* Puff, Stoss, Schlag; (beverage) Punsch; (mech.) Stanze, Locheisen; Pfrieme; **Punch** Hanswurst, Kasperle; — *v.* puffen, stossen, schlagen; (mech.) lochen, (aus)stanzen, durchschlagen

punctual *adj.* pünktlich, prompt; **–ity** *n.* Pünktlichkeit, Promptheit; Genauigkeit

punctuate *v.* mit Satzzeichen versehen

punctuation *n.* Interpunktion

puncture *n.* Stich; (tire) Loch; — *v.* perforieren, (durch)stechen; ein Loch bekommen; (med.) punktieren

pundit *n.* Gelehrter; Pandit

pungent *adj.* scharf, stechend; schmerzhaft; (fig.) beissend

punish *v.* (be)straten, züchtigen; **–able** *adj.* strafbar, straffällig; **–ment** *n.* Strafe, Bestrafung

punk *n.* Zunderholz; (sl.) Gauner

punt *n.* (cards) Punkt; (football) Treten, bevor der Ball den Boden berührt; — *v.* (football) den Ball, bevor er den Boden berührt, treten; (game) setzen

puny *adj.* winzig; schwächlich

pup *n.* Welpe, kleiner Hund; — *v.* werfen; **–py** *n.* Welpe, junger Hund, junge Robbe; (coll.) Grünschnabel

pupa *n.* Puppe, Larve

pupil *n.* Schüler, Zögling; (anat.) Pupille

puppet *n.* Puppe, Marionette; — **show** Puppenspiel, Marionettentheater

purchase *n.* Kauf, Ankauf, Erwerbung; (mech.) Hebevorrichtung; — *v.* kaufen, erwerben, erhandeln, erstehen; aufwinden; **–r** *n.* Käufer, Abnehmer

pure *adj.* rein, unverfälscht, lauter; (min.) echt, gediegen

purée *n.* Püree, Brei

purgatory *n.* Fegefeuer

purge *n.* Reinigung, Säuberung; (med.) Abführmittel; (pol.) Säuberungsaktion; — *v.* reinigen, säubern; (med.) abführen

purifier *n.* Reiniger; Reinigungsmittel; Reinigungsapparat

purify *v.* reinigen, läutern; (chem.) raffinieren, klären, desinfizieren

Puritan *n.* Puritaner

purity *n.* Reinheit, Lauterkeit

purple *n.* Purpur; — *adj.* purpurn, purpurrot; — *v.* (sich) purpurrot färben

purport *n.* Inhalt, Sinn; — *v.* enthalten, bedeuten; meiner.

purpose *n.* Vorsatz, Absicht; Zweck, Ziel; Wirkung, Erfolg; on — absichtlich, vorsätzlich; to no — zwecklos, vergebens; to the — zweckentsprechend; — *v.* beabsichtigen, bezwecken, vorhaben

purr *v.* schnurren

purse *n.* Tasche; Geldbeutel, Portemonnaie; — *v.* einstecken; **–r** *n.* Zahlmeister, Proviantmeister

pursuance *n.* Verfolgung, Fortsetzung

pursue *v.* verfolgen, nachsetzen; fortsetzen, fortfahren

pursuit *n.* Verfolgung; Nachstellung

push *n.* Stoss, Schub; Vorstoss, Angriff; Hieb, Stich; — **button** Kontaktknopf; — *v.* stossen, schieben, treiben, drücken, drängen, antreiben; betreiben, befördern; verfolgen, bedrängen; — **ahead** vorwärtsstossen; — **back** zurücktreiben; — **through** durchstossen, durchdrücken; **-ing** *adj.* drängend, strebsam; unternehmend, energisch; kühn, zudringlich

pushover *n.* leichtes Spiel; einfache Sache; Schwächling

puss(y) *n.* Kätzchen

put *n.* Stoss, Wurf; — *v.* stossen, werfen, schleudern; zwingen, nötigen; bewegen, bereden; setzen, stellen, legen; — **aside** beiseite setzen; — **away** weglegen, fortschicken; — **down** niedersetzen; niederschreiben; unterdrücken, zum Schweigen bringen; — **forth** herausstellen; ausstrecken; (bot.) treiben, keimen; — **in order** in Ordnung bringen, aufräumen; — **off** aufschieben, hinhalten; — **on** (dress, shoes) anziehen, (hat) aufsetzen; — **out** auslöschen, verwirren; — **out of action** ausser Gefecht setzen; — **over** verschieben, überweisen; beschwindeln; — **together** zusammenstellen, zusammensetzen; — **up** aufstellen, aufschlagen, aufspannen; — **up with** dulden, sich gefallen lassen; **-t** *v.* einlochen, putten; **-ter** *n.* Steller, Setzer; (min.) Karrenschlepper

putrid *adj.* faul, verfault; verdorben; — **fever** Faulfieber

putt *n.* (golf) Schlag; **-er** (golf) Ballkelle

putty *n.* Kitt; — *v.* kitten

puzzle *n.* Rätsel; Verlegenheit, Verwirrung; jigsaw — Zusammensetzspiel, Puzzle(spiel); — *v.* verwirren; in Verlegenheit sein (*or* bringen)

pyrex *n.* Pyrex, Jenaer Glas

pyrometer *n.* Hitzegradmesser

python *n.* Python, Riesenschlange

Q

quack *n.* Quacksalber; Marktschreier; — *adj.* quacksalberisch; prahlend; — *v.* quacksalbern; prahlen; quacken, schnattern

quadrangle *n.* Viereck; (arch.) viereckiger Hof, Häuserblock

quadrant *n.* Quadrant, Viertelkreis

quadrilateral *adj.* vierseitig

quadroon *n.* Viertelneger; Kind eines Mulatten und einer Weissen (*or* umgekehrt)

quadruped *n.* Vierfüssler; — *adj.* vier-

füssig
quadruple *adj.* vierfältig, vierfach; — *v.*
(sich) vervierfachen; **-ts** *n. pl.* Vierlinge
quail *n.* Wachtel; — *v.* verzagen
quaint *adj.* wunderlich, seltsam; altmodisch
quake *n.* Erdbeben; Zittern, Beben; — *v.*
zittern, beben
Quaker *n.* Quäker
qualification *n.* Qualifikation, Befähigung,
Tauglichkeit
qualify *v.* qualifizieren, befähigen; mässigen, mildern; benennen, näher bestim-
men
quality *n.* Qualität, Güte; Eigenschaft,
Beschaffenheit
qualm *n.* Anfall; Übelkeit, Schwäche,
Ohnmacht; (fig.) Skrupel, Bedenken
quandary *n.* Verlegenheit, verdriessliche
Lage
quantity *n.* Quantität, Menge; Länge,
Grösse
quarantine *n.* Quarantäne; Isolierung; —
v. unter Quarantäne stellen; — **a nation**
eine Nation in Schranken halten
quarrel *n.* Zank, Streit, Zwist; — *v.* (sich)
zanken, streiten
quarrelsome *adj.* zänkisch, streitsüchtig
quarry *n.* Steinbruch; (hunting) Beute;
(fig.) Fundgrube
quart *n.* Quart (1 1/4 Liter); (mus.) Quarte
quarter *n.* Viertel, Quartal; Stadtviertel
Himmelsrichtung; Fünfundzwanzig-
centstück; Gnade, Pardon; — **of an
hour** Viertelstunde; **-s** *pl.* Quartier,
Logis; Wohnung; — *v.* vierteilen; (mil.)
einquartieren, unterbringen; **-ly** *adj.*
quartalsweise, vierteljährig
quarterback *n.* (football) ausserhalb der
Gruppe stehender Ballfänger; (fig.)
Spielleiter
quarter-deck *n.* (naut.) Achterdeck
quartermaster *n.* Quartiermeister; (naut.)
Steuermannsmaat
quartet *n.* Quartett
quartz *n.* Quarz
quasar *adj.* quasar, quasi-stellär
quay *n.* Kai, Uferstrasse
queen *n.* Königin; (chess and cards)
Dame; — **bee** Bienenkönigin, Weisel;
-ly *adj.* königlich, wie eine Königin
queer *adj.* wunderlich, seltsam, sonderbar
quell *v.* überwältigen, unterdrücken, bezwingen
quench *v.* (aus)löschen, stillen; unterdrücken
quest *n.* Suchen, Nachforschen, Untersuchung, Prüfung
question *n.* Frage; Befragung, Untersuchung; Streitfrage, Sache, Angelegen-

heit; (law) Verhör; (math.) Aufgabe;
(pol.) Verhandlungsgegenstand; **be out
of** — nicht in Betracht kommen; **beyond** — ohne Frage; **in** — fraglich;
vorliegend; **put a** — eine Frage stellen;
— *v.* befragen; streiten; (law) untersuchen, verhören; (fig.) bezweifeln, misstrauen; **-able** *adj.* fraglich, zweifelhaft;
bedenklich, fragwürdig; **-naire** *n.*
Fragebogen
quibble *n.* Ausflucht, Vorwand; — *v.* ausweichen, Ausflüchte machen
quick *adj.* schnell, rasch, hurtig; beweglich, behend; lebendig, lebhaft; heftig,
stark; **be** —! schnell! beeil dich! — **ear**
feines Ohr; — **eye** scharfes Auge; —
fire Schnellfeuer; — **returns** schneller
Umsatz; — **time** (mil.) Schnellschritt;
— *n.* Lebende; empfindliches Fleisch;
cut to the — auf das Empfindlichste
kränken; **-en** *v.* beleben, beschleunigen;
aufleben; sich regen; **-ness** *n.* Schnelligkeit, Geschwindigkeit; Lebhaftigkeit
quick-freezing *n.* Schnellgefrierung;
schnellarbeitende Gefriermaschine
quicklime *n.* ungelöschter Kalk, Ätzkalk
quicksand *n.* Flugsand, Treibsand
quicksilver *n.* Quecksilber
quick-tempered *adj.* leidenschaftlich
quick-witted *adj.* schlagfertig, scharfsinnig
quiescent *adj.* ruhig, still; ruhend
quiet *n.* Stille, Ruhe; Ungestörtheit; (fig.)
Frieden, Seelenruhe; — *adj.* still, ruhig;
gelassen, friedlich; gemütlich, harmlos;
— *v.* (sich) beruhigen, stillen, besänftigen; (law) in Ruhe lassen; **-ness** *n.*,
-ude *n.* Ruhe, Stille; Friedfertigkeit,
Gemütsruhe, Gleichmut
quill *n.* Feder; Federkiel; (mech.) Weber-
spule; (mus.) Rohrpfeife; (spices) Rin-
denrolle; (zool.) Stachel
quilt *n.* Steppdecke; **crazy** — Flickendecke
quince *n.* Quitte; — **tree** Quittenbaum
quinine *n.* Chinin
quinsy *n.* Halsbräune
quintessence *n.* Quintessenz; (fig.) Kern,
Inbegriff
quintet *n.* Quintett
quip *n.* Witz, Stichelei; Spitzfindigkeit
quit *v.* verlassen, aufgeben; quittieren; **zurückzahlen**; — *adj.* quitt, frei, los; **-ter**
n. Weggehende, Drückeberger
quite *adv.* ganz, gänzlich; völlig, durchaus;
(coll.) ziemlich
quiver *n.* Schauer, Zittern; Köcher; — *v.*
zittern, beben
quiz *n.* Rätselfrage, Quiz; Prüfung; Nek-
kerei, Spöttelei; — *v.* (aus)fragen,
prüfen; aufziehen, necken
quorum *n.* beschlussfähige Mitgliederzahl

quota **449** **raiment**

quota *n.* Quote, Anteil, Kontingent; Beitrag

quotation *n.* Anführung, Zitierung; Zitat; (com.) Preisnotierung; — marks Anführungszeichen; Gänsefüsschen

quote *n.* Zitat; — *v.* zitieren, anführen, angeben; (com.) notieren; — a price ein Preisangebot machen

quotient *n.* Quotient; Teilzahl, Teilwert; intelligence — Intelligenzberechnungswert

R

rabbet *n.* Falz, Fuge, Nut; — *v.* falzen; einfügen

rabbi *n.* Rabbi(ner)

rabbit *n.* Kaninchen

rabble *n.* Pöbel, Haufen

rabid *adj.* wütend, rasend, toll

rabies *n.* Tollwut; Hundswut; Wasserscheu

rac(c)oon *n.* Waschbär

race *n.* Rasse, Geschlecht, Volksstamm; Wettrennen, Wettlauf; Strömung, Lauf; Strom, Rinne; — horse Rennpferd; — track Rennbahn; — *v.* rennen, wettlaufen, wettfahren, wettreiten; –r *n.* Wettläufer; Rennpferd, Rennboot, Rennwagen; (mech.) Laufschiene

racecourse *n.* Rennbahn

racial *adj.* rassenmässig; Rassen-

racism *n.* Rassenvorurteil

rack *n.* Gestell, Ständer, Stativ; Reck; Raufe; (mech.) Zahnstange; (rail.) Gepäcknetz; — railway Zahnradbahn; — *v.* recken, strecken; foltern, quälen; — one's brains sich den Kopf zerbrechen

racket *n.* Lärm, Getöse, Tumult; (tennis) Schläger; (sl.) Erpressergeschäft; –eer *n.* Schieber, Erpresser; –eer *v.* schieben, erpressen

radar *n.* Radar

radiance *n.* Strahlen, Glanz; (geom.) Strahl

radiant *adj.* strahlend, leuchtend; strahlenförmig; –*n.* (opt.) Radiationspunkt

radiator *n.* Heizkörper; Kühler

radical *adj.* radikal, gründlich; wesentlich; — *n.* (chem.) Grundstoff; (gram.) Stammwort; (pol.) Radikale; –ism *n.* Radikalismus

radio *n.* Radio, Rundfunk, directional — Funkpeilgerät; — amplifier Verstärkerröhre; — announcer Rundfunkansager; — beacon Stationszeichen; Peilturm; — beam Richtstrahl; — homing Radiopeilung; — hookup Ringsendung; Übertragung; — listener

Rundfunkhörer; — message Funkspruch, Rundfunkmeldung; — operator Funker; — receiver Rundfunkempfänger; — set Rundfunkapparat; — transcription Schallplattensendung; — *v.* funken, senden

radioactive *adj.* radioaktiv

radioactivity *n.* Radioaktivität

radiobroadcasting *n.* Rundfunksendung; — station Sender, Rundfunksender

radiology *n.* Strahlenlehre

radio(tele)gram *n.* Funkspruch

radiotherapy *n.* Radiotherapie

radish *n.* Rettich; little — Radieschen

radium *n.* Radium

radius *n.* Radius, Halbmesser; (anat. und mech.) Speiche

raffle *n.* Auswürfeln, Auslosen; (coll.) Gerümpel, Abfall; — *v.* (aus)losen, (aus)würfeln

raft *n.* Floss; — *v.* flössen

rafter *n.* Sparren, Dachsparren; Flösser

rag *n.* Lumpen, Lappen, Fetzen; *pl.* Putzwolle; –amuffin *n.* Lump(enkerl); –ged *adj.* uneben, rauh; zottig; zackig; abgerissen, zerlumpt, schäbig

rage *n.* Wut, Raserei; Ekstase; Sucht, Manie, Gier; — *v.* wüten, rasen, toben; fly into a — wütend (*or* rasend) werden; — oneself out sich austoben

raging *adj.* wütend, rasend, tobend

ragtime *n.* groteske Negermusik

ragweed *n.* Klette, wilde Aster; European — Kreuzkraut

raid *n.* Überfall, Streifzug; Raubzug; (police) Razzia; — *v.* überfallen; –er *n.* Angreifer; (avi.) Jagdflugzeug, Bombenflugzeug; (naut.) Kaperschiff; Nahkämpfer

rail *n.* Riegel, Querholz; Geländer; (orn.) Ralle; (rail.) Schiene, Schienenstrang; *pl.* Eisenbahnaktien; by — per Eisenbahn; third — Stromschiene; — *v.* umzäunen, mit einem Geländer versehen; schimpfen, schelten; –ing *n.* Geländer, Brustwehr; Gitter; –ing *adj.* spottend, schmähend

railroad *n.* Eisenbahn; belt — Ringbahn; electric — elektrischer Zug; elevated — Hochbahn; narrow-gauge — Schmalspurbahn; standard-gauge — Normalspurbahn; — crossing Bahnkreuzung; — stock Eisenbahnkapital; — track Schienenstrang; — *v.* per Eisenbahn befördern; (sl.) durch Verleumdung ins Unglück (*or* Gefängnis) bringen

railway *n.* Schienenweg; cable —, funicular — Drahtseilbahn

raiment *n.* Kleidung

rain *n.* Regen; — **gauge** Regenmesse;
— *v.* regnen; it never –s but it pours
ein Unglück kommt selten allein; it –s
cats and dogs es regnet in Strömen; **–y**
adj. regnerisch

rainbow *n.* Regenbogen

raincheck *n.* Eintrittskartenabschnitt
(falls wegen schlechten Wetters um-
disponiert wird); (coll.) Rückversicherung

raindrop *n.* Regentropfen

rainfall *n.* Niederschlag; Regenmenge

rainproof *adj.* wasserdicht, regenfest

raise *n.* Gehaltserhöhung; — *v.* (auf)he-
ben, erhöhen; errichten, aufrichten;
erheben, hervorrufen, erregen; züchten,
aufziehen; beschwören; (mil.) ausheben, werben; (min.) fördern, gewinnen;
(pol.) aufwerfen, vorbringen; (tax)
eintreiben, einkassieren; — **an objection** einen Einwurf machen

raisin *n.* Rosine

rake *n.* Rechen, Harke; (naut.) Überhängen, Neigung; (coll.) Müssiggänger,
Wüstling; — *v.* rechen, harken; zusammenscharren, zusammenraffen; durchstöbern; (mil.) bestreichen; (fig.) überblicken, betrachten; (coll.) liederlich
leben

rally *n.* Sammeln, Sammelsignal; (med.)
Erholung; (pol.) Massenversammlung;
— *v.* (sich) wieder sammeln; (med.)
sich erholen; (fig.) anfeuern; scherzen,
spotten

ram *n.* Widder; (mech.) Ramme; **battering** — Sturmbock, Mauerbrecher; —
jet Vorstossrakete; — *v.* (ein)rammen;
ansetzen

ramble *n.* Streifzug, Ausflug; — *v.* umherstreifen, abschweifen; (bot.) ranken,
wuchern; **–r** *n.* Umherstreicher, Nachtschwärmer; (bot.) Kletterrose

ramification *n.* Verzweigung, Abzweigung

ramp *n.* Rampe, Auffahrt; — *v.* sich zum
Sprung erheben; tollen; **–ant** *adj.*
wuchernd; (fig.) zügellos, ausgelassen

ramshackle *adj.* wackelig, baufällig; (fig.)
verworren

ranch *n.* Farm; Viehwirtschaft; **–er** *n.*
Farmer, Viehzüchter

rancid *adj.* ranzig; (fig.) widerlich[1]

random *n.* Zufall; at — blindlings, aufs
Geratewohl

range *n.* Reihe, Kette, Raum, Umfang;
Bereich, Reichweite, Tragweite, Ausdehnung, Spielraum; Bezirk; (cooking)
Kochherd; (mil.) Schussweite; Schiessplatz; (mus.) Stimmumfang; — **finder**
Entfernungsmesser; — *v.* (ein)reihen,
ordnen; durchstreifen, durchwandern;

sich erstrecken, reichen; (mil.) die
Schussweite bestimmen; (naut.) ent-
lang fahren; (rail.) rangieren; **–r** *n.*
Umherstreifer; Förster; (mil.) Jäger

rank *n.* Reihe, Linie, Glied; Rang, Stand,
Klasse, Dienstgrad; — **and file** Reihe
und Glied; gemeine Soldaten; **rise from
the** –s von der Pike auf dienen; — *adj.*
stark, rein, richtig; ranzig; üppig,
übermässig, fruchtbar; — *v.* rangieren,
rechnen zu; (sich) ordnen

ransack *v.* durchsuchen, durchstöbern;
plündern

ransom *n.* Lösegeld, Loskauf; — *v.* los-
kaufen, auslösen; (rel.) erlösen

rap *n.* Schlag, Klopfen; Heller; (sl.) un-
verdiente Strafe; — *v.* schlagen,
klopfen; raffen, fortreissen; verweisen

rapacious *adj.* raubgierig, räuberisch;
habgierig, unverschämt

rape *n.* Raub, Entführung; (bot.) Raps,
Rübsen; (law) Notzucht, Vergewalti-
gung; — *v.* rauben; (law) vergewaltigen, notzüchten

rapid *adj.* schnell, rasch; reissend; rapid;
— **consumption** (med.) galoppierende
Schwindsucht; — **fire** Schnellfeuer; —
march (mil.) Laufschritt; **–s** *n. pl.*
Stromschnellen, Strudel; **–ity** *n.* Schnelligkeit, Geschwindigkeit; Ungestüm

rapine *n.* Raub, Plünderung

rapt *adj.* geraubt, entführt; (fig.) entrückt, hingerissen, entzückt; versunken; **–ure** *n.* Entrückung, Verzük-
kung, Ekstase; **–urous** *adj.* hinreissend,
entzückend; leidenschaftlich

rare *adj.* selten, rar; dünn, fein; locker,
porös; **–fied** *adj.* verdünnt

rarity *n.* Rarität, Seltenheit

rascal *n.* Spitzbube, Halunke, Schuft; **–ly**
adj. gemein, schuftig, erbärmlich

rash *n.* Hautausschlag; — *adj.* hastig,
übereilt; unvorsichtig, vorschnell;
–ness *n.* Hastigkeit, Übereiltheit,
Unbesonnenheit; Ungestüm

rasp *n.* Raspel, Reibeisen; — *v.* reiben,
raspeln, kratzen; (mus.) krächzen;
(fig.) kränken, verletzen

raspberry *n.* Himbeere

rat *n.* Ratte; (sl.) Überläufer; Streikbrecher; — *v.* Ratten fangen; (sl.) verraten, überlaufen

rate *n.* Rate, Anteil; Mass, Verhältnis;
Preis, Betrag; Dosis; Veranschlagung;
Abgabe, Steuer; Geschwindigkeit; **at a
low** — wohlfeil; **at any** — auf jeden
Fall, um jeden Preis; — **of discount**
Diskontsatz; — **of exchange** Wech-
selkurs; — **of interest** Zinsfuss; — *v.*
schätzen, taxieren; ansehen, bestim-

men; besteuern; regulieren; ausschelten

rather adv. eher, lieber; ziemlich; vielmehr

ratification n. Ratifizierung, Bestätigung

ratify v. ratifizieren, bestätigen

rating n. Schätzung; Rang, Klasse; Verweis

ratio n. Verhältnis

ration n. Ration, Anteil, Bedarf; **-ing** n. Rationierung

rational adj. vernunftgemäss, vernünftig; rational

Ratisbon n. Regensburg

rattle n. Gerassel; Klapper, Knarre; — v. rasseln, klirren; klappern, knarren; röcheln; (fig.) verwirren

rattlesnake n. Klapperschlange

ravage n. Verwüstung, Verheerung; — v. verwüsten, verheeren

rave v. rasen, toben; schwärmen, faseln

ravel v. verwirren; (sich) auftrennen, ausfassern

raven n. Rabe; **-ous** adj. gefrässig, heisshungrig

ravine n. Hohlweg; Bergschlucht

ravish v. rauben, entführen; schänden; (fig.) hinreissen; **-ing** adj. entzückend, hinreissend

raw adj. roh, ungekocht; rauh; unerfahren; unreif; unbearbeitet; (med.) wund-(gerieben); — **materials** Rohstoffe, Rohmaterial

rawhide n. ungegerbtes Leder; Reitpeitsche

ray n. Strahl; (ichth.) Roche

rayon n. Rayon, Kunstseide

razor n. Rasiermesser, Rasierapparat; — **blade** Rasierklinge; — **strop** Streichriemen; **electric** — Trockenrasierer

reach n. Bereich, Strecke; Hörweite; Schussweite, Reichweite; Ausdehnung; — v. (er)reichen; erlangen, greifen; ausstrecken; (sich) erstrecken

react v. reagieren, rückwirken; entgegenwirken; **-ion** n. Rückwirkung, Gegenwirkung; Reaktion; **-ionary** n. Reaktionär; **-ionary** adj. reaktionär; **-ivate** v. reaktivieren

read v. (ab)lesen; (an)zeigen; auslegen; studieren; — adj. belesen, bewandert (in); **-able** adj. lesbar, lesenswert; **-er** n. Leser, Vorleser; Erklärer; Lesebuch; **-ing** n. Lesen, Lesung; Vorlesung; Lektüre, Lesestoff; Lesart, Auffassung; Belesenheit; Durchsicht, Korrektur; **-ing room** Lesezimmer

readily adv. bereitwillig; gleich; leicht; gern

readiness n. Schnelligkeit, Raschheit; Bereitwilligkeit; Bereitschaft

ready adj. bereit, fertig; schnell, gewandt; (com.) bar, prompt; (naut.) klar

ready-made adj. (gebrauchs)fertig; — **clothes** Konfektionskleidung

real adj. wirklich, tatsächlich, real; wahr, echt; (law) unbeweglich; — **estate** Grundbesitz; — **wages** Reallöhne; **-sim** n. Realismus; **-ist** n. Realist; **-istic** adj. realistisch; **-ity** n. Wirklichkeit, Realität; **-ization** n. Verwirklichung, Realisierung; (com.) Geldanlage; **-ize** v. verwirklichen, ausführen, realisieren; sich vorstellen, erkennen; (com.) anlegen, verwerten; einbringen, erzielen; zu Geld machen; **-ly** adv. wirklich, in der Tat

realm n. Reich; Gebiet

ream n. Ries; — v. erweitern

reap v. schneiden, mähen; ernten; **-er** n. Schnitter; Mähmaschine

rear n. Hinterseite, Hintergrund; Rückseite; (mil.) Nachhut, Nachtrab; — adj. Hinter-, Rück-; — **admiral** Konteradmiral; — v. aufheben, aufrichten; errichten; aufziehen, grossziehen; sich bäumen

rearmament n. Wiederbewaffnung, Wiederaufrüstung

rearrange v. neu ordnen

rearview n. Rückansicht

rear-vision mirror n. Rückspiegel

reason n. Vernunft, Verstand; Grund, Ursache; Recht, Billigkeit; Einsicht, Überlegung; by — of wegen; for this — aus diesem Grunde; in — massvoll; it is against all — es ist gegen alle Vernunft; it stands to — es ist vernünftig; listen to — Vernunft annehmen; without — ohne Grund; **-able** adj. vernünftig, verständig; billig, mässig; **-ing** n. Urteil(en); Beweisführung

reassurance n. wiederholte Versicherung, Beruhigung; (com.) Rückversicherung

rebate n. Rabatt, Abzug; (arch.) Kannelierung; Falz

rebel n. Rebell, Aufrührer, Empörer; — adj. rebellisch, aufrührerisch; — v. rebellieren, sich empören (or auflehnen); **-lion** n. Aufruhr, Empörung; Widerspenstigkeit; **-lious** adj. aufständisch, widerspenstig

rebirth n. Wiedergeburt

rebound n. Rückprall; Rückstoss; Widerhall; — v. zurückspringen, zurückprallen, abprallen; widerhallen

rebroadcast n. wiederholte Rundfunksendung

rebuild v. wieder aufbauen, wiederherstellen; **-ing** n. Umbau

rebuke n. Tadel, Vorwurf; — v. tadeln, schelten, zurechtweisen

rebut *v.* (law) widerlegen

recall *n.* Zurückrufung; Widerruf; Hervorruf; — *v.* zurückrufen; wieder wachrufen; widerrufen

recap *n.* (tire) neuer Belag; — *v.* neu vulkanisieren; –itulate *v.* rekapitulieren, kurz wiederholen

recapture *n.* Wiedereinnahme, Wiederfestnahme; — *v.* wieder einnehmen (*or* festnehmen)

recast *v.* umgiessen, umformen

recede *v.* zurücktreten, zurückweichen; abstehen

receipt *n.* Annahme; Quittung, Empfangsschein; (med.) Rezept; *pl.* Eingänge; **acknowledge** — den Empfang bestätigen; — *v.* quittieren, bestätigen

receivable *adj.* annehmbar; — bills offen stehende Rechnungen

receive *v.* empfangen, erhalten; einnehmen; aufnehmen; annehmen; anerkennen; **–r** *n.* Empfänger; Einnehmer; (chem.) Rezipient; (mech.) Behälter, Sammelgefäss; (tel.) Hörer; **–r in bankruptcy** Konkursverwalter; **–r of stolen goods** Hehler; **–rship** *n.* Konkursverwaltung

recent *adj.* neu, frisch; **–ly** *adv.* kürzlich, vor kurzem, unlängst

receptacle *n.* Behälter; (anat.) Gefäss; (coll.) Schlupfwinkel

reception *n.* Empfang; Annahme; Aufnahme; **–ist** *n.* Empfangsdame

receptive *adj.* aufnahmefähig, empfänglich

recess *n.* Unterbrechung, Ferien; (arch.) Nische, Vertiefung; (fig.) Winkel; **–ion** *n.* wirtschaftlicher Stillstand

recipe *n.* Rezept

recipient *n.* Empfänger

reciprocal *adj.* wechselseitig, gegenseitig; reziprok

reciprocate *v.* austauschen, erwidern; abwechseln(d wirken)

reciprocity *n.* Gegenseitigkeit

recital *n.* Vortrag, Vorlesung; (mus.) Konzert

recitation *n.* Rezitation, Deklamation; Vortrag

recitative *n.* (mus.) Rezitativ

recite *v.* rezitieren, vortragen, deklamieren, aufsagen

reckless *adj.* tollkühn, verwegen; rücksichtslos; leichtsinnig, unbekümmert

reckon *v.* rechnen, zählen; schätzen, meinen, vermuten; **–ing** *n.* Berechnung, Abrechnung; Zählung; Schätzung

reclaim *v.* reklamieren, rückfordern; bessern, zivilisieren; (agr.) urbarmachen; abgewinnen; (law) protestieren; (zool.) zähmen

reclamation *n.* Reklamation, Rückforderung; Besserung; (agr.) Urbarmachung, Gewinnung; (law) Protest, Einspruch

recline *v.* (sich) lehnen, ausruhen

recognition *n.* Anerkennung, Beglaubigung; Erkennen

recognize *v.* anerkennen, beglaubigen; wiedererkennen

recoil *n.* Rückstoss, Rücklauf; — *v.* zurückfahren, zurückweichen, zurückstossen, zurückschaudern; sich zurückziehen

recollect *v.* sich fassen (*or* wieder sammeln); sich erinnern; **–ion** *n.* Erinnerung, Gedächtnis

recommend *v.* empfehlen; **–ation** *n.* Empfehlung

recommission *v.* wieder in Dienst stellen

recompense *n.* Entschädigung, Ersatz; Belohnung

reconcile *v.* versöhnen, schlichten; in Einklang bringen

reconciliation *n.* Versöhnung, Aussöhnung

recondition *n.* Wiederinstandsetzung, Reparatur; — *v.* wieder instandsetzen, reparieren

reconnaissance *n.* Aufklärung

reconsider *v.* von neuem betrachten (*or* erwägen)

reconstruct *v.* wieder aufbauen (*or* herstellen)

record *n.* Bericht, Aufzeichnung; Urkunde, Dokument; Verzeichnis, Protokoll, Register; Schallplatte; (pol.) Vergangenheit, Ruf; (sports) Rekord, Höchstleistung; *pl.* Archiv, Papiere, Geschichtsbücher; **off the** — im Vertrauen, ohne Aufzeichnungen zu machen; — *v.* eintragen, registrieren; verzeichnen, aufzeichnen, protokollieren; überliefern; (sports) einen Rekord aufstellen; **–er** *n.* Registrator, Protokollführer; Archivar; Geschichtsschreiber; (mech.) Zähler; Aufnahmeapparat; (sports) Zeitnehmer

record-breaking *adj.* rekordbrechend

recount *v.* wieder erzählen

re-count *v.* wieder zählen, nochmals berechnen

recoup *v.* schadlos halten, ersetzen

recourse *n.* Zuflucht; Regressrecht

recover *v.* wieder erlangen (*or* erobern); wiederfinden; wiedergutmachen; einholen, nachholen; herauskommen; sich erholen; — **one's senses** wieder zum Bewusstsein (*or* zu Verstand) kommen; — **property** Eigentum zurückerhalten; **–y** *n.* Wiedererlangung, Wiedereroberung; (law) Schadenersatz; (med.) Wiederherstellung, Genesung, Rekonvaleszenz

recreate *v.* sich erholen; erfrischen; neu gestalten, umschaffen

recreation *n.* Erholung, Erfrischung; Neugestaltung

recruit *n.* Rekrut, Neuling; — *v.* rekrutieren, ergänzen, wiederherstellen; erneuern; **-ing** *n.* Rekrutierung; — **office** Bezirkskommando, Werbebüro

rectangle *n.* Rechteck

rectangular *adj.* rechteckig, rechtwinkelig

rectifier *n.* Entzerrungsgerät, Gleichrichter

rectify *v.* berichtigen, verbessern; (rad.) gleichrichten, entzerren

rector *n.* Rektor; Pfarrer; **-y** *n.* Rektorat; Pfarre, Pfarrhaus

recuperate *v.* sich erholen; wieder herstellen (*or* kräftigen)

recur *v.* zurückkommen; wieder einfallen; periodisch wiederkehren; **-rence** *n.* Wiederkehr, Rückkehr; Zurückfliessen; **-rent** *adj.* wiederkehrend; rückläufig, zurückfliessend

red *n.* Rot; (art.) Rötel; — *adj.* rot; (pol.) rot, kommunistisch; (fig.) blutig, blutgefärbt; — **herring** getrockneter Hering; (coll.) Vorspieglung, Finte; — **lead** Mennig; — **man** Rothaut, Indianer; — **pepper** Piment, Paprika, roter (*or* spanischer) Pfeffer; — **tape** Bürokratie, Amtsschimmel; **-den** *v.* röten, rot färben (*or* werden); erröten; **-dish** *adj.* rötlich; **-ness** *n.* Röte, Rötung

redbird *n.* Kardinal

red-blooded *adj.* vital, mutig; (coll.) waschecht

redbreast *n.* Rotkehlchen

redcap *n.* Gepäckträger; (orn.) Stieglitz, Distelfink

redeem *v.* auslösen, zurückkaufen; tilgen; wiedergutmachen, wieder einbringen; ersetzen; befreien, erlösen; **-er** *n.* Einlösende; **Redeemer** Erlöser, Heiland

redemption *n.* Rückkauf; Auslösung; Wiedergutmachung; (rel.) Erlösung

red-haired *adj.* rothaarig

redhead *n.* Rotkopf

red-hot *adj.* rotglühend; (coll.) heftig, hitzig; (news) neuste

red-letter day *n.* Festtag, Glückstag, Freudentag

redskin *n.* Rothaut, Indianer

red-tape *adj.* bürokratisch

reduce *v.* verkleinern, vermindern; herabsetzen, abschwächen; zurückführen (auf); (chem.) reduzieren; (med.)

abnehmen (durch Diät)

reducing agent *n.* Reduktionsmittel; (med.) Abmagerungsmittel

reduction *n.* Verringerung, Verminderung, Abschwächung

redundant *adj.* überfliessend; übermässig, üppig; weitschweifig; (fig.) überflüssig

redwood *n.* Rotholz

reed *n.* (arch.) Kannelierung; (bot.) Ried, Rohr; (mech.) Weberkamm; (mus.) Mundstück, Zunge; Rohrflöte

reef *n.* Riff, Klippe; — *v.* raffen, einziehen

reek *n.* Rauch, Dunst; — *v.* rauchen, dampfen; räuchern, ausdunsten

reel *n.* Haspel, Rolle, Spule; (coll.) Taumel, Wirbel; — *v.* haspeln, rollen; taumeln, wirbeln; — **off** herunterleiern

re-elect *v.* wiederwählen; **-ion** *n.* Wiederwahl

re-enforce *v.* (sich) verstärken; wieder inkraftsetzen

re-enter *v.* wieder eintreten (or eindringen); wiedereintragen

re-entry *n.* Wiedereintritt in die Erdatmosphäre

re-establish *v.* wiederherstellen

refer *v.* verweisen, hinweisen; — **to** hinweisen auf, sich beziehen auf; **-ee** *n.* Schiedsrichter, Unparteiische; (law) Sachverständige; **-ee** *v.* als Schiedsrichter tätig sein; **-ence** *n.* Referenz, Verweisung; Empfehlung, Auskunft; Erwähnung, Anspielung; **works of -ence** Nachschlagewerke; **-endum** *n.* Volksentscheid

refill *n.* Nachfüllung; Ersatzbatterie; — *v.* neu füllen, auffüllen, nachfüllen

refine *v.* verfeinern, reinigen, läutern; (mech.) raffinieren; **-ment** *n.* Verfeinerung, Veredlung, Feinheit; (mech.) Raffinierung; **-ry** *n.* Raffinerie

reflect *v.* zurückwerfen, reflektieren, widerspiegeln, widerstrahlen; **-ion** *n.* Reflexion, Zurückstrahlung; Reflex; (fig.) Überlegung; Tadel; **-or** *n.* Reflektor; Rückstrahler

reflex *n.* Reflex, Widerschein; — *adj.* reflektiert, zurückgebogen; Reflex-

reforest *v.* wiederaufforsten

reform *n.* Reform, Verbesserung; — *v.* verbessern; (eccl.) reformieren; **-ation** *n.* Umgestaltung; (eccl.) Reformation; **-atory** *n.* Besserungsanstalt; **-atory** *adj.* bessernd, reformatorisch; **-er** *n.* Verbesserer; (eccl.) Reformator

refrain *n.* Refrain, Kehrreim; — *v.* sich enthalten, zurückhalten, bezähmen, zügeln

refresh *v.* (sich) erfrischen, auffrischen; erquicken; **-er** *n.* Erfrischung; Auf-

frischung; (law) Zuschlagshonorar; –er
adj. erfrischend, auffrischend; –er
course Wiederholungskurs; –ment *n.*
Erfrischung

refrigeration *n.* Abkühlung, Kühlung

refrigerator *n.* Kühlschrank, Eisschrank;
Kühlapparat

refuel *v.* tanken; wieder füllen

refuge *n.* Zuflucht; Ausflucht, Ausweg;
Schutzinsel; –e *n.* Flüchtling

refund *n.* Ersatz, Zurückzahlung; — *v.*
zurückzahlen, zurückerstatten, ersetzen

refusal *n.* Weigerung, Verweigerung;
Ablehnung; Vorkaufsrecht

refuse *n.* Abfall, Kehricht, Müll; (fig.)
Abschaum, Ausschuss; — *v.* verweigern, ablehnen, abschlagen, zurückweisen

refute *v.* widerlegen

regain *v.* wiedergewinnen, wiedererreichen

regal *adj.* königlich, fürstlich; –ia *n.*
Abzeichen; Krönungsschmuck

regard *n.* Achtung, Ansehen; Aufmerksamkeit, Rücksicht; Hinsicht; *pl.*
Grüsse, Empfehlungen; give –s Grüsse
übermitteln; in — to hinsichtlich, was
mich betrifft; with — to mit Rücksicht
auf; — *v.* achten, ansehen, betrachten;
beachten; betreffen; –ing *prep.* betreffs;
in Anbetracht, hinsichtlich; –less *adj.*
unachtsam, unaufmerksam; unbekümmert; rücksichtslos; –less *adv.* –less of
ohne Rücksicht auf

regency *n.* Regierung, Regentschaft

regenerate *v.* (sich) erneuern; nachladen

regeneration *n.* Regenerierung, Wiederherstellung; Wiedergeburt

regent *n.* Regent, Herrscher

regime *n.* Regime, Regierung(sform); –n
n. Regierung; (gram.) Rektion

regiment *n.* Regiment; (pol.) Herrschaft;
— *v.* in Regimente einteilen; organisieren; –ation *n.* Einteilung in Regimente;
Organisation; Disziplinierung

region *n.* Region, Gegend, Bezirk; (anat.)
Stelle; –al *adj.* regional, örtlich, strichweise

register *n.* Register, Verzeichnis; (mech.)
Registriervorrichtung, Schieber; (mus.)
Register; cash — Registrierkasse; — *v.*
einschreiben, registrieren, verzeichnen;
eintragen, aufzeichnen, buchen; –ed
adj. registriert, eingeschrieben; –ed
letter Einschreibebrief, Einschreiben

registrar *n.* Registrator

registration *n.* Registrierung, Eintragung

registry *n.* Registratur; Register; Eintragung

regression *n.* Rückbildung, Rückfall

regret *n.* Bedauern, Schmerz; –s *pl.* Ableh-

nung, Absage; — *v.* bedauern; vermissen; –ful *adj.* bedauernd; kummervoll;
–table *adj.* bedauerlich

regular *n.* aktiver Soldat; (eccl.) Ordens-
geistliche; (coll.) Stammkunde, Stamm-
gast; — *adj.* regulär, regelmässig;
pünktlich, richtig, ordentlich; (geom.)
normal, symmetrisch; — army aktives
Heer; –ity *n.* Regelmässigkeit; Richtigkeit, Ordnung

regulate *v.* regulieren; ordnen, regeln;
einrichten, stellen

regulation *n.* Regulierung, Regelung;
Anordnung

rehabilitate *v.* rehabilitieren; wiedereinsetzen

rehabilitation *n.* Rehabilitierung; Wiedereinsetzung

rehash *v.* wiederkäuen, aufwärmen

rehearsal *n.* Wiederholung; Vortrag;
(theat.) Probe

rehearse *v.* wiederholen, rezitieren;
(theat.) proben

reign *n.* Regierung(sdauer); (fig.) Macht,
Herrschaft; — *v.* regieren, herrschen

reimburse *v.* wiedererstatten, entschädigen; –ment *n.* Wiedererstattung; Dek-
kung, Entschädigung

rein *n.* Zügel; give — to die Zügel schiessen lassen; — *v.* zügeln, zurückhalten

reincarnation *n.* Reinkarnation, Wieder-
verkörperung

reindeer *n.* Renntier

reinforce *v.* verstärken; –d *adj.* verstärkt;
–d concrete Eisenbeton; –ment *n.*
Verstärkung

reinstate *v.* wiedereinsetzen, wiederherstellen, wiederinstandsetzen

reiterate *v.* (dauernd) wiederholen

reject *v.* ablehnen, zurückweisen; aus-
mustern; verwerfen, verschmähen; –ion
n. Ablehnung, Abweisung; Ausmuste-
rung

rejoice *v.* erfreuen, sich freuen (über)

rejoicing *n.* Freude; *pl.* Freudenbezeigun-
gen, Lustbarkeiten; — *adj.* erfreulich,
freudig

rejuvenate *v.* verjüngen

relapse *n.* Rückfall; — *v.* zurückfallen;
rückfällig werden, einen Rückfall
bekommen

relate *v.* erzählen, berichten; sich beziehen, in Verbindung bringen; –d *adj.*
berichtet, erzählt; verwandt

relation *n.* Bericht, Erzählung; Verhältnis, Bezug; Verwandtschaft, Verwandte; –ship *n.* Verwandtschaft

relative *n.* Verwandte; (gram.) Relativ-
pronomen; — *adj.* relativ, verhältnismässig, bedingt; bezüglich; **verwandt**

relativity *n.* Relativität

relax *v.* lockern, schwächen; erschlaffen, nachlassen; entspannen, zerstreuen, erheitern; **-ation** *n.* Lockerung, Nachlassen, Erlass; Entspannung, Zerstreuung, Erholung

relay *n.* Wechsel, Ablösung; (sports) Stafette; (tel.) Relais; — **race** Stafettenlauf

release *n.* Entlassung, Freilassung, Freigabe, Befreiung; Ausklinken; — *v.* entlassen, freilassen; freigeben; auslösen; erlösen

relent *v.* nachgeben; sich erweichen lassen; **-less** *adj.* unnachgiebig, unerbittlich; unbarmherzig

relevant *adj.* erheblich; angemessen; einschlägig

reliability *n.* Zuverlässlichkeit, Verlässlichkeit

reliable *adj.* zuverlässlich, verlässlich

reliance *n.* Verlass, Vertrauen, Zutrauen

reliant *adj.* vertrauensvoll, zuversichtlich

relic *n.* Reliquie; Andenken; Überrest; *pl.* sterbliche Hülle

relief *n.* Erleichterung, Linderung; Abhilfe; Unterstützung; (art) Relief; (mil.) Ablösung, Entsatz; (fig.) Hervorhebung; — **map** Reliefkarte

relieve *v.* erleichtern, lindern; helfen, unterstützen; ablösen, ersetzen

religion *n.* Religion

religious *adj.* religiös; — **instruction** Religionsunterricht

relinquish *v.* verlassen, aufgeben, verzichten auf, überlassen

relish *n.* Geschmack, Wohlgefallen; Beigeschmack, Würze; — *v.* gerne essen; schmackhaft machen; schmekken, munden; würzen

reload *v.* wieder beladen

reluctance *n.* Widerstreben, Widerstand, Abneigung

reluctant *adj.* widerstrebend, widerwillig; unwillig; zögernd

rely *v.* sich verlassen; bauen auf

remain *v.* (ver)bleiben, übrigbleiben; dauern; **-der** *n.* Rest; (books) Restauflage; (com.) Rückstand, Saldo; (law) Anwartschaft; **-s** *n. pl.* Überreste, sterbliche Reste; (lit.) hinterlassene Werke

remake *v.* wiedermachen, erneuern

remark *n.* Bemerkung, Anmerkung; — *v.* bemerken, beobachten; äussern; **-able** *adj.* bemerkenswert, merkwürdig; auffallend

remedy *n.* Heilmittel; Hilfsmittel, Gegenmittel; Rechtsmittel; — *v.* heilen; (ab)helfen

remember *v.* sich erinnern, eingedenk sein, behalten

remembrance *n.* Erinnerung, Andenken; Gedächtnis

remind *v.* erinnern, mahnen; **-er** *n.* Verweis, Mahnung; Wink

remit *v.* übersenden; verzeihen; erlassen, nachlassen; **-tance** *n.* Sendung; Verzeihung; **-ter** *n.* Absender, Übersender

remnant *n.* Überbleibsel, Rest

remodel *v.* umbilden

remonstrance *n.* Einwand, Vorstellung, Einspruch

remonstrate *v.* einwenden, Vorstellungen machen

remorse *n.* Gewissensbiss, Zerknirschung; **-ful** *adj.* reuevoll, reumütig; **-less** *adj.* reuelos, gefühllos, hartherzig

remote *adj.* entfernt, entlegen; **-ness** *n.* Entfernung, Entlegenheit

removable *adj.* fortschaffbar; abnehmbar, auswechselbar; absetzbar

removal *n.* Beseitigung, Wegräumen; Entfernung, Entlassung

remove *v.* wegschaffen, wegräumen; beseitigen, entfernen; absetzen, entlassen; **-r** *n.* Spediteur; **spot -r** Fleckenentferner

remunerate *v.* belohnen, entlohnen

remuneration *n.* Belohnung, Entschädigung

rend *v.* (zer)reissen; spalten, bersten

render *v.* zurückgeben, vergelten; abstatten, leisten; einreichen; übersetzen; (lit.) vortragen; (mech.) ausschmelzen

rendezvous *n.* Rendezvous, Stelldichein; Treffpunkt

rendition *n.* Übergabe, Ergebung; Auslieferung; (theat.) Vortrag

renew *v.* erneuern; **-al** *n.* Erneuerung

renounce *v.* entsagen, verzichten auf; verleugnen; (cards) nicht bedienen

renovate *v.* renovieren, erneuern

renown *n.* Ruhm, Ruf; Name; **-ed** *adj.* berühmt, namhaft

rent *n.* Miete, Pacht; (geol.) Riss, Spalte, Kluft; — *v.* mieten; (ver)pachten; **-al** *n.* Rentenverzeichnis, Zinsregister; Miete; **-al** *adj.* Miets-, Pachts-; **-er** *n.* Mieter, Pächter

renunciation *n.* Verzichtleistung, Entsagung

reopen *v.* wieder(er)öffnen

reorder *v.* neuordnen; erneut bestellen

reorganize *v.* reorganisieren, neugestalten

repair *n.* Reparatur, Ausbesserung, Instandsetzung; — *v.* reparieren, ausbessern, instandsetzen; wiedergutmachen; — **shop** Reparaturwerkstatt; **-ed** *adj.* repariert, ausgebessert

reparable adj. wiederherstellbar; wiedergutzumachend

reparation n. Wiederherstellung; Ersatz, Entschädigung; (pol.) Reparation

repast n. Mahl(zeit)

repatriate v. repatriieren, in die Heimat zurückbringen

repay v. zurückzahlen, entschädigen; belohnen, vergelten

repeal n. Widerruf, Aufhebung; — v. widerrufen, aufheben

repeat v. (sich) wiederholen; -ed adj. wiederholt; -er n. Wiederholer; (law) Vorbestrafte; (pol.) Doppelwähler

repeating decimal n. periodischer Dezimalbruch

repel v. zurücktreiben, zurückstossen; abstossen; -lent adj. abstossend; zurückstossend

repent v. bereuen; -ance n. Reue; -ant adj. reuig; bussfertig

repercussion n. Rückprall; (fig.) Widerhall, Rückwirkung

repertoire n. Repertoire, Spielplan

repetition n. Wiederholung; Vortrag

replace v. ersetzen; wieder hinstellen (or einsetzen); -ment n. Ersatz

replenish v. ergänzen; wieder füllen

reply n. Antwort, Entgegnung; Erwiderung; — v. antworten, entgegnen

report n. Bericht; Schulzeugnis; Gericht; Knall; — v. (sich) melden, berichten, Bericht erstatten; -er n. Reporter, Berichterstatter

repose n. Ruhe, Schlaf; — v. (sich) ausruhen, schlafen; ruhen; vertrauen; beruhen

represent v. darstellen, vorstellen; vertreten; -ation n. Schilderung, Darstellung; Vorstellung; Vertretung; -ative n. Repräsentant, Vertreter; Stellvertreter; House of Representatives Abgeordnetenhaus; -ative adj. bezeichnend, vorstellend; (stell)vertretend

repress v. unterdrücken, einschränken

reprimand n. Tadel, Verweis; — v. tadeln, einen Verweis erteilen

reprint n. Neudruck, Nachdruck; — v. neudrucken, neuauflegen

reproach n. Vorwurf, Tadel; Schande; — v. vorwerfen, tadeln; schelten

reprobate n. Verworfene, Schuft; — adj. verworfen, ruchlos, verdammt; — v. verwerfen, missbilligen; (rel.) verdammen

reproduce v. reproduzieren, nachbilden

reproduction n. Reproduktion, Nachbildung

reproof n. Vorwurf, Verweis

reprove v. missbilligen, tadeln, rügen

reptile n. Reptil

republic n. Republik; -an n. Republikaner; -an adj. republikanisch

repudiate v. verwerfen, zurückweisen; verstossen

repudiation n. Verwerfung; Nichtanerkennung; Verstossung

repugnant adj. widersprechend, zuwider; widerstrebend

repulse n. Zurücktreiben; Zurückweisung; — v. zurückschlagen; zurücktreiben; zurückweisen, abschlagen

repulsion n. Zurücktreibung; (phy.) Abstossung; (fig.) Abscheu, Widerwille

repulsive adj. abstossend; widerwärtig

reputable adj. achtbar, anständig; angesehen

reputation n. Ansehen, Ruf

repute v. halten für, hochschätzen

request n. Bitte, Gesuch; Anspruch, Forderung; (com.) Nachfrage; on — auf Verlangen; — v. bitten, ersuchen

require v. verlangen, (er)fordern; nötig haben; -ment n. Forderung, Bedürfnis; Erfordernis; -ments pl. Ansprüche

requisite n. Werkzeug, Zubehör; (fig.) Notwendigkeit; — adj. erforderlich, notwendig

requisition n. Anforderung; (mil.) Requirierung

resale n. Wiederverkauf, Weiterverkauf

rescind v. aufheben, umstossen; für ungültig erklären

rescue n. Rettung, Befreiung; — v. retten, befreien; (law) gewaltsam befreien

research n. Forschung; Nachforschung

resemblance n. Ähnlichkeit

resemble v. ähneln, ähnlich sein, gleichen

resent v. übelnehmen; -ful adj. empfindlich; grollend, rachsüchtig; -ment n. Empfindlichkeit; Unwille, Rachsucht

reservation n. Vorbehalt; Naturschutzgebiet, Reservat

reserve n. Reserve, Vorrat; Vorsicht, Zurückhaltung; — v. reservieren, aufsparen, aufbewahren; zurückhalten, belegen; -d adj. reserviert, vorsichtig; zurückhaltend; belegt, vorgemerkt

reservoir n. Reservoir, Behälter

reset v. wiedereinsetzen; (typ.) neu setzen

reside v. wohnen, ansässig sein, residieren; -nce n. Wohnsitz; Aufenthaltsort; Residenz; -nt n. Bewohner, Ortsansässige; -nt adj. wohnhaft, ansässig; sich aufhaltend; -ntial adj. wohnend; Wohn-

residue n. Überrest, Abfall; (chem.) Rückstand; (com.) Restbestand

resign v. entsagen, verzichten; aufgeben, niederlegen; sich abfinden; -ation n.

Amtsniederlegung, Rücktritt; Ergebung; –ed *adj.* ergeben, resignierend, resigniert

resin *n.* Harz; –ous *adj.* harz(art)ig; (elec.) negativ

resist *v.* widerstehen, sich widersetzen; –ance *n.* Widerstand; –ance coil Widerstandsspule; –ant *adj.* widerstehend, gegnerisch

resolute *adj.* resolut, entschlossen, entschieden

resolution *n.* Auflösung; Entschluss; (pol.) Resolution, Beschluss

resolve *n.* Entschluss; Beschluss; — *v.* beschliessen; (auf)lösen; –d *adj.* entschlossen, fest

resonance *n.* Resonanz; Widerhall

resonant *adj.* nachklingend, widerhallend

resort *n.* Zuflucht; Badeort, Kurort; **summer** — Sommerfrische

resource *n.* Hilfsquelle, Hilfsmittel; Zuflucht; *pl.* Geldmittel; –ful *adj.* reich an Hilfsquellen; findig

respect *n.* Respekt, Achtung, Ehrfurcht; Rücksicht, Hinsicht; Beziehung; *pl.* Grüsse, Empfehlungen; — *v.* verehren, schätzen, respektieren, achten; betreffen, sich beziehen; berücksichtigen; –ability *n.* Achtbarkeit, Ansehnlichkeit; –able *adj.* achtbar, ansehnlich; (com.) solid, reell; –ed *adj.* angesehen; –ful *adj.* respektvoll, ehrerbietig; –ing *prep.* in Bezug auf, hinsichtlich; –ive *adj.* jedesmalig, jeweilig; –ively *adv.* beziehungsweise

respiration *n.* Atmen, Atemzug

respond *v.* antworten, erwidern; reagieren; (law) haften

response *n.* Antwort, Erwiderung; Reaktion, Erfolg

responsibility *n.* Verantwortlichkeit, Verantwortung; Verpflichtung

responsible *adj.* verantwortlich, vertrauenswürdig

responsive *adj.* empfänglich, entsprechend; beantwortend; Antwort-

rest *n.* Rest; Stütze, Gestell; Rast, Ruhe, Schlaf; (fig.) Friede, Tod; — **room** Toilette; — **cure** Liegekur; — *v.* rasten, ruhen; liegen, schlafen; (sich) stützen, (sich) lehnen; –ful *adj.* ruhig; beruhigend; –ive *adj.* widerspenstig, störrisch; –less *adj.* rastlos, ruhelos, schlaflos; unruhig; –lessness *n.* Rastlosigkeit; Unruhe

restaurant *n.* Restaurant

restitution *n.* Wiederherstellung, Wiedererstattung

restoration *n.* Wiederherstellung; Wiedereinsetzung; (art) Restaurierung, Erneuerung

restore *v.* wiederherstellen, wiedereinsetzen; (art) restaurieren, erneuern; (med.) heilen, gesund machen

restrain *v.* abhalten, zurückhalten, in Schranken halten; unterdrücken, hemmen, hindern; –t *n.* Zurückhaltung; Hindernis, Hemmung, Zwang; Einschränkung; Haft, Gefangenschaft

restrict *v.* beschränken, einschränken; –ion *n.* Verbot, Einschränkung, Vorbehalt

result *n.* Resultat, Ergebnis, Folge; — *v.* folgen, sich ergeben

resume *v.* wiederaufnehmen, wiederanfangen

resurrect *v.* wiedererwecken; –ion *n.* Auferstehung

resuscitate *v.* wiederbeleben (durch künstliche Atmung)

retail *n.* Kleinhandel; Einzelhandel; **at** — im kleinen (or Detail); einzeln; — *v.* im Einzelhandel verkaufen; (coll.) umständlich erzählen; –er *n.* Kleinhändler, Einzelhändler

retain *v.* zurück(be)halten; festhalten, beibehalten; –er *n.* Anhänger, Dienstmann; Vorschuss; (law) Prozessvollmacht, Anwaltshonorar

retaliate *v.* vergelten, Vergeltung üben

retaliation *n.* Wiedervergeltung

retard *v.* verzögern, verspäten; aufhalten

retention *n.* Zurückhalten; Beibehaltung

retina *n.* Retina, Netzhaut

retire *v.* (sich) zurückziehen; pensionieren; (sports) ausscheiden; –ment *n.* Rücktritt, Ausscheiden; Pensionierung; Zurückgehen

retiring *adj.* zurückhaltend, bescheiden

retort *n.* Erwiderung, Entgegnung; (chem.) Retorte; — *v.* zurückgeben, erwidern

retrace *v.* zurückverfolgen, zurückführen

retract *v.* zurückziehen, widerrufen; (med.) zusammenziehen, verkürzen; –able *adj.* einziehbar, zurückziehbar

retread *n.* (tire) neuer Belag; — *v.* neu vulkanisieren; wieder betreten, zurückschreiten

retreat *n.* Rückzug; Zapfenstreich; Zufluchtsort, Zurückgezogenheit; — *v.* zurücktreten, sich zurückziehen; sich zur Ruhe setzen

retrench *v.* beschneiden, verkürzen; auslassen; (sich) einschränken; (mil.) sich verschanzen

retrieve *v.* wiedererlangen, wiederherstellen; ersetzen, gutmachen; (dog) apportieren

retroactive *adj.* rückwirkend

retrogression *n.* Rückgang, Rückwärtsgehen; rückläufige Bewegung

return *n.* Rückkehr, Wiederkehr; Antwort, Erwiderung; (arch.) Seitenflügel; (com.) Rückgabe, Rückzahlung; (law) Wiedervorladung; (med.) Rückfall; (mil.) Bericht, Meldung; (pol.) Wiederwahl; *pl.* Einnahmen, Gewinne; Statistiken; Wahlberichte, Wahlergebnisse; **in** — als Vergeltung; **in** — **for** als Ersatz für; **without** — unentgeltlich, umsonst; **by** — **mail** postwendend; — **match** Revanchepartie; — **ticket** Rückfahrkarte; — **trip** Rückfahrt, Rückreise; — **visit** Gegenbesuch; — *v.* zurückkommen, wiederkehren; antworten, erwidern; (cards) nachspielen; (com.) zurückzahlen, zurückerstatten; (fencing) zurückschlagen; (law) wieder vorladen; (med.) rückfällig sein (*or* werden); (mil.) berichten, melden; (pol.) wählen; **-able** *adj.* zurückzugebend

reunion *n.* Wiedervereinigung; Gesellschaft

reunite *v.* wiedervereinigen, wieder versöhnen

revaluation *n.* Aufwertung, Umwertung

reveal *v.* aufdecken, enthüllen, offenbaren

revel *n.* Trinkgelage, Schwelgerei; — *v.* schwelgen, schwärmen; **-(l)er** *n.* Schwärmer; Nachtschwärmer; **-ry** *n.* lärmende Festlichkeit

revelation *n.* Enthüllung, Offenbarung

revenge *n.* Rache, Revanche; Genugtuung; — *v.* rächen, revanchieren; **-ful** *adj.* rachsüchtig, rächend

revenue *n.* Einkommen; Zoll; *pl.* Einkünfte; — **cutter** Zollkutter; — **stamp** Steuermarke, Banderole

revere *v.* verehren; **-nce** *n.* Verehrung; Verbeugung; **-nce** *v.* hochachten, ehrerbietig grüssen; **-nd** *adj.* ehrwürdig, hochwürdig; **Reverend** *n.* Hochwürden; **-nt(ial)** *adj.* ehrerbietig, ehrfurchtsvoll

reverie, revery *n.* Träumerei, Schwärmerei

reversal *n.* Umkehrung, Umstossung; (mech.) Umsteuerung

reverse *n.* Umkehrung; Rückseite; (fig.) Rückschlag, Schicksalsschlag; Gegenteil; — *adj.* umgekehrt, verkehrt, entgegengesetzt; — *v.* umkehren, umstellen; umstossen; (mech.) umsteuern

revert *v.* umkehren; zurückkommen; wenden; (law) heimfallen

review *n.* Durchsicht, Prüfung; Rückblick, Überblick; (educ.) Wiederholung; (law) Revision; (lit.) Kritik, Rezension; (kritische) Zeitschrift; Rundschau; (mil.) Parade, Truppenschau; (theat.) Revue; — *v.* durchsehen, prüfen; zurückblicken auf; (law) revidieren; (lit.) rezensieren, kritisieren; (mil.) mustern, Parade **abhalten; -er** *n.* Kritiker, Rezensent

revile *v.* schmähen, verun|limpfen

revise *n.* nochmalige Durchsicht, **Revi**sion; — *r.* revidieren, nochmals **durch**sehen

revision *n.* Revision, nochmalige **Durch**sicht

revival *n.* Wiederbelebung, **Wiederauf**leben; Erneuerung; (law) Wiederinkrafttreten; (rel.) Erweckung; **Wieder**geburt; (theat.) Wiederaufführung

revive *v.* wiederbeleben; erneuern, **wieder** einführen; wieder aufleben; erwecken

revoke *v.* widerrufen, aufheben, zurücknehmen; abschwören; (cards) **nicht** bedienen

revolt *n.* Revolte, Empörung, Aufruhr; — *v.* revoltieren, (sich) empören; **-ing** *adj.* aufrührerisch; (fig.) **empörend,** abstossend

revolution *n.* Revolution, Umsturz, Umbruch, Umschwung; Umdrehung; (ast.) Umlauf, Kreislauf; **-ary** *n.* Revolutionär; **-ary** *adj.* revolutionär, Umsturz-; **-ist** *n.* Revolutionär; **-ize** *v.* revolutionieren, aufwiegeln; umgestalten

revolve *v.* sich drehen um, **rotieren,** kreisen; (fig.) erwägen, überlegen

revolver *n.* Revolver

revolving *adj.* sich drehend, Dreh-

revue *n.* Revue

reward *n.* Belohnung, Vergeltung; **Preis;** — *v.* belohnen, vergelten

rewrite *v.* nochmals schreiben, **umschrei**ben

rhapsody *n.* Rhapsodie

Rhenish Palatinate *n.* Rheinpflaz

rhetoric *n.* Rhetorik; **-al** *adj.* **rhetorisch**

rheumatic *adj.* rheumatisch

rheumatism *n.* Rheumatismus

RH-factor *n.* (med.) Rhesusfaktor

rhinoceros *n.* Rhinozeros, **Nashorn**

rhubarb *n.* Rhabarber

rhyme *n.* Reim, Vers, Gedicht; — *v.* **(sich)** reimen, dichten; **-ster** *n.* Verseschmied

rhythm *n.* Rhythmus; **-ic(al)** *adj.* rhythmisch

rib *n.* Rippe; (naut.) Spant; — *v.* rippen; (coll.) spotten; **-bed** *adj.* gerippt, geriffelt

ribbon *n.* Band, Borte; Streifen; **-s** *pl.* Zügel; Fetzen; **typewriter** — Farbband; — *v.* bebändern

rice *n.* Reis; — **paper** Reispapier

rich adj. reich; nahrhaft, kräftig, fett; ergiebig, fruchtbar; (mus.) voll.; (coll.) gepfeffert, gelungen; -es n. pl. Reichtümer, Vermögen; -ness n. Reichtum; Reichhaltigkeit, Gehalt; Pracht

rickety adj. rachitisch; (fig.) gebrechlich, hinfällig, schwach

rid v. befreien, freimachen; get — of loswerden; -dance n. Befreiung

riddle n. Rätsel; Sieb; — v. enträtseln, erraten; sieben

ride n. Ritt, Fahrt; — v. reiten, fahren; — a bicycle radfahren; — at anchor vor Anker liegen; -r n. Reiter; Fahrer, Fahrende; (arch.) Strebe; (com.) Beiblatt; (law) Zusatz

ridge n. Rückgrat, Rücken; (agr.) Furche, Rain; (arch.) First; (geol.) Kamm, Grat; Kette; — v. (sich) furchen

ridgepole n. Dachpfosten

ridicule n. Lächerliches; Spott, Hohn; — v. lächerlich machen, bespötteln

ridiculous adj. lächerlich

riding n. Reiten; Fahren; reitend, fahrend; — boot Reitstiefel; — breeches Reithose; — master Reitlehrer, Stallmeister; — school Reitbahn

riffraff n. Abfall, Ausschuss; (coll.) Gesindel

rifle n. Gewehr, Büchse, Stutzen; — barrel Gewehrlauf; — corps Schützenabteilung; — range Schiessplatz, Scheibenstand; Schussweite; — v. rauben, plündern

rifleman n. Scharfschütze; (mil.) Jäger

rift n. Riss, Spalte, Ritze, Sprung

rig n. Takelung; — v. aufputzen; ausrüsten; (naut.) auftakeln; -ging n. Takelage

right n. Recht; Richtige; Rechte, rechte Seite; Anrecht, Vorrecht, Anspruch; all -s reserved alle Rechte vorbehalten; by -s von Rechts wegen, eigentlich; — and wrong Gutes und Böses; to the — nach rechts; — adj. recht, richtig; gerade; (law) rechtmässig, gesetzmässig, gerecht; — angle rechter Winkel; — adv. ganz, gänzlich; gerade, genau; augenblicklich; geradeswegs; richtig; all — schon gut, einverstanden; be — recht haben; übereinstimmen; it serves him — es geschieht ihm recht; — against gerade gegenüber; — ahead geradeaus; — away sofort, sogleich; — off gleich (fort), gleich davon; — on geradezu, set — berichtigen, zurechtweisen; reparieren; —! interj. recht! gut! richtig! — v. (avi.) abfangen, abschiessen; (law) Recht verschaffen; (naut.) aufrichten; -eous adj. recht-

schaffen, redlich; gerecht; -ist n. Rechtsradikale

rightabout n. Rechtswendung

right-angled adj. rechtwinklig

right-hand adj. rechtshändig; recht, rechtschaffen; to the — side nach rechts, zur rechten Seite (or Hand)

rigid adj. starr, steif; unbeugsam, nachsichtslos; -ity n. Starrheit, Steifheit; Festigkeit; Strenge, Härte; Unbeugsamkeit

rigmarole n. Geschwätz, Salbaderei

rigor n. Strenge, Härte; (med.) Schüttelfrost; — mortis Leichenstarre, Totenstarre; -ous adj. streng, hart; scharf, genau

rim n. Rand, Krempe; Radkranz, Felge

rime n. Reif, Rauhfrost

rind n. Rinde, Borke; Schale

ring n. Ring; Kreis, Reif; Öse, Öhr; (mus.) Schall, Klang; Geläute; — finger Ringfinger; — v. beringen; umringen; kreisen; klingen, klingeln, läuten; — in einläuten; — out ausläuten; — the bell die Glocke läuten; (coll.) Lärm schlagen; — up anrufen; -ing n. Klingeln; -ing adj. klingelnd; brausend

ringleader n. Rädelsführer, Anführer

ringworm n. Ringelflechte

rink n. Eisbahn; Rollschuhbahn

rinse v. (aus)spülen, ausschwenken

riot n. Aufstand, Aufruhr; Lärm, Tumult; — r. Aufruhr stiften; lärmen, toben; schwelgen; -er n. Aufrührer, Meuterer; Schwelger; -ous adj. aufrührerisch; lärmend, schwelgerisch; liederlich

rip n. Riss; (coll.) Kerl; — cord Reissleine; — v. (zer)reissen; auftrennen; -ping adj. aufreissend; (sl.) famos

ripe adj. reif; -n v. reifen

ripple n. kleine Welle; Kräuselung; Geriesel; — v. (sich) kräuseln; plätschern, rieseln

rise n. Aufstehen; Aufsteigen; Aufstieg; Erhöhung, Steigung; Zuwachs, Zunahme; Steigerung; Ursprung; (arch.) Bogenhöhe, Durchgang; (com.) Steigen, Aufschlag; (mus.) Anschwellen; (sun) Sonnenaufgang; — v. aufstehen, sich erheben, aufsteigen; emporkommen, heraufkommen; aufgehen; entstehen, wachsen, zunehmen; (mus.) anschwellen; — above übertreffen; -r n. Aufstehende; Frühaufsteher; Aufständische

risk n. Risiko, Gefahr, Wagnis; — v. riskieren, wagen, aufs Spiel setzen; -y adj. riskant, gefährlich, gewagt

ritual n. Ritual; — adj. rituell, feierlich

rival n. Rivale, Nebenbuhler, Konkurrent; — *adj.* wetteifernd, nebenbuhlerisch, Konkurrenz-; — *v.* rivalisieren, wetteifern, konkurrieren; -ry *n.* Rivalität, Konkurrenz; Wetteifer

river *n.* Fluss, Strom; — **bed** Flussbett; — **horse** Flusspferd

riverside *n.* Flussufer; Flussseite

rivet *n.* Niet(e); — *v.* (ver)nieten; befestigen, heften

roach *n.* Küchenschabe; (ichth.) Plötze, Rotauge

road *n.* Strasse, Weg; Fahrbahn; (min.) Strecke; (naut.) Reede; (coll.) Eisenbahn; **main** — Hauptstrasse; **paved** — Pflasterstrasse; — **metal** Schotter; -ster *n.* Tourenwagen

roadblock *n.* Strassensperre; Hindernis

roadway *n.* Fahrdamm; Strassendamm; (min.) Förderbahn

roam *v.* umherstreifen, durchstreifen

roar *n.* Gebrüll; Brausen, Krachen; Rollen, Donnern; — *v.* brüllen; brausen, krachen; rollen, donnern; -ing *adj.* brüllend; geräuschvoll; (coll.) kolossal

roast *n.* Braten; — *adj.* — **beef** Roastbeef, Rinderbraten; — *v.* braten, rösten; (mech.) brennen, backen; -er *n.* Röster; Bratrost; Spanferkel, Brathuhn

rob *v.* (be)rauben; -ber *n.* Räuber; -bery *n.* Raub; **highway** -bery Strassenraub

robe *n.* Robe, Staatskleid; Talar, Amtskleid; — *v.* (sich) kleiden; schmücken

robin *n.* Rotkehlchen

robot *n.* Robot; Maschinenmensch

robust *adj.* robust, derb, kräftig

rock *n.* Fels; Stein; Klippe; (coll.) Schaukel; — **bottom** Urboden; Wirklichkeit; — **crystal** Bergkristall; — **garden** Steingarten; — **salt** Steinsalz; — *v.* schwanken, wiegen, schaukeln; -er *n.* Kufe; -er *adj.*, -er **arm** Kipphebel; -ing *adj.* schaukelnd, wiegend; -ing **chair** Schaukelstuhl; -y *adj.* felsig

rocket *n.* Rakete; — **base** *n.* Raketenbasis; **circumlunar** — Mondrakete; **ferry** — Raketenfähre; **multi-stage** — Vielstufenrakete; **retro-** Rückfeuerungsrakete; Bremsrakete; **secondary** — Landerakete

rocket-propelled *adj.* raketengetrieben; — **plane** Raketenflugzeug

rod *n.* Rute, Stab, Stange; **connecting** — Verbindungsstange

rodent *n.* Nagetier

Roger! *interj.* (avi.) Viktor-Viktor!

rogue *n.* Landstreicher· Schurke, Spitzbube

roll *n.* Rolle; Walze, Welle; Semmel, Brötchen; Verzeichnis, Liste; Rollen; Wirbel; (naut.) Schlingern; **call the** —

namentlich aufrufen; — **call** Namensaufruf; (mil.) Appell; — *v.* rollen, walzen; wälzen; wirbeln; (naut.) schlingern; — **the drum** Trommelwirbel schlagen; -er *n.* Rollende, Walzer; Walze, Rolle; (naut.) Sturzsee; (orn.) Roller; Tümmlertaube; -er **bearing** Rollager; -er **coaster** Fahruntersatz; Berg- und Talbahn; -er **skate** Rollschuh; -er **towel** endloses Handtuch; -ing *adj.* rollend; wellenförmig; -ing **mill** Walzwerk; -ing **pin** Nudelholz; -ing **stock** rollendes Material, Wagenpark

rollicking *adj.* ausgelassen, übermütig

roll-top desk *n.* Rollschreibtisch

roly-poly *n.* Teigrolle; (coll.) rundliche Person; — *adj.* kugelrund

Roman *n.* Römer; — *adj.* römisch; — **type** Antiquaschrift

romance *n.* Romanze; Erdichtung, Erzählung; Romantik; **Romance** *adj.* romanisch; — *v.* erdichten; aufschneiden

romantic *adj.* romantisch; -ism *n.* Romantik

romp *n.* Balgerei; (coll.) Range; — *v.* tollen, toben; sich balgen; -ers *n. pl.* Spielanzug

roof *n.* Dach, First; — **of the mouth** Gaumen; — **garden** Dachgarten; — *v.* bedachen, überdachen; (fig.) bergen, schützen; -ing *n.* Dachdeckerarbeit; Bedachung; Dachmaterial

rook *n.* (chess) Turm; (orn.) Saatkrähe; (coll.) Bauernfänger, Betrüger; — *v.* (chess) rochieren; (coll.) betrügen

rookie *n.* Neuling, Anfänger

room *n.* Raum, Platz; Zimmer, Stube; (fig.) Gelegenheit, Spielraum; -er *n.* Mieter, Mitbewohner; -y *adj.* geräumig, weitläufig

roommate *n.* Stubengenosse

roost *n.* Hühnerstange; Hühnerstall; (coll.) Ruheplatz; — *v.* (wie Hühner auf der Stange) sitzen (*or* schlafen); -er *n.* Hahn

root *n.* Wurzel; (gram.) Stammwort; (mus.) Grundton; (fig.) Quelle, Ursache, Ursprung; **take** — Wurzel fassen (*or* schlagen); — *v.* (ein)wurzeln; (um)wühlen; (fig.) einprägen; — **out** ausroden, ausjäten; vertilgen; -ed *adj.* eingewurzelt, verwurzelt; eingebettet, eingelagert; -er *n.* Ausrotter, Vertilger; (sl.) Anhänger

rope *n.* Tau, Seil, Strick, Strang, Schnur; (naut.) Reep; — *v.* mit einem Seil zusammenschnüren (*or* fangen); anseilen

ropedancer, ropewalker *n.* Seiltänzer

rosary *n.* Rosengarten, Rosenbeet; (eccl.) Rosenkranz

rose *n.* Rose; Rosa, Rosenfarbe; Windrose; Rosette; (mech.) Brause; **-tte** *n.* Rosette

rosebud *n.* Rosenknospe

rosebush *n.* Rosenstock, Rosenstrauch

rosewood *n.* Rosenholz

rosin *n.* Geigenharz, Kolophonium; — *v.* mit Harz einreiben (*or* überziehen) harzen

roster *n.* Verzeichnis, Liste; (mil.) Diensttabelle

rostrum *n.* Tribüne, Rednerpult; Schnabel

rosy *adj.* rosig, rosenrot; (fig.) blühend

rot *n.* Fäule, Fäulnis; Verwesung; (sl.) Unsinn, Gewäsch; — *v.* (ver)faulen, verwesen, vermodern, verrotten; (coll.) verkommen; **-ten** *adj.* faul(ig), verfault; stinkend; eitrig; morsch, verfallen; (coll.) verdorben, niederträchtig

rotary *adj.* rotierend, kreisend; sich drehend; — **press** Rotationsmaschine

rotate *v.* rotieren, sich drehen, kreisen; (ab)wechseln

rotation *n.* Rotation, Umdrehung; Abwechslung, Folge

rote *n.* Routine; **by** — durch blosse Übung, rein mechanisch

rotogravure *n.* Fotogravüre

rotor *n.* drehender Zylinder

rotund *adj.* rund, kreisförmig; abgerundet; (mus.) volltönend

rouge *n.* rote Farbe (*or* Schminke), Rouge; (mech.) Polierrot, Englischrot

rough *n.* Rohe, Unbearbeitete, Grobe; — *adj.* roh, erstmalig; rauh, holprig, uneben; ungebildet; (naut.) stürmisch; — **draft** erster Überschlag (*or* Entwurf); **-en** *v.* rauhen; rauh machen (*or* werden); (fig.) verwildern; **-ness** *n.* Rauheit, Roheit; Heftigkeit

rough-and-ready *adj.* grob aber zuverlässig; gerade recht

round *n.* Runde; Kreis; Kreislauf, Umlauf; (arch.) Rundgang; (mil.) Salve, Ladung; (mus.) Rundgesang; — *adj.* rund, kreisförmig; abgerundet; voll, ganz; beträchtlich; offen; gründlich; **make** — abrunden; — **number** runde Zahl; — **steak** rundes Steak (vom Rindsschenkel); — **table** grüner Tisch; Forum; Diskussionsgruppe; — **trip** Rundreise; — *adv.* ringsumher, in der Runde; **all the year** — das ganze Jahr hindurch; — *v.* (ab)runden; umgeben, einfassen; umfahren, umbiegen; (naut.) umsegeln; — **up** zusammentreiben,

einkreisen; **-ness** *n.* Rundung, Rundheit; (fig.) Geradheit, Offenheit

roundabout *adj.* weitläufig, umständlich; (fig.) umfassend, weitschauend

roundhouse *n.* (rail.) Lokomotivenschuppen; (naut.) Hinterdeckkajüte

roundup *n.* Zusammentreiben, Einkreisung

rouse *v.* (auf)wecken, aufwachen; (hunting) aufjagen, aufstöbern; (fig.) erregen, anregen

roustabout *n.* Dockarbeiter; Gelegenheitsarbeiter; Handlanger

rout *n.* Bande, Rotte; Rudel; Flucht; — *v.* aufstöbern; in die Flucht schlagen, vernichten

route *n.* Route, Strasse; Strecke

rove *v.* umherstreifen, umherwandern; **-r** *n.* Landstreicher, Vagabund

row *n.* Rudern; Reihe, Linie; Lärm, Prügelei; — *v.* rudern; (auf)reihen, anreihen; lärmen, prügeln; (coll.) ausschelten; verderben; **-dy** *n.* Rowdy, Raufbold, Strolch; **-dy** *adj.* lärmend, händelsüchtig; gewalttätig, roh

rowboat *n.* Ruderboot

royal *adj.* königlich; (fig.) fürstlich, prächtig; **-ist** *n.* Royalist; **-ty** *n.* Königtum; Königshaus; Mitglied der königlichen Familie; (lit.) Tantieme

rub *n.* Reiben, Abreibung; (coll.) Klemme; Stichelei; — *v.* reiben; (ab)wischen, einreiben; (ab)scheuern, putzen; — **against** anstossen, anstreifen; — **down** abreiben, striegeln; (coll.) ausschimpfen; **-ber** *n.* Reiber; Waschlappen

rubber *n.* Gummi; Gummireifen; **-s** *n. pl.* Gummischuhe; **hard** — Hartgummi; — **band** Gummiband; — **cement** Klebestoff; — **gasket** Gummidichtung; — **plant** Gummipflanze; (mech.) Kautschukfabrik; — **stamp** Gummistempel; (coll.) automatische Zustimmung; **-ize** *v.* gummieren, mit Gummi beziehen

rubbish *n.* Schutt, Kehricht; Plunder, Schund; Wirrwarr; (coll.) Unsinn

rubble *n.* Geschiebe, Geröll; Trümmergestein

rubdown *n.* Abreibung; — *v.* abreiben

ruby *n.* Rubin; Rubinrot

rudder *n.* Ruder; Steuerruder; (avi.) Seitensteuer

rude *adj.* grob, unhöflich, roh; wild, heftig; rauh; (fig.) ungebildet, kunstlos; **-ness** *n.* Grobheit, Roheit; Rauheit

rudiment *n.* Rudiment, Ansatz

ruffian *n.* Grobian, Raufbold; Schuft, Lump; — *adj.* roh, wüst, rauflustig

ruffle *n.* Manschette; Halskrause; Kräu-

seln; (mil.) Trommelwirbel; (fig.) Unruhe, Aufregung; — v. falten, kräuseln;
zerknittern, zerdrücken; (fig.) beunruhigen

rug n. Decke, Teppich; Vorleger; — v.
zerren

rugged adj. rauh; zottig, zerzaust; uneben, gefurcht

ruin n. Ruin; Zusammenbruch, Untergang, Verderben; pl. Ruinen; — v.
ruinieren, verderben; zerstören, verheeren; –ous adj. verfallen, baufällig,
schadhaft; verderblich

rule n. Lineal; Masstab; Regel, Verordnung, Verfügung, Vorschrift; Norm,
Richtschnur; (law) Rechtsgrundsatz;
(pol.) Regierung, Geschäftsordnung; as
a — in der Regel; — of three Regelde-
tri; standard — Normalmass; — v.
linieren; regeln, anordnen, festsetzen;
leiten, regieren, beherrschen; entscheiden, verfügen; –r n. Lineal; Herrscher

ruling n. Regelung; (law) Entscheidung;
— adj. herrschend; vorherrschen !

rum n. Rum; — adj. seltsam, wunderlich

rumba n. Rumba; — v. Rumba tanzen

rumble v. rumpeln, rasseln

ruminant n. Wiederkäuer; — adj. wieder-
käuend; (coll.) nachdenklich

ruminate v. wiederkäuen; (coll.) grübeln,
nachdenken

rummage n. Durchsuchen, Kramen;
Umwälzung; — sale Ramschverkauf;
— v. durchsuchen, durchstöbern; wühlen

rumor n. Gerücht, Gerede; — v. Gerüchte
verbreiten (or aussprengen)

rump n. Rumpf; Rest; (orn.) Bürzel;
(zool.) Hinterteil, Kreuz, Steiss

run n. Lauf; Laufen, Rennen; Verlauf,
Gang; Ausflug, Reise; Bach, Fluss;
(com.) Sorte; Andrang, Zulauf, Nachfrage; (mech.) Betrieb, Leistung;
(mus.) Lauf; (naut.) Route; Geschwindigkeit; (theat.) Aufführungsserie; in
the long — auf die Dauer; am Ende;
— v. rennen, laufen, eilen; fliessen;
strömen, rinnen; umlaufen, zirkulieren;
leiten, betreiben; lauten; — across
zufällig treffen, in die Quere kommen;
— aground auflaufen, scheitern; —
away durchgehen, davonlaufen; —
down (her)ablaufen; abhetzen; (naut.)
auf Grund setzen; (coll.) schlecht
machen; — for office sich um ein Amt
bewerben; — into sich belaufen; treffen;
— off davonlaufen, durchgehen; —
over überfahren; überlaufen; — out of
sich ausgeben, sich erschöpfen; — the
risk Gefahr laufen, riskieren; –ner n.

Renner, Läufer; (bot.) Ausläufer;
(mech.) Schieber; Kufe; –ning n.
Rennen; Lauf, Gang; –ning adj. laufend, rennend, fliessend; ununterbrochen; –ning board Trittbrett; –ning
gear Getriebe; –ning mate (pol.)
Nebenkandidat; (race) Schrittmacher;
–ning water fliessendes Wasser

runaway n. Flüchtling, Ausreisser; Durchgänger

run-down adj. abfliessend, ablaufend;
erschöpft, heruntergebracht

rung n. Sprosse

runner-up n. Zweite (im Endkampf)

runway n. Lauf; Tierpfad; (avi.) Rollbahn

rupture n. Bruch; — v. brechen; sprengen

rural adj. ländlich; bäuerlich; Land-

ruse n. List, Kunstgriff

rush n. Anstrum, Andráng; (bot.) Binse;
— hours Hauptverkehrsstunden,
Hauptgeschäftsstunden; — order
Eilauftrag; — v. (sich) stürzen, drängen; eilen, jagen, stürmen; schiessen,
rauschen

Russia n. Russland

Russian n. Russe; — adj. russisch

rust n. Rost, Moderfleck; (bot.) Brand;
(fig.) Untätigkeit; — v. (ver)rosten;
modern; –y adj. rostig, verrostet;
moderfleckig; (bot.) brandig; (fig.)
rostfarben, abgetragen, verschossen

rustic n. Landmann; (arch.) Bossenwerk;
— adj. ländlich, bäuerisch

rustle n. Rascheln, Rauschen; — v.
rascheln, rauschen; (coll.) sich rühren
(or dranhalten)

rustproof adj. rostsicher

rut n. Geleise; (zool.) Brunst, Brunft; —
v. furchen; brunsten, brunfften

rutabaga n. Kohlrübe

ruthless adj. unbarmherzig, grausam

rye n. Roggen; — field Roggenfeld

S

sabbath n. Sabbat; (fig.) Ruhetag

saber, sabre n. Säbel, Schwert

sable n. Zobel; Zobelfell

sabotage n. Sabotage

saboteur n. Saboteur

SAC (Strategic Air Command) n. Strate-
gisches Luftkommando

saccharine n. Sacharin

sack n. Sack, Tasche; (mil.) Plünderung;
(coll.) Laufpass, Entlassung; — v. einsacken; plündern; entlassen

sackcloth n. Sackleinen

sacrament n. Sakrament

sacred adj. heilig; geweiht; sakral, geistlich

sacrifice n. Opfer; — v. opfern, aufs Spiel setzen; mit Verlust verkaufen; — oneself sich aufopfern

sacrilege n. Sakrileg, Kirchenschändung

sad adj. traurig, kläglich, jämmerlich; schlimm; dunkel; — **sack** (sl.) nasser Sack, trübe Tasse, Kaczmarek; –den v. (sich) betrüben; schwärzen; –ness n. Traurigkeit, Schwermut

saddle n. Sattel; — horse Reitpferd; — v. satteln

saddlebag n. Satteltasche

safari n. Safari, Expedition

safe n. Safe, Bankfach; Geldschrank; — adj. sicher, unversehrt; ausser Gefahr; gesund; zuverlässig; — and sound frisch und gesund; –ty n. Sicherheit; –ty belt Rettungsgürtel; (avi.) Anschnallgurt; –ty catch Sicherheitskette; –ty island Schutzinsel; –ty pin Sicherheitsnadel; –ty valve Sicherheitsventil

safebreaker n. Geldschrankknacker

safe-conduct n. sicheres Geleit; Schutzbrief

safe-deposit adj. gesichert; — box einbruchssicherer Schrank

safeguard n. Schutz; Eskorte, Konvoy; — v. beschützen, schirmen

safelight n. Farbfilter; Dunkelkammerlampe

saffron n. Safran

sag n. Senkung; — v. sacken, sich senken, durchhängen, nachgeben; (naut.) nach Lee treiben

saga n. Sage

sage n. Weise; (bot.) Salbei; — adj. weise, verständig

sagebrush n. Wermut, Edelraute

Sagittarius n. Schütze

sail n. Segel; Segelfahrt; — v. segeln; fahren, durchsegeln; –ing n. Segeln; Segelschiffahrt; –ings n. pl. Schiffsabfahrtzeiten; –ing adj. segelnd; –or n. Matrose, Seemann

sailboat n. Segelboot

sailfish n. fliegender Fisch

saint n. Heilige; guardian — Schutzheilige; Saint adj. Sankt, Heilige; — v. heiligsprechen; –ly adj. heilig, geheiligt; fromm

sake n. for God's — um Gottes willen; for my — meinetwegen

salad n. Salat; — bowl Salatschüssel; — dressing Salatsosse

salamander n. Salamander, Molch

salary n. Gehalt, Besoldung

sale n. Verkauf, Absatz; Umsatz; Auktion; clearance — Räumungsausverkauf; –s tax Verkaufssteuer; — price Verkaufspreis

salesclerk n. Verkäufer(in)

salesman n. Vertreter; traveling — Geschäftsreisende; –ship n. Verkaufsgewandtheit, Kunst des Verkaufens

salesroom n. Verkaufsraum

saliva n. Speichel

sallow adj. blass, gleich, gelblich

salmon n. Salm, Lachs; Lachsfarbe; — adj. lachsfarben; — trout Lachsforelle

saloon n. Salon, Empfangszimmer; Saal; (coll.) Kneipe

salt n. Salz; (fig.) Würze, Witz; — adj. salzig, gesalzen, gepökelt; — mine Saline; — water Salzwasser, Seewasser; — v. (ein) salzen, pökeln; –y adj. salzig; pikant

saltpeter, saltpetre n. Salpeter

saltshaker n. Salzstreuer

salutation n. Begrüssung; Gruss

salute n. Gruss; (mil.) Salut, Salutieren; — v. grüssen, salutieren

salvation n. Erlösung; Rettung

salve n. Salbe, Heilmittel; — v. salben, heilen; beruhigen; retten

same adj. nämlich, gleich; ebenerwähnt, vorerwähnt, besagt; derselbe, dieselbe, dasselbe; (fig.) einförmig, eintönig; all the — dessenungeachtet, gleichwohl; it's all the — to me es ist mir einerlei (or ganz gleich); –ness n. Gleichheit, Identität; Eintönigkeit

sample n. Probe, Muster; — v. (aus)probieren, kosten; Proben zeigen (or nehmen); –r n. Probennehmer; Mustersticktuch

sanatorium n. Sanatorium, Heilanstalt

sanctify v. weihen; heiligen

sanctimonious adj. frömmelnd, scheinheilig

sanction n. Sanktion, Sühnemassnahme; Genehmigung, Bestätigung; Gesetz; — v. sanktionieren, gutheissen, bestätigen

sanctuary n. Heiligtum, Freistätte; Tempel

sanctum n. heilige Stätte; (fig.) Privatgemach

sand n. Sand; — pit Sandgrube; –y adj. sand(art)ig

sandal n. Sandale

sandalwood n. Sandelbaum, Sandelholz

sandbag n. Sandsack; — v. mit Sandsäcken verstopfen (or niederschlagen)

sandblast n. Sandstrahlgebläse

sandbox n. Sandkiste; (rail.) Sandstreuer

sandpaper n. Sandpapier

sandstone n. Sandstein

sandstorm n. Sandsturm

sandwich n. Sandwich; belegtes Brot; — man Plakatträger; — v. zusammenklappen, aufeinanderlegen; einlegen sane *adj.* geistig gesund, vernünftig

sanguine *adj.* vollblütig, blutreich; (fig.) sanguinisch, zuversichtlich

sanitary *adj.* sanitär; Gesundheits-

sanitation *n.* Gesundheitswesen

sanity *n.* geistige Gesundheit

sap *n.* Saft; (mil.) Sappe, Laufgraben; (fig.) Lebenskraft, Mark; (coll.) Schwachkopf; — *v.* untergraben; -ling *n.* junger Baum; (coll.) Grünschnabel

sapphire *n.* Saphir; Saphirblau

sarcasm *n.* Sarkasmus, bitterer Spott

sarcastic *adj.* sarkastisch

sardine *n.* Sardine

sash *n.* Fensterrahmen; (mil.) Feldbinde, Schärpe

Satan *n.* Satan

satanic *adj.* satanisch

satchel *n.* Schulmappe; Umhängetasche

sateen *n.* Satin

satelite *n.* Satellit, Trabant

satin *n.* Atlas

satire *n.* Satire

satiric(al) *adj.* satirisch

satirize *v.* verspotten, bespötteln

satisfaction *n.* Genugtuung, Befriedigung; Zufriedenheit; Bezahlung, Tilgung

satisfactory *adj.* befriedigend, zufriedenstellend; genügend

satisfy *v.* genügen, befriedigen; zufriedenstellen; bezahlen; sühnen; überzeugen

saturate *v.* sättigen, völlig durchdringen

saturation *n.* (chem.) Sättigung; Durchwässerung; (phot.) Leuchtkraft; — point Sättigungspunkt

Saturday *n.* Sonnabend, Samstag

satyr *n.* Satyr

sauce *n.* Sosse, Tunke; (coll.) Würze; — *v.* mit einer Sosse versehen, würzen

saucer *n.* Untertasse; Untersatz

saucy *adj.* frech, unverschämt; (coll.) pikant

sauerkraut *n.* Sauerkraut

sausage *n.* Wurst

savage *n.* Wilde, Barbar; — *adj.* wild, wüst; roh, barbarisch; -ry *n.* Wildheit, Roheit; Barbarei

save *v.* retten, bergen; aufbewahren; erlösen; (er)sparen, schonen; — *prep.* ausser, ausgenommen; unbeschadet, ohne; -r *n.* Retter; Sparer

saving *n.* Rettung; *pl.* Ersparnisse; -s bank Sparkasse; — *adj.* rettend; sparsam, haushälterisch; vorbehaltend

savio(u)r *n.* Retter, Erlöser; Savior Heiland

saw *n.* Säge; — *v.* sägen

sawdust *n.* Sägespäne, Sägemehl

sawmill *n.* Sägemühle, Schneidemühle

Saxony *n.* Sachsen

saxophone *n.* Saxophon

say *n.* Rede, Meinung, Wort; — *v.* sagen, sprechen; berichten; aufsagen, vortragen; anführen, erwähnen; entscheiden; widersprechen, bestreiten; meinen; — **mass** Messe lesen; **that is to** — das heisst; -ing *n.* Redensart, Ausspruch; Gerede; Sprichwort

scab *n.* Schorf, Räude; (coll.) Lump; (sl.) Streikbrecher

scabbard *n.* Scheide

scaffold *n.* Schaffott; (arch.) Gerüst; (theat.) Schaubühne, Zuschauertribüne; -ing *n.* Gerüst; Rüstmaterial

scald *n.* Verbrühung, Brandwunde; — *v.* verbrennen, verbrühen; abkochen, ausbrühen

scale *n.* Schuppe; (math.) Gradeinteilung, Masstab, Zahlensystem; (mech.) Waage, Waagschale; (mus.) Tonleiter, Skala; (fig.) Stufenleiter, Abstufung; platform — Brückenwaage; — *v.* schuppen, abschaben, abscharren; (ab)wiegen, wägen; (art) richtig darstellen; (mil.) erstürmen, ersteigen; (fig.) prüfen

scallop *n.* Kammuschel; Muschelform; Langette, Auszackung; — *v.* in der Schale (*or* mit geriebener Semmel) zubereiten

scalp *n.* Skalp, Kopfhaut; (coll.) Perücke; — *v.* skalpieren; (com.) schwarzhandeln, spekulieren, schachern; -er *n.* Skalpierende; Spekulant; **ticket -er** Schwarzhändler für Eintrittskarten

scamp *n.* Schuft; Taugenichts; -er *n.* Pfuscher; Ausreisser

scandal *n.* Skandal; -ize *v.* Ärgernis geben; -ous *adj.* skandalös

Scandinavian *n.* Skandinavier; — *adj.* skandinavisch

scant(y) *adj.* knapp, kärguen, _ _ug; beschränkt

scapegoat *n.* Sündenbock

scar *n.* Narbe, Schramme; Klippe, Steilhang; — *v.* schrammen; vernarben

scarab(aeous) *n.* Mistkäfer; Skarabäus

scarce *adj.* selten, rar; spärlich, knapp; -ly *adv.* kaum

scarcity *n.* Seltenheit; Teuerung, Mangel

scare *n.* Schrecken, Panik; — *v.* erschrecken, scheuchen

scarecrow *n.* Vogelscheuche; Schreckbild

scarf *n.* Schal, Halstuch; Schärpe; (mech.) Lasche

scarfpin *n.* Schalnadel; Krawattennadel

scarlet *n.* Scharlach, Scharlachrot; — *adj.* scharlachrot, scharlachfarben; — **fever** Scharlachfieber

scatter *v.* (sich) zerstreuen, verbreiten; ausstreuen

scatterbrained *adj.* flatterhaft, zerstreut, faselig

scavenger *n.* Strassenkehrer; (enth.) Aaskäfer; Mistkäfer; (zool.) Aasgeier

scenario *n.* Drehbuch, Filmmanuskript

scenarist *n.* Drehbuchautor

scene *n.* Szene, Auftritt; Schauplatz; *pl.* Kulissen, Dekoration; –ry *n.* Szenerie, Gegend, Bild; (theat.) Dekoration

scenic(al) *adj.* szenisch, dramatisch; malerisch

scent *n.* Geruch; Duft, Wohlgeruch; (hunting) Witterung, Fährte; — *v.* riechen; durchduften; wittern

scepter, sceptre *n.* Zepter

sceptic(al) *adj.* skeptisch, zweifelnd

schedule *n.* Zettel; Verzeichnis, Tabelle; Fahrplan; — *v.* aufzeichnen, festlegen; anhängen

schematic *adj.* schematisch

scheme *n.* Schema; Plan, System; — *v.* schematisieren, planen, entwerfen; (coll.) Ränke schmieden; –r *n.* Plänemacher, Projektemacher; (coll.) Ränkeschmied

schism *n.* Schisma

scholar *n.* Schüler; Gelehrte; (educ.) Stipendiat; –ly *adj.* gelehrt; –ship *n.* Gelehrsamkeit; (educ.) Stipendium

school *n.* Schule; (ichth.) Zug; (whales) Herde; **high** — Mittelschule, höhere Schule; — *v.* schulen, unterrichten, bilden; –ing *n.* Schulunterricht; Schulzucht

schoolhouse *n.* Schulhaus, Schulgebäude

schoolteacher *n.* Schullehrer

schooner *n.* Schoner

science *n.* Wissenschaft; Kenntnis, Kunst

scientific *adj.* wissenschaftlich, gelehrt; systematisch

scientist *n.* Gelehrte, Wissenschaftler; Forscher

scissors *n. pl.* Schere

sclerosis *n.* Sklerose, Verkalkung; Gewebeverhärtung

scold *n.* Schelter; — *v.* schelten, zanken, keifen; –ing *n.* Schelte

scoop *n.* Schaufel, Schippe; Schöpfkelle; (geol.) Höhlung, Vertiefung; (med.) Spatel; (newspaper sl.) Sensationsnachricht; (coll.) Gewinn; — *v.* (aus)schaufeln; (aus)schöpfen; aushöhlen; (coll.) zusammenscharren

scooter *n.* Segelschlitten; (toy) Roller

scope *n.* Ausdehnung, Reichweite, Spielraum; Gesichtskreis; Absicht, Zweck, Ziel

scorch *v.* rösten, versengen, verbrennen; (coll.) spotten; (sl.) dahinsausen

score *n.* Kerbe; Rechnung, Zeche; Schuld,

Posten; zwanzig Stück; (mus.) Partitur; (sports) Spielstand **what's the** —? wie steht das Spiel? — *v.* kerben; aufschreiben; (mus.) instrumentieren; (sports) Spielstand verzeichnen, Punkte gewinnen

scorn *n.* Verachtung; Hohn, Spott; — *v.* geringschätzen, verachten; verhöhnen; –ful *adj.* verächtlich; höhnisch, spöttisch

scorpion *n.* Skorpion

Scot *n.* Schotte; –ch *adj.*, –tish *adj.* schottisch

scoundrel *n.* Schurke, Schuft, Lump

scour *v.* scheuern, reinigen; entfetten; eilen, jagen; durchstöbern; –ge *n.* Geissel; **Peitsche; Rute;** –ge *v.* geisseln, peitschen; strafen

scout *n.* Späher, Kundschafter; Aufklärer; **boy** — Pfadfinder; **girl** — Pfandfinderin; — *v.* spähen, kundschaften; aufklären

scoutmaster *n.* Pfadfinderführer

scowl *n.* mürrischer Blick, finsteres Aussehen; — *v.* finster (*or* mürrisch) blicken

scramble *v.* strampeln; klettern, sich reissen (um); — *n.* (mil.) Alarmstart; –d *adj.*, –d **eggs** Rühreier

scrap *n.* Stückchen, Brocken; Bruchstück; Bild, Ausschnitt; *pl.* Grieben; Abfall; — **heap** Abfallhaufen; — **iron** Abfalleisen, Alteisen; — *v.* kämpfen; boxen; sich prügeln

scrape *n.* Schaben, Kratzen, Scharren; Kratzfuss; (coll.) Klemme, Patsche; — *v.* (ab)schaben, (ab)kratzen, (ab)scharren; (mus.) fiedeln; –r *n.* Kratzer; Schaber; Fussabtreter; (mus.) Fiedler

scratch *n.* Ritz, Riss, Schramme; Ausgangspunkt; (sports) Strich, Linie; — **paper** Schmierpapier; — *v.* (zer)kratzen, ritzen, schrammen; (aus)streichen; (coll.) kritzeln, schmieren

scrawl *n.* Gekritzel; — *v.* (be)kritzeln

scrawny *adj.* dünn, mager, knochig

scream *n.* Geschrei, Gekreisch; — *v.* schreien, kreischen

screech *n.* Schrei, Gekreisch; — *v.* kreischen, schrillen, schreien

screen *n.* Schirm; Schutz(wand); (arch.) Lettner, Schranke; (film) Leinwand, Bildfläche; (mech.) Sieb; — *v.* beschirmen, (be)schützen; decken; geheimhalten; (film) verfilmen; abblenden; (mech.) (durch)sieben

screw *n.* Schraube; Schraubengewinde; Korkenzieher; (fig.) Druck; — **driver** Schraubenzieher; — **propeller** Schiffsschraube; — *v.* (fest)schrauben; (fig.)

verdrehen, verzerren, verziehen; bedrängen, drücken; klemmen

scribble *n.* Gekritzel, Geschmiere; — *v.* kritzeln, beschmieren

scribe *n.* Schreiber, Sekretär; (mech.) Markierinstrument; — *v.* schreiben; markieren

scrimmage *n.* Gedränge; Handgemenge, Getümmel

scrip *n.* Zettel; (com.) Interimsaktie; (coll.) Papiergeld; -t *n.* Schrift; Handschrift; Manuskript; (film) Drehbuch; (law) Originaldokument; (theat.) Rollenbuch, Textbuch; -tural *adj.* schriftmässig, biblisch

Scripture *n.* Heilige Schrift, Bibel; Bibelstelle

scroll *n.* Pergamentrolle; Papierrolle; Liste, Entwurf; (arch.) Spirale, Schnecke, Schnörkel; — **saw** Bogensäge; — *v.* eintragen; entwerfen, aufsetzen; (auf)rollen

scrollwork *n.* Verschnörkelung

scrub *n.* Gestrüpp, Busch(werk); (coll.) Packesel; — *v.* schrubben, scheuern; (coll.) sich plagen; -ber *n.* Schrubber, Scheuerbürste

scruple *n.* Skrupel, Zweifel, Bedenklichkeit; (fig.) Kleinigkeit; — *v.* Bedenken haben; Anstand nehmen

scrupulous *adj.* allzu bedenklich, ängstlich; gewissenhaft, peinlich

scrutinize *v.* erforschen, prüfen, untersuchen

scrutiny *n.* Nachprüfung; Forschen, genaue Untersuchung

scuff *n.* watschelnder Gang, Schlurfen; — *v.* schlurfen, schlorren; abnutzen; -le *n.* Balgerei, Handgemenge, Getümmel; -le *v.* sich balgen, raufen, handgemein werden

sculptor *n.* Bildhauer; Bildschnitzer

sculpture *n.* Bildhauerarbeit, Skulptur; Bildhauerkunst, Holzschnitzkunst; — *v.* meisseln, aushauen; modellieren

scum *n.* Schaum; (mech.) Schlacke; (coll.) Abschaum; — *v.* abschäumen; (mech.) entschlakken

scurrilous *adj.* gemein, pöbelhaft, zotig

scurvy *n.* Skorbut; — *adj.* schändlich, niederträchtig

scuttle *n.* Kohlenkiste, Kohleneimer; rascher Schritt; (arch.) Luke; (naut.) Bullauge; — *v.* eilen; (naut.) versenken, anbohren

scuttlebutt *n.* (naut.) Trinkwasserbrunnen; (sl.) Latrinengerücht

scythe *n.* Sense, Sichel

sea *n.* See; Meer; Seegang; **heavy** (*or* **rough**) — hochgehende See; — **breeze**

Seewind; — **food** Seefische; — **gull** Seemöve; — **horse** Seepferdchen; — **level** Meeresspiegel; — **urchin** Seeigel; — **wall** Uferdamm, Mole

seaboard *n.* Meeresufer, Seeküste; — *adj.* am Meer gelegen

seacoast *n.* Meeresküste

seagoing *adj.* die offene See befahrend; — **vessel** Ozeanschiff

seal *n.* Siegel, Stempel; (mech.) Verschluss; (zool.) Seehund, Robbe; — *v.* versiegeln, verschliessen; (fig.) besiegeln bestätigen; -ing *n.* Siegeln; -ing *adj* -ing **wax** Siegellack

sealskin *n.* Seehundsfell; Seal

seam *n.* Saum, Naht; (geol.) Schicht, Flöz; (med.) Narbe; Falte; — *v.* säumen, zusammennähen; schrammen, furchen; -less *adj.* nahtlos; -stress *n.* Näherin

seaplane *n.* Seeflugzeug

seaport *n.* Seehafen, Hafenstadt

sear *v.* brennen, versengen; (fig.) brandmarken

search *n.* Suche; Untersuchung, Durchsuchung; Forschung, Nachforschung; **in** — **of** auf der Suche nach; — *v.* suchen; untersuchen, durchsuchen; (nach)forschen; sondieren

searchlight *n.* Scheinwerfer

seashore *n.* Seeküste

seaside *n.* Strand; Meeresküste

season *n.* Jahreszeit; Saison; — **ticket** Dauerkarte, Abonnementskarte; — *v.* würzen; trocknen; gewöhnen, akklimatisieren; -able *adj.* zeigemäss, passend; -al *adj.* der Jahreszeit entsprechend; Saison-; -ed *adj.* gewürzt; getrocknet

seat *n.* Sitz, Stuhl; Platz; Wohnsitz; Schauplatz; Gesäss; front — Vordersitz; — **cover** Sitzüberzug; — *v.* (hin)setzen; (pol.) einsetzen, anstellen; **be** -ed sitzen; sich setzen; -ing *n.* Bestuhlung; -ing *adj.* -ing **capacity** Zahl der Sitzplätze

seaward *adj.* seewärts gerichtet; -s *adv.* seewärts

seaweed *n.* Tang; Alge

seaworthy *adj.* seefest, seetüchtig; **seeklar**

secede *v.* abfallen, ausscheiden; sich trennen

secession *n.* Abfall, Absonderung; Spaltung

seclude *v.* absondern; ausschliessen

seclusion *n.* Zurückgezogenheit, Abgeschiedenheit

second *n.* Sekunde; Sekundant, Beistand; Zweite; — *adj.* zweite; nächst, folgend, nachstehend, untergeordnet; — **childhood** zweiter Frühling; — **hand** Sekun-

denzeiger; — **lieutenant** Leutnant; —
v. sekundieren, beistehen, unterstützen; **-ly** *adv.* zweitens; **-ary** *adj.* sekundär; untergeordnet; Neben-, Hilfs-;
-ary school Höhere Schule

second-degree burn *n.* Verbrennung zweiten Grades

secondhand *adj.* aus zweiter Hand, gebraucht; antiquarisch; — **dealer** Alt-
warenhändler; Antiquar; — **shop** Alt-
warenhandlung; (books) Antiquariat

second-ráte *adj.* zweitrangig, minderwertig

secrecy *n.* Verschwiegenheit, Heimlichkeit; Verborgenheit

secret *n.* Geheimnis; **in** — insgeheim, im
Vertrauen; — *adj.* geheim, heimlich;
verborgen; — **service** Geheimdienst;
-ly *adv.* im geheimen, im verborgenen;
-ive *adj.* verschwiegen, geheimtuerisch;
(med.) ausscheidend

secretariat *n.* Sekretariat; Kanzlei

secretary . *n.* Sekretär; Schriftführer;
(orn.) Sekretärvogel; (pol.) Minister;
private — Privatsekretär

secrete *v.* verstecken, verbergen; (med.)
ausscheiden, absondern

secretion *n.* Absonerung, Ausscheidung

sect *n.* Sekte; **-arian** *n.,* **-ary** *n.* Sektierer;
-arian *adj.* sektiererisch

section *n.* Sektion; Schnitt, Durchschnitt;
Abschnitt, Abteilung; (med.) Sezie-
rung; (mil.) Zug; (rail.) Strecke

sector *n.* Sektor; (mil.) Abschnitt

secular *adj.* hundertjährig; (fig.) weltlich

secure *adj.* sicher, gewiss; gesichert, befe-
stigt: — *v.* sichern; befestigen, festmachen; sicherstellen; sich verschaffen

security *n.* Sicherheit, Gewissheit; Schutz;
Bürgschaft; — **risk** *n.* Sicherheitsrisiko;
(pol.) unzuverlässiger Regierungsbe-
amte

sedan *n.* (auto.) Sedan

sedate *adj.* gelassen, gesetzt; ruhig

sedative *n.* Beruhigungsmittel

sediment *n.* Sediment; Bodensatz, Niederschlag; (geol.) Ablagerung; **-ary** *adj.*
sedimentär; Ablagerungs-

sedition *n.* Aufruhr, Aufstand, Empörung

seduce *v.* verführen, verlocken, verleiten

seductive *adj.* verführerisch

see *n.* erzbischöflicher Stuhl, Erzbistum;
Holy See päpstlicher Stuhl, Papsttum;
— *v.* sehen, ansehen; wahrnehmen, erblicken, beobachten; einsehen, begreifen; besuchen, empfangen; **I don't**
— **it** ich sehe das nicht ein; **live to** —
erleben; — **to it** dafür sorgen (*or*
achten); — **to the door** zur Tür begleiten; **—!** *interj.* schau! sieh da! **-ing**

n. Sehen, Sehvermögen; **-ing** *conj.* **-ing**
that angesichts; da ja; **-ing** *adj.* **worth**
-ing sehenswert; **-r** *n.* Seher, Prophet

seed *n.* Same, Saat; (ichth.) Milch,
Rogen; (fig.) Geschlecht, Abkunft, Ursprung; — *v.* säen, Samen ausstreuen;
besäen; entkernen; (bot.) Samen tragen, in Samen schiessen; **-ling** *n.* Säm-
ling, Steckling; **-y** *adv.* voller Samen,
in Samen schiessend; (coll.) schäbig

seek *v.* suchen; durchsuchen, durchforschen; begehren, verlangen; trachten, streben

seem *v.* (er)scheinen; **-ing** *n.* Anschein;
-ingly *adj.* anscheinend, scheinbar;
-ingly *adv.* zum Schein, dem Anschein
nach; **-ly** *adj.* anständig, geziemend,
schicklich

seep *v.* durchlaufen, durchsickern

seersucker *n.* kreppartiger Leinendruck
(*or* Baumwolldruck)

seesaw *n.* Schaukel, Wippe; — *v.* schaukeln, wippen

seethe *v.* sieden, kochen; einweichen, aufweichen

segment *n.* Segment, Abschnitt

segregate *adj.* abgesondert; — *v.* trennen;
(sich) absondern

segregation *n.* Absonderung, Trennung

seismograph *n.* Seismograph, Erdbeben-
messer

seize *v.* ergreifen, fassen, packen; festnehmen; beschlagnahmen; sich bemächtigen, in Beschlag nehmen

seizure *n.* Ergreifung, Festnahme; Be-
schlagnahme; (med.) plötzlicher Anfall

seldom *adv.* selten

select *v.* auswählen, auslesen; — *adj.*
auserlesen, auserwählt; **-ion** *n.* Auswahl; **-ive** *adj.* wahlweise, auswählend;
Auswahl-

selenium *n.* Selen

self *adj.* derselbe, dieselbe, dasselbe; —
pron. selbst; — *n.* Selbst, Ich

self-acting *adj.* selbsttätig, automatisch

self-addressed *adj.* mit Anschrift versehen

self-confident *adj.* selbstvertrauend, sich
auf sich selbst verlassend

self-conscious *adj.* selbstbewusst; befangen

self-contained *adj.* zurückhaltend, verschlossen; beherrscht; (mech.) unabhängig

self-control *n.* Selbstbeherrschung

self-defense *n.* Selbstverteidigung; (law)
Notwehr

self-denial *n.* Selbstverleugnung

self-evident *adj.* selbstverständlich,
augenscheinlich

self-explanatory *adj.* sich selbst erklärend; selbstverständlich

self-expression *n.* (art) Ausdruck der Persönlichkeit, Persönlichkeitsstempel

self-governing *adj.* sich selbst regierend; selbständig

self-help *n.* Selbsthilfe

self-indulgence *n.* Nachsicht gegen sich selbst; zügellose Genussucht

selfish *adj.* selbstsüchtig, eigennützig; egoistisch; **-ness** *n.* Selbstsucht, Eigennutz; Egoismus

self-made *adj.* selbstgemacht; **— man** Selfmademan; durch eigene Kraft emporgestiegener Mann

self-possession *n.* Selbstbeherrschung, Geistesgegenwart; Fassung

self-preservation *n.* Selbsterhaltung; Selbstschutz

self-propelling *adj.* Selbstfahr-, Selbstantrieb-

self-protection *n.* Selbstschutz

self-reliance *n.* Selbstvertrauen

self-reliant *adj.* selbstvertrauend, selbstsicher

self-respect *n.* Selbstachtung

self-righteous *adj.* selbstgerecht; pharisäisch

self-sacrifice *n.* Selbstaufopferung

selfsame *adj.* ebenderselbe, ebendieselbe, ebendasselbe

self-satisfied *adj.* selbstzufrieden

self-seeking *adj.* selbstsüchtig, eigennützig

self-service *n.* Selbstbedienung

self-starter *n.* Selbstanlasser

self-stopping *n.* Selbstsperrung

self-sufficient *adj.* selbstgenügsam; selbstversorgend, dünkelhaft

self-support *n.* Selbsterhaltung; Selbstversorgung

self-taught *adj.* autodidaktisch

sell *n.* (coll.) Betrug, Täuschung; **—** *v.* verkaufen, veräussern, absetzen; sich verkaufen, gehen; verraten; (coll.) täuschen, betrügen; **— out** ausverkaufen, Lager räumen; **-er** *n.* Verkäufer

seltzer *n.* Selters, Selterwasser

selvage *n.* Kante, Borte; Webekante

semantics *n. pl.* Semantik, Wortbedeutungslehre

semaphore *n.* Zeichentelegraf; Flaggenwinken

semblance *n.* Ähnlichkeit; Ebenbild, Gestalt, Erscheinung; Anschein

semester *n.* Semester

semiannual *adj.* halbjährig

semicircle *n.* Halbkreis

semicircular *adj.* halbkreisförmig, halb-rund

semicolon *n.* Semikolon; Strichpunkt

semifinal *adj.* halbbeendet; **-s** *pl.* Vorschlussrunde, Vorschlussspiele

seminar *n.* Seminar, Arbeitsgruppe; **-y** *n.* Seminar, Erziehungsanstalt; (bot.) Pflanzenschule

semiofficial *adj.* halbamtlich

semiweekly *adj.* halbwöchentlich, zweimal wöchentlich

semiyearly *adj.* halbjährlich

senate *n.* Senat

senator *n.* Senator; **-ial** *adj.* senatorisch

send *v.* senden; aussenden, entsenden; schicken; **— for** holen lassen; **-er** *n.* Absender; (mech.) Taste; (rad.) Sender; **-ing** *n.* Sendung, Senden

senile *adj.* senil, altersschwach

senior *n.* Senior, Ältere, Rangältere; **—** *adj.* älter; Senior-, Ober-; **-ity** *n.* höheres Alter (*or* Dienstalter)

sensation *n.* Empfindung, Eindruck; (fig.) Sensation, Aufsehen; **-al** *adj.* sensationell, aufsehenerregend; Empfindungs-

sense *n.* Sinn; Gefühl; Bedeutung; Vernunft; common **—** gesunder Menschenverstand; **— of sight** Gesichtssinn; talk **—** vernünftig reden; **—** *v.* wahrnehmen, empfinden; (coll.) verstehen; **-less** *adj.* besinnungslos; unempfindlich, gefühllos, leblos; sinnlos, unvernünftig

sensibility *n.* Sensibilität, Empfindungsvermögen, Empfindlichkeit

sensible *adj.* fühlbar, empfänglich; verständig

sensitive *adj.* empfindlich, sensitiv; empfänglich, feinfühlig; **— plant** Mimose

sensitization *n.* (phot.) Lichtempfindlichmachen

sensitize *v.* empfindlich machen

sensory *adj.* Empfindungs-, Sinnes-

sensual *adj.* sinnlich, fleischlich; **-ity** *n.* Sinnlichkeit

sensuous *adj.* sinnlich, sinnenfreudig

sentence *n.* Spruch; (gram. and mus.) Satz; (law) Rechtsspruch, Urteil, Entscheidung; **—** *v.* (ver)urteilen; (fig.) verdammen

sentiment *n.* Empfindung, Gefühl; Meinung; **-al** *adj.* sentimental, gefühlvoll, empfindsam; **-ality** *n.* Sentimentalität, Rührseligkeit

sentinel *n.* Wachthabende, Posten

sentry *n.* Wache, Wachposten; Schildwache

separable *adj.* trennbar, ablösbar

separate *v.* (sich) trennen, (sich) scheiden, (sich) absondern, auseinandergehen, sortieren; — *adj.* getrennt, abgesondert, einzeln; separat; geschieden; **under — cover** (com.) mit derselben Post; **-ly** *adv.* einzeln, besonders

separation *n.* Trennung, Scheidung

separator *n.* Scheidemaschine; **cream —** Zentrifuge, Entsahner

September *n.* September

septic *adj.* septisch, Fäulnis erregend; **— poisoning** Blutvergiftung; **— tank** Klärbecken

sepulchre *n.* Grab, Grabstätte, Gruft

sequel *n.* Folge, Fortsetzung; Ergebnis

sequence *n.* Reihenfolge, Anordnung

sequoia *n.* Rotholzbaum, Sequoia

seraph *n.* Seraph

Serbia *n.* Serbien

serenade *n.* Serenade, Ständchen; **—** *v.* ein Ständchen bringen

serene *adj.* hell, klar, heiter; ungetrübt, ruhig

serf *n.* Sklave, Leibeigene

sergeant, serjeant *n.* Sergeant, ‹Feldwebel, Wachtmeister

serial *n.* Fortsetzungsroman; Serienaufführung; Sendereihe; **—** *adj.* reihenweise, periodisch, serienweise

series *n. pl.* Reihe; Reihenfolge, Serie

serious *adj.* ernst(haft), seriös; feierlich, wichtig, schwer

sermon *n.* Predigt; Sermon

serpent *n.* Schlange; **-ine** *n.* Serpentine, Schlangenlinie; (min.) Serpentin; **-ine** *adj.* schlangenartig, schlangenförmig; schlängelnd

serum *n.* Serum: Blutwasser

servant *n.* Diener, Bediente; Magd; **public —** Staatsbeamte

serve *v.* dienen; servieren, bedienen, aufwarten, auftragen; verwalten, genügen; verbüssen; (tennis) anspielen; **— a warrant** die Klageschrift (*or* Vorladung) zustellen; **that —s him right** das geschieht ihm recht

service *n.* Dienst; Arbeitsleistung, Bedienung; Stellung; Gehorsam, Unterwerfung; Service, Tafelgeschirr; (com.) Nutzen, Vorteil; (eccl.) Gottesdienst; (law) Zustellung; (mil.) Dienstpflicht, Heeresdienst; (rail.) Verkehr; (tennis) Aufschlag, Anspiel; **at your —** zu Ihrer Verfügung; **be of —** zu Diensten stehen; **night —** Nachtdienst, Nachtverkehr; **— station** Tankstelle; **-able** *adj.* zweckdienlich, nützlich; diensttauglich, brauchbar, dienstbereit

servitude *n.* Dienstbarkeit, Knechtschaft

servomotor *n.* Hilfsmotor; Kraftverstärker; Stellmotor

sesame *n.* Sesam

session *n.* Tagung, Sitzung; Sitzungsperiode

set *n.* Satz; Garnitur, Service, Besteck; Reihe, Folge; Richtung; (ast.) Sinken, Untergang; (film) Standfoto; (horses) Gespann; (rad.) Apparat; (tennis) Partie; (sl.) Pack, Bande; **—** *v.* (hin)setzen, (hin)stellen, legen; wenden; (ein)richten, ordnen, zurechtmachen; befestigen; (agr.) pflanzen; (ast.) sinken, untergehen; (hunting) (vor)stehen, hetzen; (jewels) fassen; (med.) einrenken; (mech.) schärfen; (mus.) komponieren, in Noten setzen; **— aside** beiseitesetzen; verwerfen; **— back** zurücksetzen, zurückstossen; **— on fire** anzünden; **— the table** den Tisch decken; **— up** aufsetzen, aufstellen; erheben, erwecken; einrichten; **-ter** *n.* Setzer; (zool.) Setter, Vorstehhund; **-ting** *n.* Setzen, Stellen; Umgebung, Umrahmung; (ast.) Untergang; (chem.) Erstarrung, Gerinnung; (jewels) Fassung; (mech.) Erhärten; Einstellung; (naut.) Richtung; (theat.) Inszenierung

setback *n.* Rückschlag; Zurückverlegung

setscrew *n.* Stellschraube

setting-up exercises *n.* Bodengymnastik

settle *n.* Sitztruhe; **—** *v.* bestimmen, entscheiden; bezahlen; beilegen, schlichten; abmachen; sich niederlassen (*or* ansiedeln); sich senken, sich setzen; nachlassen, sich legen; **-ment** *n.* Regelung, Abmachung, Verabredung; Ansiedlung, Niederlassung; **-r** *n.* Ansiedler, Kolonist

setup *n.* Haltung, Aufmachung; (sl.) abgekartetes Spiel

seven *n.* Sieben(er); **—** *adj.* sieben; **-teen** *n.* Siebzehn(er); **-teen** *adj.* siebzehn; **— -teenth** *n.* Siebzehnte, Siebzehntel; **-teenth** *adj.* siebzehnt; **-th** *n.* Siebente; Siebentel; **-th** *adj.* siebent; **-ty** *n.* Siebzig(er); **-ty** *adj.* siebzig

sever *v.* (ab)trennen, absondern; abhauen, zerschneiden, aufbrechen, auseinanderreissen; **-ance** *n.* Trennung, Scheidung

several *adj.* getrennt, gesondert; einzeln, besonder, verschiedene, mehrere; **-ly** *adv.* getrennt; besonders, einzeln; **jointly and —** samt und sonders

severe *adj.* streng, nachsichtslos; ernst; hart, heftig; rauh

severity *n.* Strenge, Härte; Genauigkeit

sew *v.* nähen, heften; **-er** *n.* Näher; **-ing** *n.* Nähen, Näherei

sewage *n.* Abwasser

sewer *n.* Abzugskanal, Siel, Kloake

sex *n.* Geschlecht; **-ual** *adj.* sexuell, ge-

schlechtlich; Geschlechts-
sextant *n.* Sextant
sexton *n.* Küster
shabby *adj.* schäbig, abgetragen; (coll.)
gemein
shack *n.* Bretterbude, Hütte
shackle *n.* Fessel; **-s** *n. pl.* Handschellen;
— *v.* fesseln, anketten
shade *n.* Schatten, Schattierung; Schirm;
(fig.) Kleinigkeit; — *v.* beschatten, verdunkeln; schützen; (art) abstufen,
schattieren
shadow *n.* Schatten(bild); Schutz; — *v.*
verdunkeln, beschatten; andeuten; bergen, schützen; heimlich beobachten;
-y *adj.* schattig, dunkel; wesenlos
shadowboxing *n.* Trainings boxen (ohne
Gegner)
shady *adj.* schattig; zweifelhaft, anrüchig
shaft *n.* Schaft, Stiel; Pfeil, Speer; (mech.)
Achse, Spindel, Welle; (min.) Schacht,
Grube
shaggy *adj.* zottig, langhaarig; rauh
shake *n.* Schütteln, Erschütterung;
(mus.) Triller; *pl.* Zittern, Schüttelfrost; — *v.* schütteln, rütteln; erschüttern; zittern, beben; (mus.) trillern; —
hands die Hand schütteln (*or* geben);
zu einem Abkommen gelangen; **-r** *n.*
Schüttler, Zitterer; Streuer; **cocktail -r**
Mixbecher; **salt -r** Salzstreuer
shakedown *n.* Notbett, Notlager; (coll.)
Erpressung
shake-up *n.* Aufruhr, Erregung; (coll.)
Reorganisierung, Personalwechsel
shaky *adj.* zitternd, unsicher; wackelig,
hinfällig; unzuverlässlich
shale *n.* Schiefer(ton)
shall *v.* werden, sollen; — **we go for a
walk?** wollen wir spazieren gehen?
shallow *adj.* seicht, flach; (fig.) oberflächlich
sham *n.* Imitation, Schein, Täuschung;
Überzug; — **battle** Scheingefecht;
— **jewelry** Talmischmuck; — *v.*
vortäuschen, betrügen, hintergehen;
sich verstellen, simulieren
shame *n.* Scham; Schande, Schmach; —
v. sich schämen; beschämen; schänden,
verunehren; **-ful** *adj.* schändlich,
schimpflich, schmachvoll; **-less** *adj.*
schamlos; unverschämt
shamefaced *adj.* schamhaft, schüchtern
shampoo *n.* Kopfwäsche; — *v.* den Kopf
waschen, schampunieren
shamrock *n.* Feldklee; (fig.) Kleeblatt
shank *n.* Schenkel, Unterschenkel; (bot.)
Stiel, Stengel; (mech.) Schaft, Rohr
shanty *n.* Hütte, Bude
shape *n.* Gestalt, Form; (coll.) Zustand,

Verfassung; — *v.* bilden gestalten;
formen, anpassen, einrichten; ersinnen;
-less *adj.* formlos, ungestalt; **-ly** *adj.*
wohlgestaltet, ebenmässig; **-r** *n.* (mech.)
Fräsmaschine
share *n.* Teil, Anteil; Beitrag; (com.)
Aktie, Anteilschein; Kux; Kontingent,
Quote; — *v.* teilen; verteilen, austeilen;
gemeinsam geniessen (*or* erdulden);
teilhaben, teilnehmen; **-r** *n.* Teiler,
Teilhaber
shareholder *n.* Aktienbesitzer, Aktionär
shark *n.* Hai(fisch); (sl.) Gauner
sharp *n.* (mus.) Kreuz; (sl.) Gauner,
Bauernfänger; (sports sl.) Eingeweihte;
— *adj.* scharf, schneidend, spitz; hitzig;
hart, hell; streng, bitter, beissend;
rasch, heftig; (coll.) spitzfindig, verschlagen; **two o'clock** — genau zwei
Uhr; **-en** *v.* (ver)schärfen, spitzen;
reizen; (mus.) erhöhen; **-ener** *n.*
Schärfer; **pencil -ener** Bleistiftanspitzer; **-er** *n.* Gauner, Schwindler; **-ness**
n. Schärfe, Strenge, Härte; Heftigkeit;
(fig.) Scharfsinn
sharpshooter *n.* Scharfschütze
shatter *n.* Bruchstück, Scherbe; — *v.* zerbrechen, zerschmettern, zerrütten
shatterproof *adj.* bruchsicher
shave *n.* Rasieren; **close** — knappes Entkommen; — *v.* (sich) rasieren; **-r** *n.*
Rasierer; Leuteschinder, Wucherer;
(coll.) Grünschnabel
shawl *n.* Schal, Umschlagetuch
she *pron.* sie
sheaf *n.* Garbe, Bündel; — *v.* in Garben
binden, bündeln
shear *n.* Schur; (mech.) Schneidema-
schine; — *v.* scheren, abschneiden;
(coll.) rupfen, übervorteilen
sheath *n.* Scheide, Futteral; (ent.) Flügeldecke; **-e** *v.* in die Scheide stecken; einhüllen, bedecken
shed *n.* Schuppen; Hütte; — *v.* vergiessen; verbreiten; verlieren, abwerfen
sheen *n.* Schein, Glanz
sheep *n.* Schaf; (coll.) Schafskopf; **-ish**
adj. schafsmässig; einfältig, blöde
sheepman *n.* Schafzüchter
sheepskin *n.* Schaffell, Schafleder; (coll.)
Diplom
sheer *adj.* rein, lauter; bloss; dünn, zart;
steil, senkrecht; — *adv.* gänzlich, völlig;
— *v.* (naut.) scheren
sheet *n.* Bettuch, Laken; Blatt, Platte,
Bogen; Fläche; **blank** — unbeschrie-
bener Bogen (*or* Wahlzettel); — **anchor**
Notanker; — **glass** Tafelglas; — **iron**
Eisenblech, Weissblech; — **lightning**
Wetterleuchten; — **metal** Blech; —

music Notenblatt; — *v.* überziehen, einhüllen; **–ing** *n.* blattweise Anordnung; Laken

shelf *n.* Brett; Regal, Fach; Gestell; (geol.) Felsvorsprung; (naut.) Riff; **corner —** Eckregal; **on the —** (coll.) ausrangiert

shell *n.* (bot.) Schale, Hülse, Schote; (ent.) Flügeldecke; (mech.) Mantel, Gerippe, Gerüst; (mil.) Granate, Bombe; (zool.) Muschel, Schale, Schild, Panzer; (fig.) Gehäuse; **cartridge —** Patronenhülse; **turtle —** Schildkrötenschale, Schildpatt; **— room** (naut.) Granatenmagazin; **— shock** (mil.) Nervenerschütterung (nach einer Granatexplosion); — *v.* schälen, enthülsen; (ichth.) abschuppen; (mil.) bombardieren, beschiessen

shellproof *adj.* bombensicher

shelter *n.* Schutzraum; Schuppen; Schutz, Obdach, Unterschlupf; **air-raid —** Luftschutzkeller; — *v.* (be)schützen; (be)schirmen

shelve *v.* mit Brettern (*or* Regalen) versehen; auf ein Brett (*or* Regal) stellen; sich neigen, abschüssig sein; (coll.) ausrangieren, unberücksichtigt lassen

shepherd *n.* Schäfer, Schafhirt; (bibl.) Seelenhirt

sherbet *n.* Scherbett, Sorbett

sheriff *n.* Sheriff, Bezirkspolizeibeamte

shield *n.* Schild; Schirm, Schutz; Beschützer; Schutzdach; — *v.* (be)schirmen, (be)schützen; bedecken, behüten

shift *n.* Schicht; Veränderung, Wechsel; Behelf; Auskunftsmittel; Notlüge, List, Kniff; — *v.* (ver)schieben; wechseln, verändern; sich davonmachen; sich heraushelfen, sich herauslügen; sich durchschlagen; sich umziehen; (naut.) wenden, umspringen; **–less** *adj.* hilflos; ungewandt; faul; **–lessly** *adv.* unzuverlässig; **–y** *adj.* schlau, verschlagen

shimmer *n.* Schimmer; — *v.* schimmern, flimmern

shin(bone) *n.* Schienbein

shine *n.* Schein, Glanz; (coll.) Neigung; — *v.* scheinen, leuchten; (coll.) putzen; (fig.) glänzen

shingle *n.* Schindel; (coll.) Praxistafel; *pl.* (med.) Gürtelrose; — *v.* mit Schindeln decken; kurz schneiden

shining *n.* Scheinen, Glänzen; — *adj.* scheinend, glänzend

shiny *adj.* blank; schimmernd; hell

ship *n.* Schiff; **–'s papers** Schiffspapiere; — *v.* schiffen; an Bord bringen (*or* nehmen); verladen, verschiffen, versenden; anheuern; **–ment** *n.* Verladung,

Vorschiffung; Warensendung; (naut.) Schiffsladung; **–per** *n.* Verschiffer, Verlader; (com.) Absender; **–ping** *n.* Verschiffung, Verladung; (com.) Versand; (naut.) Schiffe, Flotte; Gesamttonnenzahl; **–ping clerk** Versandabteilungsangestellte; **–ping room** Versandabteilung, Versandraum

shipboard *n.* Bord, Schiff(sseite); **on —**

shipbuilding *n.* Schiffbau, Schiffsbaukunst

shipmate *n.* Schiffskamerad; Mitreisende

shipowner *n.* Reeder, Schiffsbesitzer

shipwreck *n.* Schiffbruch; Wrack; **–ed** *adj.* gestrandet, gescheitert; schiffbrüchig; **–ed person** Schiffbrüchige, Gestrandete

shipyard *n.* Schiffswerft

shirk *n.* Drückeberger; — *v.* sich drücken; (educ.) schwänzen

shirr *v.* Gummifäden einziehen; kräuseln

shirt *n.* Hemd; **— cuff** Manschette; **— sleeve** Hemdsärmel; **— stud** Manschettenknopf

shiver *n.* Splitter, Bruchstück; Schauer, Erzittern; *pl.* Fieberschauer, Schüttelfrost; — *v.* zerbrechen, zersplittern; schau(d)ern, zittern; **–ing** *adj.* erzitternd, schaudernd

shoal *n.* Menge, Masse, Schwarm; (naut.) Untiefe, Sandbank; **— of fish** Fischzug, Fischschwarm; — *v.* flacher werden; wimmeln, sich drängen

shock *n.* Stoss, Zusammenstoss, Erschütterung; (geol.) Erdstoss; (med.) Schock, Nervenerschütterung; (mil.) Angriff, Anfall; **electric —** elektrischer Schlag; **— absorber** Stossdämpfer; **— wave** Stosswelle; — *v.* (an)stossen; zusammenstossen, erschüttern; Anstoss geben, beleidigen; **–ing** *adj.* anstössig, verletzend; unangenehm, empörend

shockproof *adj.* stossfest, stossicher

shoe *n.* Schuh; Hufeisen; Beschlag; Hemmschuh; **rubber —** Gummischuh; **— polish** Schuhkrem, Schuhwichse; — *v.* beschuhen; beschlagen

shoeblack *n.* Schuhputzer, Stiefelputzer

shoehorn *n.* Schuhanzieher

shoemaker *n.* Schuhmacher

shoestring, shoelace *n.* Schnürsenkel

shoestring potatoes *n. pl.* Kartoffelstäbchen

shoot *n.* Schiessen; Gleitbahn; Stromschnelle; (bot.) Spross; (min.) Erzlager, Rutsche; — *v.* schiessen; fliegen, stürzen, strömen; (bot.) keimen, treiben; (film) aufnehmen, drehen; (mil.) (ab)schiessen, (ab)feuern; **–ing gallery** Schiesstand; **–ing star** Sternschnuppe

shop *n.* Laden, Geschäft; Werkstatt, Betrieb; (fig.) Fach, Beruf; **pastry** —, confectionery — Konditorei; **talk** — fachsimpeln; — *v.* einkaufen; **-per** *n.* Käufer, Kunde; Einkäufer; **-ping** *n.* Einkaufen, Besorgung; go **-ping** Einkäufe machen, Geschäfte besuchen

shopkeeper *n.* Ladeninhaber, Geschäftsbesitzer

shoplifter *n.* Ladendieb

shopwindow *n.* Schaufenster

shore *n.* Strand, Ufer, Küste; Gestade; (arch.) Stütze, Strebe; — **leave** Landurlaub; — **line** Küstenstrich

short *adj.* klein, kurz; beschränkt, knapp; sparsam; trocken, barsch; (cake) mürbig, knusprig; (sl.) unverdünnt; **a —while ago** vor kurzem; **for** — abgekürzt; **on** — notice in kurzer Zeit, kurzfristig; **run** — knapp werden, ausgehen; — **circuit** Kurzschluss; — **sale** schneller Absatz; Baissespekulation; — **temper** Ungeduld, Reizbarkeit; — **wave** Kurzwelle; — *n.* Kurze; kurze Silbe, kurzer Vokal; *pl.* Shorts kurze Hosen; **-age** *n.* Mangel, Knappheit; Fehlbetrag, Abgang, Gewichtsverlust; **-en** *v.* (ab)kürzen, vermindern, verringern; abnehmen; (bot.) beschneiden; **-ening** *n.* Verkürzung; Backfett; **-ly** *adv.* kürzlich; kurz, bald

shortcake *n.* Mürbekuchen,

shortchange *v.* zu wenig herausgeben

short-circuit *v.* kurzschliessen

shortcoming *n.* Unzulänglichkeit, Pflichtversäumnis; Mangel, Schwäche

shorthand *n.* Stenografie, Kurzschrift; — *adj.* stenografisch; — *v.* stenografieren

shortsighted *adj.* kurzsichtig; **-ness** *n.* Kurzsichtigkeit

shortstop *n.* Innenspieler zwischen zweitem und drittem Mal

short-term *adj.* kurzfristig

shot *n.* Schuss; Geschoss, Kugel; Schütze; Stoss, Schlag, Wurf; (sl.) Spritze; bird — Schrot

shotgun *n.* Jagdflinte, Schrotflinte

should *v.* sollte, würde

shoulder *n.* Schulter, Achsel; (meat) Kamm, Bug; — **blade** Schulterblatt; — **knot** —, **loop** —, **mark** Achselstück, Achselklappe; — **strap** Achselriemen; — *v.* schultern; drängen; (fig.) auf sich nehmen

shout *n.* Geschrei, Gejauchze; Ruf; — *v.* rufen, schreien, jauchzen

shove *n.* Schub, Stoss; — *v.* schieben, stossen; drängen; — **off** abstossen, absetzen

shovel *n.* Schaufel, Schippe, Spaten; — *v.* schaufeln, häufeln

show *n.* Schau(stellung); Ausstellung; (theat.) Schauspiel, Aufführung; (fig.) Angabe, Prunk; — **bill** Plakat; — **card** Musterkarte; — **window** Schaufenster, Auslage; — *v.* zeigen; bekanntmachen, erklären, deuten; ausstellen, darstellen; beweisen, erscheinen; — **off** hervorstechen, sich grosstun; — **oneself superior to** sich überlegen zeigen; — **one's true colors** sein wahres Gesicht zeigen; — **up** blosstellen, entlarven; **-y** *adj.* prächtig, prunkvoll, glänzend; auffällig

showboat *n.* Theaterschiff

showcase *n.* Schaukasten, Glaskasten

shower *n.* Schauer; (fig.) Erguss, Fülle, Menge; — **bath** Brause, Dusche; — *v.* (sich) ergiessen, hageln, regnen

showman *n.* Schausteller, Aussteller; (theat.) Komödiant; **-ship** *n.* Darstellungskunst

showroom *n.* Ausstellungsraum, Vorführraum

shred *n.* Schnitzel; Fetzen, Streifen; — *v.* zerschneiden, zerfetzen, zerreissen

shrewd *adj.* scharfsinnig; klug, schlau; **-ness** *n.* Scharfsinn, Schlauheit; Verschlagenheit

shriek *n.* Gekreisch, Angstschrei; — *v.* kreischen, schreien

shrill *adj.* schrill, gellend, durchdringend

shrimp *n.* Garnele, Krabbe; (coll.) Knirps

shrine *n.* Schrein, Heiligtum; Kapelle

shrink *v.* schrumpfen, einlaufen, sich zusammenziehen; abnehmen, schwinden; (fig.) zurückschrecken; **-age** *n.* Einlaufen, Schrumpfen; Abnahme, Schwund

shrivel *v.* einschrumpfen, runzeln; falten, zerknittern; (fig.) vergehen

shroud *n.* Leichentuch, Sterbehemd; (naut.) Want(tau); (fig.) Gewand, Kleidung; *pl.* (naut.) Wanten; — *v.* einhüllen; verbergen

shrub *n.* Strauch, Busch, Staude; **-bery** *n.* Gebüsch, Gesträuch, Buschwerk

shrug *n.* Achselzucken; — *v.* schaudern; mit der Achsel zucken

shudder *n.* Erzittern; Schauder; — *v.* (er)beben, erzittern, schaudern

shuffle *n.* Schieben, Stossen; Ausflucht; Schiebung; (cards) Mischen; (walk) schleppender Gang; — *v.* schieben, stossen; verwirren, durcheinanderbringen; (cards) mischen; (walk) schwerfällig gehen, schlürfen, scharren

shuffling *adj.* schiebend, mischend; schleppend; (fig.) unredlich, ausweichend

shun *v.* (ver)meiden, ausweichen; beiseite

schieben (*or* drängen)

shut *v.* (ver)schliessen, zumachen; zuziehen; ausschliessen, aussperren; -ter *n.* Schliesser; Deckel, Klappe, Schieber; Rolladen, Jalousie, Fensterladen; Schalter; (mech.) Verschluss

shutdown *n.* Stillstand, Arbeitsniederlegung

shut-in *n.* Patient, Bettlägrige

shuttle *n.* Weberschiffchen; — **service** Zubringerverkehr, Pendelverkehr

shy *adj.* scheu, schüchtern, zurückhaltend; behutsam; argwöhnisch, misstrauisch; -**ness** *n.* Scheu, Schüchternheit, Zurückhaltung; Behutsamkeit; Argwohn

sick *adj.* krank; unwohl, übel; schwach, kraftlos; überdrüssig; -**en** *v.* kränkeln, erkranken, dahinsiechen; krank machen, anekeln; -**ly** *adj.* schwächlich, kränklich; unpässlich, krankhaft, ungesund; blass; schmerzlich; widerlich; -**ness** *n.* Krankheit; Übelkeit, Schwäche

sickbed *n.* Krankenbett

sickle *n.* Sichel

side *n.* Seite; Rand, Ufer, Grenze; (geol.) Abhang; (geom.) Schenkel; (pol.) Partei, Bezirk; — **by** — dichtbeieinander, nebeneinander; — *adj.* seitlich, indirekt; Seiten-, Neben-; — **aisle** Seitenschiff; — **arms** Seitenwehr; — **dish** Nebengericht, Vorspeise, Nachspeise; — **issue** Nebensache, Nebenpunkt; — **light** Seitenlicht; Streiflicht; — **line** Nebenerwerb, Nebenberuf; — **show** Nebenschau; — **view** Seitenansicht; — *v.* Partei ergreifen; beiseitelegen

sideboard *n.* Anrichte(tisch), Büffet

sideburns *n.* Kotelette, Backenbart

sidecar *n.* Beiwagen

sidesaddle *n.* Damensattel

side-step *v.* beiseitetreten, ausweichen

sidetrack *n.* Nebengeleis(e); — *v.* verschieben; (rail.) rangieren

sidewalk *n.* Bürgersteig, Trottoir

sidewards, sideways, sidewise *adv.* seitwärts

siding *n.* (rail.) Nebengeleis; Weiche

siege *n.* Belagerung

sierra *n.* Sierra, Gebirgskette

siesta *n.* Siesta, Mittagsruhe

sieve *n.* Sieb; — *v.* (durch)sieben, sichten

sift *v.* sieben, sichten; aussondern, auslesen; prüfen, untersuchen

sigh *n.* Seufzer; — *v.* seufzen (nach)

sight *n.* Sehen, Gesicht; Sehkraft; Blick, Anblick; Einsicht; (gun) Visier, Korn; (fig.) Menge, Masse, Schauspiel, Erscheinung, Merkwürdigkeit, Sehenswürdigkeit; **at first** — im ersten Augenblick; **at** — sogleich, augenblicklich; **bomb** — Bombenzielgerät; **by** — vom Sehen; bei Vorlage; **on** — bei Sicht (*or* Vorlage); **out of** — ausser Sicht; aus den Augen; **play at** — vom Blatt spielen; — **draft** Sichtwechsel; -**less** *adj.* blind; unsichtbar; -**ly** *adj.* ansehnlich, stattlich

sight-seeing *n.* Besichtigung der Sehenswürdigkeiten; — *adj.* schaulustig; — **car** Rundfahrtenwagen

sight-seer *n.* Schaulustige, Besucher der Sehenswürdigkeiten, Tourist

sign *n.* Zeichen, Gebärde, Wink; Anzeichen, Kennzeichen, Merkmal; Schild; (ast.) Tierkreiszeichen; (com.) Firmenzeichen, Unterschrift; (med.) Symptom; (mus.) Vorzeichen; — **language** Zeichensprache; — *v.* unterzeichnen, unterschreiben; Zeichen geben, winken; -**al** *n.* Signal; **busy** -**al** Besetztzeichen; -**al box** Feuermelder; (rail.) Stellwerk; -**al code** Signalcode; -**al light** Signallicht, Signalfeuer; -**al mast** Signalmast; -**alize** *v.* deutlich machen, auszeichnen; -**atory** *adj.* unterzeichnend; -**ature** *n.* Unterschrift, Namenszug; (mus.) Vorzeichen; -**et** *n.* Siegel, Handzeichen

signalman *n.* (rail.) Weichensteller; (naut.) Signalgast

signboard *n.* Aushängeschild, Firmenschild

significant *adj.* bedeutsam, bezeichnend

signify *v.* bezeichnen, bedeuten, andeuten; bekanntmachen

signpost *n.* Schilderpfosten, Wegweiser

silence *n.* Schweigen, Stille, Ruhe; Schweigsamkeit, Verschwiegenheit; — *v.* beruhigen, beschwichtigen; zur Ruhe bringen; -**r** *n.* Schalldämpfer; (auto.) Auspufftopf

silent *adj.* still, ruhig, schweigend; schweigsam, verschwiegen; (gram.) stumm; — **partner** stiller Teilhaber

Silesia *n.* Schlesien

silica, silex *n.* Kieselerde

silk *n.* Seide; Seidenstoff; Seidenzeug; — **stockings** Seidenstrümpfe; -**en** *adj.* seiden, seidig; -**iness** *n.* Seid(enart)ige; -**y** *adj.* seid(enart)ig; (fig.) weich, zart

silkworm *n.* Seidenraupe

sill *n.* Schwelle; Fensterbrett

silliness *n.* Torheit; Albernheit

silly *adj.* einfältig, dumm; albern, töricht

silo *n.* Speicher; (mil.) Raketenbunker

silver *n.* Silber; Silbergeld; Silbergerät; — *adj.* silbern; silberhell; — **fir** Silbertanne, Edeltanne; — **foil**, — **leaf** Blattsilber; — **fox** Silberfuchs; — **glance**

Silberglanz, Schwefelsilber; — grey
Silbergrau; — paper Silberpapier,
Staniolpapier; — plating Silberplat-
tierung; — thistle Bärenklau; — wedding silberne Hochzeit; — v. versilbern;
–y adj. silbern, silberglänzend; silberhell; Silber-
silversmith n. Silberschmied, Silberar-
beiter
silverware n. Silberwaren, Silberzeug
similar adj. ähnlich, gleich(artig); –ity n.
Gleichartigkeit, Ähnlichkeit
simile n. Gleichnis, Vergleich
simmer v. sieden, brodeln, wallen
simple adj. einfach, schlicht; einfältig,
arglos, simpel; –ton n. Einfaltspinsel,
Tropf
simplicity n. Einfachheit, Schlichtheit;
Unbefangenheit, Einfalt
simplify v. vereinfachen, erleichtern
simply adv. einfach, schlicht, klar; bloss,
nur; schlechthin
simultaneous adj. gleichzeitig, simultan
sin n. Sünde; — v. sündigen; sich versündigen; –ful adj. sündig, sündhaft;
–ner n. Sünder
since adv. seitdem, vorher; — prep. seit;
— conj. da, weil, seit(dem)
sincere adj. aufrichtig; lauter, wahr;
ernst; –ly adv. gänzlich; –ly yours Ihr
(sehr) ergebener, hochachtungsvoll
sincerity n. Aufrichtigkeit, Redlichkeit
sine n. (math.) Sinus
sinew n. Sehne; (fig.) Stärke, Stütze; –y
adj. sehnig; nervig, kräftig
sing v. singen, klingen; summen; (lit.)
besingen; –er n. Sänger; –ing n. Singen,
Gesang
singe n. leichte Verbrennung; — v. (ver)
sengen
single adj. einzig, einzeln, einfach; unverheiratet, ledig; **bookkeeping by** — **entry**
einfache Buchführung; — **fight** Zweikampf; — **file** Gänsemarsch; –**ness** n.
Alleinsein; Einfachheit
single-breasted adj. einreihig
singlehanded adj. einhändig; allein, eigenhändig, selbständig
single-minded adj. aufrichtig, grundehr-
lich, ohne Falsch
single-track adj. eingleisig, einspurig
singly adv. einzeln, allein; besonders
singular adj. einzigartig, sonderbar, ungewöhnlich; (gram.) Singular-; — n. Ein-
zahl, Singular
sinister adj. unheilvoll, finster; böse,
schlecht, unrecht
sink n. Ausguss; Abzugskanal, Senkgrube,
Kloake; (theat.) Versenkung; — v.
sinken, untertauchen, untergehen; ein-

fallen, sich senken; abnehmen, erliegen,
entarten; verfallen; graben; (naut.)
versenken; –er n. Schachtarbeiter;
(naut.) Senkblei
sinus n. Krümmung, Höhlung; **Bucht**;
(anat.) Höhle; (math.) Sinus
sip n. Schluck; Nippen, Schlürfen; — v.
nippen, schlürfen
siphon n. Siphon, Saugheber
sir n. Herr; **dear** — sehr geehrter **Herr**
siren n. Sirene
sirloin n. Lendenstück
sissy n. Weichling; femininer **Junge** (or
Mann)
sister n. Schwester; (eccl.) Nonne; –**hood**
n. Schwesternschaft; –ly adj. schwester-
lich
sister-in-law n. Schwägerin
sit v. sitzen, sich setzen; (pol.) tagen; –**ting**
n. Sitzung, Tagung; (orn.) Brüten;
–**ting room** Wohnzimmer
site n. Lage; Platz; Sitz; Schauplatz
sit-in (strike) n. Sitzstreik
situate v. unterbringen; –d adj. unterge-
bracht, gelegen
situation n. Situation, **Lage, Stellung,**
Zustand, Umstand
six n. Sechs(er); — adj. sechs; –**fold** adj.
sechsfach; –**teen** n. Sechzehn(er); –**teen**
adj. sechzehn; –**teenth** n. Sechzehnte;
Sechzehntel; –**teenth** adj. sechzehnt;
–th n. Sechste; Sechstel; (mus.) Sexte;
–th adj. sechst; –**tieth** n. Sechzigste,
Sechzigstel; –**tieth** adj. sechzigst; –**ty**
n. Sechzig(er); –**ty** adj. sechzig
six-shooter n. sechsläufiger Revolver
size n. Grösse, Gestalt; Format, Umfang;
(com.) Nummer, Mass; (mil.) Kaliber;
(min.) Mächtigkeit; — v. einordnen,
sortieren; Mass nehmen; (coll.) beurteilen; –d adj. angemessen, **in der**
Grösse von; geleimt
sizzle n. Zischen; — v. zischen
skate n. Schlittschuh, Rollschuh; (ichth.)
Glattroche; **roller** — Rollschuh; — v.
Schlittschuh (or Rollschuh) laufen;
–r n. Schlittschuhläufer, Rollschuh-
läufer
skating rink n. Kunsteisbahn; Rollschuhbahn
skeleton n. Skelett, Gerippe; **Rahmen,**
Gestell
skeptic n. Skeptiker; — adj. skeptisch
sketch n. Skizze, Entwurf, Handzeich-
nung; (theat.) Sketch; — v. skizzieren,
entwerfen
skewer n. Speiler, Fleischspiess; — v. aufspiessen
ski n. Ski; — **jump** Sprungschanze; Ski-
sprung; — v. skilaufen

skid n. Ausrutschen; (avi.) Kufe; (mech.) Hemmschuh, Hemmkette; (naut.) Ladebord; — v. hemmen, bremsen; ausrutschen, abrutschen; gleiten, schleudern

skilful adj. geschickt, gewandt, bewandert

skill n. Geschicklichkeit, Fertigkeit, Gewandtheit; **-ed** adj. geschickt, erfahren; kundig, geübt

skillet n. Bratpfanne

skim n. Abschäumen; Dahingleiten; — adj. — milk Magermilch; — v. abschöpfen, absahnen; flüchtig durchsehen (or durchlesen); dahingleiten; **-mer** n. Schaumlöffel

skimp v. knapp halten, knausern; **-y** adj. knauserig, sparsam

skin n. Haut, Fell, Pelz; (bot.) Schale, Hülse; (mech.) Leder. Decke; — v. bedecken, überziehen; häuten, abbalgen; abschälen; (sl.) filzen, prellen; **-ny** adj. hautartig; fleischlos, mager

skin-deep adj. oberflächlich

skintight adj. dicht anliegend, prall

skip n. Sprung; — v. springen, hüpfen; überspringen, auslassen

skipper n. (avi.) Flugzeugkommandant; (naut.) Schiffer, Kapitän

skirmish n. Scharmützel, Geplänkel; — v. plänkeln

skirt n. Frauenrock; Rand, Saum; — v. umsäumen; umgeben; (sich) entlangziehen

skull n. Schädel, Hirnschale; (coll.) Kopf

skullcap n. Hausmütze; (bot.) Helmkraut; (mil.) Sturmhaube

skunk n. Skunk, Stinktier; Skunkpelz; (sl.) Schuft

sky n. Himmel; Luftraum; — blue himmelblau

skylark n. Feldlerche; — v. Unfug treiben, Dummheiten machen

skylight n. Oberlicht, Lichthof; (naut.) Deckfenster

skyline n. Horizontlinie; Silhouette; Wolkenkratzerkette

skyrocket n. Raumrakete; — v. raketengleich aufsteigen, in die Höhe schiessen

skyscraper n. Wolkenkratzer, Hochhaus

slab n. Platte, Fliese; Schalbrett

slack n. Flaute; (min.) Grus; (naut.) loses Tauende; pl. Slacks; lange, weite Hosen; — adj. schlaff, lose, locker; matt; (nach)lässig; (com.) flau; **-en** v. erschlaffen, ermatten, nachlassen, (sich) verlangsamen; entspannen; **-er** n. Drückeberger, Schlappschwanz

slag n. Schlacke

slam n. Schlag, Knall; (cards) Schlemm, Durchmarsch; — v. zuschlagen, zu-

knallen; (cards) Schlemm bieten (or machen)

slander n. Verleumdung; — v. verleumden, schmähen; **-er** n. Verleumder

slang n. Slang; Jargon; Berufssprache

slant n. Abhang, Schräge; Neigung, Richtung; — v. sich neigen, abfallen; schräg liegen (or legen), abschrägen; (coll.) angleichen; **-ing** adj. schief, schräg; quer, geneigt; abschüssig

slap n. Klaps, Schlag; — adv. stracks; — v. klapsen, schlagen

slash n. Hieb, Schlitz, Schmarre, Schnitt; — v. hauen, schlitzen, schneiden

slat n. Querholz, Leiste, Schiene

slate n. Schiefer; (educ.) Schiefertafel; (pol.) Kandidatenliste; — adj. schieferfarbig, blaugrau; — v. mit Schiefer decken; (pol.) auf die Kandidatenliste setzen

slaughter n. Schlachten; Gemetzel, Blutbad; Ermordung; — v. (ab)schlachten; niedermetzeln

slaughterhouse n. Schlachthaus

slave n. Sklave; — v. sich schinden (or plagen); **-ry** n. Sklaverei, Knechtschaft; Schinderei; white **-ry** Mädchenhandel

slaw n. Krautsalat

slay v. erschlagen, umbringen; vernichten; **-er** n. Totschläger, Mörder

sled(ge) n. Schlitten, Schleife

sledge (hammer) n. Schmiedehammer, Vorschlaghammer

sleek adj. glatt, blank; geschmeidig; — v. glätten, putzen; gleiten

sleep n. Schlaf; — v. schlafen; — soundly fest schlafen; schlafen; **-er** n. Schläfer; (rail.) Schlafwagen; Querträger, Schwelle; **-iness** n. Schläfrigkeit; (fig.) Trägheit; **-ing** n. Schlafen; Ruhen; **-ing** adj. schlafend; **-ing bag** Schlafsack; **-ing room** Schlafzimmer; **-ing sickness** Schlafkrankheit; **-less** adj. schlaflos; (fig.) ruhelos; **-y** adj. schläfrig, verschlafen, träge

sleepwalker n. Nachtwandler, Somnambule

sleepyhead n. (orn.) Ruderente; (fig.) Schlafmütze

sleet n. Schlossen, Graupeln; Hagelschauer; — v. graupeln, hageln

sleeve n. Ärmel; (mech.) Muffe; **laugh in one's** — sich ins Fäustchen lachen; **-less** adj. ärmellos

sleigh n. Schlitten

sleight n. Kunststück, Taschenspielerei

slender adj. schlank, dünn, mager; schwach, dürftig

Sleswick-Holstein n. Schleswig-Holstein

sleuth *n.* Spürhund; (coll.) Detektiv

slice *n.* Schnitte, Scheibe; — *v.* abschneiden, in Scheiben schneiden

slick *adj.* gewandt, glattzüngig; glatt, geölt; — *v.* glätten, polieren; —er *n.* wasserdichter Mantel; (coll.) gerissener Gauner

slide *n.* Gleiten; Gleitbahn; (film) Diapositiv; (geol.) Erdrutsch; (mech.) Gleitbacke, Läufer, Schieber; — **rule** Rechenschieber; — **valve** Schieberventil; — *v.* (aus)gleiten, rutschen, schlittern; einschieben, laufen lassen; (fig.) hinübergleiten

sliding scale *n.* bewegliche Lohnskale (*or* Preisskala)

slight *n.* Nichtachtung, Geringschätzung; — *adj.* verächtlich, geringschätzig; gering, unbedeutend; dünn, schwach, leicht; — *v.* geringschätzig behandeln, vernachlässigen; -ness *n.* Geringfügigkeit, Nachlässigkeit; Schwäche, Dünnheit

slim *adj.* schlank, schmächtig; unbedeutend, unwesentlich; gerissen; -ness *n.* Schlankheit

slime *n.* Schleim, Schlamm

sling *n.* Schleuder; Tragriemen, Gewehrriemen; Wurf, Stoss; (med.) Schlinge, Binde; — *v.* schleudern; überhängen, umschlingen; (mil.) schultern

slingshot *n.* Schleuder

slink *v.* schleichen

slip *n.* Gleiten, Rutschen; Entschlüpfen, Entwischen; Unterrock; Kissenbezug; (bot.) Spross, Steckling; (naut.) Helling; (fig.) Fehler, Versehen; — **of paper** Zettel; — **of the tongue** Versprechen; — *v.* gleiten, rutschen; ausgleiten; schleudern; entwischen, entschlüpfen; (fig.) sich irren (*or* versprechen); -pery *adj.* schlüpfrig, glitschig, glatt; (fig.) unzuverlässlich, veränderlich

slipcover *n.* Möbelüberzug; Schutzumschlag

slipper *n.* Pantoffel, Hausschuhe

slipshod *adj.* latschig, nachlässig; unordentlich

slit *n.* Schlitz, Spalte; — *v.* (zer)schlitzen, spalten

sliver *n.* Splitter; — *v.* abreissen, abspalten, splittern

slobber *n.* Geifer; — *v.* geifern, sabbern

slogan *n.* Schlagwort, Reklametext

sloop *n.* Schaluppe, Korvette

slop *n.* Pfuhl, Pfütze; Schmutzfleck; *pl.* Spülwasser; Gesöff; Krankensuppe; fertiggekaufte Kleidungsstücke; — **pail** Spüleimer; -py *adj.* nass, wässrig;

(coll.) schmutzig, nachlässig

slope *n.* Abhang, Neigung, Böschung; Abschrägung, Fall; — *v.* abfallen; (sich) neigen (*or* abschrägen)

slot *n.* Öffnung, Einwurf, Schlitz; (mech.) Kerbe, Nut; — **machine** Automat

slouch *n.* schlaffe Haltung; Müssiggänger; — *adj.* — **hat** Schlapphut; — *v.* schlottern, schlendern; (coll.) latschen

slough *n.* Sumpf, Pfütze; (mech.) Schlauch, Balg; (med.) Schorf; (zool.) abgeworfene Schlangenhaut; (fig.) Niedergeschlagenheit

slovenly *adj.* schmutzig, schlampig, liederlich

slow *adj.* langsam, träge; spät, nachgehend; schwerfällig, bedächtig; faul, nachlässig; — **motion** Zeitlupe; — *v.* verlangsamen, hinziehen; — **down** langsamer fahren, sich mehr Zeit lassen; -ness *n.* Langsamkeit; Nachlässigkeit; Begriffsstutzigkeit

sludge *n.* Schlamm; Eisscholle

slug *n.* Schlag; (mech.) Hackblei, Metallstück; (zool.) Wegschnecke; — *v.* einen Schlag versetzen; -gard *n.* Faulenzer, Müssiggänger; -gish *adj.* träge, schwerfällig, faul; albern, dumm; (agr.) unfruchtbar; -gishness *n.* Trägheit, Schwerfälligkeit

sluice *n.* Schleuse, Siel; durchgeschleuste Wasser; — *v.* schleusen; überschwemmen, berieseln; waschen

slum *n.* Hintergasse; *pl.* Elendsviertel, Verbrechergegend; — *v.* Elendsquartiere besuchen, im Armenviertel arbeiten

slumber *n.* Schlummer; — *v.* schlummern

slump *n.* Preissturz, Nachlassen

slur *n.* Fleck, Makel; Vorwurf, Verleumdung; (mus.) Bindezeichen; — *v.* beschmutzen, beflecken; verleumden; vertuschen, übergehen; (mus.) binden, schleifen

slush *n.* Matsch, Schlamm; (mech.) Schmiere

small *n.* Kleine; Kurzwaren, Kleingebäck; — **of the back** Kreuz, Lendengegend; — *adj.* klein, schmal, gering, dünn, schlank; (fig.) kleinlich, beschränkt; — **arms** Handwaffen; — **change** Kleingeld; — **fry** kleines Gemüse, Kinder; — **hours** erste Morgenstunden; — **intestine** Dünndarm; — **talk** Plauderei; -ish *adj.* winzig, schmächtig; -ness *n.* Kleinheit, Schmalheit; Unbedeutenheit

smallpox *n.* Pocken, Blattern

smart *n.* Schmerz, Stich; — *adj.* gewandt, gerissen, schlau, pfiffig; elegant, fein; schmerzhaft, heftig, stechend, schneidend; — **money** Schmerzensgeld; **–ness** *n.* Schlauheit, Gescheitheit; Eleganz; Schneidigkeit

smash *n.* Zerschmettern; Krach; Zerstörung; (tennis) Schmetterball; (sl.) Zusammenbruch, Bankrott; — *v.* zerschmeissen, zertrümmern, (zer)schmettern

smashup *n.* schrecklicher Zusammenstoss (*or* Zusammenbruch)

smattering *n.* oberflächliche Kenntnis

smear *n.* Schmiere; Schmiererei; (coll.) Verleumdung; — *v.* schmieren, beschmieren, besudeln; (coll.) anschwärzen

smell *n.* Geruch; Duft; **sense of** — Geruchssinn; — *v.* riechen; duften; (coll.) aufspüren

smile *n.* Lächeln; — *v.* lächeln, schmunzeln

smirch *v.* beschmieren, besudeln

smite *v.* (er)schlagen, treffen, eindringen; heimsuchen, vernichten

smith *n.* Schmied; **black–** Grobschmied, Hufschmied; **–(er)y** *n.* Schmiede; Schmiedehandwerk

smock *n.* Frauenhemd; Kittel; — **frock** Staubmantel, Arbeitskittel

smog *n.* Rauchschleier, Dunstschleier; russige Atmosphäre

smoke *n.* Rauch, Qualm, Dunst; (coll.) Rauchware; — **consumer** Rauchverzehrer; — **pipe** Abzugsrohr; — **screen** Rauchvorhang; künstliche Nebelschleier; — *v.* rauchen, räuchern; qualmen, dampfen; (mil.) einnebeln; **–less** *adj.* rauchlos; **–less powder** rauchschwaches Pulver; **–r** *n.* Raucher; Räucherer; (coll.) Raucherabteil

smokehouse *n.* Räucherhaus

smokestack *n.* Schornstein, Rauchfang

smoking *n.* Rauchen; Räuchern; — *adj.* rauchend, räuchernd; — **car** Raucherabteil; **no** —! Rauchen verboten!

smoky *adj.* rauchig, qualmig; dampfend, nebelig

smolder *n.* Qualm; — *v.* schwelen, qualmen; glimmen

smooth *adj.* glatt; mild, schlicht, sanft; poliert; (fig.) fliessend, geschmeidig, schmeichlerisch; — *v.* glätten, polieren, ebnen; plätten; (fig.) mildern, schlichten; **–ly** *adv.* sanft, weich; geschoren; klumpenfrei; fliessend; **–ness** *n.* Glätte, Ebenheit; (fig.) Sanftheit, Freundlichkeit

smother *n.* Qualm, Dunst; — *v.* ersticken; dämpfen, schmoren

smudge *n.* Fleck, Schmutz; — *v.* (be)schmieren, beschmutzen

smug *adj.* schmuck, sauber; (fig.) eitel, selbstzufrieden

smuggle *v.* schmuggeln; **–r** *n.* Schmuggler

smuggling *n.* Schmuggel

smut *n.* Russ(fleck); Schmutz; Zote; (agr.) Brand; — *v.* berussen, beschmutzen; (agr.) den Brand bekommen; **–ty** *adj.* russig, schmutzig; (agr.) brandig; (fig.) schlüpfrig, zotig

snack *n.* Bissen, Imbiss; Anteil; **go –s** teilnehmen, teilhaben

snag *n.* Knoten, Knorren; Baumstumpf; (zool.) Geweihsprosse; Raffzahn

snail *n.* Schnecke

snake *n.* Schlange, Natter; — *v.* schlängeln, winden

snap *n.* Zuschnappen, Schnapper; Knall, Knack(s); Bruch, Sprung; (coll.) etwas Leichtes; — *v.* schnappen, zuschnappen; (zer)springen, abbrechen; (coll.) anschnauzen; — **one's fingers at** someone jemandem ein Schnippchen schlagen; **–per** *n.* Schnapper; **–py** *adj.* schnippig, bissig; beissend; (coll.) lebhaft, elegant

snapdragon *n.* Löwenmaul

snapshot *n.* Schnappschuss, Momentaufnahme

snare *n.* Schlinge, Fallstrick; — *v.* verstrikken, umgarnen; mit einer Schlinge fangen

snarl *n.* Knurren; — *v.* knurren, brummen

snatch *n.* schneller Griff, Ruck; Stückchen, Bissen; Augenblick; — *v.* schnell ergreifen, erhaschen, erschnappen; **an** sich reissen

sneak *n.* Schleicher, Kriecher; Duckmäuser; — *v.* schleichen, kriechen; stibitzen; angeben

sneer *n.* Hohnlächeln, Naserümpfen; Stichelei; — *v.* hohnlächeln, spötteln, die Nase rümpfen

sneeze *n.* Niesen; — *v.* niesen

snicker *n.* Gekicher; — *v.* kichern

sniff *n.* Schnüffeln, Naserümpfen; — *v.* schnüffeln, schnuppern, riechen; die Nase rümpfen; (fig.) spionieren, wittern; **–le** *n.* Näseln; **–le** *v.* näseln; schnupfen, triefen; wimmern

snip *n.* Schnippen; Schnitzel; — *v.* schnippen; schnipseln, schneiden

snipe *n.* Schnepfe, Bekassine; — *v.* Schnepfen schiessen; (mil.) aus dem Hinterhalt (*or* grosser Entfernung) schiessen; **–r** *n.* Scharfschütze

snivel *n.* Nasenschleim, Rotz; — *v.* Schnupfen haben, schnüffeln, triefen; schluchzen, wehleidig tun; **–ly** *adj.* triefnasig, schnüffelnd

snob *n.* Snob, Grosstuer, Protz; **–bish** *adj.*

snobistisch, eingebildet; protzig

snood *n.* Haarband, Haarnetz

snoop *n.* Schnüffler; (coll.) Detektiv; — *v.* schnüffeln, aufspüren; (coll.) spionieren

snooze *n.* Schlummer, Schläfchen; — *v.* schlummern, ein Schläfchen tun

snore *n.* Schnarchen; — *v.* schnarchen

snorkel *n.* Schnorchel; Feuerleiter

snout *n.* Schnauze, Maul; Rüssel; (mech.) Mundstück, Tülle; (coll.) Nase

snow *n.* Schnee; — line Schneegrenze; — owl Schneeule; — *v.* schneien; -y *adj.* schneeig, beschneit; schneeweiss

snowball *n.* Schneeball; — tree Schneeballstrauch

snowbound *adj.* eingeschneit

snowdrift *n.* Schneewehe

snowdrop *n.* Schneeglöckchen

snowflake *n.* Schneeflocke

snowplow *n.* Schneepflug

snowshed *n.* Lawinenschutzwand

snowslide *n.* Lawine

snowstorm *n.* Schneesturm

snowsweeper *n.* Schneepflug

snow-white *adj.* schneeweiss; Snow-white *n.* Schneewittchen

snub *n.* Zurechtweisung, Rüge, Verweis; — *v.* rügen, verweisen, schelten

snub-nosed *adj.* stumpfnasig

snuff *n.* Schnupftabak; Schnauben; — *v.* schnauben, schnüffeln, schnupfen; näseln, verschnupft sein; -er *n.* Tabakschnupfer; Lichtputzschere; -le *v.* schnuppern, beschnüffeln; näseln; -les *n. pl.* (med.) festsitzender Schnupfen

snuffbox *n.* Schnupftabakdose

snug *adj.* schmuck, nett; eng; behaglich, wohnlich; -gle *v.* (sich) anschmiegen, liebkosen

so *adv.* so, also; derartig, indem; wie, auch; and — forth und so weiter; I hope — ich hoffe es; — as solange als; — much (gerade) soviel; — much more um so mehr; — then darum, daher

soak *n.* Einweichen; (coll.) Kneiperei, Sauferei; — *v.* einweichen, einsaugen, durchnässen; (coll.) sich vollaufen lassen

soap *n.* Seife; (sl.) Schmus; Bestechungsgeld; — bubble Seifenblase; — factory Seifenfabrik; — opera Schmalzoper, schmalziges Programm; (rad.) Programm für die Hausfrauen; — *v.* (ein)seifen; (sl.) schmeicheln, bestechen, schmieren; -less *adj.* seifenlos; (coll.) ungewaschen; -y *adj.* seifig; (coll.) aalglatt, glattzüngig

soapbox *n.* Seifenkiste; (coll.) improvisierte Plattform

soapstone *n.* Speckstein

soapsuds *n. pl.* Seifenlauge, Seifenwasser

soar *v.* sich erheben (or aufschwingen); -ing *n.* Aufstieg; -ing *adj.* hochfliegend, erhaben

sob *n.* Schluchzen, Schluchzer; — *v.* schluchzen

sober *adj.* nüchtern, mässig; ernst, besonnen

so-called *adj.* sogenannt

soccer *n.* Rugbyart

sociability *n.* Geselligkeit

sociable *adj.* gesellig

social *adj.* sozial; gesellschaftlich, gesellig; — science Sozialwissenschaft, Soziologie; — security Sozialversicherung; — services soziale Einrichtungen; — work Fürsorge; — worker Fürsorger; -ism *n.* Sozialismus; -ist *n.* Sozialist; -istic *adj.* sozialistisch; -ize *v.* sozialisieren

society *n.* Gesellschaft; Verein, Bund

sociological *adj.* soziologisch

sociology *n.* Soziologie, Sozialwissenschaft

sock *n.* Socke; Einlegesohle; (sl.) Prügel

socket *n.* (anat.) Höhle, Pfanne; (elec.) Fassung; (mech.) Röhre

sod *n.* Rasen(decke); — *v.* mit Rasen belegen

soda *n.* Soda, kohlensaures Natron; baking — Backpulver; — bicarbonate doppelkohlensaures Natron; — cracker Salzkeks; — fountain Siphon; — water Selterwasser

sodium *n.* Natrium; — chloride Chlornatrium, Kochsalz

sofa *n.* Sofa, Ruhebett

soft *adj.* weich, sanft; mild, zart; zärtlich; (coll.) einfältig; — coal Braunkohle; — drink alkoholfreies Getränk; -en *v.* erweichen; mildern, lindern; (fig.) besänftigen; -ening *n.* Erweichen; -ening of the brain Gehirnerweichung; -ness *n.* Weichheit, Sanftmut, Milde

softball *n.* Baseballart

soft-boiled *adj.* weichgekocht; — eggs weich(gekocht)e Eier

soft-pedal *v.* zurücknehmen, leiser treten

soft-spoken *adj.* leise sprechend; (fig.) sanft, mild

soggy *adj.* durchweicht, nass, feucht; sumpfig

soil *n.* Boden, Erde; Suhle; Schmutz, Fleck; (agr.) Dünger; — *v.* beschmutzen, besudeln, beflecken; (agr.) düngen, Grünfutter geben; -ed *adj.* beschmutzt, besudelt, befleckt

solac·*n.* Trost, Erquickung; — *v.* trösten, erquicken, aufheitern; beruhigen

solar *adj.* solar; Sonnen-; — plexus Sonnengeflecht; — system Sonnensystem;

–ium *n.* sonniger Raum. Glasveranda

solder *n.* Lot; Lötzinn; Kitt, Bindemittel; — *v.* löten, kitten; (fig.) verbinden, zusammenfügen; **–ing** *n.* Löten; **–ing iron** Lötkolben

soldier *n.* Soldat; **–ly** *adj.* soldatisch, militärisch; Soldaten-

sole *n.* Sohle; (ichth.) Seezunge; — *adj.* allein, einzig; (law) ledig, unverheiratet; — *v.* besohlen

solemn *adj.* feierlich, würdevoll; **–ity** *n.* Ernst, Feierlichkeit, Würde; Festlichkeit; **–ize** *v.* feiern, festlich begehen; feierlich stimmen

solicit *v.* nachsuchen, ersuchen; (dringend) bitten, sich bewerben; erfordern; ansprechen, belästigen; **–ation** *n.* Ersuchen, dringende Bitte; **–or** *n.* Antragsteller; Bittsteller; (law) Anwalt; **–ous** *adj.* besorgt, bekümmert; **–ude** *n.* Besorgnis, Sorge; Sorgfalt

solid *adj.* fest, dicht, massiv, dauerhaft; echt, gediegen; stark, gesund; (com.) kreditfähig, solide; (geom.) körperlich, kubisch; (pol.) einstimmig, einhellig; (fig.) zuverlässig; **in — color** einfarbig; **— geometry** Stereometrie; **— state physics** Festkörperphysik; **–arity** *n.* Solidarität; **–ify** *v.* (sich) verdichten, verhärten; **–ity** *n.* Solidität, Gediegenheit; Festigkeit

soliloquise *n.* Monologisierende

soliloquy *n.* Monolog, Selbstgespräch

solitary *n.* Einsiedler, Eremit; — *adj.* allein, einsam, abgesondert; abgelegen; zurückgezogen; einzeln

solitude *n.* Einsamkeit

solstice *n.* Sonnenwende

solution *n.* Lösung

solve *v.* (auf)lösen; **–ncy** *n.* Zahlungsfähigkeit; **–nt** *adj.* (auf)lösend; zahlungsfähig; **–nt** *n.* Lösungsmittel

somatic *adj.* physisch, körperlich

some *adj.* and *pron.* irgendein, ein gewisser; etwas; einige, etliche, manche; etwa, ungefähr; — *adv.* etwas, sehr

somebody *n.* jemand; — *adj.* and *pron.* jemand, irgendein

somehow *adv.* irgendwie, auf irgendeine Art

someone *pron.* irgendjemand, irgendein

somersault, somerset *n.* Purzelbaum; — *v.* einen Purzelbaum schiessen

something *n.* etwas; — *adv.* etwas, ein wenig; ziemlich; — **else** etwas anderes

sometime *adv.* einmal, einst; ehemals; — *adj.* ehemalig, früher; **–s** *adv.* zuweilen, manchmal

somewhat *n.* etwas Bedeutendes; — *adv.* etwas, ein wenig; einigermassen, ziemlich

somewhere *adv.* irgendwo(hin); — **else** anderswo

somnambulism *n.* Nachtwandeln, Somnambulismus

son *n.* Sohn

sonar *n.* Sonar-Gerät (ein speziell amerikanisches Gerät, eine Verbesserung des Echolot)

song *n.* Lied; Gesang; (lit.) Gedicht; **buy for a** — spottbillig kaufen; **Song of Solomon** Hohe Lied Salomons; — **sparrow** Rohrsperling; — **thrush** Singdrossel; — **writer** Liederdichter, Liederkomponist; **–ster** *n.* Sänger; Singvogel

songbook *n.* Liederbuch, Gesangbuch

sonic *adj.* mit Schallgeschwindigkeit; — **barrier** Schallgrenze; — **boom** Schallexplosion

son-in-law *n.* Schwiegersohn

sonorous *adj.* klangvoll, wohltönend

soon *adv.* bald, schnell; früh(zeitig); **as —** **as** sobald wie; **–er** *adv.* eher, früher; lieber; **no –er than** kaum . . . als; **–er or later** früher oder später

soot *n.* Russ; — *v.* (be)russen; **–y** *adj.* russig, berusst; russend; (fig.) düster

soothe *v.* beruhigen, besänftigen, lindern

soothsayer *n.* Wahrsager

sophism *n.* Sophismus; Trugschluss

sophist *n.* Sophist; **–ic(al)** *adj.* sophistisch; **–icate** *v.* unnatürlich (*or* gekünstelt) werden; aufklären; anders darstellen; **–icate(d)** *adj.* gekünstelt, unnatürlich; anspruchsvoll, weltklug; **–ication** *n.* Sophisterei, Trugschluss; Verfälschung; **–ry** *n.* Sophistik, Spitzfindigkeit

sophomore *n.* Student (im zweiten Jahr)

sopping *adj.* durchweicht; — **wet** klatschnass

soprano *n.* Sopran; — **singer** Sopranistin

sorcerer *n.* Zauberer, Hexenmeister

sorceress *n.* Zauberin, Hexe

sorcery *n.* Zauberei, Zauberkunst; **Hexerei**, Magie

sordid *adj.* schmutzig; gemein; geizig

sore *n.* wunde Stelle; Übel; — *adj.* wund, schmerzhaft, entzündet; empfindlich; schlimm; — **throat** Halsschmerzen, Halsweh

sorehead *n.* Sauertopf, Missvergnügte

sorghum *n.* chinesisches Zuckerrohr

sorority *n.* Schwesternschaft; Mädchenverein, Frauenklub

sorrel *n.* Sauerampfer; (zool.) Rotfuchs; — *adj.* rotbraun, fuchsrot

sorrow *n.* Sorge, Trübsal; Gram, Kummer, Leid; — *v.* trauern, sich grämen (*or* grämen, betrüben); **–ful** *adj.* sorgenvoll, kummervoll; betrübt, jämmerl͟i͟.

sorry *adj.* traurig, bekümmert, betrübt; **be — etwas** bedauern; **I am very —** es tut mir leid; entschuldigen Sie, bitte

sort *n.* Sorte, Art, Gattung, Qualität; Weise; **in some — of** gewissermassen; **out of —s** unpässlich, verdriesslich; **something of the —, that — of thing** etwas Derartiges; **—** *v.* sortieren, aussuchen; klassifizieren, aussondern; übereinstimmen

so-so *adv.* soso, leidlich, einigermassen

sot *n.* Trunkenbold; **-tish** *adj.* versoffen, dumm

soul *n.* Seele; **-ful** *adj.* seelenvoll

sound *n.* Ton, Laut, Schall, Klang; (ichth.) Schwimmblase; (med.) Sonde; (naut.) Sund, Meerenge; **—** *adj.* gesund, unversehrt, unbeschädigt; unverdorben; tadellos; stark, tüchtig, gründlich; (sleep) fest; **— track** Tonspur; **— wave** Schallwelle; **—** *v.* (er)tönen, (er)schallen, (er)klingen; erschallen lassen; (med.) sondieren; abhorchen; (naut.) loten; **-ing** *n.* Lotung; **-ing** *adj.* tönend, klingend, klangvoll, wohlklingend; (er)schallend; (gram.) stimmhaft; (fig.) bombastisch; **-ing line** Lotleine, Senkschnur; **-ness** *n.* Gesundheit, Unversehrtheit; Stärke; Gründlichkeit, Zuverlässigkeit, Richtigkeit

soundboard *n.* Resonanzboden

sounder key *n.* Morsetaste

soundproof *adj.* schalldicht; **—** *r.* schalldicht machen

soup *n.* Suppe, Brühe; (avi.) Milchsuppe, Nebel

sour *n.* Säure, Saure; **—** *adj.* sauer; scharf, bitter, geronnen; (agr.) kalt, nass; (fig.) sauertöpfig, mürrisch; **—** *v.* säuern; (fig.) erbittern, erzürnen, versauern

source *n.* Quelle, Ursprung; Urheber

souse *n.* Salzlake, Pökelbrühe; **—** *v.* einsalzen, einpökeln, durchnässen

south *n.* Süden; Südseite; Südwind; **—** *adj.* südlich, Süd-; **-ern** *adj.* südlich; **-erner** *n.* Südländer, Südstaatler

southernmost *adj.* südlichst

South Pole *n.* Südpol

southward *adv.* südwärts

southwest *n.* Südwest(en); **-(ern)** *adj.* südwestlich; **-er** *n.* Südwestwind; (hat) Südwester

souvenir *n.* Souvenir, Andenken

sovereign *n.* Souverän, Herrscher; Sovereign, Pfund Sterling; **—** *adj.* souverän, unumschränkt; höchst, vornehmst; unübertrefflich, unfehlbar; **-ty** *n.* Souveränität, Oberherrschaft

Soviet *n.* Sowjet

sow *n.* Sau, Bache, Mutterschwein; (mech.) Mulde; **—** *v.* (aus)säen, ausstreuen; **-er** *n.* Säemann, Säemaschine; **-ing** *n.* Aussaat; Saatkorn

soybean *n.* Sojabohne

spa *n.* Heilbad, Kurort

space *n.* Raum, Platz; Zwischenraum; Zeitraum; Flächeninhalt; **— capsule** Kapsel des Astronauten; Weltraumschiff; **— command** Fernlenkung, Fernsteuerung; **— control** Photogrametrie; **— suit** Überdruckkombination, Raumanzug des Astronauten; **—** *v.* einteilen, in Zwischenräume setzen; (typ.) durchschiessen, sperren

spaceship *n.* Raumschiff

spacious *adj.* geräumig, umfassend; weit

spade *n.* Spaten; (cards) Pik; **call a — a —** das Kind beim richtigen Namen nennen; **—** *v.* graben; umgraben

span *n.* Spanne; (agr.) Gespann; (arch.) Spannweite; **— of a bridge** Brückenweite, Brückenbogen; **—** *v.* (um)spannen, überspannen; (naut.) zurren

spangle *n.* Flitter; **—** *v.* mit Flitter besetzen; flimmern, funkeln; (fig.) übersäen

spaniel *n.* Spaniel, Wachtelhund

spank *n.* Schlag, Klaps; **—** *v.* klapsen; eilen, flitzen

spar *n.* Sparren; (min.) Spat; (naut.) Spiere; (fig.) Finte; **—** *v.* Scheinhiebe machen; (boxing) trainieren; (fig.) sich streiten

spare *v.* (er)sparen, schonen; erübrigen; entbehren; **—** *adj.* sparsam, spärlich; mager, karg; verfügbar; **— anchor** Reserveanker; **— bed** Gastbett; **— money** Sparpfennig, Notgroschen; **— parts** Ersatzteile; **— time** Freizeit, Mussezeit; **— tire** Ersatzreifen; **-ly** *adv.* sparsam, spärlich; kaum

sparerib *n.* Rippespeer, Rippenstück

sparing *n.* Sparen, Sparsamkeit; **—** *adj.* sparsam, karg; spärlich, knapp; voraussehend

spark *n.* Funke(n); **— plug** Zündkerze; **-le** *n.* Funke(n); **-le** *v.* funkeln, blitzen, sprühen; (wine) schäumen

sparrow *n.* Sperling, Spatz; **— hawk** Sperber

spasm *n.* Krampf; **-odic** *adj.* krampfhaft

spastic *adj.* zuckend

spatial *adj.* räumlich

spatter *n.* Spritzer; Geknatter; **—** *v.* (be)spritzen

spatula *n.* Spatel; (orn.) Löffelente

spawn *n.* Laich, Rogen, Fischbrut; **—** *v.* laichen; (coll.) aushecken; **-ing** *n.*

Laichen

speak *v.* sprechen, reden; äussern; (mus.) erschallen, erklingen; (naut.) anpreien; **so to** — sozusagen; — **for** bitten, ein Wort einlegen für; — **for oneself** sich verteidigen; — **in torrents** sich in einem Wortschwall ergiessen; — **out** laut sprechen; offen reden, aussprechen; — **plainly** freiheraus sprechen; — **to** anreden, ins Gewissen reden; — **up!** heraus mit der Sprache! **-er** *n.* Sprecher, Redner; Vorsitzende; **-ing** *n.* Sprechen, Reden; **-ing** *adj.* sprechend, ausdrucksvoll

spear *n.* Speer, Spiess, Lange; — *v.* durchbohren, (auf)spiessen

spearhead *n.* Speerspitze, Lanzenspitze; (mil.) Vortrupp, Spitze

special *adj.* speziell; besonder, eigen, ausserordentlich; Spezial-; — **delivery** Eilzustellung; **-ist** *n.* Spezialist, Fachmann, Facharzt; **-ize** *v.* spezialisieren; einzeln anführen; besonders ausbilden; **-(i)ty** *n.* Spezialität

special-delivery letter *n.* Eilbrief

species *n. pl.* Art, Gattung, Sorte

specific *adj.* spezifisch; eigen(tümlich), besonder; — **gravity** spezifisches Gewicht; — *n.* (med.) besonderes Heilmittel; **-ation** *n.* Spezifizierung; Einzelangabe, Beschreibung; **-ations** *pl.* Bestimmungen

specify *v.* einzeln angeben (*or* benennen); spezifizieren

specimen *n.* Probe(stück), Muster, Exemplar

spectacle *n.* Anblick; Schauspiel, Schau; *pl.* Brille, Augengläser

spectacular *adj.* schauspielerisch; lärmend; — *n.* (TV) Fernsehgrossprogramm

spectator *n.* Zuschauer, Beobachter

spectral *adj.* geisterhaft, gespenstisch; (phy.) Spektral-

spectrogram *n.* fotografische Aufnahme eines Spektrums

spectroscope *n.* Spektroskop, Spektralapparat

spectrum *n.* Spektrum, Farbenbild; **solar** — Sonnenspektrum

speculate *v.* spekulieren

speculation *n.* Spekulation

speech *n.* Sprache; Rede, Vortrag; Unterredung, Unterhaltung; **-less** *adj.* sprachlos, stumm

speed *n.* Eile, Schnelligkeit, Geschwindigkeit; (mech.) Gang, Lauf; (fig.) Beschleunigung, Fortgang, Erfolg; **average** — Durchschnittsgeschwindigkeit; **good** —! viel Glück! (*or* Erfolg!); **initial** — Anfangsgeschwindigkeit; — **limit**

(zulässige) Höchstgeschwindigkeit; — *v.* (be)eilen; beschleunigen, fördern; (fig.) glücken, gelingen; **-ily** *adv.* schnellfüssig; eilfertig; rasch bereit; baldig; förderlich; **-y** *adj.* eilig, schnell, rasch; (fig.) glücklich

speedboat *n.* Rennboot; Schnellboot

speedometer *n.* Tachometer, Geschwindigkeitsanzeiger

speed-up *n.* Beschleunigung

speedway *n.* Schnellstrasse

spell *n.* Zauber; Zauberformel; **Ablösung**; (med.) Anfall; (coll.) Unterbrechung, Atempause; — *v.* bezaubern; ablösen; ausruhen; (gram.) buchstabieren, richtig schreiben; (fig.) entziffern, ergründen; **-er** *n.* Fibel; Buchstabierer; **-ing** *n.* Buchstabieren; Orthographie, Rechtschreibung

spellbound *adj.* (fest)gebannt, bezaubert

spelunker *n.* Höhlenforscher

spend *v.* spenden, ausgeben, verwenden; erschöpfen, verschwenden; (time) verbringen

spendthrift *n.* Verschwender; — *adj.* verschwenderisch

spent *adj.* verausgabt, verbraucht; erschöpft, entkräftet; matt

sperm *n.* (männlicher) Same

spermatozoon *n.* Samenfädchen

spew *v.* (aus)speien; (coll.) erbrechen

sphere *n.* Sphäre, Wirkungskreis; **Kugel**; Erdkugel, Himmelskugel

spice *n.* Gewürz; (fig.) Würze, Beigeschmack; — *v.* würzen

spick-and-span *adj.* blitzblank; funkelnagelneu; schmuck

spicy *adj.* würzig, aromatisch; gewürzt; (coll.) pikant

spider *n.* Spinne; (mech.) Dreifuss

spigot *n.* Zapfen, Hahn

spike *n.* Nagel, Stift; (bot.) Ähre; **Kolben**; Dorn, Stachel; (zool.) Geweihsprosse; *pl.* (sports) Spikes

spill *n.* Umwerfen, Abfluss; Fidibus; (coll.) Sturz; — *v.* verschütten, verspritzen, vergiessen; (naut.) brassen; (coll.) abwerfen

spin *n.* Wirbeln; Drehung; rasche Fahrt; — *v.* wirbeln, kreiseln, trudeln, drehen; spinnen; **-dle** *n.* Spindel, Spule; **-ning** *n.* Spinnerei; Gespinst; **-ning** *adj.* **-ning frame** Spinnmaschine; **-ning jenny** Mehrspulmaschine; **-ning mill** Spinnerei; **-ning wheel** Spinnrad

spinach *n.* Spinat

spinal *adj.* spinal, Rücken-; — **columa** Rückgrat, Wirbelsäule; — **cord** Rükkenmark

spine *n.* (anat.) Rückgrat; (bot.) Dorn,

Stachel; (geol.) Grat; (ichth.) Stachel

spinster n. alte Jungfer

spiral adj. Spiral-; schneckenförmig, schraubenförmig; — **stairs** Wendeltreppe; — n. Spirale, Schneckenlinie

spire n. Spitze, Gipfel; (arch.) Turmspitze; Kirchturm

spirit n. Geist; Gespenst; Genie; Sinn, Mut; Seele, Gemütsart; pl. Spiritus; Spirituosen; **in high —s** guter Laune; — v. begeistern, aufmuntern; — **away** verschwinden lassen, wegzaubern; entführen; **—ed** adj. geistvoll, lebhaft, feurig; mutig; **—ism** n. Spiritismus, Geisterglaube; **—ual** adj. geistig, geistlich; geistreich; **—ualism** n. Spiritualismus; Spiritismus; **—ualist** n. Spiritualist; Spiritist

spirit v. (hervor)spritzen; (hervor)strömen

spit n. Speichel, Spucke; Sprühregen; (geol.) Landzunge; (mech.) Spiess; — v. spucken, speien; (auf)spiessen; **—tle** n. Speichel; (coll.) Spucke; **—toon** n. Spucknapf

spite n. Groll, Ärger, Verdruss; Bosheit; **in —** of trotz, ungeachtet; **out of spite** aus Groll, zum Ärger; — v. grollen, ärgern; kränken; **—ful** adj. boshaft, gehässig; feindselig

spitfire n. Hitzkopf

spitz n. (dog) Spitz

splash n. Fleck, Spritzer; — v. (be)spritzen, platschen

splayfoot n. Spreizfuss

spleen n. Spleen, Verschrobenheit, üble Laune; (anat.) Milz

splendid adj. glänzend, prächtig, herrlich

splendo(u)r n. Glanz, Pracht, Herrlichkeit

splice n. Verbinden, Einfügen; (naut.) Spleissen; (sl.) Heirat; — v. verbinden, einfügen; verweben; (naut.) spleissen; (sl.) verheiraten

splint n. Splitter, Span; (mech.) Splint; (med.) Schiene; — v. schienen; **—er** n. Span, Splitter; **—er** v. (zer)splittern, zerspalten

split n. Spalt, Riss, Bruch; Spaltung; — adj. gespalten, gespaltet; — v. spalten, zereissen; bersten; (sich) entzweien; — **one's sides with laughter sich totlachen; —ting** adj. spaltend; sehr heftig, schnell; **—ting headache** rasende Kopfschmerzen

spoil n. Raub; (mech.) Schlacke; pl. Beute, — v. (be)rauben, plündern; verderben; verwöhnen; stören; **—er** n. Räuber, Plünderer; Verderber; Störenfried

spoke n. Speiche, Sprosse; (mech.) Hemmvorrichtung

spokesman n. Wortführer, Fürsprecher

sponge n. Schwamm; (coll.) Schmarotzer; **throw up the —** (sports) sich für besiegt erklären; — v. abwischen, auslöschen; reiben; aufsaugen; (coll.) schmarotzen; — **up** sich vollsaugen; **—r** n. Wischer; Anfeuchter; (naut.) Schwammfischer; (coll.) Schmarotzer

spongecake n. Biskuitkuchen

spongy adj. schwammig, porös

sponsor n. Förderer, Gönner; Bürge; Pate; (rad.) reklamemachende Firma

spontaneity n. Spontanietät; Freiwilligkeit

spontaneous adj. spontan, freiwillig; Selbst-; — **combustion** Selbstverbrennung

spook n. Spuken; — v. spuken

spool n. Spule; — v. (auf)spulen

spoon n. Löffel; — v. (aus)löffeln; **-ful** n. Löffelvoll

spore n. Spore

sport n. Sport; Spiel, Unterhaltung; — **shirt** Sporthemd; — v. spielen, sich belustigen, scherzen; Sport treiben; **—ing** adj. spielend; sporttreibend; Sport-; **—ive** adj. lustig, scherzhaft; kurzweilig; sportlich

sportsman n. Sportler; Sportliebhaber; Weidmann; **-ship** n. Sportlichkeit

spot n. Fleck(en), Klecks; Tupfen, Punkt; Stelle, Ort; (cards and dice) Auge; — **cash** Bargeld; — **remover** Fleckenentferner; — v. (be)flecken; tüpfeln, sprenkeln; feststellen; **—ting** adj. **—ting system** Meldesystem; **-less** adj. fleckenlos; unbefleckt; **—ted** adj., **-ty** adj. gefleckt, fleckig; gesprenkelt, getupft; (fig.) befleckt, besudelt; **—ted fever** Flecktyphus

spotlight n. Schweinwerfer(licht)

spouse n. Gemahl; Gatte; Gattin

spout n. Wasserstrahl; Ausguss, Traufe; Tülle, Schnabel; (naut.) Wasserhose; — v. hervorspritzen, hervorquellen, heraussprudeln, herausspringen; (fig.) deklamieren, vortragen

sprain n. Verrenkung; — v. verrenken

sprawl v. sich spreizen (or rekeln)

spray n. Sprühregen; (bot.) Zweig, Reis; (mech.) Zerstäuber, Spritze; (naut.) Gischt; — **gun** Spritzpistole, Zerstäuber; — v. bestäuben, (be)sprühen, zerstieben; (med.) ausspritzen

spread n. Verbreitung; Ausdehnung, Umfang, Fläche; Bettdecke, Tischtuch; (mil.) Streuung; — adj. ausgebreitet, breit; — v. (aus)breiten, verbreiten;

entfalten, ausspannen, ausdehen; (be)-
decken; bestreichen

spree *n.* Spass, Streich, Jux; Zechgelage,
Bummel

sprig *n.* Spross, Schössling; (mech.)
Zwecke, Stift; (fig.) Sprössling

sprightly *adj.* lebhaft, heiter, munter;
mutig

spring *n.* Frühling; Frühjahr; (geol.)
Quelle; (mech.) Feder; Federkraft;
(fig.) Triebfeder, Ursprung; — **balance**
Federwage; — **gun** Selbstschuss; —
mattress Sprungfedermatratze; — *v.*
springen; emporschiessen; sprudeln;
(fig.) entspringen, entstehen; befreien;
— **back** zurückspringen; — **from** entspringen von (*or* aus); **-er** *n.* Springer;
(arch.) Gewölbetragstein; (zool.)
Springbock; **-like** *adj.* frühlingshaft; **-y**
adj. elastisch, federnd

springboard *n.* Sprungbrett

sprinkle *n.* Sprühregen; Sprenkelmuster;
— *v.* (be)sprengen, bespritzen, sprühen;
sprenkeln; **-r** *n.* Rasensprenger; Giesskanne; Sprengwagen

sprinkling *n.* Sprengen, Spritzen; (coll.)
Anflug, Anstrich

sprint *n.* Sprint; kurzer, scharfer Wettlauf; — *v.* sprinten

sprite *n.* Geist, Kobold

sprocket *n.* Radkranzstift; — **wheel**
Kettenrad

sprout *n.* Spross(e), Sprössling, Keim; —
v. spriessen, wachsen, keimen

spruce *n.* Fichte; — *adj.* nett, sauber,
schmuck; geputzt; — *v.* herausputzen

spry *adj.* flink, hurtig, munter; rüstig

spun glass *n.* gesponnenes Glas

spur *n.* Sporn; Steigeisen; Antrieb; (geol.)
Ausläufer; **on the — of the moment**
ohne Überlegung, spornstreichs; **win
one's —s** sich die Sporen verdienen; —
stone Prellstein; — **wheel** Kammrad

spurn *v.* mit dem Fuss wegstossen; verschmähen

spurt *n.* Strahl; Ausbruch; Ruck; plötz-
liche Anstrengung; Spurt; — *v.* heraus-
spritzen; spurten

sputter *n.* Gesprudel; (fig.) Getue, Lärm;
— *v.* spritzen, sprühen; hervorsprudeln

sputum *n.* Auswurf, Speichel

spy *n.* Spion, Späher, Kundschafter; —
v. spionieren, spähen; kundschaften

spyglass *n.* Fernglas, Fernrohr

squabble *n.* Zank, Streit; — *v.* (sich)
zanken, streiten

squad *n.* Trupp, Rotte; Mannschaft; —
car Funkwagen; **-ron** *n.* Schwadron;
(avi.) Staffel; (naut.) Geschwader

squalid *adj.* schmutzig, abstossend; armselig

squall *n.* Schrei; (naut.) Bö, Windstoss;
— *v.* aufschreien; plötzlich wehen

squalor *n.* Schmutz, Unflat

squander *v.* verschwenden, verschleudern;
umherschweifen; — *n.* Verschwendung

square *n.* Platz; Viereck, Quadrat; (chess)
Feld; (mech.) Winkelmass; Reiss-
schiene; — *adj.* viereckig, quadratisch;
redlich, rechtschaffen; passend; **be —**
quitt sein; — **dance** Quadrille; — **deal**
faires Spiel; — **inch** Quadratzoll; —
foot Quadratfuss; — **mile** Quadrat-
meile; — **number** Quadratzahl; — **root**
Quadratwurzel; — *v.* ausgleichen, abrechnen; (geom.) abmessen, anpassen;
(math.) ins Quadrat erheben

square-built *adj.* vierschrötig

squash *n.* Brei; Ausgepresstes; Platsch,
Fall; Gedränge; (bot.) Kürbis; **lemon
—** Zitronenlimonade; — *v.* zerquet-
schen, zerdrücken; (fig.) unterdrücken

squat *n.* Hocken, Kauern; (min.) Erznest; — *adj.* kauernd; plattgedrückt;
untersetzt; — *v.* sich ohne Rechtstitel
ansiedeln; **-ter** *n.* Hockende, Kauernde;
(fig.) Ansiedler ohne Rechtstitel

squaw *n.* Squaw, Indianerfrau; Frau

squawk *n.* schriller Aufschrei; — *v.* schrill
aufschreien

squeak *n.* Gequiek; — *v.* quieken, quietschen

squeal *v.* quieken, quäken, schreien; (coll.)
protestieren; verraten, ausplaudern

squeeze *n.* Druck; Quetschen; Gedränge;
— *v.* (sich) drücken, pressen, quetschen,
drängen; **-r** *n.* Presse

squelch *n.* heftiger Schlag (*or* Fall); — *v.*
zerdrücken, zermalmen; (fig.) unterdrücken

squint *n.* Schielen; Neigung, Hang; —
adj. schielend; schräg, schief; — *v.*
schielen; schräg (*or* verstohlen) anblicken

squire *n.* Gutsherr; (fig.) Begleiter; — *v.*
begleiten

squirm *v.* sich krümmen (*or* winden)

squirrel *n.* Eichhörnchen

squirt *n.* Spritze; Strahl; (coll.) Emporkömmling, Wichtigtuer; — *v.* spritzen

stab *n.* Stich, Stoss; Stichwunde; (fig.)
Streich; — *v.* (er)stechen; verwunden

stability *n.* Stabilität, Dauerhaftigkeit;
Festigkeit; Standfestigkeit, Beständigkeit

stabilize *v.* stabilisieren

stable *n.* Stall; — *adj.* stabil, dauerhaft,
beständig; — *v.* (ein) stallen

stack *n.* Haufen, Schober; Meiler; Stapel,
Stoss; Schornstein; (mil.) Gewehrpyra-

mide; — *v.* schichten, stapeln; aufstellen

stadium *n.* Stadium, Kampfbahn

staff *n.* Stab; Stock, Knüttel, Pfahl; (mech.) Stange, Welle; (fig.) Stab, Personal, Mitarbeiter; editorial — Redaktionspersonal; **music** — Notensystem, Notenlinien; — **officer** Stabsoffizier

stag *n.* Hirsch; (coll.) Strohwitwer; — **party** Herrengesellschaft

stage *n.* Gerüst, Gestell; Bühne, Schauplatz; (fig.) Stadium, Station, Stufe; **landing** — Landungsbrücke; — **box** Proszeniumsloge; — **direction** Inszenierung; — **effect** Bühnenwirkung; — **fright** Lampenfieber; — **scenery**, — **setting** Bühnendekoration; — **whisper** Bühnengeflüster; — *v.* auf die Bühne bringen, inszenieren

stagger *n.* Schwanken, Taumeln; -s *pl.* Schwindel Drehkrankheit; — *v.* taumeln, schwanken; verblüffen; stutzig werden

staging *n.* (theat.) Inszenierung

stagnancy *n.*, **stagnation** *n.* Stagnierung, Stockung, Stillstand

stagnant *adj.* stagnierend, stillstehend, stokkend

stagnate *v.* stagnieren, stillstehen, stocken

stain *n.* Fleck; Beize; (fig.) Makel, Schandfleck; — *v.* (be)flecken; färben; **-less** *adj.* fleckenlos, unbefleckt; (fig.) tadellos; **-less steel** rostfreier Stahl

stair *n.* Stufe; *pl.* Treppe; **back—s** Hintertreppe

staircase, **stairway** *n.* Treppenhaus

stake *n.* Pfahl, Stange; Marterpfahl; (bet) Einsatz, Preis; **be at** — auf dem Spiel stehen; — *v.* pfählen; einsetzen, aufs Spiel setzen, wagen, wetten; — **out** (*or* **off**) abstecken

standpoint *n.* Standpunkt, Gesichtspunkt

stale *n.* Urin, Harn; — *adj.* schal, matt, abgestanden, fade; altbacken, abgenutzt; (sports) übertrainiert; — *v.* schal werden, verflauen; wertlos machen; urinieren; **-ness** *n.* Schalheit, Abgestandenheit; Plattheit, Abgenutztheit

stalemate *n.* Unentschieden, Stillstand; (chess) Patt; — *v.* zum Stillstand bringen, lähmen; (chess) Patt setzen

stall *n.* Abteilung, Stand; Bude; Chorstuhl; (theat.) Sperrsitz; — *v.* einstallen; festfahren, festsitzen; steckenbleiben; (avi.) sacken

stallion *n.* Hengst, Zuchthengst

stalwart *adj.* standhaft; stark, kräftig, handfest

stamen *n.* (bot.) Staubfaden

stamina *n.* Ausdauer, Widerstandskraft

stammer *n.* Stottern, Stammeln; — *v.* stottern, stammeln; **-er** *n.* Stotterer, Stammler

stamp *n.* Stampfen; (mail) Briefmarke, Poststempel; (mech.) Stampfer, Stanze, Stempel; **postage** — Briefmarke, Postwertzeichen; **revenue** — Zollstempel, Zollmarke; — *v.* (auf)stampfen; zerstossen; (mail) frankieren, abstempeln; (mech.) prägen; lochen, stanzen, stempeln; eichen

stampede *n.* Panik, wilde Flucht; — *v.* in wilder Flucht davonjagen, durchgehen

stand *n.* Stand, Stehen; Stillstand, Widerstand; Standpunkt, Höhepunkt; Halteplatz; Stativ, Ständer, Gestell; Lesepult; Tribüne; — *v.* stehen, sich befinden; stillstehen; anhalten, aushalten, ausstehen, ertragen; bestehen; stellen; — **aside** beiseitestehen, beiseitetreten; — **back** zurücktreten; — **by** aufhelfen, bereitstehen; — **in** vertreten; — **in line** in der Reihe stehen; — **off** abstehen, zurücktreten; — **one's ground** sich behaupten; — **out** hervorragen; widerstehen; — **still** stillstehen; — **treat** die Zeche bezahlen; — **up** aufstehen, sich erheben; **-ing** *n.* Stand, Stellung; Rang, Ruf; Dauer; **-ing** *adj.* stehend; fest, dauernd; **-ing room** Stehplatz

standard *n.* Standard, Muster, Masstab, Norm, Durchschnitt; Ständer, Pfosten; (mil.) Standarte; (orn.) Blütenblatt; Stamm; **gold** — Goldwährung; — **of living** Lebenshaltung; — *adj.* massgebend; aufrecht, gerade; hochstämmig; **Normal-, Muster-; — measure** Standardmass; — **time** Normalzeit; Durchschnittszeit; — **works** klassische Werke; **-ization** *n.* Normung; **-ize** *v.* normen, vereinheitlichen

standard-gauge *adj.* Normalspur-

standstill *n.* Stillstand, Pause

stanza *n.* Stanze, Strophe

staple *n.* Stapelung; Stapelplatz; Haupterzeugnis, Rohstoff; Heftklammer; — *adj.* stapelnd, heftend; — *v.* stapeln, heften; **-r** *n.* Heftmaschine

star *n.* Stern, Gestirn; (film) Star; **-'s and stripes** Sternenbanner; — *v.* besäen; mit einem Stern versehen; (theat.) glänzen, in der Hauptrolle auftreten; gastieren; **-let** *n.* Sternchen, kleiner Star; **-red** *adj.*, **-ry** *adj.* sternenbesät; gestirnt; **Stern(en)-**

starboard *n.* Steuerbord

starch *n.* Stärke; (fig.) Steifheit; — *adj.* gestärkt; (fig.) steif, förmlich; — *v.*

stärken

stare *n.* Starren; — *v.* (an)starren

stark-naked *adj.* splitter(faser)nackt

starlight *n.* Sternenlicht; (fig.) schwächliches Licht; — *adj.* sternenhell

star-spangled *adj.* sternenbesät

start *n.* Sprung, Satz, Ruck, Stoss; Aufschrekken, Zusammenfahren, Stutzen; Start, Anfang, Aufbruch, Abfahrt, Abflug; get a — einen Anfang machen, einen Vorsprung erhalten; **make a new — ein' neues Leben** beginnen; — *v.* aufspringen, aufschrecken, stutzen, zusammenfahren; aufbrechen, abfahren, abfliegen; starten; (mech.) anlassen, in Gang setzen; — **a business** ein Geschäft anfangen (*or* errichten); — **an objection** einen Einwand machen; — **off**, — **out** abfahren, aufbrechen; abweichen; **–er** *n.* Starter, Anlasser; Erreger; **–ing** *n.* Anlassen, Starten; Ablauf; **–ing point** Ausgangspunkt; Startlinie; **–le** *n.* Bestürzung, Schreck; **–le** *v.* erschrecken, bestürzt sein; **–ling** *adj.* erschreckend, ergreifend, aufsehenerregend; bestürzt

starvation *n.* Hungerleiden, Verhungern; (med.) Hungertod

starve *v.* verhungern, aushungern; (mech.) stehenbleiben; (fig.) verkümmern

state *n.* Stand, Zustand, Beschaffenheit; (pol.) Staat, Macht; **–'s evidence** Zeuge (*or* Beweismaterial) für den Staatsanwalt; — *v.* angeben, darlegen, feststellen; **–ly** *adj.* staatlich, prächtig, erhaben; pomphaft; **–ment** *n.* Darlegung, Angabe, Aussage; Vermögensstand; (com.) Voranschlag, Überschlag; Aufstellung, Auszug

Statehouse *n.* Regierungsgebäude, Parlament

stateroom *n.* Staatszimmer; (naut.) Luxuskajüte; (rail.) Luxuswagen

statesman *n.* Staatsmann, Politiker; **–ship** *n.* Staatskunst, Regierungskunst

static *adj.* statisch; (rad.) störend; — *n.* (rad.) Sendestörung; **–s** *n.* Statik, Gleichgewichtslehre

station *n.* Standort, Standpunkt; Stelle, Rang, Stand, Stellung; Geschäft, Posten; Station; — **agent** Stationsbeamte; — **hall** Bahnhofshalle; — **house** Polizeiwache; — **wagon** Tourenwagen; **–ary** *adj.* stationär, stillstehend, beständig, fest

stationery *n.* Papierwaren, Schreibwaren

statistic *adj.* **–al** *adj.* statistisch; **–ian** *n.* Statistiker; **–s** *n. pl.* Statistik

statue *n.* Statue, Standbild, Bildsäule

stature *n.* Statur, Wuchs

status *n.* Status, Zustand; Stellung, Rang

stave *n.* Daube; (lit.) Stanze, Strophe; (naut.) Steven; — *v.* ein Loch einschlagen; verdichten; brechen; — **off** abwehren

stay *n.* Aufenthalt, Stockung; Träger, Stütze, Strebe; (naut.) Stag; *pl.* Korsett; — *v.* bleiben, verweilen, sich aufhalten; hindern, hemmen; stützen; (naut.) stagen; **–er** *n.* Steher

stay-at-home *n.* (mil.) Heimatkrieger

stead *n.* Statt, Stelle; Nutzen, Vorteil; — *v.* nutzen, dienen

steadfast *adj.* unentwegt, standhaft; unverwandt, unerschütterlich

steady *adj.* fest, unerschütterlich, sicher; regelmässig, stetig; zuverlässig, beständig; — *v.* festmachen, festhalten

steady-state universe *n.* gleichbleibendes Weltall, unveränderliches Weltall

steak *n.* Steak, Schnitzel

steal *n.* Diebstahl; — *v.* stehlen, entwenden; — **away** sich fortschleichen

stealth *n.* Heimlichkeit; **by —** heimlich(erweise); **–y** *adj.* verstohlen, heimlich

steam *n.* Dampf, Dunst; Ausdünstung; — *adj.* dampfend, dunstend; — **bath** Schwitzbad; — **boiler** Dampfkessel; — **cooker** Dampfkochapparat; — **engine** Dampfmaschine, Lokomotive; — **gauge** Manometer; — **heating** Dampfheizung; — **pressure** Dampfdruck; — **roller** Dampfwalze; — *v.* dampfen, ausdunsten; dünsten; (coll.) schnauben, rasen; **–er** *n.* Dampfer; Dämpfer

steamboat *n.* Dampfschiff, Dampfer

stearin(e) *n.* Stearin

steed *n.* (lit.) Schlachtross

steel *n.* Stahl; — *adj.* stählern; — **filings** Stahlstaub; — **helmet** Stahlhelm; — **plate** Stahlblech; — **wool** Stahlspäne; — *v.* stählen; stahlhart machen; (ver)härten

steel-clad *adj.* stahlgepanzert

steel-colored *adj.* stahlfarben, stahlblau

steelworks *n. pl.* Stahlhütte, Stahlhammer

steelyard *n.* Schnellwaage

steep *n.* Steilhang; Eintauchen; Lauge; — *adj.* steil, jäh, abschüssig; (coll.) schwierig, sehr gross; — *v.* eintauchen, einweichen, tränken, imprägnieren

steeple *n.* spitzer Turm; Kirchturm; — **jack** Turmdecker

steeplechase *n.* Hindernisrennen

steer *n.* Steuern; (zool.) Stier; — *v.* steuern, lenken; **–age** *n.* Steuerung; Kurs; **–ing** *n.* Steuerung; Steuermannskunst; **–ing** *adj.* steuernd, lenkend; — **whee**

Steuer(rad)
stein *n.* Bierglas, Masskrug, Humpen
stem *n.* Stamm; Stengel, Stiel; — *v.* von
Stengeln befreien; stemmen; eindämmen, stauen
stench *n.* Gestank, übler Geruch
stencil *n.* Schablone, Matritze; — *v.* mit
einer Schablone (*or* Matritze) arbeiten
stenographer *n.* Stenograf
stenography *n.* Stenografie, Kurzschrift
stenotyping *n.* Druck in Kurzschrift
step *n.* Schritt, Tritt; Fusstapfe; Stufe;
be in — Schritt halten; by –s Schritt
für Schritt, stufenweise; false — Fehltritt; — *v.* schreiten, treten, gehen;
fortschreiten; abschreiten, ausmessen;
— aside ausweichen; — in einsteigen;
einen Besuch machen; — out austreten,
aussteigen; — up hinaufgehen
stepbrother *n.* Stiefbruder
stepdaughter *n.* Stieftochter
stepfather *n.* Stiefvater
stepladder *n.* Stehleiter
stepmother *n.* Stiefmutter
stepsister *n.* Stiefschwester
stepson *n.* Stiefsohn
stereophonic *adj.* volltönend; sterephon-
isch
stereoscope *n.* Stereoskop
stereotype *n.* Stereotypie, Plattendruck;
— *adj.* stereotyp; feststehend, unveränderlich; — *v.* abdrucken; (fig.) eine
bleibende Form geben
sterile *adj.* steril, unfruchtbar
sterility *n.* Sterilität, Unfruchtbarkeit
sterilize *v.* sterilisieren, unfruchtbar machen
sterling *n.* Sterling; — *adj.* echt, hochgradig; hervorragend; zuverlässig
stern *n.* Heck; — *adj.* finster, ernst,
streng; unnachgiebig
stet *v.* (typ.) stehenlassen
stethoscope *n.* Stethoskop
stevedore *n.* Staumeister; Lader, Stauer
stew *n.* Gedämpfte, Geschmorte; (coll.)
Verwirrung, Aufregung; — *v.* dämpfen,
schmoren; (educ. sl.) büffeln
steward *n.* Verwalter; (avi. and naut.)
Steward; –ess *n.* Stewardess, Aufwärterin
stick *n.* Stock, Stange, Stab; (avi.)
Steuerknüppel; Bombenabzug; — *v.*
stecken; kleben, heften; ertragen;
stocken, (stehen)bleiben; — to festhalten an, bleiben bei; anstecken,
ankleben; — together zusammenhal-
ten; ◂er *n.* Stecker, Stecher; Ankleber;
(com.) Ladenhüter; Klebezettel; –y
adj. klebrig, zäh; feucht. dunstig
stickle *v.* hartnäckig streiten; –r *n.* Eiferer,

Verfechter; –r for ceremony Formen-
mensch
stickpin *n.* Krawattennadel
stiff *adj.* steif, starr; dicht; schwierig,
hartnäckig; stark; –en *v.* steif werden;
verhärten, versteigen; erstarren (lassen); stärken; –ness *n.* Steifheit; Widerstandsfähigkeit; Halsstarrigkeit; Ge-
zwungenheit
stifle *v.* ersticken, unterdrücken; vertuschen
stifling *adj.* erstickend
stigma *n.* Stigma
still *n.* Stille, Ruhe; (chem.) Destillierap-
parat; — *adj.* still, ruhig, regungslos;
— *adv.* noch (immer); — *conj.* (je)doch,
dennoch; — *v.* destillieren; stillen;
–ness *n.* Stille, Ruhe
stillborn *adj.* totgeboren
stilt *n.* Stelze; (orn.) Stelzvogel; –ed *adj.*
gestelzt; (fig.) gespreizt, hochtrabend
stimulant *n.* Reizmittel; — *adj.* stimu-
lierend
stimulate *v.* (an)reizen
stimulation *n.* Reizung; Antrieb
stimulus *n.* Reizmittel
sting *n.* Stachel; Stich, Biss; (fig.) Schärfe,
Spitze; Antrieb; — ray Stachelrochen;
— *v.* stechen; (fig.) schmerzen; verwunden; anstacheln; –iness *n.* Geiz;
Kargheit; –ing *adj.* stechend; scharf,
schmerzhaft; –ing nettle Brennessel;
–y *adj.* geizig; kärglich, knapp
stink *n.* Gestank; — *adj.* — bomb Stinkbombe; — *v.* stinken; verstänkern
stipulate *v.* (aus)bedingen, festsetzen
stipulation *n.* Abmachung; Festsetzung;
Klausel
stir *n.* Bewegung, Aufregung; Getümmel,
Auflauf; — *v.* rühren; anschüren, bewegen, aufstören; sich rühren; — up
aufrühren, reizen; –ring *adj.* anregend;
aufregend; belebend, begeisternd
stirrup *n.* Steigbügel; (arch.) Steigeisen
stitch *n.* Stich, Masche; — *v.* stechen;
nähen, sticken, heften; häkeln; (agr.)
furchen
stock *n.* Stamm, Stock; Block, Klotz;
(agr.) Vieh(stand); (bot.) Stengel,
Strunk; (com.) Vorrat, Lager, Stamm-
kapital; *pl.* Inventar; Barvermögen;
Aktien, Staatspapiere, Effekten; Stapel; in — lagernd, vorrätig; rolling —
(rail.) Betriebsmaterial; — on hand
Warenbestand; — *adj.* lagernd, (bereit)
stehend, ständig; — book Aktienver-
zeichnis; Zuchtregister; — company
Aktiengesellschaft; — dove Holztaube;
— exchange Börse; — list Kurszettel;
— market Effektenbörse; Viehmarkt;

— **play** (theat.) Repertoirestück; —
raiser Viehzüchter; — *v.* lagern, aufspeichern; vorrätig haben, versorgen;
(cards) betrügerisch mischen; **–ade** *n.*
Staket, Einpfählung, Palisaden; **–y** *adj.*
stämmig. untersetzt

stock-blind *adj.* stockblind

stockbroker *n.* Börsenmakler

stockholder *n.* Aktionär

stocking *n.* Strumpf

stockpile *n.* Materialreserve, Vorrat-
shaufen; **atomic** — Atomkernreserve;
— *v.* Rohmaterial aufspeichern

stockroom *n.* Lagerraum

stockyard *n.* Viehhof

stoke *v.* schüren, stochern; **–r** *n.* Heizer;
Schürhaken

stole *n.* Stola

stolid *adj.* unerschütterlich, gleichmütig

stomach *n.* Magen; (fig.) Appetit, Neigung; — *v.* verdauen; vertragen, (fig.)
sich gefallen lassen

stone *n.* Stein; (bot.) Kern; (min.) Edelstein; — *adj.* steinern. steinig; Stein-;
— **coal** Steinkohle, Anthrazit; — **falcon**
(orn.) Merlin; — **fruit** Kernobst; —
marten Steinmarder; — **pit** Steinbruch;
— *v.* steinigen; mit Steinen einfassen;
entkernen; (fig.) versteinern, verhärten

stone-broke *adj.* bankrott, vollkommen
abgebrannt

stonecutter *n.* Steinhauer, Steinklopfer;
Steinschleifer

stone-dead *adj.* mausetot

stone-deaf *adj.* stocktaub

stonemason *n.* Steinmetz

stony *adj.* steinig, steinern; versteinert

stooge *n.* Stichwortbringer, Double;
Schreiberseele; Neuling in der Unterwelt

stool *n.* Schemel; Stuhl; (med.) Stuhl-
gang; — **pigeon** Lockspitzel, Zeichen-
geber; (orn.) Locktaube

stoop *n.* gebeugte Haltung; Demütigung;
(arch.) Verande; — *v.* sich beugen (*or*
herablassen); neigen; demütigen; (orn.)
herabstossen

stop *n.* Halt; Einhalt, Stillstand, Pause,
Unterbrechung; Haltestelle; Hem-
mung, Hindernis; (mus.) Klappe, Ventil; Register; Griff; — **light** Bremslicht;
— **order** begrenzter Auftrag; — **signal**
Haltesignal, Haltezeichen; — **watch**
Stoppuhr; — *v.* (ver)stopfen, (ver)-
sperren; aufhalten, einhalten, einstellen; (stehen)bleiben. anhalten, ruhen;
unterbrechen; hemmen, hindern; (bot.)
beschneiden; (med.) stillen; (mus.)
greifen; **–page** *n.* Hemmung, Einstellung, Anhalten, Stockung; Verstop-

fung; **–per** *n.* Stöpsel, Pfropfen; Auf-
halter; Hemmung, Versperrung; **–per**
v. verstopfen, zustöpseln; **–ping** *n.*
Halt, Anhalten; (dent.) Plombe, Fül-
lung; **–ping** *adj.* **–ping place** Haltestelle

stopover *n.* Zwischenaufenthalt

storage *n.* Lagerung, Aufspeichern;
Lagergeld, Lagermiete; — **battery** Ak-
kumulator

store *n.* Geschäft, Laden; Lager. Magazin, Speicher; Vorrat, Menge; **department** — Kaufhaus; — *v.* aufhäufen,
aufspeichern; einlagern; versehen, versorgen

storehouse *n.* Lagerhaus; Warenniederla-
lage; (fig.) Schatzkammer

storekeeper *n.* Magazinverwalter; Geschäftsbesitzer; (naut.) Proviantmeister

storeroom *n.* Vorratskammer, Lagerraum

stork *n.* Storch; **–'s bill** Storchenschnabel

storm *n.* Sturm; Gewitter; — **center**
Sturmzentrum; — **door** Doppeltür; —
troops Sturmtruppen; — **window** Dop-
pelfenster; — *v.* stürmen; toben, wüten;
–y *adj.* stürmisch

story *n.* Geschichte, Erzählung; Handlung; (arch.) Stock(werk), Geschoss;
(fig.) Flunkerei; **short** — Novelle; —
v. erzählen, erfinden; (fig.) flunkern

stout *n.* Dickwanst; Porterbier; — *adj.*
dick, beleibt; stämmig, kräftig; derb;
(fig.) standhaft, mannhaft

stove *n.* Ofen; Kochherd

stowaway *n.* (naut.) blinder Passagier

straddle *n.* Spreizen; (pol.) Schwanken;
— *adv.* rittlings; — *v.* spreizen, grät-
schen; (pol.) schwanken

straggle *v.* umherstreifen; abweichen; zer-
streut liegen; **–r** *n.* Herumstreicher;
Nachzügler, Versprengte; (bot.)
Schössling

straight *n.* Gerade; — *adj.* gerade, direkt;
vollständig, rückhaltlos; — **line** Gerade, gerade Linie; — *adv.* gerade-
(wegs); sogleich; **–en** *v.* gerade machen;
glatt ziehen; straffen; (fig.) in Ordnung
bringen

straightaway *adj.* gerade, gradlinig

straightedge *n.* Lineal; Richtscheit

straightforward *adj.* geradsinnig; ehrlich
redlich; — *adv.* geradeaus

straightway *adv.* geradeswegs, auf der
Stelle

strain *n.* Spannung, Anstrengung; Verdrehung, Formveränderung; (biol.) Geschlecht; (med.) Verrenkung; (mus.)
Ton, Weise; — *v.* (an)spannen, straffen;
ausdehnen, strecken; anstrengen, überanstrengen; verrenken; verdrehen;

(mech.) durchpressen; filtrieren; — to one's breast umarmen; -er n. Durchschlag, Seiher, Filter

strait n. Meerenge, Strasse; (fig.) Zwangslage; — adj. eng. knapp, schmal, begrenzt; — jacket Zwangsjacke; -en v. verengen, einengen, beschränken

strand n. Strand, Ufer; Strähne, Strang; — v. stranden

strange adj. fremd; ungewöhnlich, seltsam; auffallend; -r n. Fremde, Ausländer; (law) Unbeteiligte; (fig.) Neuling

strangle v. erdrosseln, erwürgen, strangulieren; (fig.) ersticken; (pol.) zu Fall bringen; — adj. — hold Würgegriff

strap n. Riemen, Gurt; (mech.) Treibriemen, Tragriemen; (mil.) Achselschnur; — v. mit Riemen befestigen, festschnallen, verschnüren; züchtigen; -ping adj. stämmig, robust

strategic adj. strategisch

stratified adj. aufgeschichtet, schichtförmig

stratocruiser n. Stratosphärenflugzeug

stratosphere n. Stratosphäre

straw n. Stroh; Strohhalm; (fig.) Belanglosigkeit; — adj. strohig; Stroh-; (fig.) wertlos, leer; falsch; — hat Strohhut; — vote Probeabstimmung

strawberry n. Erdbeere

stray n. Verirrte; — adj. irre, verirrt, verlaufen; — v. irregehen, abirren; umherschweifen

streak n. Strich, Streifen; (min.) Ader; (fig.) Anflug, Anwandlung; — v. streifen

stream n. Strom, Fluss; Bach, Wasserlauf; Strömung; — v. strömen, fliessen; -er n. Wimpel, Fahne; Strahl

streamline n. Stromlinie(nform); — v. in Stromlinienform bauen; modernisieren; -d adj. stromlinienförmig, schnittig, modernisiert

street n. Strasse; Gasse

streetcar n. Strassenbahn, Elektrische

strength n. Stärke, Kraft, Festigkeit; Widerstandsfähigkeit; (mil.) Mannschaftsbestand; gain — wieder zu Kräften kommen; -en v. (ver)stärken, kräftigen; (fig.) bekräftigen

strenuous adj. tätig, eifrig; anstrengend

streptococcus n. (med.) Streptokokkus

streptomycin n. Streptomyzin

stress n. Druck, Gewicht, Nachdruck; Betonung; Heftigkeit; — v. betonen, unterstreichen

stretch n. Ausdehnung; Spannung; Strecke, Weite, Umfang; Anstrengung; (fig.) Übertreibung; — v. strecken,

dehnen, spannen; recken, weiten; sich ausdehnen; sich anstrengen; (fig.) überschreiten, übertreiben; -er n. Strecker; (med.) Tragbahre; (naut.) Rippe, Spant; Fussbrett; (sl.) Flunkerei

strict adj. strikt, streng; genau, pünktlich; — order ausdrücklicher Befehl; -ly adv. strenggenommen, ausschliesslich

stride n. langer Schritt; Schrittweite; (fig.) Fortschritt; — v. schreiten; durchschreiten

strife n. Streben; Wettbewerb; Streit

strike n. Streik, Aufstand; (baseball) Nichttreffer; — v. streiken, die Arbeit einstellen; treffen, schlagen, stossen; abschliessen; anzünden; (flag) streichen; (min.) schürfen; — a balance eine Bilanz ziehen; -r n. Streikende

strikebreaker n. Streikbrecher

striking adj. Schlag-; streikend; überraschend, auffallend; treffend; (bot.) wurzelschlagend

string n. Schnur, Band, Bindfaden; (anat.) Nerv, Sehne; (bot.) Rippe, Ader, Faser; (mus.) Saite; — adj. — bean grüne Bohne; — v. aufreihen, aufziehen; verschnüren; anspannen, überanstrengen; bespannen; -ed adj. geschnürt, angebunden; (mus.) Saiten-; — instrument Streichinstrument; — quartet Streichquartett; -y adj. faserig, sehnig; saitenartig; klebrig, zäh

strip n. Streifen; Zerstörung, Abbruch; Entkleidung; — v. abstreifen, entkleiden, entblössen; auseinandernehmen

stripe n. Streifen, Strich; Strieme; — v. streifen, streifig machen; -d adj. streifig, gestreift

striptease n. Nacktschau, (coll.) Fleischmarkt

strive v. streben, sich bemühen (or anstrengen); sich sträuben; streiten

stroboscope n. Wunderscheibe, optisches Gerät

stroke n. Schlag, Streich, Hieb, Stoss; Strich; (mech.) Hub; (med.) Schlaganfall; — of a pen Federstrich

stroll n. Schlendern; Spaziergang; — v. umherziehen, schlendern, bummeln; -er n. Umherstreifende; Landstreicher, Strolch

strong adj. stark, kräftig, tüchtig; fest, schwer; überzeugend, gewaltig; energisch, lebhaft; — room Stahlkammer; -ly adv. sehr; durchaus; stark

strongbox n. Geldkassette

strontium n. Strontium (Metall)

struck adj. betroffen, ergriffen

structural adj. organisch, baulich; — iron Gusseisen; Stahlgerippe

structure *n.* Bau, Struktur, Gefüge; Aufbau

struggle *n.* Ringen, Kampf; Anstrengung; — *v.* ringen, streiten, kämpfen; sich abmühen

strychnine *n.* Strychnin

stub *n.* Stumpf, Stubben; Abschnitt; — *v.* anstossen; (agr.) roden; **-ble** *n.* Stoppel; **-by** *adj.* stämmig, untersetzt; borstig, stachelig

stubborn *adj.* widerspenstig, halsstarrig; hartnäckig

stucco *n.* Stuck, Stukkatur

stuck-up *adj.* hochnäsig, hochmütig

stud *n.* Nagel, Stift; Knopf; Buckel, Knauf; (arch.) Pfosten, Eckpfeiler; (zool.) Gestüt; — **book** Zuchtbuch; — **mare** Zuchtstute; — *v.* verzieren, besetzen, besäen

student *n.* Student, Studierende; Gelehrte

studied *adj.* einstudiert, vorsätzlich

studio *n.* Studio, Atelier

studious *adj.* fleissig; bemüht, beflissen

study *n.* Studium, Studieren; Untersuchung; Studierzimmer; (art.) Studie; — *v.* studieren; (er)forschen; (theat.) einstudieren

stuff *n.* Stoff; Zeug; (com.) Ware; —! *interj.* dummes Zeug! — *v.* (voll)stopfen, ausstopfen; polstern; (cooking) füllen, spicken; (fig.) vorflunkern, weismachen; — **up** verstopfen; **-ing** *n.* Füllung; Polsterung; **-y** *adj.* dick; dumpf, schwül; (fig.) eigensinnig

stumble *n.* Stolpern, Straucheln; Fehltritt; — *v.* stolpern, straucheln

stumbling block *n.* Hindernis; Stein des Anstosses

stump *n.* Stumpf, Stummel, Strunk; (pol.) Plattform; — **speech** Wahlrede; — *v.* stampfen; abstumpfen, stutzen; roden

stun *v.* betäuben; verblüffen; **-ning** *adj.* betäubend; verblüffend, famos

stunt *n.* Kunststück, Bravourstück, Trick, Sensation; (biol.) Verkümmerung; — *v.* Sensationen vollbringen; (avi.) kunstfliegen; (biol.) verkümmern

stupendous *adj.* erstaunlich, riesig

stupid *adj.* dumm, beschränkt, stupid; langweilig; **-ity** *n.* Stupidität, Dummheit

stupor *n.* Erstarrung, Betäubung; Stumpfsinn

sturdily *adv.* handfest, derb, kräftig; standhaft

sturdy *adj.* stark, derb; starr, hart

sturgeon *n.* Stör

stutter *n.* Stottern, Stammeln; — *v.* stottern, stammeln

sty *n.* Schweinestall; (med.) Gerstenkorn

style *n.* Stichel, Griffel; (med.) Sonde; (fig.) Stil, Ausdrucksweise; Mode; in — stilvoll; modisch; — *v.* (be)nennen, betiteln

stylish *adj.* stilgerecht, modisch, elegant

stylist *n.* Stilist

stylographic *adj.* stylografisch; — **pen** Füllfeder(halter)

sub *n.* Vorschuss; (coll.) Ersatz; Untergebene; U-boot

subcommittee *n.* Unterausschuss

subconscious *n.* Unterbewusstsein; — *adj.* unterbewusst

subdivide *v.* unterteilen

subdivision *n.* Unterabteilung

subdue *v.* unterwerfen, überwältigen; unterdrücken; dämpfen

subhead *n.* Untertitel

subject *n.* Gegenstand, Thema, Vorwurf; Untertan; (gram.) Subjekt; — *adj.* untergeben, untertan, unterworfen; ausgesetzt; — **matter** Gegenstand, Hauptinhalt; — *v.* unterwerfen; aussetzen; **-ion** *n.* Unterwerfung; Abhängigkeit; **-ive** *adj.* subjektiv, persönlich, einseitig, voreingenommen

subjunctive *n.* Konjunktiv; — *adj.* Konjunktiv-

sublease *n.* Untermiete; — *v.* untervermieten

sublet *v.* unterverpachten

sublime *n.* Erhabene; — *adj.* erhaben, grossartig; — *v.* sublimieren, läutern, veredeln

submarine *n.* Unterseeboot; — *adj.* unterseeisch; — *v.* (coll.) versenken, torpedieren

submerge, submerse *v.* überschwemmen; (naut.) untertauchen, versenken

submission *n.* Unterwerfung, Ehrerbietung

submissive *adj.* ehrerbietig, unterwürfig

submit *v.* unterwerfen, unterbreiten, vorlegen; anheimstellen; sich fügen

subnormal *adj.* unternormal

subordinate *n.* Untergebene; — *adj.* untergeordnet; Neben-; — *v.* unterordnen, abstufen

subordination *n.* Unterordnung, Subordination

suborn *v.* verleiten, anstiften

subpoena *n.* Vorladung unter Strafandrohung; — *v.* unter Strafandrohung vorladen

subscribe *v.* abonnieren; unterschreiben, zeichnen; anerkennen; **-r** *n.* Abonnent; Unterzeichner; (tel.) Teilnehmer

subscription *n.* Abonnement; Unterschrift, Unterzeichnung

subsequent *adj.* (nach)folgend, nachherig, später

subservient *adj.* dienlich, nützlich, förderlich; unterwürfig

subside *v.* sinken; sich senken; abnehmen, nachlassen

subsidiary *n.* Hilfe, Beistand; — *adj.* behilflich, mitwirkend; Hilfs-; Neben-

subsidize *v.* subventionieren, mit Geld unterstützen

subsidy *n.* Unterstützung, Subvention

subsist *v.* bestehen; sich ernähren, auskommen; erhalten; **-ence** *n.* Dasein, Bestand; Unterhalt

substance *n.* Substanz, Stoff, Wesen; Vermögen

substantial *adj.* wesentlich; kräftig, nahrhaft; vermögend

substantiate *v.* verwirklichen; beweisen; beglaubigen

substitute *n.* Stellvertreter; Ersatz; — *v.* ersetzen, vertreten

substitution *n.* Einsetzung; Stellvertretung, Ersetzung; Unterschiebung

substructure *n.* Unterbau

subterranean *adj.* unterirdisch

subtilize *v.* verfeinern; ausklügeln

subt(i)le *adj.* subtil, fein, zart; spitzfindig

subtitle *n.* Untertitel, Nebentitel

subtract *v.* subtrahieren, abziehen; **-ion** *n.* Abnahme, Wegnahme, Entziehung; (math.) Subtraktion, Abziehen

suburb *n.* Vorstadt; *pl.* Vororte, Umgebung; **-an** *adj.* vorstädtisch; (fig.) unfein; **-anite** *n.* Vorstädter

subvention *n.* Subvention, Beihilfe, Unterstützung

subversive *adj.* subversiv, umstürzlerisch, unterminierend, zerstörend

subway *n.* Tunnel, unterirdischer Gang; Unterführung; Untergrundbahn

succeed *v.* gelingen, glücken; (nach)folgen

success *n.* Erfolg, Gelingen; Fortgang, Ausgang; **-ful** *adj.* erfolgreich, glücklich; **-ion** *n.* Folge, Nachfolge, Reihenfolge; Thronfolge, Erbfolge; **-ive** *adj.* aufeinanderfolgend, ununterbrochen; (law) erbberechtigt; **-or** *n.* Nachfolger; Thronfolger

succor *n.* Hilfe, Beistand, Unterstützung; (mil.) Entsatz; — *v.* helfen, beistehen, unterstützen; (mil.) entsetzen

succotash *n.* junger Mais mit Bohnen

succulent *adj.* saftig; strotzend

succumb *v.* unterliegen, erliegen

such *pron.* and *adj.* solch; so ein; derartig; **no — thing** nichts dergleichen, mitnichten; **— as** diejenigen, welche; **— like** dergleichen; — *adv.* auf diese Art (*or* Weise)

suck *n.* Saugen; — *v.* saugen, säugen; auf-

saugen; (fig.) aussaugen; **-er** *n.* Sauger; Säugling; (bot.) Saugwurzel; (ichth.) Lumpfisch; (coll.) Gimpel, Einfaltspinsel; **-ing** *adj.* saugend, Saug-; **-le** *v.* säugen, nähren, stillen

suction *n.* Ansaugen; — **pump** Saugpumpe

sudden *adj.* plötzlich, unerwartet, unvermutet

suds *n. pl.* Sud; Seifenwasser, Seifenlauge

sue *v.* (ver)klagen, nachsuchen

suede *n.* Wildleder

suet *n.* Talg, Nierenfett

suffer *v.* (er)leiden, (er)dulden; ertragen, ausstehen; erlauben; **-ing** *n.* Leiden; **-ing** *adj.* leidend, duldend

suffice *v.* genügen, befriedigen

sufficient *adj.* genügend, ausreichend; fähig

suffocate *v.* ersticken

suffocation *n.* Erstickung

suffrage *n.* Stimmrecht, Wahlrecht

sugar *n.* Zucker; (coll.) Süsse; Geld; **— beet** Zuckerrübe; **— bowl** Zuckerdose; **— cane** Zuckerrohr; **— mill** Zuckerpresse; — *v.* zuckern; verzuckern, versüssen; **-y** *adj.* zuckersüss, zuckerig

sugar-cane *adj.* Rohrzucker-

sugar-coated *adj.* überzuckert, verzuckert

suggest *v.* vorschlagen; anregen, eingeben; **-ion** *n.* Anregung, Vorschlag, Wink, Rat; Suggestion; **-ive** *adj.* andeutend, inhaltvoll; suggestiv

suicidal *adj.* selbstmörderisch

suicide *n.* Selbstmord; Selbstmörder

suit *n.* Anzug; Kostüm; (cards) Farbe; (law) Prozess; (fig.) Bewerbung; — *v.* passen, kleiden, stehen; anpassen, einrichten; entsprechen; zufriedenstellen; **-or** *n.* Bewerber; Bittsteller; (law) Prozessierende

suitability *n.* Geeignetheit, Angemessenheit

suitable *adj.* passend, geeignet; schicklich

suitcase *n.* Handkoffer

suite *n.* Gefolge; Reihe, Folge; **— of rooms** Zimmerflucht

sulfa drugs *n. pl.* Sulfanomiden

sulk *n.* Schmollen, mürrische Laune; — *v.* schmollen, verdriesslich sein; **-y** *adj.* verdriesslich, ärgerlich, launisch; trotzig

sullen *adj.* mürrisch, unfreundlich; feindselig

sulphur *n.* Schwefel; **— dioxide** Schwefelsauerstoff

sultry *adj.* schwül, drückend

sum *n.* Summe; Betrag; (math.) Exempel; (fig.) Inhalt, Inbegriff, Vollendung; **— total** Gesamtsumme, Endsumme; — *v.* summieren, zusammenrechnen, zusammenzählen; **–marize** v. (kurz) zusammenfassen; **–mary** n. Zusammenfassung, Übersicht; Inhaltsangabe; Auszug; **–mary** adj. summarisch, kurz zusammengefasst; **–mation** n. Summierung, Zusammenfassung

summer n. Sommer; — adj. sommerlich; — **house** Sommerhaus, Landhaus; — **resort** Sommerfrische; — **sausage** getrocknete Wurst

summertime n. Sommerzeit

summit n. Gipfel, Höhe, Spitze

summit conference n. Gipfelkonferenz

summon v. auffordern; (be)rufen, zitieren; aufbieten; (law) vorladen; **–s** n. pl. Aufforderung, Mahnung; (law) Vorladung

sumptuous adj. kostbar, prächtig

sun n. Sonne; — **bath** Sonnenbad; — **parlor** Glasveranda; — **porch** Veranda; — **visor** Sonnenschutz; — v. (sich) sonnen; **–less** adj. sonnenlos, schattig; **–ny** adj. sonnig; strahlend, freundlich; **–ny side** Sonnenseite

sunbeam n. Sonnenstrahl

sunbonnet n. leichter Frauenhut

sunburn n. Sonnenbrand; **–t** adj. sonn(en)verbrannt

sundae n. Fruchtspeiseeis

Sunday n. Sonntag; Sonntags-

sunder v. absondern; (sich) trennen

sundial n. Sonnenuhr

sundown n. Sonnenuntergang

sundries n. pl. Verschiedenes; Diverse; Kleinigkeiten

sundry adj. mannigfaltig; allerlei; verschiedene, mehrere

sunfast adj. lichtecht

sunfish n. Sonnenfisch

sunflower n. Sonnenblume

sunglass n. Brennglas; pl. Sonnenbrille

sunlamp n. Höhensonne

sunlight n. Sonnenlicht

sunproof adj. gegen Sonnenbestrahlung geschützt

sunrise n. Sonnenaufgang

sunroom n. sonniger Raum; Glasveranda

sunset n. Sonnenuntergang

sunshade n. Sonnenschirm; Markise

sunshine n. Sonnenschein; (fig.) Frohsinn, Heiterkeit

sunshiny adj. sonnig, heiter

sunspot n. Sonnenfleck

sunstroke n. Sonnenstich

sup n. Schluck, Mundvoll; — v. schlucken; (ein)schlürfen; auskosten

superabundant adj. überreichlich, überschwenglich

superb adj. prächtig, vorzüglich, herrlich

supercilious adj. hochmütig, arrogant, anmassend

supererogatory adj. überflüssig

superficial adj. oberflächlich

superfluous adj. überflüssig, unnötig

superhighway n. Autostrasse

superhuman adj. übermenschlich

superimpose v. darüberlegen; überlagern

superintend v. beaufsichtigen, überwachen; verwalten; **–ent** n. Oberaufseher, Inspektor; Vorsteher, Verwalter

superior n. Vorgesetzte, Höherstehende; — adj. ober, höher; vorzüglich, überlegen; **–ity** n. Überlegenheit, Vorrecht

superlative n. Superlativ; — adj. unübertrefflich, höchst

superman n. Übermensch

supermarket n. Selbstbedienungsladen

supernatural adj. übernatürlich

supersede v. verdrängen, ersetzen; **absetzen**; (law) für ungültig erklären

supersonic adj. Überschall-

superstition n. Aberglaube

superstitious adj. abergläubisch

superstructure n. Überbau, Oberbau, Hochbau

supervise v. beaufsichtigen, überwachen

supervision n. Beaufsichtigung, Aufsicht, Oberaufsicht

supervisor n. Aufseher, Inspektor, Kontrolleur; Vorsteher

supper n. Abendessen, Abendmahl; Nachtmahl; **Lord's Supper** das Heilige Abendmahl

supplant v. verdrängen, vertreiben; ausstechen

supplement n. Ergänzung, Nachtrag, Anhang; Beilage; — r. ergänzen; beilegen; **–al** adj., **–ary** adj. nachträglich; Ergänzungs-, Nachtrags-

supply n. Vorrat, Versorgung; Proviant; — **and demand** Angebot und Nachfrage; — v. ergänzen, ersetzen, abhelfen; versorgen, liefern

support n. Stütze, Unterlage; Stativ, Gestell; Träger; (mus.) Begleitung; (fig.) Unterstützung, Unterhalt; — v. (unter)stützen; unterhalten, beistehen; (chess) decken; (mus.) begleiten; (fig.) auskommen; **–er** n. Unterstützer, Beistand, Gönner; (pol.) Anhänger; (med.) Träger

suppose v. voraussetzen, vermuten, annehmen; **–d** adj. vorausgesetzt, mutmasslich; scheinbar, vermeintlich

supposing conj. unter der Voraussetzung, — **that** für den Fall, dass

supposition n. Voraussetzung, Vermutung

suppress v. unterdrücken, verheimlichen; **–ion** n. Unterdrückung

supremacy n. Obergewalt, Vorrang

supreme adj. höchst, vornehmst; oberst,

grösst

surcharge n. Zuschlag, Verteuerung; — v. überladen, verteuern; mehr berechnen; mit einer Geldstrafe belegen

sure adj. sicher, gewiss; **make** — **sich vergewissern**; **to be** — allerdings, freilich; **-ly** adv. sicherlich, zuverlässlich; wahrhaftig; **-ty** n. Bürgschaft, Bürge; Sicherheit, Gewissheit

sure-footed adj. standfest; (fig.) zuverlässlich

surf n. Brandung; — **riding** Wellenreiten

surface n. Oberfläche, Aussenseite; (geom.) Fläche(ninhalt); (min.) Tag; — adj. oberflächlich; — **mining** Tagebau; — **tension** Oberflächenspannung; — v. auftauchen, emporkommen; (mech.) flachdrehen

surfboard n. Wellenreiter(brett)

surfboat n. besonders starkes Boot

surfeit n. Übersättigung, Überladung; Ekel; — v. (sich) überladen, übersättigen; sich ekeln

surge n. Aufwallung; (naut.) Woge, Sturzsee, Brandung; — v. wogen, wallen, branden; anschwellen

surgeon n. Chirurg

surgery n. Chirurgie

surly adj. mürrisch, unfreundlich, sauertöpfisch, finster

surmise n. Vermutung, Argwohn, Verdacht; — v. vermuten, argwöhnen, verdächtigen

surname n. Zuname, Familienname; — v. beim Zunamen nennen

surpass v. übersteigen, überschreiten

surplice n. Chorhemd, Stola

surplus n. Überschuss; Überfluss; Überrest

surprise n. Überraschung; (mil.) Überrumplung; — v. überraschen, erschrecken; (mil.) überrumpeln, überfallen

surprising adj. überraschend, erstaunlich

surrender n. Auslieferung, Übergabe, Ergebung; (law) Abtretung; — v. ausliefern, übergeben; sich ergeben; abtreten

surrogate n. Surrogat, Ersatzstoff; Stellvertreter; (law) Nachlassverwalter

surround v. umgeben; (mil.) umzingeln; **-ing** n. Einschliessung; **-ings** pl. Umgegend, Umgebung, Nachbarschaft; **-ing** adj. umgebend

surtax n. Steuerzuschlag

surveillance n. Überwachung; Aufsicht

survey n. Überblick, Übersicht; Besichtigung; Vermessung; — v. überblicken, übersehen; besichtigen; vermessen, ausmessen; **-ing** n. Inspektion, Verwaltung; Ausmessung; Feldmesskunst; **-or** n. Aufseher, Inspektor, Verwalter; Feldmesser, Landmesser

survival n. Überleben; Fortleben; Überrest

survive v. überleben, fortleben; übrig bleiben

surviving adj. überlebend, fortlebend; übrig bleibend

survivor n. Überlebende; (law) Hinterbliebene

susceptible adj. empfänglich, empfindlich; erregbar; fähig

suspect n. Verdächtige, Beargwöhnte; — adj. verdächtig; — v. verdächtigen; (be)argwöhnen, vermuten

suspend v. aufhängen; entlassen, entheben, suspendieren; aufschieben; (com.) einstellen; (mus.) anhalten; (pol.) vertagen; **-er** n. Aufschiebende; **-ers** pl. Hosenträger

suspense n. Aufschub, Unterbrechung; Spannung; Unentschiedenheit, Ungewissheit; (law) Urteilsaussetzung

suspension n. Einstellung, Aufschub; (einstweilige) Amtsentsetzung; Aufhebung; (mech.) Aufhängen; — **bridge** Hängebrücke

suspicion n. Verdacht, Argwohn

suspicious adj. verdächtig, argwöhnisch, misstrauisch

sustain v. stützen, tragen; aufrechterhalten, unterhalten; **-ing** adj. beistehend; **-ing program** (rad.) nicht kommerzielles Programm

sustenance n. Lebensunterhalt, Nahrung; (coll.) Lebensmittel

suture n. Naht; — v. nähen

swab n. Scheuerlappen, Kehrwisch; Schwamm; (med.) Abstrich; — v. aufwischen

Swabia n. Schwaben

swaddling clothes n. pl. Windeln

swagger n. Grosstun, Prahlen; — adj. — **stick** kurzer Offiziersstab; — v. stolzieren; grosstun, prahlen; **-er** n. Grosstuer, Renommist

swain n. Schäfer; Liebhaber

swallow n. Schlund, Kehle; Schluck, Trunk; (orn.) Schwalbe; — v. verschlingen, (ver-)schlucken; zurücknehmen

swallow-tailed adj. schwalbenschwänzig; — **coat** Frack; (coll.) Schwalbenschwanz

swamp n. Sumpf, Morast, Moor; — v. überschwemmen; unterdrücken; (naut.) versenken

swan n. Schwan; — **song** Schwanengesang; — **dive** Auerbachsprung

swank n. Aufschneiderei, Spiegelfechterei; — adj. prahlerisch, schick, fesch; — v. renommieren, aufschneiden; -y adj. elegant, luxuriös

swap n. Tausch, Handel; — v. tauschen; umsetzen, losschlagen

swarm n. Schwarm, Haufen, Gewimmel; — v. schwärmen, wimmeln

swart(hy) adj. schwärzlich, dunkelfarbig

swastika n. Hakenkreuz

swath(e) n. Binde, Wickelband; (agr.) Schwaden, Sensenhieb; — v. (ein)-wicken, einhüllen

sway n. Schwingen, Schwung; Ausschlag, Übergewicht; Einfluss, Macht; — v. schwingen, schwenken, schwanken; herrschen; beeinflussen

swear v. (be)schwören; fluchen; — in vereidigen

sweat n. Schweiss; — v. schwitzen; sich abmühen; (coll.) ausbeuten

sweater n. Sweater

sweatshop n. Ausbeutungsbetrieb

Sweden n. Schweden

sweep n. Fegen, Kehren; Schwung; Krümmung, Windung; Bereich, Spielraum; Schornsteinfeger, Strassenkehrer; (mil.) Schussweite; **make a clean — reinen** Tisch machen; — v. fegen, kehren; schleppen; krümmen, winden; (mil.) bestreichen; -er n. Feger, Kehrer; -ing n. Ausfegen; -ings pl. Kehricht, Abfall; -ing adj. ausgedehnt, schwungvoll; umfassend, durchgreifend

sweepstake(s) n. Wettrennen (Prämie aus Wetteinsätzen)

sweet adj. süss, lieblich, hübsch; frisch, rein; sanft, freundlich; — **alyssum** (bot.) Lobelie; — **basil** Basilikum; — **potato** Batate, süsse Kartoffel; **have a — tooth** ein Leckermaul (or eine Naschkatze) sein; — n. Süsse; (fig.) Annehmlichkeit; pl. Süssigkeiten, Leckereien, Zuckerwerk; -en v. (ver)-süssen; angenehm machen; -ness n. Süssigkeit, Wohlgeschmack; Lieblichkeit, Freundlichkeit; Annehmlichkeit

sweetbread n. Thymusdrüse; Bauchspeicheldrüse; (meat) Kalbsmilch

sweetbrier, sweetbriar n. Heckenrose

sweetheart n. Geliebte, Liebchen, Schatz

sweetmeats n. pl. Zuckerwerk, Süssigkeiten; Eingemachtes

swell n. Anschwellung; (geol.) Anhöhe; (mech.) Ausschweifung; (med.) Geschwulst; (mus.) Crescendo; Anwachsen; (coll.) Hauptkerl; — adj. flott, famos; — v. (an)schwellen, aufwallen; sich blähen (or aufbauschen); aufblasen; vergrössern; -ing n. Schwel-len; (med.) Beule

swelter v. verschmachten, hinschmelzen, versengen

swept adj. gefegt, gekehrt

swerve n. Seitenbewegung, Abweichung; — v. abweichen, abschweifen, ablenken

swift n. (mech.) Haspel; (orn.) Mauerschwalbe, Turmsegler; — adj. schnell, eilig; geschwind, flüchtig; voreilig

swig n. Schluck; — v. schlucken, zechen

swim n. Schwimmen; — **bladder** Schwimmblase; — v. schwimmen; gleiten, schweben; -mer n. Schwimmer; -ing n. Schwimmen, Gleiten; -ing adj. schwimmend, gleitend; -ing **pool** Schwimmbassin; Schwimmbad

swindle n. Schwindel(ei); — v. (be)-schwindeln; -r n. Schwindler

swine n. Schwein; (coll.) Schweinehund

swing n. Schwung; Schaukel; (boxing) Schwinger; (mech.) Freilauf, Spielraum; (mus.) Swing; — v. schwingen; schaukeln, schwanken, baumeln; sich drehen; -ing n. Schwingen, Schaukeln; Schwankung; -ing adj. schwingend, schaukelnd

swipe n. Schlag, Stoss; (mech.) Schwengel; (coll.) Schluck; — v. schlagen, stossen; (coll.) stehlen; heruntergiessen

swirl n. Strudel, Wirbel; — v. (herum)-wirbeln

switch n. Gerte, Rute; (elec.) Schalter; **ignition —** Zündschalter; — **box** Schaltkasten; (rail.) Weichenbock; — v. peitschen; (elec.) umschalten, schalten; — **off** ausschalten, ausknipsen

switchback n. Berg- und Talbahn; Zickzackbergbahn

switchblade n. Federtaschenmesser

switchboard n. Klappenschrank, Schalttafel, Schaltbrett

switchman n. (rail.) Weichensteller

Switzerland n. die Schweiz

swivel n. Drehring, Drehzapfen; (mil.) Karabinerhaken; — **chair** Drehstuhl; — v. sich drehen

swollen adj. angeschwollen

swoon n. Ohnmacht; (coll.) Begeisterungsdusel; — v. in Ohnmacht fallen; vor Begeisterung die Sinne verlieren

swoop n. Stoss, Sturz; — v. (herab)stossen

sword n. Schwert; Degen, Säbel; — **belt** Degengehenk, Säbelkoppel

swordfish n. Schwertfisch

sycamore n. Sykomore; **Maulbeerfeigenbaum**

syllable n. Silbe

symbol n. Symbol, Sinnbild; -ic(al) adj. symbolisch, sinnbildlich; -ism n. Symbolik; -ize v. symbolisieren, sinnbildlich darstellen

symmetric(al) *adj.* symmetrisch, gleichmässig, ebenmässig

symmetry *n.* Symmetrie, Ebenmass

sympathetic *adj.* sympathisch, mitfühlend; harmonierend, seelenverwandt

sympathize *v.* sympathisieren; — **with** übereinstimmen mit; mitfühlen, mitempfinden; **–r** *n.* Sympathisierende, Mitfühlende; Anhänger

sympathy *n.* Sympathie; Mitgefühl

symphony *n.* Symphonie, Sinfonie

symposium *n.* Gastmahl; Symposium

symptom *n.* Symptom, Anzeichen

synagogue *n.* Synagoge

synchronize *v.* synchronisieren; (watch) gleichgehend machen; gleichzeitig sein

syncopation *n.* Synkopieren; Verkürzung

syndicate *n.* Syndikat, Konsortium, Konzern; — *v.* zu einem Syndikat zusammenschliessen

synonym *n.* Synonym; sinnverwandtes Wort; **–ous** *adj.* synonym, sinnverwandt

synopsis *n.* Übersicht, Zusammenfassung; Synopsis

synthetic *adj.* synthetisch, künstlich

syphilis *n.* Syphilis

Syria *n.* Syrien

syringe *n.* Spritze, Injektionsnadel; — *v.* (aus)spritzen, einspritzen

syrup *n.* Sirup

system *n.* System; Verfahren; **–atic** *adj.* systematisch, planmässig

T

tab *n.* Streifen; Riemen, Aufhänger; Klappe; (coll.) Anweisung; Scheck

tabernacle *n.* Tabernakel; (Jewish) Stiftshütte

table *n.* Tisch; Tafel; Platte; Tabelle; Register; Tischgesellschaft; **folding —** Klapptisch; **round —** Tafelrunde; **side —** Seitentisch; **set the —** den Tisch decken; — **d'hôte** Hoteltafel; feste Speisenfolge; — **of contents** Inhaltsverzeichnis; **turn the –s** den Spiess umdrehen; **wait at the —** aufwarten, servieren; — **cover** Tischdecke; — **linen** Tischzeug; — **manners** Tischmanieren; — **service** Tafelaufsatz; Tischbedienung; — **tennis** Tischtennis; — *v.* verzeichnen, katalogisieren; auf den Tisch legen; vorschlagen

tableau *n.* Gemälde; Bild

tablecloth *n.* Tischtuch

tablespoon *n.* Esslöffel; **–ful** *n.* Esslöffelvoll

tablet *n.* Tablette, Pastille; Täfelchen

tableware *n.* Tischgeschirr

Tabloid *n.* Tablette; Zeitung im Halbformat, Sensationsblatt

taboo, tabu *n.* Tabu, Verbot; — *adj.* tabu, verboten, verrufen; — *v.* verbieten, untersagen, in Verruf bringen

tabular *adj.* tafelförmig; blättrig; tabellarisch

tabulate *v.* katalogisieren; zusammenfassen

tabulation *n.* Tabellarisierung

tachometer *n.* Tachometer

tacit *adj.* stillschweigend

tack *n.* Stift, Zwecke, Reissnagel; — *v.* (an-)heften; (naut.) lavieren, wenden

tackle *n.* Gerät, Geschirr; (football) Griff; (mech.) Flaschenzug; (naut.) Takel, Tauwerk; — *v.* befestigen; packen, festhalten

tact *n.* Takt, Feinfühligkeit; **–ful** *adj.* taktvoll; **–less** *adj.* taktlos

tactics *n.* Taktik

tadpole *n.* Kaulquappe

taffeta *n.* Taf(fe)t

tag *n.* Ende, Stück; Stift; Etikett, Preisschild; Troddel, Quaste; — *v.* etikettieren; auszeichnen; (coll.) anheften

tail *n.* Schwanz, Schweif; Rute, Wedel; Ende, Schluss, Anhang; Kehrseite

taillight *n.* Schlusslicht

tailor *n.* Schneider; **–ing** *n.* Schneidern, Schneiderei

tailor-made *adj.* vom Schneider angefertigt

taint *n.* Fleck(en), Makel; (med.) Ansteckung; (fig.) Verderbnis; — *v.* beflecken, verderben, vergiften; (med.) anstecken

take *n.* Einnahme; (film) Szene; (typ.) Manuskript; — *v.* (an)nehmen, abnehmen, aufnehmen, einnehmen, mitnehmen, übernehmen, wegnehmen; ergreifen; machen; erfordern; verstehen, ansehen; — **aback** verwirren, erstaunen; — **after** ähneln, nacharten; — **apart** auseinandernehmen; — **a walk** spazierengehen; — **away** wegnehmen, entfernen; — **care of** in Verwahrung nehmen; sorgen für; — **charge of** Verantwortung übernehmen für; — **effect** in Kraft treten; gelingen; — **fire** Feuer fangen; — **for granted** als selbstverständlich annehmen; — **heart** Mut fassen; — **it easy** es sich leicht machen; — **off** abnehmen, ausziehen; kopieren; (avi.) abfliegen; — **out** herausnehmen; — **place** stattfinden; — **the liberty** sich die Freiheit nehmen; — **to it** sich angewöhnen, liebgewinnen; — **upon oneself** sich anmassen; aufsichnehmen;

-r n. Abnehmer
take-home adj., — **pay** n. Nettogehalt
take-in n. (coll.) Einnahme; Betrug
take-off n. Nachahmung, Karikatur;
(avi.) Abflug; Start
taking adj. einnehmend, reizend; (med.)
ansteckend; — n. Einnahme; (phot.)
Aufnahme; pl. Gesamteinnahme, Gewinn
talc(um) n. Talk; — **powder** Körperpuder
tale n. Erzählung, Geschichte; Märchen;
tell -s aus der Schule plaudern
talebearer n. Zuträger, Angeber
talent n. Talent, Begabung; **-ed** adj.
talentiert, begabt
talk n. Gespräch; Geschwätz, Gerücht;
— v. reden, sprechen, plaudern, klatschen; sich unterhalten; **-ative** adj.
geschwätzig, gesprächig, redselig; **-er**
n. Redner, Sprecher; Schwätzer; **-ie** n.
(coll.) Sprechfilm, Tonfilm; **-ing** n.
Unterhaltung, Geplauder; **-ing** adj.
redend, sprechend; plaudernd; geschwätzig; **-ing machine** Sprechmaschine, Grammofon; **-ing picture**
Sprechfilm, Tonfilm
tall adj. gross, hoch, lang; ausserordentlich; (coll.) fabelhaft
tallow n. Talg; (mech.) Schmiere; — v.
einfetten; schmieren
tally n. Abrechnung; (fig.) Kerbholz,
Gegenstück; — adj. — **sheet** Abrechnungsbogen; — v. abrechnen, nachzählen; übereinstimmen; einkerben
talon n. Kralle, Klaue; (cards) Talon
tambourine n. Tamburin
tame adj. zahm; (fig.) matt, schal, eindruckslos; — v. (be)zähmen, bändigen;
mildern; (fig.) demütigen
taming n. Zähmung, Bändigung
tamper v. sich vergreifen, hineinpfuschen;
intrigieren
tan n. Lohe; Gelbbraun; Sonnenbräune;
— adj. lohfarben, gelbbraun; — v.
gerben; bräunen; (coll.) durchwalken;
-ned adj. lohfarben; sonnenverbrannt;
-ner n. Gerber; **-nery** n. Gerberei; **-nic**
adj. gerbend, Gerb-; **-nin** n. Tannin,
Gerbsäure; **-ning** n. Gerberei; (coll.)
Prügel
tandem n. Tandem; — adv. hintereinander
tangerine n. Mandarine
tangible adj. greifbar, fühlbar; körperlich
tangle n. Verwicklung, Gewirr; Knoten;
(bot.) Riementang; — v. (sich) verwirren, verwickeln
tango n. Tango
tank n. Behälter; (mil.) Tank; **water** —
Zisterne; — **car** Tankwagen, Kessel-

wagen; — v. tanken, füllen
tantrum n. üble Laune, Rappel, Koller
tap n. Zapfen, Spund; Hahn; Gewindebohrer; Pochen; pl. (mil.) Zapfenstreich; — **dance** Steptanz; — v.
anzapfen, anstecken, anbohren; anschliessen, abzweigen; pochen, klopfen
tape n. Band, Streifen, Schnur; (sl.)
Branntwein; **adhesive** — Leukoplast;
red — Bürokratismus; — **recording**
Tonbandaufnahme; — v. bebändern,
binden, heften
tapeline n. Bandmass
taper n. Wachskerze; (geom.) Verjüngung; — adj. spitz zulaufend; konisch,
verjüngt; — v. spitz zulaufen, sich verringern; (sich) zuspitzen
tapestry n. Wandteppich, Gobelin
tapeworm n. Bandwurm
tapioca n. Tapioka
taproom n. Schenkstube, Bar
tar n. Teer; (sl.) Teerjacke, Matrose; —
v. teeren; **-ry** adj. teerig
tarantula n. Tarantel(spinne)
tardiness n. Langsamkeit, Verspätung
tardy adj. langsam, säumig, spät
target n. Ziel(scheibe)
tariff n. Tarif
tarnish n. Trübung, Anlaufen; Belag; —
v. trüben, beflecken; anlaufen, matt
werden
tarpaulin n. (geteerte) Wagendecke;
(naut.) Persenning, Ölzeug
tarry v. zögern, säumen, warten; — adj.
zögernd, wartend
tart n. Fruchttörtchen; Pastete; — adj.
scharf, sauer, herb; schroff
tartar n. Weinstein, Zahnstein
task n. Aufgabe; Tagewerk; (educ.)
Arbeit; — v. beschäftigen, anstrengen
tassel n. Quaste, Troddel; — v. mit
Quasten (or Troddeln) verzieren
taste n. Geschmack, Kostprobe; (fig.)
Neigung, Lust; — v. kosten, probieren,
schmecken; (fig.) empfinden, geniessen;
— **of** schmecken nach; einen Nachgeschmack haben; **-ful** adj. schmackhaft;
(fig.) geschmackvoll; **-less** adj. unschmackhaft; geschmacklos
tasty adj. köstlich; appetitlich; (fig.)
stilvoll, modisch
tatter n. Lumpen, Fetzen; **-ed** adj.
zerlumpt, zerfetzt
tatting n. Spitzenarbeit
tattle n. Geschwätz, Plauderei; — v.
schwatzen, plaudern
tattletale n. Klatschgeschichte
tattoo n. Tätowierung; (mil.) Zapfenstreich; — v. tätowieren; (fig.) trommeln

taunt n. Hohn, Spott; Stichelei; — v. verhöhnen, spotten; sticheln

taupe n. Mausgrau; — adj. mausgrau

Tauris n. Tauris

taut adj. steif, straff; stramm; (fig.) herausgeputzt

tavern n. Taverne, Schenke, Wirtshaus; **roadside** — Wegschenke, Rasthaus

tawdry adj. auffallend, prahlerisch, aufgeputzt, billig

tax n. Steuer, Gebühr, Abgabe, Zoll; (fig.) Bürde, Last; **additional** — Steuerzuschlag; — **collector** Steuereinnehmer; — **rate** Steuerbetrag; — v. taxieren, abschätzen, veranschlagen; besteuern; (fig.) in Anspruch nehmen; beschuldigen; –able adj. steuerbar, steuerpflichtig; zollpflichtig, verzollbar; –ation n. Besteuerung; (law) Schätzung

tax-exempt adj. steuerfrei, nicht steuerpflichtig

taxi n. Taxe; — v. mit einer Taxe fahren; (avi.) in Position rollen

taxicab n. Taxe

taxidermy n. Kunst des Ausstopfens

taximeter n. Fahrpreisanzeiger an öffentlichen Fahrzeugen

taxonomy n. Klassifizierung

taxpayer n. Steuerzahler; Bürger

tea n. Tee; Teestrauch; Teegesellschaft

teacart n. Teewagen

teach v. lehren, unterrichten, unterweisen; –er n. Lehrer; –ing n. Lehren, Unterricht; Lehre; –ing adj. belehrend, unterrichtend; –ing staff Lehrkörper

teacup n. Teetasse, Teeschale

teakettle n. Teekessel; Teemaschine

team n. Team, Mannschaft; Gespann

teamwork n. Zusammenarbeit; (sports) Zusammenspiel

teapot n. Teekanne, Teetopf

tear n. Träne, Tropfen; Riss; Abnutzung; — **bomb** Tränengasbombe; — **gas** Tränengas; — v. tränen, tropfen; (zer)reissen, zerfleischen; dahinrasen, dahinstürmen; –ful adj. tränenvoll; (fig.) beklagenswert

teardrop n. Träne

tearoom n. Teestube, Teeraum

tease v. plagen, quälen; necken, hänseln; (mech.) kämmen, zupfen

teaspoon n. Teelöffel; –ful n. Teelöffelvoll

technical adj. technisch, gewerblich; fachlich; –ity n. technische Eigentümlichkeit; Fachausdruck

technician n. Techniker

technicolor n. Technicolor; Farbfilmtechnik

technics, technique n. Technik, Kunstfertigkeit

technology n. Technologie, Gewerbekunde

tedious adj. langweilig, weitschweifig; lästig; –ness n., tedium n. Langeweile; Langweiligkeit, Weitläufigkeit

tee n. Mal, Marke, Ziel; (golf) Erdhaufen; — v. — **off** (golf) wegschlagen, das Spiel eröffnen

teem v. erzeugen; wimmeln, übervoll sein

teen-age n. Entwicklungszeit; Flegeljahre; — adj. teen-age-, halbwüchsig; –r n. Backfisch; Halbwüchsige

teens n. pl. Entwicklungsalter; (math.) Zehner (von 10 bis 19)

teeth n. pl. Zähne; **set of** — Gebiss; –ing n. Zahnen; –ing ring Beissring

teetotaler n. Abstinenzler, Temperenzler, Enthaltsame

telautogram n. Bildtelegramm

telecast v. (tv.) Fernsehsendungen übertragen

telegram n. Telegramm, Depesche

telegraph n. Telegraf; — **operator** Telegrafist(in); — v. telegrafieren

telepathy n. Telepathie

telephone n. Telefon, Fernsprecher; **dial** — Selbstanschlusstelefon; Selbstwählapparat; — **booth** Fernsprechzelle; — **directory** Telefonbuch; — **exchange** Fernsprechamt; — **operator** Telefonist(in); — **receiver** Telefonhörer

teleprompter n. Textband

telescope n. Teleskop, Fernrohr

teletype n. Fernschreiber, Fernschreiben; — v. fernschreiben

television n. Fernseher

tell v. erzählen, sagen, mitteilen; benachrichtigen; unterscheiden; herausfinden, erkennen; zählen; befehlen; –er n. Erzähler; Zähler; (com.) Kassengehilfe; **paying** –er Kassierer am Auszahlungsschalter; **receiving** –er Kassierer am Einzahlungsschalter; –ing adj. wirkungsvoll, eindrucksvoll

telltale n. Ausplauderer, Zuträger

temper n. Stimmung, Laune; Gemüt- (sart); Wut, Ärger; (mech.) Mischung; Härtegrad; **lose one's** — die Geduld verlieren, heftig werden; — v. mässigen, mildern; anpassen; (mech.) härten, mischen; –ament n. Temperament; Art; –amental adj. temperamentvoll; (fig.) launenhaft; –ance n. Mässigkeit, Enthaltsamkeit; –ate adj. mässig, massvoll, gemässigt, ruhig; –ate zone gemässigte Zone; –ature n. Temperatur; –ed adj. gestimmt, gelaunt; gleichmütig, gelassen; (mech.) gehärtet

tempest n. Sturm; Gewitter; –uous adj; stürmisch, ungestüm

temple n. Tempel, Gotteshaus; (anat.) Schläfe

tempo n. Tempo; Zeitmass

temporal adj. zeitlich; weltlich; (anat.) Schläfen-

temporary adj. zeitweilig, vorläufig; vorübergehend

temporize v. hinhalten, zaudern, zögern

tempt v. versuchen, verlocken; (fig.) herausfordern; -ation n. Versuchung, Reiz; (fig.) Herausforderung; -ing adj. versuchend, verführerisch, verlockend; reizend

ten n. Zehn(er); — adj. zehn

tenacious adj. festhaltend, treu, beharrlich, zäh, hartnäckig

tenant n. Mieter, Insasse; Pächter; — v. mieten, pachten; bewohnen

tend v. (be)dienen, pflegen; (be)hüten; (fig.) neigen, gerichtet sein, abzielen; -ency n. Richtung, Tendenz, Neigung; Zweck; -er n. (naut. and rail.) Tender

tender adj. zart, zärtlich; weich, schwach; empfindlich; — n. Angebot; legal — gesetzliches Zahlungsmittel; — v. hochschätzen, hochachten; anbieten; -ness n. Zartheit, Weichheit; Zärtlichkeit

tenderfoot n. Neuling, Anfänger

tenderhearted adj. weichherzig, kleinmütig

tenderloin n. Lendenstück, Filet

tendon n. Sehne

tendril n. Ranke

tenement n. Haus; Wohnung; — house Mietshaus

tenet n. Grundsatz, Lehrsatz

tennis n. Tennisspiel; — court Tennisplatz; — player Tennisspieler

tenor n. (law) Inhalt, Abschrift; (mus.) Tenor; (fig.) Wesen, Beschaffenheit, Fortgang, Verlauf

tense (gram.) Zeitform; **past** — Vergangenheit; — adj. straff, gespannt; -ness n. Straffheit, Spannung

tension n. Spannung; Gespanntheit; (phys.) Expansion, Spannkraft; **high** — Hochspannung

tent n. Zelt; **oxygen** — Sauerstoffzelt; — v. zelten

tentacle n. Fühler, Fühlhorn

tentative adj. versuchend, Versuchs-

tenth n. Zehnte; Zehntel; (mus.) Dezime; — adj. zehnt; -ly adv. zehntens

tenuous adj. dünn, fein, zart; geringfügig, dürftig

tenure n. Besitz(anspruch); Amtszeit

tepid adj. lau(warm); -ity n. Lauheit

term n. Termin, Frist; Zeitdauer; (educ.) Semester, Studienjahr; (gram.) Aus-

druck, Wort; (law) Sitzungsperiode; (math.) Glied; pl. Bestimmungen, Bedingungen; Preise; Honorare, Schulgeld; Beziehungen; **be on good -s auf gutem Fusse stehen; come to -s sich einigen** (or vergleichen); **-s of payment** Zahlungsbedingungen; — v. benennen; -inal n. Grenze, Spitze, Ende; (rail.) Endstation; -inal adj. End-, Termin-; letzt; (bot.) gipfelständig; -inate v. beendigen, schliessen; begrenzen; beilegen; -ination n. Ausgang, Grenze; Ende; (gram.) Endung; -inology n. Terminologie, Fachsprache; -inus n. Grenze, Endpunkt; (rail.) Endstation

termite n. Termite

terrace n. Terrasse; — v. (terassenförmig) aufsteigen

terrestrial adj. irdisch; Erden-

terrible adj. schrecklich, furchtbar

terrier n. Terrier

terrific adj. fürchterlich, schreckenerregend; (coll.) ungeheuer, kolossal

terrify v. erschrecken, entsetzen

territory n. Gebiet, Bezirk; Territorium

terror n. Terror, Schrecken, Entsetzen; -ism n. Gewaltherrschaft; -ist n. Terrorist; -ize v. terrorisieren

terror-stricken adj. von Schrecken ergriffen

terse adj. bündig, kurz, markig

test n. Test, Probe; Prüfung, Untersuchung; (chem.) Reagens; (fig.) Prüfstein; — **case** Schulbeispiel, Präzedenzfall; — **pilot** Testpilot; — **tube** Probierröhre; Reagensglas; -ament n., Testament (bibl.) Testament; -er n. Prüfer; (arch.) Baldachin, Himmel; -ify v. (be)zeugen; -imonial n. Zeugnis, Attest; -imonial adj. beglaubigend, bezeugend; -imony n. Zeugnis, Beweis; Zeugenaussage; -ing n. Versuch; Kennzeichen, Merkmal; -y adj. eigensinnig, mürrisch; reizbar

tetanus n. Tetanus, Wundstarrkrampf

tether n. Spannseil; (fig.) Spielraum; — v. kurz halten, anbinden, begrenzen

text n. Text; (rel.) Bibelstelle; -ual adj. textmässig, textlich, Text-

textbook n. Lehrbuch, Schulbuch; Leitfaden; (mus.) Textbuch

textile adj. gesponnen, gewebt; webbar; Textil-, Web-; -s n. pl. Textilien, Webwaren

texture n. Struktur, Gewebe

than conj. als, denn; damals, darauf

thank n. Dank; pl. Danke! — v. danken, verdanken; -ful adj. dankbar, erkenntlich; -fulness n. Dankbarkeit, Erkenntlichkeit; -less adj. undankbar

thanksgiving n. Danksagung; (rel.) Dankgebet; **Thanksgiving (Day)** Dankfest; Erntedankfest

that adj. and pron. jene, diese, solche, welche; der, die, das; — conj. dass, damit, weil, da; — adv. dermassen; so

thatch n. Dachstroh; — v. mit Stroh decken; **-ed** adj. strohgedeckt; **-ed roof** Strohdach

thaw n. Tau; Tauwetter; — v. (auf)tauen

the art. der, die, das; pl. die; — adv. desto, um so, nur noch

theater n. Theater; — **of war** Kriegsschauplatz

theatrical adj. theatralisch, bühnenmässig; Theater-

thee pron. dich, dir, deiner

theft n. Diebstahl

their pron. ihr; pl. ihre; der (or die, das) ihrige

them n. pron. sie; ihnen; **-selves** pron. sie (or sich) selbst; allein

theme n. Thema, Gegenstand; (gram.) Stamm; (mus.) Motiv

then adv. darauf, (als)dann; damals, da; nun; denn, daher, darum, also, folglich; doch, freilich; **every now and —** alle Augenblicke; **now and —** dann und wann, hier und da

thence adv. von dort, dorther; daher, daraus; seitdem; **-forth** adv. seitdem, von da ab

theocracy n. Gottesherrschaft, Theokratie

theologian n. Theologe

theologic(al) adj. theologisch

theology n. Theologie

theorem n. Lehrsatz

theoretical adj. theoretisch

theory n. Theorie

theosophy n. Theosophie

therapeutics n. Therapeutik, **praktische** Heilkunde

therapy n. Therapie, Heilverfahren

there adv. da, dort; darin; dorthin; —! interj. so ist's recht! schon gut!

thereabouts adv. da herum; ungefähr (soviel)

thereafter adv. danach, demgemäss

thereby adv. dadurch, damit, dabei, daran

therefore adv. deswegen, deshalb, darum, folglich

therefrom adv. davon, daran, daraus

therein adv. darin, dadurch; in dieser Beziehung

thereof adv. davon, dessen, deren

thereon adv. darauf, daran, darüber

there(un)to adv. dazu, noch dazu; ausserdem

thereupon adv. darauf(hin), hierauf; demzufolge

therewith adv. damit, darauf

thermal, thermic adj. Thermal-, Wärme-, Heiz-; **— waters** heisse Quellen

thermionics n. Thermoionik

thermite n. Thermit (Füllung für Bomben)

thermodynamics n. Thermodynamik

thermometer n. Thermometer

thermonuclear adj. thermonuklear

Thermos bottle n. Thermosflasche

thermostat n. Thermostat

thesaurus n. Wörterbuch

these pron. diese

thesis n. These, Leitsatz

they pron. sie, die(jenigen), solche; **man**

thiamin n. Vitamin B1

thick n. Dicke, Mitte; (coll.) Dummkopf; — adj. dick, gross, dicht; trübe, undeutlich; vertraut; (voice) heiser; **-ly** adv. oft, häufig; schnell hintereinander; schwerfällig; **-en** v. verdicken, (sich) verdichten (or trüben); verstärken; **-et** n. Dickicht; **-ness** n. Dicke, Stärke; Dichtheit

thickheaded adj. dickköpfig

thick-skinned adj. dickhäutig, dickschalig; (coll.) dickfellig

thief n. Dieb; (fig.) Schelm, Spitzbube

thievish adj. diebisch; spitzbübisch

thigh n. Schenkel, Oberschenkel

thighbone n. Schenkelknochen

thimble n. Fingerhut; **-ful** n. Fingerhutvoll

thin adj. dünn, mager; spärlich, schwach, leicht; — v. verdünnen, lichten, vermindern; abnehmen; **-ness** n. Dünne, Dünnheit; Zartheit; (coll.) Seichtheit

thine pron. dein; der (or die, das) deinige

thing n. Ding, Sache, Wesen, Geschöpf; pl. Kleider, Gepäck; Angelegenheiten

think v. denken, meinen, glauben; gedenken; sich besinnen; **-er** n. Denker; **-ing** n. Denken, Nachdenken; Denkvermögen; Meinung

thin-skinned adj. dünnhäutig; (fig.) feinfühlend, empfindlich

third n. Dritte; Drittel; (mus.) Terz; — adj. dritt

thirst n. Durst; (fig.) Begierde, Verlangen; — v. dursten; (fig.) verlangen; **-y** adj. durstig; (agr.) dürr, versengt; (fig.) gierig

thirteen n. Dreizehn(er); — adj. dreizehn; **-th** n. Dreizehnte, Dreizehntel; **-th** adj. dreizehnt

thirtieth n. Dreissigste, Dreissigstel; — adj. dreissigst

thirty n. Dreissig(er); — adj. dreissig

this adj. and pron. dies, das; laufend, gegenwärtig; heutig, letzt; hier(her)

thistle n. Distel

thither *adv.* dorthin, dahin

thong *n.* Riemen, Peitschenschnur

thorn *n.* Dorn; (mech.) Stachel; — **in the side** der Dorn im Auge, der Pfahl im Fleisch; **-y** *adj.* dornig, stach(e)lig; (fig.) beschwerlich

thorough *adj.* gründlich, vollkommen, vollendet, vollständig, gänzlich, völlig; **-ly** *adv.* durchgreifend, durch und durch; **-bred** *n.* Vollblut; **-bred** *adj.* vollblütig, reinblütig; **-ness** *n.* Gründlichkeit, Vollständigkeit

thoroughfare *n.* Durchgang, Durchfahrt; **no** —! Durchfahrt verboten!

those *adj.* and *pron.* jene, die(jenigen), solche

thou *pron.* du; — *v.* duzen

though *conj.* obgleich, obschon, obwohl, wenn auch; — *adv.* allerdings, freilich, immerhin, übrigens, doch

thought *n.* Gedanke, Einfall; Nachdenken; **-ful** *adj.* gedankenvoll; nachdenklich; aufmerksam, rücksichtsvoll; **-fulness** *n.* tiefes Nachdenken; Aufmerksamkeit, Rücksichtsnahme, Sorgfalt; **-less** *adj.* gedankenlos; achtlos, sorglos, rücksichtslos

thousand *n.* Tausend; — *adj.* tausend; **-th** *n.* Tausendste, Tausendstel; **-th** *adj.* tausendst

thrash *n.* Dreschen; — *v.* dreschen; (coll.) verdreschen; **-er** *n.* Drescher; Dreschmaschine; **-ing** *n.* Dreschen; (coll.) Prügel

thread *n.* Faden; Zwirn, Garn; Faser, Fiber; (mech.) Gewinde; (min.) Ader; **-bare** *adj.* fadenscheinig, abgetragen, schäbig

threat *n.* Drohung; **-en** *v.* (be)drohen, androhen; **-ening** *adj.* drohend

three *n.* Drei(er); — *adj.* drei; **-fold** *adj.* dreifach

three-legged *adj.* dreibeinig; — **stool** Dreifuss; dreibeiniger Stuhl

thresh *v.* dreschen; **-er** *n.* Drescher; **-ing** *adj.* dreschend; **-ing machine** Dreschmaschine

threshold *n.* Schwelle

thrice *adv.* dreimal

thrift *n.* Wirtschaftlichkeit, Sparsamkeit; Gedeihen; (bot.) Grasnelke; **-less** *n.* verschwenderisch; **-y** *adj.* sparsam, haushälterisch; gedeihend

thrill *n.* Schauer, Zittern, Erbeben; — *v.* durchbohren, durchdringen, durchschauern, erschüttern; packen, aufregen; **-er** *n.* Schauergeschichte; **-ing** *adj.* erregend, spannend; sensationell

thrive *v.* gedeihen, geraten, wachsen; Glück (or Erfolg) haben

throat *n.* Kehle, Gurgel, Schlund; Hals; Rinne; **clear one's** — sich räuspern; **sore** — Halsschmerzen, Halsweh

throb *n.* Pochen, Klopfen, Schlagen; Pulsschlag; — *v.* pochen, klopfen, schlagen

throne *n.* Thron; (fig.) Herrschaft; — *v.* thronen; **an der Macht sein; auf den Thron setzen; erheben**

throng *n.* Gedränge, Menge, Schar; — *v.* drängen, strömen; bedrängen

throttle *n.* (anat.) Luftröhre; (mech.) Hals; Drosselklappe; Drosselung; — *v.* (er)drosseln, abdrosseln

through *prep.* durch; aus, vor; mittels; überall in; während; — *adv.* hindurch; durchaus, ganz und gar; — *adj.* offen, frei; durch(gehend)

throughout *prep.* ganz, hindurch; während; — *adv.* in jeder Beziehung, durchaus, überall

throw *n.* Wurf; Wurfweite; (geol.) Verwerfung; (mech.) Kolbenhub; — *v.* werfen, schleudern; giessen, schütten; (chem.) fällen; (dice) würfeln; (mech.) einschalten, ausschalten; — **down** niederwerfen, unterdrücken, zerstören; — **into gear** den Gang einschalten, in Gang bringen; — **out of gear** den Gang ausschalten

thrush *n.* Drossel; (med.) Mundfäule

thrust *n.* Stoss, Schub, Stich; Angriff, Anfall; (mech.) Druck; — *v.* stossen, stechen; (ein)drängen, einwerfen

thud *n.* Dröhnen; — *v.* (er)dröhnen

thug *n.* Meuchelmörder

thumb *n.* Daumen; (mech.) Zapfen; — **notches** Daumenabdrücke, Fingerabdrücke; — *v.* beschmutzen, abgreifen; durchblättern; (mus.) klimpern, leiern; — **a ride** durch Fingerzeichen eine Mitfahrt erbitten

thumbnail *n.* Daumennagel; — *adj.* haargenau

thumbscrew *n.* Flügelschraube, Flügelmutter; Daumenschraube

thumbtack *n.* Reissnagel

thump *n.* Schlag, Puff; (coll.) Plumps, Bums; — *v.* schlagen, puffen; (coll.) hämmern; plumpsen, knuffen; schwerfällig gehen

thunder *n.* Donner; — *v.* donnern, toben; **-ing** *adj.* donnernd, tobend; **-ous** *adj.*, **-y** *adj.* donnernd; gewitterschwül; gewaltig

thunderbolt *n.* Donnerkeil; Blitz(strahl)

thunderclap *n.* Donnerschlag

thundershower *n.* Gewitterschauer, Gewitterregen

thunderstorm *n.* Gewitter(sturm)

thunderstruck adj. vom Blitz getroffen; (fig.) wie vom Donner gerührt

Thuringia n. Thüringen

Thursday n. Donnerstag

thus adv. so, also; daher, so sehr; auf diese Weise

thwack n. derber Schlag; — v. schlagen; prügeln

thwart n. (naut.) Ducht, Ruderbank; — v. durchkreuzen, vereiteln

thy pron. dein; **-self** pron. du selbst; dir, dich (selbst)

thyme n. Thymian

thyroid n. Schilddrüse

tick n. Ticken; Punkt, Haken; (ent.) Zecke; (coll.) Tick; Pump; Klaps; — v. ticken; punktieren; anhaken; (coll.) borgen, pumpen klapsen; **-er** n. Börsentelegraf; (coll.) Herz, Uhr; **-er tape** Papierstreifen des Börsentelegrafen (or Zeitungstelegrafen); **-ing** n. Ticken; Drillich, Drell

ticket n. Zettel; Schein; Eintrittskarte; Billet, Fahrkarte; Pfandschein; (com.) Etikette, Preiszettel; (pol.) Kandidatenliste, Wahlzettel; (police) Strafmandat; **roundtrip** — Hin- und Rückfahrkarte; **season** — Dauerkarte, Abonnement; — **collector** Fahrkartenkontrolleur; — **office** Fahrkartenausgabe; — **scalper** Schwarzhändler mit Eintrittskarten; — **seller** Billettverkäufer; — **window** Fahrkartenschalter

tickle n. Kitzel(n); — v. kitzeln; reizen, schmeicheln

tickling adj. kitzelnd; reizend

ticklish adj. kitzlig; (fig.) wankelmütig, unzuverlässig, heikel

tidal adj. flutartig; Flut-; — **wave** Flutwelle, Springflut

tidbit n. Leckerbissen

tide n. Gezeiten; Ebbe, Flut; (fig.) Strömung; **high** — Hochwasser; Flut; — v. fluten; (mit dem Strom) treiben; glücklich überwinden

tidewater n. Flut(wasser)

tidings n. pl. Nachrichten; Neuigkeiten

tidy adj. nett, reinlich; schmuck; — v. — **up** wegräumen, aufräumen; zurechtmachen

tie n. Band, Schleife, Knoten; Krawatte; Verbindung, Bindung; (rail.) Schwelle; (sports) Unentschieden; — **beam** Verbindungsbalken; — v. (ver)binden, (ver)knüpfen; vereinigen; (med.) unterbinden; (rail.) mit Schwellen versehen; (sports) gleich stehen

tier n. Reihe, Lage; (theat.) Sitzreihe, Rang

tie-up n. Verkehrsstörung; Geschäfts-störung; Maschinenstörung

tiger n. Tiger; — **lily** Tigerlilie; — **moth** Bärenspinner

tight adj. dicht, fest; straff; gespannt, eng, knapp, prall; undurchlässig; energisch, fähig; schwierig; (sl.) beschwipst; — **squeeze** Klemme; **-s** n. pl. Trikot; knapp anliegende Hosen; **-en** v. straff spannen (or festziehen); zusammenziehen, verengen; **-ness** n. Festigkeit, Dichtheit

tightrope n. straffgespanntes Seil; Seiltänzerseil

tigress n. Tigerin

tile n. Ziegel, Kachel, Fliese; (coll.) Zylinderhut; — v. mit Ziegeln decken, kacheln, Fliesen legen

till prep. bis zu (or auf); — **now** bis jetzt; — conj. bis; — n. Ladenkasse, Schalterkasse; — v. bestellen; ackern, pflügen; **-er** n. (agr.) Pflüger

tiller n. (bot.) Wurzelspross; (naut.) Pinne; — adj. — **rope** (naut.) Steuerleine

tilt n. Neigung, Kippe; Auseinandersetzung; Stoss; Geschwindigkeit; — v. neigen, kippen; überdecken; stossen; streiten

timber n. Holz, Baumbestand; **building** — Bauholz; — **line** Baumgrenze; — **wolf** grauer Wolf; — v. zimmern, bauen

timberland n. Nutzwald

timberwork n. Zimmerwerk; Holzbau

timbre n. Timbre, Klangfarbe

time n. Zeit; Zeitpunkt, Zeitabschnitt, Zeitalter; Lebenszeit; Frist; Mal; (mus.) Takt, Tempo; Zeitmass; **at all -s** stets, immer; **at no** — niemals; **at some** — or other irgendwann; **at the same** — zur gleichen Zeit; **at -s hin und wieder** manchmal; **before one's** — verfrüht; **behind** — hinter der Zeit, veraltet; verspätet; **for the** — **being** für den Augenblick; unter den Umständen; **from** — **to** — gelegentlich; **in no** — im Nu; **in** — im Takt (or Schritt); rechtzeitig; **keep** — pünktlich abkommen; Takt halten; die Zeit kontrollieren; **on** — pünktlich; **out of** — zur Unzeit; **spare** — Mussestunden; **take** — sich Zeit nehmen; **what is the** —? wie spät ist es? — adj. — **and again** wieder und wieder; — **ball** (naut.) Zeitball; — **bomb** Zeitbombe; — **clock** Kontrolluhr; — **exposure** Zeitaufnahme; — **fuse** Zeitzünder; — **lens** Zeitlupe; — **limit** Frist; — **sheet** Kontrollblatt (für geleistete Arbeitsstunden); — **signal** Zeitzeichen; — v. die Zeit abmessen (or einteilen, bestimmen); (mus.) Takt halten (or angeben); **–less** adj. zeitlos, ewig; **–liness** n. Rechtzeitigkeit; **–ly** adj. (recht)zeitig, frühzeitig; passend; aktuell; **–r** n. Zeitnehmer, Unparteiische; (mech.) Stoppuhr

timecard n. Kontrollkarte

timekeeper n. Uhr; (mus.) Metronom; (sports) Stoppuhr

timepiece n. Zeitmesser, Uhr

timesaver n. Zeitersparer

timetable n. Zeittabelle; (educ.) Stundenplan; (rail.) Fahrplan

timeworn adj. abgenutzt, veraltet

timid adj. furchtsam, schüchtern; **–ity** n. Furchtsamkeit, Schüchternheit

timing n. Zeiteinteilung, Einstellung

timothy n. Timotheusgras

tin n. Zinn; Weissblech; Zinngerät; **— can** Konservendose; **— foil** Zinnfolie, Staniol; **— plate** verzinntes Eisenblech; v. verzinnen; **–ned** adj. verzinnt; **–ner** n. Zinngiesser, Verzinner; Klempner; **–ny** adj. blechern

tine n. Zinke, Zacken

tinge n. Tünche; Färbung, Anstrich; **— v.** tünchen, einen Anstrich geben, färben

tingle n. Prickeln, Kribbeln; **— v.** klingen; prickeln, kribbeln

tinker n. Kesselflicker; **— v.** Kessel flicken; herumflicken

tinsel n. Rauschgold, Rauschsilber; Flitter; falscher Glanz; **— adj.** flitternd, glänzend; **— v.** mit Flitterwerk schmücken

tinsmith n. Blechschmied

tint n. Farbe, Tönung, Schattierung; **— v.** färben; abtönen, schattieren

tiny adj. winzig, sehr klein

tip n. Spitze, Ecke, Zwinge; Mundstück; Trinkgeld; leichter Stoss, leichte Neigung; Wink, Rat; **have at the — of** one's fingers aus dem Handgelenk schütteln; **— v.** beschlagen, bekleiden; tippen, kippen, umwerfen, umstürzen; Winke (or Ratschläge) geben; Trinkgeld geben; **–ple** n. Getränk; **— v.** zechen, picheln; **–sy** adj. berauscht, angeheitert; benebelt

tiptoe n. Zehenspitze

tirade n. Tirade; Wortschwall

tire n. Ermüdung, Abspannung; (mech.) Reifen; (rail.) Radkranz; pl. Bereifung; **flat — Reifenpanne; spare — Ersatzreifen; — v.** erschöpfen, ermüden, (über)anstrengen; (mech.) bereifen, beschienen; **–d** adj. müde, verbraucht; (fig.) überdrüssig; **–less** adj. unermüdlich; **–some** adj. ermüdend, langweilig; verdriesslich

tissue n. Gewebe; **— paper** Seidenpapier

tit n. Kleine; (anat.) Zitze; **— for tat wie** du mir, so ich dir; Wurst wider Wurst

titanic adj. titanisch, riesenhaft

tithe n. Zehnte; Zehntel; (fig.) unbedeutender Teil

title n. Titel; Überschrift, Aufschrift; (law) Rechtstitel, Anspruch; **— deed** Besitztitel, Eigentumsurkunde; **— page** Titelseite; **— role** Titelrolle

titmouse n. (orn.) Kohlmeise

tittle n. Pünktchen, Tüttelchen

to prep. and adv. an, in, nach, zu; auf, gegen, für; bis, bis auf (or zu); damit; um zu; vorwärts, weiter; dazu, deswegen; **— and fro** hin und her, auf und ab

toad n. Kröte

toadstool n. Giftpilz

toast n. Toast, geröstetes Brot; Trinkspruch; **— v.** toasten, Brot rösten; trinken auf; **–ed** adj. geröstet; **–er** n. Brotröster

toastmaster n. Toastleiter

tobacco n. Tabak(pflanze); **cut — Schnittabak; — pouch** Tabaksbeutel

toboggan n. flacher Schlitten; **— v.** rodeln; (com.) fallen

today adv. heute, heutiger Tag; **a week from — heute in einer Woche; — adv.** heute, heutigentages

toddy n. Grog

to-do n. Geschäftigkeit, Lärm, Aufsehen

toe n. Zehe; Spitze; **— dancer** Spitzentänzer; **— v.** mit den Zehen berühren; **— the line** sich am Start aufstellen; die Regeln (or seine Verpflichtungen) einhalten

toenail n. Zehennagel

tog n. Kleidung; **— v.** (coll.) sich fein machen

together adv. zusammen, miteinander; beisammen, beieinander; zugleich, gleichzeitig; nacheinander, hintereinander

toil n. Mühsal, Plackerei, Schererei; **— v.** sich abmühen (or plagen); **–ful** adj., **–some** adj. mühsam

toilet n. Toilette; (med.) Säuberung; **— paper** Toilettenpapier; **— water** Gesichtswasser

token n. Zeichen, Merkmal; Andenken; Münze; **— payment** Anzahlung

tolerable adj. erträglich, leidlich

tolerance n. Toleranz, Duldung, Duldsamkeit

tolerant adj. tolerant

tolerate v. dulden, leiden, tolerieren

toleration n. Duldung, Nachsicht

toll n. Zoll; Wegegeld, Brückengeld; **— bridge** Zollbrücke; **— call** Fernge-

spräch; — v. Zoll (or Steuern) erheben;
läuten; (fig.) ködern; -ing n. Geläute
tollgate n. Schlagbaum
tomato n. Tomate
tomb n. Grab(mal); — v. bestatten,
begraben
tomboy n. Range, Wildfang
tombstone n. Grabstein, Leichenstein
tomcat n. Kater
tome n. Band, Buch
tomfoolery n. Narretei
tomorrow adv. morgen; day after — übermorgen; — adj. — morning morgen
früh; — adv. morgen
tom-tom n. Tamtam
ton n. Tonne; (fig.) Ton; -nage n. Tonnage, Tonnengehalt, Lastigkeit
tone n. Ton, Klang, Laut; Sprechweise;
Betonung; Tönung, Färbung; (med.)
Spannkraft; — v. tönen, klingen; (art)
abtönen, färben; (mus.) stimmen;
erschallen; (phot.) tonen; — down
herabstimmen; — up höher stimmen
tongs n. pl. Zange
tongue n. Zunge; (geol.) Landzunge;
(mech.) Klöppel; (fig.) Sprache; hold
one's — den Mund halten, schweigen;
slip of the — Sprachfehler; Versprechen
'ongue-tied adj. sprachlos; mundfaul
ınic n. (med.) Stärkungsmittel, Toni-
kum; (mus.) Grundton, Tonika; — adj.
ʼnisch; stärkend
ʼht adv. heute nacht; (fig.) heute
ʼd
toʼ.ʼ. .. Mandel; -lectomy n. Mandel-
operation; -litis n. Mandelentzündung
too adv. zu, allzu; auch, noch, dazu,
ebenfalls, gleichfalls; überdies
tool n. Werkzeug, Gerät, Instrument; —
bag Werkzeugtasche; — chest Werk-
zeugkasten; — v. mit Werkzeugen
arbeiten
toot n. Tuten; Hornstoss; — v. tuten,
blasen; -le v. dudeln; schwatzen
tooth n. Zahn; molar — Backenzahn; —
paste Zahnpaste, Zahnpasta; — powder
Zahnpulver; -ed adj. gezahnt; -less
adj. zahnlos
toothache n. Zahnschmerzen, Zahnweh
toothbrush n. Zahnbürste
toothpick n. Zahnstocher
top n. Spitze, Höhe; (head) Scheitel,
Schopf; Haupt; (house) Giebel, First;
(mech.) Kappe, Deckel; (mountain)
Gipfel, Kuppe; (naut.) Topp, Mars;
(toy) Kreisel; (tree) Wipfel, Krone; —
adj. oberst, vornehmst; grösst, höchst,
äusserst; — hat Zylinderhut; — v.
bedecken; übertreffen, überragen; kappen; -ple v. (um)kippen, umstürzen;

überhängen, vorstehen
topaz n. Topas; smoky — Rauchtopas;
yellow — Goldtopas
topcoat n. Überrock, Überzieher; leichter
Mantel
toper n. (coll.) Säufer, Trinker
topflight adj. hervorragend, vorzüglich;
erstklassig, prima
top-heavy adj. oberlastig
topic n. Thema, Gegenstand; -al adj.
örtlich, lokal; aktuell
topknot n. Haarknoten; (orn.) Haube
topmost adj. höchst, oberst
topnotch adj. erstklassig, ausgezeichnet,
prima
top-secret adj. streng geheim
topsoil n. Ackerkrume, Humusboden
topsy-turvy adv. kopfüber, halsüberkopf;
— adj. umgestürzt, verkehrt, verdreht
torch n. Fackel
torchbearer n. Fackelträger
torchlight n. Fackelschein; — procession
Fackelzug
toreador n. Torero, Stierkämpfer
torment n. Folter, Qual, Marter; — v.
foltern, quälen, peinigen, martern; -or
n., -er n. Peiniger, Quälgeist; Folter-
knecht
torn adj. zerrissen, zerfetzt, geschlitzt
tornado n. Tornado, Wirbelsturm
torpedo n. Torpedo; (ichth.) Zitterrochen;
— boat Torpedoboot; — tube Torpedo-
rohr; — v. torpedieren; (fig.) unwirksam machen
torque n. Drehung
torrent n. Wolkenbruch; Sturzbach; (fig.)
Wortschwall; -ial adj. strömend, reissend; (fig.) wortreich
torrid adj. verdorrt, verbrannt; heiss; —
zone heisse Zone
torso n. Torso, Rumpf
tort n. Unrecht; untrue n. Tortur, Folter;
— v. foltern, martern
tortoise n. Schildkröte; — shell Schildpatt, Schildkrötenpanzer
tortoise-shell adj. Schildpatt-
Tory n. Tory; Loyalist; — adj.
toryistisch; loyalistisch
toss n. Werfen; Wurf, Stoss; Würfeln,
Losen; — v. bewegen; (herum)werfen,
stossen; würfeln, losen
tossup n. Hochwerfen; (fig.) Ungewissheit
tot n. Kleine; -ter v. wanken, wackeln,
schwanken; -tering adj. wankend,
wackelnd, schwankend
total adj. total, ganz gänzlich; — loss
Totalverlust; — war totaler Krieg; —
weight Gesamtgewicht; — n. Gesamt-
betrag; — v. sich belaufen auf; -itarian
adj. totalitär

touch *n.* Berührung; Tastsinn. Gefühl; Anflug; (art) Pinselstrich; (mus.) Anschlag; — *v.* berühren, anrühren; anstossen; erreichen; betreffen; spielen; färben, angreifen; sich berühren; **–able** *adj.* berührbar, fühlbar; **–ing** *adj.* (be)rührend, ergreifend; **–ing** *prep.* in betreff, wegen, betreffend; **–y** *adj.* empfindlich, reizbar

touch-and-go *adj.* leicht hingeworfen, oberflächlich, flüchtig

touchback *n.* (football) Ball hinter der eigenen Ziellinie

touchdown *n.* (football) Ball an (*or* hinter) der feindlichen Ziellinie

touchiness *n.* Empfindlichkeit

touch-me-not *n.* Rührmichnichtan

touchstone *n.* (mech.) Probierstein; (mech.) Kieselschiefer; (fig.) Prüfstein

tough *n.* Raufbold; — *adj.* zäh, fest, hart; robust; unnachgiebig; schwierig; **–en** *v.* zäh machen (*or* werden)

toupee, toupet *n.* Toupet; unechtes Haar

tour *n.* Tour; Reise, Rundreise; Reihenfolge; — *v.* durchreisen, bereisen; an einer Tour teilnehmen; **–ing** *n.* Reisen; **–ist** *n.* Tourist

tourist court *n.* Motorhotel; Zeltplatz

tournament *n.* Turnier, Wettkampf, Wettspiel

tourniquet *n.* (med.) Abbindematerial

tousle *v.* zerzausen, verwirren

tow *n.* Tau; Schleppen; Werg; — *v.* (ab)schleppen

toward(s) *prep.* and *adv.* gegen, nach, zu, betreffend; gegenüber; fast, ungefähr; bevorstehend

towel *n.* Handtuch; **roller** — endloses Handtuch

tower *n.* Turm; — *v.* sich emportürmen (*or* erheben, hervorragen, aufschwingen)

towline *n.* Schlepptau, Bugsiertau

town *n.* Stadt; **home** — Heimatstadt; Stadt; städtisch; — **council** Stadtverordnetenversammlung; — **crier** Ausrufer; — **hall** Rathaus; — **planning** Städtebau

townsman *n.* Bürger, Stadtbewohner

toxin *n.* Giftstoff, Toxin

toy *n.* Spielzeug; Tand; — *v.* spielen, tändeln, liebäugeln

trace *n.* Spur, Fährte; Grundriss; Strang, Zugseil; **kick over the** **–s** über die Stränge schlagen; — *v.* nachspüren, verfolgen; herausfinden; zeichnen; durchpausen; abstecken; anspannen; **–able** *cdj.* auffindbar; nachweisbar; zurückzuverfolgen(d); **–r** *n.* Verfolger; (mech.) Vorzeichner, Pauser

trachea *n.* Luftröhre; (bot.) Spiralgefäss

tracing *n.* Durchzeichnen; Pauszeichnung; — *adj.* — **paper** Pauspapier

track *n.* Spur; Bahn; Geleis(e); Fährte, Pfad; **race** — Rennbahn; **–less** *adj.* spurlos, pfadlos

tract *n.* Strecke, Gegend; Ausdehnung; (lit.) Traktat, Abhandlung; **–able** *adj.* handlich, lenksam, folgsam; **–ion** *n.* Zug(kraft); Spannung; (med.) Zusammenziehung; **–or** *n.* Zugmaschine, Trecker; Schlepper

trade *n.* Handel; Handwerk, Gewerbe; Geschäft; Verkehr; **board of** — Handelsamt; — **price** Engrospreis, Grosshandelspreis; — **school** Handelsschule, Gewerbeschule; — **union** Gewerkschaft; — **winds** Passatwinde; **–r** *n.* Händler, Handelsmann; (naut.) Handelsschiff

trade-in *n.* Eintauschobjekt

trademark *n.* Schutzmarke; Fabrikzeichen

tradesman *n.* Geschäftsmann, Kleinhändler

tradespeople *n. pl.* Geschäftsleute, Kleinhändler

trade-unionism *n.* Gewerkschaftswesen

trading *n.* Handel(n)

tradition *n.* Tradition, Überlieferung; **–al** *adj.* traditionell, überliefert, herkömmlich

traffic *n.* Verkehr, Handel; **heavy** — starker Verkehr; — **lane** Autoreihe; Fahrbahn; — **light** Verkehrslicht; — **sign** Verkehrszeichen; — *v.* handeln; (coll.) verschachern

tragedy *n.* Tragödie, Trauerspiel

tragic *adj.* tragisch

trail *n.* Spur, Fährte; Schwanz, Schweif; Schleppe; — *v.* verfolgen, nachspüren; (nach) schleppen, (nach)schleifen; sich hinziehen, nachfolgen; **–er** *n.* (bot.) Kriechpflanze, Ranke; (car) Wohnwagen; Anhänger; (film) Vorschau, Beiprogramm; (mech.) Hemmstange; (coll.) Spürnase; **–ing** *adj.* nachschleppend, verfolgend, nachfolgend; **–ing arbutus** (bot.) kriechender Grindstrauch

train *n.* Zug; (dress) Schleppe; (mech.) Kette, Räderwerk; (mil.) Train; Lafettenschwanz; (fig.) Reihe, Folge; Gefolge; — **conductor** Zugführer; — **oil** Tran; — *v.* ziehen; (nach)schleppen; schulen, erziehen, ausbilden, trainieren; dressieren; (mil.) exerzieren, drillen; (mus.) harmonieren; **–er** *n.* Trainer, Ausbilder; Erzieher; Dompteur; **–ing** *n.* Training, Übung, Ausbildung; Erziehung; Dressur; (bot.) Spalierzucht; (mil.) Exerzieren, Drillen

trainload n. Zugladung

trainman n. Mitglied des Zugpersonals

trait n. Strich, Zug; Umriss

traitor n. Verräter; **–ous** adj. verräterisch, treulos

trajectory n. Flugbahn, Fallkurve; Geschossbahn

tramp n. Landstreicher, Vagabund; Getrampel; (fig.) Wanderung; — **steamer** unfahrplanmässiger Frachter; — v. wandern, vagabondieren; trampeln; **–le** n. Getrampel; **–le** v. trampeln

trance n. Trance, Traumzustand; Verzückung

tranquil adj. ruhig, gelassen; **–lity** n. Ruhe

tranquilizer n. medizinisches Beruhigungsmittel

transact v. verrichten, durchführen, abwickeln; (ab)machen; **–ion** n. Transaktion, Geschäft

transatlantic adj. transatlantisch; Ozean-

transcontinental adj. transkontinental

transcribe v. abschreiben, kopieren; (rad.) Schallplatten (or Tonbandaufnahmen) senden

transcript n. Abschrift, Umschrift; Übertragung; **–ion** n. Abschreiben; Umsetzen; (rad.) Bandaufnahme, Schallplattenwiedergabe; Umschnitt

transept n. Querschiff

transfer n. Übertragung, Transfer; Verlegung, Versetzung; Abzug, Umdruck; (mil.) Transferierung; (rail.) Umsteiger; — v. übertragen, versetzen; verlegen; umdrucken; transferieren; (rail.) umsteigen; **–able** adj. übertragbar; **–ence** n. Übertragung, Versetzung

transfiguration n. Umgestaltung; (rel.) Verklärung

transfigure v. umgestalten, umbilden; (rel.) verklären

transfix v. durchstechen, durchbohren

transform n. umwandeln, umformen; sich umbilden; **–ation** n. Verwandlung, Umformung; Umgestaltung; **–er** n. Transformator, Umformer

transgress v. überschreiten, übertreten; sich vergehen; **–ion** n. Überschreitung, Übertretung; Vergehen; **–or** n. Übertreter, Schuldige, Missetäter; Sünder

transient n. Durchreisende; — adj. vorübergehend, vergänglich, flüchtig

transistor n. Transistor; Verstärker (Elektronensystem) ·

transit n. Transport; Durchgang, Durchfuhr; Transit; Verkehrsstrasse; — v. passieren; **–ion** n. Übergang; **–ional** adj.

Übergangs-; **–ive** adj. transitiv; **–ory** adj. vergänglich, flüchtig

translate v. übersetzen, übertragen; auslegen, umsetzen, versetzen

translation n. Übersetzung

translator n. Übersetzer

transmission n. Übertragung, Übermittlung; Vererbung, Fortpflanzung; (mech.) Transmission; (rad.) Sendung

transmit v. übermitteln übertragen; senden; **–ter** n. Sender; Übermittler

transmute v. verwandeln; umgestalten

transoceanic adj. überseeisch, Ozean-

transom n. Querholz; Oberfenster

transparency n. Durchsichtigkeit; Transparent

transparent adj. transparent, durchsichtig

transpiration n. Ausdünstung, Schweiss; Transpirieren

transpire v. ausdunsten, transpirieren, ausschwitzen; (fig.) ruchbar werden, geschehen

transplant v. verpflanzen

transport n. Transport, Beförderung; Spedition; (naut.) Transportschiff; — v. transportieren, befördern; **–ation** n. Transport, Beförderung, Versendung

transpose v. transponieren, versetzen; (gram.) umstellen

transposition n. Transponierung, Umstellung

transship v. umladen

transubstantiate v. stofflich umwandeln

trap n. Falle, Fussangel; Klappe; pl. Siebensachen; — **door** Falltür; (theat.) Versenkung; — v. Fallen stellen, in einer Falle fangen; (fig.) ertappen; **–per** n. Trapper, Fallensteller; **–pings** n. pl. Schmuck, Staat, Putz

trapeze n. Trapez

trash n. Abfall, Plunder; (coll.) Unsinn, Blech; **–y** adj. wertlos, unnütz; kitschig

travail n. mühevolle Arbeit; (med.) Wehen; — v. sich abarbeiten; (med.) in den Wehen liegen

travel n. Reise; (mech.) Bewegung, Lauf, Hub; — v. reisen; durchwandern; **–er** n. Reisende; (mech.) Laufvorrichtung; **–ing** adj. reisend, fahrend, wandernd; (mech.) Lauf-; **–ing companion** Reisegefährte; **–ing expenses** Reisespesen; **–ing salesman** ·Handelsreisende; **–og(ue)** n. Reisevortrag mit Illustrationen

traveler's check n. Reisescheck

traverse n. Durchquerung; Querbalken, Quergang, Querträger; — adj. kreuzweise, quer; — v. durchqueren, durchgehen; durchforschen; (fig.) durchkreuzen

trawl *n.* Schleppnetz; Grundnetz; — *v.* mit Schleppnetz fischen; **-er** *n.* Schleppnetzfischer; Schleppnetzboot

tray *n.* Servierbrett, Tablett; Schale

treacherous *adj.* verräterisch, treulos, unzuverlässig

treachery *n.* Verrat, Treulosigkeit; Untreue

tread *n.* Tritt, Schritt; Gangart; — *v.* treten, gehen, schreiten; betreten, begehen; **-le** *n.* Pedal

treason *n.* Verrat, Treubruch; **high —** Hochverrat

treasure *n.* Schatz; — *v.* (Schätze) sammeln, aufhäufen; (fig.) hochschätzen; **-r** *n.* Schatzmeister, Zahlmeister; Kassierer

treasury *n.* Schatzkammer; (pol.) Finanzministerium; — note Schatzanweisung

treat *n.* Bewirtung, Schmaus; Hochgenuss; Runde, Lage; — *v.* behandeln; bewirten, freihalten; — **a patient** einen Patienten behandeln; — **of** handeln von; **-ise** *n.* Abhandlung; **-ment** *n.* Behandlung, Verfahren; **-y** *n.* Vertrag

tree *n.* Baum; (mech.) Schaft, Stamm; (fig.) Galgen; **family —** Familienstammbaum; **— frog** Laubfrosch; **-less** *adj.* baumlos

trek *n.* Treck; — *v.* trecken, im Ochsenwagen reisen

trellis *n.* Spalier, Gitter; — *v.* vergittern, verflechten; (bot.) am Spalier ziehen

tremble *n.* Zittern; — *v.* zittern

tremendous *adj.* furchtbar, schrecklich; kolossal

tremor *n.* Zittern, Beben

trench *n.* Graben; — *v.* umgraben, Gräben ziehen

trend *n.* Neigung, Richtung, Lauf; Tendenz; — *v.* sich neigen (*or* erstrecken, richten); streben

trespass *n.* Vergehen; Übertretung, Verletzen, Eingriff; — *v.* sich vergehen; übertreten; unbefugt eindringen; über Gebühr in Anspruch nehmen; **-er** *n.* Übertreter, Rechtsverletzer; unbefugt Eindringende

tress *n.* Locke, Haarflechte, Haarsträhne

Treves *n.* Trier

triad *n.* Dreiheit, Dreizahl; (mus.) Dreiklang

trial *n.* Versuch, Probe, Prüfung; Experiment; (law) Untersuchung, Verhör, Verhandlung; (fig.) Versuchung; Heimsuchung; — **balance** Rohbilanz; — **order** Probebestellung

triangle *n.* Dreieck; (mus.) Triangel

triangular *adj.* dreieckig

tribal *adj.* den Stamm betreffend; Stammes-

tribe *n.* Stamm, Geschlecht, Sippe

tribulation *n.* Trübsal, Drangsal, Quälerei

tribunal *n.* Tribunal, Gericht(shof); Richterstuhl

tribune *n.* Tribüne; Rednerbühne

tributary *n.* Tributpflichtige; (geol.) Nebenfluss; — *adj.* tributpflichtig; steuerbar; untergeordnet; (geol.) zufliessend; (fig.) helfend

tribute *n.* Tribut, Zins, Abgabe; Beitrag; (fig.) Bezeugung

trick *n.* Trick, Kniff, Kunstgriff, Streich; (cards) Stich; — *v.* überlisten, betrügen, hereinlegen, zum besten haben; verleiten; (cards) stechen; **-ery** *n.* Betrügerei, Gaunerei; **-iness** *n.* Mutwilligkeit; **-ster** *n.* Betrüger, Gauner; Taschenspieler; **-y** *adj.* heikel, verwickelt; (hinter)listig

trickle *n.* Tropfeln; — *v.* tröpfeln, träufeln, rieseln

tricycle *n.* Dreirad

tried *adj.* erprobt, treu, zuverlässig

triennial *adj.* dreijährig, dreijährlich

trifle *n.* Kleinigkeit, Lappalie; (cooking) Auflauf; — *v.* scherzen, spassen, tändeln

trifling *adj.* tändelnd; geringfügig, unbedeutend, wertlos

trigger *n.* Drücker, Abzug; (phot.) Auslöser

trigonometry *n.* Trigonometrie

trillion *n.* Trillion; (USA) 1,000.000.000.-000; (Europe) 1,000.000.000.000.000

trilogy *n.* Trilogie

trim *adj.* geputzt, gepflegt, ordentlich, nett; — *v.* in Ordnung (*or* ins Gleichgewicht) bringen, zurechtmachen, ausrüsten; pflegen, putzen, schmücken, garnieren; trimmen; — *n.* Ordnung, Zustand, Ausrüstung, Putz; **-ming** *n.* Putzen; Garnieren; Ausarbeitung; **-mings** *pl.* Besatz; Garnierung; Ausstaffierung

trinity *n.* Dreiheit; (ec.) Dreieinigkeit

trinket *n.* Schmuckstück; (fig.) Kram, Tand

trio *n.* Trio

trip *n.* Trippeln, Stolpern; Fehltritt, Fehler; Ausflug, Reise, Fahrt; **one way** — einfache Fahrt; **return** — Rückfahrt; **round** — Rundreise, Hin- und Rückfahrt; — *v.* trippeln, stolpern, straucheln; einen Fehler machen; einen Ausflug machen; loslassen, losmachen; **-ping** *n.* Trippeln, Hüpfen; — *adj.* trippelnd; munter, flink

triphase current *n.* Drehstrom

triple *adj.* dreifach, dreimaltig; — *v.* (sich) verdreifachen; **-t** *n.* drei Dinge (*or* Personen) derselben Art; (mus.) Triole, Trio; **-ts** *pl.* Drillinge

triplicate *adj.* dreifach; — *v.* dreifach ausfertigen

tripod *n.* Dreifuss; Stativ

trisyllable *n.* dreisilbiges Wort

trite *adj.* abgenutzt, abgedroschen; alltäglich

triumph *n.* Triumph; — *v.* triumphieren, frohlocken; **-ant** *adj.* triumphierend

trivial *adj.* trivial, alltäglich, gewöhnlich; **-ity** *n.* Trivialität, Plattheit

troll *v.* rollen, (sich) drehen; vor sich hin trällern

trolley *n.* Rollwagen, Draisine; — **bus** Oberleitungsbus; — **car** Oberleitungswagen

trombone *n.* Posaune

troop *n.* Trupp(e), Schar, Haufen; — *v.* sich sammeln (*or* scharen); haufenweise ziehen; **-er** *n.* Kavallerist; (theat.) Schauspieler

troopship *n.* Truppentransporter

trophy *n.* Trophäe, Siegeszeichen

tropic *n.* Wendekreis; *pl.* Tropen; — *adj.* Wendekreis-; **-(al)** *adj.* tropisch

trot *n.* Trott, Trab; — *v.* trotten, traben; **-ter** *n.* Traber; (coll.) Fuss, Treter; **-ting** *adj.* trottend, trabend

trouble *n.* Unruhe, Störung; Verdruss, Belästigung, Beschwerde, Plage; Unannehmlichkeit; **be in** — in Verlegenheit (*or* Sorge) sein; — **shooter** Störungssucher; — *v.* beunruhigen, stören; verdriessen, belästigen; Kummer verursachen, quälen, ängstigen; **-ed** *adj.* gestört, betrübt, beunruhigt; **-some** *adj.* lästig, beschwerlich, störend

troublemaker *n.* Störenfriend

trough *n.* Trog, Mulde, Wanne; Kanal, Strombett; — **of a wave** Wellental

troupe *n.* (theat.) Truppe

trousers *n. pl.* Hosen, Beinkleider

trousseau *n.* Brautausstattung

trout *n.* Forelle

trowel *n.* Maurerkelle, Hohlspatel

troy (weight) *n.* Goldgewicht

Troy *n.* Troja

truant *n.* Müssiggänger, Faulenzer; (educ.) Schwänzer; — *adj.* träge, müssig, bummelnd; (educ.) schwänzend

truce *n.* Waffenstillstand, Ruhe

truck *n.* Lastwagen, Güterwagen; Tausch(handel); (sl.) Plunder; **small** — Handwagen; — **farm** Gemüsefarm; — **frame** Lokomotivrahmen, Waggonrahmen; — *v.* in Lastwagen (*or* Güterwagen versenden; tauschen, handeln; **-age** *n.*

Lastwagenbeförderung; Güterwagenverkehr; Fuhrlohn

truckman *n.* Tauschhändler; Lastwagenfahrer

trudge *n.* Fusswanderung; — *v.* wandern, gehen; sich fortschleppen

true *adj.* wahr, echt, wirklich; treu; genau, (regel)recht; **come** — sich bewahrheiten; — **bill** (law) Anklagebestätigung; — *v.* in die richtige Form (*or* **Lage**) bringen, berichtigen

truehearted *adj.* treuherzig

truelove *n.* Herzliebste

truism *n.* Binsenwahrheit, Binsenweisheit

truly *adv.* aufrichtig, wahrhaftig, wirklich

trump *n.* Trumpf; (mus.) Trompete; (fig.) Prachtmensch; — *v.* auftrumpfen; übertrumpfen; — **up** erdichten; überstechen; **-et** *n.* Trompete; (mil.) Signalhorn; (coll.) Ausposauner; **-et** *v.* trompeten, die Trompete blasen; (coll.) ausposaunen; **-eter** *n.* Trompeter; (mil.) Hornist; (orn.) Trompetertaube

truncate *v.* stutzen, verstümmeln; (math.) abstumpfen; — *adj.* gestutzt, verstümmelt; stumpf

trunk *n.* Stamm, Stumpf; (anat.) Rumpf; (arch.) Säulenschaft; (zool.) Rüssel; (coll.) Schrankkoffer; — *adj.* Stamm-, Rüssel-; — **line** (rail.) Hauptlinie; (tel.) Fernleitung

trunnion *n.* Drehzapfen

truss *n.* Bund, Bündel; (arch.) Kragstein, Stütze; (bot.) Büschel; (med.) Bruchband; — *adj.* untersetzt, stämmig; — *v.* schnüren, bündeln; stützen

trust *n.* Trust, Unternehmerverband; Vertrauen, Glauben; Verwahrung, Pflegschaft, Pfand; **in** — in treuen Händen; **on** — auf Kredit; — *v.* (ver)trauen, anvertrauen; glauben; **-ee** *n.* Sachverwalter, Treuhänder, Kurator; **-eeship** *n.* Treuhandverwaltung, Kuratorium; **-ful** *adj.* vertrauend, zutraulich; **-iness** *n.* Zuverlässigkeit, Glaubwürdigkeit; Redlichkeit; **-ing** *adj.* vertrauensvoll, vertrauensselig; **-y** *adj.* treu, redlich; sicher, beharrlich

trustworthy *adj.* vertrauenswürdig, zuverlässig, glaubwürdig

truth *n.* Wahrheit, Wahrhaftigkeit; Wirklichkeit, Genauigkeit; **-ful** *adj.* wahrhaft(ig); **-fulness** *n.* Wahrhaftigkeit

try *n.* Versuch, Probe; — *v.* versuchen, probieren; prüfen; anprobieren; sich bemühen; **-ing** *adj.* prüfend; (fig.) kritisch, peinlich

try-on *n.* Anprobe; (sl.) Versuch

tryout *n.* Ausprobieren; Ausscheidungsspiel

tub *n.* Bad(ewanne), Kübel, Zuber; — *v.* ein Wannenbad nehmen, baden; (bot.) in Kübel pflanzen; (sl.) im Rudern unterrichten; **-bing** *n.* Wannematerial, Wannenfabrikation; Rudertraining

tuba *n.* Tuba, Bombardon

tube *n.* Tube; Rohr, Röhre; Pfeife; (med.) Kanüle; (rail.) Tunnel; **amplifying** — Verstärkerröhre; **electronic** — Elektronenröhre; **inner** — Luftschlauch; **test** — Probierröhre, Reagensglas; **vacuum** — Vakuumröhre; — *v.* in Tuben (*or* Röhren) füllen

tuber *n.* Knoten, Schwellung; (bot.) Knolle; (sl.) Kartoffel

tubercle *n.* Tuberkel, Knötchen; Warze, Höcker

tuberculosis *n.* Tuberkulose

tubing *n.* Röhrenmaterial; Röhrenanlage

tubular *adj.* röhrenförmig; Röhren-

tuck *n.* Falte, Einschlag, Umschlag; (sl.) Näscherei; — *v.* falten, einschlagen, umschlagen; umkrempeln; einwickeln

Tuesday *n.* Dienstag

tuft *n.* Büschel; Quaste, Franse; (orn.) Haube, Schopf; — *v.* mit Büscheln (*or* Quasten, etc.) schmücken; **-ed** *adj.* buschig, buschreich; mit Büscheln (*or* Quasten) geschmückt; Hauben-

tug *n.* Ruck; Mühe, Anstrengung; — **of war** Tauziehen; — *v.* ziehen, zerren, zausen, zupfen; schleppen; (sich) abmühen

tugboat *n.* Schlepper, Schleppdampfer

tuition *n.* Unterricht, Anleitung, Belehrung

tulip *n.* Tulpe

tulle *n.* Tüll

tumble *n.* Sturz, Fall; (fig.) Wirrwarr; — *v.* stürzen, fallen, purzeln; taumeln, umstürzen, umwerfen; durchwühlen, stopfen, zerknüllen; **-r** *n.* Gaukler; Wassergla ; (mech.) Gewehrverschluss; (orn.) Tümmler; (toy) Stehaufmännchen

tumble-down *adj.* hinfällig, verfallen

tummy *n.* (coll.) Bauch

tumor *n.* Tumor

tumult *n.* Tumult, Lärm, Aufruhr; **-uous** *adj.* lärmend, stürmisch, ungestüm

tuna *n.* (bot.) Fackeldistel, indianische Feige; (ichth.) Thunfisch

tune *n.* Melodie, Lied; Tonstück; Stimmung; — *v.* (ab)stimmen; tönen, klingen; anstimmen; — **in** (rad.) einstellen; **-ful** *adj.* wohlklingend, lieblich; melodisch; **-r** *n.* Stimmer; (rad.) Abstimmskala

tungsten *n.* Wolfram

tuning *n.* Stimmen; — *adj.* — **dial**

Stationsskala; — **fork** Stimmgabel

tunnel *n.* Tunnel; Stollen; — *v.* durchbohren, einen Tunnel anlegen

turban *n.* Turban

turbid *adj.* trübe, wolkig, schmutzig; (fig.) verworren

turbine *n.* Turbine; **blast** — Gebläseturbine

turbojet *n.* Turbinen-Luftstrahlmotor

turboprop *n.* Propeller-Turbinenmotor

turbulent *adj.* turbulent, stürmisch

tureen *n.* Terrine

turf *n.* Turf, Rennbahn, Rennsport; Rasen(narbe); Torf; — *v.* mit Rasen belegen; Torf stechen

turkey *n.* Truthahn; — **buzzard** amerikanischer Geier

Turkey *n.* die Türkei

Turkish *n.* Türkisch; — *adj.* türkisch; — **bath** Dampfbad; — **towel** Frottiertuch

turmoil *n.* Aufruhr, Unruhe; Getümmel

turn *n.* Umdrehung; Krümmung, Kurve, Richtung, Wendung; Neigung, Hang, Veränderung; Art, Gestalt; Reihenfolge; Dienst(leistung); Wechsel, (com.) Turnus, Geschäftsgang; (min.) Schicht; (mus.) Doppelschlag; (coll.) Schock, Schreck; **a good** — eine gute Wendung; **by** **-s** der Reihe nach, abwechselnd; **it is his** — er ist an der Reihe; **sharp** — scharfe Biegung; — *v.* (um)drehen, (um)wenden, umkehren; lenken, richten; neigen; formen, verändern, gestalten; abwechseln; an der Reihe sein; trudeln; drechseln; — **against** aufbringen gegen; sich wenden gegen; — **away** abwenden, abweisen, wegjagen; — **back** zurückdrehen; umwenden, umkehren: (sich) abwenden; — **down** herunterschrauben, kleinstellen; ablehnen; — **off** ableiten, abwenden, ablenken, ausdrehen, abschalten; — **on** anleiten; anstellen, aufdrehen; sich wenden (*or* richten) auf; — **out** wegjagen; (sich) nach aussen wenden; ausfallen, sich herausstellen; — **over** umwenden, umschlagen; überdenken; übertragen, übergeben; umsetzen; übergehen; purzeln; — **pale** erbleichen, erblassen; — **the corner** um die Ecke biegen; — **to** (sich) wenden an; lenken (*or* richten) auf; umwandeln in; sich verwandeln in; hinauslaufen auf; **-ing** *n.* Umwenden; Drehung, Biegung, Krümmung, Ecke; Abweichung; **-ing** *adj.* drehend, drehbar; **-ing point** Wendepunkt, Entscheidung

turnbridge *n.* Drehbrücke

turndown *n.* Umlegekragen; Zurückweisung; — *adj.* umgelegt turnip n. weisse Rübe, Steckrübe

turnout n. Versammlung; Ausstaffierung, Aufputz; (com.) Gesamtproduktion; Aussperrung; (mil.) Ausrücken; (rail.) Ausweichstelle

turnover n. Umwerfen; Umschlag; (com.) Umsatz; — adj. umgeschlagen

turnpike n. Schlagbaum; Strasse, deren Benutzung bezahlt werden muss

turnstile n. Drehkreuz

turntable n. Drehscheibe; Plattenteller

turnup adj. umklappbar

turpentine n. Terpentin

turquoise n. Türkis

turret n. Türmchen; (mil.) Panzerturm; (rail.) Ventilationsaufsatz

turtle n. Schildkröte

turtledove n. Turteltaube

tusk n. Fangzahn, Stosszahn, Eckzahn

tussle n. Rauferei, Zank; — v. raufen, sich balgen; zanken

tutelage n. Vormundschaft; (educ.) Unterricht

tutor n. Hauslehrer, Privatlehrer; Vormund; — v. unterrichten, belehren; nachhelfen; zurechtweisen

tuxedo n. Smoking; — coat Gesellschaftsanzug

twaddle n. Geschwätz, Geplapper; — v. schwatzen, plappern

twang n. Singsang; Schwirren; — v. schwirren; (mus.) klimpern

tweak n. Zwicken, Kniff; — v. zwicken, kneifen

tweed n. Tweed

tweezers n. pl. Pinzette

twelfth n. Zwölfte; Zwölftel; — adj. zwölft

Twelfth-night n. Dreikönigsabend

twelve n. Zwölf; — adj. zwölf

twelvemonth n. Jahr; this day — heute in einem Jahr

twentieth n. Zwanzigste; Zwanzigstel; — adj. zwanzigst

twenty n. Zwanzig(er); — odd zwanzig und darüber; — adj. zwanzig; -fold adj. zwanzigfach

twice adv. zweimal, zweifach, doppelt

twice-told adj. nacherzählt; abgedroschen

twiddle n. Drehen; — v. drehen; tändeln; vibrieren

twig n. Zweig, Rute; Wünschelrute; — v. (coll.) beachten, bemerken, verstehen

twilight n. Zwielicht, Dämmerung; — adj. dämmern, dämmerig; Dämmerungs-

twill n. Köper; — v. köpern

twin n. Zwilling; — adj. doppelt, Zwillings-; — screw Doppelschraube; — v. paaren; Zwillinge gebären

twine n. Zwirn, Schnur, Bindfaden, Garn; Windung, Geflecht, Gewirr; (bot.) Ranke; — v. zwirnen, zusammendrehen; schnüren, weben, schlingen; (sich) winden; verflechten; (bot.) ranken

twin-engined adj. zweimotorig

twinkle n. Flimmern, Funkeln, Glitzern; Blinzeln, Zwinkern; — v. flimmern, funkeln, glitzern; blinzeln, zwinkern

twinkling n. Augenblick; in the — of an eye im Nu

twirl n. Wirbel; (dance) Pirouette; — v. wirbeln

twist n. Drehung, Windung; Verdrehung, Verrenkung; (mech.) Geflecht, Maschinengarn, Twist; (mil.) Drall; (fig.) Verwicklung; — v. drehen, winden; verdrehen, verrenken; wickeln, spinnen, (ver)flechten; -ed adj. gewunden

twitch n. Zupfen, Ruck; Zwicken, Kneifen; (med.) Zuckung; — v. zupfen, zerren, kneifen, zwicken; (med.) zucken

twitter n. Gezwitscher, Gezirpe; (fig.) Aufregung; — v. zwitschern, zirpen; (fig.) zittern

two n. Zwei(er); Paar; — adj. zwei; -fold adj. zweifach, doppelt

two-by-four n. Brett (zwei zu vier Zoll)

two-cycle adj. Zweitakt; — n. Zweitakt

two-faced adj. doppelzüngig, falsch

two-fisted adj. (coll.) kräftig, handfest

two-handed adj. zweihändig; für zwei Personen

two-piece adj. zweiteilig

two-seater n. Zweisitzer

two-step n. Twostep, Zweierschritt

tycoon n. Industriemagnat

type n. Typ(us), Urbild, Vorbild, Muster; Art, Gestalt, Charakter, Persönlichkeit; Merkmal; (typ.) Type, Druckbuchstabe; — bar Schreibmaschinentaste; — founder Schriftgiesser; — v. Schreibmaschine schreiben, tippen

typesetter n. Schriftsetzer; Setzmaschine

typesetting n. Schriftsetzen

typewrite v. Schreibmaschine schreiben, tippen; -r n. Schreibmaschine; portable -r Reiseschreibmaschine; -r ribbon Farbband

typhoid adj. typhös; — fever Unterleibstyphus

typhoon n. Taifun

typhus n. Flecktyphus

typic(al) adj. typisch, charakteristisch

typify v. typisieren, (vor)bildlich darstellen

typing n. Maschineschreiben, Tippen

typist n. Maschineschreiber(in)

typographer n. Buchdrucker

typography n. Buchdruckerkunst, Typographie

tyrannic(al), tyrannous *adj.* tyrannisch, grausam, ungerecht, streng
tyrannize *v.* als Tyrann herrschen; — **over** tyrannisieren
tyrant *n.* Tyrann
Tyrol *n.* Tirol

U

ubiquitous *adj.* allgegenwärtig
udder *n.* Euter
ugliness *n.* Hässlichkeit, Widerwärtigkeit
ugly *adj.* hässlich, widerwärtig; ekelhaft
ukase *n.* Ukas; Edikt, Befehl
ukulele *n.* Ukulele; Hawaiguitarre
ulcer *n.* Geschwür; **-ate** *v.* schwären
ulster *n.* Ulster
ulterior *adj.* jenseitig; weiter, anderweitig
ultimate *n.* Endgültige, Grundsätzliche; — *adj.* endlich, (aller)letzt; **-ly** *adv.* zu guter Letzt
ultimatum *n.* Ultimatum
ultimo *n.* Ultimo; — *adj.* im letzten (*or* vorigen) Monat
ultrahigh frequency *n.* Ultra-Hochfrequenz
ultramodern *adj.* übermodern
ultrasonic *adj.* in Überschallgeschwindigkeit
ultraviolet *adj.* ultraviolett, infrarot
umber *n.* Umbra, Umbererde; (art.) Bergbraun; — *adj.* dunkelbraun
umbilical cord *n.* Nabelschnur
umbra *n.* Kernschatten, Schlagschatten; **-ge** *n.* Schatten, Anstoss, Verdacht; **take -ge** Anstoss nehmen, übelnehmen
umbrella *n.* Schirm; (pol.) Kompromiss; — **stand** Schirmständer
umlaut *n.* Umlaut
umpire *n.* Schiedsrichter, Unparteiische; — *v.* Schiedsrichter (*or* Unparteiischer) sein
unabashed *adj.* unverschämt, unverfroren
unabated *adj.* unvermindert; **-ly** *adv.* unablässig
unable *adj.* unfähig; **be — ausserstande** sein
unabridged *adj.* unverkürzt
unaccented *adj.* unbetont
unacceptable *adj.* unannehmbar
unaccomodating *adj.* unnachgiebig, ungefällig
unaccountable *adj.* unverantwortlich; unerklärlich, sonderbar
unaccustomed *adj.* ungewohnt; ungewöhnlich
unacquainted *adj.* unbekannt, unkundig, unerfahren
unadulterated *adj.* unverfälscht, rein
unadvised *adj.* unbedacht, unbesonnen

unaffected *adj.* unberührt, ungerührt; unbefangen, ungekünstelt; natürlich, einfach
unaided *adj.* ohne Unterstützung; unbewaffnet, bloss
unaltered *adj.* unverändert
unanimity *n.* Einstimmigkeit, Einmütigkeit
unanimous *adj.* einstimmig, einmütig
unapproachable *adj.* unzugänglich; unvergleichlich
unapt *adj.* untauglich, ungeeignet
unarmed *adj.* unbewaffnet; wehrlos
unassailable *adj.* unangreifbar; unerschütterlich
unassisted *adj.* ohne Beistand (*or* Unterstützung)
unassuming *adj.* anspruchslos, bescheiden
unattached *adj.* ungebunden, lose; (educ.) extern; (law) herrenlos; (mil.) zur Verfügung
unattainable *adj.* unerreichbar
unattended *adj.* unbegleitet; ungepflegt, vernachlässigt, verwahrlost
unattractive *adj.* nicht anziehend, reizlos
unavailing *adj.* nutzlos, vergeblich
unavoidable *adj.* unvermeidlich, unumgänglich; (law) unumstösslich
unawares *adv.* unvermutet, plötzlich, unversehens
unbalanced *adj.* unausgeglichen; aus dem Gleichgewicht gebracht
unbearable *adj.* unerträglich
unbecoming *adj.* unpassend; unkleidsam
unbelief *n.* Unglaube; Misstrauen
unbeliever *n.* Ungläubige
unbeloved *adj.* ungeliebt
unbend *v.* (sich) entspannen; nachlassen; **-ing** *adj.* unbiegsam; unbeugsam
unbiased *adj.* unbefangen, vorurteilsfrei; unparteiisch
unbid(den) *adj.* ungeheissen, ungeladen, ungebeten; (cards) nicht angesagt
unbind *v.* abbinden; entbinden, befreien
unblemished *adj.* unbefleckt, makellos; rein
unbolt *v.* aufriegeln; **-ed** *adj.* unverriegelt, offen; (fig.) rauh, grob
unborn *n.* ungeboren; zukünftig
unbosom *v.* sich offenbaren
unbound *adj.* ungebunden; (book) geheftet; **-ed** *adj.* unbegrenzt, schrankenlos, zügellos
unbreakable *adj.* unzerbrechlich
unbroken *adj.* ungebrochen, ungebändigt; ununterbrochen
unbuckle *v.* losschnallen, abschnallen
unburden *v.* entladen; entlasten; erleichtern
unbutton *v.* aufknöpfen

uncalled-for *adj.* ungerufen, unaufgefordert; nicht verlangt (*or* gerechtfertigt)

uncanny *adj.* unheimlich, nicht geheuer; (fig.) ungeschickt

unceasing *adj.* unaufhörlich

uncertain *adj.* ungewiss, unsicher; unbestimmt; unbeständig, unzuverlässig; unentschlossen; **-ty** *n.* Ungewissheit; Unzuverlässigkeit

unchangeable *adj.* unveränderlich

unclaimed *adj.* nicht beansprucht (*or* gefordert); — **letters** unbestellbare Briefe

uncle *n.* Onkel

unclean *adj.* unrein, unsauber; unkeusch

unclouded *adj.* unbewölkt, wolkenlos; heiter

uncomfortable *adj.* unbequem, unbehaglich, ungemütlich; unerfreulich

uncommon *adj.* ungewöhnlich, ungemein; selten

uncommunicative *adj.* verschlossen

uncompromising *adj.* unnachgiebig; (fig.) unleugbar

unconcern *n.* Gleichgültigkeit; **-ed** *adj.* gleichgültig sorglos; unbekümmert, unbeteiligt, unbetroffen

unconditional *adj.* unbedingt, bedingungslos

unconfined *adj.* ungehindert, unbegrenzt

unconscientious *adj.* gewissenlos

unconscious *adj.* unbewusst, unwissend; (med.) bewusstlos

unconstitutional *adj.* verfassungswidrig

uncontested *adj.* unbestritten

uncontrollable *adj.* unkontrollierbar; unumschränkt, zügellos

unconventional *adj.* unkonventionell; formlos, zwanglos; natürlich

uncork *v.* entkorken

uncorrupt *adj.* unverdorben; unbestochen

uncouple *v.* loskoppeln; (aus)lösen

uncouth *adj.* ungeschlacht, roh, linkisch; wunderlich, seltsam

uncover *v.* enthüllen, aufdecken; entblössen

unction *n.* Salbe, Einreibung; **extreme —** letzte Ölung

uncultured *adj.* unkultiviert, ungebildet

uncut *adj.* un(auf)geschnitten, unbehauen

undamaged *adj.* unbeschädigt

undated *adj.* nicht datiert; ohne Datum

undecided *adj.* unentschieden; unschlüssig

undefined *adj.* unbegrenzt; unbestimmt

undeniable *adj.* unleugbar, unbestreitbar

under *prep.* unter(halb), weniger; — *adv.* unten; darunter; — *adj.* niedrig, untergeordnet; Unter-

underage *adj.* unmündig, minderjährig

underbid *v.* unterbieten

underbrush *n.* Unterholz, Gesträuch

undercarriage *n.* Fahrgestell

undercharge *v.* nicht genügend berechnen (*or* beladen)

underclothes *n. pl.,* **underclothing** *n.* Unterkleidung, Leibwäsche

undercurrent *n.* Unterströmung, Gegenströmung

undercut *n.* Unterhöhlung; (meat) Filet; — *v.* unterhöhlen; unterbieten

underdog *n.* Benachteiligte; Unterliegende

underdone *adj.* nicht gar, halb roh

underestimate *v.* unterschätzen

underexposure *n.* (phot.) Unterbelichtung

underfed *adj.* unterernährt

underfoot *adv.* unter den Füssen; von unten

undergo *v.* erdulden, ertragen; sich unterziehen

undergraduate *n.* Student (ohne Universitätsgrad)

underground *n.* Untergrund; — *adj.* unterirdisch; Untergrund-

underhand(ed) *adj.* unter der Hand; heimlich, versteckt; hinterlistig, unehrlich

underline *v.* unterstreichen

underling *n.* Untergebene; Kriecher

underlying *adj.* zugrundeliegend; Grund-

undermine *v.* unterminieren, untergraben

underneath *prep.* unter; — *adv.* unten; unterwärts, unterhalb, darunter

undernourished *adj.* unterernährt

underpass *n.* Unterführung

underpay *v.* ungenügend (*or* schlecht) bezahlen

underpin *v.* unterlegen, unterbauen, stützen

underrate *v.* unterschätzen; herabsetzen; zu niedrig ansetzen

underscore *v.* unterstreichen

undersell *v.* verschleudern, unter dem Wert verkaufen

undershirt *n.* Unterhemd

underside *n.* Unterseite

undersigned *n.* Unterzeichnete; — *adj.* unterzeichnet

understand *v.* verstehen, begreifen; vernehmen; annehmen; sich verstehen auf; **that is understood** das ist selbstverständlich; **-ing** *n.* Verstand, Verständigung; Einvernehmen, Einverständnis; Voraussetzung; **-ing** *adj.* verständig, einsichtsvoll

understatement *n.* Unterschätzung; **zu geringe Angabe**

understudy *n.* (theat.) zweite Besetzung; Ersatzschauspieler; — *v.* einstudieren (*or* einspringen) für
undertake *v.* unternehmen, übernehmen; **–r** *n.* Leichenbestatter; Unternehmer
undertaking *n.* Leichenbestattung; Unternehmen, Unterfangen; Unternehmung
undertone *n.* Unterton; Flüsterton
undervalue *v.* unterschätzen; geringschätzen
underwater *adj.* Unterwasser-
underwear *n.* Unterzeug, Leibwäsche
underweight *n.* Untergewicht
underwood *n.* Unterholz, Gestrüpp
underworld *n.* Unterwelt
underwrite *v.* unterschreiben; versichern; **–r** *n.* Versicherer
undeserved *adj.* unverdient
undeserving *adj.* unwürdig
undesirable *adj.* unerwünscht
undeveloped *adj.* unentwickelt; — **country** unterentwickeltes (*or* unerschlossenes) Land
undiluted *adj.* unverdünnt, unverfälscht
undiminished *adj.* unvermindert
undismayed *adj.* unverzagt, unerschrocken
undisputed *adj.* unbestritten
undisturbed *adj.* ungestört; unerschüttert
undivided *adj.* ungeteilt; nicht verteilt
undo *v.* aufmachen, aufbinden, aufdecken, auftrennen, aufknöpfen; ungeschehen machen, aufheben; **–ing** *n.* Aufmachen; (fig.) Verderben
undoubted *adj.* unbestritten; zweifellos
undress *n.* Hauskleid, Negligé, Morgenrock; (mil.) Halbuniform; — *v.* (sich) entkleiden, ausziehen, ablegen
undue *adj.* ungebührlich; unangemessen, unverhältnismässig; (com.) noch nicht fällig
undulant fever *n.* Mittelmeerfieber, subtropisches Wechselfieber
undulate *v.* sich wellenförmig bewegen; wogen, wallen; — *adj.* wellenförmig, gewellt
unduly *adv.* unziemlich, ungehörig; übertrieben
undying *adj.* unsterblich, unvergänglich
unearth *v.* ausgraben, aufstöbern; ans Licht bringen
unearthly *adj.* unheimlich; überirdisch
uneasiness *n.* Unruhe, Unbehagen; Unbequemlichkeit
uneasy *adj.* unruhig, unbehaglich; unbequem
uneducated *adj.* unerzogen, ungebildet
unemotional *adj.* leidenschaftslos, passiv
unemployed *adj.* arbeitslos, erwerbslos; unbeschäftigt; — **capital totes** (*or*

brachliegendes) Kapital
unemployment *n.* Arbeitslosigkeit, Erwerbslosigkeit
unending *adj.* endlos, unendlich
unequal *adj.* ungleich(mässig), unverhältnismässig; **–ed** *adj.* unvergleichlich, unübertroffen, unerreicht
unerring *adj.* unfehlbar, untrüglich
unessential *adj.* unwesentlich
uneven *adj.* uneben, ungleich; **ungerade**
unexampled *adj.* beispiellos
unexceptionable *adj.* untad(e)lig, vortrefflich
unexpected *adj.* unerwartet, unvermutet; unvorhergesehen
unexplored *adj.* unerforscht
unfading *adj.* unverwelkbar; (color) echt
unfailing *adj.* unfehlbar, untrüglich; unerschöpflich
unfair *adj.* unfair; unehrlich, unbillig
unfaithful *adj.* ungetreu, treulos; wortbrüchig; nicht wortgetreu
unfaltering *adj.* nicht schwankend; unerschrocken
unfamiliar *adj.* unbekannt, ungewohnt, ungewöhnlich
unfavorable *adj.* ungünstig, unvorteilhaft
unfeigned *adj.* unverhohlen
unfinished *adj.* unvollendet
unfit *adj.* untauglich, ungeeignet, **unfähig;** — *v.* untüchtig (*or* untauglich) machen
unfold *v.* (sich) entfalten; ausbreiten, aufschlagen; enthüllen
unforeseen *adj.* unvorhergesehen
unforgettable *adj.* unvergesslich
unforgiving *adj.* unversöhnlich
unfortunate *adj.* unglücklich, unglückselig
unfounded *adj.* unbegründet, grundlos
unfrequented *adj.* unbesucht; einsam, verlassen
unfurl *v.* entfalten, aufspannen, ausspannen; (naut.) losmachen
unfurnished *adj.* nicht ausgerüstet; unmöbliert
ungainly *adj.* ungeschickt, linkisch, **plump**
ungodly *adj.* gottlos; verrucht
ungrateful *adj.* undankbar
ungratified *adj.* unbefriedigt
ungrounded *adj.* unbegründet, **grundlos**
unhandy *adj.* ungeschickt, unbequem
unhappy *adj.* unglücklich, un(glück)selig, elend
unharmed *adj.* unbeschädigt, unverletzt, unversehrt; ungekränkt
unhealthy *adj.* ungesund, schädlich; krankhaft
unheard-of *adj.* ungehört, unerhört; unbekannt
unheeded *adj.* unbeachtet, unbemerkt; unerwogen

unhesitating *adj.* ohne Zögern
unhinge *v.* aus den Angeln heben; zer- rütten
unhook *v.* aufhaken, aushaken
unhurt *adj.* unbeschädigt, unverletzt, un- versehrt
unification *n.* Vereinheitlichung, Ver- einigung
uniform *n.* Uniform; — *adj.* einförmig, einheitlich; Einheits-; — *v.* uniformie- ren; –ity *n.* Gleichförmigkeit, Gleich- mässigkeit; Einheitlichkeit, Übereín- stimmung
unify *v.* verein(ig)en, vereinheitlichen
unilateral *adj.* einseitig
unimpaired *adj.* unvermindert, unge- schwächt
unimpeachable *adj.* vorurteilsfrei; un- anfechtbar
unimpeded *adj.* ungehindert
unimportant *adj.* unwichtig
uninformed *adj.* ununterrichtet
uninjured *adj.* unbeschädigt, unverletzt, unversehrt; ungekränkt; unverdorben
unintelligible *adj.* unverständlich
unintentional *adj.* unabsichtlich
uninterrupted *adj.* ununterbrochen
uninviting *adj.* wenig einladend
union *n.* Einheit, Eintracht, Übereinstim- mung; Vereinigung, Verbindung, Ver- ein; (pol.) Gewerkschaft; –ism *n.* Gewerkschaftswesen; –ist *n.* Gewerk- schaftler; –ize *v.* eine Gewerkschaft bilden; einer Gewerkschaft zuführen
unique *adj.* einzig(artig), ungewöhnlich
unison *n.* Einklang, Gleichklang; Über- einstimmung; in — unisono, einstimmig
unit *n.* Einheit; Abteilung; –ary *adj.* Ein- heits-, Einer-; –y *n.* Einheit, Einigkeit, Eintracht
unite *v.* (sich) vereinigen, verbinden; –d *adj.* vereinigt; einig; **United States** Vereinigte Staaten
Univac *n.* Elektronengehirn
universal *adj.* allgemein, allumfassend; Universal-; –ity *n.* Vielseitigkeit
universe *n.* Universum, Weltall
university *n.* Universität
unjust *adj.* ungerecht, unbillig; –ifiable *adj.* unverantwortlich; nicht zu recht- fertigen
unkempt *adj.* ungekämmt; ungepflegt, roh
unkind *adj.* unfreundlich; lieblos
unknowingly *adv.* unwissentlich, unbe- wusst
unknown *n.* Unbekannte; — *adj.* unbe- kannt; unerkannt; unbewusst, unge- wöhnlich
unlace *v.* aufschnüren, aufbinden; lösen
unlaid *adj.* ungelegt; ungestillt

unlawful *adj.* ungesetzlich; unerlaubt
unleash *v.* losbinden, loskoppeln; ent- fesseln
unless *conj.* wenn nicht; ausser, ausge- nommen; es sei denn, dass
unlettered *adj.* unbelesen, ungelehrt; un- wissend; (lit.) nicht mit Buchstaben bezeichnet
unlicensed *adj.* nicht konzessioniert; un- berechtigt
unlike *adj.* ungleich, unähnlich; — *adv.* anders als; nicht wie
unlikely *adj.* unwahrscheinlich; ungeeig- net; aussichtslos
unlimited *adj.* unbegrenzt, grenzenlos; unbeschränkt, schrankenlos
unload *v.* abladen, entladen, ausladen; erleichtern; (com.) massenhaft auf den Markt werfen; (naut.) löschen, aus- schiffen
unlock *v.* aufschliessen; (fig.) aufdecken
unloose *v.* (auf)lösen, losmachen, loslassen
unlovable *adj.* unliebenswürdig
unlovely *adj.* reizlos, abstossend
unlucky *adj.* unglücklich, unheilbringend, verhängnisvoll
unmanageable *adj.* unlenksam; unfolg- sam, widerspenstig; unhandlich
unmannerly *adj.* unmanierlich, ungezo- gen, unartig
unmarked *adj.* unbezeichnet; unbemerkt
unmarried *adj.* unverheiratet, ledig
unmask *v.* (sich) demaskieren, entlarven
unmatched *adj.* ungepaart; unvergleich- lich
unmentionable *adj.* unaussprechlich; nicht zu erwähnen, unnennbar
unmerciful *adj.* unbarmherzig
unmindful *adj.* unbedacht, ohne Rück- sicht, sorglos
unmistakable *adj.* unverkennbar
unmixed *adj.* unvermischt, unverfälscht; rein
unmodified *adj.* unverändert
unmoved *adj.* unbewegt, ungerührt
unnamed *adj.* ungenannt
unnatural *adj.* unnatürlich
unnavigable *adj.* nicht schiffbar
unnecessary *adj.* unnötig, überflüssig
unnerve *v.* entnerven, entmutigen
unnot(ic)ed *adj.* unbemerkt, unbeachtet
unnumbered *adj.* ungezählt, unzählig, zahllos; unnummeriert
unobjectionable *adj.* einwandfrei
unobserved *adj.* unbe(ob)achtet, un- bemerkt; unbefolgt
unobtainable *adj.* unerreichbar
unobtrusive *adj.* unaufdringlich, beschei- den
unoccupied *adj.* unbesetzt, unbenutzt; un-

beschäftigt
unofficial *adj.* unoffiziell, nicht amtlich
unorthodox *adj.* unorthodox; nicht (recht) gläubig
unpack *v.* auspacken; entlasten, entladen
unpaid *adj.* unbezahlt, unbelohnt; (letter) unfrankiert
unpalatable *adj.* unschmackhaft, ungeniessbar
unparalleled *adj.* beispiellos
unpleasant *adj.* unangenehm
unpolished *adj.* unpoliert; (fig.) ungebildet
unpopular *adj.* unpopulär, unbeliebt
unpractical *adj.* unpraktisch
unprecedented *adj.* beispiellos, unerhört; noch nie dagewesen
unprejudiced *adj.* unbefangen, vorurteilsfrei
unpremeditated *adj.* unüberlegt, unvorbereitet; aus dem Stegreif; (law) unvorbedacht
unpretending, unpretentious *adj.* anspruchslos, bescheiden
unprincipled *adj.* skrupellos, gewissenlos; unsittlich, gottlos
unproductive *adj.* unproduktiv, unfruchtbar, unergiebig
unprofessional *adj.* nicht berufsmässig, laienhaft
unprofitable *adj.* uneinträglich, unvorteilhaft; nutzlos, vergeblich
unprotected *adj.* ungeschützt, unbeschützt; schutzlos
unprovided *adj.* nicht vorgesehen, unvorbereitet
unpunished *adj.* ungestraft, straflos
unqualified *adj.* ungeeignet, unberechtigt; unbeschränkt
unquenchable *adj.* un(aus)löschbar; unersättlich
unquestionable *adj.* unbestreitbar, unzweifelhaft
unravel *v.* entwirren, aufräufeln; lösen
unreadable *adj.* unleserlich
unready *adj.* nicht fertig; unentschlossen
unreal *adj.* unwirklich, wesenlos
unreasonable *adj.* unvernünftig; grundlos; unmässig
unrecognizable *adj.* nicht wiederzuerkennen
unreconciled *adj.* unversöhnt
unrelenting *adj.* unerbittlich
unreliable *adj.* unzuverlässig
unremitting *adj.* unablässig, unaufhörlich
unremunerative *adj.* nicht lohnend
unrequited *adj.* unerwidert
unreserved *adj.* unnummeriert, nicht reserviert; vorbehaltlos, rückhaltlos, unbeschränkt

unresponsive *adj.* unempfänglich
unrest *n.* Unruhe, Ruhelosigkeit; –ing *adj.* rastlos, ruhelos
unrestrained *adj.* ungehemmt, uneingeschränkt; unbeherrscht
unripe *adj.* unreif, unzeitig, unfertig
unrivaled *adj.* ohne Nebenbuhler; unvergleichlich
unroll *v.* abrollen, entrollen; entfalten
unruled *adj.* unbeherrscht; (paper) unliniiert
unruly *adj.* unbändig, ungestüm; widerspenstig, störrisch; ausgelassen, stürmisch
unsafe *adj.* unsicher, gefährlich
unsanitary *adj.* unhygienisch
unsatisfactory *adj.* unbefriedigend
unsavory *adj.* unschmackhaft, geschmacklos; widerwärtig, widerlich
unscathed *adj.* unbeschädigt, unverletzt
unschooled *adj.* ungeschult
unscientific *adj.* unwissenschaftlich
unscrew *v.* abschrauben, aufschrauben, losschrauben
unscrupulous *adj.* gewissenlos, bedenkenlos
unseasonable *adj.* unzeitig; (fig.) ungelegen
unseat *v.* vom Sitz heben, aus dem Sattel werfen; (pol.) absetzen; für ungültig erklären
unseemly *adj.* unziemlich, unschicklich, unpassend
unseen *adj.* ungesehen, unbemerkt; unsichtbar
unselfish *adj.* selbstlos, uneigennützig
unsettled *adj.* ungeordnet, ungeregelt, unbestimmt; unbeständig, schwankend; unbesiedelt; — accounts unbezahlte Rechnungen, unbeglichene Konten
unshakable *adj.* unerschütterlich; standhaft
unsightly *adj.* unansehnlich; hässlich
unskilful *adj.* ungeschickt
unskilled *adj.* unerfahren, ungeschult, ungelernt
unsociable *adj.* ungesellig
unsolved *adj.* ungelöst, ungeklärt
unsophisticated *adj.* unverfälscht, ungekünstelt; natürlich, schlicht
unsound *adj.* ungesund, kränklich; angegangen, verdorben, faul; brüchig, wurmstichig
unsparing *adj.* freigebig, reichlich; schonungslos; unbarmherzig, streng, hart
unspeakable *adj.* unaussprechlich, unsagbar; unsäglich
unspoken *adj.* ungesagt, unerwähnt
unstable *adj.* unbeständig, unstet,

schwankend; labil
unsteady *adj.* unstet, unbeständig, unsolide
unstressed *adj.* unbetont
unsubdued *adj.* unbesiegt, unbezwungen
unsubstantial *adj.* unkörperlich, wesenlos; unsolide
unsuccessful *adj.* erfolglos
unsuitable *adj.* unpassend, ungeeignet, unziemlich, unstatthaft, unschicklich; untauglich, unfähig
unsullied *adj.* unbeschmutzt, unbesudelt, unbefleckt; lauter, rein
unsurpassable *adj.* unübertrefflich
unsuspected *adj.* unverdächtig
unswerving *adj.* standhaft, fest
untamed *adj.* ungezähmt, ungebändigt
untangle *v.* entwirren
untarnished *adj.* ungetrübt, glänzend
untaught *adj.* ungelehrt, unwissend
untenable *adj.* unhaltbar
unthinkable *adj.* undenkbar
unthinking *adj.* gedankenlos, sorglos, unachtsam
untidy *adj.* unordentlich
untie *v.* aufbinden, aufknoten, auflösen; aufknüpfen; (er)lösen
until *prep.* bis; — *conj.* bis (dass)
untilled *adj.* unbebaut
untimely *adj.* unzeitig, unpassend, ungelegen, ungünstig; frühzeitig
untiring *adj.* unermüdlich
unto *prep.* (poet.) zu, an, nach; für, auf, gegen
untold *adj.* ungesagt, unerzählt; unerwähnt, ungezählt, unermesslich; unbeschreiblich
untouched *adj.* unberührt, unangetastet; ungerührt
untoward *adj.* ungünstig, widrig; widerspenstig; ungeschickt, verkehrt
untried *adj.* unversucht; ungeprüft, unerprobt; unerfahren; unerledigt; (law) noch nicht verhört
untrod(den) *adj.* unbetreten
untroubled *adj.* ungestört, unbelästigt; ungetrübt
untrue *adj.* unwahr; untreu
untrustworthy *adj.* unzuverlässig
untruth *n.* Unwahrheit
untutored *adj.* ununterrichtet, ungebildet
unused *adj.* ungebraucht, unbenutzt; ungewohnt
unusual *adj.* ungewöhnlich, ungebräuchlich; ungewohnt
unvarying *adj.* unveränderlich, unwandelbar
unveil *v.* (sich) entschleiern, enthüllen
unversed *adj.* unbewandert, unerfahren
unwanted *adj.* unerwünscht

unwarranted *adj.* unberechtigt; **unverbürgt**
unwelcome *adj.* unwillkommen
unwholesome *adj.* ungesund, schädlich
unwieldy *adj.* unbeholfen, ungelenk; unhandlich, sperrig
unwilling *adj.* unwillig, abgeneigt, widerwillig
unwind *v.* loswinden, loswickeln; (sich) abwickeln, aufgehen; lösen
unwise *adj.* unklug, töricht
unwittingly *adv.* unwissentlich, unbeabsichtigt
unwonted *adj.* ungewohnt, ungewöhnlich
unworkable *adj.* unpraktisch; unbrauchbar
unworthy *adj.* unwürdig
unwounded *adj.* unverwundet, unverletzt
unwrap *v.* aufwickeln, auswickeln; auspacken
unwritten *adj.* ungeschrieben, unbeschrieben; mündlich überliefert; — **law** Gewohnheitsrecht
unyielding *adj.* unnachgiebig, unbeugsam; unergiebing
up *adv.* auf, hinauf, in die Höhe, empor, aufwärts; herauf; oben; aufgestanden, aufgegangen, aufgestiegen; angeschwollen; aufgeregt; aus, vorbei; **be — to** something einer Sache gewachsen sein; it is — to me es hängt von mir ab, es liegt bei mir; — *prep.* herauf, hinauf; — to bis auf (*or* an); —! *interj.* auf! herauf! hinauf! — *n. pl.* the — **and** downs of life die Wechselfälle des Lebens
upbraid *v.* vorwerfen, vorhalten; **-ing** *adj.* vorwurfsvoll, tadelnd, scheltend
upbringing *n.* Erziehung; **Aufziehen, Grossziehen**
upbuild *v.* aufbauen, errichten
upgrade *n.* Abstufung; Aufstieg, Steigung; — *v.* abstufen, abteilen
upheaval *n.* Erhebung; Umwälzung
uphill *adj.* bergan, bergauf; (fig.) mühsam
uphold *v.* hochhalten; aufrecht(er)halten, stützen
upholster *v.* dekorieren; (auf)polstern; ausstatten; **-er** *n.* Polsterer, Dekorateur; **-y** *n.* Dekorierung; Polsterung; Möbelbezüge
upkeep *n.* Instandhaltung; **Unterhaltungskosten**
upland *n.* Hochland; — *adj.* Hochlands-; hochgelegen
uplift *v.* emporheben; erheben
upon *prep.* an, auf, in, über, **zu; aus,** durch, nach, unter, von; gemäss, **zufolge;** — *adv.* darauf, hinterher; beinahe

upper *adj.* höher, ober; Ober-; — **end** Kopfende; — **deck** Oberdeck; — **hand** Oberhand; — **jaw** Oberkiefer; — **lip** Oberlippe

upper-case *adj.* (typ.) gross gedruckt

upper-class *adj.* den oberen Gesellschaftsschichten angehörend

uppermost *adj.* oberst, höchst; vorherrschend, hauptsächlich

uppish *adj.* (coll.) anmassend, arrogant

upright *adj.* aufrecht, gerade; aufrichtig, rechtschaffen

uprising *n.* Erhebung, Aufstand; Aufstehen, Aufsteigen; Entstehen

uproar *n.* Getümmel, Lärm, Unruhe; Aufruhr; **-ious** *adj.* aufrührerisch, lärmend, tobend

uproot *v.* entwurzeln, ausreissen; vertilgen

upset *n.* Umwerfen, Umsturz; Misserfolg, Fehlschlag; Streit; — *adj.* festgesetzt, angesetzt; — *v.* umstürzen; in Unordnung (*or* aus der Fassung) bringen; aufregen, stören

upshot *n.* Ausgang, Ende; Beschluss; Ergebnis

upside-down *adj.* auf den Kopf stellend; verkehrt, umgekehrt; — *adv.* drunter und drüber; auf dem Kopf

upstairs *adv.* oben; nach oben; hinauf

upstanding *adj.* gerade, aufrichtig; (coll.) vorzüglich

upstart *n.* Emporkömmling, Neureiche

upstream *adv.* stromauf(wärts); gegen den Strom

up-to-date *adj.* zeitgemäss, modern, modisch

uptown *n.* Wohnbezirk (vom Zentrum entfernt); obere Stadtteile

upturn *n.* Umsturz; (com.) Heraufschnellen; — *v.* aufwerfen, hochwerfen; umstürzen

upward *adv.* aufwärts, steigend, in die Höhe; darüber

uranium *n.* Uran

urban *adj.* städtisch, Stadt-; **-ite** *n.* Grosstädter; **-ization** *n.* Verstädterung

urbane *adj.* artig, höflich, gebildet

urbanity *n.* Höflichkeit; Urbanität

urchin *n.* (zool.) Igel; (coll.) Schlingel, Schelm

uremia *n.* Harnvergiftung

urethra *n.* Harnröhre

urge *n.* Trieb; — *v.* drängen, (an)treiben; dringen, nötigen, zusetzen; **-ncy** *n.* Dringlichkeit; **-nt** *adj.* dringend, dringlich

urinal *n.* Harnglas, Ente; (coll.) Pissoir

urinate *v.* urinieren, harnen; Urin lassen

urine *n.* Urin, Harn

urn *n.* Urne; Gefäss

us *pron.* uns; **of** — unser

usable *adj.* brauchbar, benutzbar

usage *n.* Gebrauch; Brauch, Herkommen; Behandlung

use *n.* Gebrauch, Benutzung, Anwendung, Verwendung; Nutzen; Gewohnheit; — *v.* anwenden, verwenden, gebrauchen, (ver)brauchen; (be)nutzen; ausüben, betreiben; **she -d to do** sie pflegte zu tun, sie tat gewöhnlich; **-d** *adj.* gewohnt; gebräuchlich, üblich; verbraucht, abgenutzt; **-ful** *adj.* nützlich, dienlich, brauchbar; **-fulness** *n.* Nützlichkeit; **-less** *adj.* nutzlos, unnütz, unbrauchbar; fruchtlos, vergeblich; **-lessness** *n.* Nutzlosigkeit; **-r** *n.* Benutzer, Gebraucher

usher *n.* Türhüter; (law) Gerichtsdiener; (theat.) Platzanweiser; — *v.* einführen, ankündigen, anmelden; (theat.) Plätze anweisen; **-ette** *v.* Platzanweiserin

usual *adj.* üblich, gewöhnlich

usurer *n.* Wucherer

usurp *v.* sich aneignen, an sich reissen; usurpieren; **-ation** *n.* widerrechtliche Aneignung

usury *n.* Wucher; **practise —** Wucher treiben

utensil *n.* Gerät; Werkzeug; *pl.* Utensilien, Gerätschaften

uterus *n.* Gebärmutter, Uterus

utility *n.* Nützlichkeit, Nutzen; **public utilities** gemeinnützige Betriebe

utilization *n.* Nutzbarmachung, Nutzanwendung, Verwertung

utilize *v.* verwerten, nutzbar machen

utmost *adj.* äusserst, fernst, höchst, grösst

Utopian *n.* Utopist; — *adj.* utopisch

utter *adj.* äusserst, gänzlich; — *v.* äussern, aussprechen, ausstossen; **-ance** *n.* Ausserung, Ausdruck, Ausspruch, Wort; Aussprache

uttermost *adj.* äusserst, fernst, höchst, grösst

uvula *n.* Zäpfchen

V

vacancy *n.* freie Stelle, Vakanz; Leere, Lücke

vacant *adj.* frei, offen, unbesetzt, vakant; leer, unbewohnt

vacate *v.* leeren, räumen, freimachen; aufgeben; aufheben

vacation *n.* Ferien, Urlaub

vaccinate *v.* impfen

vaccination *n.* Impfung

vaccine *n.* Impfstoff, Lymphe

vacillate *v.* schwanken, wanken; unschlüssig sein

vacuous *adj.* leer, ausdruckslos

vacuum *n.* Vakuum; (luft)leerer Raum; — bottle Thermosflasche; — cleaner Staubsauger; — filter Vakuumfilter; — tube Vakuumröhre, Geisslersche Röhre

vagabond *n.* Vagabund, Landstreicher; — *adj.* umherstreifend, vagabundierend; — *v.* vagabundieren

vagina *n.* (nat.) Scheide

vagrancy *n.* Landstreicherei

vagrant *adj.* unstet, ziellos, wandernd

vague *adj.* vag, unbestimmt ungewiss; schwankend

vain *adj.* eitel; nichtig, leer, vergeblich; in — vergebens, umsonst

valance *n.* kurzer Vorhang; (fabric) halbseidener Damast

valence *n.* Wertigkeit

valentine *n.* am St. Valentinstag gewählter Schatz (*or* gesandter Gruss)

valet *n.* Kammerdiener

valiant *adj.* tapfer, mutig

valid *adj.* wirksam, triftig; rechtsgültig; –ate *v.* legalisieren, für rechtsgültig erklären; –ity *n.* Gültigkeit

valise *n.* Reisetasche

valley *n.* Tal; (arch.) Dachkehle

valor *n.* Wert, Gehalt; Tapferkeit, Mut; –ous *adj.* tapfer, kühn

valuable *adj.* wertvoll, hochwertig, kostbar; — *n. pl.* Kostbarkeiten, Schmucksachen, Wertsachen

valuation *n.* Abschätzung, Wertbestimmung, Veranschlagung; (fig.) Wertschätzung, Würdigung

value *n.* Wert, Preis; (com.) Valuta; face — Nennwert; real — Realwert; — *v.* (ab)schätzen, veranschlagen; (fig.) schätzen, achten; –less *adj.* wertlos

valve *n.* Ventil, Klappe; air — Luftventil; exhaust — Auslassventil

vamp *n.* (shoe) Oberleder; (sl.) Vamp; — *v.* zurechtflicken; (mus.) improvisieren

vampire *n.* Vampir

van *n.* Möbelwagen; Gepäckwagen; (agr.) Getreideschwinge; (min.) Erzschwinge; cattle — Viehtransportwagen

Van Allen Radiation Belt *n.* Van Allens Radiationsgürtel

vandal *n.* Vandale; –ism *n.* Vandalismus

vane *n.* Wetterfahne, (mech.) Flügel

vanguard *n.* Vorhut, Vortrab

vanilla *n.* Vanille

vanish *v.* (ver)schwinden, vergehen; –ing *adj.* verschwindend; –ing line Fluchtlinie

vanity *n.* Eitelkeit, Nichtigkeit, Vergeblichkeit; — case Puderdose

vanquish *v.* besiegen, überwältigen

vapid *adj.* abgestanden, schal; matt, geistlos

vapor *n.* Dunst, Dampf; — *v.* (ver)dunsten, (ver)dampfen; (coll.) prahlen; –ize *v.* (ver)dampfen, (ver)dunsten; –ous *adj.* dunstig, dampfartig; (fig.) nebelhaft, duftig

variable *adj.* veränderlich, veränderbar; verstellbar

variance *n.* Veränderung; Uneinigkeit

variant *adj.* verschieden, veränderlich; unbeständig

variation *n.* Variation, Abweichung; Abänderung; Abwechslung, Unterschied

varicose *adj.* krampfadrig; — vein Krampfader

varied *adj.* variiert, verändert; verschiedenartig, mannigfaltig

variety *n.* Mannigfaltigkeit, Auswahl, Menge; Spielart

various *adj.* mannigfaltig, verschieden-(artig); abwechslungsreich

varnish *n.* Firnis, Lack; Anstrich; — *v.* firnissen, lackieren; (fig.) beschönigen

varsity *n.* (coll.) Universität; — crew Rudermannschaft der Universität

vary *v.* variieren, (ver)ändern, (ab)wechseln, abweichen; veränderlich sein; –ing *adj.* variiert; abwechselnd; veränderlich

vase *n.* Vase

Vaseline *n.* Vaseline

vassal *n.* Vasall, Lehnsmann

vast *adj.* ungeheuer, gewaltig, riesig, unermesslich

vat *n.* Fass; Bottich, Kufe

vaudeville *n.* Schlager; Vaudeville, Varieté

vault *n.* Sprung; (arch.) Stahlkammer; Gewölbe, Wölbung; — *v.* (über)wölben; springen, hinwegspringen über

veal *n.* Kalbfleisch; — chop Kalbskotelett

vector *n.* (avi.) Winkel der Luftverdrängung beim Fliegen

veer *v.* (sich) drehen, wenden; (naut.) halsen, fieren

vegetable *n.* Gemüse; — *adj.* Pflanzen-, Gemüse

vegetarian *n.* Vegetarier; — *adj.* vegetarisch

vegetate *v.* vegetieren

vegetation *n.* Vegetation

vehemence *n.* Vehemenz, Heftigkeit, Leidenschaft

vehement *adj.* vehement, heftig, leidenschaftlich

vehicle *n.* Fuhrwerk, Fahrzeug; (fig.) Träger, Ausdrucksmittel

veil *n.* Schleier, Hülle; — *v.* (sich) ver-

schleiern, verhüllen; bemänteln
vein *n.* Ader; — *v.* ädern, marmorieren;
–ed *adj.*, –y *adj.* geädert; marmoriert,
gemasert
vellum *y.* Pergament
velocity *n.* Geschwindigkeit
velvet *n.* Samt; — *adj.* samten, samtweich: –y *adj.* Samt-; (fig.) sanft, mild
venal *adj.* käuflich, feil
vend *v.* verkaufen, feilbieten; –or *n.* Verkäufer, Händler; Verkaufsautomat
veneer *n.* Furnier; Anstrich, Tünche; —
v. furnieren, einlegen, auslegen; (fig.)
umkleiden; den Anstrich geben
venerable *adj.* ehrwürdig, verehrungswürdig
veneration *n.* Verehrung
venereal *adj.* wollüstig; Liebes-, Geschlechts-; (med.) venerisch
Venetian *n.* Venezianer; Venezianisch; —
adj. venezianisch; — blind Jalousie
vengeance *n.* Rache; Strafe
venial *adj.* verzeihlich, entschuldbar
venison *n.* Wildbret
venom *n.* Gift; –ous *adj.* giftig, vergiftet
vent *n.* Öffnung, Loch; Abzug, Ausweg;
(mil.) Zündloch; (zool.) After; give —
sich Luft machen (or aussprechen); —
v. lüften; ziehen; auslassen
ventilate *v.* ventilieren, lüften; (fig.)
erörtern
ventilation *n.* Ventilation, Lüftung(sanlage); (fig.) Erörterung
ventilator *n.* Ventilator
ventriloquist *n.* Bauchredner
venture *n.* Wagnis, Risiko; Einsatz;
Spekulation; — *v.* wagen, aufs Spiel
setzen, riskieren; spekulieren; –some
adj. unternehmend, wagend, verwegen
veracious *adj.* wahrhaftig, wahrheitsliebend; glaubwürdig
veracity *n.* Wahrhaftigkeit, Wahrheit
veranda(h) *n.* Veranda
verb *n.* Verb, Zeitwort; –al *adj.* wörtlich,
mündlich; buchstäblich; Wort-, Verbal-; –atim *adv.* wörtlich, wortgetreu;
–iage *n.* Wortschwall; Ausdruck
(sweise); –ose *adj.* wortreich; weitschweifig
verdant *adj.* grün(end), blühend; (coll.)
unreif
verdict *n.* Urteil, Meinung; (law) Geschworenenspruch
verdigris *n.* Grünspan
verdure *n.* Grün; Frische
verge *n.* Rand, Einfassung; Stab; (mech.)
Spindel; — *v.* sich neigen, streifen,
übergehen; begrenzen
verification *n.* Nachprüfung, Bestätigung
verify *v.* (nach)prüfen, beweisen, bestäti

gen
verily *adv.* wahrlich, wahrhaftig, wirklich;
vollkommen
veritable *adj.* wahr(haftig), wirklich, echt
verity *n.* Wahrheit, Wirklichkeit
vermicelli *n.* Fadennudeln
vermicide *n.* Wurmmittel
vermilion *n.* Zinnober(rot); — *adj.* hochrot; — *v.* zinnoberrot färben
vermin *n.* Schädling, Ungeziefer
vermouth *n.* Wermuth
vernacular *adj.* einheimisch; Landes-
vernal *adj.* Frühlings-
versatile *adj.* veränderlich, beweglich;
vielseitig, gewandt
versatility *n.* Beweglichkeit, Gewandtheit; Wandelbarkeit
verse *n.* Vers; Strophe; blank — Blankvers; –d *adj.* versiert, bewandert,
erfahren
versify *v.* Verse machen; dichten, reimen;
in Verse bringen
version *n.* Version, Fassung, Darstellung,
Lesart; Übersetzung
versus *prep.* kontra, gegen
vertebra *n.* Wirbel; *pl.* Rückgrat, Wirbelsäule; –l *adj.*, –te *adj.* Wirbel-; –te *n.*
Wirbeltier
vertex *n.* Spitze, Scheitel
vertical *adj.* vertikal, senkrecht; Scheitel-; — fin (avi.) Seitenflosse; — line
Senkrechte; Lot(rechte)
vertigo *n.* Schwindel
very *adv.* sehr; — *adj.* derselbe; the —
thing gerade das; the — thought schon
der Gedanke; to the — bone bis auf
den Knochen; Very light Leuchtkugel
vespers *n. pl.* Vesper; Abendgottesdienst
vessel *n.* Gefäss; (naut.) Schiff
vest *n.* Weste, Jacket
vest *v.* bekleiden, bedecken, einkleiden;
einsetzen; verleihen
vested *adj.* festbegründet, festgesetzt;
erworben
vestibule *n.* Vestibül, Vorhof, Vorhalle,
Hausflur
vestige *n.* Spur; Merkmal, Überbleibsel
vestment *n.* Amtsgewand; Messgewand;
Kleid
vest-pocket edition *n.* Taschenausgabe
vestry *n.* Sakristei
vestryman *n.* Kirchenälteste
veteran *n.* Veteran; — *adj* ausgedient;
erfahren
veterinary *n.* Tierarzt; Veterinär; — *adj.*
tierärztlich
veto *n.* Veto; — *v.* sein Veto einlegen;
verbieten
vex *v.* schikanieren, quälen, ärgern;
necken; –ation *n.* Verdruss, Ärger,

Sorge, Schikane; **-atious** *adj.* quälend, ärgerlich, verdriesslich; neckend
via *prep.* via, über, bei
viaduct *n.* Viadukt, Überführung
vial *n.* Phiole, Flasche
vibrant *adj.* vibrierend
vibrate *v.* vibrieren, schwingen
vibration *n.* Vibration, Schwingung
vicar *n.* Vikar
vicarious *adj.* stellvertretend
vice *n.* Laster, Untugend; Unart
vice *prep.* an Stelle von; Vize-, Unter-
vice-admiral *n.* Vizeadmiral
vice-chairman *n.* stellvertretender Vorsitzender; Vizepräsident
vice-consul *n.* Vizekonsul
vice-president *n.* Vizepräsident
vice versa vice versa, umgekehrt
vicinity *n.* Nachbarschaft, Nähe, Umgegend
vicious *adj.* fehlerhaft, verwerflich; lasterhaft, boshaft, bösartig; — circle Kreislauf, Umlauf; (math.) Zirkelschluss; (phil.) Trugschluss
vicissitudes *n. pl.* Wechselfälle
victim *n.* Opfer; **-ize** *v.* opfern, preisgeben; hereinlegen, betrügen
victor *n.* Sieger; **-ious** *adj.* siegreich; Sieges-; **-y** *n.* Sieg
victual *v.* (sich) mit Lebensmittel versorgen; — *n. pl.* Lebensmittel
video *n.* Fernsehen; — *adj.* fernsehend; Fernseh-
vie *v.* wetteifern, überbieten
Vienna *n.* Wien
view *n.* Aussicht, Anblick; Sicht; Sehen, Auge; Ansicht, Meinung; bird's-eye — Vogelperspektive; in — of angesichts, im Hinblick auf; point of — Gesichtspunkt; — *v.* (be)sehen, betrachten; besichtigen; beabsichtigen, erwägen
viewfinder *n.* (phot.) Sucher
viewpoint *n.* Gesichtspunkt
vigil *n.* Schlaflosigkeit; Nachtwache; **-ance** *n.* Wachsamkeit; **-ant** *adj.* wachsam
vigor *n.* Lebenskraft, Energie; Nachdruck; **-ous** *adj.* stark, kräftig; nachdrücklich
vile *adj.* niedrig, gemein; abscheulich
villa *n.* Villa
village *n.* Dorf; **-r** *n.* Dorfbewohner
villain *n.* Schurke, Schuft, Bösewicht; **-ous** *adj.* schurkisch, schändlich; abscheulich; **-y** *n.* Schurkerei; Schändlichkeit
vim *n.* Tatkraft, Energie
vindicate *v.* rechtfertigen, verteidigen; beanspruchen
vindication *n.* Rechtfertigung; Anspruch

vine *n.* Wein(stock), Rebe; Ranke; — louse Reblaus
vinegar *n.* Essig
vineyard *n.* Weinberg; **keeper of a —** Winzer
vintage *n.* Weinlese, Traubenernte; **Jahrgang**
vinyl *n.* Vinyl
viol *n.* Viola, Bratsche
viola *n.* Viola
violate *v.* schänden, entweihen; **(law)** verletzen, übertreten, brechen
violation *n.* Schändung, Entweihung; (law) Verletzung, Übertretung, Bruch
violator *n.* Schänder; (law) Rechtsbrecher
violence *n.* Gewalttätigkeit, Gewaltsamkeit, Heftigkeit
violent *adj.* gewaltsam, heftig, **gewalttätig**; unnatürlich
violet *n.* Veilchen; Veilchenblau, Violett; — *adj.* veilchenblau, violett; — **rays** ultraviolette Strahlen
violin *n.* Geige, Violine; (coll.) Fiedel; **-ist** *n.* Geiger, Violinist; (coll.) Fiedler
violoncello *n.* Violoncello, Cello
viper *n.* Viper, Natter, Otter
virgin *n.* Jungfrau; — *adj.* jungfräulich; Jungfern-; unberührt; **-al** *adj.* jungfräulich; **-ity** *n.* Jungfräulichkeit
virtual *adj.* dem Wesen nach, eigentlich
virtue *n.* Tugend; Vortrefflichkeit, Wirksamkeit; **by — of** kraft, vermöge
virtuosity *n.* Virtuosität; Virtuosentum
virtuous *adj.* virtuos; vortrefflich, wirksam; tugendhaft
virulence *n.* Bösartigkeit, Giftigkeit
virulent *adj.* bösartig; giftig; eiternd
virus *n.* Virus, Krankheitserreger
visa *n.* Visum, Sichtvermerk; — *v.* **mit einem Visum versehen**
visage *n.* Gesicht, Angesicht
viscera *n. pl.* Eingeweide; **-l** *adj.* innerlich
viscose *n.* Viskose, Kunstseide; — *adj.* zähflüssig
viscosity *n.* Zähegrad
viscount *n.* Erbgraf
vise *n.* Schraubstock
visibility *n.* Sicht(barkeit)
visible *adj.* sichtbar, ersichtlich; **augenscheinlich**
vision *n.* Sehkraft; Vision, Erscheinung; **-ary** *n.* Träumer; Geisterseher; Phantast; **-ary** *adj.* visionär, phantastisch
visit *n.* Besuch; — *v.* besuchen; besichtigen; **-ation** *n.* Besichtigung, Besuch; Durchsuchung; Heimsuchung; **-ing** *adj.* Besuchs-; **-ing card** Visitenkarte; **-or** *n.* Besucher; Inspektor
visor, vizor *n.* Visier; (cap) Schirm
vista *n.* Sicht

Vistula *n.* Weichsel
visual *adj.* visuell; Seh-, Gesichts-; **-ize** *v.*
sichtbar machen; sich vorstellen (*or*
vergegenwärtigen)
vital *adj.* vital, lebenswichtig; — **statistics**
Lebensdauerstatistik; — **parts**, — *n. pl.*
lebenswichtige Körperteile, edle Teile;
-ity *n.* Vitalität, Lebenskraft
vitamin *n.* Vitamin
vitreous *adj.* gläsern; Glas-
vituperate *v.* tadeln, schmähen
vivacious *adj.* lebhaft, munter; (bot.) ausdauernd
vivacity *n.* Lebhaftigkeit, Munterkeit
vivid *adj.* lebhaft, lebendig; (fig.) anschaulich; **-ness** *n.* Lebendigkeit, Anschau-
lichkeit
vivisection *n.* Vivisektion
vixen *n.* Füchsin, Fähe; (fig.) Zänkerin
viz. *abbr.* nämlich, d.h.
vocabulary *n.* Wörterverzeichnis; Wort-
schatz
vocal *adj.* Stimm-, Vokal-; stimmlich;
laut, mündlich; — **cords** Stimmbänder;
-ist *n.* Sänger(in)
vocation *n.* Beruf(ung); Neigung, Anlage;
-al *adj.* beruflich; **-al school** Berufsschule
vociferous *adj.* schreiend, brüllend, laut
vogue *n.* Beliebtheit, Mode; Bewegung
voice *n.* Stimme; Sprache; (gram.) Form;
— *v.* aussprechen, äussern; **-less** *adj.*
stimmlos; schweigend, stumm
void *adj.* leer, unbesetzt; ungültig;
zwecklos, nichtig; — of frei von; arm
an; — *v.* leeren, verlassen; ungültig
machen, aufheben
volatile *adj.* flüchtig; flatterhaft
volcanic *adj.* vulkanisch
volcano *n.* Vulkan
volition *n.* Willenskraft, Wollen; Entschluss
volley *n.* Schwall, Hagel; (mil.) Salve,
Ladung; (tennis) Flugball
volleyball *n.* Ball über die Schnur
volt *n.* Volte, Wendung; (elec.) Volt; **-age**
n. (elec.) Spannung; **-aic** *adj.* voltaisch
voluble *adj.* beweglich; geläufig, fliessend;
geschwätzig
volume *n.* Band; Volumen, Menge,
Masse, Umfang
voluminous *adj.* umfangreich; ausführlich
voluntary *adj.* freiwillig; unabhängig;
absichtlich
volunteer *n.* Volontär, Freiwillige; — *v.*
volontieren, sich freiwillig anbieten (*or*
melden); freiwillig dienen
voluptuous *adj.* wollüstig, sinnlich; üppig
vomit *n.* Erbrechen; Brechmittel; — *v.*
erbrechen, ausspeien, sich übergeben;

auswerfen
voracious *adj.* gefrässig, gierig
Vosges Mountains *n.* Vogesen
votary *n.* Verehrer, Anhänger, Jünger;
(eccl.) Geweihte
vote *n.* Wahlstimme; Abstimmung; Vo-
tum; Wahlzettel, Wahlkugel; — *v.*
(ab)stimmen; vorschlagen; beschliessen, wählen; **-r** *n.* Wähler, Stimm-
berechtigte
vouch *v.* (ver)bürgen, bezeugen; **-er** *n.*
Zeuge, Bürge; Quittung, Gutschein;
Zeugnis
vouchsafe *v.* gewähren, bewilligen
vow *n.* Gelübde, Schwur; — *v.* geloben;
weihen, widmen
vowel *n.* Vokal, Selbstlaut
voyage *n.* Seereise, Luftreise; — *v.* eine
Seereise (*or* Luftreise) machen; bereisen, befahren; **-r** *n.* Seereisende,
Luftreisende
vulcanize *v.* vulkanisieren
vulgar *adj.* vulgär, gemein, gewöhnlich,
niedrig, pöbelhaft; **-ity** *n.* Gemeinheit,
Gewöhnlichkeit; Pöbelhaftigkeit
vulnerable *adj.* verwundbar, verletzlich
vulture *n.* Geier
vying *adj.* wetteifernd

W

wad *n.* Pfropf(en), Bausch; Polster;
(min.) Manganschaum; (coll.) Bank-
notenbündel; — *v.* (aus)stopfen, füllen;
wattieren, polstern; **-ding** *n.* Wattierung, Watte
waddle *v.* watscheln, wackeln
wade *v.* (durch)waten; (fig.) sich durcharbeiten
wafer *n.* Oblate, Waffel; (eccl.) Hostie
waffle *n.* Waffel
wag *n.* Schütteln; (coll.) Spassvogel; — *v.*
wackeln, wedeln, schütteln; signalisieren
wage *v.* wagen; aufs Spiel setzen; (war)
führen
wager *n.* Wette, Wetteinsatz; — *v.*
riskieren, wagen; wetten
wages *n. pl.* Lohn, Gehalt; Diäten
waggish *adj.* schelmisch, schalkhaft; mutwillig
wagon *n.* Waggon, Güterwagen; Lastwagen; (min.) Förderwagen; **-er** *n.*
Fuhrmann
waif *n.* Heimatlose; herrenloses Gut;
Strandgut
wail *n.* Klage, Jammer; — *v.* (weh)klagen,
jammern
wainscoting *n.* Täfelung, Getäfel
waist *n.* Taille; Mieder; schmalste Stelle;

(naut.) Mitteldeck

waistcoat n. Weste

waistline n. Taillenweite

wait n. Warten; Wartezeit; Hinterhalt; (theat.) Pause, Zwischenakt; — v. (er)warten, abwarten; aufwarten; begleiten; lauern; -er n. Kellner, Aufwärter; Präsentierteller; -ing n. Warten; Erwartung; Aufwartung, Bedienung, Dienst; -ing adj. wartend; aufwartend, bedienend; begleitend; lauernd; -ing room Wartezimmer; (rail.) Wartesaal; -ress n. Kellnerin

waiver n. Verzicht, Aufgabe

wake n. Totenwache; (naut.) Kielwasser; — v. wachen; erwachen; (er)wecken; -ful adj. wachend, wachsam; (fig.) schlaflos; -n v. (auf)wachen; (auf)wecken; (fig.) anregen

waking n. Wachen; Nachtwache; Totenwache

walk n. Schritt, Gang; Spaziergang; Weg; Laufbahn; — v. gehen, wandern; umhergehen, spazieren führen; (fig.) wandeln; -er n. Fussgänger, Spaziergänger; -ing n. Gehen; Fussweg

walkie-talkie n. Feldtelefon, Sprechfunkgerät; Kleinfunkgerät

wall n. Wand, Mauer; Wall; — v. einmauern, ummauern; (fig.) einschliessen, abschliessen

wallet n. Brieftasche; Reisetasche; Rucksack

wallflower n. Goldlack; (fig.) Mauerblümchen

wallop v. (coll.) prügeln, schlagen

wallow v. sich wälzen; (fig.) schwelgen

wallpaper n. Tapete

walnut n. Walnuss

walrus n. Walross

waltz n. Walzer

wand n. Rute, Gerte, Stab, Stock

wander v. wandern; umherirren, umherstreifen; -er n. Wanderer

wane n. Abnahme, Verfall; in the — of the moon bei abnehmendem Mond; — v. abnehmen, sinken; (fig.) verfallen

want n. Mangel, Bedürfnis, Armut; — v. (er)mangeln, bedürfen; verlangen, wünschen; -ing adj. fehlend, (er)mangelnd

wanton n. Schelm; (fig.) Wüstling; liederliches Frauenzimmer; — adj. mutwillig, ausgelassen; frevelhaft, ausschweifend; wollüstig, geil

war n. Krieg; — v. Krieg führen; streiten; — like adj. kriegerisch, Kriegs-; — fare n. Kriegsführung; Kampf

warble n. Getriller, Schmettern, Schlagen; — v. trillern, schmettern, schlagen; -r n. Sänger; Singvogel

ward n. Wache; Krankensaal; Gefängnisabteilung; (law) Vormundschaft, Mündel; (pol.) Wahlkreis, Bezirk; — v. behüten, bewahren; — off abwehren, abwenden; parieren

warden n. Wärter, Wächter, Aufseher; Vormund, Pfleger; Vorsteher

wardrobe n. Garderobe; Kleiderschrank, Kleiderkammer

ware n. Ware

warehouse n. Warenlager, Lager; Speicher

warehouseman n. Lagerverwalter

warily adv. vorsichtig, behutsam, bedächtig

warm adj. warm, heiss; feurig, leidenschaftlich; — v. wärmen; (sich) erwärmen; -ing adj. erwärmend; -ing pan Wärmflasche, Anwärmer; -ing n. Erwärmung; -th n. Wärme; Herzlichkeit; Lebhaftigkeit, Feuer, Eifer

warm-blooded adj. heissblütig; (zool.) warmblütig

warmhearted adj. warmherzig, herzlich, teilnehmend

warmonger n. Kriegshetzer

warn v. warnen; ermahnen; benachrichtigen; -ing n. Warnung; Mahnung; Benachrichtigung; Kündigung; air-raid -ing Fliegeralarm, Luftwarnung

warp n. Kette, Aufzug; (naut.) Bugsiertau; (wood) Verwerfung; — v. sich verziehen (or werfen); verzerren; (naut.) verholen, bugsieren

warrant n. Vollmacht; Berechtigung, Erlaubnis; (law) Haftbefehl; Haussuchungsbefehl; Vollstreckungsbefehl; — v. bevollmächtigen, berechtigen; verbürgen, garantieren; rechtfertigen; -y n. Garantie, Gewähr; Bürgschaft(sschein); Berechtigung

warrior n. Krieger

warship n. Kriegsschiff

wart n. Warze, Auswuchs; -y adj. warzig

wartime n. Kriegszeit

wary adj. bedachtsam, vorsichtig, wachsam; sparsam

wash n. Wäsche; Abwaschen; Spülwasser; Wellenschlag; Tünche, Anstrich; (geol.) Schwemmland; (naut.) Kielwasser, Ruderblatt; — v. waschen; (be)spülen; reinigen; schwemmen; schlämmen; waschecht sein; -able adj. waschbar, waschecht; -er n. Wäscher; Waschmaschine; Spülmaschine; (mech.) Dichtungsscheibe, Manschette; -ing n. Wäsche, Waschung; (mech.) Plattierung; (phot.) Wässern; -ing adj. waschend; -ing machine Waschmaschine

washbowl n. Waschbecken, Waschschüssel

washerwoman n. Wäscherin, Waschfrau

washout n. (geol.) Auswaschung; (coll.) Reinfall, Durchfall

washstand n. Waschständer, Waschschüssel

wasp n. Wespe

waste n. Abfall, Schwund, Verlust; Verwüstung, Verödung; Vergeudung, Verschwendung; Abnutzung; (law) Vernachlässigung, Verfall; — pipe Abzugsrohr; Abflussrohr; — adj. wüst, öde, unbebaut; unnütz, unbrauchbar; überflüssig; — v. verwüsten, verheeren, veröden; vergeuden, verschwenden; — away hinschwinden, sich verzehren, verfallen; -ful adj. verheerend; verschwenderisch; -r n. Verschwender; Verwüster; Ausschuss; (coll.) Tunichtgut •

wastebasket n. Papierkorb

wastepaper n. Altpapier, Makkulatur

watch n. Wache, Wachsamkeit; Taschenuhr; (mil.) Posten; night — Nachtwache; stop — Stoppuhr; wrist — Armbanduhr; — v. wachen, bewachen; achtgeben, beobachten; — out! interj. Achtung! gib acht! -ful adj. wachsam, aufmerksam, achtsam; (fig.) schlaflos

watchdog n. Hofhund, Kettenhund; (fig.) Zerberus

watchmaker n. Uhrmacher

watchman n. Wächter, Nachtwächter; (rail.) Bahnwärter

watchtower n. Wachtturm, Warte

watchword n. Parole, Losung

water n. Wasser; Gewässer; be in low — auf dem Trockenen sitzen; — bird Wasservogel; — cask Wasserfass; — closet Wasserklosett; — color Aquarellfarbe, Wasserfarbe; — cress Brunnenkresse; — cure Wasserkur; — front Hafengegend; — gap Felsbachspalte; — gas Wassergas; — gate Schleusentor; — gauge Wasserstandsanzeiger, Pegel; — glass Wasseruhr; (chem.) Wasserglas; — level Wasserstand(slinie); (mech.) Wasserwaage; — lily Seerose; — main Hauptwasserrohr, Hauptwasserader; — meter Wassermesser; — moccasin Mokassinwasserschlange; — polo Wasserpolo; — power Wasserkraft; — tower Wasserturm; — wing Brückenmauer; Schwimmgürtel; — v. (be)wässern, berieseln; begiessen, besprengen; verwässern, verdünnen; tränken; tränen; -ing n. Wässern, Bewässern, Begiessen; -ing place Schwemme, Tränke; -ing pot Giesskanne; -y adj. wässerig, feucht, nass; Wasser-; wasserreich

water-cooled adj. wassergekühlt

waterfall n. Wasserfall

waterlogged adj. wassergefüllt; sinkend, leck

watermark n. Wassermarke, Wasserzeichen

watermelon n. Wassermelone

waterproof adj. wasserdicht, imprägniert

watershed n. Wasserscheide

water-skiing n. Wasserskilaufen

waterspout n. Wasserhose; Wasserstrahl

waterworks n. pl. Wasserwerk(e); Wasserkünste; (sl.) Tränenschleusen

watt n. Watt

wave n. Welle, Woge; Wellenlinie; Schwenken, Wink(en); short — Kurzwelle; sound — Schallwelle; — length Wellenlänge; — v. wellig machen, wellen; wogen; wehen, flattern; winken, schwenken; -d adj. gewellt, wellenförmig; -r v. wanken, schwanken; zaudern, unschlüssig sein; flackern

waving adj. wankend, schwankend; unschlüssig

wavy adj. wogig, wogend; wellig, gewellt

wax n. Wachs; — adj. wächsern; — candle Wachskerze; — paper Wachspapier; — v. wachsen, bohnen, polieren; wichsen; pichen; -en adj. wächsern, wachsfarben; (fig.) nachgiebig; -y adj. wachsartig, weich; (med.) wachsbleich

waxwork n. Wachsfigur

way n. Weg, Strasse; Bahn, Kurs, Richtung, Strecke; Fahrt; Weite, Entfernung; Wandel, Benehmen; Zustand; Mittel, Methode, Art und Weise, Verfahren; by the — nebenbei, beiläufig; by — of über; force one's — sich gewaltsam eindrängen; give — aus dem Wege gehen, weichen; in no — keineswegs; on the — unterwegs, auf dem Wege; out of the — ungewöhnlich; entlegen; -s and means Mittel und Wege

wayfarer n. Reisende, Wanderer; Hotelpächter

waylay v. auflauern, nachstellen

wayside n. Strassenrand, Wegseite; by the — an der Strasse (or am Wege) gelegen

wayward adj. launisch, eigensinnig, widerspenstig; unregelmässig

we pron. wir

weak adj. schwach; kränklich; -en v. schwächen; schwach werden; verdünnen; entkräften; nachlassen; -ling n. Schwächling; -ness n. Schwäche,

Schwächlichkeit; Schlaffheit
weak-minded *adj.* schwachsinnig; charakterschwach
wealth *n.* Wohlstand, Reichtum; (fig.) Fülle, Überfluss; **-y** *adj.* reich, vermögend, begütert, wohlhabend
wean *n.* entwöhnen; abgewöhnen, abbringen von
weapon *n.* Waffe; Wehr
wear *n.* Tragen; Tracht, Mode; Abnutzung; — *v.* tragen, anhaben, aufhaben; abtragen, abnutzen, erschöpfen; — out a person jemanden ermüden (*or* langweilen); **-ing** *adj* **-ing apparel** *n.* Kleidung(sstücke)
weariness *n.* Müdigkeit, Ermüdung; (fig.) Überdruss
wearisome *adj.* mühsam, beschwerlich, ermüdend; (fig.) langweilig, belästigend
weary *adj.* müde, matt; (fig.) überdrüssig; ermüdend, lästig
weasel *n.* Wiesel
weather *n.* Wetter, Witterung; (naut.) Luv; — **forecast** Wettervoraussage; — **report** Wetterbericht; — **strip** Dichtungsleiste, Dichtungsstreifen; — *v.* lüften; dem Wetter aussetzen, verwittern; (arch.) abschrägen; (naut.) luvwärts umschiffen; (fig.) widerstehen, wetterfest sein
weather-beaten *adj.* wettergebräunt, abgehärtet, wetterfest; mitgenommen
weathercock *n.* Wetterhahn, Wetterfahne
weatherman *n.* Wetterberichterstatter, Meteorologe
weather-strip *v.* (gegen Wettereinflüsse) abdichten
weather-tight *adj.* wetterdicht
weave *n.* Gewebe; Weberei; — *v.* weben, wirken; flechten; (fig.) ersinnen; **-r** *n.* Weber
web *n.* Gewebe, Netz; (orn. and zool.) Schwimmhaut; — *v.* weben, wirken; (zool.) einspinnen; **-bed** *adj.* (orn. and zool.) mit Schwimmhäuten versehen
web-footed *adj.* schwimmfüssig
wed *v.* heiraten, ehelichen; verheiraten, trauen; **-ded** *adj.* verheiratet, angetraut, ehelich; (fig.) ergeben, eng verbunden; **-ding** *n.* Heirat, Hochzeit, Trauung; **-ding cake** Hochzeitskuchen; **-ding ring** Trauring
wedge *n.* Keil; — *v.* (ver)keilen, spalten
wedlock *n.* Ehe(stand)
Wednesday *n.* Mittwoch
wee *adj.* klein, winzig
weed *n.* Unkraut; (coll.) Kraut, Tabak; **widow's** — Witwentrauer; — *v.* jäten; säubern, auslesen; **-y** *adj.* unkrautartig, verkrautet

week *n.* Woche; **by the** — wochenweise, wöchentlich; — **end** Wochenende; **-ly** *adj.* wöchentlich; **-ly publication** Wochenschrift
weep *v.* (be)weinen, beklagen; feucht sein, tröpfeln; **-ing** *adj.* weinend; Trauer-; **-ing willow** Trauerweide; **-ing** *n.* Weinen, Klagen
weigh *v.* (ab)wiegen; (ab)wägen, erwägen; gelten, den Ausschlag geben; (naut.) lichten; **-t** *n.* Gewicht; Wucht, Schwere, Last, Druck; Bedeutung; **inspector of -ts and measures** Eichamtsinspektor; **-ty** *adj.* gewichtig, schwer(wiegend), erheblich; drückend
weightlessness *n.* Schwerelosigkeit
weird *adj.* unheimlich, geisterhaft, überirdisch; merkwürdig; Schicksals-; **the Weird Sisters** die Parzen
welcome *n.* Willkomm(en); — *adj.* willkommen, angenehm; — *v.* willkommen heissen, bewillkommnen; **you are — es ist gern geschehen; —! *interj.* herzlich willkommen!
weld *v.* (zusammen)schweissen; — *n.* Schweissnaht; **-er** *n.* Schweisser; **-ing** *n.* Schweissen
welfare *n.* Wohlfahrt, Wohlergehen, Wohlstand; — **society** Fürsorgeverein; — **state** Nation mit verstaatlichter Fürsorge; — **work** Wohlfahrtspflege, Fürsorgewerk
well *n.* Brunnen, Quelle; Schacht; — *adj.* wohl
well *adv.* gut, schön, richtig; wohl; gänzlich, völlig; **as — as** so gut wie, sowohl als auch; **very —!** sehr gut! — **then!** nun gut! wohlan!; — *adj.* wohl, gesund; —! *interj.* gut! schön! richtig! nun!
well-behaved *adj.* wohlerzogen, anständig
well-being *n.* Wohlergehen, Wohlstand, Wohlfahrt
wellborn *adj.* hochgeboren, von guter Herkunft
well-bred *adj.* wohlerzogen; artig, manierlich; (zool.) von guter Abstammung
well-defined *adj.* gut definiert
well-disposed *adj.* wohlgesinnt, wohlmeinend
well-done *adj.* gut gemacht; **(cooking)** gar, gut gebraten
well-groomed *adj.* gut gepflegt; elegant
well-intentioned *adj.* wohlmeinend, wohlgemeint
well-known *adj.* wohlbekannt
well-nigh *adv.* beinahe, fast
well-off *adj.* gut situiert, wohlhabend
well-timed *adj.* rechtzeitig; angebracht
well-to-do *adj.* wohlhabend, begütert
well-wisher *n.* Gönner, Freund

welter *n.* Rollen; Wälzen; (fig.) Aufruhr; — *v.* rollen, sich wälzen; schwimmen
welterweight *n.* Weltergewicht
wench *n.* Mädchen, Frauenzimmer; Strassenmädchen
wend *v.* (sich) wenden, lenken
west *n.* West(en); (fig.) Abendland; — *adj.* westlich, westwärts; (fig.) abendländisch; West-; **-erly** *adj.*, **-ern** *adj.* westlich, West-; (fig.) abendlich; **-ward** *adv.* westwärts
Westphalia *n.* Westfalen
West Prussia *n.* Westpreussen
wet *n.* Nässe, Feuchtigkeit; — **blanket** *adj.* feuchtes Tuch; (coll.) Spielverderber; — **nurse** Amme; — *adj.* nass, feucht; (coll.) benebelt; — *v.* nass machen, durchnässen; benetzen, anfeuchten; begiessen
wether *n.* Hammel
whack *n.* Schlag, Stoss; (sl.) Versuch; Anteil; Zustand; — *v.* (coll.) durchschlagen; (sl.) verteilen; prügeln; —! *interj.* klaps! schwaps!
whale *n.* Wal(fisch); — **oil** Tran
whalebone *n.* Fischbein
wharf *n.* Kai; Landeplatz; — *v.* löschen
what *pron.* was (für ein), wer; wie(viel); welch; — **is the matter?** was ist los?
what(so)ever *pron.* and *adj.* was auch (immer); welch auch (immer); was nur
wheat *n.* Weizen; **winter —** Winterweizen
wheatear *n.* Weizenähre
wheel *n.* Rad; Getriebe; Umdrehung; **driving —** Triebrad; **gambling —** Glücksrad; **paddle —** Schaufelrad; **potter's —** Töpferscheibe; **spinning —** Spinnrad; **steering —** Steuerrad; **base —** Radstand; — **chair** Rollstuhl; — **rope** (naut.) Steuerreep; — *v.* rollen, (sich) drehen; (mil.) schwenken
wheelbarrow *n.* Schubkarren
wheeze *v.* keuchen, schnauben, röcheln
whelm *v.* bedecken, verschütten; (fig.) erdrücken
when *adv.* wann, zu welcher Zeit; — *pron.* seit wann, wie lange; — *conj.* wenn, während, als; sobald
whence *adv.* von wo, woher; woraus, weshalb
when(so)ever *adv.* wann auch immer, so oft als
where *adv.* wo(hin), woher, da
whereabouts *n.* Aufenthalt, Wohnort; — *adv.* woherum, worüber, weswegen; wo ungefähr
whereas *conj.* da nun, während doch; wohingegen
whereat *adv.* worüber, wobei, worauf, woran

whereby *adv.* wobei, wodurch, wovon, womit
wherefore *adv.* warum, weshalb, weswegen, wozu
wherein *adv.* worin (auch immer)
whereof *adv.* wovon; dessen, deren
where(up)on *adv.* worauf(hin), wonach
wherever *adv.* wo auch (immer); wohin auch (immer)
wherewith *adv.* womit, mit wem; **-al** *adv.* and *pron.* womit; nötig; **-al** *n.* Erforderliche, Mittel
whet *v.* wetzen, schärfen, schleifen
whether *conj.* ob
whetstone *n.* Schleifstein, Wetzstein
whey *n.* Molke
which *pron.* welch; der, die, das
which(so)ever *pron.* and *adj.* welch (*or* was) auch immer
whiff *n.* Zug, Paff; Hauch; (coll.) Nu
while *n.* Weile, Zeitraum; — *conj.* während, indem, so lange (wie)
whim *n.* Einfall, Laune, Grille; **-sical** *adj.* grillenhaft, launenhaft; wunderlich; **-sy** *n.* Laune; Grille(nhaftigkeit)
whimper *n.* Gewimmer, Winseln; — *v.* wimmern, winseln
whine *n.* Gewimmer, Gewinsel; — *v.* weinen, wimmern, winseln; jaulen, jammern
whinny *n.* Gewieher; — *v.* wiehern
whip *n.* Peitsche; Geissel; (pol.) Einpeitscher; — **hand** Oberhand; — *v.* peitschen; schlagen, geisseln; (pol.) einpeitschen, durchpeitschen; **-ped** *adj.* geschlagen, gepeitscht; **-ped cream** Schlagsahne
whippoorwill *n.* Ziegenmelker
whirl *n.* Wirbel, Strudel; (bot.) Quirl; (zool.) Gewinde; — *v.* (sich) drehen, wirbeln; kreisen
whirlpool *n.* Wirbel, Strudel
whirlwind *n.* Wirbelwind, Windhose
whisk *n.* Wedel; kleiner Besen, Handfeger; Schneeschläger; — *v.* wischen, fegen, kehren; abstauben; schwingen, wirbeln; schlagen
whisker *n.* Wischer, Feger; — *pl.* Backenbart
whisk(e)y *n.* Whisky
whisper *n.* Wispern, Geflüster; — *v.* wispern, flüstern, raunen
whistle *n.* Pfiff, Pfeifen; Pfeife, Flöte; — *v.* pfeifen
whit *n.* Jota, Punkt; Bisschen
white *n.* Weiss(e); Eiweiss(körper); (fig.) Reinheit, Wahrheit; — *adj.* weiss; farblos; (fig.) rein, unbefleckt; — **ant** Termite; — **feather** weisse Feder; Feigheitszeichen; — **gold** Weissgold;

— **heat** Weissglut; — **lead** Bleiweiss; — **lie** Notlüge; — **matter** (anat.) Gehirnhaut; Rückenmark; — **oak** Silbereiche; — **pine** Silberkiefer; — **poplar** Silberpappel; — **sauce** Mehlschwitze, Einbrenne; — **slavery** Mädchenhandel; -n v. weissen, tünchen; weiss machen; weiss (or grau, blass) werden, ergrauen; bleichen; -ness n. Weisse, Blässe; (fig.) Reinheit

white-collar worker n. Büroangestellte

white-haired adj. weisshaarig

white-hot adj. weissglühend

whitewash n. Tünche; — v. tünchen, weissen; (fig.) rein waschen, übertünchen

whither adv. wohin

whittle v. schnitze(l)n; — **away** (or **down**) beschneiden

whiz n. Zischen, Sausen; — v. zischen, sausen

who pron. wer; welch; der, die, das

whodunit n. (coll.) Kriminalroman, Detektivgeschichte

who(so)ever pron. wer auch (immer); ein jeder, der

whole n. Ganze, Gesamtheit; — adj. ganz, ungeteilt; voll(ständig); heil, unversehrt

wholehearted adj. aufrichtig, ernst

whole-meal bread n. Vollkornbrot, Schrotbrot

wholesale n. Grosshandel; (fig.) in Bausch und Bogen; — adj. Gross-, en gros; -r n. Grosshändler, Engroshändler

wholesome adj. heilsam, zuträglich, bekömmlich; gesund; nützlich

whole-wheat adj. Weizenschrot-

wholly adv. ganz, gänzlich; ganz und gar; vollkommen, völlig

whoop n. Schrei, Geschrei; — v. (auf)schreien; -ing cough Keuchhusten

whop v. vertobaken, prügeln

whore n. Hure

whose pron. wessen; dessen, deren

why adv. warum, weshalb, weswegen; that is — deshalb, darum

wick n. Docht

wicked adj. böse, schlecht; gottlos; verrucht, lasterhaft

wide adj. weit, breit, fern; umfassend, abweichend; far and — weit und breit; -n v. erweitern, (aus)weiten; verbreitern; verbreiten

wide-awake adj. hell wach; (fig.) aufmerksam, schlau

wide-eyed adj. mit weitgeöffneten Augen

widespread adj. weit verbreitet (or ausgebreitet)

widow n. Witwe; -ed adj. verwitwet; verwaist; -er n. Witwer; -hood n. Wit-

wenstand

width n. Weite, Breite

wield v. handhaben, schwingen, führen; beherrschen, leiten; ausüben; (er)tragen

wife n. Weib, Ehefrau, Gattin, Gemahlin

wig n. Perücke; — v. (coll.) schelten, ausschimpfen

wiggle n. Schwänzeln, Schlängeln; — v. schwänzeln, schlängeln

wild n. Wildnis, Wüste, Einöde; — adj. wild, stürmisch; toll, zügellos, ausschweifend; ziellos; abenteuerlich; ungezähmt, verwildert; (bot.) wild wuchernd (or wachsend); — **boar** Wildschwein, Keiler; — **oats** (coll.) Jugendstreich; -erness n. Wildnis, Wüste, Einöde; (fig.) Unmenge

wildcat n. Wildkatze; (com.) unsolides (or ungesetzliches) Unternehmen; (rail.) führerlose Lokomotive; — adj. planlos; schwindelhaft; (com.) unsolid, ungesetzlich; (rail.) nicht fahrplanmässig, unkontrolliert

wildfire n. Feuersbrunst; **spread like** — sich wie ein Lauffeuer verbreiten

wild-goose chase n. vergebliche Bemühung (or Jagd); Querfeldeinritt

wile n. List, Tücke; Kniff

wilful adj. eigensinnig, eigenwillig; (law) vorsätzlich

will n. Wille, Wunsch; Macht, Willkür; (law) letzter Wille, Testament; at — nach Belieben, ohne Einschränkung; — v. wollen, wünschen, verlangen; (law) letztwillig verfügen, hinterlassen; -ing adj. (bereit)willig; willens; -ingness n. Bereitwilligkeit, Geneigtheit

willow n. Weide

will-o'-the-wisp n. Irrlicht

willy-nilly adv. wohl oder übel

win n. Gewinn, Sieg; — v. gewinnen, siegen, den Sieg davontragen; erlangen; (mil.) erobern, einnehmen; -ner n. Gewinner, Sieger; -ning n. Gewinn, Nutzen, Ausbeute; -ning adj. gewinnend, einnehmend

winch n. Winde, Kran, Kurbel

wind n. Wind; Luftzug; Hauch, Atem; — **instrument** Blasinstrument; — **tunnel** (avi.) Windkanal; — v. ausser Atem sein (or bringen); -ed adj. ausser Atem; **short** -ed kurzatmig; -ward n. Windseite, Luv(seite); -ward adv windwärts, luvwärts; -y adj. windig, stürmisch; (med.) blähend; (fig.) aufgeblasen, prahlerisch

wind v. (sich) winden, wickeln; (bot.) ranken; — **up** schliessen, end(ig)en; aufwickeln; (watch) aufziehen; (fig.)

abwickeln; (com.) liquidieren; –ing n.
Windung, Krümmung; Wicklung; Gewinde; –ing adj. sich windend; –ing
sheet Leichentuch, Sterbehemd; –ing
stairs Wendeltreppe

windbag n. Blasebalg; (coll.) Windbeutel

windfall n. Fallobst; Windbruch; (fig.)
Glücksfall, unerwarteter Gewinn

windlass n. Winde; Kran

windmill n. Windmühle

window n. Fenster; (com.) Schaufenster,
Auslage; Schalter; — **blind**, — **shade**
Jalousie, Rouleau; — **shutter** Fenster-
laden; — **sill** Fenstersims, Fensterbrett;
French — Flügelfenster

windowpane n. Fensterscheibe

windpipe n. Luftröhre

windshield n. Windschutzscheibe; —
wiper Scheibenwischer

wine n. Wein; — **bag** Weinschlauch

wing n. Flügel; Seite; (arch.) Seitenflügel;
(avi.) Tragfläche; Staffel; (football)
Aussenstürmer; (mil.) Flanke; pl.
(theat.) Kulissen, Seitendekoration; —
case (ent.) Flügeldecke; — **spread**
Flügelweite; — **stroke** Flügelschlag; —
v. mit Flügeln versehen; beflügeln,
beschwingen; durchfliegen, überfliegen

wink n. Wink; Blinzeln, Blinken; (fig.)
Augenblick; **not get a** — **of sleep** kein
Auge zutun; — v. winken; blinzeln,
blinken

winsome adj. gefällig, angenehm; anziehend

winter n. Winter; — **wheat** Winterweizen;
— v. überwintern, Winterquartiere
beziehen

wintry adj. winterlich; kalt, frostig

wipe n. Wischen, Putzen; (sl.) Schlag,
Hieb; — v. (ab)wischen, putzen; aus-
wischen, reinigen; (ab)trocknen; (sl.)
prügeln; — **out** (coll.) ausrotten

wire n. Draht; (coll.) Telegramm; **barbed**
— Stacheldraht; **conducting** — Lei-
tungsdraht; **live** — geladener Draht;
screen — Netzdraht; — **bridge** Hängebrücke; — **fence** Drahtzaun, Draht-
gitter; — **gauge** Drahtmass; — **photo**
Bildtelegramm; — **rope** Drahtseil; —
screen Drahtnetz, Drahtsieb; — **tap-
ping** Anzapfen (der Leitung); Abhören
(telefonischer or telegrafischer Mit-
teilungen); — v. mit Draht versehen
(or befestigen); (mech.) Leitungen
legen; (coll.) drahten; –less adj. draht-
los; Funk-

wirepuller n. Drahtzieher

wiring n. Leitung, elektrische Anlage

wiry adj. drahtig; sehnig, zäh

wisdom n. Weisheit, Klugheit; Einsicht;

Gelehrsamkeit, Wissen; — **tooth** Weis-
heitszahn

wise n. Weise; — adj. weise, klug; verständig, einsichtig; erfahren; gelehrt

wisecrack n. witzige Bemerkung; — v.
witzige Bemerkungen machen

wish n. Wunsch, Verlangen; Glückwunsch; — v. wünschen, verlangen,
wollen; beglückwünschen; –ful adj.
sehnsüchtig, verlangend

wishbone n. (orn.) Brustbein

wishy-washy adj. wässrig, schwach;
gegenstandslos, kraftlos

wisp n. Wisch; Strähne; Irrlicht

wistful adj. sehnsüchtig, sehnlich; gedankenvoll

wit n. Witz; Verstand, Geist; Witzbold;
be at one's — **'s end** sich nicht mehr zu
helfen wissen; **to** — nämlich, das heisst;
–less adj. witzlos, geistlos; gedankenlos; –tingly adv. wissentlich, geflissentlich; –ty adj. witzig, geistreich; (fig.)
beissend

witch n. Hexe, Zauberin; — v. verhexen,
verzaubern; –ery n. Zauberei; Entzücken

witchcraft n. Hexerei; Zauberkunst,
Zauberei

with prep. mit; bei, nebst, durch, von,
über

withdraw v. (sich) zurückziehen, weg-
ziehen, abziehen; herausziehen, herausnehmen; entfernen, abwenden;
(law) zurücknehmen, widerrufen; –al
n. Zurückziehung, Abhebung; Zurück-
nahme; Entziehung; (law) Widerruf;
(mil.) Rückzug

wither v. (ver)welken; austrocknen, verdorren; (fig.) vergehen

withhold v. zurückhalten, abhalten, vorenthalten

within prep. innerhalb, binnen, in; — adv.
im Innern, drin(nen), darin; inwendig;
daheim, zu Hause; — **bounds** (mil.)
erlaubt, gestattet

without prep. ohne; ausserhalb, ausser;
— adv. aussen, draussen; äusserlich;
auswendig; nicht daheim (or zu Hause);
that goes — **saying** das versteht sich
von selbst

withstand v. widerstehen, widersetzen,
widerstreben

witness n. Zeuge; Zeugnis; — v. bezeugen,
Zeuge sein; zugegen sein

wizard n. Zauberer, Hexenmeister,
Magier

wobble n. Schlottern, Torkeln; — v.
schlottern, torkeln, schwanken,
wackeln

wobbly adj. wackelnd, wackelig; torkelnd.

schlotternd

woe *n.* Leid, Elend; Pein, Weh; **-ful** *adj.* kummervoll, elend, jämmerlich; bedauernswert, leiderfüllt

wolf *n.* Wolf; **cry** — blinden Alarm schlagen

woman *n.* Frau, Weib; (coll.) Weibsbild; **—'s rights** Frauenrechte; **-hood** *n.* Weiblichkeit; (coll.) Frauenwelt; **-kind** *n.* weibliches Geschlecht, Frauen(welt); **-ly** *adj.* weiblich, fraulich; (coll.) weibisch

womb *n.* Leib, Schoss; (anat.) Gebärmutter

wonder *n.* Wunder; Verwunderung; — *v.* (sich) wundern, bewundern, verwundern, staunen; gern wissen wollen, neugierig sein; **-ful** *adj.* wundervoll, wunderbar, wunderschön; erstaunlich

wonderland *n.* Wunderland

wont *n.* Gewohnheit, Gebrauch; **-ed** *adj.* gewöhnlich, gewohnt

woo *v.* freien, werben, anhalten; (fig.) suchen; locken; drängen

wood *n.* Holz; Wald(ung), Forst, Gehölz; Brennholz; (typ.) Holzblock; **— alcohol** Holzalkohol; **— anemone** Waldanemone, Windröschen; **— louse** Holzwurm, Assel; **— pigeon** Holztaube; **— pulp** Holzschliff, Zellulose; **— wind** (mus.) Holzblasinstrument; — *v.* aufforsten; mit Brennholz versehen; **-ed** *adj.* waldig, bewaldet; **-en** *adj.* hölzern; Holz-; **-y** *adj.* waldig; holzig; Wald-, Holz-

woodbine *n.* Geissblatt

woodchuck *n.* Murmeltier

woodcraft *n.* Weidwerk, Jägerei

woodcut *n.* Holzschnitt; **-ter** *n.* Holzfäller; Holzschnitzer

woodland *n.* Waldland, Waldung

wood(s)man *n.* Waldbewohner; Förster

woodpecker *n.* Specht; **spotted — Bunt**specht

woodpile *n.* Holzhaufen, Holzstoss

woodruff *n.* Waldmeister

woodshed *n.* Holzschuppen

woodwork *n.* Holzwerk; Holzarbeit

wool *n.* Wolle; **-en** *adj.* wollen; Woll-; **-y** *adj.* wollig; Woll-; (coll.) verschwommen, verschleiert

word *n.* Wort; Nachricht, Bescheid, Meldung, Botschaft; Rede; Spruch; Zusage, Versprechen; (mil.) Losungswort; Kommando; *pl.* Wörter, Worte; Wortwechsel, Rede; Text; **by — of mouth** mündlich; **-iness** *n.* Wortfülle, Wortschwall; **-ing** *n.* Ausdruck(sweise), Stil; Wortlaut; **-y** *adj.* wortreich, weitschweifig

work *n.* Werk, Arbeit; Tat, Tätigkeit; Beruf, Beschäftigung; Leistung, Erzeugnis; (mech.) Gang, Getriebe; *pl.* Fabrik, Anlage, Betrieb; Werke; — *v.* arbeiten, bearbeiten; wirken; in Gang bringen (or setzen), bewirken; **-able** *adj.* ausführbar, brauchbar; schmiegsam, bearbeitbar; **-er** *n.* Arbeiter; Urheber; **-ers** *pl.* Arbeiterschaft; **-ing** *n.* Arbeit, Wirken; Bewegung; Arbeitsprozess, Bearbeitung; (chem.) Gärung; **-ing day** Werktag, Arbeitstag; **-ing** *adj.* arbeitend

workbench *n.* Werkbank, Arbeitstisch

workhouse *n.* Besserungsanstalt, Arbeitshaus

work(ing)man *n.* Arbeiter; Handwerker

workmanship *n.* Geschicklichkeit, Kunstfertigkeit

workout *n.* Geschicklichkeitsprobe; (sports) Training; Leistungsprüfung

workshop *n.* Werkstatt, Werkstätte

world *n.* Welt; Erde; (fig.) Menge; **-ly** *adj.* weltlich, irdisch, Welt-; zeitlich

world-wide *adj.* weltberühmt, allgemein anerkannt, weitverbreitet

worm *n.* Wurm; (mech.) Gewinde; **— gear** Schneckengetriebe; **—, powder** Wurmpulver; — *v.* sich krümmen (or winden); kriechen; nach Würmern graben; Würmer entfernen; **-y** *adj.* wurmig, madig, wurmstichig, von Würmern befallen; (fig.) kriechend

worm-eaten *adj.* wurmstichig, vermottet

wormwood *n.* Wermut

worn(-out) *adj.* abgenutzt, abgetragen; verbraucht

worry *n.* Sorge; Quälerei, Plage; — *v.* (sich) sorgen; plagen, quälen; zerren

worse *adj.* schlechter, schlimmer, übler, ärger; **so much the —** umso schlimmer

worship *n.* Anbetung, Verehrung; Gottesdienst; — *v.* verehren, anbeten

worst *n.* Schlimmste, Ärgste; **at (the) —** im schlimmsten Falle (or Zustand); — *adj.* schlechtest, schlimmst, ärgst; — *adv.* am schlechtesten (or schlimmsten, ärgsten)

worsted *n.* (fabric) Kammgarn, Wollgarn

worth *n.* Wert; — *adj.* wert, würdig; **be — wert sein, gelten, kosten; **-iness** *n.* Würdigkeit, Verdienst; **-less** *adj.* wertlos; unwürdig, nichtswürdig; **-y** *n.* Ehrenmann, Würdenträger; **-y** *adj.* würdig; verdienstvoll, trefflich; ehrbar; schätzbar, rühmlich

worth-while *adj.* **be —** sich lohnen, der Mühe wert sein

would-be *adj.* angeblich, vermeintlich, scheinbar, sogenannt; Schein-

wound n. Wunde; Verwundung, Verletzung; (fig.) Kränkung; — v. verwunden, verletzen; (fig.) kränken

wrangle n. Zank, Streit; — v. zanken, streiten

wrap v. (ein)wickeln, einschlagen, einhüllen; verpacken; -per n. Packer; Hülle, Überzug, Umschlag; Packpapier; Umhüllung; Morgenrock; -ping n. Hülle, Mantel; Packmaterial

wrath n. Zorn, Grimm, Wut; -ful adj. zornig, grimmig, wütend

wreath n. Kranz; Girlande; Gewinde; -e v. winden, flechten; bekränzen, umwinden; sich ringeln

wreck n. Wrack; Schiffbruch; (fig.) Ruin, Verfall, Untergang; — v. zum Scheitern bringen; zerstören, zertrümmern; zugrunde richten; **be -ed** scheitern; -age n. Schiffstrümmer, Strandgut; (fig.) Trümmer, Reste; **-er** n. Strandräuber; (fig.) Abbrucharbeiter

wren n. Zaunkönig

wrench n. Drehung, Verrenkung; (mech.) Schraubenschlüssel; — v. winden, drehen; verdrehen, verrenken

wrest v. zerren; entwinden, entreissen

wrestle n. Ringen; — v. ringen, kämpfen; (coll.) sich herumbalgen; **-r** n. Ringer

wrestling n. Ringkampf

wretch n. Unglückliche, Elende; **poor —!** armer Teufel! **-ed** adj. unglücklich, armselig, erbärmlich; nichtswürdig, verächtlich

wriggle v. sich winden (or schlängeln), sich hin und her drehen

wring v. (aus)ringen; (aus)pressen; (um)drehen; entreissen; (hands) ringen; **-er** n. Auswringer; (mech.) Wringmaschine; (coll.) Erpresser

wrinkle n. Runzel, Falte; Kniff; — v. (sich) runzeln; falten

wrist n. Handgelenk; — **watch** Armbanduhr

wristband n. Manschette; Armband

writ n. Schrift; (law) gerichtlicher Befehl, Vorladung, Klageschrift; (pol.) behördlicher Erlass

write v. schreiben; — **down** niederschreiben, aufschreiben; — **off** abschreiben; — **poetry** Verse schreiben, dichten; — **up** (coll.) anpreisen, herausstreichen; **-r** n. Schreiber; Schriftsteller

write-up n. (coll.) Anpreisung, lobender Artikel

writhe v. sich winden (or krümmen)

writing n. Schreiben; Schrift; Handschrift; Aufsatz, Werk; Schreibart, Stil; Schriftstellerei; (law) Urkunde, Dokument; **in —** schriftlich; **the**

present — das vorliegende Schreiben, **— desk** Schreibtisch, Schreibpult; Schreibmappe; — **paper** Schreibpapier

wrong n. Unrecht; Kränkung, Beleidigung; Irrtum; Schaden; — adj. unrecht, falsch; verkehrt, unrichtig, irrig; unbillig; — v. Unrecht tun, benachteiligen, Schaden zufügen; kränken, beleidigen; **-ful** adj. ungerecht; beleidigend, kränkend; nachteilig; **-ly** adv. mit Unrecht, fälschlich, versehentlich, auf ungerechte (or verkehrte, falsche) Weise

wrongdoer n. Missetäter, Übeltäter; Beleidiger

wrong-sided adj. (phot.) seitenverkehrt

wrought adj. bearbeitet, verarbeitet; — **iron** Schmiedeeisen

wry adj. schief, krumm; verdreht; — **face** schiefes Gesicht, Grimasse

Wurtemberg n. Württemberg

X

Xanthippe n. Xanthippe; (fig.) zänkisches Weib

Xmas, Christmas n. Weihnachten, Weihnachtsfest

X ray n. Röntgenstrahl; Röntgenbild, Röntgenplatte; **X-ray** adj. Röntgen-; — **specialist** Röntgenologe; — v. röntgen, durchleuchten

xylograph n. Holzschnitt

xylophone n. Xylofon

Y

yacht n. Jacht, Segelboot

yam n. Yamswurzel

yank v. (coll.) zerren, wegreissen; fortschnellen

Yankee n. Yankee, Nordamerikaner; — adj. yankeemässig

yap n. Gekläff; — v. kläffen

yard n. Hof(raum); (agr.) Viehhof; (measure) Elle; (rail.) Rangierbahnhof

yardmaster n. (naut.) Werftaufseher; (rail.) Rangiermeister

yardstick n. Zollstock; (fig.) Masstab

yarn n. Garn; (naut.) Kabelgarn, Ducht

yaw n. & v. Kursabweichung; abtreiben; wenden; gieren

yawing n. Seitenbewegung

yawl n. Jolle

yawn n. Gähnen; — v. gähnen, klaffen

yea adv. ja, gewiss; — **or nay** ja oder nein; **the -s have it** die Jastimmen sind in der Mehrheit

year n. Jahr; pl. Jahre; Alter; **all — around** das ganze Jahr (hindurch); **many -s ago** vor vielen Jahren; **-ling**

n. Jährling, einjähriges Tier; **–ly** *adj.* jährlich, jährig; ein Jahr dauernd

yearbook *n.* Jahrbuch

yearn *v.* sich sehen, verlangen, schmachten; **–ing** *n.* Verlangen, Sehnsucht

yeast *n.* Hefe; (water) Gischt, Schaum

yell *n.* gellender Schrei, Geheul; Erkennungsruf; — *v.* gellen, schreien, heulen

yellow *n.* Gelb; Eigelb; — *adj.* gelb; — **fever** gelbes Fieber; — **jacket** (ent.) gelbe Wespe; — **press** Hetzpresse, Schundpresse; — *v.* gelb werden; vergilben; **–ish** *adj.* gelblich, fahlgelb

yelp *n.* Gekläff; — *v.* kläffen, bellen

yen *n.* (Japanese coin) Yen; (coll.) Sehnsucht, Verlangen

yes *adv.* ja; — indeed ja wahrhaftig; — truly ja freilich; — **man** Jasager

yesterday *n.* gestriger Tag; — *adv.* gestern; **day before** — vorgestern; **I was not born** — ich bin nicht von gestern

yet *adv.* noch; jetzt (noch), bis jetzt; nunmehr, schon, selbst, sogar; — *conj.* doch, dennoch, obwohl, obgleich, gleichwohl, trotzdem

yield *n.* Ertrag, Ausbeute, Ernte; — *v.* einbringen, tragen, abwerfen; überlassen, aufgeben, übergeben; gewähren, zugeben; sich fügen, nachgeben; (mil.) sich ergeben; **–ing** *adj.* ergiebig, einträglich; nachgiebig, dehnbar; willfährig

yodel *n.* Jodler; — *v.* jodeln

yoke *n.* Joch; — *v.* ins Joch spannen; (fig.) unterjochen

yokel *n.* Tölpel

yolk *n.* Eidotter, Eigelb

yon(der) *adv.* dort, drüben; jenseits; an jener Stelle; — *adj.* jene, jenseitig

yore *adv.* — of ehemals, vormals, ehedem

you *pron.* du, Sie, man, ihr

young *adj.* jung; frisch, neu; unerfahren; Young Men's Christian Association,

Y.M.C.A. Christlicher Verein junger Männer; **Young Women's Christian Association, Y.W.C.A.** Christlicher Verein junger Mädchen; **–ster** *n.* Junge, Bursche; Kind

your *pron.* dein, Ihr, euer; **–s** *pron.* der (or die, das) deinige (or Ihrige, eurige); **sincerely –s** Ihr ganz ergebener; **–s truly** Ihr ergebener; **–self, –selves** (*pl.*) (du, Sie, ihr, sich) selbst; (dich, Sie, euch) selbst

youth *n.* Jugend; Jüngling, **junger Bursche**; junge Leute; — **hostel** Jugendherberge; **–ful** *adj.* jugendlich, jung

yucca *n.* Yukka, Palmlilie

Yule *n.* Weihnacht(en), Julfest

Yuletide *n.* Weihnachtszeit

Z

zeal *n.* Eifer; Wärme; **–ous** *adj.* eifrig; warm, innig, herzlich

zebra *n.* Zebra

zephyr *n.* Zephir

zero *n.* Null; Nullpunkt; (phys.) Gefrierpunkt; — **hour** Entscheidungsstunde

zest *n.* Behagen, Wohlgefallen; Würze, Beigeschmack

zigzag *n.* Zickzack; — *adj.* zickzackförmig; — *v.* im Zickzack laufen

zinc *n.* Zink; — *v.* verzinken

zipgun *n.* selbsthergestelltes, primitives Gewehr

zipper *n.* Reissverschluss

zither *n.* Zither

zodiac *n.* Tierkreis

zone *n.* Zone; Gebiet; Bezirk, Bereich

zoo *n.* Zoo, zoologischer Garten; **–logic(al)** *adj.* zoologisch; **–logy** *n.* Zoologie, Tierkunde

zoom *v.* (avi.) senkrecht in die Höhe steigen, hochreissen

zyme *n.* Gärungsstoff, Ferment

Traveler's Conversation Guide

ENGLISH-GERMAN

STATION OR AIRPORT
DER BAHNHOF ODER DER FLUGHAFEN

Here is my passport.	Hier ist mein Pass.
Here is my baggage.	Da ist mein Gepäck.
Here are the checks.	Hier sind die Scheine.
Where is the porter?	Wo ist der Träger?
Please put my bags in a taxi.	Bitte, schaffen Sie die Koffer in ein Taxi.
I have nothing to declare.	Ich habe nichts zu verzollen.
Must I pay duty on this?	Ist das zollpflichtig?
How much?	Wieviel?
How many pieces of baggage?	Wieviele Gepäckstücke?
Where is the baggage room?	Wo ist die Gepäckaufbewahrung?
I want to check my baggage.	Ich möchte mein Gepäck aufgeben.
Where is the ticket office?	Wo ist der Fahrkartenschalter?
I want a ticket to _____.	Ich möchte eine Fahrkarte nach _____ haben.
Where can I get change money?	Wo kann ich Geld wechseln?
Please give me Deutsche Marks.	Bitte, geben Sie mir Deutsche Mark.
Where is the men's room? (ladies' room?)	Wo ist die Herrentoilette? (Damentoilette?)
Here is a tip.	Hier ist ein Trinkgeld.
Is that all?	Ist das alles?
That is all.	Das ist alles.

TAXI

Porter, please take my luggage to a taxi.

What is your rate to _____?

Take the shortest way.

Where is the shopping district?

Stop here.

Please wait for me.

Drive more slowly (faster).

To the Hotel _____.

Where is a good hotel?

Is it expensive?

Is there a good restaurant?

TRAIN

Where is the railroad station?

What is the fare to _____?

I want a ticket to _____?

One way.

Round trip.

Where are the first- (second-) class cars?

Please put my baggage on the train (in my compartment).

At what time does the train for _____ leave?

On what track does the train leave?

TAXI

Träger, laden Sie mein Gepäck bitte in ein Taxi.

Wieviel kostet es nach _____?

Bitte, fahren Sie den kürzesten Weg.

Wo ist das Geschäftsviertel?

Halten Sie hier.

Bitte, warten Sie auf mich.

Bitte, fahren Sie langsamer (schneller).

Zum Hotel _____.

Wo gibt es ein gutes Hotel?

Ist es teuer?

Gibt es ein gutes Gasthaus?

DER ZUG

Wo ist der Bahnhof?

Was kostet die Fahrt nach _____?

Ich möchte eine Fahrkarte nach _____?

Hinfahrt.

Hin-und Rückfahrt.

Wo sind die Wagen erster (zweiter) Klasse?

Bitte, tragen Sie mein Gepäck in den Zug (in mein Abteil).

Um wieviel Uhr fährt der Zug nach _____ ab?

Von welchem Bahnsteig fährt der Zug?

Is there a dining-car on this train?	Hat dieser Zug einen Speisewagen?
Is there a sleeping-car on this train?	Hat dieser Zug einen Schlafwagen?
Does the train stop at _____?	Hält der Zug in _____ ?
All aboard!	Alle einsteigen!
Are you the conductor?	Sind Sie der Zugführer?
Where is the dining-car?	Wo ist der Speisewagen?
Is there time to get something to eat?	Habe ich genug Zeit um etwas zu essen?
Where is the smoking compartment?	Wo ist das Raucherabteil?
Is the train on time?	Ist der Zug pünktlich?
Why are we stopping?	Warum halten wir?

AIRPLANE

DAS FLUGZEUG

I am flying to _____.	Ich fliege nach _____.
Is there motor service to the airport?	Gibt's einen Zubringerdienst?
Here is the airport.	Hier ist der Flugplatz.
What planes are there to _____?	Wann gehen Flugzeuge nach _____?
How much luggage is each passenger allowed?	Wieviel Gepäck darf jeder Passagier mitnehmen?
What is the charge for extra luggage?	Wieviel kostet weiteres Gepäck?
Please put my luggage on the plane for _____.	Bitte laden Sie mein Gepäck in das Flugzeug nach _____.
At what time do we leave (arrive)?	Um wieviel Uhr fliegen wir ab (kommen wir an)?
Which is the plane to _____?	Welches ist das Flugzeug nach _____?

The plane leaves on runway No. _____.

Das Flugzeug fliegt von Position Nummer _____ ab.

Here is the waiting room.

Hier ist der Wartesaal.

Where is the stewardess (hostess)?

Wo ist die Stewardess (Kellnerin)?

Wait for me at the gate.

Warten Sie auf mich bei der Schranke.

How high are we flying?

Wie hoch fliegen wir?

How fast are we flying?

Wie schnell fliegen wir?

I feel sick.

Mir ist schlecht.

We are thirty minutes late.

Wir haben dreissig Minuten Verspätung.

When do we arrive at _____?

Wann kommen wir in _____ an?

Where is the airline office?

Wo ist das Fluglinienbüro?

BUS OR STREETCAR

DER AUTOBUS ODER DIE STRASSENBAHN

Does this streetcar (bus) go to _____?

Geht diese Strassenbahn (dieser Autobus) nach _____?

Wait at the car (bus) stop.

Warten Sie bei der Strassenbahn (Autobus) Haltestelle.

How much is the fare, please?

Was kostet die Fahrt, bitte?

Will you please tell me where to get off?

Sagen Sie mir, bitte, wo ich aussteigen muss.

I want to go to _____.

Ich möchte nach _____ fahren.

Do I need a transfer?

Brauche ich ein Umsteigebillet?

When does this car (bus) return?

Wann fährt diese Strassenbahn (dieser Autobus) zurück?

SHIP

DAS SCHIFF

Which way to the quay?

Wie kommt man zu der Landestelle?

When does the ship sail?	Um wieviel Uhr geht das Schiff ab?
May visitors come on board?	Können Besucher an Bord kommen?
I am going to my stateroom.	Ich gehe in meine Kabine.
I am going on deck.	Ich gehe auf Deck.
I want to rent a deck chair.	Ich möchte einen Liegestuhl mieten.
I want to speak to the purser (deck steward).	Ich möchte gern mit dem Zahlmeister (Decksteward) sprechen.
Where are the lifeboats (life preservers)?	Wo sind die Rettungsboote (Rettungsringe)?
Where is the dining salon?	Wo ist der Speisesaal?
When are meals served?	Wann wird serviert?
I am seasick.	Ich bin seekrank.
Have you a remedy for seasickness?	Haben Sie ein Mittel gegen Seekrankheit?
We are landing at _____.	Wir gehen in _____ an Land.

AUTOMOBILE   DAS AUTO

Do you have a road map?	Haben Sie eine Autokarte?
Can you draw me a map?	Können Sie mir eine Zeichnung machen?
Which is the road to _____?	Welche Strasse führt nach _____?
How far is _____?	Wie weit ist es bis _____?
Is the road good?	Ist die Strasse gut?
Is there a good restaurant (hotel) in _____?	Gibt es ein gutes Gasthaus (Hotel) in _____?
Where is the garage?	Wo ist die Garage?
Fill her up.	Machen Sie den Tank voll.
Do I need oil (water, air)?	Brauche ich Öl (Wasser, Luft)?
How much is a liter?	Was kostet ein Liter?
Give me thirty liters.	Geben Sie mir dreissig Liter.

Please check the tires (the oil, the battery, the water, the spark plugs).

Bitte, sehen Sie die Reifen (das Öl, die Batterie, das Wasser, die Zündkerzen) nach.

Please wash the car.

Bitte, waschen Sie den Wagen.

Please grease the car.

Bitte, schmieren Sie die Maschine ab.

Please tighten the brakes.

Bitte, ziehen Sie die Bremse an.

Is there a mechanic here?

Ist ein Mechaniker hier?

The engine overheats (stalls).

Der Motor überhitzt (bleibt stehen).

Can you tow me?

Können Sie mich abschleppen?

Where may I park?

Wo kann ich parken?

ROAD SIGNS

DIE STRASSENZEICHEN

Stop	Halt!
Slow	Langsam!
Caution	Vorsicht!
Detour	Umleitung
Danger	Gefahr
Notice	Achtung!
Road closed (open)	Strasse geschlossen (offen)
Crossroads	Kreuzung
One way	Einbahnstrasse
(Dangerous) curve	(Gefährliche) Kurve
Speed limit 30 km. an hour	Geschwindigkeitsgrenze 30 Km.
Ladies	Damen
Gentlemen	Herren
lavatory	der Waschraum
Entrance	Eingang
Exit	Ausgang
No smoking (admittance, parking, spitting).	Rauchen (Eintritt, Parken, Spucken) verboten

Tourist Information Office	(Touristen) Auskunftsstelle
Extreme caution	Ausserste Vorsicht
Keep right (left)	Rechts (links) fahren
Grade crossing	Bahnübergang
Watch out for trains	Vorsicht, Zugverkehr!
Narrow bridge	Enge Brücke
No thoroughfare	Keine Durchfahrt
No right (left) turn	Nicht rechts (links) einbiegen
Steep grade (up)	Starke Steigung
Steep grade (down)	Starkes Gefälle
No trespassing	Unbefugtes Betreten verboten
School	Schule

HOTEL

DAS HOTEL

Where is a good hotel?	Wo gibt es ein gutes Hotel?
Is it expensive?	Ist es teuer?
I want a room.	Ich wünsche ein Zimmer.
Have you a room with bath?	Haben Sie ein Zimmer mit Bad?
I made a reservation.	Ich habe eine Vorbestellung gemacht.
Have you a single (double) room with bath (with shower)?	Haben Sie ein Einzel- (Doppel-) zimmer mit Bad (mit Brause)?
How much is it by the day (week, month)?	Wieviel kostet es täglich (wöchentlich, monatlich)?
I should like to see the room.	Ich möchte das Zimmer sehen.
It is too small (large, noisy, hot, cold).	Es ist zu klein (gross, laut, heiss, kalt).
Are meals included?	Sind Mahlzeiten einbegriffen?
Where is the bathroom (the telephone, the lavatory, the dining room)?	Wo ist das Badezimmer (das Telephon, die Toilette, der Speisesaal)?

What is the room number?	Was ist die Zimmernummer?
Open the window.	Machen Sie das Fenster auf.
Close the door.	Machen Sie die Tür zu.
Please bring towels (soap).	Bringen Sie Handtücher (Seife), bitte.
Please send the chambermaid (the valet, the waiter).	Bitte, schicken Sie das Zimmermädchen (den Hausdiener, den Kellner).
I want these shoes shined.	Ich möchte diese Schuhe putzen lassen.
I want it pressed.	Ich will ihn nur bügeln lassen.
Please take these suits (these dresses) to be cleaned.	Lassen Sie diese Anzüge (diese Kleider) bitte reinigen
Is there any mail for me?	Ist Post für mich da?
Please mail these letters for me.	Bitte, senden Sie diese Briefe für mich ab.
Some stamps.	Einige Briefmarken.
Some writing paper.	Etwas Schreibpapier.
An envelope.	Einen Briefumschlag.
Please change the sheets (pillow cases, towels).	Bitte, wechseln Sie die Laken (die Kissenbezüge, die Handtücher).
Call me at 6 a.m.	Wecken Sie mich um sechs Uhr morgens.
Who is there?	Wer ist es?
Wait a minute.	Bitte, warten Sie eine Minute!
Do not disturb.	Bitte, nicht stören!
I want an interpreter (guide, secretary) who speaks English.	Ich möchte einen Dolmetscher (einen Führer, eine Sekretärin) der (die) Englisch spricht.
Prepare my bill, please.	Meine Rechnung, bitte.

RESTAURANT

Where is a good restaurant?

A table for two, please, (near the window).

Let me have the menu (wine list).

What do you recommend?

Do you have a table d'hôte dinner (lunch, breakfast)?

What wine do you recommend?

Give us an aperitif (whiskey, gin, liqueur).

Bring us this, please.

Bring us two orders of soup.

We should like to have dinner (lunch) German style.

Bring us orders of _____.

eggs	Eier
toast	Toast
chops	Koteletten
omelet	Omeletten
chicken	Huhn
duck	Ente
oysters	Austern
shrimps	Krabben
salad	Salat
liver	Leber
beans	Bohnen

DAS RESTAURANT

Wo ist ein gutes Restaurant?

Ein Tisch für zwei, bitte, (nah dem Fenster).

Bitte geben Sie mir die Speisekarte (Weinkarte).

Was empfehlen Sie?

Haben Sie ein Table d'Hôte Abendessen (Mittagessen, Frühstück)?

Welchen Wein empfehlen Sie?

Geben Sie uns ein Aperitif (Whisky, Wacholderbranntwein, einen Likör).

Bringen Sie uns das, bitte.

Bringen Sie uns zwei Portionen Suppe.

Wir mochten gern Abendessen (Mittagessen) auf deutsche Art haben.

Bringen Sie uns Portionen _____

roast beef	Rostbraten
roast pork	Schweinebraten
pork chops	Schweinekoteletten
steak (rare, medium, well done)	Englisch, halb durchgebraten, gut durchgebraten)
fish	Fisch
lobster	Hummer
lamb	Lamm
radishes	Radieschen

carrots	Karotten	tomatoes	Tomaten
peas	Erbsen	cucumber	Gurke
lettuce	Kopfsalat	cabbage	Kohl
spinach	Spinat	stringbeans	Schnittbohnen
rice	Reis	onions	Zwiebeln
potatoes	Kartoffeln		
(fried,	(gebraten,		
mashed)	Püree)		

Please bring _____:

Bitte, bringen Sie mir _____:

milk and cream	Milch und Sahne
vinegar and oil	Essig und Öl
lemon	Zitrone
salt and pepper	Salz und Pfeffer
cheese	Käse
tea	Tee
coffee	Kaffee
a napkin	eine Serviette
fork	Gabel
knife	Messer
teaspoon	Teelöffel

What have you for dessert?

Was haben Sie zum Nachtisch?

ice cream	Eis	cake	Kuchen
pastry	Backwerk	pie	Torte
fruits	Obst		

I would like a cup of tea (black coffee, coffee with milk)

Ich möchte eine Tasse Tee (schwarzen Kaffe, Milchkaffee).

The check, please

Die Rechnung, bitte!

THE MARKET

DER MARKT

I should like to go shopping.

Ich möchte einkaufen gehen.

Can you tell me where I can buy _____?

Können Sie mir sagen wo ich _____ kaufen kann?

I should like to go to a department store.

  a shoeshop

  a bookstore

  a cigar store

  a stationer's

I should like to see _____.

How much is this?

What size (color)?

Do you have it in white? (black, red, brown, green, blue, yellow)

Do you have something larger (smaller)?

May I try this on?

Have you a better quality?

This is too expensive.

I like this one.

Sale

Bargain sale

It does not fit.

I shall take it with me.

Send it to the Hotel, _____, please.

THE POST OFFICE

Can you direct me to the post office?

Where can I get some stamps?

How much is the postage?

Ich möchte gern zu einem Warenhaus gehen.

  einem Schuhladen

  einer Buchhandlung

  einem Tabakladen

  einem Papiergeschäft

Ich möchte gern _____ sehen.

Wieviel kostet dies?

Welche Grösse (Farbe)?

Haben Sie das in weiss? (schwarz, rot, braun, grün, blau, gelb)

Haben Sie etwas Grösseres (Kleineres)?

Kann ich dies anprobieren?

Haben Sie eine bessere Qualität?

Es ist zu teuer.

Mir gefällt dies hier.

Verkauf

Ausverkauf

Es passt nicht.

Ich werde es mitnehmen.

Senden Sie es zum Hotel _____, bitte.

DAS POSTAMT

Können Sie mir den Weg zum nächsten Pastamt zeigen?

Wo kann ich Briefmarken bekommen?

Was ist die Gebühr?

What is the local postage here?	Was kostet ein einfacher Brief?
What is the regular postage to the U.S.A.?	Was kostet ein einfacher Brief nach U.S.A.?
What is the airmail postage to the U.S.A.?	Was kostet Luftpost nach U.S.A.?
I want to send this package.	Ich möchte dieses Paket absenden.
I want it insured.	Ich möchte es versichern.
Here is the (my) address.	Hier ist die (meine) Adresse.

PHOTOGRAPHER

DER PHOTOGRAPH

I should like some camera film No. _____. (a roll of color film)	Ich möchte Kamerafilm Nummer _____. (eine Rolle Farbfilm)
Please develop the films (plates).	Bitte, entwickeln Sie diese Filme (Platten).
How much does it cost to develop a roll?	Wieviel kostet es eine Rolle zu entwickeln?
I want one print (enlargement) of each.	Ich möchte einen Abzug (Vergrösserung) von jedem.
I want these pictures developed for tomorrow.	Ich möchte diese Bilder für morgen entwickeln lassen.
When will it be ready?	Wann wird es fertig sein?

EVERYDAY EXPRESSIONS

ALLTÄGLICHE AUSDRUCKE

Good morning.	Guten Morgen.
Good day.	Guten Tag.
Good afternoon.	Guten Tag.
How are you?	Wie geht es Ihnen?
Good evening.	Guten Abend.
Goodbye.	Auf Wiedersehen.
Well, thank you.	Danke, gut.
And you?	Und Ihnen?

Pleased to meet you.	Sehr angenehm.
Yes.	Ja.
No.	Nein.
Please.	Bitte.
Thank you.	Danke schön.
All right.	Sehr gut.
Don't mention it.	Nichts zu danken.
Pardon me.	Entschuldigen Sie.
Not at all.	Sicher nicht.
O.K.	Schön! (or Machen wir!)
I am sorry.	Es tut mir leid.
Isn't it so?	Nicht wahr?
I'm glad.	Es freut mich.
Perhaps.	Vielleicht.
I agree.	Ich bin einverstanden.
I (don't) think so.	Ich glaube ja (nicht).
You're right (wrong).	Sie haben recht (unrecht).
Would you like _____?	Möchten Sie gern _____?
Do you like _____?	Gefällt Ihnen _____?
Do you want _____?	Wünschen Sie _____?
I (do not) understand.	Ich verstehe (nicht).
Can anyone here speak _____?	Kann hier jemand _____ sprechen?
Please speak slowly.	Bitte sprechen Sie langsam.
Not so fast.	Nicht so schnell.
I see.	Ich verstehe.
I (don't) know.	Ich weiss (nicht).
I am glad.	Es freut mich.
I am ready.	Ich bin fertig.
Don't forget.	Vergessen Sie nicht.
Gladly.	Gerne.
Certainly.	Gewiss.

Of course.	Natürlich.
I am most grateful.	Ich bin sehr dankbar.
The pleasure is mine.	Gleichfalls.
May I introduce you to _____?	Darf ich Ihnen _____ vorstellen?
My name is _____.	Ich heisse _____.
Here is my card.	Hier ist meine Karte.
Give my regards to _____.	Besten Gruss an _____.
Please sit down.	Bitte setzen Sie sich.
Make yourself at home.	Machen Sie es sich bequem.
What time is it?	Wieviel Uhr ist es?
Do you mind my smoking?	Stört es Sie, wenn ich rauche?
May I open (close) the window (the door)?	Darf ich das Fenster (die Türe) öffnen (schliessen)?
Bring me _____.	Bringen Sie mir _____.
Take this away.	Nehmen Sie das weg.
I am tired.	Ich bin müde.
I am hungry.	Ich habe Hunger.
I am thirsty.	Ich habe Durst.
Please send for a doctor.	Bitte rufen Sie einen Arzt.
I am going out.	Ich gehe aus.
I shall return at _____ o'clock.	Ich komme um _____ Uhr zurück.
Has anyone asked for me?	Hat jemand nach mir gefragt?
Where are we (you) going?	Wohin gehen wir (Sie)?
Which way?	Welche Richtung?
To the right (left).	Nach rechts (links).
This way.	Diese Richtung.
That way.	Dorthin.
Notice!	Achtung!
Entrance.	Eingang.
Can you tell me _____.	
Exit.	Ausgang.
Pedestrians.	Fussgänger
Knock.	(An)klopfen.
Ring the bell.	Bitte läuten.
	Können Sie mir _____ sagen?

I am looking for _____. Ich suche _____.

Push.	Drücken!	Free.	Frei.
Pull!	Ziehen!	Occupied.	Besetzt.
Quiet.	Ruhig.	A pleasant stay.	Angenehmen Aufenthalt!

As quickly as possible. So schnell wie möglich.

How long have you been waiting? Wie lang warten Sie schon?

You have been very kind. Sie waren äusserst gütig.

A pleasant journey. Glückliche Reise.

Let me hear from you. Lassen Sie von sich hören!

I want an interpreter. Ich möchte einen Dolmetscher haben!

THE WEATHER   DAS WETTER

What is the weather like today? Wie ist das Wetter heute?

It is a fine day. Es ist ein schöner Tag.

It is (very) warm (cold). Es ist (sehr) warm (kalt).

It is raining (snowing). Es regnet (es schneit).

The wind is blowing from the north (south, east, west). Der Wind bläst von Norden (Süden, Osten, Westen).

What is the weather likely to be tomorrow? Wie wird das Wetter morgen sein?

TIME   DIE ZEIT

What time is it? Wieviel Uhr ist es?

It is five o'clock. Es ist fünf Uhr.

It is a quarter past six. Es ist viertel nach sechs.

It is half-past seven. Es ist halb acht.

It is a quarter to eight. Es ist viertel vor acht.

It is twenty past nine. Es ist zwanzig na h neun.

It is ten to ten. Es ist zehn vor zehn.

Midday   Mittag   January   Januar

Midnight	Mitternacht	February	Februar
Sunday	Sonntag	March	März
Monday	Montag	April	April
Tuesday	Dienstag	May	Mai
Wednesday	Mittwoch	June	Juni
Thursday	Donnerstag	July	Juli
Friday	Freitag	August	August
Saturday	Samstag	September	September
Spring	Frühling	October	Oktober
Summer	Sommer	November	November
Autumn	Herbst	December	Dezember
Winter	Winter		

THE NUMERALS   DIE ZAHLEN

nought	null	sixteen	sechzehn
one	eins	seventeen	siebzehn
two	zwei	eighteen	achtzehn
three	drei	nineteen	neunzehn
four	vier	twenty	zwanzig
five	fünf	twenty-one	einundzwanzig
six	sechs	thirty	dreissig
seven	sieben	forty	vierzig
eight	acht	fifty	fünfzig
nine	neun	sixty	sechzig
ten	zehn	seventy	siebzig
eleven	elf	eighty	achtzig
twelve	zwölf	ninety	neunzig
thirteen	dreizehn	one hundred	hundert
fourteen	vierzehn	one thousand	tausend
fifteen	fünfzehn	one million	eine Million

THE *NEW CENTURY* DICTIONARIES

VELAZQUEZ SPANISH/ENGLISH DICTIONARY

VEST-POCKET DICTIONARIES

French

German

Italian

Spanish

INSTANT CONVERSATION GUIDES

French

German

Spanish